CRIMINAL EVIDENCE

Fifth Edition

AUSTRALIA
Law Book Co.
Sydney

CANADA and USA
Carswell
Toronto

HONG KONG
Sweet & Maxwell Asia

NEW ZEALAND
Brookers
Wellington

SINGAPORE and MALAYSIA
Sweet & Maxwell Asia
Singapore and Kuala Lumpur

CRIMINAL EVIDENCE

Fifth Edition

RICHARD MAY
*Judge of the International Criminal Tribunal
for the Former Yugoslavia 1997–2004;
Circuit Judge on the Midland and Oxford Circuit 1987–1997;
Bencher of the Inner Temple;
Honorary Fellow, Selwyn College, Cambridge*

STEVEN POWLES
*LL.B. (London), LL.M. (Cantab.)
of Middle Temple, Barrister*

London
Sweet & Maxwell
2004

Published in 2004 by
Sweet & Maxwell Ltd of
100 Avenue Road, Swiss Cottage,
London, NW3 3PF
www.sweetandmaxwell.co.uk
Computerset by YHT Ltd, London
Printed and bound in Great Britain by
TJ International Ltd, Padstow, Cornwall

No natural forests were destroyed to make this product,
only farmed timber was used and replanted

A CIP catalogue record for this book is available from the British Library

ISBN 0 421 796 60X

Preface

There have been two significant statutory developments in the law of criminal evidence since the last edition of this work was published. First and foremost, the Criminal Justice Act 2003 has substantially reformed the law of hearsay, character and disclosure. It also introduces for the first time trial on indictment by judge alone. The innovations of the Criminal Justice Act 2003 are the most far-reaching (and controversial) in the law of criminal evidence for the last century—even more so than the great reforming Police and Criminal Evidence Act 1984 and many other lesser statutory changes. Although it is anticipated that the relevant sections of the Act will not come into effect until April 2005, the changes to the law of evidence are such that they have been included in this edition to allow time to digest them and because of their immense importance to practitioners. Secondly, the Youth Justice and Criminal Evidence Act 1999 has provided a new statutory scheme governing the competence of witnesses, and sets out new and important procedures for the protection of vulnerable witnesses testifying in criminal trials.

There have also been important decisions of the appellate courts relating to criminal evidence, for example the decisions of the House of Lords in *Forbes* (identification), *H and C* (public interest immunity), *Lambert* (reverse burden of proof) and those of the Privy Council in *Brown v Stott* (privilege against self incrimination) and *Benedetto and Labrador* (cell confessions). Discussion of these cases, together with much other new material, is incorporated in this edition. In particular, as a result of the coming into force of the Human Rights Act 1998 in October 2000 and the incorporation of the European Convention on Human Rights into domestic law, considerable attention is given to the effect of Strasbourg jurisprudence on the law of evidence. Thus, reference is made to significant recent decisions of the European Court of Human Rights such as *Edwards and Lewis v UK* (public interest immunity), *Rowe and Davis v UK* (disclosure) and *JB v Switzerland* (protection against self-incrimination). Notice is also taken of the comprehensive review of the criminal justice system and subsequent recommendations made by Lord Justice Auld in the Auld Review.

As a result in the growth of the material and amendments to the law, parts of the work have been restructured for this edition. Thus the Chapters on similar facts and character have been amalgamated into one Chapter on character to reflect the wide-ranging reform of this area of the law by the

Criminal Justice Act 2003. Similarly, the Chapters on common law exceptions to the rule against hearsay and the exceptions connected with documents have been merged into one Chapter on hearsay under the Criminal Justice Act 2003. Parts have been re-written: for instance, the section on disclosure to incorporate the new disclosure regime following amendment of the Criminal Procedure and Investigations Act 1996 by the Criminal Justice Act 2003; the section on identification setting out the new procedure under the new Code of Practice; and the discussion on vulnerable witnesses.

The purpose of this book (as earlier prefaces have stated) is "to provide a concise and readable guide for the practitioner, concentrating on the problems which arise in all trials, whether summary or on indictment". It is also hoped that the book will be of assistance to those whose work or study brings them into contact with criminal evidence and those who have an interest in the subject.

There are many who have contributed to the production of this edition of the book—to all we give our most sincere thanks. Special thanks are due to Radmila May for all her preparatory and editorial work on the text which enabled the work to be completed after Richard May's illness and retirement as Judge from the ICTY in 2004. Her support and encouragement during this time has been invaluable. Special thanks also to Nicholas May for his preparatory work on Chapter 7. Much appreciation also to Janice Looman-Kearns and Ros Capron for their assistance with typing and to Tonia Gillett and Laura Janes for assistance with research. Thanks to Paul Bogan for his review and comments on Chapter 14 (identification) and to Kate Beattie (Co-ordinator of Doughty Street Human Rights Unit) for her helpful human rights law updates. Thanks also to Steven's clerks at Doughty Street for their patience during the months of preparation of this work. Finally, special thanks are due to the staff of Sweet and Maxwell for seeing the work through the press.

The law is stated as at March 1, 2004.

Richard May and Steven Powles

Contents

	Page
Preface	v
Table of Cases	xiii
Table of International Cases	lxxi
Table of Statutes	lxxv
Table of Statutory Instruments	lxxxvii
Table of European Convention on Human Rights	lxxxix

PART 1: INTRODUCTORY

	Para.

CHAPTER 1: INTRODUCTION

1. The Meaning and Classification of Evidence	1–01
2. The Best Evidence Rule	1–11
3. Admissibility and Relevance	1–12

CHAPTER 2: REAL EVIDENCE

1. Chattels	2–02
2. Documents	2–05
3. Inspection and View	2–06
4. The Admissibility of Photographs and Recordings: General Principles...	2–09
5. Photographs	2–11
6. Tape Recordings	2–16
7. Video Recordings	2–31
8. Automatic Recordings..	2–43

CHAPTER 3: DOCUMENTS

1. Meaning and Classification	3–02
2. Private Documents	3–04

3. Public Documents 3–18
4. Judicial Documents 3–21

PART 2: BURDEN AND STANDARD OF PROOF

CHAPTER 4: BURDEN AND STANDARD OF PROOF

1. Burden of Proof 4–02
2. Standard of Proof 4–36

CHAPTER 5: PROOF WHERE EVIDENCE IS NOT NECESSARY

1. Presumptions 5–02
2. Formal Admissions 5–07
3. Judicial Notice 5–08
4. The Effect of Previous Acquittals and Convictions 5–13

PART 3: EXCLUSIONARY RULES AND EXCEPTIONS

CHAPTER 6: EVIDENCE OF OPINION

1. General Rule 6–02
2. Exceptions to the General Rule 6–07

CHAPTER 7: CHARACTER

1. Introduction 7–01
2. Good Character 7–06
3. Bad Character 7–27

CHAPTER 8: HEARSAY 1: HEARSAY GENERALLY

1. Introduction 8–01
2. Admissibility—General Principle 8–12
3. The Principal Categories of Admissibility 8–16

CHAPTER 9: HEARSAY 2: CONFESSIONS

1. What Amounts to a Confession?............................ 9–04
2. When is a Confession Admissible?......................... 9–15
3. Rules Concerning the Use of Confessions.................. 9–51
4. Evidence Obtained in Consequence of an Inadmissible Con- 9–60
    fession ....

PART 4: EXCLUSION THROUGH DISCRETION PRIVILEGE OR
CONVENTION RIGHTS

CHAPTER 10: THE DISCRETION TO EXCLUDE EVIDENCE

1. The Common Law Discretion 10–02
2. The Discretion under s.78............................... 10–13
3. Recommendations of the Royal Commission 10–32
4. Recommendations of the Auld Review 10–33

CHAPTER 11: PRIVILEGE

1. The Privilege against Self-incrimination.................. 11–02
2. Legal Professional Privilege 11–27
3. Other Confidential Communications....................... 11–37

CHAPTER 12: PUBLIC INTEREST

1. Information for the Detection of Crime 12–02
2. Public Interest Immunity 12–12

CHAPTER 13: CONVENTION

1. Introduction.. 13–01
2. The Human Rights Act 1998 13–03
3. The Convention Rights 13–09
4. Violations of Convention Rights......................... 13–27

PART 5: IDENTIFICATION AND CORROBORATION

CHAPTER 14: IDENTIFICATION

1. Visual Identification 14–02
2. Identification in Court: Dock Identification 14–13
3. Identification Out of Court 14–16
4. The Use of Photographs for Identification 14–35
5. Admissibility of Identification Based on Photographic Images 14–38
6. Admissibility of Photofits and Sketches 14–39
7. Other Forms of Identification 14–41

CHAPTER 15: CORROBORATION AND SUSPECT EVIDENCE

1. The Corroboration Rules 15–01
2. The Evidence of Suspect Witnesses 15–14

PART 6: RULES CONNECTED WITH THE TRIAL

CHAPTER 16: FUNCTIONS OF JUDGE, JURY AND JUSTICES

1. Trials on Indictment by both Judge and Jury: The Functions of 16–02
   Judge and Jury ....
2. Trials on Indictment Without a Jury 16–25
3. Summary Trials: Functions of Justices 16–27

CHAPTER 17: COMPETENCE AND COMPELLABILITY OF WITNESSES

1. The General Rule 17–01
2. Children 17–03
3. Persons of Unsound Mind 17–06
4. Incapacitated Witnesses 17–08
5. The Defendant 17–11
6. The Defendant's Spouse 17–26

CHAPTER 18: DISCLOSURE

1. Trials on Indictment 18–01

2. Summary Trial 18–03
3. Unused Material: The Criminal Procedure and Investigation 18–05
   Act 1996, Pts I and II Unused Material ....
4. Other Statutory Rules.. 18–31

Chapter 19: Course of Evidence

1. Calling Witnesses 19–01
2. Swearing Witnesses 19–08
3. Vulnerable and Intimidated Witnesses 19–11
4. The Order of Evidence....................................... 19–34

Chapter 20: Previous Consistent Statements

1. The Rule Against Previous Consistent Statements 20–02

Chapter 21: Examination of Witnesses

1. Introduction... 21–01
2. Examination-in-Chief 21–04
3. Cross-examination 21–15
4. Re-examination 21–32

                                                                Page
Index... 631

Table of Cases

A [1997] Crim.L.R. 883, CA 15–13, 17–18, 17–19
A (No.2) [2001] 2 Cr.App.R. 351 1–13
A (Complainant's Sexual History); sub nom. Y and A (No.2) [2001] UKHL
    25; [2002] 1 A.C. 45; [2001] 2 W.L.R. 1546; [2001] 3 All E.R. 1;
    [2001] 2 Cr.App.R. 21; 165 J.P. 609; [2001] H.R.L.R. 48; [2001]
    U.K.H.R.R. 825; 11 B.H.R.C. 225; [2001] Crim.L.R. 908; 165 J.P.N.
    750, HL 7–80, 13–05, 13–08
A (Criminal Proceedings: Disclosure), Re [1996] 1 F.L.R. 221; [1996] Fam.
    Law 142, CA 12–23
A (Joinder of Appropriate Minister) [2001] 1 W.L.R. 789; *The Times*,
    March 21, 2001; *Independent*, March 27, 2001, HL 13–07
Abadom (Steven) [1983] 1 W.L.R. 126; [1983] 1 All E.R. 364; 76 Cr.App.R.
    48; [1983] Crim.L.R. 254; 79 L.S.G. 1412; 133 N.L.J. 132; 126 S.J.
    562, CA 6–38, 6–39, 6–40, 6–41
Abraham (Alan) [1973] 1 W.L.R. 1270; [1973] 3 All E.R. 694; 57
    Cr.App.R. 799; [1974] Crim.L.R. 246; 117 S.J. 663, CA 4–27
Absolam (Calvin Lloyd) (1989) 88 Cr.App.R. 332; [1988] Crim.L.R. 748;
    The Times, July 9, 1988, CA 9–31, 9–42, 18–27
Ackinclose (Karl) [1996] Crim.L.R. 747, CA 17–17, 17–19
Acton Justices Ex p. McMullen and Tower Bridge Magistrates' Court Ex p.
    Lawlor (1991) 92 Cr.App.R. 98; 154 J.P. 901; 154 J.P.N. 563, DC   8–19, 8–28
Adams (Denis John) (No.1) [1996] 2 Cr.App.R. 467; [1996] Crim.L.R. 898;
    The Times, May 9, 1996, CA 14–42, 14–43
Adams (Denis John) (No.2) [1998] 1 Cr.App.R. 377; *The Times*, November
    3, 1997, CA 14–42
Adams (Junior Barrington) [1994] R.T.R. 220; [1993] Crim.L.R. 525; *The
    Times*, January 26, 1993, CA 16–03
Adams (Mark Barry) (1992) 13 Cr.App.R. (S.) 180, CA 5–18
Adams (Peter) and Robinson (Michael) [1997] Crim.L.R. 292, CA 12–08
Adams v Lloyd (1858) H. & N. 351 11–06
Adel Muhammed El Dabbah v Att-Gen of Palestine [1944] A.C. 156, PC
    (Pal) 19–01
Agar (Vincent Raymond) [1990] 2 All E.R. 442; (1990) 90 Cr.App.R. 318;
    154 J.P. 89; [1990] Crim.L.R. 183; 139 N.L.J. 1116, CA 12–07
Aickles (1784) 1 Leach 294 3–13
Air Canada v Secretary of State for Trade (No.2) [1983] 2 A.C. 394; [1983]
    2 W.L.R. 494; [1983] 1 All E.R. 910, HL 12–12
Aitken (Ian Murray) (1992) 94 Cr.App.R. 85, CA 2–25
Ajodha v Trinidad and Tobago [1982] A.C. 204; [1981] 3 W.L.R. 1; [1981]
    2 All E.R. 193; 73 Cr.App.R. 129; [1981] Crim.L.R. 555; 125 S.J. 305,
    PC (Trin) 9–49, 16–08
Ajula [1998] 2 Cr.App.R. 16, CA 13–24
Akaidere [1990] Crim.L.R. 808, CA 14–09
Akhtar v Grout (1998) 162 J.P. 714; 162 J.P.N. 786, QBD 6–13

Alath Construction Ltd and Brightman [1990] 1 W.L.R. 1255; 154 J.P. 911; 60 P. & C.R. 533; [1991] 1 P.L.R. 25; [1991] 1 E.G.L.R. 285; [1990] Crim.L.R. 516; 154 J.P.N. 505; 134 S.J. 735, CA 4–23
Albarus and James [1989] Crim.L.R. 905, CA 2–06
Alconbury v Secretary of State for the Environment [2001] 2 W.L.R. 1389 13–06
Algar (Reginald Horace) [1954] 1 Q.B. 279; [1953] 3 W.L.R. 1007; [1953] 2 All E.R. 1381; 37 Cr.App.R. 200; 118 J.P. 56; 97 S.J. 833, CCA .. 17–34
Ali [2001] 6 *Archbold News* 2, CA 11–22
Ali (Maqsud) and Hussain (Ashiq) [1966] 1 Q.B. 688; [1965] 3 W.L.R. 229; [1965] 2 All E.R. 464; 49 Cr.App.R. 230; 129 J.P. 396; 109 S.J. 331, CCA 2–09, 2–11, 2–12, 2–17, 2–20, 2–30, 10–23
Alladice (Colin Carlton) (1988) 87 Cr.App.R. 380; [1988] Crim.L.R. 608; 138 N.L.J. Rep. 141; *The Times*, May 11, 1988, CA 9–26, 9–30, 9–33, 9–34, 10–21
Allen [1992] Crim.L.R. 297, CA 9–52
Allen (Cynthia) [1995] Crim.L.R. 643, CA 14–29
Allen (Richard William) [1996] Crim.L.R. 426, CA 14–36
Allen v Ireland; sub nom. Allan v Ireland [1984] 1 W.L.R. 903; 79 Cr.App.R. 206; 148 J.P. 545; [1984] Crim.L.R. 500; 81 L.S.G. 2618; 128 S.J. 482, Dc 14–49
Alliance & Leicester Building Society v Ghahremani [1992] R.V.R. 198; 142 N.L.J. 313; *The Times*, March 19, 1992, Ch D 3–02
Amado-Taylor [2000] 2 Cr.App.R. 189 16–16
Anastasiou (Michael) [1998] Crim.L.R. 67, CA 14–17, 14–25
Anderson (1930) 21 Cr.App.R. 178 .... 16–06, 21–25
Anderson [1995] Crim.L.R. 831, CA 19–01
Anderson (James) [1972] 1 Q.B. 304; [1971] 3 W.L.R. 939; [1971] 3 All E.R. 1152; 56 Cr.App.R. 115; [1972] Crim.L.R. 40; 115 S.J. 847, CA .. 6–04, 6–22
Anderson v Secretary of State for the Home Department; sub nom. R. v Secretary of State for the Home Department Ex p. Anderson; R. v Secretary of State for the Home Department Ex p. Taylor [2002] UKHL 46; [2003] 1 A.C. 837; [2002] 3 W.L.R. 1800; [2002] 4 All E.R. 1089; [2003] 1 Cr.App.R. 32; [2003] H.R.L.R. 7; [2003] U.K.H.R.R. 112; 13 B.H.R.C. 450; 100(3) L.S.G. 31; 146 S.J.L.B. 272; *The Times*, November 26, 2002; *Independent*, November 27, 2002, HL 13–06
Anderson (Rupert) v R. [1972] A.C. 100; [1971] 3 W.L.R. 718; [1971] 3 All E.R. 768; 115 S.J. 791, PC (Jam) 6–43
Andover Justices Ex p. Rhodes [1980] Crim.L.R. 644, DC 3–17
Andrews (Donald Joseph) [1987] A.C. 281; [1987] 2 W.L.R. 413; [1987] 1 All E.R. 513; 84 Cr.App.R. 382; [1987] Crim.L.R. 487; 151 J.P.N. 254, HL 8–52, 8–53, 8–54, 8–55, 8–56
Angeli (Solon Lucien) [1978] 3 All E.R. 950; 68 Cr.App.R. 32; [1979] Crim.L.R. 388; 122 S.J. 591, CA 4–48
Antrim Justices (1895) 2 I.R. 603 5–10
Apicella (Alfred Robert) (1986) 82 Cr.App.R. 295; [1986] Crim.L.R. 238, CA 10–07
Argent (Brian) [1997] 2 Cr.App.R. 27; 161 J.P. 190; [1997] Crim.L.R. 346; 161 J.P.N. 260; *The Times*, December 19, 1996, CA 11–23
Arif, *The Times*, June 17, 1993 20–24
Arthurs (John Edward) v Att-Gen of Northern Ireland (1971) 55 Cr.App.R. 161; 114 S.J. 824, HL 14–03
Ashford Ex p. Hilden [1993] Q.B. 555; [1993] 2 W.L.R. 529; [1993] 2 All E.R. 154; 96 Cr.App.R. 92; 156 J.P. 869; [1992] Crim.L.R. 879; [1993] C.O.D. 29; 156 J.P.N. 636, DC 8–27, 8–28

Aspinall (Paul James) [1999] 2 Cr.App.R. 115; 49 B.M.L.R. 82; [1999]
   Crim.L.R. 741; 96(7) L.S.G. 35; *The Times*, February 4, 1999, CA ..   9–22
Associated Provincial Picture Houses Ltd v Wednesbury Corp. [1948] 1 K.B.
   223; [1947] 2 All E.R. 680; 63 T.L.R. 623; 112 J.P. 55; 45 L.G.R. 635;
   [1948] L.J.R. 190; 177 L.T. 641; 92 S.J. 26, CA 15–11
Ataou (Yiannis) [1988] Q.B. 798; [1988] 2 W.L.R. 1147; [1988] 2 All E.R.
   321; 87 Cr.App.R. 210; 152 J.P. 201; [1988] Crim.L.R. 461, CA 11–32
Atkinson (1934) 24 Cr.App.R. 123 15–03
Attard (Anthony) (1959) 43 Cr.App.R. 90, CCC 19–34
Att-Gen v Briant (1846) 15 M. & W. 169 12–02
Att-Gen v Clough [1963] 1 Q.B. 773; [1963] 2 W.L.R. 343; [1963] 1 All
   E.R. 420; 107 S.J. 96, QBD 11–01, 11–37, 11–38
Att-Gen v Guardian Newspapers Ltd, Observer Ltd and Times Newspapers
   Ltd (No.2) [1990] 1 A.C. 109; [1988] 3 W.L.R. 776; [1988] 3 All E.R.
   545; [1989] 2 F.S.R. 181; 85(42) L.S.G. 45; 138 N.L.J. Rep. 296; 132
   S.J. 1496; *The Times*, October 14, 1988; *Independent*, October 14,
   1988, HL 13–02
Att-Gen v Hitchcock (1847) 1 Ex. 91 .... 21–28, 21–30
Att-Gen v Le Merchant (1772) 2 T.R. 201   3–12
Att-Gen v Lundin (1982) 75 Cr.App.R. 90; [1982] Crim.L.R. 296, DC ... 11–39
Att-Gen v Mulholland and Foster [1963] 2 Q.B. 477; [1963] 2 W.L.R. 658;
   [1963] 1 All E.R. 767; 107 S.J. 154, CA 11–37, 11–38
Att-Gen v Radloff (1854) 10 Ex. 84 11–04
Att-Gen of the Cayman Islands v Roberts [2002] UKPC 18; [2002] 1 W.L.R.
   1842; [2002] 2 Cr.App.R. 28; 146 S.J.L.B. 93, PC (CI)   5–08
Att-Gen of South Australia v Brown [1960] A.C. 432; [1960] 2 W.L.R. 588;
   [1960] 1 All E.R. 734; 44 Cr.App.R. 100; 104 S.J. 268, PC (Aus)   6–18
Att-Gen's Guidelines: Disclosure of Information to the Defence in Cases to
   be Tried on Indictment (1982) 74 Cr.App.R. 302 ...... 12–03, 18–06, 18–08,
                                                                   18–11, 18–12, 18–24
Att-Gen's Reference (No.3 of 1977), Re [1978] 1 W.L.R. 1123; [1978] 3 All
   E.R. 1166; 67 Cr.App.R. 393; 122 S.J. 641, CA   6–23
Att-Gen's Reference (No.3 of 1979), Re (1979) 69 Cr.App.R. 411; [1979]
   Crim.L.R. 786; 123 S.J. 70, CA 20–28, 20–30, 20–31
Att-Gen's Reference (No.3 of 1999), Re; sub nom. R. v B [2001] 2 A.C. 91;
   [2001] 2 W.L.R. 56; [2001] 1 All E.R. 577; [2001] 1 Cr.App.R. 34;
   [2001] H.R.L.R. 16; [2001] Crim.L.R. 394; 98(7) L.S.G. 39; 150 N.L.J.
   1889; 145 S.J.L.B. 8, HL 10–20, 10–21
Att-Gen's Reference (No.3 of 2000) [2001] 2 Cr.App.R. 472 10–16
Att-Gen's Reference (No.3 of 2000), Re; sub nom. G (Entrapment); Loosley
   (Grant Spencer) (No.2); Loosely (Grant Spencer) [2001] UKHL 53;
   [2001] 1 W.L.R. 2060; [2001] 4 All E.R. 897; [2002] 1 Cr.App.R. 29;
   [2002] H.R.L.R. 8; [2002] U.K.H.R.R. 333; [2002] Crim.L.R. 301;
   98(45) L.S.G. 25; 145 S.J.L.B. 245, HL 10–16, 10–27
Att-Gen's Reference (No.7 of 2000), Re [2001] EWCA Crim 888; [2001] 1
   W.L.R. 1879; [2001] 2 Cr.App.R. 19; [2001] H.R.L.R. 41; [2001]
   B.P.I.R. 953; [2001] Crim.L.R. 736; 98(22) L.S.G. 35; 145 S.J.L.B. 109;
   The Times, April 12, 2001, CA 11–11, 11–12
Att-Gen's Reference (Criminal Justice Act 1977, s.36) (No.2 of 2002),
   unreported, October 7, 2002 14–38
Att-Gen's Reference (No.4 of 2002), Re [2003] EWCA Crim 762; [2003] 3
   W.L.R. 1153; [2004] 1 All E.R. 1; [2003] 2 Cr.App.R. 22; [2003]
   H.R.L.R. 15; 100(21) L.S.G. 29, CA   4–18

Att-Gen's Reference (No.5 of 2002) [2004] 1 Cr.App.R. 11 2–21
Att-Gen's Reference (No.1 of 2003) [2003] 2 Cr.App.R. 453 8–57
Aves (John Robert) [1950] 2 All E.R. 330; 34 Cr.App.R. 159; 114 J.P. 402;
    48 L.G.R. 495; [1950] W.N. 342; 94 S.J. 475, CCA 1–08, 4–26
Aveson v Kinnaird (1805) 6 East 188 8–59
Aziz (Kazim) [1996] A.C. 41; [1995] 3 W.L.R. 53; [1995] 3 All E.R. 149;
    [1995] 2 Cr.App.R. 478; 159 J.P. 669; [1995] Crim.L.R. 897; 159
    J.P.N. 756; 92(28) L.S.G. 41; 145 N.L.J. 921; [1995] 139 S.J.L.B. 158,
    HL 7–13, 7–15, 7–16, 7–18, 20–18

B [2000] Crim.L.R. 50 18–11
B or D [2001] 2 Cr.App.R. 601 8–22
B (K) [2002] 10 *Archbold News* 1 19–30
B (MT) [2000] Crim.L.R. 181 .... 11–20, 15–12
BT [2002] 1 Cr.App.R. 254 7–81
B v Auckland District Law Society; sub nom. Russell McVeagh McKenzie
    Bartleet & Co. v Auckland District Law Society [2003] UKPC 38;
    [2003] 2 A.C. 736; [2003] 3 W.L.R. 859; 100(26) L.S.G. 38; 147
    S.J.L.B. 627; *The Times*, May 21, 2003, PC (NZ) 11–28
Bacon (1915) 11 Cr.App.R. 90 14–41
Badjan (Keith Kebba) (1966) 50 Cr.App.R. 141; [1966] Crim.L.R. 288; 110
    S.J. 146, CCA 16–15
Bailey [1989] Crim.L.R. 723, CA 7–25
Bailey (Jason Gregory) and Smith (Steven Simon) [1993] 3 All E.R. 513; 97
    Cr.App.R. 365; 143 N.L.J. 579; *The Times*, March 22, 1993; *Inde-*
    pendent, March 29, 1993, CA 10–23
Bailey (Paula) [1995] 2 Cr.App.R. 262; [1995] Crim.L.R. 723, CA 9–57
Bailey (Rodney William) (1978) 66 Cr.App.R. 31, CCA 6–43, 6–44
Bailey v DPP (1999) 163 J.P. 518; 95(31) L.S.G. 36; 142 S.J.L.B. 198, QBD 3–25
Baines [1987] Crim.L.R. 508, CA 17–08
Baldwin (1925) 18 Cr.App.R. 173 21–16
Baldwin [1978] Crim.L.R. 104, CA 19–01, 19–06
Baldwin [1986] Crim.L.R. 681, CA 21–10
Balmforth [1992] Crim.L.R. 825, CA 19–01
Banghera [2001] 1 Cr.App.R. 299 10–20
Barclays Bank plc v Eustice [1995] 1 W.L.R. 1238; [1995] 4 All E.R. 511;
    [1995] B.C.C. 978; [1995] 2 B.C.L.C. 630; 145 N.L.J. 1503; *The Times*,
    August 3, 1995, CA 11–31
Barker (1973) 65 Cr.App.R. 287 16–11
Barking and Dagenham Justices Ex p. DPP (1995) 159 J.P. 373; [1995]
    Crim.L.R. 953; 159 J.P.N. 318; *The Times*, November 22, 1994;
    Independent, November 14, 1994, QBD 16–30
Barnes (Anthony) [1995] 2 Cr.App.R. 491; 139 S.J.L.B. 174; *The Times*,
    July 6, 1995; *Independent*, August 14, 1995, CA 14–05, 14–08
Barnes v Chief Constable of Durham. *See* Barnes v DPP
Barnes v DPP; sub nom. Barnes v Chief Constable of Durham [1997] 2
    Cr.App.R. 505; 162 J.P. 126; 162 J.P.N. 121; *The Times*, May 6, 1997,
    DC 14–14
Barratt (Paul Henry) and Sheehan (Eugene Patrick) [1996] Crim.L.R. 495,
    CA 17–07
Barry (Patrick Valentine) (1992) 95 Cr.App.R. 384, CA 9–21
Barsoum [1994] Crim.L.R. 194 16–18

Barton [1973] 1 W.L.R. 115; [1972] 2 All E.R. 1192; [1974] Crim.L.R. 43;
    117 S.J. 72, Crown Ct 11–32
Bashir (Mohammed) and Manzur (Mohammed) [1969] 1 W.L.R. 1303;
    [1969] 3 All E.R. 692; 54 Cr.App.R. 1; 133 J.P. 687; 113 S.J. 703,
    Assizes 21–24
Baskerville [1916] 2 K.B. 658, CCA 14–08, 15–01, 15–06
Bass [1992] Crim.L.R. 647, CA 16–15
Bass (Ronald Dennis) [1953] 1 Q.B. 680; [1953] 2 W.L.R. 825; [1953] 1 All
    E.R. 1064; 37 Cr.App.R. 51; 117 J.P. 246; 97 S.J. 282, CCA 20–29,
                                                                      20–32, 20–34
Bastin v Carew (1825) Ry. & M. 127 21–12
Bath (1990) 154 J.P. 849; [1990] Crim.L.R. 716; 154 J.P.N. 596, CA 14–05
Bathurst (Eric Wilfred) [1968] 2 Q.B. 99; [1968] 2 W.L.R. 1092; [1968] 1
    All E.R. 1175; 52 Cr.App.R. 251; 112 S.J. 272, CA 17–25
Batley v DPP, *The Times*, March 5, 1998, QBD 9–43
Bayliss (Roy Alfred) (1994) 98 Cr.App.R. 235; 157 J.P. 1062; [1994]
    Crim.L.R. 687; 157 J.P.N. 522; *The Times*, March 16, 1993, CA 9–28
Beard (Jason Robert) [1998] Crim.L.R. 585, CA 7–77
Beattie (Alan James) (1989) 89 Cr.App.R. 302; *The Times*, February 15,
    1989, CA 20–10, 21–26, 21–33
Beck (Barry Alexander) [1982] 1 W.L.R. 461; [1982] 1 All E.R. 807; 74
    Cr.App.R. 221; [1982] Crim.L.R. 586, CA 15–13, 15–15, 15–16
Beckford (Junior) (1992) 94 Cr.App.R. 43; [1991] Crim.L.R. 918; *The
    Times*, June 12, 1991; *Independent*, June 21, 1991; *Guardian*, June 25,
    1991, CA 16–24
Beckford and Daley [1991] Crim.L.R. 833; *The Times*, April 3, 1991, CA 9–03
Beckles (Keith Anderson) and Montague (Rudolph Leopold) [1999]
    Crim.L.R. 148, CA 11–17, 14–05
Bedi (Balwinder Singh) and Bedi (Kamal) (1992) 95 Cr.App.R. 21; [1992]
    Crim.L.R. 299, CA 8–35, 16–05
Bedingfield (1878) 14 Cox C.C. 341 8–53
Beech v Jones (1848) 5 C. B. 696 20–32
Bell [1967] Crim.L.R. 545; 117 N.L.J. 706, CA 4–44
Bellamy (John Alfred) (1986) 82 Cr.App.R. 222; [1986] Crim.L.R. 54, CA 17–06
Bellis (Ivor Edward) [1966] 1 W.L.R. 234; [1966] 1 All E.R. 552n; 50
    Cr.App.R. 88; 130 J.P. 170; 110 S.J. 169, CCA 7–13
Belmarsh Magistrates' Court Ex p. Gilligan [1998] 1 Cr.App.R. 14; [1997]
    C.O.D. 342, DC 8–28
Benedetto (Alexander) and Labrador (William) v R. [2003] UKPC 27;
    [2003] 1 W.L.R. 1545; [2003] 2 Cr.App.R. 25; 100(24) L.S.G. 35; 147
    S.J.L.B. 539; *The Times*, April 28, 2003, PC (BVI) 9–24, 15–17
Benjamin (1913) 8 Cr.App.R. 146 20–11
Bennett (1989) 153 J.P. 317; [1988] Crim.L.R. 686; 153 J.P.N. 434, CA . 5–30
Bennett v Brown (1980) 71 Cr.App.R. 109, DC 16–31
Bentley (Derek) [2001] 1 Cr.App.R. 21; [1999] Crim.L.R. 330; *The Times*,
    July 31, 1998, CA 4–03, 4–40, 16–16
Bentum (1989) 153 J.P. 538; 153 J.P.N. 611, CA 2–28, 6–41
Bernard (1858) 1 F. & F. 240 21–27
Berrada (Rachid) (1990) 91 Cr.App.R. 131; *The Times*, February 20, 1989,
    CA 7–23, 16–15
Berriman (1854) 6 Cox C.C. 388 9–60
Berryman v Wise (1792) 4 Term Rep. 366 5–05
Bessela v Stern (1876–77) L.R. 2 C.P.D. 265, CA 9–07

Bethall, 2000, Crown Ct 17–11
Bethelmie (Luke Davis), *The Times*, November 27, 1995, CA 10–03
Betts (Raymond Christopher) and Hall (John Anthony) [2001] EWCA Crim
    224; [2001] 2 Cr.App.R. 16; [2001] Crim.L.R. 754, CA 11–20
Beveridge (Thomas Henry) (1987) 85 Cr.App.R. 255; [1987] Crim.L.R.
    401, CA 10–31, 14–29, 16–07
Bexley Justices Ex p. King [1980] R.T.R. 49, DC 19–05
Bey (Mehmet) [1994] 1 W.L.R. 39; [1993] 3 All E.R. 253; 98 Cr.App.R.
    158; 143 N.L.J. 639; *The Times*, March 18, 1993, CA 16–17
Bingham (Graham Carlo) and Cooke (Samuel David) [1999] 1 W.L.R. 598;
    [1999] N.I. 118; 96(15) L.S.G. 29; *The Times*, March 15, 1999, HL
    (NI) 17–12, 21–15
Birch (1924) 18 Cr.App.R. 26 .... 21–12, 21–26
Birchall (Keith) [1999] Crim.L.R. 311; *The Times*, February 10, 1998,
    CA 13–17, 17–22, 17–24
Bircham [1972] Crim.L.R. 430, CA 21–16
Bird v Adams [1972] Crim.L.R. 174, DC 9–59
Birks (Dene) [2002] EWCA Crim 3091; [2003] 2 Cr.App.R. 7; [2003]
    Crim.L.R. 401, CA 20–06
Birmingham Justices Ex p. Shields (1994) 158 J.P. 845; 158 J.P.N. 666; *The
    Times*, August 3, 1994, DC 17–30
Bishop (Roger Anthony) [1975] Q.B. 274; [1974] 3 W.L.R. 308; [1974] 2
    All E.R. 1206; 59 Cr.App.R. 246; [1974] Crim.L.R. 546; 118 S.J. 515,
    CA 7–66
Black (1922) 16 Cr.App.R. 118 8–59
Blackburn (Albert Raymond) (No.1) (1955) 39 Cr.App.R. 84, CCA 4–05
Blackledge (William Stuart) (No.2) [1996] 1 Cr.App.R. 326; 8 Admin. L.R.
    361; *The Times*, November 8, 1995; *Independent*, November 8, 1995,
    CA 18–29
Blackstock (Stuart) (1980) 70 Cr.App.R. 34, CA 7–52
Blake and Austin v DPP (1993) 97 Cr.App.R. 169; [1993] Crim.L.R. 283;
    The Times, November 26, 1992, DC 12–10
Blake and Tye (1844) 6 Q.B. 126 8–64
Blastland (Douglas) [1986] A.C. 41; [1985] 3 W.L.R. 345; [1985] 2 All E.R.
    1095; 81 Cr.App.R. 266; [1985] Crim.L.R. 727, HL 8–60
Bleakley [1993] Crim.L.R. 203, CA 14–35, 14–36
Blenkinsop (David Richard) [1995] 1 Cr.App.R. 7, CA 2–14, 14–38
Blick (Brian Anthony) (1966) 50 Cr.App.R. 280; [1966] Crim.L.R. 508; 110
    S.J. 545, CCA 5–10
Bliss (1837) 7 A. & E. 550 8–58
Blunt v Park Lane Hotel Ltd [1942] 2 K.B. 253, CA 11–02
Boal (William Gerald) [1965] 1 Q.B. 402; [1964] 3 W.L.R. 593; [1964] 3
    All E.R. 269; 48 Cr.App.R. 342; 128 J.P. 573; 108 S.J. 694, CCA ... 17–13
Boardman v DPP. *See* DPP v Boardman
Bone (Michael Edward) [1968] 1 W.L.R. 983; [1968] 2 All E.R. 644; 52
    Cr.App.R. 546; 132 J.P. 420; 112 S.J. 480, CA 4–27
Bonnick (Derek Denton) (1978) 66 Cr.App.R. 266; [1978] Crim.L.R. 246;
    121 S.J. 79, CA 4–30
Bonython (1984) 38 S.A.S.R. 45 6–39
Booth (Alan William) (1982) 74 Cr.App.R. 123; [1981] Crim.L.R. 700,
    CA 9–48, 21–09, 21–11, 21–12, 21–14, 21–24, 21–34
Borrett (1833) 6 C. & P. 124 5–05
Borthwick v Vickers [1973] R.T.R. 390; [1973] Crim.L.R. 317, Dc 5–11

Bottomley, Ex p. [1909] 2 K.B. 14, KBD 21–07

Bow Street Magistrates' Court Ex p. Choudhury [1991] 1 Q.B. 429; [1990]
3 W.L.R. 986; 91 Cr.App.R. 393; [1990] Crim.L.R. 711; [1990]
C.O.D. 305; 87(24) L.S.G. 40; 140 N.L.J. 782, QBD 13–02

Bowden (Brian Thomas) [1999] 1 W.L.R. 823; [1999] 4 All E.R. 43; [1999]
2 Cr.App.R. 176; 163 J.P. 337; 163 J.P.N. 387; 96(10) L.S.G. 28; 143
S.J.L.B. 73; *The Times*, February 25, 1999, CA 11–29

Bowers (Victor John) (1999) 163 J.P. 33; [1998] Crim.L.R. 817; 162 J.P.N.
1006; *Independent*, March 24, 1998, CA 11–20

Bowman v DPP (1990) 154 J.P. 524; [1991] R.T.R. 263; [1990] Crim.L.R.
600; 154 J.P.N. 441, DC 5–11, 5–12

Boyes (1861) 1 B. & S. 311 .... 11–06, 11–07

Boyle v Wiseman (1855) 11 Exch. 306 3–06

Bozkurt v Thames Magistrates' Court [2001] EWHC Admin 400; [2002]
R.T.R. 15; *The Times*, June 26, 2001; *Independent*, July 2, 2001; *Daily
Telegraph*, May 22, 2001, DC 11–29

Bracegirdle v Apter (1951) 49 L.G.R. 790 3–13

Bracegirdle v Oxley [1947] K.B. 349; [1947] 1 All E.R. 126; 63 T.L.R. 98;
111 J.P. 131; [1947] L.J.R. 815; 176 L.T. 187; 91 S.J. 27, KBD 16–24,
16–31

Bracewell (Michael Geoffrey) (1979) 68 Cr.App.R. 44; [1979] Crim.L.R.
111, CA 4–37

Bradshaw (Colin) (1986) 82 Cr.App.R. 79; [1985] Crim.L.R. 733, CA 6–41,
8–59

Braham v DPP (1995) 159 J.P. 527; [1996] R.T.R. 30; *The Times*, December
29, 1994, QBD 10–29

Braithwaite (Frank Wilson) and Girdham (Ralph) [1983] 1 W.L.R. 385;
[1983] 2 All E.R. 87; 77 Cr.App.R. 34; 147 J.P. 301; [1983] Crim.L.R.
468, CA 4–12

Brannan v Peek [1948] 1 K.B. 68; [1947] 2 All E.R. 572; 63 T.L.R. 592; 112
J.P. 10; 45 L.G.R. 654; [1948] L.J.R. 405; 91 S.J. 654, DC 10–07

Brannigan v Davison [1997] A.C. 238; [1996] 3 W.L.R. 859; 2 B.H.R.C.
395; 140 S.J.L.B. 231, PC (NZ) 11–02

Brasier (1779) 1 Leach 199 .... 17–04, 20–04, 20–05

Bratty v Att-Gen of Northern Ireland [1963] A.C. 386; [1961] 3 W.L.R.
965; [1961] 3 All E.R. 523; 46 Cr.App.R. 1; 105 S.J. 865, HL 4–09,
4–27, 4–30, 6–18

Bray (Robin John) (1989) 88 Cr.App.R. 354; 153 J.P. 11; [1988] Crim.L.R.
829; 153 J.P.N. 43, CA 8–24, 8–35

Breslin (Martin Anthony) (1985) 80 Cr.App.R. 226, CA 14–08

Brewster v Sewell (1820) 3 B. & Ald. 296 3–12

Briggs (1930) 22 Cr.App.R. 68 19–05

Bright v Central Criminal Court. *See* Central Criminal Court Ex p. Bright

Brine [1992] Crim.L.R. 122, CA 9–26

Briscoe v Briscoe [1968] P. 501; [1966] 2 W.L.R. 205; [1966] 1 All E.R.
465; 130 J.P. 124; 109 S.J. 996; *The Times*, November 17, 1965, DC 19–04

British Airways Board v Taylor [1976] 1 W.L.R. 13; [1976] 1 All E.R. 65;
[1976] 1 Lloyd's Rep. 167; 62 Cr.App.R. 174; [1977] Crim.L.R. 372;
18 Man. Law 146; 120 S.J. 7; *The Times*, December 11, 1975, HL .. 16–03

British Steel Corp. v Granada Television Ltd [1981] A.C. 1096; [1980] 3
W.L.R. 774; [1981] 1 All E.R. 417; 124 S.J. 812, HL .. 11–37, 11–38, 12–06

Britton (Stanley Richard) [1987] 1 W.L.R. 539; [1987] 2 All E.R. 412; 85
Cr.App.R. 14; 151 J.P. 473; [1987] Crim.L.R. 490, CA 20–33

Broadhurst v R. [1964] A.C. 441; [1964] 2 W.L.R. 38; [1964] 1 All E.R.
111; 107 S.J. 1037, PC (M) 16–17
Bromley Justices Ex p. Haymills (Contractors) Ltd [1984] Crim.L.R. 235   4–03
Bromley Magistrates' Court Ex p. Smith; sub nom. Bromley Justices Ex p.
Wilkins; Wells Street Stipendiary Magistrate Ex p. King [1995] 1
W.L.R. 944; [1995] 4 All E.R. 146; [1995] 2 Cr.App.R. 285; 159 J.P.
251; [1995] Crim.L.R. 248; [1995] C.O.D. 257; 159 J.P.N. 179; 92(2)
L.S.G. 36; 139 S.J.L.B. 16, DC 18–08
Brook, *The Times*, March 31, 2003 21–16
Brophy (Edward Manning) [1982] A.C. 476; [1981] 3 W.L.R. 103; [1981] 2
All E.R. 705; 73 Cr.App.R. 287; [1981] Crim.L.R. 831; 125 S.J. 479,
HL 9–54, 16–08
Brower (Lionel) [1995] Crim.L.R. 746, CA 16–15
Brown (1960) 44 Cr.App.R. 181 7–66
Brown [1991] Crim.L.R. 368, CA 14–25
Brown (Daniel William) (1971) 55 Cr.App.R. 478; 115 S.J. 708, CA .. 4–12, 4–46
Brown (Daniel) and Brown (Matthew) [1997] 1 Cr.App.R. 112; [1996]
Crim.L.R. 659, CA 19–02
Brown (Davina) [2001] EWCA Crim 961; [2002] 1 Cr.App.R. 5; [2001]
Crim.L.R. 675; *The Times*, May 1, 2001, CA
Brown (Jamie) [1998] Crim.L.R. 196; *The Times*, December 13, 1997, CA 16–10
Brown (Milton) [1998] 2 Cr.App.R. 364; *The Times*, May 7, 1998; *Inde-
pendent*, May 8, 1998, CA 21–18
Brown (Richard Bartholomew) and Daley (Desmond Roy) (1988) 87
Cr.App.R. 52; [1988] Crim.L.R. 239, CA 12–11
Brown (Winston) [1998] A.C. 367; [1997] 3 W.L.R. 447; [1997] 3 All E.R.
769; [1998] 1 Cr.App.R. 66; 161 J.P. 625; [1998] Crim.L.R. 60; 161
J.P.N. 838; 94(33) L.S.G. 28; 147 N.L.J. 1149; 141 S.J.L.B. 198; *The
Times*, July 25, 1997; *Independent*, October 15, 1997, HL; affirming
[1994] 1 W.L.R. 1599; [1995] 1 Cr.App.R. 191; 91(31) L.S.G. 36; 138
S.J.L.B. 146, CA 13–22, 18–07, 18–08
Brown and Routh [1983] Crim.L.R. 38, CA 17–36
Brown v Dunn (1869) 6 R. 67 21–16
Brown v Stott; sub nom. Stott (Procurator Fiscal) v Brown [2003] 1 A.C.
681; [2001] 2 W.L.R. 817; [2001] 2 All E.R. 97; 2001 S.C. (P.C.) 43;
2001 S.L.T. 59; 2001 S.C.C.R. 62; [2001] R.T.R. 11; [2001] H.R.L.R.
9; [2001] U.K.H.R.R. 333; 11 B.H.R.C. 179; 3 L.G.L.R. 24; 145
S.J.L.B. 100; 2000 G.W.D. 40–1513, PC (Sc) 4–14, 10–29, 11–11,
11–12, 11–13
Brown v Woodman (1834) 6 C. & P. 206 3–07
Browne (1943) 29 Cr.App.R. 106 19–42
Browning (Edward Owen) (1992) 94 Cr.App.R. 109; [1992] R.T.R. 49; *The
Times*, June 12, 1991, CA 14–12
Browning (Edward) [1995] Crim.L.R. 227; *Independent*, May 17, 1994;
Guardian, May 20, 1994, CA 21–03
Browning v JWH Watson (Rochester) Ltd [1953] 1 W.L.R. 1172; [1953] 2
All E.R. 775; 117 J.P. 479; 51 L.G.R. 597; 97 S.J. 591, DC 10–07
Brushett [2001] Crim.L.R. 471 12–17
Brutus v Cozens [1973] A.C. 854; [1972] 3 W.L.R. 521; [1972] 2 All E.R.
1297; 56 Cr.App.R. 799; [1973] Crim.L.R. 56; 116 S.J. 647, HL 16–02,
16–31
Bryant (Horace Henry) and Dickson (Victor Richard) (1946) 31 Cr.App.R.
146, CCA 18–06

Bryce (Paul Andrew) [1992] 4 All E.R. 567; 95 Cr.App.R. 320; [1992]
  Crim.L.R. 728; 142 N.L.J. 1161, CA 9–40, 9–44
Buchan (Henry Femister)[1964] 1 W.L.R. 365; [1964] 1 All E.R. 502; 48
  Cr.App.R. 126; 128 J.P. 239; 108 S.J. 121, CCA 10–23
Buckingham (Michael) (1994) 99 Cr.App.R. 303; [1994] Crim.L.R. 283,
  CA 5–32
Buckley (1873) 13 Cox C.C. 293 8–60
Buckley (Robert John) (1999) 163 J.P. 561; 163 J.P.N. 672; 96(23) L.S.G.
  34; The Times, May 12, 1999, CA 14–41
Bullard v R. [1957] A.C. 635; [1957] 3 W.L.R. 656; 42 Cr.App.R. 1; 121
  J.P. 576; 101 S.J. 797, PC (Trin) 4–27, 4–28
Bullivant v Att-Gen of Victoria [1901] A.C. 196, HL 11–30
Burge (Sean Gary), Hurst (Carl) and Pegg (David Graham) [1996] 1
  Cr.App.R. 163; 139 S.J.L.B. 99; The Times, April 28, 1995, CA 16–19,
                                                                        16–20
Burgess (Henry George) [1968] 2 Q.B. 112; [1968] 2 W.L.R. 1209; [1968] 2
  All E.R. 54n; 52 Cr.App.R. 258; 132 J.P. 314; 112 S.J. 272, CA 9–58
Burgess v Bennett (1872) 20 W.R. 720 20–32
Burke and Kelly (1847) 2 Cox C.c. 295 14–33
Burnal and Moore, April 28, 1997, PC 6–26
Burrell, October 3, 2002, CCC 12–14
Burrough v Martin (1809) 2 Camp. 112 .... 20–28, 20–31
Burrows [2000] Crim.L.R. 48 15–18
Bursill v Tanner (1885) 16 Q.B.D. 1 11–28
Burton v Gilbert (1983) 147 J.P. 441; [1984] R.T.R. 162, DC 15–04
Burton v Plummer (1834) 2 A. & E. 341 20–30
Burut v Public Prosecutor of Brunei [1995] 2 A.C. 579; [1995] 3 W.L.R. 16;
  [1995] 4 All E.R. 300; 92(24) L.S.G. 38; 139 S.J.L.B. 116; The Times,
  April 28, 1995, PC (Bru) 9–17
Busby (Charles Jonathan) (1982) 75 Cr.App.R. 79; [1982] Crim.L.R. 232,
  CA 21–28, 21–29
Butler (Diana Helen) [1999] Crim.L.R. 835, CA 7–13
Butler v Board of Trade [1971] Ch. 680; [1970] 3 W.L.R. 822; [1970] 3 All
  E.R. 593; 114 S.J. 604, Ch D 11–30, 11–35, 11–36
Butterwasser (Abraham) [1948] 1 K.B. 4; [1947] 2 All E.R. 415; 63 T.L.R.
  463; 32 Cr.App.R. 81; 111 J.P. 527; 91 S.J. 586, CCA 7–09, 7–11, 7–14
Buzalek and Schiffer [1991] Crim.L.R. 115; [1991] Crim.L.R. 116, CA ... 7–16
Byrne [2002] Cr.App.R. 311, CA 1–14
Byrne (Patrick Joseph) [1960] 2 Q.B. 396; [1960] 3 W.L.R. 440; [1960] 3
  All E.R. 1; 44 Cr.App.R. 246; 104 S.J. 645, CCA 6–18
Byrne and Trump [1987] Crim.L.R. 689, CA 14–37
Byron (Darren), The Times, March 10, 1999, Ca 14–49

C (A Minor) (Care Proceedings: Disclosure), Re; sub nom. EC (A Minor)
  (Care Proceedings: Disclosure), Re; EC (Disclosure of Material), Re
  [1997] Fam. 76; [1997] 2 W.L.R. 322; [1996] 2 F.L.R. 725; [1996] 3
  F.C.R. 521; [1997] Fam. Law 160; The Times, October 22, 1996, CA 11–09
CAZ (1990) 91 Cr.App.R. 203, CA 17–05
Cain (Jason Sylvester) [1994] 1 W.L.R. 1449; [1994] 2 All E.R. 398; 99
  Cr.App.R. 208, CA 7–20
Caird (1970) 54 Cr.App.R. 499; [1970] Crim.L.R. 656; 114 S.J. 652; The
  Times, August 20, 1970, CA 14–13, 14–15
Cairns (Alison Louise), Zaidi (Samina)and Chaudhary (Abdul Qavai) [2002]

EWCA Crim 2838; [2003] 1 W.L.R. 796; [2003] 1 Cr.App.R. 38; [2003] Crim.L.R. 403; 100(3) L.S.G. 31; *The Times*, December 2, 2002, CA 15–17, 18–18

Calcraft v Guest [1898] 1 Q.B. 759, CA 11–36

Calder & Boyars Ltd [1969] 1 Q.B. 151; [1968] 3 W.L.R. 974; [1968] 3 All E.R. 644; 52 Cr.App.R. 706; 133 J.P. 20; 112 S.J. 688, CA 6–04, 6–22

Caldwell (Paul) and Dixon (Terence) (1994) 99 Cr.App.R. 73; [1993] Crim.L.R. 862, CA 2–37, 14–38

Callaghan (Brian Terence) (1979) 69 Cr.App.R. 88, CA 21–17

Callender (David Peter) [1998] Crim.L.R. 337, CA 8–55

Callis v Gunn [1964] 1 Q.B. 495; [1963] 3 W.L.R. 931; [1963] 3 All E.R. 677; 48 Cr.App.R. 36; 128 J.P. 41; 107 S.J. 831, DC 10–06

Calvert v Flower (1836) 7 C. & P. 386 21–21

Camelleri [1922] 2 K.B. 122, CCA 20–04

Camelot Group plc v Centaur Communications Ltd [1999] Q.B. 124; [1998] 2 W.L.R. 379; [1998] 1 All E.R. 251; [1998] I.R.L.R. 80; [1998] E.M.L.R. 1; 94(43) L.S.G. 30; 147 N.L.J. 1618; 142 S.J.L.B. 19, CA 11–37

Cameron (Leon) [2001] EWCA Crim 562; [2001] Crim.L.R. 587; *The Times*, May 3, 2001, CA 16–04, 16–09, 19–07

Campbell (Oliver Keith) [1995] 1 Cr.App.R. 522; [1995] Crim.L.R. 157, CA 9–56, 9–57

Campbell (Stephen) [1996] Crim.L.R. 500, CA 14–12

Campbell v Wallsend Slipway & Engineering Co. Ltd [1978] I.C.R. 1015; [1977] Crim.L.R. 351; 121 S.J. 334, DC 5–05

Canale (Ramon Michael) [1990] 2 All E.R. 187; 91 Cr.App.R. 1; 154 J.P. 286; [1990] Crim.L.R. 329; 154 J.P.N. 45, CA 9–31, 9–37

Canning (Derek William) [1996] 2 Cr.App.R. (S.) 202, CA 4–24

Cannings (Angela) [2004] EWCA Crim 1; [2004] 1 All E.R. 725; [2004] 1 F.C.R. 193; (2004) 101(5) L.S.G. 27; (2004) 148 S.J.L.B. 114; *The Times*, January 23, 2004 6–12

Cannon (Terence Francis) (1986) 82 Cr.App.R. 286, CA 7–53

Cape (Jason Bradley), Jackson (Stephen Anthony) and Gardner (David Kevin) [1996] 1 Cr.App.R. 191; 146 N.L.J. 918, CA 14–11

Carass (Clive Louden) [2001] EWCA Crim 2845; [2002] 1 W.L.R. 1714; [2002] 2 Cr.App.R. 4; [2002] B.P.I.R. 821; 99(9) L.S.G. 28; 146 S.J.L.B. 28, CA 4–16

Carnall (Jason James) [1995] Crim.L.R. 944, CA 8–55

Carr-Briant [1943] K.B. 607, CCA 4–45, 4–46

Carrington (Roger Vincent) (1994) 99 Cr.App.R. 376; [1994] Crim.L.R. 438, CA 8–35

Carroll (Deborah Louise) (1994) 99 Cr.App.R. 381; [1993] Crim.L.R. 613, CA 15–03

Carter (Colin Mark) (1997) 161 J.P. 207; [1997] Crim.L.R. 505; 161 J.P.N. 236; *The Times*, November 14, 1996, CA 7–68

Carter v Eastbourne BC (2000) 164 J.P. 273; [2000] 2 P.L.R. 60; [2000] C.O.D. 263, QBD 5–11

Cartwright (1914) 10 Cr.App.R. 219 14–13

Cascoe (Handel Barrington) [1970] 2 All E.R. 833; 54 Cr.App.R. 401, CA .. 4–27

Case (Matthew) (1992) 13 Cr.App.R. (S.) 20; [1991] Crim.L.R. 192, CA ... 8–19

Case Statements made under s.9 of Criminal Justice Act 1987, Re (1993) 97 Cr.App.R. 417; *The Times*, December 18, 1992, CA 18–02

Cassidy (1858) 1 F. & F. 79 19–01

Castillo (Luis Angel) [1996] 1 Cr.App.R. 438; 140 S.J.L.B. 12; *The Times*,
    November 2, 1995, CA 8–23
Castle [1989] Crim.L.R. 567, CA 5–33
Castle v Cross [1984] 1 W.L.R. 1372; [1985] 1 All E.R. 87; [1985] R.T.R.
    62; [1984] Crim.L.R. 682; 81 L.S.G. 2596; 128 S.J. 855, DC 2–44, 8–75
Castleton (1909) 3 Cr.App.R. 74, CA 14–41
Causley (Russell) [1999] Crim.L.R. 572, CA 15–16, 15–17
Cavanagh (James Michael) and Shaw (William Anthony) [1972] 1 W.L.R.
    676; [1972] 2 All E.R. 704; 56 Cr.App.R. 407; [1972] Crim.L.R. 389;
    116 S.J. 372, CA 19–02
Central Criminal Court Ex p. Bright [2001] 1 W.L.R. 662; [2001] 2 All E.R.
    244; [2001] E.M.L.R. 4; [2000] U.K.H.R.R. 796; [2002] Crim.L.R. 64;
    97(38) L.S.G. 43; *The Times*, July 26, 2000, QBD 11–37
Central Criminal Court Ex p. Garnier [1988] R.T.R. 42 19–37
Chadwick [1998] 7 *Archbold News* 3, CA 17–19
Chalkley (Tony Michael) and Jeffries (Tony Brisbane) [1998] Q.B. 848;
    [1998] 3 W.L.R. 146; [1998] 2 All E.R. 155; [1998] 2 Cr.App.R. 79;
    [1999] Crim.L.R. 214; 95(5) L.S.G. 29; 142 S.J.L.B. 40, CA .. 10–17, 10–19
Challinor (Robert) (1985) 80 Cr.App.R. 253; 149 J.P. 358; [1985] R.T.R.
    373; [1985] Crim.L.R. 53, CA 16–23
Chan Kau (alias Chan Kai) v Queen, The [1955] A.C. 206; [1955] 2 W.L.R.
    192; [1955] 1 All E.R. 266; 99 S.J. 72, PC (HK) 4–07, 4–27
Chan Wei Keung v R. [1967] 2 A.C. 160; [1967] 2 W.L.R. 552; [1967] 1 All
    E.R. 948; 51 Cr.App.R. 257; 111 S.J. 73, PC (HK) 9–58
Chan Wai-Keung v R. [1995] 1 W.L.R. 251; [1995] 2 All E.R. 438; [1995] 2
    Cr.App.R. 194; [1995] Crim.L.R. 566; 139 S.J.L.B. 44; *The Times*,
    December 21, 1994; *Independent*, January 10, 1995, PC (HK) 15–17,
                                                                                    17–14
Chandler (Roy Frank) [1976] 1 W.L.R. 585; [1976] 3 All E.R. 105; 63
    Cr.App.R. 1; [1976] Crim.L.R. 308; 120 S.J. 96, CA 9–08
Chandler (Terence Norman) v DPP [1964] A.C. 763; [1962] 3 W.L.R. 694;
    [1962] 3 All E.R. 142; 46 Cr.App.R. 347; 106 S.J. 588, HL ... 16–15, 16–22
Chapman (1838) 8 C. & P. 558 19–06
Chapman (1911) 7 Cr.App.R. 53 14–22
Chapman [1980] Crim.L.R. 42, CA 19–08
Chapman (David) [1969] 2 Q.B. 436; [1969] 2 W.L.R. 1004; [1969] 2 All
    E.R. 321; 53 Cr.App.R. 336; 133 J.P. 405; 113 S.J. 229, CA 8–04
Chapman v Ingleton (1973) 57 Cr.App.R. 476; [1973] Crim.L.R. 296, DC   8–79
Chapple (1892) 17 Cox 453 8–64
Chard (Peter John) (1972) 56 Cr.App.R. 268, CA 6–04, 6–14
Cheema (Julie Mary) [1994] 1 W.L.R. 147; [1994] 1 All E.R. 639; 98
    Cr.App.R. 195; [1994] Crim.L.R. 206; 143 N.L.J. 1439; 137 S.J.L.B.
    231; *The Times*, October 6, 1993; *Independent*, October 5, 1993;
    Guardian, October 8, 1993, CA 15–08, 15–18
Cheltenham Justices Ex p. Secretary of State for Trade [1977] 1 W.L.R. 95;
    [1977] 1 All E.R. 460, DC 3–14
Cheng (Kwok Si) (1976) 63 Cr.App.R. 20; [1976] Crim.L.R. 379; 120 S.J.
    198, CA 20–30
Chief Constable of Norfolk v Clayton; sub nom Clayton, Re; R. v Hun-
    stanton Justices Ex p. Clayton [1983] 2 A.C. 473; [1983] 2 W.L.R. 555;
    [1983] 1 All E.R. 984; 77 Cr.App.R. 24; [1983] Crim.L.R. 552, HL .   7–54
Chief Constable of the Royal Ulster Constabulary Ex p. Begley [1997] 1

W.L.R. 1475; [1997] 4 All E.R. 833; [1997] N.I. 275; 3 B.H.R.C. 173;
    94(42) L.S.G. 32; 147 N.L.J. 1545; 141 S.J.L.B. 218, HL 9–33
Chief Constable of South Wales Ex p. Merrick [1994] 1 W.L.R. 663; [1994]
    2 All E.R. 560; [1994] Crim.L.R. 852; [1994] C.O.D. 284; 144 N.L.J.
    423; *The Times*, February 17, 1994, QBD 9–33
Chief Constable of the West Midlands Ex p. Wiley [1995] 1 A.C. 274;
    [1994] 3 W.L.R. 433; [1994] 3 All E.R. 420; [1995] 1 Cr.App.R. 342;
    [1994] C.O.D. 520; 91(40) L.S.G. 35; 144 N.L.J. 1008; 138 S.J.L.B.
    156; *The Times*, July 15, 1994; *Independent*, July 15, 1994, HL 12–13,
    12–14
Ching (Yap Chuan) (1976) 63 Cr.App.R. 7; [1976] Crim.L.R. 687, CA4–06, 4–43
Chisnell [1992] Crim.L.R. 507, CA 9–27
Christie [1914] A.C. 545, HL 8–50, 9–06, 10–03, 14–31, 14–32, 14–33,
    14–34, 20–12
Christon [1996] 2 W.L.R. 620; [1996] 2 All E.R. 927; [1996] 2 Cr.App.R.
    360; [1996] Crim.L.R. 911; 93(20) L.S.G. 30; 146 N.L.J. Rep. 750, HL 7–53
Christou (Anastasis) and Wright (Christopher) [1992] Q.B. 979; [1992] 3
    W.L.R. 228; [1992] 4 All E.R. 559; 95 Cr.App.R. 264; [1992]
    Crim.L.R. 729; 142 N.L.J. 823; 136 S.J.L.B. 182, CA 9–27, 9–43, 9–44,
    10–24
Chung (Howard) (1991) 92 Cr.App.R. 314; [1991] Crim.L.R. 622, CA ... 9–38
Churchill [1993] Crim.L.R. 285, CA 8–29
Clare (Richard) and Peach (Nicholas William) [1995] 2 Cr.App.R. 333; 159
    J.P. 412; [1995] Crim.L.R. 947; 159 J.P.N. 424; 92(17) L.S.G. 47; 139
    S.J.L.B. 117, CA 2–09, 2–38, 2–39, 6–12, 6–27, 14–38
Clark (George Thomas) [1955] 2 Q.B. 469; [1955] 3 W.L.R. 313; [1955] 3
    All E.R. 29; 39 Cr.App.R. 120; 119 J.P. 531; 99 S.J. 527, CCA 7–66
Clarke (James Frederick) [1969] 2 Q.B. 91; [1969] 2 W.L.R. 505; [1969] 1
    All E.R. 924; 53 Cr.App.R. 251; 133 J.P. 282; 113 S.J. 109, CA 3–19
Clarke (Robert Lee) [1995] 2 Cr.App.R. 425, CA 2–15, 6–12, 6–17, 6–42,
    14–38
Clarke and Hewins [1999] 6 *Archbold News* 2, CA 16–12
Clarke v Saffery (1824) Ry. & M. 126 21–12
Clarksons Holidays Ltd (1973) 57 Cr.App.R. 38; 71 L.G.R. 1; [1972]
    Crim.L.R. 653; 116 S.J. 728, CA 16–03
Cleghorn (John Robert) [1967] 2 Q.B. 584; [1967] 2 W.L.R. 1421; [1967] 1
    All E.R. 996; 51 Cr.App.R. 291; 131 J.P. 320; 111 S.J. 175, CA 19–06
Clemo [1973] R.T.R. 176n, CA 16–22, 16–24
Clewer (Brian Edward) (1953) 37 Cr.App.R. 37, CCA 19–07
Clift v Long [1961] Crim.L.R. 121, DC 5–11
Cockley (Wayne Edward) (1984) 79 Cr.App.R. 181; 148 J.P. 666; [1984]
    Crim.L.R. 429; 148 J.P.N. 667; 81 L.S.G. 1437, CA 16–12
Cocks (Eugene George) (1976) 63 Cr.App.R. 79, CA 4–39
Cole (Michael Patrick) [1990] 1 W.L.R. 865; [1990] 2 All E.R. 108; 90
    Cr.App.R. 478; 154 J.P. 692; [1990] Crim.L.R. 333; 154 J.P.N. 562;
    87(13) L.S.G. 42; 134 S.J. 908, CA 8–74
Coleman (MA), *The Times*, November 21, 1987, CA 19–38
Coll (1889) 24 I.R. 522 .... 20–02, 20–10
Collins (Albert Patrick) (1960) 44 Cr.App.R. 170, CCA 3–09
Collinson (1931) 23 Cr.App.R. 49 16–22
Collinson v Mabbott, *The Times*, October 10, 1984, CA 15–04
Coltress (Courtney Anthony)(1979) 68 Cr.App.R. 193; [1979] Crim.L.R.
    170; *The Times*, October 27, 1978, CA 10–12

Commonwealth Shipping Representative v Peninsular and Oriental Branch
    Service; sub nom. Peninsular & Oriental Branch Service v Common-
    wealth Shipping Representative [1923] A.C. 191; 13 Ll. L. Rep. 455,
    HL 5–08
Comptroller of Customs v Western Lectric Co; sub nom. Comptroller of
    Customs v Western Electric Co. [1966] A.C. 367; [1965] 3 W.L.R.
    1229; [1965] 3 All E.R. 599; 109 S.J. 873, PC (Fiji) 9–59
Condron (Karen) and Condron (William) [1997] 1 W.L.R. 827; [1997] 1
    Cr.App.R. 185; 161 J.P. 1; [1997] Crim.L.R. 215; 161 J.P.N. 40; The
    Times, November 4, 1996, CA 11–21
Connelly v DPP [1964] A.C. 1254; [1964] 2 W.L.R. 1145; [1964] 2 All E.R.
    401; 48 Cr.App.R. 183; 128 J.P. 418; 108 S.J. 356, HL .. 5–14, 5–16, 5–18,
                                                                         5–19, 5–20
Constantinou (Richard) (1990) 91 Cr.App.R. 74; 153 J.P. 619; [1989]
    Crim.L.R. 571; 153 J.P.N. 658, CA 14–39, 14–40
Conti (Victor Lawrence) (1974) 58 Cr.App.R. 387; [1974] Crim.L.R. 247,
    CA 17–13
Conway (John Patrick) (1990) 91 Cr.App.R. 143; [1990] Crim.L.R. 402,
    CA 14–17
Conway v Rimmer [1968] A.C. 910; [1968] 2 W.L.R. 998; [1968] 1 All E.R.
    874; 112 S.J. 191, HL 12–04, 12–12, 12–13
Cook [1982] Crim.L.R. 670, Crown Ct 6–16
Cook (Albert Samuel John) [1959] 2 Q.B. 340; [1959] 2 W.L.R. 616; [1959]
    2 All E.R. 97; 43 Cr.App.R. 138; 123 J.P. 271; 103 S.J. 353, CCA .. 7–66,
                                                                              7–67
Cook (Christopher) [1987] Q.B. 417; [1987] 2 W.L.R. 775; [1987] 1 All
    E.R. 1049; 84 Cr.App.R. 369; [1987] Crim.L.R. 402, CA 2–11, 14–39,
                                                                              14–40
Cooke (Gary) (1987) 84 Cr.App.R. 286, CA 5–25
Coombes (Peter Michael) (1961) 45 Cr.App.R. 36; 125 J.P. 139, CCA
Cooper (Warwick John) (1986) 82 Cr.App.R. 74; [1985] Crim.L.R. 592,
    CA 21–20
Cooper and Schaub. See Schaub (Mark Tony)
Cooper v Slade (1858) 6 H.L. Cas. 746, HL 4–45
Coote (1873) L.R. 4 P.C. 599 11–04
Corelli (Ernesto) [2001] EWCA Crim 974; [2001] Crim.L.R. 913, CA 7–24
Corke v Corke and Cook [1958] P. 93; [1958] 2 W.L.R. 110; [1958] 1 All
    E.R. 224; 102 S.J. 68, CA 20–02
Corless (Raymond Francis) (1972) 56 Cr.App.R. 341; [1972] Crim.L.R.
    314, CA 19–42
Coshall (Richard Edward) (1995) 92(12) L.S.G. 34; 139 S.J.L.B. 66; The
    Times, February 17, 1995, CA 19–27
Cottrill (Philip) [1997] Crim.L.R. 56, CA 11–36
Coulson v Disborough [1894] 2 Q.B. 316, CA 21–15
Coulthread (1933) 24 Cr.App.R. 4 20–04
Courteen v Touse (1807) 1 Camp. 43 21–07
Courtie (Thomas) [1984] A.C. 463; [1984] 2 W.L.R. 330; [1984] 1 All E.R.
    740; 78 Cr.App.R. 292; 148 J.P. 502; [1984] Crim.L.R. 366, HL 4–42
Couzens and Frankel (No.1) [1992] Crim.L.R. 822; The Times, April 17,
    1992, CA 16–21
Coventry Justices Ex p. Bullard (1992) 95 Cr.App.R. 175; [1992] R.A. 79;
    [1992] C.O.D. 285; 142 N.L.J. 383; 136 S.J.L.B. 96, QBD 8–77
Cowan (Donald), Gayle (Ricky) and Ricciardi (Carmine) [1996] Q.B. 373;

[1995] 3 W.L.R. 818; [1995] 4 All E.R. 939; [1996] 1 Cr.App.R. 1; 160
J.P. 165; [1996] Crim.L.R. 409; 160 J.P.N. 14; 92(38) L.S.G. 26; 145
N.L.J. 1611; 139 S.J.L.B. 215; *The Times*, October 13, 1995; *Independent*, October 25, 1995, CA 17–17, 17–19, 17–20, 17–22,
                                                                    17–23, 18–21
Cowell [1940] 2 K.B. 49, CCA 16–08, 17–11
Cox [1898] 1 Q.B. 179, CCR 6–08
Cox (Rodney William) (1993) 96 Cr.App.R. 464; 157 J.P. 785; [1993]
    Crim.L.R. 382; 157 J.P.N. 188, CA 9–37, 9–38
Cox and Railton (1884) 14 Q.B.D. 153, CCR 11–30
Crampton (Kenneth) (1991) 92 Cr.App.R. 369; [1991] Crim.L.R. 277; *The
    Times*, November 22, 1990, CA 9–20, 9–23
Creamer (George Robert) (1985) 80 Cr.App.R. 248, CA 14–20
Crees (Graham Peter) [1996] Crim.L.R. 830, CA 19–43
Creevy v Carr (1835) 7 C. & P. 64 21–12
Critchley [1982] Crim.L.R. 524, DC 4–29, 4–30
Crosdale v R.; sub nom. Crosland v R. [1995] 1 W.L.R. 864; [1995] 2 All
    E.R. 500; [1995] Crim.L.R. 958; 92(24) L.S.G. 38; 145 N.L.J. 594; 139
    S.J.L.B. 143, PC (Jam) 16–11
Cross (John Morris) [1990] B.C.C. 237; [1991] B.C.L.C. 125; 91 Cr.App.R.
    115, CA 21–20
Crossland v DPP [1988] 3 All E.R. 712; 153 J.P. 63; [1988] R.T.R. 417;
    [1988] Crim.L.R. 756, DC 15–04
Crouch (1850) 4 Cox 163 6–10
Crown Prosecution Service Ex p. Warby; sub nom. DPP Ex p. Warby (1994)
    158 J.P. 190; [1994] Crim.L.R. 281; [1994] C.O.D. 98; 158 J.P.N.
    108; *The Times*, October 20, 1993; *Independent*, September 16, 1993,
    DC 12–25
Croydon Magistrates' Court Ex p. DPP. See DPP v Croydon Magistrates'
    Court
Crush [1978] Crim.L.R. 357, Crown Ct 8–40
Cruttenden (Roger Christian) [1991] 2 Q.B. 66; [1991] 2 W.L.R. 921;
    [1991] 3 All E.R. 242; 93 Cr.App.R. 119; 155 J.P. 798; [1991]
    Crim.L.R. 537; 155 J.P.N. 236; *The Times*, February 15, 1991, CA . 17–34
Culbertson (Robert Keith) (1970) 54 Cr.App.R. 310; [1970] Crim.L.R. 302,
    CA 16–16
Cummings [1948] 1 All E.R. 551; 92 S.J. 284, CCA 20–06
Cunningham [1988] Crim.L.R. 543; *The Times*, March 21, 1988, CA 17–11
Curry [1988] Crim.L.R. 527, CA 5–33
Curry (Brian William), *The Times*, March 23, 1998, CA 8–74
Curtin (Joseph) [1996] Crim.L.R. 831, CA 16–15
Customs and Excise Commissioners v Harz and Power; sub nom. Harz
    (Samuel Mendel) and Power (Jack) [1967] 1 A.C. 760; [1967] 2 W.L.R.
    297; [1967] 1 All E.R. 177; 51 Cr.App.R. 123; 131 J.P. 146; 111 S.J.
    15, HL 9–04, 11–09

D and S, 166 J.P. 792 19–30
D v Camberwell Green Youth Court; R v Balham Youth Court; N v
    Camberwell Green Youth Court; DPP) v Camberwell Green Youth
    Court [2003] EWHC (Admin) 227; [2003] 2 Cr.App.R. 16; 167 J.P.
    210; [2003] Crim.L.R. 659; 167 J.P.N. 317; *The Times*, February 13,
    2003, QBD 19–16
D v DPP (1998) 142 S.J.L.B. 254; *The Times*, August 7, 1998, QBD 14–28

D v National Society for the Prevention of Cruelty to Children (NSPCC)
[1978] A.C. 171; [1977] 2 W.L.R. 201; [1977] 1 All E.R. 589; 76
L.G.R. 5; 121 S.J. 119, HL 12–01, 12–02, 12–03, 12–04, 12–05, 12–14
DJN (1992) 95 Cr.App.R. 256, CA 17–05
DPP Ex p. J; sub nom. X Justices Ex p. J; Crown Prosecution Service Ex p. J
[2000] 1 W.L.R. 1215; [2000] 1 All E.R. 183; *The Times*, July 8, 1999;
Independent, July 5, 1999, DC 13–23, 18–01
DPP Ex p. Kebilene [2000] 2 A.C. 326; [1999] 3 W.L.R. 972; [1999] 4 All
E.R. 801; [2000] 1 Cr.App.R. 275; [2000] H.R.L.R. 93; [2000]
U.K.H.R.R. 176; 2 L.G.L.R. 697; 11 Admin. L.R. 1026; [2000]
Crim.L.R. 486; 96(43) L.S.G. 32; *The Times*, November 2, 1999, HL;
reversing [1999] 3 W.L.R. 175; 11 Admin. L.R. 785; [1999] Crim.L.R.
994; [1999] C.O.D. 207, DC 4–13, 13–21, 13–28, 13–29
DPP Ex p. Lee [1999] 1 W.L.R. 1950; [1999] 2 All E.R. 737; [1999] 2
Cr.App.R. 304; 163 J.P. 569; 163 J.P.N. 651; 143 S.J.L.B. 174; *The
Times*, April 26, 1999, QBD 18–01, 18–11
DPP Ex p. Mansfield; sub nom. DPP v Mansfield (1996) 160 J.P. 472;
[1997] R.T.R. 96, DC 3–25
DPP Ex p. Warby. *See* Crown Prosecution Service Ex p. Warby
DPP v A & BC Chewing Gum Ltd [1968] 1 Q.B. 159; [1967] 3 W.L.R. 493;
[1967] 2 All E.R. 504; 131 J.P. 373; 111 S.J. 331, DC 6–06, 6–23
DPP v Acton Youth Court [2001] 1 W.L.R. 1828 12–25
DPP v Blake [1989] 1 W.L.R. 432; 89 Cr.App.R. 179; 153 J.P. 425; [1989]
C.O.D. 407; 153 J.P.N. 483; 133 S.J. 483, DC 9–28, 9–30
DPP v Boardman [1975] A.C. 421; [1974] 3 W.L.R. 673; [1974] 3 All E.R.
887; 60 Cr.App.R. 165; [1975] Crim.L.R. 36; 118 S.J. 809, HL 7–02,
7–03, 7–69, 7–70, 14–47
DPP v British Telecommunications plc (1991) 155 J.P. 869; [1991]
Crim.L.R. 532; 155 L.G. Rev. 298, DC 2–02
DPP v Cornish, *The Times*, January 27, 1997, QBD 9–30
DPP v Croydon Magistrates' Court [2001] EWHC Admin 552; [2001]
Crim.L.R. 980; *Independent*, October 22, 2001, DC 18–03
DPP v Curtis [1993] R.T.R. 72; 157 J.P.N. 266, DC 5–11
DPP v Godwin (1992) 156 J.P. 643; [1991] R.T.R. 303; 155 J.P.N. 554, DC   10–19
DPP v Hester; sub nom. Hester (John James) [1973] A.C. 296; [1972] 3
W.L.R. 910; [1972] 3 All E.R. 1056; 57 Cr.App.R. 212; [1973]
Crim.L.R. 43; 116 S.J. 966, HL 15–01
DPP v Humphrys (Bruce Edward) [1977] A.C. 1; [1976] 2 W.L.R. 857;
[1976] 2 All E.R. 497; 63 Cr.App.R. 95; [1976] R.T.R. 339; [1977]
Crim.L.R. 421; 120 S.J. 420, HL 5–14, 5–18, 5–19, 5–20
DPP v Hutchings (1992) 156 J.P. 702; [1991] R.T.R. 380; 156 J.P.N. 522,
DC 3–05
DPP v Jordan and Staniforth [1977] A.C. 699; [1976] 3 W.L.R. 887; [1976]
3 All E.R. 775; 64 Cr.App.R. 33; [1977] Crim.L.R. 109; 120 S.J. 817,
HL 6–22, 6–23
DPP v Kavaz [1999] R.T.R. 40, QBD 4–19
DPP v Kilbourne [1973] A.C. 729; [1973] 2 W.L.R. 254; [1973] 1 All E.R.
440; 57 Cr.App.R. 381; [1973] Crim.L.R. 235; 117 S.J. 144, HL 1–13,
7–70, 15–01
DPP v M [1998] Q.B. 913; [1998] 2 W.L.R. 604; [1997] 2 All E.R. 749;
[1997] 2 Cr.App.R. 70; 161 J.P. 491; [1997] 2 F.L.R. 804; [1998] Fam.
Law 11, DC 17–03, 17–05

DPP v Marshall (Robert Dennis) [1988] 3 All E.R. 683; [1988] Crim.L.R.
    750, DC 10–22
DPP v Mooney [1997] R.T.R. 434; [1997] Crim.L.R. 137, DC 3–25
DPP v P; sub nom. P (A Father) [1991] 2 A.C. 447; [1991] 3 W.L.R. 161;
    [1991] 3 All E.R. 337; 93 Cr.App.R. 267; 156 J.P. 125; [1992]
    Crim.L.R. 41; 155 J.P.N. 572; 141 N.L.J. 928; 135 S.J.L.B. 69, HL . 7–03
DPP v Ping Lin [1976] A.C. 574; [1975] 3 W.L.R. 419; [1975] 3 All E.R.
    175; 62 Cr.App.R. 14; [1976] Crim.L.R. 53; 119 S.J. 627, HL 4–47
DPP v Roberts, *The Times*, June 1, 1992, DC 5–09
DPP v Rous (1992) 94 Cr.App.R. 185 9–42
DPP v Stonehouse [1978] A.C. 55; [1977] 3 W.L.R. 143; [1977] 2 All E.R.
    909; 65 Cr.App.R. 192; [1977] Crim.L.R. 544; 121 S.J. 491, HL 16–22,
    16–23, 16–24
DPP v Walker [1974] 1 W.L.R. 1090; [1974] Crim.L.R. 368; 118 S.J. 532,
    PC (Jam) 4–30
DPP v Wilson (1992) 156 J.P. 916; [1991] R.T.R. 284; [1991] Crim.L.R.
    441; 156 J.P.N. 732; *The Times*, February 12, 1991, DC 10–21
DS [1999] Crim.L.R. 911, CA 21–01
Dadson (Peter Ernest) (1983) 77 Cr.App.R. 91; [1983] Crim.L.R. 540, CA 3–15
Daley v R. [1994] 1 A.C. 117; [1993] 3 W.L.R. 666; [1993] 4 All E.R. 86;
    98 Cr.App.R. 447; [1994] Crim.L.R. 931; 143 N.L.J. 1331; 137
    S.J.L.B. 210; *The Times*, October 12, 1993, PC (Jam) 16–11
Dallagher (Mark Anthony) [2002] EWCA Crim 1903; [2003] 1 Cr.App.R.
    12; [2002] Crim.L.R. 821, CA 6–17
Dallagher, unreported, July 25, 2002 14–49
Dallison v Caffery [1965] 1 Q.B. 348; [1964] 3 W.L.R. 385; [1964] 2 All
    E.R. 610; 128 J.P. 379; 108 S.J. 560, CA 18–06
Daniel [2003] 1 Cr.App.R. 99, CA 4–16
Daniel (Anthony Junior) [1998] 2 Cr.App.R. 373; 162 J.P. 578; [1998]
    Crim.L.R. 818; 162 J.P.N. 663; *The Times*, April 10, 1998, CA 11–17,
    11–21
Darby [1989] Crim.L.R. 817; *The Times*, June 20, 1989, CA 19–06, 21–10,
    21–12
Darby v Ouseley (1856) 1 H. & N. 1 21–27
Dartey (Alexander Kwame) (1987) 84 Cr.App.R. 352, CA 19–38
Da Silva (Michael Reginald) [1990] 1 W.L.R. 31; [1990] 1 All E.R. 29; 90
    Cr.App.R. 233; 153 J.P. 636; [1990] Crim.L.R. 192; 153 L.G. Rev.
    676; 133 S.J. 1234, CA 20–25, 20–27
Davey v Harrow Corp. [1958] 1 Q.B. 60; [1957] 2 W.L.R. 941; [1957] 2 All
    E.R. 305; 101 S.J. 405, CA 5–08
David R. *See* R (David)
Davie (James Pennycook) v Edinburgh Corp. (No.2); sub nom. Davie v
    Edinburgh Magistrates, 1953 S.C. 34; 1953 S.L.T. 54, 1 Div 6–42
Davie v Edinburgh Magistrates. *See* Davie (James Pennycook) v Edinburgh
    Corp. (No.2)
Davies (Lewis John) [1962] 1 W.L.R. 1111; [1962] 3 All E.R. 97; (1962) 46
    Cr.App.R. 292; 126 J.P. 455; 106 S.J. 393, CMAC 6–04, 6–08, 6–28
Davies v Health and Safety Executive [2002] EWCA Crim 2949; [2003]
    I.C.R. 586; [2003] I.R.L.R. 170; 100(9) L.S.G. 27; 147 S.J.L.B. 29, CA 4–17
Davis (Desmond John) [1998] Crim.L.R. 659, CA 11–21
Davis (George John) (1976) 62 Cr.App.R. 194, CA 19–43
Davis (Michael George), Rowe (Raphael George) and Johnson (Randolph
    Egbert) (No.1) [1993] 1 W.L.R. 613; [1993] 2 All E.R. 643; 97

Cr.App.R. 110; 137 S.J.L.B. 19; *The Times*, January 19, 1993; *Independent*, January 22, 1993, CA 12–12, 12–21, 12–22, 12–23, 12–24, 12–25

Davis (Michael George), Rowe (Raphael George) and Johnson (Randolph Egbert) (No.3) [2001] 1 Cr.App.R. 8; [2000] H.R.L.R. 527; [2000] U.K.H.R.R. 683; [2000] Crim.L.R. 1012; *The Times*, July 25, 2000, CA 2–06

Day (1940) 27 Cr.App.R. 168 .... 19–06, 19–37

Daye [1908] 2 K.B. 333 3–02

Deakin (Richard Albin) [1994] 4 All E.R. 769; [1995] 1 Cr.App.R. 471; [1995] Crim.L.R. 411; 91(21) L.S.G. 41; 144 N.L.J. 707; *The Times*, May 3, 1994; *Independent*, May 2, 1994, CA 17–07

Deen, *The Times*, January 10, 1994, CA 14–42

Delaney (Joseph Patrick) (1989) 88 Cr.App.R. 338; 153 J.P. 103; [1989] Crim.L.R. 139; 153 J.P.N. 169, CA 2–22, 9–27, 9–29, 9–37

Dempster (Andrew David) (1980) 71 Cr.App.R. 302; [1980] Crim.L.R. 659, CA 2–27

Denney [1963] Crim.L.R. 191; *The Times*, December 21, 1962, CCA 4–27

Denton (Clive) [2001] 1 Cr.App.R. 16; [2001] Crim.L.R. 225; *The Times*, November 22, 2000, CA 8–28, 10–31

Derby & Co. Ltd v Weldon (No.9), *The Times*, November 9, 1990, CA; [1991] 1 W.L.R. 652; [1991] 2 All E.R. 901, Ch D 3–02

Derby Magistrates' Court Ex p. B [1996] A.C. 487; [1995] 3 W.L.R. 681; [1995] 4 All E.R. 526; [1996] 1 Cr.App.R. 385; 159 J.P. 785; [1996] 1 F.L.R. 513; [1996] Fam. Law 210; 159 J.P.N. 778; 145 N.L.J. 1575; [1995] 139 S.J.L.B. 219; *The Times*, October 25, 1995; *Independent*, October 27, 1995, HL 11–32, 21–23, 21–24, 21–25

Derbyshire CC v Times Newspapers Ltd [1993] A.C. 534, HL; affirming [1992] Q.B. 770; [1992] 3 W.L.R. 28; [1992] 3 All E.R. 65; 90 L.G.R. 221; 4 Admin. L.R. 469; [1992] C.O.D. 305; 142 N.L.J. 276, CA 13–02

Derwentside Magistrates' Court Ex p. Heaviside (1996) 160 J.P. 317; [1996] R.T.R. 384; [1995] R.L.R. 557; 159 J.P.N. 703, DC 3–25, 3–26

Derwentside Magistrates' Court Ex p. Swift; sub nom. Derwentside Justices Ex p. Swift (1996) 160 J.P. 468; [1997] R.T.R. 89; [1996] C.O.D. 203, DC 3–25

De Silva (Marc Anthony) [2002] EWCA Crim 2673; [2003] 2 Cr.App.R. 5; [2003] Crim.L.R. 474, CA 9–04, 9–26, 9–45

Devonport (Derrick) [1996] 1 Cr.App.R. 221; [1996] Crim.L.R. 255, CA   8–64

Dexter, Laidler and Coates (1899) 19 Cox C.C. 360 20–28

Dibble (1908) 1 Cr.App.R. 155 21–12

Diedrick [1997] 1 Cr.App.R. 361; [1997] Crim.L.R. 58, CA 8–63, 9–12

Dillon (Robert William) (1987) 85 Cr.App.R. 29; 149 J.P. 182; [1984] Crim.L.R. 100, CA 20–35

Director of the Serious Fraud Office Ex p. Smith; sub nom. Smith v Director of the Serious Fraud Office [1993] A.C. 1; [1992] 3 W.L.R. 66; [1992] 3 All E.R. 456; [1992] B.C.L.C. 879; 95 Cr.App.R. 191; [1992] Crim.L.R. 504; [1992] C.O.D. 270; 89(27) L.S.G. 34; 142 N.L.J. 895; 136 S.J.L.B. 182; *The Times*, June 16, 1992; *Independent*, June 12, 1992; *Financial Times*, June 17, 1992; *Guardian*, July 1, 1992, HL .. 11–14

Dix (Trevor Glyn) (1982) 74 Cr.App.R. 306; [1982] Crim.L.R. 302, CA . 4–12, 6–18

Dixon (Sarah Louise) [2001] Crim.L.R. 126, CA 5–31

Docherty (Michael) [1999] 1 Cr.App.R. 274, CA 10–30

Dodson (Patrick) and Williams (Danny Fitzalbert) [1984] 1 W.L.R. 971; 79
    Cr.App.R. 220; [1984] Crim.L.R. 489; 81 L.S.G. 1677; 128 S.J. 364,
    CA 2–12, 2–14, 14–38
Doe d. France v Andrews (1850) 15 Q.B. 756   8–42
Doe d. Gilbert v Ross (1840) 7 M. & W. 102   3–07
Doheny (Alan James) and Adams (Gary Andrew) [1997] 1 Cr.App.R. 369;
    [1997] Crim.L.R. 669, *The Times*, August 14, 1996, CA 6–45, 14–43,
                                                                               14–46
Dolan (Edward George) [2002] EWCA Crim 1859; [2003] 1 Cr.App.R. 18   7–38
Doldur [2000] Crim.L.R. 178 .... 11–21, 14–18
Donaldson (Robin Clive), Watson (Raymond) and Reed (Ronald Michael)
    (1977) 64 Cr.App.R. 59, CA 20–14, 20–17
Donat (Rinaldo William) (1986) 82 Cr.App.R. 173, CA   8–64
Donoghue (Raymond) (1988) 86 Cr.App.R. 267; [1988] Crim.L.R. 60, CA   4–06
Doosti (Reza) (1986) 82 Cr.App.R. 181; [1985] Crim.L.R. 665, CA   5–23
Doran (Richard) (1972) 56 Cr.App.R. 429; [1972] Crim.L.R. 392; 116 S.J.
    238, CA   19–38
Downer (1880) 14 Cox 486 .... 8–63, 9–11, 11–29
Downes (Bernard) (1994) 15 Cr.App.R. (S.) 435; *The Times*, December 10,
    1993; *Independent*, October 25, 1993, CA   20–17
Downey (James) [1995] 1 Cr.App.R. 547; [1995] Crim.L.R. 414, CA   2–14
Downie v Coe, *The Times*, November 28, 1997, CA   11–05
Dragic (Filip) [1996] 2 Cr.App.R. 232; (1996) 160 J.P. 771; [1996]
    Crim.L.R. 580; 160 J.P.N. 936; *The Times*, March 7, 1996, CA   8–19
Drake [1996] Crim.L.R. 109   14–08
Draper [1962] Crim.L.R. 107, CCA   16–22
Drummond (Andrew) [2002] EWCA Crim 527; [2002] 2 Cr.App.R. 25;
    [2002] R.T.R. 21; [2002] Crim.L.R. 666, CA   4–16
Drury (Christopher), Clark (Robert), Reynolds (Thomas), O'Connell (Ter-
    ance) and Kingston (Thomas) [2001] EWCA Crim 975; [2001]
    Crim.L.R. 847, CA 16–07, 16–08
Duchess of Kingston's case (1776) 20 St. Tr. 355   11–37
Duffin v Markham (1918) 82 J.P. 281   19–37
Duffy (Paula) (No.1) [1999] Q.B. 919; [1998] 3 W.L.R. 1060; [1999] 1
    Cr.App.R. 307; [1998] Crim.L.R. 650; 95(20) L.S.G. 33; 142 S.J.L.B.
    149; *The Times*, May 2, 1998, CA   19–34
Dunbar (Ronald Patrick) [1958] 1 Q.B. 1; [1957] 3 W.L.R. 330; [1957] 2
    All E.R. 737; 41 Cr.App.R. 182; 121 J.P. 506; 101 S.J. 594, CCA ...   4–12,
                                                                               4–46
Duncan (Findlay) (1981) 73 Cr.App.R. 359; [1981] Crim.L.R. 560, CA .. 20–17,
                                                                              20–18
Duncan v Cammell Laird & Co Ltd [1942] A.C. 624; [1942] 1 All E.R. 587;
    73 Ll. L. Rep. 109; 86 S.J. 287, HL   12–13
Dunford (Nicholas James) (1990) 91 Cr.App.R. 150; [1991] Crim.L.R. 370;
    140 N.L.J. 517, CA   9–35
Dunn v Aslett (1828) 2 M. & R. 122   21–30
Dunne (1929) 21 Cr.App.R. 176 .... 16–06, 17–07
Dunning [1965] Crim.L.R. 372, CCA   17–06
Durbin (Barry Henry) [1995] 2 Cr.App.R. 84, CA 7–13, 7–16
Dures (Thomas), Williams (Florence Elizabeth) and Dures (Steven) [1997] 2
    Cr.App.R. 247; [1997] Crim.L.R. 673, CA 9–58, 10–29
Dwyer (Thomas) and Ferguson (Allen) [1925] 2 K.B. 799; 18 Cr.App.R.
    145, CCA   14–35

Dye, Williamson and Davies [1992] Crim.L.R. 449; *The Times*, December
    19, 1991, CA 21–04
Dyer (Antony James) [1997] Crim.L.R. 442, CA 8–32

E [1995] 1 W.L.R. 1348, CA 15–13
Ealing LBC v Woolworths plc [1995] Crim.L.R. 58, DC 10–22
Early (John) [2002] EWCA Crim 1904; [2003] 1 Cr.App.R. 19; 99(39)
    L.S.G. 38; *The Times*, August 2, 2002, CA 12–08
Eastwood [1961] Crim.L.R. 414, CCA 16–22
Ebrahim v Feltham Magistrates' Court; sub nom. Feltham Magistrates'
    Court Ex p. Ebrahim [2001] EWHC Admin 130; [2001] 1 W.L.R.
    1293; [2001] 1 All E.R. 831; [2001] 2 Cr.App.R. 23; [2002] R.T.R. 7;
    [2001] Crim.L.R. 741; 151 N.L.J. 304; *The Times*, February 27, 2001;
    Independent, February 27, 2001, DC 18–24, 18–27
Edwards (1837) 8 C. & P. 26 20–28
Edwards (1848) Cox C.C. 82 .... 19–01, 19–06
Edwards (1991) 93 Cr.App.R. 48 .... 21–27, 21–29
Edwards (Errington) [1975] Q.B. 27; [1974] 3 W.L.R. 285; [1974] 2 All
    E.R. 1085; 59 Cr.App.R. 213; [1974] Crim.L.R. 540; 118 S.J. 582, CA   4–21
Edwards (John) [1991] 1 W.L.R. 207; [1991] 2 All E.R. 266; 93 Cr.App.R.
    48; [1991] Crim.L.R. 372; 141 N.L.J. 91, CA 5–23, 5–24
Edwards (Martin John) [1997] Crim.L.R. 348, CA 9–44
Edwards (Nicholas Webb) (1983) 77 Cr.App.R. 5; 147 J.P. 316; [1983]
    Crim.L.R. 484, CA 4–39, 4–40
Edwards (Robert Hamilton) (1983) 5 Cr.App.R. (S.) 145; [1983] Crim.L.R.
    539, CA 9–10
Effik (Godwin Eno) and Mitchell (Graham Martin) [1995] 1 A.C. 309;
    [1994] 3 W.L.R. 583; [1994] 3 All E.R. 458; 99 Cr.App.R. 312; [1994]
    Crim.L.R. 832; 158 J.P.N. 552; 91(39) L.S.G. 39; 138 S.J.L.B. 167; *The
    Times*, July 22, 1994; *Independent*, July 29, 1994, HL 12–05
Elahee [1999] Crim.L.R. 399, CA 21–29
Eldridge [1999] Crim.L.R. 166, CA 21–23
Eleftheriou (Costas and Lefterakis) [1993] Crim.L.R. 947; *The Times*,
    March 2, 1993; *Independent*, February 26, 1993; *Guardian*, March 8,
    1993, CA 20–29
Elleray (Colin Woods) [2003] EWCA Crim 553; [2003] 2 Cr.App.R. 11;
    167 J.P. 325; 167 J.P.N. 471; *The Times*, February 28, 2003, CA 9–26
Ellis v Jones [1973] 2 All E.R. 893; [1973] Crim.L.R. 361, CA 14–07
Elworthy (1865–72) L.R. 1 C.C.R. 103 3–13
Ely Justices Ex p. Burgess (1993) 157 J.P. 484; [1992] Crim.L.R. 888;
    [1993] C.O.D. 21; 157 J.P.N. 189; 89(34) L.S.G. 34; 136 S.J.L.B. 244,
    DC 2–08
Emmerson (Geoffrey) (1991) 92 Cr.App.R. 284; [1991] Crim.L.R. 194,
    CA 2–26, 2–27
English Exporters (London) Ltd v Eldonwall Ltd [1973] Ch. 415; [1973] 2
    W.L.R. 435; [1973] 1 All E.R. 726; 25 P. & C.R. 379; 117 S.J. 224, Ch
    D 6–40
Enoch and Zaretsky, Re [1901] 1 K.B. 32 21–15
Ensor (Maxie Angus Anderson) [1989] 1 W.L.R. 497; [1989] 2 All E.R.
    586; 89 Cr.App.R. 139; [1989] Crim.L.R. 562; 86(15) L.S.G. 36; 139
    N.L.J. 575; 133 S.J. 483, CA 15–19
Evans [1981] Crim.L.R. 699; *The Times*, May 6, 1981, CA 8–63, 9–11
Evans (David John) (1990) 91 Cr.App.R. 173; 87(24) L.S.G. 40, CA 16–15

Evans (Terrance Roy) (1992) 156 J.P. 539; [1992] Crim.L.R. 125; 156
    J.P.N. 154, CA 7–24
Everett [1988] Crim.L.R. 826, CA 9–21
Ewens [1967] 1 Q.B. 322; [1966] 2 W.L.R. 1372; [1966] 2 All E.R. 470; 50
    Cr.App.R. 171; 110 S.J. 483, CCA 4–19
Ewer v Ambrose (1825) 3 B. & C. 746 21–08
Ewing (Terence Patrick) [1983] Q.B. 1039; [1983] 3 W.L.R. 1; [1983] 2 All
    E.R. 645; 77 Cr.App.R. 47; [1984] E.C.C. 234; [1983] Crim.L.R. 472;
    127 S.J. 390, CA 4–48
Exall (1866) 4 F. & F. 922 1–06

F [1996] Crim.L.R. 257 7–53
F (An Infant) v Chief Constable of Kent [1982] Crim.L.R. 682, DC 16–27
Fairfax (Kenneth) (No.1) [1995] Crim.L.R. 949, CA 8–28
Falconer-Atlee (Joan Olive) (1974) 58 Cr.App.R. 348, CA 7–13
Farnham Justices Ex p. Gibson (1991) 155 J.P. 792; [1991] R.T.R. 309;
    [1991] Crim.L.R. 642; [1991] C.O.D. 497; 155 J.P.N. 362; *The Times*,
    March 14, 1991; *Daily Telegraph*, March 18, 1991, DC 17–12
Farr (Roger John) (1999) 163 J.P. 193; [1999] Crim.L.R. 506; 163 J.P.N.
    172; *The Times*, December 10, 1998, CA 16–16
Faryab (Frank) [1999] B.P.I.R. 569; [2000] Crim.L.R. 180, CA 11–10, 16–19
Faversham and Sittingbourne Justices Ex p. Stickings (1996) 160 J.P. 801;
    [1996] C.O.D. 439; 160 J.P.N. 811; *The Times*, May 9, 1996, QBD   16–29
Feely (David) [1973] Q.B. 530; [1973] 2 W.L.R. 201; [1973] 1 All E.R. 341;
    57 Cr.App.R. 312; [1973] Crim.L.R. 193; 117 S.J. 54, CA 16–24
Fenlon (Kevin), Neal (Raymond Frank) and Neal (Gary Steven) (1980) 71
    Cr.App.R. 307; [1980] Crim.L.R. 573; 124 S.J. 478, CA 20–35, 21–16
Fergus [1992] Crim.L.R. 363; *The Times*, November 11, 1991; *Guardian*,
    November 20, 1991, CA 14–15
Fergus (Ivan) (1994) 98 Cr.App.R. 313; 157 J.P.N. 699; *The Times*, June
    30, 1993; *Independent*, June 29, 1993, CA 14–05, 14–30
Fernandez, Ex p. (1861) 10 C.B. (N.S.) 3 17–01
Fidelitas Shipping Co. Ltd v V/O Exportchleb [1966] 1 Q.B. 630; [1965] 2
    W.L.R. 1059; [1965] 2 All E.R. 4; [1965] 1 Lloyd's Rep. 223; 109 S.J.
    191, CA 5–19
Finley [1993] Crim.L.R. 50, CA 14–27
Fitzpatrick (Gerald) [1999] Crim.L.R. 832; *The Times*, February 19, 1999,
    CA 6–43
Flanagan v Fahy [1918] 1 I.R. 361 20–09
Flemming (Desmond John) (1988) 86 Cr.App.R. 32; [1987] Crim.L.R. 690;
    131 S.J. 972, CA 14–06, 16–07
Folkes v Chadd (1782) 3 Doug. K.B. 157 6–12
Folley [1978] Crim.L.R. 556, CA 4–27
Foote [1964] Crim.L.R. 405, CCA 4–28
Forbes (Anthony Leroy) [2001] 1 A.C. 473; [2001] 2 W.L.R. 1; [2001] 1 All
    E.R. 686; [2001] 1 Cr.App.R. 31; 165 J.P. 61; [2001] Crim.L.R. 649;
    165 J.P.N. 664; 98(8) L.S.G. 43; 145 S.J.L.B. 44; *The Times*, December
    19, 2000; *Independent*, December 21, 2000, HL 13–05, 14–17, 14–24,
    14–25, 14–29
Forsyth (Elizabeth) [1997] 2 Cr.App.R. 299; [1997] Crim.L.R. 581; *The
    Times*, April 8, 1997, CA 19–20
Foster [1995] Crim.L.R. 333, CA 19–18
Fotheringham [1975] Crim.L.R. 710; 119 S.J. 613, CA 20–31

Fowden and White [1982] Crim.L.R. 588, CA 2–37
Fowkes, *Digest of the Law of Evidence* (12th ed., 1948), p.8 20–08
Fox (Leslie Raymond); sub nom. Fox v Chief Constable of Gwent [1986]
    A.C. 281; [1985] 1 W.L.R. 1126; [1985] 3 All E.R. 392; 82 Cr.App.R.
    105; [1985] R.T.R. 337; [1986] Crim.L.R. 59, HL 10–05
Fox v Chief Constable of Gwent. *See* Fox (Leslie Raymond)
Fox v General Medical Council [1960] 1 W.L.R. 1017; [1960] 3 All E.R.
    225; 124 J.P. 467; 104 S.J. 725, PC 20–02, 20–10
Foxley (Gordon) [1995] 2 Cr.App.R. 523; (1995) 16 Cr.App.R. (S.) 879;
    [1995] Crim.L.R. 636, CA 8–32
Francis (1874) L.R. 2 C.C.R. 128 2–04
Francis (Peter Robert) [1990] 1 W.L.R. 1264; [1991] 1 All E.R. 225; 91
    Cr.App.R. 271; 154 J.P. 358; [1990] Crim.L.R. 431; 154 J.P.N. 265;
    134 S.J. 860, CA 14–09, 19–35
Francom (Mark Frank) [2001] 1 Cr.App.R. 17; [2000] Crim.L.R. 1018; *The
    Times*, October 24, 2000, CA 11–20
Frank Truman Export Ltd v Commissioner of Police of the Metropolis
    [1977] Q.B. 952; [1977] 3 W.L.R. 257; [1977] 3 All E.R. 431; 64
    Cr.App.R. 248; [1977] Crim.L.R. 476; 121 S.J. 512; *The Times*,
    December 22, 1976, QBD 11–34
Franklin, *The Times*, June 6, 1994, CA 9–33
Fraser (Francis) and Warren (Robert) (1956) 40 Cr.App.R. 160, CCA 21–10
French (Lee Ernest) and Gowhar (Walid Mohammed) (1993) 97 Cr.App.R.
    421; *The Times*, March 25, 1993, CA 8–24
French's Dairies (Sevenoaks) v Davis [1973] Crim.L.R. 630, DC 8–79, 19–44
Fricker (Clive Frederick) (1999) 96(30) L.S.G. 29; *The Times*, July 13, 1999,
    CA 5–10
Friend (Billy-Joe) [1997] 1 W.L.R. 1433; [1997] 2 All E.R. 1012; [1997] 2
    Cr.App.R. 231; [1997] Crim.L.R. 817, CA 16–20, 17–18
Frost (1839) 9 C. & P. 159 19–39
Fulcher (Dominic Josef) [1995] 2 Cr.App.R. 251; [1995] Crim.L.R. 883, CA   7–37
Fulling (Ruth Susan) [1987] Q.B. 426; [1987] 2 W.L.R. 923; [1987] 2 All
    E.R. 65; 85 Cr.App.R. 136; 151 J.P. 485; [1987] Crim.L.R. 492; 151
    J.P.N. 364; 131 S.J. 408, CA 9–18, 9–24, 10–13
Funderburk (Roy) [1990] 1 W.L.R. 587; [1990] 2 All E.R. 482; 90
    Cr.App.R. 466; [1990] Crim.L.R. 405; 87(17) L.S.G. 31; 134 S.J. 578,
    CA 21–24, 21–29, 21–30
Fursey (1833) C. & P. 81 3–12
Fuschillo (1940) 27 Cr.App.R. 193 9–59

G v DPP [1998] Q.B. 919; [1998] 2 W.L.R. 609; [1997] 2 All E.R. 755;
    [1997] 2 Cr.App.R. 78; 161 J.P. 498; [1997] 2 F.L.R. 810; [1998] Fam.
    Law 12, DC 17–03, 19–30
G (An Infant) v Coltart; sub nom. G (An Infant), Re [1967] 1 Q.B. 432;
    [1967] 2 W.L.R. 333; [1967] 1 All E.R. 271; 110 S.J. 888, DC 5–15
Gainsborough Justices Ex p. Green (1984) 78 Cr.App.R. 9; 147 J.P. 434;
    [1983] Crim.L.R. 627, DC 19–37
Galbraith (George Charles) [1981] 1 W.L.R. 1039; [1981] 2 All E.R. 1060;
    73 Cr.App.R. 124; [1981] Crim.L.R. 648; 125 S.J. 442, CA 8–72, 14–06,
    16–10, 16–11, 16–12, 16–30
Gale [1994] Crim.L.R. 208 16–16
Gale, *The Times*, June 2, 1993; *Guardian*, June 11, 1993, CA 16–16
Galizadeh [1995] Crim.L.R. 232 6–33

Gall (Gerald) (1990) 90 Cr.App.R. 64; [1989] Crim.L.R. 745; *The Times*,
    May 2, 1989, CA 5–14, 14–27
Gallagher (Robert John) [1974] 1 W.L.R. 1204; [1974] 3 All E.R. 118; 59
    Cr.App.R. 239; [1974] Crim.L.R. 543; 118 S.J. 680, CA 16–21, 17–37,
                                                                        19–02
Garbett (1847) 1 Den. 236 .... 11–04, 11–05
Garland v British Rail Engineering Ltd (No.2) [1983] 2 A.C. 751; [1982] 2
    W.L.R. 918; [1982] 2 C.M.L.R. 174; [1982] I.C.R. 420; [1982]
    I.R.L.R. 257; 126 S.J. 309, HL 13–02
Garner v Chief Constable of Manchester, *The Times*, May 14, 1983, DC   14–07
Garrod (John Trevor) [1997] Crim.L.R. 445, CA 20–19
Garton v Hunter (Valuation Officer) (No.1) [1969] 2 Q.B. 37; [1968] 2
    W.L.R. 86; [1969] 1 All E.R. 451; 133 J.P. 162; 67 L.G.R. 229; 15
    R.R.C. 145; (1968) S.J. 924, CA 3–07
Gaskin v Liverpool City Council [1980] 1 W.L.R. 1549; 124 S.J. 498, CA   12–14
Gatland v Commissioner of Police of the Metropolis [1968] 2 Q.B. 279;
    [1968] 2 W.L.R. 1263; [1968] 2 All E.R. 100; 132 J.P. 323; 66 L.G.R.
    519; 112 S.J. 336, DC 4–19, 4–21
Gayle (Michael) [1999] Crim.L.R. 502, CA 11–17
Gayle (Nicholas Nehemiah) [1999] 2 Cr.App.R. 130, CA 14–18
Gazard (1838) 8 C. & P. 595 12–01
Gearing (Jack William) [1968] 1 W.L.R. 345n; 50 Cr.App.R. 18; [1966]
    Crim.L.R. 438; 109 S.J. 872; *The Times*, October 26, 1965, CCA 19–42
Gent (Stuart Brian) [1990] 1 All E.R. 364; 89 Cr.App.R. 247; *The Times*,
    March 30, 1989, CA 16–23
Ghosh (Deb Baran) [1982] Q.B. 1053; [1982] 3 W.L.R. 110; [1982] 2 All
    E.R. 689; 75 Cr.App.R. 154; [1982] Crim.L.R. 608; 126 S.J. 429, CA   16–24
Gibbins v Skinner; sub nom. Boyd Gibbins v Skinner [1951] 2 K.B. 379;
    [1951] 1 All E.R. 1049; [1951] 1 T.L.R. 1159; 115 J.P. 360; 49 L.G.R.
    713, DC 5–05
Gibson (Ivano) [1983] 1 W.L.R. 1038; [1983] 3 All E.R. 263; 77 Cr.App.R.
    151; 147 J.P. 683; [1983] Crim.L.R. 679; 80 L.S.G. 2133; 127 S.J. 509,
    CA 4–06, 4–44
Gibson (Rodney Douglas) (1991) 93 Cr.App.R. 9; [1991] Crim.L.R. 705;
    135 S.J.L.B. 574, CA 7–19
Gibson v Wales [1983] 1 W.L.R. 393; [1983] 1 All E.R. 869; 76 Cr.App.R.
    60; 147 J.P. 143; [1983] Crim.L.R. 113; 80 L.S.G. 153, DC 5–10
Gilbert (Raymond Sidney) (1978) 66 Cr.App.R. 237; [1978] Crim.L.R. 216,
    CA 11–15
Gilbey, unreported, January 26, 1990 16–15
Gilfoyle (Norman Edward) (Appeal against Conviction) [2001] 2 Cr.App.R.
    5; [2001] Crim.L.R. 312; *The Times*, February 13, 2001, CA 6–17, 8–60
Gill (Samuel James) [1963] 1 W.L.R. 841; [1963] 2 All E.R. 688; 47
    Cr.App.R. 166; 127 J.P. 429; 107 S.J. 417, CCA 4–27
Gill (Sewa Singh) [2003] EWCA Crim 2256; [2004] 1 W.L.R. 469; [2003] 4
    All E.R. 681; [2004] 1 Cr.App.R. 20; *The Times*, August 29, 2003 ..   9–28
Gill (Stephen Ian) [2001] 1 Cr.App.R. 11; [2000] Crim.L.R. 922; *The
    Times*, August 17, 2000, CA 11–21
Gill and Ranuana [1989] Crim.L.R. 358, CA 10–15
Gillard (Margaret Beatrice) and Barrett (Ivor) (1991) 92 Cr.App.R. 61; 155
    J.P. 352; [1991] Crim.L.R. 280; 154 L.G. Rev. 770; *The Times*, Sep-
    tember 5, 1990, CA 9–41

Gillespie (Gaenor Pearl) and Simpson (Rebecca Heslop) (1967) 51
  Cr.App.R. 172; [1967] Crim.L.R. 238; 117 N.L.J. 100; 111 S.J. 92, CA 21–20
Gillie v Posho Ltd [1939] 2 All E.R. 196, PC (EA) 20–02
Glaves [1993] Crim.L.R. 685, CA 9–41
Gloster (1888) Cox C.C. 471 8–59
Glover [1991] Crim.L.R. 48, CA 8–52
Goddard [1994] Crim.L.R. 46, CA 9–43
Goldenberg (Meir) (1989) 88 Cr.App.R. 285; 152 J.P. 557; [1988]
  Crim.L.R. 678; 152 J.P.N. 654; *The Times*, May 27, 1988, CA 9–20,
                                                                           9–21
Golder (Sidney Elmer) [1960] 1 W.L.R. 1169; [1960] 3 All E.R. 457; 45
  Cr.App.R. 5; 124 J.P. 505; 104 S.J. 893, CCA 21–12
Gonzales de Arango (Maria Neza) (1993) 96 Cr.App.R. 399; [1992]
  Crim.L.R. 180, CA 8–24
Goodway (Gary Michael) [1993] 4 All E.R. 894; 98 Cr.App.R. 11; [1993]
  Crim.L.R. 948; 143 N.L.J. 1159; 137 S.J.L.B. 203; *The Times*, August
  11, 1993; *Independent*, August 27, 1993, CA 16–17
Goold v Evans & Co. [1951] 2 T.L.R. 1189, CA 2–07
Gordon (1781) 1 Leach 505; 21 How St. Tr. 435 .... 5–05, 8–64
Gordon (1987) 92 Cr.App.R. 50n 16–23
Gordon (Michael) [1995] 1 Cr.App.R. 290; [1995] Crim.L.R. 413; *The
  Times*, May 27, 1994; *Independent*, June 9, 1994, CA 14–42
Gordon (Stafford George) [1995] 2 Cr.App.R. 61; [1995] Crim.L.R. 142,
  CA 1–14, 16–05
Gough v Chief Constable of Derbyshire; sub nom. Miller v Leeds Magis-
  trates Court [2002] EWCA Civ 351; [2002] Q.B. 1213; [2002] 3
  W.L.R. 289; [2002] 2 All E.R. 985; [2002] 2 C.M.L.R. 11; [2002] Eu.
  L.R. 359; [2002] H.R.L.R. 29; [2002] A.C.D. 75; 99(18) L.S.G. 36; 152
  N.L.J. 552; 146 S.J.L.B. 94; *The Times*, April 10, 2002; *Independent*,
  March 27, 2002; *Daily Telegraph*, March 28, 2002, CA 13–14
Governor of Pentonville Prison Ex p. Osman (No.1); sub nom. Osman
  (No.1), Re [1990] 1 W.L.R. 277; [1989] 3 All E.R. 701; 90 Cr.App.R.
  281; [1988] Crim.L.R. 611; 87(7) L.S.G. 32; 134 S.J. 458, QBD 3–06,
                                                                           11–30
Governor of Brixton Prison Ex p. Osman [1991] 1 W.L.R. 281; [1992] 1 All
  E.R. 108; 93 Cr.App.R. 202; 3 Admin. L.R. 225; [1991] Crim.L.R.
  533; [1991] C.O.D. 103; 88(7) L.S.G. 36; *The Times*, December 17,
  1990, DC 12–16
Governor of Pentonville Prison Ex p. Voets [1986] 1 W.L.R. 470; [1986] 2
  All E.R. 630; 83 L.S.G. 1058; 130 S.J. 245, DC 14–37
Grafton (John Peter) [1993] Q.B. 101; [1992] 3 W.L.R. 532; [1992] 4 All
  E.R. 609; 96 Cr.App.R. 156; 156 J.P. 857; [1992] Crim.L.R. 826; 156
  J.P.N. 490; 89(21) L.S.G. 27; 136 S.J.L.B. 113; *The Times*, April 13,
  1992, CA 19–06
Graham [1973] Crim.L.R. 628, CA 20–24, 20–31
Grannell (Robert James) (1990) 90 Cr.App.R. 149; *The Times*, August 16,
  1989, CA 14–28
Grant (1944) 30 Cr.App.R. 99 17–11
Grant (Richard Francis) [1996] 2 Cr.App.R. 272, CA 14–12
Grant v Southwestern and County Properties Ltd [1975] Ch. 185; [1974] 3
  W.L.R. 221; [1974] 2 All E.R. 465; 118 S.J. 548, Ch D 3–02
Gray (Darren John) and Evans (Gareth) [1998] Crim.L.R. 570; *The Times*,
  March 9, 1998, CA 9–54, 21–21

Gray (David John), Liggins, Riding (Mark)and Rowlands (Catherine Mary) [1995] 2 Cr.App.R. 100; [1995] Crim.L.R. 45; 91(39) L.S.G. 38; 138 S.J.L.B. 199, CA 8–64
Gray (Paul Edward) [2003] EWCA 1001 .... 6–06, 6–42
Gray (Richard Michael) (1974) 58 Cr.App.R. 177, CA 4–43
Greasby [1984] Crim.L.R. 488, CA 5–21
Greenhough v Eccles (1859) 5 C.B. (N.S.) 786 ...... 21–08, 21–09, 21–12, 21–14
Greer (James) [1998] Crim.L.R. 572, CA 8–28, 8–74
Gregory v DPP [2002] EWHC 385 (Admin); 166 J.P. 400; 166 J.P.N. 509, QBD 6–13
Gregory v Tavernor (1836) 6 C. & P. 280 .... 20–32, 20–33
Grimer [1982] Crim.L.R. 674; 126 S.J. 641, CA 2–37
Grossman (Joseph Henry) (1981) 73 Cr.App.R. 302; [1981] Crim.L.R. 396, CA 3–17
Grundy & Co. Excavations Ltd and Sean Parry v Halton Division Magistrates' Court [2003] EWHC 272; (2003) 167 J.P. 387; (2003) 167 J.P.N. 534 13–21
Gummerson (James Wesley) and Steadman [1999] Crim.L.R. 680, CA 14–48
Gunewardene (Sumatalage Reginald) [1951] 2 K.B. 600; [1951] 2 All E.R. 290; [1951] 2 T.L.R. 315; 35 Cr.App.R. 80; 115 J.P. 415; 95 S.J. 548, CCA 9–54
Guney (Erkin Ramadan) [1998] 2 Cr.App.R. 242; [1999] Crim.L.R. 485; 95(15) L.S.G. 30; 142 S.J.L.B. 99; The Times, March 9, 1998; Independent, March 6, 1998, CA 18–12
Gunning (Mervyn Whitfield) (1994) 98 Cr.App.R. 303, CA 19–07
Gurney [1977] R.T.R. 211; [1976] Crim.L.R. 567, CA 2–06
Gutteridge [1973] R.T.R. 135 16–22
Guttridge (1840) 9 C. & P. 471 20–05
Guyll v Bright (1987) 84 Cr.App.R. 260; [1987] R.T.R. 104, QBD 4–19

H [1987] Crim.L.R. 47, Crown Ct 10–23
H [1994] Crim.L.R. 205, CA 7–15
H (A Minor) (Originating Application in Adoption Proceedings), Re; sub nom. H (Criminal Proceedings: Disclosure of Adoption Records), Re [1995] 1 F.L.R. 964; [1995] 2 F.C.R. 711; [1995] Fam. Law 470, Fam Div 12–17
H (Evidence: Corroboration); sub nom. Hepburn [1995] 2 A.C. 596; [1995] 2 W.L.R. 737; [1995] 2 All E.R. 865; [1995] 2 Cr.App.R. 437; 159 J.P. 469; [1995] Crim.L.R. 717; 92(24) L.S.G. 39; 139 S.J.L.B. 144, HL 7–70
H (Harry) (A Juvenile) [2001] Crim.L.R. 227; The Times, May 5, 2000, CA 5–31
H (Joseph Robert) (1990) 90 Cr.App.R. 440; [1990] Crim.L.R. 51, CA ... 5–26
HM Coroner for Newcastle upon Tyne Ex p. A (1998) 162 J.P. 387; [1998] C.O.D. 163; The Times, January 19, 1998, QBD 19–18
H (Minors) (Sexual Abuse: Standard of Proof), Re; sub nom. H (Minors) (Child Abuse: Threshold Conditions), Re; H and R (Child Sexual Abuse: Standard of Proof), Re [1996] A.C. 563; [1996] 2 W.L.R. 8; [1996] 1 All E.R. 1; [1996] 1 F.L.R. 80; [1996] 1 F.C.R. 509; [1996] Fam. Law 74; 145 N.L.J. 1887; 140 S.J.L.B. 24, HL 4–37
H (Special Measures), The Times, April 15, 2003, CA 19–13
H (Witness Reprisals); sub nom. A (Witness Reprisals) [2001] Crim.L.R. 815; The Times, July 6, 2001, CA 8–28

H and C [2003] 1 W.L.R. 3006; *The Times*, February 6, 2004 .... 12–17, 12–18,
    12–19, 12–25
H and M v DPP [1998] Crim.L.R. 653, CA 9–30
Hackney (David John) (1982) 74 Cr.App.R. 194, CA 3–13, 21–22
Hadwen [1902] 1 K.B. 882, CCR 21–15
Hagan (Sean) [1997] 1 Cr.App.R. 464; [1997] Crim.L.R. 583, CA 2–27
Halawa v Federation Against Copyright Theft [1995] 1 Cr.App.R. 21; 159
    J.P. 816; [1995] Crim.L.R. 409; 159 J.P.N. 797, QBD 9–49, 10–13,
    10–31, 16–28
Hall [1993] Crim.L.R. 527; *The Times*, March 5, 1993, CA 5–27, 5–30
Hall (Peter Barnabas) [1973] Q.B. 496; [1972] 3 W.L.R. 974; [1973] 1 All
    E.R. 1; 57 Cr.App.R. 170; [1973] Crim.L.R. 48; 116 S.J. 901, CA ... 8–85
Hallett [1986] Crim.L.R. 462, CA 12–07
Halpin (John Francis) [1975] Q.B. 907; [1975] 3 W.L.R. 260; [1975] 2
    All E.R. 1124; 61 Cr.App.R. 97; [1975] Crim.L.R. 453; 119 S.J. 541,
    CA 8–42
Ham (Benjamin Albert) (1997) 36 B.M.L.R. 169; *The Times*, December 12,
    1995, CA 9–57
Hamand (Graham Alan) (1986) 82 Cr.App.R. 65; [1985] Crim.L.R. 375; 82
    L.S.G. 1561, CA 20–17
Hamid (Ahmed Youssef) and Hamid (Beebee Nazmoon) (1979) 69
    Cr.App.R. 324, CA 15–03, 15–07
Hamilton [1969] Crim.L.R. 486; 113 S.J. 546, CA 7–61
Hammond (1941) 28 Cr.App.R. 84 16–05
Hampshire (David Peter) [1996] Q.B. 1; [1995] 1 W.L.R. 260; [1995] 2 All
    E.R. 1019; [1995] 2 Cr.App.R. 319; [1995] Crim.L.R. 644, CA 17–03,
    19–26
Hardwick (Gary Kevin) [2001] EWCA Crim 369; *The Times*, February 28,
    2001, CA 8–21
Hardwicke (Joseph Philip) and Thwaites (Stefan Peter) [2001] Crim.L.R.
    220; *The Times*, November 16, 2000, CA 10–16
Hardy (1794) 24 How. St. Tr. 199 12–02
Hardy [2003] 1 Cr.App.R. 494 2–21
Haringey Justices Ex p. DPP [1996] Q.B. 351; [1996] 2 W.L.R. 114; [1996]
    1 All E.R. 828; [1996] 2 Cr.App.R. 119; 160 J.P. 326; [1996]
    Crim.L.R. 327; [1996] C.O.D. 115; 160 J.P.N. 684; *The Times*, Sep-
    tember 5, 1995, QBD 19–01, 19–02
Harman (1984) 148 J.P. 289; [1985] Crim.L.R. 326, CA 21–33
Harmony Shipping Co. SA v Davis [1979] 1 W.L.R. 1380; [1979] 3 All E.R.
    177; [1980] 1 Lloyd's Rep. 44, CA 6–29, 11–33, 17–01
Harris [1986] Crim.L.R. 123, CA 16–16
Harris [2001] Crim.L.R. 227 5–31
Harris (Dora) [1927] 2 K.B. 587, CCA 19–06
Harris (Frank Herbert) v DPP [1952] A.C. 694; [1952] 1 All E.R. 1044;
    [1952] 1 T.L.R. 1075; 36 Cr.App.R. 39; 116 J.P. 248; 96 S.J. 312,
    HL 10–04
Harris v Tippett (1811) 2 Camp. 637 .... 21–12, 21–28
Harron (Robert David) [1996] 2 Cr.App.R. 457; [1996] Crim.L.R. 581,
    CA 4–08, 16–18, 16–19
Hart (Richard Charles) (1958) 42 Cr.App.R. 47, CCA 21–11, 21–24
Hart (Walter Berkley) (1932) 23 Cr.App.R. 202, CCA 21–16
Harvey [1988] Crim.L.R. 241, CCC 9–24
Harwood [1989] Crim.L.R. 285, CA 10–15

Hay (1860) 2 F. & F. 4 11–37
Hay (Christopher Paul) (1983) 77 Cr.App.R. 70; [1983] Crim.L.R. 390, CA   5–24
Hayes (Geoffrey) [1977] 1 W.L.R. 234; [1977] 2 All E.R. 288; 64 Cr.App.R.
    194, CA
Hayter (Paul Ali) [2003] EWCA Crim 1048; [2003] 1 W.L.R. 1910; [2003]
    2 Cr.App.R. 27; 100(25) L.S.G. 45; 147 S.J.L.B. 537; *The Times*, April
    18, 2003, CA 9–54
Head (Elsie) and Warrener (Ivy) (1961) 45 Cr.App.R. 225; 105 S.J. 552,
    CCA 4–41
Heath 9–22
Heath, *The Times*, February 10, 1994, CA 7–26
Hedges (1909) 3 Cr.App.R. 262 20–06
Hendrie, *The Times*, July 27, 1994, CA 5–23
Hendry (Wayne Russell) (1989) 88 Cr.App.R. 187; 153 J.P. 166; [1988]
    Crim.L.R. 766; 153 J.P.N. 185; *The Times*, June 14, 1988, CA 16–06
Hennessey (1978) 68 Cr.App.R. 419, CA 12–02, 12–05
Hennessy v Wright (1888) 21 Q.B.D. 509 12–02
Hepworth (George Alfred) and Fearnley (Norman) [1955] 2 Q.B. 600;
    [1955] 3 W.L.R. 331; [1955] 2 All E.R. 918; 39 Cr.App.R. 152; 119
    J.P. 516; 99 S.J. 544,   CCA 4–41, 4–42
Hersey (Ian) [1998] Crim.L.R. 281, CA 14–48
Hertfordshire CC Ex p. Green Environmental Industries Ltd; sub nom.
    Green Environmental Industries Ltd, Re; Green Environmental Indus-
    tries Ltd v Hertfordshire CC [2000] 2 A.C. 412; [2000] 2 W.L.R. 373;
    [2000] 1 All E.R. 773; [2000] Eu. L.R. 414; [2000] Env. L.R. 426;
    [2000] E.H.L.R. 199; [2000] H.R.L.R. 359; [2000] U.K.H.R.R. 361; 2
    L.G.L.R. 754; [2000] B.L.G.R. 215; [2000] 1 P.L.R. 108; [2000]
    C.O.D. 223; [2000] E.G.C.S. 27; 97(9) L.S.G. 42; 150 N.L.J. 277;
    [2000] N.P.C. 15; *The Times*, February 22, 2000; *Independent*, Feb-
    ruary 22, 2000, HL 11–02, 11–11
Hester. *See* DPP v Hester
Hetherington [1972] Crim.L.R. 703, CA 16–07
Hewett [1978] R.T.R. 174; [1977] Crim.L.R. 554, CA 14–10
Hewitt (Peter) and Davis (Reginald Anthony) (1992) 95 Cr.App.R. 81;
    [1992] Crim.L.R. 650; 142 N.L.J. 160; *The Times*, January 1, 1992;
    Independent, January 24, 1992, CA 12–09
Hickmet (Mustapha) [1996] Crim.L.R. 588, CA 7–19
Higgins, *The Times*, February 16, 1989; *Independent*, February 13, 1989,
    CA 19–43
Higgins [1996] 1 F.L.R. 137; [1996] 2 F.C.R. 612; [1996] Fam. Law 144;
    146 N.L.J. 918, CA 12–17
Higgins (Brian George) and Litchfield (Elizabeth), *The Times*, August 11,
    1995; *Independent*, July 31, 1995, CA 16–14
Highbury Magistrates' Court Ex p. Boyce (1984) 79 Cr.App.R. 132; [1984]
    Crim.L.R. 294; 148 J.P.N. 332; 81 L.S.G. 733, DC 14–14
Hill (1851) 2 Den. 254 17–06
Hill (1912) 7 Cr.App.R. 1 19–34
Hill (Valerie Mary) and Hall (Jennifer) (1989) 89 Cr.App.R. 74; [1989]
    Crim.L.R. 136; *The Times*, October 6, 1988, CA 16–23
Hill v Baxter [1958] 1 Q.B. 277; [1958] 2 W.L.R. 76; [1958] 1 All E.R. 193;
    61 T.L.R. 452; 42 Cr.App.R. 51; 122 J.P. 134; 56 L.G.R. 117; 102 S.J.
    53, DC 4–27, 6–18

Hilton (Keith) [1972] 1 Q.B. 421; [1971] 3 W.L.R. 625; [1971] 3 All E.R. 541; 55 Cr.App.R. 466; 115 S.J. 565, CA 17–12, 21–15
Hindson v Ashby [1896] 2 Ch. 1 2–11
Hipson [1969] Crim.L.R. 85; 112 S.J. 945, CA 6–30
Hirst v Chief Constable of West Yorkshire (1987) 85 Cr.App.R. 143; 151 J.P. 304; [1987] Crim.L.R. 330; 151 L.G. Rev. 130, DC 4–19
Hobbs v CT Tinling & Co. Ltd [1929] 2 K.B. 1, CA 21–27
Hocking v Ahlquist Bros Ltd [1944] K.B. 120, KBD 2–02, 2–03
Hodges (Kevin John) and Walker (John) [2003] EWCA Crim 290; [2003] 2 Cr.App.R. 15; [2003] Crim.L.R. 472, CA 6–39
Hogan (James Faulkner) [1974] Q.B. 398; [1974] 2 W.L.R. 357; [1974] 2 All E.R. 142; 59 Cr.App.R. 174; [1974] Crim.L.R. 247; 118 S.J. 218, Crown Ct 5–19
Hogan (Kevin Barry) [1997] Crim.L.R. 349, CA 3–13, 8–32
Holden (1838) 8 C. & P. 606 19–06
Hollington v F Hewthorn & Co. Ltd [1943] K.B. 587, CA 5–27
Holmes (1871) L.R. 1 C.C.R. 334 21–28
Holmes (Joseph) [1953] 1 W.L.R. 686; [1953] 2 All E.R. 324; 37 Cr.App.R. 61; 117 J.P. 346; 97 S.J. 355, CCA 6–05
Homes v Newman [1931] 2 Ch. 112, Ch D 8–61
Honeyghon (Jason Norman) [1999] Crim.L.R. 221, CA 21–10
Hookway [1999] Crim.L.R. 750 14–38
Hopes and Lavery v HM Advocate, 1960 J.C. 104; 1960 S.L.T. 264; [1960] Crim.L.R. 566, HCJ 2–28
Hopper [1915] 2 K.B. 431, KBD 4–31
Horne v Mackenzie (1839) 6 Cl. & F. 628 20–30
Horseferry Road Magistrates' Court Ex p. Bennett (No.2) [1994] 1 All E.R. 289; 99 Cr.App.R. 123; [1994] Crim.L.R. 370; The Times, November 26, 1993; Independent, November 12, 1993, DC 12–12
Horseferry Road Magistrates' Court Ex p. Hillier (1998) 162 J.P. 783; 162 J.P.N. 983, DC 19–37
Horsford, The Times, June 2–6, 1898 8–59
Horsham Justices Ex p. Bukhari (1982) 74 Cr.App.R. 291; [1982] Crim.L.R. 178, DC 14–13, 14–14
Hoskyn v Commissioner of Police of the Metropolis [1979] A.C. 474; [1978] 2 W.L.R. 695; [1978] 2 All E.R. 136; 67 Cr.App.R. 88; [1978] Crim.L.R. 429; 122 S.J. 279, HL 17–31
House and Meadows [1994] Crim.L.R. 682, CA 16–18
Howe v Malkin (1878) 40 L.T. 196 8–58
Howick [1970] Crim.L.R. 403, CA 14–13
Hudson [1912] 2 K.B. 464, CCA 7–66
Hudson [1994] Crim.L.R. 920, CA 5–21
Hudson v DPP (1992) 156 J.P. 168; [1992] R.T.R. 27; [1992] C.O.D. 22; 156 J.P.N. 28; The Times, May 28, 1991, DC 10–14
Hughes, The Times, November 8, 1977 14–15
Hughes [1988] Crim.L.R. 519, CA 10–17, 10–28
Hui Chi-Ming v R. [1992] 1 A.C. 34; [1991] 3 W.L.R. 495; [1991] 3 All E.R. 897; 94 Cr.App.R. 236; [1992] Crim.L.R. 446, PC (HK) ... 5–21, 5–23
Hulbert (Lilian Juliet) (1979) 69 Cr.App.R. 243, CA 9–59
Hulusi (Kolliari Mehmet) and Purvis (Maurice Malcolm) (1974) 58 Cr.App.R. 378, CA 19–07
Hunjan (Mohinder Singh) (1979) 68 Cr.App.R. 99; [1979] Crim.L.R. 110, CA 14–36

Hunt [1992] Crim.L.R. 582, CA 9–42
Hunt (Richard Selwyn) [1987] A.C. 352; [1986] 3 W.L.R. 1115; [1987] 1
    All E.R. 1; 84 Cr.App.R. 163; [1987] Crim.L.R. 263, HL 2–06, 4–12,
                                                    4–21, 4–22, 4–23, 4–24, 4–25
Hunter [1969] Crim.L.R. 262; 113 S.J. 161, CA 14–13
Hurst (Marnie Michelle) [1995] 1 Cr.App.R. 82; *The Times*, February 2,
    1994, CA 8–23, 8–24
Hutchinson (Arthur) (1986) 82 Cr.App.R. 51; [1985] Crim.L.R. 730; 82
    L.S.G. 2332; 129 S.J. 700, CA 8–63, 9–11, 9–12, 19–40
Hutton (Martin) and Aslam (Mohammed) (1987) 9 Cr.App.R. (S.) 484;
    [1988] Crim.L.R. 258, CA 20–16
Hutton (Michael Anthony) [1999] Crim.L.R. 74, CA 14–20

ITC Film Distributors Ltd v Video Exchange Ltd (No.1) [1983] E.C.C. 43,
    CA; affirming [1982] Ch. 431; [1982] 3 W.L.R. 125; [1982] 2 All E.R.
    241; [1982] Crim.L.R. 237; 125 S.J. 863, Ch D 11–36
Ilyas (Mohammed) and Knight (Paul) [1996] Crim.L.R. 810, CA 8–32
Imran (Mohammed) and Hussain (Sajid) [1997] Crim.L.R. 754, CA .. 2–32, 11–23
Inch (Christopher) (1990) 91 Cr.App.R. 51, CMAC 6–28
Ingram v Percival [1969] 1 Q.B. 548; [1968] 3 W.L.R. 663; [1968] 3 All
    E.R. 657; 133 J.P. 1; 112 S.J. 722, DC 5–11
Inhabitants of Llanfaethly (1853) 2 E. & B. 940 3–14
Inquiry under the Company Securities (Insider Dealing) Act 1985 (No.1), Re
    [1988] A.C. 660; [1988] 2 W.L.R. 33; [1988] 1 All E.R. 203; (1988) 4
    B.C.C. 35; [1988] B.C.L.C. 153; [1988] P.C.C. 133; 85(4) L.S.G. 33;
    137 N.L.J. 1181; 132 S.J. 21, HL 11–37
Ioannou [1999] Crim.L.R. 586, CA 11–17
Irish Society v Bishop of Derry (1846) 12 Cl. & F. 641 8–41
Iroegbu, *The Times*, August 2, 1988, Ca 16–16
Islam (Abdul Khair) [1999] 1 Cr.App.R. 22; 162 J.P. 391; [1998] Crim.L.R.
    575; 162 J.P.N. 445; 95(17) L.S.G. 29; 142 S.J.L.B. 123; *The Times*,
    March 18, 1998, CA 20–04
Islington LBC v Panico [1973] 1 W.L.R. 1166; [1973] 3 All E.R. 485; 72
    L.G.R. 51; [1973] Crim.L.R. 536; 117 S.J. 648, DC 4–46
Ismael [1990] Crim.L.R. 109 9–41

JM (A Minor) v Runeckles (1984) 79 Cr.App.R. 255, DC 5–04
Jackson [1992] Crim.L.R. 214, CA 16–13
Jackson (Terry Paul) [1996] 2 Cr.App.R. 420; [1996] Crim.L.R. 732, CA   6–33,
                                                                                6–41
James (Colin Richard) [1996] Crim.L.R. 650; *The Times*, March 18, 1996,
    CA 9–28
James v South Glamorgan CC (1994) 99 Cr.App.R. 321; 157 J.P. 561;
    [1992] R.T.R. 312; 156 J.P.N. 618, DC 19–35
Jarvis v DPP [1996] R.T.R. 192, DC 5–09
Jayasena (Rajapakse Pathurange) v R. [1970] A.C. 618; [1970] 2 W.L.R.
    448; [1970] 1 All E.R. 219; 114 S.J. 56, PC (Cey) 4–29
Jefferson (Andrew Steven) [1994] 1 All E.R. 270; 99 Cr.App.R. 13; 158 J.P.
    76; [1993] Crim.L.R. 880; 157 J.P.N. 699; *The Times*, June 22, 1993,
    CA 9–30, 9–54
Jeffrey v Black [1978] Q.B. 490; [1977] 3 W.L.R. 895; [1978] 1 All E.R.
    555; 66 Cr.App.R. 81; [1977] Crim.L.R. 555; 121 S.J. 662, DC 10–05,
                                                                        10–06, 16–27

Jeffries (Mark Thomas) [1997] Crim.L.R. 819, CA 6–04
Jelen (Lawrence) and Katz (Anthony) (1990) 90 Cr.App.R. 456, CA 9–27,
    10–22, 10–23
Jenkins (1945) 31 Cr.App.R. 1 .... 7–66, 7–68
Jenkins (Nigel) and Starling (Mark) [2002] EWCA Crim 2475; [2003]
    Crim.L.R. 107, CA 8–32
Jennings (Gary) and Miles (John) [1995] Crim.L.R. 810, CA 8–29
Jiminez-Paez (Carmenza); sub nom. Carmenza Jiminez-Paez (1994) 98
    Cr.App.R. 239; [1993] Crim.L.R. 596; *The Times*, March 16, 1993,
    CA 8–24
Johanssen (1977) 65 Cr.App.R. 101; [1977] Crim.L.R. 677; 121 S.J. 423,
    CA 7–70
John [1973] Crim.L.R. 113, CA 14–15
John M. *See* M (John)
John v Express Newspapers [2000] 1 W.L.R. 1931; [2000] 3 All E.R. 257;
    [2000] E.M.L.R. 606; 97(21) L.S.G. 38; 150 N.L.J. 615; 144 S.J.L.B.
    217; *The Times*, April 26, 2000; *Independent*, May 2, 2000, CA 11–37
John v Humphreys [1955] 1 W.L.R. 325; [1955] 1 All E.R. 793; 53 L.G.R.
    321; 99 S.J. 222, DC 4–19, 4–24
Johnson (Anthony Hugh) [1961] 1 W.L.R. 1478; [1961] 3 All E.R. 969; 46
    Cr.App.R. 55; 126 J.P. 40; 105 S.J. 1108, CCA 4–27
Johnson (Beverley) [1996] Crim.L.R. 504, CA 14–22
Johnson (Kenneth) [1988] 1 W.L.R. 1377; [1989] 1 All E.R. 121; 88
    Cr.App.R. 131; [1988] Crim.L.R. 831; 139 N.L.J. 643, CA ... 12–09, 12–10
Johnstone (Robert Alexander) [2003] UKHL 28; [2003] 1 W.L.R. 1736;
    [2003] 3 All E.R. 884; [2003] 2 Cr.App.R. 33; 167 J.P. 281; [2004]
    E.T.M.R. 2; [2003] H.R.L.R. 25; [2003] U.K.H.R.R. 1239; [2003]
    F.S.R. 42; 167 J.P.N. 453; 100(26) L.S.G. 36; 147 S.J.L.B. 625; *The
    Times*, May 29, 2003; *Independent*, June 5, 2003, HL 13–21
Jolly v DPP [2000] Crim.L.R. 471 19–41
Jones (1923) 17 Cr.App.R. 117 7–66
Jones (Brian) [1997] 2 Cr.App.R. 119; [1996] Crim.L.R. 901, CA 8–64
Jones (Keith) (1997) 161 J.P. 597; [1998] Crim.L.R. 56; 161 J.P.N. 838; *The
    Times*, April 24, 1997, CA 4–22
Jones (Kerry Michael) [1988] Crim.L.R. 579 21–10
Jones (Mark Anthony), Dowling, Jones (DH) and Brown (1994) 158 J.P.
    293; 138 S.J.L.B. 51; *The Times*, January 13, 1994, CA 14–26, 14–27
Jones (Reginald Watson) [1970] 1 W.L.R. 16; [1969] 3 All E.R. 1559; 54
    Cr.App.R. 63; [1970] R.T.R. 35; 113 S.J. 962, CA 5–09
Jones (Reginald William). *See* Jones (Reginald Watson)
Jones and Nelson, *The Times*, April 21, 1999, CA 14–22
Jones v DPP [1962] A.C. 635; [1962] 2 W.L.R. 575; [1962] 1 All E.R. 569;
    46 Cr.App.R. 129; 126 J.P. 216; 96 I.L.T. 207; 106 S.J. 192, HL 7–32,
    7–54
Jones v National Coal Board [1957] 2 Q.B. 55; [1957] 2 W.L.R. 760; [1957]
    2 All E.R. 155; 101 S.J. 319, CA 19–07
Jones v Owen (1870) 34 J.P. 759 10–05
Jones v South Eastern & Chatham Railway (1918) 87 L.J. K.B. 775 20–02
Jones v Stroud (1825) 2 C. & P. 196 20–31
Joseph [1993] Crim.L.R. 206, CA 9–37
Joseph (Sheldon) [1994] Crim.L.R. 48; *The Times*, May 25, 1993, CA 14–23
Joy v Federation against Copyright Theft [1993] Crim.L.R. 588, DC 9–28
Juett [1981] Crim.L.R. 113, CA 16–10

K [1999] Crim.L.R. 980 20–04

K (Minors) (Disclosure of Privileged Material), Re; sub nom. Kent CC v K
[1994] 1 W.L.R. 912; [1994] 3 All E.R. 230; [1994] 1 F.L.R. 377;
[1994] 2 F.C.R. 805; [1994] Fam. Law 247; *Independent*, November
23, 1993, Fam Div 11–09

K (Minors) (Wardship: Criminal Proceedings), Re [1988] Fam. 1; [1987] 3
W.L.R. 1233; [1988] 1 All E.R. 214; 152 J.P. 185; [1988] 1 F.L.R. 435;
[1988] Fam. Law 166; 84 L.S.G. 3501; 138 N.L.J. 388; 131 S.J. 1697,
Fam Div 17–05

K (TD) (1993) 97 Cr.App.R. 342; [1993] 2 F.L.R. 181; [1993] Crim.L.R.
281; [1993] Fam. Law 515; 136 S.J.L.B. 328; *The Times*, December 8,
1992, CA 12–14, 12–15, 12–16, 12–20

Kabariti (Wared Mhaywi) (1991) 92 Cr.App.R. 362; [1991] Crim.L.R. 450,
CA 7–23

Kachikwu (Augustine Achuzia) (1968) 52 Cr.App.R. 538; [1968] Crim.L.R.
375; 112 S.J. 460, CA 16–15

Kajala v Noble (1982) 75 Cr.App.R. 149; [1982] Crim.L.R. 433, DC 2–28,
2–31, 3–04, 3–06

Kalia (Daya) (1974) 60 Cr.App.R. 200; [1975] Crim.L.R. 181, CA 21–16

Kansal (Yash Pal) (No.2) [2001] UKHL 62; [2002] 2 A.C. 69; [2001] 3
W.L.R. 1562; [2002] 1 All E.R. 257; [2002] 1 Cr.App.R. 36; [2002]
H.R.L.R. 9; [2002] U.K.H.R.R. 169; [2002] B.P.I.R. 370; [2002]
Crim.L.R. 498; 99(3) L.S.G. 25; 145 S.J.L.B. 275; *The Times*,
December 4, 2001; *Independent*, December 4, 2001; *Daily Telegraph*,
December 6, 2001, HL 13–03

Karamat v R. [1956] A.C. 256; [1956] 2 W.L.R. 412; [1956] 1 All E.R. 415;
40 Cr.App.R. 13; 120 J.P. 136; 100 S.J. 109, PC (BG) 2–06

Karia v DPP, unreported, October 14, 2002 14–14

Kaul (Natasha) and Collin (Peter John) [1998] Crim.L.R. 135; *The Times*,
November 10, 1997, CA 19–42

Keane [1992] Crim.L.R. 306, CA 9–45, 16–16

Keane (Peter Paul) (1977) 65 Cr.App.R. 247, CA 14–04, 14–08

Keane (Stephen John) [1994] 1 W.L.R. 746; [1994] 2 All E.R. 478; 99
Cr.App.R. 1; [1995] Crim.L.R. 225; 144 N.L.J. 391; 138 S.J.L.B. 75;
The Times, March 15, 1994; *Independent*, March 16, 1994, CA 12–16,
12–21, 18–07

Kearley (Alan Robert) [1992] 2 A.C. 228; [1992] 2 W.L.R. 656; [1992] 2 All
E.R. 345; 95 Cr.App.R. 88; [1992] Crim.L.R. 797; 89(21) L.S.G. 28;
142 N.L.J. 599, HL 5–32

Keaton (1970) 54 Cr.App.R. 267 10–23

Keenan (Graham) 1990] 2 Q.B. 54; [1989] 3 W.L.R. 1193; [1989] 3 All E.R.
598; 90 Cr.App.R. 1; 154 J.P. 67; [1989] Crim.L.R. 720; 153 J.P.N.
802; 87(1) L.S.G. 30; 134 S.J. 114, CA 9–29, 9–31, 9–38, 18–27

Keeton (Geoffrey Wayne) [1995] 2 Cr.App.R. 241; *The Times*, July 21,
1994, CA 16–18

Kelly (Francis William) [1970] 1 W.L.R. 1050; [1970] 2 All E.R. 198; 54
Cr.App.R. 334; 114 S.J. 357, CA 16–22

Kelly (Liam Paul) (1998) 162 J.P. 231; 162 J.P.N. 243; *The Times*, February
23, 1998, CA 14–27

Kelsey (Alan) (1982) 74 Cr.App.R. 213; [1982] R.T.R. 135; [1982]
Crim.L.R. 435; 126 S.J. 97, CA 20–29, 20–31

Kemble (Peter) [1990] 1 W.L.R. 1111; [1990] 3 All E.R. 116; 91 Cr.App.R.
178; 154 J.P. 593; [1990] Crim.L.R. 719; 154 J.P.N. 547; *The Times*,

June 12, 1990; *Independent*, June 25, 1990; *Daily Telegraph*, September 3, 1990, CA 19–08

Kempster (Mark John) [1989] 1 W.L.R. 1125; 90 Cr.App.R. 14; [1989] Crim.L.R. 747, CA 5–33, 5–35

Kennedy [1992] Crim.L.R. 37, CA 8–74

Kennedy (John) v HM Advocate (Murder), 1944 J.C. 171; 1945 S.L.T. 11, HCJ Appeal 4–28

Kennedy and Burrell [1994] Crim.L.R. 50, CA 8–74

Kenny (David) [1994] Crim.L.R. 284; *The Times*, July 27, 1993, CA 9–56

Kent v Stamps [1982] R.T.R. 273, DC 5–11

Kent CC v K. *See* K (Minors) (Disclosure of Privileged Material), Re

Khan [1993] Crim.L.R. 54, CA 9–45

Khan (Junaid) (1987) 84 Cr.App.R. 44, CA 17–35

Khan, Sakkaravej and Pamarapa [1997] Crim.L.R. 508, CA 10–19

Khan (Shakeel) [2001] EWCA Crim 486; [2001] Crim.L.R. 673, CA 16–21

Khan (Sultan) [1997] A.C. 558; [1996] 3 W.L.R. 162; [1996] 3 All E.R. 289; [1996] 2 Cr.App.R. 440; [1996] Crim.L.R. 733; 93(28) L.S.G. 29; 146 N.L.J. 1024; 140 S.J.L.B. 166, HL 10–05, 10–26, 13–02, 13–06

Khan (Umer), Dad (Afran) and Afsar (Shakeel) [2002] EWCA Crim 945; [2003] Crim.L.R. 428, CA 21–10

Khan v Khan [1982] 1 W.L.R. 513 11–08

Kilbourne. *See* DPP v Kilbourne

Kilgour v Owen (1889) 88 L.T. 7 3–14

King (David Andrew) [1983] 1 W.L.R. 411; [1983] 1 All E.R. 929; 77 Cr.App.R. 1; 147 J.P. 65; [1983] Crim.L.R. 326, CA ... 6–29, 11–33, 11–34

King v Kucharz (1989) 153 J.P. 336; [1989] C.O.D. 469; 153 J.P.N. 390, DC 18–03

Kinglake (1870) Cox C.C. 499 11–04

King's Lynn Justices Ex p. Holland [1993] 1 W.L.R. 324; [1993] 2 All E.R. 377; 96 Cr.App.R. 74; 156 J.P. 825; [1992] Crim.L.R. 880; [1993] C.O.D. 30; 156 J.P.N. 588, DC 10–14

Kingston upon Hull Justices Ex p. McCann (1991) 155 J.P. 569; 155 J.P.N. 394, DC 18–04

Kirk (Alfred Alexander) [2000] 1 W.L.R. 567; [1999] 4 All E.R. 698; [2000] 1 Cr.App.R. 400, CA 10–20

Kitchen [1994] Crim.L.R. 684, CA 14–35

Knowlden (Derek James) (1983) 77 Cr.App.R. 94, CA 15–18

Kolton (Grzegorz) [2000] Crim.L.R. 761, CA 5–07

Konscol [1993] Crim.L.R. 950, CA 10–21

Korniak (Anthony John) (1983) 76 Cr.App.R. 145; [1983] Crim.L.R. 109, CA 9–59

Kray [1970] 1 Q.B. 125; [1969] 3 W.L.R. 831; [1969] 3 All E.R. 941; 53 Cr.App.R. 569; 133 J.P. 719; 113 S.J. 793, CA 7–52

Kritz (Abraham Barnett) [1950] 1 K.B. 82; [1949] 2 All E.R. 406; 65 T.L.R. 505; 33 Cr.App.R. 169; 113 J.P. 449; 48 L.G.R. 88; [1949] L.J.R. 1535; 93 S.J. 648, CCA 4–05, 4–41, 4–42

Kunnath v Mauritius [1993] 1 W.L.R. 1315; [1993] 4 All E.R. 30; 98 Cr.App.R. 455; 143 N.L.J. 1332; 137 S.J.L.B. 195; *The Times*, July 30, 1993; *Guardian*, August 20, 1993, PC (Mau) 19–34

Kurshid [1984] Crim.L.R. 288, CA 20–14

Kuruma v R. [1955] A.C. 197; [1955] 2 W.L.R. 223; [1955] 1 All E.R. 236; 119 J.P. 157; [1955] Crim.L.R. 339; 99 S.J. 73, PC (EA) 10–05, 10–06

L [1994] Crim.L.R. 839, CA 9–17

L (A Minor) (Police Investigation: Privilege), Re; sub nom. L (Minors) (Disclosure of Medical Reports), Re; L (Minors) (Police Investigation: Privilege), Re [1997] A.C. 16; [1996] 2 W.L.R. 395; [1996] 2 All E.R. 78; [1996] 1 F.L.R. 731; [1996] 2 F.C.R. 145; 32 B.M.L.R. 160; [1996] Fam. Law 400; 160 L.G. Rev. 417; 93(15) L.S.G. 30; 146 N.L.J. 441; 140 S.J.L.B. 116; The

L v DPP [2002] 1 Cr.App.R. 420, DC 4–15, 4–16

L (Fraser Martin) v DPP [1998] 2 Cr.App.R. 69; [1998] C.O.D. 96, QBD 19–29, 19–34

Lam Chi-Ming v R. [1991] 2 A.C. 212; [1991] 2 W.L.R. 1082; [1991] 3 All E.R. 172; 93 Cr.App.R. 358; [1991] Crim.L.R. 914; 135 S.J.L.B. 445, PC (HK) 9–01, 9–60

Lamb (Peter David John) (1980) 71 Cr.App.R. 198; [1980] Crim.L.R. 433, CA 14–23, 14–35, 14–36, 14–37

Lamb v Munster (1882–83) L.R. 10 Q.B.D. 110; 5 L.J. Q.B. 46, QBD 11–02

Lambert (Steven), Ali (Mudassir Mohammed) and Jordan (Shirley) [2001] UKHL 37; [2002] 2 A.C. 545; [2001] 3 W.L.R. 206; [2002] 1 All E.R. 2; [2001] 3 All E.R. 577; [2001] 2 Cr.App.R. 28; [2001] H.R.L.R. 55; [2001] U.K.H.R.R. 1074; [2001] Crim.L.R. 806; 98(33) L.S.G. 29; 145 S.J.L.B. 174; The Times, July 6, 2001; Independent, July 19, 2001; Daily Telegraph, July 17, 2001, HL; affirming [2002] Q.B. 1112; [2001] 2 W.L.R. 211; [2001] 1 All E.R. 1014; [2001] 1 Cr.App.R. 14; [2001] H.R.L.R. 4; [2000] U.K.H.R.R. 864; 97(35) L.S.G. 36, CA ... 4–14, 4–15, 4–17, 4–18, 4–26, 13–03, 13–08, 13–21

Lambeth Metropolitan Stipendiary Magistrate Ex p. McComb [1983] Q.B. 551; [1983] 2 W.L.R. 259; [1983] 1 All E.R. 321; 76 Cr.App.R. 246; [1983] Crim.L.R. 266; 127 S.J. 35, CA 2–02

Lamont [1989] Crim.L.R. 813, CA 9–56

Landau (1944) 60 L.Q.R. 201 .... 6–01, 6–03

Landon [1995] Crim.L.R. 338, CA 16–18, 16–19

Lanfear (Colin) [1968] 2 Q.B. 77; [1968] 2 W.L.R. 623; [1968] 1 All E.R. 683; 52 Cr.App.R. 176; 132 J.P. 193; 112 S.J. 132, CA 6–43

Langley (Dean Ronald) [2001] EWCA Crim 732; [2001] Crim.L.R. 651, CA 18–13

Langton (1877) 2 Q.B.D. 296 20–31

Larkin [1943] K.B. 174; [1943] 1 All E.R. 217, CCA 20–02

Latif (Khalid) and Shahzad (Mohammed Khalid) [1996] 1 W.L.R. 104; [1996] 1 All E.R. 353; [1996] 2 Cr.App.R. 92; [1996] Crim.L.R. 414; 93(5) L.S.G. 30; 146 N.L.J. 121; 140 S.J.L.B. 39; The Times, January 23, 1996; Independent, January 23, 1996, HL; affirming [1995] 1 Cr.App.R. 270; 15 Cr.App.R. (S.) 864; [1994] Crim.L.R. 750; 91(18) L.S.G. 37; 138 S.J.L.B. 85; The Times, March 17, 1994, CA 10–25

Lau Pak Ngam v R. [1966] Crim.L.R. 443, CA (HK) 20–23, 20–24, 20–28

Law [1961] Crim.L.R. 52; 110 L.J. 816, CCA 4–41

Law (Anthony), The Times, August 15, 1996, CA 18–23

Lawless (Alan); sub nom. Alan Lawless (1994) 98 Cr.App.R. 342; [1994] Crim.L.R. 974, CA 17–09

Lawrence (Alan) [1968] 1 W.L.R. 341; [1968] 1 All E.R. 579; 52 Cr.App.R. 163; 132 J.P. 173; 112 S.J. 109, CA 2–06, 19–43

Lawrence (Irvin) [1995] Crim.L.R. 815, CA 7–24

Lawrence (Stephen) [2002] Crim.L.R. 584, CA 13–26

Lawrenson [1961] Crim.L.R. 398, CCA 14–36

Lawson (Anthony) (1990) 90 Cr.App.R. 107; [1990] Crim.L.R. 62; *The Times*, June 21, 1989, CA 18–06
Law-Thompson (Howard James) [1997] Crim.L.R. 674, CA 9–30
Leadbeater [1988] Crim.L.R. 463, CA 16–10
Lean (1923) 17 Cr.App.R. 204, CCA 7–68
Leathem (1861) 8 Cox C.C. 498 10–05
Lee (1911) 7 Cr.App.R. 31 20–07
Lee (Robert Paul) [1996] 2 Cr.App.R. 266; 160 J.P. 462; [1996] Crim.L.R. 412; 140 S.J.L.B. 38; *The Times*, December 28, 1995; *Independent*, February 5, 1996, CA 19–15
Lee Kun [1916] 1 K.B. 337 19–34
Leggett [1970] 1 Q.B. 67; [1969] 2 W.L.R. 29; 133 J.P. 98; [1969] 1 All E.R. 47, CA 19–07
Lennard (Michael) [1973] 1 W.L.R. 483; [1973] 2 All E.R. 831; 57 Cr.App.R. 542; [1973] R.T.R. 252; [1973] Crim.L.R. 312; 117 S.J. 284, CA 5–07
Lesley (Leroy Owen) [1996] 1 Cr.App.R. 39; [1995] Crim.L.R. 946, CA . 4–08, 16–19
Leung Kam-Kwok v R. (1985) 81 Cr.App.R. 83; [1985] Crim.L.R. 227; 82 L.S.G. 687, PC (HK) 20–17
Levy (Reginald George Cecil) and Tait (John William) (1966) 50 Cr.App.R. 198; [1966] Crim.L.R. 454; 116 N.L.J. 921, CCA 19–39
Lewis (Albert Roy) [1969] 2 Q.B. 1; [1969] 2 W.L.R. 55; [1969] 1 All E.R. 79; 53 Cr.App.R. 76; 133 J.P. 111; 112 S.J. 904, CA 18–16
Lewis (Robert Alexander) (1971) 55 Cr.App.R. 386; [1971] Crim.L.R. 414; 115 S.J. 385, CA 5–07
Leyfield's Case (1611) 10 Co.Rep. 88a 3–12
Li Shu-Ling v R. [1989] A.C. 270; [1988] 3 W.L.R. 671; [1988] 3 All E.R. 138; 88 Cr.App.R. 82; [1989] Crim.L.R. 58; 85(32) L.S.G. 34; 132 S.J. 1268, PC (HK) 2–41, 2–42, 2–42
Lilley v Pettit [1946] K.B. 401, KBD 8–42
Lillyman [1896] 2 Q.B. 167, CCR 20–04, 20–05, 20–06
Lin, Hung and Tsui [1995] Crim.L.R. 817, CA 9–44
Lister v Quaife [1983] 1 W.L.R. 48; [1983] 2 All E.R. 29; 75 Cr.App.R. 313, DC 8–79
Liverpool City Justices Ex p. Topping [1983] 1 W.L.R. 119; [1983] 1 All E.R. 490; 76 Cr.App.R. 170; 147 J.P. 154; [1983] Crim.L.R. 181; 127 S.J. 51, DC 16–29
Liverpool Juvenile Court Ex p. R [1988] Q.B. 1; [1987] 3 W.L.R. 224; [1987] 2 All E.R. 668; 86 Cr.App.R. 1; 151 J.P. 516; [1987] Crim.L.R. 572; 151 J.P.N. 364, DC 9–49, 9–50, 16–27
Lloyd (David) [2000] 2 Cr.App.R. 355; [2001] Crim.L.R. 250, CA 7–18
Loak (1911) 7 Cr.App.R. 71 6–03
Lobban v R. [1995] 1 W.L.R. 877; [1995] 2 All E.R. 602; [1995] 2 Cr.App.R. 573; [1995] Crim.L.R. 881; 92(21) L.S.G. 37; 145 N.L.J. 688; 139 S.J.L.B. 140; *The Times*, April 28, 1995, PC (Jam) ... 9–54, 10–02
Lobell (Harry Lazarus) [1957] 1 Q.B. 547; [1957] 2 W.L.R. 524; [1957] 1 All E.R. 734; 41 Cr.App.R. 100; 121 J.P. 282; 101 S.J. 268, CCA ... 4–08, 4–27
Lock [1975] Crim.L.R. 35, CA 4–05
Lockheed-Arabia v Owen [1993] Q.B. 806; [1993] 3 W.L.R. 468; [1993] 3 All E.R. 641; 143 N.L.J. 654; 137 S.J.L.B. 108, CA 6–10

Long (Robert William) (1973) 57 Cr.App.R. 871; [1973] Crim.L.R. 577;
117 S.J. 728, CA 14–08
Longden (Mark), *The Times*, May 31, 1995, CA 21–25
Loughran [1999] Crim.L.R. 404, CA 6–20
Loveridge (William) (Appeal against Conviction) [2001] EWCA Crim 973;
[2001] 2 Cr.App.R. 29; 98(23) L.S.G. 36; 145 S.J.L.B. 120, CA 10–20,
10–27, 13–26
Lowery (Christopher Russell) v R. [1974] A.C. 85; [1973] 3 W.L.R. 235;
[1973] 3 All E.R. 662; 58 Cr.App.R. 35; [1973] Crim.L.R. 523; 117 S.J.
583, PC (Aus) 6–19, 6–25, 7–58
Lucas (Lyabode Ruth) [1981] Q.B. 720; [1981] 3 W.L.R. 120; [1981] 2 All
E.R. 1008; 73 Cr.App.R. 159; [1981] Crim.L.R. 624, CA 16–17, 16–19,
16–20
Ludlow v Commissioner of Police of the Metropolis [1971] A.C. 29; [1970]
2 W.L.R. 521; [1970] 1 All E.R. 567; (1970) 54 Cr.App.R. 233; 114
S.J. 148, HL 7–52
Ludlow v Metropolitan Police Commissioner. *See* Ludlow v Commissioner
of Police of the Metropolis
Lui Mei Lin v R. [1989] A.C. 288; [1989] 2 W.L.R. 175; [1989] 1 All
E.R. 359; 88 Cr.App.R. 296; [1989] Crim.L.R. 364; 132 S.J. 1553, PC
(HK) 21–16
Lunnon (Keith) (1989) 88 Cr.App.R. 71; [1988] Crim.L.R. 456, CA . 5–30, 5–33
Lushington v Otto [1894] 1 Q.B. 420 2–02
Lydon (Sean Michael) (1987) 85 Cr.App.R. 221; [1987] Crim.L.R. 407, CA 8–05
Lyell v Kennedy (No.3) (1884) L.R. 27 Ch. D. 1; 50 L.T. 730, CA
Lyell v Kennedy and Kennedy v Lyell (No.4) (1889) L.R. 14 App. Cas. 437,
HL 8–41

M [1995] Crim.L.R. 336, CA 19–28
M (A Child)) and La Rose v Commissioner of Police of the Metropolis
[2001] EWHC Admin 553; [2002] Crim.L.R. 215; [2001] A.C.D. 91;
98(34) L.S.G. 40; 151 N.L.J. 1213; 145 S.J.L.B. 215; *The Times*,
August 17, 2001, DC 13–22
M (John) (Criminal Evidence: Replaying Video) [1996] 2 Cr.App.R. 56; 140
S.J.L.B. 37; *The Times*, November 29, 1995; *Independent*, January 15,
1996, CA 19–28
McAndrew-Bingham (Victor John) [1999] 1 W.L.R. 1897; [1999] 2
Cr.App.R. 293; [1999] Crim.L.R. 830; 96(5) L.S.G. 35; 143 S.J.L.B.
38; *The Times*, December 28, 1998, CA 17–04, 19–15
McCarthy (Colin Paul) [1998] R.T.R. 374, CA 3–19
McCarthy (Gerald Joseph) (1980) 71 Cr.App.R. 142, CA 20–14
McCarthy (June Patricia), Bullen (Philip Mark)and Lewis (Peter) [1996]
Crim.L.R. 818, CA 9–30
McCartney [2003] 6 *Archbold News* 2, CA 18–12
McCay (Graham Steven) [1990] 1 W.L.R. 645; [1991] 1 All E.R. 232; 91
Cr.App.R. 84; 154 J.P. 621; [1990] Crim.L.R. 338; 154 J.P.N. 489;
87(19) L.S.G. 39; 134 S.J. 606, CA 8–58, 14–33
McDonald, *The Times*, April 10, 1987 4–05
McDonald [1991] Crim.L.R. 122; *The Times*, August 29, 1990, CA 9–26
Macdonnell (1909) 2 Cr.App.R. 322 17–13
McFadden (Cornelius Michael) (1976) 62 Cr.App.R. 187; [1976] Crim.L.R.
193; 120 S.J. 46, CA 21–17
McGarry (Patrick John) [1999] 1 W.L.R. 1500; [1998] 3 All E.R. 805;

[1999] 1 Cr.App.R. 377; [1999] Crim.L.R. 316; 95(35) L.S.G. 36; 142 S.J.L.B. 239; *The Times*, August 7, 1998; *Independent*, July 23, 1998, CA 11–20

McGee (Francis) and Cassidy (Kevin Gerrard) (1980) 70 Cr.App.R. 247; [1980] Crim.L.R. 172, CA 7–67

McGillivray (Charles) (1993) 97 Cr.App.R. 232; 157 J.P. 943; 157 J.P.N. 394; *The Times*, January 3, 1993, CA 8–21

McGlinchey (Michael) (1984) 78 Cr.App.R. 282; 148 J.P. 73; [1988] Crim.L.R. 808, CA 7–52

McGovern (Cherie) (1991) 92 Cr.App.R. 228; [1991] Crim.L.R. 124, CA   9–41

McGreevy v DPP [1973] 1 W.L.R. 276; [1973] 1 All E.R. 503; 57 Cr.App.R. 424; [1973] Crim.L.R. 232; 117 S.J. 164, HL 1–10, 4–41, 4–42

McGregor (John) [1968] 1 Q.B. 371; [1967] 3 W.L.R. 274; [1967] 2 All E.R. 267; 51 Cr.App.R. 338; 131 J.P. 366; 111 S.J. 454, CA 9–04

McGuinness (Cyril) [1999] Crim.L.R. 318, CA 11–17, 16–20

McIntosh [1992] Crim.L.R. 651, CA 8–05

McIvor (Neil) [1987] Crim.L.R. 409, CC 9–33

McKenna (John) (1956) 40 Cr.App.R. 65, CCA 19–37

MacKenney (Henry Jeremiah) and Pinfold (Terence Joseph) (1983) 76 Cr.App.R. 271, CA 6–27

McKenzie (David Stuart) (Practice Note) [1993] 1 W.L.R. 453; 96 Cr.App.R. 98; 89(34) L.S.G. 34; 142 N.L.J. 1162; 136 S.J.L.B. 260, CA ... 9–23, 16–10

MacLean [1978] Crim.L.R. 430, CA 7–66

McLernon (Brian Gerard) [1992] N.I. 168, CA (NI); [1990] N.I.J.B. 91 .. 17–22

McManus (Paul) and Cross (Andrew John) [2001] EWCA Crim 2455, CA 11–20

McNab [2002] Crim.L.R. 129 10–21

McQuaker v Goddard [1940] 1 K.B. 687, CA 5–08

McQuiston (James Wallace) [1998] 1 Cr.App.R. 139; [1998] Crim.L.R. 69; 161 J.P.N. 1173; *The Times*, October 10, 1997; *Independent*, October 6, 1997, CA 19–29

McShane v Chief Constable of Northumbria (1981) 72 Cr.App.R. 208; [1980] R.T.R. 406, DC 14–04

Machin v Ash (1950) 49 L.G.R. 87; [1950] W.N. 478; 94 S.J. 705, DC .. 3–13

Madden [1986] Crim.L.R. 804, CA 21–20

Maggs (Edwards) (1990) 91 Cr.App.R. 243; [1990] R.T.R. 129; [1990] Crim.L.R. 654; 87(12) L.S.G. 39; 134 S.J. 933, CA 19–44

Maguire (Anne Rita) [1992] Q.B. 936; [1992] 2 W.L.R. 767; [1992] 2 All E.R. 433; 94 Cr.App.R. 133, CA 6–37, 18–08, 18–13, 18–22

Maguire (Jason) (1990) 90 Cr.App.R. 115; [1989] Crim.L.R. 815; *The Times*, August 23, 1989, CA 9–42

Mahmood (Khalid) and Manzur (Nanah) [1997] 1 Cr.App.R. 414; [1997] Crim.L.R. 447, CA 5–32

Makanjuola (Oluwanfunso) and Easton (Christopher John) [1995] 1 W.L.R. 1348; [1995] 3 All E.R. 730; [1995] 2 Cr.App.R. 469; 159 J.P. 701; 92(22) L.S.G. 40; 139 S.J.L.B. 179; *The Times*, May 17, 1995; *Independent*, June 6, 1995, CA 15–11, 15–12, 15–13, 15–16, 15–19

Makanjuola v Commissioner of Police of the Metropolis [1992] 3 All E.R. 617, CA 12–12

Makin v Att-Gen of New South Wales [1894] A.C. 57, PC (Aus) 7–03

Malik (Waseem) (Appeal against Conviction) [2000] 2 Cr.App.R. 8; [2000] Crim.L.R. 197, CA 5–26

Maloney [1994] Crim.L.R. 525, CA 8–23

Manchester Crown Court Ex p. R (Legal Professional Privilege) [1999] 1

W.L.R. 832; [1999] 4 All E.R. 35; [1999] 2 Cr.App.R. 267; [1999]
  Crim.L.R. 743; 96(10) L.S.G. 31; *The Times*, February 15, 1999;
  Independent, February 15, 1999, QBD 11–28
Manchester Crown Court Ex p. Williams [1985] R.T.R. 49; [1985]
  Crim.L.R. 237; 82 L.S.G. 929, DC 3–14
Mancini [2002] 2 Cr.App.R. 377 3–27
Mancini v DPP [1942] A.C. 1; [1941] 3 All E.R. 272, HL . 4–07, 4–10, 4–26, 4–31
Manji [1990] Crim.L.R. 512, CA 9–29
Manley v Shaw (1840) C. & M. 361 5–10
Mann (Brian Peter) (1972) 56 Cr.App.R. 750; [1972] Crim.L.R. 704, CA .. 9–55,
                                                                      10–11, 21–11
Mansfield (Edward Reginald) [1977] 1 W.L.R. 1102; [1978] 1 All E.R. 134;
  65 Cr.App.R. 276; 121 S.J. 709, CA 16–11
Maqsud Ali. *See* Ali (Maqsud)
Marcus (1923) 17 Cr.App.R. 191 1–09
Marks v Beyfus (1890) 25 Q.B.D. 494 .... 12–02, 12–03
Marlborough Street Stipendiary Magistrate Ex p. Simpson (1980) 70
  Cr.App.R. 291; [1980] Crim.L.R. 305, DC 3–16, 3–17
Marr (Fraser) (1990) 90 Cr.App.R. 154; [1989] Crim.L.R. 743, CA 16–15,
                                                                      21–32
Marrin (Keith Ian) [2002] EWCA Crim 251; *The Times*, March 5, 2002, CA 14–20
Marsh [1991] Crim.L.R. 455, CA 9–43
Marsh, *The Times*, July 6, 1993, CA 16–09, 19–07
Marsh (Stephen Leslie) (1986) 83 Cr.App.R. 165; [1986] Crim.L.R. 120,
  CA 21–28, 21–29
Marshall (Mark), *The Times*, December 28, 1992, CA 9–35
Martin (1872) L.R. 1 C.C.R. 378 2–06
Martin [2001] 2 Cr.App.R. 2 7–19
Martin (Ellis Anthony) and White (James Robert) [1998] 2 Cr.App.R. 385;
  The Times, March 17, 1998; *Independent*, February 24, 1998, CA ... 21–26
Martin (Peter John) (1973) 57 Cr.App.R. 279; [1973] R.T.R. 171; [1973]
  Crim.L.R. 583, CA 16–22
Martin and Nicholls [1994] Crim.L.R. 218, CA 14–29
Masih [1986] Crim.L.R. 395, CA 6–19, 6–20
Mason (Carl) [1988] 1 W.L.R. 139; [1987] 3 All E.R. 481; 86 Cr.App.R.
  349; 151 J.P. 747; [1987] Crim.L.R. 757; 151 J.P.N. 542; 131 S.J. 973,
  CA 9–25, 9–26, 10–13, 10–14, 10–19, 10–21, 10–22
Mason, Wood, McClelland and Tierney, unreported, February 3, 2002, CA 10–27
Matheson (Albert Edward) [1958] 1 W.L.R. 474; [1958] 2 All E.R. 87; 42
  Cr.App.R. 145; 102 S.J. 309, CA 6–43, 6–44
Mattey (Jimmy Cyril) and Queeley (Juanita Amelia) [1995] 2 Cr.App.R.
  409; [1995] Crim.L.R. 308; 91(41) L.S.G. 41; 138 S.J.L.B. 208, CA . 8–19
Matthews [2003] 2 Cr.App.R. 302, CA 4–15
Matthews (Sarah) (1990) 91 Cr.App.R. 43; 154 J.P. 177; [1990] Crim.L.R.
  190; 153 J.P.N. 835, CA 9–39, 9–32
Matthews v Morris [1981] Crim.L.R. 495, DC 19–37
Mattison [1990] Crim.L.R. 117; (1989) 139 N.L.J. 1417, CA 5–33
Matto v Wolverhampton Crown Court; sub nom. Matto (Jit Singh) v DPP;
  Matto v DPP [1987] R.T.R. 337; [1987] Crim.L.R. 641, DC 10–21
Mauricia (Richard Audberto)[2002] EWCA Crim 676; [2002] 2 Cr.App.R.
  27; [2002] Crim.L.R. 655; 99(13) L.S.G. 26; 146 S.J.L.B. 62, CA 7–11
Maw [1994] Crim.L.R. 841, CA 21–10, 21–13
Maxwell v DPP [1935] A.C. 309; 24 Cr.App.R. 152, HL 7–02

Mayhew (1834) 6 C. & P. 315 15–03
Maynard (Robert John), Dudley (Reginald John), Clarke (Charles Edwin)
   and Dudley (Kathleen) (1979) 69 Cr.App.R. 309, CA 14–36, 21–16
Mears v R. [1993] 1 W.L.R. 818; (1993) 97 Cr.App.R. 239; [1993]
   Crim.L.R. 885; 137 S.J.L.B. 133, PC (Jam) 16–15
Mechanical and General Inventions Co. Ltd v Austin; sub nom. Mechanical
   and General Inventions Co. Ltd v Austin Motor Co. Ltd; Lehwess v
   Austin [1935] A.C. 346, HL 21–17
Mehrban (Razia)and Mehrban (Mohammed)[2001] EWCA Crim 2627;
   [2002] 1 Cr.App.R. 40; [2002] Crim.L.R. 439, CA 19–10
Mendy (Eileen) (1977) 64 Cr.App.R. 4; [1976] Crim.L.R. 686, CA 19–39,
   21–31
Menhard [1995] 1 Cr.App.R. 306 9–42
Mercer v Denne [1905] 2 Ch. 538, CA 8–42
Miah (Badrul) and Akhbar (Showkat) [1997] 2 Cr.App.R. 12; [1997]
   Crim.L.R. 351, CA 7–18
Middleton (Ronald) [2001] Crim.L.R. 251; The Times, April 12, 2000, CA 16–18
Middleton v Rowlett; sub nom. Middleton v Rowlatt [1954] 1 W.L.R. 831;
   [1954] 2 All E.R. 277; 118 J.P. 362; 52 L.G.R. 334; 98 S.J. 373, DC   19–37
Milford (David John) [2001] Crim.L.R. 330, CA 11–20, 11–21
Miller (Keith Glenn) [1998] Crim.L.R. 209, CA 9–42, 10–29
Miller v Howe [1969] 1 W.L.R. 1510; [1969] 3 All E.R. 451; 133 J.P. 665;
   113 S.J. 706, DC 2–02
Miller v Ministry of Pensions; sub nom. Miller v Minister of Pensions [1947]
   2 All E.R. 372; 63 T.L.R. 474; [1947] W.N. 241; [1948] L.J.R. 203;
   177 L.T. 536; 91 S.J. 484, KBD 4–38, 4–45
Milliken (James) (1969) 53 Cr.App.R. 330, CA 19–39
Mills (Clifford Ernest) and Rose (Peter Samuel) [1962] 1 W.L.R. 1152;
   [1962] 3 All E.R. 298; 46 Cr.App.R. 336; 126 J.P. 506; 106 S.J. 593,
   CCA 10–23, 20–28, 20–29
Mills (Gary) and Poole (Anthony Keith) [1998] A.C. 382; [1997] 3 W.L.R.
   458; [1997] 3 All E.R. 780; [1998] 1 Cr.App.R. 43; 161 J.P. 601;
   [1998] Crim.L.R. 64; 161 J.P.N. 858; 94(39) L.S.G. 39; 141 S.J.L.B.
   211; The Times, July 30, 1997, HL 18–06
Mills v Cooper [1967] 2 Q.B. 459; [1967] 2 W.L.R. 1343; [1967] 2 All E.R.
   100; 131 J.P. 349; 65 L.G.R. 275; 111 S.J. 273, DC 5–19
Mills v Oddy (1834) 6 C. & P. 728 3–14
Mills v R. [1995] 1 W.L.R. 511; [1995] 3 All E.R. 865; [1995] Crim.L.R.
   884; 139 S.J.L.B. 84; The Times, March 1, 1995, PC (Jam) 14–04, 14–05
Minihane (1921) 16 Cr.App.R. 38 11–02
Minors (Craig) and Harper (Giselle Gaile) [1989] 1 W.L.R. 441; [1989] 2
   All E.R. 208; 89 Cr.App.R. 102; [1989] Crim.L.R. 360; 133 S.J. 420,
   CA 4–48, 8–19, 8–32, 8–35
Mitchell (1892) 17 Cox C.C. 508 9–07
Mitchell (David) v R. [1998] A.C. 695; [1998] 2 W.L.R. 839; [1998] 2
   Cr.App.R. 35; [1998] Crim.L.R. 422; 142 S.J.L.B. 61; The Times,
   January 24, 1998, PC (Bah) 16–06, 16–08
Moghal (Mohammed Ilias) (1977) 65 Cr.App.R. 56; [1977] Crim.L.R. 373,
   CA 8–60
Mohammed (Allie) v Trinidad and Tobago [1999] 2 A.C. 111; [1999] 2
   W.L.R. 552; 6 B.H.R.C. 177; The Times, December 10, 1998, PC
   (Trin) 9–26

Mokrecovas (Andrius) [2001] EWCA Crim 1644; [2002] 1 Cr.App.R. 20;
    [2001] Crim.L.R. 911, CA 7–81
Molloy, unreported, July 30, 1997, CA 18–13
Montgomery (Stephen) [1996] Crim.L.R. 507, CA 14–17
Moon [1969] 1 W.L.R. 1705; [1969] 3 All E.R. 803; 133 J.P. 703; 113 S.J.
    584, CA 4–04, 4–05, 4–07, 4–27
Moor v Moor [1954] 1 W.L.R. 927; [1954] 2 All E.R. 459; 98 S.J. 438, CA .. 21–06
Moore [1992] Crim.L.R. 882, CA 8–19, 8–27
Moore (Frederick Pearson) (1956) 40 Cr.App.R. 50, CCA 5–33
Moore v Lambeth County Court Registrar (No.1); sub nom. Lambeth
    County Court Registrar v Moore [1969] 1 W.L.R. 141; [1969] 1 All
    E.R. 782; 112 S.J. 926, CA 19–05
Moran (Kevin John) (1985) 81 Cr.App.R. 51; 7 Cr.App.R. (S.) 101, CA .. 17–14
Moran v Crown Prosecution Service (2000) 164 J.P. 562, DC 3–26
Morgan (Lewis) [1925] 1 K.B. 752, CCA 3–12
Morgan Grenfell & Co. Ltd v Special Commissioner of Income Tax; sub
    nom. Inland Revenue Commissioners Ex p. Morgan Grenfell & Co.
    Ltd; Special Commissioners of Income Tax Ex p. Morgan Grenfell &
    Co. Ltd [2002] UKHL 21; [2003] 1 A.C. 563; [2002] 2 W.L.R. 1299;
    [2002] 3 All E.R. 1; [2002] S.T.C. 786; [2002] H.R.L.R. 42; 74 T.C.
    511; [2002] B.T.C. 223; 4 I.T.L. Rep. 809; [2002] S.T.I. 806; 99(25)
    L.S.G. 35; 146 S.J.L.B. 126; [2002] N.P.C. 70; The Times, May 20,
    2002, HL 11–28
Morgans v DPP [2001] 1 A.C. 315; [2000] 2 W.L.R. 386; [2000] 2 All E.R.
    522; [2000] 2 Cr.App.R. 113; [1998–99] Info. T.L.R. 415; [2000]
    Crim.L.R. 576; [2000] C.O.D. 98; 97(9) L.S.G. 39; The Times, Feb-
    ruary 18, 2000, HL 12–05
Morris [1973] R.T.R. 171 16–22
Morris [1998] Crim.L.R. 416, CA 19–27
Morrison (1911) 6 Cr.App.R. 159; 75 J.P. 272 .... 19–04, 19–41
Mortimer v M'Callan (1840) 6 M. & W. 58 .... 3–12, 3–18
Moshaid (Abdul) and Mahmood (Fadel Fanta) [1998] Crim.L.R. 420, CA 11–20
Moss (Frank) (1990) 91 Cr.App.R. 371; 140 N.L.J. 665, CA 9–24, 10–31
Moss v Moss [1963] 2 Q.B. 799; [1963] 3 W.L.R. 171; [1963] 2 All E.R.
    829; 47 Cr.App.R. 222; 127 J.P. 466; 107 S.J. 459, DC 17–34
Moulding (Richard) [1996] Crim.L.R. 440, CA 1–08
Mouqni, The Times, April 14, 1994, CA 15–15, 15–16
Mullins (1848) 32 Cox 526 20–28
Muncaster (Warwick) [1999] Crim.L.R. 409, CA 15–16, 15–17
Munnery (Vincent) (1992) 94 Cr.App.R. 164; [1992] Crim.L.R. 215,
    CA 19–35, 19–36
Murdoch v Taylor [1965] A.C. 574; [1965] 2 W.L.R. 425; [1965] 1 All E.R.
    406; 49 Cr.App.R. 119; 129 J.P. 208; 109 S.J. 130, HL 21–15
Murphy (William Francis) [1980] Q.B. 434; [1980] 2 W.L.R. 743; [1980] 2
    All E.R. 325; 71 Cr.App.R. 33; [1980] R.T.R. 145; [1980] Crim.L.R.
    309; 124 S.J. 189, CA 6–27
Murray (Anthony John) [1997] 2 Cr.App.R. 136; [1997] Crim.L.R. 506, CA   8–64
Murray (Michael) [1951] 1 K.B. 391; [1950] 2 All E.R. 925; 66 T.L.R. (Pt.2)
    1007; 34 Cr.App.R. 203; 114 J.P. 609; 49 L.G.R. 90; 94 S.J. 726,
    CCA 9–54, 16–08
Murray (Gary) v DPP (1993) 97 Cr.App.R. 151; 158 J.P. 261; [1993] R.T.R.
    209; [1993] Crim.L.R. 968; 157 J.P.N. 768; The Times, February 9,
    1993; Independent, February 12, 1993, HL 17–21

Murtagh (Dennis Patrick) and Kennedy (Kenneth) (1955) 39 Cr.App.R. 72, CCA 4–08

Mussell (Barry Charles) and Dalton [1995] Crim.L.R. 887, CA 14–05, 16–18

N, *The Times*, February 13, 1998 11–23

Nadir (Asil) and Turner (John) [1993] 1 W.L.R. 1322; [1993] 4 All E.R. 513; 98 Cr.App.R. 163; 143 N.L.J. 1026; 137 S.J.L.B. 175; *The Times*, July 2, 1993; *Independent*, July 2, 1993; *Guardian*, July 2, 1993, CA 10–12, 18–33

Nagah (Jasant Singh) (1991) 92 Cr.App.R. 344; 155 J.P. 229; [1991] Crim.L.R. 55; 154 L.G. Rev. 770, CA 14–26

Nagrecha (Chandu) [1997] 2 Cr.App.R. 401; [1998] Crim.L.R. 65, CA ... 21–29, 21–30

Napper (Barry) (1997) 161 J.P. 16; [1996] Crim.L.R. 591; 161 J.P.N. 62, CA 17–21

Nathaniel (Lonsdale) [1995] 2 Cr.App.R. 565; *The Times*, April 6, 1995; *Independent*, May 8, 1995, CA 10–21

National Association of Operative Plasterers v Smithies [1906] A.C. 434, HL 11–05

Naudeer (Philip Hoosen) [1984] 3 All E.R. 1036; 80 Cr.App.R. 9; [1984] Crim.L.R. 501, CA 17–36, 17–37

Nazeer (Mohammed Azad) [1998] Crim.L.R. 750, CA 3–07, 3–08

Neal [1962] Crim.L.R. 698, CMAC 6–08

Neale [1998] Crim.L.R. 737 21–30

Neale (Paul Michael) (1977) 65 Cr.App.R. 304, CA 6–25

Neil [1994] Crim.L.R. 441, CA 9–41

Neill v North Antrim Magistrates' Court [1992] 1 W.L.R. 1220; [1992] 4 All E.R. 846; 97 Cr.App.R. 121; 158 J.P. 197; 6 Admin. L.R. 85; [1993] Crim.L.R. 945; 158 J.P.N. 380; *The Times*, November 16, 1992, HL 8–28, 18–01

Neilson v Harford (1841) 8 M. & W. 806 16–03

Neilson v Laugharne [1981] Q.B. 736; [1981] 2 W.L.R. 537; [1981] 1 All E.R. 829; 125 S.J. 202; *The Times*, December 19, 1980, CA 12–14

Nelson [1992] Crim.L.R. 653, CA 21–12

Nelson (Sonia Eloise) and Rose (Cynthia Delores) [1998] 2 Cr.App.R. 399; [1998] Crim.L.R. 814, CA 9–43

Newis v Lark (1571) Plowd. 403 4–45

Newsome (Kevin) (1980) 71 Cr.App.R. 325, CA 20–16

Newton and Dyer [1987] Crim.L.R. 687 21–12

Nicholas (1846) 2 Car. & K. 246 8–59

Nicholas v Penny; sub nom. Penny v Nicholas [1950] 2 K.B. 466; [1950] 2 All E.R. 89; 66 T.L.R. (Pt.1) 1122; 114 J.P. 335; 48 L.G.R. 535; 21 A.L.R.2d 1193; 94 S.J. 437, DC 5–06, 15–04

Nicholls (Arthur Roy) (1976) 63 Cr.App.R. 187; [1977] Crim.L.R. 675, CA   8–19

Nicholson (Andrew Robert), *The Times*, September 7, 1999 14–18

Nickolson [1999] Crim.L.R. 61, CA 11–20

Nimmo v Alexander Cowan & Sons Ltd [1968] A.C. 107; [1967] 3 W.L.R. 1169; [1967] 3 All E.R. 187; 1967 S.C. (H.L.) 79; 1967 S.L.T. 277; 3 K.I.R. 277; 111 S.J. 668, HL 4–20, 4–23

Nixon (Stanley Leslie) and Nixon (Anne) [1968] 1 W.L.R. 577; [1968] 2 All E.R. 33; 52 Cr.App.R. 218; 132 J.P. 309; 112 S.J. 231, CA 2–06, 19–43

Nixon v Freeman (1860) 5 H. & N. 647 8–40

Nkambule v R. (No.1) [1940] A.C. 760, PC (Swa) 2–24, 3–03, 19–34

Noor Mohammed v R. [1949] A.C. 182; [1949] 1 All E.R. 365; 65 T.L.R. 134; 8 C.R. 407; [1949] 2 W.W.R. 753; 93 S.J. 180, PC (BG)   10–03, 10–11

Norbrook Laboratories (GB) Ltd v Health and Safety Executive [1998] E.H.L.R. 207; *The Times*, February 23, 1998, DC   5–12

Norcott [1917] 1 K.B. 347, CCA   20–07

North Australian Territory Co. v Goldsborough Mort & Co. [1893] 2 Ch. 381, CA   21–16

North Yorkshire Trading Standards Department v Williams (1995) 159 J.P. 383; 159 J.P.N. 317; *The Times*, November 22, 1994; *Independent*, December 19, 1994, DC 14–14, 14–15

Norton and Driver (No.1) [1987] Crim.L.R. 687, CA   21–34

Norwich Stipendiary Magistrate Ex p. Keable [1998] Crim.L.R. 510; [1998] C.O.D. 169; *The Times*, February 5, 1998, DC   18–05

Nottingham City Council v Amin [2000] 1 W.L.R. 1071; [2000] 2 All E.R. 946; [2000] 1 Cr.App.R. 426; [2000] R.T.R. 122; [2000] H.R.L.R. 280; [2000] U.K.H.R.R. 134; [2000] Crim.L.R. 174, DC   10–22

Nottingham Justices Ex p. Lynn; sub nom. Nottingham City Justices Ex p. Lynn (1984) 79 Cr.App.R. 238; [1984] Crim.L.R. 554, DC 3–16, 3–17

Nowaz (Gul); sub nom Karim (Abdul) [1976] 1 W.L.R. 830; [1976] 3 All E.R. 5; 63 Cr.App.R. 178; [1974] Crim.L.R. 510; 120 S.J. 402, CA .   3–14

Nugent (Philip Gwyn) [1977] 1 W.L.R. 789; [1977] 3 All E.R. 662; 65 Cr.App.R. 40; [1977] Crim.L.R. 375; 121 S.J. 286, CCC   19–01

Nye (Brian) and Loan (Nicholas Warde (1978) 66 Cr.App.R. 252; [1978] Crim.L.R. 94, CA 8–52, 8–55

Nye (Colin Edward) (1982) 75 Cr.App.R. 247, CA   7–25

Oakley (Trevor Alan) (1980) 70 Cr.App.R. 7; [1979] R.T.R. 417; [1979] Crim.L.R. 657, CA   6–27

Oakwell (Edward James) [1978] 1 W.L.R. 32; [1978] 1 All E.R. 1223; 66 Cr.App.R. 174; [1978] Crim.L.R. 168; 122 S.J. 32, CA   14–10

O'Brien (Michael Alan), Hall (Darren Dennis) and Sherwood (Ellis) [2000] Crim.L.R. 676; *The Times*, February 16, 2000, CA 6–18, 9–22

O'Brien, Nicholson & Nicholson [1982] Crim.L.R. 746   14–39

O'Connell v Adams [1973] R.T.R. 150; [1973] Crim.L.R. 113, DC   21–16

O'Connor [1980] Crim.L.R. 43, CA   15–03

O'Connor (Peter Stephen) (1987) 85 Cr.App.R. 298; [1987] Crim.L.R. 260, CA 5–27, 5–28, 5–30

Odeyemi (Olujimi) and Abiodun (Danny) [1999] Crim.L.R. 828, CA   11–17

O'Doherty (Anthony) [2002] N.I. 263; [2003] 1 Cr.App.R. 5; [2002] Crim.L.R. 761, CA (NI)   2–28

Ofori (Noble Julius) and Tackie (Nazar) (1994) 99 Cr.App.R. 223, CA ...   5–09, 16–02

O'hAdhmaill [1996] Crim.L.R. 509; *The Times*, February 13, 1996, CA .   19–41

Okafor (Stephen) [1994] 3 All E.R. 741; 99 Cr.App.R. 97; [1994] Crim.L.R. 221; 137 S.J.L.B. 244; *The Times*, November 10, 1993, CA   9–28

Okolie (Frank), *The Times*, June 16, 2000, CA   16–02

Okoruda [1982] Crim.L.R. 747   14–39

O'Laughlin and McLaughlin (1987) 85 Cr.App.R. 157; [1957] Crim L.R. 632   8–27

O'Leary (Terence) (1988) 87 Cr.App.R. 387; (1989) 153 J.P. 69; [1988] Crim.L.R. 827; 153 J.P.N. 90; *The Times*, May 18, 1988, CA 10–12, 10–18, 10–29

Oliphant [1992] Crim.L.R. 40, CA   9–35

Oliva (Joseph Francis) [1965] 1 W.L.R. 1028; [1965] 3 All E.R. 116; 49
    Cr.App.R. 298; 129 J.P. 500; 109 S.J. 453, CCA 19–01, 21–12
Oliver (Frank Ephraim) [1944] K.B. 68, CCA 4–19
Ollis (Thomas Edwin) [1900] 2 Q.B. 758, CCR 5–18
O'Neill [1969] Crim.L.R. 260, CA 21–24, 21–26
O'Neill and Ackers (Arthur) (1950) 34 Cr.App.R. 108; 48 L.G.R. 305,
    CCA 21–17
Onufrejczyk (Michal) [1955] 1 Q.B. 388; [1955] 2 W.L.R. 273; [1955] 1 All
    E.R. 247; 39 Cr.App.R. 1; 99 S.J. 97, CCA 1–10
Ormskirk Justices Ex p. Davies (1994) 158 J.P. 1145; [1994] Crim.L.R. 850;
    [1995] C.O.D. 28; 158 J.P.N. 602; The Times, June 23, 1994, DC ... 16–27,
                                                                              16–28
Orrell [1972] R.T.R. 14; [1972] Crim.L.R. 313, CA 2–03
Osborne (William Henry) [1905] 1 K.B. 551, CCR 20–04, 20–06, 20–07
Osbourne (Colin) and Virtue (John Graham) [1973] Q.B. 678; [1973] 2
    W.L.R. 209; [1973] 1 All E.R. 649; 57 Cr.App.R. 297; [1973]
    Crim.L.R. 178; 117 S.J. 123, CA 14–33, 14–34
O'Shea [1993] Crim.L.R. 951; The Times, June 8, 1993, CA 7–26
O'Sullivan (John David) [1969] 1 W.L.R. 497; [1969] 2 All E.R. 237; 53
    Cr.App.R. 274; 133 J.P. 338; 113 S.J. 161, CA 6–10
O'Sullivan v Commissioner of Police of the Metropolis (1995) 139 S.J.L.B.
    164; The Times, July 3, 1995, QBD 12–14
O'Toole v Knowsley MBC [1999] E.H.L.R. 420; 32 H.L.R. 420; 96(22)
    L.S.G. 36; [1999] Env. L.R. D29; The Times, May 21, 1999, DC 6–13
Owen (John) [1952] 2 Q.B. 362; [1952] 1 All E.R. 1040; [1952] 1 T.L.R.
    1220; 36 Cr.App.R. 16; 116 J.P. 244; 96 S.J. 281, CCA 19–39, 19–40,
                                                                    19–41, 19–42, 19–44
Owen v Edwards (1983) 77 Cr.App.R. 191; 147 J.P. 245; [1983] Crim.L.R.
    800, DC 20–25
Owen v Sambrook [1981] Crim.L.R. 329, DC 3–16
Owner v Beehive Spinning Co. Ltd [1914] 1 K.B. 105 3–12
Owners of the Sapporo Maru v Owners of the Statue of Liberty (The Sap-
    poro Maru and The Statue of Liberty); sub nom. Owners of Motorship
    Sapporo Maru v Owners of Steam Tanker Statue of Liberty [1968] 1
    W.L.R. 739; [1968] 2 All E.R. 195; [1968] 1 Lloyd's Rep. 429; (1968)
    112 S.J. 380, PDAD 2–09, 2–12, 2–43, 2–44
Oxford City Justices Ex p. Berry [1988] Q.B. 507; [1987] 3 W.L.R. 643;
    [1987] 1 All E.R. 1244; 85 Cr.App.R. 89; 151 J.P. 505; [1987]
    Crim.L.R. 396; 151 J.P.N. 287, DC 16–28
Oxfordshire CC v P (A Minor) [1995] Fam. 161; [1995] 2 W.L.R. 543;
    [1995] 2 All E.R. 225; [1995] 1 F.L.R. 552; [1995] 2 F.C.R. 212; 93
    L.G.R. 336; 159 J.P.N. 302; The Times, February 8, 1995; Indepen-
    dent, February 3, 1995, Fam Div 11–09
Oyesiku (Charles) (1972) 56 Cr.App.R. 240; [1972] Crim.L.R. 179, CA .. 20–09,
                                                                              2—11

P [2001] 2 Cr.App.R. 8, HL 10–21, 10–27
P (GR) [1988] Crim.L.R. 667, CA 21–33
P (Telephone Intercepts: Admissibility of Evidence); sub nom. X, Y and Z
    (Telephone Intercepts: Admissibility of Evidence) [2002] 1 A.C. 146;
    [2001] 2 W.L.R. 463; [2001] 2 All E.R. 58; [2001] 2 Cr.App.R. 8; 98(8)
    L.S.G. 43; 145 S.J.L.B. 28, HL 2–21, 13–26

Pais v Pais [1971] P. 119; [1970] 3 W.L.R. 830; [1970] 3 All E.R. 491; 114
   S.J. 72, PDAD 11–37
Palastanga v Solman (1962) 106 S.J. 176, DC 3–19
Pall (1992) 156 J.P. 424; [1992] Crim.L.R. 126; 156 J.P.N. 218; *The Times*,
   November 4, 1991, CA 9–32
Palmer (Harry Ashley) (1994) 99 Cr.App.R. 83; 158 J.P. 138; [1994]
   Crim.L.R. 122; 158 L.G. Rev. 92; *The Times*, October 5, 1993, CA . 17–14
Palmer v Maclear and M'Grath (1858) 1 Sw. & Tr. 149 21–21
Palmer v Trower (1852) 8 Exch. 247 21–28
Palmer (Sigismund) and Irving (Derrick) v R. [1971] A.C. 814; [1971] 2
   W.L.R. 831; [1971] 1 All E.R. 1077; 55 Cr.App.R. 223; 115 S.J. 264,
   PC (Jam) 4–27
Paris (Anthony) (1993) 97 Cr.App.R. 99; [1994] Crim.L.R. 361, CA 9–17
Park (Randy Alyan) (1994) 99 Cr.App.R. 270; 158 J.P. 144; 158 L.G. Rev.
   92; *The Times*, July 30, 1993, CA 9–13, 9–43
Parker [1995] Crim.L.R. 233, CA 9–18
Parker (Francis) [1996] Crim.L.R. 511, CA 19–27
Parker v DPP [2000] R.T.R. 240, DC 4–16, 5–02
Parker v Smith [1974] R.T.R. 500; [1974] Crim.L.R. 426, DC 4–29
Parkes v R. [1976] 1 W.L.R. 1251; [1976] 3 All E.R. 380; 64 Cr.App.R. 25;
   [1976] Crim.L.R. 741; 120 S.J. 720, PC (Jam) 9–07
Parkin v Moon (1836) 7 C. & P. 409 21–16
Parris (David John) (1989) 89 Cr.App.R. 68; [1989] Crim.L.R. 214; *The
   Times*, November 2, 1988, CA 9–26, 9–29, 9–34
Parry v Boyle (1986) 83 Cr.App.R. 310; [1987] R.T.R. 282; [1986]
   Crim.L.R. 551, DC 2–07, 2–08
Patel (Atul) [2001] EWCA Crim 2505; [2002] Crim.L.R. 304, CA 12–08
Patel (Framroze) [1951] 2 All E.R. 29; [1951] 1 T.L.R. 1018; 35 Cr.App.R.
   62; 115 J.P. 367; [1951] W.N. 258; 95 S.J. 854, CCA 16–05
Paterson v DPP [1990] R.T.R. 329; [1990] Crim.L.R. 651, DC 8–79
Pattinson (Dean) and Exley (Warren) [1996] 1 Cr.App.R. 51, CA 14–05
Paul (James) and McFarlane (Robert) [1920] 2 K.B. 183, CCA 17–12, 21–15
Paul v DPP (1990) 90 Cr.App.R. 173; [1989] Crim.L.R. 660; [1990] C.O.D.
   59; 153 J.P.N. 435, DC 5–11
Payne (William John) [1963] 1 W.L.R. 637; [1963] 1 All E.R. 848; 47
   Cr.App.R. 122; 127 J.P. 230; 107 S.J. 97, CCA 10–06
Peach (Geoffrey Tom) [1990] 1 W.L.R. 976; [1990] 2 All E.R. 966; 91
   Cr.App.R. 279; [1990] Crim.L.R. 741, CA 15–03
Pearce (David Anthony) (1979) 69 Cr.App.R. 365; [1979] Crim.L.R. 658,
   CA 20–14, 20–15, 20–16, 20–17
Pearce (Gary James) [2001] EWCA Crim 2834; [2002] 1 W.L.R. 1553;
   [2002] 1 Cr.App.R. 39; 166 J.P. 103; [2002] 3 F.C.R. 75; 166 J.P.N.
   190; 99(8) L.S.G. 34; 146 S.J.L.B. 37; *The Times*, January 21, 2002,
   CA 13–25, 17–27, 17–28
Pemberton (Jason Clive) (1994) 99 Cr.App.R. 228, CA 14–09
Penman (James) (1986) 82 Cr.App.R. 44, CA 4–08, 16–17
Penny (Steven Charles) (1992) 94 Cr.App.R. 345; [1992] Crim.L.R. 184;
   141 N.L.J. 1555; *The Times*, October 17, 1991, CA 14–17, 14–28
Pentonville Prison Governor Ex p. Schneider and Holloway Prison Governor
   Ex p. Newall (1981) 73 Cr.App.R. 200, DC 17–15
Perry (Stephen Arthur), *The Times*, April 28, 2000, CA 13–01
Pestano [1981] Crim.L.R. 397, CA 21–10

Peterborough Justices Ex p. Hicks [1977] 1 W.L.R. 1371; [1978] 1 All E.R. 225; [1977] Crim.L.R. 621; 121 S.J. 605, DC 11–34
Peters (1886) 16 Q.B.D. 636 8–40
Petrie (Dudley Leighton) [1961] 1 W.L.R. 358; [1961] 1 All E.R. 466; 45 Cr.App.R. 72; 125 J.P. 198; 105 S.J. 131, CCA 4–12
Pettnam, unreported, May 2, 1985 7–37
Phelan v Back [1972] 1 W.L.R. 273; [1972] 1 All E.R. 901; 56 Cr.App.R. 257; 116 S.J. 76, DC 19–06
Philcox v Carberry [1960] Crim.L.R. 563, DC 4–19
Phillips (1936) 26 Cr.App.R. 17 21–30
Phillips (Alun Charles) [2003] EWCA Crim 1379; [2003] 2 Cr.App.R. 35 7–38
Phillips (Daniel Mark) (1988) 86 Cr.App.R. 18; 151 J.P. 467; 151 J.P.N. 286, CA 9–24
Phillipson (Bridget Phillipson) (1990) 91 Cr.App.R. 226; [1990] Crim.L.R. 407, CA 18–13
Pico [1971] R.T.R. 500, CA 16–22
Pieterson (Matthew Theodore) and Holloway (James) [1995] 1 W.L.R. 293; [1995] 2 Cr.App.R. 11; [1995] Crim.L.R. 402; 92(2) L.S.G. 36; 138 S.J.L.B. 228; *The Times*, November 11, 1994, CA 14–49
Piggott v Sims [1973] R.T.R. 15; [1972] Crim.L.R. 595, DC 19–37
Pigram (Charles Howard) [1995] Crim.L.R. 808, CA 7–14
Pipe (William Augustine) (1967) 51 Cr.App.R. 17; [1967] Crim.L.R. 42; 110 S.J. 829; *The Times*, October 25, 1966, CA 17–15
Pitt (Ian Barry) [1983] Q.B. 25; [1982] 3 W.L.R. 359; [1982] 3 All E.R. 63; 75 Cr.App.R. 254; [1982] Crim.L.R. 513; 12 Fam. Law 152; 79 L.S.G. 953; 126 S.J. 447, CA 17–29, 21–09
Plato Films Ltd v Speidel; sub nom. Speidel v Plato Films Ltd; Speidel v Unity Theatre Society [1961] A.C. 1090; [1961] 2 W.L.R. 470; [1961] 1 All E.R. 876; 105 S.J. 230, HL 7–07
Platt [1981] Crim.L.R. 332, CA 6–45
Podola (Guenther Fritz Erwin) [1960] 1 Q.B. 325; [1959] 3 W.L.R. 718; [1959] 3 All E.R. 418; 43 Cr.App.R. 220; 103 S.J. 856, CCA 4–11, 4–47
Pointer (John) [1997] Crim.L.R. 676, CA 11–17
Popat (Chetan) (No.1) [1998] 2 Cr.App.R. 208; 162 J.P. 369; [1998] Crim.L.R. 825; 162 J.P.N. 423; *The Times*, April 10, 1998, CA 14–24
Poplar Housing & Regeneration Community Association Ltd v Donoghue; sub nom. Donoghue v Poplar Housing & Regeneration Community Association Ltd; Poplar Housing & Regeneration Community Association Ltd v Donaghue [2001] EWCA Civ 595; [2002] Q.B. 48; [2001] 3 W.L.R. 183; [2001] 4 All E.R. 604; [2001] 2 F.L.R. 284; [2001] 3 F.C.R. 74; [2001] U.K.H.R.R. 693; 33 H.L.R. 73; 3 L.G.L.R. 41; [2001] B.L.G.R. 489; [2001] A.C.D. 76; [2001] Fam. Law 588; [2001] 19 E.G.C.S. 141; 98(19) L.S.G. 38; 98(23) L.S.G. 38; 145 S.J.L.B. 122; [2001] N.P.C. 84; *The Times*, June 21, 2001; *Independent*, May 2, 2001; *Daily Telegraph*, May 8, 2001, CA 13–08
Porritt (George Anthony) [1961] 1 W.L.R. 1372; [1961] 3 All E.R. 463; 45 Cr.App.R. 348; 125 J.P. 605; 105 S.J. 991, CCA 16–15
Porter v Magill; sub nom. Magill v Porter; Magill v Weeks [2001] UKHL 67, HL; reversing [2000] 2 W.L.R. 1420, CA; reversing (1998) 30 H.L.R. 997; 96 L.G.R. 157, DC 13–29
Powell [1985] Crim.L.R. 592, CA 21–34
Powell v DPP (1993) 157 J.P. 700; [1992] R.T.R. 270; [1992] C.O.D. 191; 156 J.P.N. 460, DC 14–25

Powers [1990] Crim.L.R. 586, CA 1–09
Practice Direction (Criminal Proceedings: Consolidation); sub nom. Practice
    Statement (CA (Crim Div): The Consolidated Criminal Practice
    Direction) [2002] 1 W.L.R. 2870; [2002] 3 All E.R. 904; [2002] 2
    Cr.App.R. 35, CA 2–25, 7–22, 7–23, 7–24, 8–63, 9–12, 19–26
Practice Direction: Crown Court (Defendant's Evidence) [1995] 2
    Cr.App.R. 192 17–17
Practice Direction (QBD: Crime: Evidence by Written Statements); sub nom.
    Practice Direction (QBD: Evidence: Written Statements) [1986] 1
    W.L.R. 805; [1986] 2 All E.R. 511; 83 Cr.App.R. 212; [1986]
    Crim.L.R. 620, QBD 8–82
Practice Direction (QBD: Rehabilitation of Offenders Act 1974: Imple-
    mentation: Reference to Spent Convictions during Trial) [1975] 1
    W.L.R. 1065; 61 Cr.App.R. 260; [1975] Crim.L.R. 520 .... 7–21, 7–24,
                                                                    7–25, 10–11
Practice Direction (Submission of No Case) [1962] 1 W.L.R. 227; [1962] 1
    All E.R. 448, QBD 16–30
Practice Direction (Ward: Witness at Trial) [1987] 1 W.L.R. 1739 17–05
Practice Direction (Ward: Witness at Trial) (No.2) [1988] 1 W.L.R. 989 . 17–05
Prager (Nicholas Anthony) (No.2) [1972] 1 W.L.R. 260; [1972] 1 All E.R.
    1114; 56 Cr.App.R. 151; 116 S.J. 158, CA 9–18
Prasad v R.; sub nom. Ragho Prasad S/O Ram Autar Rao v R. [1981] 1
    W.L.R. 469; [1981] 1 All E.R. 319; (1981) 72 Cr.App.R. 218; [1981]
    Crim.L.R. 172; 124 S.J. 864, PC (Fiji) 9–58
Prayag, *The Times*, July 31, 1991, CA 7–14
Preece v Parry [1983] Crim.L.R. 170, DC 9–05
Prefas (Takis) and Pryce (Daniel) (1988) 86 Cr.App.R. 111; [1987]
    Crim.L.R. 327, CA 21–10
Preston (Stephen) [1994] 2 A.C. 130; [1993] 3 W.L.R. 891; [1993] 4 All
    E.R. 638; 98 Cr.App.R. 405; [1994] Crim.L.R. 676; 137 S.J.L.B. 256,
    HL 12–05
Price (Julian Lewis) [1996] Crim.L.R. 738, CA 17–17
Price v Manning (1889) L.R. 42 Ch. D. 372, CA 10–11
Pridmore (1913) 29 T.L.R. 330 8–64
Priestley (Martin) (1967) 51 Cr.App.R. 1n; 50 Cr.App.R. 183; [1966]
    Crim.L.R. 507; 116 N.L.J. 948, CCA 9–18
Prince v Samo (1837) 7 L.J.Q.B. 123 21–33
Process Church of the Final Judgment (A Corporate Body) v Hart-Davis
    (Rupert), *The Times*, January 29, 1975, CA 8–09
Proulx v Governor of Brixton Prison and Bow Street Magistrates' Court Ex
    p. Proulx [2001] 1 All E.R. 57; [2000] Crim.L.R. 997; [2000] C.O.D.
    454, QBD 9–20
Pryce [1991] Crim.L.R. 379, CA 15–13
Pullen [1991] Crim.L.R. 457, CA
Pydar Justices Ex p. Foster (1996) 160 J.P. 87, QBD 2–02

Quinn [1983] Crim.L.R. 475, CA 4–39
Quinn [1990] Crim.L.R. 581, CA 10–21
Quinn (Francis Joseph) [1995] 1 Cr.App.R. 480; [1995] Crim.L.R. 56; 138
    S.J.L.B. 76; *The Times*, March 15, 1994; *Independent*, April 4, 1994,
    CA 10–29, 14–19, 14–29
Quinn (Geoffrey Anthony) and Bloom (Samuel) [1962] 2 Q.B. 245; [1961] 3

W.L.R. 611; [1961] 3 All E.R. 88; 45 Cr.App.R. 279; 125 J.P. 565; 105
S.J. 590, CCA 1–11, 2–41, 2–42

R, unreported, February 6, 1995, CA 19–27, 21–11
R. [1996] Crim.L.R. 815 15–11
R (A Minor) (Wardship: Criminal Proceedings), Re [1991] Fam. 56; [1991]
    2 W.L.R. 912; [1991] 2 All E.R. 193; [1991] 2 F.L.R. 95; [1991] F.C.R.
    642; [1991] Fam. Law 315; 141 N.L.J. 164; 135 S.J.L.B. 164; *The
    Times*, January 24, 1991; *Independent*, February 13, 1991; *Daily
    Telegraph*, January 31, 1991, CA 17–05
R (Blood Sample: Privilege) [1994] 1 W.L.R. 758; [1994] 4 All E.R. 260;
    [1995] 1 Cr.App.R. 183; 138 S.J.L.B. 54; *The Times*, February 2, 1994;
    Independent, February 21, 1994, CA 11–33
R (David) [1999] Crim.L.R. 909, CA 21–29
Radford v Kent CC (1998) 162 J.P. 697; 162 J.P.N. 606; *The Times*, March
    11, 1998, DC 17–17
Rafique [1973] Crim.L.R. 777, CA 4–44
Raghip, *The Times*, December 9, 1991 .... 6–18, 9–22
Rampling [1987] Crim.L.R. 823, CA 2–25, 2–29
Rankine (Elliston) [1986] Q.B. 861; [1986] 2 W.L.R. 1075; [1986] 2 All
    E.R. 566; 83 Cr.App.R. 18; [1986] Crim.L.R. 464; 130 S.J. 315, CA   12–09
Rantzen v Mirror Group Newspapers (1986) Ltd [1994] Q.B. 670; [1993] 3
    W.L.R. 953; [1993] 4 All E.R. 975; 143 N.L.J. 507; *The Times*, April 6,
    1993; *Independent*, April 1, 1993, CA 10–26, 13–02
Raphaie (Daniel) [1996] Crim.L.R. 812, CA 10–30
Ratten (Leith McDonald) v R. [1972] A.C. 378; [1971] 3 W.L.R. 930;
    [1971] 3 All E.R. 801; 56 Cr.App.R. 18; 115 S.J. 889, PC (Aus) 1–15,
                                         8–06, 8–50, 8–52, 8–53, 8–54,
                                                 8–55, 8–56, 8–61
Raviraj (Thaneran) (1987) 85 Cr.App.R. 93, CA 1–08, 1–09, 9–55
Rawlings (Royston George) and Broadbent (Timothy Charles) [1995] 1
    W.L.R. 178; [1995] 1 All E.R. 580; [1995] 2 Cr.App.R. 222; 92(2)
    L.S.G. 36; 144 N.L.J. 1626; 138 S.J.L.B. 223; *The Times*, October 19,
    1994; *Independent*, October 18, 1994, CA 19–28, 19–29
Raynor (Stephen) (2001) 165 J.P. 149; 165 J.P.N. 664; *The Times*, Sep-
    tember 19, 2000, CA 18–01
Read v Bishop of Lincoln (No.3) [1892] A.C. 644; 56 J.P. 725; 62 L.J. P.C.
    1; 67 L.T. 128, PC 8–40
Reader, unreported, April 7, 1998, CA 11–20
Reading (Albert) [1966] 1 W.L.R. 836; [1966] 1 All E.R. 521n; 50
    Cr.App.R. 98; 130 J.P. 160; 110 S.J. 368, CCA 14–47
Reader v Bunyard (1987) 85 Cr.App.R. 185; [1987] R.T.R. 406; [1987]
    Crim.L.R. 274, DC 4–20
Reading and West Berkshire Stipendiary Magistrates Ex p. Dyas (2000) 164
    J.P. 117, QBD 21–32
Redgrave (Scott) (1982) 74 Cr.App.R. 10; [1981] Crim.L.R. 556, CA 7–09
Regan (1887) 16 Cox C.C. 203 3–05
Reid, *The Times*, August 17, 1999 16–15
Reid (Sonni Lee) [2001] EWCA Crim 1806; [2002] 1 Cr.App.R. 21; [2002]
    Crim.L.R. 211; *The Times*, November 12, 2001, CA 18–12
Reid v R. [1990] 1 A.C. 363; [1989] 3 W.L.R. 771; [1993] 4 All E.R. 95n;
    90 Cr.App.R. 121; [1990] Crim.L.R. 113; 133 S.J. 1062, PC (Jam) .. 14–04
Reynolds, Re (1882) 20 Ch.D. 294 11–06

Reynolds [1989] Crim.L.R. 220, CA 6–20
Reynolds (Ernest Albert) [1950] 1 K.B. 606; [1950] 1 All E.R. 335; 66
    T.L.R. (Pt.1) 333; 34 Cr.App.R. 60; 114 J.P. 155; 48 L.G.R. 239; 94
    S.J. 165, CCA 16–06, 17–07
Reynolds v Llanelly Associated Tin Plate Co. [1948] 1 All E.R. 140, CA . 5–12
Rhodes [1959] Crim.L.R. 138, CCA 9–54
Riaz (Raqaiya) and Burke (Martin) (1992) 94 Cr.App.R. 339; 156 J.P. 721;
    [1992] Crim.L.R. 366; 156 J.P.N. 348, CA 2–27
Rice (Anthony John) [1963] 1 Q.B. 857; [1963] 2 W.L.R. 585; [1963] 1 All
    E.R. 832; 47 Cr.App.R. 79; 127 J.P. 232; 107 S.J. 117, CCA 9–52,
                                            10–11, 19–35, 19–38, 21–16
Richards (Randall) (1999) 163 J.P. 246; [1999] Crim.L.R. 764, CA 13–19
Richards v Curwen [1977] 1 W.L.R. 747; [1977] 3 All E.R. 426; 65
    Cr.App.R. 95; [1977] Crim.L.R. 356; 121 S.J. 270, DC 16–31
Richardson (1994) 98 Cr.App.R. 174 19–01
Richardson (David Ernest) [1971] 2 Q.B. 484; [1971] 2 W.L.R. 889; [1971]
    2 All E.R. 773; 55 Cr.App.R. 244; 115 S.J. 263, CA 20–23, 20–24,
                                                    20–28, 20–31
Richardson (Jean) (1967) 51 Cr.App.R. 381; [1968] Crim.L.R. 165, CCC   17–13
Richens (Andrew Ronald) [1993] 4 All E.R. 877; 98 Cr.App.R. 43; [1993]
    Crim.L.R. 384; *The Times*, November 25, 1992, CA 16–17
Rickard (1918) 13 Cr.App.R. 140 6–10
Rider (Theresa Ann) (1986) 83 Cr.App.R. 207; [1986] Crim.L.R. 626, CA 15–03
Riley (1866) 4 F. & F. 964 21–25
Rimmer (Patrick) [1972] 1 W.L.R. 268; [1972] 1 All E.R. 604; 56
    Cr.App.R. 196; [1972] Crim.L.R. 98; 116 S.J. 158, CA 10–12, 16–07
Rimmer and Beech [1983] Crim.L.R. 250, CA 6–25
Rivett (James Frank) (1950) 34 Cr.App.R. 87, CA 6–43
Robb (Robert McCheyne) (1991) 93 Cr.App.R. 161; [1991] Crim.L.R. 539;
    135 S.J. 312, CA 2–28, 6–28, 10–28
Roberts (1942) 28 Cr.App.R. 102 .... 20–02, 20–08
Roberts (1984) 80 Cr.App.R. 89 19–01
Roberts [1992] Crim.L.R. 375, CA 4–05
Roberts [2000] Crim.L.R. 183 14–48
Roberts (John Marcus) (1985) 80 Cr.App.R. 89, CA 19–06
Roberts (Michael) (1998) 162 J.P. 691; [1998] Crim.L.R. 682; 162 J.P.N.
    544, CA 2–33
Roberts (Stephen Paul) [1997] 1 Cr.App.R. 217; [1997] Crim.L.R. 222,
    CA 9–30, 10–23
Robertson (Eric John) [1968] 1 W.L.R. 1767; [1968] 3 All E.R. 557; 52
    Cr.App.R. 690; 133 J.P. 5; 112 S.J. 799, CA 4–11, 4–47
Robertson (Malcolm) and Golder (Martin) [1987] Q.B. 920; [1987] 3
    W.L.R. 327; [1987] 3 All E.R. 231; 85 Cr.App.R. 304; 151 J.P. 761;
    [1987] Crim.L.R. 627; 151 J.P.N. 558; 84 L.S.G. 2044; 131 S.J. 1002,
    CA 5–27, 5–29, 5–30, 5–33, 5–35, 16–21
Robinson (1897) 61 J.P. 520 21–07
Robinson (Michael) [2001] EWCA Crim 214; [2001] Crim.L.R. 478, CA   7–61
Robinson (Raymond) [1994] 3 All E.R. 346; 98 Cr.App.R. 370; [1994]
    Crim.L.R. 356; 143 N.L.J. 1643, CA 6–25
Roble (Ali Hersi) [1997] Crim.L.R. 449, CA 11–21
Robson (Bernard Jack) and Harris (Gordon Frederick) [1972] 1 W.L.R. 651;
    [1972] 2 All E.R. 699; 56 Cr.App.R. 450; [1972] Crim.L.R. 316; 116
    S.J. 313, CCC 2–18, 2–19, 2–26, 16–07

Rogers v Secretary of State for the Home Department [1973] A.C. 388;
    [1972] 3 W.L.R. 279; [1972] 2 All E.R. 1057; 116 S.J. 696, HL 12–02,
                                                                        12–03, 12–12
Rose v R. [1995] Crim.L.R. 939, PC (Jam) 14–05
Rosser (1836) 7 C. & P. 648 5–10
Rowson (James) [1986] Q.B. 174; [1985] 3 W.L.R. 99; [1985] 2 All E.R.
    539; 80 Cr.App.R. 218; [1985] Crim.L.R. 307; 82 L.S.G. 1330; 129
    S.J. 447, CA 21–16
Rowton [1865] Le. & Ca. 520, CCR 7–01, 7–07, 7–08, 7–10, 7–11
Royal v Prescott-Clarke [1966] 1 W.L.R. 788; [1966] 2 All E.R. 366; 130
    J.P. 274; 110 S.J. 312, DC 19–37
Rudd (Leonard) (1948) 64 T.L.R. 240; (1948) 32 Cr.App.R. 138; 92 S.J.
    206, CCA 17–12
Rumping v DPP [1964] A.C. 814; [1962] 3 W.L.R. 763; [1962] 3 All E.R.
    256; 46 Cr.App.R. 398; 106 S.J. 668, HL 9–04
Rush (1896) 60 J.P. 777 20–06
Russell v McAdams [2001] N.I. 157, CA 10–21
Russell-Jones (Kenneth) [1995] 3 All E.R. 239; [1995] 1 Cr.App.R. 538;
    [1995] Crim.L.R. 833, CA 19–02
Ruston (1786) 1 Leach 408 17–08
Rutherford (Osborne Alexander) and Palmer (1994) 98 Cr.App.R. 191,
    CA 14–17
Rutherford (Wayne) [1998] Crim.L.R. 490, CA 8–28
Ryan [1992] Crim.L.R. 187, CA 14–28

S [1995] 2 Cr.App.R. 313, CA 19–28
S and C [1996] Crim.L.R. 346, CA 16–11
S (Children) (Care Order: Implementation of Care Plan), Re; sub nom. W
    and B (Children) (Care Plan), Re; W (Children) (Care Plan), Re [2002]
    UKHL 10; [2002] 2 A.C. 291; [2002] 2 W.L.R. 720; [2002] 2 All E.R.
    192; [2002] 1 F.L.R. 815; [2002] 1 F.C.R. 577; [2002] H.R.L.R. 26;
    [2002] U.K.H.R.R. 652; [2002] B.L.G.R. 251; [2002] Fam. Law 413;
    99(17) L.S.G. 34; 146 S.J.L.B. 85, HL 13–08
S v Havering LBC, *The Times*, December 2, 2002 4–17
Saifi v Governor of Brixton Prison; sub nom. R. v Governor of Brixton
    Prison Ex p. Saifi [2001] 1 W.L.R. 1134; [2001] 4 All E.R. 168; [2001]
    Crim.L.R. 653; *The Times*, January 24, 2001, DC 10–30
Salsbury v Woodland [1970] 1 Q.B. 324; [1969] 3 W.L.R. 29; [1969] 3 All
    E.R. 863; 113 S.J. 327, CA 2–07
Sambasivam v Public Prosecutor, Malaya [1950] A.C. 458; 66 T.L.R. (Pt.2)
    254, PC (FMS) 5–14, 5–16, 5–22
Samuel (Cornelius Joseph) [1988] Q.B. 615; [1988] 2 W.L.R. 920; [1988] 2
    All E.R. 135; 87 Cr.App.R. 232; [1988] Crim.L.R. 299; 152 J.P.N. 238,
    CA 9–26, 9–34, 10–17, 10–19,
                                                                             10–29
Samuel (Norman) (1956) 40 Cr.App.R. 8, CCA 7–61
Sanderson (Andrew John) [1953] 1 W.L.R. 392; [1953] 1 All E.R. 485; 37
    Cr.App.R. 32; 97 S.J. 136, CCA 19–41
Sandhu (Major) [1998] 1 P.L.R. 17; [1997] J.P.L. 853; [1997] Crim.L.R.
    288; [1996] N.P.C. 179, CA 1–14
Sang (Leonard Anthony) and Mangan (Matthew) [1980] A.C. 402; [1979] 3
    W.L.R. 263; [1979] 2 All E.R. 1222; 69 Cr.App.R. 282; [1979]

Crim.L.R. 655, HL; affirming [1979] 2 W.L.R. 439; [1979] 2 All E.R.
    46; 68 Cr.App.R. 240; [1979] Crim.L.R. 389; 123 S.J. 232, CA 4–42,
                    10–04, 10–05, 10–07, 10–08, 10–11, 10–14,
                    10–15, 16–05, 16–08, 16–27
Sat-Bhambra (Ajit Singh) (1989) 88 Cr.App.R. 55; (1988) 152 J.P. 365;
    [1988] Crim.L.R. 453; 152 J.P.N. 383; 132 S.J. 896, CA 9–13, 9–46,
                    9–48, 9–49, 10–30
Saunders, unreported, September, 1990, CCC 18–07, 18–09
Saunders (Ernest Walter) (No.2) [1996] 1 Cr.App.R. 463; [1996] Crim.L.R.
    420; 140 S.J.L.B. 22; *The Times*, November 28, 1995; *Independent*,
    November 28, 1995, CA 11–09
Savage v Chief Constable of Hampshire; sub nom. Savage v Hoddinot
    [1997] 1 W.L.R. 1061; [1997] 2 All E.R. 631; *The Times*, February 14,
    1997, CA 12–02
Sawoniuk (Anthony) [2000] 2 Cr.App.R. 220; [2000] Crim.L.R. 506, CA .. 7–38,
                    14–09
Sbarra (1918) 13 Cr.App.R. 118 9–59
Scaife (1851) 5 Cox C.C. 8–85
Scarrott (Ernest Theodore) [1978] Q.B. 1016; [1977] 3 W.L.R. 629; [1978]
    1 All E.R. 672; 65 Cr.App.R. 125; [1977] Crim.L.R. 745; 121 S.J. 558,
    CA 7–37
Schaub (Mark Tony); sub nom. Cooper (Joey) [1994] Crim.L.R. 531; 91(5)
    L.S.G. 35; 138 S.J.L.B. 11; *The Times*, December 3, 1993, CA 19–18
Scott (1856) Dears. & B. 47 11–09
Scott (Anthony Stanley) (1984) 79 Cr.App.R. 49; 148 J.P. 731; [1984]
    Crim.L.R. 235, CA 19–39
Scott v Baker [1969] 1 Q.B. 659; [1968] 3 W.L.R. 796; [1968] 2 All E.R.
    993; 52 Cr.App.R. 566; 132 J.P. 422; 112 S.J. 425, DC 5–05
Scott (Richard) v R. [1989] A.C. 1242; [1989] 2 W.L.R. 924; [1989] 2 All
    E.R. 305; 89 Cr.App.R. 153; [1989] Crim.L.R. 820; 86(23) L.S.G. 40;
    133 S.J. 421, PC (Jam) 8–74, 10–03
Seaman v Netherclift (1877) 2 C.P.D. 53 21–27
Seamark v Prouse [1980] 1 W.L.R. 698; [1980] 3 All E.R. 26; 70 Cr.App.R.
    236; [1980] Crim.L.R. 240; 124 S.J. 167, DC 16–31
Secretary of State for the Home Department Ex p. Brind [1991] 1 A.C. 696;
    [1991] 2 W.L.R. 588; [1991] 1 All E.R. 720; 3 Admin. L.R. 486; 141
    N.L.J. 199; 135 S.J. 250; *The Times*, February 8, 1991; *Independent*,
    February 8, 1991; *Guardian*, February 8, 1991, HL 13–02
Seelig (Roger Hugh) and Baron Spens [1992] 1 W.L.R. 149; [1991] 4 All
    E.R. 429; [1991] B.C.C. 569; [1991] B.C.L.C. 869; 94 Cr.App.R. 17;
    141 N.L.J. 638, CA 9–28
Sekhon (Malkiat Singh) (1987) 85 Cr.App.R. 19; [1987] Crim.L.R. 693; 84
    L.S.G. 736; 131 S.J. 356, CA 20–34, 20–35
Selvey (Wilfred George) (No.1); sub nom. Selvey (Wilfred George) v DPP
    (No.1) [1970] A.C. 304; [1968] 2 W.L.R. 1494; [1968] 2 All E.R. 497;
    52 Cr.App.R. 443; 132 J.P. 430; 112 S.J. 461, HL 7–67, 10–04, 10–11,
                    10–12
Senat (Martin) and Sin (Christopher Cho Him) (1968) 52 Cr.App.R. 282;
    [1968] Crim.L.R. 269; 112 S.J. 252, CA 2–20
Senat v Senat [1965] P. 172; [1965] 2 W.L.R. 981; [1965] 2 All E.R. 505,
    PDAD 20–33, 21–21
Seneviratne v R. [1936] 3 All E.R. 36; [1936] 3 W.W.R. 360, PC (Cey) .. 19–01

Senior v Holdsworth Ex p. Independent Television News [1976] Q.B. 23;
    [1975] 2 W.L.R. 987; [1975] 2 All E.R. 1009; 119 S.J. 393, CA   3–02
Serious Fraud Office Ex p. Maxwell (Kevin), *The Times*, October 9, 1992;
    Independent, October 7, 1992; *Guardian*, October 20, 1992, DC   18–03
Shah [1994] Crim.L.R. 125, CA   9–43
Shand v R. [1996] 1 W.L.R. 67; [1996] 1 All E.R. 511; [1996] 2 Cr.App.R.
    204; [1996] Crim.L.R. 422; 140 S.J.L.B. 24; *The Times*, November 29,
    1995, PC (Jam)   14–11
Shannon (John James); sub nom. Alford (John James) [2001] 1 W.L.R. 51;
    [2001] 1 Cr.App.R. 12; [2000] Crim.L.R. 1001; 97(40) L.S.G. 41; 144
    S.J.L.B. 257; *The Times*, October 11, 2000, CA 10–15, 10–16, 18–12,
                                                                    21–05
Sharman (Peter Edward) [1998] 1 Cr.App.R. 406; 162 J.P. 110; [1998] 1
    F.L.R. 785; [1998] Fam. Law 315; 162 J.P.N. 187; *The Times*,
    December 18, 1997, CA 17–03, 19–08
Sharp (Colin) [1988] 1 W.L.R. 7; [1988] 1 All E.R. 65; 86 Cr.App.R. 274;
    152 J.P. 164; [1988] Crim.L.R. 303; 152 J.P.N. 142; 138 N.L.J. Rep. 6;
    132 S.J. 21; *Guardian*, January 11, 1988, HL   20–18
Sharp (Frank) [1994] Q.B. 261; [1994] 2 W.L.R. 84; [1993] 3 All E.R. 225;
    98 Cr.App.R. 144; *The Times*, February 10, 1993, CA   16–17
Sharrock (1974) 32 Cr.App.R. 124   17–11
Shaw (1888) 16 Cox 503   21–30
Shaw (Deborah Ann) (1993) 97 Cr.App.R. 218; *The Times*, December 31,
    1992, CA   7–19
Sheldrake v DPP [2003] EWHC 273 (Admin); [2003] 2 W.L.R. 1629;
    [2003] 2 All E.R. 497; [2003] 2 Cr.App.R. 14; 167 J.P. 333; [2004]
    R.T.R. 3; 167 J.P.N. 514; 100(13) L.S.G. 29; *The Times*, February 25,
    2003, DC   4–16
Shephard (Hilda) [1993] A.C. 380; [1993] 2 W.L.R. 102; [1993] 1 All E.R.
    225; 96 Cr.App.R. 345; 157 J.P. 145; [1993] Crim.L.R. 295; 143 N.L.J.
    127; 137 S.J.L.B. 12, HL   8–35
Shillingford (Holly) and Vanderwall (Rayonne Niel) [1968] 1 W.L.R. 566;
    [1968] 2 All E.R. 200; 52 Cr.App.R. 188; 132 J.P. 264; 112 S.J. 170,
    CA   15–07
Silcott [1987] Crim.L.R. 765, CCC   9–54
Silcott (Winston), Braithwaite and Raghip, *The Times*, December 9, 1991,
    CA   9–34
Silverlock [1894] 2 Q.B. 766, QBD   6–28
Simbodyal, *The Times*, October 10, 1991, CA   6–13
Simmonds (Bernard Harry) [1969] 1 Q.B. 685; [1967] 3 W.L.R. 367; [1967]
    2 All E.R. 399; 51 Cr.App.R. 316; 131 J.P. 341; 111 S.J. 274, CA ...   21–16
Simmonds (Robin) [1996] Crim.L.R. 816, CA   17–03
Simpson (Calvin) [1983] 1 W.L.R. 1494; [1983] 3 All E.R. 789; 78
    Cr.App.R. 115; 148 J.P. 33; [1984] Crim.L.R. 39; 127 S.J. 748, CA .   5–10
Simpson (Montgomery Robert) (1994) 99 Cr.App.R. 48, CA   17–10
Sims (1834) 6 C. & P. 540   9–04
Sims [1946] K.B. 531; [1946] 1 All E.R. 699; 62 T.L.R. 431; [1947] L.J.R.
    160; 175 L.T. 72; 90 S.J. 381, CCA   1–14
Sinclair, *The Times*, September 9, 1992   2–25
Sittingbourne Justices Ex p. Stickings. *See* Faversham and Sittingbourne
    Justices Ex p. Stickings
Skegness Magistrates' Court Ex p. Cardy [1985] R.T.R. 49; [1985]
    Crim.L.R. 237; 82 L.S.G. 929, DC   3–14

Skinner (Gary) (1994) 99 Cr.App.R. 212; 158 J.P. 931; [1994] Crim.L.R. 676; 158 J.P.N. 701; 158 L.G. Rev. 701; 137 S.J.L.B. 277, CA 20–24
Skirving (Donald William) and Grossman (Beth Susan) [1985] Q.B. 819; [1985] 2 W.L.R. 1001; 81 Cr.App.R. 9; [1985] Crim.L.R. 317; 82 L.S.G. 1409; 129 S.J. 299, CA 6–22
Slater (Robert David) [1995] 1 Cr.App.R. 584; [1995] Crim.L.R. 244, CA 14–10
Slatterie v Pooley (1840) 6 M. & W. 664 .... 3–05, 9–01
Sloggett (1856) Dears 656 11–04
Smallman [1982] Crim.L.R. 175, CA 7–23
Smith (1968) 52 Cr.App.R. 848 6–10
Smith [1971] Crim.L.R. 53 7–13
Smith (1990) 148 J.P. 216 1–08
Smith (Joan) [1968] 1 W.L.R. 636; [1968] 2 All E.R. 115; 52 Cr.App.R. 224; 132 J.P. 312; 112 S.J. 231, CA 19–04
Smith (John Anthony James) [1973] 1 W.L.R. 1510; [1974] 1 All E.R. 376; 58 Cr.App.R. 106; [1973] Crim.L.R. 700; 117 S.J. 774, CA 6–38
Smith (Joe) [2001] 1 W.L.R. 1031; [2001] 2 Cr.App.R. 1; *The Times*, December 20, 2000, CA 12–18, 12–19
Smith (Patrick Joseph) [2000] 1 All E.R. 263; [1999] 2 Cr.App.R. 238; 96(23) L.S.G. 34 Times, May 31, 1999, CA 16–12
Smith (Percy) [1976] Crim.L.R. 511, CA 14–40
Smith (Stanley Ivan) [1979] 1 W.L.R. 1445; [1979] 3 All E.R. 605; 69 Cr.App.R. 378; [1979] Crim.L.R. 592; 123 S.J. 602, CA 6–18, 6–29
Smith (Wallace Duncan) [1994] 1 W.L.R. 1396; 99 Cr.App.R. 233, CA .. 9–28, 18–26
Smith (William) and Doe (Henry) (1987) 85 Cr.App.R. 197; [1987] Crim.L.R. 267; *The Times*, December 3, 1986, CA 2–33, 14–07, 14–31, 16–11
Smurthwaite (Keith) and Gill (Susan) [1994] 1 All E.R. 898; 98 Cr.App.R. 437; 158 J.P. 165; [1994] Crim.L.R. 53; 158 L.G. Rev. 92; 143 N.L.J. 1568; 137 S.J.L.B. 235, CA 10–07, 10–13, 10–25
Smyth (1980) 72 Cr.App.R. 86 1–08
Smyth (Paul), *The Times*, September 16, 1998, CA 2–06
Sneddon v Stevenson [1967] 1 W.L.R. 1051; [1967] 2 All E.R. 1277; 131 J.P. 441; 111 S.J. 515, DC 10–07
Soames-Waring (Jonathan Drew) [1999] Crim.L.R. 89; *The Times*, July 20, 1998, CA 16–15
Sodeman v The King [1936] W.N. 190, PC 4–11, 4–46
Somers (Mark) [1999] Crim.L.R. 744, CA 21–30
Somers (Patrick) [1963] 1 W.L.R. 1306; [1963] 3 All E.R. 808; (1964) 48 Cr.App.R. 11; 128 J.P. 20; 61 L.G.R. 598; 107 S.J. 813, CCA 6–38
South Ribble Stipendiary Magistrate Ex p. Cochrane [1996] 2 Cr.App.R. 544; 160 J.P. 517; [1996] Crim.L.R. 741; [1996] C.O.D. 359; 160 J.P.N. 730; *The Times*, June 24, 1996; *Independent*, July 22, 1996, QBD 20–27
South Worcestershire Magistrates Ex p. Lilley [1995] 1 W.L.R. 1595; [1995] 4 All E.R. 186; [1996] 1 Cr.App.R. 420; 159 J.P. 598; [1995] Crim.L.R. 954; [1996] C.O.D. 109; 92(13) L.S.G. 31; 139 S.J.L.B. 67; *The Times*, February 22, 1995, DC 12–25
Sparrow (Peter George) [1973] 1 W.L.R. 488; [1973] 2 All E.R. 129; 57 Cr.App.R. 352; [1973] Crim.L.R. 233; 117 S.J. 283, CA 16–16
Spencer (Alan Widdison) [1987] A.C. 128; [1986] 3 W.L.R. 348; [1986] 2 All E.R. 928; 83 Cr.App.R. 277; 130 S.J. 572, HL 15–15, 15–16

Spencer (John) [1995] Crim.L.R. 235; *The Times*, July 14, 1994, CA 14–12
Spens (No.1); sub nom. Lord Spens; Rex (Patrick Michael); Baron Spens
 [1991] 1 W.L.R. 624; [1991] 4 All E.R. 421; [1991] B.C.C. 140; 93
 Cr.App.R. 194; *The Times*, January 31, 1991; *Independent*, February
 8, 1991; *Daily Telegraph*, February 15, 1991, CA 16–03
Spinks (Mark Lee) [1982] 1 All E.R. 587; 74 Cr.App.R. 263; [1982]
 Crim.L.R. 231, CA 9–54
Spokes v Grosvenor Hotel [1897] 2 Q.B. 124 3–12
Spurge (Frederick Albert) [1961] 2 Q.B. 205; [1961] 3 W.L.R. 23; [1961] 2
 All E.R. 688; 45 Cr.App.R. 191; 125 J.P. 502; 59 L.G.R. 323; 105 S.J.
 469, CCA 4–27
Stagg, unreported [1994] 9 *Archbold News*, September 14, 1994, CCC ... 6–17,
 10–25, 14–49
Stamford (John David) [1972] 2 Q.B. 391; [1972] 2 W.L.R. 1055; [1972] 2
 All E.R. 430; 56 Cr.App.R. 398; [1972] Crim.L.R. 374; 116 S.J. 313,
 CA 6–22
Stannard (1837) 7 C. & P. 673 .... 7–12, 7–17
Statue of Liberty. *See* Owners of the Sapporo Maru v Owners of the Statue
 of Liberty
Steele (Kevin Munro) and Forbes v HM Advocate, 1992 J.C. 1; 1992 S.L.T.
 847; 1992 S.C.C.R. 30, HCJ Appeal 2–39
Stephens (Alan Edwin) [2002] EWCA Crim 1529; *The Times*, June 27,
 2002, CA 4–41
Stephens v Foster (1833) 6 C. & P. 289 20–33
Stevenson (Ronald), Hulse (Barry) and Whitney (Raymond) [1971] 1
 W.L.R. 1; [1971] 1 All E.R. 678; 55 Cr.App.R. 171; 115 S.J. 11, Assizes 2–19
Stewart [1995] Crim.L.R. 500 9–29
Stewart (Angela Claudette) and Sappleton (Marcia Angela) (1989) 89
 Cr.App.R. 273; [1989] Crim.L.R. 653; *The Times*, March 23, 1989;
 Independent, April 17, 1989, CA 19–44
Stipendiary Magistrate for Norfolk Ex p. Taylor (1997) 161 J.P. 773; [1998]
 Crim.L.R. 276; 161 J.P.N. 976, DC 12–25
Stirland v DPP [1944] A.C. 315; 30 Cr.App.R. 40, HL 7–01, 16–04, 16–05
Stockwell (Christopher James) (1993) 97 Cr.App.R. 260; *The Times*, March
 11, 1993, CA 2–15, 6–06, 6–12, 14–38
Stoke, *The Times*, August 6, 1987, CA 3–22
Stokes, unreported, February 2, 2000 9–26
Stoneley v Coleman [1974] Crim.L.R. 254, DC 16–30
Storey (Stephanie) and Anwar (Rashid) (1968) 52 Cr.App.R. 334; [1968]
 Crim.L.R. 387; 112 S.J. 417, CA 20–14, 20–15
Straffen (John Thomas) [1952] 2 Q.B. 911; [1952] 2 All E.R. 657; [1952] 2
 T.L.R. 589; 36 Cr.App.R. 132; 116 J.P. 536; 96 S.J. 749, CCA 7–42
Stratford Justices Ex p. Imbert [1999] 2 Cr.App.R. 276; 163 J.P. 693; 163
 J.P.N. 771; *The Times*, February 25, 1999, DC 18–04
Stratford Youth Court [2001] EWHC Admin 615; 165 J.P. 761; 165 J.P.N.
 926, QBD 9–30
Stretton (1986) 86 Cr.App.R. 7, CA 17–09
Stroud v Stroud (Practice Note) (No.1) [1963] 1 W.L.R. 1080; [1963] 3 All
 E.R. 539; 107 S.J. 273, PDAD 21–21
Sturla v Freccia; sub nom. Polini v Gray (1879–80) L.R. 5 App. Cas. 623,
 HL 3–18, 8–41, 8–42
Subramaniam v Public Prosecutor [1956] 1 W.L.R. 965; 100 S.J. 566, PC
 (FMS) 8–07

Sullivan [1923] 1 K.B. 47, CCA 19–07
Sullivan v Maidstone Crown Court [2002] EWHC 967; [2002] 1 W.L.R. 2747; [2002] 4 All E.R. 427; [2002] 2 Cr.App.R. 31; [2002] Crim.L.R. 646; [2003] A.C.D. 3; 99(26) L.S.G. 36; 146 S.J.L.B. 151; *The Times*, June 5, 2002; *Independent*, July 15, 2002, DC 18–21
Summers (Alfred) [1952] 1 All E.R. 1059; [1952] 1 T.L.R. 1164; 36 Cr.App.R. 14; 116 J.P. 240; [1952] W.N. 185; 96 S.J. 281, CCA 4–42
Sumner (Matthew) [1977] Crim.L.R. 362; [1977] Crim.L.R. 614, Crown Ct 6–23
Sumner & Lievesley v John Brown & Co. (1909) 25 T.L.R. 745 21–08
Sunair Holidays Ltd [1973] 1 W.L.R. 1105; [1973] 2 All E.R. 1233; 57 Cr.App.R. 782; [1973] Crim.L.R. 587; 117 S.J. 429, CA 16–03
Surujpaul v R. [1958] 1 W.L.R. 1050; [1958] 3 All E.R. 300; 42 Cr.App.R. 266; 102 S.J. 757, PC (BG) 9–59
Sutton, unreported 16–20
Sutton (Margaret Anne) (1969) 53 Cr.App.R. 128, CA 10–12
Sutton (Richard John) (1992) 94 Cr.App.R. 70; [1991] Crim.L.R. 836, CA 20–27, 21–33
Swain v Gillett [1974] R.T.R. 446; [1974] Crim.L.R. 433, DC 15–04
Sweet-Escott (Robin Patrick Bickham) (1971) 55 Cr.App.R. 316, Assizes . 21–27
Sweeting (Dawn Karen) and Thomas (David Howard) [1999] Crim.L.R. 75, CA 8–70
Sykes (1913) 8 Cr.App.R. 233 9–54
Sykes (Richard Lee) [1997] Crim.L.R. 752, CA 14–49
Symonds (1924) 18 Cr.App.R. 100, CCA 17–12

T and H (Complainant's Sexual History); sub nom. RT; MH [2001] EWCA Crim 1877; [2002] 1 W.L.R. 632; [2002] 1 All E.R. 683; [2002] 1 Cr.App.R. 22; [2002] Crim.L.R. 73, CA 7–81
Tagg (Heather Susan) [2001] EWCA Crim 1230; [2002] 1 Cr.App.R. 2; [2001] Crim.L.R. 900, CA 6–09
Tameshwar and Seokumar v R. [1957] A.C. 476; [1957] 3 W.L.R. 157; [1957] 2 All E.R. 683; 41 Cr.App.R. 161; 121 J.P. 477; 101 S.J. 532, PC (BG) 2–06
Tang (Koon Cheung) [1995] Crim.L.R. 813; *The Times*, May 23, 1995, CA 3–19
Tariq, Re [1991] 1 W.L.R. 101; [1991] 1 All E.R. 744; 92 Cr.App.R. 276; 35 S.J. 184; *The Times*, January 4, 1991, CA 18–33
Taylor [1978] Crim.L.R. 92, CA 9–55
Taylor [1999] Crim.L.R. 77 .... 11–17, 17–17, 17–19
Taylor (Gary) [1995] Crim.L.R. 253; *The Times*, August 17, 1994; *Independent*, September 12, 1994, CA 19–18, 21–02
Taylor (Michael Anthony) (1993) 157 J.P. 1147; 157 J.P.N. 636; *The Times*, June 15, 1993, CA 16–14
Taylor (Michelle Ann) and Taylor (Lisa Jane) (1994) 98 Cr.App.R. 361; *The Times*, June 15, 1993; *Independent*, June 15, 1993, CA 16–14
Taylor (Nicholas James) and Goodman (Donald Walter) [1999] 2 Cr.App.R. 163; 163 J.P. 168; [1999] Crim.L.R. 407; 163 J.P.N. 112; 95(46) L.S.G. 33; *The Times*, November 3, 1998; *Independent*, November 16, 1998, CA 15–13
Taylor, Weaver and Donovan (1928) 21 Cr.App.R. 20 1–06
Taylor v Anderton; sub nom. Taylor v Chief Constable of Greater Manchester [1995] 1 W.L.R. 447; [1995] 2 All E.R. 420; 92(11) L.S.G. 37; 139 S.J.L.B. 66; *The Times*, January 19, 1995; *Independent*, February 28, 1995, CA 12–14

Taylor v Chief Constable of Cheshire [1986] 1 W.L.R. 1479; [1987] 1 All
    E.R. 225; 84 Cr.App.R. 191; 151 J.P. 103; [1987] Crim.L.R. 119; 151
    J.P.N. 110; 84 L.S.G. 412; 130 S.J. 953, DC 2–31, 14–38
Taylor v Chief Constable of Greater Manchester. *See* Taylor v Anderton
Taylor-Sabori (Sean Marc) [1999] 1 W.L.R. 858; [1999] 1 All E.R. 160;
    [1999] 1 Cr.App.R. 437; [1999] Masons C.L.R. 65; [1999] Crim.L.R.
    322; 95(39) L.S.G. 34; 142 S.J.L.B. 259, CA 2–21
Teper v R. [1952] A.C. 480; [1952] 2 All E.R. 447; [1952] 2 T.L.R. 162;
    116 J.P. 502; 96 S.J. 493, PC (BG) 1–10, 8–50, 8–53
Terrelonge [1977] Crim.L.R. 218, CA 16–07
Theodosi (Marios Andreas) [1993] R.T.R. 179; *The Times*, April 13, 1992,
    CA 6–16
Thomas (Horatio Gerald), *The Times*, February 9, 1987, CA 19–43
Thomas (Steven) [1986] Crim.L.R. 682, Crown Ct 2–33
Thomas [1994] Crim.L.R. 745, CA 20–24
Thomas v Connell (1834) 4 M. & E. 267 8–58
Thomas v David (1836) 7 C. & P. 350 21–30
Thomas v DPP [1991] R.T.R. 292; *The Times*, October 17, 1989, DC 10–21
Thomas v Thomas [1961] 1 W.L.R. 1; [1951] 1 All E.R. 19; 125 J.P. 95; 105
    S.J. 17, DC 5–12
Thompson [1912] 3 K.B. 19 .... 21–16, 21–26
Thompson (Marcellus) [1893] 2 Q.B. 12, CCR 4–33
Thompson (Michael) [1984] 1 W.L.R. 962; [1984] 3 All E.R. 565; 79
    Cr.App.R. 191; [1984] Crim.L.R. 427; 81 L.S.G. 1438; 128 S.J. 447,
    CA 16–23
Thompson (Robert Charles) [1982] Q.B. 647; [1982] 2 W.L.R. 603; [1982]
    1 All E.R. 907; 74 Cr.App.R. 315; [1982] Crim.L.R. 303; 126 S.J. 206,
    CA 8–85
Thompson v R. [1918] A.C. 221, HL 14–47
Thompson (Eversley) v R. [1998] A.C. 811; [1998] 2 W.L.R. 927; 142
    S.J.L.B. 102, PC (StV) 7–14
Thompson v Trevanion (1693) Skin. 402 8–52
Thomson [1967] Crim.L.R. 62; 110 S.J. 788, CA 19–05
Thorne [1981] Crim.L.R. 702, CA 14–19
Thorne (John Francis) (1978) 66 Cr.App.R. 6, CA 5–23
Thornton (Brian) [1995] 1 Cr.App.R. 578; 158 J.P. 1155; 158 J.P.N. 587,
    CA 14–10
Threlfall (1914) 10 Cr.App.R. 112 15–03
Thwaites and Brown (1991) 92 Cr.App.R. 106 9–28
Tibbs (John) [2000] 2 Cr.App.R. 309; [2001] Crim.L.R. 759; *The Times*,
    February 28, 2000, CA 18–15, 18–21
Tilley (Leonard Thomas) and Tilley (George Richard) [1961] 1 W.L.R.
    1309; [1961] 3 All E.R. 406; 45 Cr.App.R. 360; 125 J.P. 611; 105 S.J.
    685, CCA 6–10
Timson and Hales [1993] Crim.L.R. 58, CA 7–14
Tingle Jacobs & Co. v Kennedy [1964] 1 W.L.R. 638n; [1964] 1 All E.R.
    888n; 108 S.J. 196, CA 5–06
Tiplady (Gary) (1995) 159 J.P. 548; [1995] Crim.L.R. 651; *The Times*,
    February 23, 1995, CA 14–21
Tiverton Justices Ex p. Smith [1980] R.T.R. 280, DC 6–13
Tobi v Nicholas (1988) 86 Cr.App.R. 323; [1988] R.T.R. 343; [1987]
    Crim.L.R. 774, DC 8–56

Togher (Kenneth) [2001] 3 All E.R. 463; [2001] 1 Cr.App.R. 33; [2001]
    Crim.L.R. 124; *The Times*, November 21, 2000, CA .. 10–29, 13–05, 13–06
Tolson (1864) 4 F. & F. 103 .... 2–11, 2–13
Tomey (1909) 2 Cr.App.R. 329 17–14
Tomlinson [1895] 1 Q.B. 706 8–40
Tompkins (George Edward) (1978) 67 Cr.App.R. 181; [1978] Crim.L.R.
    290, CA 11–36, 21–20
Toner (John) (1991) 93 Cr.App.R. 382; [1991] Crim.L.R. 627, CA 6–18
Tonge (John William) (1993) 157 J.P. 1137; [1993] Crim.L.R. 876; 157
    J.P.N. 637, CA 2–26
Toohey v Commissioner of Police of the Metropolis [1965] A.C. 595; [1965]
    2 W.L.R. 439; [1965] 1 All E.R. 506; 49 Cr.App.R. 148; 129 J.P. 181;
    109 S.J. 130, HL 6–25, 17–07
Tooke (Mark Adrian) (1990) 90 Cr.App.R. 417; 154 J.P. 318; [1990]
    Crim.L.R. 263; *The Times*, October 25, 1989, CA 20–16
Treacey (1944) 30 Cr.App.R. 93; [1944] 2 All E.R. 229 ..... 9–52, 21–16, 21–20
Tregear (Terence William) [1967] 2 Q.B. 574; [1967] 2 W.L.R. 1414;
    [1967] 1 All E.R. 989; 51 Cr.App.R. 280; 131 J.P. 314; 11 J.P. 314; 111
    S.J. 175, CA 19–01, 19–06
Triplex Safety Glass Co. Ltd v Lancegaye Safety Glass (1934) Ltd [1939] 2
    K.B. 395, CA 11–01, 11–06
Trust Houses Ltd v Postlethwaite (1844) 109 J.P. 12, DC 3–14
Turnbull (Raymond) [1977] Q.B. 224; [1976] 3 W.L.R. 445; [1976] 3 All
    E.R. 549; 63 Cr.App.R. 132; [1976] Crim.L.R. 565; 120 S.J. 486,
    CA 2–14, 14–03, 14–04, 14–05, 14–06, 14–07, 14–08, 14–09,
                        14–10, 14–11, 14–12, 14–15, 14–48, 16–11
Turnbull (Ronald) (1985) 80 Cr.App.R. 104; [1984] Crim.L.R. 620, CA . 8–54,
                                                                          8–55
Turner (1975) 61 Cr.App.R. 67 .... 17–14, 17–15
Turner [1991] Crim.L.R. 57, CA 5–28
Turner (Bryan James) (1975) 61 Cr.App.R. 67; [1975] Crim.L.R. 525;
    [1975] Crim.L.R. 451; 119 S.J. 422; 119 S.J. 575 CA 8–63, 9–12
Turner (Paul David) [1995] 1 W.L.R. 264; [1995] 3 All E.R. 432; [1995] 2
    Cr.App.R. 94; *The Times*, October 11, 1994, CA 12–07, 12–21, 12–23
Turner (Terence Stuart) [1975] Q.B. 834; [1975] 2 W.L.R. 56; [1975] 1 All
    E.R. 70; 60 Cr.App.R. 80; [1975] Crim.L.R. 98; 118 S.J. 848, CA ... 6–12,
                                                        6–14, 6–19, 6–25, 6–40
Turner v Underwood [1948] 2 K.B. 284; [1948] 1 All E.R. 859; 112 J.P.
    272; 46 L.G.R. 357; [1949] L.J.R. 680; 92 S.J. 379, DC 9–54, 16–27
Turpin [1990] Crim.L.R. 514, CA 5–33
Tutton v Darke (1860) 5 H. & N. 647 8–40
Tyndale [1999] Crim.L.R. 320, CA 20–11
Tyrer (Josephine Lesley) (1990) 90 Cr.App.R. 446; *The Times*, July 26,
    1989, CA 9–20

Ugorji (John Nwangkugi), *Independent*, July 5, 1999, CA 21–13
Umoh (Mfongbong) (1987) 84 Cr.App.R. 138; [1987] Crim.L.R. 258,
    CA 11–37, 11–38
Underwood (Dennis Bernard) [2003] EWCA Crim 1500; 147 S.J.L.B. 657,
    CA 18–13
Uxbridge Justices Ex p. Sofaer (1987) 85 Cr.App.R. 367, DC 2–02, 2–03
Uxbridge Magistrates' Court Ex p. Patel; sub nom. Uxbridge Justices Ex p.
    Patel; London City Justices Ex p. Cropper (2000) 164 J.P. 209; [2000]

Crim.L.R. 383; [2000] C.O.D. 104; 97(1) L.S.G. 22; 144 S.J.L.B. 27;
  The Times, December 7, 1999, QBD 18–05, 18–24

Valentine (Anthony) [1996] 2 Cr.App.R. 213, CA 20–06, 20–07
Van Tattenhove (Frans Willem) and Doubtfire (Robert Henry) (No.1)
  [1996] 1 Cr.App.R. 408; [1996] 2 Cr.App.R. (S.) 91, CA 12–23
Vasiliou [2000] Crim.L.R. 845 18–13
Vel v Owen; sub nom. Vel (Kevin) v Chief Constable of North Wales (1987)
  151 J.P. 510; [1987] Crim.L.R. 496; 151 J.P.N. 287, DC 9–49, 10–30,
                                                                  10–31, 16–28
Vickers (Richard John) [1975] 1 W.L.R. 811; [1975] 2 All E.R. 945; 61
  Cr.App.R. 48; [1975] Crim.L.R. 337; 119 S.J. 300, CA 16–22
Virgo (Wallace Harold) (1978) 67 Cr.App.R. 323; [1978] Crim.L.R. 557,
  CA 20–33, 20–34
Voisin (Louis Marie Joseph) [1918] 1 K.B. 531; 1 A.L.R. 1298, CCA 9–61
Vye (John Arthur) [1993] 1 W.L.R. 471; [1993] 3 All E.R. 241; 97
  Cr.App.R. 134; 157 J.P. 953; 12 Tr. L.R. 62; 157 J.P.N. 380; 143
  N.L.J. 400, CA 7–13, 7–17, 7–18, 7–19, 7–20

W [1994] Crim.L.R. 130, CA 9–30
W (G) and W (E). *See* Whittle (George Alfred)
Wahab [2003] 1 Cr.App.R. 232/252 .... 6–14, 9–20
Wainwright (1871) 13 Cox C.C. 171 8–60
Wait (Delme Gareth) [1998] Crim.L.R. 68, CA 14–25
Waldeman (1934) 24 Cr.App.R. 204 7–11
Walker (Haughton Alfonso) [1996] Crim.L.R. 742, CA 15–11
Walker (Rebecca) [1998] Crim.L.R. 211, CA 8–28, 9–21
Walkers Snack Foods Ltd v Coventry City Council [1998] 3 All E.R. 163;
  [1998] E.H.L.R. 260; *The Times*, April 9, 1998, DC 9–43, 11–02
Wallace (Sonia) and Sayles [1990] Crim.L.R. 433; *The Times*, November
  15, 1989, CA 19–43
Wallace and Fuller v R. [1997] 1 Cr.App.R. 396; [1997] Crim.L.R. 356; 141
  S.J.L.B. 12; *The Times*, December 31, 1996, PC (Jam) 16–05
Wallwork (William Evans) (1958) 42 Cr.App.R. 153; 122 J.P. 299,
  CCA 17–04, 17–05, 19–06, 20–04, 20–05
Wallworth v Balmer [1966] 1 W.L.R. 166; [1965] 3 All E.R. 721; 63 L.G.R.
  524, DC 6–08
Walsh (Gerald Frederick) (1990) 91 Cr.App.R. 161; [1989] Crim.L.R. 822,
  CA 9–26, 9–35, 10–28, 18–27
Walshe (Barry Robert) (1982) 74 Cr.App.R. 85, CA 14–29, 16–07
Walters (Henry) v R. [1969] 2 A.C. 26; [1969] 2 W.L.R. 60; 113 S.J. 14, PC
  (Jam) 4–41, 4–43
Waltham Forest LBC v Mills [1980] R.T.R. 201; 78 L.G.R. 248; [1980]
  Crim.L.R. 243, DC 16–31
Walton v R. [1978] A.C. 788; [1977] 3 W.L.R. 902; [1978] 1 All E.R. 542;
  66 Cr.App.R. 25; [1977] Crim.L.R. 747; 121 S.J. 728, PC (Bar) 6–44
Ward (Judith Theresa) [1993] 1 W.L.R. 619; [1993] 2 All E.R. 577; 96
  Cr.App.R. 1; [1993] Crim.L.R. 312; 89(27) L.S.G. 34; 142 N.L.J. 859;
  136 S.J.L.B. 191, CA 6–18, 6–37, 9–22, 12–07, 12–12,
                                                12–21, 14–30, 18–05, 18–07, 18–09, 18–13
Ward (Michael), Andrews (Russell) and Broadley (Wayne) [2001]
  Crim.L.R. 316; *The Times*, February 2, 2001, CA 9–04
Ward (Wayne) (1994) 98 Cr.App.R. 337; *The Times*, July 29, 1993, CA . 9–43

Warickshall (1783) 1 Leach 263 9–60

Warnell (1923) 17 Cr.App.R. 53 20–04

Warner (Gary David) and Jones (Kevin Lloyd) (1993) 96 Cr.App.R. 324;
The Times, November 16, 1992, CA 5–32

Warren v Warren [1997] Q.B. 488; [1996] 3 W.L.R. 1129; [1996] 4 All E.R.
664; [1996] 2 F.L.R. 777; [1997] 1 F.C.R. 237; [1996] Fam. Law 720,
CA 17–01

Waters (Scott Martin) (1997) 161 J.P. 249; [1997] Crim.L.R. 823; 161
J.P.N. 388; 94(9) L.S.G. 33; 141 S.J.L.B. 58, CA 8–28

Watford Magistrates' Court Ex p. Lenman [1993] Crim.L.R. 388; [1992]
C.O.D. 474; The Times, June 10, 1992, DC 19–18

Watson (1788) 2 T.R. 199 3–14

Watson [1992] Crim.L.R. 434, CA 4–31

Watson (Campbell Louis) [1980] 1 W.L.R. 991; [1980] 2 All E.R. 293; 70
Cr.App.R. 273; [1980] Crim.L.R. 307; 124 S.J. 167, CA 9–49

Wayte (William Guy) (1983) 76 Cr.App.R. 110, CA 3–07, 3–08, 3–09

Weaver (George) and Weaver (John Henry) [1968] 1 Q.B. 353; [1967] 2
W.L.R. 1244; [1967] 1 All E.R. 277; 51 Cr.App.R. 77; 131 J.P. 173;
111 S.J. 174, CA 9–54

Webb [1954] Crim.L.R. 49 14–49

Webb v Leadbetter [1966] 1 W.L.R. 245; [1966] 2 All E.R. 114; 130 J.P.
277; 110 S.J. 90, DC 19–06, 19–44

Weeder (Thomas Henry) (1980) 71 Cr.App.R. 228; [1980] Crim.L.R. 645,
CA 14–08

Weekes [1988] Crim.L.R. 244, CA 20–10

Weekes (Alan John) (1982) 74 Cr.App.R. 161; 2 Cr.App.R. (S.) 377, CA   17–14

Weekes (Trevor Dave) (1993) 97 Cr.App.R. 222; [1993] Crim.L.R. 211;
The Times, May 15, 1992, CA 9–30

Weeks [1995] Crim.L.R. 52, CA 9–48

Weerdesteyn (Gerritt Johannes) [1995] 1 Cr.App.R. 405; [1995] Crim.L.R.
239; The Times, March 17, 1994, CA 9–43

Weightman (Beverley Anne) (1991) 92 Cr.App.R. 291; [1991] Crim.L.R.
204, CA 6–21

Welch [1992] Crim.L.R. 368, CA 9–55

Wellingborough Justices Ex p. François (1994) 158 J.P. 813; [1994] C.O.D.
462; 158 J.P.N. 587; The Times, July 1, 1994, DC 19–01

Welstead (Stephen Paul) [1996] 1 Cr.App.R. 59, CA 19–27

West (Rosemary Pauline) [1996] 2 Cr.App.R. 374; The Times, April 3,
1996, CA 21–05

Western v DPP [1997] 1 Cr.App.R. 474; [1997] C.O.D. 181, DC 20–19

Westinghouse Electric Corp. Uranium Contract Litigation MDL Docket 235
(No.1); sub nom. Rio Tinto Zinc Corp. v Westinghouse Electric Corp.
(No.1) [1977] 3 W.L.R. 430; [1977] 3 All E.R. 703; [1977] 2 C.M.L.R.
420; 121 S.J. 491, CA 11–03, 11–05, 11–06, 11–07

Westminster City Council v Croyalgrange Ltd [1986] 1 W.L.R. 674; [1986]
2 All E.R. 353; 83 Cr.App.R. 155; 150 J.P. 449; 84 L.G.R. 801; [1986]
Crim.L.R. 693; 83 L.S.G. 2089; 136 N.L.J. 491; 130 S.J. 409, HL ...   4–20

Weston-super-Mare Justices Ex p. Townsend [1968] 3 All E.R. 225n; 132
J.P. 526; 112 S.J. 541, DC 7–68

Westwell (Stephen) [1976] 2 All E.R. 812; 62 Cr.App.R. 251; [1976]
Crim.L.R. 441; 120 S.J. 283, CA 20–23, 20–24, 20–25

Wetherall v Harrison [1976] Q.B. 773; [1976] 2 W.L.R. 168; [1976] 1 All
E.R. 241; [1976] R.T.R. 125; [1976] Crim.L.R. 54; 119 S.J. 848, DC   5–12

Wharam v Routledge (1805) 5 Esp. 235 21–21
Wheeler [1917] 1 K.B. 283, CCA 17–11
Wheeler (Leslie) [2001] 1 Cr.App.R. 10; 164 J.P. 565; [2001] Crim.L.R.
    744; 165 J.P.N. 66; 97(42) L.S.G. 43; *The Times*, July 7, 2000, CA . 18–21
Wheeler (Paul Howard Francis) [1967] 1 W.L.R. 1531; [1967] 3 All E.R.
    829; 52 Cr.App.R. 28; 132 J.P. 41; 111 S.J. 850, CA 16–21
Whitaker (Charles Hildyard) [1914] 3 K.B. 1283; 10 Cr.App.R. 245, CCA 8–64
White (1922) 17 Cr.App.R. 60 21–12
White [1991] Crim.L.R. 779, CA 9–38
White (Kory) v R. [1999] 1 A.C. 210; [1998] 3 W.L.R. 992; [1999] 1
    Cr.App.R. 153; 142 S.J.L.B. 260; *The Times*, September 25, 1998, PC
    (Jam) 20–06, 20–07
Whitehead (1866) L.R. 1 C.C.R. 33 17–08
Whittle (George Alfred); sub nom. W (G); W (E) [1997] 1 Cr.App.R. 166;
    [1996] Crim.L.R. 904; 93(28) L.S.G. 29; 140 S.J.L.B. 168, CA 3–14
Whitton (Miriam) [1998] Crim.L.R. 492, CA 17–36
Whybrow and Saunders (1994) 144 N.L.J. 124; *The Times*, February 14,
    1994; *Independent*, January 28, 1994, CA 19–07
Wiedemann v Walpole [1891] 2 Q.B. 534, CA 9–10
Wilbourne (1917) 12 Cr.App.R. 279 20–06
Wilkinson v Crown Prosecution Service; sub nom. Wilkinson v DPP (1998)
    162 J.P. 591; [1998] Crim.L.R. 743; [1998] C.O.D. 367; 162 J.P.N.
    625, QBD 18–01
William (1912) 8 Cr.App.R. 84 14–22
Williams (1853) 6 Cox 343 20–28
Williams (Gary John) v DPP [1993] 3 All E.R. 365; 98 Cr.App.R. 209;
    [1994] R.T.R. 61; [1993] Crim.L.R. 775; *The Times*, March 9, 1993,
    DC 10–24
Williams (Gladstone) [1987] 3 All E.R. 411; 78 Cr.App.R. 276; [1984]
    Crim.L.R. 163; 81 L.S.G. 278, CA 4–07
Williams (Noel) v R. [1997] 1 W.L.R. 548; 141 S.J.L.B. 84, PC (Jam) 14–22
Williams (Winston Anthony) (1994) 99 Cr.App.R. 163; 91(2) L.S.G. 41;
    The Times, November 11, 1993, CA 4–29
Williams v Mohamed [1977] R.T.R. 12; [1976] Crim.L.R. 577, DC 16–27
Williams v Russell (1983) 149 L.T. 190 4–19
Williams v Summerfield [1972] 2 Q.B. 512; [1972] 3 W.L.R. 131; [1972] 2
    All E.R. 1334; 56 Cr.App.R. 597; [1972] Crim.L.R. 424; 116 S.J. 413,
    DC 3–16
Willis (George Arthur) [1960] 1 W.L.R. 55; [1960] 1 All E.R. 331; 44
    Cr.App.R. 32; 124 J.P. 111; 103 S.J. 1029, CCA 8–08
Wilmot (Alan) (1989) 89 Cr.App.R. 341, CA 16–21
Wilson (1913) 9 Cr.App.R. 124 21–06
Wilson, 18 Cr.App.R. 108, CCA 16–09
Wilson (Donald Theodore) (1984) 78 Cr.App.R. 247, CA 4–12
Wilson (Joseph) (1957) 41 Cr.App.R. 226, CCA 19–42
Wilson v Rastall (1792) 4 T.R. 753 11–28
Windass (Walter James) (1989) 89 Cr.App.R. 258, CA 21–21
Winfield (1939) 27 Cr.App.R. 139 7–63
Wink (1834) 6 C. & P. 397 20–04
Winsor (1866) L.R. 1 Q.B. 289 17–14
Wong [1986] Crim.L.R. 683, Crown Ct 21–34
Wong Kam-Ming v R. [1980] A.C. 247; [1979] 2 W.L.R. 81; [1979] 1 All

E.R. 939; 69 Cr.App.R. 47; [1979] Crim.L.R. 168; 123 S.J. 47, PC
(HK) 9–48, 9–54
Wood (1877) 14 Cox C.C. 46 20–04
Wood (Alan George) (1968) 52 Cr.App.R. 74; [1968] Crim.L.R. 104,
CA 4–08, 4–27
Wood (Stanley William) (1983) 76 Cr.App.R. 23; [1982] Crim.L.R. 667,
CA 2–44, 8–75
Wood v DPP (1989) 153 J.P. 20; 152 J.P.N. 786, DC 6–14
Wood v Mackinson (1840) 2 M. & R. 273 21–12
Woodcock [1963] Crim.L.R. 273, CCA 20–31
Woodhead (1847) 2 C. & K. 520 .... 19–01, 19–02
Woodhouse v Hall (1981) 72 Cr.App.R. 39; [1980] Crim.L.R. 645, DC .. 8–06
Woods [1961] Crim.L.R. 324, CCA 4–41
Woolgar [1991] Crim.L.R. 545, CA 17–33
Woolmington v DPP [1935] A.C. 462, HL 4–03, 4–07, 4–10, 4–37,
4–42, 16–22
Worley v Bentley [1976] 2 All E.R. 449; 62 Cr.App.R. 239; [1976]
Crim.L.R. 310, DC 20–25
Wright (1866) 4 F. & F. 967 21–25
Wright (1934) 25 Cr.App.R. 35, CA 14–35, 14–36
Wright [1994] Crim.L.R. 131, CA 14–35
Wright (Albert Edward) and Ormerod (Sidney George) (1990) 90 Cr.App.R.
91, CA 17–04, 20–05
Wright (Derek) [2000] Crim.L.R. 851; *The Times*, May 31, 2000, CA 16–07
Wright (Shani Ann) [2000] Crim.L.R. 510; *The Times*, March 3, 2000, CA 17–37
Wright v Kerrigan [1911] 2 I.R. 301 8–59
Wyatt [1990] Crim.L.R. 343, CA 17–09

X Ltd v Morgan Grampian (Publishers) Ltd [1991] 1 A.C. 1; [1990]
2 W.L.R. 1000; [1990] 2 All E.R. 1; 87(17) L.S.G. 28; 140
N.L.J. 553; 134 S.J. 546, HL 11–37
XYZ (1990) 91 Cr.App.R. 40, CA 19–17, 19–18
XYZ. *See* P (Telephone Intercepts: Admissibility of Evidence)

Yacoob (David Shik) (1981) 72 Cr.App.R. 313; [1981] Crim.L.R.
248, CA 4–34, 16–07, 17–02
Young (Eric Rutherford) [1964] 1 W.L.R. 717; [1964] 2 All E.R. 480; 48
Cr.App.R. 292; 128 J.P. 352; 108 S.J. 339, CCA 16–11
Young and Robinson [1978] Crim.L.R. 163, CA 9–52
Younis and Ahmed [1990] Crim.L.R. 425, CA 9–42
Yousry (1916) 11 Cr.App.R. 13 21–20

Z (Children) (Disclosure: Criminal Proceedings), Re [2003] EWHC 61;
[2003] 1 F.L.R. 1194; [2003] Fam. Law 472, Fam Div 18–12
Z (Prior Acquittal); sub nom. X (Prior Acquittal) [2000] 2 A.C. 483; [2000]
3 W.L.R. 117; [2000] 3 All E.R. 385; [2000] 2 Cr.App.R. 281; 164 J.P.
533; 164 J.P.N. 824; 97(28) L.S.G. 31; 150 N.L.J. 984, HL 5–15, 7–28
Z [2003] 2 Cr.App.R. 173 9–14
Zielinski (Edmund Wladyslaw Brotow) [1950] 2 All E.R. 1114n; 66 T.L.R.
(Pt.2) 956; 34 Cr.App.R. 193; 114 J.P. 571; 49 L.G.R. 45; [1950] W.N.
494, CCA 16–05
Zoppola-Barraza [1994] Crim.L.R. 833; *The Times*, May 6, 1994, CA 7–15
Times, March 22, 1996, HL 11–32, 11–33

Table of International Cases

European Court of Human Rights

Aksoy v Turkey (1997) 23 E.H.R.R. 553; 1 B.H.R.C. 625 13–10
Allen v United Kingdom (Admissibility) (76574/01), 74 T.C. 263; [2003]
    Crim.L.R. 280; (2002) 35 E.H.R.R. CD289 11–12
Atlan v United Kingdom (36533/97) (2002) 34 E.H.R.R. 33; [2001]
    Crim.L.R. 819; *The Times*, July 3, 2001 12–23
Averill v United Kingdom (36408/97) (2001) 31 E.H.R.R. 36; 8 B.H.R.C.
    430; [2000] Crim.L.R. 682; *The Times*, June 20, 2000 11–24

B v Austria (A/175) (1991) 13 E.H.R.R. 20 13–13
Barbera v Spain (A/146); sub nom. Barbera, Messegue, Jabardo v Spain;
    Barbera v Spain (10588/83); Messegue v Spain (10589/83); Jabardo v
    Spain (10590/83) (1989) 11 E.H.R.R. 360 .... 10–10, 13–15, 13–18,
                                                     13–20, 13–23
Beckles v United Kingdom (44652/98) (2003) 36 E.H.R.R. 13; 13 B.H.R.C.
    522; *The Times*, October 15, 2002 .... 11–22, 13–17
Benham v United Kingdom (19380/92) (1996) 22 E.H.R.R. 293; *The Times*,
    June 24, 1996; *Independent*, June 19, 1996 13–14
Borgers v Belgium (A/214) (1993) 15 E.H.R.R. 92 13–16
Boyle v United Kingdom (A/282–B) [1994] 2 F.C.R. 822; 19 E.H.R.R.
    179 13–25
Brennan v United Kingdom (39846/98) (2002) 34 E.H.R.R. 18; [2002]
    Crim.L.R. 216; *The Times*, October 22, 2001 13–22
Brogan v United Kingdom (A/145–B) (1989) 11 E.H.R.R. 117 13–12

Chahal v United Kingdom (22414/93) (1997) 23 E.H.R.R. 413; 1 B.H.R.C.
    405 12–23
Condron v United Kingdom (35718/97) (2001) 31 E.H.R.R. 1; 8 B.H.R.C.
    290; [2000] Crim.L.R. 679; *The Times*, May 9, 2000 .... 11–22, 13–17

Doorson v Netherlands (1996) 22 E.H.R.R. 330 .... 12–17, 13–23, 21–02

Edwards v United Kingdom (A/247B) (1993) 15 E.H.R.R. 417; *The Times*,
    January 21, 1993 .... 10–10, 13–15, 13–18, 18–30
Edwards v United Kingdom (39647/98); sub nom. Lewis v United Kingdom
    (40461/98) 15 B.H.R.C. 189; *The Times*, July 29, 2003 .... 12–18, 12–19,
                                                   12–25, 13–18, 18–30
Engel v Netherlands (A/22) (1979–80) 1 E.H.R.R. 647 13–14
Ezeh and Connors v United Kingdom (39665/98) and (40086/98) (2002) 35
    E.H.R.R. 28; 12 B.H.R.C. 589; [2002] Crim.L.R. 918; *The Times*, July
    30, 2002 13–14

Fitt v United Kingdom (2000) 30 E.H.R.R. 480 .... 12–23, 18–30

Foucher v France (1998) 25 E.H.R.R. 234 13–18
Fox, Campbell and Hartley v United Kingdom (A/182) (1991) 13 E.H.R.R.
  157; *The Times*, October 16, 1990; *Guardian*, October 4, 1990 13–12
Funke v France (A/256–A) [1993] 1 C.M.L.R. 897; 16 E.H.R.R. 297 11–26,
                                                                                          13–17

Garcia Alva v Germany (23541/94) (2003) 37 E.H.R.R. 12 .... 12–18, 13–13,
                                                                                          18–29
Gaskin v United Kingdom (A/160) [1990] 1 F.L.R. 167; 12 E.H.R.R. 36;
  The Times, August 28, 1989 13–25
Goodwin v United Kingdom (17488/90) (1996) 22 E.H.R.R. 123; 1
  B.H.R.C. 81; *The Times*, March 28, 1996 11–38

Halford v United Kingdom (20605/92) [1997] I.R.L.R. 471; 24 E.H.R.R.
  523; 3 B.H.R.C. 31; [1998] Crim.L.R. 753; 94(27) L.S.G. 24; *The
  Times*, July 3, 1997 .... 13–24, 13–25
Heaney v Ireland (34720/97) (2001) 33 E.H.R.R. 12; [2001] Crim.L.R. 481 11–12
Hutchinson-Reid v United Kingdom, February 20, 2003 13–13

IJL and AKP v United Kingdom, *The Times*, October 13, 2000 11–10
Ireland v United Kingdom (A/25) (1979–80) 2 E.H.R.R. 25 13–10

JB v Switzerland (31827/96), 3 I.T.L. Rep. 663; [2001] Crim.L.R. 748 11–12,
                                                                                          11–13
Jablonski v Poland (33492/96) (2003) 36 E.H.R.R. 27 13–13
Jasper v United Kingdom (2000) 30 E.H.R.R. 441; [2000] Crim.L.R.
  586 .... 12–23, 18–30
Johnston v Ireland (A/112) sub nom. Johnston v Ireland (9697/82) (1987) 9
  E.H.R.R. 203; *The Times*, January 7, 1987 13–27

Kalashnikov v Russia (47095/99) (2003) 36 E.H.R.R. 34 13–13
Khan v United Kingdom (35394/97) (2001) 31 E.H.R.R. 45; 8 B.H.R.C.
  310; [2000] Crim.L.R. 684; *The Times*, May 23, 2000 .... 10–09, 10–26,
                                                                                          10–27
King v United Kingdom (Admissibility) (13881/02), 5 I.T.L. Rep. 963;
  (2003) 37 E.H.R.R. CD1 13–20
Klass v Germany (A/28) (1979–80) 2 E.H.R.R. 214 .... 13–24, 13–25, 13–27
Kostovski v Netherlands (A/166) (1990) 12 E.H.R.R. 434; *The Times*,
  November 22, 1989 .... 13–15, 13–23, 21–02
Kroon v Netherlands (A/297–C) [1995] 2 F.C.R. 28; 19 E.H.R.R. 263 13–25

Lawless v Ireland (No.3) (A/3) (1979–80) 1 E.H.R.R. 15 13–27
Letellier v France (A/207) (1992) 14 E.H.R.R. 83 13–13
Lingens v Austria (No.2) (A/103); sub nom. Lingens v Austria (9815/82)
  (1986) 8 E.H.R.R. 407 13–20
Ludi v Switzerland (A/238) (1993) 15 E.H.R.R. 173; *The Times*, August 13,
  1992 10–09

Magee v United Kingdom (28135/95) (2001) 31 E.H.R.R. 35; 8 B.H.R.C.
  646; [2000] Crim.L.R. 681; *The Times*, June 20, 2000 .... 11–24, 13–22
Marckx v Belgium (A/31) (1979–80) 2 E.H.R.R. 330 13–25
Miailhe v France (No.2) (1997) 23 E.H.R.R. 491 .... 10–09, 13–15, 18–30

Moustaquim v Belgium (A/193) (1991) 13 E.H.R.R. 802; *The Times*, May
8, 1991 13–25
Murray v United Kingdom (Right to Silence) (18731/91); sub nom. John
Murray v United Kingdom (1996) 22 E.H.R.R. 29; *The Times*, February 9, 1996 .... 9–33, 11–23, 13–17, 17–24

Neumeister v Austria, Series A, No.8 (1968) 13–13
Niemietz v Germany (A/251B) (1993) 16 E.H.R.R. 97 13–24

Open Door Counselling Ltd v Ireland (A/246) (1993) 15 E.H.R.R. 244; *The
Times*, November 5, 1992 13–05
Ozturk v Germany (A/73) (1984) 6 E.H.R.R. 409 13–14

PG and JH v United Kingdom (44787/98) [2002] Crim.L.R. 308; *The
Times*, October 19, 2001 .... 10–09, 10–26, 10–27, 13–25
Pisano v Italy (36732/97) (2002) 34 E.H.R.R. 27 13–16
Pretto v Italy (A/71) (1984) 6 E.H.R.R. 182 13–19

Ribitsch v Austria (A/336) (1996) 21 E.H.R.R. 573 13–10
Rowe and Davis v United Kingdom (28901/95) (2000) 30 E.H.R.R. 1; 8
B.H.R.C. 325; [2000] Crim.L.R. 584; *The Times*, March 1, 2000 12–17,
12–22, 12–23, 18–30

Sadik v Greece (1997) 24 E.H.R.R. 323 13–28
Saidi v France (1994) 17 E.H.R.R. 251 13–23
Salabiaku v France (1988) 13 E.H.R. R. 379 .... 4–13, 5–02, 13–20
Saunders v United Kingdom (19187/91) [1997] B.C.C. 872; [1998] 1
B.C.L.C. 362; 23 E.H.R.R. 313; 2 B.H.R.C. 358; *The Times*, December
18, 1996 .... 10–09, 11–10, 11–11, 11–26, 13–14, 13–17
Schenk v Switzerland (A/140) (1991) 13 E.H.R.R. 242; *The Times*, August
2, 1988 .... 10–09, 10–26, 13–15, 13–23, 13–26
Scott v Spain (1997) 24 E.H.R.R. 391 13–13
Serves v France (1999) 28 E.H.R.R. 265; 3 B.H.R.C. 446; [1998] H.R.C.D.
4 13–14

Telfner v Austria (33501/96) (2002) 34 E.H.R.R. 7; [2001] Crim.L.R.
821 .... 4–13, 11–13, 11–21
Teixeira de Castro v Portugal (1999) 28 E.H.R.R. 101; 4 B.H.R.C. 533;
[1998] Crim.L.R. 751; [1998] H.R.C.D. 8 .... 10–09, 10–16, 10–27
Tomasi v France (A/241–A) (1993) 15 E.H.R.R. 1 13–10
Tyrer v United Kingdom (A/26) (1979–80) 2 E.H.R.R. 1 13–27

Unterpringer v Austria (1986) 13 E.H.R.R. 175 13–23

Van Mechelen v Netherlands (1998) 25 E.H.R.R. 647; 2 B.H.R.C. 486 ... 12–17,
13–15, 13–23, 21–02

W v Switzerland (A/254) (1994) 17 E.H.R.R. 60 13–13
Windisch v Austria (A/186) (1991) 13 E.H.R.R. 281 .... 13–23, 21–02
Winterwerp v Netherlands (A/33) (1979–80) 2 E.H.R.R. 387 13–11
Wood (2314/02) January 20, 2004 13–26

X v Austria (1987) 11 E.H.R.R. 112 13–12

Z v Finland (1998) 25 E.H.R.R. 371; 45 B.M.L.R. 107 13–25

European Commission of Human Rights

Austria v Italy (1963) 6 Y.B. 740 13–23
Blastland v United Kingdom (12045/86) (1988) 10 E.H.R.R. CD528 8–60
X v Federal Republic of Germany (9411/81) (1983) 5 E.H.R.R. CD276 .. 13–12
X v Federal Republic of Germany (1986) 11 E.H.R.R. 84 10–09
X v United Kingdom (1972) 42 C.D. 135 4–12

European Court of Justice

Orkem SA (formerly CdF Chimie SA) v Commission of the European
    Communities (C-374/87) [1989] E.C.R. 3283; [1989] E.C.R. 3355;
    [1991] 4 C.M.L.R. 502 11–11

Australia

Benz v R. (1989) 168 C.L.R. 110 8–61
Butera v DPP (Vic.) (1988) 76 A.L.R. 45, HC 2–29, 2–30
Driscoll v R. (1977) 51 A.L.J.R. 731, HC 21–13
McGuinness v Att-Gen for Victoria (1940) 63 C.L.R. 73 11–37
Mraz (1956) 30 A.L.J. 604 5–19
Nominal Defendant v Clements (1961) 104 C.L.R. 476 .... 20–09, 20–11
Pollit (1992) 174 C.L.R. 558 18–13
Schultz [1982] W.A.R. 171 6–21
Stephens v R. (1978) 21 A.L.R. 680, HC 16–03
Tripoli (1961) 104 C.L.R. 1 8–64
Wilkes (1948) 77 C.L.R. 511 5–19

Canada

Lupien, 1970 S.C.R. 263 6–21

New Zealand

Dehar [1969] N.Z.L.R. 763 16–18
Howe [1982] N.Z.L.R. 618 .... 2–38, 2–39, 6–12, 6–27
Lindsay [1970] 1 N.Z.L.R. 1002 14–49
McCarthy [1976] 1 N.Z.L.R. 472 14–49
Uljee [1982] 1 N.Z.L.R. 561, CA 11–36

United States

Bevan (1993) 82 C.C.C. (3d) 310 18–13
Dodds v State of Oklahoma, 993 P 2d 778 18–13
Sealfo v United States 332 U.S. 575 (1947) 5–19

Table of Statutes

1795 Treason Act (35 Geo. 3 c.7)
s.1 15–05

1843 Evidence Act (6 & 7 Vict. c.85)
s.1 17–01

1845 Evidence Act (8 & 9 Vict. c.113)
s.3 3–19

1851 Evidence Act (14 & 15 Vict. c.99)
s.7 3–27
s.13 3–24
s.14 3–20

1865 Criminal Procedure Act (28 & 29 Vict. c.18) 4–48, 20–20
s.3 .... **21–09**, 21–10, 21–11, 21–12, 21–14, 21–24
s.4 ... 21–14, **21–23**, 21–24, 21–26
s.5 ... 21–23, **21–25**, 21–26, 21–33
s.6 .... 3–24, 21–31
s.8 .... 4–48, 6–10

1868 Documentary Evidence Act (31 & 32 Vict. c.37)
s.2 3–19

1871 Prevention of Crimes Act (34 & 35 Vict. c.112)
s.18 3–24

1872 Licensing Act (35 & 36 Vict. c.94) 16–31

1879 Bankers' Books Evidence Act (42 & 43 Vict. c.11)
s.3 3–14
s.6 17–01
s.7 .... 3–16, 3–17
s.9 3–15

1882 Documentary Evidence Act (45 & 46 Vict. c.9)
s.2 3–19

1898 Criminal Evidence Act (61 & 62 Vict. c.36) 7–30, 7–32, 7–43
s.1 .... 7–01, 7–03, 7–27, 17–01, 17–11, 17–13, 17–25
(b) 17–36
(e) 7–32, 11–02
(f) 3–28
(ii) 7–60, 7–65, 7–66, 7–73, 10–04, 10–11
(iii) 7–56
(h) 17–11
(8)(ii) 7–60

1911 Perjury Act (1 & 2 Geo. 5 c.6)
s.13 15–03
Official Secrets Act (1 & 2 Geo. 5 c.28)
s.6 11–08

1913 Forgery Act (3 & 4 Geo. 5 c.27)
s.16(1) 11–34

1915 Indictments Act (5 & 6 Geo. 5 c.90)
s.5(3) 7–52

1916 Prevention of Corruption Act (6 & 7 Geo. 5 c.64)
s.2 4–12

1925 Criminal Justice Act (15 & 16 Geo. 5 c.86)
s.13(3) 8–27
s.41 .... 10–20, 10–27

1933 Children and Young
Persons Act (23 &
24 Geo. 5 c.12)
s.1 21–18
s.38 17–01
(1) 15–02, 17–04
s.42 8–82
s.43 8–82
s.50 5–03
s.99 6–08
Sch.1 8–82
1936 Public Order Act ((1
Edw. 8 & 1 Geo.
6, c.6)
s.5 .... 14–49, 16–02
1939 Offences Against the
State Act
s.52 11–12
1946 Statutory Instruments
Act (9 & 10 Geo.
6 c.36)
ss.2–4 3–19
1948 Companies Act (11 &
12 Geo. 6 c.38) .. 11–35
Criminal Justice Act
(11 & 12 Geo. 6
c.58)
s.39 3–27
s.80(3) 6–08
1949 Marriage Act (12, 13 &
14 Geo. 6 c.76)
s.65(3) 3–19
1952 Vehicle and Excise
Registration Act
s.52 3–19
Magistrates' Courts
Act (15 & 16 Geo.
6 & 1 Eliz. 2 c.55)
s.81 4–46
1953 Prevention of Crime Act
(1 & 2 Eliz 2 c.14)
s.1 .... 4–46, 5–10
(i) 4–12
Births and Deaths
Registration Act
(1 & 2 Eliz 2 c.20)
s.34(6) 3–19
Post Office Act (1 & 2
Eliz 2 c.)
s.11 6–22
1954 Criminal Procedure
(Insanity) Act)
s.4 4–12

1956 Sexual Offences Act (4
& 5 Eliz. 2 c.69)   17–26,
21–18
ss.2–4 15–05
s.22 15–05
s.23 15–05
s.30(2) 4–12
1957 Homicide Act (5 & 6
Eliz. 2 c.11)
s.2(2) 4–12, 4–14, 4–46
1958 Public Records Act (6
& 7 Eliz. 2 c.51)
s.9(2) 3–19
1959 Highways Act (7 & 8
Eliz. 2 c.26)
s.127 16–31
Obscene Publications
Act (7 & 8 Eliz. 2
c.66) 6–22
s.1 6–04
s.4(1), (2) 6–23
1960 Indecency with Children
Act (8 & 9 Eliz. 2
c.33) 17–26, 21–18
1961 Factories Act (9 & 10
Eliz. 2 c.34)
s.29(1) 4–20
1963 Children and Young
Persons Act (c.37)
s.16 5–03
(2) 7–31
s.28(1) 19–08
(2) 19–08
1964 Diplomatic Privileges
Act (c.81) 17–01
Criminal Procedure
(Insanity) Act
(c.84) 7–70
s.4A(2) 8–71
1965 Criminal Evidence Act
(c.20) 8–19, 8–32
Criminal Procedure
(Attendance of
Witnesses) Act
(c.69)
s.1 18–02
s.2 3–14
1967 Sexual Offences Act
(c.60) 17–26, 21–18
Criminal Justice Act
(c.80)
s.9 .... 3–25, 3–28, 8–79,
8–82, 14–07, 19–37

1967 Criminal Justice Act —
        cont.
    s.9(2) 8–79
    (4) 8–79
    s.10 ...... 3–28, 5–07, 9–01
    (1) 5–07
    (2) 5–07
    (4) 5–07
    s.11 18–16
    (1) 18–08
    (8) 18–16
    s.39 3–28
1968 Criminal Appeal Act
        (c.19)
    s.2 .... 4–05, 10–29
    (1) . 4–39, 13–05, 15–07
    Sch.2 8–81
    paras 1, 1A 8–85
    Firearms Act (c.27)
    s.58(2) 16–31
    Theft Act (c.60)
    s.27(4) 8–80
    s.30(2) 17–28
    s.31 11–08
    Civil Evidence Act
        (c.64) 8–01,
                                11–03
    Pt I 3–03
    s.10 2–10
    s.11 5–27
    s.14 11–02
    (1) 11–02
    s.16(1) 11–03
1970 Taxes Management Act
        (c.9)
    s.6 12–12
    s.101 13–20
    Sch.1 12–12
1971 Misuse of Drugs Act
        (c.38)
    s.5(1) 4–14
    (2) 4–22
    s.28 .... 4–14, 4–15
    (2) .. 4–12, 4–15, 13–21
    (3) 13–21
1972 Road Traffic Act (c.20)
    s.172 .... 11–11, 11–12
    (2) 11–11, 11–13
    European Communities
        Act (c.68) 11–03
    Local Government Act
        (c.70)
    s.238 3–19

1974 Health & Safety at
        Work Act (c.37)
    s.40 4–17
    Rehabilitation of
        Offenders Act
        (c.53) 7–25,
                        7–32, 10–11
    s.4(1) 7–21
    Town and Country
        Planning Act
        (c.78) 4–23
1976 Sexual Offences
        (Amendment) Act
        (c.82) 7–78, 21–28
1977 Criminal Law Act
        (c.45)
    s.7 18–03
    s.48 18–03
    s.54 .... 17–26, 21–18
1978 Oaths Act (c.19) 19–08
    s.1 19–08
    (1) 19–08
    (2) 19–09
    s.4(1) 19–09
    (2) 19–09
    s.5 .... 17–01, 19–09
    (2) 19–09
    (3) 19–09
    Interpretation Act
        (c.30)
    s.3 3–19
    Protection of Children
        Act (c.37) . 17–26, 21–18
1979 Banking Act 1979
        (c.37)
    Sch.6 3–15
1980 Magistrates' Courts
        Act (c.43) 18–01
    s.5A 18–01
    (3)(a) 18–01
    s.6(2) 18–01
    s.97 3–14
    s.101 .... 4–19, 4–20, 4–21,
                        4–25, 4–46
    s.150(4) 6–08
1981 Criminal Attempts Act
        (c.47)
    s.2(1) 15–02
    (2)(g) 15–02
    Contempt of Court Act
        (c.49) 11–38
    s.2(1) 11–37
    s.10 11–37

1982 Criminal Justice Act
(c.48)
s.72 .... 17–11, 17–12
Insurance Companies
Act (c.50)
s.43A 11–10
s.44 11–10
1983 Mental Health Act
(c.20) 19–12
1984 Road Traffic Regula-
tion Act (c.27)
s.89(2) 6–08, 15–04
County Courts Act
(c.28)
s.12(2) 3–22
Child Abduction Act
(c.37)
s.1 21–18
s.2 .... 19–15, 21–18
Video Recordings Act
(c.39) 10–22
Police and Criminal
Evidence Act
(c.60) 8–13,
9–19, 11–01,
17–28, 17–29
Pt VIII 9–46, 10–11,
16–04
s.3 5–30
s.30 9–45
s.54A 14–49
s.58 ...... 9–33, 9–35, 9–41
(8) 9–33, 9–34
s.60 2–22
(A) 2–22
s.64 10–21
(1) 10–20
(3B)(b) 10–20
s.66 .... 9–27, 9–33,
14–16, 14–33,
18–24
s.67(7) 9–27
(9) 9–28, 18–26
(11) 2–22, 9–27,
9–28, 14–28, 14–33,
18–27
s.68 .... 8–24, 8–32
s.69 8–76
s.71 3–11
s.73 ...... 3–24, 3–26, 3–27
(1), (2) **3–23**
(3) 3–26, 3–28
(4) 3–28

1984 Police and Criminal
Evidence Act—
cont.
s.74 ..... 3–26, **5–27**, 5–28,
5–30, 5–31, 5–32, 5–33,
5–34, 5–36, 9–54, 10–18
(1) 5–33
(2) 4–12, 5–35
(3) .. 4–12, 5–30, 5–31,
5–35
s.75 5–36
(1) 5–36
(2) 5–36
(4) 5–36
s.76 ..... 8–37, **9–02**, 9–03,
9–04, 9–13, 9–15, 9–16,
9–17, 9–18, 9–26, 9–27,
9–30, 9–31, 9–35, 9–37,
9–46, 9–49, 16–07
(2) .. 4–33, 4–47, 9–15,
9–17, 9–47, 9–49, 16–27
(2)(a) 9–17, 9–18
(b) 9–20
(3) 9–47
(4)(a) 9–60
(b) 9–61
(5) 9–60
(6) 9–60
(a) 9–60
(b) 9–60
(7) 9–17
(8) 9–17
s.76A ... 8–37, 9–02, 9–03,
9–04, 9–13, 9–16, 9–17,
9–18, 9–24, 9–27, 9–30,
9–31, 9–46, 9–61, 21–16
(1) 9–53
(2) 4–47, 9–03,
9–15, 9–17, 9–18,
9–47, 9–53
(a) 9–17
(b) 9–20
(3) 9–04, 9–16, 9–20,
9–24, 9–46, 9–47,
9–53
(4) 9–53
(a) 9–60
(b) 9–61
(5) 9–60, 9–61
(6) 9–60
(a) 9–60
(b) 9–60
s.77(1) 9–56

1984 Police and Criminal
　　　Evidence Act—
　　　cont.
　　　s.77(2) 9–56
　　　　(3) 9–56
　　　s.78 ..... 2–11, 2–31, 5–15,
　　　　5–33, 5–34, 7–49, 8–20,
　　　　8–35, 8–37, 8–73, 9–15,
　　　　9–25, 9–26, 9–27, 9–30,
　　　　9–31, 9–33, 9–35, 9–37,
　　　　9–41, 9–45, 9–49, 10–01,
　　　　10–07, 10–10, 10–11, **10–13**,
　　　　10–14, 10–15, 10–16, 10–17,
　　　　10–19, 10–20, 10–21, 10–22,
　　　　10–23, 10–24, 10–25, 10–26,
　　　　10–29, 10–30, 10–31, 11–09,
　　　　11–11, 11–28, 11–36, 12–18,
　　　　13–26, 13–29, 14–23, 14–27,
　　　　14–28, 14–29, 14–48, 16–07,
　　　　16–28, 17–05, 19–30, 20–33,
　　　　　　　　　　　　　20–34
　　　　(1) 9–25, 10–12,
　　　　　10–14, 10–30, 10–33,
　　　　　　　　　　　　　14–29
　　　　(2) 10–11, 10–12,
　　　　　　　　　　　　　10–30
　　　s.79 19–04
　　　s.80 .... 17–01, **17–26**,
　　　　　　　　　17–34, 17–35
　　　　(2) 17–33
　　　　(2A) 17–28
　　　　　(a) 17–33
　　　　(3) 17–33
　　　　　(a) 17–30
　　　　　(b) 17–30
　　　　　(c) 17–30, 17–33
　　　　(4) 17–28, 17–33
　　　　(5) 17–34
　　　　(8) 17–36
　　　s.80A 17–36
　　　s.81 .... 6–35, 6–36, 11–15,
　　　　18–05, 18–08, 18–31
　　　s.82 10–14
　　　　(1) ... 9–04, 9–13, 9–45
　　　　(3) 9–46, 9–49,
　　　　　10–11, 10–12,
　　　　　10–30, 16–04
　　　s.101(1)(c) 11–33
　　　s.118(1) 3–03
1985 Companies Act (c.6)
　　　s.434 .... 11–09, 11–10
　　　　(5) 11–09
　　　s.447 11–10

1985 Interception of Com-
　　　munications Act
　　　(c.56) 2–21
　　　ss.1–10 2–21
　　　s.9 12–05
1986 Insolvency Act (c.45) . 3–22
　　　s.206(4) 4–16
　　　s.291(b) 11–11
　　　s.433 11–10
　　　Company Directors
　　　Disqualification
　　　Act (c.46)
　　　s.20 11–10
　　　Building Societies Act
　　　(c.53)
　　　s.57 11–10
　　　Financial Services Act
　　　(c.60)
　　　s.105 11–10
　　　s.177 11–10
　　　Public Order Act (c.64)
　　　s.4 8–04
1987 Banking Act (c.22)
　　　s.39 11–10
　　　s.41 11–10
　　　s.42 11–10
　　　Criminal Justice Act
　　　(c.38) 18–02
　　　s.1(1) 18–02
　　　s.2 .... 11–10, 11–15
　　　s.6 11–16
　　　s.9 ..... 8–84, 18–02, 18–05
　　　　(3) 18–32
　　　　(4) 18–02
　　　　(5) 18–08, 18–32, 18–33
　　　　(7) 18–32
　　　s.10(1) 18–32
1988 Criminal Justice Act
　　　(c.33) 8–28, 8–69
　　　Pt II 3–03, 8–12,
　　　　　　　　　　　　　8–86
　　　s.23 ..... 8–19, 8–24, 8–27,
　　　　　　　　8–29, 21–09
　　　　(1) 19–34
　　　　(3) 8–27, 8–28
　　　　　(a) 8–27
　　　　　(b)(i)(ii) . 8–23, 8–74
　　　s.24 .... 8–30, 8–32,
　　　　　　　　　　　　　8–35
　　　s.27 3–11
　　　s.28 8–69
　　　s.29 8–86

1988   Criminal Justice Act—
            cont.
            s.30   6–31
            s.31   8–84
            s.32 .... 19–15, 19–24
                (1)(a)   19–20
                (3)   19–20
            s.32A 19–11, 19–15,
                            19–26, 19–30,
                            21–33
                (3)(c)   19–26
            s.33A 17–01, 17–04
            s.34(1)   15–02
                (2) **15–08**
            s.34A   19–11
            s.139   4–15
            Sch.2   8–12
                    para.1   8–69
            Sch.13, para.6   8–33
            Sch.16   15–02
        Legal Aid Act (c.34)
            s.38   12–12
        Road Traffic Act (c.52)
            s.5(1), (2)   4–16
                (2)   4–12
            s.15(2) 4–12, 4–16
        Copyright, Designs and
            Patents Act (c.48)
            s.280   11–37
1989   Prevention of Terror-
            ism Act (c.4)
            s.2(A)(4)-(6)   11–24
            s.16(A) 4–13, 13–21
        Football Spectators Act
            (c.37)   13–14
        Companies Act (c.40)
            s.83   11–10
        Children Act (c.41) ...   11–32
            Pt IV   11–09
            Pt V   11–09
            s.98   11–09
                (1)   11–09
                (2)   11–09
1990   Criminal Justice (Inter-
            national Co-oper-
            ation) Act (c.5) ..   8–83
        Food Safety Act (c.16)   9–43,
                                    11–02
        Environmental Protec-
            tion Act (c.43) ...   6–13
            s.71   11–11
                (2)   11–11

1991   Criminal Justice Act
            (c.53)
            ss.52–55   17–04
            Sch.6, para.5   11–16
1992   Friendly Societies Act
            (c.40)
            s.67   11–10
1993   Sexual Offences Act
            (c.30)   5–03
1994   Trade Marks Act (c.26)   6–13
            s.92   4–17
                (5) 4–17, 13–21
        Criminal Justice and
            Public Order Act
            (c.33)   11–14
            s.31   7–65
            s.32 .... 15–08, **15–09**,
                            15–10, 15–13,
                            15–16
                (1)   15–11
                (2)   15–08
            s.33   15–05
            s.34 ..... 9–09, 9–33, 9–55,
                        11–16, 11–17, 11–18,
                        11–20, 11–21, 11–22,
                        11–23, 13–17
            ss.34–37 .... 9–06, 11–25
            ss.34–38   11–26
            s.35 .... 13–17, 16–28,
                        17–16, 17–17, 17–18,
                        17–19, 17–20, 17–21,
                        17–24, 18–21, 19–03
                (1) 17–18, 17–19
                (2)   17–17
                (3) 17–17, 17–21
                (4)   17–17
                (5)   17–19
            s.36 ....   **11–24**
                (1)   11–25
                (4)   11–25
            ss.36–38   9–33
            s.37 ....   **11–24**
                (1)   11–25
                (3)   11–25
            s.38(3) 11–25, 17–20
                (5)   11–25
            s.142   20–04
            s.168   17–25
            Sch.11   17–25
1995   Civil Evidence Act
            (c.38) 8–47, 8–48,
                            8–49, 20–21
            s.7   8–38

1995 Criminal Law (Con-
      solidation) Act
      (c.39)
      s.28 11–10
1996 Criminal Procedure
      and Investigations
      Act (c.25) 14–30,
          18–04, 18–10, 18–15,
          18–18, 18–19, 18–28,
          18–29, 18–30, 21–21
      Pt I 18–05, 18–09,
                              18–10
      Pt II 18–22
      s.1(3) 18–05
      s.3 ... 14–30, 18–11, 18–12,
          18–14, 18–15, 18–22
          (1) **18–11**
          (2) **18–11**, 18–12
              (a) 18–12
      s.5 .... 18–14, 18–15,
                      18–17, 18–22
          (7) 18–16
          (8) 18–16
      s.6 .... 18–15, 18–17, 18–22
          (2) 18–15
      s.6A **18–14**, 18–15,
                      18–17, 18–20
          (2) 18–16, 18–18
          (3) 18–16
      s.6B 18–17, 18–22
          (1)(a) 18–17
          (3) 18–17
          (4) 18–17
      s.6C 18–18
          (1) **18–18**
          (2) 18–18
          (4) 18–18
      s.6D 6–35, 18–19
          (1) **18–19**
      s.6E 18–21
      s.7A 18–22, 18–23
          (1) 18–22
          (2) 18–22
          (4) 18–22
          (5) 18–22, 18–23
          (6) 18–22
          (8) 18–22
          (9) 18–22
      s.8 18–23
          (1) **18–23**
          (2) **18–23**
      s.11 .. 18–18, 18–20, 18–21
          (5) 18–20, 18–21

1996 Criminal Procedure
      and Investigations
      Act—*cont.*
      s.11(6) 18–20
          (7) 18–20
          (8) 18–20
          (9) 18–20
          (10) 18–21
      s.14 12–25
      s.15 12–24
          (4) 12–24
          (5) 12–24
      s.16 12–15
      s.20 18–31
          (1) 18–05
          (3) 6–36
      s.21 .... 18–05, 18–10
          (2) 12–12
      s.21A 18–18
      s.23 18–24
          (1) 18–24
              (a) 18–26
      s.26(1) 18–26
          (3) 18–27
          (4) 18–27
      s.29 18–02
      s.31 18–02
      s.35 12–19
      s.40(1) 16–06
          (3), (4) 16–06
          (5) 16–06
      s.47 18–01
      s.65 18–02
      s.66 3–14
      s.68 8–78
      s.74 18–16
      Sch.1 18–01
      Sch.2 8–78
      Sch.5 18–02
1997 Special Immigration
      Appeals Commis-
      sion Act (c.68) ... 12–23
1998 Data Protection Act
      (c.29) 12–15
      Crime and Disorder
      Act (c.37)
      s.34 5–04
      s.35 .... 17–16, 17–18
      s.36(3) 15–05
      s.51 18–01
      s.51B 16–25
      Sch.3, para.1 18–01
      Sch.9 5–04

1998 Criminal Justice (Ter-
        rorism   and
        Conspiracy)   Act
        (c.40)
        s.1 11–24
     Human   Rights   Act
        (c.42) 2–21, 4–13,
              4–18, 8–10, 9–15,
              10–16, 10–33, 11–18,
              13–01, 14–14, 17–25
        s.1(1)(a) 13–04
            (b) 13–04
        s.2 13–06
            (2) 13–06
        s.3 .... **13–07**, 13–08, 13–21
        s.4 13–07
        s.6 .... **13–03**
            (1) 13–04
        s.7 .... **13–04**
            (6) 13–05
        s.8 13–28
            (1) **13–05**
        s.11(a) 13–05
        s.12 13–29
        s.13 13–29
        s.18 13–01
        s.19 13–01
        s.21(5) 13–01
        s.22 13–01
        s.76 10–27
        s.78 10–27
1999 Access to Justice Act
        (c.22)
        s.90(1) 8–82
        Sch.13(9) 8–82
     Youth   Justice   and
        Criminal Evidence
        Act (c.23) 17–01,
              19–13, 19–17, 19–18,
              19–20, 19–22, 19–24,
                    19–27, 19–28
        Pt II, Ch.I 19–11
        Pt II, Ch.II 21–18
        Ch.V . 17–03, 17–06, 17–08
        s.4(1) 7–80
        s.16 .... 19–12, 19–14
            (1)(a) 19–12, 19–15
            (b) 19–12
            (2)(a)(i) 19–12
               (ii) 19–12
            (b) 19–12
            (3) 19–12
            (4) 19–12

1999 Youth   Justice   and
        Criminal Evidence
        Act—*cont.*
        s.16(5) 19–12
        s.17 .... 19–12, 19–14
            (1) 19–12
            (2)(a) 19–12
            (b) 19–12
            (c) 19–12
            (d) 19–12
            (3) 19–12
            (4) 19–13
        s.19 .... 8–26, 19–11,
                    19–14, 21–19
            (1) 19–14
            (2)(a) 19–14
            (b) 19–14
            (3) 19–14
            (6)(a) 19–14
            (b) 19–14
        s.20(2) 19–14
            (5) 19–14
            (6) 6–24
        s.21 .... 19–15, 19–16
            (1)(b) 19–15
            (3)(a) 19–15
            (b) 19–15
            (4) 19–15
            (6) 19–15
            (7) 19–15
            (8) 19–15
        s.22 .... 19–15, 19–16
        s.23 .... 19–17, 19–18
            (2) 19–17
        s.24 19–15
            (2) 19–20
            (5) 19–20
            (8) 19–20
        s.25 19–22
            (2) 19–22
            (3) 19–22
            (4) 19–22
        s.26 19–23
        s.27 .... 19–15, 19–24,
              19–26, 19–30, 19–31,
                    19–33, 21–33
            (2) 19–24
            (3) 19–24
            (4) 19–26
            (5) 19–26
            (9) 19–26
        s.28 . 19–15, 19–31, 19–33
        s.29 .... 17–08, 19–32

1999 Youth Justice and
    Criminal Evidence
    Act—*cont.*
    s.29(2) 19–32
    s.30 .... 17–08, 19–32
    s.31 19–33
      (2) 19–33
      (3) 19–33
      (4) 19–33
    s.32 19–33
    s.34 .... 21–18, 21–19
    s.35 .. 19–15, 21–18, 21–19
      (2) 21–18
      (3) 21–18
      (5) 21–18
    s.36 .... 21–18, 21–19
      (1) 21–19
      (2) 21–19
        (b) 21–19
      (3) 21–19
    s.37 21–18
    s.38 21–18
      (2) 21–19
      (3) 21–19
      (4) 7–64, 21–19
      (5) 21–19
    s.39 21–19
    s.41 ..... 7–73, **7–78**, 7–79,
        7–81, 7–82, 13–08
      (2) 7–81
      (3)(c) 7–80
    s.42 7–79
      (1)(b) 7–80
    s.43 7–82
    s.53 .... 8–22, 8–68, 17–03,
        17–11
      (1) **17–01**, 17–05,
        17–13
      (3) **17–01**, 17–06,
        17–08
      (4) 17–01, **17–11**
      (5) 17–01
    s.54(1) **17–02**
      (2) 4–34, 17–02
      (4) 17–02
      (5) 6–24, 17–02, 17–03
    s.55 .... 17–11, 19–08
      (2) 17–03, 17–08
      (4) 17–03
      (6) 6–24
      (8) 17–03
    s.56 .... 17–03, 17–06,
        17–11, 19–08

1999 Youth Justice and
    Criminal Evidence
    Act—*cont.*
    s.58 .. 9–33, 11–16, 11–17,
        11–24
    s.59 .... 9–33, 11–10
    s.60 8–78
    s.67(1) 17–11, 17–26,
        17–35
      (3) 17–26
    Sch.3 11–10
    Sch.4 .... 7–27, 17–01
      para.1 17–11
      para.3 17–26
      para.14 17–35
    Sch.6 17–26
2000 Electronic Communi-
    cations Act (c.7)
    s.7(1) 3–03
      (2) 3–03
      (3) 3–03
    s.15(1) 3–03
      (3) 3–03
    Terrorism Act (c.11)
    s.11(1), (2) 4–18
    s.18(2) 4–18
    s.118 4–18
      (1) 4–18
      (5) 4–18
    s.120 3–08
    Regulation of Investi-
    gatory Powers Act
    (c.23) 10–09
    s.1 2–21
      (1) 2–21
    s.2(1) 2–21
      (2) 2–21
    s.17 .... 2–21, 12–05,
        18–22, 18–31
    s.17(1)(a), (b) 2–21
    s.18 .... 2–21, 18–31
      (1)(a) 2–21
      (4) 2–21
      (7) 2–21
      (8) 2–21
      (9) 2–21
    s.82 2–21
    Sch.5 2–21
2001 Criminal Justice and
    Police Act (c.16)
    s.76 2–22
    s.82 10–21

2001	International Criminal Court Act (c.17)		
	s.28		11–02
	Sch.3		11–02
2003	Crime (International Co-operation) Act (c.32)		
	s.3		8–83
	s.7		8–33, 8–83
	(4)(a)		8–83
	s.8		8–83
	s.9		8–83
	ss.11–25		8–83
	Sexual Offences Act (c.42)		
	s.76		5–04
	s.77		5–04
	(3)		5–04
	Criminal Justice Act (c.44)		3–12, 3–14, 7–05, 8–01, 12–18, 16–01, 16–25, 18–05, 18–08, 18–11, 18–12, 18–14, 18–15, 18–18, 18–21, 18–22, 18–23, 18–28, 20–21, 21–21
	Pt II, Ch.1		9–53
	Ch.2		8–01, 8–12, 8–13
	Pt V		18–10
	Pt VII		16–25
	Pt VIII		19–21
	Pt 11, Ch.1		5–17, 7–05, 7–27, 7–28, 7–30, 7–31, 7–51
	Ch.2		8–12
	Ch.2		8–66, 8–73, 8–87
	s.6A(2)		11–15
	s.20(1)		8–12
	s.28		9–61
	s.32		18–11, 18–12
	s.33		18–14, 18–17
	s.34		18–18, 18–19
	s.35		6–35
	s.39		18–20
	s.41		18–01
	s.43		16–25
	(4)		16–25
	(5)		16–25
	(6)		16–25
	(7)		16–25
	s.44		16–25
	(4)		16–25

2003	Criminal Justice Act—cont.		
	s.44(5)		16–25
	(6)		16–26
	s.46(3)		16–26
	(4)		16–26
	(5)		16–26
	s.48(3)		16–26
	(5)(a)		16–26
	s.51		19–21
	(3)		19–21
	(4)(a)		19–21
	(6)		19–21
	(7)		19–21
	(8)		19–21
	s.54		19–21
	s.55		19–21
	s.98		7–01, 7–28, 7–31, 7–65, 11–02, 11–08, 17–12
	s.99(1)		7–27
	(2)		7–27
	s.100		7–72, 7–78
	(4)		7–66
	s.101		7–27, 7–72
	s.101(1)		7–33, 7–34, 7–73
	(a)		7–35, 7–75
	(b)		7–36, 7–76
	(c)		7–37, 7–69
	(d)		7–32, 7–40, 7–44, 7–49, 7–69
	(e)		7–46, 7–55, 7–69
	(f)		7–11, 7–36, 7–60, 7–62, 7–69, 10–04, 10–11
	(g)		7–49, 7–64, 7–69
	(2)		7–34
	(3)		7–44, 7–46, 7–49, 7–50, 7–51, 7–68, 7–72, 7–76
	(c)		7–76
	(d)		7–76
	(4)		7–50, 7–51
	ss.101–108		7–33, 17–12
	s.102		7–37
	ss.102–106		7–34
	s.103(1)		7–40
	(a)		7–41, 7–42, 7–45
	(b)		7–43
	(2)		7–45

2003 Criminal Justice Act—
        cont.
        (3) 7–46
        (4) **7–45**
    s.103(6) 7–40, 7–46
    s.104 .... **7–55**
        (1) 7–56
    s.105(1) 7–11, **7–60**
        (2) 7–62
            (a) 7–62
            (b) 7–62
            (c) 7–62
            (d) 7–62
            (e) 7–62
        (3) 7–62
        (4), (5) 7–60
        (6) 7–62, 7–62
        (7) 7–62
    s.106(1) **7–64**
        (2) 7–64
        (3) 7–64
    s.107 .... 7–34, 7–72
        (1) 7–69, 7–70
        (2) 7–70
        (3) 7–70
        (4) 7–72
        (5) **7–69**
    s.108(1) 7–31
        (2) 7–31
            (a) 7–31
            (b) 7–31
    s.109 7–51
        (1) 7–71
        (2) 7–71
    s.110(1) 7–72
        (2) 7–72
    s.111 7–59
        (2) 7–59
        (4) 7–59
    s.112 ..... 4–47, 7–41, 7–55
        (1) 7–28, 7–33,
                        7–46, 7–55
        (2) 7–51
    s.114 ..... 3–07, 8–12, 8–66
        (1) 8–13, 8–15
            (d) 8–35, 8–85
        (2) 8–15
        (3) 8–13
    s.115 8–14
        (1) **8–14**
        (2) 8–14, 8–30,
                        8–75
        (3) 8–30

2003 Criminal Justice Act—
        cont.
    s.116 .... 8–19, 8–29, **8–66**,
                    8–85, 21–09
        (1) **8–17**, 8–18
            (a) 8–18, 8–60
            (b) 8–18
        (2) 8–34
            (a) 8–21
            (a)-(e) 8–17
            (b) 8–22
            (c) 8–23, 8–24
            (d) 8–25, 8–26
            (e) **8–26**, 8–28
        (3) 8–26
        (4) **8–26**, 8–27
        (5) **8–20**
    s.117 .... 3–13, 6–33, 8–30,
                    8–32, 8–35, 8–66,
                        8–69
        (1) 8–30
        (2) 8–30, 8–31
            (a) 8–31
            (b) 8–31
            (c) 8–31
        (3) 8–31
        (4) 8–30, 8–33
            (a) 8–33
            (b) 8–33
        (5) 8–33, 8–34
            (a) 8–34
            (b) 8–34
        (6) **8–36**
        (7) **8–36**
    s.118 ..... 6–12, 8–13, 8–66
        (1) . 7–27, 8–38, 9–02
        (2) 8–38
    s.119 8–66
    s.120 8–66
    s.123 .... **8–68**
        (3) 8–68
    s.124 .... **8–69**
        (2)(a) 8–69
            (b) 8–69
            (c) 8–69
        (3) 8–70
        (4) 8–69
    s.125 .... **8–71**
        (1) 8–71, 9–46
    s.125(2) 8–71
    s.126 ..... 8–35, 8–37, **8–73**
        (1) 9–46
        (2) 8–73

2003	Criminal Justice Act—*cont.*	
	s.127	6–33
	(1)(a)	6–33
	(b)	6–33
	(c)	6–33
	(2)	6–33
	(3)	6–33
	(4)	6–33
	(5)	6–33
	(6)	6–33
	s.128	9–02, 9–03, 9–13, 9–15, 9–53
	s.129	2–44, **8–75**
	(1)	5–06, 8–75, 8–76
	(2)	5–06, 8–76
	s.131	8–85
	s.132	6–34, 8–87
	(5)(a)	8–87
	(b)	8–87
	(6)	8–87
	(7)	8–87
2003	Criminal Justice Act—*cont.*	
	s.133	3–09, 3–11, **8–86**
	s.134	3–02, 8–13, 8–30, 8–71
	s.137	19–24, 19–25
	(1)(a), (f)	19–24
	(b)	19–24
	(d)	19–24
	(3)(a)	19–24
	(b)(i)	19–25
	(4)	19–25
	s.138(1)	19–25
	(3)	19–25
	(4)	19–24
	s.139	20–22, **20–26**, 20–27
	s.336(3)	16–25, 19–21, 19–24, 20–26
	Sch.3	18–01
	Sch.25, Pt 4	5–27, 5–30
	Sch.37	18–14

Table of Statutory Instruments

1965 Rules of the Supreme Court (SI 1965/1776)
  Ord.38, r.10(11) ... 3–22
1970 Food Hygiene Regulations (SI 1970/1172) 3–19
1971 Indictment Rules (SI 1971/1253) 7–52
1973 Misuse of Drugs Regulations (SI 1973/797) 4–22
  Sch.1 4–22
1981 Magistrates' Courts Rules (SI 1981/553)
  r.68 3–22
  r.71 5–07
1982 Crown Court Rules (SI 1982/1109)
  r.22E 21–18
  r.23 12–15
  r.23B 19–20
  r.23B(10) 19–20
  rr.24B–24D 21–18
1985 Magistrates' Courts (Advance Information) Rules (SI 1985/601) . 18–03, 18–04
  r.4(3) 18–03
  Control of Trade in Endangered Species (Enforcement) Regulations (SI 1985/1155) 4–24
1986 Companies (Northern Ireland) Order (SI 1986/1032)
  art.427, 440 11–10
  Insolvency Rules (SI 1986/1925)
  r.12.20 3–22

1987 Crown Court (Advance Notice of Expert Evidence) Rules (SI 1987/716) ... 6–35, 6–36, 18–08
1988 Criminal Justice (Evidence) (Northern Ireland) Order (SI 1988/2159 11–25
  art.4 .... 17–21, 17–24
1989 Companies (Northern Ireland) Order (SI 1989/2404)
  art.23 11–10
  Insolvency (Northern Ireland) Order (SI 1989/2405)
  art.373 11–10
1997 Crown Court (Advance Notice of Expert Evidence) (Amendment) Rules (SI 1997/700) 6–35
1996 Proceeds of Crime (Northern Ireland) Order (SI 1996/1299)
  Sch.2, para.6 11–10
1997 Magistrates' Courts (Criminal Procedure and Investigations Act 1996 (Disclosure) Rules (SI 1997/703 12–25
  Magistrates' Courts (Advance Notice of Expert Evidence) Rules (SI 1997/705) 6–36

2000 Human Rights Act 1998 (Commencement No.2) Order (SI 2000/1851) ... 13–01

Crown Court (Amendment) Rules (SI 2000/2093) 21–18

Crime and Disorder Act 1998 (Service of Prosecution Evidence) Regulations (SI 2000/3305) ... 18–01

2002 Magistrates' Courts (Special Measures Directions) Rules (SI 2002/1687) ... 19–14

Crown Court (Special Measures, Directions and Directions Prohibiting Cross-Examination) Rules (SI 2002/1688) 19–14, 21–18

2002 Regulation of Investigatory Powers (Interception of Communications: Code of Practice) Order (SI 2002/1693) 2–21

Youth Justice and Criminal Evidence Act 1999 (Commencement No.7) Order (SI 2002/1739) ... 19–11, 21–18

2003 Police and Criminal Evidence Act 1984 (Codes of Practice) (Codes B to E) (No.2) Order (SI 2003/703) 14–16

Table of European Convention on Human Rights

1950 European Convention
    on Human Rights
    and Fundamental
    Freedoms 4–13, 4–18,
      10–02, 10–05, 10–09,
      10–21, 10–26, 13–01,
      13–02
Art.1 13–01
Arts 2–12 13–04
Art.3 .... 13–09, 13–29
Art.5 .... 13–09, 13–11,
      13–12, 13–13, 13–27
   (1) 13–12
     (c) 13–12
   (3) 13–12, 13–13
   (4) 12–18, 13–13,
      18–29
Art.6 .... 4–13, 7–80, 8–60,
      10–09, 10–10, 10–15,
      10–26, 10–27, 10–31,
      11–11, 11–12, 11–24,
      11–26, 12–18, 12–19,
      12–23, 13–05, 13–08,
      13–09, 13–14, 13–16,
      13–17, 13–18, 13–20,
      13–23, 13–26, 13–29,
      14–14, 17–24, 17–25,
      18–30, 19–16, 21–02
   (1) 10–09, 10–10,
      10–22, 10–26, 10–27,
      11–10, 11–12, 11–22,
      11–23, 11–26, 12–17,
      12–18, 12–21, 13–14,
      13–15, 13–16, 13–17,
      13–19, 13–23, 13–26,
      17–24, 18–30, 19–22

1950 European Convention
    on Human Rights
    and Fundamental
    Freedoms—*cont.*
Art.6(2) 4–03, 4–12,
      4–13, 4–15, 4–16,
      4–17, 11–12, 11–21,
      11–26, 13–14, 13–17,
      13–20, 13–21
   (3) 9–33, 13–14,
      13–22
     (b) 13–22
     (c) 13–22
     (d) ... 8–22, 13–16,
      13–22, 13–23,
      18–18
   (6) 9–33
Art.8 10–10,
      10–20, 10–26, 10–27,
      13–09, 13–24, 13–25,
      13–26, 13–29, 17–28,
      18–30
   (1) 13–24, 13–25,
      17–28
   (2) 10–09, 13–25
Art.9 13–29
Art.10 .... 11–38, 13–29
Art.11 13–29
Art.14 13–04
Arts 16–18 13–04
Art.25 13–05
Art.34 .... 13–04, 13–05
1st Protocol, Arts
    1–3 13–04
11th Protocol 13–05,
      13–09

PART 1

Introductory

CHAPTER 1

Introduction

1. THE MEANING AND CLASSIFICATION OF EVIDENCE

The law of evidence establishes rules to determine: 1–01

    (a) what facts may be proved in a trial; and

    (b) what evidence may be called to prove those facts.

While such rules play an important part in every trial, they are of particular importance in criminal trials. The major part of this book is concerned with these rules. It is, however, necessary at the outset to consider some introductory matters concerning the meaning and classification of evidence and questions of relevance and admissibility.

    Evidence is something which tends to prove or disprove any fact or   1–02
conclusion. In a trial it means the information which is put before the court in order to prove the facts in issue, *i.e.* in a criminal trial those facts which the prosecution must establish in order to prove their case and the defendant must establish in order to raise a defence. Evidence may take the following forms:

    — testimony, *i.e.* oral statements by witnesses on oath;

    — documents produced for the inspection of the court;

    — real evidence, *i.e.* exhibits and other material objects;

    — and admissions of fact.

    Evidence has been classified in various ways: the most common classifications are considered below.

A. Direct and indirect evidence

Direct evidence may be: 1–03

    (a) the evidence of a witness of what he himself saw, heard or perceived. Thus on a charge of wounding, direct evidence may be given by the victim who describes the circumstances in which he was attacked and by eye-witnesses who identify the attacker;

3

(b) the evidence of a witness as to his own physical or mental state; or

(c) the production of anything.

Direct evidence is to be contrasted with "indirect" evidence in the sense of either hearsay (*i.e.* that which the witness heard from another) or circumstantial evidence (*i.e.* evidence from which inferences may be drawn). Indirect evidence is as much evidence as direct evidence. Direct evidence may, however, have more or less weight according to the judgment of the tribunal of fact. Its only virtue may be said to be that there is only one area of possible doubt about it, namely the truth and accuracy of the witness; whereas in the case of indirect evidence problems of judging the weight of hearsay or deciding on proper inferences arise.

B. Original and hearsay evidence

1–04 Evidence of statements made out of court by any person may either be original evidence and therefore admissible as evidence, or hearsay and, subject to exception, inadmissible.

The distinction is as follows. Statements tendered as original evidence are tendered as evidence of what was said irrespective of whether what was said is true or not. On the other hand, hearsay evidence consists of the evidence of statements made out of court which are tendered as evidence of the truth of what was said. Thus if A is charged with wounding B, it would be hearsay for B to say in evidence that C had told him that A was responsible for wounding him.

C. Primary and secondary evidence

1–05 These expressions commonly relate to the proof of the contents of a document.[1] Primary evidence is the best which can be given, *i.e.* the original document. Secondary evidence is any other inferior evidence of the document, *i.e.* a copy or oral evidence of what the document contained. Nowadays both types are admitted.

D. Circumstantial evidence

1–06 Circumstantial evidence is evidence of circumstances surrounding an event or offence from which a fact in issue may be inferred. Thus, suppose it is alleged that A burgled a jeweller's shop in a "smash and grab" raid. B gives evidence that he was in a nearby street at the material time: he heard a crash of glass; he then saw A running down the street from the direction from which the sound of breaking glass had come; B saw that A had some jewellery hanging out of his pocket; B also noticed that there was a cut on one of A's hands. B's evidence of what he saw and heard would be cir-

---

[1] See paras 3–04 *et seq.*, below for a discussion.

cumstantial. The inference to be drawn from it is that A burgled the jeweller's shop.

Because crimes are committed very often when witnesses are not present, circumstantial evidence may be a crucial ingredient in a prosecution. The individual items of such evidence may by themselves be insufficient to establish guilt, but taken together, the cumulative effect may be very telling. In *Exall*[2] Pollock C. B. described circumstantial evidence as like a rope composed of several strands, none of which was sufficient on its own to bear weight, but taken all together would be sufficiently strong. The suggestion, sometimes made, that circumstantial evidence is of less substance than direct evidence is misconceived. "It is no derogation of evidence to say that it is circumstantial."[3]

Examples of circumstantial evidence occur daily in criminal trials. Some   **1–07** of the more common examples are listed below.

Motive

Evidence of motive often forms part of a prosecution case. Thus, suppose it is alleged that a company director had his company's warehouse burnt to the ground in order to obtain the insurance; evidence that the company was in financial difficulties would be admissible to show motive from which the jury may draw an inference of guilt.

Acts preparatory to the commission of the offence

Evidence of such acts are admissible to show an intention on the part of the defendant to commit the offence charged. Thus if the defendant were charged with others with the robbery of a bank, evidence that prior to the robbery he had attempted to acquire plans of the bank would be admissible to identify him as one of those participating in the plan to rob the bank.

Fingerprints

As will be seen when evidence of identification is considered, the finding of fingerprints is powerful evidence from which a jury may infer the identity of the perpetrator of an offence.

Lies told by the defendant

The fact that a defendant told lies when interviewed by the police about the   **1–08** offence charged may give rise to an inference of guilt in the absence of an explanation (or an explanation which may be true) as to why the lies were told.

---

[2] (1866) 4 F. & F. 922, 929.
[3] *Taylor, Weaver and Donovan* (1928) 21 Cr.App.R. 20, 21, *per* Lord Hewart C.J.

Possession of recently stolen goods

(This example of circumstantial evidence is called by a misnomer "the doctrine of recent possession.") If a person is found in possession of recently stolen goods and offers no explanation to account for the possession, or offers an explanation which the jury are satisfied is not true the jury may infer that he either stole the goods or dishonestly handled them. Which of the two inferences is correct may depend upon the circumstances. On a charge of theft, the jury should be directed that the inference only arises if the circumstances of the case point exclusively to the defendant being the thief rather than a handler.[4] On a charge of handling stolen goods, the jury should be directed[5] that they may infer that the defendant knew or believed that the goods were stolen if (i) the defendant offered no explanation to account for his possession of the goods; or (ii) they are satisfied that his explanation is untrue; *but* (iii) if an explanation is offered which they find might be true[6] or which leaves them in reasonable doubt as to whether he knew the goods were stolen or not, they should acquit.[7]

1–09   Whether or not the goods have been stolen sufficiently recently to give rise to the inference will depend upon the circumstances of the case. In one case a period of eight months between the theft of goods and their first being seen in the defendant's possession was held to be too long.[8] In another case the Court of Appeal said that in relation to stolen cars a time span of a matter of months (four to six in the instant case) between theft and acquisition could not be said to be recent.[9] It is submitted that these are extreme examples and a period of hours or days is more usually involved. However, there can be no hard and fast rules since the whole doctrine depends upon the application of common sense to the facts of the particular case. As the Court of Appeal said:

> "The doctrine is only a particular aspect of the general proposition that where suspicious circumstances appear to demand an explanation and no explanation or an extremely incredible explanation is given, the lack of any explanation may warrant an inference of guilty knowledge in the defendant. This again is only part of a wider proposition that guilt may be inferred from unreasonable behaviour of a defendant when confronted with facts which seem to accuse."[10]

---

[4] *Smith* (1990) 148 J.P. 216.
[5] *Aves* (1950) 34 Cr.App.R. 159; *Smith*, above; *Smyth* (1980) 72 Cr.App.R. 86.
[6] *Moulding* [1996] Crim.L.R. 440.
[7] In an appropriate case it may be necessary to remind the jury of the defendant's right of silence. It would be a misdirection to tell them that the right was over-ridden in these circumstances; see *Raviraj* (1987) 85 Cr.App.R. 93, 107. For the right of silence, see paras 11–14 *et seq.* below.
[8] *Marcus* (1923) 17 Cr.App.R. 191.
[9] *Powers* [1990] Crim.L.R. 586.
[10] *Raviraj* (1987) 85 Cr.App.R. 93, 103.

The House of Lords has held that no special direction need be given to a   **1–10**
jury in a case where the prosecution case depends upon circumstantial
evidence provided that the jury are adequately directed that they must not
convict unless they are satisfied of the defendant's guilt beyond reasonable
doubt.[11] However, it may well be appropriate to warn the jury in such a
case not to convict unless they are sure that the facts proved are not only
consistent with the guilt of the accused but are also such as to be inconsistent with any other reasonable conclusion.[12]

Presumptions of fact

A presumption of fact is a type of circumstantial evidence which from its
common occurrence is said to give rise to a presumption. It is an inference
of fact which a court may draw as a matter of common experience once a
particular fact is proved. The inferred fact is then said to be presumed until
the contrary is proved. For instance, a presumption of guilty knowledge
arises once it is proved that the defendant was in possession of recently
stolen goods. However, such a presumption may always be contradicted.
Even if it is not contradicted, the jury or magistrates are not bound to draw
the inference indicated by common experience. Since such presumptions
involve pure questions of fact there is nothing to be gained by further
elaboration.

2. The Best Evidence Rule

The best evidence rule was that a party must produce the best evidence   **1–11**
which the nature of the case would permit. At one time the rule was an
important part of the law of evidence. The only vestige of it now remaining,
however, is that if the original of a document is available it must be produced.[13] The court will now admit all evidence whether it is the best or not.
The only significance of a failure to produce the best evidence is that the
weight of the evidence may be diminished. The rule has made an occasional, untypical appearance in the last 50 years. In *Quinn and Bloom*,[14]
for instance, a film showing a reconstruction of a striptease act was held to
be inadmissible because it was not the best evidence. In fact, the reason for
this ruling may be said to have nothing to do with the rule. It would have
been wrong to admit the film because it would not have been a true
reconstruction of the act.

---

[11] *McGreevy v DPP* (1973) 57 Cr.App.R. 424.
[12] See *Lejzor Teper* [1952] A.C. 480, 489, *per* Lord Normand; *Onufrejczyk* [1955] 1 Q.B.
388, 400–401, *per* Lord Goddard C.J.
[13] See para.3–05, below.
[14] [1962] 2 Q.B. 245.

3. ADMISSIBILITY AND RELEVANCE

1–12   The law of evidence is concerned primarily with admissibility, *i.e.* what evidence is admissible. Evidence is admissible if it may lawfully be admitted at a trial. Questions of admissibility in trials by jury are matters for the judge alone to decide, usually in the absence of the jury. On the other hand, questions relating to the "weight" of evidence are normally matters for the jury to decide. (There may be exceptional occasions when a judge may have to investigate the weight of evidence, for example in deciding whether to admit a confession or tape-recording.)

The golden rule of admissibility is that all evidence which is relevant is admissible and that which is irrelevant is inadmissible.

1–13   It is not easy to define the meaning of "relevance" in general terms: it will depend in each case upon the circumstances and the way in which the case is being conducted. However, definitions have been attempted. Two examples may be given:

(a)   Stephen defined the word "relevant" (and thus, the effect of relevant evidence) as

"Any two facts to which it is applied are so related to each other that according to the common course of events one either taken by itself or in connection with other facts either proves or renders probable the past, present or future existence or non-existence of the other."[15]

(b)   Lord Simon of Glaisdale said:

"Evidence is relevant if it is logically probative or disprobative of some matter which requires proof ... '[L]ogical probativeness' ... does not of itself express the element of expedience which is so significant of its operation in law ... It is sufficient to say ... that relevant evidence, *i.e.* logically probative of disprobative evidence is evidence which makes the matter which requires proof more or less probable."[16]

The matter may be summarised in this way. For the purpose of a criminal trial, evidence is relevant if its effect is to make more or less probable the existence of any fact which is in issue, *i.e.* upon which guilt or innocence depends. Or, as Lord Steyn recently put it: "[to] be relevant the evidence need merely have some tendency in logic and common sense to advance the proposition in issue".[17]

---

[15] *Digest of the Law of Evidence* (12th ed., 1948 (revised)), art.1.
[16] *Kilbourne* [1973] A.C. 729, 756.
[17] *A (No.2)* [2001] 2 Cr.App.R. 351, 362.

The facts in issue are those facts which the prosecution must establish in **1–14** order to prove its case and the defendant must establish in order to raise a defence. In a criminal trial "everything is in issue and the prosecution must prove the whole of their case, including the identity of the accused, the nature of the act and the existence of any necessary knowledge or intent."[18] For instance, in a theft trial the prosecution must prove that the defendant dishonestly appropriated goods belonging to another and that he did so with the intention of permanently depriving the loser of them. Each of these separate elements must be proved. Evidence rendering any fact relating to them more probable is relevant to a fact in issue. Thus, if the defence is that although the defendant appropriated the goods he did not do so dishonestly, any evidence which makes that conclusion more probable is relevant to a fact in issue. Similarly, in a case alleging possession of drugs with intent to supply (once the fact that the defendant was in possession of the drugs has been proved), the remaining evidence must be logically probative of the defendant's intent to supply, *i.e.* making that intention more or less probable.[19] On the other hand, in the case of an offence involving strict liability, evidence which goes beyond that necessary to prove the specific elements in the offence is irrelevant and inadmissible.[20]

Facts may also be relevant to the issue because they form part of the **1–15** story, or (as it is sometimes still called) *res gestae*:[21] "when a situation of fact [such as a killing] is being considered, the question may arise when does the situation begin and when does it end. It may be arbitrary and artificial to confine the evidence to the firing of the gun or the insertion of the knife, without knowing in a broader sense, what was happening."[22]

Facts such as those concerning the credibility of a witness are said tobe collateral facts and evidence relevant to such an issue is admissible subject to the rule that no evidence may be called to rebut a witness's evidence in cross-examination as to credit.[23]

The rule that all relevant evidence is admissible is subject to certain **1–16** exceptions for it is a feature of the English law of evidence that not all matters which are logically relevant are admissible, usually for reasons of policy. These exclusionary rules form an important part of the law of evidence and are dealt with elsewhere. The main exclusionary rules relate to:

---

[18] *Sims* [1946] K.B. 531, 539, *per* Lord Goddard C.J.
[19] *Gordon* [1995] 2 Cr.App.R. 61, 64.
[20] *Sandhu* [1997] Crim.L.R. 288. In *Byrne* [2002] Cr.App.R. 311, 312, the Court of Appeal, applying *Sandhu*, reiterated that the prosecution is only entitled to adduce evidence which is sufficiently relevant to an issue in its case; and all that is irrelevant, or not sufficiently relevant, to the case as advanced by the prosecution, should be excluded.
[21] The expression in this context adds nothing to the concept that evidence to be admissible must be relevant: Stone, "Res gestae Reagitata" (1939) 55 L.Q.R. 66, 71.
[22] *Ratten v R* [1972] A.C. 378, 388, *per* Lord Wilberforce.
[23] For cross-examination as to credit, see para.21–27, below.

(a) hearsay statements, including confessions;

(b) evidence of a witness's opinion;

(c) evidence of the defendant's character;

(d) privilege and public interest;

(e) the discretion of the court to exclude evidence.

1–17 All the above matters may well be relevant, but may be excluded as too prejudicial to be admitted if the trial is to be fair, or because the matter is for the court, not the witness, to decide.

Evidence may also be excluded because it would cloud the issue being tried and would only serve to confuse the jury. Thus, a witness may be cross-examined about his conduct in order to attack his credibility, but evidence is not admissible to disprove his denials. If such evidence were admitted it would lead to the opening of a multiplicity of side issues which might blur the issues which the jury had to resolve.

1–18 While these general principles remain true, there has been a trend in recent years towards dispensing with exclusionary rules in favour of admitting all relevant evidence. Thus, Sir Robin Auld in his Review of the Criminal Courts ("Auld Report") in 2001 criticised "the blight" in the law of evidence attributable to incoherence, confusion and conflict in aims and policy and, also, criticised its neglect of summary trials.[24] The Report called for a comprehensive review of the law of criminal evidence "to make it a simple and efficient agent for ensuring that all criminal courts are told all and only what they need to know",[25] and, therefore, recommended that the law should move away from technical rules of admissibility to trusting judicial and lay fact-finders to give relevant evidence the weight it deserves.[26] This view was echoed in 2002 in a government White Paper which complained that the current rules are difficult to understand and complex to apply.[27] The Paper also referred to growing public concern that evidence relevant to the search for truth is being wrongly excluded and stated that magistrates, judges and juries should be trusted to give appropriate evidence the weight it deserves: "[to] enable them to do so, the rules of evidence need to be re-written to ensure that they have all relevant material to reach a just verdict."[28]

1–19 All the above criticisms may be justified, particularly in the eyes of a

---

[24] Review of the Criminal Courts of England and Wales Report (London, The Stationery Office, October 2001), Ch.11, para.76, p.546.

[25] *ibid.*, para.77. Such a view was beyond the scope of the Auld Report which recommended that it be part of an exercise of reform and codification of the criminal law: *ibid: op.cit.*, Ch.1, paras 35–36.

[26] *ibid.*, para.78.

[27] *Justice for All* (2002), CM 5563, para.4.52.

[28] *ibid.*, paras 4.52–53. The Government has also supported the introduction of a criminal evidence code and the formation of a Criminal Procedure Rules Committee.

public which cannot understand why any piece of evidence is withheld from a court. But, however complex these rules may appear, many have stood the test of time and play their part in ensuring the balance necessary for a fair trial. It is therefore to be hoped that any proposed reform does not disturb that balance unnecessarily. Whether the changes brought about by the Criminal Justice Act 2003 will have that effect remains to be seen.

CHAPTER 2
Real Evidence

2–01   Real evidence consists of the production of material objects for the inspection of the court or to which it can listen. This includes chattels, documents, photographs, films and recordings.[1] It also includes information obtained by the court at an inspection or view. Each category will be considered separately.

1. CHATTELS

2–02   The general rule is that objects which may be evidence of crime and which come into the possession of the prosecuting authorities should be preserved and retained for use in court.[2] For instance, in a theft case the recovered property will be produced and exhibited unless it is perishable or too large (in which case it can be retained and photographs of it produced). However, it is not always possible to maintain this desirable standard: exhibits go astray or are tested to destruction.[3] In these circumstances it may be possible for the prosecution to rely on secondary evidence: see below.

   Once an article has become an exhibit the court has jurisdiction over it and it remains available to the court to examine it and its contents whenever the court pleases.[4] The court, also, has a responsibility to preserve and retain an exhibit so that it may always be available for the purposes of justice until the trial is concluded.[5]

2–03   An object does not have to be produced in order that evidence may be given about it.[6] The following are examples:

   (a) In a shoplifting case, the stolen articles may not be produced if they are perishable. The store detective can still give evidence that she saw the defendant stealing them.

---

[1] Electronic communications are documents and may also be classed as real evidence, see para.3–03, below.
[2] *Lushington v Otto* [1894] 1 Q.B. 420, 423 *per* Wright J.; *Uxbridge JJ. Ex p. Sofaer* (1987) 85 Cr.App.R. 367, 377.
[3] *Uxbridge JJ.*, above, at 377; or altered irretrievably: *DPP v British Telecommunications plc* [1991] Crim.L.R. 532.
[4] *Pydar JJ. Ex p. Foster* (1996) 60 J.P. 87.
[5] *Lushington Ex p. Otto* [1894] 1 Q.B. 420, 423, *per* Wright J., quoted with approval by Court of Appeal in *Lambeth Stipendiary Magistrate Ex p. McComb* [1983] Q.B. 551.
[6] *Hocking v Ahlquist* [1944] K.B. 120, DC; *Miller v Howe* [1969] 1 W.L.R. 1510, DC.

(b) The police are not obliged to produce the very breath test device used in a particular case.[7]

(c) In *Orrell*,[8] secondary evidence of the label of a bottle containing a urine sample was held to have been correctly admitted although neither bottle nor label was produced.

(d) The prosecution may be entitled to rely on photographs of goods which have been lost or destroyed.[9]

In some cases the article itself is unimportant. For instance in a shop-   2–04
lifting case, if the case is straightforward and the article commonplace, the
jury or magistrates may not be much assisted by seeing the article. On the
other hand, the article may itself be of importance, for example if the thief
had hidden the object in his clothes and a question arises as to whether this
would be possible or not.

Non-production of an article may not affect its admissibility as evidence,
but may affect its weight and the judge may comment on this.[10]

2. DOCUMENTS

A document may be admissible as real evidence: the document is then   2–05
produced, not to prove its contents, but to prove its existence. Thus, a
stolen cheque bearing a fingerprint will be admissible for this reason. A
further example would be as follows: A, a trespasser, walks into B's office
while the office is unoccupied. He finds B's coat and steals a wallet from it.
The wallet contains B's cheque book and driving licence. In due course the
cheque book and driving licence are recovered from A's house. A is charged
with burglary of the office. The cheque book and driving licence would be
admissible as real evidence. (For proof of existence of documents, see Ch.3.)

3. INSPECTION AND VIEW

The court may also obtain information by means of an inspection or view.   2–06
The term "view" is applied to two situations. In the first case it may simply
be an inspection of something which is too large to be produced in court,
for instance, a piece of machinery. In this case the object is very often
brought into the precincts of the court and the jury may leave court to see it.
Such an inspection may properly be regarded as real evidence in the same
way as the inspection of any exhibit. In the second case the jury may go to

---

[7] *Miller v Howe*, above.
[8] [1972] R.T.R. 14, CA.
[9] See, *e.g.*, *Uxbridge JJ. Ex p. Sofaer*, above.
[10] *Francis* (1874) L.R. 2 C.C.R. 128.

see the *locus in quo* of an incident.[11] A view or inspection may take place at any time during the trial until the retirement of the jury.[12]

The judge and the defendant should always be present at a view,[13] whether witnesses are present or not.[14] Normally, the whole court will adjourn to the place where the view is being held including counsel and the shorthand writer. The jury then examine the place or thing without anything being said. A witness or defendant may give a demonstration, but must make no communication to the jury.[15] If any questions arise on the view or if the jury have any questions about it, the usual course is for such questions to be asked in court after the view is over. The fact that a witness has already given evidence does not prevent him taking part in a view, provided that he may be recalled to be cross-examined.

2–07   Inspection of the *locus in quo* may not be delegated to one of the jury in order that he may report back to the rest[16]; and the jury should not be invited to visit the scene of a crime on their way home during an adjournment of the trial.[17] Problems may arise when jurors decide, of their own initiative, to visit the scene of a crime. This is understandable. A juror may feel that he or she would be assisted by a visit to the scene and not appreciating the dangers, decides on making a visit. Those dangers may arise from the fact that the juror may see something which was not referred to in court and was not part of the evidence, and then the juror (and the rest of the jury, if they are told of it) may rely, in reaching a verdict, on something that was not part of the evidence. Thus, it was held in *Davis, Rowe and Johnson*[18] to have been a material irregularity for the foreman of the jury to have visited the scenes of the crime alone. The Court of Appeal said that in future judges should consider whether in the particular case

---

[11] The Juries Act 1974, s.14 provides that rules may be made as respects views by jurors. None have so far been made. The section also provides that the places to which a juror may be called to go on a view shall not be restricted to any particular county or area.

[12] *Lawrence* (1968) 52 Cr.App.R. 163. In *Nixon* (1968) 52 Cr.App.R. 218, the jury were allowed to inspect a car after retirement. Since the inspection was at the express wish of the defence the proviso was applied and the conviction confirmed.

[13] *Tameshwar v R* [1957] A.C. 476. If the defendant has been allowed by the judge to be absent from the view, he cannot afterwards allege that his absence made the trial illegal: see *Karamat*, below, n.14.

[14] *Hunt* [1987] A.C. 352.

[15] *Martin* (1872) L.R. 1 C.C.R. 378; *Karamat* [1956] A.C. 256.

[16] *Gurney* [1977] R.T.R. 211. In *Gurney* it was held to have been an irregularity for the judge to have invited one of the jury to inspect street lighting and report on it to his colleagues. On the other hand, in a more recent case, a juror similarly had visited the scene of a crime to assess the street lighting. The Court of Appeal said that the irregularity would only render the conviction unsafe if it could have significance to the issues to be determined by the jury (which in the instant case it did not, since the colour of the lighting was not relevant to the identification evidence in the case): *Smyth, The Times*, September 16, 1998. The distinction between the cases must be (a) that in *Smyth* the juror's visit was voluntary effort by the juror whereas in *Gurney* it was at the invitation of the court; and (b) that the significance of the visit in *Gurney* was far greater than that in *Smyth*.

[17] *Albarus and James* [1989] Crim. L.R. 905.

[18] *The Times*, July 25, 2000.

there is a risk of anyone acting on his or her own initiative and to give an appropriate direction.[19]

The practice to be adopted by magistrates when visiting the *locus in quo* was considered by the Divisional Court in *Parry v Boyle*.[20] The court, commenting that justices, like the judge in a civil case, are judges both of law and fact, said that the principles in two civil cases, *Salsbury v Woodland*[21] and *Goold v Evans & Co.*,[22] should be followed by magistrates. Those principles may be summarised as follows: (i) a view is part of the evidence; (ii) the judge must take a view in the presence of both parties; or (iii) both parties must be given the opportunity of being present; (iv) the only exception is where the judge goes to see some public place, for example the scene of a road accident; (v) the judge should not attend anything in the form of a demonstration or reconstruction in the absence of the parties.

The court in *Parry v Boyle* held that the justices in that case, who had   2–08 viewed the scene of a road accident in the absence of the parties, had complied with the principles because they told the parties what they were doing and thus impliedly invited the parties to come. However, the court said that, as a general rule, justices should not have a view without being accompanied by the parties or their representatives and that a view should take place before the conclusion of the evidence so that the parties may have the opportunity of commenting on any feature which they have observed. Unless there are special circumstances, the absence of the defendant at a view will normally be fatal to a conviction.[23] He should be present because he might be able to point out something of which his lawyer was unaware or about which the justices were making a mistake.

4. The Admissibility of Photographs and Recordings: General Principles

In the *Statue of Liberty*[24] Sir Jocelyn Simon said that the law is now bound   2–09 to take cognisance of the fact that mechanical means replace human effort. As a result, evidence of recordings plays an increasing part in criminal trials, particularly with the introduction of tape recording of police interviews and the wider use of videotapes. The law of evidence has had to adapt to these techniques of recording as they have been invented. Thus, photographs

---

[19] For a discussion of the view as a species of real evidence and argument as to the need for statutory regulation, see Ormerod, "A Prejudicial View" [2000] Crim.L.R. 452.
[20] (1986) 83 Cr.App.R. 310.
[21] [1970] 1 Q.B. 324.
[22] [1951] 2 T.L.R. 1189.
[23] *Ely JJ. Ex p. Burgess* (1992) 136 S.J. (LB) 244.
[24] [1968] 1 W.L.R. 739, 740. Part of the material for this chapter is based on the author's article, "The Admissibility of Photographic and Videotape Evidence" (1987) 51 J.C.L. 437.

were admitted in the nineteenth century, and tape recordings and videotape evidence were admitted in the twentieth. These techniques are capable of providing the court with the most immediate evidence, for instance, a video recording of the crime itself being committed or a tape recording of a conversation between conspirators. It is clearly desirable that, if available, such evidence should be put before the court. Marshall J., giving the judgment of the Court of Criminal Appeal in *Maqsud Ali*,[25] said that it appeared wrong to deny to the law of evidence advantages to be gained by new techniques and new devices. More recently, Lord Taylor C.J. said that as technology develops, evidential practice will need to be evolved to accommodate it: "[whilst] the Courts must be vigilant to ensure that no unfairness results, they should not block steps which enable the jury to gain full assistance from the technology."[26]

2–10   The essential principle on which the admissibility of photographs and recordings is based is as follows:

(a) The fact that a witness has been aided by a device in seeing or hearing something (for example binoculars or a loudspeaker), does not make the evidence of what he saw or heard inadmissible.

(b) The fact that a machine is used to assist the senses of the viewer or witness makes no difference.

(c) Similar principles apply if the machine is capable of recording what would have been seen or heard.

(d) The recording is admissible as real evidence to prove what has been recorded. (No question of hearsay arises.)

While the underlying principle of admissibility is the same in each case, different considerations apply to photographs, tape recordings, videotape and automatic recordings.[27]

5. PHOTOGRAPHS

A. Admissibility

2–11   Photographs are admissible as real evidence for the inspection of the court. Thus in 1864, Willes J. admitted a photograph in order to prove a person's identity.[28] This ruling, as has recently been observed, has never been

---

[25] [1966] 1 Q.B. 688, 701.
[26] *Clare and Peach* [1995] 2 Cr.App.R. 333, 339.
[27] Photographs, tape recordings, film and video recordings may also be admissible as documentary evidence: Civil Evidence Act 1968, s.10.
[28] *Tolson* (1864) 4 F. & F. 103.

16

doubted.[29] Since then, photographs have been admitted in evidence so that today their production in criminal trials is a normal and frequent occurrence. Cinematic film makes a less frequent appearance, but the same principles of admissibility apply.

Before a photograph may be admitted, its authenticity must be proved.[30] The photographer must prove that he took the photograph and when and where he did so: he or another person must prove that the prints were taken from untouched negatives. It is unusual for there to be dispute about these matters which are normally proved by the service of a statement made by an appropriate witness.

To be admissible, the photograph must be relevant to an issue in the case and must not be subject to any of the general exclusionary rules. The judge has a discretion to exclude a photograph if it would be unfair to admit it under the provisions of s.78 of the Police and Criminal Evidence Act 1984 or in the exercise of the court's discretion retained by the Act.[31] For instance, a photograph of the defendant produced from police files (indicating that he was known to the police) might be excluded if, in the circumstances of the particular case, the effect of producing it would be more prejudicial than probative.

B. Photographs as evidence

Inspection of the photograph may itself reveal what is sought to be proved, for example a victim's injuries, stolen goods or scenes of crime. Occasionally, photographs are admitted which show offences being committed. Thus, a newspaper photographer may take photographs of a riot. Such photographs would be admissible to show what happened in the riot. Similarly, a police photographer may take a photograph of a body as it was found; or photographs may be taken of the scene in a house after a drugs raid. Such photographs are admissible as evidence relating to the scenes which they represent. They are scenes or situations "reproduced by mechanical and chemical devices."[32] The court may therefore inspect them and draw whatever inferences are proper.

A witness may, of course, refer to a photograph to assist in giving his evidence and may point out things in the photograph, for example something which is not readily visible. However, there are cases where inspection of the photograph will not by itself reveal what a party seeks to prove: the evidence of a witness is necessary to make good the deficiency. This most commonly occurs in cases where it is sought to prove a person's

2–12

---

[29] *Cook* [1987] 2 W.L.R. 775, 781, *per* Watkins L.J.
[30] *Hindson v Ashby* [1896] 2 Ch. 1, 21, *per* A.L. Smith L.J.; *Maqsud Ali* [1966] 1 Q.B. 688 at 701, *per* Marshall J.
[31] For a discussion of this discretion, see paras 10–13 *et seq.*, below.
[32] *Maqsud Ali*, above, at 701.

identity by means of a photograph. Similar principles apply to photographs taken by a security camera[33] or film taken automatically.[34]

C. Proving identity by photographs

2–13   A distinction may be made between cases where a photograph is produced to a witness who identifies the person shown in it and cases in which the jury themselves are invited to make the identification.

Tolson[35] is an example of the former case. The prisoner was charged with bigamy. Willes J. permitted witnesses to look at a photograph of the prisoner's first husband to identify him as the person named in the certificate of marriage. As a further example, a witness who knows the defendant may be shown a photograph and identify the person shown in it as the defendant. In these circumstances, the jury are not required to make any identification themselves. However, before relying on the evidence, they must be satisfied that the witness was correct in his identification. If the person to be identified is the defendant, it is submitted that the jury may, in deciding whether the witness was correct, compare the person in the dock with the person shown in the photograph: see discussion below.

2–14   In some cases there is no witness to identify the man in the photograph as the defendant. In these cases the jury must themselves make the identification. In doing so they are entitled to use the evidence of their own eyes. There is no rule to stop them. Thus, in Dodson[36] the Court of Appeal refused to prevent a jury from comparing the men in the dock with the men in the photographs. In that case the defendants concerned were involved in an attempted armed robbery at the offices of a building society. During the attempt two security cameras were activated and began taking photographs of the men involved in the raid. The Court held that the photographs had been rightly admitted in evidence and rejected a submission that they should have been excluded because they had not been identified as depicting the defendants by a witness competent to make any identification. However, the Court said that the judge must warn the jury of the perils of convicting on such evidence and direct them as to the significance of factors such as the quality of the photographs, exposure of the person depicted and any change in the defendant's appearance. In Downey[37] a differently constituted Court of Appeal said that there was no invariable rule that a warning had to be given: the appropriate direction depended on the circumstances of each case and, if no special factors arose, the absence of a specific direction could not amount to a misdirection. On the other hand, it is submitted that it is usually prudent to give a direction, if only to bring

---

[33] Dodson (1984) 79 Cr.App.R. 220, cited para.2–14, below.
[34] Statue of Liberty [1968] 1 W.L.R. 739, cited para.2–43, below.
[35] [1864] 4 F.&.F. 103.
[36] (1984) 79 Cr.App.R. 220.
[37] [1995] 1 Cr.App.R. 547, 556.

home to the jury the importance of being sure about the identification. Thus, in *Blenkinsop*[38] the Court of Appeal held that a *Turnbull* direction on identification (para.14–03, below) is not appropriate or necessary in such cases provided that the jury are warned of the risk of mistaken identification and of the need to exercise particular care in any identification which they make for themselves.

An expert witness may assist the jury in making an identification. It is for the judge to decide whether the jury would be assisted by expert evidence and whether the witness is sufficiently expert to give it: *Stockwell*[39] (in which "facial mapping" evidence was admitted to identify a defendant in a case where photographs of a robber in disguise had been taken by a security camera and identification was more difficult because the defendant had grown a beard shortly before arrest). In *Clarke*[40] the Court of Appeal said that "facial mapping" was a species of real evidence in the interpretation of which assistance could be given by an expert.

2–15

If such evidence is admitted the judge must direct the jury that it is for them, not the expert, to decide whether the defendant is the offender. In these circumstances it is submitted that it will be unusual for expert evidence to be admitted and that juries can normally be left to decide issues of identification for themselves.

6. TAPE RECORDINGS

The Royal Commission on Criminal Procedure in 1981 recommended the introduction of tape recording of police interviews.[41] The arguments in favour of such a course were: (a) to produce an accurate record of the interview; (b) to provide a check on police conduct; and (c) to prevent lengthy disputes as to admissibility. Tape recording of police interviews is now in force throughout England and Wales. This development was welcome. It has the additional advantage that the jury is much better able to judge the quality of an interview when they can actually hear it. As a result of these developments the use of tape recordings became a common feature of criminal trials.

2–16

A. Admissibility

Tape recordings of conversations or other sounds are admissible to prove the conversations or sounds recorded on the tape. They are admissible because the tape recorder provides a means of recording and reproducing

2–17

---

[38] [1995] 1 Cr.App.R. 7.
[39] (1993) 97 Cr.App.R. 260.
[40] [1995] 2 Cr.App.R. 425 at 429.
[41] Report, Cmnd. 8092 (1981), paras 4.25–4.30.

sounds. Thus, once a tape recording has been proved, it is evidence of the sounds or conversation recorded.

It was established that this evidence was admissible in *Maqsud Ali*.[42] In that case M and A were charged with the murder of A's wife. They went voluntarily to the police station where they were taken to a room in which there was a hidden microphone. A tape recording was made of a conversation in Punjabi between them. The recording was imperfect, but part was decipherable and amounted to a confession to murder. The Court of Appeal held that a tape recording is admissible in evidence providing (i) that the evidence is relevant, and is otherwise admissible, and (ii) that the accuracy of the recording can be proved and the voices properly identified. The Court said that there could be no question of laying down rules by which admissibility could be judged. However, a court must first apply the usual rules relating to relevance and admissibility. If the material on a tape is irrelevant or falls foul of any of the exclusionary rules, it cannot be admitted.

2–18   If there is a challenge to the accuracy of a tape the court must satisfy itself of its provenance and authenticity before admitting it. This may require the judge to hear evidence and to conduct an inquiry into these matters (involving a departure from the usual rule that the weight of evidence is for the jury to determine). In *Robson and Harris*[43] Shaw J. conducted such an inquiry. He heard evidence on both sides about the history and condition of certain tapes and directed himself that he was required to do no more in relation to determining their provenance than to satisfy himself that a prima facie case of originality had been made out. It is submitted, with respect, that this direction is correct: to do more, as Shaw J. remarked, would be to trespass on the function of the jury.

2–19   The burden of establishing a condition of admissibility normally falls on the party seeking to adduce the evidence. There is no reason why these circumstances should form an exception to the general rule. Accordingly, since the prosecution generally wish to adduce evidence of tape recordings, the burden of establishing the conditions of admissibility will generally be on them. There is no clear authority as to what standard of proof should be applied in these circumstances. In *Stevenson*,[44] a trial at Nottingham Assizes, it was contended that the prosecution had to establish admissibility beyond reasonable doubt, but no decision was made on the point.

In *Robson and Harris* Shaw J. accepted that he should decide the question of admissibility on the balance of probabilities. However, as a general rule, where questions of fact have to be determined in relation to admissibility the prosecution have to establish admissibility beyond reasonable doubt. It is not clear why this case should be an exception. It is submitted

---

[42] [1966] 1 Q.B. 688.
[43] (1972) 56 Cr.App.R. 450.
[44] (1971) 55 Cr.App.R. 171.

that the criminal standard should apply when the prosecution seek to produce tapes (a) for reasons of consistency; and (b) because if the authenticity of a tape cannot be established beyond reasonable doubt a case based on it cannot be said to be proved.

On the other hand, the burden of proof of an issue when it falls on the defence in a criminal trial is not as high as that which falls on the prosecution. As a result, the civil standard would appear to be appropriate when the defence seek to produce tapes.

The judge has a discretion to exclude a tape recording if it would be prejudicial or unfair to admit it. The Court of Appeal said in *Maqsud Ali* that the method of taking the recording cannot affect admissibility as a matter of law, although it must remain very much a matter of discretion for the judge. However, in *Maqsud Ali* the tape recording was admitted although obtained by eavesdropping, while in *Senat and Sin*[45] tape recordings of conversations obtained by telephone tapping by a private individual were admitted. In these circumstances admissibility would now be governed by s.78 of the Police and Criminal Evidence Act 1984 which obliges the Court to consider all the circumstances, including the circumstances in which the evidence was obtained, in deciding whether it would be unfair to admit the evidence: see para.10–13, below for a discussion of s.78.

The admissibility into evidence in any legal proceedings of interceptions of postal and telephone communications, "intercepts" is now governed by the Regulation of Investigatory Powers Act 2000.[46] The effect of ss.17 and 18 of the Act is to provide (with exceptions) that no evidence should be adduced, disclosure made or questions asked which disclose an intercept made as a result of an unlawful interception (an offence under s.1 of the Act) or the issue of a warrant under the Act[47]; or that anything has or may have occurred in relation to such actions.[48] The exceptions include proceedings for any offence under the Act[49] or where the intercept was lawful

2–20

2–21

---

[45] (1968) 52 Cr.App.R. 282.
[46] This Act repeals ss.1–10 of the Interception of Communications Act 1985: 2000 Act, s.82, Sch.5. The 1985 Act is, however, preserved as regards actions lawfully undertaken under it, *e.g.* interception warrants issued under the Act. For a full discussion of the effect of the Human Rights Act 1998 on this legislation, see Mirfield, "Regulation of Investigatory Powers Act 2000: Evidential Aspects" [2000] Crim.L.R. 91. For the 1985 Act, and cases decided under it, see the 4th edition of this work and the Online Supplement, ss.2–21. There is now in force, as from July 1, 2002, a Code of Practice relating to the interception of communications: Regulation of Investigatory Powers (Interception of Communications: Code of Practice) Order (SI 2002/1693). The Court of Appeal, in *Att-Gen's Reference (No.5 of 2002)* [2004] 1 Cr.App.R. 11 criticised RIPA as being "puzzling" and "difficult". See also Ormerod and Mackay, "Telephone Intercepts and their Admissibility" [2004] Crim.L.R. 15.
[47] s.17(1)(a) of the Act. The section also covers warrants under the 1985 Act.
[48] s.17(1)(b). s.17 makes "wholly inadmissible the result of interception, properly so-called, where it is conducted under warrant of the Home Secretary ... or where an offence has been committed under section 1 ... Apart from that, however, it is a fallacy to submit that s.17 makes inadmissible the contents of an interception. It does so only where s.17(1) applies ...", *Hardy* [2003] Cr.App.R. 494, 504.
[49] s.18(1)(a).

for a reason not involving a warrant.[50] The effect of the section is to provide for the inadmissibility of intercepts and their contents: this is because it will usually be impossible to adduce evidence about the contents of an intercept without adducing evidence about its origins which the section forbids in most cases. However, to prevent injustice in the individual case, disclosure is permitted to a prosecutor for the purpose of enabling him to determine what is required of him by his duty to secure the fairness of the prosecution, and to a judge who has ordered disclosure to himself alone[51]: if the judge is then of the opinion that there are exceptional circumstances requiring him to do so, he may direct the prosecutor to make such admission of fact as the judge thinks essential in the interests of justice.[52] Thus, the prosecutor and judge will be under a duty to ensure that relevant, exculpatory evidence is not withheld by reason of the prohibitions under the Act and, if necessary, can be put before the jury by means of a proper admission.

Finally, it may be noted that the Act relates to intercepts in the UK[53] and to systems and services located in the UK.[54] Under the predecessor Act of 1985[55] it was held that pager messages transmitted from Holland were not transmitted by a public telecommunications system within the Act[56]; and that where an intercept was made in a foreign country by the authorities of that country, the Act did not apply and public policy did not make this evidence inadmissible in England.[57] Likewise, "interception" does not include, under the 2000 Act, the recording of a telephone call by one party to the call.[58]

B. Procedure for recording and documentation

2–22   The Code of Practice E on Tape Recording issued by the Home Secretary under s.60 of the Police and Criminal Evidence Act 1984 establishes a procedure to be followed by police officers when recording interviews.[59] There is provision in the Code for the suspect to be told formally about the tape recording and to be cautioned. The Code also lays down procedures

---

[50] s.18(4).
[51] s.18(7). The judge may only order disclosure if satisfied that the exceptional circumstances of the case make it essential in the interests of justice: s.18(8).
[52] s.18(9).
[53] s.1(1) of the Act.
[54] s.2(1). Note that RIPA, s.1 includes private telecommunication systems (subs.(2)).
[55] Interception of Communications Act 1985.
[56] *Taylor-Sabori* [1999] 1 Cr.App.R. 437.
[57] *P* [2001] 2 Cr.App.R. 8 (HL).
[58] *Hardy* [2003] 1 Cr.App.R. 494.
[59] A revised Code was brought into operation on April 10, 1995. S.76 of the Criminal Justice and Police Act 2001 enacted a new section (60A) of the Police and Criminal Evidence Act 1984 enabling the Secretary of State to issue a Code of Practice for the visual recording of interviews at police stations and to make requiring such recording to be in accordance with the Code.

for interviewing the suspect, recording any objections and recording the interview.

There may be objection to the admissibility of a tape on the ground that the police have not followed the Code of Practice. The court must then take account of any relevant breach in deciding whether the tape should be admitted or not: s.67(11) of the Police and Criminal Evidence Act 1984. However, in *Delaney*[60] the Court of Appeal held that the fact that the Code of Practice relating to the questioning of suspects had not been followed did not necessarily mean that a confession should be excluded: it was a matter for the judge's discretion as to the weight to be given to the breach. It would appear that the same principle should apply to tape recordings.

In the case of a police interview which has been tape recorded, the interviewing officer should have a written record prepared, summarising the interview and containing a balanced account of it.[61] The defendant's solicitors and unrepresented defendants have the right of access to such tapes provided the right is exercised reasonably.[62] If the solicitor requests it, he should normally be sent a copy. There is no requirement that the solicitor listen to the tape in every case.[63] It may well be necessary in many contested cases but not all, *e.g.* where the defendant accepts that the police summary is correct and says that he added nothing material in the interview.

2–23

Producing a balanced summary may not be an easy matter. Even an experienced lawyer may find it difficult. Accordingly, the summary should be checked to ensure that it reflects what was said in interview. On the other hand, in many cases, a summary will be of greater assistance to the jury than the playing of the tape which may be repetitive and difficult to follow.

It is not anticipated that a transcript (*i.e.* a written record of what is heard on the tape), will be produced in the ordinary case. The Royal Commission on Criminal Procedure recommended that such preparation be kept to a minimum.[64] However, in some cases the preparation of a transcript will be necessary, for example those involving interviews containing complicated detail which can only be followed satisfactorily with the assistance of a transcript.

In the case of tape recordings of conversations other than police inter-

2–24

---

[60] (1989) 88 Cr.App.R. 338, 341.
[61] The summary is to be prepared in accordance with national guidelines approved by the Home Secretary: Code E 5A. The guidelines are to be found in the Home Office Circular 26/1995, an amended version of the Home Office Circular 21/1992 (now withdrawn). The main change is to allow for the involvement of other persons than the interviewing officer (including civilian staff) in the preparation of the record.
[62] The Tape Recording of Police Interviews with Suspects: Field Trials: Procedural Guidance, Home Office, 1983.
[63] Statement approved by the Standing Committee on Criminal Law of the Law Society, quoted in the procedural guidance mentioned above.
[64] Cmnd. 8092 (1981), para.4.23.

views, transcripts are frequently provided. In these cases the recordings are not usually made in circumstances as ideal as those to be found in the police interviewing room. As a result, the voices may be indistinct or there may be extraneous noise on the tape. In such cases a transcript is necessary to assist the jury in understanding what was said.

If a recording is made of a conversation in a foreign language or a suspect is interviewed through an interpreter an English translation must be prepared. Indeed, the recording can only be put before the jury with an accompanying translation. In the circumstances, the translator must prove in evidence that his translation is a record of what he heard on the tape, correctly rendered into English.[65]

C. Procedure at trial

2–25   1. In most cases, it is anticipated that the summary of the tape recorded interview contained in the interviewing officer's statement will be sufficient for evidential purposes. In these cases it will not be necessary to play the tape. The fact that counsel agree that a summary should be put before the jury will not prevent the tape itself being played. For instance, if an issue emerges during the trial which can only be resolved by playing the tape, it should be admitted.[66] Indeed, the tape may be played after the speeches of counsel (provided that no injustice would be done thereby to the defendant).[67]

2. In other cases where a transcript of the tape recording has been prepared, the defence will agree that the transcript is correct. In these cases the transcript can be read and the tape need not be played.

3. The procedure for the preparation of transcripts and editing of tapes is now governed by the *Practice Direction (Evidence of Tape Recorded Interviews)*.[68] The *Practice Direction* lays down a timetable to be followed if the parties are unable to agree a record of interview and specifies that editing should be based on the usual principles: discussed at para.9–54, below.

4. If it is necessary to produce the tape, the interviewing officer or any other officer present at the interview should produce and prove it: *Practice Direction*, above. The officer should listen to the tape before the trial. He can then give evidence as to who spoke the recorded words and deal with questions of accuracy and suggestions of falsification.[69] In the case of recordings other than police interviews, the person who made the tape recording must produce it.

---

[65] *Fakisandhla Nkambule v R* [1940] A.C. 760, 771.
[66] *Sinclair, The Times,* September 9, 1992.
[67] *Aitken* (1992) 94 Cr.App.R. 85.
[68] Consolidated Criminal Practice Direction 43 [2002] 2 Cr.App.R. 533, 568.
[69] *Rampling* [1987] Crim.L.R. 823. The Court of Appeal in *Rampling* provided the courts with guidance concerning tape recorded interviews and the use of transcripts.

5. The tape is then played to the jury.[70] In this way the court obtains the **2–26**
evidence of the conversation or other sounds recorded. If the authenticity of
the tape is in issue, the jury must be satisfied of its authenticity beyond
reasonable doubt before relying on its contents.[71] It is then for the jury to
determine what was said, if this be in dispute. It is also for the jury to decide
what weight to give to the evidence.

6. Once the tape has been played, it is normally made an exhibit. It is
then available for reference during the trial. Parts can be played during
counsel's speeches and the summing-up. The jury, if they wish, should be
able to hear it after they have retired to consider their verdict.[72] In an
appropriate case they may be able to hear it in their room. It is not
improper for the judge to allow them to do so.[73] On the other hand, it may
be more appropriate for the parts which they wish to hear to be played to
them in court, for example if there is a danger that they will receive a partial
or misleading impression of the evidence on a particular point unless all the
relevant parts are played to them.

In *Emmerson*[74] the Court of Appeal said that if any part of the tape had **2–27**
been played in court the jury could take (a) the whole tape if they had a
transcript, but (b) only that part played in court if they had no transcript.
The Court of Appeal also said that there was no need for the trial judge to
re-assemble the court to hear passages already heard in open court. However, in *Riaz and Burke*,[75] a differently constituted Court of Appeal
disagreed and said that, while it was a matter for the judge's discretion, the
better practice was for the jury to be brought back and for the tape to be
played in open court. While it is submitted that this is the appropriate
course in most cases, particularly where a tape has been edited, it must be
doubted whether it is necessary if the interview is straightforward and
neither side objects. Thus in *Tonge*[76] the Court said the judge should
normally require the tape to be played in open court unless he thought it
more convenient for the jury to hear it in their room.

If the tape is to be heard in the jury room, the court must make
arrangements. Normally this will present no difficulty. It will be a matter
for the court to ensure that no injustice is done. In *Dempster*[77] the Court of
Appeal held that there had been no material irregularity in a case where
arrangements had been made for the jury to communicate by radio to a
technician in court who played the required part to them in their room. The

---

[70] Counsel should indicate the parts which it is necessary to play in order to avoid the playing
of irrelevant matter: *Practice Direction*, above.
[71] *Robson and Harris* [1972] 1 W.L.R. 651.
[72] *Emmerson* (1991) 92 Cr.App.R. 284.
[73] In *Tonge* [1993] Crim.L.R. 876, the Court of Appeal said that this course was not improper
when the jury had heard the tape and had a transcript.
[74] Above, at 287.
[75] (1992) 94 Cr.App.R. 339, 344.
[76] [1993] Crim.L.R. 876.
[77] (1980) 71 Cr.App.R. 302.

Court said that some system had to be devised for the jury to hear the tape in order to assess the evidence given by experts about it and it was impracticable for them to have to come into court every time they wished to hear it.

7. If, after retirement, a jury who have been provided with a transcript wish to hear a tape which has not been played in open court they should be allowed to do so: *Riaz and Burke,* above. They may wish to do so, for instance, to assess the tone of voice on the recording. However, the judge must first consider whether in the particular circumstances of the case it is fair to allow the tape to be played for the first time after the jury have retired.[78]

2–28   8. If the tape is available, secondary evidence of its contents should not be admitted (except in the circumstances mentioned above, where there is no dispute about the contents). If it is available the tape should be played.

On the other hand, if there is difficulty in deciphering what is said on the tape, the evidence of a person who has heard it several times may be admissible to assist the jury.[79] In *Hopes and Lavery v H.M. Advocate*[80] the High Court of Justiciary doubted whether the evidence of an unskilled person was admissible for this purpose. (In that case a tape recording of a conversation between a blackmailer and his victim had been played to the jury. A typist made a shorthand analysis of what she heard on the tape after hearing it played several times.) However, as was pointed out, the difficulty would be overcome if the prosecution could call a witness skilled in the interpretation of tape recordings. Such an expert may be able to decipher the sounds on the recording by using machinery which repeats particular parts of the tape. Thus, in *Robb*[81] the Court of Appeal held that evidence of voice identification given by a suitably qualified expert was admissible even if he used a technique supported by a minority of his profession.

9. If the original tape is not available, the court may admit a copy in order to prove the sounds or conversation recorded, provided that the court is satisfied of the provenance and authenticity of the original tape and the copy tape. Thus, the Divisional Court held in *Kajala v Noble*[82] that justices were entitled to rely on a copy of a film shown on a BBC television news bulletin provided that they were satisfied that it was an authentic copy of the original. The court said that the old rule that a party must produce the

---

[78] *Hagan* [1997] 1 Cr.App.R. 464.
[79] If an expert gives evidence about voice identity the tapes on which he has worked in forming his opinion are admissible in evidence: *Bentum* (1989) 153 J.P. 583.
[80] 1960 S.C.(J). 104.
[81] (1991) 93 Cr.App.R. 161. It may be noted that *Robb* was not followed by the Court of Appeal in Northern Ireland in *O'Doherty* [2002] Crim.L.R. 761: that Court expressed no confidence (in the present state of scientific knowledge) in voice identification solely based on auditory analysis (*i.e.* one dealing principally with accent or dialect), as opposed to acoustic analysis which examined the acoustic properties of the speech. However, the emphasis must be on the suitability of the qualification of the witness rather than its type.
[82] (1982) 75 Cr.App.R. 149.

best evidence was limited to written documents and had no relevance to tapes and films.

10. If neither original nor copy is available it would seem that the court, if satisfied that the absence of the tape can be explained satisfactorily, may receive secondary evidence of its contents from a witness who has heard it. This evidence would not be hearsay because A is not repeating what B told him, but what he (A) heard on the tape.[83]   **2–29**

11. If a transcript has been prepared, the interviewing officer (or other officer present at the interview) may produce it, provided that he has first checked its accuracy against the tape: there is no need to call the audio-typist.[84] Of course, if the typist is called he can produce the transcript and prove it as an accurate record of what he heard on the tape.

12. Once a transcript is produced, copies are usually given to the jury to assist them in following the evidence and to take with them into the jury room when they retire. In most cases copies go before the jury without dispute. However, if there is a dispute, the judge will have to decide whether to allow the jury to have copies or not. In *Rampling*[85] the defence objected to a transcript going before the jury on the ground that it was not evidence and could not be produced to the jury without the consent of the defence. The Court of Appeal held that the judge had correctly exercised his discretion in allowing the jury to have the transcript: the consent of the prosecution and defence was not required; the transcript is an administrative convenience comparable to a schedule and its use is a matter to be decided within the judge's discretion.

In many cases it is essential that the jury have a transcript. If they did not,   **2–30** the recording would have to be played over time and again, for example cases where the sound quality is poor. In *Maqsud Ali*[86] the Court of Appeal held that the jury may have a copy of the transcript, properly proved, provided that they are guided by what they hear themselves and base their decisions upon that.

13. If a translation is produced, it will usually be appropriate for it to be exhibited and for the jury to have copies.[87] This is for reasons of practicality. If the jury do not have copies, they cannot follow the case. Thus, in the Australian case of *Butera v DPP (Vic.)*[88] a tape recording had been made of a conversation in English and other languages. Two interpreters listened to the tape and prepared English translations. At the trial the tape was played to the jury and the interpreters listened to the tape and produced and verified their respective translations in evidence. The translations were exhibited and copies given to the jury. The High Court of Australia held

[83] *Butera v DPP (Vic.)* (1988) 76 A.L.R. 45, 48 (High Court of Australia).
[84] *Rampling* [1987] Crim.L.R. 823.
[85] Above.
[86] [1966] 1 Q.B. 688.
[87] *Maqsud Ali*, above.
[88] (1988) 76 A.L.R. 45.

that this course was appropriate because if the jury had not had the copies it would have been impossible for the jury to follow the lengthy cross-examination relating to the translations.

7. VIDEO RECORDINGS

A. Admissibility

2–31   Video recordings are admissible as real evidence to prove what is recorded on the tape, *i.e.* what was to be seen happening at a particular place and time.[89] They are admissible on the same principles and for the same reasons as photographs and tape recordings. (For a discussion of the admissibility of video recordings of interviews with vulnerable witnesses see paras 19–24 *et seq.*, below.)

The same principles of admissibility apply both to video and tape recordings. These principles have already been considered at paras 2–17 *et seq.*, above. They may be summarised in relation to video recordings as follows:

(a) the authenticity and provenance of the recording must be established;

(b) the recording must be relevant to an issue in the case;

(c) the usual exclusionary rules apply;

(d) the judge has a discretion to exclude a recording which it would be unfair to admit under the provisions of s.78 of the Police and Criminal Evidence Act 1984 or the common law discretion retained by the Act.[90]

If the original recording is not available, a copy is admissible provided that the court is satisfied of its authenticity.[91] If neither original nor copy is available, a witness may give evidence of what he saw on the recording. In *Taylor v Chief Constable of Cheshire*[92] the Divisional Court held that the evidence of witnesses who had seen a video recording of the defendant shoplifting was admissible although the tape had been accidentally erased before the trial. The court said that there was no distinction as far as admissibility was concerned between a direct view, a view on the visual display unit of a camera and a view on a recording.

---

[89] For a discussion of the use of video-technology in England and Canada, see Goldstein, "Video-technology in the Criminal Courts of the United Kingdom and Canada" (1989) 53 J.C.L. 215.

[90] The exercise of the discretion is discussed in Ch.12, below.

[91] *Kajala v Noble* cited at para.2–28, above.

[92] [1986] 1 W.L.R. 1479; (1986) 84 Cr.App.R.191.

When a witness gives evidence of what he has seen on a video recording, **2–32** no question of hearsay arises. The witness gives evidence of what he has seen in the same way that a witness gives evidence of something which he has seen when he had a direct view of an occurrence. It would therefore appear contrary to common sense to exclude such evidence. However, questions of its weight and reliability are matters which the court will have to consider. In *Taylor* the Divisional Court said that the court must hesitate and consider very carefully before convicting on such evidence. It would seem right to give a jury a warning in similar terms.

Once a recording is produced it becomes an exhibit in the case. It may then be referred to at other stages of the trial. The jury may see parts of it again during their retirement. This will normally mean their returning to court. This has the advantage that the recording is shown in the presence of the parties and all the parts relevant to a particular incident can be shown so that the jury has a full—and not a partial—picture of the incident; and to ensure that no improper use of the recording is made by the jury. Thus in *Imran and Hussain*[93] the Court of Appeal said that there can be no objection to a jury seeing a police surveillance video (played in evidence) again after they have retired: however, it should be played in open court.

B. Video recordings as evidence

A video recording may be made which shows the commission of crime, for **2–33** example television film of a riot. Such a recording is then admissible in evidence to prove both that the crime was committed and the identity of the offenders. A recording may show the aftermath of a crime or something connected with the investigation, for example the scene of a crime, an identification parade,[94] or the route of a car chase.[95] The tape will then speak for itself and may be shown in court without comment. It will be for the jury to determine what weight to give the evidence and what inferences to draw from it. A witness may not, of course, give his opinion that what he saw on a video recording amounted to the commission of a crime: that is a matter for the jury to decide.

If a video recording of an event comes to light after a witness has made a statement, he may be shown the recording and, if necessary, modify his statement provided that the procedure adopted did not taint the evidence or amount to rehearsal of the evidence.[96]

---

[93] [1997] Crim.L.R. 754.
[94] While it is permissible to film an identification parade or group identification so that the court will have an impression of the circumstances in which a witness made an identification, the witness should not be shown the recording before giving evidence to try to improve his evidence as to identification: see *Smith and Doe* (1987) 85 Cr.App.R. 197.
[95] *e.g. Thomas* [1986] Crim. L.R. 682.
[96] *Roberts* [1998] Crim.L.R. 682. Lord Bingham C.J. said in *Roberts* that the growing use of video evidence merited detailed consideration with a view to devising a code of practice.

C. Interpreting the recording

2–34   Once a tape is admitted in evidence any question relating to its interpretation is ultimately for the tribunal of fact, *i.e.* the jury or magistrates, to
determine. It is for them to decide what the tape reveals, for example
whether the activities shown amount to the commission of an offence or
whether the offender shown is the defendant. It is also for the tribunal to
decide what weight to give the evidence shown and what inferences to draw
from it. As a general rule, no evidence is admissible to explain the tape and
it is produced and played or shown to the court without comment. In most
cases no other evidence is needed and none should be given. There are
exceptions to this rule as follows:

(1) Eye-witnesses

2–35   If a witness himself made a videotape of an event he is entitled to
authenticate it, produce it in evidence and describe what he saw by reference to it. Similarly, if the tape was made by another witness and produced
in evidence by him, an eye-witness of the events shown on the tape may be
asked about incidents which he saw. Such a witness may be asked to look at
the tape and say what is happening; he may also be asked to identify people
he knows. He is not then giving evidence of opinion since he is describing
(a) something he himself saw and (b) somebody he recognises.

(2) Experts

2–36   An expert may give evidence about incidents within his field of expertise
which are shown on a tape. Thus, if a video recording of a game of cards or
chance were shown to a jury, a suitably qualified expert could give evidence
explaining how the game was played and explaining the steps in the game
as they appeared on the recording. Without such evidence the jury would be
completely in the dark.

(3) Identifying witnesses

2–37   If the identification of a defendant on a video recording is in dispute, a
witness who knows him may give evidence identifying him as the person on
the recording. This is because there is no distinction between the evidence
of a witness who sees an occurrence and recognises somebody he knows
and a witness seeing somebody he knows on videotape. In *Grimer*[97] a
security officer saw the tape and recognised the thief as the defendant whom
he knew. The Court of Appeal held that the evidence of the security officer
was admissible to identify the defendant. But where the prejudicial effect
outweighs probative value, the court should exclude the evidence, as in

---

[97] [1982] Crim.L.R. 674.

Fowden and White[98] where the witnesses who identified the defendants knew them from a similar offence committed a week later. However, the mere fact that a police officer's knowledge of a defendant comes from the latter's criminal activities cannot operate to bar this type of evidence: that would give an unfair advantage to criminals.[99]

There is clearly a danger of misidentification in such cases, particularly if the tape recording is not clear or the suspect is under arrest at the police station. Accordingly, the Court of Appeal in *Caldwell*[1] recommended that procedures be instituted for regulating the showing of recordings in cases where there were known suspects. (The Court pointed out that there was an analogy with the showing of photographs to a witness in order to identify a suspect (para.14–35, below).)

The same rules may also apply in the case of a witness who does not   2–38
know the accused, provided that by close study he has made himself sufficiently familiar with the material on which the identification is based so that he can assist the court with his special knowledge. In *Clare and Peach*[2] a number of defendants were charged with offences involving violent disorder following a football match. There was an unclear video recording of the actual events together with better quality film and photographs taken before and during the match. A police constable made a lengthy and detailed comparison of the video and the film and photographs and was thus able to identify the defendants as being among the perpetrators of the violent acts. The Court of Appeal held that the constable's evidence was admissible because he had acquired special knowledge which the Court did not possess by lengthy and studious application to material which was itself admissible evidence; and to afford the jury the time and facilities to conduct the same research would be impracticable. The Court said that it was legitimate to allow the constable to assist the jury by pointing to what he asserted was happening on the film and to identify the individual actors: such identifications were not secondary evidence and, although the officer did not know the defendants, he was well-qualified to identify them as a result of his repeated study of their likenesses on the colour film and photographs.[3]

A further example is to be found in a similar case in New Zealand, *Howe*.[4] In that case a police officer, having viewed video-tapes of a riot and studied films and photographs, was allowed to give evidence identifying individual defendants and describing what they appeared to be doing. The New Zealand Court of Appeal said that the police officer should be regarded as sufficiently "expert ad hoc" to give identification evidence and

---

[98] [1982] Crim.L.R. 588.
[99] *Caldwell* (1994) 99 Cr.App.R. 73.
[1] *ibid.*
[2] [1995] 2 Cr.App.R. 333.
[3] At 338–339.
[4] [1982] N.Z.L.R. 618.

held that his evidence was admissible as an aid to the jury in a case where the action was confused. In *Clare and Peach* the Court of Appeal (although not commenting on whether the phrase "expert ad hoc" was appropriate or not) said that the trial judge was right to follow *Howe*.[5]

D. Commentary by non-experts

2–39   The general rule is that a witness must not state an opinion about the evidence. He may say what he saw, heard or did but not what he believes or thinks (see Ch.6). Should there be an exception in cases where the tape may be difficult to interpret without assistance, for example a tape showing a confused piece of action? In *Clare and Peach*, above, the Court of Appeal held that such evidence was admissible from a witness (who had made a close study of the material) in order to assist the jury: the Court pointed out that the witness was subject to cross-examination and the jury, after proper direction and warnings, were free to accept or reject his assertions. A commentary has also been admitted for practical reasons in New Zealand and Scotland. In *Howe*[6] the New Zealand Court of Appeal said that while a commentary would not be proper for a film of activities of a simple kind, it was a field where much was to be left to the trial judge's discretion and that economy, convenience and despatch would commend the admission of a commentary in a case where the action was more complicated and confused. Similarly, in a Scottish case, *Steele v H.M. Advocate*,[7] witnesses, apparently without challenge, gave evidence of what they believed they saw on videotapes of police surveillance. The Lord Justice General said that it was undesirable for a trial to be prolonged by a long series of re-playings of the tape and it was likely to be of advantage for witnesses to give their own opinion as to what is being shown on the tape in order that the minds of the jury can be directed to the relevant points while the tape is being played.

2–40   It is submitted that a similarly practical approach should be normally adopted in order to prevent the jury being deprived of necessary assistance. Accordingly, the judge has a discretion to admit such evidence provided (a) the jury require assistance in interpreting the tape because, without it, the significance of what is shown would not be apparent; (b) the witness is thoroughly familiar with the material; and (c) the jury are directed that ultimately it is for them to decide whether they accept the witness's evidence or not.

---

[5] The decision in *Clare and Peach* has been criticised (a) as allowing the witness (effectively) to give evidence about the ultimate issue which the court has to decide; see Munday, "Videotape Evidence and the Advent of the Expert Ad Hoc" (1995) 159 J.P. 547; and (b) as allowing the witness too great an influence on the issue of identification; see Elliott, "Video Tape Evidence: The Risk of Over-Persuasion" [1998] Crim.L.R. 159. However, those difficulties can normally be overcome by appropriate direction to the jury; and (in the case of summary trial) by the justices keeping in mind that they are the ultimate judges of fact.
[6] Above.
[7] 1992 S.C.C.R. 30.

E. Re-enactments

Re-enactments of crime on film or video recording are regarded by the courts with caution because of the danger that they may give a false or misleading impression of the actual event. In *Quinn and Bloom*[8] Quinn was charged with keeping a disorderly house. The prosecution alleged that an obscene striptease act was performed at his club. He sought to adduce in evidence a film of a striptease act intended to be a reconstruction of the act on which the prosecution was based. The Court of Criminal Appeal held that this evidence was inadmissible because it would be impossible to make an accurate reconstruction.[9]

2–41

However, different considerations may apply when a defendant re-enacts a crime to which he has already confessed. In *Li Shu-Ling v R*[10] the defendant had made an oral confession to the murder of a woman. Two days later the police invited the defendant to re-enact the killing at the scene of the crime while a video recording was made. The defendant agreed to this course. He then re-enacted the killing with a woman police officer playing the part of the victim. A video recording was made with a running commentary by the defendant explaining his movements. At the trial the video recording was admitted in evidence. The Privy Council held that a video recording of the re-enactment of a crime by the defendant is admissible in evidence even if another person participated in it. The Privy Council said that there was no distinction in principle between admitting a video recording of a confession including a re-enactment, and admitting a recording of a re-enactment at the scene of the crime. Such a recording must be made reasonably soon after the confession. The defendant must be given a warning that he need not take part and must do so voluntarily. The Privy Council also said that the recording should be shown to the accused as soon as practicable after it has been completed and he should be given the opportunity to make and have recorded any comments he wishes about the film.

The Privy Council in *Li Shu-Ling* distinguished *Quinn and Bloom* on the ground that the film in the latter case was self-serving evidence which would be suspect because of the ease with which the performance could be altered. It is submitted, with respect, that the Privy Council's decision accords with common sense and principle. It is common for a defendant to demonstrate to police officers during an interview. He may, for instance, get up from the table and show them how he did something, if necessary using one of the officers to show what he did. If he volunteered to take the officers to the scene of the crime to demonstrate what he had done, they could give evidence of his demonstration. The video recording merely records what he

2–42

---

[8] [1962] Q.B.245.
[9] The court said that the evidence was not the "best evidence". However, the best evidence rule is now in disuse: para.1–11, above.
[10] (1988) 88 Cr.App.R. 82.

did. The court may then see it, instead of having to rely on the verbal description of a witness.

Accordingly, if it is proposed to adduce a video recording of a re-enactment in evidence, it is submitted that the court will have to be satisfied before admitting it, either (a) that the conditions mentioned in *Li Shu-Ling* have been met, or (b) that it is such an accurate reconstruction that it can be put before the jury without the risk of creating a misleading impression.

8. AUTOMATIC RECORDINGS

2–43   The principles applicable to tape recordings apply to recordings made automatically by recording or measuring machines. The fact that the recording is produced mechanically without human intervention makes no difference.

In the *Statue of Liberty*,[11] an action arising from a collision between two ships, the plaintiff sought to adduce in evidence film of echoes recorded by radar apparatus on shore. The defendant objected on the grounds that it (a) was evidence produced mechanically without human intervention and (b) offended the hearsay rule. Sir Jocelyn Simon P. held that it was admissible as real evidence. He said:

> "If tape recordings are admissible it seems that a photograph of radar reception is equally admissible or indeed any other type of photograph. It would be an absurd distinction that a photograph should be admissible if the camera were operated manually by a photographer, but not if it were operated by a trip or clock mechanism. Similarly, if evidence of weather conditions were relevant, the law would affront common sense if it were to say that those could be proved by a person who looked at a barometer from time to time, but not by producing a barograph record. So, too, with other types of dial recordings. Again, cards from clocking in and out machines are frequently admitted in accident cases"[12]

2–44   The same principles apply to recordings produced by a computer, provided that it is being used as a recording machine or calculator. Thus in *Wood*[13] the Court of Appeal held that a computer printout showing the results of certain calculations made by the computer was admissible as real evidence: the computer was being used as a calculator and the printout showed the result of its calculations. Similarly, the Divisional Court held in *Castle v Cross*[14] that a printout produced as a result of a test by an

---

[11] [1968] 1 W.L.R. 739.
[12] At 740.
[13] (1982) 76 Cr.App.R. 23.
[14] [1984] 1 W.L.R. 1372.

Intoximeter breach testing device was admissible as real evidence: it was "the product of a mechanical device which falls into the same category of real evidence as that indicated by Sir Jocelyn Simon in the *Statue of Liberty*."[15]

In these cases information had not been entered into the computer by means of human intervention. If a human had entered information the recording would have been hearsay and not real evidence. See new s.129 of the Criminal Justice Act 2003,[16] paras 8–75 to 8–76, below.

---

[15] At 1378–1379.
[16] At the time of writing, the section is due to come into effect on April 1, 2005.

CHAPTER 3

Documents

3–01 A party wishing to rely on the contents of a document must first prove it, *i.e.* adduce it in evidence. In general, the proof of documents does not create difficulties in criminal trials. Their admissibility is not usually disputed.

For this reason, the provisions for proving documents may be considered concisely. The general rule is that primary evidence of the document must be given. This rule is subject to a number of exceptions, in particular in the case of public and judicial documents. The meaning and classification of documents is first considered.

1. Meaning and Classification

3–02 In general speech, a document is taken to mean something written which furnishes information.[1] The writing is usually thought of as being on a piece of paper. However, it is the writing which is of significance, not the object on which it is written. Darling J. said that any written thing capable of being evidence is properly described as a document, no matter what material it was written on.[2] (As Darling J. pointed out, it was once common to write on parchment and, before that, on stone, marble or clay.) Accordingly, the definition of "document" is not confined to writing on paper. It is, also, not restricted to things written. The essential feature of a document is that it should convey information.[3] Accordingly, photographs of tombstones and houses have been accepted as documents for the purposes of discovery,[4] a tape recording has been held to be a document for the same purposes[5] and a film has been held to be a document for the purposes of a *subpoena duces tecum*.[6] In two recent cases information stored upon a hard disk has been held to come within the meaning of "documentary".[7]

A similar broad definition is given in the Police and Criminal Evidence Act 1984. "Document" is defined for the purposes of that Act by s.118(1) (the general interpretation section) as having the same meaning as in Pt I of

---

[1] See *Shorter Oxford English Dictionary*.
[2] *Daye* [1908] 2 K.B. 333, 340.
[3] *Grant v Southwestern Properties* [1975] Ch. 185, 193, *per* Walton J.
[4] *Lyell v Kennedy (No.3)* (1884) 50 L.T. 730, CA.
[5] *Grant v Southwestern Properties*, above.
[6] *Senior v Holdsworth Ex p. ITN* [1976] Q.B. 23.
[7] *Derby & Co. Ltd v Weldon* [1991] 1 W.L.R. 652 (Vinelott J.); *Alliance & Leicester Building Society v Ghahremani, The Times*, March 19, 1992 (Hoffmann J.).

the Civil Evidence Act 1968. "Document" is defined for the purposes of Pt I of that Act to include *inter alia* any photograph, tape or film. For the purposes of the law relating to hearsay, "document" is defined as being "anything in which information of any description is recorded".[8]

Electronic communications and data stored electronically are documents and admissible in criminal proceedings. The Electronic Communications Act 2000 makes provision for the admissibility of electronic signatures and related certificates in legal proceedings in relation to any question as to the authenticity of such communications or data.[9] This includes communications and data which have been encrypted.[10] It will be for the court to decide whether the electronic signature has been correctly used and what weight it should be given.[11] "Document" is defined by the Act to include *inter alia* any plan, design or other image[12]; "communication" to include a communication comprising sounds or images or both[13]; "electronic communication" means a communication transmitted either by means of a telecommunications system or by other means but while in an electronic form.[14]

3–03

If a document is written in a foreign language, it must be translated into English before it is admitted in evidence. The translator must himself swear to the accuracy of the translation.[15]

Documents are usually classified as follows:

(i) *private, i.e.* documents emanating from a private person[16];

(ii) *public, i.e.* documents made by a public officer for the purpose of the public making use of them;

(iii) *judicial, i.e.* documents recording the proceedings and judgments of courts of law.

---

[8] Criminal Justice Act 2003, s.134. At the time of writing, the section is expected to come in to effect in April 2005.

[9] s.7(1). For the definition of "electronic signature" see s.7(2). The signature is required to be certified by a person who has made a statement confirming it: s.7(3).

[10] Encryption is the process of turning normal test into a series of letters or numbers which can only be deciphered by someone with the correct password or key: Explanatory Notes to the Act, para.5. Such communications and data may be put into intelligible form, for instance, restored to the condition in which it was before any encryption or similar process was applied to it: s.15(3) of the Act.

[11] Explanatory Notes to the Act, the Stationery Office, 2000, para.43.

[12] s.15(1).

[13] *ibid.*

[14] *ibid.*

[15] *Fakisandhla Nkambule v R* [1940] A.C. 760, 771.

[16] See Nokes, *An Introduction to Evidence* (4th ed.), pp.353–354. For these purposes a corporate body is a private person. Thus documents produced by the police are private.

2. PRIVATE DOCUMENTS

A. Primary Evidence

3–04   The general rule is that private documents must be proved by primary evidence.[17] The Divisional Court, however, has said that this rule is limited to written documents and in the strict sense of the term is not relevant to tapes and films.[18] The reason for the distinction would appear to be that originally copies of documents could only be made by hand: with the attendant risks of error through transcription. As a result, strict rules were necessary to limit the use of copies, save in particular circumstances. Such rules are not necessary in the case of copies made by mechanical devices.

Primary evidence in this context usually means the production of the original document.[19] The operation of the rule may be illustrated as follows. Suppose a defendant to have made a written confession to the police. The confession was written as a statement by a police officer at the defendant's dictation. In order to adduce the confession in evidence, the prosecution must call the officer to produce the original handwritten statement. If the original is not produced, the prosecution cannot normally rely on a typewritten copy and the confession will not be admitted in evidence.

3–05   Two points should be made about original documents.

(a)   Normally there is only one original document; but, in some cases, there may be more than one, for example the counterparts of a lease or the second set of printouts from an intoximeter.[20]

(b)   In some cases the question as to which document is the original will depend on the circumstances. Thus, in the case of a telegram, the original (as against the sender) was the message handed in at

---

[17] A person wishing to rely on a private document must prove that it has been duly executed, *i.e.* that it was signed by the person who purported to have signed it and (where attestation is necessary) that it was attested. (Evidence of attestation is only necessary in the case of wills and other testamentary documents.) Execution is usually proved by calling a person to identify his own signature on the document. In his absence it may be proved by calling somebody who saw him sign the document or can identify his handwriting (see para.6–10, below, for evidence as to handwriting).

[18] *Kajala v Noble* (1982) 75 Cr.App.R. 149, 152; cited at para.3–06 below.

[19] In certain unusual instances, primary evidence may be given by other means, *e.g.* (i) in a few cases copies of private documents made under public authority are receivable as primary evidence; (ii) an admission of the truth of the contents of an inadmissible document may be evidence of the contents against the party making the admission: *Slatterie v Pooley* (1840) 6 M. & W. 664.

[20] *DPP v Hutchings* [1991] R.T.R. 380. In that case the first set of printouts had been lost and a police officer took a second set. This amounted to a second "reading" of the same material, resulting from the further operation of the device. The Divisional Court commented that the second set was as much an original as the first. Presumably the same test could be applied to any printouts taken from a machine operating in the same way as the Intoximeter.

the Post Office.[21] Sometimes a carbon copy may be the relevant original, for example if the offence alleged is that a carbon copy has been falsified.

The rule has a long history. It is now seen as the last surviving aspect of the best evidence rule, *i.e.* that a party must produce the best evidence of which the nature of the case permits.

The best evidence rule was considered by the Divisional Court in *Kajala v Noble*.[22] The defendant in that case was charged with using threatening behaviour during the course of a disturbance in which a group of youths threw missiles at the police. The defendant was identified as one of those participating in the missile-throwing by a witness who had recognised him on a BBC television news bulletin concerning the disturbance. At the trial before the magistrates, the prosecution relied on a cassette recording of the film. The defendant appealed on the ground that since the original film existed, the prosecution should not have been allowed to rely on a copy. The Divisional Court did not agree. Ackner L.J. giving the judgment of the court said:

3–06

> "The old rule, that a party must produce the best evidence that the nature of the case will allow, and that any less good evidence is to be excluded, has gone by the board long ago. The only remaining instance of it is that, if an original document is available in one's hands, one must produce it; that one cannot give secondary evidence by producing a copy. Nowadays we do not confine ourselves to the best evidence. We admit all relevant evidence. The goodness or badness of it goes only to weight, and not to admissibility."[23]

The general rule does not affect the admissibility of documents as real evidence (discussed at para.2–05, above) or for the purposes of identification. Thus, a document may be identified by looking at its contents.[24] For instance, a cheque book or a driving licence may be identified by the name upon it.

B. Secondary evidence

Secondary evidence usually takes the form of a copy. At one time (when the best evidence rule prevailed) there were degrees of secondary evidence. Thus, if the original document could not be produced, the next best evi-

3–07

---

[21] *Regan* [1887] 16 Cox C.C. 203.

[22] (1982) 75 Cr.App.R. 149.

[23] At 152. The same point was also made by Lloyd L.J. in *R. v Governor of Pentonville Prison Ex p. Osman* [1990] 1 W.L.R. 277, 308, when he said that all remains of the best evidence rule is that if a party has an original document and does not produce it without reasonable explanation the court will infer the worst.

[24] *Boyle v Wiseman* (1855) 11 Exch. 306, 367, *per* Martin B.

dence had to be adduced. However, there are now no degrees of secondary evidence.[25] Accordingly, oral evidence of the contents of a document may be given. Thus, a witness may give evidence of the contents of a document which he has himself read.[26] A statement which has been read to him may be admissible under the new hearsay legislation: see s.114 of the Criminal Justice Act 2003.[27] In *Nazeer*[28] three employees of the Record Department of the D.S.S. checked the computer records in the Department for payable orders from lost or stolen pension or allowance books which had passed through the defendant's sub post-office during a particular period. The orders were individually examined and compared with the entries on the computer screen and a schedule setting out more than 7,000 such entries was produced. It was argued that the evidence of the employees relating to the comparison between the orders and the entries on the screen was inadmissible as secondary evidence. The Court of Appeal held that secondary evidence was itself admissible because it was impracticable to produce the computers in court and (there being no degrees of secondary evidence) such evidence might be given in a number of ways which meant that this evidence was admissible: questions of accuracy were only relevant to the weight of the evidence.

(1) Copies

3–08   Copies may take a number of forms such as (i) the certified copy which has been certified as true by an officer to whose custody the original document has been entrusted[29]; (ii) the examined copy which has been proved to have been examined and checked with the original.

Today, since most copies are produced by photocopiers, disputes rarely arise.

In *Wayte*,[30] the Court of Appeal laid down guidelines on the procedure to be adopted if there is a dispute about the admissibility of photocopies. The guidelines may be summarised as follows:

(a)   As a general rule, documents should not be handed to nor seen by the jury until questions of admissibility have been determined.

(b)   Warning should be given before such documents are produced to counsel for the parties likely to be affected by admission of the

---

[25] *Brown v Woodman* (1834) 6 C. & P. 206, *per* Parke B.; *Doe d. Gilbert v Ross* (1840) 7 M. & W. 102, 106–107; *Garton v Hunter* [1969] 2 Q.B. 37, 44, *per* Lord Denning M.R.; *Wayte* (1983) 76 Cr.App.R. 110, 116.

[26] *Brown v Woodman*, above.

[27] At the time of writing, the section is expected to come into effect in April 2005.

[28] [1998] Crim.L.R. 750.

[29] For instance, under s.120 of the Terrorism, Act 2000, a document bearing a certificate signed by the Secretary of State, or on his behalf, and stating that the document is a true copy of a notice or direction under the Act and signed by him is evidence of the document.

[30] (1983) 76 Cr.App.R. 110, 118.

document so that they may have a fair chance of considering their admissibility.

(c) If the defendant is unrepresented, the guidance of the court should be sought before the document is put before the jury.

The Court said that on very rare occasions there would have to be a trial-within-a-trial on the question of admissibility; but in the end the issue of the genuineness of the document will have to be left to the jury. Whether copies are first or secondhand goes only to the weight of the evidence.[31]

(2) Copies of copies

A copy of a copy is admissible in a case where secondary evidence may be given. Usually a witness is called who can verify that the copy is not only a true copy of the original copy but is also in the same terms as the original document.[32] Even if such evidence cannot be given, the copy of the copy may still be admitted. The fact that a false document can be constructed by photocopying techniques does not render a photocopy inadmissible: that is a matter of weight, not admissibility.[33] Where a statement in a document is hearsay but is also admissible it may be proved by production of a copy.[34]

3–09

(3) Microfilm copies

The contents of a document may be proved by production of a microfilm copy of it or of a material part of it which must be authenticated in such matter as the court approve.[35]

Thus, once a document has been microfilmed, a copy may be produced in any proceedings, provided that it is authenticated in such manner as the court may approve. This provision applies whether or not the document is in existence. No indication is given of the manner in which the document should be authenticated. However, in many cases the authenticity of a document is proved by a witness who has had custody or control of it.

3–10

(4) Hearsay statements

Section 133 of the Criminal Justice Act 2003 provides that where a hearsay statement in a document is admissible as evidence it may be proved by producing either the document or a copy of it (or the material part) authenticated in whatever way the court may approve. This section replaces s.27 of the Criminal Justice Act 1988 and is in very similar terms. Its

3–11

---

[31] *Nazeer* [1998] Crim.L.R. 750.
[32] *Collins* (1960) 44 Cr.App.R. 170.
[33] *Wayte*, above.
[34] Criminal Justice Act 2003, s.133; see below.
[35] Police and Criminal Evidence Act 1984, s.71.

purpose is to cover all forms of copying, including the use of imaging technology.[36]

C. Admissibility of secondary evidence

3–12   Secondary evidence of documents may be admissible in the following circumstances. (This is not an exhaustive list of all the circumstances in which secondary evidence may be given but outlines the main exceptions to the general rule.)

> (1)   Where the original has been destroyed, for example by fire,[37] or lost, so long as there is evidence that a search has been made for it.[38]
>
> (2)   Where it is impossible or inconvenient to produce the original.[39] Examples would be a placard on a wall[40] or a notice in a factory.[41]

Where a party wishes the original of a document to be produced, but it is in the hands of the opposite side, he must serve a notice to produce on the opposing party or his solicitors.

The rule in criminal cases is the same as in civil cases,[42] save that civil rules as to discovery do not apply in criminal proceedings.[43] Failure to serve a notice may make secondary evidence inadmissible (unless the evidence is admissible by reason of the hearsay provisions of the Criminal Justice Act 2003.[44] In 1925, a conviction was quashed because copies of letters had been produced without notice to produce having been served.[45] However, copies of documents are produced today without notice and without objection. Thus, if a defendant is charged with a hire purchase fraud, the prosecution will produce copies of the relevant hire purchase agreement without giving notice to produce the original. Objection will usually not be taken to this course. If the original document is relevant, the defendant may be in a position to produce it or procure its production.

3–13   Indeed, it may be that in the above example, no objection could properly be taken because there is no need for the prosecution to serve a notice when

---

[36] Explanatory Notes to the Criminal Justice Bill, para.366.
[37] *Leyfield's Case* (1611) 10 Co.Rep. 88a, 92b.
[38] *Brewster v Sewell* (1820) 3 B. & Ald. 296.
[39] The principle was laid down in *Mortimer v M'Callan* (1840) 6 M. & W. 58, 72 which concerned the books of the Bank of England but which suggested inscriptions on tombstones or on a wall as examples. Graffiti on a wall inciting to racial hatred would be a modern example.
[40] *Fursey* (1833) C. & P. 81.
[41] *Owner v Beehive Spinning Co. Ltd* [1914] 1 K.B. 105.
[42] *Att-Gen v Le Merchant* (1772) 2 T.R. 201.
[43] *Spokes v Grosvenor Hotel* [1897] 2 Q.B. 124. For rules as to disclosure in criminal proceedings, see Ch.20.
[44] At the time of writing, these are expected to come into effect in April 2005. See Ch.8 below.
[45] *Morgan* [1925] 1 K.B. 752.

the document is the subject matter of the proceedings, for example where the defendant was charged with theft of a bill of exchange, it was held that there was no need for the prosecution to serve a notice in relation to the bill.[46] This is because "[by] the form of the indictment the prisoner has notice that he is charged with possession of the very document and will be required to produce it."[47] Thus, in cases where the defendant was charged with driving a motor vehicle without insurance, it was held that notice to produce the certificate was not necessary and secondary evidence of it was admitted.[48] "The summons itself is a notice to the defendant to have his policy in court."[49]

The defence often request the prosecution without notice during the trial to produce records made during a defendant's detention in the police station. Such requests are usually complied with. However, in *Hackney*[50] the Court of Appeal appeared to deprecate this practice and said that such records did not prove themselves. "The prosecution do not have to produce them without some notice which allows proper opportunity of proving and explaining their contents by the evidence of officers who actually made the records." (However, it should be noted that custody records are also admissible under s.117 of the Criminal Justice Act 2003: para.8–32, below.[51])

If a notice to produce a document has been served, the court has no power to compel an accused to comply with it[52]: to do so would be to require the defendant to produce evidence against himself. On the other hand, failure to comply with a notice to produce will allow secondary evidence of the documents to be given.[53]   **3–14**

If a document is in the hands of a stranger to the proceedings, a witness summons may be issued requiring the stranger to attend before the court and to produce the document.[54]

However, the document in question must be material to the proceedings. The Divisional Court has accordingly held that summonses should not have been issued in a disguised attempt to obtain discovery[55] or to obtain material for use in cross-examination.[56] Where a summons is issued

---

[46] *Aickles* (1784) 1 Leach 294.
[47] *Elworthy* (1867) L.R. 1 C.C.R. 103, 106, *per* Kelly C.B.
[48] *Machin v Ash* (1950) 49 L.G.R. 87; *Bracegirdle v Apter* (1951) 49 L.G.R. 790.
[49] *Machin v Ash* at 89, *per* Lord Goddard C.J.
[50] (1982) 74 Cr.App.R. 194, 198.
[51] *Hogan* [1997] Crim.L.R. 349. At the time of writing, the section is expected to come into effect in April 2005.
[52] *Trust Houses Ltd v Postlethwaite* (1944) 109 J.P. 12, DC.
[53] *Watson* (1788) 2 T.R. 199.
[54] For proceedings in the Crown Court the procedure is governed by the Criminal Procedure [Attendance of Witnesses] Act 1965, s.2 (as amended by the Criminal Procedure and Investigations Act 1996, s.66); and for the magistrates' court: Magistrates' Courts Act 1980, s.97.
[55] *Skegness Magistrates' Court Ex p. Cardy* [1985] R.T.R. 49; *Manchester Crown Court Ex p. Williams* [1985] R.T.R. 49.
[56] *Cheltenham Justices Ex p. Secretary of State for Trade* [1977] 1 W.L.R. 95.

requiring a third party (for instance a local authority) to disclose a large number of documents and the party applies to set the summons aside, it is proper for the judge to accept the assurance of the party (for instance the local authority, based on the opinion of independent counsel instructed by the authority) that certain documents are irrelevant.[57]

Secondary evidence will be admissible if the document is in the possession of somebody who (a) is outside the jurisdiction[58] or (b) has successfully claimed privilege in respect of the document[59]; or (c) has diplomatic immunity.[60] If, on the other hand, no summons has been served or the summons is disobeyed, secondary evidence may not be admissible[61] unless a copy which has been authenticated in whatever way the court may approve is admitted under the Criminal Justice Act 2003.[62]

D. Bankers' books

3–15 Special provisions have been enacted to protect banks from the disruption caused by the removal of ledgers and accounts. Accordingly, s.3 of the Bankers' Books Evidence Act 1879 provides that a copy of any entry in a banker's book shall be received as prima facie evidence of such entry and the matters, transactions and accounts therein recorded. The word "book" is not used in its normal sense but is given a wide definition in the Act which has been amended to include modern methods of recording transactions.[63] However, it does not extend to letters in a file of bank correspondence.[64]

For a copy to be admissible under the Act, it must be proved that:

(a) the book was at the time of the making of the entry one of the ordinary books of the bank;

(b) the entry was made in the ordinary course of business;

(c) the book is in the custody or control of the bank[65]; and

(d) the copy has been examined with the original entry and is correct.[66]

---

[57] W(G) and W(E) [1997] 1 Cr.App.R. 166.

[58] Kilgour v Owen (1889) 88 L.T.7.

[59] Mills v Oddy (1834) 6 C. & P. 728.

[60] Nowaz (1976) 63 Cr.App.R. 178.

[61] Inhabitants of Llanfaethly (1853) 2 E. & B. 940.

[62] s.133. At the time of writing, the section is expected to come into effect in April 2005.

[63] The Bankers' Books Evidence Act 1879, s.9 (as substituted by paras 1 and 13 of Sch.6 to the Banking Act 1979) provides that the expression includes ledgers, day-books, cashbooks, account-books and other records used in the ordinary business of the bank, whether those records are in written form or are kept on microfilm, magnetic tape or any other form of mechnical or electronic data retrieval mechanism.

[64] Dadson (1983) 77 Cr.App.R. 91.

[65] s.4.

[66] s.5.

Section 7 of the Bankers' Books Evidence Act 1879 provides that on the application of any party to a legal proceeding, a court may order that such party be at liberty to inspect and take copies of any entries in a banker's book for any of the purposes of such proceedings. Accordingly, once legal proceedings are in being against a particular defendant, the police may apply for an order under this section to inspect the defendant's bank account if it is relevant to the proceedings to do so.

3–16

The person affected by an order cannot object on the ground that he may incriminate himself.[67] However, care should be taken before such an order is made because it is an interference with the liberty of the subject. In *Williams v Summerfield*,[68] Lord Widgery C.J., laying down guidelines for magistrates, said that they should limit the period of disclosure of the account to a period strictly relevant to the charge; and consider whether the prosecution has other evidence to support the charge before making the order.

The latter consideration is to prevent the prosecution from going on a "fishing expedition" in order to try to find material for a case. An order should only be made where there is evidence of the commission of an offence and the purpose of the application is to add to that evidence.[69] The reason for these restrictions is to prevent the oppression of the person affected. Thus the Divisional Court has quashed orders which were not limited in time[70] or covered a longer period than was relevant to the charge.[71]

The following points should also be noted:

3–17

(a) An order may be made to inspect a person's bank account although the person is not a party to the proceedings. Thus, in *Andover Justices Ex p. Rhodes*,[72] Mrs R was charged with the theft of some money. She told the police that the money was in her husband's bank account. Magistrates made an order allowing the police to inspect the account. The Divisional Court held that the order was proper, despite the fact that the husband was not a party to the proceedings. In this case the order was necessary because inspection of the husband's account was relevant to the charge and he could not be compelled to give evidence and produce the account. In *Grossman*,[73] the Court of Appeal said that such an order should be made only in exceptional circumstances in criminal cases; and only where the public interest in assisting a

---

[67] *Williams v Summerfield*, below.
[68] [1972] 2 Q.B. 512, 518–519.
[69] *Nottingham City JJ. Ex p. Lynn* (1984) 79 Cr.App.R. 238, 243.
[70] *Marlborough Street Stipendiary Magistrate Ex p. Simpson* (1980) 70 Cr.App.R. 291.
[71] *Nottingham City JJ. Ex p. Lynn*, above; *Owen v Sambrook* [1981] Crim.L.R. 329.
[72] [1980] Crim.L.R. 644.
[73] (1981) 73 Cr.App.R. 302, 307.

prosecution outweighed the private interest in keeping a bank account confidential.

(b) There must be legal proceedings in being before an order is made. The order itself cannot constitute the proceedings. *Nottingham City Justices Ex p. Lynn*[74] is an example of a case where it was held that proceedings were in being. In that case a person was charged with an offence connected with the importation of drugs. He was subsequently twice remanded in custody by the magistrates. An order under s.7 was then made. It was argued that there were no proceedings in being. The Divisional Court commented that this was an idle suggestion.

(c) There is no requirement that notice of an application should be given to the party affected. However, Lord Widgery observed that there was much to be said for giving notice.[75] Shaw L.J. made similar observations in the case of persons not party to the proceedings unless considerations of urgency or secrecy make it imperative that the application should be dealt with *ex parte*.[76] It is submitted that if the considerations mentioned by Shaw L.J. do not exist, it is better practice to give notice, if only so that any objection may be canvassed at the earliest stage.

3. PUBLIC DOCUMENTS

3–18 A public document is a document made by a public officer for the purpose of the public making use of it and being able to refer to it.[77] In general, the originals of such documents do not have to be produced. The reason for the rule is that the production of the originals would cause public inconvenience.[78] Public documents do not require evidence of execution. For admissibility, see paras 8–41 *et seq.*, below.

3–19 The production of many public documents is governed by statute. The following may be cited by way of example.

(a) Private Acts of Parliament and entries in the journals of both Houses of Parliament may be proved by copies printed by the Queen's Printers or under the authority of HMSO.[79] All statutes of the UK are public Acts and to be judicially noticed as such,

---

[74] Above.
[75] *Marlborough Street Stipendiary Magistrate*, above, at 294.
[76] *Grossman*, above, at 308.
[77] *Sturla v Freccia* (1880) 5 App.Cas. 623, 643, *per* Lord Blackburn.
[78] *Mortimer v M'Callan* (1840) 6 M. & W. 58, 63, *per* Alderson B.
[79] Evidence Act 1845, s.3; Documentary Evidence Act 1882, s.2.

unless the contrary is provided in the Act: Interpretation Act 1978, s.3.

(b) Royal proclamations and orders or regulations issued by the Government may be proved by copies printed by the Queen's Printer or under the authority of HMSO: Documentary Evidence Act 1868, s.2; Documentary Evidence Act 1882, s.2. In *Clarke*[80] the Court of Appeal said that the word "order" in the 1868 Act should be given a wide meaning covering "any executive act of Government performed by the bringing into existence of a public document for the purpose of giving effect to an Act of Parliament." The Court, therefore, held that an order printed by HMSO stating that the Home Secretary had approved a breath test device was an order within s.2 of the Act.

(c) Statutory instruments may be proved by a copy printed by the Stationery Office.[81] In *Koon Cheung Tang*[82] the defendant was charged with offences under the Food Hygiene General Regulations 1970. At the trial the Regulations were proved by the production in the form of a photocopy from a commercial publication rather than the Queen's Printer's copy. It was argued on appeal that this procedure failed to comply with s.2 of the Documentary Evidence Act 1868. The Court of Appeal held that technically the judge was probably wrong to hold that the provisions of s.2 had been satisfied. (The Court said that this was only "probably" so because some Regulations have attained such notoriety that judicial notice may be taken of them: *Jones*.[83]) However, it was not suggested that there was any inaccuracy in the text before the court; and the Court dismissed the appeal on the ground that no miscarriage of justice had actuallly occurred.

(d) Byelaws may be proved by a printed copy purporting to be made by the local authority making the bye-law and endorsed with a certificate signed by the proper office of the authority.[84]

(e) Public records may be proved by a certified copy of a public record in the Public Records Office.[85]

(f) Births and deaths may be proved by a certified copy of an entry

---

[80] [1969] 2 Q.B. 91, 97.
[81] Documentary Evidence Act 1868, s.2; Documentary Evidence Act 1882. See also, Statutory Instruments Act 1946, ss.2–4; *Palastanga v Solman* (1962) 106 S.J. 176.
[82] [1995] Crim.L.R. 813.
[83] [1970] 1 W.L.R. 16, see para.5–09, below.
[84] Local Government Act 1972, s.238.
[85] Public Records Act 1958, s.9(2).

purporting to be sealed or stamped with the Seal of the General Register Office.[86]

(g) Marriages may be proved by similar means.[87]

(h) The records of the Driver and Vehicle Licensing Authority (DVLA) may be proved under s.52 of the Vehicle and Excise Registration Act 1952.[88]

3–20   If there is no statute providing for the admissibility of a particular document, it may be admissible under s.14 of the Evidence Act 1851. This section provides that whenever any book or other document is of such a public nature as to be admissible in evidence on its mere production from the proper custody and no statute exists which renders its contents provable by means of a copy, an examined or certified copy is admissible.

4. JUDICIAL DOCUMENTS

3–21   Convictions, acquittals, judgments and connected documents are usually proved by certified copies. For proof of convictions and acquittals, see below.

A. Civil proceedings

3–22   The following provisions relating to civil proceedings should first be noted.

(a) All writs, records, pleadings and documents filed in the High Court are proved by office copies.[89]

(b) Proceedings in the County Court may be proved by a certified copy of an entry in the district judge's book.[90]

(c) Proceedings in the magistrates' court may be proved by a certified extract from the court register.[91]

(d) Orders of the court required to be gazetted under the Insolvency Act 1986 or the Insolvency Rules 1986 may be proved by the

---

[86] Births and Deaths Registration Act 1953, s.34(6) as amended.

[87] Marriage Act 1949, s.65(3).

[88] *McCarthy* [1998] R.T.R. 374.

[89] RSC Ord.38, r.10(11). An office copy is one made by an officer of the court.

[90] County Courts Act 1984, s.12(2). In *Stoke, The Times*, August 6, 1987, the Court of Appeal held that an oral admission by the defendant that County Court judgments had been entered against him was evidence of the entry of the judgment. The court described s.12(2) as a piece of machinery providing a means of proof and said that proof by some other method was perfectly acceptable.

[91] Magistrates' Courts Rules 1981, r.68. For convictions and acquittals in the magistrates' court, see below.

production of a copy of the *London Gazette* containing the relevant notice.[92]

Despite these provisions it is submitted that in cases relating to the forgery of a court record or perjury in an affidavit, the original document should be produced. Indeed, it is difficult to see how the prosecution could proceed without production of the original.

B. Proof of convictions and acquittals

Proof of convictions and acquittals in all proceedings is now governed by s.73(1) and (2) of the Police and Criminal Evidence Act 1984 which provides: **3–23**

"(1)   Where in any proceedings the fact that a person has in the United Kingdom been convicted or acquitted of an offence otherwise than by a Service court is admissible in evidence, it may be proved by producing a certificate of conviction or, as the case may be, of acquittal relating to that offence, and proving that the person named in the certificate as having been convicted or acquitted of the offence is the person whose conviction or acquittal of the offence is to be proved.

(2)   For the purposes of this section a certificate of conviction or of acquittal—

(a)   shall, as regards a conviction or acquittal on indictment, consist of a certificate, signed by the clerk of the court where the conviction or acquittal took place, giving the substance and effect (omitting the formal parts) of the indictment and of the conviction or acquittal; and

(b)   shall, as regards a conviction or acquittal on a summary trial, consist of a copy of the conviction or of the dismissal of the information, signed by the clerk of the court where the conviction or acquittal took place or by the clerk of the court, if any, to which a memorandum of the conviction or acquittal was sent;

and a document purporting to be a duly signed certificate of conviction or acquittal under this section shall be taken to be such a certificate unless the contrary is proved."

The section thus provides for proof of convictions or acquittals in both trials on indictment and summary trials by: **3–24**

---

[92] Insolvency Rules 1986, r.12.20.

(a) production of a certificate duly signed by the clerk of the appropriate court; and

(b) proof that the person named in the certificate is the person whose conviction or acquittal is to be proved.

Section 73 is based on a clause in the draft Bill annexed to the Eleventh Report of the Criminal Law Revision Committee.[93] The Committee described the section as a modernised provision for the proof of convictions or acquittals. It supersedes a number of nineteenth-century provisions.[94]

3–25 In *Derwentside JJ. Ex p. Heaviside*[95] the Divisional Court emphasised that strict proof that the accused was the person named in the certificate was required in order to avoid mistakes. The Court held that it was insufficient to produce the court register showing that person of the same name, date of birth and address had been disqualified and that the identity of the person convicted must be proved by an admission, fingerprints or the evidence of a person in court on that occasion. The Court listed these three methods as providing the necessary proof. However, in subsequent cases the Court made it clear that it is an error of law to consider that these three methods are exhaustive: it is for the justices to determine in the individual case whether other means are sufficient.[96] These methods may include proof of an admission to a witness in the case or proof by means of a written statement under s.9 of the Criminal Justice Act 1967.[97] Similarly, justices were held to have been wrong in ignoring evidence of admissions to a police officer on the ground that it did not fall into one of the three above categories.[98] The position was summarised by Simon Brown L.J. in *Bailey v DPP*[99]:

(a) the link between the certificate and the defendant must be proved beyond reasonable doubt;

(b) this link can be proved by any admissible means;

(c) the list in *Heaviside* is not exhaustive and other methods can be envisaged; but

(d) there must be "some evidence which plainly demonstrates that a previous conviction in the defendant's name is not possibly

---

[93] Cmnd. 4991.

[94] Evidence Act 1851, s.13; part of the Criminal Procedure Act 1865, s.6; and Prevention of Crimes Act 1871, s.18.

[95] [1996] R.T.R. 384.

[96] *Derwentside Justices Ex p. Swift* [1997] R.T.R. 89; *DPP v Mansfield* [1997] R.T.R. 96; *DPP v Mooney* [1997] R.T.R. 434.

[97] *Derwentside Justices Ex p. Swift.*

[98] *DPP v Mooney*, above.

[99] (1999) 163 J.P. 518, 523.

explicable ... by some other person having given the defendant's details both to the police and to the Court...".[1]

A conviction may be proved by admission even in the absence of a certificate. This is illustrated by *DPP v Moran*[2] where the Divisional Court upheld a conviction in circumstances where no certificate of disqualification was produced to the Court, but the accused had admitted to the police that he was disqualified and gave details; and, at trial, accepted that his admission was correct.

3–26

The following should also be noted:

(a) References in s.73 to the clerk of a court include references to his deputy and to any other person having the custody of the court records (s.73(3)).

(b) If a defendant denies a conviction lawfully put to him in cross-examination the prosecution may prove the conviction in the manner provided for in this section.

(c) For proof of the *facts* upon which a conviction is based (as applied to the conviction itself) see Police and Criminal Evidence Act 1984, s.74, discussed at paras 5–27 *et seq.*, below.

Section 73 of the 1984 Act and *Heaviside*, above, apply only to convictions in the UK. Foreign convictions must be proved under s.7 of the Evidence Act 1851. This was established in *Mancini*[3] in which the Court of Appeal accepted, as "examined copies" under the Act, certificates of convictions in the Netherlands produced by a Dutch liaison officer called to give evidence by the Crown. The Court said that it was open to the Crown to prove that the "examined copies" related to the defendant in the ordinary way, in the instant case, by means of admissible fingerprint evidence.[4]

3–27

The following should also be noted:

3–28

(a) A person disputing the correctness of a conviction bears the burden of proving that it is incorrect.

(b) The method of proving a conviction or acquittal authorised by the section is in addition to and not to the exclusion of any other authorised manner of proving a conviction or acquittal (s.73(4)), *i.e.* evidence by a person in court; proof by means of fingerprints

---

[1] *ibid.*
[2] (2000) 164 J.P. 562.
[3] *Mancini* [2002] 2 Cr.App.R. 377.
[4] The method of proof of convictions by fingerprints under s.39 of the 1948 Act only applies to convictions in Great Britain.

under s.39 of the Criminal Justice Act 1967; written statements under s.9 of the same Act or admissions under s.10 of that Act.

(c) References in the section to the clerk of a court include references to his deputy and to any other person having the custody of the court record (s.73(3)).

(d) If a defendant denies a conviction lawfully put to him in cross-examination (for example under the Criminal Evidence Act 1898, s.1(f)), the prosecution may prove the conviction in the manner provided for in this section.

PART 2

Burden and Standard of Proof

CHAPTER 4

Burden and Standard of Proof

Questions relating to the incidence of the burden of proof and the standard of proof lie at the heart of the criminal trial. Directions on these issues must form part of every summing-up. Justices are bound by the same rules. A discussion on both questions follows. **4–01**

1. BURDEN OF PROOF

The expression "burden of proof" is used in two senses in a criminal trial: **4–02** (a) the obligation on the prosecution to prove all the facts necessary to establish guilt; and (b) the obligation on either prosecution or defence to establish the facts upon a particular issue.

In the first sense, it is known as the "persuasive" or "legal" burden,[1] meaning the duty of persuading the tribunal of fact, in this case, the jury or justices. In the second sense, the burden is called "evidential", meaning the burden of adducing evidence.

The expression is also used to describe the duty of establishing the admissibility of evidence.

A. The persuasive burden

(1) The rule

In a criminal trial the prosecution bear the persuasive burden. Therefore, **4–03** the rule is that the duty of persuading the tribunal of fact, *i.e.* the burden of proving the defendant's guilt, is upon the prosecution. This is the cardinal principle of all criminal trials. It forms an essential part of the directions which every jury must receive and which magistrates must apply.[2] It encapsulates the presumption of law that the defendant remains innocent until he is proved guilty (now enshrined in Art.6.2 of the European Convention on Human Rights: see para.13–14, below). The only exceptions to the rule that the prosecution bear the persuasive burden occur in cases where a defence of insanity is raised or in cases involving statutory exceptions.

---

[1] Both expressions are in common use. "Persuasive" is used in this work.
[2] Thus, if justices feel unable to reach a decision, the prosecution have not proved the case and the defendant must be acquitted: *Bromley JJ. Ex p. Haymills (Contractors) Ltd* [1984] Crim.L.R. 235.

The rule was firmly established by the House of Lords in *Woolmington v DPP*[3] The accused in that case was charged with murdering his wife. He admitted shooting her. The defence was that he had fired the fatal shot by accident. The trial judge directed the jury that once it was established that she died as a result of the accused's act he had the burden of establishing it was an accident. The House of Lords held this to be a misdirection and Viscount Sankey L.C. stated the law in a celebrated passage in his speech:

> "While the prosecution must prove the guilt of the prisoner, there is no ... burden laid on the prisoner to prove his innocence and it is sufficient for him to raise a doubt as to his guilt.
>
> Throughout the web of the English Criminal Law one golden thread is always to be seen, that it is the duty of the prosecution to prove the prisoner's guilt subject ... to the defence of insanity and subject also to any statutory exception. If, at the end of and on the whole of the case, there is a reasonable doubt, created by the evidence given by either the prosecution or the prisoner, as to whether the prisoner killed the deceased with a malicious intention, the prosecution has not made out the case and the prisoner is entitled to an acquittal. No matter what the charge or where the trial, the principle that the prosecution must prove the guilt of the prisoner is part of the common law of England and no attempt to whittle it down can be entertained."[4]

4–04   More recently, Lord Bingham C.J. reiterated the principle and said that for many years it had been a "cardinal requirement of a properly conducted trial" to instruct the jury unambiguously that the burden of proof lay on the Crown and ordinarily there was no burden on the accused to prove anything.[5]

Accordingly, the prosecution must prove all the elements in the offence necessary to establish guilt. For instance, a person is guilty of theft if he dishonestly appropriates property belonging to another with the intention of permanently depriving the other of it. A jury in such a case will therefore be told that the prosecution must prove (a) that the defendant appropriated the property belonging to another and (b) if they find that he did appropriate the property, that he did so dishonestly and with the intention of depriving the other of it permanently. If the prosecution do not prove any of these elements, the prosecution fails and the defendant must be acquitted. Similarly, the burden of proving negative averments falls on the prosecution. A negative averment is a negative allegation. For instance, in a case of rape the prosecution must prove that when sexual intercourse took place the complainant did not consent to it.

---

[3] [1935] A.C. 462.
[4] At 481.
[5] *Bentley, The Times*, July 31, 1998.

The defendant, therefore, has to prove nothing unless, as mentioned above, he raises insanity or certain statutory exceptions apply. He does not have to prove his defence. Even where the evidential burden shifts to the defendant the persuasive burden remains on the prosecution.[6]

Every jury must be directed upon the burden of proof. Nothing should be said which detracts from the principle that the burden of proof rests with the prosecution.[7] Any misdirection by the judge in the course of his summing-up to the effect that the defendant bears an onus when he does not, must be put right in the plainest possible terms.

4–05

> "It would be necessary ... to repeat the direction which had been given, to acknowledge that the direction was quite wrong, to tell the jury to put out of their minds all that they had heard ... about the burden of proof and then in clear terms which would be incapable of being misunderstood, tell them very plainly and simply what the law is.[8]

In *Lock*,[9] the Court of Appeal said that if there were no direction on the burden and standard of proof an unfair trial was likely to result and the verdict might be regarded as unsafe. (It is hard to conceive of circumstances where the verdict would *not* be unsafe. However, in one case the Court of Appeal held that the omission was not necessarily fatal to the conviction and it could properly consider applying the proviso to s.2 of the Criminal Appeal Act 1968 on the ground that no miscarriage of justice had actually occurred.)[10]

No particular formula of words for instructing the jury on the nature of the burden of proof is prescribed.[11] The usual direction is to tell the jury that the prosecution must prove the defendant's guilt and that he does not have to prove his innocence.[12] This direction is usually given at the beginning of the summing-up.[13]

4–06

No repetition of this direction is necessary unless it appears from a

---

[6] *Moon* [1969] 1 W.L.R. 1705, CA.

[7] Thus, in a case where there is no burden on the defendant, it will be a misdirection if the judge uses an expression such as "the defence, if it is established." Such a direction might suggest to the jury that it was for the defendant to prove the particular defence: see *McDonald*, *The Times*, April 10, 1987.

[8] *Moon* at 1707, *per* Salmon L.J.

[9] [1975] Crim.L.R. 35.

[10] *Roberts* [1992] Crim.L.R. 375.

[11] *Blackburn* (1955) 39 Cr.App.R. 84; *Kritz* [1950] 1 K.B. 82.

[12] This direction is based on the direction in the *Specimen Directions* published by the Judicial Studies Board (4th ed., 1996) and approved by Lord Taylor C.J. An earlier version of the Direction was approved by the Court of Appeal in *Donoghue* (1988) 86 Cr.App.R. 267, 272. For the current version, which adds nothing to the above, see *www.jsboard.co.uk*.

[13] The best place to deal with it, according to the Court of Appeal in *Ching* (1976) 63 Cr.App.R. 7, 9.

question that the members of the jury have not understood it, in which case a further direction should be given.[14]

(2) The burden on the prosecution to negative the defence

4–07 The rule in *Woolmington* extends throughout the criminal law. It is of "general application in all charges under the criminal law"[15] and "permits of no exceptions save only in the case of insanity which is not strictly a defence."[16]

Therefore, the general rule is that if a defence is raised, the onus is on the prosecution to disprove it and not on the defendant to prove it. Self-defence is a frequently recurring example. In cases of violence, the defendant often says that he was acting in self-defence or the prosecution evidence may be such as to put self-defence in issue. The jury must then be directed in clear terms as to the burden of proof. They must be told that it is not for the defendant to prove that he was acting in self-defence but that the burden is on the prosecution to prove that he was not.[17] The same rule applies to any defence, justification or explanation put forward by the defendant, for example alibi, accident, automatism or duress.

This has led some judges to protest at the description of such "defences" as defences in law and to prefer to treat such issues in purely evidential terms where the burden is on the prosecution. Their description as "defences", however, is so well established in practice that they will be described below as such.

4–08 The general practice is to direct the jury that the defendant does not have to prove such a defence: the prosecution must prove that it does not arise. In *Wood*[18] Lord Parker C.J. said that although there was no general rule of law that in every case where an alibi is raised a particular direction should be given, if there was a danger of the jury thinking that there was a burden on the defence the judge should give a specific direction. In most cases, this is the safer course.[19] It should be made clear to the jury that they must

---

[14] *Gibson* (1983) 77 Cr.App.R. 151, see also para.4–44, below.

[15] *Mancini v DPP* [1942] A.C. 1, 11, *per* Lord Simon.

[16] *per* Lord Tucker in *Chan Kau v R* [1955] A.C. 206, 211.

[17] *Moon* [1969] 1 W.L.R. 1705, 1706, *per* Salmon L.J. If the defence is that the defendant acted under a belief that another person was being unlawfully assaulted, it is for the prosecution to negative the possibility that he was acting under a genuine mistake of fact: *Williams* (1984) 78 Cr.App.R. 276.

[18] (1968) 52 Cr.App.R. 74, 78.

[19] In *Lesley* [1996] 1 Cr.App.R. 39, 50, the Court of Appeal said that the direction should routinely be given and that reliance should no longer be placed on *Penman* (1986) 82 Cr.App.R. 44 (where the Court had said that there was no rule requiring a judge to direct the jury that the fact that they reject the defendant's alibi is not indicative of guilt). On the other hand, a differently constituted Court of Appeal held that no such direction was necessary in *Harron* [1996] 2 Cr.App.R. 457 because the alleged lies about the alibi in that case did not constitute a matter which the jury might have to take into account separately from their determination of the main issue in the case. It is, nonetheless, submitted that it is the safer course to give the direction. (See paras 16–17 to 16–20, below, for discussion of the appropriate direction in cases where lies told by the defendant are relied on by the prosecution.)

acquit if either they accept the evidence which would constitute a defence, or short of accepting it, the evidence leaves them in doubt as to the defendant's guilt.[20]

The prosecution is under no obligation to negative any such defence or explanation until it is raised.[21] It does not have to disprove a theoretical possibility. There must, therefore, be sufficient evidence of the defence before the prosecution has to negative it beyond reasonable doubt. It is for this reason that it is sometimes said that there is an *evidential* burden on the defence to put the "defence" in issue, whereas, when it is so put in issue, the *persuasive* burden is on the prosecution to disprove it beyond reasonable doubt.

However, until such time as the defence or explanation is a live issue, the prosecution do not have to lead evidence to rebut it. In *Bratty v Att-Gen*,[22] Lord Morris of Borth-y-Gest illustrated this proposition by the example of a man who committed an act of violence, but alleged that he did it while sleepwalking. If the man were genuinely unconscious he would not be criminally liable for his act. It would not be the duty of the prosecution in these circumstances to adduce evidence at the outset of the trial negativing the possibility of the act having been committed while the man was sleepwalking. But once the explanation had "sufficient substance to merit consideration by the jury, then the onus which is upon the prosecution would not be discharged unless the jury, having considered the explanation, were sure that guilt ... was established beyond reasonable doubt."   4–09

(3) Exceptions to the rule

Woolmington established that there were only two exceptions to the rule that the prosecution bore the persuasive burden, namely, insanity and statutory exceptions. The House of Lords in *Mancini*[23] confirmed that these were the only exceptions.   4–10

Insanity. The defence bears the persuasive burden of establishing insanity (thus encapsulating the presumption of sanity), although the standard of proof is not as high as that borne by the Crown and is proof on the balance of probabilities[24]: see para.4–45.   4–11

Where the issue of fitness to plead is raised by the prosecution and the defence contests it, the burden of proving unfitness is upon the prosecu-

---

[20] See, *e.g.*, *Murtagh and Kennedy* (1955) 39 Cr.App.R. 72, 83.
[21] *Lobell* [1957] 1 Q.B. 547.
[22] [1963] A.C. 386, 416.
[23] [1942] A.C. 1.
[24] *Sodeman v R* [1936] W.N. 190, PC. For criticsm of the rule as an anomaly which conflicts with the presumption of innocence, see Jones, "Insanity, Automatism, and the Burden of Proof on the Accused" (1995) 111 L.Q.R. 475.

tion.[25] *Per contra*, if the defence raises the issue and the prosecution contests it, the defence bears the burden.[26] If the judge raises the issue,[27] the prosecution bears the burden.

4–12   **Express statutory exceptions.** Statutes on occasion put the burden of proving certain matters upon the accused For instance, the burden of establishing that he had lawful authority or reasonable excuse to have a offensive weapon in a public place is specifically put on the defendant.[28] Similarly, in a case of driving with a concentration of alcohol in the blood above the prescribed limit, the burden of proving that there was no likelihood of his driving while the concentration remained above the prescribed limit is on the defendant.[29] Other examples are:

(a) proving diminished responsibility in cases of murder[30];

(b) the presumption that a man who lives with a prostitute or exercises control over her movements is living on the earnings of prostitution unless he proves to the contrary[31];

(c) the provision that in cases of corruption a consideration shall be deemed to have been given corruptly unless the contrary is proved[32];

(d) proving in a drugs case that the defendant did not know or suspect that the substance in question was a controlled drug[33];

[25] *Robertson* (1968) 52 Cr.App.R. 690. See also *Podola* [1960] 1 Q.B. 325; Criminal Procedure (Insanity) Act 1964, s.4.
[26] *Podola*, above.
[27] Criminal Procedure (Insanity) Act 1954, s.4.
[28] Prevention of Crime Act 1953, s.1(i); *Petrie* (1961) 45 Cr.App.R. 72; *Brown* (1971) 55 Cr.App.R. 478. For argument that the legal burden is too frequently placed on the accused by statute, see Ashworth and Blake, "Innocence in English Criminal Law" [1996] Crim.L.R. 306.
[29] Road Traffic Act 1988, s.5(2).
[30] Homicide Act 1957, s.2(2); *Dunbar* [1958] 1 Q.B.1; *Dix* (1982) 74 Cr.App.R. 306 (in which the Court of Appeal held that medical evidence was essential to establish diminished responsibility).
[31] Sexual Offences Act 1956, s.30(2). In *Wilson* (1984) 78 Cr.App.R. 247, 249 the Court of Appeal approved a direction to the jury in these terms: "if this woman is a prostitute and if [the defendant] was living with her, then he must be presumed to be living on immoral earnings unless he proves to the contrary." In *X v U.K.* (1972) 42 C.D. 135 the European Commission of Human Rights rejected as ill-founded a complaint that a conviction under this provision violated Art.6(2) of the European Convention: see paras 13–14, 13–20 to 13–21, below, for Art.6(2).
[32] Prevention of Corruption Act 1916, s.2; *Carr-Briant* [1943] K.B. 607; *Braithwaite* [1983] 1 W.L.R. 385 in which Lord Lane C.J. set out the judge's duty in such a case as "to direct the jury first of all that they must decide whether they are satisfied so as to feel sure that the defendant received money or gift or consideration, and then to go on to direct them that if they are so satisfied, then ... the burden of proof shifts" (389).
[33] Misuse of Drugs Act 1971, s.28(2).

(e) proving that a person did not commit an offence of which he has been convicted[34];

(f) assuming where a specimen of breath is provided by a defendant in relation to a driving offence connected with drink that the proportion of alcohol at the time of the offence was not less than in the specimen.[35]

The introduction of the European Convention of Human Rights into **4–13** English law under the Human Rights Act 1988 has led to consideration whether the placing of a persuasive burden on the defendant is in violation of Art.6(2) of the Convention which contains the presumption of innocence. The European Court of Human Rights in *Telfer v Austria*[36] commented that legal presumptions are not in principle incompatible with Art.6. Such a presumption may effectively move a burden of proof to the defence. Thus, it may be taken that a reverse onus does not necessarily infringe Art.6(2) and in some cases may be justifiable. However, in *Salabiaku v France*[37] the European Court had also said that although the Convention does not prohibit presumptions in principle, Art.6(2) does not regard them with indifference and requires States to confine them within reasonable limits which take into account the importance of what is at stake and maintain the rights of the defence.

This view has been taken by the House of Lords. In *DPP v Kebilene*[38] in the House of Lords (reversing the Divisional Court) held that s.16(A) of the Prevention of Terrorism Act 1989 did not place a reverse burden on the accused and was not inconsistent with Art.6(2) of the European Convention on Human Rights. (The section provided that a person was guilty of an offence if he had any article in his possession in circumstances giving rise to a reasonable suspicion that the purpose was connected with the commission of acts of terrorism; but it was a defence for the person to prove that the article was not in his possession for such a purpose.) The Divisional Court had held that the section undermined the presumption of innocence and placed a reverse burden on the defendant to prove lawful authority or reasonable excuse for his possessing the articles: the section thus violated Art.6(2) of the Convention. The House of Lords did not agree but said that it was arguable that the effect of the use of the word "prove" in s.16(A) was merely to place an *evidential* burden on the accused.

Similarly, the Court of Appeal held that ss.2(2) of the Homicide Act 1957 **4–14** and 28 of the Misuse of Drugs Act 1971 are not in breach of Art.6(2) of the European Convention on Human Rights since Parliament could displace

---

[34] Police and Criminal Evidence Act 1984, s.74(2) and (3).
[35] Road Traffic Act 1988, s.15(2).
[36] (2002) 34 E.H.R.R. 7.
[37] (1998) 13 E.H.R.R. 379, para.28.
[38] [2002] 2 A.C. 326.

the burden of proof provided it used clear words.[39] Moreover, in both these cases, the accused were not being required to prove an essential ingredient of the offence but being given the opportunity to establish a special defence. The sections were well balanced and proportionate and accordingly did not breach Art.6(2). These decisions reflect what Lord Bingham, giving the judgment of the Privy Council, said in *Brown v Stott*[40] when dealing with interpretation of the Convention:

> "The jurisprudence of the European Court clearly establishes that while the overall fairness of the criminal trial cannot be compromised, the constituent rights, express or implied, within Article 6, are not themselves absolute. Limited qualification of those rights is acceptable if reasonably directed by national authorities towards a clear and proper public objective and if representing no greater qualification than the situation calls for."

The House of Lords upheld the decision of the Court of Appeal in *Lambert*,[41] albeit with an evidential and not a legal burden. The House of Lords held that there was justification for legislative interference with the presumption of innocence in the circumstances of the case. Thus Lord Steyn said that there was justification for interference with the burden of proof in prosecutions under s.5(1) of the Misuse of Drugs Act 1971 because drug dealers, etc. secrete the drugs in some container, thereby enabling the possessor to say he was unaware of the container: "such defences are commonplace and they pose real difficulties for the police and prosecuting authorities".[42]

4–15   In *Lambert* the majority of the House of Lords also held that it was possible to read the words of s.28(2) of the Misuse of Drugs Act 1971 as imposing only an evidential burden which would be compatible with the E.C.H.R.[43] However, Lord Hope pointed out that the practical effect would be minimal (of imposing an evidential and not a persuasive burden) since it is not what the accused must do by way of calling evidence but the state of mind of the judge or jury which is affected; and it would be in the interests of clarity and convenience, as well as on grounds of principle, to impose an evidential burden.[44] "To prove" in s.28 should be read as meaning "to give sufficient evidence".[45]

Lambert has been followed by similar decisions relating to other statu-

---

[39] *Lambert, Ali and Jordan* [2001] 1 Cr.App.R. 205.
[40] [2001] 2 W.L.R. 817, 836.
[41] [2001] Cr.App.R. 511.
[42] [2001] 2 Cr.App.R. 511, 527.
[43] *per* Lord Slynn, p.517; Lord Steyn, p.530; Lord Hope, p.547; and Lord Clyde, pp.569–70. (Lord Hutton dissented, p.588.)
[44] pp.546–47.
[45] *ibid.*

tory provisions although there is no unanimity as to whether the evidential burden should be applied. The Divisional Court in *L v DPP*[46] held that the reverse onus of proof in s.139 of the Criminal Justice Act 1988, which provides that it is for an accused to prove that he had good reason or lawful authority to have an article with him (in this case, a lock-knife) was not in violation of Art.6(2) of the European Convention on Human Rights. There was a strong public interest in bladed weapons not being carried in public, and Parliament, without infringing the Convention, was entitled to deter the carrying of such articles in public, which anyway required a defendant to prove something within his own knowledge. Therefore, Pill L.J. said, a fair balance permits the existence of a reverse onus in the context of s.139.[47] Pill L.J., however, also said that it is better not to speak of an evidential burden of proof since all it does is to raise an issue and, therefore, is no proof at all.[48]

L was approved by the Court of Appeal in *Matthews*.[49] The Court in that case held that the burden under s.139 was the legal burden and not merely evidential. The reverse onus provisions were proportionate and struck a fair balance between the general interest of the community in the realisation of a legitimate legislative aim and the fundamental rights of the individual and went no further than is necessary to accomplish Parliament's objective in protecting the public from the menace posed by persons having bladed articles in public places without good reason.[50]

Similarly, in *Parker v DPP*,[51] the Divisional Court held that there was no incompatibility between s.15(2) of the Road Traffic Act 1988, above, and Art.6(2) because the defendant was not prevented from adducing evidence that his condition as alleged on the road did not in fact exist. But, in *Carcass*,[52] the Court of Appeal held that the burden on the accused to prove that he had no intent to defraud under the Insolvency Act 1986, s.206(4) was not the legal burden and to "prove" in the subsection meant to "adduce sufficient evidence".

4–16

Likewise, in *Sheldrake v DPP*,[53] the Divisional Court held by a majority that, while the requirement under s.5(2) of the Road Traffic Act 1988 for a person charged under s.5(1) of the Act with being in charge of a vehicle with excess alcohol to prove that there was no likelihood of his driving was not an infringement of Art.6(2), the burden was evidential.

However, the view that such acts only involve an evidential burden of

---

[46] [2002] 1 Cr.App.R. 420.
[47] At 430.
[48] At 430.
[49] [2003] 2 Cr.App.R. 302.
[50] At 313.
[51] [2000] R.T.R. 240.
[52] [2002] 2 Cr.App.R. 77. In *Daniel* [2003] 1 Cr.App.R. 99 a differently constituted Court of Appeal held that it was bound by the decision in *Carcass*, but had reservations about the imposition of an evidential burden when the statute spoke of "prove".
[53] *The Times*, February 25, 2003.

proof has not always been followed: *L v DPP*, above. The Court of Appeal in *Drummond*[54] reiterated that the burden of proof under s.15(2) of the Road Traffic Act 1988 is the persuasive one and this is not an infringement with the presumption of innocence in Art.6(2). The Court said that the legislative interference in s.15(2) with the presumption of innocence was justified and no greater than necessary. If an accused drunk after an offence he made the scientific test potentially unreliable; furthermore, evidence concerning the consumption of alcohol after an alleged offence was within the knowledge of, or obtainable by, the accused rather than the Crown.

4–17   Similarly in *S v Havering LBC*[55] it was held that the defence under s.92(5) of the Trade Marks Act 1994 (to a charge, under s.92 of the Act, of trading in counterfeit goods) of holding a reasonable belief that the use of the mark was not an infringement of the section imposes a legal burden on the accused. Because the defence did not relate to an essential element of the offence, the presumption of innocence under Art.6(2) had no application since, regardless of the efforts of the accused to prove his defence, the burden of proof remained on the prosecution to prove the essential element of sale of infringing goods. Section 92(5) was also discussed by the House of Lords in *Johnstone*[56] the House considered that there must be "compelling reasons" to justify a reverse onus of proof and that public interest considerations in combating counterfeiting and piracy by means of bootleg compact discs of recordings by well-known performers could constitute such a reason.

Finally, in *Davies v Health and Safety Executive*[57] the Court of Appeal held that the imposition of a reverse legal burden under s.40 of the Health and Safety at Work Act 1974 was compatible with Art.6(2) and justified, necessary and proportionate. (Section 40 provides a defence to certain offences under the Act for failing to comply with a duty for an accused to prove that it was not reasonably practicable to do more than was, in fact, done.) The Court held that the burden was legal since the focus of the statutory scheme would be altered and enforcement difficulties arise if the burden was evidential and the only source of evidence the defendant himself or an inaccessible associate.

The upshot is that no hard and fast rule can be said to exist as to whether the burden is legal or evidential. The courts have generally approached the matter since *Lambert* practically and considered the proportionality of the burden, the mischief aimed at and the problems of disproving it, in order to determine whether the burden should be legal or not. The decision in each case of each statute will depend on its circumstances. However, there may

---

[54] [2002] 2 Cr.App.R. 25.
[55] *The Times*, December 2, 2002.
[56] [2004] Crim.L.R. 244.
[57] (2003) 67 Jo.Crim.L. 97.

be a tendency to say that the burden generally should be no more than adducing sufficient evidence.

This now is reflected in the Terrorism Act 2000, s.118(1), which provides **4–18** that the reverse onus of proof is satisfied if the person adduces evidence which is sufficient to raise an issue with respect to the matter unless the prosecution can prove to the contrary beyond reasonable doubt. This provision applies to those offences to which s.118 applies, including possession, for terrorist purposes and collection of information: s.118(5). However, there are other sections of the Act to which s.118 does not apply and which impose a burden on the defendant of proof on a balance of probabilities, for example membership (s.11(2)), money laundering (s.18(2)) and disclosure of information (s.19(3)).[58] Thus, in *Att-Gen's Reference (No.4 of 2002)*[59] the Court of Appeal held that the burden in relation to the defence under s.11(2) of the Act was legal rather than evidential. Section 11(2) provides a defence to a charge of belonging to a proscribed organisation under s.11(1) for a person to prove that the organisation was not proscribed on the last occasion on which he became a member and that he had not taken any part in the activities of the organisation at any time while it was proscribed. The Court of Appeal said that the varying consequences of the application of the views of the House of Lords in *Lambert* makes it clear that the first task of the Court in this type of case is to determine the meaning of the statutory provision in question on ordinary canons of construction and to identify the context in terms of the mischief to which the statutory provisions are directed before turning to determine the effect of the Human Rights Act 1998 and the Convention.[60] On the ordinary principles of construction, the burden in this case was the legal one and the intention was to criminalise membership of a proscribed organisation: the defence was open to two limited categories of person. The imposition of the burden imposed no interference with the presumption of innocence.

Implied statutory exceptions. Some statutes prohibit the doing of acts **4–19** subject to provisos, exceptions and the like, for example driving without a licence or selling liquor without a licence. In these circumstances the statute may impliedly put the burden of proving the exception upon the defendant.[61] If these circumstances arise, the court must analyse the enactment to determine whether it places a burden on the defence or not. The rules governing such cases at summary trial and at trials on indictment are similar, but in the former case the rules are statutory.

---

[58] For comment, see Rowe, "The Terrorism Act 2000" [2000] Crim.L.R. 527.
[59] [2003] 2 Cr.App.R. 346.
[60] At 351–352.
[61] In *Hunt* [1987] A.C. 352; (1987) 84 Cr.App.R. 163 the House of Lords rejected a submission that the "statutory exceptions" mentioned by Lord Sankey were express statutory exceptions and said that a statute may place a burden of proof expressly or by implication.

The position at summary trial is governed by s.101 of the Magistrates'
Courts Act 1980 which provides that where the defendant relies for his
defence on "any exception, exemption, proviso, excuse or qualification",
the burden of proving it shall be on him.

Thus, for instance, in cases of driving without a licence or driving
without insurance, it is for the driver to prove that he has a licence[62] or
insurance.[63] For further examples where the exception has been held to
apply, see *Oliver*[64] (selling sugar without a licence required by wartime
legislation), *Ewens*[65] (possessing drugs without a doctor's certificate),
Gatland v Metropolitan Police Commissioner[66] (depositing a skip on the
highway without lawful authority or excuse), *Guyll v Bright*[67] (keeping a
vehicle without an excise licence). On the other hand, in *Hirst and Agu v
Chief Constable of West Yorkshire*[68] the Divisional Court held that it was
for the prosecution to prove that the obstruction of a highway was without
lawful authority or excuse. It is difficult to reconcile this decision with the
other authorities. However, it is to be noted that neither they nor s.101
were referred to the court.

4–20   When does the defendant rely on any exception, exemption, proviso,
excuse or qualification? The best guide is to be found in the speech of Lord
Pearson in *Nimmo v Alexander Cowan*,[69] a Scottish case decided in the
House of Lords and turning on the construction of s.29(1) of the Factories
Act 1961. Lord Pearson said that "an exemption or exception or proviso
would be easily recognisable from the drafting of the enactment ... an
exception would naturally begin with the word 'except' and a proviso with
the words 'Provided always that'." He said that the addition of the words
"excuse" and "qualification" showed an intention to widen the provision
and to direct attention to the substance and effect rather than the form of
the enactment to which it is to be applied. He continued:

> "There is no usual formula for an 'excuse'. A 'qualification', if
> understood in a grammatical sense, might cover any adjective, adverb
> or adjectival or adverbial phrase. More probably it means some qua-
> lification, such as a licence, for doing what would otherwise be
> unlawful. There is no usual formula for 'qualification' in that sense.
> You have to look at the substance and effect of the enactment, as well

[62] *John v Humphreys* [1955] 1 W.L.R. 325.
[63] *Williams v Russell* (1983) 149 L.T. 190; *Philcox v Carberry* [1960] Crim.L.R. 563; *DPP v Kavaz* [1999] R.T.R. 40.
[64] [1944] K.B. 68.
[65] [1967] 1 Q.B. 322.
[66] [1968] 2 Q.B. 279.
[67] [1987] R.T.R. 104.
[68] (1987) 85 Cr.App.R. 143.
[69] [1968] A.C. 107.

as its form, in order to ascertain whether it contains an 'excuse or qualification' within the meaning of the section."[70]

Before deciding to cast a burden on the defence, the court must analyse the offence charged to ensure that the matter in issue is not an element of that offence. If it is an element of the offence, the prosecution bears the burden of proving it.[71] The court must also analyse the enactment to ensure that s.101 is applicable to the particular case. Thus in *Westminster City Council v Croyalgrange Ltd*[72] the House of Lords said that s.101 did not apply in the circumstances of that case because the exception relied on by the defence qualified a prohibition in the relevant enactment and not the offence charged.

Once the exception operates, the *persuasive* burden is on the defendant.   **4–21**
In *Gatland v Metropolitan Police Commissioner*,[73] Lord Parker C.J. said that it was for the accused "to raise and *prove* lawful authority or excuse."[74] (It was accepted in *Hunt*[75] that *Gatland* had been correctly decided: see para.4–22, below). The defendant must prove the exception on the balance of probabilities.

The law in trials on indictment is similar to that governing summary trials. In *Edwards*[76] the Court of Appeal decided that s.101 was a statutory statement of the common law rule, reflecting the rule in trials on indictment. This decision was approved by the House of Lords in *Hunt*.[77] The appellant in *Edwards* had been convicted of selling liquor without a licence. He appealed on the ground that the prosecution did not call evidence to show that there was no justices' licence in force. The Court, dismissing the appeal, said that the common law had evolved an exception to the rule that the prosecution must prove every element of the offence charged. The Court expressed the exception to be:

"limited to offences arising under enactments which prohibit the doing of an act save in specified circumstances or by persons of specified classes or with specified qualifications or with the licence or permission of specified authorities."[78]

---

[70] At 135.
[71] *e.g. Reader v Bunyard* [1987] R.T.R. 406; (1987) 85 Cr.App.R. 185, where the defendant was charged with driving a motor vehicle while disqualified: the magistrates wrongly put on the defence the burden of proving an essential element of the offence, *i.e.* that the vehicle was a motor vehicle within the meaning of the Act.
[72] [1986] 1 W.L.R. 674; (1986) 83 Cr.App.R. 155.
[73] [1968] 2 Q.B. 279, 286.
[74] Emphasis supplied by author.
[75] See [1987] A.C. 352, *per* Lord Ackner at 385.
[76] [1975] Q.B. 27.
[77] Above.
[78] [1975] Q.B. 27, 40.

4–22   However, the House of Lords in *Hunt* said that this statement was better regarded as a guide to construction rather than as an exception to a rule.[79] The House thus rejected the notion that the incidence of the burden of proof is always to be determined by the wording of the enactment. Where the statute does not make the incidence clear, other considerations may be taken into account.

In *Hunt*[80] the defendant was charged with possession of a controlled drug, morphine, contrary to s.5(2) of the Misuse of Drugs Act 1971. The police recovered from his house a paper fold containing powder. On analysis the powder was found to contain morphine mixed with caffeine and atropine (neither of which were controlled drugs). The prosecution called no evidence as to the proportion of morphine in the powder. At the close of the prosecution case, the defence submitted that there was no case to answer because the prosecution had not proved that the powder was not a preparation specified in Sch.1 to the Misuse of Drugs Regulations 1973, *i.e.* a preparation containing not more than 0.2 per cent of morphine and from which the morphine was not readily recoverable. Such a preparation is excepted from the provisions of s.5. The judge ruled against the submission and the Court of Appeal upheld his ruling on the ground that the defendant bore the burden of proving that the powder fell within the exception. However, the House of Lords held that the prosecution had the burden of proving that the powder did *not* come within the exception. This was because the offence, properly analysed, consists not of being in possession of morphine, but being in possession of morphine other than in a preparation as specified in Sch.1 to the 1973 Regulations. As a result, it was for the prosecution to prove that the morphine was in its prohibited form and not in a specified preparation.[81]

4–23   The majority of the House of Lords in *Hunt*[82] concluded that if a statute does not clearly indicate on whom the burden lies, the court may look to other considerations to determine the intention of Parliament. Those considerations include the seriousness of the offence and the practical

---

[79] [1987] A.C. 352, *per* Lord Griffiths at 375 and Lord Ackner at 386.

[80] Above. For academic discussion of the decision in *Hunt*, see Zuckerman (1987) 103 L.Q.R. 170; Healy, "Proof and Policy: No Golden Threads" [1987] Crim.L.R. 355; Mirfield, "The Legacy of Hunt" [1988] Crim.L.R. 19; and Birch, "Hunting the Snark: the Elusive Statutory Exception" [1988] Crim.L.R. 221.

[81] The Court of Appeal in *Hill* (1993) 96 Cr.App.R. 456, 460 did not accept that the effect of the decision in *Hunt* is to require scientific evidence to be adduced in every case to identify a prohibited drug. However, Waterhouse J. said that it was clear from *Hunt* that the prosecution must establish the identity of a drug (the subject of a charge) with sufficient certainty to achieve the criminal standard of proof. In *Jones (Keith)*, *The Times*, April 24, 1997, the Court of Appeal emphasised the importance of clarity in an analyst's report in order to exclude the possibility that the substance did not come within the exception. The Court said that the sooner the prosecuting authorities took to heart the observations to this effect in *Hunt*, the better.

[82] Lords Keith, Griffiths, Mackay and Ackner.

consequences of holding that one party or the other should bear the burden.[83]

The court should take the seriousness of the offence into account because the more serious the offence, the graver the consequences of holding that the defendant bears a burden of proof. Thus, Lord Griffiths said in *Hunt*[84] that he had regard to the fact that "offences involving the misuse of hard drugs were among the most serious in the criminal calendar" and that it seemed right "to resolve any ambiguity in favour of the defendant and to place the burden of proving the nature of the substance involved in so serious an offence upon the prosecution."

In considering the practical consequences the court must take into account the ease or difficulty which a party might have in discharging the burden.[85] In some cases it may be relatively simple to determine which party would have the greater difficulty. Thus, in *Hunt* the prosecution could without difficulty have called the analyst to give evidence as to the proportion of morphine in the powder. Similarly, in cases where a person is charged with driving without insurance, it is easier for him to prove that he had insurance than for the prosecution to prove that he did not. In *Alath Construction Ltd*[86] the Court of Appeal held that in a prosecution under the Town and Country Planning Act 1974 for cutting down a tree, the subject of a tree preservation order, the burden of proving that the tree was dying or dead (and, hence, no preservation order could apply) was on the defence since this was a true exception from liability and the owner and not the local authority was in the best position to discover the true condition of the tree.

On the other hand, had it not already been decided that the defendant **4–24** bears the burden of proving that he has a licence to drive,[87] it might be argued that under the present computerised system, the prosecution would have no difficulty in shouldering the burden. In cases of doubt, the court should bear in mind Lord Griffiths' comment in *Hunt*[88] that he regarded this consideration to be of great importance because Parliament can never lightly be taken to have intended to impose a duty on a defendant to prove his innocence in a criminal case and a court should be very slow to draw any such inference from the language of a statute.

---

[83] This conclusion was based on the earlier decision of the House in *Nimmo v Alexander Cowan & Sons Ltd* [1968] A.C. 107 where Lord Pearson said that in construing an enactment there were factors to be taken into account other than its arrangement and the form of expression used in it, in particular the parties' means of knowledge and spheres of responsibility (pp.132–133).
[84] Above, at 378.
[85] *Nimmo v Alexander Cowan & Sons Ltd*, above, at 152, *per* Lord Pearson; *Hunt*, above, at 374, *per* Lord Griffiths and 383, *per* Lord Ackner.
[86] [1990] 1 W.L.R. 1255.
[87] *John v Humphreys*, see para.4–19, above.
[88] Above, at 364.

Accordingly, in deciding if a statute places a burden on the accused the court should:

    (a) analyse the enactment to determine whether the wording makes the incidence of the burden clear; and (if it does not),

    (b) consider the seriousness of the offence and the practical consequence of holding that the burden falls on one party or another.

An example is to be found in *Canning*.[89] The Court of Appeal held in that case that the burden of proving an exception to the prohibition on trade in endangered species in the Control of Trade in Endangered Species (Enforcement) Regulations 1985 rested on the defence. The Court said that it was not clear from the Regulations on whom the burden lay and it was necessary (applying *Hunt*) to consider the mischief at which the legislation was aimed and the ease of proof on either side. In this case the mischief was taking species from the wild and (since the defendant relied on an exemption which provided for the keeping of birds for teaching or breeding) the prosecution would find the burden more difficult than the defence.

4–25   If a burden is placed on the defendant, it is the same burden whether in a summary trial or trial on indictment, *i.e.* the burden of proof on the balance of probabilities.[90] There is considerable support for the view that the defence should only bear an evidential burden in these circumstances.[91] However, the House of Lords in *Hunt* did not accept this view for these reasons: (a) when Parliament imposes a burden, it is the persuasive burden and it should not be different when the burden is placed by necessary implication; (b) s.101 places the persuasive burden on the defendant and the nature of the burden should not vary according to the type of trial; and (c) the discharge of the evidential burden proves nothing, but merely raises an issue.[92]

B. The evidential burden

4–26   The expression "evidential burden" may be defined as the burden of adducing sufficient evidence to put a matter in issue. The decision in the House of Lords in *Lambert*[93] (discussed at paras 4–14 to 4–15, above) does not alter the position.

The expression is in one sense a misnomer since it is not a burden of *proof*. It is not, however, a misnomer in the sense that if the evidential burden is not satisfied, a burden of proof in relation to the matter in

---

[89] [1996] 2 Cr.App.R.(S.) 202.
[90] *Hunt*, above.
[91] Eleventh Report of the Criminal Law Revision Committee: Cmnd. 4991 (1972), para.140; [1974] Crim.L.R. 541–542.
[92] See 385, *per* Lord Ackner.
[93] [2001] 2 Cr.App.R. 522, see *per* Lord Steyn at 526.

question does not arise. Thus, for instance, unless sufficient evidence to put self-defence in issue is given (whether by the defence or otherwise) the prosecution are under no burden to negative it.

The expression "prima facie case" is related but distinct: unless the prosecution have adduced sufficient evidence to allow a reasonable jury, properly directed, to convict on that evidence alone, the defendant will be acquitted. To the extent that it must adduce sufficient evidence to make a prima facie case, the prosecution may be said to be under an evidential burden. The remainder of this discussion is concerned with the evidential burden on the defence.

The expression "evidential burden on the defence" needs to be treated with care. This is because (subject to the exceptions above), the defendant bears no burden in a criminal case. However, facts may be proved by the prosecution which, if unexplained by the defendant, would warrant an inference of guilt. Furthermore, in many cases an explanation may well, as a matter of common sense, be required from the defendant. An example is to be found in the case of the alleged handler of stolen property where the only evidence against the defendant is the possession of recently stolen property. The jury will be told that if the defendant offers no explanation to account for his possession, they *may* infer guilty knowledge.[94] If the handler does have an explanation, he would therefore be well advised to give it. At that stage the evidential burden may be described as having shifted to him. The jury are not obliged to convict if he does not give an explanation, but they may well do so.

In many cases the defence will depend upon an issue being raised *in the defendant's favour*, as to the existence of a defence, usually but not always by adducing evidence. In these cases the evidential burden is said to have "shifted" to the defence. Self-defence is an example which has already been referred to.[95] There are many other examples: defences of alibi,[96] provocation (in murder),[97] automatism,[98] duress,[99] mechanical defect,[1] and drunkenness,[2] among them. Again, however, the language may tend to mislead. The only effect of the failure on the defendant's part to satisfy the evidential "burden" on him in relation to the issue is that it will simply not arise as an issue to be negatived by the prosecution.

4–27

---

[94] *Aves* (1950) 34 Cr.App.R. 159.
[95] See, *e.g. Mancini v DPP* [1942] A.C. 1, HL; *Lobell* [1957] 1 Q.B. 547, CA; *Palmer v R* [1971] A.C. 814, PC; *Moon* [1969] 1 W.L.R. 1705, CA; *Abraham* (1973) 57 Cr.App.R. 799; and *Folley* [1978] Crim.L.R. 556.
[96] *Johnson* [1961] 1 W.L.R. 1478; *Denney* [1963] Crim.L.R. 191; *Wood* (1968) 52 Cr.App.R. 74.
[97] *Chan Kau v R* [1955] A.C.206; *Bullard v R* [1957] A.C. 635; *Cascoe* (1970) 54 Cr.App.R. 401.
[98] *Hill v Baxter* [1958] 1 Q.B. 277; *Bratty v Att-Gen* [1963] A.C. 386; para.4–30, below.
[99] *Gill* (1963) 47 Cr.App.R. 166; *Bone* (1968) 52 Cr.App.R. 546.
[1] *Spurge* [1961] 2 Q.B. 205; 45 Cr.App.R. 191.
[2] *Kennedy v H.M. Advocate* 1944 S.C.(J) 171; *Foote* [1964] Crim.L.R. 405.

4-28   The issue must be raised in a way which makes it fit to be considered by the jury. The decision whether an issue is fit for the jury to consider is a matter of law for the judge. It will depend on the circumstances of the case. In some cases, for instance self-defence, the issue may be raised during the prosecution case. Prosecution witnesses may give evidence-in-chief in such a way that it is clear that the accused *may* have been acting in self-defence, or they may make admissions to the same effect in cross-examination. In this way the issue is raised without any evidence being given by the defence. In *Gill*[3] (a case of duress) Edmund Davies J. said:

> "The accused, by the cross-examination of prosecution witnesses or by evidence called on his behalf, or by a combination of the two, must place before the court such material as makes duress a live issue, fit and proper to be left to the jury. But, once he has succeeded in doing this, it is then for the Crown to destroy that defence in such a manner as to leave in the jury's minds no reasonable doubt that the accused cannot be absolved on the grounds of the alleged compulsion."

Edmund Davies J. was almost certainly speaking with reference to the facts of the case before him and not intending to lay down any limiting principle. Thus, in *Bullard*,[4] Lord Tucker said:

> "It has long been settled law that if on the evidence, whether of the prosecution or of the defence, there is any evidence of provocation fit to be left to a jury, and whether or not this issue has been specifically raised at the trial by counsel for the defence and whether or not the accused has said in terms that he was provoked, it is the duty of the judge, after a proper direction, to leave it open to the jury to return a verdict of manslaughter if they are not satisfied beyond reasonable doubt that the killing was unprovoked."

4-29   The crucial question is whether *on the evidence as a whole* there is any evidence which would put in issue the existence of any defence, explanation or excuse which, if accepted by the jury as true or possibly true, would lead to the defendant's acquittal. As Lord Devlin said of the "burden": "the only burden that is laid upon the accused is to collect from the evidence enough material to make it possible for a reasonable jury to acquit.[5]"

A distinction must be drawn between an issue raised on the evidence and matters which are not raised on the evidence at all, for instance a contention by a defence advocate unsupported by evidence.[6] In the latter case

---

[3] (1963) 47 Cr.App.R. 166, 172.
[4] [1957] A.C. 635, 642.
[5] *Jayasena v R* [1970] A.C. 618, 623.
[6] *Parker v Smith* [1974] R.T.R. 500; *Critchley* [1982] Crim.L.R. 524, CA.

there is no issue proper for the jury to consider. If an issue is not raised on the evidence the judge will not leave it to the jury. On the other hand, if the issue is raised, it is his duty to leave it. This is so, even if it involves the judge directing the jury on a version of the facts which neither prosecution nor defence had advanced.[7]

There are cases where, in practice, an issue will not arise unless the defence calls evidence in support of it. The defence of automatism is an obvious example. It is difficult to conceive of such a defence arising unless some evidence is called in support. In *Bratty v Att-Gen*,[8] Lord Denning said the necessity of laying a *proper foundation* for the defence of automatism is on the defence: "If it is not so laid, the defence of automatism need not be left to the jury, any more than the defence of drunkenness, provocation or self-defence." Lord Denning emphasised that the Crown was entitled to rely on the presumption that every man has sufficient mental capacity to be responsible for his crimes. Thus, in order to displace that presumption the defence must give sufficient evidence from which it may reasonably be inferred that the act was involuntary. "The evidence of the man himself will rarely be sufficient unless it is supported by medical evidence which points to the cause of mental incapacity.[9]" In *Stripp*[10] the Court of Appeal said that *Bratty* should be carefully followed and that the court should ensure that there is a proper foundation for the defence before leaving it to the jury.[11]

The question whether there is sufficient evidence for a defence or explanation to be left to the jury is for the trial judge to decide by applying common sense to the evidence.[12] The judge is not under a duty to leave to the jury defences which are fanciful or speculative[13] or for which there is not a scintilla of evidence.[14]

On the other hand, he is under a duty to direct the jury to consider any defences which may reasonably arise upon the evidence, notwithstanding that it was not the defence put forward by the defendant.[15] This situation does arise occasionally. Suppose an assault case where the defence is alibi. During the prosecution case it becomes apparent (from the evidence) that the alleged attacker may have been acting in self-defence. Evidence of alibi is given on behalf of the defence. Defence counsel may well not refer to self-

4–30

4–31

---

[7] *Williams, The Times*, November 11, 1993.
[8] (1962) 46 Cr.App.R. 1, 21.
[9] At 22.
[10] (1978) 69 Cr.App.R. 318.
[11] In *Pullen* [1991] Crim.L.R.457 the Court of Appeal said that before hypoglycaemia and automatism could be left to the jury as a defence, some foundation must be laid in evidence by the defence.
[12] *Bonnick* (1978) 66 Cr.App.R. 266. See also, *Bratty v Att-Gen* [1963] A.C. 386, 416, 417, *per* Lord Morris of Borth-y-Gest.
[13] *Bratty*, above, at 416, 417; *Critchley*, above.
[14] *DPP v Walker* [1974] 1 W.L.R. 1090, PC.
[15] *Hopper* [1915] 2 K.B. 431, 435, *per* Lord Reading C.J. approved in *Mancini v DPP* [1942] A.C. 1.

defence in his speech. The judge must nonetheless direct the jury to consider self-defence. This duty has been described as the "invisible burden" on the trial judge, *i.e.* to put before the jury a possible defence although not expressly raised by either party.[16]

Justices are under a similar obligation to consider defences which may reasonably arise on the evidence.

4-32   The law as to the evidential burden falling on the accused can be summarised as follows:

(i)   The "burden" on the accused is to put before the court such material as to oblige the judge to leave a possible defence to the jury.

(ii)   The material must be collected from the evidence in the case: a theoretical possibility will not suffice.

(iii) The issue as to the existence of the defence may be put before the court in an appropriate case without the defendant adducing evidence in support of it.

(iv)   In some cases in order to ensure a proper evidential foundation to put the matter in issue, the defendant will have to adduce evidence.

(v)   A defence should be left to the jury if, properly directed, a reasonably jury might acquit as a result of it.

C. The burden of establishing the admissibility of evidence

Confessions

4-33   It was established at common law that the burden of proving the admissibility of confessions is on the prosecution.[17] This rule is preserved by statute. The Police and Criminal Evidence Act 1984, s.76(2) provides that the burden of proving beyond reasonable doubt that a confession was not obtained by oppression or in consequence of anything said or done which was likely to render it unreliable is on the prosecution.[18]

Competence of witnesses

4-34   The burden of proving the competence of a prosecution witness is on the prosecution. This was the position at common law, as the Court of Appeal

---

[16] Doran, "Alternative defences: the 'invisible burden' on the trial judge" [1991] Crim.L.R. 878, quoted in *Watson* [1992] Crim.L.R. 434.
[17] *Thompson* [1893] 1 Q.B. 12 (CCR).
[18] See paras 9–16 *et seq.*, below.

held in *Yacoob*.[19] The Court held in that case that it is for the prosecution, once the issue of the competence of one of its witnesses is raised, to prove that the person is competent to testify. Although there was no authority directly on the point, it was generally assumed that the same rule applied to witnesses called by the defence, *i.e.* the defence bore the burden of establishing competence. The Youth Justice and Criminal Evidence Act 1999, s.54(2) has now restated and clarified the common law by providing that "[it] is for the party calling the witness to satisfy the court that, on a balance of probabilities, the witness is competent to give evidence...".

The admissibility of other evidence

The burden of establishing the conditions of admissibility of other evidence will fall on whichever side is seeking to adduce it. That side is in the better position to do so since it alone will know what the evidence is and what relevance it has to the issues in the case.

4–35

2. Standard of Proof

The expression "standard of proof" means the standard or degree to which proof must be established. There are only two standards of proof in criminal proceedings: proof "beyond reasonable doubt", and proof "on the balance of probabilities".

4–36

A. Proof beyond reasonable doubt

In a criminal trial the prosecution must establish the defendant's guilt beyond reasonable doubt. This principle together with that relating to the burden of proof is central to all criminal trials. This standard of proof, accordingly, is called the "criminal standard": it is to be applied by justices and juries alike. Thus, Lord Sankey L.C. said that if there is a reasonable doubt created by the evidence given by either the prosecution or the prisoner the prosecution has not made out the case and the prisoner is entitled to be acquitted.[20] (The defendant is, of course, not merely entitled to be acquitted in these circumstances; he *must* be acquitted.)

4–37

Many attempts have been made to define a reasonable doubt. Some of those definitions when given to juries have caused problems. The standard of proof is a high one, but it is important that it should not be confused with absolute certainty: nor with scientific proof.[21] Thus, in *Re H (Minors)*,[22] Lord Nicholls said: "The law looks for probability, not certainty. Certainty

---

[19] (1981) 72 Cr.App.R. 313. The Court said that the appropriate time to raise the issue of competence was at the beginning of the trial.
[20] *Woolmington v DPP* [1935] A.C. 462, 481.
[21] *Bracewell* (1979) 68 Cr.App.R. 44, CA.
[22] [1996] 2 W.L.R. 8, 24.

is seldom attainable. But probability is an unsatisfactorily vague criterion because there are degrees of probability. In establishing principles regarding the standard of proof, therefore, the law seeks to define the degree of probability appropriate for different types of proceedings."

4–38   In *Miller v Minister of Pensions*[23] Denning J. said of the degree of proof required in a criminal case:

> "That degree is well settled. It need not reach certainty, but it must carry a high degree of probability. Proof beyond doubt does not mean proof beyond the shadow of a doubt. The law would fail to protect the community if it admitted fanciful possibilities to deflect the course of justice. If the evidence is so strong against a man as to leave only a remote possibility in his favour which can be dismissed with the sentence, 'of course it is possible but not in the least probable', the case is proved beyond reasonable doubt but nothing short of that will suffice."

However, that definition is open to the following criticism: if the jury found that the defence was possible but not in the least probable, can it be said that the prosecution has proved the case beyond reasonable doubt? The jury must surely consider the possibilities however remote they may appear to be, *unless* they are so remote that the jury feel sure that they can be safely disregarded. The expression is therefore better left to speak for itself, undefined.

B. Directions to the jury

4–39   The judge's duty is to direct the jury so that they understand that they must not return a verdict of guilty unless they are sure of the defendant's guilt.[24] This duty was restated by the Court of Appeal in *Edwards*.[25] In that case, the judge failed to direct the jury on the standard of proof. The Court held that this was a serious defect in the summing up which could not be cured by the fact that reference had been made to the standard of proof by counsel in their speeches to the jury, or by the fact that the jury was experienced. However, the evidence for the prosecution was overwhelming and the Court applied the proviso to s.2(1) of the Criminal Appeal Act 1968 on the ground that no miscarriage of justice had occurred and dismissed the appeal. A further point arises from this case. At the trial defence counsel had noticed the judge's omission. Prosecuting counsel had not. Defence counsel did not bring the judge's attention to the omission. They were not

[23] [1947] 2 All E.R. 372, 373.
[24] The Court of Appeal said that if judges, in summing up on the standard of proof, told juries that they must be satisfied of the accused's guilt, so that they could be sure of it, and then refrained from developing it again and again when summing up, many cases would not reach the Court: *Quinn* [1983] Crim.L.R. 474.
[25] (1983) 77 Cr.App.R. 5.

obliged to do so.[26] The Court of Appeal, however, said that it was fortified in its conclusion that no miscarriage of justice had occurred by the fact that defence counsel had not drawn the judge's attention to the omission: from which the Court deduced that defence counsel, too, must have formed the view that the case was overwhelming. The Court said that, if counsel ever found themselves placed as counsel for the defence were placed at the trial of the appellant, they might find the judgment in the present case of assistance.

This is no place for a discussion of the duty of counsel in these circum-   **4–40** stances, but the comments of the Court of Appeal, albeit *obiter*, make it plain, at the least, that if defence counsel do not draw the judge's attention to a failure on the part of the judge to direct the jury on the standard of proof, the Court of Appeal are likely to take the view that this indicates an acknowledgement by counsel of the strength of the prosecution case and accordingly the proviso is likely to be applied.

However, in *Bentley*[27] the Court of Appeal (on a reference by the Criminal Cases Review Commission) allowed an appeal against a conviction for murder in 1952 on the ground *inter alia* that the summing up had contained no direction on the standard of proof. Lord Bingham C. J. said that although in the light of *Edwards* such a conviction could be regarded as safe if the case was overwhelming, it was to be questioned whether a conviction in a capital case could ever be so regarded in the absence of an adequate direction. It is submitted that this must also apply to other grave cases.

There is no particular formula to be used in directing the jury on the   **4–41** standard of proof. It is the effect of the summing up as a whole that matters.[28] The Privy Council has said that it is best left to the discretion of the judge, who has had an opportunity of observing the jurors, to choose the most appropriate set of words to make *that* jury understand that they must not return a verdict against the defendant unless they are sure of his guilt.[29] The law was put succinctly by Lord Goddard in *Hepworth and Fearnley*.[30]

> "I should be very sorry if it were thought that cases should depend on the use of a particular formula or a particular word or words. The point is that the jury should be directed first, that the onus is always on the prosecution; secondly, that before they convict they must feel sure of the accused's guilt. If that is done, that will be enough."

---

[26] James L.J. in *Cocks* (1976) 63 Cr.App.R. 79, 82, said that defence counsel were under no duty to draw the judge's attention to any error of law in the summing up. In *Edwards*, the Court of Appeal, without deciding the point, proceeded on the basis that this dictum was correct.
[27] [1999] Crim.L.R. 330.
[28] *Kritz* [1950] 1 K.B. 82, 90. See also, *per* Lord Morris of Borth-y-Gest in *McGreevy v DPP* [1973] 1 W.L.R. 276, 284.
[29] *Walters v R* [1969] 2 A.C. 26, 30.
[30] [1955] 2 Q.B. 600, 603.

Although there is no formula, there are two directions which are used by judges. Juries are directed either that they "must be satisfied so that they are sure of the defendant's guilt"[31] or "that they must be satisfied beyond a reasonable doubt of the defendant's guilt." Both directions are in constant use (sometimes combined). Both have the support of authority.

4–42   The "reasonable doubt" direction has the authority of *Woolmington*[32]; and in *McGreevy v DPP*[33] Lord Morris of Borth-y-Gest said that:

"the basic necessity before guilt in a criminal charge can be pronounced is that the jury are satisfied of guilt beyond all reasonable doubt. This is a conception that a jury can readily understand and by clear exposition can readily be made to understand."

However, problems connected with the phrase "reasonable doubt" and its exposition led Lord Goddard C.J. to state his preference for the direction that the jury should be "sure"[34] which he said was the direction which he constantly gave juries.[35] In *Hepworth and Fearnley*,[36] Lord Goddard returned to the point:

"the explanations given as to what is and what is not a reasonable doubt are so very often extraordinarily difficult to follow and it is very difficult to tell a jury what is a reasonable doubt. To tell a jury that it must not be a fanciful doubt is something that is without any real guidance. To tell them that a reasonable doubt is such a doubt as to cause them to hesitate in their own affairs never seems to me to convey any particular standard."

4–43   Despite these remarks, problems were still encountered with definitions of "reasonable doubt". Thus, in 1968 the Privy Council approved of a definition as "that quality and kind of doubt which when you are dealing

---

[31] Not "reasonably" sure; *Head and Warrener* (1961) 45 Cr.App.R. 225; nor "pretty certain": *Law* [1961] Crim.L.R. 52; nor "pretty sure": *Woods* [1961] Crim.L.R. 324. The Court has recently reiterated that it is not of assistance to the jury for the judge to attempt to clarify the established phrase "satisfied so that you are sure". In the instant case the jury had asked how certain they had to be and the judge had responded "not certain, but sure, something which is less than being certain". The Court said that such an attempt at guidance was unhelpful: *Stephens, The Times*, June 27, 2002.
[32] [1935] A.C. 462.
[33] [1973] 1 W.L.R. 276, 285. See also, the speeches of Lords Salmon and Diplock in *Sang* [1980] A.C. 402 where both refer to the need for the case against the accused to be proved beyond all reasonable doubt and the speech of Lord Diplock in *Courtie* [1984] 2 W.L.R. 330, 332 which is in similar terms.
[34] *Summers* [1952] 1 All E.R. 1059, 1060.
[35] *Kritz* [1950] 1 K.B. 82, 90.
[36] [1955] 2 Q.B. 600, 603.

78

with matters of *importance* in your own affairs, you allow to influence you one way or another."[37]

On the other hand, in 1973 the Court of Appeal disapproved of a definition as: "the sort of doubt which might affect you in the conduct of your *everyday* affairs" since it might suggest to a jury too low a standard of proof.[38] The distinction between what the Privy Council approved and the Court of Appeal disapproved lies between "important" and "everyday" affairs. In substance the Court of Appeal must have been concerned that in their everyday affairs jurors would be likely to act routinely, unaffected by doubts, whereas in their important affairs they would be more reflective and likely to be affected by doubts.

In *Ching*[39] the Court of Appeal did not disapprove of a judge's use of an analogy of a reasonable doubt being the sort of matter which might influence a person considering a mortgage of his house. The Court said that in most cases judges would be well advised not to attempt any gloss on what is meant by "sure" and "reasonable doubt", but that in some cases the jury may need help which was best left to the discretion of the trial judge.

However, the substitution of "sure" for "absence of reasonable doubt" may not by itself produce any greater precision or clarity of expression. In any case, the notion of proving guilt "beyond reasonable doubt" is so much part of our culture that a jury might be troubled if it formed no part of the judge's direction. On the other hand, "sure" is probably a word which jurors find easier to understand and apply. Both these considerations are therefore satisfied by a direction that "you should not convict unless you are satisfied so that you are sure of the defendant's guilt which is the same thing as being satisfied beyond reasonable doubt."   **4–44**

Usually no repetition of a direction relating to the burden and standard of proof is necessary. However, there may be cases when a question from the jury makes it plain that the members of the jury have not grasped the meaning of the direction. In such cases a further direction should be given.[40]

C. Proof on the balance of probabilities

On the rare occasion when the burden of proof of an issue is on the defence, the standard of proof is not as high as the standard on the Crown in proving the guilt of the accused. The standard to which the defence have to prove an issue is on the *balance of probabilities*, the standard applicable in civil cases. This means that the burden is discharged by evidence satisfying the jury of the probability of the issue which the defence has to prove.   **4–45**

This burden was defined most clearly by Denning J. in *Miller v Minister*

---

[37] *Walters v R* [1969] 2 A.C. 26.
[38] *Gray* (1974) 58 Cr.App.R. 177, 183.
[39] (1976) 63 Cr.App.R. 7.
[40] *Gibson* [1983] 1 W.L.R. 1038; *Rafique* [1973] Crim.L.R. 777; *Bell* [1967] Crim.L.R. 545.

of Pensions[41] when he said that it must carry a reasonable degree of probability, but not as high as required in a criminal case. If the evidence is such that the tribunal say: "we think it more probable than not," the burden is discharged, but if the probabilities are equal it is not. In *Carr-Briant*[42] the Court of Criminal Appeal referred to the same proposition:

> "What is the burden resting on a plaintiff or defendant in civil proceedings can, we think, best be stated in the words of the classic pronouncement on the subject by Miles J. in *Cooper v Slade*.[43] That learned judge referred to an ancient authority in support of what he termed 'the elementary proposition that in civil cases the preponderance of probability may constitute sufficient ground for a verdict.' "[44]

4–46   Authority for the proposition that the civil standard should be applied to burdens falling on the defence is to be found: (a) in *Sodeman v R*,[45] in which Lord Hailsham L.C. said that the burden of proof resting on the accused to prove insanity was not as heavy as the burden resting on the Crown[46] and (b) in *Carr-Briant*[47] in which Humphreys J. giving the judgment of the Court of Criminal Appeal said:

> "In our judgment, in any case where, either by statute or at common law, some matter is presumed against an accused person 'unless the contrary is proved,' the jury should be directed that it is for them to decide whether the contrary is proved, that the burden of proof required is less than that required at the hands of the prosecution in proving the case beyond a reasonable doubt, and that the burden may be discharged by evidence satisfying the jury of the probability of that which the accused is called upon to establish."

There is also authority to the same effect in respect of specific statutes which put a persuasive burden on the defendant.[48]

---

[41] [1947] 2 All E.R. 372.

[42] [1943] 1 K.B. 607, 611, 612.

[43] (1857–58) 6 HL Cas. 746.

[44] The authority in question was the judgment of Dyer C.J. and a majority of the justices of the Common Pleas in *Newis v Lark* (1571) Plowd. 403, 412 decided in the reign of Queen Elizabeth I. The report contains this passage: "where the matter is so far gone that the parties are at issue ... so that the jury is to give a verdict one way or another, there, if the matter is doubtful, they may found their verdict upon that which appears the most probable."

[45] [1936] W.N. 190.

[46] At 191.

[47] [1943] K.B. 607, 612.

[48] *Brown* (1971) 55 Cr.App.R. 478 (Prevention of Crime Act 1953, s.1); *Islington LBC v Panico* [1973] 1 W.L.R. 1166 (Magistrates Courts Act 1952, s.81, re-enacted in the Magistrates' Courts Act 1980, s.101); *Dunbar* [1958] 1 Q.B. 1 (Homicide Act 1957, s.2(2)).

D. Standard of proof on other issues

Fitness to plead

If the prosecution raise the issue and bear the burden, the criminal standard   **4–47**
is applied.[49] *Per contra*, if the defence raise the issue and bear the burden,
the civil standard applies.[50]

Confessions

The Police and Criminal Evidence Act 1984, s.76(2), provides that if the
issue is raised the court shall not allow the confession to be given in evidence by the prosecution unless the prosecution proves *beyond reasonable
doubt* that the confession was not obtained by oppression of the accused or
anything said or done likely to render the confession unreliable.[51] Section
76A (2) of the 1984 Act[52] makes similar provision in relation to confessions
given in evidence for a co-accused.

Other questions of admissibility of evidence[53]

It is a general rule that whenever the admissibility of evidence in a criminal   **4–48**
trial turns upon an issue of fact and depends upon a rule of common law,
the prosecution has to prove admissibility to the criminal standard.[54]

There are, however, two conflicting decisions of the Court of Appeal as
to whether the rule applies when the admissibility of documents for the
purpose of the comparison of handwriting is in issue under s.8 of the
Criminal Procedure Act 1865.

The section provides that comparison of a disputed writing with any
writing "proved to the satisfaction of the judge" to be genuine shall be
permitted. The Court in *Angeli*[55] decided that the judge had only to be
satisfied to the civil standard. This was because the 1865 Act applied the
provisions of an earlier Act (which operated in the civil courts) to the
criminal courts. The Court said that the standard of proof applicable in the
civil courts became applicable in the criminal courts when the same provision was made operative in criminal courts. On the other hand, a
differently constituted court in *Ewing*[56] held that the criminal standard
applied. The Court in that case disagreed with the reasoning of the Court in

---

[49] *Robertson* [1968] 1 W.L.R. 1767; 52 Cr.App.R. 690; para.4–11, above.
[50] *Podola* [1960] 1 Q.B. 325; para.4–11, above.
[51] The statute preserved the common law rule: for the rule see *DPP v Ping Lin* [1975] 3 W.L.R. 419, *per* Lord Hailsham L.C. at 425.
[52] As inserted by s.128 of the Criminal Justice Act 2003. At the time of writing, the section is expected to come into effect in April 2005.
[53] When the prosecution has to establish the competence of one of its witnesses, it has to do so beyond reasonable doubt: see para.4–43, above.
[54] *Minors* [1989] 1 W.L.R. 441, 448; *Ewing*, below.
[55] (1979) 68 Cr.App.R. 32.
[56] (1983) 77 Cr.App.R. 47.

Angeli and said that, since the section was silent about the standard of proof, the common law applied: were it otherwise, the case could not be said to be proved beyond reasonable doubt. It is submitted that *Ewing* is to be preferred as a matter of principle and as a decision on the statute. The fact that a provision has a civil law origin does not warrant the implication of a civil standard of proof into a criminal statute concerned with the admissibility of evidence to prove guilt.

CHAPTER 5
Proof Where Evidence is Not Necessary

In certain cases facts may be proved without the necessity of calling   5–01
evidence. These cases arise when facts are proved either because they are
presumed, admitted or judicially noticed, or as a result of previous
acquittals and convictions.

1. PRESUMPTIONS

Facts may be inferred from the surrounding circumstances of an event or   5–02
alleged offence. Such facts are sometimes said to be presumed either as a
matter of fact or as a matter of law. This discussion is concerned with
presumptions of law, but two points should first be noted.

(a) Presumptions of fact are no more than a species of circumstantial
    evidence and have been considered under that heading (para.
    1–06).

(b) In two cases the term "presumption" is used to indicate no more
    than the incidence of the burden of proof. These cases are the
    presumption of innocence and the presumption of sanity. The
    presumption of innocence means that the defendant is presumed
    innocent until the prosecution has proved its case against him
    beyond reasonable doubt.[1] Likewise, the presumption of sanity
    means no more than that a man is presumed to be sane and
    responsible for his actions until the contrary is proved.[2]

(c) The European Court of Human Rights has held that presumptions
    of fact or law are not contrary to the convention in principle, but
    that Art.6(2) requires states to confine them within reasonable
    limits which take into account the importance of what is at stake

---

[1] The presumption of innocence is provided for in Art.6(2) of the European Convention on
Human Rights: see para.13–14, below.
[2] McNaghten Rules (1843) to be found in editions of *Archbold: Criminal Pleading, Evidence
and Practice.*

and maintain the rights of the defence.[3] (It is not thought that any of the presumptions, discussed here, offend these criteria.)

5–03   Presumptions of law are divided into irrebuttable presumptions and rebuttable presumptions. Irrebuttable presumptions are rules of substantive law which require the court in particular circumstances to come to a particular conclusion. Thus, for instance, a child under 10 is conclusively presumed to be incapable of committing a crime.[4] Similarly, every man is presumed to know the law. More recently, Parliament has enacted a "conclusive" presumption that there was no consent in relation to certain sexual offences where the defendant has used deception or impersonation.[5] These matters are more properly the concern of substantive law.

Where a rebuttable presumption of law arises, once a particular fact has been established the *presumed* fact must be presumed to exist in the absence of evidence to the contrary. The most common examples are as follows:

(a)   if it is established that a person has not been heard of for seven years, his death will be presumed;

(b)   once there is evidence of the celebration of a marriage, it will be presumed that the marriage was valid in the absence of evidence to the contrary;

(c)   it is presumed that a child born during lawful wedlock is legitimate in the absence of evidence to the contrary.

5–04   These presumptions are given as examples, since they may make an occasional appearance in a criminal trial. The effect of such a presumption is to indicate upon which party the burden of proof on the issue lies. The burden, however, is not the same in all cases. If the prosecution wishes to challenge the presumption it bears a persuasive burden. In *J.M. v Runeckles*[6] the Divisional Court held that in order to rebut the presumption that a child was *doli incapax* the prosecution must prove that the child knew what he or she was doing was seriously wrong,[7] and Mann J. said

---

[3] *Salabiaku v France* [1988] 13 E.H.R.R. 379. See also *Parker v DPP* [2001] R.T.R. 240.
[4] Children and Young Persons Act 1933, s.50, as amended by the Children and Young Persons Act 1963, s.16. (It may be noted that s.1 of the Sexual Offences Act 1993 removed the irrebuttable presumption that a boy under 14 is incapable of sexual intercourse.)
[5] Sexual Offences Act 2003, s.76. As the Minister of State in the Home Office pointed out, this presumption reflected the existing law. HL Debs, June 17, 1003, col.672. The presumption, furthermore, is confined to two very specific situations which are both unusual: House of Commons Home Affairs Committee, Fifth Report of Session 2002–03, H.C. 639, para.34.
[6] (1984) 79 Cr.App.R. 255.
[7] The presumption that a child aged between 10 and 14 years is *doli incapax*, *i.e.* incapable of forming a criminal intent, was abolished by the Crime and Disorder Act 1998, s.34, but by Sch.9 to the Act the section does not apply to anything done before the commencement of the section.

that he had no doubt that the standard to which the prosecution must satisfy the court is the criminal standard, that is, beyond reasonable doubt. If, on the other hand, the defence challenge the presumption, the burden is not so heavy. The burden in the case of the defence is the evidential burden.

This approach has been followed in a new rebuttable presumption introduced by s.77 of the Sexual Offences Act 2003. This presumption requires a defendant in certain specified circumstances[8] to put forward evidence in order to raise an issue about consent in relation to certain sexual offences, or his belief in consent to put the matter before the jury. Thus, an evidential burden on this issue is placed on an accused: see paras 4–26 to 4–32, above, for a discussion of the evidential burden. As the Minister of State in the Home Office said, it would be for the accused to satisfy the judge that there is a real issue about consent, or belief in consent, which could be done, for instance, by evidence given by the accused or on his behalf, or by cross-examination of the complainant.[9]

One further example of a rebuttable presumption needs to be considered, namely, the presumption of regularity which is expressed in the maxim "*omnia praesumuntur rite esse acta*". The effect of the presumption is that if there is evidence that a person acted in a particular office, it will be presumed that he had been duly appointed to it.[10] Thus, evidence that a police constable acted in that capacity is sufficient proof of his appointment.[11] A similar rule applies to other public officials or servants, for instance, a postman,[12] or an Inspector of the Health and Safety Executive.[13]

5–05

The presumption has also been applied to infer that a direction was given by a local authority to justify the erection of speed limit signs.[14] However, in *Scott v Baker*[15] Lord Parker C.J. said that in a criminal case, very great care should be taken in applying the presumption. In that case the Divisional Court held that the presumption could not be applied to prove that the Secretary of State had approved a breath test device.

It is submitted that the burden of proof necessary to rebut this presumption varies according to the party seeking to rebut it. Thus, the prosecution bears the persuasive burden; whereas in the case of the defence, the evidential burden should suffice. The question arises as to whether the defence must call evidence in order to rebut the presumption. In *Campbell v*

---

[8] The specified circumstances include those where the defendant has used, or threatened, violence against, or unlawfully detained the complainant, or the complainant was asleep, unconscious or disabled and unable to communicate consent: s.77(3).
[9] HL Deb, June 17, 2003, col.670.
[10] *Gordon* (1781) 1 Leach 505; *Berryman v Wise* (1792) 4 Term Rep. 366; *Borrett* (1833) 6 C. & P. 124.
[11] *Gordon*, above.
[12] See *Borrett*, above.
[13] *Campbell v Wallsend Slipway and Engineering Co. Ltd* [1978] I.C.R. 1015.
[14] *Gibbins v Skinner* [1951] 2 K.B. 379.
[15] [1969] 1 Q.B. 659, 672. *Gibbins v Skinner*, above was distinguished in *Scott v Baker* on two grounds: there was a statutory duty upon the local authority to erect signs and signs were erected in pursuance of that duty.

Wallsend Slipway and Engineering Co. Ltd[16] the majority of the Divisional Court appeared to think that evidence must be called. They said that the presumption could be displaced only by rebutting evidence and not by mere challenge. However, if there is other material in the case (not limited to rebutting evidence) which indicates that the presumption should not apply, it is submitted that this would suffice to oblige the court to leave the issue of fact (*i.e.* whether the presumption had been rebutted) to the jury.

5–06   The courts have also applied a similar presumption to that of regularity in relation to mechanical instruments. Thus, if a watch records a particular time or a speedometer records a particular speed, that is prima facie evidence of that time or speed, notwithstanding that no evidence is adduced of the accuracy of the device.[17] The courts will similarly presume that devices such as traffic lights are in working order.[18] "Where you have a device of this kind [traffic lights] set up for public use in active operation ... the presumption should be that it is in proper working order unless there is evidence to the contrary."[19] Section 129(2) of the Criminal Justice Act 2003 specifically provides that s.129(1) (which deals with representations other than by a person, *i.e.* a machine) does not affect "the operation of the presumption that a mechanical device has been properly set or calibrated".[20] This presumption applies to computers.

2. FORMAL ADMISSIONS

5–07   A "formal admission" is to be distinguished from an "informal admission" made by a defendant, which may be proved against him as an exception to the hearsay rule. Informal admissions are considered in Ch.10 below.

Provision is made for formal admission by statute, namely s.10 of the Criminal Justice Act 1967 which provides that "any fact of which oral evidence may be given in any criminal proceedings may be admitted for the purpose of those proceedings by or on behalf of the prosecutor or defendant, and the admission by any party of any such fact under this section shall as against that party be conclusive evidence in those proceedings."[21]

If a fact is formally admitted the judge should direct the jury that they must find what has been admitted as a fact. Such an admission may, however, with the leave of the court, be withdrawn.[22] The Court of Appeal has said that such leave would be unlikely to be granted unless there is

---

[16] Above.
[17] *Nicholas v Penny* [1950] 2 K.B. 466.
[18] *Tingle Jacobs & Co. v Kennedy* [1964] 1 All E.R. 888. The Law Commission saw no reason why the presumption of regularity should not be applied to computers: L.C. Consultation Paper No.138 (1995), para.14–28.
[19] At 889, *per* Lord Denning M.R.
[20] The section is due to come into effect in April 2005.
[21] s.10(1).
[22] s.10(4).

cogent evidence from the defendant and his lawyers that the admission had been made by mistake or due to a misunderstanding.[23] If the admission is made before a magistrates' court for the purpose of a summary trial the admission must be written down and signed by the party making the admission.[24] At a trial on indictment an admission must be in writing if made otherwise than in court.[25] If made during the trial, the admission is often made orally[26] the absence of the jury when it is made is immaterial.[27] If the admission is in any way complicated, it is better to reduce it into writing. However made, such admissions result in considerable savings of time.

3. JUDICIAL NOTICE

The doctrine of judicial notice allows the tribunal of fact (the magistrates or jury in a criminal case) to find that a fact exists without evidence being called to establish it.   5–08

The expression "judicial notice" is, however, used in a number of different ways.[28] In its best-known form the doctrine refers to the notice taken of facts which are so well known or notorious as to render proof unnecessary. A party will not have to prove that Christmas Day is on December 25. Judicial notice will also be taken of facts which may be established from an authoritative source, for example that January 1, 2003 was a Wednesday. "Judicial notice refers to facts which a judge can be called upon to receive and to act upon, either from his general knowledge of them or from inquiries to be made by himself from his own information from sources to which it is proper for him to refer."[29] Thus, there may be judicial notice of Ordnance Survey practice (in relation to maps)[30] or books of reference.[31] (However, questions of foreign law cannot be the subject of judicial notice in criminal proceedings.[32])

---

[23] *Kolton* [2000] Crim.L.R. 761.
[24] Magistrates' Court Rules 1981, r.71.
[25] s.10(2).
[26] It must however, in a trial on indictment be in a form that causes it to appear clearly on the shorthand note; (*Lennard* (1973) 57 Cr.App.R.542) and in such a way that the jury can understand what has been admitted (see *Lewis* (1971) 55 Cr.App.R. 386).
[27] *Lewis* [1989] Crim.L.R. 61, CA.
[28] See P.B. Carter's essay, "Judicial Notice: Related and Unrelated Matters", in *Well and Truly Tried*; and Nokes, "The Limits of Judicial Notice" (1958) 74 L.Q.R. 59.
[29] *Commonwealth Shipping Representative v P. & O. Branch Services* [1923] A.C. 191, 212, *per* Lord Sumner. As a recent simple example, the Privy Council in *AG for Cayman Islands v Roberts* [2002] Crim.L.R. 368 said that it was within judicial knowledge that cocaine hydrochloride was a form of cocaine.
[30] *Davey v Harrow Corporation* [1957] 2 W.L.R. 941, 944.
[31] Stephen's *Digest of the Law of Evidence* (12th ed., 1948), Art.62, quoted with approval in *McQuaker v Goddard* [1940] 1 K.B. 687, 700, *per* Clauson L.J.
[32] *Ofori* (1994) 99 Cr.App.R. 223.

5–09   Knowledge of facts may be gained from other cases. In *Jones (Reginald William)*[33] the Court of Appeal held that, since the breathalyser Alcotest R 80 device had been formally proved in a large number of cases to be of a type approved by the Secretary of State, the court was entitled to take judicial notice of its approval. On the other hand, the Divisional Court in *DPP v Roberts*[34] held that justices were not entitled to take judicial notice that a radar gun (used to measure speed) was a device approved by the Home Secretary on the basis of evidence that a police official regularly used it. The court said that the considerations which led to the decision in *Jones* were not applicable. The distinction between these cases may not be immediately apparent. It may lie in the widespread use of the breathalyser device and the courts' consequent familiarity with it (and the Minister's approval of it) when contrasted with the then comparative novelty of the radar gun.

It follows that knowledge gained in other cases can only rarely be used; and only when it is appropriate to do so. In *Jarvis v DPP*[35] a stipendiary magistrate (relying on evidence which he had heard in other cases) found that there was only one Intoximeter device available at Fulham Police Station at the relevant time. The Divisional Court held that it was wrong in principle for the magistrate to have used the evidence which he had heard in other cases to supplement the evidence in the case which he was trying: this was not a case where it was appropriate to use judicial knowledge to fill a gap in the evidence. (As the Court pointed out, it did not follow that because there was only one device available on one date, there was not more than one on another date.)

5–10   If judicial notice is taken of a fact in a criminal trial, the judge will direct the jury to find the fact to exist (and magistrates will so find). For example, the courts will take judicial notice that flick knives are offensive weapons per se for the purposes of s.1 of the Prevention of Crime Act 1953 and juries should be directed accordingly.[36]

The expression, "judicial notice", is also used to describe the use which magistrates or jurors may make of knowledge acquired out of court. The rule is that while a jury or justices may make use of their *general* knowledge they may not use their *personal* knowledge.[37] Thus in *Rosser*[38] it was said that in a criminal prosecution jurors may use general knowledge which any man can bring to the subject, but if any juror has a particular knowledge of the subject he ought to be sworn and examined as a witness. In *Manley v*

---

[33] [1970] 1 W.L.R. 16.
[34] *The Times*, June 1, 1992.
[35] [1996] R.T.R. 192.
[36] *Gibson v Wales* (1983) 76 Cr.App.R. 60; *Simpson* (1984) 78 Cr.App.R. 115.
[37] *Rosser* (1836) 7 C. & P. 648; *Manley v Shaw* (1840) C. & M. 361; *Antrim JJ.* (1895) 2 I.R. 603. See Manchester, "Judicial Notice and Personal Knowledge" (1979) 42 M.L.R. 22, 23.
[38] Above.

Shaw,[39] a juror said that a bill of exchange was a forgery. It was held that before the jury could act on his opinion he should be sworn as a witness to prove the forgery. It is most unlikely that a juror would today be sworn as a witness. However, the principle is that jurors must not rely on specialist knowledge without giving the parties notice of it; and if it is discovered that a juror has been providing the jury with such knowledge, and the parties are not able to deal with the issue by calling evidence or making submissions, it may be necessary to discharge the jury.[40] On the other hand, a juror's personal knowledge may be made known and affect the course of a trial. For instance, a juror may interject that to his knowledge a piece of evidence is wrong; or, more likely, pass a note to that effect. This happened in *Blick*[41] where a juror passed a note to the judge which (from the juror's local knowledge) contradicted alibi evidence given by the defendant. As a result, the judge allowed the prosecution to call evidence to rebut the alibi. The Court of Criminal Appeal upheld the judge's decision. This case illustrates the effect which a juror's local knowledge may have on a trial. It does not follow that the juror can, in effect, give evidence.

The rule with regard to justices is that they may use their *local* knowledge within reasonable limits. In *Ingram v Percival*[42] the Divisional Court held that justices were entitled to use their local knowledge as to whether a particular stretch of water was tidal. Lord Parker C.J. said that it has always been recognised that justices may and should take into consideration matters which they know of their own knowledge and particularly matters in regard to the locality.[43]   5–11

The Divisional Court has held that justices were entitled to use their local knowledge: (a) that a car park was a public place[44] or open at night[45]; (b) that a journey involved travelling on public roads[46]; (c) that a vehicle could not have been travelling at 40 m.p.h. at a particular place[47]; and (d) that a particular area was frequented by prostitutes.[48]

How far are justices entitled to go in the use of personal or local knowledge?

First, they should not ordinarily depart from or supplement the evidence in the case by relying upon their own experience.[49] For instance, if the evidence is that a building is at a certain place the justices cannot use their

---

[39] Above.
[40] *Fricker, The Times*, July 13, 1999 (CA). It should be noted that the Court also said in *Fricker* that in some circumstances it may be possible to deal with the matter by means of further direction from the judge.
[41] (1966) 50 Cr.App.R. 280.
[42] [1969] 1 Q.B. 548.
[43] At 555.
[44] *Clift v Long* [1961] Crim.L.R. 121.
[45] *Bowman v DPP* [1991] R.T.R. 263.
[46] *Borthwick v Vickers* [1973] Crim.L.R. 317.
[47] *Kent v Stamps* [1982] R.T.R. 273.
[48] *Paul v DPP, The Times*, May 1, 1989.
[49] *DPP v Curtis* [1993] R.T.R. 72; *Carter v Eastbourne B.C.* (2000) 164 J.P. 273.

personal experience to find otherwise. Likewise, they are not entitled to rely on their own experience of their gardens and woodlands to determine the rate at which trees grow.[50] (Their proper course in these circumstances is to inform the parties of their experience and have the matter further investigated in evidence.)

5–12   Secondly, the use of personal knowledge should not amount to the giving of evidence in the absence of the prosecution and defence. In *Reynolds v Llanelly Tinplate Co.*[51] the Court of Appeal held that a county court judge acting as an arbitrator may rely on his personal knowledge of local matters provided that such use was properly applied and within reasonable limits. However, in *Wetherall v Harrison*[52] Lord Widgery C.J. said that such an approach was not appropriate for justices. In that case the defendant was charged with failing to supply a specimen for a laboratory test. His defence was that he had a reasonable excuse for his failure to supply a specimen in that he had had a fit. A doctor called on behalf of the prosecution alleged that the fit was simulated. The justices retired. One of their number was a doctor. He gave his opinion that the defendant's behaviour may have been genuine. The justices dismissed the case. The prosecutor appealed on the ground that the justices should not have used the doctor's specialised knowledge. The Divisional Court, dismissing the appeal, said that a justice who has specialised knowledge may draw on it in interpreting the evidence and give his own view on how the case should be decided but he must not give evidence behind closed doors contradicting the evidence given in court.

Thus, if justices do propose to use special or local knowledge, it is as well if that fact is brought to the parties' attention so that they may deal with it by calling evidence or otherwise.[53]

4. THE EFFECT OF PREVIOUS ACQUITTALS AND CONVICTIONS

5–13   In certain cases the effect of previous acquittals and convictions is to prove matters without calling evidence. Thus, the prosecution may not adduce evidence inconsistent with a previous acquittal of a defendant except in very limited circumstances; and statute now provides that the fact that a person has been convicted of an offence is admissible as evidence that he committed it. These rules and related rules are now discussed.

---

[50] *Carter v Eastbourne B.C.*, above.
[51] [1948] 1 All E.R. 140.
[52] [1976] Q.B. 773.
[53] *Thomas v Thomas* [1961] 1 W.L.R. 1; *Bowman v DPP*, above. In *Norbrook Laboratories (GB) Ltd v Health and Safety Executive, The Times*, February 23, 1998, an appeal was allowed where magistrates had failed to inform the parties that they were bringing their own knowledge to bear on reaching a decision. The Divisional Court said that it was perfectly legitimate for local knowledge to be relied on by magistrates, but the parties should be informed and have the opportunity to comment on the knowledge which the magistrates have.

A. Acquittals

(1) Acquittals cannot be challenged

Once a man has been acquitted of an offence, he cannot be prosecuted   5–14
again for the same offence. This is known as the rule against double jeopardy and is expressed in the maxim *nemo debet bis puniri pro uno delicto*.

It had been thought that a corollary was that the prosecution in a subsequent trial against the same defendant may not challenge the validity of
the acquittal by adducing evidence which was inconsistent with it.[54] Thus
in *Sambasivam v Public Prosecutor, Federation of Malaya*,[55] the accused
was tried before a judge and two assessors under emergency regulations of
carrying a firearm and possessing ammunition. At his first trial he was
acquitted of possessing ammunition but the Court failed to agree on the
charge of carrying a firearm. At the re-trial the prosecution produced for the
first time a confession made by the accused to the police both of carrying a
firearm and being in possession of ammunition. However, the trial judge
failed to warn the assessors that the prosecution could not assert that the
part of the statement dealing with the ammunition was untrue or tell them
that the accused had been acquitted of being in possession of the ammunition. As a result of these misdirections, the Privy Council quashed the
conviction. However, Lord MacDermott, giving the judgment of the Board
also said: "The effect of a verdict of acquittal pronounced by a competent
court on a lawful charge and after a lawful trial is not completely stated by
saying that the person acquitted cannot be tried again for the same offence.
To that it must be added that the verdict is binding and conclusive in all
subsequent proceedings between the parties to the adjudication. The maxim
res judicata pro veritate accipitur is no less applicable to criminal than civil
proceedings."[56]

An illustration of this principle is to be found in a decision of the Divi-   5–15
sional Court. In *G v Coltart*,[57] the Divisional Court held that magistrates
had wrongly admitted evidence relating to the larceny on which the prosecution had offered no evidence (the loser having returned to South Africa)
on another larceny (from the owner of the house in which the first loser had
been a guest and the defendant was a servant), since the only relevance was
to show that the defendant had been guilty of larceny of the first loser's

---

[54] *Sambasivam*, below; *DPP v Humphrys* [1977] A.C. 1, 41, *per* Lord Hailsham, 43, *per* Lord
Salmon; *Gall* (1990) 90 Cr.App.R. 64. The rule was described as (i) an extension of the
doctrine of *autrefois acquit* (the plea in bar to an indictment for an offence of which a man has
previously been acquitted): see *Connelly v DPP* [1964] A.C. 1254, 1341, *per* Lord Devlin,
1288 (the argument of the Solicitor General); or (ii) based on the rule against double jeopardy:
see *Humphrys*, above, at 41, *per* Lord Hailsam. It should be noted that the plea of *autrefois
acquit* and the related plea of *autrefois convict* are matters of procedure and are accordingly
not further considered here.
[55] [1950] A.C. 458.
[56] At 479.
[57] [1967] 1 Q.B. 432.

property and she had been acquitted of that offence. However, *G v Coltart* was overruled by the House of Lords in *Z*,[58] see below.

In *Z*[59] the House of Lords held that, provided a defendant was not placed in double jeopardy (*i.e.* being prosecuted on the same or substantially the same facts as had given rise to an earlier acquittal), evidence relevant in a subsequent prosecution was not admissible because it tended to show that the defendant was, in fact, guilty of the offence for which he had been earlier acquitted. In that case the defendant was charged with rape and his defence was that the complainant had consented or he believed that she had. The Crown sought leave to adduce evidence from complainants in four earlier rape trials in order to rebut this defence: in three of these cases, the accused had been acquitted. The House of Lords held that this evidence was admissible because:

(a) the defendant was not placed in double jeopardy since the facts giving rise to the present prosecution were different from those giving rise to the earlier prosecutions;

(b) the evidence was relevant and came within the similar facts rule;

(c) the evidence was therefore not inadmissible because it showed that he was guilty of the offences of which he had been acquitted;

(d) any question of admissibility was subject to the trial judge's discretion to exclude unfair evidence under s.78 of the Police and Criminal Evidence Act 1984 or because its prejudicial effect outweighed its probative value.

5–16   Lord Hutton, in a speech with which the other members of the House agreed, said:

"The distinction drawn between the prosecution adducing evidence on a second trial to seek to prove that the defendant was, in fact, guilty of an offence of which he had been earlier acquitted and the prosecution adducing evidence on a second trial to seek to prove that the defendant is guilty of the second offence charged in that trial even though the evidence may tend to show that he was, in fact, guilty of an earlier offence of which he had been acquitted is a difficult one to maintain. The reality is that when the Crown adduces evidence in a criminal trial for a second offence it does so to prove the guilt of the defendant in respect of that offence. In order to prove the guilt in respect of the second offence it may wish to call evidence which, in fact, shows or tends to show that the defendant was guilty of an earlier offence, but

---

[58] [2000] 3 W.L.R. 117; [2000] 2 Cr.App.R. 281.
[59] Above.

the evidence is adduced not for the purpose of showing that the defendant was guilty of the first offence but for the purpose of proving that the defendant is guilty of the second offence. Moreover I think that a distinction cannot realistically be drawn between evidence relating to a specific issue (such as intention or knowledge) and evidence which shows that, in fact, the defendant was guilty of the offence of which he had been acquitted because in some trials the proof of a single disputed issue will establish the guilt of the defendant. I also think that it is difficult to draw a distinction between evidence which shows that the defendant was, in fact, guilty of an earlier offence of which he has been acquitted and evidence which tends to show that he was, in fact, guilty of that offence."[60]

Lord Hutton concluded, that in *Sambasivam*:

"it was right to set aside the conviction, and that the proper ground for doing so was for the reason given by Lord Pearce in *Connelly v Director of Public Prosecutions*,[61] namely that a man should not be prosecuted a second time where the two offences were in fact founded on one and the same incident and that man ought not to be tried for a second offence which was manifestly inconsistent on the facts with a previous acquittal. The carrying of the revolver and the carrying of the ammunition constituted one and the same incident, and having been acquitted of having possession of the ammunition the allegation of carrying the revolver (in which some of the ammunition was loaded) was manifestly inconsistent with the previous acquittal. But I consider that provided a defendant is not placed in double jeopardy in the way described by Lord Pearce, evidence which is relevant on a subsequent prosecution is not inadmissible because it shows or tends to show that the defendant was, in fact, guilty of an offence of which he had earlier been acquitted. Therefore, I think that in the relevant passage of Lord MacDermott's judgment, at p.479, the second sentence commencing 'To that it must be added' requires the qualification which I have ventured to state".[62]

Lord Hope agreed that the second of the two statements by Lord Mac-   5–17
Dermott was in need of qualification in order to confine its application to its proper context.

"The principle which underlies both statements is that of double jeopardy. It is obvious that this principle is infringed if the accused is put

---

[60] At 296.
[61] (1964) 48 Cr.App.R. 183, 276, 279; [1964] A.C. 1264, 1362, 1364.
[62] P. 301.

on trial again for the offence of which he has been acquitted. It is also infringed if any other steps are taken by the prosecutor which may result in the punishment of the accused on some other ground for the same offence. But it is not infringed if what the prosecutor seeks to do is to lead evidence which was led at the previous trial, not for the purpose of punishing the accused in any way for the offence of which he has been acquitted, but in order to prove that the defendant is guilty of a subsequent offence which was not before the court in the previous trial."[63]

Thus the rule may be stated in this way:

(1) An accused may not be put in double jeopardy, *i.e.* be prosecuted again for the same offence.

(2) If relevant, evidence may be admitted despite the fact that it tends to show that the accused was guilty of an offence of which he has been acquitted.

This rule is now affirmed in statutory form by Chapter 1 of Pt 11 of the Criminal Justice Act 2003, discussed in Ch.7 below.

5–18   The rule was in any case subject to the exception that evidence of an offence of which a defendant has been acquitted may be admissible at a subsequent trial for another offence if it is relevant to the proof of the second offence.[64] An example is to be found in *Ollis*.[65] The defendant, O, had been acquitted of obtaining property by falsely pretending that a cheque which he had given the complainant, R, was good and valid. O's defence was that when he gave R the cheque he believed that he would receive another cheque to meet it. O was subsequently tried on a second indictment alleging the obtaining of money by false pretences relating to three other cheques. These offences occurred at about the same time as the case involving R. The prosecution was allowed to call R to give the same evidence as he gave in the first trial. The Court of Criminal Appeal upheld the admission of R's evidence because it showed an intention to defraud on O's part in relation to the offences being tried. The evidence was admitted not to challenge the validity of the acquittal but as relevant to O's knowledge and state of mind when he gave the three other cheques.[66] More

---

[63] P. 283.

[64] *Connelly v DPP*, above, at 1302 *per* Lord Morris; *Humphrys*, above at 43, *per* Lord Salmon.

[65] [1900] 2 Q.B. 758.

[66] The difficulty about *Ollis* as an example is that while the prosecution may have been able to assert that R's evidence was relevant to the offence being tried, the prosecution case must also have been that O was intending to defraud R; and O had been acquitted of any such offence. However, whatever doubts there may be about the circumstances in *Ollis* the principle underlying the decision cannot be questioned.

recently, it has been held that evidence relating to a statute-barred count was admissible to support the evidence on other counts in the indictment provided it had probative value.[67] The Court of Appeal commented that it was one thing to be acquitted on the merits and quite another to be acquitted because a count was statute-barred.

In *DPP v Humphrys*,[68] the House of Lords decided that the doctrine of issue estoppel (which applies in civil cases) had no application in the criminal law. This doctrine provides that once an issue has been raised, and determined between two parties, neither party may raise the issue again.[69] This doctrine is to be contrasted with the rule under consideration which applies to verdicts. The rule prevents the general verdict of a jury being challenged. Issue estoppel, on the other hand, prevents separate issues of fact from being raised again.

5–19

In *Humphrys*, H was charged with driving a motor vehicle while disqualified on July 18, 1972. Evidence was given for the prosecution by a police officer who identified H as driving a motor cycle on that day. H denied that he had driven any motor vehicle at all during 1972. He was acquitted. H was later charged with perjury relating to his statement that he had not driven any motor vehicle in 1972. At the trial, three neighbours gave evidence to the effect that H had ridden a motor cycle in 1972; and the police officer was allowed to give evidence again identifying H as the driver of the motorcycle on July 18, 1972. H was convicted of perjury. The Court of Appeal quashed the conviction on the ground that issue estoppel applied and since the jury at the first trial had determined the issue of the identity of the driver on July 18, 1972 in H's favour, the evidence of the police officer at the second trial was inadmissible. The House of Lords restored the conviction for perjury. The House held that issue estoppel did not apply in criminal proceedings and the police officer's evidence was admissible because it was directed to proving that H had committed perjury at the first trial.

The most compelling reason for rejecting issue estoppel in criminal proceedings is the difficulty of identifying (from a general verdict of not guilty) the issues which the jury have determined. Thus, Lord Devlin said, in *Connelly v DPP*[70]:

5–20

---

[67] *Adams, The Times*, April 8, 1993, CA.
[68] [1977] A.C. 1.
[69] *Fidelitas Shipping Co. Ltd v Exportchleb* [1966] 1 Q.B. 630, 640; see also *Mills v Cooper* [1967] 2 Q.B. 459, 468, *per* Diplock L.J. The doctrine has been applied to criminal proceedings in Australia (*Wilkes* (1948) 77 C.L.R. 511; *Mraz* (1956) 30 A.L.J. 604) and the USA (*Sealfon v United States* 332 U.S. 575 (1947)). For a time there was some doubt as to whether the doctrine existed here. In *Connelly v DPP* [1964] A.C. 1254, Lord Morris, Lord Pearce and Lord Hodson considered that it did apply. See also *Hogan* [1974] Q.B. 398 (Lawson J.), the only case in which it was held that the prosecution could rely on issue estoppel. *Hogan* was overruled by the *House of Lords in DPP v Humphrys*.
[70] [1964] A.C. 1254, 1345.

"[For] estoppel on issues to work satisfactorily, the issues need to be formulated with some precision. In civil suits this is usually done as a matter of record: in the criminal process it is not. If issue estoppel is going to be introduced into the criminal law, the proper basis for it is a system of special verdicts on separate issues. But that would be to introduce a profound change into the working of our law which I am not prepared at present to countenance."[71]

(2) Defence entitled to rely on previous acquittal

5–21   The fact that a defendant has been acquitted of an offence on an earlier occasion is usually irrelevant and the jury are not told about it.[72]

Two examples may be given. In *Greasby*[73] A and B were charged with robbery. In the first trial the jury acquitted A, but could not reach a verdict in the case of B. When B was subsequently re-tried the judge ruled that the jury in that case should not be told of A's acquittal in the earlier trial. The Court of Appeal ruled that this was a matter for the discretion of the trial judge and upheld the ruling. In *Hui Chi Ming*[74] A, B (the ring-leader) and others went in search of a man to redress some bullying. B had a metal pipe (a fact known to A). B hit the victim on the head with the pipe, causing injuries from which he subsequently died. A then disappeared. B and three others were tried for murder: B was acquitted but convicted of man-slaughter. Two years later, A was arrested and tried for murder. At his trial the judge refused to admit evidence of B's acquittal. A was convicted of murder. The Privy Council upheld the judge's decison. Lord Lowery said that the verdict in the first trial was irrelevant and inadmissible because it amounted to no more than evidence of the opinion of that jury.[75]

There is a further reason why such evidence is not normally admitted: namely, the need not to clutter a trial with side issues. It is important that the minds of the jury are brought to bear on the central issues. Introducing evidence about other trials may only result in making their task harder.

5–22   However, there are occasions when reference may be made to a previous acquittal. The test is whether it is relevant. The principle was stated by Lord Macdermott:

"The mere fact that there has been a previous trial is usually irrelevant and, therefore, inadmissible on a re-trial. This does not mean that it is

---

[71] See also, for reasons for not applying issue estoppel, *DPP v Humphrys* [1977] A.C. 1, 43, *per* Lord Salmon, and Lanham, "Issue Estoppel in English Criminal Law" [1970] Crim.L.R. 428.

[72] The fact that the acquittal is not as the result of the verdict of a jury, but by the direction of the judge (on the grounds of insufficient evidence) makes no difference: the effect of the acquittal is the same: *Hudson* [1994] Crim.L.R. 921.

[73] [1984] Crim.L.R. 488.

[74] (1990) 94 Cr.App.R. 236.

[75] At 240.

never permissible to refer to an earlier trial, for it may be necessary to do so to establish some relevant fact as, for example, in identifying the occasion on which some particular statement or admission was made."[76]

Thus, as has been seen in *Sambasivam*, the Privy Council held that the assessors should have been told of S's previous acquittal and Lord Macdermott said that S was entitled to rely on his acquittal so far as it might be relevant to his defence.

In *Hui Chi Ming*[77] the Privy Council said that some exceptional feature is needed in order to make evidence of what happened in an earlier case relevant. Thus, the fact that a police officer has been involved in earlier cases where juries have acquitted is not in itself sufficient for evidence of those acquittals to be given. Lord Lane C.J. said that the acquittal of a defendant in case A, where the prosecution depended largely or entirely upon the evidence of a police officer, does not normally render that officer liable to cross-examination as to credit in case B.[78] "The fact that a jury returns a verdict of not guilty does not go to prove that an important witness for the prosecution, albeit the sole witness, is a liar."[79] For example, in *Doosti*[80] the defendant was charged with conspiracy to supply heroin. He had been acquitted six months earlier of drugs offences occurring at the same premises at which he was arrested. The same police officer gave evidence at both trials. The trial judge refused to allow defence counsel to cross-examine the officer about the previous acquittal. The Court of Appeal upheld this ruling because the cross-examination was not directed to any relevant issue. The Court said that the previous acquittal did not mean the officer had been lying or was unreliable but was consistent with the jury not being sure that the case had been made out.

On the other hand, if an acquittal has an effect on the credibility of a prosecution witness or the reliability of a confession, it may well amount to that type of a feature which requires evidence of the acquittal to be admitted. In *Edwards*[81] Lord Lane C.J. said that if a police officer had given evidence of an admission in case A (and the defendant's acquittal demonstrated that the officer's evidence was not believed) evidence of that

5–23

5–24

---

[76] *Sambasivam* [1950] A.C. 458, 471.
[77] Above, at 241.
[78] *Edwards* (1991) 93 Cr.App.R. 48, 57.
[79] *Thorne* (1978) 66 Cr.App.R. 6, 15, *per* Lawton L.J.
[80] (1986) 82 Cr.App.R. 181. See also *Hendrie, The Times,* July 27, 1994. The defendants in that case were charged with conspiring to supply drugs. They sought to adduce evidence of acquittals in a connected trial in Scotland in order to discredit police officers who had given evidence in both trials. The Court of Appeal upheld the trial judge's refusal to admit the evidence. There appears to have been two grounds for this decision. First, the evidence was of observation, which, as the Court commented, raises questions not only of honesty but also of honest mistake. Secondly, the verdicts in the Scottish trial (including verdicts of guilty) indicated that some of the officers' evidence must have been accepted.
[81] Above.

acquittal should be admitted in case B if it is alleged that the officer fabricated an admission. Two cases, below, illustrate the proposition.

1. In *Hay*[82] the defendant was charged with arson and burglary. He had made a statement to the police confessing to both offences. The two offences were unconnected and were tried separately. The arson charge was tried first. Before the confession statement was put in evidence, it was edited to remove all references to the burglary. H alleged that the statement had been fabricated by the police. The jury acquitted him of arson. At his subsequent trial for burglary, H required the whole statement to go before the jury in order to use his acquittal of arson to support his contention that the police had also fabricated that part of the statement concerning the burglary. However, the judge did not allow him to tell the jury about the acquittal. The Court of Appeal, applying *Sambasivam*, held that this ruling was wrong and that the jury should have been told of the acquittal. The Court said that the jury should have been directed that (a) the acquittal was conclusive evidence that H was not guilty of arson and that his confession to that offence was untrue and (b) when considering the statement they should keep in mind that the part of the statement relating to the arson must be regarded as untrue.

5–25　　2. In *Cooke*,[83] the defendant was charged with conspiring with others including S and C to commit offences of forgery and deception. S and C pleaded guilty to these offences. S and C had also been charged in the same indictment with robbery. They had been tried separately on this count and had been acquitted. The fact and circumstances of the acquittal of S and C was said to be relevant to issues raised at the defendant's trial for the following reasons. S, C and the defendant had all been arrested on the same day and interviewed by the same detective constable, A. It was alleged that S and C then made admissions to the robbery. At the defendant's trial counsel sought to cross-examine A to elicit (a) that at the trial of S and C he had given evidence of these admissions, (b) that the only other evidence had related to recent possession and (c) that S and C had been acquitted. Leave to cross-examine was refused. The Court of Appeal held that it should have been given because A's credibility was a vital issue and the offences and interviews were so closely connected that the defence should have been allowed to refer to them.

Accordingly, in deciding whether evidence of a previous acquittal should be admitted on the ground that it affects the credibility of a witness, the judge must determine:

(a) whether the evidence is relevant to the issues in the instant trial; and, if so,

---

[82] (1983) 77 Cr.App.R. 70.
[83] (1987) 84 Cr.App.R. 286.

(b) whether the acquittal necessarily indicates that the jury in the previous trial disbelieved the witness.

If the evidence passes both tests it is likely (but not certain) to be admitted. In these circumstances no hard and fast rules can be applied. Thus, Lord Lane C.J. said that the judge had to balance the interests of the defendant and the prosecution and determine what was fair: fairness rather than any remote abstruse legal principle being the matter which had to actuate a judge's reasoning, coupled with the necessity of ensuring that the jury did not have their minds clouded by issues which were not the true issues they had to determine.[84] It is not a ground for refusing to allow cross-examination that the type of malpractice on the part of the police in issue is different to that alleged in the earlier case. The Court of Appeal so held in *Malik*.[85] The Court held that the trial judge had been wrong to refuse cross-examination of a police officer as to his reliability on the ground that he had allegedly fabricated an interview in an earlier case whereas the allegation in the instant case was that he had suborned a witness. The Court said that it is necessary to consider how significant the police officer's evidence is and what past misconduct he is alleged to have committed.

B. Convictions as evidence of the offence charged

(1) Admissibility under s.74

At common law the fact that a person has been convicted of an offence is not admissible as evidence that the person committed the offence. This principle was known as the rule in *Hollington v Hewthorn*.[86] This rule was abolished in civil proceedings by s.11 of the Civil Evidence Act 1968. The rule, however, remained for some years in criminal proceedings. The results were sometimes anomalous.

Section 74 of the Police and Criminal Evidence Act 1984 eventually abolished the rule in *Hollington v Hewthorn* in criminal proceedings.

Section 74[87] provides:

"(1) In any proceedings the fact that a person other than the accused has been convicted of an offence by or before any court in the United Kingdom or by a Service court outside the United Kingdom shall be admissible in evidence for the purpose of proving, where to do so is relevant to any issue in those proceedings, that that person committed that offence, whether or not any other evidence of his having committed that offence is given.

5–26

5–27

---

[84] *H* (1990) 90 Cr.App.R. 440, 445.
[85] [2000] 2 Cr.App.R. 8.
[86] [1943] K.B. 587.
[87] As amended by Sch.25, Pt 4, of the Criminal Justice Act, 2003.

(2) In any proceedings in which by virtue of this section a person other than the accused is proved to have been convicted of an offence by or before any court in the United Kingdom or by a Service court outside the United Kingdom, he shall be taken to have committed that offence unless the contrary is proved.

(3) In any proceedings where evidence is admissible of the fact that the accused has committed an offence, if the accused is proved to have been convicted of the offence—

(a) by or before any court in the United Kingdom; or
(b) by a Service court outside the United Kingdom,

he shall be taken to have committed that offence unless the contrary is proved.

(4) Nothing in this section shall prejudice—

(a) the admissibility in evidence of any conviction which would be admissible apart from this section; or
(b) the operation of any enactment whereby a conviction or a finding of fact in any proceedings is for the purposes of any other proceedings made conclusive evidence of any fact."

5–28   Thus where A's conviction of an offence is relevant to any issue in the trial of B, A's conviction is admissible to prove that he committed that offence even if no other evidence of his having committed the offence is given.[88] For the method of proof of convictions, see paras 3–23, 3–24, above. There is no generic discretion to admit, for instance, a co-defendant's plea of guilty: admissibility is governed by s.74.[89]

The Court of Appeal at first appeared to take a restricted view of the applicability of s.74. Thus the Court said in O'Connor[90] that the object of the section was to deal with cases where it was necessary as a preliminary matter to prove the conviction of another as a condition precedent to the conviction of the defendant, for example to prove another person guilty of theft against a defendant charged with handling or harbouring.[91] (In O'Connor the defendant and B were charged with conspiring together to obtain money by deception. B pleaded guilty. Evidence of B's pleas was admitted under s.74 at the defendant's trial. The Court of Appeal held that the evidence should have been excluded because its admission was tanta-

---

[88] It should be noted that "conviction" in s.74 means a finding of guilt or a formal plea of guilty. Whether or not the defendant has been sentenced is irrelevant: *Robertson and Golder*, below.
[89] *Hall* [1993] Crim.L.R. 527.
[90] (1987) 85 Cr.App.R. 298, 302.
[91] It has been suggested that this represented the true intention of Parliament: Munday, "Proof of Guilt by Association" [1990] Crim.L.R. 236. A further example might be to prove the conviction of a principal in a trial against an aider and abettor: *Turner* [1991] Crim.L.R. 57.

mount to admitting, unchallenged, a statement by B from which the jury may have inferred that the defendant had conspired with B.)

However, in the leading case of *Robertson and Golder*[92] the Court took a less restricted view. Lord Lane C.J. giving the judgment of the Court said that the word "issue" in s.74 is apt to cover not only an issue which is an essential ingredient in the offence charged (the "restricted meaning"), but also less fundamental issues, for instance, evidential issues arising during the course of the proceedings (the "extended meaning"). Lord Lane said that provided the conviction is relevant to an issue in the case, it is admissible.

5–29

In *Robertson and Golder* the Court heard two similar cases. In *Robertson* R was charged with conspiring with P and L to commit burglary at premises belonging to Comet plc. On arraignment P and L pleaded guilty to counts involving 15 burglaries at Comet premises. The Crown was allowed to adduce evidence of these convictions in order to prove the existence of a conspiracy between P and L. The Court of Appeal held that the evidence had been properly admitted because it was relevant to the issue of whether there was a conspiracy between P and L, since it was that conspiracy to which the prosecution sought to prove R was a party. Similarly, in *Golder* the defendant was charged with two others, M and F, with robbing a garage attendant. G confessed to the police, but challenged the confession at his trial. M and E both pleaded guilty and the prosecution were permitted to adduce evidence of these convictions. The Court of Appeal upheld this ruling because the evidence was relevant to two issues: (a) to prove that the robbery had been committed; and (b) to show that G's confession was in accordance with the facts and therefore was more likely to be true.

The Court in *Robertson and Golder* said that s.74 may well be at its most useful in dealing with cases where the restricted meaning (above) may be applied. (For instance, the section should not be used merely to explain why co-defendants are not on trial.[93]) On the other hand, the Court of Appeal has applied the extended meaning subsequently and held, for instance, that evidence of a conviction of a co-defendant was admissible to prove that a theft had been committed[94] or that a conspiracy existed.[95]

5–30

The problems of admissibility have been much simplified by the amendment to s.74(3) by Sch.25, Pt 4, of the Criminal Justice Act, 2003. Section 3, as originally drafted, provided that the evidence was admissible if the fact that the accused has committed an offence in so far as it was

---

[92] (1987) 85 Cr.App.R. 304, 311.
[93] *Hall* [1993] Crim.L.R. 527.
[94] *Bennett* [1988] Crim.L.R. 686.
[95] *Lunnon* (1989) 88 Cr.App.R. 71. In *Lunnon* the evidence of the plea of guilty of one conspirator, L, was admitted at the trial of three co-conspirators. The Court of Appeal said that this evidence could be adduced as relevant to the existence of the conspiracy rather than to the question of whether any particular defendant was a party to it. The Court distinguished *O'Connor*, above, n.78 because in that case two men alone were indicted jointly in one count with having conspired together and with no one else.

"relevant to any matter in issue in the proceedings for a reason other than a tendency to show in the accused a tendency to commit the kind of offence with which he is charged". These words have now been omitted by Sch.25 to the 2003 Act. This Act is fully discussed in Ch.7; however, for these purposes, it is sufficient to note that the Act abolishes the common law rule that evidence of a person's disposition is not normally admissible in criminal proceedings as evidence of guilt. The amendment to s.74(3) follows from that abolition.[96] The result should be that evidence of convictions should be more freely admissible, but this is still subject to the requirement of relevance, on which the earlier authorities still have a bearing.

5–31   In particular, care must be taken in a case where it is disputed that the offence was committed at all. This is because in a trial involving several defendants charged with the same offence, it does not necessarily follow from the fact that one has pleaded guilty, that the facts constituting the offence can be accepted as proved in respect of the others, if they deny that the offence had been committed. Thus, in *Dixon, Sarah Louise*[97] the defendant and several others were charged with attempted burglary. One of the co-defendants pleaded guilty to the offence, but Dixon denied that the offence had ever been committed. The Court of Appeal held that it had been wrong of the trial judge to suggest that the guilty plea was evidence that the offence was committed: since Dixon's defence was that no offence had been committed she was entitled to have the issue considered, although the onus was on her to prove that there had been no offence.

Furthermore, it has been held that the purpose of the section is to assist in the mode of proof of the fact that the accused had committed an offence; and not to define or enlarge the circumstances in which the fact was admissible.[98]

The fact that the conviction sought to be proved under s.74 is a conviction on the same indictment as that on which the defendant is standing trial does not prevent its being adduced. In *H (Harry) v Juvenile*,[99] the defendant was charged on an indictment with two counts: violent disorder and inflicting grievous bodily harm. At his trial *H* was convicted of violent disorder but the jury failed to agree on the other count. At his retrial, evidence of his conviction for violent disorder was admitted. *H* appealed on the ground that s.74(3) did not apply to a conviction on a count in the same indictment. The Court of Appeal held that s.74(3) was not so restricted.

5–32   Convictions of third parties are also admissible provided that it is relevant to an issue in the instant proceedings to prove that the parties had committed the offence. Thus, in *Warner*[1] the defendants were charged with conspiracy to supply Class A drugs. The police observed callers at the house

---

[96] At the time of writing, the amendment is expected to come into effect in April 2005.
[97] [2001] Crim.L.R. 126.
[98] *Harris* [2001] Crim.L.R. 227.
[99] *The Times*, May 5, 2000.
[1] (1993) 96 Cr.App.R. 324.

of one of the defendants. The Court of Appeal held that it was admissible under s.74 to prove that the callers had convictions for possessing or dealing in heroin; the evidence was admissible to prove that the character of transactions at the house was not innocent but in order to obtain heroin.[2] Anything which enables a jury better to understand the relevant factual background against which the issue arises has been said to be relevant to that issue within the terms of s.74.[3]

It is not possible to formulate a general rule as to when evidence will be admissible, since the question whether a conviction is relevant or not to an issue in the case will depend on the facts of the particular case. In order to identify the issue to which a conviction is said to be relevant, it may be essential in some cases to discover the basis on which a defendant pleaded guilty. Thus, in *Manzur and Mahmood*[4] the issues at a rape trial were (a) whether the complainant was incapable (by reason of drunkenness) of consenting to sexual intercourse, (b) whether she did consent, or, alternatively, (c) whether the defendants believed she was consenting. The plea of guilty by a co-defendant was admitted in evidence, but no indication was given as to the basis on which he had pleaded guilty. The Court of Appeal said that the jury may have assumed that the co-defendant knew that the complainant did not consent and concluded that the defendants must have known it also. As a result, the conviction was quashed.

(2) Discretion to exclude

If the evidence is admissible under s.74(1) it would appear that the court has no discretion to exclude it since the section states that "it shall be admissible."[5] The discretion to exclude the evidence is derived from s.78 of the Act. Thus, in almost every case in which an application is made under s.74, the court must consider whether, in the exercise of its discretion under s.78, the admission of the evidence would so adversely affect the fairness of the proceedings that it should be excluded.[6] Thus, Lord Lane C.J. said that s.74 should be sparingly used: evidence adduced under it may on occasion be technically admissible, but its effect will be so slight that it would be wiser not to use it, particularly if there is a danger of contravention of s.78.[7]

5–33

---

[2] *Kearley* (1992) 95 Cr.App.R. 88 was distinguished on the grounds that the evidence about the callers in the instant case was not hearsay since it was not based on what the callers said but on their convictions.
[3] *Buckingham* (1994) 99 Cr.App.R. 303.
[4] [1997] 1 Cr.App.R. 414.
[5] See the dictum of the Court of Appeal to this effect as reported in *Castle* [1989] Crim.L.R. 567.
[6] In *Kempster*, below, the Court of Appeal quashed the conviction in circumstances where the judge had not made a clear and informed decision as to any adverse effect the admission of evidence of the pleas of guilty of three co-defendants might have on the fairness of the proceedings.
[7] *Robertson and Golder*, above, p.312.

The exercise of the discretion under s.78 is discussed, generally, below.[8] However, in this connection it should be noted that the Court of Appeal has said that it is important to ascertain the purpose for which evidence admitted under s.74 is to be adduced before deciding whether to exclude it under s.78.[9] If the sole purpose of admitting the evidence is to invite the jury to convict the defendant because of a co-defendant's plea of guilty, it is submitted that the evidence should be excluded. This is because at common law, the plea of guilty of one of two co-defendants is not evidence against the other[10] and s.74 would not appear to have been designed to alter that rule. Thus, in *Curry*[11] the Court of Appeal is reported as saying that where the evidence expressly or by necessary inference imports the complicity of the person on trial it should not be used.

5–34   Accordingly, it is submitted that in deciding whether a conviction should be admitted under s.74 the court should:

(a) identify the issues to which the evidence is relevant;

(b) determine whether the effect is more than slight, for example more than to invite the jury to convict because of a co-defendant's plea of guilty;

(c) bear in mind that s.74 should be sparingly used; and

(d) decide, if the evidence is admissible, whether it should be excluded under s.78.

(3) Other rules

5–35   1. If the evidence of a conviction is admitted the judge should explain to the jury the effect of the evidence and its limitations.[12] An appropriate direction would be to explain the purpose for which it has been admitted and to tell them that it is not to be used for any other purpose (for example inferring the defendant's guilt merely because another defendant has pleaded guilty).

2. Where a conviction is proved under the section, the person convicted shall be taken to have committed the offence unless the contrary is proved: s.74(2). Thus, the defendant may challenge the validity of a conviction. However, if he does so, he has to prove its invalidity on the balance of probabilities. The burden is placed on the defendant because a conviction is a result of a judicial decision (beyond reasonable doubt) and it would be

---

[8] Paras 10–13 *et seq.*
[9] *Kempster* (1989) 90 Cr.App.R. 14; *Lunnon*, above.
[10] *Moore* (1956) 40 Cr.App.R. 50. It is usual for the judge to direct the jury accordingly, but he is not required to do so: *Turpin*, *The Times*, February 2, 1990.
[11] [1988] Crim.L.R. 527. See also, *Mattison* [1990] Crim. L.R. 117 where the Court of Appeal held that the judge should have exercised his discretion to exclude the evidence of a plea of guilty by a co-defendant to gross indecency with the defendant when the latter was charged with gross indecency with the former.
[12] *Robertson and Golder*, above at 312; *Kempster*, above.

contrary to the interests of justice to impose a burden on the prosecution of proving that the conviction was valid.[13]

3. The same rules apply to cases where it is admissible to prove that the defendant has committed an offence: s.74(3). The section, however, specifically excludes evidence relating to a tendency to show in the accused a disposition to commit the kind of offence charged, thereby preserving the common law rule that such evidence is inadmissible.

4. In order to identify the facts on which a conviction admissible under s.74 is based, certain documents are made admissible by s.75 of the Act. Section 75(1) provides that for this purpose the contents of any document which is admissible as evidence of the conviction and the contents of the relevant indictment or information shall be admissible.   5–36

5. The documents admitted by s.75(1) will give no more than an indication of the facts on which a conviction is based. However, such an indication will be sufficient for the purposes of s.74, for example in a case of handling a stolen camera, that X had been convicted of stealing the camera. Such information may enable the court to decide whether the fact that a person committed the particular offence is relevant to the proceedings before the court. The section does, however, allow other admissible evidence to be given (for example oral evidence of the trial which resulted in the conviction).

6. The following provisions of s.75 should also be noted:

   (i)   A certified copy of the document is admissible: s.75(2).

   (ii) Admissibility is limited to subsisting convictions. Convictions quashed on appeal or cancelled by a free pardon are therefore excluded: s.75(4).

---

[13] Criminal Law Revision Committee, Eleventh Report *op.cit.* para.219.

PART 3

Exclusionary rules and exceptions

CHAPTER 6
Evidence of Opinion

"Opinion" may be defined as an inference drawn from perceived facts.[1]   6–01
The general rule is that evidence of opinion is not admissible. However, the
rule is subject to certain well-known exceptions, particularly relating to
expert evidence.

1. GENERAL RULE

The general rule is that while evidence of fact is admissible, evidence of   6–02
opinion is not. This rule flows from the principle that while witnesses give
evidence as to facts, the inferences to be drawn from those facts are matters
for the jury. Thus, in a murder case, a witness may say "A shot B." He may
not say "A killed B" because it is for the jury to determine whether A killed
B, *i.e.* whether the shot caused B's death.

The rule may be further illustrated as follows. Suppose a smash and grab
raid to have taken place at a jeweller's shop. A witness in a nearby street
heard the crash of the breaking glass. Shortly afterwards he saw a man
running into the street from the direction of the jeweller's shop. The man
was carrying jewellery and his hands were bleeding. The obvious inference
is that the man was the thief. In ordinary speech the witness would say "I
saw the thief." However, when giving evidence the witness may only say
what he saw. He may not say that the man was the thief. That is an
inference for the jury to draw.

There are essentially two reasons for the rule excluding evidence of opinion.   6–03
They are as follows:

1. The opinion of the witness is irrelevant. Thus, in the example given
above, the opinion of the witness that the man he saw was the thief does not
matter. The relevant parts of his evidence are those involving what he saw
and heard. A familiar example of the same principle is the eye-witness in a
case of dangerous driving. He may give evidence of what he saw. He may
not, however, give his opinion as to whether the defendant's driving was
dangerous.

Similarly, the opinion of the non-expert witness as to a matter requiring
expert evidence is irrelevant and inadmissible. Thus, if a person is
attempting to establish a defence of insanity, he may not call his friends and

---

[1] Landau (1944) 60 L.Q.R. 201.

relations to give evidence of their opinion on the subject. In *Loak*[2] a friend of the defendant and a magistrate were not allowed to give evidence of their opinion that the defendant was insane.

2. If evidence of opinion is admitted, the function of the jury, *i.e.* to decide on the "ultimate issue", will be usurped. This is the primary reason for the rule. It is thought that it is the reason why the rule was developed.[3]

6–04   A witness cannot, therefore, say that in his opinion the defendant is guilty. Thus, a bystander cannot say that A was driving dangerously, a store detective cannot say that B stole the goods from the shops; an eye-witness cannot say C murdered D. These are all issues which the jury have to decide. For example, evidence is not admissible as to (a) whether an article is such as to "tend to deprave and corrupt" under s.1 of the Obscene Publications Act 1959[4]; or (b) whether a driver is unfit to drive through drink or drugs[5]; or (c) whether a defendant intended to commit a particular crime or not.[6] In *Chard*[7] a prison doctor was not permitted to say that in his opinion the defendant who was charged with murder had not intended at the time of the offence to commit murder. The Court of Appeal held that this evidence had been rightly excluded because it went to the very issue which the jury had to decide. The Court said: "It is not permissible to call a witness, whatever his personal experience, merely to tell the jury how he thinks an accused man's mind—assumedly a normal mind—operated at the time of the alleged crime with reference to the crucial question of what the man's intention was."[8]

An example is to be found in *Jeffries*.[9] The defendant in that case was charged with possessing drugs with intent to supply them. At trial a detective constable gave evidence that in her opinion certain lists found at the defendant's flat related to the sale of drugs. The Court of Appeal held that this evidence should not have been admitted because the officer was essentially giving her opinion on the ultimate issue, namely whether the defendant had the drugs in his possession with intent to supply them (although she was entitled to give evidence, based on her experience, as to value and prices).

6–05   It follows that questions must be framed in such a way as to avoid the risk that the witness will give an opinion on the ultimate issue which the jury have to decide. Thus, if a victim has died of gunshot wounds, an eye-witness should be asked "Did A shoot at B?"; "Did the shot hit B?"; and *not* "Did A kill B?"

---

[2] (1911) 7 Cr.App.R. 71.
[3] Landau (1944) 60 L.Q.R. 201.
[4] *Calder & Boyars Ltd* [1969] 1 Q.B. 151; *Anderson* [1972] 1 Q.B. 304.
[5] *Davies* (1962) 46 Cr.App.R. 292.
[6] *Chard* (1972) 56 Cr.App.R. 268.
[7] Above.
[8] At 270–271.
[9] [1997] Crim.L.R. 819.

However, the rule that witnesses may not be asked questions as to the "ultimate issue" is subject to modification in the case of expert witnesses. Thus, questions on the ultimate issue are allowed if it would be artificial for the witness not to express his opinion on that issue. In the case of insanity, for instance, a medical witness may be asked in cross-examination whether in his opinion the conduct of the defendant immediately after a murder would indicate that he knew (a) the nature and quality of the act; (b) that the act was contrary to law.[10]

The reasons for allowing such questions may be summarised:

(i) Since the expert's opinion may have been obvious from his evidence, it would be artificial not to allow him to express it merely because it is on an ultimate issue.

(ii) The defence may be hampered in presenting their case if the expert may not be asked about that issue in the most direct way.

In fact, the tendency to allow experts to give evidence on the ultimate issue had been recognised by the courts as long as 50 years ago.[11] The practice was sanctioned by the Court of Appeal in *Stockwell*.[12] In that case the defendant was charged with robbery. The only issue was identification. The prosecution were permitted to call a "facial mapping" expert who gave his opinion that the defendant was the robber as shown on photographs taken by security cameras. The Court of Appeal held that this evidence was admissible although it was on the very issue which the jury had to decide. Lord Taylor C.J. said that the old rule was more a matter of form than substance and had been more honoured in the breach than the observance. The Lord Chief Justice said that an expert should be allowed to give his opinion on an ultimate issue subject to a direction by the judge to the jury that they are not bound by it.

6–06

A witness may, similarly, state an opinion on an ultimate issue if it is a way of conveying relevant facts perceived by him. The statement is then admissible as evidence of what the witness perceived. Thus, a witness in a case of wounding may say that he saw several people attack the defendant who then took up a weapon "to defend himself". He will not be stopped if he says this, although the question whether the defendant was defending himself or not is one for the jury to decide. To say that the defendant took up the knife in self-defence is merely to describe the way in which a weapon was taken up under pressure of attack.

---

[10] *Holmes* (1953) 37 Cr.App.R. 61.
[11] *DPP v A. & B.C. Chewing Gum* [1968] A.C. 159, 164, *per* Lord Parker C.J.
[12] *Stockwell* (1993) 97 Cr.App.R. 20. Doubts have been expressed as to the advisability of admitting expert evidence as to image analysis and facial mapping, see *Gray (Paul Edward)*, para.6–42n below.

2. EXCEPTIONS TO THE GENERAL RULE

A. The opinions of non-experts

6–07   Evidence of the opinion of non-experts is not generally admissible. However, such evidence is admitted on certain topics. The most common example is a witness's opinion as to a person's identity (considered in Ch.14). Four other exceptions are considered below.

(1) Matters of impression and narrative

6–08   Evidence of the opinion of a witness who is not an expert may be admissible if (a) the impression received by the witness is too vague to be otherwise described; or (b) if made as a way of conveying relevant facts perceived by him.

A witness may say that the person he saw was a "young woman" or a "child of about five".[13] He may state the impression as to the speed of the car[14] or (provided he states the facts upon which he relies) whether a person has taken a drink or not.[15] Therefore, if an eye-witness of an accident says "there was nothing the driver could do to avoid the accident", he has described accurately the impression which the event made on him.

(2) Witness's own condition

6–09   A witness may give evidence of his own condition, whether physical or mental. Such evidence may include evidence of opinion. Thus a witness may say "I had seven pints of beer to drink, but I was not drunk" or "I was well until I ate the food given me by the defendant: then I fell ill."

A witness may likewise give evidence (a) as to his motive for doing a particular act; or (b) as to what his feelings were. For example, in a case of robbery the witness may say that he handed over the goods to the defendant because he was frightened that if he did not, he would be injured or a witness may state that in his opinion a threat that he would "suffer as before" was a threat to burn his house down.[16]

(3) Handwriting

6–10   Whether a particular sample of handwriting is that of a particular person is one matter where the evidence of a non-expert witness may be admitted. In

---

[13] *Cox* [1898] 1 Q.B. 179; *Wallworth v Balmer* [1966] 1 W.L.R. 166. The court may determine a person's age: Children and Young Persons Act 1933, s.99; Criminal Justice Act 1948, s.80(3); Magistrates' Courts Act 1980, s.150(4).

[14] But the Road Traffic Regulation Act 1984, s.89(2) provides that a person shall not be liable to be convicted solely on the evidence of one witness that in his opinion the person prosecuted was driving the vehicle at a speed exceeding the specified limit.

[15] *Davies* (1962) 46 Cr.App.R. 292; *Neal* [1962] Crim.L.R. 698; *Tagg* [2002] 1 Cr.App.R. 22.

[16] (1850) 4 Cox 243.

practice, such evidence is rarely tendered. However, the Criminal Procedure Act 1865, s.8, provides that comparison of a disputed writing with any writing proved to be genuine shall be permitted and the evidence of witnesses on the subject is admissible as evidence of the genuineness or otherwise of the disputed writing.

The witness must be acquainted with the defendant's writing and is open to cross-examination as to the extent of his acquaintance. He may have seen the particular person write; he may have received letters from him; or he may have seen, in the ordinary course of business, documents purporting to be in the particular person's handwriting. But he must not have become acquainted with the person's handwriting simply for the purposes of the trial.[17]

A jury must not be asked to compare two pieces of handwriting; in such circumstances they must have the opinion of an expert witness to guide them.[18] In some cases, however, in which no expert has been called, jurors have before them specimens of handwriting, one of which is disputed. The Court of Appeal in *O'Sullivan*[19] recognised that, in such circumstances, it is unavoidable that the jury may try to make comparisons; but there must never be an invitation or exhortation to a jury to look at disputed handwriting (and try to make comparisons). "There should be a warning of the dangers; further than that, as a matter of practical reality, it cannot be expected that the court will go."[20]

B. The opinions of experts

The chief exception to the general rule that evidence of opinion is not admissible relates to the evidence of experts. The remainder of the Chapter is concerned with a discussion of this exception.   **6–11**

(1) Admissibility

The opinion of experts is admissible on those matters which require such evidence, that is, where the subject is one which competency to form an opinion can only be acquired by a course of special study or experience. "In matters of science, no other witnesses can be called."[21] Such evidence is preserved by s.118(1) of the Criminal Justice Act 2003, which preserves certain common law categories of admissible hearsay, including "any rule of law under which in criminal proceedings an expert may draw on the body of expertise relevant to his field".[22]   **6–12**

---

[17] *Crouch* (1850) 4 Cox 163; *Rickard* (1918) 13 Cr.App.R. 140. The opinion may be based on comparison from a photocopy: *Lockheed Arabia v Owen* [1993] Q.B. 806.
[18] *Tilley* (1961) 45 Cr.App.R. 360; *Smith* (1968) 52 Cr.App.R. 848.
[19] [1969] 2 All E.R. 237.
[20] At 242, *per* Winn L.J.
[21] *Folkes v Chadd* (1782) 3 Doug. K.B. 157, *per* Lord Mansfield.
[22] At the time of writing, the section is expected to come into effect in April 2005.

The purpose of expert evidence is to provide the court with information which is outside the experience and knowledge of a judge or jury.[23]

It is for the court to decide whether or not a particular point requires expert evidence; if the court decides that it does not, then the point in question must be proved either without the admission of opinion evidence at all or by non-expert evidence. "In each case it must be for the judge to decide whether the issue is one on which the jury could be assisted by expert evidence."[24]

Account must be taken of advances in scientific expertise. In *Clarke*[25] the Court of Appeal said that there were no closed categories where expert evidence may be placed before the jury. It would be wrong to deny the law of evidence the advantages to be gained from new techniques and advances in science. Accordingly, the tendency is to admit expert evidence on a point unless it is apparent that it is not a matter for expertise. However, in *Cannings*[26] it was held that juries should not be placed in a position where they must choose between the opinion of expert witnesses where there was no cogent evidence supporting either expert's stance. The Court of Appeal held that the prosecution of a parent for murder should not be commenced if the outcome of the trial depended exclusively on a serious disagreement between distinguished and reputable experts as to the cause of death, unless there was evidence—additional to the expert evidence—supporting the conclusion that the infant was deliberately harmed.

In *Clare and Peach*[27] a police officer who had made a study of video recordings depicting scenes of violence after a football match was allowed to give evidence in order to identify offenders shown on the recordings. The Court of Appeal referred to a New Zealand case in which such a witness was described as "sufficiently expert ad hoc to give identification evidence."[28] The Court of Appeal did not comment on whether the expression "expert ad hoc" was suitable in these circumstances. It is submitted that it is not, since such a witness cannot be described as an expert.[29]

6–13   If, however, the matter is one upon which an expert *should* give evidence, the court should refrain from acting as its own expert. Thus, the Divisional Court held that justices acted wrongly when, in a case concerning defective tyres, they called for a tyre gauge and then retired with the tyres and the

---

[23] *Turner* [1975] 1 Q.B. 834.

[24] *Stockwell* (1993) 97 Cr.App.R. 260, 264, *per* Lord Taylor C.J.

[25] [1995] 2 Cr.App.R. 425. The expertise in this case was facial mapping by video superimposition. But certain types of expert evidence are not yet of sufficient scientific status to be acceptable see para.6–17, below. In some cases of voice identification expert evidence may be of assistance, but not all: *Hersey* [1998] Crim.L.R. 281. See also para.14–48 for voice identification.

[26] *The Times*, January 23, 2004.

[27] [1995] 2 Cr.App.R. 333, cited at para.2–39, above.

[28] *Howe* [1982] 1 N.Z.L.R. 618.

[29] For further discussion of this topic, see Elliott, "Video Tape Evidence: The Risk of Over Persuasion" [1998] Crim.L.R. 159.

gauge without any evidence being given as to how the gauge should be operated.[30] Similarly, the Court of Appeal has criticised a judge for appearing to turn himself into a handwriting expert by comparing examples of the defendant's handwriting.[31] In *Akhtar v Grout*,[32] a prosecution under the Trade Marks Act 1994, it was held that expert evidence was admissible to supplement the knowledge and experience of justices as to whether or not certain clothing was not genuinely what the trade marks indicated that it should be. As a matter of law, the mere fact that, if justices accept the evidence of the expert it would be conclusive of the question put to the court, is not by itself a reason for excluding the evidence. In *O'Toole v Knowsley MBC*[33] the Divisional Court held that justices should not have refused to accept the uncontradicted advice of experts (in a case of statutory nuisance under the Environmental Protection Act 1990). The issue was pre-eminently a matter of expert evidence which the justices should have taken into account and they had been wrong in refusing to do so.

If expert evidence is to be rejected there must be some logical basis for doing so: *Gregory v DPP*[34] in which it was held that the evidence of a toxicologist which raised significant doubts as to the accuracy of blood alcohol tests should not have been rejected.

On the other hand, if information is within the knowledge of the court or the issue is one which the court can decide of its own experience, expert evidence will not be admitted.

6–14

> "If on the proven facts a judge or jury can form their own conclusion without help, then the opinion of the expert is unnecessary. In such a case if it is dressed up in scientific jargon it may make judgment more difficult. The fact that an expert witness has impressive scientific qualifications does not by that fact alone make his opinion in matters of human nature or behaviour within the limits of normality any more helpful than that of the jurors themselves; but there is a danger that they may think it does."[35]

Thus, in *Chard*[36] the evidence of a prison doctor was not admitted when the purpose was to show that the defendant did not have the necessary *mens rea* to commit murder and in *Turner*[37] the evidence of a psychiatrist

---

[30] *Tiverton JJ. Ex p. Smith* [1980] R.T.R. 280.
[31] *Simbodyal, The Times*, October 10, 1991.
[32] (1998) 162 J.P. 714.
[33] *The Times*, May 21, 1999.
[34] [2002] 166 J.P. 400 (QBD).
[35] *Turner* [1975] 2 Q.B. 834, *per* Lawton L.J.
[36] (1972) 56 Cr.App.R. 268, 270. See also *Wood* (1989) 153 J.P. 20 where the Divisional Court held that magistrates were right to reject certain evidence given by a consultant psychiatrist on the ground, *inter alia*, that it dealt with matters within the knowledge and experience of the court.
[37] Above.

was not admitted when the purpose was to show that a man charged with murder was likely to have been provoked.

The same applies where the issue in question is not a scientific matter. Thus, in *Wahab*[38] it was held to be inappropriate to call expert evidence of one solicitor criticising the competence of another since the judge did not need the expert legal evidence to form a view about the reliability of the confession.

6–15 There are difficulties sometimes in disentangling questions of opinion from questions of fact.[39] This distinction is particularly important when considering the evidence of experts. This is because the function of the expert witness is twofold.

First, he may give his opinion upon an issue in the case (*i.e.* inferences which he draws from perceived facts as a result of his knowledge and experience). Secondly, he may give evidence of facts which his training has equipped him to perceive, but which would not be observed by a layman, *i.e.* "something perceptible upon physical examination but which would be recognised only by someone possessed of special knowledge or experience."[40]

These functions are often combined. Thus, the fingerprint expert points out the "ridge" characteristics of a certain print. These are matters of fact. He compares the print with the defendant's fingerprint and draws the inference that the defendant made the print in question. That is a matter of opinion. This distinction between evidence of fact and evidence of opinion may be of importance when assessing the expert's evidence.

6–16 The expert may, like any other witness, give evidence of fact. He may give evidence of fact which is *not* within his field of expertise. In this case, the jury must be directed that the witness was not speaking as an expert. Thus, in *Cook*[41] the defence to a charge of murder was provocation. A pathologist gave evidence that, as a matter of personal (but not medical) opinion, the blows to the victim were not consistent with having been inflicted by someone in a frenzy. There was held to have been a material irregularity in the case in that the judge in summing up had indicated that the pathologist had spoken as an expert and the jury might have attached far greater weight to his view than it merited.[42]

An expert's inadmissible opinion (outside his area of expertise) does not become admissible when adduced on behalf of a co-defendant. In *Theodosi*[43] T and a co-defendant were both charged with causing death by dan-

---

[38] [2003] 1 Cr.App.R. 232.

[39] Landau: *op.cit.*

[40] Law Reform Committee, 17th Report, *Evidence of Opinion and Expert Evidence*, Cmnd. 4489, para.7.

[41] [1982] Crim.L.R. 670.

[42] Since the pathologist was speaking outside his field of expertise, it must be doubtful whether his view should have *any* weight.

[43] *The Times*, April 13, 1992.

gerous driving. Each blamed the other for the offence. A police officer gave evidence of the estimated speed of T's car. In cross-examination counsel for the co-defendant adduced the police officer's opinion that T was wholly to blame for the accident. The Court of Appeal held that the trial judge should have discharged the jury because inadmissible and very prejudicial evidence had been given.

The subjects of expert evidence fall into a number of broad categories; **6–17** the most common are matters of science, art or skill, for example the evidence of medical practitioners as to the cause of injury or death; mechanical experts as to the functioning of a motor car; handwriting or fingerprint experts on the subject of their expertise. The categories of expert evidence will expand as new techniques are developed and new advances in science are made.[44] So long as the field of expertise is sufficiently well-established to pass ordinary tests of relevance and reliability no enhanced tests need be applied: *Dallagher*.[45] Not all topics on which expert opinions are available are admissible as evidence. For instance, in *Gilfoyle*,[46] it was held that the evidence of a psychologist relating to a "psychological autopsy" was not expert evidence of a kind properly to be put before the court since *inter alia* the academic status of such autopsies was not such as to permit them to be admitted as a basis for expert opinion. And in *Dallagher*[47] evidence of earprints was not admitted: although there was no objection in principle, the expertise was in its infancy and conclusions could not be expressed in terms of statistical probability. It is for the court to decide whether a point requires expert evidence.

Subjects will now be considered where there are particular considerations in relation to expert evidence, namely psychiatric evidence, cases of obscenity, special measures directions, and credibility of witnesses.

Psychiatric evidence. In some cases psychiatric evidence is a neces- **6–18** sity.[48] Thus, it is a practical necessity in order to establish a defence of automatism[49] or diminished responsibility.[50] Despite authority to the

---

[44] See *Clarke*, above, at para.6–13.
[45] [2003] 1 Cr.App.R. 195.
[46] [2001] 2 Cr.App.R. 57. See also *Stagg*, C.C.C. September 14, 1994, Ognall J., unreported, *Archbold News*, issue 9, November 4, 1994, where it was doubted whether psychological profiling could properly be described as expert evidence.
[47] Above, n.43.
[48] For a discussion of psychiatric evidence, see Kenny, "The Expert in Court" (1983) 99 L.Q.R. 197; and for a discussion of the role of the expert, see Gee, "The Expert Witness in the Criminal Trial" [1987] Crim.L.R. 307. Not all categories of psychiatric evidence are admissible: see *Gilfoyle* and *Stagg*, above.
[49] *Hill v Baxter* [1958] 1 Q.B. 277, 285, *per* Devlin J.; *Smith* (1979) 69 Cr.App.R. 378, 385, *per* Geoffrey Lane L.J., *Bratty v Att-Gen* [1963] A.C. 386, 413, *per* Lord Denning.
[50] *Byrne* [1960] 2 Q.B. 396; *Dix* (1982) 74 Cr.App.R. 306. "While the subsection does not in terms require that medical evidence be adduced in support of a defence of diminished responsibility, it makes it a practical necessity if that defence is to begin to run at all": *Dix*, above, at 311, *per* Shaw L.J.

contrary[51] it is also difficult to see how a defence of insanity could succeed in the absence of medical evidence. Where the possible effect of hypoglycaemia on intent has to be considered, expert evidence is required since the matter is outside the experience of ordinary jurors.[52]

Expert evidence may also be admissible to assist the judge and jury in assessing the reliability of a confession. In *O'Brien, Hall and Sherwood*,[53] the Court of Appeal said that, where expert evidence of the abnormality of a defendant's personality is to be admitted as being relevant to the reliability of a confession, there must be a significant deviation from the norm and also a history predating the confession (not based solely on the history given by the subject) which pointed to or explained the abnormality. The jury should be directed that they were not obliged to accept the evidence but should consider it, if they think right, as throwing light on the personality of the defendant and bringing to their attention aspects of his personality of which they might otherwise be unaware. In *Raghip*[54] the defendant was aged 19 but was of low I.Q. and had the reading age and level of functioning of a child under 10 years old. In these circumstances the Court of Appeal said that psychological evidence was necessary and admissible to assist the jury in assessing the reliability of a confession made by R. The Court drew a distinction between evidence admissible for this purpose and such evidence relating to a defendant's *mens rea* (which is generally inadmissible). In *Ward*[55] the Court of Appeal held that expert evidence of a psychiatrist or psychologist may be admitted if it is to the effect that the defendant is suffering from a condition not properly described as mental illness, but from a personality disorder so severe as to be categorised as a mental disorder.

6–19   In *Lowery v R*[56] the Privy Council upheld the evidence of a psychologist, called by one of two co-defendants charged with murder, to the effect that the defendant was less likely on the grounds of personality to have committed the murder.[57]

On the other hand, psychiatric evidence will not be admitted if the issue is one which the jury should determine without assistance. The question is whether the jury require the help of a psychiatrist in deciding the issue or not. Will the psychiatrist tell the jury something which they do not know from their own knowledge and experience?

In all the following examples the essential point is that the issue of the

---

[51] *Att-Gen for S. Australia v Brown* [1960] A.C. 432; (1960) 44 Cr.App.R. 100, 112, 113.
[52] *Toner* (1991) 93 Cr.App.R. 382.
[53] *The Times*, February 16, 2000.
[54] *The Times*, December 9, 1991.
[55] (1993) 96 Cr.App.R. 1, 66.
[56] [1974] A.C. 85.
[57] *Lowery* has been distinguished as a decision on its own special facts because the evidence was called on behalf of one defendant to rebut the evidence of his co-defendant: *Turner*, below at 842: *Masih*, below. Accordingly it would appear that *Lowery* cannot be taken as establishing any general rule relating to the admissibility of psychiatric evidence.

defendant's state of mind is one that the members of the jury can judge for themselves.

The leading case is *Turner*[58] in which the defendant was charged with murdering his girlfriend who admitted to sleeping with other men and to being pregnant by another man. The defendant's defence was provocation and he sought to admit psychiatric evidence to the effect that he had had a deep emotional relationship with his girlfriend and that her admissions were likely to have caused a blind explosion of rage. He was not, however, suffering from a mental illness. The Court of Appeal held that the trial judge had been right to exclude the psychiatric evidence.

The Court said that (i) the question whether the defendant suffered from mental illness was within the expert's province, but was not relevant since it was not in issue; (ii) the remaining points in the psychiatrist's opinion were matters which were well within ordinary human experience. The Court commented that "Jurors do not need psychiatrists to tell them how ordinary folk who are not suffering from a mental illness are likely to react to the stresses and strains of life."[59]

If there is an underlying medical condition which the defendant claims made him unable to commit the crime alleged there must be an organic or psychiatric connection between the condition and the inability to commit the crime. In *Loughran*[60] where the defendant was charged with rape and robbery he sought to adduce psychiatric evidence that, due to an underlying physical condition, he suffered from pathological anxiety at the prospect of sexual intercourse which tended to confirm his contention that he was incapable of sexual intercourse. The Court of Appeal held that the evidence had been rightly excluded since it went to the defendant's credibility and did not furnish information outside the jury's own experience.

6–20

In *Masih*[61] the defendant, who was charged with rape, sought unsuccessfully to adduce psychiatric evidence to the effect that his low intelligence and immaturity made him easily led by his two co-defendants. However, although his intelligence was low, it was within the scale of normality. The Court of Appeal, upholding the trial judge, said that in these circumstances expert evidence was not as a rule necessary and should be excluded, but that if a person came into the class of mental defective (*i.e.* with an I.Q. of 69 and below) and mental defectiveness was relevant to an issue, expert evidence should be admitted; the evidence should be confined to an assessment of the defendant's I.Q. and an explanation of any relevant abnormal characteristics which such an assessment involved.

In *Reynolds*,[62] a defendant charged with murder wished to call a psychiatrist to give evidence that his ability to separate reality from fantasy was

[58] [1975] Q.B. 834.
[59] At 841.
[60] [1999] Crim.L.R. 404.
[61] [1999] Crim.L.R. 395.
[62] [1989] Crim.L.R. 220.

flawed. The trial judge refused to admit the evidence. The Court of Appeal held that this ruling was correct: the evidence was irrelevant. This was because the issue in the case was whether the defendant had the necessary intention or not and there was no suggestion in the evidence that he had been fantasising at the time of the killing. The Court said that even if there had been such a suggestion, it amounted to a personal trait, about which the jury could use their common sense and did not require psychiatric evidence.

6–21   Some Commonwealth courts have taken a less restrictive view.[63] In *Lupien*[64] a majority of the Supreme Court of Canada held that psychiatric evidence should have been admitted to show that a defendant would react violently to homosexual advances.[65] In *Schultz*[66] the Supreme Court of Western Australia held that psychiatric evidence was admissible on the issue of intent in a case of murder to establish that the appellant was of borderline mentally-defective intelligence with an I.Q. of between 69 and 78. Burt C.J. said that the evidence, if accepted, would "take the appellant outside the range of the ordinary and would alert the jury to the fact ... that he was in a class apart."[67] However, the Court of Appeal said in *Masih* that *Schultz* went too far and would not be followed.

Thus, as a general rule, it would appear that the court should distinguish between a case where the defendant suffers from mental illness or abnormality of mind (in which case psychiatric evidence is admissible to assist the jury) and a case in which there is no mental illness or abnormality of mind (in which case the jury can draw on its own knowledge and experience without assistance). It is sometimes argued that this test cannot be applied because mental abnormality and illness cannot be precisely defined.[68] However, the question whether mental illness or abnormality exists in a particular case is for the court to determine on the evidence before it. Each case must be decided on its own facts.[69]

6–22   **Cases of obscenity.** The general rule is that expert evidence is not admissible to prove that material is obscene under the Obscene Publications Act 1959, *i.e.* whether it tends to deprave and corrupt the class of persons

---

[63] See Pattenden, "Conflicting Approaches to Psychiatric Evidence" [1986] Crim.L.R. 92 for a comparison of the approaches in England, Canada and Australia.

[64] 1970 S.C.R. 263. For a discussion of recent decisions on this topic and a plea that *Turner*, above, should be reconsidered, see Mackay and Colman, "Equivocal Rulings on Expert Psychological and Psychiatric Evidence" [1996] Crim.L.R. 88.

[65] *per* Ritchie, Spence and Hall JJ. The author is grateful to Judge Gordon Killeen, Senior Judge for the County of Middlesex, District Court of Ontario, for pointing out this result.

[66] [1982] W.A.R. 171.

[67] At 174.

[68] See, *e.g.* Pattenden, *op.cit.*, pp.99–100 and Mackay and Colman, "Excluding Expert Evidence" [1991] Crim.L.R. 800, where the authors suggest that the present rule is too restrictive and that expert evidence should be admitted if the defendant exhibits any abnormality of mind or personality.

[69] *Weightman* (1991) 92 Cr.App.R. 291, 297, CA.

likely to read it.[70] The issue whether it has that tendency is for the jury to decide. The rationale of the rule is that the jury has been given the responsibility of making the decision as representing the ordinary man. It should not, therefore, be taken away from the jury and given to experts.[71]

However, there may be cases where expert evidence is admissible because it is not aimed at establishing that material has a tendency to deprave and corrupt, but at providing information to assist the jury to decide whether it has such a tendency. Thus, in *Skirving and Grossman*[72] the defendants were charged with having an obscene article for publication for gain. The article was a pamphlet concerned with the different ways of taking cocaine. The Court of Appeal held that expert evidence relating to the taking of cocaine had rightly been admitted because the expert was not usurping the function of the jury but informing them of something which they could not be expected to know, *i.e.* the effects of taking cocaine.

There may be an exception to the rule if the material is to be read by an exceptional class of reader, "such that a jury cannot be expected to understand the likely impact of the material upon its members without assistance."[73] In *DPP v A. & B.C. Chewing Gum Ltd*,[74] the Divisional Court held that evidence from a psychiatrist was admissible as to the effect of certain "battle cards" upon the minds of children aged from five years upwards. The reason for the decision was that while an adult jury is perfectly capable of considering the effect of something on an adult, the jury or justices need help when considering the effect upon children.[75]

6–23

The correctness of the decision has been doubted,[76] but it has not been overruled. But there must be doubt whether there is sufficient cogency in the reason given by the court to justify such a departure from principle. Most parents, do not need assistance from an expert on the question whether material was likely to deprave and corrupt children.

Section 4(2) of the Obscene Publications Act 1959 provides that expert evidence is admissible to establish or negative the defence[77] that publication of an obscene article is for the public good on the grounds that it is in the interests of science, literature, art, or learning or other subjects of general interest. However, that evidence is to be limited to "the literary, artistic, scientific or other merits" of the articles.[78] It does not extend to evidence that the publication of the obscene material would be of therapeutic benefit

---

[70] *Calder & Boyars Ltd* [1969] 1 Q.B. 151; *Anderson* [1972] 1 Q.B. 304, 313; *cf.* Post Office Act 1953, s.11; *Stamford* [1972] 2 Q.B. 391.
[71] *DPP v Jordan* [1977] A.C. 699, 717, *per* Lord Wilberforce.
[72] [1985] Q.B. 819.
[73] *Jordan*, above, at 718, *per* Lord Wilberforce.
[74] [1968] 1 Q.B. 159.
[75] At 164–165, *per* Lord Parker C.J.
[76] *Jordan*, above, at 722, *per* Lord Dilhorne.
[77] Provided by s.4(1) of the Act.
[78] s.4(2).

to a minority of the public with certain sexual tendencies or difficulties[79] or would tempt young people to read it,[80] or would promote sex education.[81]

6-24   **Special measures directions.**   An expert witness may now give evidence in connection with an application for a special measures direction under s.20(6)(c) of the Youth Justice and Criminal Evidence Act 1999. An expert may also give evidence as to whether a witness is competent (*ibid.*, s.54(5)), and can give sworn or unsworn evidence (*ibid.*, s.55(6)).

6-25   **Credibility of witnesses.**   Medical evidence may be called to show that a witness through disease or defect or abnormality of mind is not capable of giving true or reliable evidence. The House of Lords held in *Toohey v Metropolitan Police Commissioner*[82] that such evidence was admissible. Lord Pearce stated the principle thus:

> "Medical evidence is admissible to show that a witness suffers from some disease or defect or abnormality of mind that affects the *reliability* of his evidence. Such evidence is not confined to a general opinion of the unreliability of the witness, but may give all the matters necessary to show, not only the foundation of and reasons for the diagnosis, but also the extent to which the credibility of the witness is affected."[83]

This principle appeared to have been extended by the decision of the Privy Council in *Lowery v R*, above, para.6-19. However, the scope of this decision has been considerably restricted by subsequent decisions.[84] In *Turner*,[85] the Court of Appeal said that the Court did not consider it "authority for the proposition that in all cases psychologists and psychiatrists can be called to prove the probability of the accused's veracity."[86] Thus, it will only be in an exceptional case that such evidence will be admitted. For instance, it is not permissible for the prosecution to call a psychiatrist or psychologist to give evidence as to why a witness's evidence should be accepted as reliable (unless the defence is calling a witness to say that it is unreliable).[87]

6-26   Evidence of the assessment of the credibility of witnesses by means of a

---

[79] *DPP v Jordan* [1977] A.C. 699.
[80] *Sumner* [1977] Crim.L.R. 614.
[81] *Att-Gen's Ref. (No.3 of 1977)* (1978) 67 Cr.App.R. 393.
[82] [1965] A.C. 595.
[83] At 609; emphasis supplied by author.
[84] *Turner*, below; *Neale*, below, and *Rimmer and Beech*, below.
[85] [1975] Q.B. 834.
[86] At 842. Attempts to call psychiatric evidence in circumstances where one defendant blamed the other for an offence failed in *Neale* (1977) 65 Cr.App.R. 304 and *Rimmer and Beech* [1983] Crim.L.R. 250. In both cases, the evidence was held not to be relevant.
[87] *Robinson* (1994) 98 Cr.App.R. 370.

lie detector machine (polygraph) has not been admitted in this country.[88] There is no reported authority on the subject and in the unreported case of *Burnal and Moore* the Privy Council said that polygraph evidence should only be made admissible, if at all, as a result of legislation based on full scientific and legal research.[89]

The question of admissibility of such evidence bristles with difficulty. First, the evidence of the operator of the machine concerning statements by a witness relating to any incident or offence must be hearsay. Secondly, if a defendant seeks to introduce evidence of a test which he has taken, he will be in contravention of the rule prohibiting previous consistent statements.[90] There are also practical difficulties since there are doubts about the accuracy of the test. Thus, the Royal Commission on Criminal Procedure concluded that the machine's "lack of certainty from an evidential point of view" told against its introduction in this country.[91] A yet more fundamental objection to its introduction is that it would make considerable inroads into the jury's function of assessing the credibility of witnesses. It can hardly be in the interests of justice that this important function be handed over to a machine, the accuracy of which is in doubt.

Qualifications of experts. It is for the court to decide whether a witness is qualified to give expert evidence or not. Such competence may have been derived either from a course of study or from experience. Thus, a medical practitioner or a scientist will give evidence of his qualifications and thereby establish his expertise. On the other hand, the witness may be an expert, but not in the relevant subject. In that case, his opinion will not be admissible. Thus a witness with training in psychology was not allowed to give medical evidence.[92]

6–27

However, the expertise may be derived from experience and not formal study. Such experience may have been gained in a trade or business, for example an antique dealer. Alternatively, it may have been gained simply during the course of work. Thus, an experienced police officer was allowed to give expert evidence as to how an accident had occurred.[93] In *Murphy*[94] the Court of Appeal held that a police officer could give evidence of any

---

[88] For use of the polygraph in the USA, see D. W. Elliott's essay in *Well and Truly Tried* (1983) and for its use in Israel see Harnon, "Evidence Obtained by Polygraph: an Israeli Perspective" [1982] Crim.L.R. 340.
[89] April 28, 1997 ("Polygraph Evidence in Jamaica—The Door Left Ajar", Broadbent, 62 Jo.Crim.L. 585).
[90] See D. W. Elliott, *op.cit.* for a discussion of these difficulties.
[91] Cmnd. 8092 (1981), para.4–76.
[92] *Mackenney* (1983) 76 Cr.App.R. 271.
[93] *Oakley* (1979) 70 Cr.App.R. 7.
[94] [1980] Q.B. 434.

matter that was within his expertise. In *Clare and Peach*[95] a police officer who had made a lengthy study of a poor quality, confused video which purported to show the defendants committing offences was allowed to give evidence as to what, in his opinion, was happening on the video. As the court pointed out, the witness was open to cross-examination and the jury, after proper directions and warnings, would be free to accept or reject his assertions.

6–28   On the other hand, ordinary experience is not sufficient to make a witness an expert. Thus, the fact that a witness is a driver himself does not entitle him to give an opinion as to whether another driver is unfit through drink.[96] Likewise, in *Inch*[97] the Courts-Martial Appeal Court held that a medical orderly should not have been allowed at a court-martial to give evidence of his opinion that a wound was the result of a blow from an instrument and was not consistent with a clash of heads: such evidence should have been given by a person qualified to provide a medical opinion. There may, however, be occasions when the opinions of amateurs are admissible. Thus, in *Silverlock*[98] a solicitor was allowed to give evidence as an expert on handwriting, having gained his experience during the course of his practice. However, such circumstances must be very rare. It must be very doubtful if an amateur would now be allowed to give evidence on a subject when there are experts available.

In practice, provided (a) the subject is one on which expert evidence is admissible[99]; and (b) the witness has specialised knowledge or experience of the subject, the witness's evidence will usually be admitted and questions as to his qualifications then go to the weight of the evidence rather than its admissibility.[1] For instance, the Court of Appeal in *Robb*[2] held that a phonetician, qualified by academic training and practical experience, was qualified to express an opinion on voice identification, although he relied on a technique which had minority support in his profession.

(2) The expert as witness

6–29   **Compellability and privilege.** Expert witnesses are, like other witnesses, compellable.[3] They may also be required to produce documents as

---

[95] [1995] 2 Cr.App.R. 333. The Court of Appeal referred, in the absence of English authority, to Commonwealth cases, in particular to *Howe* (1982) 1 N.Z.L.R. 618 where the facts were very similar. See also Munday, "Videotape Evidence and the Advent of the Expert Ad Hoc" (1995) 159 J.P. 547.

[96] *Davies* (1962) 46 Cr.App.R. 292.

[97] (1990) 91 Cr.App.R. 51.

[98] (1894) 2 Q.B. 766. See para.6–10, above, for a discussion concerning the opinion of non-experts as to handwriting.

[99] This does not apply to all topics. See para.6–19, above.

[1] Law Reform Committee, 17th Report, *Evidence of Opinion and Expert Evidence*, Cmnd. 4489, para.19.

[2] (1991) 93 Cr.App.R. 161.

[3] *Harmony Shipping Co. v Davis* [1979] 3 All E.R. 177, CA. For the compellability of witnesses, see Ch.17, below.

the result of a *subpoena*.[4] There is no property in an expert witness. Therefore, if a psychiatrist interviews a defendant in prison, he may be called as an expert by the prosecution or defence.[5]

Confidential communications between a solicitor and an expert are protected by legal professional privilege.[6] There is, however, no privilege in relation to (i) the documents or materials upon which the expert's opinion is based or (ii) the independent opinion of the expert himself.[7] Thus, in *King*[8] the defence solicitor had sent various documents to a handwriting expert for his opinion. The prosecution served a *subpoena* on the expert requiring him to produce the documents. The defence objected to the production of the documents on the ground of privilege. The judge ruled that no privilege attached to the documents and allowed the prosecution to call the expert to produce the documents. The Court of Appeal upheld this ruling.

In many cases, the expert's evidence is not in dispute and there is no need to call him. In some cases, however, it may be essential to do so. *Hipson*[9] is an example of such a case. An expert was called at the committal proceedings. He said, without giving reasons, that in his opinion the handwriting on an endorsement of a cheque was the defendant's. He was conditionally bound as a witness. His deposition was read at the trial. There was no other evidence against the defendant. A submission of no case was refused. The subsequent appeal was allowed on the ground that the undisputed evidence fell short of the required standard of proof. The Court of Appeal said that in such cases the jury should have the assistance of the expert witness in court in order to help them make a decision as to the weight and reliability of the evidence.

Expert reports. Section 30 of the Criminal Justice Act 1988 provides that a report by an expert is admissible as evidence in criminal proceedings of any fact or opinion of which the expert could have given oral evidence. This is so, whether or not the expert gives evidence. But if he is not to give oral evidence, the leave of the court is required before his report is admitted. The section defines an "expert report" as a written report by a person dealing wholly or mainly with matters on which he is or would, if living, be qualified to give expert evidence. The section provides that in determining whether to give leave, the court shall have regard to the contents of the report; the reason why it is proposed that the expert shall not give oral evidence; the risk, having regard in particular to whether it is

6–30

6–31

---

[4] *King* (1983) 77 Cr.App.R. 1.
[5] See, *e.g.*, *Smith* (1979) 69 Cr.App.R. 378.
[6] *Harmony Shipping Co. v Davis*, above, at 181. For legal professional privilege, see para.11–33.
[7] *Harmony Shipping Co.*, above, at 181, *per* Lord Denning M.R.; *King*, above.
[8] Above.
[9] 112 S.J. 945; [1969] Crim.L.R. 85.

likely to be possible to controvert statements in the report without oral evidence, of unfairness to the accused; and any other relevant circumstances.

Accordingly, if the expert gives evidence, his report is admissible as evidence of the facts and opinions stated in it. This means that the court and jury can have copies of the report while the expert is giving evidence. It is thus possible to avoid the laborious process of the expert reading out his report when giving evidence. He can simply produce his report and be cross-examined upon it.

6–32   Whether leave is granted for the report to be admitted when the expert does not give evidence depends on the circumstances of the particular case. The court must consider all the matters set out in the section. In some cases it may be proper to admit the report without oral evidence because its contents are not in dispute or not substantially in dispute. On the other hand, in most cases where there is a substantial dispute about the contents, it is difficult to see how it will be possible properly to controvert the statements in the report unless the maker gives oral evidence and is cross-examined. It may be said that the statements can be controverted by other evidence. However, the jury will not be able to assess the evidence properly unless they have seen the expert cross-examined on his report.

6–33   **Preparatory work.** Before the coming into effect of s.127 of the Criminal Justice Act 2003 an expert was not permitted to give an opinion based on scientific facts run by assistants unless all those assistants were called upon to give supporting evidence in court.[10] This situation could in theory affect all such evidence since experts almost invariably depend on primary facts provided by machines or derived from the evidence of others or from their own earlier observations[11] and had considerable potential for the waste of public time and money.[12]

The position has now been rectified by s.127 of the 2003 Act[13] as follows. An expert giving evidence in criminal proceedings may base an opinion or inference on a statement prepared by another person for the purposes of criminal proceedings or a criminal investigation.[14] That person must have, or be reasonably supposed to have had, personal knowledge of

---

[10] Report of the Royal Commission on Criminal Justice, Cm.2263 (1993), para.9.78, quoted Law Commission Report, "Evidence in Criminal Proceedings: Hearsay and Related Topics", Law Com. No.245, 1997, para.9.1. The situation was also criticised in the Law Commission Consultative Paper No.138, 1995, "Evidence in Criminal Proceedings: Hearsay and Related Topics".

[11] Morland J. in *Galizadeh* [1995] Crim.L.R. 232.

[12] Illustrated by *Jackson* [1996] Crim.L.R. 732, Law Com. Rep. at para.9.11. At the time of writing, the section is expected to come into effect in April 2005.

[13] Based on cl.16 of the Draft Bill appended to the Law Commission Report.

[14] s.127(1)(a)(2)(6).

the matters stated,[15] and notice must be given that the expert will be basing his opinion or inference on that statement.[16]

Such a statement is to be treated as evidence of what it states,[17] but the court may, if applied to by one of the parties to the proceedings, order in the interests of justice that the statement not be admitted.[18] In deciding whether or not to call the original maker of statement, the court should take into consideration the expense of calling the statement maker, whether he could give relevant evidence which the expert could not, and whether he could reasonably be expected to remember the matters stated well enough to give oral evidence of them.[19]

The Law Commission Report anticipated that the expert's report would 6–34 be accompanied by a list of the persons involved in its preparation, together with a list of the tasks carried out by each one of them; the onus would then pass to the other side to indicate which of them it proposed to cross-examine and why. Leave of the court would be required to allow cross-examination because otherwise there would be no effective sanction where no, or no adequate, reason was given.[20] Where it was the defence which wished to cross-examine, only the general line of inquiry need be given. The requirement that it would be for the court to allow cross-examination would prevent defendants who did not seriously wish to challenge the expert evidence from disrupting or prolonging the trial by demanding that witnesses attend for no good reason.[21]

Disclosure of expert evidence. *Advance notice.* The Crown Court 6–35 (Advance Notice of Expert Evidence) Rules 1987, made under s.81 of the Police and Criminal Evidence Act 1984, require the parties to proceedings in the Crown Court to disclose any expert evidence (whether of fact or opinion) which they intend to adduce in evidence.[22] The obligation is to supply the other party with a written statement of any expert finding or opinion which it is proposed to adduce and, on request, provide a copy of, or opportunity to examine, the material on which it is based. The rules permit oral disclosure (if the other party consents) and non-disclosure (if a party has reasonable grounds for believing that disclosure might lead to the intimidation of witnesses or interference with justice). Section 6D of the

---

[15] subs.(1)(b).
[16] subs.(1)(c); "under the appropriate rules" as to advance evidence: by subs.(7). No such rules have been made to date.
[17] subs.(3).
[18] subs.(4).
[19] subs.(5).
[20] Law Commission Report, para.9.19. By s.132, Rules of Court are to be issued which will make provision.
[21] Law Commission Report, para.9.22.
[22] The Crown Court (Advance Notice of Expert Evidence) (Amendment) Rules (SI 1997/700) apply the above provisions where a notice of transfer of the preferment of the bill of indictment has been issued in cases where no criminal investigation was begun before April 1, 1997.

Criminal Procedure and Investigative Act 1996 requires an accused who instructs an expert to notify the court of the name and address of that expert.[23]

A party who fails to disclose expert evidence is not permitted to adduce it without leave of the court. In deciding whether to give leave, the court will be required to exercise its discretion by balancing the interests of the public represented by the Crown and the interests of the defendant. The result may be that it is necessary to admit evidence (albeit at the last minute) because of its importance in relation to the issues in the trial. On the other hand, if the defence keeps expert evidence to itself and then seeks to "ambush" the prosecution it is likely to be excluded.

6–36   The purpose of these rules is to ensure that a party is not taken by surprise by expert evidence being adduced without notice at trial. In particular, the prosecution is thus afforded an opportunity to evaluate any such evidence and thereby avoid the delay which may be occasioned by an adjournment to consider evidence during the trial. If delay is occasioned in these circumstances a "wasted costs" order may appropriately be made against the party responsible.

Section 20(3) of the Criminal Procedure and Investigations Act 1996 permits similar rules relating to the disclosure of expert evidence as apply to trials on indictment (under s.81 of the Police and Criminal Evidence Act 1984 and the Crown Court (Advance Notice of Expert Evidence) Rules 1987) to apply to summary trials also.[24] Such a provision is to be welcomed as lessening the opportunity for "trial by ambush" by springing expert evidence on the other party with the consequent unfairness and the potential for waste of time if an adjournment has to be granted for the other party to meet the evidence.

6–37   *Unused material.* There is a requirement that forensic scientists make full disclosure of unused material: *Ward*.[25] The duty extends to anything casting doubt on the scientists' opinions and includes anything that might arguably assist the defence. It exists irrespective of requests by the defence. The Royal Commission on Criminal Justice[26] interpreted the decision to mean that, if expert witnesses are aware of experiments or tests (even if not carried out by them), they are under an obligation to bring the records of the experiments to the attention of the police and prosecution.

As to disclosure of unused material, see further generally paras 18–05 to 18–30.

---

[23] See further para.18–19, below. The section was inserted by the Criminal Justice Act 2003, s.35, which is expected to come into effect in April 2005.
[24] The rules which have been issued are the Magistrates' Courts (Advance Notice of Expert Evidence) Rules 1997.
[25] *Ward* (1992) 94 Cr.App.R. 1. Also *Maguire* (1992) 94 Cr.App.R. 133.
[26] Cm. 2263 (1993), paras 9–46–9–48.

Written material, experiments, personal experience. Experts, when 6–38
giving evidence of opinion, may make reference to text books and other
material written in their field of expertise. The material does not have to be
in published form.[27] The Law Reform Committee summarised the principle
succinctly. "Experts may refer to a text book or other written material if it
is regarded as authoritative by those qualified in their speciality."[28] It is
obviously essential that experts should be allowed to refer to such written
material in order to give authority for their opinions and keep abreast with
developments in the subject of their expertise.

The expert may thus rely on the accepted work of others. He may rely on
experiments conducted by others. He is not required to have conducted an
experiment himself in order to make his evidence about it admissible. Thus,
a doctor may refer to recognised tables relating to the rates of conversion
and destruction of alcohol in the body, although he himself has not conducted the experiments on which the tables are based.[29] The fact that he
himself has not made the experiments *may* go to the weight of the evidence:
it does not go to admissibility.[30]

Similarly, the expert may rely on statistics collated by others. In *Abadom*[31] the Court of Appeal held that an expert was entitled to rely on
statistics of the refractive index of broken glass collated by the Home Office
in giving his opinion that glass samples found on the defendant's shoes
came from a window broken during the course of an armed robbery. It was
argued in *Abadom* that the evidence based on the statistics was hearsay and
therefore inadmissible. The Court rejected this argument because (a) it was
inevitable that such statistics would result from the work of others; and (b)
to exclude reliance upon such information would lead to the distortion of
unreliability of the expert's opinion.

If the expert does rely on such information (whether published or 6–39
unpublished) he should refer to the material in his evidence so that his
opinion can be assessed by reference to it.[32]

An expert may also rely on his own experience. Thus, in *Hodges and
Walker*,[33] the evidence of an experienced drugs officer as to the method of
the supply of heroin, the local purchase price and that a certain amount
would have been more than would have been used for personal use was
rightly admitted as expert evidence. This was consistent with the approach
outlined in *Bonython*[34] and was of the type envisaged in *Abadom*.[35]

---

[27] *Abadom* (1983) 76 Cr.App.R. 48.
[28] 17th Report, above, para.20. The same rule applies to professional practice: see *Smith*
(1974) 58 Cr.App.R. 106.
[29] *Somers* (1963) 48 Cr.App.R. 11.
[30] *Somers*, above.
[31] Above.
[32] *Abadom*, above, at 52–53.
[33] [2003] Crim.L.R. 472.
[34] (1984) 38 S.A.S.R. 45.
[35] *Above*, n.3.

(3) Proving facts upon which expert opinion is based

6–40 There is a distinction in the evidence given by experts between (i) evidence of fact, for example the characteristics of a fingerprint and (ii) evidence of opinion, *i.e.* inferences drawn from certain facts.

In the former case the expert gives evidence of his own findings and the facts are thereby proved. In this case the person who carried out any work upon which such findings are based must himself give evidence. Thus, if it is to be proved that the blood found in some stains was of a similar grouping to that of the defendant, the forensic scientist who carried out the tests to establish the grouping must be called. If another scientist were to give evidence of the tests (which he had not himself carried out), that evidence would be hearsay and inadmissible.

In the latter case ((ii) above) the expert must, in giving his opinion, rely on certain facts. These facts must be proved in the trial by admissible evidence.[36] Furthermore, the witness should state the facts upon which his opinion is based. The Court of Appeal has said that the witness should do this in examination in chief.[37] The jury will thereby discover whether the witness has been correctly informed about the facts, and has taken the relevant facts into consideration. The jury will then be in a position to assess the witness's evidence properly.

6–41 The witness's statement of facts may lead to the introduction of some secondhand evidence, for example a doctor may rely upon what a patient has told him. This will not be hearsay since, whether true or false, it is merely part of the information upon which the doctor's opinion was formed.[38] Thus, the Court of Appeal in *Bradshaw*[39] said that a doctor may not state what a patient told him about past symptoms as evidence of those symptoms because that would infringe the rule against hearsay, but he may give evidence as to what the patient told him in order to explain the grounds on which he came to a conclusion with regard to the patient's condition.

The facts may be proved by the expert himself. Thus, the fingerprint expert will give evidence of his findings of similarity in "ridge" character-istics between the defendant's fingerprint and that found at the scene of the crime. In giving evidence the expert produces the materials on which he has worked, for example blown-up photographs of fingerprints or handwriting samples. He can then demonstrate how he has arrived at his opinion. He can also be cross-examined about both the opinion and his materials.

---

[36] *Abadom* [1983] 1 W.L.R. 126; (1983) 76 Cr.App.R. 48, applying dicta in *English Exporters (London) Ltd v Eldonwall Ltd* [1973] Ch. 415, 421, *per* Megarry J. and *Turner* [1975] 1 Q.B. 834, 840. See also *Hodges and Walker*, para.6–39, above.

[37] *Turner*, above, at 840.

[38] Wigmore, *A Treatise on the Anglo-American System of Evidence* (3rd ed., 1940), Vol.vi, para.1320 quoted in Pattenden, "Expert Opinion Evidence on Hearsay" [1982] Crim.L.R. 85, 87. See also, para.8–59, below.

[39] (1985) 82 Cr.App.R. 79, 83.

Indeed, in the absence of the materials, it may not be possible for the jury to see how the expert arrived at his opinion. In a case where an expert gave evidence about voice identity, the Court of Appeal held that a judge was wrong to have excluded the tapes on which the expert's opinion was based.[40]

The facts must be proved, if not by the expert, then by someone else, as, for instance, when the finding of a fingerprint at the scene of crime is proved by another witness such as the Scenes of Crime Officer. If the facts are not proved, the opinion of the expert is worthless. Where the expert relies on facts which are not proved by him, it is for the prosecution (or the party calling the expert) to fill the evidential gap.[41] Once the facts have been proved by admissible evidence, experts are "entitled to draw on the work of others as part of the process of arriving at their conclusion."[42]

(4) Function and weight of expert evidence

The function of expert evidence is to assist the court by providing information which is outside the experience and knowledge of the judge or jury. The expert's function in giving his opinion is to assist the jury in the interpretation of evidence where such evidence might not otherwise be intelligible to them. (In *Clarke*[43] the evidence concerned was facial mapping by way of video superimposition: the court pointed out that this new, and valuable, crime detection technique was just as much evidence as blown-up photographs of fingerprint evidence.) On the other hand, questions relating to the weight of the evidence are for the jury to determine. These issues involve the consideration of two apparently conflicting principles.

6–42

The first principle is that the expert does not decide the case. He assists the jury or justices to do so. This principle was stated by Lord President Cooper:

> "[The duty of the expert witness] is to furnish the Judge or jury with the necessary scientific criteria for testing the accuracy of their conclusions, so as to enable the Judge or jury to form their own independent judgment by the application of these criteria to the facts proved by the evidence. The scientific opinion evidence, if intelligible, convincing and tested, becomes a factor (and often an important factor) for consideration along with the whole other evidence in the case."[44]

---

[40] *Bentum* (1989) 153 J.P. 538.
[41] *Jackson* [1996] 2 Cr.App.R. 420.
[42] *Abadom* (1983) 76 Cr.App.R. 48, 52.
[43] [1995] 2 Cr.App.R. 425. In *Gray (Paul Edward)* [2003] EWCA 1001, the court said that unless or until there was a national database or an agreed formula for determining the occurrence of facial characteristics was established, expert evidence involving image analysis and facial mapping could only be viewed as a subjective opinion.
[44] *Davie v Edinburgh Magistrates*, 1953 S.C. 34, 40.

Thus, the fact that an expert says that in his opinion, fingerprints found at the scene of a burglary were made by the defendant, does not, itself, decide the defendant's guilt. It is for the jury to say whether he is guilty or not.

6–43 The jury must also be allowed to decide what weight to give to the expert's evidence. While it is important to direct the jury that they were not bound by an expert's opinion, the direction need not be given in a particular way (such as that promulgated by the Judicial Studies Board): *Fitzpatrick (Gerald)*.[45] Nor should the jury be directed that the evidence of an expert "*ought*" to be accepted as it gives a misleading impression of the weight of the evidence.[46] A further example is to be found in the defence of insanity. This is an issue for the jury to decide. In *Rivett*,[47] the Court of Criminal Appeal would not interfere with a verdict of guilty despite medical evidence that the defendant was insane.

The second principle is that if there is nothing to contradict the expert's evidence the jury should accept it. For example, it was held to be a misdirection to invite the jury to disregard the uncontradicted evidence of an expert that there was no blood on certain boots and to substitute their own opinion.[48] Similarly, if there is uncontradicted medical evidence in support of a defence of diminished responsibility, the jury should not reject it, and convict of murder. In *Matheson*[49] and *Bailey*[50] there was uncontradicted medical evidence to this effect, but the jury convicted of murder. In both cases the Court of Criminal Appeal substituted verdicts of manslaughter. The rationale for these decisions is to be found in the judgment of Lord Goddard C.J. in *Matheson*:

"While it has often been emphasised and we would repeat, that the decision in these cases, as in those in which insanity is pleaded, is for the jury and not for the doctors, the verdict must be *founded on evidence*. If there are facts which would entitle a jury to reject or differ from the opinions of the medical men, the court would not, and indeed could not, disturb their verdict, but if the doctor's evidence is unchallenged and there is no other on this issue, a verdict contrary to their opinion would not be 'a true verdict in accordance with the evidence.' "[51]

[45] [1999] Crim.L.R. 832.
[46] *Lanfear* (1968) 52 Cr.App.R. 176.
[47] (1950) 34 Cr.App.R. 87.
[48] *Anderson* [1972] A.C. 100.
[49] [1958] 1 W.L.R. 474.
[50] (1978) 66 Cr.App.R. 31.
[51] At 478; emphasis supplied by author.

On the other hand, in *Walton v R*,[52] the Privy Council held that a jury   **6–44**
was entitled to reject the uncontradicted evidence of a psychiatrist in support of a defence of diminished responsibility when:

(a)   the quality and weight of medical evidence fell a long way short of
      that in *Bailey* and *Matheson*;

(b)   evidence of the conduct of the defendant at the time of the killing
      did not indicate a person bordering on insanity; and

(c)   there was no objective evidence of a history of mental disorder on
      the part of the defendant.

Reconciling these cases is not easy; but the position may be summarised
in this way:

(a)   if the expert evidence is clear and uncontradicted by any other
      evidence, the jury should accept it.

(b)   If, however, the evidence is not clear or there is evidence which
      tends to contradict the expert's opinion, the jury may reject it.

Where two or more expert witnesses give evidence for opposing sides, the   **6–45**
direction to the jury should be to convict *only* if it is satisfied beyond
reasonable doubt that it should accept the expert evidence adduced by the
prosecution and reject that adduced by the defence. Accordingly, a direction to the jury to decide on the balance of probabilities is wrong.[53]

In *Doheny and Adams*[54] Phillips L.J. said that when the judge comes to
sum up, the jury are likely to need careful directions in respect of any issues
of expert evidence that may have been engendered. That case was concerned with DNA evidence, but the principle must surely apply generally
where expert evidence is concerned.

(5) Proposals for reform

The Royal Commission on Criminal Justice considered the admissibility   **6–46**
and presentation of expert evidence in some detail.[55] The Commission
rejected the suggestion that a court expert should give the evidence. It did so
on the grounds that there was no guarantee that such an expert would be
nearer the truth and the parties would thereby be deprived of the oppor-

---

[52] [1978] A.C. 788.
[53] *Platt* [1981] Crim.L.R. 332.
[54] [1997] 1 Cr.App.R. 369. For the procedure laid down by that decision in cases where DNA
evidence is to be considered by the jury, see paras 14–44 to 14–46, below.
[55] Cm. 2263 [1993], Ch.9.

tunity of calling expert evidence.[56] The Commission said that the aim should be the objective presentation of expert evidence in a way which jurors can reasonably be expected to follow. To this end it recommended that:

(a) in cases where the defence is calling its own expert, the witnesses on each side be required to meet to draw up for the court a report of the scientific facts and their interpretation[57];

(b) in cases where there is no dispute about the evidence a written statement of it be provided for the jury.[58]

It is regrettable that these recommendations have not been enacted since it must be very difficult for a jury to follow evidence (which is often complex) without a written summary or report before it. (For the Commission's recommendations for the re-call of expert witnesses, see para.21–34, below.)

6–47   The Royal Commission also recommended that professional bodies should assist the courts by maintaining a register of members, suitably qualified to give evidence in their particular areas of expertise.[59]

The Royal Commission[60] and the Law Commission[61] expressed concern that, because of the hearsay rule, expert witnesses could not be permitted to give an opinion based on scientific tests run by assistants unless the latter were to give evidence. This has now been rectified by s.111 of the Criminal Justice Act 2003 (above, para.6–33).

The Auld Report recommended[62] that new Criminal Procedure Rules contain a rule that the expert's duty is to the court and any report should contain a declaration to this effect. The new Rules should formalise the court's powers to control the admission of expert evidence and to restrict it to that which is reasonably required to resolve any issue of importance in the proceedings, but the court should not have power to appoint an expert. In addition the parties should arrange for experts to discuss and identify issues and produce a joint statement for use in evidence as to those issues.

---

[56] *ibid.*, para.9–74.
[57] *ibid.*, para.9–63.
[58] *ibid.*, para.9–71.
[59] *ibid.* para.9–77.
[60] *ibid.* para.9–78.
[61] "Evidence in Criminal Proceedings: Hearsay and Related Topics" (1995) Law Comm. Consultation Paper No.138.
[62] Review of the Criminal Courts of England and Wales, 2001, pp.571–582.

CHAPTER 7

Character

1. INTRODUCTION

"Character" may bear two meanings in law. According to common law   7–01
rules, it meant general reputation,[1] *i.e.* the general reputation which a man
or woman bears. However, under s.1 of the Criminal Evidence Act 1898
the word was said to combine both the concept of reputation and the
concept of disposition, *i.e.* a disposition to act or think in a particular way.[2]

These concepts are similarly combined in s.98 of the Criminal Justice Act
2003 in which the law in relation to bad character is now to be found.[3] As
to bad character, see now Section C "Bad Character" of this Chapter, paras
7–27 *et seq.*

It should also be borne in mind that when a practitioner speaks of a man
having a "good" character he usually means that the man has no previous
convictions for criminal offences. Conversely, when the practitioner speaks
of a man having a "bad" character, he means that he has previous convictions. Thus a man's reputation or disposition is measured by whether he
has previous convictions or not. The terminology is liable to confuse jurors
who, on hearing a defendant described as "a man of good character", may
well think that this connotes moral rectitude, as it does in everyday speech.
However, the usage is so well-established that there is little point in considering whether it ought to be changed.

The rules discussed in this Chapter are concerned with the admissibility   7–02
of evidence relating to the character of both defendants and witnesses. The
former general rule was that evidence of a person's disposition or reputation was generally inadmissible. In particular, evidence that the accused had
been guilty of misconduct other than that charged or had a disposition to
commit the kind of offence charged (or crimes in general) was inadmissible
for the purpose of showing that he committed the offence charged. Two
reasons were usually given for this exclusionary rule: (a) evidence of previous misconduct is generally irrelevant; and (b) such evidence is so
prejudicial that a fair trial is impossible.

This rule was considered to be fundamental to all criminal trials. It was

---

[1] *Rowton* [1865] Le. & Ca. 520.
[2] *Stirland v DPP* [1944] A.C. 315, 325 *per* Lord Simon L.C.
[3] See paras 7–27 to 7–82, below. At the time of writing, the section is due to come into effect
in April 2005.

described by Lord Sankey L.C. as "one of the most deeply rooted and jealously guarded principles of our common law"[4] and Lord Hailsham said that its force should not be reduced or diminished.[5] This was because it was thought that if this were to happen the evidence of propensity on the part of the defendant to commit offences might so influence the minds of the jury that all other considerations would be set aside and the jury might reason that simply because the defendant had committed one or more offences in the past he must have committed the offence which they were trying.

7–03   The effect of the exclusionary rule was that evidence of a defendant's disposition was normally inadmissible and the prosecution was not permitted to adduce evidence of the bad character of the defendant, *i.e.* evidence of his bad reputation, disposition and previous misconduct. However, there were numerous exceptions to this rule. The common law, for instance, developed a rule known as the "similar fact" rule which permitted evidence of the disposition and previous misconduct of an accused to be given if sufficiently relevant to an issue in the case to outweigh its prejudicial effect. This antithesis received its most famous expression in *Makin v Att-Gen*.[6]

> "It is undoubtedly not competent for the prosecution to adduce evidence tending to show that the accused has been guilty of criminal acts other than those covered in the indictment, for the purpose of leading to the conclusion that the accused is a person likely from his criminal conduct or character to have committed the offence for which he is being tried. On the other hand, the mere fact that the evidence adduced tends to show the commission of other crimes does not render it inadmissible if it be relevant to an issue before the jury, and it may be so relevant if it bears upon the question of whether the acts alleged to constitute the crime charged in the indictment were designed or accidental, or to rebut a defence which would otherwise be open to the accused."

The evidence thus admitted was known as "similar fact" evidence.

Likewise the Criminal Evidence Act 1898, s.1 permitted the accused to be cross-examined as to his character in certain prescribed circumstances. Both of these exceptions created a great deal of case law which became increasingly complex and convoluted.[7] There followed a period in which the various categories of case into which such evidence could be fitted became central to admissibility. This approach was rejected by the House of Lords in *Boardman*.[8] In that case the House held that it was the degree of

---

[4] *Maxwell v DPP* [1935] A.C. 309, 317.
[5] *Boardman v DPP* [1975] A.C. 421, 456.
[6] [1894] A.C. 57, 65 *per* Lord Herschell.
[7] For discussion of these exceptions, see the fourth edition of this work, Chs 6 and 7.
[8] [1975] A.C. 421.

relevance which made similar fact evidence admissible. The question in each case was whether the evidence was sufficiently relevant and had the necessary probative force to outweigh its prejudicial effect. As Lord Mackay L.C. said in *DPP v P*[9]: "the essential feature of such evidence is that its probative force is sufficiently great for it to be just for the evidence to be admitted notwithstanding the prejudice to the accused in tending to show that he was guilty of another offence."

The complications and seeming illogicality of the law led to calls for reform. There followed a number of reports concentrating on the admissibility of previous convictions. In 2001 the Law Commission issued a Report on Evidence of Bad Character[10] which recommended reform of the law. The Commission summarised its criticism of the law as a haphazard mixture of statute and common law rules which produced inconsistent and unpredictable results, distorted the trial process, made tactical considerations paramount and inhibited the defence in presenting its true case while exposing witnesses to exposure of long-forgotten misconduct.[11]

7–04

In its Report the Law Commission proposed a scheme based on the concept of "a central set of facts" in the trial, about which evidence of character would normally be admissible, *i.e.* evidence connected with the offence charged or misconduct connected with the investigation or prosecution. Evidence of bad character outside this category would only be admissible if the court gave leave and might only be given in the case of witnesses where the evidence had substantial probative value to an important issue. In the case of defendants leave would only be granted if it were in the interests of justice in four situations relating to circumstances where the evidence was relevant: (a) as having substantial probative value in relation to an important issue; (b) to credibility; (c) to correct a misleading impression about the defendant; or (d) where the evidence had substantial probative value in relation to an issue between co-defendants.[12]

In the same year as the Law Commission Report Sir Robin Auld in his Review of the Criminal Courts said that the law in this area was highly unsatisfactory in its complexity and uncertainty and was not an honest system; it was not logical or effective for a rule to keep a defendant's previous convictions from lay but not professional fact-finders and the Law Commission's recommendations should be considered in the context of a wider review.[13] Meanwhile, a Home Office White Paper suggested, as an

---

[9] (1991) 93 Cr.App.R. 267, 279.
[10] Law Commission Report (No.273) on Evidence of Bad Character in Criminal Proceedings (2001) Cm. 5257.
[11] *ibid.*, para.1.7.
[12] This is an abbreviated summary of the conclusions to be found in Part XVIII of the Report. For an article welcoming the report of the Law Commission and calling for Implementation see: McEwan, "Previous Misconduct at the Cross-Roads; Which Way Ahead?" [2002] Crim.L.R. 180.
[13] Review of Criminal Courts in England and Wales, Report by Lord Justice Auld (2001, Stationery Office, London), paras 563–568.

option for simplifying the rules, permitting the admission of previous convictions, where relevant and provided the prejudicial effect did not outweigh its probative value.[14] Finally, the government issued a White Paper in 2002 favouring an approach which would permit the judge to determine whether the convictions of an accused or a witness were sufficiently relevant to the issues in the case to be admitted (despite their prejudicial effect); and would permit the jury to decide in the circumstances what weight to give the evidence.[15]

7–05   The changes brought about by the Criminal Justice Act 2003 broadly follow this latter approach rather than the carefully constructed approach of the Law Commission (although some features of its report have been incorporated). The advantage is a simplification of the law. However, it remains to be seen whether this is outweighed by the disadvantage from the danger that previous convictions may be used to prove an offence, a route towards proof which was always previously discouraged. Part 11, Chapter 1, of the Criminal Justice Act 2003 relating to evidence will be discussed.

First, it is necessary to discuss the rules relating to good character which remain unchanged by the new Act.

2. GOOD CHARACTER

7–06   The common law has for many years allowed the defendant to call evidence of his good character. Such a character may be established by:

(a) the defendant's own evidence; or

(b) by witnesses called on his behalf; or

(c) by cross-examination of prosecution witnesses such as, for instance, a police officer.

A. What evidence may be given?

7–07   When evidence of character is given it should be directed to that part of the man's character which is relevant.[16] Thus, if the charge is theft, the relevant part is his character for honesty; and if the charge is assault, his character for violence. If the defendant gives evidence of his own character, however, he is usually given a fairly wide latitude.

The rule at common law is that evidence of character is confined to evidence of general reputation. Evidence of (a) opinion or, (b) particular acts or examples of conduct should, as a matter of law, be excluded. As will

---

[14] Home Office White Paper, *Criminal Justice: The Way Ahead*, T50, Com. 5074 (2001).
[15] *Justice for All*, issued by the Lord Chancellor's Department at the Home Office, July 2002, para.4.53.
[16] *per* Lord Denning in *Plato Films Ltd v Speidel* [1961] A.C. 1090, 1140.

be seen, in practice, such evidence is often admitted. It is, however, admitted as an act of indulgence.

This rule was established by the Court of Crown Cases Reserved in the well-known case of *Rowton*.[17] In that case, Rowton was charged with indecent assault upon a boy of 14. During the trial, he called witnesses as to his good character. In rebuttal, the prosecution called a witness who said that he knew nothing of the neighbourhood's opinion of Rowton because the witness had only been a boy at school when he had known Rowton; but the witness said that in his opinion and that of his brothers (who were also pupils of the accused) the latter was a man capable of the grossest indecency and the most flagrant immorality.

A court of 13 judges sitting in the Court of Crown Cases Reserved held (with two dissentients) that the evidence should not have been admitted because it was based on the opinion of the witness and was not evidence of the general reputation of the accused.[18] The two dissenting judges did not consider that examples of conduct could be given. They thought, however, that evidence of disposition and not merely reputation should be admitted.

The decision in *Rowton* has been criticised on two grounds:　　　　7–08

(a)　A general reputation may well be inaccurate. "A witness may with perfect truth swear that a man who, to his knowledge, has been a receiver of stolen goods for years, has an excellent character for honesty, if he has the good luck to conceal his crimes from his neighbours."[19]

(b)　Evidence of general reputation may well lack cogency compared with the opinion of a witness who knows the defendant well.[20]

In practice, the rule is persistently ignored.[21] Evidence is often given by a witness who says that he knows the defendant well and holds a high opinion of him. An employer, for example, may give evidence that he has employed the defendant for a number of years and during that time no money has gone missing while the defendant had charge of the cash. Such evidence will usually be given without objection. It is, however, admitted as an indulgence to the defendant for it is technically inadmissible.

From time to time, the courts are reminded of the rule, for instance, by　7–09

---

[17] (1865) Le. & Ca. 520.
[18] It is to be noted that the evidence in *Rowton's* case was evidence of "bad" character adduced by the prosecution and not evidence of "good" character adduced by the defence.
[19] Sir James Fitzjames Stephen, *Digest of Law of Evidence* (12th ed., 1948), p.201.
[20] "To my mind personal experience gives cogency to the evidence; whereas such a statement as, 'I have heard some persons speak well of him,' or, 'I have heard general report in favour of the prisoner' has a very slight effect in comparison." *Rowton*, above, at 534, *per* Erle C.J., dissenting.
[21] As noted by the Criminal Law Revision Committee in 1972 in their Eleventh Report: Cmnd. 4991, para.134.

the Court of Appeal in *Redgrave*.[22] The defendant in that case was charged with importuning for immoral purposes. The defence sought to produce a number of letters, cards and photographs in order to prove that the defendant had relationships of a heterosexual nature and to show that he was not making homosexual advances to the prosecution witnesses. The judge refused to admit this evidence. The Court of Appeal upheld the judge's ruling. The Court held that the defendant was trying to give evidence of particular facts, *i.e.* examples of conduct and he was not allowed to do this:

> "In our judgment the defendant is bound by the same rules as the prosecution. He can call evidence that he did not commit the acts which are alleged against him, but he is not allowed by reference to particular facts, to call evidence that he is of a disposition which makes it unlikely that he would have committed the offence charged."[23]

Therefore, the Court said that although a disposition to commit the kind of offence charged was relevant, the defendant could do no more than say or call witnesses to prove that he was not by general repute the kind of young man who would have behaved in the kind of way that the Crown alleged. The Court did, however, say that it was not seeking to stop a defendant from saying in this class of case that he was having a normal sexual relationship with his wife or girlfriend.

7–10   The law, therefore, remains as decided in *Rowton*, tempered in practice by an indulgence to defendants. There would appear to be five reasons for limiting evidence as to character, namely that such evidence: (a) is easy to fabricate; (b) is often irrelevant[24]; (c) may lead to the investigation of side issues of little relevance to the case; (d) amounts frequently to evidence of opinion which is generally excluded; and (e) may create a risk that the function of the jury will be usurped.[25]

On the other hand, the interests of justice have often required a more liberal attitude. The result is the present unsatisfactory situation. It should be clarified by the House of Lords.

B. Evidence in rebuttal

7–11   At common law where the defendant put his character in issue by giving or calling evidence of his good character or cross-examining witnesses to that

---

[22] (1982) 74 Cr.App.R. 10; see also *Butterwasser* [1948] 1 K.B. 4, 6, *per* Lord Goddard C.J.
[23] At 14.
[24] *e.g.* the fact that a man is capable of acts of personal generosity is usually irrelevant when he is charged with armed robbery.
[25] *i.e.* by a witness who, in saying that the accused is not of such a character as to commit the offence charged, says in effect that he is not guilty: the opinion of the witness may then become a substitute for the verdict of the jury.

effect, the prosecution were entitled to call evidence of his bad character in rebuttal.[26] If he called witnesses as to his good character, they might be cross-examined as to his bad character.[27] These rules are retained by the Criminal Justice Act 2003, ss.101(1)(f) and 105(1), see paras 7–60 *et seq*, below.

However, the old rule was that, if the defendant attacked prosecution witnesses but did not himself give evidence, the prosecution was not allowed to adduce evidence of his bad character.[28] This rule has now been abolished by the above sections of the 2003 Act and such evidence is not admissible.[29]

It should also be noted that the prosecution may rely on attested copies of a conviction by a foreign court in order to rebut a claim of good character by an accused.[30]

C. Directions to the jury

Evidence of good character is relevant to two issues in a criminal trial, namely: (a) whether it is likely that a person with such a character committed the offence charged; and (b) whether the defendant's evidence should be believed, *i.e.* his credibility.   7–12

The relevance of good character to the first of these issues was recognised at a time before the defendant was permitted to give evidence. It was acknowledged then that good character was capable of being evidence for the jury to consider since the accused, in effect, invited the jury to infer that by reason of his good character he was unlikely to have committed the offence charged. Thus, in *Stannard*[31] Williams J. said: "I have no doubt ... that evidence to character must be considered evidence in the cause. It is evidence ... to be submitted to the jury, to induce them to say whether they think it likely that a person with such a character would have committed the offence."

Later, after the accused was permitted to give evidence, the courts placed emphasis upon the relevance of good character to the second issue and it was considered to be relevant primarily to the credibility of the defendant.[32] Judges normally directed juries in these terms, *i.e.* that when the jury were considering whether the defendant had told the truth his good character should be put in the scales in his favour. At one time it was said that the judge had no duty to give a direction on this subject.[33] However, the   7–13

---

[26] *Rowton* [1865] Le. & Ca.520, cited at para.7–09 above.
[27] *Waldeman* (1934) 24 Cr.App.R. 204.
[28] *Butterwasser* [1948] 1 K.B. 4.
[29] At time of writing, the sections are expected to come into effect in April 2005.
[30] *Mauricia* [2002] 2 Cr.App.R. 27.
[31] (1837) 7 C. & P. 673.
[32] *Bellis* (1966) 50 Cr.App.R. 88; *Falconer-Atlee* (1974) 58 Cr.App.R. 348, 358.
[33] *Smith* [1971] Crim.L.R. 53.

modern practice is to give a direction. In *Berrada*[34] the Court of Appeal confirmed that this was so and said that the judge should give a clear direction as to the relevance of the defendant's good character: failure to do so amounts to a major defect in the summing-up. In that case the Court quashed a conviction where issues of credibility were at the heart of the trial and no proper direction was given. Waterhouse J., giving the judgment of the Court, said that the appellant was entitled to have put to the jury from the judge herself a correct direction about the relevance of his previous good character to his credibility. "That is a conventional direction and it is regrettable that it did not appear in the summing-up in this case."[35] (This became known as a "first limb direction".)

Accordingly, a direction relating to credibility must be given in every case where the defendant has given evidence. It must also be given in a case where the defendant relies on answers or a statement given or made to the police or others during the course of investigation.[36] A direction (modified as necessary) must be given, even if the defendant has told lies during the course of the investigation[37]; or has made "mixed" statements containing both admissions and self-exculpatory explanations.[38] The direction must be given clearly and normally without qualification. Thus in *Butler*[39] it was held to have been a misdirection for the judge to have directed the jury that the good character of the accused was somehow tarnished by earlier acts of violence about which the prosecution had adduced evidence. The Court of Appeal said that where credibility was in issue it was doubtful whether any qualification should be put in a direction. On the other hand, if the defendant does not give evidence and has not given pre-trial answers or statements no direction is required since there is no issue concerning the defendant's credibility.

7–14   The following points may also be noted:

1. If counsel does not adduce any evidence of a defendant's good character the judge is not required to raise it in his summing-up.[40] Thus, the Privy Council held in *Thompson*[41] that where the issue of good character is not raised by the defence the judge is under no duty to raise it (saying that it was a duty to be discharged by the defence), and if it is intended to rely on the good character of the defendant, the issue must be raised by calling evidence or putting questions on the issue to the witness.[42] However, if the issue is not raised the judge may often raise this issue with counsel in the

---

[34] (1990) 91 Cr.App.R. 131 (Note).
[35] At 134.
[36] *Vye* (1993) 97 Cr.App.R. 134.
[37] *Kabariti* (1991) 92 Cr.App.R. 362; *Durbin* [1995] 2 Cr.App.R. 84.
[38] *Aziz* [1995] 2 Cr.App.R. 478, HL.
[39] [1999] Crim.L.R. 835.
[40] *Prayag, The Times,* July 31, 1991.
[41] [1998] 2 W.L.R. 927.
[42] Approving a dictum of Lord Goddard C.J. in *Butterwasser* [1948] 1 K.B. 4, 6, to this effect.

absence of the jury. Then, if the defendant's character has not been mentioned due to an oversight, evidence of it may be given by way of admission.

2. If a defendant has an isolated conviction for an offence of a different nature to that charged he may in certain circumstances be treated as being of good character. It is for the judge to decide in his discretion whether those circumstances arise in the individual case. In *Timson and Hales*[43] a previous conviction for driving with excess alcohol was not relevant where charges relating to deception were concerned. In *Pigram*[44] the defendant, charged with handling stolen goods, had a previous conviction for criminal damage. The Court of Appeal held that it was not enough for the trial judge to tell the jury that the previous conviction bore no resemblance to the offence for which he was on trial and did not help to decide whether he was guilty as charged, and they should put it out of their minds. She should have told the jury that the previous conviction was irrelevant and should have treated him as being of effectively good character.

3. In *Aziz*[45] the House of Lords held that a trial judge has a residual **7–15** discretion whether to give a direction in the case of a defendant without previous convictions but who is shown during the trial to have been guilty of serious criminal misbehaviour.

Lord Steyn described the discretion as limited: "Prima facie the directions must be given." However, his Lordship also said[46]: "A good starting point is that a judge should never be compelled to give meaningless or absurd directions. And cases occur from time to time where a defendant, who has no previous convictions, is shown *beyond doubt* to have been guilty of *serious criminal behaviour similar to the offence charged*. A sensible criminal justice system should not compel a judge to go through the charade of giving [good character] directions in a case where the defendant's claim to good behaviour is spurious. [A] trial judge has a *residual*[47] discretion to decline to give any character directions in the case of the defendant without previous convictions ... [T]he judge will often be able to place a fair and balanced picture before the jury by giving [good character] directions and then adding words of qualification concerning other *proved or possible* criminal conduct of the defendant which emerged during the course of the trial. On the other hand, if it would make no sense to give [good] character directions, the judge may in his discretion dispense with them." Lord Steyn went on to say that it was not desirable to generalise about this essentially practical subject which should be left to the good sense of trial judges. But he did suggest that if a trial judge proposed to give a direction which was

---

[43] [1993] Crim.L.R. 58.
[44] [1995] Crim.L.R. 808.
[45] [1995] 2 Cr.App.R. 428.
[46] At 488–489. Italics and words in square brackets supplied.
[47] Lord Steyn referred to two earlier cases where the Court of Appeal had ruled that there was such a residual discretion: *H* [1994] Crim.L.R. 205, and *Zoppola-Barraza* [1994] Crim.L.R. 833.

not likely to be anticipated by counsel, he should initiate submissions on his directions.

7–16   In *Durbin*[48] the Court of Appeal held that a defendant was entitled to a good character direction, although he admitted smuggling goods across the frontiers of European countries during the course of a visit out of which a charge of importing a large amount of drugs into the UK arose. However, it is submitted that (following *Aziz*) this decision went too far and that the judge is not required to give a direction relating to the defendant's credibility when his claim to be of good character is contradicted by the evidence in the case. In *Buzalek and Schiffer*[49] the defendants were charged with fraudulent trading. They had no previous convictions but both admitted dishonesty in the subject matter of the case. The judge reminded the jury of their lack of convictions, but did not relate it to their credibility. The Court of Appeal held that in the difficult circumstances this was not a misdirection. It is submitted that this must be correct since the conventional direction would fly in the face of the evidence in the case. As the Court of Appeal observed, if a defendant has been dishonest, although not convicted of an offence, he could hardly be regarded as a man of good character.[50]

7–17   For some time there was doubt whether a direction was required along the lines suggested in *Stannard*, above, *i.e.* the relevance of good character to the likelihood of the defendant having committed the offence (a "propensity" or second limb direction). The Court of Appeal resolved the issue in *Vye*[51] by holding that whether or not the defendant gives evidence, such a direction must be given. Lord Taylor C.J. said that it must be for the trial judge in each case to decide how he tailors his direction to the particular circumstances:

> "He would probably wish to indicate, as is commonly done, that good character cannot amount to a defence. In cases such as that of [a] long-serving employee [who having carried out his duties impeccably is finally charged with stealing from the till] he may wish to emphasise 'the second limb' direction more than in the average case. By contrast, he may wish in a case such as [that of a defendant charged with murder who admits manslaughter] to stress the very limited help the jury may feel they can get from the absence of any propensity to violence in the defendant's history. Provided that the judge indicates to the jury the two respects in which good character may be relevant, *i.e.* credibility

---

[48] [1995] 2 Cr.App.R. 84
[49] [1991] Crim.L.R. 116.
[50] For vigorous criticism of the law and a call for less rigidity, see Munday, "What Constitutes a Good Character?" [1997] Crim.L.R. 247; and on the need for adherence to specimen directions, see Munday, "Judicial Studies Board Specimen Directions and the Enforcement of Orthodoxy" [2002] Jo.Crim.L. 158.
[51] (1993) 97 Cr.App.R. 134.

and propensity, this court will be slow to criticise any qualifying remarks he may make based on the facts of the individual case."[52]

The decision of the Court of Appeal in *Vye* has subsequently been approved by the House of Lords in *Aziz*.[53] The House in that case held that a defendant who gives evidence or who has made pre-trial statements is entitled to a direction both in respect of the relevance of good character to credibility *and* to propensity to commit the offence charged (subject to the judge's residual discretion, discussed at para.7–15, above). The defendants in *Aziz* were charged with fraudulent evasion of income tax and VAT by using false invoices. Two of the defendants (who were of good character) gave evidence denying dishonesty in relation to the invoices, but admitting making false mortgage applications: one also admitted lying to customs officers in interview and the other admitted that he had not declared his full earnings for income tax purposes. The judge gave a direction in relation to credibility but not to propensity when dealing with these two defendants. The Court of Appeal held this to be a misdirection; a decision affirmed by the House of Lords.

Lord Steyn said: "The question might ... be posed: Why should a judge be obliged to give directions on good character? The answer is that in modern practice a judge almost invariably reminds the jury of the principal points of a prosecution case. At the same time he must put the defence case in a fair and balanced way. Fairness requires that the judge should direct the jury about good character because it is evidence of probative significance."[54]

There is no need for the direction on either limb to be given in a particular form of words although "you must take into account" is a better expression than "you are entitled to".[55] However, it should be given in the form of an affirmative statement, rather than rhetorical questions.[56]

The need for fairness and balance must be taken into account. In *Hickmet*[57] the defendant was charged with rape and with supplying a Class A drug. The judge referred to Hickmet's previous spent convictions, but also to the fact that the complainant and another witness had consumed drugs: he was endeavouring to treat the complainant and the defendant on a basis of complete equality. The Court of Appeal commented that had he given the standard direction that H's lack of previous relevant convictions made it less likely that he would have committed a rape, "the intelligent jury asking themselves the question 'Why?' might find that question difficult to answer, and consequently a dangerous question to ask on the facts of the case."

7–18

7–19

---

[52] At 139.
[53] [1995] 2 Cr.App.R. 478.
[54] At 486.
[55] *Miah and Akbar* [1997] 2. Cr.App.R. 12 at 22.
[56] *Lloyd* [2000] 2 Cr.App.R. 355.
[57] [1996] Crim.L.R. 588.

The fact that a defendant has been cautioned by the police may be relevant to his good character. In *Martin*[58] the court held that, in giving a direction as to good character, the judge in the exercise of his discretion is entitled to take into account the fact that the accused had been cautioned by the police. In these circumstances, it is quite proper to give the first half of the direction relating to credibility but to omit the second limb relating to propensity.

There had been a difference of view as to the direction to be given in a case where a defendant of good character is charged with a defendant of bad character. Should the judge say little about good character in order to avoid highlighting the bad character of the other defendant?[59] On the other hand, is the defendant with a good character entitled to insist that the jury be given a full direction?[60] The issue was resolved in *Vye*,[61] where the Court of Appeal held that where a defendant of good character is charged together with a defendant of bad character, the defendant of good character is entitled to a direction as to the relevance of good character.

7–20   In the above circumstances the judge will be left with the problem of what to say about the defendant of bad character. In *Vye* Lord Taylor C.J. said that any comment about the defendant of bad character will depend upon the circumstances of the individual case: for instance, how great an issue has been made of character during the evidence and speeches.

> "In some cases the judge may think it best to [...] tell the jury they must try the case on the evidence, there has been no evidence about [that defendant's] character, they must not speculate and must not take the absence of information as to [the defendant's] character as any evidence against [him]. In other cases the judge may ... think it best to say nothing about the absence of evidence as to [that defendant's] character."[62]

It is submitted that the latter is not infrequently the better course. Any other direction, no matter how carefully worded, may have the effect of encouraging speculation.

On the other hand, if there is evidence that the defendant *has* previous convictions, a direction will be necessary. In these circumstances the judge must direct the jury as to the limited relevance of previous convictions, *i.e.* they are relevant to the defendant's credibility, but irrelevant to his guilt.[63]

If an issue arises whether defendants in these circumstances should have separate trials, it is a matter for the judge to decide on a case-by-case basis

[58] [2001] 2 Cr.App.R. 2.
[59] *Gibson* (1991) 93 Cr.App.R. 9, *per* Lord Lane C.J.
[60] *Shaw* (1993) 97 Cr.App.R. 218.
[61] (1993) 97 Cr.App.R. 134.
[62] At 140.
[63] *Cain* (1994) 99 Cr.App.R. 208.

according to the usual principles, *i.e.* by weighing the prejudice to the accused against the interest of the Crown in having persons charged with the same offence tried together.[64] Lord Taylor said that that there is no rule in favour of separate trials in the circumstances and that generally, those jointly indicted should be jointly tried.[65]

D. Spent convictions

(1) The practice

The effect of s.4(1) of the Rehabilitation of Offenders Act 1974 is that once   **7–21**
a conviction is spent the rehabilitated person shall be treated in law as a person who has not been convicted or charged with the offence. A conviction becomes spent after a period specified in the Act. Some convictions are excluded from the Act altogether, *i.e.* those resulting in sentences of life imprisonment or custody for life or sentences of more than 30 months' imprisonment or detention.[66] The rehabilitation period is 10 years for a conviction resulting in a sentence of more than six but not exceeding 30 months' imprisonment or detention; seven years when the sentence is six months' or less imprisonment or detention; five years for a fine, probation, or community service, one year in the case of a conditional discharge,[67] six months for an absolute discharge.

Section 4(1) does not apply to evidence given in criminal proceedings; but   **7–22**
in 1975 the Lord Chief Justice made a Practice Direction, now consolidated in the consolidated Criminal Practice Direction (2002), which provides that:

> "... both court and advocates should give effect to the general intention of Parliament by never referring to a spent conviction when such reference can reasonably be avoided;
> ...no one should refer in open court to a spent conviction without the authority of the judge, which authority should not be given unless the interests of justice so require."[68]

The effect of the Practice Direction is that in criminal proceedings,   **7–23**
reference to spent convictions should not be made if it can be reasonably avoided. If a reference is to be made, the leave of the judge should be sought first, which leave will not be granted unless the interests of justice so require. Although the Practice Direction is for the guidance of Crown Courts, magistrates will no doubt follow it.
The result is that before a reference to a spent conviction can be made,

---

[64] *Vye*, above.
[65] *ibid.*, at 141.
[66] In a young offender institution.
[67] Or the period of the order or discharge, whichever is longer.
[68] [2002] 2 Cr.App.R. 35, paras 6.4, 6.6.

the leave of the judge must be sought, a requirement which is sometimes overlooked when witnesses are being cross-examined as to previous convictions. This happened in *Smallman*,[69] where prosecuting counsel, without leave, revealed the spent conviction of a defence witness when cross-examining him. The judge directed the jury to leave out of account the prejudice resulting from the disclosure. The defendant appealed on the ground that the prejudicial effect of the disclosure had made a fair trial impossible. The Court of Appeal held that although there had been a breach of the *Practice Direction*, that could not be a ground for upsetting a conviction which was otherwise perfectly proper.

However, it is not difficult to envisage situations in which a fair trial *would* be prejudiced by the unauthorised disclosure of a spent conviction. Suppose a case where the defendant is charged with wounding. He calls a man who was not involved at all in the violence but who was an eyewitness to what occurred. The evidence of this man is crucial to the defence. The man has a spent conviction for inflicting grievous bodily harm, an offence committed many years before. The revelation of such a conviction might, because of its similarity to the offence being tried, disproportionately affect the credibility of the witness in the eyes of the jury. If such a conviction was disclosed without leave, it is difficult to see how a fair trial would not be prejudiced.

7–24   In *Lawrence (Irvin)*[70] the Court of Appeal said that the effect of the Practice Direction was to give the judge a wide discretion as to when, and in what manner, it is appropriate for reference to be made to spent convictions: any discretion had to be excercised with the intent and spirit of the Act in mind, and it was undesirable to go further than was necessary for the justice of the case. In *Lawrence* the defendant was charged with unlawfully wounding W. The trial judge refused to allow the defence to question W about 20 spent convictions (mainly for dishonesty) and only allowed questions on four more recent convictions (also for dishonesty). The Court of Appeal said that the judge had not erred in principle and was right not to have allowed the defence to cross-examine W about matters going back to 1966: on the other hand he had ensured that the defence were given sufficient opportunity to elicit information about W so that the jury could decide how much of his evidence to believe. The Court said that the judge should not give the same latitude to counsel as would be afforded if the convictions were live.

On the other hand, a refusal to allow disclosure of spent convictions may also lead to unfairness. In *Evans*[71] credibility was at the heart of the issue in the trial. However, the judge refused to allow defence counsel to cross-examine a witness about her spent convictions. The Court of Appeal held

---

[69] [1982] Crim.L.R. 175.
[70] [1995] Crim.L.R. 815.
[71] (1992) 156 J.P. 539.

that the judge's refusal amounted to a material irregularity because it was relevant for the jury to know that the witness had been dishonest in the past.

In any case a defendant has the right to cross-examine a co-defendant as to his or her spent convictions where the co-defendant has given evidence against him: this right was not taken away by the Practice Direction of 1975.[72]

(2) Spent convictions and good character

The Act does not confer on a rehabilitated person the right to be called a man of good character. If the defence wants to put such a person forward as being of good character, it must first apply to the judge. It is then a matter of the judge's discretion to decide whether such a course is to be followed or not.[73] The judge should be asked for his ruling at the outset of the trial.[74] **7–25**

No rules can be laid down as to the exercise of the discretion. If the defendant is adult and has been convicted long ago of a trivial offence, no doubt the judge will allow the defendant to be treated as a man of good character. But if, on the other hand, the defendant has been convicted of some more serious offence and the conviction has only recently been spent the judge is not likely to take such a lenient view. It will depend on the circumstances of the case.

In *Nye*[75] the defendant was charged with three counts of assault occasioning actual bodily harm. He had been involved in a collision in his car and thereafter assaulted three police officers. The defendant, who was 32, had two previous convictions. Both convictions occurred 10 years before the trial and had been spent for some five years. They were for criminal damage and burglary. At the beginning of the trial, his counsel applied to the judge for a ruling that the defendant should be treated as a man of good character. The judge ruled that there should be no reference to character. The Court of Appeal upheld this ruling. The Court, although not sure that it would not have been better for the defendant in the circumstances to have been put forward as a man of good character, found no reason to criticise the judge for the way he exercised his discretion. The Court said:

"The essence of this matter is that the jury must not be misled and no lie must be told to them about this matter. The exercise of discretion of the trial judge ... must be carried out having regard to the 1974 Act and to the Practice Direction. It should be exercised, so far as it can be, favourably towards the accused person."[76]

---

[72] *Corelli* [2001] Crim.L.R. 913.
[73] *Nye* (1982) 75 Cr.App.R. 247; *Bailey* [1989] Crim.L.R. 723.
[74] *Nye*, above.
[75] *Nye*, above.
[76] At 250–251.

7-26   While the jury must not be told that the defendant has no convictions (when he has) for that would be to mislead them,[77] a formula sometimes used is to say that the defendant is "a man of good character with no relevant convictions".

On the other hand, where a defendant's spent convictions are so immaterial that the court decides that he should be treated as a man of good character, a full good character direction should be given[78]: paras 7–12, 7–13, above.

3. BAD CHARACTER

7-27   The admissibility of evidence of bad character is now governed by Pt 11, Chapter 1, of the Criminal Justice Act 2003. These provisions govern the admissibility of evidence relating to the character of both defendants and witnesses. The common law rules governing the admissibility of evidence of bad character in criminal proceedings are abolished: s.99(1) of the Criminal Justice Act 2003.[79] The effect is to repeal the common law rules on this topic[80] For instance, the common law immunity for a defendant who alleges consent in a rape case no longer exists.[81]

The Criminal Evidence Act 1898, s.1, which formerly governed the cross-examination of the accused as to character is amended, making the admissibility of character evidence subject to s.101 of the Criminal Justice Act 2003 and repealing subs.(3), formerly s.1(f) of the 1898 Act.[82]

Note that the provisions of the Criminal Justice Act 2003 discussed in this section of the book are expected, at the time of writing, to come into effect in April 2005. Before that date the fourth edition of this book should be referred to.

A. Bad character defined

7-28   Section 98 of the Criminal Justice Act 2003 provides:

"References in this Chapter to evidence of a person's 'bad character'

---

[77] *O'Shea, The Times,* June 8, 1993.

[78] *Heath, The Times,* February 10, 1994.

[79] This abolition is subject to the preservation of the rule under which evidence of reputation is admissible for the purposes of proving good or bad character: s.118(1) (see below).

[80] The exception is the rule under which a person's reputation is admissible for the purposes of proving his bad character which is preserved under ss.99(2) and 118(1) of the 2003 Act. The purpose in retaining the rule was explained by the Parliamentary Secretary at the Home Office to be avoid an inconsistency in retaining it for the purposes of the hearsay rule (Ch.8, below) and abolishing all the common law rules on this topic: HC Debs Standing Committee B, col.561.

[81] See para.7–57 of the fourth edition of this work for the rule.

[82] s.1 of the 1898 Act was previously amended by Sch.4 to the Youth Justice and Criminal Evidence Act 1999.

are to evidence of, or of a disposition towards, misconduct on his part, other than evidence which—

    (a) has to do with the alleged facts of the offence with which the defendant is charged, or

    (b) is evidence of misconduct in connection with the investigation or prosecution of that offence."

Section 98 thus provides that references to evidence of a "person's bad character" in Chapter 1 of Pt II of the Act "are to evidence of, or of a disposition towards, misconduct on his part", other than evidence relating to the offence charged or the investigation or prosecution (see below).

The effect of the section is to define evidence of a person's bad character as evidence of either misconduct on his or her part or a disposition towards misconduct, and for these purposes, "misconduct" means "the commission of an offence or other reprehensible behaviour": s.112(1). The first issue for the court to determine, then, is whether there is evidence of misconduct in the sense of commission of an offence.

Evidence that a person has committed an offence may take a number of forms. The first and most common way is by proof of a previous conviction. If the person has a conviction for an offence it plainly shows that he committed the offence and is evidence of bad character under the Act. There is little difficulty in admitting this sort of evidence. In practice, the vast majority of instances of bad character have been proved in the past in this way and will no doubt continue to be so.

However, this is not the only evidence that a person has committed an offence. Evidence which suggests that a person has committed an offence, even if there has been no charge or conviction, may also be admissible. This would include cases where a person has been acquitted (thus retaining the rule in Z),[83] provided that the evidence is otherwise admissible. Evidence, therefore, that an accused had been implicated in a series of rapes would not necessarily be inadmissible in a subsequent rape charge on the grounds that he had been acquitted of the earlier rapes. It will be a matter of establishing the relevance of the earlier rapes to the subsequent charge.

The second part of the definition relates to evidence of a disposition on   **7–29** the part of a person towards misconduct, *i.e.* the commission of offences or other reprehensible behaviour, on his part. This sort of evidence was formerly covered by the "similar fact" rule, now abolished. Deciding what is reprehensible behaviour these days may not be as entirely a straightforward proposition as it once was. Nonetheless, there will be clear cases. For instance, a person with a sexual interest in children, even if he has not acted on it in a criminal way, may still show a disposition towards reprehensible behaviour.

---

[83] [2000] 2 A.C. 483; [2000] 2 Cr.App.R. 281, cited at para.5–15, above.

The subsection is based on the Law Commission recommendation that "bad character" cannot be defined solely in terms of committing an offence. Evidence of conduct can be demonstrative of a person's bad character, even if that conduct is not a crime. Nonetheless, the concept of bad character evidence should, as far as possible, be defined according to objective criteria. The Law Commission thought that the most appropriate criterion for this purpose is whether a reasonable person might disapprove of what the evidence reveals about the person to whom it relates.[84] As originally drafted, the Bill provided that evidence of conduct which would be disapproved of by the reasonable person would be evidence of bad character.

7–30   The difficulty with this definition lay in its breadth and vagueness. The House of Lords and House of Commons Joint Committee on Human Rights expressed its concern about it by noting that it could permit a generalised attack on a defendant's or witness's morals and undermine the presumption of innocence on the basis of vague or impressionistic evidence as to matters on which moral opinions may differ, the Committee was not reassured by the assertion of the Minister of State that the type of evidence would have been potentially admissible as evidence of bad character under the Criminal Evidence Act 1898 and would be subject in any event to the restrictions under the 2003 Act (discussed below).[85] It is submitted that the Committee was right to be concerned about the breadth of this provision. In practice, under the Criminal Evidence Act 1898 such evidence was almost invariably limited to evidence of previous convictions. The present definition spreads the net much wider. Thus, although "reprehensible" is defined as "deserving of reprehension, censure or rebuke"[86] and, therefore, referring to more serious conduct, nonetheless, it could be taken to include offences for which a person was cautioned or bound over. Suppose an accused has been bound over for creating a minor disturbance; many might disapprove of such conduct, consider it reprehensible and the evidence of the bind-over hence be admissible. Likewise, breaches of civil injunctions not to molest spouses and children could well be similarly admissible since it might be difficult to say that such behaviour would not be regarded as a tendency towards reprehensible behaviour. A further extension might consist of evidence of neighbours concerning alleged anti-social behaviour by an accused in the locality in which he lives. The old practice had the advantage of certainty. The danger of the present law lies in its potential breadth. A further danger is that in admitting evidence of such past misbehaviour there is a danger that juries will be diverted from consideration of the main issue with regard to the offence charged. It will require careful supervision by the courts to meet the concerns expressed above.

---

[84] Law Commission Report, Evidence of Bad Character in Criminal Proceedings (No.273), Cm.5257, paras 8.10–8.16.
[85] House of Lords and House of Commons Joint Committee on Human Rights, Eleventh Report of Session 2002–03, June 2003, HL Paper 118, HC 724, paras 10 and 11.
[86] Shorter Oxford English Dictionary, 1993.

It should be noted that the previous convictions of a person for offences 7–31 committed while a child under 14 are now admissible under s.108(1) of the 2003 Act.[87] This is the rule except in the case of an offence committed by a defendant, aged 21 or over, when evidence of conviction for an offence when under the age of 14 is not admissible unless both offences are triable on indictment and the court is satisfied that it is in the interests of justice to require the evidence to be admitted: s.108(2). Thus, in the case of an offence committed by an accused under 21 the evidence of a previous conviction will normally be admissible provided that it is also otherwise admissible. However, limitations apply in proceedings for an offence committed by a defendant aged over 21. For the evidence to be admissible in such cases, both offences, the one being tried and the earlier conviction, must be for offences triable only on indictment (s.108(2)(a)), *i.e.* they must both be serious; and the court must be satisfied that the interests of justice require the evidence to be admissible (s.108(2)(b)). There is thus a discretion for the court to restrict the giving of such evidence when it is unnecessary and unduly prejudicial. This should prevent the giving of evidence such as that for convictions which have little to do with the case, but which would simply lower the defendant in the eyes of the jury. This should allow relevant convictions to be given.

Section 98 also provides that references in Chapter 1 to evidence of a person's bad character are to evidence other than that which:

"(a) has to do with the alleged facts of the offence with which the defendant is charged, or

(b) is evidence of misconduct in connection with the investigation or prosecution of that offence."

The effect of the subsection is that evidence may be admitted about the 7–32 facts of the offence charged (for example forensic evidence or closely related facts) together with any evidence connected with the investigation, for example intimidating witnesses or striking a police officer when faced with an awkward question in interview.[88] Such evidence is admissible outside the scheme in this Act. It follows that a defendant may be cross-examined about the offence charged and cannot refuse to answer relevant questions on the ground that they might incriminate him.

Under a similar provision of the Criminal Evidence Act 1898, s.1(2),

---

[87] Repealing s.16(2) of the Children and Young Persons Act 1963 which prohibited the asking of questions of a person aged over 21, relating to any offence while he was under 14.
[88] Explanatory Notes to the Bill (Stationery Office, London, 2002), para.290. "Spent" convictions under the Rehabilitation of Offenders Act 1974 (para.7–21, above) are not excluded under the Act since as the Parliamentary Under-Secretary at the Home Office explained in the Committee Debate in the House of Commons there may be circumstances in which a spent conviction is relevant to a current charge, *e.g.* to show a pattern of offending or to correct a false impression given by the defendant: HC Debs. Standing Committee B, col.554.

which permitted cross-examination of an accused although "it would tend to criminate him as to the offence charged", the issue arose as to whether an accused might be asked questions which were *indirectly* relevant to the offence charged. In *Jones*[89] the defendant was charged with the murder of a Girl Guide. During the investigation of the murder, the defendant gave a false alibi to the police. When explaining why he had done so in evidence in chief at his trial, the defendant admitted that he had previously been in trouble with the police. He also gave an account of his movements on the night of the murder. In order to show that this account had not been recently invented, the defendant described a conversation with his wife shortly after the event. He said that during the conversation his wife asked him if he were connected with an incident reported in the Sunday newspapers. The defendant's evidence about this conversation was almost word for word similar to evidence of a conversation with his wife which the defendant gave at an earlier trial when he was charged with the rape of a girl. He was cross-examined about the similarities between these conversations. No mention was made of an earlier trial. However, there was an obvious inference that the defendant had been in trouble for an offence which had been reported in the Sunday newspapers. The majority of the House of Lords held that the cross-examination was not admissible under para.(e) of s.1 of the Criminal Evidence Act 1898 because it was not directly relevant to the offence charged.[90]

B. Bad character of the defendant

7-33 The admissibility of evidence of the bad character of the defendant is now governed by ss.101–108 of the Criminal Justice Act 2003 which set out the circumstances in which such evidence is admissible. ("Bad character" is to be read in accordance with s.98, para.7–28, above)[91]

Section 101(1) provides that in criminal proceedings[92] evidence of the defendant's bad character is admissible "if, but only if—

    (a) all parties to the proceedings agree to the evidence being admissible,

    (b) the evidence is adduced by the defendant himself or is given in an answer to a question asked by him in cross-examination and intended to elicit it,

[89] [1962] A.C. 635.
[90] The evidence would now be admissible since it was relevant to an important issue between the prosecution and the defence: see s.101(1)(d) of the Criminal Justice Act 2003, below, para.7–40.
[91] s.112(1) Criminal Justice Act 2003.
[92] In s.112(1) "criminal proceedings" are defined as "criminal proceedings in relation to which the strict rules or evidence may apply" and "defendant" in relation to criminal proceedings as "a person charged with an offence in those proceedings".

(c) it is important explanatory evidence,

(d) it is relevant to an important matter in issue between the defendant and the prosecution,

(e) it has substantial probative value in relation to an important matter in issue between the defendant and a co-defendant,

(f) it is evidence to correct a false impression given by the defendant, or

(g) the defendant has made an attack upon another person's character."

The effect of this section is that evidence of the bad character of the defendant is admissible "if, but only if" the circumstances in s.101(1) apply. If they do not apply such evidence is not admissible. The aim of this Part of the Act is to create an inclusionary approach to the admissibility of a defendant's previous convictions and other misconduct rather than the exclusionary approach of the old law. The new law makes such evidence admissible subject to exclusion in certain circumstances if the court considers that the adverse effect that it would have on the fairness of the proceedings required this.[93]

Section 101(1) provides the "gateways" (as they are termed in the   **7–34** Explanatory Notes) through which such evidence may be admitted.[94] Sections 102–106 supplement s.101(1): s.101(2). Section 107 provides a statutory limitation upon admissibility (see below paras 7–69 to 7–70).

The White Paper preceding the Act states that it should be for the judge to decide whether previous convictions are sufficiently relevant to the case, bearing in mind the prejudicial effect, to be heard by the jury and for the jury to decide what weight should be given to that evidence in the circumstances of the case. And this should be the case of the previous convictions of witnesses as well as defendants.[95]

(1) Agreement between the parties

Evidence of a defendant's bad character is admissible if all the parties to the   **7–35** proceedings agree to its admissibility: s.101(1)(a). This will require prosecution and defence (and any co-defendants) to agree formally on its admissibility. The Law Commission recommended that agreement between the parties as to the admissibility of evidence of the defendant's bad char-

---

[93] Explanatory Notes to the Bill (Stationery Office, London, 2002), para.298.
[94] Explanatory Notes to the Bill (Stationery Office, London, 2002), para.298.
[95] Home Office White Paper, *Justice for All*, Cm.5563, T50 (Stationery Office, London, 2002), para.4.56.

acter was one of the few situations where such evidence should be auto-matically included.[96] Practice suggests this to be a relatively rare occurrence. But there may be occasions where it may be expedient for both parties to agree, for instance, on the form in which an accused's bad character is put into evidence if both sides agree that part, at least, of that character is relevant and admissible.

(2) Adduced by the defendant

7–36 Evidence of a defendant's bad character is admissible if adduced by the defendant himself or elicited in cross-examination by him or, as is most usually the case, on his behalf: s.101(1)(b).

This subsection reflects the common law which permitted a defendant to give evidence of his own bad character or previous misconduct, or elicit the evidence from a witness (such as a police officer) in cross-examination. This, again, is a relatively rare occurrence, but not one which usually gives rise to problems. However, problems may arise if the defence seek to be selective as to which convictions should be adduced into evidence. In these circumstances, if the prosecution do not agree with the selectivity of the defence's approach, this subsection does not apply: indeed, if the defence did adduce the evidence, it would be open to the prosecution to rely on subs.101(1)(f) which permits evidence of bad character to be given to correct a false impression given by the defendant.

(3) Important explanatory evidence

7–37 Evidence of a defendant's bad character is admissible if it is important explanatory evidence: s.101(1)(c). Section 102 provides that evidence is

"important explanatory evidence" if—

(a) without it, the court or jury would find it impossible or dif-ficult properly to understand other evidence in the case, and
(b) its value for understanding the case as a whole is substantial."

The purpose of this provision is to allow evidence of a defendant's bad character to be adduced where it is necessary for the understanding of the case as a whole. It is based on recommendations of the Law Commission (see para.7–39 below).

The common law allowed such evidence to be given because "some surrounding circumstances have to be considered in order to understand either the offence charged or the nature of the ... evidence which it is sought to adduce."[97] Likewise, evidence may be relevant in describing the

[96] Law Commission Report, "Evidence of Bad Character in Criminal Proceedings" (No.273) Cm.5257, para.8.31.
[97] *Scarrott* [1978] Q.B. 1016, *per* Scarman.

context and circumstances in which offences were committed. Thus in *Fulcher*[98] evidence of the defendant's irritation towards his crying baby son was held admissible as showing that on the critical occasion he struck a fatal blow; and the court quoted from *Pettnam*[99]—

> "Where it is necessary to place before the jury evidence of part of a continual background of history relevant to the offence charged in the indictment and without the totality of which the account placed before the jury would be incomplete or incomprehensible, then the fact that the whole account involves including evidence establishing the commission of an offence with which the accused is not charged is not of itself a ground for excluding the evidence."

These dicta were approved in *Sawoniuk*[1] where the Court of Appeal **7–38** pointed out that offences cannot be fairly judged in a factual vacuum. In that case the accused *was* convicted of two murders committed in German-occupied Poland during World War II, fifty years before the trial. In holding the applicant's complaints inadmissible, the European Court of Human Rights held that, in relation to the defendant's complaint about evidence being given concerning the context of the complaints, in the trial of a person for war crimes it is not realistic to expect that evidence can be restricted to the specific counts alleged without the context of the incidents being examined.[2]

Relevant background evidence may be admissible. In *Phillips*[3] the defendant was charged with murdering his wife. He claimed that the marriage was happy but evidence was admitted to show that the marriage had in reality broken down so that the jury could make a properly informed assessment of the entire evidence. But the evidence must relate to the type of offence: in *Dolan*,[4] where the defendant was charged with murdering his baby son by shaking him there was evidence that he lost his temper and damaged inanimate objects but no evidence of violence towards human beings.

The Law Commission noted in its report that the common law approach **7–39** allowed evidence of the defendant's bad character to be included in these circumstances without consideration of its potentially prejudicial effect.[5] Once the court was satisfied that the evidence was of an important nature, it was admissible irrespective of its potential effect on the jury. Thus the

---

[98] [1995] 2 Cr.App.R. 251.
[99] Unreported, May 2, 1985, *per* Purchas L.J.
[1] [2000] 2 Cr.App.R. 220.
[2] [2001] Crim.L.R. 918 (No.637/6100; Decision 29/5/2001).
[3] [2003] Crim.L.R. 629.
[4] [2003] Crim.L.R. 41.
[5] Law Commission Report, "Evidence of Bad Character in Criminal Proceedings" (No.273) Cm.5257, paras 10.6–10.12.

Law Commission recommended that a twofold test should be introduced when determining whether evidence of a defendant's bad character, which was of an important explanatory nature, should be admitted. The first limb is that the court must be satisfied that, without the evidence, the court or jury would find it impossible or difficult properly to understand other evidence in the case, and that its value for understanding the case as a whole was substantial. The second limb of the test provides that the interests of justice require the evidence to be adduced notwithstanding any prejudicial potential it might have.

This approach emphasises the importance of examining the value of the evidence for understanding the case as a whole, not solely its probative value. The new test would also allow the court to consider any potential prejudicial effect the evidence might have, and, if appropriate, disallow it on that basis.

(4) Matter in issue between the defendant and prosecution

7–40 Evidence of a defendant's bad character is admissible if it is relevant to an important matter in issue between the defendant and prosecution: s.101(1)(d).[6]

For the purposes of this subsection, s.103(1) provides that the matters in issue between the defendant and the prosecution "include—

(a) the question whether the defendant has a propensity to commit offences of the kind with which he is charged, except where his having such a propensity makes it no more likely that he is guilty of the offence;

(b) the question whether the defendant has a propensity to be untruthful, except where it is not suggested that the defendant's case is *untruthful* in any respect".

Thus the matters in issue may include the propensity to commit similar offences to that charged and a propensity to be untruthful. These topics will be considered separately.

7–41 **Propensity to commit the crime charged.** The effect of s.103(1)(a) is to make admissible the evidence of an accused's propensity to commit the very type of offence with which he is charged where it has substantive probative value to an important issue between the parties. (Such a matter is one of substantial importance in the context of the case as a whole: s.112.)

The Explanatory Notes to the Bill explain that this provision will enable evidence over and above convictions for the same or a similar offence to be admitted and would cover, for example, evidence that did not amount to

---

[6] Only prosecution evidence is admissible under this provision: s.103(6).

criminal conduct or for which the defendant had been acquitted previously.[7] It would also cover circumstances where evidence might be relevant even though it related to a different type of offence (for example evidence that the defendant had previously committed various crimes with a particular group of people might be relevant to a charge of conspiracy to commit a different type of offence with the same group).

In determining whether to admit evidence under this provision it will first be necessary for the court to identify the matter in issue to which the propensity of the accused is relevant. It must next be determined whether that matter is an "important matter in issue between the defendant and the prosecution". If it is not relevant to an important issue the evidence must be excluded.

It must then be determined whether "his having a such propensity makes   **7–42** it no more likely that he is guilty of the offence", *i.e.* the evidence of propensity adds nothing more than prejudice to the prosecution evidence. For instance, this might be the case where there is no dispute about the facts of the case and the issue is simply whether those facts constitute the offence.

A case decided under the common law illustrates the point. In *Straffen*[8] the accused had escaped from Broadmoor. A small girl, Y, was murdered during the short time that he was at large. Y had been strangled and there was no attempt either at sexual interference or to conceal the body. Evidence was admitted that the accused had strangled two other little girls in similar circumstances with in each case features similar to the murder for which he was being tried. The reason that the evidence was admissible under the common law was not to show that he was a professional strangler but that he had strangled Y. It would have been contrary to common sense for the jury not to have heard the evidence of the previous murders because it clearly had the strongest probative force. Such evidence would be admissible *now* under s.103(1)(a) to show that the accused was a professional strangler, but the case illustrates how the evidence added something more than mere propensity.

Propensity for untruthfulness. The effect of s.103(1)(b) is to make   **7–43** admissible a defendant's propensity for untruthfulness when it has substantial probative value in relation to an important issue between the parties. This provision replaces the complicated rules which formerly existed under the Criminal Evidence Act 1898 in relation to credibility. This provision makes admissible an accused's bad character for untruthfulness if there is an important issue of credibility between the prosecution and defence. This is intended to cover evidence of convictions for offences such as perjury or offences involving deception, *i.e.* showing that the accused has a propensity to dishonesty and is not, therefore, to be regarded as a credible

---

[7] Explanatory Notes to the Bill (Stationery Office, London, 2002), para.304.
[8] [1952] 2 Q.B. 911.

witness. However, the provision is not intended to cover a conviction for *any* criminal offence.[9] As s.103(1)(b) makes clear, the provision is not applicable in a case where it is *not* suggested that the defendant's case is *untruthful* in any respect.

A number of examples were provided in the White Paper to show how this provision may work in practice. In the first a doctor is charged with indecent assault against a patient.[10] He denies that any indecency took place. However, separate patients in the last five years have made similar complaints resulting in similar trials. On both occasions the doctor has been acquitted. The matter in issue is whether the complainant is telling the truth when she says that the indecency took place or the accused when he says it did not. According to the White Paper, it defies belief that that it could only be an unlucky coincidence that this number of patients have made this kind of allegation and therefore the previous allegations are of clear probative value. The judge should therefore be able to rule that the jury should hear of the previous allegations, taking into account the other evidence in the case and the risk that undue weight might be put on them.

7–44   In another example the defendant is charged with assaulting his wife.[11] He has a history of violence, including a number of convictions for assault occasioning actual bodily harm, and there are witness accounts of his striking his wife in the past. He claims that she received her injuries while falling down the stairs. In this case, his previous conduct could be thought relevant to determining whether the allegations of violence, or the defendant's version of events, are true. The judge should therefore be able to rule whether this is admissible, provided he is satisfied that it can be put in its proper context by the jury.

Admissibility under s.101(1)(d) is subject to the power under s.101(3) to exclude such evidence if it appears to the court that the admission of the evidence would have such an adverse effect on the proceedings that the court ought not to admit it.

7–45   **Ancillary matters.** Section 103(2) provides that where s.103(1)(a) applies (*i.e.* propensity to commit the crime charged) a defendant's propensity to commit offences of the kind charged may be "established"[12] by evidence that he has been convicted of—

(a)   an offence of the same description as the one with which he is charged, or

---

[9] Explanatory Notes, para.306.
[10] Home Office White Paper, *Justice For All*, Cm. 5563, T50 (Stationery Office, 2002), Example 1, p.80.
[11] Home Office White Paper, *Justice For All*, Cm. 5563, T50 (Stationery Office, 2002), p.80, Example 2.
[12] This provision is specifically stated to be "without prejudice to any other way of doing so": s.103(2).

(b) an offence of the same category as the one with which he is charged".

However, s.103(3) provides the court with a discretion to exclude such evidence if "the court is satisfied, by reason of the length of time since the conviction or for any other reason, that it would be unjust for it to apply" in the instant case. Thus, if the conviction is too old to have any probative value the court should not admit it, or, if there are other reasons which would make it unjust to admit it, the evidence should be excluded. This provides the court with a discretion to exclude evidence of little probative value, but much prejudicial effect. The court must be so satisfied before excluding the evidence, but once satisfied, must do so.

Further definition is to be found in s.103(4) which provides that:

"(a) Two offences are of the same description as each other if the statement of the offence in an information or an indictment would, in each case, be in the same terms;

(b) two offences are of the same category as each other if they belong to the same category of offences prescribed for the purposes of this section by an order made by the Secretary of State."

The effect of this section is to enable convictions for the same type of offence, or similar, to be admitted. There should be little difficulty in showing that offences are of the same description, *i.e.* in the same terms in any indictment or information. On the other hand, offences of the same category are defined by reference to categories of offences drawn up by the Home Secretary in secondary legislation. The purpose was that the categories should contain offences that were of the same type, for example offences involving violence or sexual offences.[13] The four categories in the secondary legislation are theft-related offences, violent offences against the person, non-consensual sexual offences, and child sex offences, and the list of offences is comprehensive, for example the theft-related offences include theft, handling, robbery, burglary, aggravated burglary and aggravated vehicle taking.[14]

7-46

The following matters should also be noted. Evidence that a defendant may wish to give about a co-defendant is dealt with in s.101(1)(e), paras 7–55 *et seq.* below. Thus, s.103(6) provides that only prosecution evidence is admissible under this heading.[15]

---

[13] Explanatory Notes to the Bill (Stationery Office, London, 2002), para.303.
[14] At the time of writing, the relevant statutory instrument had not yet been published.
[15] "Prosecution evidence" is defined as "evidence which is to be (or has been) adduced by the prosecution, or which a witness is to be invited to give (or has given) in cross-examination by the prosecution": s.112(1).

Evidence admissible under this head is subject to the defendant's right to apply to exclude it under s.101(3), discussed below, paras 7–49 to 7–52.

7–47   **General considerations.** The Government originally proposed in the Bill, sent by the House of Commons to the House of Lords, that evidence of a defendant's bad character should be admissible if the prosecution has evidence of a defendant's conviction for an offence of the same description or category as the offence charged. This proposal proved controversial and was defeated in the House of Lords. The suggestion has been modified and added as a consideration for the court in determining whether a defendant's propensity has been established.

This provision is the most controversial of all those in this part of the Act. Thus the White Paper preceding the Act had considered a number of possible procedures concerning the admissibility of a defendant's bad character under this heading. The first procedure was for a defendant's previous convictions to be read out at the beginning of a trial as a matter of routine.[16] This approach was dismissed; principally because it would distract the jury and would have immense prejudicial effect.

The White Paper instead favoured the approach whereby any relevant information, including evidence of a defendant's convictions for offences of a similar description or category should, as far as possible, be entrusted to those determining the case. The basis of the argument was that it should be for the judge to decide whether previous convictions are sufficiently relevant to the case, bearing in mind the prejudicial effect, to be heard by the jury and for the jury to decide what weight should be given to that information in all the circumstances of the case.

7–48   A number of examples were provided in the White Paper to illustrate how this approach might work in practice. (Although the proposals have changed, it is submitted that the examples remain apt for the current legislation.) In the first a defendant is charged with assaulting his wife.[17] He has a history of violence, including a number of convictions for assault occasioning actual bodily harm, and there are witness accounts of his striking his wife in the past. He claims that she received her injuries while falling down the stairs. In this case, his previous conduct could be thought relevant to determining whether the allegations of violence, or the defendant's version of events, are true. The judge should therefore be able to rule whether to admit the evidence of previous misconduct provided, of course, that the evidence can be put in its proper context by the jury. (This latter will require careful direction by the judge to ensure that this is done.)

In another example, a 19-year-old man is stopped at 2 a.m. driving a car

---

[16] Home Office White Paper, *Justice For All*, Cm. 5563, T50 (Stationery Office, 2002) paras 4.54–56.
[17] Home Office White Paper, *Justice For All*, Cm. 5563, T50 (Stationery Office, 2002), p.80, Example 2.

that has been reported stolen.[18] He tells the arresting officer that the car belongs to a friend of a friend and that he has been given permission to borrow the vehicle. Upon investigation it transpires that he has three recent previous convictions for taking without consent (TWOC). There is a statutory defence to TWOC if the court is satisfied that the accused acted in the belief that he had lawful authority, or that the owner would have consented had he or she known of the circumstances of the taking. In this case the young man's previous convictions are clearly relevant to whether his version of events is true and it would be for the magistrate to determine whether they are likely to have a disproportionate effect, in the context of other evidence in the case.

The danger, however, in admitting this kind of evidence is that it allows a potentially misleading shortcut to conviction. The danger is that which the original rule was designed to guard against, *i.e.* because the accused has committed this sort of offence in the past, he has committed the offence charged. As noted above, in order to avoid miscarriages of justice, juries must be directed as to the significance of the evidence and this danger pointed out to them. Magistrates, likewise, must have it in mind.   **7–49**

A further safeguard against miscarriage of justice is to be found in s.101(3) of the Act which provides that the court must not admit evidence under subs.(1)(d) or (g) if, on an application by the defendant to exclude it, it appears to the court that the admission of the evidence would have such an adverse effect on the fairness of the proceedings that the court ought not to admit it.

Thus, admission of evidence under this heading is subject to such an application by the defendant. The application will be successful and the court must exclude the evidence if it appears that the evidence would have such an adverse effect on the fairness of the proceedings that the court ought not to admit it. Thus, it is mandatory to exclude the evidence if it appears that it would have such an effect.

The test (of an adverse effect on the proceedings) is familiar from s.78 of the Police and Criminal Evidence Act 1984 which is in similar terms. No doubt, similar principles will apply (discussed at paras 9–27 *et seq.* below). It should, however, be borne in mind that the exclusionary power under s.78 is only discretionary.

It follows that in considering an application under s.101(3) the court must first consider whether the admission of the evidence would have an adverse effect on the fairness of the proceedings. Thus, the court will be required to balance the probative nature of the convictions (that is, the extent to which they are relevant to an issue in the case) against the prejudicial effect of admitting the evidence[19]; and ask itself in the   **7–50**

---

[18] Home Office White Paper, *Justice For All*, Cm. 5563, T50 (Stationery Office, 2002), p.80, Example 3.
[19] Explanatory Notes to the Bill (Stationery Office, London, 2002), para.303.

circumstances of the particular case: does the prejudicial effect of evidence of the previous convictions of the accused outweigh its probative value? This, it should be said, is a balancing exercise with which the courts are thoroughly familiar.

In deciding this issue the court must also have regard to the age of the convictions.[20] Plainly this will bear on issues of probative value and prejudicial effect. A conviction as a juvenile for grievous bodily harm will be of little assistance to a court hearing a case of shoplifting, when the same juvenile is grown up, but it might have a seriously prejudicial effect.

A further example given by the White Paper is that of a defendant with a conviction for indecent assault.[21] Many years later he is charged with possession of cannabis with intent to supply. He claims that the police have framed him and planted the drugs and the money. Under the previous law, this defence opened the way for his own record to be put to him when he gave evidence, and this was likely to include his previous conviction even though it had little bearing on the issues in the case. Alternatively, the fear of his record coming out might prevent the defendant from presenting his full defence to the court. The White Paper thought it unlikely that evidence of the indecent assault conviction would be considered sufficiently relevant to be admitted now.

7–51   The following matters may also be noted:

(1) On an application to exclude evidence under s.101(3) the court must have regard, in particular, to the length of time between the matters to which that evidence relates and the matters which form the subject of the offence charged: s.101(4).

(2) In considering issues of relevance and probative value the court must bear in mind the assumption of truth provided for in s.109, para.7–71 below.

(3) Section 112(2) provides that, where a defendant is charged with two or more offences in the same proceedings, Chapter 1 of Pt 11 of the Act (except s.101(3)) has effect as if each offence were charged in separate proceedings (and references to the offence with which the defendant is charged are to be read accordingly). The effect is that where the defendant is charged with more than one offence the court must consider the admissibility of the evidence for each offence separately. The result is that evidence may be admissible in relation to one offence, but inadmissible in relation to another. This may require a separate trial for the offences since the balancing exercise of treating convictions as

---

[20] s.101(4), below.
[21] Home Office White Paper, *Justice For All*, Cm. 5563, T50 (Stationery Office, 2002), p.80, Example 5.

relevant to one offence but not another may involve an impossible task. For severance, see paras 7–52 to 7–54, below.

Severance. In a case involving a series of offences, an application may   7–52
be made for severance of the indictment, *i.e.* to have each count tried separately. The judge must then decide whether the charges are founded on the same facts, or form, or are part of, a series of offences of the same or similar characters within r.9 of the Indictment Rules 1971. If they do not fall within the rule the indictments must be severed. If they do fall within the rule the counts are triable together. If the judge decides that one count is so connected to another as to be admissible in relation to the other count, he will almost certainly rule against severance.

However, the court has a discretion to order separate trials even if the counts are properly joined. The Indictments Act 1915, s.5(3) provides that where the court is of the opinion that an accused person may be "prejudiced or embarrassed in his defence by reason of being charged with more than one offence in the same indictment ... the court may order a separate trial of any count or counts of such indictment".

But if the judge excludes the evidence as inadmissible, does this mean that he must order separate trials on each count to avoid prejudice to the defendant? The answer is that he has a discretion to do so but is not obliged to do so. *Kray*[22] and *Ludlow v Metropolitan Police Commissioner*[23] show that provided there is a sufficient nexus between the offences alleged there may be a single trial provided that the jury is directed that the evidence on one offence is not evidence on any other. The judge, however, has a discretion to sever in any case where he is of the opinion that the accused would be unfairly prejudiced if all the counts were tried together.[24]

In *Cannan* the defendant was charged in an indictment containing counts   7–53
involving offences against three women. The judge did not order severance although the evidence on the various counts was not admissible in others. The Court of Appeal refused to interfere with the judge's exercise of discretion. Lord Lane C.J. said that the judge in sexual cases may often order severance but s.5(3) gives the judge a discretion with which the court would not interfere unless the judge had failed to exercise his discretion on the usual and proper principles.

Lord Lane's dictum was approved by the House of Lords in *Christou*.[25] In that case the accused was charged with sexual offences against his two female cousins. The trial judge held that the evidence of one complainant was not admissible on the charges concerning the other, but did not order severance. The House of Lords upheld this decision, stating that there was a

---

[22] 17 [1970] 1 Q.B. 125
[23] (1970) 34 Cr.App.R. 233. *Kray* and *Ludlow* were applied in *McGlinchey* (1984) 78 Cr.App.R. 282. See also *Blackstock* (1979) 70 Cr.App.R. 34
[24] Indictments Act 1915, s.5(3).
[25] [1996] 2 Cr.App.R. 360

statutory discretion to order that all the charged be tried together and that the position in cases involving the sexual abuse of children was no different. Lord Taylor C.J. said that the things which the judge should take into account would vary from case to case but the essential requirement was the achievement of a fair resolution of the issues:

> "That requires fairness to the accused but also to the prosecution and those involved in it. Some, but by no means an exhaustive list, of the factors which may need to be considered are: how discrete or inter-related are the facts giving rise to the counts; the impact of ordering two or more trials on the defendant and his family, on the victims and their families, on press publicity; and importantly, whether directions the judge can give to the jury will suffice to secure a fair trial if the counts are tried together ... Approaching the question of severance as indicated above, judges will often consider it right to order separate trials. But I reject the argument that either generally or in respect of any class of case, the judge must so order."[26]

7–54   It follows that the judge is not obliged to order severance because inadmissible evidence would be given. Nor can there be any special rule for sexual offences any more than for burglary or shoplifting unless it is thought that there is a particular risk of prejudice where such offences are alleged. This must be a matter for the discretion of the judge in every case.

If the counts are properly tried together the judge must direct the jury that they must give separate consideration to the separate counts and, if appropriate, warn the jury of the risk of collusion.[27]

The same rules apply in magistrates' courts.[28]

It is submitted that the common law should be applied in the following respect. If the prosecution considers that proof of the commission or the conviction of some other offence is admissible, it should be proved as part of the prosecution case[29] and the defendant should not be asked about it, unless it has been so proved. Thus, in *Coombes*[30] the prosecution was allowed to cross-examine a defendant charged with indecent assault on a woman about a previous conviction of indecent assault on a girl. The defendant admitted the assault on the girl. No evidence had been given of this assault during the prosecution case and the Court of Criminal Appeal held that the evidence of the conviction should not have been given.

---

[26] At 371.
[27] *e.g. F* [1996] Crim.L.R. 257.
[28] *Chief Constable of Norfolk* [1983] 2 A.C. 473.
[29] *Jones v DPP* [1962] A.C. 635, 685 *per* Lord Morris.
[30] (1961) 45 Cr.App.R. 36.

(5) Matter in issue between the defendant and a co-defendant

Evidence of a defendant's bad character is admissible if it has substantial probative value in relation to an important matter in issue between the defendant and a co-defendant: s.101(1)(e).   **7–55**

As noted, "important matter" means a matter of substantial importance in the context of the case as a whole: s.112(1). "Co-defendant" in relation to a defendant means a person charged with an offence in the same proceedings: *ibid*.

Supplementing s.101(1)(e), s.104 provides—

> "(1) Evidence which is relevant to the question whether the defendant has a propensity to be untruthful is admissible on that basis under section 101(1)(e) only if the nature or conduct of his defence is such as to undermine the co-defendant's defence.
>
> (2) Only evidence—
>
>   (a) which is to be (or has been) adduced by the co-defendant, or
>   (b) which a witness is to be invited to give (or has given) in cross-examination by the co-defendant,
>
>   is admissible under s.101(1)(e)."

The effect of this section is to make evidence of the defendant's bad character admissible if adduced by a co-defendant only, and not by the prosecution. Its characteristic application will be in a case where the co-defendant's defence is that the offence was committed by the other defendant, and not himself.

Under this section, evidence is admissible on issues between the defendant and a co-defendant if it has substantial probative value in relation to an important issue in the case, *i.e.* the evidence must relate to a significant issue and not to a minor or insignificant one. However, once this threshold has been passed, there is no power for the courts to exclude the evidence.[31]   **7–56**

In one significant limitation, s.104(1) restricts the admissibility of evidence of a defendant's bad character which only shows that he has a propensity to be untruthful to circumstances in which the defendant has undermined the co-defendant's defence (thus, in this regard, retaining the common law).

This section is based largely on recommendations by the Law Commission. Previously, evidence of a co-defendant's bad character could be adduced under both the common law, if the evidence was relevant to the defendant's defence, and under s.1(f)(iii) of the Criminal Evidence Act 1898, where such evidence could be adduced in cross-examination if the co-defendant had given evidence against the defendant. The Law Commission

---

[31] Explanatory Notes to the Bill (Stationery Office, London, 2002), para.307.

noted a number of problems with this approach towards a "cut-throat" defence, for example the court had no discretion to consider the prejudicial effect of the evidence, the difficulties jurors faced when asked to consider the evidence in terms of credibility alone, the restrictions it placed on a defendant presenting his entire defence out of fear his own record would become admissible, and the unbalanced picture it produced by revealing the bad character evidence of one defendant and not the other.[32] As a result, the Law Commission recommended that the evidence of a co-defendant's bad character should be limited to matters substantially relevant to important issues in the case and where evidence was admitted on the issue of faithfulness, but impinging on the issue of propensity, the judge should address the problem in a straightforward manner by warning the jury of the dangers of inferring guilt from past conduct.[33]

7–57   The approach favoured by the Law Commission was that a co-defendant should be able to adduce evidence of the defendant's bad character as a right, *i.e.* in order to ensure that his full defence was presented.[34] The Law Commission recommended that a co-defendant who wished to adduce this evidence should seek leave of the court, which would be given if the evidence was of substantive probative value to an issue between the defendants. This would prevent any unnecessary prejudice against the defendant's character. Once the test had been met the co-defendant would be able to adduce the evidence as a right, and no attempts could be made to exclude it. If the co-defendant wished to adduce evidence relating to the defendant's credibility, he might only do so where the defendant had sought to undermine his defence.

When evidence of the co-defendant's bad character was adduced, the Law Commission recommended that no specific limits should be put on the use to which the jury put that evidence. If the evidence was adduced solely in relation to credibility then the judge, in summing up, should seek to place the evidence in its correct context and warn the jury against inferring guilt from it.

The Law Commission gave an example of how the approach might work in practice. D1 and D2 are jointly charged with robbery.[35] Dl's defence is that D2 committed the offence on her own. In order to have Dl's criminal record admitted on the basis that D1 has undermined D2's case, D2 must demonstrate that Dl's convictions show that he is likely to lie on oath. What is in issue is Dl's propensity to tell the truth, not his propensity to rob. Thus,

---

[32] Law Commission Report, *Evidence of Bad Character in Proceedings*, No.273, Cm. 5257, para.14.3.
[33] Law Commission Report, *Evidence of Bad Character in Proceedings*, No.273, Cm. 5257, para.14.35.
[34] Law Commission Report, *Evidence of Bad Character in Proceedings*, No.273, Cm. 5257, para.14.39–43.
[35] Law Commission Report, *Evidence of Bad Character in Proceedings*, No.273, Cm. 5257, para.14.49–51.

only evidence of Dl's bad character which was relevant to his credibility would be admissible, and there would be no danger of bad character evidence of little probative value (but significant prejudicial effect) being admitted.

A further example of how the approach might work is to be found in a leading case decided by the Privy Council under the common law. In that case, *Lowery v R*,[36] two men were charged with the murder of a young girl, the motive for which was purely sadistic. The two accused were the only people present at the time and each blamed the other. K was allowed to call the evidence of a psychologist to the effect that, whereas he (K) was immature and likely to be dominated, L was aggressive and had sadistic tendencies. The Privy Council upheld the admission of his evidence as relevant to K's case and in negativing L's case Lord Morris said that such evidence was relevant as showing that the version of facts put forward by one defendant was more probable than that put forward by his co-defendant.   **7–58**

The scheme proposed by the Law Commission has largely been followed in the Act. There is a requirement for the co-defendant to serve on the defendant notice of his intention to adduce evidence of the defendant's bad character, see below. The court will then have the ability to consider an application by the defendant to exclude the evidence whether it is admissible under this section or not.

Since the evidence under this heading may be used by a co-defendant to show that the defendant committed the offence, it will be necessary to warn juries, and magistrates must remind themselves, of the dangers of inferring from past misconduct that the defendant is guilty of the offence charged.[37]   **7–59**

Section 111 provides for Rules of Court[38] to require a party who proposes to adduce evidence of a defendant's bad character or proposes to cross-examine a witness with a view to eliciting such evidence, to give notice and particulars to the defendant as may be prescribed. The court may, while considering its discretion as to costs, take into account any failure by a defendant to comply with s.111(2): s.111(4).

(6) Evidence to correct a false impression

Evidence of a defendant's bad character is admissible if it is evidence to correct a false impression given by the defendant: s.101(1)(f). This section, which is based on Law Commission recommendations, replaces s.1(f)(ii) of the Criminal Evidence Act 1898 which permitted the prosecution to adduce evidence of a defendant's bad character if he adduced evidence of his good character. The purpose of the exception is to prevent fact-finders being left   **7–60**

---

[36] [1974] A.C. 85.
[37] As the Law Commission recommended in relation to their proposals on this topic; Law Commission Report, *Evidence Bad Character in Criminal Proceedings*, No.273, Cm. 5257.
[38] At the time of writing, no such Rules have been promulgated.

with a misleading impression of the defendant's character.[39] As the Law Commission said, the essence of the exception is to allow evidence to be adduced for its "corrective value".[40]

Supplementing s.101(1)(f), s.105(1) provides that, for these purposes:

"(a) the defendant gives a false impression if he is responsible for the making of an express or implied assertion which is apt to give the court or jury a false or misleading impression about the defendant;

(b) evidence to correct such an impression is evidence which has probative value in correcting it."

As the Explanatory Notes to the Bill state, for this provision to apply the defendant must have been responsible for an assertion that gives a false or misleading impression about himself.[41] This might be done expressly, for example, by claiming to be of good character when this is not the case, or impliedly, for example, by leading evidence of his conduct that carries an implication that he is of a better character than is actually the case. A defendant may also create a false or misleading impression about himself non-verbally through his conduct (other than in giving evidence) in court, for instance, appearance or dress: s.105(4) and (5).

7–61 Under s.1(8)(ii) of the Criminal Evidence Act 1898, it was held that a defendant may put his character in issue by implied assertion. Thus, in *Samuel*,[42] the defendant was charged with stealing a camera which had been left by a young girl at the Natural History Museum. Some weeks later the camera was discovered in his possession. At his trial for larceny, his defence was that he meant to hand the camera back. In support of this story he said that on two previous occasions when he had found property he had handed it to the police. The Court of Criminal Appeal held that the defendant had put his character in issue since he was asking the jury to infer that he was a man who dealt honestly with property which he found.

On the other hand, the Court of Appeal said that a judge was not justified in obliging a man charged with indecent assault to take off his regimental blazer[43]; the wearing of such a blazer does not amount to an assertion of good character. Whether any piece of evidence does amount to an assertion of good character is ultimately a matter for the good sense of the court.

However, care must be taken to distinguish between giving a false impression and over-enthusiasm in the giving of evidence. Thus, under the

---

[39] Law Commission Report, *Evidence Bad Character in Criminal Proceedings*, No.273, Cm. 5257, para.13.1.

[40] Law Commission Report, *Evidence Bad Character in Criminal Proceedings*, No.273, Cm. 5257, para.13.1.

[41] Explanatory Notes to the Bill (Stationery Office, London, 2002), para.308.

[42] (1956) 40 Cr.App.R. 8.

[43] *Hamilton* [1969] Crim.L.R. 486.

old law, in *Robinson*,[44] the accused gave evidence while holding and ges-
ticulating with a small Bible. The Court of Appeal held that he had not put
his character in issue, commenting that an accused did not put his character
in issue by reminding the jury of an oath he had sworn on the Bible.

Section 105(6) provides that evidence is only admissible to the extent that   **7–62**
is necessary to correct the false impression. Only prosecution evidence is
admissible under s.101(1)(f): s.105(7).

Section 105(2) provides that a defendant is treated as being responsible
for making an assertion if it is made by him in the proceedings (whether or
not in evidence given by him: s.105(2)(a)); on being questioned under
caution, on being questioned about the offence or being charged with it[45]
and the evidence is adduced in the proceedings (s.105(2)(b)). The defendant
will also be responsible for making the assertion if it is made by a witness
called by him (s.105(2)(c)), in cross-examination of a witness by him in
response intended or likely to elicit it (s.105(2)(d)), or it was made by a
person out of court and the defendant adduces evidence of it (s.105(2)(e)).

The effect of the section is to allow the prosecution to introduce evidence
of a defendant's misconduct that has probative value in correcting a false
impression created by the defendant,[46] *i.e.* evidence which is relevant to
correcting the false impression. Exactly what evidence is admissible will
turn on the facts of the case, in particular, the nature of the misleading
impression he has given. Evidence is only admissible to the extent that it is
necessary to correct that impression; s.105(6). A defendant may withdraw
or disassociate himself from a false or misleading impression by, for
example, correcting the impression himself in evidence or through cross-
examination of witnesses. Evidence to correct the impression is not then
admissible: s.105(3). Thus the opportunity for a defendant to exclude evidence of his bad character under s.105(3) is not applicable.

This section is based largely on Law Commission recommendations. The   **7–63**
Law Commission proposed that a defendant would be responsible for
creating a false impression about himself where his conduct is intended to
give the impression that he posses a specific attribute, and had the defendant expressly claimed to posses that attribute, he would have been
regarded as implicitly asserting that he is of good character.[47] Under the
common law there was authority that character was indivisible, thus an
assertion about a particular aspect of a person's character can be rebutted
by evidence about some other aspect.[48] The Law Commission noted that
this could lead to injustice as parts of the defendant's character which were
not relevant to the assertion in question were admissible, irrespective as to

---

[44] [2001] Crim.L.R. 478.
[45] Or being officially informed that he might be prosecuted for it, *ibid.*
[46] Explanatory Notes to the Bill (Stationery Office, London, 2002), paras 309–310.
[47] Law Commission Report, *Evidence of Bad Character in Criminal Proceedings*, No.273 Cm.
5257, para.13.16.
[48] *Winfield* (1939) 27 Cr.App.R. 139.

which part of his character the defendant had made an assertion. Thus the Law Commission recommended that the interests of justice should require that evidence should only be admitted under this head only so far as is necessary to correct the false impression created by the defendant.

If evidence is admitted under this section the question arises as to what direction to the jury is appropriate. The Law Commission took the view that the old direction, which directed the jury to consider the defendant's bad character only in terms of credibility, and not his propensity to commit an offence, was both illogical and unrealistic.[49] The Law Commission recommended that a more appropriate direction would be to remind the jury of the purpose for which the evidence has been admitted, and, if appropriate, apply the following direction; that evidence in relation to previous convictions or misconduct does not prove the guilt on the charge they are trying, but they must be cautious in their approach to that evidence, and must not place undue weight on it.[50]

(7) Attack on another person's character

7–64   Evidence of a defendant's bad character is admissible if the defendant has made an attack on another person's character: s.101(1)(g). However, only prosecution evidence is admissible under this subsection: s.106(3).

Section 106(1) provides that for these purposes "a defendant makes an attack on another person's character if:

(a)   he adduces evidence attacking the other person's character,

(b)   he[51] asks questions in cross-examination that are intended to elicit such evidence, or are likely to do so, or

(c)   evidence is given of an imputation about the other person made by the defendant—

  (i)   on being questioned under caution, before charge, about the offence with which he is charged, or
  (ii)   on being charged with the offence or officially informed that he might be prosecuted for it."

Section 106(2) provides that "evidence attacking the other person's character" in s.106(1), above, means evidence to the effect that the other person:

---

[49] Law Commission Report, *Evidence of Bad Character in Criminal Proceedings*, No.273 Cm. 5257, para.13.39.

[50] *per* Swinton Thomas L.J.'s response to the Law Commission, Law Commission Report, *Evidence of Bad Character in Criminal Proceedings*, No.273 Cm. 5257, para.13.47.

[51] Or any legal representative appointed under s.38(4) of the Youth Justice and Criminal Evidence Act 1999 to cross-examine a witness in his interests (see para.21–19, below: s.106(1)(b)).

"(a) has committed an offence (whether a different offence from the one with which the defendant is charged or the same one), or

(b) has behaved, or is disposed to behave, in a way, that, in the opinion of the court, might be viewed with disapproval by a reasonable person."

The effect of these sections is to permit the prosecution to adduce evidence of a defendant's bad character where he has put his character in issue by attacking the credibility of another witness. They replace s.1(f)(ii) of the Criminal Evidence Act 1898 which permitted the prosecution to cross-examine a defendant if the nature and conduct of the defence was such as to invoke imputations on the character of prosecution witnesses or the deceased victim of the alleged crime.[52] These provisions led to many problems over the admissibility of "tit-for-tat" evidence[53] which, it is to be hoped, the legislation will rectify.   7–65

The Explanatory Notes to the Bill give examples of a defendant attacking another person's character, for instance, if he gives evidence that he or she committed an offence (either the one charged or another one) or has behaved, or is disposed to behave, in a way that might be disapproved of by a reasonable person.[54] These are straightforward enough examples similar to the definition of evidence of bad character in s.98. But, in this case, it does include evidence relating to the facts of the offence charged and its investigation and prosecution. Thus, a defendant may be attacking prosecution witnesses if he claims that they are lying in their version of events or adduces evidence of their previous misconduct to undermine their credibility.

Under s.1(f)(ii) of the Criminal Evidence Act 1898 allegations of misconduct or impropriety (subject to the court's discretion) usually, but not always, rendered the accused liable to cross-examination. The following imputations, for example, were held rightly to have resulted in loss of the protection of the Act and consequent cross-examination: the crime was committed by prosecution witness[55]; a prosecution witness has fabricated evidence[56]; a prosecution witness was a homosexual[57]; police officers concocted a statement[58]; an admission was extorted by threatening that the prisoner's wife would be charged[59]; a person was drunk in charge of a   7–66

---

[52] The reference to the deceased victim was added by the Criminal Justice and Public Order Act 1994, s.31.
[53] See fourth edition of this work, paras 7.60–7.62, for discussion.
[54] Explanatory Notes to the Bill (Stationery Office, London, 2002), para.311.
[55] *Hudson* [1912] 2 K.B. 464.
[56] *Jones* (1923) 17 Cr.App.R. 117.
[57] *Bishop* [1975] Q.B. 274.
[58] *Clark* [1955] 2 Q.B. 469.
[59] *Cook* [1959] 2 Q.B. 340.

car[60]; a married woman had slept with the defendant and allowed him to take photographs of her in the nude[61]; the police obtained four remands in order to manufacture a confession.[62]

On the other hand, it was not every allegation of misconduct or impropriety which would necessarily amount to an imputation. For instance, in *MacLean*,[63] an allegation that a man was intoxicated and swearing was said by the Court of Appeal not to amount to the sort of imputation on which the Act was based.

A defendant also attacks another person's character if he asks questions that are intended, or likely, to elicit evidence of this sort or if the defendant makes an allegation of this nature when questioned under caution or on being charged with the offence and this is heard in evidence.[64]

7–67 It may be noted that the accused will only be in a position to attack the credibility of the witness if he has received leave to do so: s.100(4).

It was the practice at common law for the judge often to give a warning when it became apparent that the defendant was taking a course which would put his character in evidence. Lord Dilhorne in *Selvey*[65] said that it was desirable that such a warning be given. However, the judge was not required to do so[66] unless the defendant was unrepresented.[67] In magistrates' courts when a defendant was unrepresented the proper course was for the prosecution to ask for an adjournment and when the justices had retired to explain with the help of the clerk the risk which he ran if he continued on the course he was pursuing.[68]

In any event, under the common law practice, the prosecution usually made an application to the judge before embarking on cross-examination of an accused as to his bad character.[69] Such an application in trial on indictment was normally made in the absence of a jury. In the magistrates' court the magistrates had either to rule and, if they refused leave, put the matter out of their minds; or the matter would have to be resolved between prosecution and defence with the assistance of the clerk.

7–68 Where a defendant has attacked another person's character, evidence of his own bad character becomes generally admissible.[70] Evidence admissible on this basis may, however, be excluded on the application of the defendant under s.101(3), if it may have a prejudicial effect on the proceedings. Evi-

---

[60] *Brown* (1960) 44 Cr.App.R. 181.
[61] *Jenkins* (1945) 31 Cr.App.R. 1.
[62] *Jones* (1923) 17 Cr.App.R. 117.
[63] [1978] Crim.L.R. 430.
[64] Explanatory Notes to the Bill (Stationery Office, London, 2002), para.312.
[65] (1968) 52 Cr.App.R. 445, 468.
[66] *McGee and Cassidy* (1980) 70 Cr.App.R. 247, 255.
[67] *Cook* (1959) 43 Cr.App.R. 138, 147, *per* Devlin J., CA.
[68] *Weston-super-Mare JJ Ex p. Townsend* [1968] 3 All E.R. 225n.
[69] *Lean* (1923) Cr.App.R. 204 (Court of Criminal Appeal); *Jenkins* (1945) 31 Cr.App.R. 1 Singleton J; *Carter* [1997] Crim.L.R. 505.
[70] Explanatory Notes to the Bill (Stationery Office, London, 2002), para.313.

dence admissible under this section will primarily go to the credit of the defendant and allow his character to be known by the jury. It is not, however, intended that the jury should be expected to put all knowledge of these matters out of their minds when considering other issues in the case. However, the judge may wish to consider directing the jury that care should be taken about the level of weight to be placed on the evidence in any other respect.

The Law Commission recommended that the jury should be directed, and magistrates should direct themselves, that the purpose of any such evidence is to shed light on the defendant's propensity to tell the truth, and a judge would probably remind the jury of that.[71] It may be that, in cases where the evidence also shows that the defendant has previously done the same kind of thing, it will also be appropriate for the judge to explain why it is not being put forward for that purpose and to remind the jury they should not place undue weight on it.

(8) *Contaminated evidence*

Section 107(1) provides that in a jury trial where evidence of bad character   **7–69**
has been admitted under s.101(1)(c)–(g), above:

"(b)   and the court is satisfied at any time after the close of the case for the prosecution that;

    (i)   the evidence is contaminated, and

    (ii)   the contamination is such that, considering the importance of the evidence to the case against the defendant, his conviction of the offence would be unsafe,

  the court must either direct the jury to acquit the defendant of the offence or, if it considers that there ought to be a retrial, discharge the jury."

Section 107(5) provides that a person's evidence is contaminated where—

"(a)   as a result of an agreement or understanding between the person and one or more others, or

  (b)   as a result of the person being aware of anything alleged by one or more others whose evidence may be, or has been, given in the proceedings,

  the evidence is false or misleading in any respect, or is different from what it would otherwise have been."

---

[71] Law Commission Report, *Evidence or Bad Character in Criminal Proceedings*, No.273, Cm. 5257, paras 12.11–12.13.

This section is aimed at dealing with situations where it emerges that evidence which has already been admitted may have been affected by agreement between witnesses or others, or by what he or she has heard of allegations by other witnesses. At common law this was sometimes known as the "group objection" referring to the danger which arises when a number of witnesses who know each other well, or who come from the same group, give apparently corroborative evidence. If there is any danger that the evidence may be the result of concoction, collaboration or collusion between the witnesses, it should be excluded. As Lord Wilberforce pointed out, the danger arises, not only from deliberate invention, but also as a result of stories in the media or from fashions.[72] It is for the judge to determine whether there is such a danger or not.

7–70   There are obvious difficulties in deciding whether evidence should be excluded as a result of this exception. The objection will be made before the evidence is given and therefore the only information available will be the statements made by the witnesses. In *Kilbourne*[73] the trial judge excluded evidence from witnesses within the same group because of the possibility, as it appeared to him, of collaboration between boys who knew each other well. Lord Cross in *Boardman* approved of this approach "rather than to admit the evidence unless a case of collaboration or concoction is made out."[74] The Court of Appeal in *Johanssen*[75] took a more robust view. While acknowledging that Lord Cross's comment, although *obiter*, should be followed unless there were sound reasons for not doing so, the Court said that the judge should not act on a speculative possibility.

The House of Lords in *H(A)*[76] established that where the question of collusion is raised, the judge must draw its importance to the attention of the jury and leave it to them to decide whether the evidence is free from collusion. As the Explanatory Notes point out, this will continue to be the case as there may be cases where it is not possible to expect the jury to put this evidence completely out of their mind. Section 107 builds on the existing common law powers by conferring a duty on the judge to stop the case if the contamination is such that, considering the importance of the evidence to the case, a conviction would be unsafe.[77]

Having stopped the case, the judge may consider that there is still sufficient uncontaminated evidence against the defendant to merit his retrial or may consider that the prosecution case has been so weakened that the defendant should be acquitted. Section 107(1) provides for the judge to take either of these courses. If, however, an acquittal is ordered then the defendant is also to be acquitted of any other offence for which he could

[72] *Boardman* [1975] A.C. 421, 441 *per* Lord Wilberforce.
[73] [1973] A.C. 729.
[74] *Boardman*, above at 459.
[75] (1977) 65 Cr.App.R. 101.
[76] [1995] 2 Cr.App.R. 437.
[77] Explanatory Notes to the Bill (Stationery Office, London, 2002), para.312.

have been convicted, if the judge is also satisfied that the contamination would affect a conviction for that offence in the same way: s.107(2).[78]

(9) Ancillary rules

1. Section 109(1) provides that (subject to s.109(2) below) any reference in the Act to the relevance or probative value of evidence is a reference to its relevance or probative value on the assumption that it is true. Thus, in determining the relevance or probative value of any evidence, the court must proceed on the basis that the evidence is true. This is because, as the Law Commission explained, the quality of evidence is normally not a factor for the court to consider when deciding on the admissibility of evidence.[79]

    7–71

However, there may be exceptional circumstances when, in the interests of fairness of the proceedings, the court is required to consider the quality of the evidence. Thus, s.109(2) provides that in these circumstances the court "need not assume that the evidence is true if it appears, on the basis of any material before the court (including any evidence it decides to hear on the matter) that no court or jury could reasonably find it to be true". Thus it is open to the court to decide on the statements or any evidence in a trial not to accept the evidence as true. However, it is submitted that the court should be slow to adopt this approach since, as noted above, issues relating to the quality of evidence are normally a matter for the fact-finder at the end of the trial.

2. Section 110(1) provides that where the court makes a "relevant ruling", it must state in open court (but in the absence of the jury, if there is one) its reasons for the ruling. If the court is a magistrates' court, it must cause the ruling and the reasons for it to be entered in the register of the court's proceedings.

    7–72

Under s.110(2), a "relevant ruling" means: (a) a ruling on whether an item of evidence is evidence of a person's bad character; (b) a ruling on whether an item of such evidence is admissible under s.100 or 101 (including a ruling on an application under s.101(3)); (c) a ruling under s.107.

This requirement for the court to give reasons forms a trend, which it is submitted, is to be welcomed. This is particularly so when dealing with questions of admissibility of evidence as important as those relating to bad character which may have a pivotal effect on a trial. Such rulings may be brief and concise but must include the reasons for the court's decision.

---

[78] *ibid.*, para.318: s.107(3) extends the duty to the situation where a jury is determining under the Criminal Procedure (Insanity) Act 1964 whether a person, who is deemed unfit to plead, did the act or omission charged. S.107(4) makes it clear that the section does not affect any existing court powers in relation to ordering an acquittal or discharging a jury; *ibid.*

[79] The Law Commission Report, para.15.25.

C. Bad character of others

7–73 At common law, witnesses might be (and were) cross-examined as to their previous convictions or bad character. In the case of prosecution witnesses imputations of that sort made the accused liable to cross-examination as to his own bad character under s.1(f)(ii) of the Criminal Evidence Act 1898. On the other hand, defence witnesses might be so cross-examined without any hindrance and no leave was required. However, the judge was under a duty to stop vexatious questioning; and questions which were designed purely to blacken the witnesses' character and which had no material bearing on his standing after cross-examination would be disallowed.[80] Nonetheless, witnesses might still be unnecessarily humiliated by such cross-examination. The aim of the present law is to restrict it.

The admissibility of evidence relating to the bad character of persons other than defendants is now governed by s.100(1) of the Criminal Justice Act 2003[81] which provides that such evidence is admissible "if, and only if—

(a) it is important explanatory evidence;

(b) it has substantial probative value in relation to a matter which — (i) is a matter in issue in the proceedings, and (ii) is of substantial importance in the context of the case as a whole, or

(c) all parties agree to the evidence being admissible."

7–74 Thus evidence of bad character is admissible only if it is important explanatory evidence, is of substantial probative value in relation to an important issue, or the parties agree that it should be admitted. The purpose is to offer substantial protection to witnesses against unnecessarily wide-ranging and humiliating attacks on their character and ensure that only evidence that is clearly relevant is admissible.[82]

Two matters should be noted at the outset. First, the provision applies both to witnesses and to others. This will extend to dead victims. Secondly, except in a case where such evidence is being given by agreement, evidence of the bad character of witnesses and other persons may not be given without leave of the court: s.100(4). There is thus an important safeguard against attempts at the gratuitous blackening of the character of witnesses or others.

---

[80] For discussion, see fourth edition of this work, para.7.77.
[81] This section does not apply to evidence of a complainant's previous sexual history in trials of sexual offences, which is governed by s.41 of the Youth Justice and Criminal Evidence Act 1999 (para.7–78, below).
[82] Parliamentary Under Secretary, Home Office, Standing Committee B, HC Debs. col.566.

(1) Important explanatory evidence

Evidence of the bad character of witnesses and other persons is admissible if   **7–75**
it is important explanatory evidence: s.100(l)(a). The term "explanatory
evidence" is used to describe evidence which, whilst not going to the
question of whether the defendant is guilty, is necessary for the jury to have
an understanding of other evidence being given in the case by putting it in
its proper context.[83] The Law Commission noted that such evidence may
not have significant probative value, in that it does not prove anything in
itself, but it may be of significant value in understanding other evidence.[84]
The example given by the Law Commission was a case of intra-familial
abuse, where it was not only abusive behaviour by the defendant on
occasions other than that charged which was valuable in explaining the case
as a whole to the jury, but also abusive behaviour by other members of the
family.

For evidence to be admissible as "important explanatory evidence", it
must be such that, without it, the magistrates or jury would find it
impossible or difficult to understand other evidence in the case.[85] If,
therefore, the facts or account to which the bad character evidence relates
are largely understandable without this additional explanation, then the
evidence should not be admitted. The explanation must also give the court
some substantial assistance in understanding the case as a whole; it will not
be enough for the evidence to assist the court to understand some trivial
piece of evidence.

(2) Substantial probative value

Evidence is of probative value, or relevant, to a matter in issue where it   **7–76**
helps to prove that issue one way or the other.[86] In respect of non-defen-
dants evidence of bad character is most likely to be relevant where a
question is raised about the credibility of a witness (as this is likely to affect
the court's assessment of the issue on which the witness is giving evidence).
It might, however, also be relevant to support a suggestion by the defendant
that another person was responsible for the offence.

Evidence which is of probative value is admissible if it meets an
"enhanced relevance test": s.100(1)(b).[87] That is, it must be of substantial
probative value and the matter in issue to which it relates must be of
substantial importance in the context of the case. Thus evidence which has
no real significance to an issue or is marginally relevant would not be

---

[83] Explanatory Notes to the Bill (Stationery Office, London, 2002), para.293.
[84] Law Commission Report, *Evidence of Bad Character in Criminal Proceedings*, No.273,
Cm. 5257, paras 9.41–42.
[85] Explanatory Notes to the Bill (Stationery Office, London, 2002), para.294.
[86] Explanatory Notes to the Bill (Stationery Office, London, 2002), para.295.
[87] Explanatory Notes to the Bill (Stationery Office, London, 2002), para.296.

admissible, nor would evidence that goes only to a trivial or minor issue in the case.

Section 100(3) directs the court to take into account a number of factors when assessing the probative value of a non-defendant's bad character. These include the nature and number of the events to which it relates and when those events occurred.[88] When considering evidence that is probative because of its similarity with evidence in the case (which might be the case if the defendant were suggesting that that other person was more likely to have committed the offence), the court is directed by s.100(3)(c) to consider the nature and extent of the similarities and dissimilarities. Similarly, where the evidence is being tendered to suggest a particular person was responsible, s.100(3)(d) requires the court to consider the extent to which the evidence shows or tends to show that the same person was responsible each time.

(3) Evidence in rebuttal

7–77 The rule at common law was that if the character of a witness was attacked, evidence could not be called in rebuttal to prove his good reputation. Thus in *Wood*,[89] the defendant, charged, with robbery, alleged that the prosecutor had committed an act of gross indecency against him. The prosecution applied to call evidence in rebuttal to prove that the prosecutor was a man of good general reputation. Morris J. did not allow the evidence to be admitted. If such evidence were allowed, it would obviously open a multiplicity of new issues and result in an unduly complicated trial. More recently, in *Beard*[90] the Court of Appeal quashed the conviction in a case where the prosecution had been permitted to call a social worker to give evidence that the complainant was an honest and truthful person to rebut the suggestion made by the defendant that the former was a compulsive liar.

(4) Complainants in proceedings for sexual offences

7–78 The limitations upon the cross-examination of complainants in cases of rape introduced by the Sexual Offences (Amendment) Act 1976 have now been extended to complainants in all proceedings for sexual offences by s.41 of the Youth Justice and Criminal Evidence Act 1999.[91]

Section 41 of the Youth Justice and Criminal Evidence Act 1999 provides that—

> "(1) if a person is charged with a sexual offence, then, except with the leave of the court,

---

[88] Explanatory Notes to the Bill (Stationery Office, London, 2002), para.297.
[89] [1969] 1 Q.B. 299, 305.
[90] [1998] Crim.L.R. 585.
[91] s.41 is unaffected by s.100 of the Criminal Justice Act 2003, above, paras 7–74 to 7–76.

(a) no evidence may be adduced, and

(b) no question may be asked in cross-examination by or on behalf of any accused at the trial, about any sexual behaviour of the complainant.

(2) The court may give leave in relation to any evidence or question only on an application made by or on behalf of an accused, and may not give such leave unless satisfied;

(a) that subsection (3) or (5) applies, and

(b) that a refusal of leave might have the result rendering unsafe a conclusion of the jury or (as the case may be) the court on any relevant issue in the case.

(3) This subsection applies if the evidence or question relates to a relevant issue in the case and either—

(a) that issue is not an issue of consent; or

(b) it is an issue of consent and the sexual behaviour of the complainant to which the evidence relates is alleged to have taken place at or about the same time as the event which is the subject matter of the charge against the accused; or

(c) it is an issue of consent and the sexual behaviour of the complainant to which the evidence or question relates is alleged to have been, in any respect, so similar—

(i) to any sexual behaviour of the complainant which (according to evidence adduced or to be adduced by or on behalf of the accused) took place as part of the event which is the subject matter of the charge against the accused, or

(ii) to any other sexual behaviour of the complainant which (according to such evidence) took place at or about the same time as that event,

that the similarity cannot be reasonably explained as a coincidence.

(4) For the purposes of subsection (3) no evidence or question shall be regarded as relating to an issue in the case if it appears to the court to be reasonable to assume that the purpose (or main purpose) for which it is to be adduced or asked is to establish or elicit material for impugning the credibility of the complainant as a witness.

(5) This subsection applies if the evidence or question—

(a) relates to any evidence adduced by the prosecution about any sexual behaviour of the complainant; and

(b) in the opinion of the court, would go no further than is necessary to enable the evidence adduced by the prosecution to be rebutted or explained by or on behalf of the accused.

(6) For the purposes of subsections (3) and (5) the evidence or question must relate to a specific instance (or specific instances) of alleged sexual behaviour on the part of the complainant (and accordingly nothing in those subsections is capable of in relation to the evidence or question to the extent that it does not so relate)."

7–79   Section 42 provides that a "relevant issue in the case" means any issue falling to be proved by the prosecution or defence in the trial; an "issue of consent" means any issue whether the complainant in fact consented to the conduct constituting the offence with which the accused is charged (and accordingly does not include any issue as to the belief of the accused that the complainant so consented); and "sexual behaviour" means any sexual behaviour or other sexual experience, whether or not involving any accused or other person, but excluding anything alleged to have taken place as part of the event which is the subject matter of the charge against the accused.

The effect of s.41 is that no evidence may be adduced at the trial and no question may be asked in cross-examination by the accused about any sexual behaviour of the complainant. This goes further than the 1976 Act which referred only to the sexual experience of the complainant with a person other than the defendant. Such cross-examination will only be undertaken with leave of the court and then only if the evidence in question either:

(a) does not relate to consent as an issue; or

(b) it does relate to consent and

(i)   refers to sexual behaviour by the complainant at or about the same time as the alleged sexual offence, or
(ii) is so similar to such sexual behaviour as to be unlikely to be a coincidence.

7–80   Questions which appear to the court to be intended to impugn the credibility of the complainant may not be asked. It should also be noted that the allegations of sexual behaviour must relate to specific incidents.

In debates in the House of Lords the Government spokesman said that the section provides a statutory framework for determining relevance. He pointed out that consensual sex does not mean consent to sex in general or consent with a particular person, it means consent to sex with a particular person on a particular occasion (HL Debs. March 23, 1999, col.1217).

Where there is an issue of consent arising from the complainant's sexual behaviour this refers to the complainant's consent in fact and not to any belief that the accused may have had as to consent: s.42(l)(b).

In *A (No.2)*[92] the House of Lords held that there was no need to answer the question whether the defendant's right to a fair trial under European Convention on Human Rights, Art.6 was contravened due to the exclusion of evidence under s.4(1). This was because evidence of a complainant's sexual history was admissible where the evidence was so relevant to the issue of consent that by not including it the fairness of the trial would be brought into question. The relevance of the previous sexual experience was a matter for the trial judge to determine. Section 41(3)(c) should be construed where necessary by having regard to the interpretative obligation under s.3 of the 1998 Act and giving consideration to the need to seek to protect a complainant from indignity and humiliating questions.

Furthermore, in *T&H*[93] the Court of Appeal held that s.41 must be given a purposive interpretation and questions concerned with a complainant's credibility were not automatically to be excluded because contrary to s.41. It is important to distinguish between questions "about" sexual behaviour and those which referred to previous sexual experiences but would not require verification of the truth of them.   **7–81**

Lord Woolf C.J. said in *Mokrecovas*[94] that the purpose of s.41 is to protect complainants from being subjected to unnecessary and embarrassing cross-examination and that s.41(2) does not require the court to give leave, it merely gives the court a discretion to grant leave, conditional on the court being satisfied of the two matters referred to (above). In the instant case the Court of Appeal upheld the trial judge's ruling that the complainant could not be cross examined about an allegation that she had had sexual intercourse with the defendant's brother two hours before the alleged rape since it would add nothing to the case for the defence and "would invade the privacy [of the complainant] and subject her to unnecessary, humiliating questions and accusations."

In *BT*[95] it was held that questions relating to a complainant's failure to complain about alleged sexual assaults or having told lies about such matters were not automatically excluded by s.41 since they were not "about" the sexual behaviour of the complainant but related to a failure to complain or false statements in the past. The court said that s.41 was not so incompatible with a fair trial given this interpretation.

Section 43 provides that an application for leave under s.41 shall be heard in private and in the absence of the complainant. Where such an application has been determined, the court must state in open court (but in the absence of the jury) its reasons for giving or refusing the leave, and, if it   **7–82**

---

[92] [2001] 2 W.L.R. 1546.
[93] [2002] 1 W.L.R. 632.
[94] [2002] 1 Cr.App.R. 20.
[95] [2002] 1 Cr.App.R. 254.

gives leave, the extent to which evidence may be adduced or questions asked in pursuance of the leave. If the proceedings are in a magistrate's court, the court must cause the reasons to be entered in the register of proceedings.

Section 43 also provides that Rules of Court may make provision requiring applications for leave to specify, in relation to each item of evidence or question to which they relate, particulars of the grounds on which it is asserted that leave should be given. Rules of Court may also enable the court to request a party to the proceedings to provide the court with information which it considers would assist it in determining an application for leave; and for the manner in which confidential or sensitive information is to be treated in connection with such an application, and in particular as to its being disclosed to, or withheld from, parties to the proceedings.

CHAPTER 8
Hearsay: 1. Hearsay Generally

1. INTRODUCTION

What is hearsay?

8–01

When A tells a court what B has told him, that evidence is called hearsay. At common law such statements were inadmissible to prove the truth of the matters stated in the statement. There were three reasons for the rule[1]:

(1) as second-hand evidence hearsay was likely to be less dependable;

(2) not being given on oath and not being subject to cross-examination it was more likely to be unreliable—and if admitted, it could not be tested so that it would be more difficult for the jury or the magistrates to assess;

(3) if the rule were relaxed there would be a proliferation of evidence directed to proving or negating hearsay.[2]

In civil proceedings the rule was relaxed by the Civil Evidence Act 1968. In criminal proceedings the rule, although criticised, in particular by the Law Commission Consultation Paper on Hearsay,[3] the Auld Report[4] and the Law Commission Report, "Evidence in Criminal Proceedings: Hearsay and Related Topics,"[5] continued, albeit with some statutory interventions, until the coming into force of the Criminal Justice Act 2003.[6] That Act substantially remodelled the law relating to hearsay. The topic of hearsay is dealt with in this chapter with the exception of Confessions, which is the subject of the next chapter.

---

[1] This statement is based on the Thirteenth Report of the Law Reform Committee, *Hearsay in Civil Proceedings*, Cmnd. 2964, para.7.
[2] Criminal Law Reform Committee, *op.cit.*
[3] "Evidence in Criminal Proceedings: Hearsay and Related Topics" (1995) Law Comm. Consultation Paper No.138. See further below, para.8–10.
[4] Review of the Criminal Courts of England and Wales, October 2001, Lord Chancellor's Department and HMSO. See further below, para.8–11.
[5] Law Commission Report No.245, June 1997, Lord Chancellor's Department and HMSO, para.8–10.
[6] Part 11, Chapter 2, ss.114–136.

8–02   Hearsay evidence distinguished from evidence of previous consistent statements

Hearsay evidence should be distinguished from evidence by a witness of what he himself said on a previous occasion which was inadmissible under the rule forbidding evidence of previous consistent statements (sometimes called the rule against narrative or self-serving statements), which is dealt with in Ch.12, below.

8–03   Hearsay distinguished from "original evidence"

Hearsay evidence should also be distinguished from "original evidence". Original evidence of a statement is admissible, not to prove that a statement is true, but to prove that it was *made*.

The following are examples of original evidence.

8–04   *(1) A statement as a fact in issue*

A statement may be admissible because it is itself a fact in issue, for example words of provocation when provocation is the defence to a murder charge or threatening abusive or insulting words in a case under s.4 of the Public Order Act 1986. Thus, in *Chapman*[7] the issue was whether or not a doctor had objected to a breath specimen being taken from the defendant, and it was held that a police officer could give evidence to that effect.

8–05   *(2) A statement in a document as circumstantial evidence*

A document may be admissible not to prove the truth of its contents but as circumstantial evidence tending to implicate the defendant in the offence charged. In *Lydon*[8] papers and a gun were found near the scene of a robbery. The papers bore the name Sean (the name of the defendant) and this was held to be a statement of fact, not an assertion as to the truth of the document. In *McIntosh*,[9] a concealed paper was found containing calculations of the price and weight of drugs (not in the defendant's handwriting). The Court of Appeal held that the paper was admissible as circumstantial evidence tending to connect the defendant with the crime. The Court said that before such a document was admitted the prosecution must prove that the defendant had some connection with it by means of knowledge, possession or control. In the instant case the necessary connection was established by the fact that the defendant had been occupying the premises for two months before his arrest. (It is submitted that in these circumstances a sufficient connection exists if a jury could properly draw from the evidence the inference that the defendant was implicated in the

---

[7] [1969] 2 Q.B. 436.
[8] (1987) 85 Cr.App.R. 221.
[9] [1992] Crim. L.R. 651.

186

offence charged. However, it will be for the jury to determine whether to accept the document. Accordingly, if a document is admitted the jury should be directed that they must be sure the necessary connection exists between the defendant and the document before accepting is as evidence.)

(3) Words in a statement may be relevant to an issue in the case 8–06

Such words may be admissible to prove that the defendant committed the offence. In *Ratten v R*,[10] a case of murder, a telephone operator was allowed to give evidence that a woman who had called shortly before the murder could only have been the deceased (the defendant denied that any such call had been made), and that she had been hysterical and asking for the police thus establishing that she was in a state of emotion or fear at the time. In *Woodhouse v Hall*[11] evidence by police officers that women working at a so-called sauna had offered the officers sexual services was admissible to show the sauna was actually a brothel: the relevance here was that the offers were made.

(4) A statement may explain the state of mind of the person to whom it is made 8–07

In *Subramaniam*,[12] a case under the Emergency Regulations in Malaya, it was held that words spoken to the defendants by terrorists who had captured him were admissible as possibly affording evidence of duress.

(5) A statement may explain the defendant's state of mind on some other occasion 8–08

Words spoken may be relevant and admissible in order to explain the defendant's state of mind on some other occasion. For example, in *Willis*[13] the defendant was the owner of a scrap metal business. He was charged with stealing a drum of cable. When interviewed by the police, he untruthfully said that he knew nothing about the drum. In order to explain why he had not told the truth, he sought to give evidence of what his foreman had told him about the cable. The trial judge refused to admit this evidence on the ground that it was hearsay. However, the Court of Criminal Appeal ruled that it was not hearsay and should have been admitted so that the defendant could explain why he lied to the police.

(6) A statement may explain the state of mind of the speaker 8–09

The fact that words were spoken may also explain the state of mind of the

---

[10] [1972] A.C. 378.
[11] (1981) 72 Cr.App.R. 39.
[12] [1956] 1 W.L.R. 965.
[13] (1960) 44 Cr.App.R. 32.

speaker. In *Process Church of the Final Judgment v Rupert Hart Davis Ltd* [14] —a libel action concerning a suggestion that the Process Church had exercised a malign influence over a convicted murderer called Manson and his "family"—the Court of Appeal held that evidence from a US lawyer of the beliefs of the murderer (his client) and the teachings of the Process Church (which he had studied) was admissible as original evidence. The factor here was the ability to compare the beliefs of Manson and his "family" with the philosophy and faith (of the Process Church). Thus the evidence by the lawyer was properly admitted and was not hearsay.

Proposals for reform

8–10 *(1) The Law Commission Consultation Paper (1995) and Report (1997)*

Both the Consultation Paper [15] and the Report [16] rejected the option of no change and called for reform.

The Report quoted [17] the summary of the criticisms of the rule set out in the Consultation Paper:

> "There is no unifying principle behind the rule and this gives rise to anomalies and confusion. Court time is wasted because of the lack of clarity and complicated nature of the rule. Cogent evidence may be kept from the court, however much it may exonerate or incriminate the accused, because the fact-finders are not trusted to treat untested evidence with the caution it deserves, but if hearsay is admitted there is nothing to prevent them from committing on it alone. Witnesses may be put off by interruptions in the course of their oral evidence. Whether evidence will be let in or not is unpredictable because of the reliance on judicial discretion."

However, both the Consultation Paper and the Report recommended retaining the hearsay rule as an exclusionary rule, albeit in a statutory form, to which there would be specified exceptions with an additional discretion to admit in the interests of natural justice. [18]

The writers of the Report also considered the possible effect of the European Convention of Human Rights [19] upon their proposals and decided that the safeguards they proposed would provide adequate safeguards

---

[14] *The Times*, January 29, 1975.
[15] "Evidence in Criminal Proceedings: Hearsay and Related Topics" (1995) Law Comm. Consultation Paper No.138. For criticism of the Commission's findings as insufficiently radical, see Zuckerman, "The Futility of Hearsay" [1996] Crim.L.R. 4 and Spencer, "Hearsay Reform: A Bridge Not Far Enough" [1996] Crim.L.R. 29.
[16] "Evidence in Criminal Proceedings: Hearsay and Related Topics", Cm. 3670.
[17] Report, para.5–58.
[18] *ibid.* para.1.30.
[19] Now incorporated into English law by the Human Rights Act 1998, Ch.13, below.

"unless and until the jurisprudence of Strasbourg demonstrates that out hearsay rules are incompatible with the Convention."[20]

(2) The Auld Report

8–11

The Auld Report[21] described the law as complicated, unprincipled, and arbitrary in the application of a number of the many exceptions. The Law Commission's proposals, although a useful improvement on the present law, did not go far enough and the subject should be looked at again by the body responsible for codification. Sir Robin Auld recommended[22] that consideration should be given to making hearsay generally *admissible* subject to the principle of best evidence rather than generally *inadmissible* subject to specified exceptions.

2. ADMISSIBILITY—GENERAL PRINCIPLE

Under the Criminal Justice Act 2003, Pt II, Chapter 2, s.114, hearsay evi-   8–12
dence is now admissible as a general rule provided certain conditions are met. This inclusionary approach was confirmed in Committee by the Parliamentary Under-Secretary of State: "Our general approach is that there should be automatic categories of admission and judicial discretion elsewhere. The exact terms are neither the Law Commission's [Evidence in Criminal Proceedings: Hearsay and Related Topics (1997) Law Comm. Paper No.245] nor Sir Robin Auld's."[23] Furthermore, Pt II and Sch.2 to the Criminal Justice Act 1988 which previously largely governed the admissibility of documentary evidence is repealed and replaced by Pt II, Chapter 2, of the 2003 Act: s.136(1).[24]

   Note that the provisions of the Criminal Justice Act 2003 discussed in this Chapter are expected, at the time of writing, to come into effect in April 2005. Before that date the fourth edition of this book should be referred to.

Hearsay admissible under conditions

8–13

By s.114(1) of the Criminal Justice Act 2003, in criminal proceedings,[25] a statement[26] not made in oral evidence[27] in the proceedings is admissible as evidence of any matter stated if, and only if:

---

[20] Law Commission Report, para.5.41.
[21] Review of the Criminal Courts of England and Wales, October 2001, Lord Chancellor's Department and HMSO.
[22] Recommendations 258–259.
[23] HC Standing Committee B. *Hansard*, Col. No.603.
[24] See Ch.11 of the fourth edition of this work for discussion of the 1988 Act.
[25] This "means criminal proceedings in relations to which the strict rules of evidence apply": s.134.
[26] "a statement ... matter stated ...": see para.8–14, below.
[27] This "includes evidence which, by reason of a defect of speech or hearing, a person called as a witness gives in writing or in signs or by way of any device": s.134.

(a)   it is admissible under either Chapter 2 of the Criminal Justice Act 2003 or under any other statutory provision[28];

(b)   it is admissible under any rule of law preserved by s.118 of the Criminal Justice Act 2003[29];

(c)   all parties to the proceedings agree to the evidence being admissible; or[30]

(d)   the court is satisfied that it is in the interests of justice for it to be admissible.[31]

The effect of the section is thus to render admissible out-of-court statements which are not otherwise admissible so long as they are cogent and reliable.[32] The section applies not just to first-hand hearsay but to multiple hearsay.[33]

In addition, subs.(3) of s.114 permits the exclusion of statements even if they fulfil the requirements of the section.[34] For example, confessions must meet the additional requirements of the Police and Criminal Evidence Act 1984 before admission.[35]

8–14   Statements ... Matters stated

Section 115[36] provides, by subs.(1), that—

"In this Chapter references to a statement or a matter stated are to be read as follows.

(2) A statement is any representation of fact or opinion made by a person by whatever means; and it includes a representation made in a sketch, photofit or other pictorial form.

(3) A matter stated is one to which this Chapter applies if (and only if) the purpose, or one of the purposes, of making the statement appears to the court to have been—

(a)   to cause another person to believe in the matter, or

---

[28] This "means any provision contained in, or in a instrument made under, this or any other Act, including any Act passed after this Act": *ibid.*

[29] Below, para.8–38.

[30] "Or" applies equally to paras (a) and (b) of the subsection: Under-Secretary of State, HC Standing Committee B, *Hansard*, Col. No.603, responding to drafting criticisms.

[31] In Committee the Minister said, "We expect the trial judge to give his reason for admitting evidence under [section] 90(1)(d)": HC Standing Committee B, *Hansard*, Col. No.619.

[32] As to factors to which the court must have regard, see para.8–15, below.

[33] Explanatory Notes to the Criminal Justice Bill, November 21, 2002, para.326. As to the provisions relating to multiple hearsay, see para.8–66, below.

[34] *ibid.*, para.329.

[35] *ibid.* For confessions, see Ch. 9, below.

[36] Taken from the Law Commission's Draft Bill on Hearsay: Law Commission Report No.245, June 1997, Lord Chancellor's Department and HMSO.

> (b) to cause another person to act or a machine to operate on the basis that the matter is as stated."

Section 115 thus permits the admission of hearsay evidence where the maker does not *intend* to communicate any evidence at all.[37] Previously such statements were inadmissible at common law.[38] It also permits evidence of a failure to record an event (sometimes known as negative hearsay) to be admitted if it was the purpose of the person who failed to record the event to cause anyone to believe that the event did not occur.[39]

The definition in subs.(2) of s.115 preserves the present position whereby statements which are not based on human input fall outside the ambit of the hearsay rule. Tapes, films or photographs which directly record the commission of a offence and documents produced by machines which automatically record a process or event or perform calculations are not admissible as hearsay.[40]

Hearsay admitted by leave of the court   8–15

When the court gives leave for hearsay evidence to be admitted under s.114(1) of the Criminal Justice Act 2003 it must, by s.114(2), have regard to the following factors:

(1) the probative value of the statement (assuming it to be true) in relation to a matter in issue in the proceedings, or how valuable it is for the understanding of other evidence in the case;

(2) what other evidence has been, or can be, given on the matter or evidence mentioned in paragraph (1);

(3) how important the matter or evidence mentioned in paragraph (1) is in the context of the case as a whole;

(4) the circumstances in which the statement was made;

(5) how reliable the maker of the statement appears to be;

(6) how reliable the evidence of the making of the statement appears to be;

(7) whether oral evidence of the matter stated can be given and, if not, why it cannot;

(8) the amount of difficulty involved in challenging the statement;

---

[37] The Minister pointed out that opinion evidence will only be admitted if it is admissible under the rules relating to opinion evidence: HC Standing Committee B, *Hansard*, Col. No.621.
[38] *ibid.*, para.331.
[39] *ibid.*, para.332.
[40] *ibid.* They are, however, admissible as real evidence as to which see Ch.2, above.

(9)   the extent to which that difficulty would be likely to prejudice the party facing it.

Thus, the court must take into account all these factors in deciding whether to admit the evidence. It must begin by considering the statement itself in the circumstances of the case (and assuming the statement to be true), what is its probative value and its significance to the case. Plainly, insignificant evidence of little probative value should be excluded. However, the greater the probative value, the more carefully it must be considered. If the statement has the necessary significance and probative value, the court must consider the circumstances of the making of the statement and its reliability. It is submitted that a cautious approach to excluding evidence on this ground should be taken. If the circumstances or the statement itself clearly indicate that the statement is, or may be, unreliable, then the court should not admit it. But, in the absence of clear indications, the court is not obliged to conduct a detached inquiry (or hold a *voir dire*) to determine whether there is the possibility of such indications. It may be preferable for the court then to admit the evidence, and if later evidence shows it to be, or may be, unreliable, to exclude the evidence or direct the jury to do so.

Finally, once the court has considered the probative value and reliability of the statement, it must consider whether the evidence can be given, alternatively, as oral evidence (and, therefore, subject to cross-examination). It must then consider the amount of difficulty the opposing party would have in challenging the statement and the prejudice in doing so. The means of doing so might include the cross-examination of other witnesses, putting the credibility of the maker in issue, or calling evidence to challenge the statement. However, the court must consider how practical these means are in the particular case.

3. The Principal Categories of Admissibility

8–16   The principal categories of admissibility are:

(1)   Where a witness is unavailable (paras 8–17 to 8–29, below).

(2)   Business and other documents (paras 8–30 to 8–37, below).

(3)   Where evidence was already admissible at common law (paras 8–38 to 8–65, below).

(4)   Inconsistent statements (paras 21–09 *et seq*, below).

(5)   Other previous statements (Ch.20, below).

A. When hearsay may be admitted

(1) Where a witness is unavailable
8–17

Section 116(1) of the Criminal Justice Act 2003 provides, by subs.(1), that:

> "In criminal proceedings a statement not made in oral evidence in the proceedings is admissible as evidence of any matter stated if—
>
> (a) oral evidence given in the proceedings by the person who made the statement would be admissible as evidence of that matter.
> (b) the person who made the statement (the relevant person) is identified to the court's satisfaction, and
> (c) any of the five conditions mentioned in subsection (2) is satisfied."

The circumstances in which a witness is held to be unavailable are set out in subs.(2)(a)–(e) and are dealt with in this book at the following paragraphs:

(a) he is dead (para.8–21, below);

(b) he is unfit to give evidence through his bodily or mental condition (para.8–22, below);

(c) he is outside the UK and it is not reasonably practicable to secure his attendance (paras 8–23 to 8–24, below);

(d) he cannot be found (para.8–25, below);

(e) he does not give evidence through fear (paras 8–26 to 8–29, below).

The provisions are available to the prosecution and the defence[41] (and apply to both oral and documentary evidence, *i.e.* conversations and comments as well as written statements).

The preliminary requirements set out in subs.(1) should be noted. The evidence is only admissible (a) if it would have been admissible as oral evidence[42] (this will ensure that otherwise inadmissible evidence is not admitted under the section); and (b) the person who made the statement is identified to the court's satisfaction.[43] The party seeking to have the evidence admitted will therefore have to comply with these two preliminary requirements. This may be done by submissions, based on the statements or

8–18

---

[41] Explanatory Notes to the Criminal Justice Bill, November 21, 2002, para.333.
[42] s.116(1)(a)
[43] s.116(1)(b).

other material in the case. In some cases, it may be necessary to hold a trial-within-a-trial (see below, para.8–19).

8–19   Section 116 of the Criminal Justice Act 2003 replaces s.23 of the Criminal Justice Act 1988 which applied only to statements in documents. However, it is submitted, a number of decisions under that Act and other legislation are still relevant and applicable to the 2003 Act.

The conditions laid down by the legislation for hearsay to be admitted must be proved to the court's satisfaction. Accordingly, the party seeking to adduce evidence must lay a foundation for doing so. In *Nicholls*[44] the Court of Appeal said that a sufficient foundation must be laid for the judge to draw a reasonable inference to satisfy himself that the requirements of the section had been met. The judge may need to hold a trial-within-a-trial in order to do so. If the prosecution is seeking to adduce the evidence, the criminal standard of proof applies: they must satisfy the court beyond reasonable doubt by admissible evidence that the requirements are met.[45] On the other hand, if the defence is seeking to have a statement admitted under the section, the civil standard applies, *i.e.* the court must be satisfied on the balance of probabilities.[46] In *Case*,[47] the defendant was charged with the theft of a purse from a Portuguese tourist. At the trial, witness statements made by the victim and another tourist were admitted under s.23. The Court of Appeal held that the statements had been wrongly admitted because no evidential basis had been established to show (a) that the witnesses were outside the UK and (b) that it had not been reasonably practicable for them to attend.[48] On the other hand, it was held that there was no general principle that it was unfair to admit evidence under s.23 when the defendant would be forced to go into the witness-box to controvert it[49]; or where the witness whose statement was read was the sole identifying witness and there was no other evidence against the defendant.[50]

8–20   **Deliberate unavailability.**   By s.116(5)—

"A condition set out in any paragraph of subsection (2) which is in fact satisfied is to be treated as not satisfied if it is shown that the circumstances described in that paragraph are caused—

(a)   by the person in support of whose case it is sought to give the statement in evidence, or

---

[44] (1976) 63 Cr.App.R. 187, decided under the Criminal Evidence Act 1965 but the principle still applies.
[45] *Minors* [1989] 1 W.L.R. 441.
[46] *Mattey* [1995] 2 Cr.App.R. 409.
[47] [1991] Crim. L.R. 192.
[48] See also *Acton JJ.*, below, at 104, *per* Watkins L.J.
[49] *Moore* [1992] Crim.L.R. 882.
[50] *Dragic* [1996] 2 Cr.App.R. 232.

(b) by a person acting on his behalf,

in order to prevent the relevant person giving oral evidence in the proceedings (whether at all or in connection with the subject matter of the statement)."

This provision is aimed at those who seek to manufacture pretexts for witnesses not to appear in court and thereby avoid potentially embarrassing cross-examination. It will apply to witnesses for both cross-examination and defence. It will be for the party opposing admission to establish that this has happened.[51] It is submitted that if there is a real possibility of this having occurred, the court should not admit the evidence.

In any event, the court retains the discretion under s.78 of the Police and Criminal Act 1984 to exclude unfair evidence and at common law to exclude prejudicial evidence.[52]

(a) The witness is dead: s.116(2)(a). The party seeking to adduce the statement of a dead witness must establish the fact of death. This can usually be done by tendering a death certificate or calling a witness (for example a police officer) to prove the circumstances of death. Much will depend on the circumstances of the case. Provided the court is satisfied that the witness is dead, the statement is admissible.

    8–21

The Court of Appeal held in *McGillivray*[53] that an unsigned statement made by a deceased person to the police was admissible under s.23 provided that the deceased had clearly acknowledged by speech or otherwise that the statement was accurate. In that case the defendant was charged with murder: he had poured petrol over the deceased and set him on fire. Before he died, the victim made a statement to a police officer in hospital. A nurse said that the statement had been read back to the victim: the latter confirmed its accuracy, but could not sign it because his hands were badly burnt and heavily bandaged. The Court of Appeal held that the statement was admissible since the deceased had indicated that it was accurate but was prevented by physical disability from signing it.

An ambiguity in a statement by a deceased person where there is no firm ground on which a jury can resolve the ambiguity will render such a statement inadmissible.[54]

The direction which a judge should give when summing up a case when a deceased person's statement is admitted is at the judge's discretion. Each

---

[51] Explanatory Notes to the Criminal Justice Bill. November 21, 2002, para.337.
[52] *ibid.*, para.338.
[53] (1993) 97 Cr.App.R. 232. The statement in this case was written. A verbal statement similarly indicated by the deceased to be accurate would now be admissible.
[54] JP [1999] Crim. L.R. 232 relating to a statement in a document.

case requires its own directions which should provide adequate warning to ensure that justice is achieved.[55]

8-22   **(b) The witness "is unfit to be a witness because of his bodily or mental condition": s.116(2)(b).**   A party seeking to adduce the statement of a witness unfit to give evidence because of his bodily or mental condition must establish that condition by way of evidence to show that the condition exists. Generally this is done by way of a medical report setting out the condition and explaining why it renders the witness unfit. A mere certificate will not suffice.

A further example is to be found in video evidence. In D^{56} video evidence by a complainant, an 81-year-old woman suffering from Alzheimer's Disease, as to indecent assault and attempted rape was held admissible: the interview had taken place within a few days of the incident; the judge had applied the test under s.53 of the Youth Justice and Criminal Evidence Act 1999 as to whether the witness had been able to understand the questions and give comprehensible answers; the interests of the complainant and the defendant had been balanced so no breach of Art.6(3)(d) of the European Convention had occurred (see para.13–23, below).

8-23   **(c) The witness "is outside the United Kingdom and it is not reasonably practicable to secure his attendance": s.116(2)(c).**   A party seeking to adduce a statement under this heading must adduce evidence both that the witness is outside the country and that it is not reasonably practical to secure his attendance at court. The first requirement will usually not be difficult to prove. For instance, it will usually appear from the statements and be undisputed that the witness is resident abroad. The second requirement may present more difficulties. In an age of air travel or video link evidence, it may be relatively simple to get a witness's evidence before the court. However, there may be cost implications. All will depend on the circumstances.

This paragraph replaces para.(b)(i)(ii) of s.23(2) of the Criminal Justice Act 1988. There are a number of decisions under the previous legislation. It is submitted that they still apply. For instance, it has been held that in determining whether it is reasonably practicable to secure the attendance of a witness outside the UK, the court must consider all the circumstances of the case. In $Hurst^{57}$ the Court of Appeal said that the words "reasonable practicability" involve a consideration of the normal steps which would be taken to secure the attendance of a witness; and the qualification of reasonableness includes other circumstances such as the costs and steps which may be available to secure the witness's attendance. The normal steps are

---

[55] *Hardwick, The Times,* February 28, 2001.
[56] [2001] 2 Cr.App.R. 601.
[57] [1995] 1 Cr.App.R. 82, 92.

the reasonable steps which a party would take, having regard to the means and resources available.[58]

Practicability is not to be confused with "physical possibility". The fact that it is physically possible for a witness to attend does not mean that it is practicable for him or her to do so.[59] Other factors must be taken into account. In *Castillo*[60] the Court of Appeal gave examples of these factors: the importance of the evidence, prejudice to the defence, and the expense and inconvenience occasioned by the witness's attendance.

Three illustrations may be given of decisions under the subsection. In **8–24** *Bray*[61] a witness had gone to Korea seven months before the trial, but had not told the prosecution that he was going. As a result, nothing had been done to secure his attendance. The Court of Appeal held that whether it is reasonable or not is to be examined against the whole background of the case and not merely at the time when the trial begins and, accordingly, the prosecution had to shown that it was not reasonably practicable to secure the witness's attendance. On the other hand in *French and Gowhar*[62] the defendants were charged with robbery of a foreign student. The student came from Mexico to give evidence at the first trial at which the jury was discharged. He did not attend the second trial. The trial judge allowed two of his statements to be read. The Court of Appeal said that the right approach was to consider the matter as at the date of the application and see whether at that date it was reasonably practicable to secure the witness's attendance. The Court held that in the instant case it was not reasonably practicable to do so.

In *Hurst*[63] the Court of Appeal said that the fact that a witness could not appear as her husband had lost his job was one of the factors to be taken into account: the fact that (a) means were available to reimburse her for the cost of air travel and hotel expenses and (b) the witness had stated her intention of attending did not necessarily determine the question, since it was for the defence (in the instant case) to satisfy the judge of the requirements; and they had failed to do so.

The court may often have to consider whether the prosecution have explored all the avenues open to them to secure the witness's attendance. In *Gonzales*[64] the Court of Appeal held that the trial judge's conclusion that it was not reasonably practicable to secure the attendance of two booking

---

[58] *Maloney* [1994] Crim.L.R. 525.

[59] [1996] 1 Cr.App.R. 438.

[60] Above.

[61] (1989) 88 Cr.App.R. 354. (*Bray* was decided under s.68 of PACE but is applicable under s.116(2)(c).)

[62] (1993) 97 Cr.App.R. 421. In *Jiminez-Pael* (1994) Cr.App.R. 239 a letter written by a consular official of a foreign embassy in the UK (who was unwilling to give evidence) was held to be inadmissible. The Court of Appeal rejected a submission that because she was immune to process the official was, in effect, at all times outside the UK.

[63] Above.

[64] (1993) 96 Cr.App.R. 399.

clerks from Bogota could not be sustained: the prosecution could have offered to pay their fares, approached higher management in their company, or got in touch with the British Embassy.

In deciding whether the requirements of the section have in fact been met, the court will have to find what steps (if any) have been taken to secure the witness's attendance and then decide whether in all the circumstances it is reasonably practicable, for the party seeking to rely on the witness, to secure his or her attendance. If it is reasonably practicable to secure his attendance the statement must be excluded; if not, it is admissible, subject to the discretion to exclude (para.8–20, above). The Court of Appeal has said that it will not lightly interfere with a decision of fact by a judge on this topic.[65]

8–25   **(d) The witness "cannot be found although such steps as is reasonably practicable to take to find him have been taken": s.116(2)(d).**   The party seeking to adduce the statement of a witness in these circumstances must prove that:

(a)   the witness cannot be found;

(b)   such steps as are reasonably practicable to take to find him, have been taken.

This provision is aimed at ensuring that the evidence of a witness who has disappeared is not lost to the court which might result in injustice. It will require the party to provide material or call witnesses to establish the fact that the witness cannot be found and to set out the steps which have been taken to find him. What is "reasonably practicable" will depend on the particular circumstances. However, considerations such as those in the case of the witness abroad (para.8–23, above) may be applicable, adapted to the situation of the witness who has disappeared. Thus, it may be necessary to establish where the witness was last seen and in what circumstances, and what steps have been taken to trace him.

8–26   **(e) The witness does not give evidence through fear: s.116(2)(e).**   Section 116(2)(e) provides that hearsay evidence is admissible if—

"Through fear the [witness] does not give (or does not continue to give) oral evidence in the proceedings, either at all or in connection with the subject matter of the statement, and the court gives leave for the statement to be given in evidence."

---

[65] *Castillo* [1996] 1 Cr.App.R. 438, 443, decided under CJA 1988, s.23.

By subs.(3) " 'fear' is to be widely construed and (for example) includes fear of the death or injury of another person or of financial loss."

By subs.(4) leave may only be given under this subsection—

"if the court considers that the statement ought to be admitted in the interests of justice, having regard—

    (a) to the statement's contents,

    (b) to any risk that its admission or exclusion will result in unfairness to any party to the proceedings (and in particular to how difficult it will be to challenge the statement if the relevant person does not give oral evidence),

    (c) in appropriate cases, to the fact that a direction under section 19 of the Youth Justice and Criminal Evidence Act 1999 (c.23) (special measures for the giving of evidence by fearful witnesses etc.[66]) could be made in relation to the relevant person, and

    (d) to any other relevant circumstances."

This provision replaces s.23(3) of the Criminal Justice Act 1988[67] with three important differences.   **8–27**

The first is that under the 1988 Act the statement had to have been given "to a police officer or some other person charged with the duty of investigating offences or charging offenders".[68] This is not required by the new legislation.[69]

The second is that there is no reference to the witness being "kept out of the way" (a phrase which added little and could cause confusion).

The third is the wider construction to be given to the word "fear" (subs.(3), above, para.8–26).[70]

---

[66] As to which see paras 19–12 to 19–14, 19–15 *et seq.* below.

[67] The purpose of s.23(3) was to widen the provisions of s.13(3) of the Criminal Justice Act 1925 which related to witnesses "kept out of the way by means of the procurement of the accused or on his behalf" (a matter often difficult to establish: Munday, "Hostile Witnesses and the Admission of Witness Statements under section 23 of the Criminal Justice Act 1988" [1991] Crim.L.R. 349, 351 (mentioned in *Ashford Magistrates' Court* (1993) 96 Cr.App.R. 92 at 97)). It may be noted that under s.13(3) it was held at first instance that the prosecution must prove beyond reasonable doubt by admissible evidence that the witness has been kept out of the way on the defendant's behalf: *O'Laughlin and McLaughlin* (1987) 85 Cr.App.R. 157 (Kenneth Jones J.).

[68] Criminal Justice Act 1988, s.23(3)(a)

[69] The Minister referred (HC Standing Committee B, *Hansard*, Col. No.630) to the Law Commission's conclusion that "the fact that a statement was not made to a police officer should not necessarily make it inadmissible." The Minister believed that subs.(4), above, para.8–26, would be an adequate safeguard.

[70] The Minister, above, cols 634, 635, said that the inclusion of financial loss in the definition of fear was based on the Law Commission recommendation that the requirements in subs.(4) that such hearsay only be admitted in the interests of justice was an "adequate safeguard against any trivialisation of the proposition".

8–28   *Fear: cases under the previous legislation.*   There were a number of cases under the Criminal Justice Act 1988, s.23(3). It is submitted that they are still applicable.

Before admitting a witness's statement on the ground that the witness does not give oral evidence through fear, the following should be noted:

(a)   The court must be satisfied that the witness is in fear in relation to the offence or of something said or done subsequently relating to it and the possibility of the witness's giving evidence.[71] (*Per contra*, if the fear is not connected to the offence, for example fear of giving evidence).

(b)   It does not have to proved that something has occurred *since* the commission of the offence to put the witness in fear so as to keep him out of the way: the words of the provision are to be read disjunctively.[72]

(c)   The fact that a witness goes into the witness-box and answers some questions does not prevent the section taking effect: the provision means that the witness has not given evidence of significant relevance.[73] Thus, in *Waters*[74] the victim gave a statement to the police, stating that he and his family would be in danger if he gave evidence and that he would be unwilling to do so. However, he attended the trial and gave evidence, but said that he could not identify the attacker because he could not remember what happened. The judge permitted his statement to the admitted on the ground that he had ceased to give evidence through fear. The Court of Appeal held that the judge was entitled to conclude that the witness had not given evidence through fear and that the section applied because there was still relevant evidence to give at the time the section was invoked.

(d)   The court is not obliged to hear evidence that a witness is in fear but may come to that conclusion by observing the witness in the witness-box.[75] If the court does hear evidence, the defence are entitled to cross-examine the witnesses relied on by the prosecution.[76]

(e)   The fact that a witness does not give evidence through fear may be

---

[71] *Acton JJ. Ex p. McMullen* (1991) 92 Cr.App.R. 98. In *Rutherford* [1998] Crim.L.R. 490 the Court of Appeal said that characterisation of s.23(3) was not intended to be conclusive and all-embracing: fear of what (and whether it is relevant) is a matter for the court's consideration.
[72] *ibid.*, at 105, *per* Watkins L.J.
[73] *Ashford Magistrates' Court Ex p. Hilden* (1993) 96 Cr.App.R. 92.
[74] [1997] Crim.L.R. 823.
[75] *Ashford Magistrates Court Ex p. Hilden*, above.
[76] *Walker* [1998] Crim.L.R. 211, and now the provisions of this section.

proved by hearsay evidence.[77] It was held under the 1988 Act that oral evidence of fear was necessary and that a statement made to the Irish Garda was held not be sufficient to meet the requirements of s.29.[78] However, the same will not necessarily be the case under s.116(2)(e): there must be *some* evidence by a witness with experience of the case and the state of mind of the fearful witness. This evidence will often necessarily be hearsay. In *Belmarsh M.C. Ex p. Gilligan*[79] the Divisional Court held that a statement by a witness himself that he was in fear was not admissible to prove that he was in fear and that evidence such as oral evidence of a police officer was required. On the other hand, in *Greer*[80] the Court of Appeal held that there was no reason, either as a matter of practice or on the wording of the statute why a witness should not give evidence of his own fear. It is submitted that the decision in *Greer* is to be preferred. Who better to give evidence than the witness himself or herself? It is then for the court to decide whether to accept the evidence or reject it.

(f) In *Denton*[81] it was held that a judge should provide valid reasons for allowing statements of witnesses to be admitted on the grounds that they were in fear: however, failure to do so was not necessarily fatal to a conviction, provided that it was shown that the judge had properly exercised his discretion. In *A*[82] it was held that a stringent approach should be adopted to the asserted absence of a witness through fear, particularly if the evidence was critical to the outcome of the case: the fear should be assessed by reference to the time at which the witness was expected to give evidence. Before granting an application the court should be informed of any efforts made to persuade the witness to attend or to alleviate his or her fears.

Difficulties may arise in the following circumstances. After a statement **8–29** has been read under s.116 the jury may ask why the witness was not called to give evidence. To tell it that the witness did not give evidence through fear would obviously be extremely prejudicial and, as a result, should be avoided. On the other hand, no set answer avoiding prejudice can be suggested. Since circumstances will vary, it may be better to tell the jury

[77] *Neill v Antrim M.C.* (1993) 97 Cr.App.R. 121; *Fairfax* [1995] Crim.L.R. 949.
[78] [1998] 1 Cr.App.R. 14.
[79] *Belmarsh M.C. Ex p. Gilligan* [1998] 1 Cr.App.R. 14.
[80] [1998] Crim.L.R. 572. In *Greer* the court said that this was a matter for the judge's judgment and, provided that he had correctly reviewed the relevant matters, the court would be reluctant to go behind it.
[81] [2001] 1 Cr.App.R. 227.
[82] *The Times*, July 6, 2001.

that the judge cannot answer the question and to add a warning that it should not speculate as to the reason.

Cases decided under s.23 of the 1988 Act give an idea of the difficulties. In *Churchill*[83] the judge's answer to the jury's question contained observations to the effect that, while precise reasons could not be given, they involved nothing to the witness's detriment. The Court of Appeal held that this was not a fair way to deal with the question since it seemed to recommend the witness and suggested her failure to give evidence may have been a matter of discredit to the defendant. The court said that the judge should have told the jury that he could not answer its question. (For a direction to the jury after a statement has been read, see para.8–74 below). In *Jennings*[84] the Court of Appeal said that any investigation as to the reasons why a witness is unwilling to give evidence should be conducted in the absence of the jury, and an innocuous form of words used to explain his absence from the witness-box.

8–30   *(2) Business and other documents*

Section 117(1) of the Criminal Justice Act 2003 makes admissible as evidence in criminal proceedings[85] a statement[86] contained in a document[87] of any matter stated[88] if oral evidence[89] given in the proceedings would be admissible as evidence of that matter.

Documents admitted under subs.(1) must fulfil the requirements of subs.(2), that is, they must have been created or received in the course of a trade, business, etc. (as to which see paras 8–31 to 8–32, below). Moreover, where such documents were prepared for criminal proceedings or a criminal investigation, additional requirements are laid down by subss.(4) and (5) (as to which see paras 8–33 to 8–34, below).

The section replaces s.24 of the Criminal Justice Act 1988. It should be noted, however, that the heading to s.117 of the 2003 Act is "Business and other documents", a clearer and modern version of s.24 of the 1988 Act's "Business etc. documents".

---

[83] [1993] Crim.L.R. 285.
[84] [1995] Crim.L.R. 810.
[85] "Criminal proceedings" means "criminal proceedings in relation to which the strict rules of evidence apply": s.134.
[86] "A statement is any representation of fact or opinion made by a person by whatever means; and it includes a representation made in a sketch, photofit or other pictorial form": s.115(2).
[87] "Document" means "anything in which information of any description is recorded": s.134.
[88] "A matter stated is one to which this Chapter [*i.e.* Chapter Two of the Act] applies if (and only if) the purpose, or one of the purposes, of making the statement appears to the court to have been (a) to cause another person to believe in the matter; or (b) to cause another person to act or a machine to operate on the basis that the matter is as stated": s.115(3).
[89] "Includes evidence which, by reason of a defect of speech or hearing, a person called as a witness gives in writing or by signs or by way of any device": s.134.

(a) Documents created, etc: in the course of a trade, business, etc.: 8–31
s.117(2)(3). Subsection (2) provides that "the document, or the part
containing the statement, must have been created or received by a person in
the course of a trade, business, profession or other occupation, or as the
holder of a paid or unpaid office" (subs.(2)(a)). The "person who supplied
the information contained in the statement (the relevant person) [...] had or
may reasonably supposed to have had personal knowledge of the matters
dealt with" (subs.(2)(b)). "Each person (if any) through whom the information was supplied from the relevant person to the person [who created or
received the document must have] received the information in the course of
a trade, business, profession or other occupation, or as the holder of a paid
or unpaid office" (subs.(2)(c)).

The person who created or received the document which the statement is
in may be the same person as whoever supplied the information which is in
the statement (subs.(3)).

Previous case law. Under the previous legislation[90] there were 8–32
numerous decisions some of which, it is submitted, may be of assistance in
relation to the interpretation of s.117.

Practically all business records, correspondence and files are admissible.
Similar documents connected with other organisations such as hospitals,
clubs and societies are also admissible. Thus, a diary found on the counter
in business premises and containing entries relating to stock received has
been held to be admissible[91]; and a Greek customs border log was assumed
to be admissible.[92] Similarly, a custody log has been found admissible.[93]
But an improperly obtained confession recorded in a file of business
documents would not be admissible, for example an employee's confession
to his employer made in oppressive circumstances. Nor would evidence
excluded by any other rule of evidence.

In *Minors*[94] the court held that the requirement of personal knowledge
could, where computer records were concerned, be supplied by circumstantial evidence of the usual habit or routine regarding the use of the
computer.

The party seeking to rely on the section must satisfy the court that the
requirements of the section have been met. However, the court may be able
to draw inferences from the document itself which will suffice to meet these
requirements. The Court of Appeal in *Foxley*[95] said that it was the purpose

---

[90] Criminal Evidence Act 1965, superseded by s.68 of the Police and Criminal Evidence Act
1984, in turn superseded by s.24 of the Criminal Justice Act 1988.
[91] *Ilyas and Knight* [1996] Crim.L.R. 810.
[92] *Dyer* [1997] Crim.L.R. 442, although the Court of Appeal did say that that particular log
should not have been admitted because it was ambiguous and not sufficiently likely to be
authentic.
[93] *Hogan* [1997] Crim.L.R. 349.
[94] [1989] 1 W.L.R. 441.
[95] [1995] 2 Cr.App.R. 523.

of the section that the document should speak for itself, and Parliament's intention was that the court could draw such inferences as it thought proper from documents and the method by which they had been produced before the court: that intention would be defeated if oral evidence was required in every case from the creator or keeper of the document.

If the prosecution seeks to rely on the section, the criminal standard of proof will apply. The judge may need to hold a trial-within-a-trial and (unless admissions are made or statements read by agreement) hear oral evidence and satisfy himself beyond reasonable doubt before admitting the statement. Thus, Steyn J., giving the judgment of the Court to Appeal in *Minors*,[96] said that "the foundation requirements of [the section] will also not be susceptible of proof by certificate."

But this does not apply in every case: there must be something that substantiates the document as evidence. In *Jenkins and Starling*[97] a document of which it was not possible to say how it had been made or discovered and as to which there was no witness who had made it or who knew of its contents was held to be inadmissible.

8–33   **(b) Documents prepared for the purposes of criminal proceedings or a criminal investigation: s.117(4)(5).**   These subsections apply to documents "prepared for the purposes of pending or contemplated criminal proceedings or for a criminal investigation" (subs.(4)(a)).

There are two exceptions (subs.(4)(b)). First, documents prepared pursuant to a request under s.7 of the Crime (International Co-operation) Act 2003, as to which see para.8–83, below. Secondly, a document prepared in accordance with an order under para.6 of Sch.13 to the Criminal Justice Act 1988. Both of these relate to overseas evidence. The subsections do not apply to either of these types of document.

8–34   *Further requirements for documents prepared for criminal proceedings or a criminal investigation.*   Subsection (5) of s.117 enacts two further requirements for documents of this nature. The document must meet either one or other of the requirements.

(1) By subs.(5)(a) the document must fulfil the conditions laid down in s.116(2) as follows:

(a) he is dead (para.8–21, above);

(a) he is unfit to give evidence through his bodily or mental condition (para.8–22, above);

(c) he is outside the UK and it is not reasonably practicable to secure his attendance (paras 8–23 to 8–24, above);

---

[96] [1989] 1 W.L.R. 441 at 447.
[97] [2003] Crim.L.R. 107.

     (d) he cannot be found (para.8–25, above);

     (e) he does not give evidence through fear (paras 8–26 to 8–29, above).

  (2) Alternatively, by subs.(5)(b)), "the relevant person cannot reasonably be expected to have any recollection of the matters dealt with in the statement (having regard to the length of time and all other circumstances)." In determining whether this requirement has been met, the court will have to consider the circumstances in which the statement was made, the nature of the events to which it relates and the length of time which has elapsed since the witness made it, and then decide whether the witness would reasonably be expected to have any recollection of the matters dealt with.

A document which does not meet these requirements is inadmissible if it   **8–35** is sought to admit it as a document prepared for criminal proceedings, etc. *Bedi*,[98] decided under the previous legislation[99] but still relevant, illustrates the proposition.

The defendants in that case were charged with offences connected with the making of false sales vouchers by the use of lost and stolen credit cards. The prosecution was permitted to adduce evidence of bank reports of lost and stolen credit cards. These reports had been made and signed by employees of the bank at a clearing office. The Court of Appeal held that the reports were business documents but that the reports were not made for the purpose of criminal proceedings but for the bank's own business. The court said that the question whether a statement was prepared for the purpose of criminal proceedings or investigation can only be determined by the judge as a matter of fact in the light of the whole of the circumstances in which the statement was made. (Before such a statement is admitted, it will also have to be shown that it is in the interests of justice to do so: s.114(1)(d), para.8–13).

The question whether the maker of a statement can reasonably be expected to have any recollection of matters dealt within it is not merely to be examined at the moment the trial opens but against the whole background of the case.[1] The fact that the maker of a statement retains a recollection of some of the matters dealt with in it does not prevent part of the statement being admitted; part of a document may be treated as an independent statement for the purposes of the section.[2]

Under s.126 of the Act, s.78 of the 1984 Act and at common law, the court has a discretion to exclude evidence admissible under s.117.[3]

---

[98] (1992) 95 Cr.App.R. 21.
[99] Criminal Justice Act 1988, s.24.
[1] *Minors* [1989] 1 W.L.R. 441, 448, applying *Bray* (1989) 88 Cr.App.R. 354.
[2] *Carrington* (1994) 99 Cr.App.R. 376.
[3] See the House of Lords decision in *Shephard* [1993] 2 W.L.R. 102.

8–36   **(c) Doubtful statements: subss.(6)(7).** The court has an important power to exclude statements of doubtful reliability under s.117(6) and (7). The subsections provide as follows:

> "(6) A statement is not admissible under this section if the court makes a direction to that effect under subsection (7).
>
> (7) The court may make a direction under this subsection if satisfied that the statement's reliability as evidence for the purpose for which it is tendered is doubtful in view of—
>
>   (a) its contents,
>   (b) the source of the information contained in it,
>   (c) the way in which or the circumstances in which the information was supplied or received, or
>   (d) the way in which or the circumstances in which the document concerned was created or received."

8–37   Thus, if the contents of the document or the circumstances of its supply, or the source or supply of the information contained give rise to doubts about its reliability as evidence for the purposes for which it is tendered, the court has a discretion to exclude it. Thus, it is not the general unreliability, but reliability for the purpose for which the statement is tendered, which will lead to exclusion and in the light of the matters set out in the section.

These powers are in addition to the court's powers to exclude evidence under s.126 of the 2003 Act (below, para.8–73), ss.76, 76A or 78 of the Police and Criminal Act 1984, and at common law.

8–38   *(3) Statements admissible at common law*

Section 118(1) of the Criminal Justice Act 2003 expressly preserves certain common law categories of admissibility. These are the rules as to:

    (1) Public information, etc. (see paras 8–39, 8–40, below)

    (2) Reputation as to character (see para.8–45, below)

    (3) Reputation or family tradition (see para.8–46, below)

    (4) *Res gestae* (see paras 8–50 to 8–61, below)

    (5) Confessions (see para.8–62 and Ch.9, below)

    (6) Admissions by agents, etc. (see para.8–63, below)

    (7) Common enterprise (see para.8–64, below)

    (8) Expert evidence (see para.8–65, below and Ch.6, above)

By s.118(2) all other common law rules governing the admissibility of hearsay evidence are abolished.

The effect of the section is that in the circumstances specified above an out-of-court statement will be admissible as evidence of any matters stated in it. The first four categories listed above do not make common appearances in criminal trials.[4] The common law rules, thus preserved, are discussed in the following paragraphs.

(1) Public information. The section preserves the common law   8–39
rule under which—

"(a)   published works dealing with matters of a public nature (such as histories, scientific works, dictionaries and maps) are admissible as evidence of facts of a public nature stated in them;

(b)   public documents (such as public registers, and returns made under public authority with respect to matters of public interest) are admissible as evidence of acts stated in them;

(c)   records (such as the records of certain courts, treaties, Crown grants, pardons and commissions) are admissible as evidence of facts stated in them; or

(d)   evidence relating to a person's age or date or place of birth may be given by a person without personal knowledge of the matter."

(i) Published works, etc. Published works of a public nature are   8–40
admissible as evidence of the facts of a public nature stated in them. The following illustrations may be given:

(a)   maps are commonly admitted in order to prove the positions of places marked on them;

(b)   standard dictionaries are admissible to prove the meaning of words[5]; and

(c)   approved histories may be admitted to prove facts of a public nature.[6]

On the other hand, Pollock C.B. said that an almanac is not admissible to prove the time of the rising or setting of the sun[7] and in a Crown Court case

---

[4] Explanatory Notes on the Criminal Justice Bill, November 21, 2002, para.326, point out that many of the common law rules were preserved under the corresponding civil evidence provisions in s.7 of the Civil Evidence Act 1995.
[5] See *Peters* (1886) 16 Q.B.D. 636, 641, *per* Lord Coleridge C.J. and *Tomlinson* [1895] 1 Q.B. 706, 709, *per* Lord Russell of Killowen C.J.
[6] *Read v Bishop of Lincoln* [1892] A.C. 644, PC.
[7] *Tutton v Darke; Nixon v Freeman* (1860) 5 H. & N. 647, 654.

Whittaker's Almanac was held inadmissible for this purpose.[8] It may be argued that judicial notice should be taken of the fact that a statement of such times in an almanac is usually correct.[9] However, difficulties may occur if the material place is some distance from the place mentioned in the almanac. In that case the evidence of an astronomer will be necessary to establish the relevant times.[10]

8–41   (ii) **Statements in public documents, etc.** Statements contained in public documents are generally admissible as evidence of the facts recorded therein. Since statute provides for the proof of the most usual events such as births, deaths and marriages,[11] the common law rule is not invoked very often. In any event, it is not possible to consider all the rules relating to public documents in a work of this size. Accordingly, the subject may be considered concisely. (For proof of public documents see paras 3–18 to 3–20, above.)

A public document has been defined as a document made by a public officer for the purposes of the public making use of it and being able to refer to it.[12] Accordingly, entries in the following have been held to be admissible:

(a) public registers[13] and foreign registers of baptisms and marriages[14] as proof of the facts recorded therein; and

(b) the public books of corporations and public companies as evidence of the public acts of the corporation or company.

On the same principle:

(a) reports and returns made under public authority may be admissible as proof of their contents in relation to matters of public interest or concern; and

(b) official certificates or returns of public officers made under a public duty are admissible as evidence of the facts authorised to be stated.

The rationale of the rule is that an entry in such a document is presumed to be true. Thus, Parke B. said that in public documents made for the information of the Crown or all the King's subjects who may require the

---

[8] *Crush* [1978] Crim.L.R. 357.
[9] See Cross and Tapper *Evidence* (9th ed., 1999, Butterworths, London).
[10] Such evidence was eventually called in *Crush*, above.
[11] para.3–19 (f) and (g), above.
[12] *Sturla v Freccia* (1880) 5 App.Cas. 623, 643, *per* Lord Blackburn.
[13] *Sturla v Freccia*, above.
[14] *Lyell v Kennedy* (1889) 14 App.Cas. 437, 448–449, *per* Lord Selborne.

information they contain, the entry by a public officer is presumed to be true when it is made.[15]

In *Sturla v Freccia*[16] Lord Blackburn considered the conditions of admissibility of such a document and said that it must be a document made by a public officer for the purpose of the public making use of it and being able to refer to it, where there is a judicial or quasi-judicial duty to inquire: "the very object of it must be that it should be made for the purpose of being kept public, so that the persons concerned in it may have access to it afterwards."   8-42

It should be noted that:

(a) for a document to be public, it must be one made for the purpose of the public making use of it and to which all concerned in it have access.[17]

(b) The document should be one which it is intended to preserve and not be made for a temporary purpose.[18]

(c) The entry must be made promptly after the event which it purports to record. (However, questions relating to promptness have been said to affect the weight of the evidence rather than its admissibility.[19])

(d) Under modern conditions the duty to inquire (*i.e.* the duty of the person making the entry to satisfy himself as to the truth of the recorded facts)[20] may have to be shared. "The common law should move with the times and should recognise that the official charged with recording matters of public import can no longer in this highly complicated world, as like as not, have personal knowledge of their accuracy."[21] Thus, the Court of Appeal in *Halpin*[22] held that an extract from a company's returns entered in the company's register is admissible as proof of its contents, although the duty to make and preserve the return was shared between the person making the return and the person responsible for preserving it.

(iii) **Records.** This little-used rule preserves the common law in relation to treaties and the like.   8-43

---

[15] *Irish Society v Bishop of Derry* [1846] 12 Cl. & F. 641, 668–669.
[16] (1880) 5 App.Cas. 623, 643–644.
[17] *Lilley v Pettit* [1946] K.B. 401.
[18] *Mercer v Denne* [1905] 2 Ch. 538.
[19] *Halpin* [1975] Q.B. 907, 913.
[20] *Doe' d. France v Andrews* (1850) 15 Q.B. 756, 759.
[21] *Halpin* [1975] Q.B. 907, 915, *per* Geoffrey Lane L.J.
[22] Above.

8-44   **(iv) Age. Date or place of birth.**   This rule permits a person to give evidence of his or her age, or date and place of birth. It is a common enough occurrence in daily life for someone to give these details and not a practice which is ever questioned. However, it is strictly hearsay for a person to say how old they are or where and when they were born, so a provision is necessary to make the statement admissible in court.

8-45   (2) REPUTATION AS TO CHARACTER.   The section preserves "any rule of law under which in criminal proceedings evidence of a person's reputation is admissible for the purpose of proving his good or bad character.
Note. The rule is preserved only so far as it allows the court to treat such evidence as proving the matter concerned."[23]

8-46   (3) REPUTATION OR FAMILY TRADITION.   The section preserves "any rule of law under which in criminal proceedings evidence of reputation or family tradition is admissible for the purpose of proving or disproving—

(a)   pedigree or the existence of a marriage,
(b)   the existence of any public or general right, or
(c)   the identity of any person or thing.

Note. The rule is preserved only so far as it allows the court to treat such evidence as proving or disproving the matter concerned."
There are similar provisions in the Civil Evidence Act 1995.

[THE NEXT PARAGRAPH IS 8–50]

8-50   (4) *RES GESTAE.*   The section preserves "any rule of law under which in criminal proceedings a statement is admissible as evidence of any matter stated if—

(a)   the statement was made by a person so emotionally overpowered by an event that the possibility of concoction or distortion can be disregarded,

(b)   the statement accompanied an act which can be properly evaluated as evidence only if considered in conjunction with the statement, or

(c)   the statement relates to a physical sensation or a mental state (such as intention or emotion)."

---

[23] See Ch.7, above, as to character.

The expression *res gestae* is a corruption of the Latin phrase *res gesta pars rei gestae*. In English, if something is said to be part of the *res gestae*, it means that it is part of the story.[24] The principle is that certain hearsay statements are admissible in evidence because they are part of the *res gestae* or story.[25] The principle is that certain hearsay statements are admissible in evidence because they are part of the *res gestae* or story.[26] This principle has been explained as follows:

> "(The rule against the admission of hearsay evidence) ... admits of certain carefully safeguarded exceptions, one of which is that words may be proved when they form part of the *res gestae* ... (The rule) appears to rest ultimately on two propositions, that human utterance is both a fact and a means of communication and that human action may be so interwoven with words that the significance of the action cannot be understood without the correlative words, and the dissociation of the words from the action would impede the discovery of truth. But the judicial applications of these two propositions, which do not always combine harmoniously, have never been precisely formulated in a general principle."

Three types of statement admissible under this principle[27] are considered here: **8–51**

(a) a statement made by a person emotionally overpowered (paras 8–52 to 8–57, below);

(b) statement accompanying an act (para.8–58, below);

(c) statement relating to physical sensation or mental state (paras 8–59 to 8–60, below).

---

[24] See note by Sir Frederick Pollock at [1931] Ch. 120.

[25] The expression *res gestae* is used in a number of senses. In one sense, to say that evidence is admissible as part of the *res gestae* means no more than that the evidence is admissible because it is relevant. Thus, it may be artificial to restrict the evidence of an incident, *e.g.* a murder, to the events of the actual killing; and it may be necessary to adduce evidence of events which occurred immediately before, or at the time of, or after, the incident. This use of the expression has already been mentioned at para.1–15 above and needs no further consideration here.

[26] *Teper v R* [1952] A.C. 480, 486–487, *per* Lord Normand.

[27] At one time it had been thought that statements under the principle of *res gestae* were original evidence: see *Christie* [1914] A.C. 545, 555, *per* Lord Atkinson. Sir Rupert Cross, however, categorised such statements as exceptions to the rule against hearsay: see Cross, *Evidence* (5th ed.), pp.575–76; Cross and Tapper, *Evidence* (8th ed.), pp.723–24. This view was apparently shared by Lord Reid when he said in argument in *Ratten v R* [1972] A.C. 378, 381: "The first point is whether the evidence is hearsay. If it is not hearsay the exception in respect of *res gestae* does not arise." The categorisation is followed here.

Criticism of the *res gestae* rule by the Law Commission is set out at para.8–61, below.

8–52   (a) **Statement made by person emotionally overpowered.**   An exclamation made spontaneously by the victim of an offence or by a bystander is admissible (as part of the *res gestae*) to prove the truth of the words spoken.[28] In order to be admissible, the exclamation must have been made:

(a)   spontaneously at the time of the offence; and

(b)   in circumstances such that the possibility of concoction may be excluded.

Thus, Holt C.J. said: "What (the wife) said immediate upon the hurt received and before that she had time to contrive any thing for her own advantage might be given in evidence."[29] A modern example might be the exclamation of a bystander at a fight: "Look what X is doing to Y."[30] In *Nye and Loan*[31] an assault occurred after a collision between two motor vehicles. The police came to the scene and the victim immediately identified L as the man who had assaulted him. At the trial, the victim did not give evidence of the identification; but the police officer did. The Court of Appeal held that this evidence had been rightly admitted as the identification was spontaneous and there was no opportunity for concoction or error.

8–53   It was once thought that the test of the admissibility of such an exclamation was whether it was part of the event or transaction. However, in *Ratten*,[32] Lord Wilberforce, giving the judgment of the Privy Council, said that the test was whether the exclamation was made: "in such conditions (always being those of approximate but not exact contemporaneity) of involvement or pressure as to exclude the possibility of concoction or distortion to the advantage of the maker or the disadvantage of the accused."[33]

This test has now been approved by the House of Lords.[34] Whether it applies to a particular case will depend upon the circumstances. Three examples may be given.

---

[28] *Ratten v R* [1972] A.C. 378; *Andrews* [1987] A.C. 281.

[29] *Thompson v Trevanion* (1693) Skin. 402.

[30] Or, as happened in one case, an attacker who says "I am David Glover": *Glover* [1991] Crim.L.R. 48.

[31] (1978) 66 Cr.App.R. 252.

[32] [1972] A.C. 378.

[33] At 391.

[34] *Andrews* [1987] A.C. 281. The cases decided prior to *Ratten* are now of historical significance only, *e.g. Bedingfield* (1878) 14 Cox C.C. 341 (overruled by the House of Lords in *Andrews*, above), and *Teper v R* [1952] A.C. 480.

1. In *Ratten*[35] the accused had been convicted of the murder of his wife   8–54
who had been shot with a shotgun. The defence was that the gun had gone
off accidentally. The prosecution called a telephone operator who said that
at a time identified as being shortly before the time of the killing she had
received a call from the defendant's address from a woman who, in a
hysterical and sobbing voice, asked for the police. The defendant denied
that the call had ever been made. The Privy Council held that the tele-
phonist's evidence of the call from a woman who could only have been the
deceased was admissible not only as original evidence that the call was
made, but also as evidence of an assertion by the deceased that she was
being attacked by the defendant. This was because the words and the
shooting were closely associated in place and time. "The way in which the
statement came to be made (in a call for the police) and the tone of the voice
used, showed intrinsically that the statement was being forced from the
deceased by an overwhelming pressure of contemporary event. It carried its
own *stamp of spontaneity* and this was endorsed by the proved time
sequence and the proved proximity of the deceased to the accused with his
gun."[36]

2. In *Turnbull*[37] evidence was admitted that a mortally wounded man
shortly before his death identified "Ronnie Tommo" as the man who had
"done it". The prosecution alleged that this was an attempt to identify
the defendant with whom the dead man had been drinking prior to his
death. The Court of Appeal held that the evidence was admissible and
rejected an argument that the judge should have excluded the evidence
because there was a possibility of "distortion" of what the dying man had
said.[38]

3. In *Andrews*[39] the defendant was charged with murder. He was
charged with another man, D, who pleaded guilty to manslaughter. The
victim had been stabbed and fatally wounded. Immediately after the attack
he went to a flat downstairs for assistance. Shortly after, the police arrived
and the victim made a statement identifying the defendant and D as his
assailants. The victim died of his injuries two months later. The Crown was
allowed to adduce the evidence of the victim's statement as part of the *res
gestae*.

The House of Lords, applying *Ratten*, held that the evidence had been   8–55
properly admitted as evidence of the truth of the facts asserted. Lord
Ackner, in a speech with which the other members of the House agreed,
said that before admitting such evidence, the trial judge must satisfy himself
that the circumstances of the attack upon the victim were sufficiently

---

[35] [1972] A.C. 378.
[36] At 391, *per* Lord Wilberforce; emphasis supplied by author.
[37] (1985) 80 Cr.App.R. 104
[38] The Court said that when Lord Wilberforce referred to the possibility of distortion in
Ratten, he was referring to the possibility of fabrication.
[39] (1987) 84 Cr.App.R. 382.

contemporaneous and were so unusual, startling or dramatic as to exclude the possibility of concoction or distortion: "in order for the statement to be sufficiently 'spontaneous' it must be so closely associated with the event ... that the mind of the declarant was still dominated by the event ... [The] judge must be satisfied that the event which provided the trigger mechanism for the statement was still operative."[40]

(Provided that he applies the principles in *Andrews* and there is material to entitle him to reach the conclusions which he did, the Court of Appeal has said that it will not interfere with the judge's decision.)[41]

In *Nye and Loan*,[42] the Court of Appeal added what was described as a gloss to the test in *Ratten*, namely was there any real possibility of error? However, there is no mention of this gloss in *Turnbull*, and since it is not mentioned in *Ratten*, it is submitted that the possibility of error goes to the weight rather than the admissibility of evidence and, accordingly, is a matter for the jury to decide. Indeed, Lord Ackner said in *Andrews* that the possibility of error caused by the fallibility of human recollection went to the weight to be attached to the statement.

The present test has been summarised in this way: "... whether the person when he or she made the statement was so emotionally overpowered by the event that he or she is almost certain to have been telling the truth as he or she perceived it."[43]

8–56 Usually there will be some other evidence beside the spontaneous exclamation itself to connect the speaker with the event which gives rise to the exclamation. Lord Wilberforce said in *Ratten*[44] that on principle it would not appear right that the connection should be shown by the statement itself, but that it was impossible to lay down any general rule: "It is difficult to imagine a case where there is no evidence at all of connection between statement and principal event other than the statement itself; but whether this is sufficiently shown must be a matter for the trial judge."

If the statement is admitted the judge must direct the jury:

(a) that it is for them to decide what was said; and

(b) that they must be satisfied that:

---

[40] At 391. The fact that the declarant has acted dishonestly in the past must be considered in the light of the real question whether there was anything to suggest that he had not told the truth in this particular situation: *Carnall* [1995] Crim.L.R. 944. It was suggested in *Callender* [1998] Crim.L.R. 337 that the *Andrews* test applies to *all* categories of *res gestae*. However, as the commentary in Criminal Law Review, above, points out, there is no authority for such a proposition which ignores well-established aspects of the rule.
[41] *Carnall*, above.
[42] (1978) 66 Cr.App.R. 252.
[43] "Evidence in Criminal Proceedings: Hearsay and Related Topics" (1995) Law Comm. Consultation Paper No.245, para.8.115.
[44] *Ratten*, above, at 391.

(i) there was no possibility of mistake (any special features giving rise to that possibility must be drawn to their attention); and

(ii) that the maker did not concoct or distort the statement and, where material, that he was not activated by malice or ill-will.[45]

Lord Ackner in *Andrews* deprecated any attempt to use the doctrine of *res gestae* as a device to avoid calling, when he is available, the maker of the statement. In *Tobi v Nicholas*[46] the Divisional Court, following *Andrews*, held that the doctrine could not be used to identify the driver of a vehicle when a witness, who was available, had not been called. The court in that case held that a statement by a driver of a coach damaged in an accident (made about 20 minutes after the accident) was not admissible because (a) the event was not so unusual or dramatic as in the ordinary way to dominate the thoughts of the victim and (b) the statement and event were not contemporaneous.

Nor can the doctrine be permitted to allow as evidence an undoubted *res*   8–57
gestae statement when the maker of the statement is available but is likely to contradict the statement. Thus, in *Att-Gen's Reference No.1 of 2003*[47] the defendant was charged with two counts of grievous bodily harm on his mother. At the time the mother had called out to witnesses who had seen her in distress and had heard her identify the defendant as her attacker. Subsequently, however, the mother had made a statement to the effect that the injuries were accidental and that she would not give evidence against her son. The Court of Appeal held that the evidence of the witnesses as to what the mother had called out could not be admitted without the evidence of the mother being given: the prosecution should have been prepared to tender a witness who would give evidence which they suspected would not be capable of belief, *i.e.* a hostile witness. This is in order that the witness can be cross-examined and the full picture put before the court.

(b) Statement accompanying an act. A statement made by a person   8–58
who is not a witness may be admissible in evidence if (a) the statement accompanies and explains an act and (b) that act is relevant to an issue in the case. The statement is then said to be admissible as part of the *res gestae*. Thus, Grove J. said "Though you cannot give in evidence a declaration *per se*, yet when there is an act accompanied by a statement

---

[45] *Andrews* above, at 392, *per* Lord Ackner.
[46] (1988) 86 Cr.App.R. 323.
[47] [2003] 2 Cr.App.R. 453.

which is so mixed up with it as to become part of the *res gestae*, evidence of such a statement may be given."[48]

In order to be admissible, the statement must (a) accompany and explain an act which is itself relevant[49]; (b) be made by the actor; (c) be contemporaneous with the act[50] and (d) relate to the act.[51]

A modern example of the rule is to be found in *McCay*.[52] In that case a witness viewed an identification parade through a two-way mirror from a separate room. The participants in the parade were numbered. The witness identified the defendant by reference to his number. (The defendant could not see or hear what occurred in the viewing room.) At the trial the witness could not remember the number. A police inspector was allowed to give evidence that the witness said "it's number 8." The Court of Appeal held that this evidence was admissible because it accompanied and explained a relevant act, namely the identification.

8–59   (c) **Statement relating to physical sensation or mental state**
(i) Physical sensation. A person's declaration as to his own contemporaneous physical condition may be admissible as evidence of that condition; there may well be no other way of proving it.[53] The statement should be confined to the maker's contemporaneous physical condition; but the "contemporaneousness" may be difficult to interpret. In *Bradshaw*[54] the Court of Appeal said that a doctor may not state what a patient told him about past symptoms as evidence of the existence of those symptoms. And in *Gloster*[55] it was held that questions should be confined to contemporaneous symptoms at the time the person is speaking. But in *Black*[56] Salter J. said: "Surely 'contemporaneous' cannot be confined to feelings experienced at the actual moment when the patient is speaking; it must include such a statement as 'yesterday, I had a pain after meals.'"

It would appear, therefore, that no hard and fast rule can be made as to the meaning of "contemporaneous" in this context. However, it has been

---

[48] *Howe v Malkin* (1878) 40 L.T. 196.
[49] *Bliss* (1837) 7 A.&E. 550; *Thomas v Connell* (1834) 4 M.&E. 267, 269, *per* Parke B.
[50] *Thomas v Connell*, above.
[51] *Bliss*, above.
[52] [1990] 1 W.L.R. 645.
[53] *Wright v Kerrigan* [1911] 2 I.R. 301, 310 *per* Cherry J. See also *Aveson v Kinnaird* (1805) 6 East 188, where a wife whose life had been insured by her husband gave the doctor who examined her when the policy was taken out to understand that she was in good health. She died a few months later and when the husband sued on the insurance policy the defendant insurers were permitted to call a friend who said that the wife had told her a few days after the consultation that she had been unwell when she went to see the doctor and was afraid she would not live.
[54] (1986) 82 Cr.App.R. 79, 83.
[55] (1888) 16 Cox C.C. 471.
[56] (1922) 16 Cr.App.R. 118, 119. Note also that in *Aveson v Kinnaird*, above, the statements to the friend were made several days after the visit to the doctor.

established since the nineteenth century that the statement describing the symptoms should not include narrative as to how those symptoms were caused. Pollock C.B. said in *Nicholas*[57]:

> "If a man says to his surgeon, 'I have a pain in the head, or a pain in such a part of the body', that is evidence, but if he says to his surgeon 'I have a wound': and was to add, 'I met John Thomas who had a sword and ran me through the body with it', that would be no evidence against John Thomas".

In *Horsford*[58] evidence was admitted to the effect that the deceased told her doctor that she believed she was poisoned and had taken a powder but evidence that she had told the doctor that she believed the defendant had sent her the poison was not admitted.[59]

(ii)   Mental state.   A declaration made by a person concerning his contemporaneous state of mind may be admissible as evidence of that state of mind. In *Moghal*,[60] M and S were indicated jointly for the murder of R, who had been killed in circumstances such that only M or S could have killed him. S sought and was granted a separate trial. S was tried before M, and was acquitted. At M's trial, defence counsel submitted that he should be allowed to question police officers as to statements made by S concerning her state of mind prior to the murder and to adduce evidence of a tape recording of a family conference at which S declared her intention to kill R. In the event, no ruling was given on either of these submissions and the evidence was not adduced. However, the Court of Appeal considered the admissibility of the evidence which counsel had sought to adduce. The Court said that (a) the evidence of what S had said to the police was not evidence of her contemporaneous state of mind and was inadmissible; but (b) the tape-recording was evidence of S's contemporaneous state of mind before the killing; and was admissible.[61] A further example is to be found in *Gilfoyle*[62] where the Court of Appeal held that the statements of three friends of the deceased to the effect that the defendant had asked her to write suicide notes to connection with a project were admissible to show that she was show that she was not in a suicidal frame of mind.

8–60

---

[57] (1846) 2 Car. & K. 246, 248.
[58] *The Times*, June 2–6, 1898.
[59] Although Hawkins J. did accept that such evidence would be admissible if made as a declaration.
[60] (1977) 65 Cr.App.R. 56.
[61] Lord Bridge in *Blastland* [1985] 3 W.L.R. 345, 356 doubted whether the Court's opinion in relation to the tape recording was correct. This was because S's threat did not appear to be relevant to the issue of whether M was implicated in the murder of R or not. However, *Moghal* remains as an illustration of the principle under consideration.
[62] [1996] 1 Cr.App.R. 302.

The House of Lords emphasised in *Blastland*[63] that such a declaration is only admissible when the state of mind evidenced by it is either itself directly in issue at the trial, or is of direct and immediate relevance to an issue which arises at the trial. In *Blastland* the defendant was charged with the murder of a boy, K. The defence was that another man, M, had murdered K. At the trial, the judge refused to allow the defence to call certain witnesses to prove that M had said (at a time before the boy's body had been found) that a boy had been murdered. The House of Lords held that the evidence had rightly been excluded because M's knowledge of the murder was neither in issue at the trial nor was it relevant to the issue at the trial, *i.e.* whether the defendant had murdered K. Lord Bridge (in a speech with which the other members of the House concurred) said: "The admissibility of a statement tendered in evidence as proof of the maker's knowledge or other state of mind must always depend on the degree of relevance of the state of mind sought to be proved to the issue in relation to which the evidence is tendered."[64]

However, there are conflicting authorities as to the scope of the rule. Thus, in *Buckley*[65] the defendant was charged with the murder of a policeman. The identity of the murderer was in issue. Lush J. admitted evidence that the deceased had told a superior officer on the day that he was murdered that he was going that night to watch the defendant's movements. On the other hand, in *Wainwright*,[66] Lord Cockburn C.J. excluded evidence that the deceased woman (when leaving home on the day she was last seen alive) said that she was going to the defendant's address. In the absence of any modern authority defining the scope of this rule, it is thought that such evidence would require a high degree of probative force to be admitted today. For instance, it must be very doubtful whether evidence such as that in *Buckley* would now be admitted. This is because the fact that a man says that he is going to watch somebody does not go far towards proving that he actually met the other person. However, were the deceased to leave a note to this effect, it would now be admissible under s.116(1)(a), para.8–17, above.

8–61   **(d) Criticisms of the res gestae rule.** The Law Commission has criticised the *res gestae* rule,[67] pointing out that the usual justification for it may not hold force:

---

[63] [1985] 3 W.L.R. 345.

[64] At 358. The European Court of Human Rights held that there is no obligation under Art.6 to admit hearsay evidence which purports to exonerate the accused: *Blastland v UK* 10 E.H.R.R. 528.

[65] (1873) 13 Cox C.C. 293.

[66] (1871) 13 Cox C.C. 171.

[67] "Evidence in Criminal Proceedings: Hearsay and Related Topics" (1995) Law Comm. Consultation Paper No.138, paras 7.10–7.12.

"Whether or not the excitement of an incident means that spontaneous exclamations are reliable has long been doubted. There may be little opportunity for concoction, but the witness may have only partial information. Their actual reliability will vary with the facts of each case. In *Benz v The Queen*,[68] Mason C.J. concluded that the criticism of the doctrine was not that it had led to miscarriages of justice but that it lacked a theoretical and principled foundation and this made it difficult to apply. He suggested that the principle required 're-examination' in the same manner as the rule itself. Our provisional view is that this is a justifiable criticism."

A further criticism was that the term *res gestae* was used to encompass associated exceptions[69] to the point where it obscured rather than clarified the extent and rationale of the exception.[70] Lord Tomlin described the phrase as one "adopted to provide a respectable legal cloak for a variety of cases to which no formula of precision can be applied".[71] Wigmore went further and said that "The phrase *res gestae* has long been not only entirely useless, but even positively harmful."[72]

Despite such criticisms the Government took the traditional view and the rule has been retained because "reported words which are very closely connected to a relevant event are reliable accounts and should therefore be admissible" in the circumstances outlined above.[73]

It is submitted that in practice the rule will remain a useful tool in unusual cases. To deny the fact-finder evidence such as that of the deceased woman's telephone call in cases such as *Ratten*[74] would be to keep out potentially very important evidence for technical reasons. It should then be left to the jury or magistrates to decide whether the evidence is reliable or not. Furthermore, it is submitted that the criticisms of the misuse of the rule, however apposite 30 years or more ago, are no longer valid.

(5) CONFESSIONS. The section preserves "any rule of law relating to the admissibility of confessions or mixed statements in criminal proceedings." See Ch.9, below. **8–62**

---

[68] (1989) 168 C.L.R. 110.
[69] See paras 3–38—3–49 of the Law Comm. Consultation Paper, above.
[70] Professor Morgan observed that seven distinct types of evidence were admissible in US law under the broad term *res gestae*: E.M. Morgan, "A Suggested Classification of Utterances Admissible as Res Gestae" (1922) 31 Yale L.J. 229, 231–33.
[71] *Homes v Newman* [1931] 2 Ch. 112, 120.
[72] *Wigmore on Evidence*, vol.6, para.1767, p.255 (1976, Chadbourn revision).
[73] Explanatory Notes to the Criminal Justice Bill, November 21, 2002, para.343.
[74] [1972] A.C. 378.

8–63   (6) ADMISSIONS BY AGENTS.   This section preserves—

"any rule of law under which in criminal proceedings—

    (a) an admission made by an agent of a defendant is admissible against the defendant as evidence of any matter stated, or

    (b) a statement made by a person to whom a defendant refers a person for information is admissible against the defendant as evidence of any matter stated."

Admissions made by the defendant's agent are only admissible if it is proved that the admissions were made on the defendant's authority. In *Evans*,[75] the Court of Appeal held that evidence of a conversation between a clerk of the defendant's solicitors and a potential witness was inadmissible since there was no admissible evidence that the clerk was acting on the defendant's authority. Similarly, in order to prove admissions in a solicitor's letter written on behalf of a defendant, it would be necessary to show that the letter was written on the defendant's specific instructions.[76] In *Hutchinson*[77] a letter written by defence solicitors to the DPP contradicting statements in an alibi notice was held by the Court of Appeal to have been rightly admitted in evidence. The Court held that the letter was admissible, *inter alia*, because it was comparable to a relevant statement made by the defendant before trial to a police officer. However, it is submitted that it must be doubtful whether such a letter would ordinarily be admissible unless it related to an alibi notice or could be shown to have been written on the specific instructions of the defendant.

In *Turner*,[78] counsel made certain admissions when addressing the court in mitigation on behalf of a defendant. The prosecution was given leave to prove these admissions in a subsequent trial against the same defendant. The Court of Appeal held that this evidence had been rightly admitted because the court is entitled to assume that what counsel says in court in the presence of his client is said that the client's authority.

On the other hand, the Court of Appeal in *Hutchinson*[79] held that admissions made by counsel for the defence at a pre-trial review were not admissible. The reason for this decision was that since the review itself does not have the force of law, nothing said or done at it should be used for evidential purposes without the consent of the party affected. The same reasoning has been applied to an answer in a questionnaire produced at a Plea and Directions Hearing: such an answer is not expected to form

---

[75] [1981] Crim.L.R. 699.
[76] *Downer* (1880) 14 Cox C.C. 486.
[77] (1985) 82 Cr.App.R. 51.
[78] (1975) 61 Cr.App.R. 67 at 81–82.
[79] Above, n.76.

220

part of the material to be used at the trial and so it would rarely be appropriate to refer to it (and then only after counsel has been given the opportunity to address the court as to whether such reference should be made).[80]

(7) COMMON ENTERPRISE. The section preserves "any rule of law **8-64** under which in criminal proceedings a statement made by a party to a common enterprise is admissible against another party to the enterprise as evidence of any matter stated."

When two or more persons are engaged in a common enterprise, the acts and declarations of one in pursuance of the common purpose are admissible against the other.[81] This rule applies whether there is a charge of conspiracy or not. For instance, if two men set out to burgle a house, one to go into the house to steal, the second to act as look-out, the acts and declarations of the man inside the house are admissible against the look-out and vice versa. A further example is to be found in *Blake and Tye*.[82] The defendants in that case were employees at the Customs House. They were charged with conspiring to pass goods through the customs without paying full duty. T made entries in a book for the purpose of carrying out the fraud. Evidence relating to these entries was held to be admissible against B. On the other hand, an entry made by T in his cheque book for his own convenience was held not to be admissible against B because it was not in furtherance of the common purpose.

The following qualifications in respect of the rule should be noted.

(1) Before the hearsay evidence is admissible there must be a prima facie case (or reasonable evidence) against the defendant of involvement in the offence charged or act concerned.[83]

(2) There must be some other evidence of common purpose. The result is that the hearsay evidence may have to be admitted conditionally, since if it transpires that there is no other evidence of common purpose the evidence will not be admissible.[84] If the

[80] *Diedrick* [1997] 1 Cr.App.R. 361. For the rules concerning Plea and Directions Hearings (which are now routinely held as a form of pre-trial review in every Crown Court case), see the Practice Direction "Crown Court Plea and Directions Hearings" now in paras 41.1–41.17 of the *Consolidated Practice Direction* [2002] 2 Cr.App.R. 533. During the course of such hearings counsel fill in questionnaires relating to the issues in the case and various procedural matters: the questionnaires are then handed in to the court.
[81] *Gordon* (1781) 21 How St.Tr. 435; *Blake and Tye* (1844) 6 Q.B. 126; *Pridmore* (1913) 29 T.L.R. 330; *Chapple* (1892) 17 Cox 453; *Whitaker* [1914] 3 K.B. 1283.
[82] Above. In *Devonport* [1996] Crim.L.R. 221 the Court of Appeal held that a document was admissible if it constituted an act or declaration by one of a number of co-conspirators in furtherance of the conspiracy, although the other conspirators did not know of the document's existence.
[83] *Jones* [1997] 2 Cr.App.R. 119.
[84] *Donat* (1986) 82 Cr.App.R. 173.

evidence is admitted the judge should warn the jury that before relying on it they must be sure that the common purpose *did* exist and that the absent party shared it.[85]

(3) In *Gray, Liggins and Others*[86] the Court of Appeal held that if individual defendants agree on a common objective but are charged with number of separate substantive offences (and there is no charge of conspiracy) evidence of acts and statements in furtherance of the common aim by one defendant in the absence of the others is admissible but limited to evidence which shows the involvement of each defendant in the commission of the offence or offences. However, in *Murray*,[87] a differently constituted Court of Appeal said that *Gray, Liggins and Others* was authority primarily for the proposition that the common law exception cannot be extended to cases where individual defendants are charged with a number of separate substantive offences and where the terms of the common enterprise are not proved or are undefined. It is submitted that this interpretation is correct: if not, the standard admissibility would be set too high.

(4) Evidence of a conversation is not admissible (except as an admission by the maker) if it is no more than a narrative statement or account of an event which has already taken place. "[Usually] the question of admissibility will relate to directions, instructions or arrangements, or utterances accompanying acts."[88]

(5) Once the common enterprise is over, the acts and declarations of one participant are not evidence against another. Thus, admissions in an interview with the police relating to a conspiracy are admissible against the maker, but not a co-defendant.

8–65   (8) EXPERT EVIDENCE. The section preserves "any rule of law under which in criminal proceedings an expert witness may draw on the body of expertise relevant to his field." See Ch.6, above.

8–66   *(4) Multiple hearsay*

Section 121 of the Criminal Justice Act 2003 permits the admission of multiple hearsay as follows:

"(1) A hearsay statement is not admissible to prove the fact that an earlier hearsay statement was made unless—

---

[85] *Jones*, above.
[86] [1995] 2 Cr.App.R. 100.
[87] [1997] 2 Cr.App.R. 136.
[88] *Tripoli* [1961] 104 C.L.R. 1, 7 *per* Dixon C.J., approved by the Court of Appeal in *Gray, Liggins and Others*, above.

(a) either of the statements is admissible under section 117, 119 or 120,

(b) all parties to the proceedings so agree, or

(c) the court is satisfied that the value of the evidence in question, taking into account how reliable the statements appear to be, is so high that the interests of justice require the later statement to be admissible for that purpose.

(2) In this section 'hearsay statement' means a statement, not made in oral evidence, that is relied on as evidence of a matter stated in it."

This section was substantially amended in the House of Lords. The original clause would have allowed the admission of multiple hearsay under the general principle set out in s.114 of the Act (above, para.8–13), cases under s.116 where a witness was unavailable (see above, paras 8–17 to 8–29), cases concerning business and other documents under s.117 (see above, paras 8–30 to 8–37) cases under s.118 which preserves the common law categories (see above, paras 8–38 to 8–65), cases under s.119 relating to inconsistent statements (see paras 21–09 *et seq.*, below), and cases under s.120 relating to other previous statements by witnesses (see Ch.20, below). There was a proviso that where evidence under ss.116 and 118 was concerned, such evidence must be proved by evidence admissible under ss.117, 119 or 120.

8–67

The section in its final form now only allows multiple hearsay where business documents or inconsistent statements or other previous statements are concerned. Furthermore, either all parties to the proceedings must agree to the admission or the court must consider that it is in the interests of justice to do so.

It is notable that nowhere else in Chapter Two of the Act is the word "hearsay" specifically defined.

B. Safeguards

(1) Capability

Section 123 of the Criminal Justice Act 2003 provides that:

8–68

"(1) Nothing in section 116, 119 or 120 makes a statement admissible as evidence if it was made by a person who did not have the required capability at the time when he made the statement.

(2) Nothing in section 117 makes a statement admissible as evidence if any person who, in order for the requirements of section 117(2) to be satisfied, must at any time have supplied or received the information concerned or created or received the document or part concerned—

    (a) did not have the required capability at that time, or

    (b) cannot be identified but cannot reasonably be assumed to have had the required capability at that time.

(3) For the purposes of this section a person has the required capability if he is capable of—

    (a) understanding questions put to him about the matters stated, and

    (b) giving answers to such questions which can be understood.

(4) Where by reason of this section there is an issue as to whether a person had the required capability when he made a statement—

    (a) proceedings held for the determination of the issue must take place in the absence of the jury (if there is one);

    (b) in determining the issue the court may receive expert evidence and evidence form any person to whom the statement in question was made;

    (c) the burden of proof of the issue lies on the party seeking to adduce the statement, and the standard of proof is the balance of probabilities."

This Part of the Act sets out certain safeguards against prejudice which may be caused by the admissibility of hearsay evidence. For instance, s.123 provides that a hearsay statement is not admissible if the witness was not capable of making the statement when he did so. For these purposes a person who understands the questions put to him and gives answers which can be understood has the required capability: s.123(3).

The section reflects the test for competence to give evidence in criminal proceedings under s.53 of the Youth Justice and Criminal Evidence Act 1999.[89] For a discussion of competence, see Ch.17, below.

(2) Credibility

8–69 Section 124 provides that:

"(1) This section applies if in criminal proceedings—

    (a) a statement not made in oral evidence in the proceedings is admitted as evidence of a matter stated, and

    (b) the maker of the statement does not give oral evidence in connection with the subject matter of the statement.

(2) In such a case—

    (a) any evidence which (if he had given such evidence) would

[89] Explanatory Notes to the Criminal Justice Bill, November 21, 2002, para.351.

have been admissible as relevant to his credibility as a witness is so admissible in the proceedings;

(b) evidence may with the court's leave be given of any matter which (if he had given such evidence) could have been put to him in cross-examination as relevant to his credibility as a witness but of which evidence could not have been adduced by the cross-examining party;

(c) evidence tending to prove that he made (at whatever time) any other statement inconsistent with the statement admitted as evidence is admissible for the purpose of showing that he contradicted himself.

(3) If as a result of evidence admitted under this section an allegation is made against the maker of a statement, the court may permit a party to lead additional evidence of such description as the court may specify for the purposes of denying or answering the allegation.

(4) In the case of a statement in a document which is admitted as evidence under section 117 each person who, in order for the statement to be admissible, must have supplied or received the information concerned or created or received the document or part concerned is to be treated as the maker of the statement for the purposes of subsections (1) to (3) above."

The purpose of this section is to provide a means for the opposing party to challenge the credibility of the maker of an oral statement who does not give evidence in the proceedings. The section replaces similar provisions in the 1988 Act.[90] It permits evidence relevant to the maker's credibility to be given (s.124(2)(a))[91]; together with evidence of any matter relevant to his credibility which could have been put to him in cross-examination, but which could not have been adduced in evidence by the cross-examining party (s.124(2)(b))[92]; and for the purpose of showing that the witness has contradicted himself, evidence that he has made a statement inconsistent with his evidence (s.124(2)(c)).[93]

---

[90] s.28 and Sch.2, para.1, of the Criminal Justice Act 1988.
[91] In the case of a statement admitted under s.117 (business documents) each person who supplied or received the information or created or received the document is to be treated as the "maker" for the purposes of the section: s.124(4).
[92] Such evidence may only be given with leave of the court: s.124(2)(b). This provision will prevent unfair, scurrilous or marginally relevant but prejudicial, material from being admitted. However, since the purpose of the provision is to compensate a party for the loss of the right to cross-examine, it is submitted that leave should not be withheld unless there is a real danger that the jury will be distracted by side issues.
[93] As the paragraph makes clear, the statement may have been made at any time.

8–70   The above provisions follow the recommendations of the Law Commission.[94] The Commission also recommended that, where an allegation has been made against the maker of a hearsay statement, the court should have power to permit a party to read additional evidence for the purpose of denying or answering the allegation.[95] This follows the practice in Scotland and the Commission considered it a useful and appropriate procedure. Section 124(3) allows the court in these circumstances to permit a party to lead additional evidence to lead evidence "of such description as the court may specify" for this purpose. The court thus retains control of the sort of material which may be introduced.

Where evidence is admitted for the purpose of testing the credibility of the maker of a statement, the judge should direct the jury that inconsistent statements were not themselves evidence but only a means of testing the witness's evidence.[96]

(3) Stopping the case where the evidence is unconvincing

8–71   Section 125 provides that:

"(1)   If on a defendant's[97] trial before a judge and jury for an offence the court is satisfied at any time after the close of the case for the prosecution that—

(a)   the case against the defendant is based wholly or partly on a statement not made in oral evidence in the proceedings, and

(b)   the evidence provided by the statement is so unconvincing that, considering its importance to the case against the defendant, his conviction of the offence would be unsafe,

the court must either direct the jury to acquit the defendant of the offence or, if it considers that there ought to be a retrial, discharge the jury.

(2)   Where—

(a)   a jury is directed under subsection (1) to acquit a defendant of an offence, and

(b)   the circumstances are such that, apart from this subsection, the defendant could if acquitted of that offence be found guilty of another offence,

---

[94] "Evidence in Criminal Proceedings: Hearsay and Related Topics", Law Com. No.245 (1997, London, Stationery Office), Cm. 3670, paras 11.12–11.13.
[95] op.cit., para.11.25.
[96] Sweeting and Thomas [1999] Crim.L.R. 75.
[97] "defendant", in relation to criminal proceedings, means a person charged with an offence in those proceedings: s.134.

the defendant may not be found guilty of that other offence if the court is satisfied as mentioned in subsection (1) in respect of it.

(3) If—

    (a) a jury is required to determine under section 4A(2) of the Criminal Procedure (Insanity) Act 1964 (c.84) whether a person charged on an indictment with an offence did the act or made the omission charged, and

    (b) the court is satisfied as mentioned in subsection (1) above at any time after the close of the case for the prosecution that—

        (i) the case against the defendant is based wholly or partly on a statement not made in oral evidence in the proceedings, and

        (ii) the evidence provided by the statement is so unconvincing that, considering its importance to the case against the person, a finding that he did the act or made the omission would be unsafe,

the court must either direct the jury to acquit the defendant of the offence or, if it considers that there ought to be a rehearing, discharge the jury.

(4) This section does not prejudice any other power a court may have to direct a jury to acquit a person of an offence or to discharge a jury."

The purpose of s.125(1) is to impose a duty on the court in trials on indictment to stop a case and either direct the jury to acquit the defendant or discharge the jury if the case against him or her is based wholly or partly on an out of court statement which is so unconvincing that, considering its importance to the case, a conviction would be unsafe.[98] Section 125(2) imposes a corresponding duty on the court to direct the acquittal of any alternative offence to that charged if the court is satisfied that a conviction would be unsafe. (These provisions only apply to jury trials since magistrates would be bound to dismiss a case, or under a retrial in the above situation.) These circumstances would arise if prima facie admissible evidence is given, but which turns out either in the manner of its giving, in cross-examination or by subsequent evidence to be so unconvincing that any conviction based on it would be unsafe.

It should be noted that the duty placed on the court to acquit or order a   **8–72** retrial in such circumstances, *i.e.* where the prosecution case is based wholly or partly on hearsay so unconvincing that a conviction based on it

---

[98] Explanatory Notes, para.353.

would be unsafe, is mandatory. A similar duty is based on the court where the defendant is insane.

This provision is based on a recommendation of the Law Commission.[99] The Commission points out that this is an exception to the rule in *Galbraith*[1] that matters of fact are for the jury: the justification for a derogation being that the jury might act upon evidence which is not to be relied upon.[2] "Experience has shown that identification evidence, and confessions, can be unreliable."[3]

(4) General discretion to exclude evidence

8–73   Section 126 provides that:

> "(1)   In criminal proceedings the court may refuse to admit a statement as evidence of a matter stated if—
>
> > (a)   the statement was made otherwise than in oral evidence in the proceedings, and
> > (b)   the court is satisfied that the case for excluding the statement, taking account of the danger that to admit it would result in undue waste of time, substantially outweighs the case of the value of the evidence.
>
> (2)   Nothing in this Chapter[4] prejudices—
>
> > (a)   any power of a court to exclude evidence under section 78[5] of the Police and Criminal Evidence Act 1984 (c.60) (exclusion of unfair evidence), or
> > (b)   any other power of a court to exclude evidence at its discretion (whether by preventing questions from being put or otherwise)."

There is plainly a danger that the freer admission of hearsay will result in unnecessary and superfluous evidence being put before the court. The purpose of this section is to provide the court with a discretion to exclude such evidence if the court is satisfied that the value of the evidence is substantially outweighed by the undue waste of time which its admission would cause.[6] This is a new power, akin to that in s.135 of the Evidence Act 1995 in Australia and Rule 463 of the US Federal Rules of Evidence which allows a court to exclude admissible evidence. While this will be a useful

---

[99] Law Com. No.245, para.11.32
[1] [1981] 1 W.L.R. 1039.
[2] *op.cit.*, para.11.31.
[3] *ibid.*
[4] *i.e.* Chapter Two of Part 11 of the Criminal Justice Act 2003.
[5] See Ch.9, paras 9–25 to 9–26, below.
[6] Explanatory Notes, para.355.

power to exclude time-wasting evidence, it should be noted that the court must be satisfied that this danger not only outweighs but "substantially" outweighs the value of the evidence.[7]

Section 126(2) makes clear that the provisions in Chapter 2 do not affect the court's discretion under s.78 of the Police and Criminal Evidence Act and at common law to exclude unfair or prejudicial evidence.

These provisions are based on a recommendation of the Law Commission which anticipated that the exercise of the power under them would be exceptional, *i.e.* where the probative value of evidence was so slight that almost nothing would be gained by admitting it. However, the Commission observed that it would serve to meet the point that the admission of hearsay would lead to a lot of barely relevant evidence being adduced.[8]

(5) Directions to the jury

A further safeguard is to be found in the direction which the judge must give the jury. If a statement is read or hearsay relied on it will be necessary to warn the jury to bear in mind, when deciding whether they can rely on it, that they have not had the benefit of hearing the evidence of the maker tested in cross-examination. The Privy Council in *Scott*[9] said that such a warning is necessary in every case where a deposition is read. The same rule applies to cases where a statement is read. Thus, in *Curry*[10] the Court of Appeal quashed the conviction in a case where the judge had failed to give a warning: the Court said that the jury should be warned to use particular care in these circumstances and failure to do so was a fatal omission. Further, the jury should be warned that they have not had the opportunity of seeing the witness in the witness-box.[11]

In *Scott*[12] Lord Griffiths said that while in many cases it will be appropriate for the judge to develop the warning by pointing out features of the deposition which conflict with other evidence and could have been explored in cross-examination, no rules could usefully be laid down to control the detail to which the judge should descend in the particular case. The Court of Appeal in *Kennedy*[13] held that a trial judge, having given a suitable warning, was not obliged to direct the jury that it should pay less attention to the statement than to the evidence of live witnesses. However, in *Kennedy and Burrrell*,[14] the Court of Appeal criticised the trial judge for not pointing out specific weaknesses in the statement of a

8–74

---

[7] Law Comm. No.245, para.11.18.
[8] *ibid.*
[9] (1989) 89 Cr.App.R. 153.
[10] *The Times*, March 23, 1998.
[11] JSB Specimen Directions (under the 1988 Act): *www.jsboard.co.uk.*
[12] Above, at 161.
[13] [1992] Crim.L.R. 37.
[14] [1994] Crim.L.R. 50.

deceased witness admitted under s.23 of the 1988 Act, for example (i) the deceased had consumed much alcohol at time of the incident, and (ii) there were important inconsistencies between his evidence and that of other witnesses. Whether it will be necessary to give more than the standard warning will depend on the facts of the particular case. In *Cole*[15] the trial judge had directed the jury that they could not pay as much attention to this evidence as other evidence: this direction was not criticised on appeal. However, more recently, the Court of Appeal has said that such a direction was not appropriate when the usual warning as to limitations has been given.[16] Although the above cases were decided under the earlier legislation, it is submitted that they still apply under the current law.

C. Miscellaneous

(1) Representations other than by a person

8–75   Section 129 provides that:

"(1) Where a representation of any fact—

(a) is made otherwise than by a person, but

(b) depends for its accuracy on information supplied (directly or indirectly) by a person, the representation is not admissible in criminal proceedings as evidence of the fact unless it is proved that the information was accurate.

(2) Subsection (1) does not affect the operation of the presumption that a mechanical device has been properly set or calibrated."

The purpose of s.129(1) is to provide that, where a statement generated by a machine is based on information supplied by a human, the statement will only be admissible if it is proved that the information is accurate.[17] This was a recommendation of the Law Commission.[18] The Commission emphasised the distinction between a statement consisting of what a machine itself has observed and one which incorporates, or is based upon, information supplied by a human being. The first use relates to a machine, for example such as a computer being used as a mechanical device or tool as a calculator, breath-testing device,[19] or to analyse the chemical composition of metal[20]; also, automatic recordings, para.2–43, above. No question of hearsay arises in relation to such evidence which is real evidence.

---

[15] *Cole* (1990) 90 Cr.App.R. 478.
[16] *Greer* [1998] Crim.L.R. 572.
[17] Explanatory Notes, para.363.
[18] Law Comm. No.245, para.7.50.
[19] *Castle v Cross* [1984] 1 W.L.R. 1327.
[20] *Wood* (1983) 76 Cr.App R. 23.

This distinction is preserved by the Act which confines "statements" to a representation "made by a person": s.115(2). Thus conclusions printed out by a machine are not a "statement" for the purposes of the Act.[21]

On the other hand, in the second case referred to above, the hearsay rule does not apply in some cases if the statement of the machine is admissible only if the facts on which it is based are proved. Thus, in *Coventry JJ. Ex p. Bullard*,[22] a computer print-out of poll-tax arrears was held to be inadmissible hearsay because it was based on information which had been fed into the computer by a human being: proof of that input was necessary, to make the evidence admissible. The Law Commission's view was that in these circumstances the statement of the computer, properly understood, is conditional on the accuracy of the data on which it is based; and if the data is not proved to be accurate, the statement has no probative value.[23] The Commission pointed out that no question of hearsay arises since the evidence is simply irrelevant: it may not therefore be necessary to complicate the hearsay rule by extending it to statements made by machines on the basis of human import, but that a separate provision was necessary, independent of the hearsay rule.

The distinction above is one of fact. If the machine is working as a calculator or tool then no additional evidence is necessary. However, if its output depends on the accuracy of data put into it, then s.129(1) will require evidence to show that the data was accurate.   8–76

Section 129(2) preserves the common law presumption that a mechanical device is in proper working order: para.5–06, above. The former restrictions upon the admission of computer records made by s.69 of the Police and Criminal Evidence Act 1984 having been abolished,[24] that presumption governs the admissibility of such records.

(2) Statements and depositions   8–77

A number of statutes allow statements, depositions and other material documents which would otherwise be hearsay, to be read at criminal trials.

(a) Criminal Procedure and Investigations Act 1996, s.68 and Sch.2.   8–78
Section 68 of the 1996 Act provides for the admissibility at trial of statements and depositions admitted in evidence at committal proceedings. This section and Sch.2 make provision for the reading (without further proof) at trial of written statements and depositions admitted in evidence in modified

---

[21] Law Commission Report, Law Comm. 245, para.7.45.
[22] (1992) 95 Cr.App.R. 175.
[23] *op.cit.*, para.7.48.
[24] Youth Justice and Criminal Evidence Act 1999, s.60.

committal proceedings. Such statements and depositions will then be admitted in evidence at the trial of the defendant for the offence for which he was committed and for any other offence arising from the same circumstances. To be admissible, the statement or deposition must be signed by a magistrate (in the case of a deposition, by the magistrate before whom it was taken). If it proves that the statement or deposition was not so signed, it will be inadmissible. A statement or deposition may not be admitted if another party objects or the court, in the exercise of its discretion, so orders.

8–79   **(b) Criminal Justice Act 1967, s.9.**   This provision allows a written statement by any person to be evidence "to the like extent as oral evidence to the like effect by that person" in any criminal proceedings except committal proceedings. This provision is of importance in saving time in criminal trials, particularly in magistrates' courts.

A statement is admissible under this section providing that the conditions set out in s.9(2) are fulfilled.[25] These conditions may be summarised as follows:

(a)   the statement must be signed by the maker;

(b)   it must contain a declaration by the maker that it is true to the best of his knowledge and belief[26];

(c)   a copy must be served before the hearing on each of the other parties; and

(d)   none of the other parties within seven days of service of the copy objects to the statement being tendered in evidence.

Notwithstanding the fact that these conditions are fulfilled and that a statement is admissible under s.9, the court may of its own motion (or on the application of any party) require the maker to give evidence[27]: s.9(4). The party tendering the written statement may also call the maker (s.9(4)).

A statement admitted under s.9 is not conclusive evidence of the matters stated in it. However, if no objection is made, it will be taken that the

---

[25] These conditions must be strictly complied with: *Paterson v DPP* [1990] Crim.L.R. 651.
[26] The declaration must also state that the declarant made the statement knowing that if it were tendered in evidence, he would be liable to prosecution if he wilfully stated in it anything which he knew to be true. However, the section does not require a separate signature on the declaration: *Chapman v Ingleton* (1973) 57 Cr.App.R. 476.
[27] Justices calling evidence under s.9(4) should observe the rules as to the time within which the evidence is called: *French's Dairies (Sevenoaks) Ltd v Davis* [1973] Crim.L.R. 630. For the rules see paras 19–34 *et seq.*, below.

matters are unchallenged. If they are challenged, the proper course is to give notice so that the witness attends the hearing and the matters in dispute may be put to him in cross-examination. Thus, in *Lister v Quaife*[28] the defendant was charged with stealing a dress from a store. She told the police that she had brought it in another branch of the same store. The prosecution in order to rebut this defence served two statements under s.9 showing that no such dress would have been available at the time. No notice was given requiring the attendance of the witnesses and the statements were read at the trial. The defendant gave evidence along the lines of her explanation to the police. The justices came to the conclusion that the explanation was reasonable and dismissed the case. The Divisional Court dismissed the prosecutor's appeal because it was open to the justices to find (despite the evidence adduced under s.9) that the defendant's explanation may have been true. (The court commented that in similar circumstances it was always open to the prosecution to apply for an adjournment so that the maker of the statement could attend.) May L.J. said that legal representatives of defendants, whether in the magistrates' court of the Crown Court, should observe the well-known practice of putting their case to the witnesses for the prosecution and that failure to give a notice under s.9 was not to be used as a device for having the defendant present, giving evidence in person, whereas the prosecution statements would merely be read: reluctance to give notice under s.9 in order to obtain such an advantage was to be deprecated.

(c) Miscellaneous statutes.

(i) Theft Act 1968, s.27(4).   In proceedings relating to the theft of goods in transmission (whether by post or otherwise) or for handling goods so stolen, a statutory declaration by the sender or recipient that the goods were dispatched or received is admissible as evidence of those facts and of the condition of the goods where and to the extent that oral evidence would have been so admissible; provided (a) a copy is given to the defendant at least seven days before the hearing; and (b) the defendant has not within at least three days before the hearing (or within such further time as the court may in special circumstances allow) given written notice requiring the attendance of the person who made the declaration. But where the hearing is before examining magistrates this restriction does not apply.[29]   **8–80**

(ii) Criminal Appeal Act 1968, Sch.2.   On a retrial ordered by the Court of Appeal under the Criminal Appeal Act 1968, a transcript of the evidence given by a witness at the original trial may, with the leave of the judge, be read as evidence either by agreement between prosecution and defence; or if the judge is satisfied that the witness is dead or unfit to give   **8–81**

[28] (1982) 75 Cr.App.R. 313, D.C.
[29] subs.(4A), inserted by the Criminal Procedure and Investigations Act 1996, s.47, Sch. 1(20).

evidence or that all reasonable efforts to find him or secure his attendance have been made without success.

8-82   *(iii) Children and Young Persons Act 1933, ss.42[30] and 43.*   These sections apply in the case of a child or young person whose attendance in court would involve serious danger to his life or health in proceedings relating to offences specified in Sch.1 to the Children and Young Persons Act 1933.

Where it is necessary to edit written statements which the prosecution propose to tender under s.9 of the 1967 Act (because a witness had made more than one statment or where a statement contains inadmissible pre-judicial or irrelevant material) reference should be made to the Practice Direction given by the Lord Chief Justice on June 3, 1986.[31] The Practice Direction provides that the editing of statements should in all circumstances be carried out by a Crown Prosecutor and not by a police officer. It provides guidance as to how statements should be edited in order to meet the requirements of the respective Acts.

8-83   *(iv) Crime (International Co-operation) Act 2003.*   Section 3 of this Act[32] provides that a "prosecuting authority"[33] may apply to a "judicial authority"[34] for the latter to request assistance in obtaining outside the UK evidence in relation to an offence or reasonably suspected offence which is being prosecuted or investigated. The request by the judicial authority will be to a court or appropriate authority in the place where the evidence is situated: s.8. However, requests for information on banking transactions made in reliance on Art.2 of the 2001 Protocol must state the grounds on which the person making it considers the evidence specified in the request to be relevant for the purposes of the investigation.[35]

By s.9 evidence obtained under s.7 may not be used for any purpose other than that specified in the request. Such evidence may be protected by a "freezing order".[36]

(3) Schedules and glossaries

8-84   For the purpose of helping members of juries to understand complicated issues of fact or technical terms, s.31 of the Criminal Justice Act 1988 allows Crown Court Rules to provide:

---

[30] As amended by the Access to Justice Act 1999, s.90(1), Sch.13(9).
[31] *Practice Direction (Evidence: Written Statements)* (1986) 83 Cr.App.R. 212.
[32] The 2003 Act replaces the Criminal Justice (International Co-operation) Act 1990.
[33] To be defined by an SI made under the Act. At the time of writing, no such SI had been made.
[34] In England and Wales, any judge or justice of the peace: s.7(4)(a).
[35] subs.(7).
[36] Further as to freezing orders, see ss.11–25 of the 2003 Act.

(a) for the furnishing of evidence "in any form", although there is admissible evidence from which the evidence in that form would be derived; and

(b) for the furnishing of glossaries "for such purposes as may be specified."

These Rules apply "in any case where the court gives leave for, or requires, evidence or a glossary to be so furnished".

The provision of s.31 were based on recommendations in the Report of the Fraud Trials Committee (the "Roskill Report").[37]

They allow for the presentation of evidence by means of schedules, glossaries of technical terms, and modern visual aids (for example showing material on an overhead projector).

Schedules play an essential part in the presentation of complex matter, particularly in fraud trials. The provisions empower the judge to permit a schedule to be admitted in evidence. The purpose of admitting glossaries is to permit the jury to have written material explaining technical terms available to them throughout the trial.

In cases of serious and complex fraud s.9 of the Criminal Justice Act 1987 permits the judge at the preparatory hearing of such a case to order the prosecution to prepare its evidence and other explanatory material in such form as appears "likely to aid comprehension by the jury".

(4) Evidence at retrial

Section 131 of the Criminal Justice Act 2003 has substituted paras 1 and 1A   8–85
of the Criminal Appeal Act 1968 to the effect that evidence given at a retrial must be given orally if it was given orally at the previous trial except in the following circumstances:

(1) all the parties agree;

(2) s.116 of the 2003 Act applies, that is, the witness is unavailable because he is dead, ill, etc. (see paras 8–17 to 8–29, above); or

(3) the witness is unavailable to give evidence for some other reason and the court admits the evidence under the residual discretion under s.114(1)(d) (see para.8–13, above), *i.e.* that it would be in the interests of justice to admit the evidence.

---

[37] (1986) HMSO, paras 5.48, 5.49 and 6.60 to 6.66.

The common law permitted transcripts to be admitted at a retrial of the evidence of witnesses who had testified in the original trial, but were unavailable to give evidence at the retrial.[38] The Law Commission recommended that evidence given at the original trial should be admissible in a retrial like any other statement if the witness is unavailable to give oral evidence.[39]

(5) Proof of statements in documents

8–86 Section 133 of the Criminal Justice Act 2003 provides that:

> "Where a statement in a document is admissible as evidence in criminal proceedings, the statement may be proved by producing either—
>
> (a) the document, or
> (b) (whether or not the document exists) a copy[40] of the document or of the material part of it,
>
> authenticated in whatever way the court may approve."

This section replaces s.29 of the Criminal Justice Act 1988 and is intended to cover all forms of copying including the use of imaging technology.[41] It appeared in the Draft Bill of the Law Commission[42] and was made necessary by the repeal of Pt II of the 1988 Act.

(6) Failure to comply with procedural requirements

8–87 Section 132 provides that rules of court[43] may make provision for the purposes of Chapter 2 (the "hearsay" Chapter) of the Criminal Justice Act 2003. These rules lay down certain requirements for the admission of hearsay evidence. Failure to comply with the requirements means that the evidence is not admissible except with leave of the court.[44] Where leave is given to admit the evidence the court or jury may draw such inferences from it as seems proper.[45] However, the court, in considering whether to exercise its powers in either of these two situations, shall have regard to whether there is any justification for the failure to comply with the

---

[38] In *Hall* [1973] 1 Q.B. 496 the witness had died, in *Thompson* (1982) 74 Cr.App.R. 315 the witness was too ill to travel, and in *Scaife* (1851) 5 Cox C.C. the witness's absence had been procured by the defendant.
[39] Law Com. 245 para.8.207.
[40] " 'Copy', in relation to a document, means 'anything on to which information recorded in the document has been copied, by whatever means and whether directly or indirectly' ": s.134.
[41] Explanatory Notes to the Criminal Justice Bill, November 21, 2002, para.366.
[42] Cm. 245. Draft Bill, cl.22.
[43] No such rules have as yet been promulgated.
[44] subs.(5)(a).
[45] subs.(5)(b).

requirement.[46] Furthermore, where the court or jury is entitled to draw an inference from a failure to produce hearsay evidence in accordance with the requirements, a person should not be convicted solely on the basis of such an inference.[47]

---

[46] subs.(6).
[47] subs.(7).

CHAPTER 9

Hearsay: 2. Confessions

9–01 Informal admissions (*i.e.* statements adverse to the maker, made out of court) were admissible under the common law.[1] They were admitted as an exception to the hearsay rule because it was thought that if a person makes a statement against his own interests, it is likely to be true.[2]

Special rules governed the admissibility of informal admissions when made to a person in authority, for example a police officer investigating an offence. These admissions were known as "confessions" and were not admitted unless they were "voluntary".

If the prosecution could not show that an alleged confession was voluntary (*i.e.* not made as a result of oppression or a threat or inducement) the confession was inadmissible. The reason for the rule would appear to have been that an involuntary confession may not be reliable.[3] If a police officer tells a suspect that he will be bailed if he confesses, the suspect may make an untrue confession in order to shorten his detention. The possibility of an untrue confession being made is the greater if the suspect is subjected to ill-treatment. In *Lam Chi-Ming v R*.[4] Lord Griffiths said that the more recent English cases established that the rejection of such confessions also depended on (a) the principle that a man cannot be compelled to incriminate himself and (b) the importance which attaches in a civilised society to proper behaviour by the police towards those in their custody.

---

[1] Such admissions are called "informal" to distinguish them from "formal" admissions made under s.10 of the Criminal Justice Act 1967, 5–07 above. Informal admissions made out of court must also be distinguished from admissions made while a person is giving evidence. The same rules do not apply to admissions in the witness-box. Such admissions are evidence against the maker and any co-defendant.

[2] "What a party himself admits to be true, may reasonably be presumed to be so": *Slatterie v Pooley* (1840) 6 M. & W. 664, 669, *per* Parke B. The Law Commission in its Report on Hearsay recommended that confessions should be admissible on the general assumption that what a person says against his or her own interest is likely to be true: "Evidence in Criminal Proceedings: Hearsay and Related Topics" Law Commission Report No.245 (1997), paras 8.84–92. However, it should be noted that Sir John Smith argued that the true rationale was that a party to litigation could not invoke the hearsay rule in respect of his own statement: "Exculpatory Statements and Confessions" [1995] Crim.L.R. 280.

[3] See Criminal Law Revision Committee Eleventh Report, Cmnd. 4991, paras 55–56.

[4] (1991) 93 Cr.App.R. 358, 362.

The rule led to the exclusion of confessions made subsequently to any inducement, however trivial, by a person in authority.

The admissibility of confessions is now governed by ss.76 and 76A of the Police and Criminal Evidence Act 1984.[5]   **9–02**

Section 76 provides that—

"(1) In any proceedings a confession made by an accused person may be given in evidence against him in so far as it is relevant to any matter in issue in the proceedings and is not excluded by the court in pursuance of this section.

(2) If, in any proceedings where the prosecution proposes to give in evidence a confession made by an accused person, it is represented to the court that the confession was or may have been obtained—

    (a) by oppression of the person who made it; or

    (b) in consequence of anything said or done which was likely, in the circumstances existing at the time, to render unreliable any confession which might be made by him in consequence thereof,

the court shall not allow the confession to be given in evidence against him except in so far as the prosecution proves to the court beyond reasonable doubt that the confession (notwithstanding that it may be true) was not obtained as aforesaid.

(3) In any proceedings where the prosecution proposes to give in evidence a confession made by an accused person, the court may of its own motion require the prosecution, as a condition of allowing it to do so, to prove that the confession was not obtained as mentioned in subsection (2) above.

(4) The fact that a confession is wholly or partly excluded in pursuance of this section shall not affect the admissibility in evidence—

    (a) of any facts discovered as a result of the confession; or

    (b) where the confession is relevant as showing that the accused speaks, writes or expresses himself in a particular way, of so much of the confession as is necessary to show that he does so.

(5) Evidence that a fact to which this subsection applies was discovered as a result of a statement made by an accused person shall

---

[5] s.76 follows the general approach of the recommendations of the Criminal Law Revision Committee, Eleventh Report, Cmnd. 4991. S.76A was inserted by s.128 of the Criminal Justice Act 2003, see below paras 9–03, 9–53. At the time of writing, s.76A was expected to come into force in April 2005. S.118(1) of the Criminal Justice Act 2003 expressly preserves the rules of law relating to confessions.

not be admissible unless evidence of how it was discovered is given by him or on his behalf.

(6) Subsection (5) above applies—

(a) to any fact discovered as a result of a confession which is wholly excluded in pursuance of this section; and

(b) to any fact discovered as a result of a confession which is partly so excluded, if the fact is discovered as a result of the excluded part of the confession.

(7) Nothing in Part VII of this Act shall prejudice the admissibility of a confession made by an accused person.

(8) In this section "oppression" includes torture, inhuman or degrading treatment, and the use or threat of violence (whether or not amounting to torture).

(9) Where the proceedings mentioned in subsection (1) above are proceedings before a magistrates' court inquiring into an offence as examining justices this section shall have effect with the omission of—

(a) in subsection (1) the words "and is not excluded by the court in pursuance of this section", and

(b) subsection (2) to (6) and (8)."

9–03   The new s.76A permits a confession by one accused to be adduced in evidence by a co-accused.[6] Such a confession is only admissible if it is also admissible under s.76.[7]

Admissibility is also subject to s.78 of the 1984 Act which gives the court a discretion to exclude evidence if its admission would adversely affect the fairness of the proceedings. The court's common law discretion has also been retained, although this must now only be of marginal significance: para.9–46, below.

1. WHAT AMOUNTS TO A CONFESSION?

A. The meaning of "confession"

9–04   Section 82(1) of the 1984 Act defines "confession" to include "any statement wholly or partly adverse to the person who made it, whether made to

---

[6] Overruling *Beckford and Daly* [1991] Crim. L.R. 833 in which the Court of Appeal held that "given in evidence" meant "given in evidence by the prosecution" and did not allow a co-defendant to put a confession by another defendant in evidence.
[7] s.128, CJA 2003, subs.(2).

a person in authority or not and whether made in words or otherwise."[8]
The following points should be noted:

(a) The definition includes any informal admission made out of court.[9] No distinction is made between a full confession and admissions falling short of a full confession.[10] For instance, it will include an admission by a suspect that he is the defendant.[11]

(b) It is immaterial to whom the confession is made. This was the rule at common law, except in the case of persons in authority. Thus, "what a person is overheard saying to his wife or even saying to himself is evidence."[12] It now makes no difference to the admissibility of a confession whether it was made to a person in authority or not, *i.e.* the same rules will apply whether the confession is made to a police officer, an officer of the Customs and Excise, a social worker, a friend or a relative.

(c) "Confession" is defined to include any statement whether made in words or otherwise. Thus, a confession may be in writing. For instance, defendants may make written statements to the police confessing their guilt. However, admissions may be made in other documents. Thus, admissions in a letter which a defendant wrote to his wife but which was intercepted by a third party were held admissible at common law.[13] Such admissions would be admissible under ss.76 or 76A.

B. Admission by conduct

The question arises whether an admission by conduct is included in the definition. Thus, suppose a police officer asks a suspect if he committed a particular offence. The person says nothing but nods in reply. At common law evidence that the suspect nodded would have been admissible as evidence from which the jury could infer that the defendant accepted that he committed the offence. It would appear that the evidence would also be admissible under the section.

9–05

Admissions by conduct are only admitted in exceptional cases. For

---

[8] A self-incriminating telephone call made by the defendant resulting from a "co-operation conversation" was a confession within the meaning of s.82(1): *de Silva* [2003] Crim. L.R. 474. As to "co-operation conversations" see para.9–45, below. By the new s.76A(3), added by the Criminal Justice Act 2003, s.112, "confession" has the meaning borne in s.82(1).

[9] An admission *in* court is admissible against a defendant. In *McGregor* [1968] 1 Q.B. 371, the prosecution was held to be entitled to prove as part of its case at a retrial that the defendant had admitted on oath at the first trial that he was in possession of certain stolen goods.

[10] The common law rule is thus preserved: *Customs and Excise Commissioners v Harz and Power* [1967] 1 A.C. 760, 817–818, *per* Lord Reid.

[11] *Ward, Andrews and Brindley* [2001] Crim.L.R. 316.

[12] *Simms* (1834) 6 C. & P. 540, *per* Alderson B.

[13] *Rumping v DPP* [1964] A.C. 814.

example in *Preece v Parry*[14] the Divisional Court held that the violent and abusive behaviour of the defendants when arrested was capable of constituting an admission of violent and abusive behaviour in a public house earlier in the evening. It is, however, submitted that this is an exceptional case and the defendant's behaviour on arrest is only rarely capable of amounting to an admission.

C. Failure to reply to an accusation

9–06   Suppose that the defendant remains silent when the allegation is made. Can his failure to reply ever amount to an admission? The common law rule is that a statement in the presence of the accused is not evidence against him except insofar as he accepts what has been said. The law was stated by Lord Atkinson in *Christie*[15] as follows:

> "[the] rule of law undoubtedly is that a statement made in the presence of an accused person, even upon an occasion which should be expected reasonably to call for some explanation or denial from him, is not evidence against him of the facts stated save so far as he accepts the statement, so as to make it, in effect, his own. If he accepts the statement in part only, then to that extent alone does it become his statement. He may accept the statement by word or conduct, action or demeanour, and it is the function of the jury which tries the case to determine whether his words, action, conduct or demeanour at the time when a statement was made amounts to an acceptance of it in whole or in part."

Accordingly, the fact that an accused person fails to reply to an accusation made in his presence is not normally evidence against him. He is entitled to maintain his "right of silence" (see paras 11–14 *et seq.*, below). However, that right is now restricted by ss.34–37 of the Criminal Justice and Public Order Act 1994. These sections allow the Court to draw inferences from the accused's silence when questioned; they modify the common law rule, but do not abolish it: see paras 11–16 *et seq.* for a discussion of the sections.

9–07   There may be certain limited circumstances when a failure to reply may amount at common law to evidence against a defendant. Such circumstances arise when a reply or an indignant rebuttal of what has been said would reasonably be expected and the circumstances are such that the failure to reply is tantamount to an acceptance of what has been said. Whether silence amounts to acceptance of a statement will depend upon the circumstances. The underlying principle was expressed by Cave J. in

---

[14] [1983] Crim.L.R. 170.
[15] [1914] A.C. 545, 554.

Mitchell[16]: "Undoubtedly, when persons are speaking on even terms, and a charge is made, and the person charged says nothing, and expresses no indignation, and does nothing to repel the charge, that is some evidence to show that he admits the charge to be true." An illustration is to be found in *Parkes*.[17] In that case the defendant was charged with the murder of a young woman. He had stabbed her. Her mother found her bleeding from the wounds. The mother then saw the defendant in the yard of the house, holding a knife. The mother accused the defendant twice of stabbing her daughter. He made no reply. She took his waistband and said that she would keep him there until the police came. He then made to strike her with the knife, and as a result cut her finger. The Privy Council upheld the judge's direction that the jury could take the defendant's reaction including his silence into account in deciding whether the defendant was guilty or not.

On the other hand, when accuser and accused are not on even terms   9–08 different considerations apply. Thus, the court may have to decide whether the parties were on even terms or not. A suspect at a police station will not usually be thought to be on even terms with the police officer interviewing him. However, in *Chandler*[18] the Court of Appeal said that a detective sergeant and a suspect interviewed in the presence of his solicitor were speaking on even terms. The Court said: "We do not accept that a police officer always has an advantage over someone he is questioning. Everything depends on the circumstances." However, it is submitted that in the normal course of events a suspect cannot be said to be on even terms with an interviewing officer, even if his solicitor is present, for example when a young offender is being interviewed by an experienced detective officer.

If evidence of a defendant's failure to reply to questioning is admitted the jury should be directed that they must determine two issues: (a) does the defendant's silence indicate acceptance of what the police officer said?; and (b) if so, whether guilt could reasonably be inferred from what he had accepted. In *Chandler* the judge did not leave these issues to the jury and suggested, instead, that the defendant's silence could indicate guilt. The Court of Appeal quashed the conviction.

These rules are not affected by the power of the court under s.34 of the   9–09 Criminal Justice and Public Order Act 1994 to draw inferences from an accused's silence when questioned by the police. Section 34(5) provides that the section does not "prejudice the admissibility in evidence of the silence or other reaction of the accused in the face of anything said in his presence relating to the conduct in respect of which he is charged" or preclude the

---

[16] (1892) 17 Cox.C.C. 503, 508.
[17] (1977) 64 Cr.App.R. 25. The classic example is the old breach of promise case of *Bessela v Stern* (1877) 2 C.P.D. 265 in which the plaintiff's sister gave evidence that, when the plaintiff upbraided the defendant for promising to marry her and failing to do so, the defendant had made no denial, which was accepted as corroboration of her evidence.
[18] (1976) 63 Cr.App.R. 1, 5.

drawing of any inference from such silence or reaction which could properly be drawn.

D. Failure to reply to written allegations

9–10   In certain limited circumstances a person's failure to reply to a written allegation may amount to an admission.

In *Wiedemann v Walpole*[19] the Court of Appeal said that a letter may so imperatively demand an answer that failure to reply will amount to an admission of allegations in the letter. *Wiedemann v Walpole* concerned breach of promise but the Court referred to business and mercantile cases in which it had been held that failure to answer letters referring to agreements made by the recipient amounts to an admission of the agreement. But the rule is much stricter in criminal cases; in *Edwards*[20] the Court of Appeal said that the court must be very careful in admitting such evidence. In that case the defendant was charged with incitement to racial hatred. It was alleged that he had committed this offence by aiding the publication of a comic which contained racially offensive matter. At his trial the prosecution adduced in evidence a letter written to the defendant referring to the comic as "your idea and your work" and an unfinished reply found in the defendant's typewriter which did not refer to the comic. The Court of Appeal doubted whether the letters had been properly admitted, but held that the jury would inevitably have reached the same conclusion if the letters had been excluded.

It is submitted that it would be exceptional for such evidence to be admitted. Before doing so, the court would have to be satisfied that the failure to reply was capable of amounting to an acknowledgement of the truth of the accusation. This would appear to be rare given the disinclination of many to reply to letters. As Kay L.J. said, the "only fair way of stating the rule of law is that in every case you must look at all the circumstances under which the letter was written and you must determine for yourself whether the circumstances are such that the refusal to reply alone amounts to an admission."[21]

E. Vicarious Admissions

9–11   Admissions made by the defendant's agent are only admissible if it is proved that the admissions were made on the defendant's authority. In *Evans*,[22] the Court of Appeal held that evidence of a conversation between a clerk of the defendant's solicitors and a potential witness was inadmissible since there was no admissible evidence that the clerk was acting on the defendant's

---

[19] [1891] 2 Q.B. 534.
[20] [1983] Crim.L.R. 539.
[21] *Wiedemann v Walpole*, above at 541.
[22] [1981] Crim.L.R.699.

authority. Similarly, in order to prove admissions in a solicitor's letter written on behalf of a defendant, it would be necessary to show that the letter was written on the defendant's specific instructions.[23] In *Hutchinson*[24] a letter written by defence solicitors to the DPP contradicting statements in an alibi notice was held by the Court of Appeal to have been rightly admitted in evidence. The Court held that the letter was admissible *inter alia* because it was comparable to a relevant statement made by the defendant before trial to a police officer. However, it is submitted that it must be doubtful whether such a letter would ordinarily be admissible unless it related to an alibi notice or could be shown to have been written on the specific instructions of the defendant.

In *Turner*,[25] counsel made certain admissions when addressing the court in mitigation on behalf of a defendant. The prosecution was given leave to prove these admissions in a subsequent trial against the same defendant. The Court of Appeal held that this evidence had been rightly admitted because the court is entitled to assume that what counsel says in court in the presence of his client is said on the client's authority. 9–12

On the other hand, the Court of Appeal in *Hutchinson*[26] held that admissions made by counsel for the defence at a pre-trial review were not admissible. The reason for this decision was that since the review itself does not have the force of law, nothing said or done at it should be used for evidential purposes without the consent of the party affected. The same reasoning has been applied to an answer in a questionnaire produced at a Plea and Directions Hearing: such an answer is not expected to form part of the material to be used at the trial and so it would rarely be appropriate to refer to it (and then only after counsel has been given the opportunity to address the court as to whether such reference should be made).[27]

F. Exculpatory statements

The Court of Appeal in *Sat-Bhambra*[28] said that exculpatory statements are not within the meaning of s.82(1). The question in that case was whether such a statement which became damaging at trial could be described as wholly or partly adverse to the maker. Lord Lane C.J. said that the provisions of s.76[29] could hardly have been aimed at statements which contained nothing apparently adverse to the maker's interests: "... it would 9–13

---

[23] *Downer* (1880) 14 Cox C.C. 486.
[24] (1986) 82 Cr.App.R. 51.
[25] (1975) 61 Cr.App.R.67 at 81–82.
[26] Above.
[27] *Diedrick* [1997] 1 Cr.App.R. 361. For the rules concerning Plea and Directions Hearings see the Consolidated Criminal Practice Direction, para.41, [2002] 2 Cr.App.R. 533 at 564.
[28] (1989) 88 Cr.App.R. 55, 61.
[29] Now also s.76A, added by the Criminal Justice Act 2003, s.128, which extends the effect of s.76 to confessions given in evidence for the co-accused. The section, at the time of writing, is expected to come into effect in April 2005.

mean that the statement 'I had nothing to do with it' might in due course become a 'confession' which would be surprising with or without section 82(1)." It is respectfully submitted that must be so because to describe an exculpatory statement as a confession is to ascribe to it the opposite of its true meaning.[30] Thus, in *Park*[31] the Court of Appeal held that s.82(1) did not apply to a statement intended to be exculpatory (and exculpatory on its face) which later turned out to be false or inconsistent with the maker's evidence.

9–14   However, an exculpatory statement may contain elements which the prosecution might wish to use as evidence against the accused. In such a case, the exculpatory statement (or, at least, the elements which the prosecution wish to use) will amount to a confession and the safeguards laid down by PACE must be adhered to. Thus, in *Z*[32] the accused was charged with burglary. His defence at trial was that he had only carried out the burglary as a result of threats against him and his family by X, *i.e.* under duress. However, in an "off-the-record" conversation with the police, conducted for the purposes of acquiring information about X in relation to other crimes, Z described the threats against him and his family but did not say that they were made in connection with burglary; moreover, the threats had been made on a date after the burglary had occurred. The "off-the-record" conversation had taken place on the basis of a promise of confidentiality and it had been agreed that no questions would be asked about the burglary; the conversation was informal and the precautions required by Code C were not in operation: the appellant was not cautioned, no contemporaneous record or tape was made, but instead the police made only brief trigger notes which were not shown to the accused or his legal representative, nor was he shown the written report nor asked to sign it. Consequently, the court held that the prosecution could not rely on the discrepancies between the "off-the-record" conversation and the defendant's evidence at trial.

2. WHEN IS A CONFESSION ADMISSIBLE?

9–15   The general rule is that a confession by an accused person may be given in evidence if:

(a)   it is relevant to any matter in issue in the proceedings; and

(b)   it is not excluded by the court in pursuance of s.76(2), s.76A(2) or s.78.

---

[30]   See commentary by Professor J.C. Smith [1987] Crim.L.R. 454.
[31]   (1994) 99 Cr.App.R. 270.
[32]   [2003] 2 Cr.App.R. 173.

The effect of restricting admissibility to a confession relevant to an issue in the proceedings is to limit admissibility to a confession to:

(a) the offence charged; or

(b) some other matter admissible in evidence, for example a case where some other misconduct on the defendant's part is admissible in evidence against him.[33]

When considering the admissibility of a confession the court must have in mind the provisions of ss.76, 76A and 78 of the Police and Criminal Evidence Act 1984. The court *must* exclude a confession under s.76 or s.76A[34] if it was or may have been obtained by oppression or in consequence of anything said or done which was likely to render unreliable a confession made as a result. The court *may* exclude a confession under s.78 if, having regard to all the circumstances, the admission of the evidence would have an unfair effect on the fairness of the proceedings, (The court must also, under the Human Rights Act 1998, exclude a confession if it was obtained in violation of convention rights: para.13–10, below.)

A. Admissibility under ss.76 and 76A

1. A confession, in order to be admissible under ss.76 and 76A, must not have been obtained:

9–16

(a) by oppression of the person who made it; or

(b) in consequence of anything said or done which was likely to render unreliable any confession made.

2. In the case of confessions admitted under s.76 the prosecution must show beyond reasonable doubt that the confession was not obtained by oppression or in consequence of anything said or done which was likely to render unreliable any confession made.[35] If the prosecution cannot prove this, the confession must be excluded, notwithstanding that it may be true. The judge has no discretion to admit it. But where confessions admitted under s.76A are concerned, the court may of its own motion require the fact that the confession was not obtained by oppression or in consequence of anything said or done which was likely to render the confession unreliable to be proved on the balance of probabilities.[36]

---

[33] See paras 6–07 *et seq.*, above.
[34] This section, added by the Criminal Justice Act 2003, s.128, allows confessions to be given in evidence for a co-accused. It is expected to come into effect in April 2005.
[35] The common law concerning the burden and standard of proof is thus retained, see paras 4–33 and 4–47, above.
[36] subs.(3).

(1) Sections 76(2)(a), 76A(2)(a): oppression

9-17   It has already been noted that a confession obtained by oppression was inadmissible at common law. Section 76 retains this rule as does s.76A.

Section 76(8) and s.76A(7) define oppression as including "torture inhuman and degrading treatment and the use or threat of violence (whether or not it amounts to torture)." It may not be difficult to recognise conduct as oppressive if it falls within that definition.[37] For instance, it is submitted that any bullying is capable of amounting to oppression. In *Paris*[38] the Court of Appeal held that it was oppressive within the meaning of s.76(2) (and now s.76A(2)) for police officers to shout at a suspect and tell him what they had wanted him to say after he had denied over 300 times his involvement in an offence. Lord Taylor C.J. said in that case that the Court was horrified at the way in which the suspect was bullied and that short of physical violence it was hard to conceive of a more hostile and intimidating approach by police officers to a suspect.[39]

The Court also indicated that the suspect's solicitor who was present during the interviews should have intervened and not remained passive. Lord Taylor C.J. referred to the guidelines published by the Law Society on "Advising the suspect at the Police Station" and said that it was of the first importance that a solicitor in these circumstances should follow the guidelines and discharge his function responsibly and courageously.[40] (The guidelines state that a solicitor may need to intervene (and give reasons for his objections) if the questions are oppressive, threatening or insulting or consist of comments, or are improper or are improperly put: if the improprieties continue the solicitor may need to remind the suspect of his right to silence.)

9-18   Greater difficulty arises in deciding whether conduct falling short of that sort of behaviour amounts to oppression. Guidance will be found in the decision of the Court of Appeal in *Fulling*.[41] The Court held in that case that oppression in s.76 (and now s.76A) means the exercise of authority or power in a burdensome, harsh or wrongful manner.

The defendant in *Fulling* was charged with obtaining property by deception. It was alleged that a bogus burglary of her flat had been staged and she had then made a false insurance claim. The defendant was taken to a police station and interviewed over two days. In the first two interviews she said nothing. During the third interview, she confessed. At her trial it was submitted that the confession had been obtained by oppression. She

---

[37] Thus in *Burut v Public Prosecutor* [1995] 3 W.L.R. 16 the Privy Council held that it was oppressive to have conducted an interview with a suspect who was both manacled and hooded.
[38] (1993) 97 Cr.App.R. 99.
[39] Where there has been aggressive and hostile police questioning, it is a matter of degree whether the threshold has been passed beyond which the behaviour of the police made a confession unreliable: *L* [1994] Crim.L.R. 839.
[40] At 110.
[41] [1987] Q.B. 426.

alleged in evidence on the voir dire that a police officer had told her that her lover was having an affair with a woman who was in the next cell to herself. As a result she confessed because she thought it was the only way she could get out of the police station. The trial judge assumed for the purposes of argument that the defendant's account was true but held that "oppression" had not been made out. He said that "oppression" meant "something above and beyond that which is inherently oppressive in police custody and must import some impropriety, some oppression actively applied in an improper manner by the police." The Court of Appeal upheld the judge's ruling. The Court said that, since the Police and Criminal Evidence Act was a codifying Act, the court had to examine the language of the statute and to ask what was its natural meaning, uninfluenced by any considerations derived from the previous state of the law. The Court accordingly held that "oppression" in s.76(2)(a) should be given the ordinary dictionary meaning: "exercise of authority or power in a burdensome, harsh or wrongful manner; unjust or cruel treatment of subjects inferiors, etc., or the imposition of unreasonable or unjust burdens."[42] The Court commented that it would be hard to envisage any circumstances in which such oppression would not entail some impropriety on the part of the interrogator. The judge, therefore, was not wrong in applying the test which he did.

No doubt the question of whether there can be oppression without impropriety on the part of the police will at some stage be tested. For instance, suppose a suspect to be suffering from a fatal illness. He has no knowledge of the illness. A police officer, not realising the suspect's ignorance, tells him about the illness. In the absence of bad faith on the part of the police officer, would such conduct be oppressive? It is submitted that usually it would not. The concept of oppression involves the misuse of power or authority. In the absence of such misuse there can be no oppression.

9–19

Thus, in *Miller*[43] the defendant was a paranoid schizophrenic. In an interview with a police officer he confessed to killing his girlfriend. The confession contained a mixture of factual and delusionary material. At his trial (held before the Police and Criminal Evidence Act 1984 came into effect) a psychiatrist gave evidence that some of the questions triggered hallucinations and flights of fancy. The judge held that the questioning had not been designed to induce a delusionary state in the defendant and was not oppressive. As a result, the judge admitted the confession. The Court of Appeal upheld this ruling and said that the fact that the questions triggered

---

[42] *Oxford English Dictionary*. The effect of the decision in *Fulling* is to render inadmissible the common law authorities on the meaning of oppression, such as *Priestley* (1967) 51 Cr.App.R. 1 (Note) and *Prager* (1971) 56 Cr.App.R. 51. The Court of Appeal in *Parker* [1995] Crim.L.R. 233 said that "wrongful" in the *Fulling* definition must be understood in the context of the rest of the definition, especially "burdensome", "harsh" and "unjust or cruel treatment" "Oppression" in s.76A(2) has the same meaning: subs.(7).
[43] (1986) 83 Cr.App.R. 192.

hallucinations was not by itself indicative of oppression, but that questions deliberately asked to induce a disordered state of mind would be oppressive. It is submitted that this decision reflects the modern law.

(2) Sections 76(2)(b) and 76A(2)(b): unreliability

9–20   If the prosecution fails to satisfy the court beyond reasonable doubt[44] that a confession made by an accused person has not been obtained in consequence of anything said or done which was likely in the circumstances existing at the time to render it unreliable the confession must be excluded.
   In applying the section the court must consider:

(a)   what was said and done;

(b)   the circumstances existing at the time; and

(c)   whether in consequence of what was said or done a confession would be likely to be rendered unreliable, defined as "cannot be relied on as being the truth".[45]

1. The essence of the test is that it applies to *any* confession which the defendant *might* have made as a result of anything said or done. The section is concerned with the nature and quality of the words spoken or things done likely to induce an unreliable confession. Whether the confession is true is immaterial: the court has to consider the likelihood of its being untrue.[46]
   2. In considering what was "said or done", the court must take account of *anything* said or done likely, in the circumstances existing at the time, to render a confession unreliable. This will usually, but not necessarily, relate to the words or conduct of the interrogating police officer or other officers with whom the defendant comes into contact. It might, in the case of a juvenile, relate to a relative or social worker. However, it does not include anything said or done by the maker of the confession.[47] A confession made in reliance on competent advice from a solicitor is admissible: *Wahab*.[48] A solicitor's duty is to give his client advice which is realistic rather than directed to "getting him off". Thus, in *Wahab*, the defendant, after his arrest, instructed his solicitor to approach the police and assess whether his family would be released if he confessed. The police response was that they

---

[44] In the case of confessions sought to be admitted under s.76A, the burden of proof is the balance of probabilities: subs.(3).
[45] *Crampton* (1991) 92 Cr.App.R. 369.
[46] *ibid.* See also *Bow St. Magistrates' Court Ex p. Proulx* [2000] Crim. L.R. 997: the test is whether whatever was said or done was, in any circumstances, existing at the time, likely to have rendered the confession unreliable. In *Tyrer* (1990) 90 Cr.App.R. 446, 449–450, the Court of Appeal said that in a trial-within-a-trial the judge must not take into account the truth of the confession, but this did not mean he had to put out of his mind the whole background of the case and try the admissibility of the confession in isolation.
[47] *Goldenberg* (1989) 88 Cr.App.R. 285.
[48] [2003] 1 Cr.App.R. 252.

would review the evidence against the family. The defendant then confessed. The Court of Appeal held that his confession was not unreliable
within s.76(2)(b).

3. It must be shown that there was a connection between what was said   **9–21**
or done and the confession. This connection has been called a "causal
link".[49] If no such connection can be shown the confession is admissible.
For instance, if it can be shown that a threat or inducement was no longer
operating on a defendant's mind when he confessed, his confession may be
admissible because it had not been obtained by anything said or done.

Everything said or done must be taken into account: a selection of events
may give a misleading impression. In *Barry*[50] a series of interviews took
place with the defendant spread over two days. In an interview on the first
day a police officer told the defendant that it would be beneficial if he were
to assist the police in recovering certain property. On the second day he
made a confession. The judge held that the comment by the police officer on
the first day had no bearing on events on the second day which had led up
to his making the confession. The Court of Appeal held this approach to be
wrong. The Court said that in determining reliability the first step was to
identify the thing said or done and for this purpose everything said or done
should be taken into account (in the instant case that included the interview
the previous day); the next step was to decide whether what was said or
done was likely to render a confession unreliable; all the circumstances
should be taken into account; the test was hypothetical; finally, the judge
should ask whether the prosecution has proved beyond reasonable doubt
that the confession had not been made as a result of what was said or done.

4. The court must consider the circumstances which existed at the time
when the confession was made. As a result, the test is objective. Thus, in
Everett[51] a defendant aged 42 with a mental age of eight confessed to
indecent assault. The Court of Appeal held that the judge had been wrong
in deciding the question of admissibility only by reference to the tapes of the
interview and in not taking account of the medical evidence concerning the
mental condition of the appellant. The Court held that when considering
the circumstances which existed at the time of the confession, the test to be
applied was an objective one: what was material in the instant case was not
what the officers thought about the defendant's mental condition, but what
his mental condition actually was. (Any mental condition or personality
disorder may be relevant in this connection.[52])

5. Psychological or psychiatric evidence is admissible to assist the court   **9–22**
when considering the defendant's medical condition at the time of interview.[53] When making a decision about such a matter the judge should rely

---

[49] *Goldenberg*, above, n.46.
[50] (1992) 95 Cr.App.R. 384.
[51] [1988] Crim.L.R. 826.
[52] *Walker* [1998] Crim.L.R. 211.
[53] *Raghip*, *The Times*, December 9, 1991, applying *Everett*, above.

on the medical evidence rather than his own assessment of the defendant's performance in interview: his approach should not be governed by which side of an arbitrary line the defendant's I.Q. falls.[54] In *Ward*[55] the defendant was suffering from a personality disorder so severe as to be categorised as a mental disorder; in such a case the evidence of a psychiatrist or a psychologist was held to be admissible. In *O'Brien, Hall and Sherwood*[56] the Court said that there must be a significant deviation from the norm and also a history pre-dating the confession (not based solely on the history given by the suspect) which points to or explains the abnormality. The jury should be directed that they were not obliged to accept the evidence, and should consider it, if they think it right, as throwing light on the personality of the defendant and bringing to their attention aspects of that personality of which they might otherwise be unaware.

When a schizophrenic is interviewed by to police an appropriate adult should be present even if he or she exhibits no acute symptoms and is able to understand the procedure and answer questions. The case illustrates the care which must be taken when interviewing a suspect with a history of mental illness.[57]

On the other hand, in *Heath*[58] hearsay evidence of the impressions of a psychiatrist was held not to be admissible in a case where there was no suggestion of mental handicap or retardation and the defendant was within the normal range of intelligence. The psychiatrist's impressions were to the effect that the defendant was not bright and was suggestible. The Court of Appeal said that such evidence was inadmissible, unless based upon scientific data or expert analysis outside the experience of judge and jury.

9–23   Two further matters should be noted:

(a) It is for those present at the time to determine whether a person is fit to be interviewed. Thus, in *Crampton*[59] the Court of Appeal said that whether a drug addict is fit to be interviewed (in the sense that his answers can be relied upon as being truthful) is a matter for the judgment of those present at the time.

(b) Where (i) the prosecution case depends wholly upon confessions, (ii) the defendant suffers from a significant degree of mental disability and (iii) the confessions are unconvincing to the point where a jury properly directed could not properly convict in reliance on them, the judge should withdraw the case from the jury.[60]

---

[54] *ibid.*
[55] *Ward* (1993) 96 Cr.App.R. 1.
[56] *The Times*, February 16, 2000.
[57] *Aspinall* [1999] 2 Cr.App.R. 115.
[58] [1993] Crim.L.R. 397.
[59] (1991) 92 Cr.App.R. 369, 373.
[60] *McKenzie* (Note) (1993) 96 Cr.App.R. 98, 108, *per* Lord Taylor C.J.

6. The burden is on the prosecution[61] to exclude the possibility that the   **9–24**
confession might be unreliable in consequence of all the circumstances. In
Moss[62] a defendant of low intelligence was held in custody for over a week
and interviewed on nine occasions in the absence of a solicitor. The Court
of Appeal held that admissions made towards the end of the series of
interviews should have been excluded as likely to have been unreliable.
Taylor L.J. said that stress had not been laid on the burden of proof on the
prosecution. Similarly, in *Phillips*[63] the trial judge misunderstood the
defendant when he was giving evidence on the *voir dire* and thought he said
that an inducement had *not* operated on his mind. The defendant had said
that it *had* operated on his mind. The Court of Appeal held that, bearing in
mind the onus and standard of proof, it was not established that the
admissions were obtained in circumstances which rendered them reliable.

7. A confession may be excluded on the grounds of unreliability where
there is no suspicion of impropriety.[64] An example may be found in *Harvey*,[65] a trial at the Central Criminal Court. The defendant was charged
with murder. She was a woman of low intelligence and suffered from a
psychopathic disorder. She was present with her lesbian lover when the
victim was killed. No one else was present. On arrest, the other woman
confessed to murder (in the presence of the defendant). On the following
day, while in police custody, the defendant herself confessed to the offence.
There was no other evidence against her except her confession. Two psychiatrists gave evidence that she might have confessed in an attempt to
protect her lover. Farquharson J. held that he was not satisfied beyond
reasonable doubt that the confession was not obtained as a result of hearing
the lover's confession and excluded the defendant's confession under
s.76(2)(b). In this case there was no impropriety on the part of the police.
The relevant thing "said or done" was the confession of the lover.[66]

B. Exclusion under s.78

The court has a discretion under s.78 of the 1984 Act to exclude evidence if   **9–25**
it appears that, having regard to all the circumstances including the circumstances in which it was obtained, the admission would have such an
adverse effect on the fairness of the proceedings that the court ought not to

---

[61] In the case of confessions to which s.76A applies, the burden is the balance of probabilities:
subs.(3).
[62] (1990) 90 Cr.App.R. 371.
[63] (1988) 86 Cr.App.R. 18.
[64] *Fulling* [1987] Q.B. 426.
[65] [1988] Crim.L.R. 241.
[66] So-called "cell confessions" are another example where impropriety is not alleged. See the
article by Dein on the subject at [2002] Crim.L.R. 630. But in *Benedetto v Labrador* [2003] 2
Cr.App.R. 25 (P.C.) it was held that the evidence of a prison informer (*i.e.* a fellow inmate) was
inherently unreliable, and that, if the prosecution sought to rely on it, it was their responsibility
to indicate the factors why it should be relied on, and the judge should warn the jury that the
evidence might be tainted.

admit it.[67] The section applies to all the evidence on which the prosecution proposes to rely including confessions.[68] The general principles on which the discretion is to be exercised are discussed in Ch.10 (paras 10–17 *et seq.*, below) and reference should be made to that Chapter for a detailed consideration of the topic. This discussion considers how the exercise of discretion bears upon the admissibility of confessions.

In exercising the discretion the court must first consider all the circumstances including the circumstances in which the confession was obtained. Then the court must consider whether to admit the confession would have such an adverse effect on the fairness of the proceedings that it should be excluded.

9–26 The fact that the police acted without impropriety will not necessarily mean that a confession should not be excluded under s.78.[69] On the other hand, impropriety on their part will not necessarily mean that a confession should be excluded. For instance, a court does not necessarily have to exclude a confession because there has been a breach of the Code of Practice, although it may do so.[70]

However, some impropriety will almost certainly have this effect. For example, in *Mason*[71] the police practised a deception upon the defendant and his solicitor by telling them untruthfully that the defendant's fingerprint had been found on a bottle used in starting a fire. The solicitor then advised the defendant to answer the police questions and the defendant confessed. The Court of Appeal held that because of the deceit practised on the solicitor the evidence should have been excluded under s.78. The Court said that the judge omitted this "vital factor" from his consideration. "If he had included that in his consideration of the matter, we have not the slightest doubt that he would have been driven to an opposite conclusion, namely that the confession be ruled out." The Court described the deception of the solicitor as the "vital factor". This may be because the solicitor, having been deceived by the police, advised the defendant to answer the questions. As a result the defendant confessed.

It would appear that a confession obtained as a result of deceit will almost always be in danger of being excluded, although this will depend upon the particular deceit and the circumstances of the case. If there is

---

[67] subs.(1).
[68] *Mason* (1988) 86 Cr.App.R. 349.
[69] *Samuel* [1988] Q.B. 615; (1988) 87 Cr.App.R. 232, 245. In *Brine* [1992] Crim.L.R. 122 the trial judge admitted a confession made by a man who suffered from paranoid psychosis. The judge did so because there had been no police misconduct. The Court of Appeal held that the decision was wrong and commented that s.78 is not exclusively concerned with police misconduct. For a Trinidad and Tobago case where the breach was a breach of that country's constitution, see *Mohammed v The State* [1999] 2 W.L.R. 552 (PC).
[70] *Parris* (1989) 89 Cr.App.R. 68, 72. See also para.9–27.
[71] (1988) 86 Cr.App.R. 349. Not all lies by the police are sufficiently serious: *de Silva* [2003] Crim.L.R. 473. But see that case, below para.9–45 as to the effect of s.78 on self-incriminating evidence brought into existence as the result of a "co-operation conversation".

impropriety in the obtaining of a confession, the court may be required to exclude it under one of the limbs of s.76; but if not, s.78 will come into play. Thus, Lord Lane C.J. said in *Alladice*[72] that if the police had acted in bad faith the court will have little difficulty in ruling any confession inadmissible under s.78, if not s.76. The question whether a particular deceit used by the police in questioning a suspect amounts to such bad faith in a particular case will be a matter for the court to decide. Normally, it would appear that it does. In *Walsh*[73] the Court of Appeal, dealing with breaches of statute and code, said that bad faith on the part of the police might make substantial or significant that which would otherwise not be so.

Section 78 also applies to admissions made to persons who are not police officers. In *Mcdonald*[74] the defendant was charged with murder to which his defence was provocation. But in an interview with a psychiatrist he admitted to the murder and said that he had made up the provocation. The grounds of his appeal against conviction were that the admission, being on a non-medical matter, had been unfairly obtained. The Court of Appeal said that the issue was not whether the statement had been unfairly obtained—it had not—but whether it was used unfairly. The Court held that it had not been used unfairly because it was relevant to the issue of provocation. In *Elleray*[75] the defendant had pleaded guilty to indecent assault as an alternative to rape. While being interviewed by probation officers for the pre-sentence report he had admitted to other rapes. The admissions were included in the report. On the basis of those admissions alone he was tried and convicted of two rapes. He appealed on the grounds that the admissions should not have been admitted but the Court of Appeal held that the probation officers were under a duty to include the admissions in their report and to adduce them in evidence was not unfair. However, where such admissions to probation officers are concerned, first, the prosecution should consider whether it is in the public interest to rely on it; secondly, if relied upon, the exercise of discretion under s.78 should ensure that is is fair to do so, bearing in mind (i) the need for frankness between the offender and the probation officer; (ii) that there may be no reliable record of what was said; (iii) the offender has not been cautioned; and (iv) the offender does not have the benefit of legal representation. The court was unwilling, however, to lay down guidelines except that if there was risk of unfairness to an offender probation officers should take appropriate action. Whether, however, probation officers, being neither lawyers nor police officers, are able to recognise an "unfair situation" is, it is submitted, another matter.

---

[72] (1988) 87 Cr.App.R. 380, 386.
[73] (1990) 91 Cr.App.R. 191.
[74] [1991] Crim.L.R. 122.
[75] [2003] 2 Cr.App.R. 11. See also *Stokes*, unreported, February 2, 2000.

C. Breaches of statute and code

(1) General principles

9–27   The fact that there have been breaches of statute and Code in a particular case may be among the matters which the court has to consider when deciding whether to exclude a confession under ss.76, 76A or 78. The general rule is that if there has been a breach a confession obtained as a result is liable to be excluded. However, it is not necessary for the court to exclude it. That will depend on whether the breach has resulted in oppression, unreliability or unfairness.

Section 67(11) of the Police and Criminal Evidence Act 1984 provides that Codes of Practice issued by the Secretary of State under s.66 of the Act are to be taken into account by a court in determining any question to which they appear to be relevant.[76] As a result, the court may take into account any relevant breach of Code when determining the admissibility of a confession.[77]

In *Jelen and Katz*[78] Auld J. said the provisions of the Code were for the protection of those who were vulnerable because they were in police custody: they were not intended to confine police investigations of crime to conduct which might be regarded as sporting to those under investigation. However, it has been noted subsequently that the Code extends beyond those in detention and is intended to protect suspects who are vulnerable to abuse or pressure from police officers: it will also apply where a police officer is questioning a suspect about an offence even if the suspect is not in detention.[79]

9–28   On the other hand, in *James*[80] the Court of Appeal said that the concept of "reasonable grounds for suspicion" (which, if the Code applies, requires a suspect to be cautioned) was not absolute, particularly where there was a possibility at the relevant time that no crime had been committed. In the instant case the Court of Appeal upheld the judge's ruling not to exclude conversations between the police and the defendant shortly after the disappearance of the latter's business partner with whose murder the defendant was susequently charged. (The Court upheld the judge's ruling that the defendant was not at the time a person whom there were grounds to suspect of an offence within the meaning of para.C.10.1).

Section 67(9) applies the Codes to all persons charged with the duty of investigating offences or charging offenders. It is submitted that these words

---

[76] Revised Codes of Practice issued under s.67(7) of the Act came into force on April 1, 2003. The relevant Code for this discussion is Code C which deals with the Detention, Treatment and Questioning of Persons by Police Officers. For a discussion of the changes in the Codes made by the 2003 revisions, see Cape, "The Revised PACE Codes of Practice: A Further Step Towards Inquisitorialism" [2003] Crim.L.R. 355.

[77] *Delaney* (1989) 88 Cr.App.R. 338, 341. In *Chisnell* [1993] Crim.L.R. 507 the Court of Appeal said that s.67(11) specifically affords the court the right to exercise its discretion as to whether any breaches of Code render evidence inadmissible.

[78] (1990) 90 Cr.App.R. 456, 464.

[79] *Christou and Wright* (1992) 95 Cr.App.R. 264, 271, *per* Lord Taylor C.J.

[80] [1996] Crim.L.R. 650.

must be given their literal meaning. Thus, the Court of Appeal in *Bayliss*[81] said that the application of the Codes was not restricted to officers of the central government or persons acting under statutory powers. In *Smith*[82] the Court of Appeal said that the question whether a person is charged with the duty of investigating offences is a question of mixed law and fact, involving an examination of the statute, contract or other authority under which he carries out his functions, and a consideration of his actual work. It is a question for the court in each case whether a person comes within the subsection: store detectives,[83] customs officers,[84] commercial investigators[85] and Special Compliance Officers of the Inland Revnue[86] have been held to do so, but not DTI inspectors.[87]

A breach of statute or Code is an important matter which the court has to take account together with the other circumstances of the particular case in determining whether a confession should be excluded.[88] (It has not yet been decided whether a court should differentiate between a breach of statute and a breach of Code. However, it is submitted that in the light of s.67(11) there is in practice no difference between the two and every breach must be treated on its merits.[89])

It will be for the court to determine, first, whether any breach or breaches **9–29** have occurred. Three situations may arise.[90]

(a) The breach may be apparent on the witness statements and may, as a result, be admitted. In these circumstances the court must hear submissions and then decide whether to exclude the confession.

(b) There may be a prima facie breach which can only be justified by evidence adduced by the prosecution. In this case the court must hold a trial-within-a-trial, hear the evidence, and determine whether the breach was justified.

(c) There may be a dispute as to whether the breach occurred or not. In such a case the court must hold a trial-within-a-trial, hear

---

[81] (1994) 98 Cr.App.R. 235.
[82] *Smith* (1994) 99 Cr.App.R. 233, 240.
[83] *Bayliss*, above.
[84] *Okafor* (1994) 99 Cr.App.R. 97. (The Court of Appeal in *Okafor* said that where a customs officer had reason to suspect that an offence had been committed he had either to avoid asking questions in relation to the offence or he had to follow the provisions of the Code and administer a caution.)
[85] *Thwaites and Brown* (1991) 92 Cr.App.R. 106 (employees of a private company investigating copyright offences also come within the subsection: *Joy v Federation Against Copyright Theft Ltd* [1993] Crim.L.R. 558).
[86] *Gill and Gill* [2003] Crim.L.R. 883.
[87] *Seelig and Lord Spens* (1992) 94 Cr.App.R. 17.
[88] *DPP v Blake* (1998) 87 Cr.App.R. 380.
[89] This discussion is based on material which first appeared in the author's article, "Admissibility of Confessions: Recent Developments" [1991] 55 J.C.L. 366.
[90] *Keenan* (1990) 90 Cr.App.R. 1, 10, *per* Hodgson J.

evidence called by either or both sides, and make a finding as to whether or not there has been a breach.[91]

If the court finds that a breach has occurred it must then decide whether to admit or exclude the confession. Not every breach will lead to exclusion. Thus, Lord Lane C.J. said in *Parris*[92] that a breach of the 1984 Act or Codes did not mean that any statement made by a defendant thereafter would necessarily be ruled out: it is no part of the duty of the court to rule a statement inadmissible to punish the police for failure to observe the Codes.[93] The fact that there have been breaches of the Code, however many and however culpable, is not itself "definitive of the judge's duty to exercise his discretion one way or the other".[94]

9–30   The court must consider all the circumstances and then ask itself whether the breach amounted to oppression, or has made the confession unreliable or could adversely affect the fairness of the proceedings. Thus, in *DPP v Blake*,[95] the defendant, a girl of 16 charged with arson, was interviewed in the presence of her estranged father. She did not want him there but wanted a social worker instead. (The Code requires that a juvenile be interviewed in the presence of an "appropriate adult" who is to be present, not just as an observer, but to advise the juvenile, observe fairness and facilitate communication).[96] The Divisional Court upheld the justices' decision to exclude the defendant's confession on the ground that it was not reliable since the father was not an appropriate adult, Mann L.J. observing that such a person cannot be someone with whom the juvenile has no empathy. (On the other hand, a father who intervened robustly in a fair interview and encouraged his son to tell the truth was held not thereby to have become an inappropriate adult.[97])

---

[91] *Manji* (1990) Crim.L.R. 512.
[92] (1988) 87 Cr.App.R. 380.
[93] *Delaney* (1989) 88 Cr.App.R. 338, 341.
[94] *Stewart* [1995] Crim.L.R. 500.
[95] (1988) 87 Cr.App.R. 380.
[96] Code C. 11–17. Although it is not obligatory to interview a young person of 17 in the presence of an appropriate adult or legal representative, consideration should be given as to whether such interviews not so conducted should be excluded under ss.76, 76A, or 78 of PACE because of the risk that a young person could give misleading, unreliable or self-incriminating information in an interview: *Stratford Youth Court* (2001) 165 J.P. 761, QBD.
[97] *Jefferson* (1994) 99 Cr.App.R. 13. If a police officer questions a juvenile in the street to obtain information or to establish whether there are grounds for making an arrest no adult need be present. However, if the questioner persists and goes beyond those purposes an adult must be present, albeit the questioning takes place in the street or a police car: *Weekes* (1993) 97 Cr.App.R. 222. In *W* [1994] Crim.L.R. 130, the Court of Appeal upheld the judge's ruling that a mentally-disordered mother was an appropriate adult for an interview with her daughter since she could deal rationally with current events. The fact that an interview takes place without an appropriate adult being present does not lead to the automatic exclusion of the evidence: *Law-Thompson* [1997] Crim.L.R. 674. The court should hear evidence about the interview (as to who was present and how the interview went) in order to determine whether a confession was unreliable due to the absence of an appropriate adult: *DPP v Cornish, The Times*, January 27, 1997. (In *Cornish* the justices had simply read a medical report and then dismissed the case: a course criticised by the Divisional Court.)

However, a trivial breach or a breach which does not lead to unreliability or unfairness will not result in exclusion.[98] Nor will a combination of such breaches. For instance, in *Alladice*,[99] a confession was admitted although, in breach of both statute and Code, the police had denied the defendant access to a solicitor. The Court of Appeal upheld this decision because the defendant only wanted a solicitor as a check on the police and the reliability of the confession was not affected. Similarly, in *McCarthy*[1] it was held that the fact that the police had not told the defendant that they were stopping and searching her car because they suspected drug trafficking (but pretended that it was a routine search) did not amount to a significant and serious breach of Code; and in *Roberts*[2] the Court of Appeal held that the trial judge had rightly decided that breaches of Code were insignificant when there was no causal link between them and the defendant's subsequent admissions.

In order to justify exclusion under ss.76, 76A or 78 the breach or breaches must be "significant and substantial."[3] Thus, in *Absolam*[4] the defendant was arrested for threatening behaviour. At the police station the custody officer, who knew him, told him to put the drugs on the table. The defendant did so. Then, without telling him of his right of access to a solicitor, the custody officer asked him about the drugs. The defendant admitted selling them. The record of the interview was not shown to the defendant or signed by him. The Court of Appeal held that the interview should have been excluded in the light of the "significant and substantial" breaches of code.   **9–31**

If the breach is so significant and substantial as to be flagrant the court should exclude the confession. In *Canale*[5] two police officers failed to record interviews contemporaneously because they thought it best not to do so. The Court of Appeal said that the officers had shown a cynical disregard of the Code which they had flagrantly breached. The Court applied s.78 and quashed the conviction.

On the other hand, not all significant and substantial breaches will lead to the exclusion of a confession. In *Pall*[6] it was held that failure (a) to caution a defendant who had been charged but wished to make a written statement, and (b) to ensure that the caution was written at the top of the   **9–32**

---

[98] For instance, in *H and M v DPP* [1998] Crim.L.R. 653, the Divisional Court upheld the ruling of justices not to exclude certain evidence despite a technical breach of Code C.II.14 (relating to the presence of an appropriate adult). The court said that the main purpose of the provision was to provide protection for young people and in the instant case this had been provided. (This provision is Code C 11.17 under the revised Code.)
[99] (1998) 87 Cr.App.R. 380.
[1] [1996] Crim.L.R. 818.
[2] [1997] Cr.App.R. 217.
[3] *Keenan* (1990) 90 Cr.App.R. 1, 13.
[4] (1989) 88 Cr.App.R. 332.
[5] (1990) 91 Cr.App.R. 1.
[6] [1992] Crim.L.R. 126.

statement amounted to significant and substantial breaches. However, the Court of Appeal held that there had been no unfairness in admitting the statement.

It will be for the court in each case to determine whether breaches are "significant and substantial": no hard and fast rules can be established on such a subject. However, the Court of Appeal has emphasised two aspects of the provisions of the Act and Code, namely those relating to (a) access to legal advice and (b) accurate recording of interviews. These provisions are important because, if they are complied with, the risks of fabrication or unreliable confessions are much reduced. Accordingly, a breach of such provisions may well be "significant and substantial." The following discussion of these matters serves to illustrate the operation of the general principles.

(2) Access to legal advice

9–33 If it is submitted that a confession should be excluded because the defendant was denied access to legal advice the court must first determine whether a request for a solicitor was made and refused,[7] and, if so, whether the delay was permissible under s.58 of the Police and Criminal Evidence Act 1984. Section 58 provides that a person in custody shall be entitled to consult a solicitor privately as soon as is practicable: delay in this entitlement may only be authorised in the case of a serious arrestable offence by a senior officer who has reasonable grounds under s.58(8) for believing that the exercise of the right by that person will lead to interference with evidence, injury, alerting of suspects or hindrance in the recovery of property.[8] Lord Lane C.J. said that the police should use their powers of delaying access to a solicitor with great circumspection.[9] Their scope for doing so is limited by s.58(8). They are not entitled to refuse access, for instance, on

---

[7] The new Code C of the Codes of Practice issued under PACE, s.66 (April 1, 2003) includes a requirement that the custody officer ask the detainee whether he wants legal advice (para.3.5); the custody officer is also responsible for determining whether a suspect is vulnerable as a result of mental disorder or some other mental condition (para.3.15).

[8] In *Chief Constable of the R.U.C. v Begley* [1997] 3 W.L.R. 1475 the House of Lords held that there was no common law right for a suspect to have a solicitor present during interviews with the police. On the other hand, Lord Browne-Wilkinson said that there was a right for a suspect to consult privately with a solicitor outside the interview room: this principle was subsequently enshrined in s.58.

[9] *Alladice* (1988) 87 Cr.App.R. 380, 386. In *Chief Constable of South Wales Ex p. Merrick, The Times*, February 17, 1994, the Divisional Court held that the right of access to a solicitor under s.58 does not extend to a person remanded in custody at a magistrates court. However, the court held that such a person has a right at common law to consult a solicitor as soon as reasonably practicable. In *Franklin, The Times*, June 6, 1994, a solicitor, contacted on behalf of a suspect, was refused access to the suspect. In breach of Annex B, Code C, the defendant was not notified of the solicitor's visit; and the visit was not noted in the custody record. The Court of Appeal held that in these circumstances the interviews with the defendant should have been excluded under s.78.

the ground that it might prejudice enquiries or because the defendant might be advised to remain silent.[10]

Where a defendant in an authorised place of detention, who has failed to mention facts when questioned or charged or has failed or refused to account for objects, substances or marks or to account for his presence in a particular place, has not been allowed to consult a solicitor before being questioned, charged or informed, no inference from such failure or refusal to inform may be drawn.[11] This change in the previous law resulted from the European Court of Human Rights decision in *Murray v UK*[12] in which it was held that to deny, under Northern Ireland emergency legislation, a suspect's access to a solicitor for the first 48 hours of his detention was a violation of Art.6(3)(c) of the European Convention on Human Rights which guarantees the right of a person charged to defend himself through legal assistance of his own choosing.[13]

If the police deny access they must be prepared to justify doing so by reference to s.58(8). It will be for the prosecution to satisfy the court that there were reasonable grounds for believing that the consequences mentioned in s.58(8) would have resulted from the defendant seeing a solicitor.[14] The Court of Appeal in *Samuel*[15] said that the task of satisfying a court that there were reasonable grounds for such a belief will prove formidable and can only be achieved by reference to specific circumstances, including evidence as to the persons detained or the actual solicitor sought to be consulted. The result of this decision is that the scope of the police to deny access to a solicitor is very restricted. It has, for instance, been pointed out that before denying access a police officer would have to believe that the solicitor, if allowed to consult the detainee, would thereafter commit a criminal offence.[16]

9–34

If there has been a breach of s.58 or Code, the court must decide whether the confession should be excluded under ss.76 or 78. The Court of Appeal has said that a breach of s.58 will prima facie have an adverse effect on the fairness of the proceedings but the court must consider in each case whether

9–35

---

[10] *McIvor* [1987] Crim.L.R. 409 (Sir Frederick Lawton, sitting as a deputy High Court Judge at Sheffield Crown Court).
[11] Youth Justice and Criminal Evidence Act 1999, ss.58, 59, amending ss.34, 36–38 of the Criminal Justice and public order Act 1994, below. In such circumstances that is a specific "new" caution, 'You do not have to say anything, but anything you do say may be given in evidence" Code C, Annex C, para.2 (revised, April, 2003).
[12] (1996) 22 E.H.R.R. 29.
[13] See paras 13–14, 13–22, below.
[14] *Samuel* (1988) 87 Cr.App.R. 232; *Parris* (1989) 89 Cr.App.R. 68.
[15] Above, at 242.
[16] *Silcott, The Times*, December 9, 1991. The Court of Appeal has said that a court may have to investigate the degree of sophistication of the detainee, the conduct of the solicitor or legal executive sent to advise him and the advice which would have been likely to have been given: *Alladice*, above, at 386.

that effect is such that the evidence should be excluded.[17] The usual rules apply as follows:

(a) A trivial breach, or a breach which does not result in unfairness or unreliability, will not lead to exclusion. For example, in *Dunford*,[18] the Court of Appeal held that the judge was entitled to conclude from the defendant's answers in interview and his previous record that the presence of a solicitor would not have added anything to the defendant's knowledge of his rights and, accordingly, the judge had been right to exercise his discretion under s.78 to admit the interview despite breaches of s.58.

(b) A significant or substantial breach will normally, but not necessarily,[19] lead to exclusion. The fact that the police acted in good faith is not an end of the matter. The Court of Appeal has said that breaches which were themselves significant or substantial were not rendered otherwise by the good faith of the police.[20]

The provisions of the Code relating to legal advice should be noted: a poster advertising the right to legal advice must be prominently displayed in the police station; a person may at any time consult or communicate privately with a solicitor (subject to the power of delay as set out in the Code); no attempt should be made to dissuade the suspect from obtaining legal advice; a suspect must be reminded of his right to legal advice before the beginning of an interview or re-commencement of it.[21]

If police officers ignore the provisions relating to legal advice they do so at peril of any subsequent confession being excluded. The provision of legal advice not only safeguards the rights of the suspect but also makes a confession more likely to be reliable.

(3) Conduct and records of interviews

9–36 The best way to ensure that a confession is reliable is to have it made at a properly conducted and properly recorded interview. To this end the introduction of the tape recording of interviews was much welcomed. This procedure alone saves dispute as to the contents of interviews and as to how confessions came to be made. However, untaped interviews can still provide fertile ground for dispute. In these circumstances it is better if the

---

[17] *Walsh* (1990) 91 Cr.App.R. 161, 163; *Dunford* (1990) 91 Cr.App.R. 150, 153.
[18] (1990) 91 Cr.App.R. 150.
[19] In *Oliphant* [1992] Crim.L.R. 40 the Court of Appeal held that the failure to allow a suspect access to a solicitor amounted to a serious breach of Code and statute but upheld the judge's ruling that the absence of a solicitor did not affect the fairness of the proceedings.
[20] *Walsh*, above.
[21] Code C6, Annex B. The Court of Appeal has said that if a suspect has been interviewed with his solicitor present and has made no admissions the police would seldom be justified in interviewing him without his solicitor: *Marshall, The Times*, December 28, 1992.

interview is held in a police station (where the Codes of Practice apply). The revised Code seeks to confine interviews there except in limited circumstances. It is to be anticipated that the courts will examine closely circumstances which it is alleged justify conducting an interview elsewhere.

In cases where it is alleged that interviews were not properly recorded the court will have to determine (a) what was said; and (b) whether there has been a breach of Code and, if so, whether, as a result, the evidence should be excluded.

Each case will turn on its own facts. However, decisions of the Court of Appeal give some guidance to courts faced with certain situations when it is alleged that there is justification for not complying with the Code or that, despite breaches, a confession should not be excluded. Four such situations are now considered.

1. The failure to record the interview may be deliberate. Thus, Lord Lane   9–37
C.J. said that the judge is entitled to ask himself why the officers broke the rules; and, if the reason was a desire to conceal the truth of the suggestions they held out to the defendant, the scales may be tipped in the defendant's favour.[22] On the other hand, the police officer may have overlooked the need to record the interview. Failure to record an interview, for whatever reason, will entail a breach of the Code which provides that an accurate record should be made of an interview whether or not it takes place at a police station.[23] The Code also provides that the record must be contemporaneous (unless it would be impractical or would interfere with the conduct of the interview) and that the suspect must be given the opportunity to read the record and to sign it as correct or indicate if he considers it inaccurate.[24] Lord Lane C.J. emphasised the importance of these provisions in order to ensure an accurate record of the suspect's remarks, an opportunity for the suspect to check the record and to provide protection for the police against allegations of impropriety.[25]

In *Joseph*[26] police officers interviewed a suspect during a search. No contemporaneous note was made. However, the officers pooled their recollections when at the police station two hours after the search. They produced a record of 48 questions and answers. The Court of Appeal held that there was a breach of Code in failing to record the interview contemporaneously and (there being no reasonable explanation for not doing so) the breach was significant and substantial, requiring the exclusion of the interview under both ss.76 and 78. The Court said that the purpose of requiring a contemporaneous note was to have the most cogent version of

---

[22] *Delaney* (1989) 88 Cr.App.R. 338, 341.
[23] Code C.11.7
[24] Code C.11.7(c), 11. The record of interview should be shown to the suspect in the presence of his solicitor. If it has been shown to him prior to the arrival of the solicitor, the latter should be informed on his arrival: *Cox* (1993) 96 Cr.App.R. 464.
[25] *Canale* (1990) 91 Cr.App.R. 1, 5.
[26] *Joseph* (1993) Crim.L.R. 206.

what had happened. The court is placed at a disadvantage by a breach such as this.

9–38   The Royal Commission on Criminal Justice thought that the Code should be extended to cover situations between the arrest of a suspect and his arrival at the police station. The Commission recommended that the suspect should be invited to comment on any confession, made outside the police station, and he should be given the opportunity to do so at the beginning of any subsequent tape recorded interview.[27] This is in fact a common practice now and is to be welcomed as giving the suspect at an early stage the chance to confirm or deny any alleged confession or comment.

Failure to comply with the Code is liable to lead to the exclusion of evidence of confession since the court will be deprived of the knowledge of what occurred. In *Keenan*[28] the Court of Appeal said that if there were significant and substantial breaches of the "verballing" provisions of the Code (*i.e.* those provisions safeguarding the prisoner against the police inaccurately recording or inventing words used in questioning) the evidence so obtained will frequently be excluded. The Court pointed out that where the rest of the evidence is weak or non-existent the temptation to do what the provisions are aimed to prevent is greatest and the protection of the rules most needed. Thus, in *Chung*,[29] the defendant was arrested and taken to a police station where he asked for a solicitor. He was then taken to his flat where in breach of statute and Code he was interviewed during a search and confessed. No contemporaneous record of the interview was made. The Court of Appeal held that the confession should have been excluded as unreliable.

The Court of Appeal has said that if the judge comes to the conclusion that the police did not act fairly the chances of exclusion are increased.[30] However, a mere technical breach may not lead to exclusion. For instance, in *White*,[31] the Court of Appeal held that it was not unfair to admit evidence of an incriminating remark made by the defendant during a search, although the police, in breach of the Code, failed to record the reason for not completing a contemporaneous record.

9–39   2. The defendant may say that he will talk but not if the officer writes it down. This is what happened in *Matthews*.[32] The police officer subsequently made a note of the conversation in her notebook, but in breach of Code she did not show it to the defendant because she thought it a waste of time. Despite the breach, the Court of Appeal held that the judge, in the exercise of his discretion, was entitled to admit the evidence since the

---

[27] Cm. 2263 (1993), para.3.14.
[28] *Keenan* (1990) 90 Cr.App.R. 1, 13.
[29] (1991) 92 Cr.App.R. 314.
[30] *Cox*, above.
[31] [1991] Crim.L.R. 779.
[32] (1990) 91 Cr.App.R. 43.

breach was not significant or substantial. The Court said that in a similar situation, if a police officer showed a prisoner a record which the prisoner refused to read or sign, it might be a wise precaution for the police to serve a photocopy of the statement on the prisoner's solicitor.

(It is to be noted that the Code makes provision for the written recording of comments, including unsolicited comments, outside the context of interview.[33] The Code provides that the suspect should be given, where practicable, the opportunity to read the record, to sign it as correct or to indicate the respects in which he considers it inaccurate. It is submitted that there must now be few occasions when it will not be practicable for the officer to show the suspect the record and that it is important to do so for the reasons given above. If the suspect refuses to read or sign the record, notification of its existence should, as a matter of prudence, be given to the defence as soon as possible.)

3. A variation of the above situation may occur in these circumstances. A suspect is interviewed at the police station, the interview being tape recorded in the normal way. During the interview he makes no admissions. When the interview has ended and the tape recorder is turned off, the suspect says he will talk, but not if a record is made. He then makes a confession. This sequence of events occurred in *Bryce*.[34] The Court of Appeal in that case held that the defendant should have been cautioned again in accordance with the Code (C. 10.5) since there had been a break in questioning and the interview should have been recorded contemporaneously. Lord Taylor C.J. said that if such an interview were admitted it would set at nought the requirements of the Code, one of the main purposes of which was to eliminate the possibility of concoction. "If it were permissible for an officer simply to assert that, after a properly conducted interview ... the suspect simply confessed off the record ... then the safeguards of the Code could readily be by-passed."[35] The Court was of the view that there would have to be some highly exceptional circumstances, perhaps involving cogent corroboration, before an "off-the-record" interview could be admitted in these circumstances without it having an adverse effect on the fairness of the trial.

4. The fact that there have been breaches of the Code in an initial interview may taint subsequent interviews, for example inducements in a first interview may affect the defendant's mind and render unreliable a confession in a second, properly-conducted, interview. In *McGovern*[36] the defendant, a woman of low I.Q., confessed at an interview at which, in breach of s.58 of the Act and of the Code, no solicitor was present. She was interviewed the next day in the presence of a solicitor and again confessed.

9–40

9–41

---

[33] Code C.11.13.
[34] (1992) 95 Cr.App.R. 320.
[35] At 326.
[36] (1991) 92 Cr.App.R. 228; for further examples see *Ismael* [1990] Crim.L.R. 109 and *Glaves* [1993] Crim.L.R. 685.

The Court of Appeal held that the breaches in the first interview rendered the contents of both interviews inadmissible and pointed out that the fact that a suspect has made an admission in a first interview is likely to have an effect upon him during a second interview.

However, there is no universal rule that when a breach of Code has occurred in one or more interviews all subsequent interviews must be excluded since such a rule would fetter the court's discretion under s.78.[37] The Court of Appeal has said that the question whether a later interview should be excluded is a question of fact and degree, depending on whether the objections to the first interview were of a fundamental and continuing nature and whether the suspect was given sufficient opportunity to make an independent and informed choice whether he should repeat, retract or say nothing about what was said in the excluded interview.[38]

(4) What amounts to an interview?

9–42 If it is submitted that what was said did not constitute an interview, the court must determine whether it did or did not, and hence, whether the Code applied. (If it is not an interview the Code does not apply.) The word "interview" in the Code has generally been given a broad meaning. In *Absolam*[39] the Court of Appeal defined it as a series of questions directed by the police to a suspect with a view to obtaining evidence on which proceedings could be founded. However, in *Matthews*,[40] the Court said that normally any discussion between a suspect and a police officer about an alleged crime would amount to an interview whether instigated by the police or the suspect. This broad approach has not always been adopted by the Court of Appeal which has found that the following conversations do not amount to interviews: (a) a police officer asking questions at or near the scene of a suspected crime to elicit an explanation from a suspect[41]; (b) a suspect at a police station volunteering information and the police doing no more than making notes for their records[42]; and (c) a conversation in a car between a defendant and escorting officers where the defendant volunteered information and the officers only asked one or two questions.[43] It is submitted that in the latter case the exception was taken as far as possible. This

---

[37] *Gillard and Barrett* (1991) 92 Cr.App.R. 61, 65.
[38] *Neil* [1994] Crim.L.R. 441. For a full review of the authorities and a call for a clear decision as to whether *McGovern* or *Gillard and Barrett* should be followed, see Mirfield, "Successive Confessions and the Poisoned Tree" [1996] Crim.L.R. 554.
[39] (1989) 88 Cr.App.R. 332.
[40] (1990) 91 Cr.App.R. 43, 48.
[41] *Maguire* (1990) 90 Cr.App.R. 115. Admissions made in the course of such questioning are prima facie admissible, even if made by a juvenile when no adult is present: *ibid.*
[42] *Menhard* [1995] 1 Cr.App.R. 306.
[43] *Younis and Ahmed* [1990] Crim.L.R. 425. A request for a specimen of breath under the Road Traffic Acts has also been held not to amount to an interview: *DPP v Rous* (1992) 94 Cr.App.R. 185.

is illustrated by *Hunt*.[44] The defendant in that case was found to be in possession of a flick-knife. He ran off and was arrested. He was put in a police car and, when there, was asked why he had the knife. The Court of Appeal held that the question and subsequent answer were an interview.

The revised code seeks to obviate these difficulties by defining an interview as the questioning of a person regarding his involvement or suspected involvement in a criminal offence, which is required to be carried out under caution (*i.e.* because there are reasonable grounds to suspect the person of an offence): Code C.11.1A. The Court of Appeal in *Miller*[45] described this definition as correct.

In *Marsh*[46] it was doubted whether a simple request for information **9–43** should properly be construed as an interview. In *Walkers Ltd v Coventry C.C.*[47] it was held that the questioning of an employee of a company did not fall within the Code since it was the company which was likely to be prosecuted. The court also held that the Code did not apply since it expressly excludes a request for information under a relevant statute (here the Food Safety Act 1990).

However, the Code may apply outside the police station when a suspect, not in detention, is being questioned about an offence.[48] For instance, it is a question of fact whether questioning in order to establish whether there are grounds for making an arrest amounts to an interview: there is a distinction between asking questions to enable an officer to decide whether to effect an arrest, and asking questions about an offence after arrest.[49] In such a case the court must take into account all the circumstances including the place of the questioning, and its nature, length and sequence: the court must then determine whether what was said amounted to an interview or not.[50] (One question and answer may suffice to amount to an interview: "the nature of the question ... rather than the length of questioning will primarily determine whether it is an interview. ...")[51] On the other hand, questions by a customs officer (not in the course of a search or structured interview) designed to elicit an incriminating response have been held to amount to an interview.[52] Similarly, a question by a police officer of a publican as to the arrangements in his public house (where the police suspected after-hours drinking) has also been held to amount to an interview.[53]

Code C.10.1 requires that a person whom there are grounds to suspect of

---

[44] [1992] Crim.L.R. 582.
[45] [1998] Crim. L.R. 209.
[46] [1991] Crim.L.R. 455.
[47] [1998] 3 All E.R. 163.
[48] *Christou and Wright* (1992) 95 Cr.App.R. 264.
[49] *Goddard* [1994] Crim.L.R. 46.
[50] It should be borne in mind that what starts out as an enquiry may turn into an interview: *Park* (1994) 99 Cr.App.R. 270.
[51] *Ward* (1994) 98 Cr.App.R. 337, 341.
[52] *Weerdesteyn* [1995] 1 Cr.App.R. 405.
[53] *Batley v DPP, The Times*, March 8, 1998.

an offence must be cautioned before questions are put to him regarding that offence. If questions are put for two purposes, partly regarding a person's involvement in that offence and partly for other purposes, a caution must be given.[54] The test to determine whether there are grounds for suspecting a person of an offence is objective: such grounds may fall well short of evidence that would support a prima facie case of guilt.[55]

9–44   **Undercover police officers.** The Court of Appeal has said that an undercover police officer must not use his pose to ask questions about an offence and thus circumvent the Code.[56] This is what happened in *Bryce*.[57] It was held in that case that the judge had been wrong to admit evidence of a conversation between an undercover officer and a suspect; the conversation related to the latter's knowledge that a car was stolen. On the other hand, in *Christou and Wright*[58] the Court of Appeal held that the Code did not apply to conversations between undercover officers and customers to a shop which was run by the officers in order to recover stolen property. The conversations in that case were not related to any offences but were such as were necessary to conduct the bartering and to maintain the officer's cover.

(It is submitted that the Code will not normally apply to conversations with undercover police officers. In *Edwards*[59] the Court of Appeal doubted whether in the circumstances of that case there had been a breach of code because the undercover police officer was not at a police station acting as a police officer and could not have complied with the code. Different considerations will apply if there has been a deliberate attempt to circumvent the code by the use of an undercover officer. The Court of Appeal has said that this would be a strong reason for excluding the evidence.[60])

9–45   A "co-operation conversation" in which a suspect is encouraged to give evidence and information and to assist law enforcement authorities by informing him of the benefit to himself of doing so, is not an interview for the purposes of supplying information against himself: *de Silva*.[61] Such a "conversation" may amount to the offering to the suspect of an inducement and it would be unfair, within the meaning of s.78, to use evidence against the suspect which was brought into existence as a result of the inducement: *ibid*. In *de Silva*, the defendant was found at an airport with suitcases containing cocaine. He was told that, if he chose to help the Customs officers, this was something that a judge, having to sentence him, might take

---

[54] *Nelson and Rose* [1998] 2 Cr.App.R. 399, 408.
[55] *Shah* [1994] Crim.L.R. 125; *Nelson and Rose*, above.
[56] *Christou and Wright*, above.
[57] (1992) 95 Cr.App.R. 320.
[58] Above.
[59] [1997] Crim.L.R. 348.
[60] *Lin Hung and Tsui* [1995] Crim.L.R. 817.
[61] [2003] Crim.L.R. 474

into account: this was the "co-operation conversation". The defendant then agreed to telephone a contact (who then arrived at the airport and was arrested. The telephone calls were recorded and were held to have constituted a confession under s.82(1) of the 1984 Act (see above, para.9–04, n.8), brought into existence as a result of the "co-operation conversation". The evidence was held to have been unfairly obtained in breach of s.78. The court said that, in order for such evidence not to be held to be unfairly obtained, a caution much stronger than the conventional caution should have been given.

Section 30 of the Police and Criminal Evidence Act 1984 requires the police to take an arrested person to a police station as soon as practicable, but does not prevent delay in so doing in order to conduct such investigation (such as a search) as is reasonable to be carried out immediately. It follows that they are entitled to ask such questions as are necessary for their investigation. However, this does not mean that they have *carte blanche* to interview the defendant in these circumstances: they are restricted to necessary questions.[62] The Court of Appeal has said that if a judge believes that the police have abused the opportunity to ask questions and thus circumvented the Code he could exclude the evidence on the grounds of unfairness under s.78.[63]

For summing up in cases where there have been breaches of statute or code, see para.9–71, below.

D. Common law discretion, statutory duty

Section 82(3) of the Act provides that nothing in Pt VIII of the Act (which includes s.76) shall prejudice any power of a court to exclude evidence at its discretion. Accordingly, a court may still as a matter of discretion exclude a confession even if it is admissible under ss.76 and 76A. Thus, for instance, in the unlikely event of a court determining that the prejudicial effect of a confession outweighed its probative value, it would appear that the court could exclude it. (See paras 10–13, *et seq.*, below). In *Sat-Bhambra*[64] the Court of Appeal said that the judge had power under s.82(3) to take steps to prevent injustice if, having admitted a confession under s.76, he reconsiders his decision in the light of further evidence: see para.9–49, below.

9–46

Where, in a jury trial, the prosecution case is based wholly or partly on hearsay evidence (including confessions) and that evidence is so unconvincing that, in the opinion of the judge, it would be unsafe to convict, he must either direct that the defendant be acquitted or discharge the jury so as to allow a re-trial.[65]

---

[62] *Keane* [1992] Crim.L.R. 306; *Khan* [1993] Crim.L.R. 54.
[63] *Khan*, above.
[64] (1989) 88 Cr.App.R. 55, 62.
[65] Criminal Justice Act 2003, s.125(1). Waste of a time is a factor that must be taken into account: s.126(1)(b).

E. Procedure for determining admissibility

9–47   The defence may represent that a confession was or may have been obtained in a way mentioned in ss.76(2) or 76A(2), above. It will then be for the prosecution to establish beyond reasonable doubt that the confession was not so obtained. Alternatively, the court may of its own motion require the prosecution to prove that the confession was not obtained as mentioned in subs.(2): ss.76(3), 76A(3).[66] Such circumstances may arise when the accused is unrepresented; or the court notes a particular point in the evidence; or where the defence decides not to contest the question of admissibility.

9–48   If the defence challenge the admissibility of a confession in a trial on indictment the procedure is as follows:

(a) Before the trial, defence counsel informs prosecuting counsel of the objection.

(b) The prosecutor does not mention the confession when opening the case.

(c) The time to make a submission is before the confession is put in evidence.[67]

(d) The question of admissibility is determined as a trial-within-a-trial or *voir dire*.

(e) The judge hears evidence relating to the confession in the absence of the jury and decides whether the confession is admissible. (The judge is entitled to take into account the defendant's evidence and demeanour when determining whether a confession is admissible.[68]) The judge is not obliged to give reasons for admitting a confession but the Court of Appeal said that in a case of any complexity it was desirable to give brief reasons.[69]

(f) The evidence at the trial-within-a-trial may cover all matters relevant to the confession including the interrogation and confession itself.

(g) Evidence for the prosecution is usually given by the police officers who conducted the interview. They may be cross-examined. The defendant may give evidence and call witnesses. He and his wit-

---

[66] Note that, by s.76A(3) relating to confessions admitted under that section, the burden of proof is on the balance of probabilities.
[67] *Sat-Bhambra* (1989) 88 Cr.App.R. 55, 62.
[68] *Weeks* [1995] Crim.L.R. 52.
[69] *Booth* (1982) 74 Cr.App.R. 123, 128–129.

nesses may be cross-examined. However, the defendant may not be cross-examined as to the truth of the confession.[70]

At common law it had been held that the judge had power to reconsider the question of admissibility of a confession even if it had been admitted in evidence.[71] However, in *Sat-Bhambra*[72] the Court of Appeal held that this was no longer the case under s.76. The Court said that the wording of the section, "proposes to give in evidence" and "shall not allow the confession to be given," was not apt to describe something which had happened in the past but was directed to the situation before the statement goes before the jury. Once the judge has ruled that it should do so, s.76 (s.78, for the same reasons) ceases to have effect.[73] The Court said that this did not mean that the judge was powerless to act in these circumstances, but had the power, if only under s.82(3), to take the necessary steps to prevent injustice. He could discharge the jury (but is not obliged to do so) or direct them to disregard the statement, or may point out to them the matters which affect the weight of the confession and leave the matter in their hands.

9–49

The Divisional Court in *Liverpool Juvenile Court Ex p. R*[74] held that in summary proceedings justices must hold a trial-within-a-trial (and give a ruling before or at the end of the prosecution case)[75] if it is represented to them that a confession was or may have been obtained in either of the two ways set out in s.76(2). There is no such obligation in the case of submissions under s.78.[76] (In these circumstances the duty of magistrates is to deal with an application when it arises, or to leave a decision to the end of the hearing with the object of ensuring that the trial is fair and just to both sides.[77])

However, the court may have to consider submissions relating to ss.76 and 78 at a trial-within-a-trial. Such a situation will arise where there is an application to exclude a confession under s.76 and an alternative application that the evidence is unfair under s.78: these applications should be examined at the same trial-within-a-trial.[78]

The Court in *Liverpool Juvenile Court*, above, gave some additional guidance on the procedure to be adopted by justices which may be summarised as follows:

9–50

(i) In a trial-within-a-trial the defendant may give evidence confined

---

[70] *Wong Kam Ming v R* (1980) A.C. 247.
[71] *Ajodha v The State* (1981) 73 Cr.App.R. 129; *Watson* (1980) 70 Cr.App.R. 129.
[72] (1989) 88 Cr.App.R. 55.
[73] At 62.
[74] [1988] Q.B. 1.
[75] The usual time for such a ruling is at the end of the trial-within-a-trial.
[76] *Vel v Owen* [1987] Crim.L.R. 496.
[77] *Halawa v Federation Against Copyright Theft* [1995] 1 Cr.App.R. 21, 34.
[78] *Halawa*, above, 35.

to the question of admissibility and the justice will not be concerned with the truth or otherwise of the confession.

(ii) If no representation as to the admissibility of a confession is made during the prosecution case a trial-within-a-trial will not take place, but the defence may raise the question of admissibility at a later stage in the trial.

(iii) The court is not bound to embark on a trial-within-a-trial merely because of a suggestion in cross-examination that the alleged confession was obtained improperly.

(iv) It should never be necessary to call the prosecution evidence relating to the obtaining of a confession twice.

3. RULES CONCERNING THE USE OF CONFESSIONS

9–51   These rules concern the use of confessions in the substantive trial, *i.e.* the trial before the jury; directions to be given to the jury, and the function of the jury.

A. General Rules

9–52   If a confession is *excluded* or not adduced by the prosecution the general rules are as follows:

(a) A person who is tried alone may not be cross-examined about an inadmissible confession.[79] The same rule obtains in favour of any co-defendant of the maker of the confession.[80] However, if defence counsel in cross-examination of a witness puts the defendant's version of a conversation, in which (according to the prosecution) the alleged confession was made, the judge may be entitled to admit the confession in order to allow the witness to give his version of what was said.[81]

(b) Information derived from an inadmissible confession may be used by the prosecution in cross-examination of any co-defendant of the maker of the confession, but the fact that it was provided in a confession may not be revealed.[82]

9–53   At common law the maker of an inadmissible confession might be cross-examined about the confession by a co-defendant and the judge had no

---

[79] *Treacey* (1944) 30 Cr.App.R. 93; *Young and Robinson* [1978] Crim.L.R. 163.
[80] *Rice* [1963] 1 Q.B. 857, 868.
[81] *Allen* [1992] Crim.L.R. 297.
[82] *Rice*, above, at 868.

discretion to prevent the cross-examination.[83] Section 76A(1) of the Police and Criminal Evidence Act now provides that a confession may be given in evidence on behalf of a co-accused in so far as it is relevant to any matter in issue and is not excluded by the court in pursuance of the section.[84] However, s.76A(2) provides that, if the confession was, or may have been, obtained by "oppression" or "in consequence of anything said or done likely in the circumstances existing at the time to render unreliable any confession which might be made in consequence thereof", the court should exclude it "except in so far as it is proved to the court on the balance of probabilities that the confession (notwithstanding that it may be true) was not so obtained."[85]

Thus, the test for admissibility is the same as in the case of a confession adduced by the prosecution. However, the co-accused need only satisfy the court on the balance of probabilities that the confession was not obtained by oppression or in circumstances likely to render it unreliable.

The rule that the exclusion of the confession does not affect the admissibility of facts discovered as a result of that confession is re-iterated in s.76A(4).

If a confession is *admitted* the general rules are as follows:

9–54

(a) The whole confession must be admitted including parts favourable to the defendant.[86]

(b) Parts which show that the defendant has committed other offences or reflect on his character adversely are as a matter of common law practice excluded, unless relevant to the offence charged.[87] Chapter 1 of Pt II of the Criminal Justice Act 2003 has made evidence of a defendant's bad character and previous misconduct much more freely admissible; see Ch.7 above. However, unless such evidence is admissible under the 2003 Act, the practice in this connection is still governed by the common law. Thus, at the trial a confession may have to be "edited" to prevent such material going before the jury. Editing is usually carried out by consent, though it may be necessary for the judge to rule on the matter.[88] For instance, in *Silcott*[89] during the trial at first instance the defendants were charged with murder, riot and affray. They had made statements implicating a number of individuals including co-defendants. Hodgson J. ruled that since the jury could not

---

[83] *Rice*, above, at 868.
[84] The new section is added by the Criminal Justice Act 2003, s.128.
[85] The Court may of its own motion require that the confession was not so obtained to be proved on the balance of probabilities: s.76A(3).
[86] *McGregor* [1968] 1 Q.B. 37.
[87] *Turner v Underwood* [1948] 2 K.B. 284.
[88] *Weaver and Weaver* [1968] 1 Q.B. 353.
[89] [1987] Crim.L.R. 765.

approach their task without prejudice unless the names were removed, the names should be replaced by letters of the alphabet. In *Jefferson*[90] the Court of Appeal said that it was a matter within the discretion of the trial judge whether to edit such interviews: in some cases it may be appropriate to do so; but in others it may confuse the jury or leave a false impression: the Court said that it would be slow to intervene in cases where, matters having been canvassed before the trial judge, he decided that editing was inappropriate. However, it should be noted that there is no discretion to edit a statement or interview of one defendant on the grounds that it prejudices a co-defendant.[91]

(c) The witnesses for the prosecution may be cross-examined before the jury about the way in which the confession was obtained.[92]

(d) The prosecution may not adduce evidence before the jury of admissions or other statements made by the defendant during the trial-within-a-trial unless the defendant's evidence was irrelevant to the issues at the trial-within-a-trial.[93]

(e) A confession is only evidence against the person who made it. Accordingly, the jury must be warned that it is not evidence against a co-defendant.[94] On the other hand, an admission made in the witness-box *is* evidence against a co-defendant if it implicates him. This must be distinguished from a situation in which an admission of guilt by one person is admissible as evidence against another under s.74 of the Police and Criminal Evidence Act 1984. In *Hayter*,[95] a case of an alleged contract killing, H was the middleman between the procurer and the hitman. All three were tried together. H's guilt depended on the procurer and the hitman being found guilty, the evidence against the latter consisting solely of an out-of-court confession on the basis of which he was found guilty. The Court of Appeal held, dismissing the appeal, that the jury had found the hitman guilty and this was sufficient to support the verdict of guilty in the case of H in spite of the fact that the hitman's admission was not admissible as evidence against H.

---

[90] (1994) 99 Cr.App.R. 13, 24–29.
[91] *Lobban v R* [1995] 2 Cr.App.R. 573, PC.
[92] *Murray* [1951] 1 K.B. 391.
[93] *Wong Kam Ming v R*, above; *Brophy* [1982] A.C. 476; (1981) 73 Cr.App.R. 287.
[94] *Gunewardene* [1951] 2 K.B. 600. In cross-examination it may occasionally be appropriate to ask a question of one defendant about what another said in interview, but it is wrong to use the interview as if it is evidence against the defendant being cross-examined: *Gray and Evans, The Times*, March 9, 1998.
[95] *The Times*, April 18, 2003, distinguishing *Rhodes* (1959) 44 Cr.App.R. 23 and *Spinks* (1982) 74 Cr.App.R. 246.

(f) A person may be convicted upon the evidence of a confession alone without corroboration.[96]

At common law if a defendant made no reply to the questions in a police interview, evidence of the interview was not usually put before the jury. It had no probative value and may have considerable prejudicial effect. For this reason the Court of Appeal in *Taylor*[97] quashed a conviction in a case where evidence was given of an incriminating statement made by a co-defendant and read to the defendant by a police officer during an interview. (But now see s.34, Criminal Justice and Public Order Act 1994, para. 11–16, below.) On the other hand, the defendant may choose to answer some questions in an interview and decline to answer others. The judge must then decide in his discretion whether the whole record of the interview should go before the jury or only part.[98]

9–55

In *Mann*[99] the defendant answered some questions and, as a result, both questions and answers were admissible. Interspersed with these questions and answers were questions which the defendant refused to answer. The Court of Appeal held that the whole dialogue should be put before the jury. The Court said that, subject to the discretion in individual cases "... we think a dialogue of this kind which is clearly admissible in part should go *in toto* in the ordinary case. We think that is a much more likely route to the truth. ..."[1] (On the other hand it may be necessary to edit questions which amount to no more than the giving of evidence by the police officer and to which there is no reply.[2])

B. Confession by mentally handicapped person

Where the case against an accused depends wholly or substantially on a confession by him and the court is satisfied (a) that he is mentally handicapped, and (b) that the confession was not made in the presence of an independent person, the judge must warn the jury that there is a special need for caution before convicting in reliance on the confession: Police and Criminal Evidence Act 1984, s.77(1).

9–56

The purpose of this section is to provide additional protection for a mentally handicapped defendant.[3] A jury should obviously take particular care before convicting such a person on his own confession, if the confes-

---

[96] *Sykes* (1913) 8 Cr.App.R. 233.
[97] (1978) Crim.L.R. 92.
[98] *Mann, below; Raviraj* (1987) 85 Cr.App.R. 93, 101–105.
[99] (1972) 56 Cr.App.R. 750.
[1] At 757.
[2] *Welch* [1992] Crim.L.R. 368.
[3] "Mentally handicapped", in relation to a person, means that he is in a state of arrested or incomplete development of mind which includes significant impairment of intelligence and social functioning: s.77(3). In determining whether a person is mentally handicapped within this definition each case should be decided on its own facts rather than figures from intelligence tests in some other case: *Kenny, The Times*, July 27, 1993.

sion was made when no independent person was present and if there is little or no other evidence against him.[4] Accordingly, the judge must warn the jury of "the special need for caution" before convicting a defendant in these circumstances; and magistrates must treat the case as one in which there is special need for caution before convicting.[5] The Court of Appeal quashed a conviction in a case where the warning was not given and said that such a warning was an essential part of a fair summing-up.[6] The wording of the warning is a matter for the discretion of the judge, save that he must explain the reasons for the need for caution.[7] Such an explanation should be tailored to the circumstances of the case. However, the judge should tell the jury why a confession from a mentally handicapped person might be unreliable, *i.e.* such a person might, without meaning to do so, provide information which was unreliable, misleading or self-incriminating.[8]

9–57 Before a warning is necessary, the court must be "satisfied" that the defendant is mentally handicapped and that the confession was not made in the presence of an independent person. In this connection, the following should be noted:

(a) A finding must be made (based on medical evidence and applying the correct statutory test) as to whether or not the defendant is a mentally handicapped person.[9]

(b) The test as to whether the case depends wholly or substantially on a confession is to ask whether the case for the Crown is substantially less strong without the confession.[10]

(c) Confessions made to friends are not made to an independent person.[11]

C. Function of the jury

9–58 Once a confession is admitted, it is the function of the jury to determine its probative value, *i.e.* whether it is true: it is not their function to determine

---

[4] "Independent person" does not include a police officer or a person employed for, or engaged on, police purposes: s.77(3).
[5] s.77(2). In *Campbell* [1995] 1 Cr.App.R. 522, 535 the Court of Appeal said that the judge did not have to follow a specific wording, but would be wise to use the phrase "special need for caution".
[6] *Lamont* [1989] Crim.L.R. 813.
[7] The Court must explain that the reasons are that (a) the accused was mentally handicapped and (b) the confession was not made in the presence of an independent person: s.77.
[8] *Campbell* [1995] 2 Cr.App.R. 522, 535.
[9] *Ham, The Times,* December 12, 1995.
[10] *Campbell* [1995] 1 Cr.App.R. 522, 535.
[11] *Bailey* [1995] 2 Cr.App.R. 262.

whether it should have been admitted. Thus, it was held that it was not the function of the jury to decide whether a confession was voluntary.[12]

However, the jury may consider the way in which a confession was made when deciding what weight to attach it. If the defence alleges that a confession was obtained by oppression or is unreliable the jury will have to consider the evidence relating to oppression or unreliability in deciding whether the confession is true or not. It is submitted that in a case where oppression is alleged an appropriate direction would be to tell the jury that if it considers the confession may have been made as a result of oppression and consequently it is not sure that it is true, it must disregard it: if on the other hand, it is sure that it is true, it may rely on it, whether it was made as a result of oppression or not.

It will be necessary for the judge to direct the jury upon the significance of any relevant breach of statute or code in the particular case. It is not necessary for him to direct the jury upon the philosophy behind the Code provided that he makes it clear that the Code is based on an Act of Parliament, that there has been a breach and it is for the jury to decide whose evidence they accept in relation to what has been said in a disputed interview.[13]

D. Matters provable by admission

In the normal course of events, a person's confession is admitted to prove the person's own acts, knowledge or intentions. In certain exceptional cases, however, a person's confession may be admitted to prove other facts, *provided* that the person making the confession has personal knowledge of the facts. For instance, in *Bird v Adams*[14] the Divisional Court held that where a drug dealer admitted that certain tablets were LSD he had sufficient knowledge of the circumstances of his conduct to make his admission prima facie evidence of its truth.

9–59

Admissions which are not based on personal knowledge are not admissible to prove such facts. The Privy Council has said that a person can confess as to his own acts, knowledge or intentions, but he cannot "confess" as to the acts of other persons which he has not seen and of which he can only have knowledge by hearsay.[15]

The distinction may be illustrated by reference to a handling case in which it is sought to prove by admission that goods were stolen. If a defendant admits that he bought the goods very cheaply in a public house or that the goods were delivered to his house late at night, he admits a fact

---

[12] *Chan Wei Keung v R* [1967] 2 A.C. 160; *Burgess* [1968] 2 Q.B. 112; *Prasad v R* (1981) 72 Cr.App.R. 218.
[13] *Dures* [1997] 2 Cr.App.R. 247, 264.
[14] [1972] Crim.L.R. 174.
[15] *Surujpaul v R* [1958] 1 W.L.R. 1050, 1056.

within his own personal knowledge; and it may be open to the jury to infer from the circumstances of acquisition that the goods were stolen.[16]

On the other hand, the authorities show that no such inference may be drawn from an admission based on the defendant's belief.[17] If a defendant says that he believes goods to be stolen or that he has been told that they have been stolen, he is not speaking from his personal knowledge. Such an admission is not evidence that goods were stolen. This is because "if a man admits something of which he knows nothing, it is of no real evidential value."[18]

4. EVIDENCE OBTAINED IN CONSEQUENCE OF AN INADMISSIBLE CONFESSION

9–60   Sections 76(4)(a) and 76A (4)(a) of the Police and Criminal Evidence Act 1984 provide that evidence of any fact discovered as a result of a confession shall be admissible notwithstanding that the confession itself has been wholly or partly excluded.

The common law rule is thus preserved. The rule may be illustrated by the leading case of *Warickshall*.[19] The defendant in that case was a woman who was charged with receiving stolen goods. She made a confession during which she said that the stolen property was in her lodgings. The property was recovered from the lodgings. The confession was held to be inadmissible as it had been obtained by promises of favour. Evidence of the finding of the property was held to be admissible. The reason was stated thus:

> "(This) principle respecting confessions has no application whatever as to the admission or rejection of *facts*, whether the knowledge of them be obtained in consequence of an extorted confession, or whether it arises from any other source; for a *fact* if it exists at all, must exist invariably in the same manner, whether the confession from which it is derived be *in other respects* true or false."[20]

However, evidence that a fact was discovered *as a result of* an inadmissible confession[21] is not admissible unless evidence is given by or on behalf of the defendant that the evidence was so discovered: ss.76(5), (6),

---

[16] *Sbarra* (1918) 13 Cr.App.R. 118; *Fuschillo* (1940) 27 Cr.App.R. 193.

[17] *Hulbert* (1979) 69 Cr.App.R. 243; *Korniak* (1983) 76 Cr.App.R. 145.

[18] *Comptroller of Customs v Western Lectric Co. Ltd* [1966] A.C. 367, 371, *per* Lord Hodson.

[19] (1783) 1 Leach 263.

[20] At 264.

[21] *i.e.* a wholly inadmissible confession: ss.76(6)(a), 76A(6)(a); or, if the fact was discovered as a result of the excluded part, a partly inadmissible confession: ss.76(6)(b), 76A(a)(b).

278

76A(5), (6). Thus, a witness may not say that he discovered something as a result of a statement made by the defendant and thereby inform the jury indirectly of a statement which has been ruled inadmissible.[22] For instance, in *Lam Chi-Ming*[23] the trial judge ruled the defendant's confessions inadmissible, but admitted a silent video recording showing the defendant indicating where the murder weapon was thrown. The Privy Council held that this evidence should have been excluded since it was part of the confessions which the trial judge had ruled were inadmissible. Lord Griffiths said that the evidence would not have been admissible in English proceedings under s.76(5) (and now s.76A (5)).

Sections 76(4)(b) and 76A(4)(b) provide that if something in a statement shows that the defendant writes, speaks or expresses himself in a particular way, so much of a confession as is necessary to show that he does so shall be admissible not withstanding that the confession itself has been wholly or partly excluded[24] It may be of importance in a case involving identification evidence. The Committee referred to *Voisin*[25] as an example. The defendant in that case was charged with the murder of a woman. Part of her body was found in a parcel in which there was a piece of paper bearing the words "Bladie Belgiam". The defendant was asked by a police officer to write down the words "Bloody Belgian". The defendant wrote "Bladie Belgiam". There was no question of an inadmissible confession in *Voisin*. The Committee commented that if the words had been written in an inadmissible confession, it seemed right that the relevant part of the confession should be admitted to identify the defendant as the offender by the peculiarity of spelling. As the Committee noted, no more of the confession than was necessary should be admitted in these circumstances and it should be understood that the part admitted was only for the purpose of identification; and not as evidence of the truth of what was said.

9–61

---

[22] There appears to have been some doubt as to whether such evidence was admissible at common law; but in *Berriman* (1854) 6 Cox.C.C. 388 Erle J. held that it was not admissible.
[23] (1991) 93 Cr.App.R. 358.
[24] s.76(4)(b) resulted from a recommendation of the Criminal Law Revision Committee, Eleventh Report, para.69. S.76A was inserted into the Police and Criminal Evidence Act 1984 by the Criminal Justice Act 2003, s.128.
[25] [1918] 1 K.B. 53.

PART 4

Exclusion through Discretion Privilege or Convention Rights

CHAPTER 10

The Discretion to Exclude Evidence

At common law the court had a general discretion to exclude relevant evidence in order to ensure a fair trial. Both the judge in a trial on indictment and justices had this discretion which could be exercised to prevent questions being put or evidence adduced. Section 78 of the Police and Criminal Evidence Act 1984 provided the courts with an additional (statutory) discretion to exclude evidence which would bear adversely on the fairness of the proceedings.

10–01

1. THE COMMON LAW DISCRETION

The court's discretion at common law to exclude relevant evidence, as recognised by the House of Lords in *Sang* (cited below), took two forms:

10–02

(a) to exclude evidence if it would be likely to have a prejudicial effect outweighing its probative value; and

(b) in a limited form, to exclude improperly or unfairly obtained evidence.

The discretion in both forms had to be exercised as part of the judge's duty to ensure a fair trial. The discretion only applies to evidence on which the prosecution seek to rely: there is no discretion to exclude relevant evidence (at the request of a defendant) tendered by a co-defendant or which tends to support the defence of a co-defendant.[1] (For the role of the European Convention on Human Rights in the exercise of the discretion, see para.10–26, below. The discussion in that paragraph relates to the exercise of the statutory discretion, but the same rules apply to the exercise of the common law discretion.)

---

[1] *Lobban v R* [1995] 2 Cr.App.R. 573.

A. Prejudicial effect outweighing probative value

10–03   The discretion to exclude evidence when its prejudicial effect[2] outweighed its probative value developed as a result of a number of rules excluding evidence in certain specific situations, for example evidence of the misconduct of the defendant on occasions other than that charged.

This development may be traced through a series of landmarks beginning with passages from the speeches of Lord Moulton and Lord Reading C.J. in *Christie*.[3] These passages indicate that the trial judge should seek to prevent the calling of evidence which, although strictly admissible, would have a prejudicial effect out of proportion to its evidential value. In those days, however, the practice was not universally accepted.[4] It took the form of an intimation by the judge to the prosecution not to press for the admission of the evidence.[5]

The first authoritative modern statement of the law is to be found in *Noor Mohamed*.[6] The defendant in that case was charged with the murder by cyanide poisoning of a woman with whom he was living. Evidence was admitted (wrongly) of the death of the defendant's wife two years previously by cyanide poisoning. It had already been recognised that if evidence of this sort were to be admitted, particular care was needed in case the evidence severely prejudiced the defendant but had little probative effect. Lord du Parcq said that in all such cases the judge:

> "ought to consider whether the evidence which it is proposed to adduce is sufficiently substantial, having regard to the purpose to which it is professedly directed, to make it desirable in the interests of justice that it should be admitted...
>
> [C]ases must occur in which it would be unjust to admit evidence of a character gravely prejudicial to the accused even though there may be some tenuous ground for holding it technically admissible. The decision must then be left to the discretion and sense of fairness of the judge."[7]

---

[2] In *Scott v R* [1989] 2 W.L.R. 924, 931 Lord Griffiths said that "prejudicial effect" was a reference to the fact that where evidence is admitted to prove collateral matters there is a danger that the jury may attach undue weight to it and regard it as probative of the offence charged. If the trial judge does admit evidence with a prejudicial element he must point out the alleged probative significance of the evidence (and tell the jury that it is for them to decide whether it has probative significance or not) and also point out the possible prejudice (and tell the jury that it has nothing to do with whether the defendant committed the offence): *Bethelmie, The Times*, November 27, 1995.
[3] [1914] A.C. 545, 559 and 564 respectively.
[4] *e.g.* the interjection of the Earl of Halsbury in *Christie*, 10 Cr.App.R. 141, 149: "I must protest against the suggestion that any judge has the right to exclude evidence which is in law admissible on the ground of prudence or discretion, and so on."
[5] *Christie*, above, at 549, *per* Lord Moulton; at 564, *per* Lord Reading.
[6] [1949] A.C. 182.
[7] At 192.

The rationale for the existence of the discretion was stated by Lord Simon **10–04** in *Harris v DPP*.[8] He said that the discretion flowed from the duty of a judge in a criminal trial to set the essentials of justice above the technical rule if the strict application of the latter would operate unfairly against the accused.

The next landmark is *Selvey v DPP*.[9] The House of Lords held in that case that the judge has a discretion to exclude cross-examination of a defendant as to his previous misconduct under s.1(f)(ii) of the Criminal Evidence Act 1898 (to be replaced by s.101(1)(f) of the Criminal Justice Act 2003, para.7–60, above). Lord Hodson said that there is abundant authority that there is a discretion to exclude evidence, admissible in law, of which the prejudicial effect outweighs its probative value in the opinion of the trial judge.[10]

The final landmark is *Sang*.[11] The question certified by the Court of Appeal in that case was: "Does a trial judge have a discretion to refuse to allow evidence being evidence other than evidence of admission to be given in any circumstances in which such evidence is relevant and of more than minimal probative value?" Four of the members of the House answered that a trial judge in a criminal trial has a discretion to refuse to admit evidence if in his opinion its prejudicial effect outweighs its probative value.[12] Their Lordships said that the discretion was founded upon the judge's duty to ensure that the defendant had a fair trial.

B. Improperly obtained evidence

The general rule of English law is that the impropriety of the method by **10–05** which evidence is obtained is irrelevant to its admissibility.[13] (The only exception to this rule is in relation to confessions, above). The view of the English courts (as opposed to those of the USA and other jurisdictions)[14] has always been that if evidence is relevant to issues in the trial, it is admissible, no matter how obtained. Thus, a nineteenth-century judge said

---

[8] [1952] A.C. 694, 707.

[9] [1970] A.C. 304.

[10] At 346.

[11] [1980] A.C. 402, cited at para.10–07, below.

[12] *per* Lord Diplock, Lord Dilhorne, Lord Scarman and Lord Fraser of Tullybelton. The answer was strictly *obiter* since the issue in the case was whether a judge might exclude evidence of an offence because it was instigated by an agent provocateur. The House of Lords held that a judge has no such discretion.

[13] *Kuruma v R* [1955] A.C. 197; *Sang* [1980] A.C. 402; *Fox v Gwent Chief Constable* [1985] 1 W.L.R. 1126. The rule was recently reaffirmed by the House of Lords in *Khan* [1996] 2 Cr.App.R. 440, cited at para.10–26, below.

[14] For the approaches of other jurisdictions: see J.D. Heydon, "Illegally Obtained Evidence" [1973] Crim.L.R. 603. For a discussion of the position under the European Convention on Human Rights, see para.10–09, below; and for argument that the common law jurisdictions are too inclined to admit evidence from abroad even if obtained irregularly or even illegally, see Mackerell and Gane, "Admitting Illegally Obtained Evidence from Abroad" [1997] Crim.L.R. 720.

that it would be a dangerous obstacle to the administration of justice if evidence obtained by illegal means could not be used against an accused person.[15] Another said: "It matters not how you get it: if you steal it even, it would be admissible."[16]

In *Kuruma*,[17] the defendant had been convicted in Kenya (under Emergency Regulations) of possession of ammunition. The ammunition had been found in a search by a police constable. The constable did not have the power to make the search under the Regulations. The Privy Council held that the evidence of the search had been rightly admitted because, provided that the evidence was relevant, the court was not concerned how it was obtained. *Kuruma* was followed by the Divisional Court in *Jeffrey v Black*.[18] In that case the defendant had been arrested for theft of a sandwich from a public house. Police officers then conducted an illegal search of his room without a warrant and found drugs there. The court held that evidence of the search was relevant and admissible against the defendant on a charge of possessing the drugs.

Accordingly, the test of the admissibility of evidence obtained by improper means is whether it is relevant or not. The function of the court is not disciplinary, *i.e.* to discipline the police for their misconduct,[19] but to control the use of evidence at trial. Lord Fraser said in *Fox v Chief Constable of Gwent*[20]: "The duty of the court is to decide whether the appellant has committed the offence with which he is charged and not to discipline the police for exceeding their powers."

10–06   The strict rule of admissibility was tempered by a discretion to exclude improperly obtained evidence if admission of the evidence would be unfair. Lord Goddard C.J. said in *Kuruma*[21]:

> "No doubt in a criminal case the judge always has a discretion to disallow evidence if the strict rules of admissibility would operate unfairly against an accused . . . If, for instance, some admission of some piece of evidence, *e.g.*, a document, had been obtained from a defendant by a trick, no doubt the judge might properly rule it out . . ."

A reported instance of the exercise of the discretion is to be found in *Payne*.[22] A doctor in that case examined the defendant at a police station.

---

[15] *Jones v Owens* (1870) 34 J.P. 759, 760, *per* Mellor J.
[16] *Leathem* (1861) 8 Cox 498, *per* Crompton J.
[17] [1955] A.C. 197.
[18] [1978] 1 Q.B. 490.
[19] *Kuruma*, above, at 203, *per* Lord Goddard C.J.; *Sang* [1980] A.C. 402, 436, *per* Lord Diplock.
[20] [1985] 3 All E.R. 392, 397.
[21] *op.cit.*, at 204, *per* Lord Goddard C.J. Similar observations were made in *Callis v Gunn* [1964] 1 Q.B. 495, 501–502, *per* Lord Parker C.J.; and *Jeffrey v Black* [1978] 1 Q.B. 490, 498, *per* Lord Widgery C.J.
[22] (1963) 47 Cr.App.R. 122.

Before the examination a police officer told the defendant that the doctor would not give his opinion as to the defendant's fitness to drive. However, when the defendant was tried for offences, including driving when unfit through drink, the doctor gave evidence that in his opinion the defendant was unfit through drink. The Court of Criminal Appeal held that, while this evidence was admissible, the judge should have excluded it in the exercise of his discretion because if the defendant had realised that the doctor was likely to give evidence as to his fitness to drive he might have refused to subject himself to examination.

Lord Widgery L.J. in a subsequent case described the discretion in these terms:

> "If the case is such that not only have the police officers entered without authority but they have been guilty of trickery, or they have misled someone, or they have been oppressive, or they have been unfair, or in other respects they have behaved in a manner which is morally reprehensible, then it is open to the justices to apply their discretion and decline to allow the particular evidence to be let in as part of the trial."[23]

In *Sang*[24] the defendant was charged with conspiracy to utter forged banknotes. His case was that he would not have committed the offence but for the activities of an agent provocateur. The trial judge ruled that he had no discretion to exclude evidence relating to the commission of the offence on the ground that it was initiated by an agent provocateur. The House of Lords upheld the judge's ruling and affirmed that there is no defence of entrapment known to English law.[25] Their Lordships recognised the existence of the discretion to exclude improperly or unfairly obtained evidence, but said that it was limited to evidence obtained after the commission of the offence.[26] This was because the exclusionary rule was analogous to that excluding unfairly obtained confessions.

It seems, therefore, that the principle underlying the discretion is the rule against self-incrimination, *i.e.* that a person should not be improperly or unfairly led into providing evidence against himself.[27]

The decision of the Court of Appeal in *Apicella*[28] shows that it will only be in exceptional circumstances that evidence will be excluded as a result of

10–07

---

[23] *Jeffrey v Black* [1978] 1 Q.B. 490, 498.

[24] [1980] A.C. 402; 69 Cr.App.R. 282.

[25] The Divisional Court had so held in *Brannan v Peek* [1948] 1 K.B. 68; *Browning v Watson JWH (Rochester Ltd)* [1953] 1 W.L.R. 1172; *Sneddon v Stevenson* [1967] 1 W.L.R. 1051. The Court of Appeal in *Smurthwaite and Gill* (1994) 98 Cr.App.R. 437 held that s.78 of the Police and Criminal Evidence Act 1984 had not altered this rule.

[26] At 291, *per* Lord Diplock, 294–295, *per* Lord Dilhorne, at 297, *per* Lord Salmon, at 307–308, *per* Lord Scarman.

[27] At 289, *per* Lord Diplock, at 307–308, *per* Lord Scarman.

[28] (1985) 82 Cr.App.R. 295.

the exercise of this discretion. The defendant in that case was charged with
the rape of three girls. Each contracted an unusual strain of venereal disease. The defendant, while in prison, was examined by a consultant for
therapeutic reasons. The consultant took a sample of bodily fluid from him
in order to assist in diagnosis. The sample showed that he suffered from the
same strain of venereal disease as the complainants. The trial judge allowed
the prosecution to adduce this evidence. The Court of Appeal upheld the
judge's exercise of discretion. The Court said that the defendant had not
been tricked into submitting to the examination (as had happened in *Payne*)
and the prosecution's use of the evidence was not unfair.

C. Justices' discretion

10–08 Justices have a similar discretion to that exercised by the judge in a trial on
indictment. Lord Scarman said in *Sang*[29] that magistrates have the same
discretion in the interests of a fair trial to exclude legally admissible evidence. ... "When asked to rule they should bear in mind it is their duty to
have regard to legally admissible evidence, unless in their judgment the use
of the evidence would make the trial unfair."

In a trial on indictment, the judge will hear argument about the admissibility of evidence in the absence of the jury. In the magistrates' court this is
not possible. The magistrates must be informed of the nature of the evidence before ruling as to whether it is admissible or not. If they decide that
it is inadmissible they must ignore it.

D. European convention on human rights

10–09 Article 6(1) of the Convention (which guarantees the right to a fair trial)
does not prescribe rules for the admissibility of evidence, which are matters
for regulation by the national law.[30] As a result, the European Court of
Human Rights has not (as a matter of principle) ruled that the admission of
unlawfully obtained evidence amounts to a violation of the right to a fair
trial. However, there may be circumstances where the Court rules that the
use of unlawfully obtained evidence in a trial has deprived a defendant of a
fair trial.

These principles are illustrated by the following cases.

> (1) In *Schenk v Switzerland*[31] the Court ruled that the admission in
> evidence of an unlawfully obtained recording of a telephone
> conversation did not deprive the applicant of a fair trial and
> therefore did not contravene Art.6(1). The Court said that it could
> not exclude as a matter of principle and in the abstract that

---

[29] Above, at 307.
[30] (1988) 13 E.H.R.R. 242; *Miailhe v France No.2* (1997) 23 E.H.R.R. 491.
[31] Above.

unlawfully obtained evidence of the present kind may be admissible: it had only to ascertain that the applicant's trial was fair.[32] In reaching its conclusion the Court noted that the applicant had the opportunity of challenging the authenticity of the recording and opposing its use and could have cross-examined the relevant witnesses. The Court also attached weight to the fact that the recording was not the only evidence on which the conviction was based and the national court took account of a combination of evidential elements before reaching its opinion.

(2) In *X v F.R.G.*[33] the applicant complained that his right to a fair trial had been violated because evidence was admitted which had been obtained unlawfully. This evidence consisted of the statement of an undercover Italian policeman who had pretended to be a remand prisoner and in front of whom the applicant spoke in German to a friend. During the conversation they spoke of a murder which they had committed together, the applicant not realising that the police agent understood German. The European Commission of Human Rights found that the application was ill-founded, noting that the conviction was mainly based on other evidence and that the ruse (employed by the police) did not, in fact, constitute an unlawful method of obtaining evidence: the responsibility for talking freely was the applicant's and the agent did not encourage him to talk about the murder. The Commission commented that in these circumstances it could not be said that the applicant's freedom of will was affected by the action of the police so as to mean that the use of the evidence deprived the applicant of his right to a fair trial. However, the Commission did note that the use of evidence obtained unlawfully by coercive measures may raise an issue as to the fairness of the proceedings.

(3) In *Teixeira de Castro v Portugal*[34] the applicant was convicted of drug dealing on the evidence of two undercover police officers to whom he had been introduced by a third party and who told him they wished to buy heroin. He then bought the drugs for them. The Court found a violation of Art.6(1) because the applicant had been deprived of a fair trial from the outset. There was no evidence that he was predisposed to crime and the officers had incited the offence which would not have been committed with out their intervention. (*Ludi v Switzerland*[35] was distinguished because the officer in that case posed as a potential purchaser in a drugs deal

---

[32] para.41. Similar views have been expressed by the Commission: see their Opinion in *Saunders v UK* (1996) 23 E.H.R.R. 313, para.67.
[33] (1986) 11 E.H.R.R. 84.
[34] [1998] Crim.L.R. 751.
[35] [1993] 15 E.H.R.R. 173.

which was already set up.) The court in *Teixeira de Castro* said that the right to a fair trial under Art.6 could not be sacrificed for the sake of expediency and the public interest could not justify the use of evidence obtained as the result of police incitement: the use of undercover agents had to be restricted and safe guards put in place even in cases concerning drug trafficking.

(4) In two cases, *Kahn (Sultan) v UK*[36] and *P.G. and J.H. v UK*[37] the issue had been whether a violation of Art.8 in the gathering of evidence could give rise to a violation of Art.6(1). In both cases the Court held that no such violation arose. In *Kahn*, a covert listening device was placed on the outside wall of a private house. The placing of the device involved civil trespass not regulated by legally binding guidelines. The Court held that the interference with Kahn's private life had not therefore been "in accordance with the law" within the meaning of Art.8(2). In *P.G. and J.H.* the applicants voices had been secretly recorded when being charged at the police station. An interference with the applicants' right to respect for private life within the meaning of Art.8(1) was found.[38]

Despite the violation of Art.8, the Court found no violation of Art.6(1) in either case on the basis that the use of the evidence did not deprive the applicants of a fair trial, as the recording of the conversations had not been unlawful in the sense of being contrary to domestic criminal law, even though obtained in breach of the ECHR. Moreover, in both cases it was observed that the applicants had ample opportunity to challenge both the authenticity and use of the recordings at trial.[39]

10–10 Accordingly, the issue which has been determinative in the Court has been whether the use of improperly obtained evidence deprived the defendant of a fair trial and, thus breached the defendant's rights under Art.6(1). The determination of this issue does not depend primarily on the question of whether the evidence was improperly obtained, but does depend on the use to which it was put in the trial. Thus in *Barbera v Spain*[40] the Court said:

---

[36] [2000] 8 B.H.R.C. 310.
[37] Application No.44787/98, September 25, 2001.
[38] The Court noted that the Regulation of Investigatory Powers Act 2000 which contains provisions concerning covert surveillance on police premises was not in force at the relevant time and there was accordingly no statutory system to regulate the use of covert listening devices by the police on their own premises.
[39] The Court held in *P.G. and J.H.* that it was of no consequence regards Art.6(1) whether existing domestic guidelines on surveillance had been complied with or not.
[40] (1988) 11 E.H.R.R. 360, para.68.

"As a general rule it is for the national courts, and in particular the courts of first instance, to assess the evidence before them ... The Court must however determine whether the proceedings considered as a whole, including the way in which the prosecution and defence evidence was taken, were fair as required by Art.6(1)."

Similarly, in *Edwards v UK*[41] the Court said that it was not within its province to substitute its own assessment of the facts for that of the domestic court: its task is to ascertain whether the proceedings in their entirety, including the way in which the evidence was taken, were fair.

Thus the European Court has not gone as far as the common law in sanctioning the use of improperly obtained evidence and is ready to find that the use of such evidence deprives an applicant of a fair trial under Art.6 if the use of the evidence makes the trial, as a whole, unfair. However, this test, as will be seen, is not very different from that which has to be applied by the English courts under s.78 of the Police and Criminal Evidence Act 1984: para.10–13, below.

The incorporation of the Convention into English law means that courts must have its provisions in mind when exercising a discretion to exclude improperly obtained evidence, in particular whether the defendant's Convention rights would be violated if the evidence were admitted: see Ch.13, below for discussion of incorporation and para.13–14 for Art.6. It is submitted that the test above should be applied and there would be no violation of Art.6 providing that the proceedings, taken as a whole, are fair.

E. Section 82(3)

Section 82(3) of the Police and Criminal Evidence Act 1984 provides that nothing in Pt VIII of the Act (relating to evidence in criminal proceedings generally) "shall prejudice any power of a court to exclude evidence (whether by preventing questions from being put or otherwise) at its discretion." The effect of this subsection together with s.78(2) of the Act (which provides that nothing in that section shall prejudice any rule of law requiring a court to exclude evidence) is to retain the court's common law discretion. Thus, the power of the court to exclude evidence at its discretion in certain specific situations (discussed elsewhere) is preserved. For instance, the court has power:

10–11

(a) to admit evidence of the misconduct of the defendant on occasions other than that charged[42];

(b) to prevent cross-examination of the defendant under s.1(f)(ii) of

---

[41] (1993) 15 E.H.R.R. 417, para.34.
[42] *Noor Mohamed v R* [1949] A.C. 182.

the Criminal Evidence Act 1898 (replaced by s.101(1)(f) of the Criminal Justice Act 2003; para.7–60, above)[43];

(c)   to exclude evidence of a dock identification[44];

(d)   to allow cross-examination of a party's witness on the ground that he is hostile[45];

(e)   to allow evidence to be admitted or questions asked of a witness or defendant relating to convictions which are "spent" under the Rehabilitation of Offenders Act 1974[46];

(f)   to allow the prosecution to call evidence in rebuttal of evidence called by the defence.[47]

On the other hand, it has been held that no discretion exists to exclude evidence of an offence instigated by an agent provocateur.[48]

While the court's discretion, outlined above (paras 10–02, *et seq.*, above) is also retained in both its forms, it would appear that in the light of s.78 (discussed below) the discretion to exclude improperly obtained evidence will have little part to play in the trial. It was rarely exercised before *Sang*; and it can only be on very rare occasions that it will be exercised in the future.

10–12   On the other hand, the discretion to exclude prejudicial evidence of little probative value still has an important part to play in the criminal trial. Thus, the Court of Appeal in *O'Leary*[49] said that as a result of ss.82(3) and 78(2) of the Act, s.78(1) (see below) was not to be taken to prejudice the court's discretion to exclude evidence if in the court's opinion its prejudicial effect outweighed its probative value. The court therefore retains a discretion, the value of which, according to the Criminal Law Revision Committee, is that it enables the court to exclude evidence in cases difficult to foresee and define when the introduction of the evidence would be undesirable in particular circumstances.[50] (Subsequent dicta have confirmed that the court still retains this general discretion.[51])

The Court of Appeal will not interfere with a judge's exercise of discretion unless:

[43]   *Selvey v DPP* [1970] A.C. 304.
[44]   para.14–13, below.
[45]   *Rice v Howard* (1886) 16 Q.B.D. 681; *Price v Manning* (1889) 42 Ch.D. 372; *Mann* (1972) 56 Cr.App.R. 750; para.21–09, below.
[46]   *Practice Direction (Crime: Spent Convictions)* [1975] 1 W.L.R. 1065; para.7–21, above.
[47]   *Rice* [1963] 1 Q.B. 857; para.19–39, below.
[48]   *Sang* [1980] A.C. 402.
[49]   (1988) 87 Cr.App.R. 387, 391–392.
[50]   Eleventh Report, Cmnd. 4991, para.278.
[51]   *Nadir and Turner, The Times*, July 2, 1993.

(a) he has failed to exercise it altogether[52]; or

(b) he has erred in principle or there was no material on which he could have exercised it.[53]

2. THE DISCRETION UNDER S.78

Section 78 of the Police and Criminal Evidence Act 1984 makes the dis-   10–13
cretion to exclude improperly obtained evidence part of a much wider
statutory discretion to exclude unfair evidence. The section provides:

"(1) In any proceedings the court may refuse to allow evidence on
which the prosecution proposes to rely to be given if it appears to the
court that, having regard to all the circumstances, including the circumstances in which the evidence was obtained, the admission of the
evidence would have such an adverse effect on the fairness of the
proceedings that the court ought not to admit it.

(2) Nothing in this section shall prejudice any rule of law requiring a
court to exclude evidence."

Parliament thus introduced a new statutory discretion to exclude evidence which would adversely affect the fairness of the proceedings.[54] The
exercise of the discretion does not operate to exclude evidence because it is
inadmissible: admissible evidence is excluded because it would be unfair to
admit it.[55]

In *Mason*[56] the Court of Appeal said that in its opinion s.78 did no more
than re-state the power which the judges had at common law. This opinion
was not shared by a differently constituted Court in *Fulling*[57]: Lord Lane
C.J., giving the judgment of the Court in *Fulling*, said that the 1984 Act was
a codifying Act and, as a result, the court had to examine its language and
ask what is its natural meaning, uninfluenced by any considerations derived
from the previous state of the law.[58] It is submitted, with respect, that this

---

[52] *Sutton* (1968) 53 Cr.App.R. 128; *Rimmer* (1971) 56 Cr.App.R. 196; *Coltress* (1978) 68
Cr.App.R. 193.
[53] *Cook* [1959] 2 Q.B. 340, 348, *per* Devlin J. (cited with approval by Lord Dilhorne in *Selvey*,
above, at 342).
[54] Parts of the following discussion first appeared in the author's article, "Fair play at trial: an
Interim Assessment of s.78 of the Police and Criminal Evidence Act 1984" [1988] Crim.L.R.
722.
[55] *Halawa v F.A.C.T.* [1995] 1 Cr.App.R. 21, 33, *per* Ralph Gibson L.J.
[56] (1988) 86 Cr.App.R. 349, 354.
[57] (1987) 85 Cr.App.R. 136, 141.
[58] This view has been reaffirmed by the Court of Appeal in *Smurthwaite and Gill* (1994) 98
Cr.App.R. 437. Lord Taylor C.J. said that the right approach to the 1984 Act was stated in
Fulling, namely to examine the language of the relevant provisions in its natural meaning and
not to strain for an interpretation which either reasserted or altered the pre-existing law.

view accords with the intention of Parliament which, as has been seen, specifically preserved the common law rules.

10–14   Accordingly, the scope of s.78 is wide. The Court of Appeal has said that "evidence" in this section means all the evidence which may be introduced by the prosecution into a trial.[59] The section may be used, for instance, to exclude evidence of a confession,[60] or identification, or a co-defendant's plea of guilty. These are merely examples. Other examples may be found elsewhere in this work.

Section 78 is not to be limited in its application. Thus, the Divisional Court held that a Crown Court was wrong to hold that the section had no application to breath test procedures.[61]

The section applies "in any proceedings": s.78(1). This means that it applies both to trials on indictment and in the magistrates' court. In each case the court has a discretion to exclude evidence. The Divisional Court held that this included committal proceedings.[62] The court said that "proceedings" as defined in s.82 of the Act meant any criminal proceedings.

As has been seen, the House of Lords held in *Sang* that the court at common law has no discretion to exclude evidence of an offence on the ground that it was instigated by an agent provocateur. May the court exclude such evidence under s.78?

10–15   In *Harwood*[63] the Court of Appeal was of the opinion that it could not. The Court in that case said that the rule of law to the effect that an offence induced by an agent provocateur was not a defence to a charge was a substantive rule of law. Accordingly, it was said, s.78 did not apply: since entrapment was not a defence, a statute dealing with evidential matters could not be interpreted so as to abrogate the substantive rule. The rule could not be evaded by the procedural device of preventing the prosecution adducing evidence of the commission of the offence.

On the other hand, in *Gill*[64] the trial judge assumed that he was entitled to take into account allegations of entrapment when exercising his discretion under s.78. He admitted the evidence, having found that the alleged agent provocateur had not in fact acted as such. The Court of Appeal (of different constitution from the Court in *Harwood*), upholding this ruling, said that it had doubts about the correctness of the observations in *Harwood*. The Court said that the speeches in *Sang* and their impact were matters to be taken into account by a judge when applying the provisions of s.78. It is submitted, with respect, that these observations reflect the present law. Section 78 applies to "the evidence on which the prosecution proposes

---

[59] *Mason*, above, at 354.
[60] *ibid.*
[61] *Hudson v DPP* [1992] R.T.R. 27.
[62] *King's Lynn JJ. Ex p. Holland* (1993) 96 Cr.App.R. 74.
[63] [1989] Crim.L.R. 285.
[64] [1989] Crim.L.R. 358.

to rely." There is no qualification. Accordingly, it is difficult to see why the section should not apply to the evidence of an agent provocateur.

In *Shannon*[65] a journalist had posed as an Arab sheikh and the accused supplied him with drugs. It was argued that the evidence should be excluded under s.78 on the grounds that it was the evidence of an *agent provocateur* which had been unfairly obtained and the accused was thereby deprived a fair trial in breach of Art.6 of the ECHR. The appeal was unsuccessful. It was reiterated that there was no general objection on policy grounds to the admission of evidence obtained by an *agent provocateur*. It was within the discretion of a judge whether to exclude evidence on the basis of the impact on the procedural fairness of the proceedings: the question was whether the admission of the evidence would compromise the fairness of the trial as it would if the prosecution evidence was unreliable or tainted in some other way. The enticement of a defendant to commit an offence was a key consideration for a judge when considering whether to exclude evidence so obtained, but it was not in itself sufficient to require exclusion.[66]

The Court of Appeal decided to consider the ECHR case of *Texeira de Castro v Portugal*, see para.10–09 above, in view of the imminence of the Human Rights Act taking effect (at the time of judgement). In their view, the case demonstrated that pursuant to the Convention, national courts were given considerable discretion in relation to the admissibility of evidence, subject to a duty to ensure the fairness of the proceedings. They further noted that *Texiera* contained no analysis or discussion of the meaning or scope of the expression "fair trial" as used in Art.6. *Shannon* was distinguished from *Texiera* on the basis that the evidence fell short of establishing actual incitement or instigation of the offences concerned, as had been the case in *Texiera*.[67] In another case the Court of Appeal stated that *Texiera* must be considered on its own facts in the setting of Portuguese criminal procedure.[68] When the same case was considered by the House of Lords on appeal, their Lordships held that they did not feel that the European Court in *Texiera* had intended to state as a general principle that there was a breach of Art.6 whenever police officers gave a person an opportunity to break the law and he took advantage of it.[69] Lord Scott went further and stated that it is difficult to follow why the facts in *Texiera* rendered the trial unfair.

In *Hardwicke and Thwaites*,[70] a case on almost identical facts as *Shan-

10–16

---

[65] [2001] 1 Cr.App.R. 168.
[66] At 187.
[67] At 189.
[68] *Att-Gen's Reference (No.3 of 2000)* [2001] 2 Cr.App.R. 472, 485.
[69] Loosely; *Att-Gen's Reference (No.3 of 2000)* [2002] 1 Cr.App.R. 29. Note: Both Lord Nicholls and Lord Mackay held that the state, through its agents, must not lure the accused into committing an act for which the state then seeks to prosecute him.
[70] [2001] Crim.L.R. 220.

non, consideration of whether evidence of the journalists actions should have been excluded under s.78 was not pursued in light of the decision in *Shannon*. However, the Court of Appeal observed, with regard to whether the proceedings should have been stayed as an abuse of process, that a balance had to be struck between ensuring that serious offences were brought to trial, and avoiding damage to public confidence by giving the impression that the ends justify the means. A potential distinction was also drawn between the activities of a private individual and those of an agent of a state authority in acting as an *agent provocateur*. Kennedy L.J. referred to a distinction between "commercial lawlessness" and "executive lawlessness". There is a stronger case for a court to intervene where the conduct of the executive is impugned. Although the issue was considered in *Hardwicke and Thwaites* in the context of abuse of process, it is submitted that the distinction may apply to an application to exclude evidence under s.78.

A. Exercise of the discretion

(1) Generally

10–17   The purpose of this discussion is to consider the general principles on which the discretion is to be exercised, rather than to discuss particular occasions on which it may be exercised (discussion of which may be found elsewhere in this work).[71]

Parliament has not prescribed a test to be applied by the courts in exerciseing the discretion, and the Court of Appeal has refrained from giving any general guidance. In *Samuel*[72] the Court said: "It is undesirable to attempt any general guidance as to the way in which a judge's discretion under section 78 or his inherent powers should be exercised. Circumstances vary infinitely."

The statutory concept is that if the circumstances, including the circumstances in which the evidence was obtained, are such as to make the trial unfair, the evidence should be excluded. Consequently, there are two stages in the court's consideration:

    (i)   the court has to consider all the circumstances in which the evidence was obtained;

---

[71] In *Chalkley and Jeffries* [1998] 2 Cr.App.R. 79, 105 the Court of Appeal pointed out that, the task of determining admissibility under s.78 does not strictly involve an exercise of discretion since, if the court is of the view that the admission of the evidence would have such an adverse effect on the fairness of the proceedings that the court ought not to admit it, the court cannot logically exercise a discretion. However, it is submitted that the description of the practice as exercising a discretion is so well-established that it is unlikely to be changed.
[72] (1988) 87 Cr.App.R. 232, 245.

(ii) it must then consider whether admitting the evidence would have an adverse effect on the fairness of the proceedings.[73]

This process was summarised by the Court of Appeal as follows: the court should take all the circumstances into account and then answer the question—will the admission of the evidence have such an effect on the fairness of the proceedings that the court should not admit it?[74]   **10–18**

In each case it is a matter for the judge to decide what circumstances to take into account. It is not possible to categorise them. However, two broad sets of circumstances may be distinguished. They correspond to the two forms of discretion mentioned in connection with the common law. In the first set of circumstances, unfairness in the proceedings may arise regardless of how the evidence was obtained. In the second set of circumstances, it is the way in which the evidence was obtained which gives rise to the presumed unfairness.

An example of the first set of circumstances would be a case in which an application is made under s.74 of the 1984 Act to adduce evidence that a co-defendant has pleaded guilty to the offence charged. In this type of case the judge must consider the circumstances and decide what effect the admission of the evidence will have on the fairness of the proceedings.[75] Further examples might be found in cases where—(a) the evidence may reveal that the defendant had previous convictions, for example the production of a photograph from police files; or (b) the evidence would reveal that the defendant had himself pleaded guilty to other offences on the indictment.

(2) Improperly obtained evidence

In the second set of circumstances, mentioned above, it is the way in which the evidence is obtained which gives rise to unfairness. Commonly, this will involve a consideration of the conduct of the police. The court will be required to consider how these matters bear upon the fairness of the proceedings. The following matters should be borne in mind.   **10–19**

1. The fact that the police have behaved without impropriety does not mean that the evidence must be admitted. In *Samuel*[76] the Court of Appeal rejected a submission that the discretion should never be exercised unless the police have been guilty of impropriety. The fact that the police have

---

[73] *Hughes* [1988] Crim.L.R. 519.
[74] *O'Leary* (1988) 87 Cr.App.R. 387, 391.
[75] For a discussion of s.74 see paras 5–27 *et seq.*, above.
[76] Above. See also *DPP v Godwin* [1991] R.T.R. 303 where the Divisional Court said that it was unnecessary for there to be bad faith before the discretion was exercised.

acted without impropriety in a particular case is one of the circumstances to which the court should have regard when exercising its discretion.

2. The fact that the police have behaved improperly will not necessarily lead to the exclusion of evidence.[77] There is nothing in the section to suggest that the court's purpose in excluding evidence should be to discipline the police for misbehaviour or for exceeding their powers. Such a suggestion would be contrary to the view which the English courts take of their function, *i.e.* to determine the guilt or innocence of the accused and not to discipline the police.[78] The Court of Appeal in *Mason*[79] has made it clear that this principle applies to the exercise of the discretion under s.78. (Of course, the exercise of the court's powers may have a deterrent effect upon the police in the sense that they may be deterred from conduct which may lead to the exclusion of evidence.)

10–20   3. A serious breach of PACE and the Codes of Practice which exist under it will, in normal circumstances, lead to evidence that might not have been obtained but for the breach being excluded under s.78 where its admission will have a seriously adverse effect on the fairness of the proceedings. In *Kirk*,[80] the appellant had been arrested for one offence but then questioned by police in relation to another, more serious, offence without being told of this. As a result answers were obtained contrary to the suspect's interests. The Act and Codes presume that suspects know why they are being interviewed and the level of offence concerned. A suspect should be made aware of the true nature of an investigation in order to inform his decision as to whether to exercise his right to free legal advice. In *Kirk*, the evidence was excluded as its admission would have resulted in unfairness to the proceedings.[81] Accordingly, the appeal was allowed and the convictions quashed.

By contrast in *Att-Gen's Reference (No.3 of 1999)*,[82] the House of Lords held that a DNA sample which had previously been taken from the defendant on a burglary charge and not destroyed as required by the Police and Criminal Evidence Act, s.64(1), *was* admissible in connection with the rape of a 66-year-old woman with which the accused was initially charged. The House of Lords allowed the Att-Gen's reference on the grounds that the court retained a discretion to admit evidence obtained as a result of an investigation prohibited under s.64(3B)(b). Section 78 gave the court a discretion to admit evidence unlawfully obtained. In cases of this sort, regard must be had to the public interest and to the position of the victim

---

[77] For instance, in *Khan* [1997] Crim.L.R. 508 the Court of Appeal held that the illegal search and arrest of a diplomat in breach of the Vienna Convention on Diplomatic Relations was correctly found not to have tainted a second legal search and even if there had been some lingering illegality in repect of the arrest it had no effect on the fairness of the proceedings.
[78] See para.10–05; see, also, *Chalkley and Jeffries* [1998] 2 Cr.App.R. 79 at 105, *per* Auld L.J.
[79] [1988] 1 W.L.R. 139; (1988) 86 Cr.App.R. 349, 354.
[80] [2000] 1 Cr.App.R. 400.
[81] At 407.
[82] [2001] 1 Cr.App.R. 475.

and the victim's family. Moreover, the admission of unlawfully obtained evidence was a matter to be regulated by national law and the discretion to admit unlawfully obtained evidence was in accordance with the law. There was therefore no breach of Art.8 of the ECHR.[83]

In *Banghera*,[84] Lord Woolf C.J. identified different situations with which the courts have to deal under s.78. In situations where there has been a complete breakdown of the proper procedures in the whole of the prosecution process, the courts may well take the view that the breakdown is so significant that it would not be appropriate to allow the evidence to be admitted. Lower down the scale there may be cases where breaches of the Code can be said to be trivial or technical and the courts will almost inevitably come to the conclusion that no injustice or unfairness is involved and will allow the evidence to be given. There are difficulties with regard to middle category cases where the breach was significant but not serious: s.78 leaves this situation to be evaluated by the judge looking at all the circumstances. "Section 78 allows the courts to ensure the fairness of the trial process, and indeed the fairness of the prosecution process. That process ... involves the court being fair" to both sides.[85]

4. If there has been bad faith on the part of the police, it appears that the **10–21** discretion should be exercised to exclude the evidence: Lord Lane C.J. said in *Alladice*[86] that, if the police have acted in bad faith, the court will have

---

[83] At 484–485. See also *Loveridge* [2001] 2 Cr.App.R. 591, where a breach of s.41 of the Criminal Justice Act 1925, prohibiting the taking of photographs in court, making the filming of the applicants in the magistrates' court unlawful, did not give rise to the video evidence being inadmissible pursuant to s.78 as it did not have such an adverse effect on the fairness of the proceedings.

[84] [2001] 1 Cr.App.R. 299.

[85] At 304–305.

[86] (1988) 87 Cr.App.R. 380, 386. See also (1) *Matto v Wolverhampton Crown Court* [1987] R.T.R. 337 where police officers acting in excess of their powers and *mala fide* requested the defendant to take a breath test. The Divisional Court held that circumstances existed for the exercising of discretion to exclude this evidence. The Crown Court had not considered those circumstances and, as a result, the appeal was allowed; (2) *Thomas v DPP* [1990] Crim.L.R. 269 where the defendant was charged with failing to provide a specimen of breath at a police station. The Divisional Court, following *Matto*, accepted that there was a discretion to exclude evidence of what happened at the police station if the procedures had been tainted by police conduct at the roadside; (3) *Nathaniel* [1995] 2 Cr.App.R. 565 where the Court of Appeal held that the DNA profile of the defendant (obtained in a case of rape of which he was acquitted) should not have been admitted in relation to a later case because the information should have been destroyed on his acquittal and the defendant had been told when he provided a blood sample that the sample would be destoyed if he were acquitted. However, in breach of s.64 of the Police and Evidence Act 1984, the sample was retained. The Court of Appeal held that the admission of the blood sample in breach of statutory duty and in breach of undertaking would have an adverse effect on the fairness of the proceedings. It is submitted that *Nathaniel* can be distinguished from *Att-Gen's Reference (No.3 of 1999)*, considered above, on the basis that an undertaking was given to the accused that the sample would be destroyed, resulting in bad faith on the part of the police. Note: when s.82 of the Criminal Justice and Police Act 2001, amending s.64 of PACE, comes into effect, fingerprints and samples may, in certain circumstances, be retained.

little difficulty in ruling any confession inadmissible.[87] For example, in *Mason*[88] the police practised a deception upon the defendant and his solicitor by telling them untruthfully that the defendant's fingerprint had been found on a bottle used in starting a fire. The Court of Appeal held that the defendant's subsequent confession should have been excluded under s.78. A trial which contained evidence obtained in this way would not be fair. That, it is submitted, is the crucial test; and, it may be noted, the test under the European Convention of Human Rights: see para.10–09, above.

5. Subject to the discretion of s.78, evidence obtained abroad in accordance with the procedures of that jurisdiction may be admissible in an English criminal trial. As a result, evidence which may not have been admissible had it been obtained in England and Wales, may, provided the procedures of the foreign jurisdiction have been complied with, be held admissible.[89] The courts have failed to lay down any clear guidelines on how trial judges should approach admissibility in such cases. It is submitted, however, that where there is evidence of bad faith by the English police in using foreign police as agents or by manipulating foreign procedures to obtain evidence that may otherwise have not been lawfully obtainable, this might warrant exclusion of the evidence or a stay of the proceedings as an abuse of process.[90]

10–22　　6. If the fairness of the proceedings is not affected there is no reason to exclude the evidence. In *DPP v Marshall*[91] the Divisional Court held that the justices were wrong to exclude under s.78 the evidence of police officers who, when making test purchases with a view to adducing evidence for the prosecution of the defendant for selling liquor without a licence, did not announce that they were police officers. The court distinguished *Mason* on the ground that it involved a clear deception. The court said that it was impossible to see how the evidence in the instant case could have an effect on the fairness of the trial.[92]

A further illustration is *Nottingham City Council v Amin*,[93] in which a taxi-driver was stopped and hired by two special constables outside his

---

[87] However, there must be grounds for making a finding of bad faith on the part of the police before exercising the discretion. Thus, in *DPP v Wilson* [1991] R.T.R. 284 the Divisional Court held that justices were not entitled to exercise their discretion under the section to exclude evidence because a police officer believed a person was driving with excess alcohol as a result of an anonymous tip-off rather than the person's standard of driving.

[88] Above.

[89] See *Quinn* [1990] Crim.L.R. 581; *Konscol* [1993] Crim.L.R. 950; *Russell v McAdams* [2001] NI 157; *P* [2001] 2 Cr.App.R. 121, HL; and *McNab* [2002] Crim.L.R. 129.

[90] See *Mackarel and Gane* [1997] Crim.L.R. 720 for a critical review of the English courts' failure to provide more guidance in such cases and of the broader dangers of "evidence process laundering".

[91] [1988] 3 All E.R. 683.

[92] Similarly, in *Ealing LBC v Woolworths plc* [1995] Crim.L.R. 58 the Divisional Court held that justices were wrong to have excluded evidence of a breach of the Video Recordings Act 1984, obtained when the 11-year-old son of a Trading Standards Officer bought a category 18 video. The Court said that these were not appropriate circumstances for exclusion under s.78.

[93] [2000] 1 Cr.App.R. 426, DC.

licensed area. The Divisional Court held that these facts did not prejudice a fair trial of the driver for plying for trade for hire outside his area. There was no pressure exerted upon him to take the fare and he was not over-borne, persuaded or incited to commit the offence. After reviewing the relevant ECHR jurisprudence, Lord Bingham C.J. held that it did not oblige the court to exclude the evidence of the special constables on the ground that the admission of the evidence would render a trial unfair.[94]

7. Accordingly, it appears that the test is to ask whether a trial containing evidence obtained as a result of a particular deceit would be fair. Otherwise, there are no hard and fast rules. Illustrations may be given, but no practice is laid down. Thus, Auld J. observed in *Jelen and Katz*[95]: "The circumstances of each case are almost always different, and judges may well take different views in the exercise of their discretion even where the circumstances are similar. This is not an apt field for hard case law and well-founded distinctions between cases."

Examples may be given from cases involving police entrapment: **10–23**

(i) In H[96] a trial at Winchester Crown Court, the defendant was charged with rape. When interviewed by the police he admitted sexual intercourse took place but alleged that the complainant consented to it. He was released pending further enquiries. The police then installed tape recording equipment on the complainant's telephone with her consent. She instigated conversations which were taped. Gatehouse J. held that the tapes had been obtained by a trap and should be excluded under s.78. This decision may be contrasted with other examples in which traps were used. For instance, in *Jelen and Katz*[97] the police arrested and interviewed D: they then arranged for him to have a conversation with J who had not yet been arrested. The conversation was tape recorded without J's knowledge. The Court of Appeal upheld the trial judge's ruling that it would not be unfair to admit the tape recording of the conversation. The Court said that there were important differences between the instant case and H, the most important being that the police were at an early stage in their enquiries and J had not been interviewed.

(ii) In *Bailey and Smith*[98] the defendants were arrested in connection

---

[94] Leave to appeal to the House of Lords was granted for consideration of whether the discretion under s.78, exercised by reference to Art.6(1) of the ECHR, required exclusion of the evidence of the enforcement officers who asked the driver if he would take them to a particular destination when the driver voluntarily agreed (in the absence of persuasion or pressure) to so carry them.
[95] [1990] 90 Cr.App.R. 456, 465.
[96] [1987] Crim.L.R. 47.
[97] Above.
[98] (1993) 97 Cr.App.R. 365.

with armed robberies. At their trial the judge admitted evidence of confessions made by the two defendants and tape recorded during the course of conversations between them while they were sharing a bugged cell at a police station after being arrested, charged and remanded in custody. The police had applied to magistrates for a remand in custody to hold identification parades. This had been granted. However, a subsidiary reason was in fact to place the two into a bugged cell and to lull them into a false sense of security by pretending that their sharing a cell was contrary to the wishes of the investigating officers. The possibility of this plan had been foreseen by a solicitor for one of the men who warned him of it, but nonetheless the plan worked. It was argued that the police had acted in breach of the spirit of the Codes of Practice, tricked the defendants into speaking and undermined their right of silence. The Court of Appeal held that the evidence was admissible. The Court pointed out that such evidence of overheard or taped conversations in police stations was held to be admissible in cases decided before the enactment of s.78[99]; the Court did not doubt the essential fairness of admitting the evidence in the instant case. While the Code prevented the men from being questioned further by police it did not mean they had to be protected from speaking incriminatingly to each other if they chose to do so. (The Court commented that this was not a stratagem to be used with any frequency and only in grave cases.)

(The distinction between *H* and the other two cases may not be readily discernible. In each case a trap was laid for the defendant and as a result he made admissions. However, the cases serve to illustrate the accuracy of Auld J.'s observation quoted above.)

10–24   The exercise of discretion is further illustrated by two cases in which defendants were convicted as a result of police tricks or ruses and the result and evidence was held to be admissible:

(i)   In *Christou and Wright*[1] police officers set up a bogus jewellery and recording shop in order to trap thieves. The shop was manned by undercover officers and equipped with concealed video cameras to record conversations with customers. The Court of Appeal held that the evidence of what happened in the shop was admissible in evidence although the defendants had been subject to a

[99] *Mills and Rose* (1962) 46 Cr.App.R. 336; *Buchan* (1964) 48 Cr.App.R. 126; *Maqsud Ali* [1966] 1 Q.B. 688 (cited at para.2–17, above); *Keaton* (1970) 54 Cr.App.R. 267. More recently, a similar conclusion was reached by the Court of Appeal in *Roberts* [1997] 1 Cr.App.R. 217 (a case which illustrates the importance of the trial judge making findings of fact). For rulings by the European Court and the Commission, see para.10–09, above.
[1] (1992) 95 Cr.App.R. 264.

trick. Lord Taylor C.J. said that not every trick produces unfairness, on occasion the police adopt tricks or ruses in the public interest (for example to trap a blackmailer) and that in the instant case the trick could not reasonably be thought to involve unfairness.[2]

(ii) In *Williams v DPP*[3] the police left an insecure and unattended van containing an apparently valuable load on display in a busy shopping area. (The load was in fact dummy cigarettes.) The police kept observation and saw the defendants stealing cartons from the van. It was argued before the Divisional Court that the police evidence about what the defendants had done should not have been admitted because the police were acting as agents provocateurs by leaving temptation in the path of the defendants. The Divisional Court held that the evidence of the thefts was admissible since the defendants had incriminated themselves through their own dishonesty: the justices were right not to exclude the evidence under s.78 or at common law.

8. The Court of Appeal has given guidance to judges when exercising their discretion whether to admit the evidence of undercover police officers. In *Smurthwaite and Gill*[4] Lord Taylor C.J. said that the fact that evidence had been obtained by entrapment or by an agent provocateur or by a trick does not of itself require the judge to exclude it unless it would have the adverse effect described in s.78. However, Lord Taylor C.J. then set out some of the factors which the trial judge might take into account in these circumstances: (a) Was the officer enticing the defendant to commit a crime which he would not otherwise commit? (b) What was the nature of the entrapment? (c) Does the evidence consist of admissions to a completed offence or the actual commission of an offence? (d) How active or passive was the officer's role in obtaining the evidence? (e) Was there an unassailable record of what occurred, or was it strongly corroborated? (f) Had the officer abused his role by asking questions which ought properly to be asked at the police station and in accordance with the Codes? Lord Taylor

10–25

---

[2] At 269.
[3] (1994) 98 Cr.App.R. 209.
[4] (1994) 98 Cr.App.R. 437, 440. *Latif* [1995] 1 Cr.App.R. 270 provides another example. The Court of Appeal in that case held that the trial judge had been right to refuse to exclude (under s.78) the evidence of an agent who had lured drug smugglers from Pakistan in order to entrap them (affirmed by the House of Lords [1996] 2 Cr.App.R. 92.). On the other hand, the evidence of correspondence and recordings of conversations between a defendant and an undercover policewoman (in which she induced him to reveal his sexual fantasies to her) was excluded in a trial at first instance: *Stagg*, C.C.C., September 14, 1994, Ognall J., unreported, *Archbold News*, Issue 9, November 4, 1994. The evidence in that case was excluded under s.78 and at common law because the judge found that it was obtained by a trick which was applied to the defendant as part of a sustained enterprise to manipulate him, involving attempts to incriminate him by deceptive conduct of the grossest kind.

said that, these considerations apart, it was not possible to give general guidance as to how a judge should exercise his discretion in this field since each case had to be determined on its own facts.

9. It is sometimes suggested that the court should be governed in the exercise of its discretion by the need to discipline the police or protect citizens' rights. However, the statutory concept is that the circumstances, including the circumstances in which the evidence was obtained, may be such as to make the trial so unfair that the evidence should not be admitted. Parliament has thus chosen to place the emphasis upon the fairness of the proceedings and not on other matters. As a result, there is nothing in the section to suggest that the courts should follow the approach of other jurisdictions, for example Scotland and Australia, in exercising the discretion by balancing the conflicting interests in protecting the citizen from illegal or undue interference with his liberties and the public interest in putting before the court all the evidence relating to the offence charged. It is submitted that if Parliament had intended the courts to apply such a test, it would have said so.

(3) The European Convention on Human Rights

10–26 The principles of the Convention may affect the exercise of the court's discretion under s.78. Even before incorporation the Court of Appeal has said that the Convention might be deployed when a court was considering how to exercise a judicial discretion.[5] More specifically, the House of Lords in *Khan*[6] held that the fact that evidence had been obtained in an apparent breach of an article of the Convention might be relevant to the exercise of the judge's discretion under s.78. In *Khan* the police (acting under Home Office Guidelines) placed a covertlistening device on the outside wall of a private house (occupied by a suspected dealer in heroin). In placing the device the police were involved in civil trespass, causing damage to the house and were in apparent breach of Art.8 of the Convention (which protects the right to privacy). By means of the device the police recorded a conversation in the house, in which the defendant participated, which revealed that he had been involved in a substantial heroin importation. The House of Lords held that even if on the facts there had been a breach of Art.8, the trial judge was entitled to hold that the circumstances in which the evidence was obtained did not require its exclusion. The speeches make plain the significance of the Convention even before its incorporation into English law. Thus, Lord Nicholls said that the discretionary powers of the trial judge to exclude evidence "march hand in hand" with Art.6(1) of the Convention (which guarantees the right to a fair trial).

---

[5] *Rantzen v Mirror Group Newspapers* [1994] Q.B. 670, 691.
[6] [1996] 2 Cr.App.R. 440.

"Both are concerned to ensure that those facing criminal charges receive a fair hearing. Accordingly, when considering the common law and discretionary powers under English law, the jurisprudence on Article 6 can have a valuable role to play.[7] In the present case the decision of the European Court of Human Rights in *Schenk v Switzerland*[8] confirms that the use of material obtained in breach of the rights of privacy enshrined in Article 8 does not of itself mean that the trial is unfair. Thus, the European Court of Human Right's case law on this issue leads to the same conclusion as English law."[9]

The European Court of Human Rights has now considered the case of *Kahn v UK* and the similar case of *P.G. and J.H. v UK*. See paras 10–09 and 10–10 above. In both cases a violation of Art.8 during the course of gathering the evidence was not held to give rise to a violation of Art.6(1).[10]

Now that the Convention has been incorporated into English law[11] the courts must have regard to it when exercising a discretion under s.78. Articles 6 and 8 have proved to be particularly relevant: for discussion, see paras 13–14 *et seq.* below.

In *Mason, Wood, McClelland, and Tierney*[12] the appellants argued that the use of covert surveillance in police cells should have been ruled inadmissible under either s.76 or s.78 of the Human Rights Act, and/or common law. The court held that the police had acted reasonably, proportionately and that there was no suggestion that the tapes had been obtained through oppression. Despite not being in force at the time the surveillance was carried out, it was assumed that the Human Rights Act applied. The court accepted that there had been a breach of Art.8 as the surveillance had not been "prescribed by law". Following *Kahn* and *P.G. and J.H.* the Court held that the remedy for a breach of Art.8 was not necessarily the exclusion of the unlawfully obtained evidence. As no unfairness was caused by the reliance on the tapes as evidence at trial, there was no breach of Art.6(1). Moreover, for the purposes of the case, it was held that Art.6 added nothing to s.78. Similarly in *Loveridge*.[13] it was held that the secret filming of the defendants in the magistrates' court in contravention of s.41 of the Criminal Justice Act 1925, gave rise to a breach of Art.8 of the Convention. However, such a breach was relevant only if it interfered with the defendants right to a fair trial which, in all the circumstances, it did not.

10–27

---

[7] See para.10–09, above, for a summary of that jurisprudence in relation to improperly obtained evidence.

[8] (1988) 13 E.H.H.R. 242, cited at para.10–09, above.

[9] At 456.

[10] For a critical review of the failure by the European Court of Human Rights to give adequate reasoning for their decision in *Kahn* see the commentary to the decision in [2000] Crim.L.R. 684.

[11] Ch.13, below.

[12] Unreported, February 13, 2002, CA.

[13] [2001] 2 Cr.App.R. 591.

Furthermore, as the total evidence against the defendants was over-whelming the Court was satisfied that the trial was perfectly fair and the convictions in no way unsafe. Finally, In P[14] Lord Hobhouse stated: "The decision of the European Court of Human Rights in *Kahn v UK* shows that the coming into effect of the Human Rights Act 1998 does not invalidate in the relevant aspects the decision of your Lordship's House in that case and that s.78 is an appropriate safeguard of the fairness of the trial."[15]

Accordingly, the effect of the Convention upon the exercise of discretion may be summarised:

(1) a judge, in exercising his discretion under s.78 must have regard to the provisions of the Convention; and

(2) if there has been an apparent breach of an article, should take the breach into account when exercising his discretion;

(3) the fact that there has been an apparent breach of the Convention means that the evidence must be excluded if to admit it would make the trial unfair;

(4) what matters is the overall effect of the apparent breach on the fairness of the proceedings. However, it would appear that both s.78 and Art.6 have a common aim and that evidence which would be excluded as being in breach of one would almost certainly be in breach of the other.

(4) Conclusion

10–28 In deciding whether the circumstances in which the evidence was obtained will affect the fairness of the trial, the court will have to ask whether a trial in which this evidence is included will be fair. It is submitted that the section must involve the concept of fair play in action so that the objective bystander would say that the defendant would not have fair play if this evidence were included in his trial. Two further points should be noted.

1. The section does not refer to "fairness to the accused." Accordingly, in deciding whether the way in which the evidence was obtained adversely affects "the fairness of the proceedings," the court will have to consider the interests of both prosecution and defence. In *Hughes*[16] the Court of Appeal said that the judge would have to balance those interests to decide what the interests of justice were. However, it is submitted that while those interests must be taken into account, the question should not be determined upon

---

[14] [2001] 2 Cr.App.R. 121.

[15] Similarly, in *Loosely; Att-Gen's Reference (No.3 of 2000)* [2002] 1 Cr.App.R. 29 the House of Lords, after reviewing the English authorities in light of the European Court of Human Rights decision in *Texeria* (see para.10–09 above) held that the principles of English law require no modification.

[16] [1988] Crim.L.R. 519.

the balance of interests but upon a consideration of the admission of the evidence upon the fairness of the proceedings.[17]

2. If the court comes to the conclusion that to admit the evidence would adversely affect the fairness of the proceedings, it does not necessarily mean that it must be excluded. The Court of Appeal in *Walsh*[18] pointed out that before the evidence is excluded, the court must consider whether it has such an adverse effect on the fairness of the proceedings that justice required its exclusion. Accordingly, the court has to determine two questions:

(a) Would the admission of evidence obtained in these circumstances have an adverse effect on the fairness of the proceedings?

(b) If so, does it have such an adverse effect that the court ought not to admit it? As a matter of practice, no doubt, these questions will usually not be treated separately but considered as a whole.

B. Review of discretion

It would appear that the Court of Appeal will not interfere with the judge's discretion unless (a) he failed to exercise it at all, or (b) he exercised it unreasonably. In *O'Leary*,[19] the Court of Appeal said that, subject to unreasonableness, the question whether the evidence should be admitted under s.78 was a matter for decision by the judge in his discretion with which the Court of Appeal would be reluctant to interfere. The Court in that case said that the judge had applied the proper test laid down by statute and his decision was not perverse in the legal sense, namely a decision to which no reasonable judge could come.[20]

10–29

In *Samuel*[21] the Court said that while reluctant to interfere with the exercise of a judge's discretion, the position is different where an error has caused him not to exercise his discretion at all. In that case the judge ruled that the refusal of the police to allow a solicitor access to the defendant was justified and as a result did not exercise his discretion to exclude evidence of a subsequent interview. The Court of Appeal held that his ruling was wrong and that if he had held, as he should, that the refusal was unjustified, he was unlikely to have exercised his discretion to admit the evidence: accordingly, the appeal was allowed. In *Miller*[22] the Court came to the same conclusion

---

[17] In *Robb* (1991) 93 Cr.App.R. 161, 167 Bingham L.J. said that fairness was "a two way street: it was the fairness of the proceedings which mattered."
[18] (1990) 91 Cr.App.R. 161.
[19] (1988) 87 Cr.App.R. 387, 391.
[20] See also *Quinn* [1995] 1 Cr.App.R. 480, 489, where Lord Taylor C.J. said, "Before this Court could reach the conclusion that the judge was wrong ... we would have to be satisfied that no reasonable judge, having heard the evidence that this learned judge did, could have reached the conclusion that he did." In *Dures* [1997] Crim.L.R. 673 the Court of Appeal said that the practice of the court was represented by this statement.
[21] Above.
[22] [1998] Crim.L.R. 209.

in a case where there had been serious breaches of the Code of Practice and the trial judge exercised his discretion using an edition of the Code which was out of date.

Ultimately, the question for the Court of Appeal is whether the improper admission of evidence has rendered the conviction "unsafe".[23] It is submitted that if a defendant has been denied a fair trial as a result of the improper admission of evidence, it is almost inevitable that a conviction will be regarded as unsafe.[24]

If no application to exclude evidence under the section is made in the magistrates' court, any issue relating to the exercise of the justices' discretion may not be raised in the Divisional Court: justices could not be criticised for not exercising a power when they had not been asked to do so.[25]

C. Procedure

10–30   There is no burden on the Crown to disprove unfairness under s.78.[26] In *Saifi*,[27] the Divisional Court held that the concept of a burden of proof has no part to play in relation to s.78. There is no reference or express provision as to the burden of proof in s.78 and the court could see no basis for implying such a burden. "The prosecution desiring to adduce and the defence seeking to exclude evidence [must] each seek to persuade the court about the impact of fairness." The fact that s.78 does not state that facts are to be established or proved to any particular standard was deliberate: the matter is left open and "untrammeled by rigid evidential considerations".[28]

Section 78 provides that the court may exclude evidence "if it appears to the court" that its admission would have an adverse effect on the fairness of the proceedings. Accordingly, the defence may simply raise the issue by reference to the witness statements or to evidence already given in the trial. There would, in fact, appear to be no reason why the court itself should not raise the issue: however, it has no duty to do so.[29]

The proper time for the defence to raise the issue under s.78(1) is before the evidence is given. The section provides that "the court may refuse to allow evidence on which the prosecution proposes to rely to be given." Accordingly, once the evidence has been given, it is too late: s.78(1) ceases to have effect.[30] However, no such limitation applies at common law. It would therefore appear that in an appropriate case the court may in its discretion, preserved by s.78(2) and s.82(3), rule that evidence already

---

[23] Criminal Appeal Act 1968, s.2.
[24] *Togher* [2001] 1 Cr.App.R. 33 and *Brown v Stott* [2003] 1 A.C. 681.
[25] *Braham v DPP* (1995) 159 J.P. 527; [1996] R.T.R. 30.
[26] *Vel v Owen* [1987] Crim.L.R. 496.
[27] *R (Saifi) v Governor of Brixton Prison* [2001] 1 W.L.R. 1134.
[28] *ibid.*, at 1155.
[29] *Raphaie* [1996] Crim.L.R. 812.
[30] *Sat-Bhambra* (1989) 88 Cr.App.R. 55.

given should be disregarded and direct the jury accordingly; or discharge them if that is the only way to prevent injustice.[31]

Once the issue is raised in the Crown Court, the court must rule on it. It will usually be possible for the court to rule by referring to the witness statements and exhibits and considering the submissions of counsel. In some cases the court may wish to hear evidence on the *voir dire*, but it would appear that the defence cannot insist on it. In *Beveridge*[32] the Court of Appeal held that a judge in a trial on indictment is not obliged to hold a trial-within-a-trial where it was submitted that evidence of identification of a suspect in an identification parade should be excluded under the provisions of s.78. The Court said that there may be occasions when the judge thinks it desirable to hold a trial-within-a-trial when such a point is taken, but those occasions will be rare and the instant case was not one of them.

10–31

In the magistrates' court justices may deal with the issue either when it arises or may leave it until the end of the hearing: in either case the object must be to secure a trial which is fair and just to both sides.[33] The justices may hear the relevant evidence either in a trial-within-a-trial or as part of the prosecution case. If they decide to exclude the evidence, they must hear and determine the case without regard to the excluded evidence.[34] The defendant does not have the right to have the issue determined in a trial-within-a-trial.[35] It will only be in an exceptional case that the justices may wish to proceed by trial-within-a-trial; in such a case they are entitled to ask the defendant what issues are to be addressed in his evidence in order to assist them in deciding what course to take.[36]

In both the Crown and magistrates' courts, reasons must be given for exercising a discretion to either exclude or refuse to exclude evidence at trial. In *Denton* it was held that this has been a rule of English law for many years and to which Art.6 of the Convention gives added emphasis.[37] Thus, it would appear that older authorities suggesting that the absence of a detailed ruling will not give rise to criticism no longer apply.[38]

---

[31] See *Docherty* [1999] 1 Cr.App.R. 274. Where a jury hears evidence which they should not have heard and the evidence was such that the jury may not be able to give an impartial verdict based on the admissible evidence in the case, the trial judge has a discretionary power to discharge the jury. In exercising that discretion the judge must decide whether there is a real danger of injustice occurring because the jury, having heard the prejudicial matter, might be biased. Furthermore, where there is more than one interpretation of the inadmissible evidence the judge, in exercising his discretion on whether to discharge the jury, should approach the issue on the basis of the more prejudicial meaning that could be placed on it rather than on some lesser prejudicial interpretation.

[32] (1987) 85 Cr.App.R. 255.

[33] *Halawa v F.A.C.T.* [1995] 1 Cr.App.R. 21, 32.

[34] *ibid.*

[35] *Vel v Owen* [1987] Crim.L.R. 479.

[36] *Halawa*, above.

[37] *Denton* [2001] Crim.L.R. 225.

[38] *Moss* (1990) 91 Cr.App.R. 371 at 375.

3. RECOMMENDATIONS OF THE ROYAL COMMISSION

10–32   The Royal Commission on Criminal Justice recommended that judges be given the power to exclude repetitious or conflicting evidence.[39] This rule would be based on r.403 of the US Federal Rules of Evidence which allows the judge to exclude relevant evidence if its probative value is out weighed (a) by the danger of prejudice, confusion of the issues or misleading the jury; or (b) by consideration of undue delay, waste of time or needless presentation of cumulative evidence. The Commission thought that such a rule would encourage judges to be more robust in excluding such evidence. While it is acknowledged that the power would be a useful addition to the judge's powers to prevent time-wasting, it must be a matter of doubt whether the judge's present powers are not sufficient. The power to exclude irrelevant evidence already covers much of this matter. The court also has power to exclude evidence which will lead to a multiplication of issues. As for the rest, the prosecution will normally heed a suggestion from the bench as to time-wasting and it will be infrequent for a power to be exercised to prevent a defendant calling evidence which he considers necessary to establish his defence.

4. RECOMMENDATIONS OF THE AULD REVIEW

10–33   The Auld Review of the Criminal Courts, noting the general satisfaction of the Royal Commission with the resultant provisions of the Police and Criminal Evidence Act 1984, stated that it has only been since the Royal Commission in 1993 that the problems with the exclusion of evidence regime have become apparent. The Review identified the confusing overlap between the various provisions, much uncertainty as to the ambit of s.78(1) and the common law power to exclude, and their relationship with one another. In particular, the Review highlighted the problems that may arise where evidence, despite its impropriety, is potentially reliable and cogent. The Review also raised the question of the overlap between the courts' power to stay proceedings as an abuse of process and its powers to exclude evidence.

The Review called for a clarification of the law in this field and possible rationalisation by combining and simplifying the various forms of jurisdiction for exclusion of unfairly obtained evidence and that of staying a prosecution for abuse of process on the same grounds. This is against the background, and perhaps in preparation for the implementation of, the Review's broad recommendation that:

---

[39] Cm. 2263 (1993), para.8.13.

"The English law of criminal evidence should, in general, move away from technical rules of inadmissibility to trusting judicial and lay fact-finders to give relevant evidence the weight it deserves."

The simplification and rationalisation of the rules of excluding evidence would be a welcome development, especially in light of the recent incorporation of European Convention jurisprudence by way of the Human Rights Act 1998. It is submitted, however, that a move to simply admit more evidence into the trial process and leave it to the fact-finders to attach due weight would be a dangerous and problematic development. First, far from reducing the complexity of proceedings, such a move would require that lay fact finders be given careful and possibly lengthy directions on the weight to attach to each piece of evidence. Secondly, and of greater concern, is whether lay fact finders would necessarily even understand such directions giving rise to the prospect of unsafe convictions and an increase in appeals.

CHAPTER 11

Privilege

11–01   Privilege in the law of evidence is the right of a witness to withhold from a court information relevant to an issue in the proceedings before the court.[1] If such a privilege arises, a person may refuse to answer a question and cannot be obliged to do so. However, privilege can only be claimed by a witness once he has gone into the witness-box. Thus, privilege may be distinguished from the law relating to the compellability of a witness (considered in Ch.17) which deals with the occasions when a person may be forced to go into the witness-box and give evidence.

Privilege is a personal right.[2] Thus:

(a)   it may be exercised only by the person entitled to claim it; and

(b)   it may be waived only by that person.

Once, however, a witness has waived his right (whether by inadvertence orotherwise) the evidence given as a result is admissible.

The right arose because the law appreciated that as a matter of policy the public interest was better served by recognising certain privileges, despite the impediments to the ascertainment of the truth which may result.[3] However, these privileges are limited and only two of any significance[4] are recognised by law:

(i)   the privilege against self-incrimination, and

(ii)   legal professional privilege.

---

[1] This definition is based on that in para.1 of the Sixteenth Report of the Law Reform Committee, *Privilege in Civil Proceedings*, Cmnd. 3472 (1967).
[2] See Law Reform Committee, Sixteenth Report, above, at para.7. It should, however, be noted that a corporate defendant may also claim privilege: *Triplex Safety Glass Co. Ltd v Lancegaye Safety Glass (1934) Ltd* [1939] 2 K.B. 395.
[3] See *Att-Gen v Clough* [1963] 1 Q.B. 773, 787, *per* Lord Parker C.J.
[4] One insignificant privilege remains in criminal proceedings, the privilege of declining to produce a document of title to land. The privileges relating to communications between spouses and evidence as to marital intercourse were abolished by the Police and Criminal Evidence Act 1984.

1. THE PRIVILEGE AGAINST SELF-INCRIMINATION

A. The general rule

A witness (other than the defendant) is not bound to answer a question if **11–02** there is, in the opinion of the court, a risk that the answer will expose him to proceedings for a criminal offence, forfeiture or recovery of a penalty.[5]

The basis of the rule is to be found in the maxim *nemo tenebatur prodere seipsum*: a man should not be his own accuser. The modern rationale has been said to be the belief that "the coercive power of the state should not be used to compel a person to disclose information which would render him liable to punishment."[6]

The privilege against self-incrimination (and the right to silence) have been described as "prophylactic rules designed to inhibit abusive power by investigatory authorities and prevent the eliciting of confessions which might have doubtful probative value".[7]

The rule is subject to these limitations:

(i) In criminal proceedings (in contrast to civil proceedings[8]) the privilege does not extend to the incrimination of a spouse.[9]

(ii) The privilege does not apply to a defendant when he is asked questions in cross-examination about the offence charged: Criminal Justice Act 2003, s.98.

(iii) The privilege does not extend to protecting the witness from liability to civil proceedings.

(iv) The privilege does not apply to the incrimination of strangers.[10]

---

[5] "The rule is that no one is bound to answer any question if the answer thereto would, in the opinion of the judge have a tendency to expose the deponent to any criminal charge, penalty, or forfeiture which the judge regards as being likely to be preferred or sued for": *Blunt v Park Lane Hotel* [1942] 2 K.B. 253, 257, *per* Lord Goddard C.J.

[6] Law Reform Committee, Sixteenth Report, above, at para.8.

[7] *Regina v Hertfordshire County Council Ex p. Green Environmental Industries Ltd. The Times*, February 22, 2000, *per* Lord Hoffmann.

[8] Civil Evidence Act 1968, s.14(1).

[9] This would seem to be the law although there is some doubt. Stephen J. thought that the privilege did extend to protect a spouse (*Lamb v Munster* (1882) 10 Q.B.D. 110, 112, 113) and the Criminal Law Revision Committee considered that the law was doubtful on this point (Eleventh Report, para.169). There is much to be said for the recommendation of that Committee that the law in criminal proceedings should be brought into line with that in civil proceedings.

[10] *Minihane* (1921) 16 Cr.App.R. 38.

(v) The privilege does not protect the witness from answering questions or giving information in relation to others, including a company by whom the person is employed.[11]

(vi) The privilege does not apply if the criminal or penal sanction arises under foreign law.[12]

11–03 The privileges relating to penalty and forfeiture are of little importance now. Actions for penalties are obsolete except in revenue cases.[13] (It has been held that a fine imposed by the European Commission, enforceable under the European Communities Act 1972, is a penalty under the Civil Evidence Act 1968 and that privilege extends to liability for it.[14])

Liability to forfeiture of property was described by the Law Reform Committee as an "historical survival" which reflected the reluctance of equity to aid such a forfeiture. The Committee recommended abolition of the privilege now that the courts possess powers to grant relief against forfeiture.[15] The privilege no longer exists in civil proceedings.[16] The Criminal Law Revision Committee recommended that in this respect the law in criminal proceedings should coincide with that in civil. No action has, as yet, been taken.[17]

B. Taking the objection

11–04 In practice, questions of privilege against self-incrimination arise rarely in criminal proceedings. This may be because the principle is so well known

---

[11] *Walkers Snack Foods Ltd v Coventry City Council* [1998] 3 All E.R. 163, 173. The Divisional Court held that the privilege granted by s.14 of the Civil Evidence Act 1968 does not apply to protect an employee from answering questions of environmental health officers or giving access to a production line, as required by the Food Safety Act 1990, since it was the company and not the employee who was to be prosecuted. Accordingly, the employee could not rely on privilege as an excuse for not complying with the requirements of the 1990 Act.

[12] *Brannigan v Davison* [1996] 3 W.L.R. 861, PC. In *Brannigan v Davison* the Privy Council said that its decision was based on principle but also on the practical consideration of the difficulty of finding out what the consequences of giving evidence would be: however, the Privy Council also said that the judge has a discretion to excuse the witness from giving self-incriminating evidence in these circumstances. Note, however, that where the Secretary of State receives a request from the International Criminal Court ("ICC") for assistance in questioning a person being investigated or prosecuted by the ICC, in accordance with s.28 and Sch.3 to the ICC Act 2001, the person shall not be compelled to incriminate himself or confess guilt. The person being investigated or prosecuted should also be informed prior to being questioned of his right to remain silent, without such silence being a consideration in the determination of guilt or innocence.

[13] Law Reform Committee, Sixteenth Report, above, at para.13. Lord Denning M.R. said, however, that the privilege had been retained in respect of liability for penalties for a good reason—"the same reason as lay behind its introduction centuries ago. No person should be compelled to expose himself to pains or penalties out of his mouth": *Re Westinghouse Electric Corp.* [1977] 3 All E.R. 703, 711.

[14] *Rio Tinto Zinc v Westinghouse* [1978] A.C. 547.

[15] Sixteenth Report, above, at para.14.

[16] Civil Evidence Act 1968, s.16(1).

[17] Eleventh Report, Cmnd. 4991, para.149.

that advocates avoid questions which may expose a witness to the risk of incriminating himself. In most cases the dangers of self-incrimination are clear. It will be obvious that if the witness answers a question in a certain way he will admit a criminal offence. In such cases the judge will usually warn the witness that he is not obliged to answer the question. It is then a matter for the witness whether to answer or not.

The principles for taking the objection are as follows.

1.   The witness must take the objection himself,[18] though it is customary for the judge to advise him of his right to do so. However, the judge is not obliged to take the objection for him. The witness is supposed to know the law sufficiently to be able to do so.[19]

2.   (i)   If the witness does not take the objection, his replies, once given, will be admissible in evidence in any proceedings against him.[20]

      (ii) If, on the other hand, the witness does take the objection, but is compelled wrongly to answer, his answers are not admissible in evidence in proceedings against him.[21]

3.   The privilege is the witness's right. It belongs to no other party. Accordingly, the witness alone can take advantage of it. The defendant cannot claim the privilege on behalf of the witness, or benefit from his being wrongly denied the privilege. If a witness is wrongly compelled to answer and the defendant is convicted, the defendant cannot use this as a ground of appeal,[22] for no injustice has been done to him.[23]

4.   A witness is not afforded protection unless he can satisfy the court   **11–05** that there is reasonable ground for the objection being made.[24] The burden of establishing the privilege would therefore appear to be on the witness claiming it. The witness does not have to describe precisely the peril which he faces (since to do so may expose him to the very peril against which the privilege is claimed). However, the claim must be made by the witness himself even if support and substantiation for it came from elsewhere.[25]

5.   The witness should, however, be afforded the protection of the

---

[18] *Att-Gen v Radloff* (1854) 10 Ex. 84, 107, *per* Parke B.
[19] *Coote* (1873) L.R. 4 P.C. 599.
[20] *Sloggett* (1856) Dears 656.
[21] *Garbett* (1847) 1 Den. 236.
[22] *Kinglake* (1870) 11 Cox 499.
[23] *Kinglake*, above.
[24] *Boyes* (1861) 1 B. & S.311; *National Association of Operative Plasterers v Smithies* [1906] A.C. 434, 438, *per* Lord James of Hereford; *Westinghouse*, below, at 728, *per* Shaw L.J.
[25] *Downie v Coe, The Times*, November 28, 1997.

court if there appears reasonable ground to believe that an answer would tend to incriminate him.[26]

6. It is for the judge to rule whether there is reasonable ground or not.[27]

11–06

7. The court has a duty to ensure that the person is entitled to the protection of the privilege. Thus, if a claim is made in bad faith it will not be allowed,[28] for example if made to avoid answering the questions for reasons unconnected with self-incrimination. The mere fact that a witness swears that his answer would tend to incriminate him is not conclusive.[29]

8. A remote possibility of legal peril is not sufficient. The danger to be apprehended must be "real and appreciable, with reference to the ordinary operation of law and in the ordinary course of things."[30] Thus, if the possibility of prosecution has in fact been removed there is no privilege. In *Boyes*,[31] a witness in a bribery trial was called to prove that he had received a bribe. He refused to answer questions. The Solicitor-General was prosecuting. He handed the witness a pardon under the Great Seal. The witness still refused to answer. The judge directed him to do so. The Court of Queen's Bench upheld this ruling because the pardon had removed the risk of prosecution. It was argued that there was a risk of impeachment by the House of Commons. The court rejected this argument because the risk was not real.

11–07

9. On the other hand, provided that the risk of proceedings being taken against him is real and not remote or insubstantial, the witness does not have to show that proceedings are likely or could probably be taken against him.[32]

10. "Reasonable ground may appear from the circumstances of the case or from matters put forward by the witness himself. He should not be compelled to go into detail because it may involve his disclosing the very matter to which he takes objection. But if it appears to the judge that, by being compelled to answer, a witness

---

[26] *Garbett* (1847) 1 Den. 236 (a court of nine judges).
[27] *Boyes*, above; *Re Westinghouse Electric Corp.* [1977] 3 All E.R. 703, 717, 721, *per* Lord Denning M.R.
[28] *Adams v Lloyd* (1858) H. & N. 351, 362, *per* Pollock C.B.; *Re Reynolds* (1882) 20 Ch.D. 294, 300, *per* Jessell M.R.; *Re Westinghouse Electric Corp.* [1977] 3 All E.R. 717, 725, *per* Roskill L.J.
[29] *Triplex Safety Glass Co. v Lancegaye Safety Glass Co. (1934) Ltd* [1939] 2 K.B. 395, 403, *per* Du Parcq L.J.
[30] *Boyes* (1861) 1 B. & S. 311, 330, *per* Cockburn C.J.; approved in *Re Reynolds* (1882) 20 Ch.D. 294.
[31] Above.
[32] *Re Westinghouse Electric Corp.*, above, at 722, *per* Lord Denning M.R.

may be furnishing evidence against himself, which could be used against him in criminal proceedings or in proceedings for a penalty, then his objection should be upheld."[33]

11. Once it appears that there is a risk of danger for the witness "great latitude" should be allowed to the witness in judging the effect of a particular question.[34] It may only be one link in a chain or only corroborative of existing material, but still he is not bound to answer if he believes on reasonable grounds that it could be used against him.[35]

C. Statutory provisions

Various statutes remove the right to privilege. Some of the more significant in relation to criminal proceedings are considered here.[36]   **11–08**

1. The most significant is s.98 of the Criminal Justice Act 2003, which provides that the defendant may be asked any questions in cross-examination notwithstanding that it would tend to criminate him as to the offence charged. See paras 7–31 and 7–32, above.

The provision is clearly essential, for if the defendant could claim privilege in respect of questions in relation to the offence charged, there would be little point in his giving evidence as his evidence would remain untested by cross-examination.

2. Section 31 of the Theft Act 1968 removes the right in proceedings for the recovery or administration of any property, or for the execution of any trust or for an account of any property or dealings with property. However, the section provides that no statement or admission made by a person in answering a question put in such proceedings is admissible against the witness (or his spouse) in proceedings under the Act.[37]

3. In proceedings under Pts IV and V of the Children Act 1989, *i.e.* in   **11–09**
relation to orders for the care, supervision and protection of children, the privilege does not apply: s.98(1) of the Act. However, a statement or admission in such proceedings is not admissible in evidence against the maker or his spouse in proceedings for an offence other than perjury: s.98(2). The purpose of s.98 is to provide protection for a witness who is required to give evidence in relation to a child when such evidence could incriminate him or his spouse.[38] The true meaning of s.98(2) has still to be

---

[33] *Re Westinghouse Electric Corp.*, above, at 717, 721, *per* Lord Denning M.R.
[34] *Boyes*, above, at 330.
[35] *Re Westinghouse Electric Corp.*, above, at 722, *per* Lord Denning M.R.
[36] See also Official Secrets Act 1911, s.6; J.D. Heydon, "Statutory Restrictions on the Privilege against Self Incrimination" (1971) 87 L.Q.R. 214.
[37] s.31 applies even if a person is liable to be prosecuted for forgery as well as theft: *Khan v Khan* [1982] 1 W.L.R. 513.
[38] *Kent C.C. v K* [1994] 1 W.L.R. 912, 916, *per* Booth J. (Booth J. held that putting inconsistent statements to a witness in order to challenge her evidence did not amount to using the statements against her within the meaning of s.98.)

resolved. However, the Court of Appeal has held that the use of the words "proceedings" and "evidence" in the subsection indicates that it encompasses court proceedings (and evidence given in those proceedings) and not a police inquiry.[39] In *Oxon C.C. v P*[40] Ward J. held that s.98(2) was not limited to statements or admissions made in oral evidence and included a written statement and an oral admission made by a mother to a guardian ad litem (during the latter's investigation in care proceedings) that the mother had caused injuries to her baby.

If a person provides information under a statute removing the right to protection from self-incrimination and the statute does not restrict the use of that information, it may be used in evidence against him.[41] Thus, in *Scott*,[42] a bankrupt had been examined under an Act which provided that he was bound to answer questions put to him. Under threat of committal for contempt he answered the questions and provided certain information. His answers were used against him in criminal proceedings. The Court of Criminal Appeal held that the answers had been rightly admitted. Alderson B. said: "if you make a thing lawful to be done, it is lawful in all its consequences and one of its consequences is, that what may be stated by a person in a lawful examination, may be received in evidence against him."[43]

Pursuant to s.434 of the Companies Act 1985, a witness was obliged to answer questions put to him by Department of Trade and Industry inspectors. This was so even if the answer might tend to incriminate him. In *Saunders*[44] the Court of Appeal rejected a submission that the trial judge should have excluded (under the provisions of s.78 of the Police and Criminal Evidence Act 1984) transcripts of interviews with DTI Inspectors. Lord Taylor CJ said that Parliament had made its intentions clear in s.434(5) (that answers were prima facie admissible in criminal proceedings) and that it could not be right for a judge to exercise his discretion to exclude simply on the ground that Parliament ought not countenance the possibility of self-incrimination.[45]

11–10   However, the European Court of Human Rights subsequently ruled that *Saunders* had been deprived of a fair trial, in violation of Art.6(1) of the Convention by reason of the use of statements obtained from him by the DTI Inspectors which amounted to an unjustifiable infringement of the right to silence and the right not to incriminate oneself: *Saunders v UK*.[46]

[39] *Re C (A Minor) (Care proceedings: Disclosure)*, The Times, October 22, 1996.
[40] [1995] 1 F.L.R. 552.
[41] *Scott* (1856) Dears. & B. 47; *Customs & Excise Commissioners v Harz and Power* [1967] 1 A.C. 760, 816, *per* Lord Reid.
[42] Above.
[43] *Scott* (1856) Dears. & B. 47, 67.
[44] [1996] 1 Cr.App.R. 463.
[45] At 478.
[46] [1997] 23 E.H.R.R. 313. See also *I.J.L. and A.K.P. v UK*, The Times, October 13, 2000 in which the European Court reached a similar conclusion to that of *Saunders*.

The Court said that the question whether the use made by the prosecution of the statements obtained by the Inspectors amounted to such an infringement must be examined in the light of all the circumstances, in particular whether the applicant had been subject to compulsion to give evidence and whether the use of the testimony at his trial offended the basic principles of a fair procedure inherent in Art.6(1). Lord Taylor had said in *Saunders* that should the latter's application succeed before the European Court, our Treaty obligations will require consideration to be given to the effect of the decision here.

In response to the European Court's decision in *Saunders*, which had criticised UK legislation that permitted evidence against an accused obtained under compulsion being subsequently used against him at trial, Parliament enacted s.59 and Sch.3 to the Youth Justice and Criminal Evidence Act 1999.[47] This remedied the situation by restricting the use of answers in criminal proceedings of answers obtained from an accused under compulsion under a whole range of legislative provisions.[48] Section 59 and Sch.3 stipulate that answers obtained under compulsion pursuant to the statutes set out cannot be adduced by the prosecution in a criminal trial, in chief or in cross-examination, except (a) where the defendant himself introduced them as evidence, or (b) the prosecution is for the failure to provide answers, refusal to do so or to disclose a material fact, or for having given an untruthful answer.

Despite the entry into force of s.59 and Sch.3 to the Youth Justice and Criminal Evidence Act 1999, there are still a number of statutory provisions that permit the use of answers obtained under compulsion in criminal proceedings that are not covered by the section.

Some of these provisions have been the subject of judicial scrutiny.

In *R v Hertfordshire County Council Ex p. Green Environmental Industries Ltd*,[49] the House of Lords considered whether a notice issued by a waste regulation authority pursuant to its powers under s.71(2) of the Environmental Protection Act 1990 offended the rule against self-incrimination. In deciding that it did not, Lord Hoffmann stated that the question whether a statute which conferred a power to ask questions or obtain

11–11

---

[47] Entered into force April 14, 2000. Prior to the entry into force of the 1999 Act, the European Court's decision in *Saunders* was given effect in the UK by guidelines issued by the Att-Gen that prosecutors ought not, except in specific circumstances, rely on evidence at trial that had been obtained under compulsion (see (1998) 148 N.L.J. 208). In *Faryab* [2000] Crim.L.R. 180, the Court of Appeal quashed a conviction where, in ignorance of the Att-Gen's guidelines, answers which should not have been relied upon were admitted at trial.

[48] Insurance Companies Act 1982, ss.43A, 44; Companies Act 1985, ss.434, 447; Insolvency Act 1986, s.433; Company Directors Disqualification Act 1986, s.20; Building Societies Act 1986, s.57; Financial Services Act 1986, ss.105, 177; Companies (Northern Ireland) Orders, Arts 427, 440; Banking Act 1987, ss.39, 41, 42; Criminal Justice Act 1987, s.2; Companies Act 1989, s.83; Companies (Northern Ireland) Order 1989, Art.23; Insolvency (Northern Ireland) Order 1989, Art.373; Friendly Societies Act 1992, s.67; Criminal Law (Consolidation) Act 1995, s.28; Proceeds of Crime (Northern Ireland) Order, Sch.2, para.6.

[49] *The Times*, February 22, 2000.

documents or information excluded the privilege against self-incrimination was one of construction. Information obtained pursuant to s.71 is not obtained as a result of any oral interrogation and the information was needed not only for the purpose of investigation but also for the broad public purpose of protecting public health and the environment. Section 71 of the 1990 Act was not one of the statutes to which Parliament had made amendments following the decision of the European Court in *Saunders*. It was presumed that this was because it contained no express provision that answers were to be admissible in criminal trials and therefore left unimpaired the judge's discretion under s.78 of the Police and Criminal Evidence Act 1984.[50]

The Court of Appeal reached a similar conclusion in *Att-Gen's Reference No.7 of 2000*[51] in holding that books and papers produced by the accused under compulsion under s.291(b) of the Insolvency Act 1986 were to be admissible. The Court held that the documentation sought contained no compulsorily made statements and to admit it did not violate the accused's right to a fair trial, but stressed, that the admissibility of the documents was subject to the judge's discretion under s.78 of PACE.[52]

In *Brown v Stott*[53] the Privy Council held that while the right to a fair trial in Art.6 of the European Convention was absolute and could not be compromised, the privilege against self-incrimination, being a right implied from Art.6, was not absolute. Accordingly, where it is necessary to achieve a legitimate aim within the public interest the privilege can be subject to limited qualifications. Any such qualification, however, must be proportionate to achieving its aim. The aim of road traffic legislation, including s.172(2) of the Road Traffic Act 1972 (under which the keeper of a vehicle is required to name the driver at the time an offence was committed), is the safety of the public and hence a legitimate aim. Since s.172(2) permits the putting of the question, the answer to which does not in itself incriminate the person who answers it, and, since no improper coercion can be used to obtain an answer and the penalty for refusing to answer is moderate and non-custodial, the use of s.172 is not a disproportionate response to a serious social problem. Thus, it is not incompatible with the defendant's

---

[50] Lord Hoffmann also considered the European Court of Justice case of *Orkem v Commission of the European Communities (Case 374/87)* [1989] E.C.R. 3283, in which the European Court held that the Commission was entitled to ask for factual information, even if it might be incriminating, but that the Commission could not compel Orkem to provide it with answers which might involve an admission of an infringement which it was incumbent upon the Commission to prove. Accordingly, *Hertfordshire* fell on the right side of the line drawn by the European Court in *Orkem* as the request was for factual information and not an invitation to admit wrongdoing.

[51] [2001] Crim.L.R. 736.

[52] *ibid.*

[53] [2001] 2 W.L.R. 817. See R. Pillay [2001] E.H.R.L.R. 78, arguing that *Brown* is limited to "regulatory" offences.

right to a fair trial under Art.6 of the Convention to rely on any admission obtained under s.172.

Shortly after the Privy Council's decision in *Brown*, the European Court of Human Rights delivered its judgment in *Heaney and McGuiness v Ireland*.[54] The Court held in that case that Irish legislation[55] making it a criminal offence (punishable by six months imprisonment) for a person detained on suspicion of a defined terrorist offence to refuse to give a full account to the police of his movements and actions (during a specified period) amounted to a violation of Art.6(1) and 6(2) of the Convention. Whilst recognising that the right to silence and privilege against self-incrimination are not absolute, the Court held that the degree of compulsion created by the threat of a prison sentence in effect destroyed the very essence of the rights conferred by Art.6 in a manner incompatible with the Convention. Similarly in *JB v Switzerland*,[56] the European Court found a violation of Art.6 where authorities had attempted to compel the applicant, with the threat of a fine, to submit documents which would have provided information that could have been used against him in a prosecution for tax evasion.[57]

11–12

It has been argued[58] that *Brown v Stott* may have to be reconsidered in light of the European Court's recent rulings. It may be that *Brown* ought to be reasoned differently with greater emphasis placed on whether the degree of compulsion under s.172, namely a fine not more than £1000, is enough to destroy the very essence of the privilege. Moreover, it has been stated that "the absence of clear guidance on the application of the European case" has lead to English courts being free to side step the full rigour of the Art.6 protection by concluding that there was only an inquiry of a "quasi" criminal or "extra-judicial" nature.[59]

It is possible to distinguish *Brown* from *JB* on the basis that, in cases pursuant to s.172(2) of the Road Traffic Act 1972, it is already known that an offence has been committed by the driver of a particular vehicle. In most cases it is fair to assume that the keeper of a vehicle will be the driver, if not it is for the keeper to be in a position to provide details of who was driving the vehicle. In those cases where the keeper was not the driver, he is not under compulsion to incriminate himself, but another.[60] By contrast in *JB*, the document sought by the authorities by way of compulsion could *only* have been used to incriminate JB. Moreover, in *JB* it had not been estab-

11–13

---

[54] [2001] Crim.L.R. 481.
[55] s.52 of the Offences Against the State Act 1939.
[56] [2001] Crim.L.R. 748. By contrast, no violation of Art.6 was found in *Allen v UK* [2003] Crim.L.R. 280, the European Court held that the privilege against self-incrimination does not amount to a blanket prohibition of compulsory and regulatory powers.
[57] Note that the fine in *JB* was 2,000 Swiss francs (around £800 at current rates).
[58] See commentaries by Professor Ashworth to *JB* and *Heaney and McGuinness* and Ashworth, "The Self-Incrimination Saga" [2001] 5 *Archbold News* 5.
[59] See commentary to *Att-Gen's Reference No.7 of 2000* [2001] Crim.L.R. 737.
[60] See para.11–02 above, there is no privilege against giving information in relation to others.

lished that an offence had actually been committed. It was production of the document itself that could have provided the basis for criminal proceedings for tax evasion.

There is support for this in *Telfner v Austria*.[61] The accused had been convicted of causing injury by negligence in a car accident. The accused denied driving the car at the relevant time and refused to make any further submissions. He was convicted, in part, on account of the fact that he had refused to answer questions on who had been driving the car. The European Court held that the drawing of inferences from an accused's refusal to answer questions might be permissible where the evidence adduced was such that the only *common-sense* inference to be drawn from the accused's silence was that he had no answer to the case against him.

D. The right of silence

11–14   This topic is conveniently discussed here because the concept of a "right of silence" is based partly on the privilege against self-incrimination (and partly on the rules relating to the burden of proof).[62] This right has been restricted by the Criminal Justice and Public Order Act 1994, which is discussed at para.11–16 below.

(1) The common law rules

11–15   The right means that a suspect is not obliged to answer questions when interrogated by the police or others charged with investigating offences. The effect at common law is that a court or jury may not draw an adverse inference from a defendant's failure to answer questions. As a further consequence at common law the defendant may (a) not generally be compelled to reveal his defence before a trial, and (b) in no circumstances be compelled to give evidence. (Various inroads were made into the right; for instance, a suspect in an investigation into serious fraud may be required to answer questions. Inroads have also been made by statutory provision relating to advance disclosure of the defence case (see para.18–14, below, on defence disclosure), for example the requirement that (a) notice be given of alibi evidence[63]; (b) experts' reports be disclosed[64]; and (c) in serious fraud cases the defence be disclosed.[65]

At common law the fact that a defendant exercises his right of silence and

---

[61] (2002) 34 E.H.R.R. 7.

[62] "This expression [the right of silence] arouses strong, but unfocused feelings. In truth it does not denote any single right, but rather refers to a disparate group of immunities, which differ in nature, origin, incidence and importance, and as to the extent to which they have already been encroached upon by statute": *Director of S.F.O. Ex p. Smith* [1992] 3 W.L.R. 66, 74, *per* Lord Mustill.

[63] Criminal Justice Act 2003, s.6A(2) and (3)—see para.18–16.

[64] Police and Criminal Evidence Act 1984, s.81. See para.6–35, above.

[65] Criminal Justice Act 1987, s.2. See para.18–32.

does not reply to questions when interviewed by the police is, as a general rule, not evidence against him.

In these circumstances, the suspect's exercise of his right of silence could not normally be held against him. Thus, Lord Dilhorne said that to invite a jury to form an adverse opinion against an accused on account of his exercise of his right of silence is a misdirection.[66]

(2) Inferences from the defendant's silence: the 1994 Act

Section 34 of the Criminal Justice and Public Order Act 1994, as amended by s.58 of the Youth Justice and Criminal Evidence Act 1999, provides as follows: **11–16**

> "(1) Where, in any proceedings against a person for an offence, evidence is given that the accused—
>
> (a) at any time before he was charged with the offence, on being questioned under caution by a constable trying to discover whether or by whom the offence had been committed, failed to mention any fact relied on in his defence in those proceedings; or
>
> (b) on being charged with the offence or officially informed that he might be prosecuted for it, failed to mention any such fact,
>
> being a fact which in the circumstances existing at the time the accused could reasonably have been expected to mention when so questioned, charged or informed, as the case may be, subsection (2) below applies.
>
> (2) Where this subsection applies—
>
> (a) a magistrates' court inquiring into the offence as examining justices;
>
> (b) a judge, in deciding whether to grant an application made by the accused under—
>
> > (i) section 6 of the Criminal Justice Act 1987 (application for dismissal of charge of serious fraud in respect of which notice of transfer has been given under section 4 of that Act); or
> >
> > (ii) paragraph 5 of Schedule 6 to the Criminal Justice Act 1991 (application for dismissal of charge of violent or sexual offence involving child in respect of which notice of transfer has been given under section 53 of that Act);

---

[66] *Gilbert* (1978) 66 Cr.App.R. 237, 244.

    (c)   the court, in determining whether there is a case to answer; and

    (d)   the court or jury, in determining whether the accused is guilty of the offence charged,

may draw such inferences from the failure as appear proper.

[(2A)   Where the accused was at an authorized place of detention at the time of the failure, subsections (1) and (2) above do not apply if he had not been allowed an opportunity to consult a solicitor prior to being questioned, charged or informed as mentioned in subsection (1) above.]

(3)   Subject to any directions by the court, evidence tending to establish the failure may be given before or after evidence tending to establish the fact which the accused is alleged to have failed to mention.

(4)   This section applies in relation to questioning by persons (other than a constables) charged with the duty of investigating offences or charging offenders as it applies in relation to questioning by constables; and in subsection (1) above "officially informed" means informed by a constable or any such person.

(5)   This section does not—

    (a)   prejudice the admissibility in evidence of the silence or other reaction of the accused in the face of anything said in his presence relating to the conduct in respect of which he is charged, in so far as evidence thereof would be admissible apart from this section; or

    (b)   preclude the drawing of any inference from any such silence or other reaction of the accused which could not properly be drawn apart from this section.

(6)   This section does not apply in relation to a failure to mention a fact if the failure occurred before the commencement of this section."

11–17   The effect of the section is that the court in determining whether the defendant is guilty of the offence charged (or a court in determining whether there is a case to answer), may draw such inferences as appear proper from evidence that on being questioned under caution by the police about the offence, before being charged (or on being charged), the defendant failed to mention any fact relied on in his defence, which, in the circumstances existing at the time, he could reasonably have been expected to mention.[67]

---

[67] s.2A was inserted by s.58 of the Youth Justice and Criminal Evidence Act 1999. It applies only to proceedings instituted on or after the commencement date of that section. The commencement date is yet to be appointed.

In determining whether to conduct an interview, police officers should have the opportunity to ask questions so that explanations may be put forward showing either that no offence has been committed by the suspect (enabling police, in appropriate cases, to pursue alternative lines of enquiry before evidence disappears) or to be sure that they are not accusing the wrong person. Where the officer is sure that there is sufficient evidence for a prosecution to succeed there should be no further questioning.[68]

In *Beckles and Montague*,[69] the Court of Appeal held that, as a matter of statutory construction, inferences under s.34 were not limited to an inference of recent fabrication, and that other inferences were open, for example that the accused was reluctant to be subject to questioning and further inquiry when in a compromising position. The Court stated that a proper inference is one relevant to determining whether the accused is guilty, but may also be one which is simply adverse to the defence, and that ultimately the jury may draw such inferences as seem proper. For example in *Taylor*,[70] it had been proper to draw an adverse inference from the defendant's failure to mention a possible alibi defence when interviewed despite the fact that to have answered questions would have resulted in admissions to other criminal offences and the fact that the accused had told his solicitor of his alibi prior to interview. Thus, an accused cannot avoid an inference being drawn by informing his solicitor of his defence prior to interview with the intention thereafter to place reliance upon it. It is for the jury to consider why the salient fact was withheld, and to draw such inferences as appear proper.

The Royal Commission on Criminal Justice recommended against any interference with the right to silence on the ground that it would work adversely against the most vulnerable suspects.[71] However, it has been pointed out that there is now greater protection for suspects than formerly existed, *i.e.* greater access to legal advice and the introduction of tape recording of interviews.[72] In fact, s.34 is based on the recommendations of the Criminal Law Revision Committee's Eleventh Report of 1972 and the wording of the section is based on that in the draft Bill attached to the Report.[73] The Committee said that a suspect would not lose the right of silence in the sense that it is no offence to refuse to answer questions, but if

11–18

---

[68] *Odeyemi* [1999] Crim.L.R. 828. See also *Pointer* [1997] Crim.L.R. 676; *Gayle* [1999] Crim.L.R. 502; *McGuinness* [1999] Crim.L.R. 318; and *Ioannou* [1999] Crim.L.R. 586. The Commentary to *Odeyemi* explains the view apparently emerging from the case law is that the interviewing officer may proceed with an interview provided he has not personally formed the opinion that there is sufficient evidence to charge. If his mind is not closed to the possibility of an innocent explanation from the suspect, there is no breach of Code C: 11.4 or 16.1.
[69] [1999] Crim.L.R. 148. See also *Daniel* [1998] Crim.L.R. 818 and *Randall* (unreported, April 3, 1998).
[70] [1999] Crim.L.R. 77
[71] Cm. 2263 (1993), paras 4.20–4.24.
[72] Home Office, Report of the Working Group on the Right of Silence (1989), para.39.
[73] Cmnd. 4991, para.28.

he chooses to exercise the right he will risk having an adverse inference drawn against him at trial. The Committee thought that to forbid the jury or magistrates from drawing whatever inferences are reasonable from the failure of the accused, when interrogated, to mention a defence put forward at trial was contrary to common sense; and, without helping the innocent, gave an unnecessary advantage to the guilty.

Section 34 of the Criminal Justice and Public Order Act 1994 was enacted in the face of considerable opposition.[74] It has remained an extremely controversial piece of legislation and been the subject of considerable academic criticism[75] and judicial scrutiny, both domestically and in Strasbourg. European jurisprudence and the effect of the Human Rights Act 1998 have considerably diminished the effect of s.34 leading some to recommend its complete repeal and a return to the common law position.[76]

11–19   To keep up with the rapid development of this area of criminal evidence the Judicial Studies Board issued a revised Specimen Direction in July 2001. The new direction is as follows:

1.   Before his interview(s) the defendant was cautioned. He was first told that he need not say anything. It was therefore his right to remain silent. However, he was also told that it might harm his defence if he did not mention when questioned something which he later relied on in court; and that anything he did say might be given in evidence.

2.   As part of his defence, the defendant has relied upon (*here specify the facts to which this direction applies*). But [the prosecution say/ he admits] that he failed to mention these facts when he was interviewed about the offence(s). [If you are sure that is so, this/ This] failure may count against him. This is because you may draw the conclusion from his failure that he [had no answer then/ had no answer that he then believed would stand up to scrutiny/ has since invented his account/has since tailored his account to fit the prosecution's case/(*here refer to any other reasonable inferences contended for*)]. If you do draw that conclusion, you must not convict him wholly or mainly on the strength of it; but you may take it into account as some additional support for the pro-

---

[74] For a detailed consideration of the background to the enactment of s.34 see Professor Birch's "Suffering in Silence: A Cost-Benefit Analysis of Section 34 of the Criminal Justice and Public Order Act 1994" [1999] Crim.L.R. 769.

[75] See R. Pattenden, "Silence: Lord Taylor's Legacy" (1998) 2 *International Journal of Evidence and Proof* 141; Professor Ashworth, "Article 6 and the Fairness of Trials" [1999] Crim.L.R. 261; Anthony Jennings *et al.* "Silence and Safety: The Impact of Human Rights Law" [2000] Crim.L.R. 879; Professor Ian Dennis, "Silence in the Police Station: the Marginalisation of Section 34" [2002] Crim.L.R. 25; and Anthony Jennings Q.C. and David Emanuel, "Adverse Inferences from Silence—an Update." [2001] 9 *Archbold News* 6.

[76] See *op.cit.* Birch, n.85.

secution's case and when deciding whether his [evidence/case] about these facts is true.

3. You may draw such a conclusion against him only if you think it is a fair and proper conclusion, and you are satisfied about three things: first, that when he was interviewed he could reasonably have been expected to mention the facts on which he now relies; second, that the only sensible explanation for his failure to do so is that he had no answer at the time or none that would stand up to scrutiny; third, that apart from his failure to mention those facts, the prosecution's case against him is so strong that it clearly calls for an answer by him.

4. (*Add, if appropriate:*) The defence invite you not to draw any conclusion from the defendant's silence, on the basis of the following evidence (*here set out the evidence*). If you [accept this evidence and] think this amounts to a reason why you should not draw any conclusion from his silence, do not do so. Otherwise, subject to what I have said, you may do so.

5. (*Where legal advice to remain silent is relied upon, add the following instead of paragraph 4:*) The defendant has given evidence that he did not answer questions on the advice of his solicitor/legal representative. If you accept the evidence that he was so advised, this is obviously an important consideration: but it does not automatically prevent you from drawing any conclusion from his silence. Bear in mind that a person given legal advice has the choice whether to accept or reject it; and that the defendant was warned that any failure to mention facts which he relied on at his trial might harm his defence. Take into account also (*here set out the circumstances relevant to the particular case, which may include the age of the defendant, the nature of and/or reasons for the advice given, and the complexity or otherwise of the facts on which he relied at the trial*). Having done so, decide whether the defendant could reasonably have been expected to mention the facts on which he now relies. If, for example, you considered that he had or may have had an answer to give, but reasonably relied on the legal advice to remain silent, you should not draw any conclusion against him. But if, for example, you were sure that the defendant had no answer, and merely latched onto the legal advice as a convenient shield behind which to hide, you would be entitled to draw a conclusion against him, subject to the direction I have given you.

Accordingly, before an adverse inference can be drawn under the section the jury must be satisfied that: **11–20**

(a) on being questioned under caution the defendant failed to mention the fact;

(b) the fact is relied on in his defence;

(c) in the circumstances existing at the time, he could reasonably have been expected to mention the fact;

(d) that the only sensible explanation for his failure to mention the fact is that he had no answer at the time that would stand up to scrutiny; and

(e) that apart from the failure to mention the fact, the prosecution's case against him was so strong that it called for an answer.

The following should be noted.

1. The Criminal Law Revision Committee said that the words "any fact relied on in his defence" are intended to apply to any definite statement made by a witness at the hearing and supporting the case for the defence, for example an alibi, consent in a case of rape, innocent association in an indecency case or, in a handling case, a belief that the goods were not stolen.[77] In *Milford*[78] the Court of Appeal stated that the word "fact" should not be read in the narrow sense of an actual deed or thing done but in the fuller sense contemplated by the Oxford English Dictionary of "something that ... is actually the case ... hence, a particular truth known by actual observation or authentic testimony, as opposed to what is merely inferred, or to conjecture or to fiction". Such a fact may be established by the defendant himself in evidence, by a witness on his behalf or by a prosecution witness.[79] Bare admissions of parts of the prosecution case, however, are not facts relied upon by the defence for the purposes of s.34.[80] Therefore, a standard direction allowing a jury to draw an inference would be inappropriate where the central facts are not in dispute.[81]

2. A careful line must be drawn between a "fact" under s.34 and something which is no more than speculation, especially in a case where a motive is suggested for the making of a false allegation by the complainant.[82] The "fact" must be one relied upon by the

---

[77] *op.cit.*, para.33.
[78] [2001] Crim.L.R. 330.
[79] *Bowers* [1998] Crim.L.R. 817.
[80] *Betts and Hall* [2001] All E.R. (D) 108.
[81] *McManus and Cross* [2001] EWCA Crim 2455.
[82] *B(MT)* [2000] Crim.L.R. 181.

defendant. Failure to mention a fact is only relevant under s.34 if it is one relied on in the defence of the accused: s.34 must be confined to its express terms.[83] The precise facts that the defendant has failed to mention and from which the jury are permitted to draw an inference should be clearly identified.[84]

3. Before any adverse inference can be drawn, the defendant must seek to rely on a fact, or facts, at trial: if he does not do so, for example if it is accepted that he did not, or if he gives or calls no evidence or otherwise raises no relevant facts in his defence and merely puts the prosecution to proof, no adverse inference can be drawn.[85]

4. Where a judge decides that that requirements of s.34 have not been met, he must direct the jury expressly not to draw an adverse inference so as to avoid the danger that the jury will draw an inference unless warned not to.[86] However, failure to give a direction when one was appropriate will not necessarily lead to the overturning of a conviction, provided no unfairness is created by the failure.[87]

Section 34 does not expressly require the prosecution to satisfy the jury of   **11–21**
a prima facie case before an inference could be drawn from a defendant's silence. In *Doldur*[88] the Court of Appeal observed that a s.34 direction would usually require a consideration of both the prosecution and defence evidence, it was held that for s.34 it is not necessary for the prosecution to satisfy the jury of a prima facie case before an adverse inference could be drawn. However, in both *Gill*[89] and *Milford*[90] after considering *Doldur*, it was held that the respective juries should have been directed that any inference would not on its own prove guilt and that the jury had to be satisfied of a prima facie case against the accused before going on to consider whether to draw any inference from the accused's silence. The new JSB Direction is such that an inference can only be drawn if the prosecution has satisfied the jury of a prima facie case strong enough to actually call for any response. This would appear to be in keeping with the requirements of Art.6 of the European Convention on Human Rights. In *Telfner v Austria*[91] (see para.11–13 above) the European Court found a violation of Art.6(2)

---

[83] *Nickolson* [1999] Crim.L.R. 61.
[84] *Reader* (unreported) April 7, 1998, CA.
[85] *Moshaid* [1998] Crim.L.R. 420.
[86] *McGarry* [1998] 3 All E.R. 805.
[87] *Francom, The Times*, October 24, 2000.
[88] [2000] Crim.L.R. 178.
[89] [2001] 1 Cr.App.R. 160.
[90] [2001] Crim.L.R. 330.
[91] (2002) 34 E.H.R.R. 7.

as, by requiring the accused to provide an explanation, without first having established a prima facie case against him the burden of proof had been shifted from the prosecution to the defence.

The fact that a solicitor advises a client not to answer questions will not, of itself, prevent an adverse inference from being drawn. Thus, in *Condron and Condron*[92] the defendants were drug addicts and when they were at the police station their solicitor advised them not to answer questions because (contrary to the opinion of the Force Medical Examiner) the solicitor thought that they were unfit to be interviewed due to symptoms of drug withdrawal. The defendants made no comment in answer to the questions put to them in interview. At their trial the prosecution were permitted to adduce evidence of these interviews. The defendants gave evidence of matters which could have been given in answer to the questions asked by the police in interview and said that they had not answered questions in interview because of the advice of their solicitor. The judge directed the jury that it was for them to decide whether any adverse inference should be drawn from the defendants' failure to answer questions. The Court of Appeal upheld this direction. The Court said that it was unlikely that the bare assertion that the defendant had not answered questions on the advice of his solicitor was by itself to be regarded as a sufficient reason for not mentioning relevant matters and it would be necessary to state the reasons for the advice if the defendant wished to avoid the court drawing an adverse inference (the court added that this would amount to a waiver of legal professional privilege and the accused or his solicitor—if called—could be asked questions to explore the nature of the advice given, the reasons for it, and whether it was given for purely tactical reasons, but that it would always be open to a defendant to attempt to rebut the inference by giving evidence that the relevant matters were revealed to a solicitor—or somebody else—at the time of the interview).[93]

Similarly, the Court of Appeal in *Roble*[94] said that advice from a solicitor is not in itself likely to be regarded as a sufficient reason for not mentioning facts relevant to the defence and the evidence generally had to go further and indicate the reason for that advice (because this would be relevant to the jury's consideration of the reasonableness of the defendant's conduct in remaining silent).

---

[92] [1997] 1 Cr.App.R. 185.

[93] At 197. For legal professional privilege, see paras 11–27 *et seq.*, below. In *Davis (Desmond)* [1998] Crim.L.R. 659 the Court of Appeal said that if a defendant wished to repeat in evidence a statement of fact made by solicitor this might infringe the hearsay rule depending on the purpose for which it was to be adduced: a judge called on to rule on the admissibility of such evidence must be told in the absence of the jury what the evidence would be. Such vidence is admissible to rebut a suggestion of recent invention: Daniel [1998] Cr.App.R. 373.

[94] [1997] Crim.L.R. 449.

Condron has now been considered by the European Court of Human   **11–22**
Rights[95] who took a different view from the Court of Appeal. The European Court found a violation of Art.6(1) as the terms of the trial judge's
direction to the jury was such that it would have left them at liberty to draw
an adverse inference even if they had been satisfied that the appellants
remained silent for good reason on the advice of their solicitor. Accordingly, the jury should have been directed to draw an adverse inference only
if they believed that the accused had no answer or none that would stand up
to cross-examination. Since the jury were not properly directed the
imperfection could not be remedied on appeal as it was not possible for the
Court of Appeal to ascertain what weight, if any, was given to the applicants' silence. Ultimately, it is not the quality of the legal representatives
advice that is the issue, but the genuineness of the defendant's explanation
that he relied upon it. This is now the basis for the JSB new Direction on
s.34. See para.11–21 on implications for legal professional privilege where
advice from a solicitor is relied upon as the reason why no inference pursuant to s.34 should be drawn.

Many defendants now, on the advice of their solicitor, opt instead of
answering questions in interview to give a prepared statement which is
handed to the police. In *Ali*[96] two defendants gave the police prepared
statements. One failed to mention two facts relied on in evidence and the
other set out an alibi in similar terms to his subsequent evidence. The Court
of Appeal held that a s.34 direction was appropriate in the first case but not
the second as inference could be drawn that the defendant's explanation at
trial was a late invention if it was not in the prepared statement. Section 34
does not create a duty to answer questions where the defendant has disclosed his defence. Section 34 is therefore to be given its literal meaning.

It will be a matter for the jury to determine whether in the circumstances   **11–23**
existing at the time the defendant could reasonably be expected to mention
a fact. In *Argent*[97] the Court of Appeal said the court should not construe
such circumstances restrictively: the time of day, the defendant's age,
experience, mental capacity, state of health, sobriety, knowledge, personality and legal advice might all be relevant; and references to "the accused"
meant to the actual accused with such qualities, apprehensions, knowledge
and advice as he is shown to have had at the time. The fact that the police
do not reveal the state of their knowledge of the offence to the defendant is
irrelevant. In *Imran and Hussain*[98] the Court of Appeal held that (while
there was a duty not to mislead the accused) there was no obligation on the
police to disclose their case, for example to tell him that he had been filmed
by a video camera taking part in an offence. On the other hand, the

---

[95] *Condron v United Kingdom* (2001) 31 E.H.R.R. 1. See also *Beckles v UK* (2003) 36
E.H.R.R. 13.
[96] [2001] 6 *Archbold News* 2.
[97] [1997] Crim.L.R. 346.
[98] [1997] Crim.L.R. 754.

application of the section must be restricted to its express terms and not extended to matters which the defendant could not reasonably have been expected to mention, for example to proffer an explanation for something which he was not asked to explain since it was not known about until after the police interview.[99]

The effect of the section is to bring to an end the mandatory direction to the jury that no inference is to be drawn against the accused because of his failure to answer questions. Instead, if satisfied of the above matters the jury must determine what (if any) inference it will be proper to draw from the defendant's failure to mention a fact.

Finally, it may be noted that in *Murray v UK*[1] a case under the Criminal Justice (Evidence) (Northern Ireland) Order 1988 (a provision in similar terms to s.34) the European Court of Human Rights held that there had been no breach of Art.6(1) of the Convention (which guarantees the right to a fair trial) arising from the drawing of adverse inferences due to the defendant's failure to answer questions during interrogation and his failure to give evidence during his trial: see para.17–24, below, for a discussion of *Murray*. It has been argued that it must be doubtful whether the European Court would agree that it is permissible to draw an inference when a suspect does not answer questions because of advice from his solicitor.[2] However, it is submitted that this is simply one of the factors which a court has to take into account when deciding whether it is proper to draw an inference; and, as such, has no bearing on whether there has been a breach of Art.6.

11–24   On the other hand the position in a case where the accused has been denied access to legal advice before being questioned is different. In these circumstances no inferences will now be drawn: see para.10–33, above, for discussion of the present position. Both *Magee v UK*[3] and *Averill v UK*[4] demonstrate that a failure to allow access to a solicitor in the early stages of questioning will amount to a breach of Art.6. Section 58 of the Youth Justice and Criminal Evidence Act 1999 was enacted to ensure that English law does not give rise to such violations.[5]

Magistrates must direct themselves in the same way as a jury is directed. It will be a matter for them in a summary trial to decide what inference may properly be drawn from the defendant's failure to mention a fact.

---

[99] N, *The Times*, February 13, 1998.
[1] (1996) 22 E.H.R.R. 29.
[2] Munday, "Inferences from Silence and European Human Rights Law" [1996] Crim.L.R. 370.
[3] [2000] Crim.L.R. 681.
[4] [2000] Crim.L.R. 682.
[5] s.58 of the Youth Justice and Criminal Evidence Act 1999 applies where an accused is being questioned at an "authorised place of detention". An authorised place of detention" means either a police station or any other place so prescribed by the Secretary of State, *e.g.* a Customs and Excise Detention Unit.

Sections 36 and 37 of the 1994 Act provide as follows[6]:

"**36.**—(1) Where—

(a) person is arrested by a constable, and there is—

    (i) on his person; or
    (ii) in or on his clothing or footwear; or
    (iii) otherwise in his possession; or
    (iv) in any place in which he is at the time of his arrest.

    any object, substance or mark, or there is any mark on any such object; and

(b) that or another constable investigating the case reasonably believes that the presence of the object, substance or mark may be attributable to the participation of the person arrested in the commission of an offence specified by the constable; and

(c) the constable informs the person arrested that he so believes, and requests him to account for the presence of the object, substance or mark; and

(d) the person fails or refuses to do so.

then if, in any proceedings against the person for the offence so specified, evidence of those matters is given, subsection (2) below applies.

(2) Where this subsection applies—

(a) a magistrates' court inquiring into the offence as examining justices;

(b) a judge, in deciding whether to grant an application made by the accused under—

    (i) section 6 of the Criminal Justice Act 1987 (application for dismissal of charges of serious fraud in respect of which notice of transfer has been given under section 4 of that Act); or

    (ii) paragraph 5 of Schedule 6 to the Criminal Justice Act 1991 (application for dismissal of charge of violent or sexual offence involving child in respect of which

---

[6] It should be noted that if an accused in a terrorist case, when questioned, fails to mention a material fact (which he could reasonably be expected to mention) the court or jury when considering any question whether the accused belonged to a specified organisation, may draw from the failure inferences relating to that question: the Prevention of Terrorism (Temporary Provisions) Act 1989, s.2(A)(4)–(6), as inserted by the Criminal Justice (Terrorism and Conspiracy) Act 1998, s.1.

333

notice of transfer has been given under section 53 of
that Act);

(c) the court, in determining whether there is a case to answer;
and

(d) the court or jury, in determining whether the accused is guilty
of the offence charged,

may draw such inferences from the failure as appear proper.

37.—(1) Where—

(a) a person arrested by a constable was found by him at a place
at or about the time the offence for which he was arrested is
alleged to have been committed; and

(b) that or another constable investigating the offence reasonably
believes that the presence of the person at that place and at
that time may be attributable to his participation in the
commission of the offence; and

(c) the constable informs the person that he so believes, and
requests him to account for that presence; and

(d) the person fails or refuses to do so.

then if, in any proceedings against the person for the offence, evidence
of those matters is given, subsection (2) below applies.

[Subsection (2) is identical to subsection (2) to section 36 above.]"

11–25   The effect of these two provisions is that if the accused fails or refuses to
account for any objects, substances or marks found on him, his clothing or
footwear at the time of his arrest (s.36) or for his presence at a particular
place at or about the time the offence for which he was arrested was
committed (s.37), the court or jury may draw such inferences from the
failure or refusal as appear proper.

Before these provisions may be brought into effect it must be shown that:

(a) the police reasonably believed that the presence of the object, etc.
or the presence of the accused at the place may be attributable to
the participation of the accused in an offence;

(b) the accused was informed of this belief and requested to account
for the presence[7]; and

(c) the accused was told in ordinary language the effect if he failed or
refused to comply with the request.[8]

---

[7] ss.36(1) and 37(1) respectively.
[8] ss.36(4) and 37(3) respectively.

(d) the accused was permitted to consult a solicitor before being questioned.

These provisions are modelled on those in the Criminal Justice (Evidence) (Northern Ireland) Order 1988. They contain (as did the 1988 Order) protection for the suspect in that:

(a) the accused may not have proceedings against him transferred to the Crown Court, have a case to answer or be convicted solely on an inference drawn under ss.34–37: s.38(3); and

(b) the rules as to the inadmissibility of evidence (and exclusion under the court's discretion) are not affected by the provisions of ss.34–37: s.38(5). For the effect of the accused's silence at trial see para.17–16 below.

(3) The European Convention on Human Rights

The European Court of Human Rights has restated the right of silence in forceful terms. Thus, in *Saunders v UK*[9] the Court said:

11–26

> "Although not mentioned in Art.6 [which guarantees the right to a fair trial] the right to silence and the right not to incriminate oneself are generally recognised international standards which lie at the heart of the notion of a fair trial. The rationale lies (*inter alia*) in the protection of the accused against improper compulsion by the authorities thereby contributing to the avoidance of miscarriages of justice and to the fulfilment of Art.6. The right not to incriminate oneself, in particular, presupposes that the prosecution ... seek to prove their case ... without resort to evidence obtained through methods of coercion or oppression in defiance of the will of the accused. In this sense the right is closely linked to the presumption of innocence in Art.6(2)..."

The reference to the right of silence and the right not to incriminate oneself as "generally recognised international standards" underlines the importance which the Court attaches to these rights. This is further illustrated by *Funke v France*.[10] In that case customs officers searched the applicant's house and seized documents in order to obtain particulars of his overseas assets. Proceedings were then taken against the applicant for disclosure of his overseas bank accounts. As a result, he was convicted and fined for failing to provide statements of those accounts. The applicant complained that the conviction infringed his rights under Art.6(1). The Court held that there had been a breach of Art.6(1) because the authorities

[9] (1997) 23 E.H.R.R. 313, para.68.
[10] (1993) 16 E.H.R.R. 297.

secured the conviction in order to obtain further documents, thereby attempting to compel the applicant himself to provide the evidence of alleged offences. The Court said that such conduct infringed the right of anyone charged with a criminal offence to remain silent and not to contribute to incriminating himself.

Accordingly, it must be anticipated that any statute or common law rule which is in conflict with the right of silence will be scrutinised with great care by the European Court to ensure that it has not led to unfairness in the particular case. Now that the Convention has been incorporated into English law the courts must scrutinise with care any provision or rule which is in conflict with the right of silence to ensure that it has not led to unfairness in the particular case.[11] (See Ch.13 for discussion of the Convention and para.13–14 for Art.6.)

2. LEGAL PROFESSIONAL PRIVILEGE

11–27   Questions of legal professional privilege arise much more frequently in civil proceedings (because of the rules relating to discovery) than in criminal trials. However, such questions do on occasion arise in criminal proceedings. An outline of the general rule and exceptions is therefore given. There is also a discussion of the position of expert witnesses and of problems associated with documents.

A. The general rule

11–28   Communications passing between a client and his legal adviser are privileged from being disclosed by the client in evidence and (unless the client consents) by the legal adviser. The purpose of the rule is to allow a person to obtain legal advice with safety. The rule is a fundamental condition upon which the administration of justice rests.[12] It cannot be overridden by general or ambiguous statutory words.[13]

It should be noted that the privilege:

(a)   is the privilege of the client and not the legal adviser,[14] and

(b)   extends only to confidential communications.[15]

---

[11] For a detailed consideration of the effect of European jurisprudence on ss.34–38 of the Criminal Justice and Public Order Act 1994, see Jennings *et al.*, "Silence and Safety: the Impact of Human Rights Law" [2000] Crim.L.R. 879.

[12] *B v Auckland District Law Society*, The Times, May 21, 2003.

[13] *ibid.* and *R. (Morgan Grenfell & Co. Ltd) v Special Commissioner of Income Tax* [2003] 1 A.C. 563.

[14] *Wilson v Rastall* (1792) 4 T.R. 753.

[15] *Bursill v Tanner* (1885) 16 Q.B.D. 1. In *Manchester Crown Court Ex p. R* [1999] 2 Cr.App.R. 267, it was held that the record of a time on a solicitor's attendance note, time sheet or fee note is not subject to legal professional privilege because it was not a communication for the purpose of seeking legal advice.

According to the Law Reform Committee,[16] the privilege extends to communications between:

(a) the client (and his agents) and the client's legal advisers;

(b) the client's legal advisers and third parties if made for the purpose of pending or contemplated litigation;

(c) the client (or his agent) and third parties, if made for the purpose of obtaining information to be submitted to the client's legal advisers for the purpose of obtaining advice upon pending or contemplated litigation.

Of these categories, (a) is the most significant in criminal trials. At the more elementary level, the rule in relation to this category prevents a defendant being asked questions about any discussion which he may have had with his solicitor or counsel.[17]

The privilege also attaches to an interpreter who is present at an interview between a client and solicitor, the interpreter is bound by a duty of confidence not to disclose what has taken place.[18]

In *Bowden*,[19] the Court of Appeal said that a suspect who says that he refuses to answer questions on legal advice does not waive legal professional privilege if evidence of that factual statement is given at trial. However, if evidence is elicited by the defence from the solicitor of the grounds on which that advice was given, then the defendant will be taken to have waived that privilege and be open to cross-examination about the information which he gave his solicitor. The position was summarised by Lord Bingham C.J.:

11–29

(i) The defendant does not waive the privilege by giving evidence or calling his legal adviser to rebut a suggestion of recent fabrication and saying that the defendant had mentioned a fact earlier.

(ii) If the suspect goes beyond saying that he declines to answer questions on legal advice and explains the basis of the advice, or his solicitor, as his authorised representative, does so, then a waiver is involved. If such evidence is elicited at trial by the

---

[16] Sixteenth Report, Cmnd. 3472, para.17.

[17] A letter written by a solicitor on behalf of a client is not normally protected by privilege: *Downer* (1880) 14 Cox 486.

[18] *Regina (Bozkurt) v Thames Magistrates' Court, The Times*, June 26, 2001. The Divisional Court held that it would not be unfair for the prosecution to rely on the evidence of an interpreter who had been acted as translator at the police station when the defendant was breath-tested and subsequently present when he was interviewed by the duty solicitor. The Court stressed that the trial judge could exclude the interpreter's evidence under s.78 of PACE and the defendant had sufficient protection for the purposes of his right to a fair trial.

[19] [1999] 2 Cr.App.R. 176.

defence, the privilege is lost and the defendant can be cross-examined about the nature of the advice and the facts upon which it was based.

B. Exceptions to the general rule

11–30 Communications which are part of a criminal or unlawful proceeding are not protected.[20] The test is to ask whether the professional advice was in furtherance of a crime or fraud or in preparation for it.[21] If the answer is yes, the evidence is not protected.

The leading case is *Cox and Railton*.[22] In that case the two defendants entered into a conspiracy to defraud a creditor. They sought the advice of a solicitor in order to facilitate the conspiracy. The solicitor gave advice not knowing the purpose for which it was sought. The Court of Crown Cases Reserved held that communication between a client and legal adviser for the purpose of facilitating or guiding the client in the commission of crime or fraud was not privileged. This was because a communication in furtherance of a criminal purpose did not "come into the scope of ordinary professional employment". If such a communication were privileged, any criminal could obtain advice as to how most advantageously to commit a crime from a legal point of view and the solicitor would not be able to give evidence about it. Stephen J. said that when such a question arises the court must decide on the particular facts of the case "whether it seems probable that the accused person may have consulted his legal adviser, not after the commission of the crime for the legitimate purpose of being defended, but before the commission of the crime for the purpose of being guided or helped in committing it."[23] In *Butler v Board of Trade*,[24] a letter had been written by a solicitor to her client, warning him that he would be liable to prosecution under the Companies Act 1948 if he persisted in a certain course of conduct. Goff J. held that the letter was not written in furtherance of crime or fraud and was accordingly privileged.

11–31 Advice sought to facilitate crime is to be distinguished from advice whether a particular object can be achieved lawfully, or whether particular means are lawful or unlawful. It is submitted that the privilege should only be lost if the defendant had decided antecedently in any event to act unlawfully or if he was ready to act unlawfully if need be.

A similar rule applies if the purpose in obtaining the advice is unlawful. Thus, in *Barclay's Bank v Eustice*[25] the Court of Appeal held that where a

---

[20] *Bullivant v Att-Gen for Victoria* [1901] A.C. 196.
[21] See *Butler v Board of Trade* [1971] Ch. 680, *per* Goff J.
[22] (1884) 14 Q.B.D. 153.
[23] When deciding this question the court may look at the communication without it being proved that it was produced for this purpose: *Governor of Pentonville Prison Ex p. Osman* [1989] 3 All E.R. 701.
[24] [1971] Ch.680.
[25] [1995] 4 All. E.R. 511.

client of a solicitor sought to enter into transactions at an undervalue (the purpose of which was to prejudice persons making claims against him) that purpose was sufficiently iniquitous for public policy to require that the communications between him and his solicitor in relation to the setting up of these transactions be discoverable. The Court said that the lifting of privilege is not limited to occasions where the solicitor was a party to the crime or where the client used the solicitor's advice for a criminal or fraudulent purpose. In the instant case the dominant purpose of the legal advice on how to structure a transaction at an undervalue was to prejudice the interests of a creditor.

C. Absolute nature of the rule

There are no exceptions to the general rule. Thus the House of Lords in **11–32** *Derby Magistrates' Court Ex p. B*[26] held that no exception to the absolute nature of the privilege, once established, can be allowed. Lord Taylor C.J. (in the leading speech) said that the privilege (if it applies) is more than an ordinary rule of evidence, but a fundamental condition on which the administration of justice as a whole rests. This is because a client has to be able to consult his lawyer in confidence and be sure that what he told the lawyer would never be revealed without his consent.[27]

It had been thought that the privilege could be overridden if the defendant's interest in breaching it outweighed the witness's in maintaining it. However, the House of Lords in *Derby Magistrates' Court* held that this was not so and overruled *Barton*[28] and *Ataou*[29] (cases which had held that the judge should weigh the public interest in securing confidentiality against the public interest in seeing that all evidence was available). Lord Taylor C.J. reviewed the authorities and referred to the long-established rule that a document protected by privilege continues to be protected so long as the privilege is not waived by the client: "once privileged always privileged".[30] Thus, the House found that the privilege had been an absolute privilege for at least 150 years and held that in the instant case a defendant could not obtain a witness summons against a prosecution witness for the latter to produce documents recording his factual instructions to his solicitor after he had admitted carrying out a murder (which confession he later retracted).

It may be noted that the sweeping nature of the decision in *Derby Magistrates' Court* has not gone without criticism[31] and that, subsequently, the House of Lords held that in care proceedings under the Children Act

---

[26] [1996] 1 Cr.App.R. 385.
[27] At 401.
[28] [1973] 1 W.L.R. 115.
[29] [1988] Q.B. 798.
[30] At 397.
[31] See, *e.g.*, Zuckerman, "Legal Professional Privilege" 112 L.Q.R. 535 and Murphy, "The Innocence at Stake Test and Legal Professional Privilege: A Logical Progression for the Law ... But Not in England" [2001] Crim.L.R. 728.

1989 legal professional privilege was overcome by the considerations that the proceedings were essentially non-adversarial and the welfare of the child was paramount: *Re L (A Minor)*.[32] In that case the House (by a majority) held that an expert's report obtained by a party to the proceedings was not protected by legal professional privilege and was discloseable to the police, distinguishing *Derby Magistrates' Court* on the ground that the privilege in the latter case was that of solicitor and client and the absolute nature of that privilege did not extend to other forms of legal professional privilege (discussed below).[33]

D. Expert witnesses

11–33   The rule in the case of an expert witness is that legal professional privilege attaches to confidential communications between an expert and a solicitor, but does not attach to the chattels or documents on which the expert based his opinion or to the independent opinion of the expert himself.[34]

Thus, in *King*,[35] the solicitor for the defence sent certain documents to a handwriting expert for his examination. The prosecution suspected that the defendant had manufactured documents for the purpose of his defence. Accordingly, the prosecution served a *subpoena* on the expert to produce the documents which had been sent to him. One of the documents was a forgery. The judge ruled that no privilege attached to this document and allowed the prosecution to call the expert to produce it. The Court of Appeal upheld this ruling and commented: "It would be strange if a forger could hide behind a claim of legal professional privilege by the simple device of sending all the incriminating documents in his possession to his solicitors to be examined by an expert."[36]

On the other hand, in *R*[37] a scientist (at the request of the defence solicitor) carried out a DNA test on a blood sample provided by the defendant for this purpose. During the prosecution case the judge permitted the prosecution to interview the scientist and call him to give evidence against the defendant. The Court of Appeal commented that the prosecution could not be prevented from calling a witness because he had been consulted by the defence; but the Court held that the sample was an item subject to legal professional privilege under s.10(1)(c) of the Police and Criminal Evidence Act 1984 and the defendant was entitled to object to its production and to the giving of opinion evidence based upon it. (See paras 6–29 *et seq.* above on compellability of experts.)

---

[32] [1996] 2 W.L.R. 395.
[33] Lord Mustill and Lord Nicholls dissented.
[34] *Harmony Shipping Co. v Davis* [1979] 3 All E.R. 177, 181, *per* Lord Denning M.R.; applied in *King*, below. The legal professional privilege in this case is not absolute: *Re L (A Minor)* [1996] 2 W.L.R. 315; cited at para.11–32, above.
[35] [1983] 1 W.L.R. 411; (1983) 77 Cr.App.R. 1.
[36] [1983] 1 All E.R. 929, 931.
[37] [1994] 4 All E.R. 260.

E. Documents in a lawyer's possession

Questions occasionally arise in criminal proceedings relating to the privi- **11–34** lege of documents in the possession or control of a defendant's solicitor. The basic rule is that the privilege is the privilege of the client and not of the solicitor.[38] Therefore, if a document would be privileged in the hands of the client, it is privileged in the hands of the solicitor (for example the client's written instructions for his defence at a pending trial). in the other hand, if the document is not privileged in the hands of the client, it is not privileged in the hands of the solicitor. If, therefore, the client has no lawful authority to prevent the seizure of the document, the solicitor cannot prevent seizure by claiming privilege. In *Peterborough Justices Ex p. Hicks*,[39] a justice issued a search warrant under s.16(1) of the Forgery Act 1913 empowering the police to search a solicitor's office and seize a forged document. On an application for certiorari to quash the search warrant, the Divisional Court held that since the client had no lawful excuse to prevent the seizure of the document, the solicitor had no excuse. Eveleigh L.J. said:

> "Right in the forefront of one's consideration of this point is that the solicitor holds this document in the right of his client and can assert in respect of its seizure no greater authority than the client himself or herself possesses. The client in this case would have possessed no lawful authority or excuse that would prevent the document's seizure. In my view the solicitor himself can be in no better position. The solicitor's authority or excuse in a case like this is the authority or excuse of the client."[40]

F. The admissibility of privileged documents

Professional privilege, if invoked, prevents the production of a document: it **11–35** does not, where the privilege is not invoked, prevent the admission of a document once it has been produced. The rule in criminal cases is that if a privileged document is produced it will be admitted if it is relevant, subject to the overriding discretion of the judge to exclude unfair evidence. The rationale of the rule is to be found in the public interest that the truth should be ascertained.

Thus, in *Butler v Board of Trade*,[41] a solicitor wrote a letter to B warning him to take care or he would be liable to prosecution under the Companies Act 1948. A copy of the letter was found among the papers of the company

---

[38] There is no special rule for criminal cases: *Peterborough JJ. Ex p. Hicks* [1977] 1 W.L.R. 1371; *King* [1983] 1 All E.R. 929, 931. Observations to the effect that such a special rule existed by Swanwick J. in *Frank Truman Export Ltd v Metropolitan Police Commissioner* [1977] Q.B. 952, 961 were doubted by the Court of Appeal in *King*, above.
[39] [1977] 1 W.L.R. 1371.
[40] [1978] 1 All E.R. 225, 228.
[41] [1971] Ch. 680.

of which B was a director. B was charged with offences under the Companies Act. He sought a direction that the prosecution was not entitled to produce the copy at his trial for those offences. Goff J. held that although the original of the letter was privileged and the copy was confidential, it was admissible in evidence because the public interest in the prosecution of offences overrode B's right to restrain a breach of confidence. Goff J. said that it would not be a right exercise of the equitable jurisdiction in confidence to make a declaration at the suit of the accused in a public prosecution in effect restraining the Crown from adducing admissible evidence relevant to the crime with which he is charged.

11–36   *Butler v Board of Trade* was applied by the Court of Appeal in *Tompkins*.[42] In that case the defendant wrote a note to his counsel during the trial. The effect of the note was to contradict the defendant's evidence in chief on a crucial point. During an adjournment the note was picked up in court by a legal assistant from the prosecuting solicitor's staff. (It was accepted that the note came properly into the hands of the prosecution and that no question of impropriety arose.) In cross-examination, prosecuting counsel asked the defendant about the point to which the note referred. When the defendant gave the same answer as before, counsel handed him the note, told him to look at it and asked him if he stuck to his answer. The defence objected. The recorder ruled that the cross-examination should proceed without any direct mention of the note. The Court upheld the recorder's ruling and said that privilege, in this context, relates only to the production of a document; it does not determine its admissibility in evidence. "The note, though clearly privileged from production, was admissible in evidence once it was in the possession of the prosecution. Admissibility depends essentially on the relevance of the document; the method by which it has been obtained is irrelevant."[43] The Court put the rationale for the decision succinctly: it would require a remarkable exercise in moral philosophy to justify the conclusion that it is contrary to natural justice that a perjurer should be exposed by producing to him a document in his own handwriting, written within hours of his perjury.[44]

The admissibility of improperly obtained evidence is discussed in Ch.10, above. However, it should be noted that in the context of evidence obtained

---

[42] (1978) 67 Cr.App.R. 181.

[43] At 184.

[44] Similarly, in *Cottrill* [1997] Crim.L.R. 56 the Court of Appeal upheld the trial judge's decision to permit cross-examination of the defendant upon a statement which he had given to his solicitors and which (without his knowledge or consent) had been sent to the prosecution in an attempt to persuade them to drop the case. On the other hand, see the decision of the New Zealand Court of Appeal in *Uljee* [1982] 1 N.Z.L.R. 561 where the Court held that evidence of a lawful privileged conversation between client and solicitor overheard by a constable was inadmissible. The Court held that the conversation was protected by legal privilege. Cooke J. said that it was a consequence of the privilege that a third party who has overheard a privileged oral communication or come into possession of a copy of a written communication should not be allowed to give evidence of it unless the client waives the privilege (at 570).

in breach of privilege, s.78 of the Police and Criminal Evidence Act 1984 provides that the court may exclude evidence if it appears that "having regard to all the circumstances, including the circumstances in which the evidence was obtained" its admission would be unfair.[45] Thus, if privileged documents are obtained improperly the court may refuse to admit them in evidence even if they are relevant to an issue in the case. Suppose, therefore, facts similar to those in *Tompkins* except that there is a suspicion of sharp practice or impropriety in the way in which the prosecution had obtained the note; or suppose that police officers executing a search warrant at A's premises improperly seize a copy of his instructions to his solicitor relating to a pending trial in which A is the defendant. It is submitted that in these circumstances it would be unfair for the prosecution to benefit from a wrongful act and that accordingly, the evidence should not be admitted. By analogy, in a civil case, *ITC Film Distributors v Video Exchange Ltd*,[46] Warner J. held that circumstances where documents were obtained by stealth or by a trick in court provided an exception to the general rule in civil cases that such evidence if relevant is admissible how ever obtained.[47]

3. OTHER CONFIDENTIAL COMMUNICATIONS

The only other professional privilege recognised by law in addition to that of legal adviser and client is that between patent agent and client. Section 280 of the Copyright, Designs and Patents Act 1988 sets out a similar privilege to that between lawyer and client. The patent agent and client privilege also extends to criminal proceedings. All other claims to privilege in order to protect confidences have been rejected.[48] Thus, as a matter of law, it would appear that a priest cannot refuse to disclose information received from a penitent,[49] nor a doctor refuse to disclose information received from a patient.[50] The reason for this restriction is that no other obligation should impede the witness in revealing the truth in the witness-box. This is of particular importance in criminal proceedings where the liberty of the subject is involved. The Criminal Law Revision Committee did not recommend any extension of professional privilege in the case of priests and medical practitioners.[51] This was partly on the grounds that it

11–37

---

[45] See s.78 as set out in para.10–13 above.
[46] [1982] 2 All E.R. 241.
[47] *Calcraft v Guest* [1898] 1 Q.B. 759.
[48] However, see para.11–38 below for the position in relation to journalist's confidential sources.
[49] Hay (1860) 2 F. & F. 4; *Pais v Pais* [1971] P. 119.
[50] *Duchess of Kingston's case* [1776] 20 St.Tr. 355 at 573; see also *McGuinness v Att-Gen for Victoria* (1940) 63 C.L.R. 73, 102–103, *per* Dixon J. The Court of Appeal has said that no privilege attaches to communications between a prisoner and a prison officer in his capacity as legal aid officer (although public interest immunity may do so—see below): Umoh (1987) 84 Cr.App.R. 138.
[51] Eleventh Report, Cmnd. 4991, paras 272–276.

was unlikely that any difficulties would occur in practice. This view is borne out by experience. It is not easy to conceive of a situation in which a prosecutor would seek to compel a doctor or a priest to divulge a professional confidence, even in the unlikely event of the prosecution knowing about the confidence. Difficulties may occur in such cases where a defendant seeks to exculpate himself by questioning a priest or doctor about statements made by his co-defendant. These difficulties are best dealt with by way of discretion.

Prior to the Contempt of Court Act 1981, journalists, writers, publishers and broadcasters had no right to claim privilege when required to disclose the sources of information.[52] Accordingly, in *British Steel Corporation v Granada Television Ltd*[53] it was held that a journalist could be held in contempt of court for refusing to disclose his source. Section 10 of the Contempt of Court Act 1981 was enacted in response to *British Steel* and provides as follows:

> "No court may require a person to disclose, nor is a person guilty of contempt of court for refusing to disclose the source of information contained in the publication for which he is responsible, unless it be established to the satisfaction of the court that disclosure is necessary in the interests of justice or national security or for the prevention of disorder or crime."[54]

What is "necessary in the interests of justice",[55] "national security"[56] and "for the prevention of crime"[57] has been considered in a number of cases. What is essentially required is a balancing exercise between "enabling the ends of justice to be attained in the circumstances of the particular case on the one hand against the importance of protecting the source on the other hand".[58]

11–38   In *Goodwin v UK*,[59] the European Court of Human Rights, found a violation of Art.10 of the Convention where a journalist had been found in contempt and fined for refusing to disclose his source. The Court stated:

---

[52] *Att-Gen v Clough* [1963] 1 Q.B. 773; *Att-Gen v Mulholland and Foster* [1963] 2 Q.B. 477; *British Steel Corp. v Granada Television Ltd* [1980] 3 W.L.R. 774, 822, *per* Lord Wilberforce.
[53] See n.52 above.
[54] s.2(1) of the Act provides that "publication" includes any "speech, writing, broadcast or other communication in whatever form, which is addressed to the public at large or any section of the public".
[55] *Camelot Group plc v Centaur Communications Ltd* [1999] Q.B. 124 and *John v Express Newspapers plc* [2000] 3 All E.R. 257.
[56] *R (Bright) v Central Criminal Court* [2001] 1 W.L.R. 662 at 681. S.10 of the Contempt of Court Act 1981 was not under consideration, however, the principles may be applicable in such proceedings.
[57] *Re An Inquiry Under the Company Securities (Insider Dealing) Act 1985* [1988] A.C. 660.
[58] *X Ltd v Morgan-Grampian (Publishers) Ltd* [1991] 1 A.C. 1 at 43.
[59] (1996) E.H.R.R. 123.

"Protection of journalistic sources is one of the basic conditions for press freedom, as is reflected in the laws and the professional codes of conduct in a number of Contracting States and is affirmed in several international instruments on journalistic freedoms. ... Without such protection, sources may be deterred from assisting the press in informing the public on matters of public interest. As a result the vital public-watchdog role of the press may be undermined and the ability of the press to provide accurate and reliable information may be adversely affected. Having regard to the importance of the protection of journalistic sources for press freedom in a democratic society and the potentially chilling effect an order of source disclosure has on the exercise of that freedom, such a measure cannot be compatible with Article 10 of the Convention unless it is justified by an overriding requirement in the public interest".[60]

In relation to the disclosure of other confidential communications, it is submitted that the judge has a discretion to prevent such disclosure. Statements in support of such a discretion are to be found in pre-Contempt of Court Act 1981 cases in which journalists claimed that they were entitled to refuse to disclose the sources of their information.[61] Some doubt was expressed as to whether such a discretion applies in criminal proceedings.[62] However, no such suggestion appears to have been made in *Umoh*,[63] a case in which the Court of Appeal said that it was in the public interest that interviews between a prisoner and a prison officer in his capacity as legal aid officer should, save in exceptional circumstances, be confidential and that public interest immunity should attach to them. Indeed, the discretion has been outlined by Lord Wilberforce in terms which do not suggest that criminal cases are excluded:

"As to information obtained in confidence, and the legal duty, which may arise, to disclose it to a court of justice, the position is clear. Courts have an inherent wish to respect this confidence, whether it arises between doctor and patient, priest and penitent, banker and customer, persons giving testimonials to employees, or in other relationships. A relationship of confidence between a journalist and his source is in no different category; nothing in this case involves or will involve any principle that such confidence is not something to be respected. But in all these cases the court may have to decide, in particular circumstances, that the interest in preserving this confidence is

---

[60] para.39.
[61] *Att-Gen v Clough*, above, at 792, *per* Lord Parker C.J.; *Att-Gen v Mulholland and Foster*, above, at 489–490, *per* Lord Denning, M.R.
[62] Criminal Law Revision Committee, Eleventh Report, para.275.
[63] (1987) 84 Cr.App.R. 138, 143.

outweighed by other interests to which the law attaches importance."[64]

11-39   In a criminal trial, therefore, the judge will have to weigh the interest in
the preservation of a confidence against the interest of ensuring that no
obstacles are put in the way of ascertainment of the truth. The circumstances and significance of the evidence are bound to vary. Thus, if a
witness were giving evidence for the prosecution in a trial where there was
ample evidence against a defendant, it is not likely that a judge would
require the witness to breach a confidence. But suppose the witness were a
journalist giving crucial evidence for the prosecution in a case involving
terrorist offences. The public interest in the proper prosecution of such
offences would appear to outweigh the preservation of any confidence. Or
suppose A and B were charged with murder. A confessed to a priest that he
alone was responsible for the murder. B called the priest in his defence. In
this case the interest in securing the acquittal of an innocent man would
appear to outweigh the preservation of the confidence of the confessional.

Where a journalist claims that he should not be required to reveal the
source of his information because it is confidential:

(a) the matter should be raised in the absence of the jury; and

(b) the judge should make a reasoned decision upon the conflicting
interests.[65]

---

[64] *British Steel Corp. v Granada Television Ltd*, above, at 821.
[65] *Att-Gen v Lundin* (1982) 75 Cr.App.R. 90, 100–101.

CHAPTER 12

Public Interest

In certain cases, relevant evidence is excluded (or disclosure of infor- **12–01**
mation withheld) on the ground that it would seriously prejudice the public
interest if the material were disclosed. Such evidence is excluded "because
its adduction might imperil the security of that civil society which the
administration of justice itself subserves."[1] Thus, for example, the public
interest in:

(a) the maintenance of national security or diplomatic relations; or

(b) the effective functioning of the public service; or

(c) the detection of crime,

may in certain circumstances require that evidence be excluded or that
information be withheld. Two facets of the public interest will be discussed
here: information given for the detection of crime, and matters prejudicial
to the state and public service ("public interest immunity").[2]

1. Information for the Detection of Crime

A. The rule

The rule is that a witness is not allowed to disclose the identity of his **12–02**
informant or the sources through which he obtained his information.[3] This
rule applies both to oral evidence and to the disclosure of evidence before a
trial. To this rule there is one exception, where the judge is of the opinion

---

[1] *D v NSPCC* [1978] A.C. 171, 233, *per* Lord Simon of Glaisdale.
[2] One other matter is mentioned in textbooks in this context, namely the rule that judges
cannot be compelled to give evidence about what occurred in cases before them, as Patteson J.
held in *Gazard* (1838) 8 C. & P. 595. However, the possibility of a judge being called to give
evidence would appear to be so remote today as to call for no further comment; unless the
judge were called to give evidence about something which he had witnessed in his court, *e.g.* a
crime being committed: see para.17–01, n.2, below.
[3] *Hardy* (1794) 24 How.St.Tr. 199; *Att-Gen v Briant* (1846) 15 M. & W. 169; *Marks v Beyfus*
(1890) 25 Q.B.D. 494; *Hennessy v Wright* (1888) 21 Q.B.D. 509; *Rogers v Home Secretary*
[1973] A.C. 388, 401, *per* Lord Reid at 407, *per* Lord Simon of Glaisdale; *D v NSPCC* [1978]
A.C. 171, 218, *per* Lord Diplock at 232, *per* Lord Simon of Glaisdale. The rule was said to
apply to public prosecutions (see *Marks v Beyfus*, cited below.), *i.e.* prosecutions by the DPP.
However, the rule applied to cases where the police prosecuted and, it is submitted, is of
general application.

that it is necessary to disclose the information in order to show the defendant's innocence.[4]

The exclusion of such evidence is not a result of privilege. Accordingly:

(a) the right may not be waived; and

(b) exclusion of the answer is not dependent upon the witness claiming privilege when asked the question.

Questions aimed at eliciting such information should not be asked. If such a question is asked, the judge should refuse to allow it as soon as it is asked.[5] In practice such questions are rarely asked. This may be either because the rule is so well known or because the answer is usually liable to be so prejudicial to the defence that no defence advocate would consider asking it.

The rule is of long standing.[6] Thus, in 1846, Pollock C.B. said:

"The rule clearly established and acted on is this, that, in a public prosecution, a witness cannot be asked such questions as will disclose the informer, if he be a third person. This has been a settled rule for 50 years, and although it may seem hard in a particular case, private mischief must give way to public convenience ... and we think the principle of the rule applies to the case where a witness is asked if he himself is the informer."[7]

12–03   The rule was again considered and the exception to it defined in *Marks v Beyfus*.[8] In that case M brought an action for malicious prosecution. He called the Director of Public Prosecutions as a witness. The Director gave evidence that the prosecution had been instituted by himself and not by the defendants. M then asked who it was that gave the information upon which the Director had acted. The Director refused to answer: he was supported in his refusal by the judge. The Court of Appeal held that the judge was right. Lord Esher M.R. quoted the words of Pollock C.B. and said:

"This rule as to public prosecutions was founded on grounds of public policy, and if this prosecution was a public prosecution the rule atta-

---

[4] *Marks v Beyfus*, above; *D v NSPCC*, above, at 218, *per* Lord Diplock at 232, *per* Lord Simon of Glaisdale; *Hennessey* (1978) 68 Cr.App.R. 419, 426.
[5] *Marks v Beyfus*, above, at 500, *per* Bowen L.J.; *Rogers v Home Secretary*, above, at 407, *per* Lord Simon.
[6] For history see Wharam, "Crown Privilege in Criminal Cases" [1971] Crim.L.R. 675.
[7] *Att-Gen v Briant* (1846) 15 M. & W. 169, 185. It may be noted that an informer may reveal his own identity by bringing civil proceedings: *Savage v Chief Constable of Hampshire* [1997] 1 W.L.R. 1061. The reason for this exception to the rule is that the purpose of the rule (*i.e.* to protect the safety of the informer) no longer exists if he chooses to reveal his identity.
[8] (1890) 25 Q.B.D. 494.

ches ... I do not say it is a rule which can never be departed from; if upon the trial of a prisoner the judge should be of opinion that the disclosure of the name of the informant is necessary or right in order to show the prisoner's innocence, then one public policy is in conflict with another public policy, and that which says that an innocent man is not to be condemned when his innocence can be proved is the policy that must prevail. But except in that case, this rule of public policy is not a matter of discretion; it is a rule of law, and as such should be applied by the judge at the trial, who should not treat it as a matter of discretion whether he should tell the witness to answer or not."[9]

The same principle applies both to oral evidence and to the disclosure of information to the defence by the prosecution before trial.[10] Thus, the guidelines issued in 1981 by the Attorney-General on the disclosure of such information provided that the prosecuting authorities had a discretion to withhold a statement if it was "sensitive" and for this reason it was not in the public interest to disclose it.[11] Among the examples of sensitive material given in the guidelines was material which disclosed the identity of an informant when there were reasons for fearing that disclosure would put him or his family in danger. (For the current regime governing disclosure, see para.12–12, below.)

The rationale of the rule is that it furthers the public interest in the detection of crime and maintenance of public order: **12–04**

(a) to protect informants who might find themselves or their families in danger if their identity were disclosed; and

(b) to protect sources of information, which, if the identity were likely to be disclosed, would dry up.[12]

The second may be the real reason for the rule. Thus, in *Conway v Rimmer*,[13] Lord Reid said: "The police are carrying on an unending war with criminals many of whom are today highly intelligent. So it is essential there should be no disclosure of anything which might give any useful information to those who organise criminal activities." Informants must be guaranteed anonymity or they will not inform.

---

[9] At 498. See also, at 495–496, *per* Bowen L.J.; *Rogers v Home Secretary* [1973] A.C. 388, 401, *per* Lord Reid, 407, *per* Lord Simon; *D v NSPCC* [1978] A.C. 171, 218, *per* Lord Diplock, 232, *per* Lord Simon. For public prosecutions, see n.3, above.
[10] For such disclosure, see paras 18–05 *et seq.*, below.
[11] *Att-Gen's Guidelines* (1982) 74 Cr.App.R. 302, para.6(v).
[12] *Conway v Rimmer*, below, 953–954, *per* Lord Reid; *D v NSPCC* [1978] A.C. 171, *per* Lord Diplock, at 218, *per* Lord Simon at 232; *Hennessey* (1978) 68 Cr.App.R. 419, 426.
[13] [1968] A.C. 910, 953–954.

B. Exceptions to the rule

12–05   As has been seen, the sole exception to the rule is the case of information which might show the innocence of a defendant. The reason for this exception is that the public interest that an innocent man should not be convicted of a criminal offence outweighs the public interest in the protection of sources of police information.[14]

If an application for disclosure is made by the defence on this ground, the court will have to balance the two public interests and decide which, in the circumstances of the particular case, should prevail. It would appear that the burden of showing that the information should be disclosed is upon the defendant because (a) he alone knows the grounds for the application; and (b) the public interest in protecting the sources of police information is strong and should only be displaced for good cause.

Some guidance is to be found in *Hennessey*.[15] In that case the judge ruled that a customs officer should not be asked questions as to whether the telephone of two defendants had been tapped. The Court of Appeal upheld the judge's ruling because the questions were "fishing", aimed at finding out whether the prosecution was in possession of any undisclosed information and were irrelevant. However, the Court also considered the public interest involved in questions about telephone tapping because, as was pointed out, a negative answer may reveal that the police obtained their information from an informer and the circumstances may be such that the accused will know who he was. The Court said that generally the identity of an informer would be protected, but "... cases may occur when for good reason the need to protect the liberty of the subject should prevail over the need to protect informers. It will be for the accused to show that there is good reason."[16]

12–06   Suppose, therefore, the following facts. A is arrested at the scene of a bank robbery at the time of the commission of the offence. His defence is that he was there innocently because he was told by B to be there at that time. B bears a grudge against him and A believes that B informed the police in order to frame him. Accordingly, A wishes to know the source of the

---

[14] *D v NSPCC*, above, at 232, *per* Lord Simon; *Agar*, below.

[15] (1978) 68 Cr.App.R. 419.

[16] At 426. S.9 of the Interception of Communications Act 1985 prohibited evidence being adduced or a question asked which tended to suggest that an unlawful interception had taken place or that a warrant under the Act had been issued. This measure was said to have been necessary so that those involved in espionage or serious crime could not discover at a trial how it was that their activities had come to light: *Effik and Mitchell* (1992) 95 Cr.App.R. 427, 432. The House of Lords has held that the material arising from telephone interceptions was not to be preserved for use at trial because the effect of the 1985 Act was that the need for surveillance and secrecy overrode the duty to make disclosure: *Preston* [1993] 3 W.L.R. 891. *Effik and Mitchell* has now been over-ruled by *Morgans v DPP* [2000] 2 Cr.App.R. 113. S.9 of the Interception of Communications Act 1985 has been repealed by the Regulation of Investigatory Powers Act 2000. See s.17 of the 2000 Act at para.2–21 below.

information which the police received. The prosecution objects to the information being given.

How is such a conflict to be resolved? The civil cases show that the courts regard the vindication of legal rights as overriding other interests. In *British Steel Corporation v Granada Television Ltd*,[17] the courts regarded British Steel's right to protect its confidential information and identify its employee who had breached his duty of fidelity as overriding the journalist's interest in protecting the anonymity of his source.

However, in a criminal case, the conflict is more acute because both sides will contend that the administration of justice is involved. The prosecution will say that proof of guilt depends upon protected sources. The defence may say that it is necessary to prove that a source is tainted.

In the example above it would be material to A's defence to know the identity of the informant because if it were B, the defence would be considerably strengthened. Accordingly, it is submitted that in the interests of justice, the source in such a case should be revealed.

This approach was adopted by the Court of Appeal in *Agar*.[18] In that case the defendant was charged with possession of a drug with intent to supply. As a result of information received from X, the police had gone to a house, knowing that the defendant was to call there to supply the occupier with drugs. When the defendant saw the police, he ran off, discarding something which turned out to be the drug. His case was that the police had planted the drug, having arranged with X that the latter would get the defendant to come to the house. At the trial prosecuting counsel informed defence counsel that X was a police informer. Both counsel went to see the judge in chambers. The judge ruled that defence counsel should make no mention of this matter or cross-examine as to how the police knew that the defendant was to call at the house. The Court of Appeal held that this ruling was wrong since it forced defence counsel to emasculate his attack upon the police by not putting that they got their information from X.

12–07

No issue of principle was raised in Agar. However, Lord Justice Mustill, giving the judgment of the Court, said that while there was strong public interest in keeping secret the source of information, there was an even stronger public interest in allowing a defendant to put forward a tenable case in the best possible light.

It will be for the defendant in these circumstances to satisfy the court that good reasons exist for disclosing the information. If the judge concludes that it should be disclosed in order to prevent a miscarriage of justice, he is under a duty so to order.[19] However, Lord Taylor C.J. pointed out that applications for disclosure multiplied after the decision of the Court of

---

[17] [1980] 3 W.L.R. 774.
[18] (1990) 90 Cr.App.R. 318.
[19] *Hallett* [1986] Crim.L.R. 462.

Appeal in *Ward*, below. As a result, the Lord Chief Justice warned judges to scrutinise such applications with great care.[20] Lord Taylor C.J. said:

> "[Judges] will need to be astute to see that assertions of a need to know such details, because they are essential to the running of the defence, are justified. If they are not so justified, then the judge will need to adopt a robust approach in declining to order disclosure. ... Even when the informant has participated [in the events relating to the crime], the judge will need to consider whether his role so impinges on an issue of interest to the defence ... as to make disclosure necessary."[21]

12–08   It is submitted that it should only be in an exceptional case that disclosure is ordered and only where cogent reasons have been given. However, where a prosecution witness was an informant in the matter which is the subject of trial, there must be strong countervailing reasons as to why this should not be disclosed.[22]

(Where an issue arises between co-defendants as to the disclosure by the prosecution to one defendant of details of another defendant's activities as an informant, there should be a hearing in chambers at which the prosecution and the defendants are represented and at which it is for the defendant seeking disclosure to show cause why it should be made.[23])

C. The rule in relation to observation posts

12–09   The rule protecting informants from disclosure has been extended to protect the identity of persons who allow their premises to be used for surveillance by the police.[24] The protection also extends to the location of the premises.[25] The reason for the extension of the rule is that members of the public who co-operate with the police must be protected from possible reprisals by criminals and, without that protection, they are unlikely to co-operate. "[The] reasons which give rise to the rule that an informer is not to be identified apply with equal force to the identification of the owner or occupier of premises used for surveillance and the identification of the premises themselves. The cases are indistinguishable and the same rule must apply to each."[26]

The Court of Appeal in *Johnson*[27] said that the prosecution must provide

---

[20] *Turner (Paul)* [1995] 2 Cr.App.R. 94.
[21] At 98.
[22] *Patel* [2002] Crim.L.R. 304 and *Early* [2003] 1 Cr.App.R. 19.
[23] *Adams* [1997] Crim.L.R. 292.
[24] *Rankine* [1986] Q.B. 861; (1986) 83 Cr.App.R. 18; *Johnson* (1988) 88 Cr.App.R. 131; *Hewitt and Davis* (1992) 95 Cr.App.R. 81.
[25] *ibid.*
[26] *Rankine* (1986) 83 Cr.App.R. 18, 22.
[27] Above, at 139.

a proper evidential basis when seeking this protection. The Court said that the "minimum evidential requirements" were as follows:

(a) The evidence of a police officer in charge of the observation of a rank no lower than sergeant that before the observation he had visited the observation places and ascertained the attitude of the occupiers to the use to be made of the premises, to the disclosure thereafter of the use made, and of facts which could lead to the identification of the premises and of the occupiers. (He may also inform the court of difficulties, if any, encountered in the particular locality of obtaining assistance from the public.)

(b) The evidence of a police officer of a rank no lower than Chief Inspector that he has visited the same places, ascertained whether the occupiers are the same as when the observations took place and, whether they are or not, their attitude to disclosure of the matters mentioned above.

The protection applies as much to an occupier in danger of harassment as it does to one in danger of violence.[28]   **12–10**

Once an application has been made, based on appropriate evidence, it will be for the judge to determine whether, in the interests of justice, the protection should be given. It is submitted that in the normal case where protection is sought by the occupiers of premises, the court should give it. However, there may be exceptional cases where disclosure must be made in order to prevent a miscarriage of justice.

If the judge gives protection he should explain to the jury the effect of his ruling.[29]

D. Other cases

An attempt to extend the rule protecting sources of information to include   **12–11**
details of a police car from which a surveillance had taken place failed in *Brown and Daley*.[30] In that case the defendants were charged with theft from a parked car. Two police officers had been on duty in an unmarked police car and said they had seen the offence carried out. The defence alleged that part of the account of the surveillance was fictitious. As a result, defence counsel cross-examined as to how the surveillance had been conducted. The trial judge on the ground of public policy allowed the prosecution to withhold evidence as to the colour and make of the police car. The Court of Appeal held that the evidence should not have been withheld. The Court said that there was no authority for holding that the

---

[28] *Blake and Austin v DPP* (1993) 97 Cr.App.R. 169.
[29] *Johnson*, above, at 139.
[30] (1988) 87 Cr.App.R. 52.

making public of police methods or techniques was a public policy ground on which relevant evidence should be excluded. However, the Court did not rule out the possibility that with the advent of sophisticated methods of criminal investigation, there may be cases where such evidence is excluded as a result of public policy. The Court said that if such an application were to be made the prosecution must identify with precision the evidence sought to be excluded and the reason for its exclusion and support the application with the independent evidence of a senior officer.

The method of detection employed in *Brown and Daley* could not be described as sophisticated or novel. However, it is submitted that when such methods or equipment are used, the courts should be slow to order disclosure unless a fair trial would be seriously prejudiced. The public interest in non-disclosure in order (a) to assist the police in detection of serious crime, and (b) to prevent criminals from gaining access to such information must weight heavily in the scales when a balance is being struck.

2. PUBLIC INTEREST IMMUNITY

A. The rule

(1) Generally

12–12 The rule is that information may not be disclosed if such disclosure would be prejudicial to the state or public services.[31] (This common law rule has been expressly preserved by s.21(2) of the Criminal Procedure and Investigations Act 1996.) This rule used to be called "Crown privilege" but it has been pointed out that this expression is wrong and may be misleading.[32] This is because the principle is not that the Crown has a privilege to withhold information but that there is immunity from disclosure when the public interest in withholding information in a particular case outweighs the normal rules requiring disclosure. The reference to privilege is also inaccurate because the immunity may not be waived by the Crown or any other party.[33] Thus Bingham L.J. said that a party's duty when holding potentially immune material is to assert that immunity since it cannot be waived.[34] Accordingly, in its development over the last 25 years the concept

---

[31] Various statutes prevent disclosure of certain facts or documents, *e.g.* s.38 of the Legal Aid Act 1988, s.6 (as amended) and Sch.1 to the Taxes Management Act 1970. The discussion here is confined to the common law principles. For statutory privilege, see Eagles, "Public Interest and Statutory Privilege" [1983] C.L.J. 118.
[32] *Rogers v Home Secretary* [1973] A.C. 388, 400, *per* Lord Reid.
[33] *Air Canada v Secretary of State for Trade* [1983] A.C. 394, 436, *per* Lord Fraser. However, in *Horseferry Road Magistrates' Court Ex p. Bennett (No.2)* (1994) 99 Cr.App.R. 123 the Divisional Court held that it is not necessary in every case for the Crown Prosecution Service to apply to the court for a ruling before disclosing such information; they may make voluntary disclosure provided that they have the express approval of the Treasury Solicitor for doing so.
[34] *Makanjuola v Commissioner of Police* [1992] 3 All E.R. 617.

of "Crown privilege" has been replaced by that of "public interest immunity".[35]

The main development (following the decision of the House of Lords in *Conway v Rimmer*[36]) is that it is now for the court to decide whether material should be withheld on the grounds of public interest immunity. Thus, in *Ward*[37] the Court of Appeal held that where the prosecution in criminal proceedings makes a claim of public interest immunity in order to withhold material from disclosure, it is for the court to decide whether the material should be disclosed. Lord Taylor C.J. said that the effect of Ward was to give the court the role of monitoring the views of the prosecution as to what material should be disclosed[38] the prosecution was no longer judge in its own cause (as it used to be) but must proceed by application to the court.

(2) "Class" or "contents" claims

Claims for public interest immunity in civil proceedings are either "class based" (*i.e.* documents belonging to a class which in the public interest ought not to be disclosed, for example government documents relating to high policy, such as Cabinet papers and Foreign Office dispatches) or "contents based" (*i.e.* documents, the contents of which it would not be in the public interest to disclose).[39] However, this approach to such claims is not appropriate to criminal cases. Thus, Sir Richard Scott V.C. found in his enquiry into the "*Matrix Churchill*" and "*Ordtech*" cases (arising from the export of defence equipment to Iraq) that until those cases there had been virtually no criminal cases in which immunity claims had been made on a "class" as opposed to a "contents" basis; that the view of the law on which they had been made was unsound (there being no judicial authority approving the making of such claims in criminal trials); and that such claims should not be made in future in criminal trials.[40] (It can, therefore, be anticipated that no such claims will be made.)

Sir Richard also recommended that "contents" claims should not be made in relation to documents which might be of assistance to the defence and should not be made unless (in the opinion of the person putting forward the claim) disclosure will cause "substantial harm"; and that if the judge is asked to rule on the immunity claim he should be asked to decide whether the documents might be of assistance to the defence and that if a document satisfied that test it ought not to be withheld on public interest

12–13

---

[35] *Ward* [1993] 1 W.L.R. 619, 647, *per* Glidewell L.J.
[36] [1968] A.C. 910.
[37] Above.
[38] *Davis* [1993] 1 W.L.R. 613, 618.
[39] *Duncan v Cammell Laird* [1942] A.C. 624; *Conway v Rimmer* [1968] A.C. 910.
[40] *Report on the Inquiry into Export of Defence Equipment and Dual-Use Goods to Iraq and Related Prosecutions* (1996) HMSO 115, paras G10.10, 18–94, K6.6 (the "Scott Report").

immentity grounds[41]; and that a sensible and practical guide that any
Minister or official (trying to decide whether or not an immunity claim
should be made) could easily follow is to be found in the guidance given by
Lord Templeman in *R. v Chief Constable of West Midlands Police Ex p.
Wiley*[42]:

> "If a document is not relevant and material it need not be disclosed and
> public interest immunity will not arise. In case of doubt as to materi-
> ality and relevance the directions of the court can be obtained before
> trial ... If a document is relevant and material then it must be disclosed
> unless it is confidential and unless a breach of confidentiality will cause
> harm to the public interest which outweighs harm to the interests of
> justice caused by non-disclosure ... For my part I consider that when a
> document is known to be relevant and material, the holder of the
> document should voluntarily disclose it unless he is satisfied that dis-
> closure will cause substantial harm. If the holder is in doubt he may
> refer the matter to the judge. If the holder decides that a document
> should not be disclosed then that decision can be upheld or set aside by
> the judge."

(3) Extension of the rule

12–14 Examples of facets of the public interest which may require non-disclosure
have already been given, *i.e.* the maintenance of national security or diplomatic relations; or the effective functioning of the public service. It had
been thought that Crown privilege was only available where an interest of
central government was involved.[43] However, in *D v NSPCC*[44] the House
of Lords held that immunity from disclosure of the identity of informants
should be extended to those who gave information about neglect or mis-
treatment of children to the NSPCC. In *D* Lord Diplock said that there was
no reason for confining the public interest against disclosure to the effective
functioning of central government and that the categories of public interest
were not closed: confidentiality itself was a public interest.[45] Lord Edmund
Davis said:

> "where a confidential relationship exists (other than that of lawyer and
> client) and disclosure would be in breach of some ethical or social
> value involving the public interest the court has a discretion to uphold
> a refusal to disclose relevant evidence provided it considers that on

---

[41] *ibid.*, para.K6.18.
[42] [1993] 3 W.L.R. 433, 436–437.
[43] Issues of the Sovereign's immunity from giving evidence were reported to have been raised
in *Burrell*, CCC, October 2002 (the "royal butler case"), leading to calls for review. See
Sunday Times November 3, 2002 and *Guardian* November 4, 2002.
[44] [1978] A.C. 171.
[45] At 220.

balance the public interest would be better served by excluding such evidence."[46]

As a result, immunity has been extended to such confidential material as social services files,[47] hospital records (including tapes of interviews with patients),[48] the pro-forma initial report of an investigation sent by the police to the Crown Prosecution Service,[49] and reports prepared by investigating officers for the Police Complaints Authority[50]; but not, as a class, to police complaints files.[51]

An application may be made to the court by or on behalf of third parties, **12–15** (not parties to the proceedings), who hold such information, for example government departments, health authorities or social service departments. This was the practice at common law when it was a commonplace of child sex abuse cases for the local social services department to appear before the court to make representations about the files which it held on a child. This practice has been preserved and made statutory by s.16 of the Criminal Procedure and Investigations Act 1996. The effect of the section is to permit a third party who has been the originator of sensitive material (for which such an application is made) to make representations to the court relating to the material. Such a party may be represented by counsel. The purpose is to allow third parties to be heard to explain whether they object to disclosure or not and if they do, why they do. The reason for giving third parties the right to be heard is that they will usually know all about the material and will be better placed than the prosecution to make representations about it. The section is brought into operation on the application of the third party who is required to show that he was involved in originating the material. The court may then not make an order in relation to disclosure of the material unless the third party has been heard. (The Court of Appeal has said that in relation to an application under the common law that it is desirable in these circumstances that the prosecution should be present at the hearing[52]: the same, it is submitted, applies to applications under s.16.)

---

[46] At 245.
[47] *Gaskin v Liverpool C.C.* [1980] 1 W.L.R. 1549.
[48] *K (TD)*, below, n.52.
[49] *Taylor v Chief Constable of Greater Manchester*, *The Times*, January 19, 1995.
[50] *O'Sullivan v Commissioner of Police*, *The Times*, July 3, 1995 (Butterfield J.).
[51] *Chief Constable of West Midlands Police Ex p. Wiley* [1993] 3 W.L.R. 433, HL, overruling *Neilson v Laugharne* [1981] Q.B. 736 and the cases following it.
[52] *K (TD)* (1993) 97 Cr.App.R. 342, 345. In certain circumstances, where a third party seeks to withhold documents or evidence on grounds of public interest immunity, the party seeking disclosure may make a direct application for such disclosure to the authority concerned pursuant to the Data Protection Act 1998. Notwithstanding the fact that the authority is not obliged to provide material relating to third parties without first obtaining their consent, an application pursuant to the Data Protection Act may yield more material than an application via the Crown Court pursuant to r.23 of the Crown Court Rules 1982.

(4) The balancing exercise

12-16   Claims of public interest immunity used to arise more frequently in civil proceedings than in criminal trials. As a result there was an abundance of authority relating to civil proceedings, but little modern authority on the extent of the exclusionary rule in criminal proceedings. It was not until 1990 that there was an authoritative statement of the principles relating to criminal trials. In that year, in *Governor of Brixton Prison Ex p. Osman*,[53] Mann L.J. said that it seemed correct in principle that public interest immunity should apply equally to criminal as to civil proceedings, but that a different "balancing exercise" would be involved:

> "[A] judge is balancing on the one hand the desirability of preserving the public interest in the absence of disclosure against, on the other hand, the interests of justice. Where the interests of justice arise in a criminal case touching and concerning liberty or conceivably on occasion life, the weight to be attached to the interests of justice is plainly very great indeed."[54]

Thus, in *K (TD)*[55] the defendant applied for the production of a video tape of a therapeutic family interview which had taken place at Great Ormond Street Hospital for Sick Children. The application was resisted by the hospital on the ground of public interest immunity. The Court of Appeal recognised the hospital's concern that interviews conducted on a confidential basis for therapeutic purposes ought not to be disclosed. However, Lord Taylor C.J. said that where the liberty of the subject was in issue and disclosure might be of assistance to the defendant, a claim for disclosure would often be strong. Lord Taylor also said (in *Keane*[56]) that if material might prove the defendant's innocence or avoid a miscarriage of justice, then the balance came down resoundingly in favour of disclosing it.

12-17   Such material may relate solely to a witness's credibility. For example, in *Higgins*[57] the defendant was charged with sexual offences against a boy. There was an issue whether statements relating to the boy's educational needs, school reports and correspondence between his mother and his school should be disclosed. The Court of Appeal held that all the material came into categories for which the local authority should claim immunity and it was for the judge to decide (by doing a balancing exercise) whether the public interest in seeing that justice was done required that the material be disclosed. In the instant case the judge had performed the exercise and produced three documents which he considered relevant to the boy's

---

[53] [1991] 1 W.L.R. 281, 288.
[54] *ibid.*
[55] (1993) 97 Cr.App.R. 342.
[56] (1994) 99 Cr.App.R. 1.
[57] [1996] 1 F.L.R. 137.

reliability and there was no doubt that he would have ordered the disclosure of other documents if they had been similarly relevant. *Higgins* was followed in *Brushett*[58] in which the headmaster of a community school was convicted of various sexual offences against his former pupils. He appealed on the basis that he was denied access to some of the social services' documents relating to the complainants and other witnesses. The Court of Appeal held that in balancing the interests of a third party and those of the defendant, the trial judge had properly identified circumstances in which the interests of a third party would not prevent disclosure, namely where there had been false accusations in the past, and where there was a suggestion that some other adult might have indulged in sexual activity with the witness.

It may be noted that the Family Division has declined to give any ruling which may bind the trial judge in criminal proceedings where a defendant seeks the disclosure of local authority records relating to the adoption of a child: the question of disclosure is for that judge to determine by balancing the relevance of the material against the strict duty of confidentiality attaching to adoption proceedings.[59]

The need for a careful balancing exercise in considering public interest immunity applications is confirmed by the jurisprudence of the European Court of Human Rights. In *Rowe and Davis v UK*[60] the European Court held that the defendant's entitlement to disclosure is not an absolute right. In criminal proceedings, competing interests, such as national security, the need to protect witnesses at risk of reprisals, and the need to keep secret police methods of investigation of crime, must be weighed against the rights of the accused.[61] The Court held that it some cases it may be necessary to withhold certain evidence from the defence so as to preserve the fundamental rights of another individual or to safeguard an important public interest. However, only such measures restricting the rights of the defence which are strictly necessary are permissible under Art.6(1).[62]

The House of Lords, in *H and C*,[63] held that in order to comply with Art.6, when any departure from the "golden rule" of full disclosure comes before a court, the court must address the following series of questions:

(1) What is the material which the prosecution seek to withhold? This must be considered by the court in detail.

(2) Is the material such as may weaken the prosecution case or strengthen that of the defence? If No, disclosure should not be

---

[58] [2001] Crim.L.R. 471
[59] *H (A Minor)* [1995] 1 F.L.R. 964.
[60] 30 E.H.R.R. 1. at para.61.
[61] *Doorson v Netherlands* (1996) 22 E.H.R.R. 330.
[62] *Van Mechelen v Netherlands*, judgment of April 23, 1997.
[63] *The Times*, February 6, 2004.

ordered. If Yes, full disclosure should (subject to (3), (4) and (5) below) be ordered.

(3) Is there a real risk of serious prejudice to an important public interest (and, if so, what) if full disclosure of the material is ordered? If No, full disclosure should be ordered.

(4) If the answer to (2) and (3) is Yes, can the defendant's interest be protected without disclosure or disclosure be ordered to an extent or in a way which will give adequate protection to the public interest in question and also afford adequate protection to the interests of the defence?

This question requires the court to consider, with specific reference to the material which the prosecution seek to withhold and the facts of the case and the defence as disclosed, whether the prosecution should formally admit what the defence seek to establish or whether disclosure short of full disclosure may be ordered. This may be done in appropriate cases by the preparation of summaries or extracts of evidence, or the provision of documents in an edited or anonymised form, provided the documents supplied are in each instance approved by the judge. In appropriate cases the appointment of special counsel (see para.12–19 below) may be a necessary step to ensure that the contentions of the prosecution are tested and the interests of the defendant protected. In cases of exceptional difficulty the court may require the appointment of special counsel to ensure a correct answer to questions (2) and (3) as well as (4).

(5) Do the measures proposed in answer to (4) represent the minimum derogation necessary to protect the public interest in question? If No, the court should order such greater disclosure as will represent the minimum derogation from the golden rule of full disclosure.

(6) If limited disclosure is ordered pursuant to (4) or (5), may the effect be to render the trial process, viewed as a whole, unfair to the defendant? If Yes, then fuller disclosure should be ordered even if this leads to or may lead the prosecution to discontinue the proceedings so as to avoid having to make disclosure.

(7) If the answer to (6) when first given is No, does that remain the correct answer as the trial unfolds, evidence is adduced and the defence advanced?

It is important that the answer to (6) should not be treated as a final, once and for all, answer but as a provisional answer which the court must keep under review.

(5) Judicial reliance on material not disclosed on grounds of public interest immunity

In *Smith (Joe)*[64] at the start of the trial, the prosecution made an *ex parte*   **12–18**
public interest immunity application, following which the judge ordered
that the material put before him should not be disclosed. After being
informed of the ruling, counsel for Smith submitted that there was no
evidence that the officers in the case had reasonable grounds to arrest Smith
or suspect him of involvement in the offence for which he was arrested. The
judge ruled that the police had had reasonable grounds, the suspicion being
based on information that could not be disclosed because of its sensitive
nature and which had been the subject of the public interest immunity
application. Smith appealed on the ground that the judge had erred in the
exercise of his discretion under s.78 of the Police and Criminal Evidence Act
1984 in relying on material which had been the subject of a public interest
immunity application and never disclosed to the defence. The appeal was
dismissed, no principle in English law prevented a trial judge from using
information received by him during a public interest immunity investigation
to determine whether or not the police had reasonable suspicion that a
defendant had committed an offence, or had reasonable cause to arrest him.
It was held that this did not offend against the principle of equality of arms
enshrined in Art.6 of the European Convention as the trial judge been
involved in both the admissibility procedure and the public interest
immunity application.[65] However, in *H and C* (see para.12–19 below), the
House of Lords held that *Smith* is no longer good law.

The European Court of Human Rights, however, came to a very different
conclusion on the question of whether a trial judge may rely on material not
disclosed on public immunity grounds. In *Edwards and Lewis v UK*[66] a
violation of Art.6(1) of the Convention was found as the trial judge, who
had viewed public interest immunity material, went on to consider applications to exclude evidence pursuant to s.78 of PACE and a stay of
proceedings. The concern was that the non-disclosed material may have
had a bearing on the judge's decision. Moreover, as the defendants were not
aware of the contents of such material, they were unable to present any
counter-arguments. The European Court reached a similar conclusion in
Garcia Alva v Germany[67] where material from anonymous witnesses was
shown to the judge determining bail, but not disclosed to the defence. This
was held to violate Art.5(4) of the Convention.

The effect of *Edwards and Lewis* is that the judge who has viewed public

[64] [2001] 2 Cr.App.R. 1.
[65] See para.12–22 below.
[66] Application Numbers 39647/98 and 40461/98. Judgment: July 22, 2003. At the time of writing it is understood that the Government have applied for *Edwards and Lewis* to be re-considered by the Grand Chamber of the European Court.
[67] (2003) 37 E.H.R.R. 335.

interest material may not go on to rule on any matter which such material may have a bearing upon as the defence would be at a clear disadvantage. This could present insurmountable problems for trials on indictment by judge alone (see para.16–25 below on the new provisions under the Criminal Justice Act 2003) and summary trials where the same tribunal that view the public interest immunity material may go on the hear the trial and determine the accused's guilt or innocence. (See para.12–25 below.) The problem being that in order to comply with Art.6, the judge who decides to withhold material on public interest grounds must keep that decision under review during any ensuing trial so as to monitor whether such material gains in relevance. See paras 12–22 and 12–24, below.

12–19   A potential solution to such difficulties is the use of "special counsel" to represent defence interests during any public interest hearing. This was recommended in the *Auld Review*[68] but is yet to be adopted. It may be, however, that draft guidelines on the use of special counsel will be issued by the Attorney-General's office.[69] In the meantime it appears that special counsel may be used on an ad hoc basis in criminal proceedings.[70]

In *H and C*,[71] an interlocutory appeal under s.35 of the Criminal Procedure and Investigation Act 1996, the judge had ruled that: (i) public interest immunity sought by the Crown should not be *inter partes*, and (ii) special counsel should by appointed, in light *Edwards and Lewis*, to avoid any possible violation of Art.6 of the European Convention. The defence appealed the first decision and the Crown the second. The Court of Appeal held that *Smith (Joe)* was binding, notwithstanding *Edwards and Lewis*, until overruled by the House of Lords. Accordingly, the defence appeal was flawed. It was further held that the appointment of special counsel was premature in that particular case as the judge was yet to consider the public interest material.

The House of Lords dismissed both appeals.[72] However, the use of special counsel in certain, limited, circumstances was endorsed. It was held that:

> "Such an appointment will always be exceptional, never automatic; a course of last and never first resort. It should not be ordered unless and until the trial judge is satisfied that no other course will adequately meet the overriding requirement of fairness to the defendant."[73]

Special counsel are to be appointed by the Attorney-General. As the Director of Public Prosecutions, the head of the Crown Prosecution Service,

---

[68] *Auld Review of the Criminal Courts of England and Wales* (2001).
[69] Waterman, "Judges Who Know Too Much" *Archbold News*, Issue 8, September 1, 2003.
[70] *Forbidden Evidence, Guardian*, December 2, 2003.
[71] [2003] 1 W.L.R. 3006.
[72] *The Times* February 6, 2004 and [2004] UKHL 3.
[73] *ibid.*, at 22.

is also appointed by and subject to the superintendence of the Attorney-General it was said that consideration could be given to the external approval of the Attorney-General's list of eligible advocates by an appropriate professional body. However, such approval is not essential to the acceptability of the procedure.[74] When instructed, special counsel will assist the court with the determination of the questions set out in *H and C* (see para.12–17 above).

(6) Conclusion

Where public interest immunity is claimed for a document or other material:

12–20

(a) it is for the court to determine whether the claim should be upheld or not;

(b) the court must rule by performing a balancing exercise (following the seven questions at para.12–17 above) between the public interest in non-disclosure and fairness to the defendant;

(c) the judge must himself examine or view the material in order to perform the balancing exercise.[75]

B. Procedure

(1) Making the application

In *Ward*[76] the Court of Appeal said that if the prosecution wish to claim public interest immunity for documents helpful to the defence they are, in law, obliged to give notice to the defence. However, in *Davis, Johnson and Rowe*[77] a differently constituted court said that *Ward* went too far in accepting that the general rule requiring notice to the defence admitted of no qualification or exception. *Davis, Johnson and Rowe* establishes that there is such an exception in circumstances where even the giving of notice would be contrary to the public interest. The Court held that in these circumstances an *ex parte* application is appropriate. To do otherwise, as Lord Taylor C.J. observed, would be to force the prosecution to choose between following the normal inter partes procedure and declining to prosecute in a serious case. The Court in *Davis, Johnson and Rowe* set out the proper procedure for making public interest immunity applications. The procedure may be summarised as follows:

12–21

1.   Where the prosecution wish to rely on public interest immunity to

---

[74] *ibid.*, at 46.
[75] *K (TD)* (1993) 97 Cr.App.R. 342.
[76] (1993) 96 Cr.App.R. 1
[77] (1993) 97 Cr.App.R. 110.

justify non-disclosure, they must notify the defence that they are applying to the court for a ruling; they must also notify the defence of the category (*i.e.* type) of material held. The defence must then have the opportunity to make representations about disclosure to the court. (This procedure will enable the defence to indicate to the court why the disclosure of the category of material is relevant and important to the particular case.)

2. Where it would not be in the public interest to reveal the category of material held the prosecution should notify the defence that an application will be made (without revealing the category): the application should then be made to the court *ex parte*. If, on hearing the application, the judge decides that the defence should be notified of the category of material and have the opportunity of making representations, he may order an inter partes hearing. (In *Keane*[78] Lord Taylor C.J. emphasised that *ex parte* applications were contrary to the general principle of open justice: they were only sanctioned to test a claim for public interest immunity and not for any other purpose.)

3. Where in an exceptional case even to reveal that an application was to be made would stultify the application and "let the cat out of the bag", the prosecution should apply to the court *ex parte* without notifying the defence. The judge may then, if he so decides, order notification or an *inter partes* hearing.

4. The conduct of each application hearing will depend on the material sought to be withheld. However, the judge is under an obligation to examine or view the material and will need to hear an explanation as to why it is sensitive in order to carry out the balancing exercise. He will also need to make a ruling which can be recorded for the purposes of any appeal. How much of the ruling may be revealed will depend on the circumstances of the application. (The Court of Appeal has said that it is essential that a verbatim record is kept of any *ex parte* application.)[79]

12–22   *Davis, Johnson and Rowe,* has now been considered by the European Court of Human Rights. In *Rowe and Davis v UK*[80] the European Court found a violation of Art.6(1) of the Convention on the basis that the prosecution had failed to place certain relevant evidence before the trial judge so as to permit him to rule on the question of disclosure. The European Court noted that at the commencement of the applicant's appeal, prosecution counsel notified the defence that certain information had been

[78] Above.
[79] *Turner (Paul),* below.
[80] 30 E.H.R.R. 1.

withheld from the trial judge. The European Court considered whether this omission could be remedied on appeal by consideration of the material by the Court of Appeal. In *Rowe and Davis* the Court of Appeal had on two separate occasions reviewed the undisclosed evidence, *ex parte*, and decided in favour of non-disclosure. The European Court were of the view that the procedure before the Court of Appeal did not remedy the unfairness caused at trial. Unlike the trial judge, the Court of Appeal had been dependent for their understanding of the possible relevance of the undisclosed material on the transcripts of the Crown Court hearings and on the account of the issues given to them by prosecution counsel. Moreover, the Court of Appeal were not able to monitor the need for disclosure throughout the trial, assessing the importance of the undisclosed evidence at a stage when new issues were emerging and it might, through cross-examination, have been possible to seriously undermine the credibility of key witnesses. Finally, the European Court noted that the Court of Appeal was forced to carry out its appraisal of the evidence *ex post facto* and may unconsciously have been influenced by the jury's verdict of guilty into underestimating the significance of the undisclosed evidence. Thus, it is now firmly established that the question of withholding disclosure on grounds of public interest immunity must be determined by the trial judge.[81]

On the same day as their judgment in *Rowe and Davis*, the European **12–23** Court delivered its final ruling in *Jasper v UK* and *Fitt v UK*.[82] Unlike *Rowe and Davis*, the prosecution in both cases had applied to the trial judge at an *ex parte* hearing for an order permitting non-disclosure of material evidence. In each case the defence were notified that an application had been made and permitted to outline their case to the judge, in other words the procedure laid down by the Court of Appeal in *Davis, Johnson and Rowe* had been followed. Accordingly, the central issue in *Jasper* and *Fitt* was whether the procedure laid down by the Court of Appeal complied with Art.6 and the right to a fair trial. The applicants argued that the procedure in question did not provide the adversarial procedure which many of the European Court's judgments have stated as being necessary. The applicants proposed an adversarial procedure that would not involve informing either the defendant or their legal representative of the nature of the public interest immunity evidence, namely the use of "special counsel" from a panel of security-cleared counsel who would contest the application on the defendant's behalf.[83] By nine votes to eight the European Court held that no such procedure was necessary as the undisclosed evidence did not form part of the prosecution case and the defence had been keep informed of the application before the trial judge. Thus, the effect of these judgments is to

---

[81] The European Court reached a similar conclusion in *Atlan v UK, The Times*, July 3, 2001.
[82] [2000] Crim.L.R. 586.
[83] A similar procedure has already been implemented for immigration appeals following the implementation of the Special Immigration Appeals Commission Act 1997, enacted as a result of European Court's decision in *Chahal v UK* (1997) 23 E.H.R.R. 413.

establish that the procedure in *Rowe, Johnson and Davis* has not been found to be in violation of Art.6 or the right to a fair trial. The use of special counsel has now been endorsed by the House of Lords (see para.12–19 above).

It is not open to the defence to make an *ex parte* application.[84]

> "There is no justification for the defence going to see the judge *ex parte*. The proper approach, where this issue arises, is for the judge, at the invitation of the Crown, to look at the material and form his view. He must keep an open mind and review his decision, if necessary, as the case progresses. Subject to that, no further *ex parte* hearings are proper in this field."[85]

Application for disclosure of information acquired in Children Act proceedings requires the leave of the family court where a balance must be struck between maintaining the confidentiality of family proceedings and making relevant information available for the purposes of a criminal trial.[86]

(2) Keeping the ruling under review

12–24 The rule at common law (now made statutory) is that the court's ruling on an application is not necessarily final and the court must keep the ruling under review during the trial. The reason is that during the course of a trial, circumstances may change, giving rise to a need for the reconsideration of the earlier ruling. Thus, Lord Taylor C.J. said in *Davis*[87] that in the course of the hearing, the situation may change: issues may emerge so that the public interest in non-disclosure may be eclipsed by the need to disclose in the interests of securing fairness to the defendant.

Section 15 of the Criminal Procedure and Investigations Act 1996 requires the court (having ordered that material should not be disclosed on public interest grounds) to keep under review until the end of the trial whether it is still not in the public interest to disclose the material. Thus, the common law rule is now made statutory, but applies only in the Crown Court. The court when deciding to conduct a review may act of its own motion. Indeed, it will normally have to do so, since only the court and the prosecution will be in possession of the material on which the original ruling was based. However, the defendant may himself apply for a review: subs.(4). Such a situation may arise where the defence is in possession of some of the material or may know or suspect that the prosecution has such material in its own possession.

---

[84] *Turner (Paul)* (1995) 2 Cr.App.R. 94.
[85] *Van Tattenhove and Doubtfire* [1996] 1 Cr.App.R. 408, 413, *per* Lord Taylor C.J. For the duty of the judge to keep a ruling under review, see para.12–22, below.
[86] *Re A (Criminal proceedings: disclosure)* [1996] 1 F.L.R. 221.
[87] Above.

If the court comes to the conclusion that public interest immunity should no longer apply, it must inform the prosecutor: subs.(5). It need not inform the defendant, since the material may be so sensitive that (following the procedure in *Davis*), he will not know that an application has been made. The prosecutor will then have the opportunity of abandoning the proceedings without the defendant knowing that an *ex parte* application has been made.

In *Davis*, Lord Taylor said that since it was necessary for the court to continue to monitor the situation, it is desirable that the same judge or constitution of the court which decides the application should conduct the hearing, and if that is not possible the judge or constitution which does conduct the hearing should be apprised at the outset of the material upon which non-disclosure was upheld.

(3) Summary trials

The rules for dealing with public interest immunity applications in summary trials are the same as the rules in trials on indictment.[88] However, magistrates' courts are exempt from the duty to keep rulings under review: Criminal Procedure and Investigations Act 1996, s.4. Accordingly, if magistrates hear an application and see material which they order should not be disclosed, they may conclude that the material is so prejudicial that they cannot come to an unbiased decision on the case. In these circumstances the magistrates should disqualify themselves and the case will be heard by another bench. Thus, in *S. Worcs. Magistrates Ex p. Lilley*[89] the Divisional Court held that magistrates had a discretion to disqualify themselves if they had heard an application and felt that as a result of hearing the evidence they would be biased in making a final decision. In that case the magistrates, having been shown a document, excluded the defendant and his solicitor from court and heard evidence from the investigating officer and representations from the prosecutor: the Divisional Court held that in these circumstances the bench should have exercised their discretion and disqualified themselves. This was because the procedure in the Crown Court did not apply to magistrates who were judges of fact; and a fair-minded person would have a reasonable suspicion that the bench might have been prejudiced. However, the Divisional Court said that it was a matter for the magistrates' discretion whether or not they continued to hear the case. It is submitted that in an exceptional case of a bench having to deal with such an application and seeing or hearing prejudicial matter, it will be right (in order to avoid the risk of the appearance of prejudice) to order the case to be heard by a new bench; but there is no rule to this effect

12–25

---

[88] A similar procedure to that is *Davis, Johnson and Rowe* (para.12–21, above) applies to applications in the magistrates' court: Magistrates' Courts (Criminal Procedure and Investigations Act 1996) (Disclosure) Rules 1997.
[89] [1995] 4 All E.R. 186.

and the defendant has no right to a hearing before a new bench.[90] Ordinarily, it will not be necessary for magistrates to disqualify themselves.[91] No test can be laid down in order to determine when it will be necessary to do so: such a decision will depend on the circumstances of the particular case and the degree of prejudice involved. In *Stipendiary Magistrate for Norfolk Ex p. Taylor*[92] the Divisional Court upheld the stipendiary magistrate's decision not to disqualify himself having made a ruling in a public interest immunity application: the Court said that there was no distinction in these circumstances between stipendiary magistrates and lay justices. See, however, para.12–18 on impact of the European Court's decision in *Edwards and Lewis* on public interest immunity applications being dealt with by magistrates.

Section 14 of the 1996 Act will not prevent the defendant from applying for a review of an earlier ruling, in which case the bench as constituted for the hearing will have to decide the application.

When a case is committed for trial the examining justices should not deal with public interest immunity applications: in these circumstances the application should be heard by the Crown Court and decisions as to disclosure should be made solely by that court.[93] If a case raises complex and contentious public interest immunity issues, and the court has discretion to send the case to the Crown Court for trial, the magistrates court should carefully consider whether such issues are best resolved in the Crown Court. The use of special counsel will rarely be appropriate.[94]

---

[90] *S. Worcs. Magistrates Ex p. Lilley*, above.
[91] *Stipendiary Magistrate for Norfolk Ex p. Taylor* (1997) 161 J.P. 773. See also *R (DPP) v Acton Youth Court* [2001] 1 W.L.R. 1828.
[92] Above. Lord Bingham C.J. said that cases involving such issues do not have to be heard in the Crown Court and magistrates may hear them (although there may be serious cases raising important issues of disclosure which are better heard in the Crown Court): *Ex p. Taylor*, above, at 779.
[93] *DPP Ex p. Warby* (1994) 158 J.P. 190.
[94] *H and C, The Times*, February 6, 2004.

CHAPTER 13
Convention Rights

1. INTRODUCTION

The term "Convention Rights" refers to rights under the European Convention on Human Rights. The Human Rights Act 1998 became law in the autumn of 1998 and came into force on October 2, 2000.[1] The Act incorporates into English law the European Convention on Human Rights. The result for the law of evidence is that evidence may be rendered inadmissible because to admit it would violate Convention rights.

Since coming into force, the Act has had a considerable impact on domestic proceedings. Lord Slynn in *Lambert* stated[2]:

> "...the 1998 Act must be given its full import ... long or well entrenched ideas may have to be put aside, sacred cows culled."

However, lawyers have also been criticised for "jumping on the bandwagon" of human rights litigation.[3] The Convention, having been promulgated following the horrors of the World War II, is said to have been intended to protect citizens from "true abuses of human rights". Warnings have therefore been given about bringing both the Convention and Human Rights Act into "disrepute".[4] The Convention is, however, a "living instrument" (see para.13–27 below). What is of concern today may not have been so fifty years ago. Thus, the rights enshrined in the Convention must be considered against present-day standards.

The Convention for the Protection of Human Rights and Fundamental Freedoms (to give it its full title) was agreed by the Council of Europe in 1950 and ratified by the UK in 1951. It came into force in 1953. The purpose of the Convention is stated in the preamble and Article 1, *i.e.* that the signatory Governments—being resolved as the Governments of European countries which are like-minded and have a common heritage of political traditions, ideals, freedom and the rule of law, to take the first steps for the collective enforcement of certain rights stated (in the UN

---

[1] Human Rights Act 1998 (Commencement No.2) Order 2000 (SI 2000/1851). ss.18, 19, 21(5) and 22 came into force with the passage of the Human Rights Act 1998: s.22(2).
[2] [2002] 2 A.C. 545.
[3] *Perry, The Times*, April 28, 2000, *per* Swinton Thomas L.J.
[4] *ibid.*

Universal Declaration of Human Rights 1948)[5]—have agreed that they shall "secure to everyone within their jurisdiction the rights and freedoms defined in ... this Convention".[6] The purpose was to secure a common interpretation and enforcement of human rights throughout Europe, these rights being based on a common heritage. The obligation on every signatory is thus to secure to everyone within its jurisdiction the rights which the Convention defines.

13–02   Prior to incorporation the Convention was not part of English domestic law. As a result the courts had no powers to enforce its rights. However, as a treaty obligation it had a limited role to play in English domestic law. Thus, it was the rule that a statute was to be constructed as being consistent with obligations under the Convention and not inconsistent with it[7]; and if there was any ambiguity in a statute the courts would presume that Parliament intended to legislate in conformity with it.[8] The Convention was applicable where the common law was unclear[9]: in these circumstances the obligations imposed on the UK by the Convention were relevant sources of public policy.[10] Finally, the Convention's principles were relevant to the exercise of a judicial discretion and could be deployed in that exercise.[11]

2. THE HUMAN RIGHTS ACT 1998

13–03   The Human Rights Act 1998 makes it unlawful for a public authority to act in a way which is incompatible with a Convention right. Section 6 of the Human Rights Act provides:

> "(1)   It is unlawful for a public authority to act in a way which is incompatible with a Convention Right.
>
> (2)   Subsection (1) does not apply to an act if—
>
>   (a)   as the result of one or more provisions of primary legislation, the authority could not have acted differently; or
>   (b)   in the case of one or more provisions of, or made under, primary legislation which cannot be read or given effect in a way which is compatible with the Convention rights, the authority was acting so as to give effect to enforce those provisions.

---

[5] Preamble of the Convention.
[6] Art.1.
[7] *Garland v B.R. Engineering* [1983] 2 A.C. 751, 771, *per* Lord Diplock.
[8] *Home Secretary v Brind* [1991] 1 A.C. 696, 747–748, *per* Lord Bridge.
[9] *Att-Gen v Guardian Newspapers (No.2)* [1990] 1 A.C. 109, 283 *per* Lord Goff; *Derbyshire CC v Times Newspapers* [1992] Q.B. 770, *per* Butler-Sloss L.J.
[10] *Chief Metropolitan Magistrate, Ex p. Choudhury* [1991] 1 Q.B. 449.
[11] *Rantzen v Mirror Group Newspapers* [1994] Q.B. 670, 671; *Khan* [1996] 2 Cr.App.R. 440. For discussion, see para.10–26, above.

(3) In this section, 'public authority' includes—

    (a) a court or tribunal, and

    (b) any person certain of whose functions are functions of a public nature,

but does not include either House of Parliament or a person exercising functions in connection with proceedings in Parliament.

(4) In subsection (3) 'Parliament' does not include the House of Lords in its judicial capacity.

(5) In relation to a particular act, a person is not a public authority by virtue only of subsection (3)(b) if the nature of the act is private.

(6) 'An act' includes a failure to act but does not include a failure to—

    (a) introduce in, or lay before, Parliament a proposal for legislation; or

    (b) make any primary legislation or remedial order."

Thus, for the purpose of the Act, "public authority" includes a court and "any person certain of whose functions are functions of a public nature". This may be taken to include the police and immigration officers (as the White Paper stated),[12] and also Customs Officers and others acting in a public capacity (for example a store detective when detaining a suspected shoplifter). It is submitted therefore that the expression "functions of a public nature" must be given a broad construction.

In *Lambert*,[13] the House of Lords held that a challenge under the Human Rights Act may only be made in relation to actions or decisions of a public authority carried out after October 2, 2000, *i.e.* when the Act came into force. This decision was questioned by the majority of the House of Lords in *Kansal (No.2)*,[14] however, in the interests of judicial certainty, the decision in *Lambert* was followed.

Section 1(1)(a) of the Act provides that "Convention rights" are defined as those set out in Arts 2–12 and 14 of the Convention.[15]   **13–04**

A person who claims that a public authority has acted in a way which is made unlawful by s.6(1) (*i.e.* in a way incompatible with a Convention right) may rely on the Convention right or rights concerned in any legal proceedings. Section 7 of the Act provides:

---

[12] "Rights Brought Home", Home Office, Cm. 3782 (1997), para.2.4.

[13] [2002] 2 A.C. 545.

[14] [2002] 2 A.C. 69.

[15] See paras 13–09 *et seq.*, below, for the articles relevant to this work. S.1(1)(b) refers to Arts 1–3 of the First Protocol as read with Arts 16–18 of Convention. None of these Articles has any relevance for this work.

"(1) A person who claims that a public authority has acted (or proposes to act) in a way which is made unlawful by section 6(1) may—

(a) bring proceedings against the authority under this Act in the appropriate court or tribunal, or

(b) rely on the Convention right or rights concerned in any legal proceedings,

but only if he is (or would be) a victim of the unlawful act.

(2) In subsection (1)(a) 'appropriate court or tribunal' means such court or tribunal as may be determined in accordance with the rules; and proceedings against an authority include a counterclaim or similar proceeding.

(3) If the proceedings are brought on an application for judicial review, the applicant is to be taken to have a sufficient interest in relation to the unlawful act only if he is, or would be, a victim of that act.

(4) ...

(5) Proceedings under subsection (1)(a) must be brought before the end of—

(a) the period of one year beginning with the date on which the act complained of took place; or

(b) such longer period as the court or tribunal considers equitable having regard to all the circumstances,

but that is subject to any rule imposing a stricter time-limit in relation to the procdure in question.

(6) In subsection (1)(b) 'legal proceedings' includes—

(a) proceedings brought by or at the instigation of a public authority; and

(b) an appeal against the decision of a court or tribunal.

(7) For the purposes of this section, a person is a victim of an unlawful act only if he would be a victim for the purposes of Article 34 of the Convention if proceedings were brought in the European Court of Human Rights in respect of that act.

(8) Nothing in this Act creates a criminal offence.

(9) In this section 'rules' means—

(a) in relation to proceedings before a Court or tribunal outside Scotland, rules made by the Lord Chancellor or the Secretary of State for the purposes of this section or rules of court,

(b) ...

(c) ...

and includes provision made by order under section 1 of the Courts and Legal Services Act 1990."

The Act thus applies to all courts, including Crown Courts and magistrates' courts. The White Paper stated that the Government preferred a system in which Convention rights can be called on as they arise in normal court proceedings so that a person aggrieved will be able to challenge the act or omission in the courts.[16] This gives effect to the Government's intention that people should be able to argue that their Convention rights have been infringed in the courts at any level. "This will enable the Convention rights to be applied from the outset against the facts and background of the particular case."[17]

13–05

The following should be noted:

(a) A person can only rely on the Convention rights if he or she is a victim of the unlawful act. The purpose of this provision is to restrict those who can complain of infringements to those who are directly affected by them.[18]

(b) A person may rely on a Convention right without prejudice to any other right or freedom conferred by law: s.11(a) of the Act. Thus, a defendant is not precluded by relying on a Convention point from also relying on the common law or statute in applying for evidence to be excluded.

In relation to any act which the court finds unlawful it may grant such relief or remedy or make such order, within its jurisdiction as it considers just and appropriate. Section 8(1) of the Act provides:

"(1) In relation to any act (or proposed act) of a public authority which the court finds is (or would be) unlawful, it may grant such relief or remedy, or make such order, within its powers as it considers just and appropriate."

---

[16] Above, Introduction and para.2.3.

[17] Above, para.2.4.

[18] s.7(6) provides that a person is a victim only if he would be a victim for the purposes of Art.34 of the Convention (as amended by the 11th Protocol) which provides that the court may receive applications from any person claiming to be the victim of the violation of a Convention right. A similar test previously applied under Art.25. It was established under that provision that a person had to be directly affected by an act or omission to be a victim (see, *e.g. Open Door v Ireland*, Series A, No.246, para.43 (1992)).

Thus, the court may grant any remedy within its power if it finds there has been a breach of Convention rights. This will include a power for any court to exclude evidence or for the Court of Appeal to quash a conviction.[19] Thus, Lord Irvine L.C. said that people may rely on Convention rights in any legal proceedings and if the court finds that a public authority has behaved in a way incompatible with those rights "it may provide whatever remedy is available to it."[20]

13–06   In determining questions which arise in connection with a Convention right a court is required to take into account relevant decisions and judgments of the European Court and decisions and opinions of the European Commission: s.2 of the Act. It had been suggested that such decisions would not be binding.[21] However, the House of Lords has held that, in most circumstances, any clear and constant jurisprudence of the European Court of Human Rights should be followed by domestic courts when considering Convention rights.[22] The interpretation of constitutional documents from other jurisdictions, which are sometimes very similar (if not identical) to the rights guaranteed in the European Convention, may also be of use when considering the application of the Convention rights. As Lord Nicholls stated:

> "... every system of law stands to benefit by an awareness of the answers given by other courts and tribunals to similar problems."[23]

Thus, jurisprudence from, for example, South Africa, New Zealand, Canada, the United States, and the Caribbean, may be of immense importance in considering matters raised pursuant to the Human Rights Act.

13–07   Acts of Parliament and secondary legislation must be read and given effect (in so far as it is possible to do so) to be compatible with Convention rights. Section 3 of the Act provides:

> "(1)   So far as it is possible to do so, primary legislation and subordinate legislation must be read and given effect in a way which is compatible with the Convention rights.

---

[19] A conviction obtained in breach of Art.6 (right to fair trial) cannot stand. Thus, such convictions will be held "unsafe" pursuant to s.2(1) of the Criminal Appeals Act 1968: *A (No.2)* [2002] 1 A.C. 45 at para.38; *Forbes* [2001] 1 A.C. 473; and *Togher* [2001] 1 Cr.App.R. 33.

[20] Second Reading Debate, *Hansard*, HL, Vol.582, col.1228, November 3, 1997.

[21] See White Paper, above, para.2.4. S.2(2) of the Act provides that evidence of such decisions is to be given in proceedings in such manner as may be provided by rules of court: no rules have been made to date.

[22] *R (Anderson) v Secretary of State for the Home Department* [2003] 1 A.C. 837 and *R (Alconbury) v Secretary of State for the Environment* [2001] 2 W.L.R. 1389. See also Court of Appeal decision in *Togher* [2001] 1 Cr.App.R. 33.

[23] *Khan (Sultan)* [1996] 3 All E.R. 289 *per* Lord Nicholls at 302.

(2) This section—

(a) applies to primary legislation and subordinate legislation whenever enacted;

(b) does not affect the validity, continuing operation or enforcement of any incompatible primary legislation; and

(c) does not affect the validity, continuing operation or enforcement of any incompatible subordinate legislation if (disregarding any possibility of revocation) primary legislation prevents removal of the incompatibility."

Thus, courts are required to interpret legislation to comply with the Convention unless impossible to do so. This reverses the ruling that the Convention may only be taken into account to resolve any ambiguity in legislation.[24] In cases where it is impossible to interpret legislation to comply with the Convention, the High Court, Court of Appeal or House of Lords may make a declaration of incompatibility (s.4). Where a court is considering whether to make a declaration of incompatibility, a Minister of the Crown is entitled to be joined as a party to the proceedings (s.5).[25] In the event of a declaration of incompatibility "a fast-track procedure" exists to amend the legislation (s.10).

Lord Woolf stated that "[i]t is difficult to overestimate the importance of section 3".[26] It applies to legislation passed both before and after the Human Rights Act came into force. The courts traditional role of interpretation of statutes is replaced by the direction in s.3. Thus, legislation which predates and conflicts with the European Convention is to be treated as being subsequently amended to incorporate the language of s.3.[27]

In *A (No.2)*[28] the House of Lords considered whether any incompatibility between s.41 of the Youth Justice and Criminal Evidence Act 1999 and Art.6 of the European Convention could be avoided with the use of s.3 of the Human Rights Act. Lord Steyn stated that the interpretive obligation under s.3 is a "strong one" and applies "even if there is no ambiguity in the language in the sense of the language being capable of two different meanings".[29] He concluded:

13–08

"In accordance with the will of Parliament as reflected in section 3 it will sometimes be necessary to adopt an interpretation which linguistically may appear strained. The techniques to be used will not only

---

[24] para.13–02, above.
[25] See *A (Joinder of Appropriate Minister)* [2001] 1 W.L.R. 789, for the procedure to be followed in criminal cases where a minister seeks to be joined in such matters.
[26] *Poplar Housing and Regeneration Community Association Ltd v Donoghue* [2001] EWCA 595 at [75].
[27] *ibid.*
[28] [2002] 1 A.C. 45.
[29] *ibid.* at para.44.

involve the reading down of express language in a statute but also the implication of provisions. A declaration of incompatibility is a measure of last resort. It must be avoided unless plainly impossible to do so."[30]

Thus, it is only if there is a clear limitation on Convention rights stated in terms that such incompatibility arises. The Human Rights Act clearly reserves the amendment of primary legislation to Parliament. Accordingly, any purported use of s.3 to produce a result which departs substantially from a fundamental feature of an Act of Parliament is likely to have crossed the boundary between interpretation and amendment.[31]

3. THE CONVENTION RIGHTS

13–09 The Convention rights relevant for the purpose of exclusionary rules of evidence in criminal proceedings are to be found in Arts 3, 5, 6 and 8 of the Convention. These Articles are now discussed together with a brief summary of the case law of the European Court of Human Rights (the Court) and the European Commission of Human Rights (the Commission).[32]

A. Article 3: prohibition of torture

13–10 Article 3 provides that no one shall be subjected to torture or to inhuman or degrading treatment or punishment.

It is unlikely that an English court will face a case of torture in the context of domestic criminal proceedings.[33] However, allegations of violations of Art.3 as a result of inhuman or degrading treatment may be more common in connection with the admissibility of confessions. The Court has found conduct to amount to inhuman and degrading treatment (and, hence, in violation of Art.3) in cases involving (a) interrogation techniques used by the police in Northern Ireland when dealing with suspected terrorists (such as depriving the detainee of sleep, food and drink, putting a bag over his head or forcing him to stand for long periods)[34]; (b) the use of violence during police interrogation[35]; and (c) the infliction of injuries while a

---

[30] *ibid. A (No.2)* is an example of the "reading in" of provisions into a Statute to safeguard Convention rights and *Lambert* [2002] 2 A.C. 545, an example of "reading down" legislation to achieve a rights compatible interpretation.

[31] *Re S (Minors) (Care Order: Implementation of Care Plan)* [2002] 2 A.C. 291.

[32] It should be noted that in 1998 the Court was re-formed and the Commission abolished. The Court may sit in Committees of three judges, Chambers of seven judges, or in a Grand Chamber of seventeen judges. The decisions of the old court are not binding on the new court: Protocol 11 to the European Convention on Human Rights.

[33] The first case in which the European Court found it to have occurred was *Aksoy v Turkey*, December 18, 1996. There is, of course, the possibility that torture may arise in domestic courts as a result of extradition proceedings, either to or from the UK.

[34] *Ireland v UK*, Series A, No.25 (1978).

[35] *Tomasi v France*, Series A, No.241A (1992).

detainee was in police custody.[36] However, such treatment must attain a minimum level of severity if it is to amount to inhuman and degrading treatment.[37]

On the other hand, "the requirements of the investigation and the undeniable difficulties inherent in the fight against crime, particularly with regard to terrorism, cannot result in limits being placed on the protection to be afforded in respect of the physical integrity of individuals."[38] It should also be noted that the approach of the Commission and the Court has been to hold that states are responsible for persons held in detention. Thus, the view of the Commission was that in the event of injuries being sustained in police custody it was for the Government to produce evidence establishing facts which cast doubt on the account of events given by the victim.[39] (This was a view from which the Court did not dissent.)

B. Article 5: right to liberty and security

1. Everyone has the right to liberty and security of person. No one shall **13–11** be deprived of his liberty save in the following cases and in accordance with a procedure prescribed by law:

(a) the lawful detention of a person after conviction by a competent court;

(b) the lawful arrest or detention of a person for non-compliance with the lawful order of a court or in order to secure the fulfilment of any obligation prescribed by law;

(c) the lawful arrest or detention of a person effected for the purpose of bringing him before the competent legal authority on reasonable suspicion of having committed an offence or when it is reasonably considered necessary to prevent his committing an offence or fleeing after having done so.

2. Everyone who is arrested shall be informed promptly, in a language which he understands, of the reasons for his arrest and of any charge against him.

3. Everyone arrested or detained in accordance with the provisions of para.1(c) of this Article shall be brought promptly before a judge or other officer authorised by law to exercise judicial power and shall be entitled to trial within a reasonable time or to release pending trial. Release may be conditioned by guarantees to appear for trial.

4. Everyone who is deprived of his liberty by arrest or detention shall be

---

[36] *Ribitsch v Austria*, Series A, No.336 (1995).
[37] *Ireland*, above.
[38] *Tomasi*, above, para.115; reiterated in *Ribitsch*, above, para.38.
[39] Quoted in *Ribitsch*, above, para.31.

entitled to take proceedings by which the lawfulness of his detention shall be decided speedily by a court and his release ordered if the detention is not lawful.

13–12   The object of Art.5(1) is to ensure that no one is dispossessed of his liberty in an arbitrary fashion.[40] The principle is set out in the first sentence. The exceptions are set out in the following list in the Article. These matters may be noted:

    (i)   The words "in accordance with a procedure prescribed by law" refers back to domestic law, whereas the reference to the lawfulness of detention also includes a reference to the present Article.[41] Thus the detention must be lawful by European standards.

   (ii)   Any person arrested may be said to be deprived of his liberty. Whether a person taken to the police station for questioning has been so deprived depends on the intention of the police.[42]

  (iii)   "Reasonable suspicion" has been held to presuppose the existence of facts or information which would satisfy an objective observer.[43] "What may be regarded as reasonable will depend on the circumstances."[44] (However, it does not have to be proved that an offence has in fact been committed.)[45]

  (iv)   The fact that a suspect is not charged or brought before a court does not necessarily mean that his detention is not in accordance with Art.5(1)(c). "The existence of such a purpose must be considered independently of its achievment and [the paragraph] does not pre-suppose that the police should have obtained sufficient evidence to bring charges either at the point of arrest or while the applicants have been in custody."[46]

Article 5(3) requires the prompt appearance of a person detained before an appropriate judicial officer. In *Brogan v UK*[47] the Court referred to case law of the Commission which established that, in cases concerning ordinary criminal offences, detention of four days before such an appearance (and of five days in exceptional cases) could be considered compatible with Art.5(3). The Commission considered that a somewhat longer period was justified in the instant case given the context of the case and the special

---

[40] *Winterwerp v Netherlands*, Series A, No.33, para.37 (1979).
[41] *ibid.*, paras 39, 45.
[42] *X v F.R.G.*, 24 D.R. 158 (1981).
[43] *Fox, Campbell and Hartley v UK*, Series A, No.182, para.32 (1990).
[44] *ibid.*
[45] *X v Austria* (1987) 11 E.H.R.R. 112.
[46] *Brogan v UK* (1988) 11 E.H.R.R. 117, para.53.
[47] Above, para.57.

problems associated with the investigation of terrorist offences. However, the Court held that the applicant's detention of four days and six hours was too long to be compatible with Art.5(3). The Court said that the assessment of "promptness" (in Art.5(3)) has to be made in the light of the object and purpose of Art.5: "Judicial control of interferences by the Executive with the individual's right of liberty is an essential feature of the guarantee embodied in Article 5(3) which is intended to minimise the risk of arbitrariness."[48]

Article 5(3) also provides that there is an entitlement to trial within a **13–13** reasonable time or to release pending trial. "The purpose of the provision is essentially to require [the accused's] provisional release once his continuing detention ceases to be reasonable."[49] The persistence of reasonable suspicion that the accused has committed an offence is essential for continued detention. In *Letellier v France*[50] the Court said that:

> "[it] falls in the first place to the national judicial authorities to ensure that in a given case the detention of the accused person does not exceed a reasonable time. To this end they must examine all the facts arguing for or against the existence of a genuine requirement of public interest justifying, with due regard to the principle of the presumption of innocence, a departure from the rule of respect for individual liberty and set them out in their decisions on the applications for release."

In the circumstances of the instant case the Court held that a period of pre-trial detention of two years and nine months amounted to a violation of Art.5(3). Similarly, in *Scott v Spain*,[51] a period of four years' detention was held to have violated Art.5(3). (Scott had been arrested in Spain on suspicion of rape. Meanwhile, a British court had issued an international arrest warrant. He was detained for four years in Spain, acquitted of the rape and then extradited to Britain. The Court held that his detention was not justified by the difficulties associated with international judicial co-operation.) On the other hand, the complexity of a case may justify a longer than normal period of detention.[52] The Court stressed, as it did in *Jablonski v Poland*,[53] the need for the judicial authorities to justify the deprivation of liberty with "relevant" and "sufficient" grounds. The mere existence of a strong suspicion of guilt of serious offences cannot alone justify a long period of pre-trial detention.[54]

---

[48] *ibid.*, para.58.
[49] *Neumeister v Austria*, Series A, No.8, para.4 (1968).
[50] Series A, No.207, para.35 (1991).
[51] (1997) 24 E.H.R.R. 391.
[52] *B v Austria*, Series A, No.175, para.45 (1990); *W v Switzerland*, Series A, No.254-A (1993).
[53] (2003) 36 E.H.R.R. 27.
[54] *Kalashnikov v Russia* (2003) 36 E.H.R.R. 34.

The European Court found a violation of Art.5 where the defence had been denied access to a file provided to the Court by the prosecution which had been taken into consideration by the Court when deciding to prolong pre-trial detention.[55] Moreover, the imposition of the burden of proof on a detained person to demonstrate why he should be released has been held incompatible with Art.5(4) of the Convention.[56]

C. Article 6: right to a fair trial

13–14 1. In the determination of his civil rights and obligations or of any criminal charge against him, everyone is entitled to a fair and public hearing within a reasonable time by an independent and impartial tribunal established by law. Judgment shall be pronounced publicly but the press and public may be excluded from all or part of the trial in the interest of morals, public order or national security in a democratic society, where the interests of juveniles or the protection of the private lives of the parties so require, or to the extent strictly necessary in the opinion of the court in special circumstances where publicity would prejudice the interests of justice.

2. Everyone charged with a criminal offence shall be presumed innocent until proved guilty according to law.

3. Everyone charged with a criminal offence has the following minimum rights:

(a) to be informed promptly, in a language which he understands and in detail, of the nature and cause of the accusation against him;

(b) to have adequate time and facilities for the preparation of his defence;

(c) to defend himself in person or through legal assistance of his own choosing or, if he has not sufficient means to pay for legal assistance, to be given it free when the interests of justice so require;

(d) to examine or have examined witnesses against him and to obtain the attendance and examination of witnesses on his behalf under the same conditions as witnesses against him;

(e) to have the free assistance of an interpreter if he cannot understand or speak the language used in court.

Article 6(1) guarantees the general right to a fair hearing in criminal proceedings, while Arts 6(2) and 6(3) guarantee specific rights. Article 6

---

[55] *Garcia Alva v Germany* (2003) 37 E.H.R.R. 12.
[56] *Hutchinson-Reid v UK*, European Court of Human Rights, February 20, 2003.

applies to all criminal offences and no level of seriousness is implied.[57] "The general requirements of fairness contained in Article 6 ... apply to criminal proceedings in respect of all types of criminal offence without distinction from the most simple to the most complex."[58]

(1) Article 6(1): The fairness of the proceedings

The concern of Art.6(1) is with the overall fairness of the proceedings. The Article does not establish any rules of evidence or principles governing admissibility. These are matters for regulation by national law.[59] Similarly, as a general rule, it is for the national courts to assess evidence.[60] Thus, in *Mialhe v France (No.2)*,[61] the European Court said that it was not for that Court to substitute its view for that of the national courts which are primarily competent to determine the admissibility of evidence. It must nevertheless satisfy itself that the proceedings as a whole were fair.

13–15

Likewise, in *Kostovski v Netherlands*[62] the Court said that its task in the instant case was not to express a view as to whether certain statements were correctly admitted and assessed, but rather to ascertain whether the proceedings—considered as a whole, including the way in which the evidence was taken—were fair.

Article 6(1) contains broad and general protections and the European Court has therefore been left with plenty of leeway to develop case law and protections.[63] Article 6(1) is concerned with the general right to a fair trial and the European Court itself has established a number of specific guarantees under the Article, for example the principle of "equality of arms", the right to silence, and rights necessary for the preparation and conduct of the defence. Article 6(1) itself guarantees a public hearing. These guarantees will now be discussed.

---

[57] *Ozturk v Germany*, Series A, No.73, para.53 (1984). To determine whether the Article applies, the test is to ask whether the national legal system defines the offence as criminal, and to consider the nature of the offence, and the severity of any potential penalty: *Engel v Netherlands*, Series A, No.22 (1976) and *Benham v UK* (1996) 22 E.H.R.R. 293. The UK has been held in breach of Art.6 for treating prison disciplinary hearings as civil rather than criminal: *Ezeh and Connors v UK* (2002) 35 E.H.R.R. 691. "Charge" in Art.6(1) has been defined as the official notification to an individual by the competent authority of an allegation that he had committed a criminal offence: *Serves v France* (1998) 3 B.H.R.C. 446. In *Gough v Chief Constable of Derbyshire* [2002] 2 All E.R. 985 it was held that football banning orders made pursuant to the Football Spectators Act 1989 do not involve a "criminal charge" within the meaning of Art.6.
[58] *Saunders v UK* (1997) 23 E.H.R.R. 313, para.74, ECHR.
[59] *Schenk v Switzerland* (1998) 13 E.H.R.R. 242, para.47, cited at para.10–09, above
[60] *Barbera v Spain* (1998) 11 E.H.R.R. 360, para.68. See also *Edwards v UK* (1993) 15 E.H.R.R. 417, para.47, where the Court said that it would not substitute its own view of the facts for that of the domestic court.
[61] (1997) 23 E.H.R.R. 491, para.43.
[62] (1989) 13 E.H.R.R. 491, para.39. See also *Van Mechelen v Netherlands* 25 E.H.R.R. 647, para.50.
[63] Ashworth, "Article 6 and the Fairness of Trials" [1999] Crim.L.R. 261.

13–16   **The principle of "equality of arms".** This principle is derived from the general concern of the Article with the fairness of the trial. The effect is that the parties should be on a level playing field and that one should not have advantages denied to the other. Thus, in *Borgers v Belgium*,[64] the appellant complained that (a) he had not been able to respond to the avocat general's submissions before the Court of Cassation and (b) the latter had retired with the Court and taken part in its deliberations. The European Court said that it was necessary to consider whether the proceedings respected the rights of the defence and the principle of the equality of arms which are features of the wider concept of a fair trial.[65] The Court found that there had been a violation of Art.6(1) having regard to those matters and "the role of appearances in determining whether they have been complied with".[66]

In determining whether the requirements of Art.6 are met, the European Court will look at the entirety of the proceedings. In *Pisano v Italy*[67] it was held that it was not necessary for every defence witness to be summoned or called to satisfy Art.6(3)(d) (see para.13–23 below). It was for the national courts to assess the evidence, including the relevance of defence evidence, with the essential aim of ensuring the equality of arms as far as possible. It followed that the complaint that the accused had not received a fair trial on the grounds that insufficient efforts had been made to locate a particular witness was dismissed. The Court said that it was not for it to express an opinion on the relevance of evidence that had been rejected by the national court or to comment on the guilt or innocence of the accused. Its function was to ensure that he had been afforded a fair trial.

13–17   **The right to silence and the privilege against self-incrimination.** This right was accepted by the European Court in *Funke v France*.[68] In that case customs officers had searched the applicant's house and seized documents relating to his overseas assets. As a result, the applicant was convicted and fined for failing to provide statements of his overseas bank accounts to the customs authorities: he was ordered to produce them and subjected to a penalty for any delay. He complained that the conviction infringed Art.6(1). The European Court held that there had been a breach of the Article because the customs officers had secured the conviction in order to obtain the documents, thereby attempting to compel the applicant himself to provide the evidence of alleged offences: such conduct infringed the right of anyone charged with a criminal offence to remain silent and not to contribute to incriminating himself.[69]

---

[64] Series A, No.214-B (1991).
[65] para.24
[66] para.29.
[67] (2002) 34 E.H.R.R. 705.
[68] (1993) 16 E.H.R.R. 297.
[69] para.44.

The Court clarified this right further in two cases concerning the UK. The first, *Murray v UK*,[70] established that the right is not absolute. *Murray* (a case from Northern Ireland) concerned the drawing of adverse inferences from the accused's silence when interrogated and at trial. The Court said that there are generally recognised standards which lie at the heart of the notion of a fair procedure. "By providing the accused with protection against improper compulsion by the authorities, these immunities contribute to avoiding miscarriages of justice and to securing the aims of Article 6."[71] The Court said that what was at stake was (a) whether the immunities were absolute (*i.e.* that the exercise of the right to silence cannot under any circumstances be used against an accused at trial), and (b) whether informing him in advance that his silence may be used at trial is always to be regarded as improper compulsion. The Court said that the right was not absolute and held that the fact that inferences had been drawn from the applicant's silence did not constitute a breach of Art.6(1). In *Saunders v UK*[72] the Court held that the right is not confined to evidence of admissions or directly incriminating remarks but extended to any evidence which may be deployed in support of the prosecution case, for example evidence used to contradict or cast doubt on the evidence of the accused: what is of the essence is the use made of the evidence in the course of the trial.

In *Condron v UK*[73] the European Court found that the accused did not receive a fair trial within the meaning of Art.6(1) by reason of the failure of the trial judge to properly direct the jury by leaving open the possibility for the jury to draw an adverse inference even though they might be satisfied as to the plausibility of the defendant's explanation for not answering questions during interview. The fairness of the trial could not be served through appeal proceedings as the Court of Appeal had no means of ascertaining the role played by the applicant's silence in the jury's decision to convict. The European Court similarly found a violation of Art.6 in *Beckles v UK*[74] as the trial judge had not stressed to the jury that they should give "due weight" to the applicant's reliance on legal advice to explain his silence.

In *Birchall*[75] the Court of Appeal made clear that carefully framed directions are required in relation to any adverse inference to be drawn under ss.34 and 35 of the Criminal Justice and Public Order Act 1994 so as to comply with Art.6(1) and (2) of the European Convention.

---

[70] (1996) 22 E.H.R.R. 29, cited at para.11–23.
[71] para.45.
[72] (1997) 23 E.H.R.R. 313, cited at paras 11–10 and 11–26, above.
[73] (2001) 31 E.H.R.R. 1, cited at para.11–22, above.
[74] (2003) 36 E.H.R.R. 13.
[75] [1999] Crim.L.R. 311.

13–18   **Rights necessary for the preparation and conduct of the defence.** The requirement that the prosecution disclose to the defence all material evidence for or against the accused was established in *Edwards v UK*.[76] This is part of the more general right to enable a defence to be presented adequately which is also provided for in Art.6(3). Thus, in *Foucher v France*,[77] the Court reiterated that, according to the principle of equality of arms as one of the features of the wider concept of a fair trial, each party must be afforded a reasonable opportunity to present his case in conditions that do not place him at a disadvantage *vis-à-vis* his opponent.

(See para.12–18 above for discussion on *Edwards and Lewis v UK*[78] and disclosure and public interest immunity, and para.18–30 for impact of Art.6 on disclosure.)

13–19   **Public hearing.** Article 6(1) guarantees a "public hearing" to the accused in the determination of any criminal charge. In *Pretto v Italy*[79] the European Court held that a public hearing is one guarantee for the fairness of a trial: it offers protection against arbitrary decisions and builds confidence by allowing the public to see justice being administered. Determination of whether there has been a public hearing within the meaning of Art.6(1) requires that the proceedings be considered as a whole. The right is not, however, absolute and Art.6(1) provides clear limitations to the right on grounds of public policy, national security, privacy, or where strictly necessary in the interests of justice. In *Richards*[80] the Court of Appeal held that there had been no violation of Art.6(1) where the judge cleared the public gallery (the press being allowed to remain) where a prosecution witness in a murder trial refused to give evidence unless this was done. It was open to the judge to conclude that the interests of justice would have been prejudiced had the witness not given her evidence.

(2) Article 6(2): The right to be presumed innocent

13–20   This Article embodies the principle of the presumption of innocence.[81] Its importance has been emphasised by the Court which has said that Art.6—by protecting the right to a fair trial, and in particular the right to be presumed innocent—is intended to enshrine the fundamental principle of the rule of law.[82] It means that, when carrying out their duties, the members of a court should not start with the preconceived idea that the accused

---

[76] (1993) 15 E.H.R.R. 417, para.36, cited at para.18–30, below.
[77] (1998) 25 E.H.R.R. 234. See also *Barbera v Spain* (1989) 11 E.H.R.R. 360, para.77, where the Court said that it is for the prosecution to inform the accused of the case that will be made against him so that he may prepare and present his defence accordingly.
[78] Application Nos 39647/98 and 40461/98. Judgment, July 22, 2003.
[79] (1984) 6 E.H.R.R. 182.
[80] (1999) 163 J.P. 246.
[81] *Barbera v Spain* (1989) 11 E.H.R.R. 360, para.77.1.
[82] *Salabiaku v France* (1988) 13 E.H.R.R. 379, para.2.8.

has committed the offence charged; the burden of proof is on the prosecution, and any doubt should benefit the accused.[83] Thus, the effect of Art.6(2) is to place the burden of proof on the prosecution, although this is not expressly provided for in the Article.

There is, similarly, no provision as to the standard of proof. However, it is clear that the burden is to provide a sufficiency of evidence to prove guilt. In *Austria v Italy*[84] the Commission, having stated that the burden of proof falls on the prosecution, said that the judges could find the accused guilty only on the basis of direct or indirect evidence sufficiently strong in the eyes of the law to establish his guilt. In these circumstances, the criminal standard in the UK more than meets the requirements.

The provisions of this Article do not prevent the transfer of the burden to the accused in appropriate circumstances in order to prove certain defences.[85] In *King v UK*[86] the European Court held that the presumption in s.101 of the Taxes and Management Act 1970—to the effect that an assessment which is no longer subject to appeal may be taken as evidence that the specified sum is owed—did not contravene Art.6(2). The Court held that "a rebuttable presumption of fact and liability is to be contrasted with an assumption of guilt so as to reverse the burden of proof". It was still open to the applicant to rebut the presumption and the Commissioners still had to prove neglect or willful default.

The impact of Art.6(2) in English criminal law was first considered n domestic courts in *R v DPP Ex p. Kebilene*[87] in relation to s.16A of the Prevention of Terrorism Act 1989 which provided that, where it was proved that an accused was in possession of an item giving rise to a reasonable suspicion that it was possessed for terrorist purposes, the accused was guilty of an offence unless he proved on the balance of probabilities that he did not possess the item for a terrorist purpose. Lord Hope suggested that some legislative techniques would be more objectionable than others. A mere evidential burden, requiring the accused to do no more than raise a reasonable doubt on the issue to which it related would not breach the presumption of innocence. However, a statute which imposes a persuasive burden, requiring the accused to prove, on a balance of probabilities, a fact which is essential to his guilt or innocence, required further examination. In *Lambert*[88] the House of Lords held that ss.28(2) and 28(3) of the Misuse of Drugs Act 1971 which provided for specific knowledge defences on a charge of possession of drugs, were incompatible with the presumption of innocence contained in Art.6(2) of the European Convention. The House of Lords held that it was immaterial whether the

13–21

---

[83] *Barbera v Spain*, above.
[84] 6 Y.B. 740, 782–784 (1963) Com. Rep.
[85] *Lingens v Austria* (1986) 8 E.H.R.R. 407, para.46.
[86] Admissibility Decision, April 8, 2003.
[87] [2000] 2 A.C. 326.
[88] [2002] 2 A.C. 545.

issue of knowledge was characterised as an essential element of the offence or as a defence; the important point was its impact on the issues before the jury. The effect of ss.28(2) and 28(3) was that the accused could be convicted if he succeeded in raising a reasonable doubt on the issue, but failed to discharge the burden of proof on the balance of probabilities. Applying s.3 of the Human Rights Act 1998, their Lordships held that the proper balance could be achieved by reading the provisions as imposing an evidential burden only. Thus, the word "prove" was interpreted to mean "adduces sufficient evidence to raise the issue". Once this hurdle is overcome, it is then for the prosecution to prove guilty knowledge to the ordinary criminal standard.

Since *Lambert* there have been a number of cases considering the compatibility of various statutory provisions with Art.6(2).[89] In *Johnstone*, it was held that the reverse onus in s.92(5) of the Trade Marks Act 1994 was justifiable as the defence did not touch an essential element of the offence. A reverse onus is justifiable where there is "a compelling reason why it is fair and reasonable to deny the accused person the protection normally guaranteed to everyone by the presumption of innocence."[90] Two such compelling reasons were identified: (i) those who trade in branded products must be on their guard against counterfeits, and (ii) that prosecutors will rarely be able to trace the person who supplied the goods to the defendant.

(3) Article 6(3): the minimum rights

13–22 The minimum rights set out in Art.6(3) are to enable the accused to conduct his defence properly by knowing the charges, having time to prepare and the opportunity to present his defence: they are all facets of the right guaranteed by Art.6(1). These rights are familiar to common lawyers. Thus, in *Brown (Winston)*,[91] Lord Hope said that the right of the accused to have adequate time and facilities for the preparation of his defence (Art.6(3)(b)) has for long been part of our law relating to the conduct of criminal trials and included time for the investigation of the credibility of defence witnesses in order to decide which to call and which to reject.

Article 6(3) might be relevant to pre-trial proceedings if the fairness of the trial is likely to be seriously prejudiced by an initial failure to comply with its provisions. In *Magee v UK*[92] the European Court of Human Rights held there to have been a violation of Art.6(3)(c) in circumstances where the accused was held for over 48 hours without access to legal advice. Similarly, in *Brennan v UK*[93] the European Court found a violation of

---

[89] This case law was reviewed by Lord Nicholls in *Johnstone* [2003] 1 W.L.R. 1736 at paras 49 and 50. See also *R. (on the application of Grundy & Co. Excavations Ltd and Sean Parry) v Halton Division Magistrates' Court, The Forestry Commission* (2003) 67 Jo.Crim.L. 363.
[90] *ibid.*
[91] [1998] 1 Cr.App.R. 66, 77.
[92] *The Times*, June 20, 2000.
[93] [2002] Crim.L.R. 216.

Art.6(3)(c) where the accused had been denied an opportunity to consult with his lawyer in private while being held in police custody. In *M and La Rose*,[94] however, the Divisional Court held that there had been no violation of Art.6 where the accused had been denied the possibility of consulting privately with a lawyer: one interview had taken place in a police cell and the other in the presence of the custody sergeant. The Court held that the conditions, although less than ideal, still provided the accused adequate time and facilities for the preparation of his defence and that there was no evidence that any police officer had eavesdropped on his conversation. The Divisional Court appears to have held that there will be no violation of Art.6 unless prejudice is shown to have resulted. It is doubtful whether this is in line with the decisions of the European Court which make plain that it is unnecessary for an accused to demonstrate prejudice in showing a violation of Art.6.

The purpose of Art.6(3)(d) is to ensure for the defence complete equality   **13–23**
of treatment in obtaining the attendance and exaination of witnesses as that enjoyed by the prosecution.[95] The effect of the Article is that, as a general rule, the defence must be given the opportunity to cross-examine all the witnesses who give evidence against the accused. Two illustrations may be given:

(i) In *Unterpringer v Austria*[96] the accused was convicted on the evidence of statements made to the police by his wife and stepdaughter which were read out in court after the witnesses had exercised their right under national law to refuse to give evidence. The Court said that in itself the reading out of the statements could not be regarded as being inconsistent with Art.6(1) and (3)(d), but the use made of them as evidence must nevertheless comply with the rights of the defence, especially where the accused has not had an opportunity at any stage to question the maker of the statement.[97] As a result the Court held that there had been a breach of Art.6(1) and (3).

(ii) In *Kostovski v The Netherlands*[98] statements made by two anonymous witnesses were admitted in evidence. Kostovski complained that he had not received a fair trial as the defence did not have the opportunity to examine the witnesses. The Court found that there had been a violation of Art.6(3)(d), since no opportunity was afforded to the applicant, although he wished to challenge and question the anonymous witnesses. The Court said that:

> "In principle all the evidence must be produced in the presence of the accused at a public hearing with a view to adversarial argument. This does not mean, however, that in order to be used as evidence state-

---

[94] [2002] Crim.L.R. 215
[95] *Austria v Italy*, 6 Y.B. 740, 772 (1963) Comm. Rep.
[96] (1986) 13 E.H.R.R. 175.
[97] para.31.
[98] (1990) 13 E.H.R.R. 454.

ments of witnesses should always be made at a public hearing in court: to use such statements obtained at the pre-trial stage is not in itself inconsistent with paragraphs 3(d) and (1) of Article 6, provided the rights of the defence have been respected. As a rule these rights require that an accused should be given an adequate and proper opportunity to challenge and question a witness against him either at the time the witness was making his statement or some later stage of the proceedings."[99]

However, in *Kostovski* the Court also observed that the admissibility of evidence is primarily a matter for regulation by national law (*Schenk*)[1] and that as a general rule it is for the national courts to assess the evidence before them (*Barbera*).[2] Accordingly, the Court said that in the instant case its task was not to express a view as to whether the statements in question were correctly admitted and assessed, but rather to ascertain whether the proceedings, considered as a whole—including the way in which the evidence was taken—was fair.

On the other hand, in *Doorson v Netherlands*,[3] the Court noted that, although Art.6 did not expressly require the interests of victims and witnesses to be taken into account, their lives, liberty and security may be at stake and in appropriate cases their interests must be balanced against those of the defence. Similarly, the Commission has said that in proceedings relating to rape and other sexual offences, measures may be taken to protect the victim providing they can be reconciled with an adequate and effective exercise of the rights of the defence.[4] In *Doorson*, after balancing the interests of witnesses with the rights of the accused, it was held that the use of anonymous witness at trial did not violate Art.6(3)(d). By contrast, in *Van Mechelen v Netherlands*[5] it was held that permitting police officers to give evidence anonymously violated both Art.6(3)(d) and 6(1). The use of anonymous witnesses may only be resorted to in exceptional circumstances. In order to protect the life, liberty and security of witnesses, States must organise criminal proceedings in such a way to ensure that such interests are not put at risk. Accordingly, it may be legitimate for police authorities to preserve anonymity of an agent in undercover operations.[6] However, a conviction should not be based either solely or to a decisive extent on anonymous statements.[7] In *Van Mechelen* the anonymity had not been strictly necessary and the conviction was based almost exclusively on the

---

[99] para.41. See also *Windisch v Austria* (1990) 13 E.H.R.R. 281, paras 25–30 and *Saidi v France* (1994) 17 E.H.R.R. 251.
[1] (1988) 13 E.H.R.R. 242.
[2] (1988) 11 E.H.R.R. 360.
[3] (1996) 22 E.H.R.R. 330, para.70.
[4] *Baegen*, Appl. No.16696190 (1994), para.77.
[5] 25 E.H.R.R. 647.
[6] *ibid.* at para.57.
[7] *ibid.* at para.55.

anonymous evidence. In J^8 the Divisional Court held, on the basis of *Van Mechelen*, that prosecuting authorities had not acted improperly in withholding copies of audio and video surveillance tapes obtained by an undercover police officer.

The right to obtain the attendance of witnesses "does not imply the right to have witnesses called without restriction".[9] In *Austria v Italy*[10] the Commission said that the Article did not mean that municipal law cannot lay down conditions for the admission and examination of witnesses provided that such conditions are identical for witnesses on both sides.

D. Article 8: right to respect for private and family life

1. Everyone has the right to respect for his private and family life, his home and his correspondence.

2. There shall be no interference by a public authority with the exercise of this right except such as is in accordance with the law and is necessary in a democratic society in the interests of national security, public safety or the economic well-being of the country, for the prevention of disorder or crime, for the protection of health or morals, or for the protection of the rights and freedoms of others.

13–24

The essential purpose of Art.8 is to protect the individual against arbitrary interference by the public authorities.[11] In *Niemietz*[12] the Court declined to attempt an exhaustive definition of the notion of "private life", but said that it would be too restrictive to limit the notion to an "inner circle" and to exclude entirely the outside world. As a result the Court found that the notion of "private life" extended to activities of a professional or business nature and held that the search of a lawyer's office (in search of material which might lead to the uncovering of the identity of the author of an insulting, anonymous letter written to a judge) amounted to a violation of Art.8(1).

The Article has been held to cover telephone conversations.[13] In *Halford v UK*[14] this cover was extended to telephone calls from business premises (in that case, calls made by the applicant on her office telephone at Merseyside Police Headquarters). However, it will not be every intercept (by any means) that violates Art.8. In *Ajula*[15] the prosecution successfully applied to admit evidence of a telephone intercept in the Netherlands of a conversation between two Dutch offenders and the defendants in England. The Court of Appeal held that there had been no breach of Art.8. The

---

[8] *The Times*, July 8, 1999.
[9] *Austria v Italy*, above.
[10] *ibid.*
[11] *Niemietz v Germany*, Series A, No.251-B, para.31 (1992).
[12] *Klass v Germany* (1979) 2 E.H.R.R. 214.
[13] (1997) 24 E.H.R.R. 523.
[14] (1997) 24 E.H.R.R. 523.
[15] [1998] 2 Cr.App.R. 16.

Court said that Art.8 did not ban interference by a public authority with a person's right to privacy: what the Article required was that (a) the interference was in accordance with the law (in the instant case, Dutch law) and (b) was necessary in a democratic society for the prevention of crime.

13–25   Courts must balance the individual's right to privacy against a public interest. For example, measures compelling the disclosure of information concerning a person's HIV status call for careful scrutiny by the court. However, the interest of the patient and the public interest in protecting medical data could be outweighed by the interest in investigation and prosecution of crime.[16]

"Family life" has been broadly interpreted by the European Court and covers a whole range of relationships, both formal and informal: *Marckx v Belgium*.[17] In *Kroon v Netherlands*[18] it was held to cover the relationship between an unmarried couple. However, in *Pearce*[19] the Court of Appeal held that Art.8(1) did not protect a cohabitee of defendant from being compelled to give evidence. The interests of the family are to be weighed against those of the community at large. It was held that there was no basis to extend the meaning of the statutory protection for spouses to non-married partners or children.

As an exception to a guaranteed right, Art.8(2) is to be narrowly interpreted.[20] The term "in accordance with law" not only necessitates compliance with domestic law but also relates to the quality required to be compatible with the rule of law: *Halford v UK*.[21] The domestic law must provide some protection to the individual against arbitrary interference with his Art.8 rights in connection with surveillance or interception of communications by public authorities: it should be clear enough to indicate the circumstances in which such measures may be taken.[22]

The European Court found a violation of Art.8 in *PG and JA v UK*[23] where the police had placed a listening device in the house of an associate of suspected robbers and conversations were monitored. Authorisation had been obtained from the Chief Constable, but the Court found that the Home Office Guidelines governing the listening devices used did not satisfy the requirement of being "in accordance with the law".

13–26   The mere fact that evidence has been obtained in violation of the Article

---

[16] *Z v Finland* (1998) 25 E.H.R.R. 371.
[17] 2 E.H.R.R. 330. See also *Moustaquim v Belgium* 13 E.H.R.R. 802, *Boyle v UK* 19 E.H.R.R. 179, and *Gaskin v UK* 12 E.H.R.R. 36.
[18] 19 E.H.R.R. 263.
[19] [2002] 1 Cr.App.R. 551.
[20] *Klass v Germany*, above, para.42.
[21] Above, para.49.
[22] *ibid.*
[23] [2002] Crim.L.R. 308. An additional violation of Art.8 was found because police had also placed listening devices in police cells in which the applicants were put (the purpose being to obtain voice samples).

does not mean that a trial is unfair. Thus, in *Schenk v Switzerland*[24] the Court held that the admission in evidence of the recording of a telephone conversation in breach of the right of privacy in Art.8 did not violate Art.6(1). Similarly, in *Wood v UK*[25] the European Court held that the covert recording of defendants conversations while in police custody could amount to a violation of Art.8, but observed that the use at trial of material obtained without a proper legal basis or through unlawful means will not, generally, without more, of itself offend the standard of fairness imposed by Art.6(1) where proper procedural safeguards are in place and the nature and source of the material is not tainted.

In *P*[26] Lord Hobhouse said that:

"the fair use of intercept evidence at trial is not in breach of Article 6 even if the evidence is unlawfully obtained. It is a cogent factor in favour of the admission of intercept evidence that one of the parties to the relevant conversation is going to be a witness at the trial and give evidence of what was said during it."

He went on:

"An assessment and adjudication under section 78 [PACE] is the appropriate and right way in which to respond to an application to exclude evidence on the ground of a breach of a right to privacy. ... The criterion to be applied is the criterion of fairness in Article 6 which is likewise the criteria to be applied by the judge under section 78."

Similarly in *Lawrence*[27] it was held that the use of intrusive probes did not amount to a violation of Art.8. Moreover, if there had been any violation of Art.8 it would only affect admissibility under s.78 if it involved unfairness. A violation of Art.8 is only relevant if it interferes with the accused's right to a fair trial. Thus, in *Loveridge*[28] it was held that, even though Art.8 was contravened as a result of the secret filming of the accused at court for identification purspuses, the trial itself had not been in anyway unfair. While a breach of Art.8 may not be regarded by itself as definitive on the question of admissibility, a trial judge, when considering an application under s.78, should attach considerable importance to any violation of Art.8 and balance all the circumstances accordingly.[29]

---

[24] (1988) 13 E.H.R.R. 242, cited at para.10–09, above.
[25] Application No.23414/02, January 20, 2004.
[26] [2002] 1 A.C. 146.
[27] [2002] Crim.L.R. 584.
[28] [2001] Cr.App.R. 591.
[29] *XYZ, The Times*, May 23, 2000.

4. VIOLATIONS OF CONVENTION RIGHTS

13–27   The object of this section is to discuss the general rules governing exclusion under this heading. (Examples of exclusion are discussed under the relevant topics, for example hearsay, illegally obtained evidence, disclosure, inferences from silence.) A Judge of the High Court of New Zealand said that the principal impact of that country's Bill of Rights Act 1980 on a day-to-day basis is in the area of criminal justice, concerning police powers of search and seizure, police questioning and jury trial.[30]

The European Court of Human Rights has employed a variety of methods of interpretation of the Convention, for example (a) to give the words of the various provisions their ordinary meaning[31]; (b) to use grammatical analysis[32]; (c) to determine the way that the provision fits into the Convention as a whole ("the interpretation ... must be in harmony with the logic of the Convention"[33] or, finally, (d) to employ a purposive interpretation, *i.e.* to consider the purpose of the provision. Thus, in *Lawless v Ireland*,[34] the Court said that the meaning arrived at by grammatical analysis (of Art.5, in the instant case) was fully in harmony with the purpose of the Convention, which is to protect the freedom and security of the individual against arbitrary detention or arrest.

The Court has always regarded the Convention as "a living instrument" which must be interpreted in the light of present-day conditions.[35] However—as Judge Martens, President of the Supreme Court of the Netherlands (and a former Judge of the European Court), has pointed out—the highly abstract form in which the norms enshrined in the Convention are worded offers little assistance when it comes to working out what a particular provision implies in a specific case: national courts, turning to the case law of the Court for guidance, often do so in vain because the Court confines its reasoning strictly to the case before it.[36]

13–28   However, national courts must keep in mind their responsibilities under the Convention. In *Sadik v Greece*[37] the Court confirmed that the supervisory machinery set up by the Convention is "subsidiary to the national human rights protection systems". The effect is that the domestic courts play the primary role in safeguarding the rights embodied in the Convention: it is their responsibility to see that Convention law is complied with,

---

[30] Mr Justice Kenneth Keith, Address to Conference of International Society for Reform of the Criminal Law, London, August 1997.
[31] *Johnston v Ireland*, Series A, No.112, para.52 (1986); *Lawless v Ireland*, Series A, No.3, para.14 (1961).
[32] *Lawless*, above.
[33] *Klass v Germany*, Series A, No.28, para.68 (1978).
[34] Above.
[35] *Tyrer v UK*, Series A, No.26, para.31 (1978).
[36] "Incorporating the European Convention: The Role of the Judiciary" [1998] E.H.R.L.R. 5, 13.
[37] (1997) 24 E.H.R.R. 323, para.30.

ensure that it has full effect, and provide effective protection of rights conferred on individuals by the Convention.[38] Accordingly, if no guidance is to be found in the Court's case law, the national court must be aware of its responsibility to provide effective protection.

The primary role afforded to national authorities in performing human rights protection is reflected by the European Court in the "margin of appreciation" doctrine. The European Court allows States a certain leeway, or "margin of appreciation", when considering allegations of human rights violations. In *Kebilene*[39] Lord Hope observed that the "margin of appreciation" doctrine had no direct application in the national courts. Nevertheless, the Convention should be seen as an expression of fundamental principles rather than a set of mere rules. Accordingly, in certain areas it is appropriate for courts to recognise that there is an area of judgment within which the judiciary will defer, on democratic grounds, to the elected body or person whose act or decision is said to be incompatible with the Convention.

The Court's powers under s.8 of the Human Rights Act 1998 to exclude evidence on the ground that an act was incompatible with the Convention must thus be exercised having regard to the wording and intention of the Convention, the relevant case law and the Court's responsibilities under the Convention.

In debate in the House of Lords on the Bill, Lord Williams of Mostyn, **13–29** Parliamentary Under-Secretary of State at the Home Office, said that the solution in a civil or criminal case where a Convention incompatibility point is raised will be "infinitely variable". By way of analogy the Minister referred to the Court's powers under s.78 of the Police and Criminal Evidence Act 1984 to take steps by way of exclusion of evidence if the case may become unfair.[40] It is submitted that the analogy is apt. The test under s.78 is to ask whether a trial containing the evidence in question would be unfair.[41] The resolution of Convention points will require that the court answer a very similar question. (It should also be noted that—since the UK played a prominent role in drafting it[42]—the Convention may be thought to express the common law and its notions of fair trial.) Thus, in *Porter v Magill*[43] the Divisional Court said that it did not consider that the concept of fairness in Art.6 differed in any way from fairness as understood in domestic law. In the Divisional Court in *Kebilene*[44] Lord Bingham C.J. said:

---

[38] Judge Martens, *op.cit.*, 8–9.
[39] [2000] 2 A.C. 326.
[40] Second Reading Debate, *Hansard*, HL, Vol.582, col.1311, November 3, 1997.
[41] See para.10–28, above.
[42] "Rights Brought Home", Home Office, Cm. 3782, para.1.2.
[43] [1998] 96 L.G.R. 157, 172.
[44] [2000] 2 A.C. 326.

"Any human rights instrument must represent a compromise between the rights of the individual and the rights of other individuals who collectively make up the community, society or state. But a human rights instrument such as the Convention is a measure to protect human rights and fundamental freedoms. This does not mean that all Convention rights are equal: some may be the subject of derogation by contracting states, others may not; some (such as Article 3) are expressed without any qualification, others (such as Articles 8, 9, 10 and 11) are subject to express qualifications; some rights have been recognized in the Act of 1998 itself as deserving enhanced protection: see sections 12 and 13. The right to a fair trial protected by Article 6 is not a right from which a contracting state is not permitted to derogate; but nor is it a right which is in any material way qualified. I can readily conceive of circumstances in which it would be doubtful whether the presence of a certain feature (in itself undesirable) was such as to render a trial unfair; but I can conceive of no circumstances in which, having concluded that that feature rendered the trial unfair, the court would not go on to find a violation of Article 6."

Thus, not all violations of the Convention will result in the exclusion of evidence. The guiding principle will, in most cases, be whether the admission of evidence is unfair.

PART 5

Identification and Corroboration

CHAPTER 14
Identification

Evidence of identification often plays a most important part in a trial. It is therefore considered as a separate subject at this stage. **14–01**

There are various means of identifying a defendant: visually, by finger prints, DNA, the possession of incriminating articles, by voice, or by the admission of similar fact evidence. Each is treated separately below.

1. VISUAL IDENTIFICATION

Experience shows that visual identification is imperfect, whether a stranger is mistaken for a friend; or a victim gains no more than a fleeting glance at his assailant. The law has therefore developed rules about identification. **14–02**

A. General rules: the Turnbull guidelines

In 1970 the House of Lords held that it would be undesirable to lay down as a rule of law that the judge had to give a specific warning to the jury of the dangers of acting on evidence of visual identification.[1] However, as a result of mounting public concern about miscarriages of justice which had occurred in cases of mistaken identity, a departmental committee was set up to report on evidence of identification. The recommendations of the committee in its Report[2] were followed by the Court of Appeal in the leading case of *Turnbull*.[3] In that case, Lord Widgery C.J., giving the judgment of the Court of Appeal, laid down the following guidelines.[4] **14–03**

> "First, whenever the case against an accused depends wholly or substantially on the correctness of one or more identifications of the accused which the defence alleges to be mistaken, the judge should warn the jury of the special need for caution before convicting the accused in reliance on the correctness of the identification or identifications. In addition, he should instruct them as to the reason for the need for such a warning and should make some reference to the pos-

---

[1] *Arthurs v Att-Gen for Northern Ireland* (1971) 55 Cr.App.R. 161.
[2] "Report on Evidence of Identification in Criminal Cases", Cmnd. (1976), para.338 (known as the "Devlin Report" after the Committee's chairman).
[3] [1977] Q.B. 224.
[4] *ibid.* at 228.

sibility that a mistaken witness can be a convincing one and that a number of such witnesses can all be mistaken. Provided this is done in clear terms the judge need not use any particular form of words.

Secondly, the judge should direct the jury to examine closely the circumstances in which the identification by each witness came to be made. How long did the witness have the accused under observation? At what distance? In what light? Was the observation impeded in anyway, as for example by passing traffic or a press of people? Had the witness ever seen the accused before? How often? If only occasionally, had he any special reason for remembering the accused? How long elapsed between the original observation and the subsequent identification to the police? Was there any material discrepancy between the description of the accused given to the police by the witness when first seen by them and his actual appearance? If in any case, whether it is being dealt with summarily or on indictment, the prosecution have reason to believe that there is such a material discrepancy they should supply the accused or his legal advisers with particulars of the description the police were first given. In all cases if the accused asks to be given particulars of such descriptions, the prosecution should supply them. Finally, he should remind the jury of any specific weaknesses which had appeared in the identification evidence.

Recognition may be more reliable than identification of a stranger; but even when the witness is purporting to recognise someone whom he knows, the jury should be reminded that mistakes in recognition of close relatives and friends are sometimes made."

14–04   *Turnbull* thus makes it clear that: (a) there is a special need for caution when the prosecution case depends on evidence of visual identification; (b) the summing-up should contain a warning of the need for caution and an explanation as to why caution is needed; (c) the summing-up should deal with the circumstances of the identification in the particular case; and (d) the judge should point out that a convincing witness may be mistaken.

Failure to follow the guidelines is likely to result in a conviction being quashed and will do so if, in the judgment of the Court of Appeal, the verdict is either unsatisfactory or unsafe.[5] The advice given by the Court of Appeal in *Turnbull* should be followed by justices.[6] It should be followed in every case involving identification (there is no exception in the case of identification by police officers).[7]

Lord Widgery C.J. said that the principles in *Turnbull* should be strictly followed.[8] However, there is no set formula which has to be followed

[5] *Turnbull* [1977] Q.B. 224, 231; *Reid v R*, below, n.7.
[6] *McShane v Northumbria Chief Constable* (1980) 72 Cr.App.R. 208, 211, *per* Lord Widgery.
[7] *Reid v R* [1990] A.C. 363, 392, PC.
[8] *ibid.*

slavishly, since each summing-up must be tailored to the particular case. "It would be wrong to interpret or apply *Turnbull* inflexibly."[9] (These admonitions were reiterated by the Privy Council when the court said that *Turnbull* was not a statute and that a mechanistic approach to the direction was to be deplored: what was required was to comply with the sense and spirit of the guidance in *Turnbull*.[10]) Accordingly, the summing-up on identification should not be the subject of fine analysis or strict construction. It is simply a warning of a particular problem and what is required is a warning sufficient to the facts. As a result, on appeal, it is the adequacy of the summing-up as a whole that should be considered against the evidence rather than simply applying a universal template.[11]

Despite these admonitions, submissions have continued to be made on the basis that the *Turnbull* guidelines have not been followed. Two points, in particular, may be noted: **14–05**

(a) Does the judge have to warn the jury that a mistaken witness may be a convincing one? Lord Griffiths described this as the fundamental danger of identification evidence.[12] However, in *Rose v R*[13] a conviction was upheld, although the Judge did not say in terms that a "convincing" witness may be mistaken. (This was not a "fleeting glance" case; a strong warning had been given and the Judge referred repeatedly to the possibility of mistaken identification; as a result, the Privy Council did not regard the absence of the word "convincing" as fatal to the summing-up.) In *Mills v R*[14] the Privy Council again said that the judge was not required to say that a mistaken witness may be a convincing one. It is, however, submitted that only in an exceptional case should this important part of the direction be omitted. This is because the whole purpose of the direction is to alert the jury to dangers of which they may not be aware and this part of the direction is, accordingly, crucial.

(b) Does the judge have to list the weaknesses in the identification evidence? In *Fergus*[15] the Court of Appeal said that the judge should summarise such weaknesses as are arguably exposed by the evidence. However, this requirement has been explained and modified by the Court of Appeal in subsequent cases. Thus, in

---

[9] *Keane* (1977) 65 Cr.App.R. 247, 248, *per* Scarman L.J. In *Keane* the Court of Appeal held that the summing-up fell short of "the requirements of sound practice" in that the warning was muffled and confused; the weaknesses in the evidence were not fully exposed; and misleading comments were made about the defendant's appearance and the effect of a false alibi.
[10] *Mills v R* [1995] 1 W.L.R. 511, 518.
[11] *Beckles and Montague* [1999] Crim.L.R. 148.
[12] [1989] 2 W.L.R. 924, 935.
[13] [1995] Crim.L.R. 939.
[14] Above.
[15] (1994) 98 Cr.App.R. 313, 321.

Barnes,[16] Lord Taylor C.J. said that every minor discrepancy should not be categorised as a weakness and that *Fergus* did not impose such a regime: it was for the judge's discretion whether such matters were referred to in his review of the evidence or categorised as potential weaknesses. It has now been held that, while the judge must remind the jury of specific weaknesses, there is no mandatory requirement that he should summarise them in every case.[17] It may be more helpful to the jury (and convenient) to deal with the weaknesses at appropriate points when reviewing the evidence.[18]

Turnbull's case is concerned with the identification of a defendant. However, an analogous direction may be required where identification is in issue, and the identification is not that of the defendant but of another person. In *Bath*[19] the Court of Appeal held that where in such a case there is evidence that at the relevant time the defendant was with another person, the purported identification of the other person should be the subject of a *Turnbull* direction.

B. Withdrawing the case from the jury

14–06   Lord Widgery said in *Turnbull*[20]:

"When in the judgment of the trial judge, the quality of the identifying evidence is poor, as for example when it depends solely on a fleeting glance or on a longer observation made in difficult conditions, the situation is very different. The judge should then withdraw the case from the jury and direct an acquittal unless there is other evidence which goes to support the correctness of the identification. This may be corroboration in the sense lawyers use that word; but it need not be so if its effect is to make the jury sure that there has been no mistaken identification."

The normal time to make such a ruling is at the end of the prosecution case. It may occasionally be made after all the evidence has been called. The Court of Appeal has said that in an exceptional case the position may be so clear on the depositions and statements that a ruling may be made earlier, but that a trial-within-a-trial should not be held for this purpose.[21]

[16] [1995] 2 Cr.App.R. 491, 520.
[17] *Mussell and Dalton* [1995] Crim.L.R. 887; *Pattinson and Exley* [1996] 2 Cr.App.R. 51, 56.
[18] *ibid.*
[19] [1990] Crim.L.R. 716.
[20] [1977] Q.B. 224, 229. There is no conflict between *Turnbull* and the principles set out in *Galbraith* [1981] 1 W.L.R. 1039 governing the court's powers when a submission of no case is made: para.16–10, below.
[21] *Flemming* (1988) 86 Cr.App.R. 32, 36.

In determining whether the case should be withdrawn from the jury, it is the quality of the evidence that matters. If the quality is good, the case can be left to the jury, even though there is no corroborative or supporting evidence. An example of such a case would be one in which there has been a long period of observation. Thus, if police officers keep observation on premises for a week, during which time a particular man is a regular visitor to the premises, that identification of the man as the defendant may be left to the jury since the officers will have had ample opportunity to learn what the man looked like and could therefore identify him at a later date more safely. A further example occurs in a case where the defendant is recognised by somebody who knows him well. In such a case the dangers of incorrect identification by a stranger are not present. There remains, however, the question of whether the recognition is correct. Such a question may usually be left to the jury unless the circumstances in which the purported recognition was made were very unsatisfactory.

If, on the other hand, the quality of the evidence is poor and there is no evidence[22] to support the identification, the judge should withdraw the case from the jury and:

> "when in the judgment of the trial judge the quality of the identifying evidence is poor, as for example when it depends on a fleeting glance or on a longer observation in difficult conditions ... the judge should then withdraw the case from the jury and direct an acquittal unless there is other evidence which goes to support the correctness of the identification."[23]

The quality of the evidence will depend in each case on the circumstances and the conditions of the identification. Thus, if the victim of a "mugging" has had no real opportunity to identify his assailant or only sees him for a split second,[24] supporting evidence of any identification made by the victim may be necessary. If there is only the identifying witness (and no supporting evidence) the judge must satisfy himself that it would be safe for the jury to convict in reliance on that evidence alone.[25]

When the judge comes to decide whether the case should be stopped, he will have had the opportunity of observing the witnesses. Such observation may greatly influence his decision. Since the Court of Appeal does not have

14–07

---

[22] A submission of no case should not succeed merely because an identifying witness has not been called but his statement has been read under the Criminal Justice Act 1967, s.9: *Ellis v Jones* [1973] 2 All E.R. 893.

[23] *Turnbull* [1977] Q.B. 224, 229–230, *per* Lord Widgery C.J.

[24] In *Garner v Chief Constable of Manchester*, *The Times*, May 14, 1983, the Divisional Court quashed a conviction which had depended on the identification of the defendant by a police officer who had only seen his assailant for a split second.

[25] In *Smith and Doe* (1987) 85 Cr.App.R. 197 the Court of Appeal held that the trial judge should have withdrawn the case where the one identifying witness (who was elderly) was confused and unclear.

this opportunity, that court may in some cases be reluctant to interfere with the judge's decision. Thus, in *Hayes*[26] the Court did not overrule the Judge's decision to allow the case to go to the jury (although it was borderline) on the ground that the Court was confident that if the Judge, having seen the witnesses, had any doubt as to the reliability of the identifying evidence, he would have stopped the case. The judge should not reveal to the jury that he has decided that there is sufficient evidence of identification available and has not withdrawn the case from them.[27]

C. Supporting evidence of a visual identification

14–08 Supporting evidence need not be corroboration in the sense lawyers use the word.[28] However, the effect of the evidence must be to make the jury sure that there has not been a mistaken identification.[29] One identifying witness can support another, provided the quality of the evidence is good enough.[30] The conduct of the defendant may also provide supporting evidence. In *Long*,[31] the defendant was identified by three witnesses during a robbery, but each had only a limited opportunity for observation. When arrested some time after the robbery the defendant claimed to know who had done it and offered to help to find those responsible. The Court of Appeal in *Turnbull* commented with reference to *Long* that "it was an odd coincidence that the witnesses should have identified a man who had behaved in this way. In our judgment odd coincidences can, if unexplained, be supporting evidence."[32]

Similarly, identification evidence may sometimes be supported by the fact that the defendant has put forward a false alibi. However, a false alibi can only be relied upon in support of identification evidence where the jury are satisfied that the sole reason for its being put forward was to deceive them on the issue of identification and the jury must be so directed.[33]

The judge should point out to the jury evidence which is capable of supporting the identification.[34] Accordingly, the judge may direct the jury that the identification by one witness can constitute support for the identification by another, provided that he warns them that even a number of honest witnesses can all be mistaken.[35] In the case of cumulative identifications, *i.e.* identification of a defendant in relation to a number of similar

---

[26] (1977) 64 Cr.App.R. 194.
[27] *Smith and Doe*, above, at 200.
[28] *i.e.* independent evidence implicating the defendant in the offence charged: *Baskerville* [1916] 2 K.B. 658. The corroboration rules have been abolished: paras 15–08, *et seq.*, below.
[29] *Turnbull* [1977] Q.B. 224, 230, *per* Lord Widgery C.J.
[30] *Weeder* (1980) 71 Cr.App.R. 228.
[31] (1973) 57 Cr.App.R. 871.
[32] [1977] Q.B. 224, 230.
[33] *Turnbull*, above, at 230; *Keane* (1977) 65 Cr.App.R. 247. Failure so to direct them is a material misdirection: *Drake* (1996) Crim.L.R. 109.
[34] *Turnbull*, above, at 230.
[35] *Weeder*, above, at 231; *Breslin* (1985) 80 Cr.App.R. 226.

offences, the jury may consider the identification evidence of all the witnesses, provided that they are satisfied (on evidence other than that of visual identification) that the same man committed all the offences.[36] Thus, if a defendant is charged with a number of street robberies which show a similar pattern (for example targeting women at night when returning to their cars in a city centre and robbing them of their handbags at knifepoint), the jury may be invited to consider whether the robberies were all the work of one man, based on the similarities in the offences. Then, if on the evidence other than the visual identifications, they are satisfied that one man committed all the offences, they may consider all the identification evidence in deciding whether the defendant is the man, *i.e.* they may use the evidence of one identifying witness to support the evidence of another.[37]

If the defence is alibi the judge should tell the jury that if they reject that **14–09** defence it does not necessarily support an identification[38] (the defendant, although innocent, may have put the alibi forward in a mistaken attempt to bolster his chances of acquittal). A similar direction should be given if the prosecution rely in support of an identification on lies told by the defendant: see para.16–17, below.

The judge should also warn the jury about circumstances which the jury may think support an identification but which in fact do not do so, for example the fact that the defendant has not given evidence,[39] or the fact that the jury reject alibi evidence.[40] The judge must make it clear that it is for the jury to decide whether they accept the evidence and, if they do, whether it in fact supports the evidence of identification.[41]

It is not always necessary for the judge to warn the jury of evidence or circumstances which the jury may think is supporting evidence when it does not have this quality. In *Sawoniuk*[42] the Court of Appeal noted that in their experience many *Turnbull* directions do not contain such a direction, perhaps because it does not feature in the succinct form of words recommended by the Judicial Studies Board. The omission of such a direction may be of little significance where no such supporting evidence, capable of being wrongly relied upon, exists.

D. Cases in which Turnbull is not applicable

Turnbull was intended primarily to deal with cases involving "fleeting **14–10**

---

[36] *Barnes* [1995] 2 Cr.App.R. 491.
[37] See paras 7–41 *et seq.*, above, for further discussion on admissibility of evidence of propensity to commit crime charged.
[38] *Francis* [1990] 1 W.L.R. 1264, 1270.
[39] *Turnbull*, above, at 230. However, the Court also said that the judge would be entitled to tell the jury that, when assessing the identification evidence, they could take into consideration the fact that it was uncontradicted by evidence coming from the defendant himself.
[40] *Pemberton* (1994) 99 Cr.App.R. 228.
[41] *Akaidere* [1990] Crim.L.R. 808.
[42] [2000] 2 Cr.App.R. 220 at 240.

encounters".[43] It is, however, sometimes argued that where identification is in issue, *Turnbull* must always be applied. This is not the case. Where, for instance, one of two known people is responsible for an offence and the issue is which of the two was the offender, it is not appropriate to apply *Turnbull*. Thus, in *Hewett*[44] offences had been committed by the driver of a car. Police officers gave evidence that they had followed a man driving this car in the King's Road. There was a woman passenger. The defendant alleged that the woman had been driving. The Court of Appeal held that, since the issue was whether the man or woman was driving, *Turnbull* was not appropriate.

Similarly, a *Turnbull* direction is not necessary when the defendant's presence at the scene of an offence is admitted and the only issue is as to what he is doing: *Slater*.[45] In *Oakwell*[46] a police constable had been assaulted and knocked to the ground. It was alleged that while he was on the ground he may have been confused and thought that because the defendant was standing beside him when he got up, the defendant must have been his assailant. The Court of Appeal held that this was not the sort of identity problem with which *Turnbull* is intended to cope.

On the other hand, a *Turnbull* direction will be necessary if there is a possibility that a witness may have mistaken one person for another. Thus, in *Thornton*[47] the Court of Appeal held that a warning was necessary in a case where the defendant admitted he was present at the scene, but there were others—similarly dressed—also present and there was a possibility that the witness may have mistaken the defendant for one of them. (The distinction between the need for a warning in *Thornton* and the absence of that need in *Slater* lies in the possibility of a mistake about identification. In the former case, there was a possibility that the witness was mistaken in his identification of the defendant. In the latter case, the possibility of mistake related to what the defendant was doing.)

14–11 A similar distinction is to be found in cases where the credibility of the identifying witnesses is in issue. In *Cape*[48] the Court of Appeal said that a *Turnbull* warning is not necessary where the only issue is whether the witness is truthful or not. (In *Cape* the witness knew all three defendants and the defence alleged that there had been a frame-up.)

On the other hand, in *Shand*[49] the Privy Council said that, even where credibility is the sole line of defence, the judge would normally have to tell the jury to consider whether they are satisfied that the witness was not mistaken in view of the dangers of mistake referred to in *Turnbull*. (In

---

[43] *Oakwell* [1978] 1 W.L.R. 32, 37 *per* Lord Widgery C.J.
[44] [1978] R.T.R. 174.
[45] [1995] 1 Cr.App.R. 584.
[46] Above.
[47] [1995] Cr.App.R. 578.
[48] [1996] 1 Cr.App.R 191.
[49] [1996] 2 Cr.App.R. 204.

Shand the defence case was that two identifying witnesses, who knew the defendant, were not mistaken, but were lying in their evidence.)

It is submitted that the distinction between these cases lies in the possibility of mistake in the identification. If there is a possibility that the witness is mistaken in his identification (albeit that the thrust of the defence is that he is lying) then a *Turnbull* direction is necessary. However, if (on the evidence and as a matter of common sense) there is no possibility of mistake and either the witness is telling the truth or he is not, then a *Turnbull* direction would only serve to confuse the jury.

A *Turnbull* direction is also necessary in the following cases: **14–12**

(a) if the prosecution rely chiefly on circumstantial evidence and, only additionally, on evidence of visual identification[50];

(b) where there are a number of identifications (all alleged to be mistaken) which are said to be support one another[51];

(c) where a person is seen on a video camera going into a place and is arrested there shortly afterwards.[52]

The Court of Appeal has held that a direction analogous to that required by *Turnbull* was not required in relation to the identification of a motor car.[53] This result is perhaps not very surprising, given the characteristics of cars, compared to those of people. However, the Court said that the judge should draw the jury's attention to the opportunity which the witness had to identify the car, his ability to distinguish between makes of car and the possibility of his thinking that he recollected something whereas in fact he did not, but had absorbed the information from elsewhere.[54]

2. IDENTIFICATION IN COURT: DOCK IDENTIFICATION

The expression "dock identification" refers to the identification of the **14–13** defendant when he is in the dock at trial. The general principle is that (unless there are exceptional circumstances) a witness should not be allowed to identify a defendant for the first time in the dock. The reason for the principle is that the witness may well be influenced in making an identification by the sight of the defendant in the dock and is therefore more likely to be mistaken. The prohibition is well established. At the beginning of the twentieth century the Court of Criminal Appeal disapproved of dock

---

[50] *Spencer* [1995] Crim.L.R. 235.
[51] *Grant* [1996] 2 Cr.App.R. 272.
[52] *Campbell* [1996] Crim.L.R. 500.
[53] *Browning* (1992) 94 Cr.App.R. 109, 121–123.
[54] Above, at 121–123.

identification in such circumstances.[55] More recently the Court of Appeal has again expressed disapproval of this course whether the dock identification was at the behest of counsel[56] or the judge.[57]

If counsel inadvertently elicits a dock identification from the witness, the judge should warn the jury of the dangers of accepting the evidence of such identification. However, it may be necessary to discharge the jury in these circumstances because of the prejudice suffered by the defendant. (This course is not infrequently adopted since a warning from the judge may not be sufficient to overcome the prejudice.)

In a doubtful case the prosecution ought to apply to the court for leave to ask a witness to make a dock identification. The court is then in this position: evidence of dock identification is legally admissible. However, there is a discretion to exclude it if the prejudicial effect of the evidence outweighs the probative value.[58]

14-14 There are conflicting decisions of the Divisional Court as to whether justices have a discretion to permit a dock identification. In *North Yorkshire Trading Standards Department v Williams*[59] the Court said that an authority with a duty to prosecute summary, non-arrestable offences and with no power to require a defendant to attend an identification parade could not rely on that lack of power to press for a dock identification. Potts J. said that it would be wrong to apply one approach to dock identification for minor offences and another for more serious offences. On the other hand, a differently constituted Court in *Barnes v The Chief Constable of Durham*[60] held that justices had a discretion to permit a dock identification although there had been no previous identification. The defendant in that case was charged with failing to provide a specimen for analysis and the only evidence that he was the man who had failed to provide the specimen was a dock identification. It was argued by the defence that it was not open to the prosecution to rely on a dock identification if there had been no identification parade. The Court said that in the magistrates' court it had long been customary for a witness to identify a defendant in court: if there had to be an identification parade in every case of disputed identity the whole process of justice in the magistrates' court would be severely impaired. It is submitted that *Barnes* is to be preferred and that the distinction between the practice in the Crown Court and that in the magistrates' court is justified by the different level of seriousness of the cases tried in the two courts. The distinction may also be justified on practical grounds: it would, for instance, be impractical to organise an identification parade every time a motorist disputes that he is the man who committed the

---

[55] *Cartwright* (1914) 10 Cr.App.R. 219.
[56] *Hunter* [1969] Crim.L.R. 262; see also *Caird*, below.
[57] *Howick* [1970] Crim.L.R. 403.
[58] See *Horsham JJ. Ex p. Bukhari* (1982) 74 Cr.App.R. 291, *per* Glidewell J. and Forbes J.
[59] (1995) 159 J.P. 383.
[60] [1997] 2 Cr.App.R. 505.

offence. A safeguard against injustice in the exceptional case is to be found in the justices' discretion to exclude the evidence of a dock identification (although it may well be that such a discretion did not exist in committal proceedings[61]). In *Karia v DPP*[62] it was held that in summary, driving, cases there was no unfairness—contrary to Art.6 of the ECHR—in an officer making a dock identification where there had been no advance indication from the defendant that identity was in issue. The procedure would not be rendered unfair if it subsequently appeared that there was such a dispute. In determining whether there is a disputed identification for the purposes of Code D, the Court stated that there is no material distinction between proceedings by way of summons and those before the Crown Court. Although the defendant in the former does not have the opportunity to mention his defence at interview, it was held not unreasonable to expect a person in such circumstances to write to the prosecution disputing the identification.[63]

The one exceptional circumstance which is established is where the defendant had refused to take part in an identification parade. In these circumstances, a dock identification may take place at trial. Thus, in *John*,[64] the defendant had refused to take part in an identification parade and a witness identified him for the first time at trial. The Court of Appeal held that, although the method of identification was unsatisfactory, it was not wrong to admit the evidence in the light of the defendant's refusal to take part in the parade.

14–15

Caird[65] is an example of a case in which a dock identification was permitted in different circumstances. A police officer in that case had been knocked unconscious during a riot, and was off duty for some time thereafter. The report is silent as to whether he had been prevented by illness from making an identification before the trial. At the trial the witness was permitted to identify the defendant in the dock for the first time. The Court of Appeal upheld the ruling. This is, however, an unusual case and it cannot be a general rule that, where a witness is prevented by illness from identifying a defendant, he should be allowed to do so by a dock identification. A further illustration may be found in a case where the defendants were members of an ethnic minority. Other members of the community were reluctant to co-operate with the police. Thus, the police could not obtain sufficient men similar in appearance to form an identification par-

---

[61] *Horsham JJ. Ex p. Bukhari*, above; *Highbury Corner Magistrates Court Ex p. Boyce* (1984) 79 Cr.App.R. 132.

[62] October 14, 2002, unreported, *Archbold News*, Issue 10, December 18, 2002.

[63] The observations relating to Art.6 in *Karia* were *obiter*, the trial having taken place before the entry into force of the Human Rights Act 1998. With the entry into force of the Act there may be further challenge to the compliance of dock indentifications in driving cases in the magistrates court with Art.6 of the European Convention.

[64] [1973] Crim.L.R. 113.

[65] *The Times*, August 20, 1970; also reported at (1970) 54 Cr.App.R. 499 and [1970] Crim.L.R. 656 but not on this point.

ade. This may be a case where the court would be prepared to allow a dock identification.

There may be cases where there is an issue of identification because the witness had to pick out one person from two or more persons known to him previously.[66] In these circumstances a dock identification may be proper.[67] However, the witness's knowledge of the defendant's identity must be more than trifling. The Court of Appeal held that a dock identification was not proper when by a witness who had only seen the defendant once and then been told his name by somebody else.[68] If a dock identification is admitted in evidence, the jury should be reminded of the dangers of identification evidence and the potential weaknesses in accordance with *Turnbull* (para.14–03, above). In a summary trial, justices should receive a similar warning from their clerk.[69]

3. IDENTIFICATION OUT OF COURT

14–16   A witness of an offence may very soon after it identify the offender. As will be seen, the witness in these circumstances will be permitted to give evidence of his previous identification and identify the offender in the dock. On the other hand, if there has been a lapse of time since the offence the witness (depending on the circumstances) may identify the defendant at a video identification, an identification parade, a "group" identification or a confrontation. Police practice in relation to such identification is governed by Code of Practice D.[70]

Code D is concerned with the principal methods used by police to identify people in connection with the investigation of criminal offences and the keeping of accurate and reliable criminal records.[71] The Code provides that identification by a witness arises if the offender is seen committing the crime and a witness is given an opportunity to identify the suspect in one of the identification procedures provided for in the Code.[72] The procedures set out in Code D are designed to:

---

[66] In an identification parade, of course, a witness will be seeking to identify one person from a number of other persons who will be unknown to him.

[67] *Hughes, The Times*, November 8, 1977.

[68] *Fergus* [1992] Crim.L.R. 363.

[69] *North Yorkshire Trading Standards Department v Williams* (1995) 159 S.P. 383.

[70] Issued by the Home Secretary under s.66 of the Police and Criminal Evidence Act 1984. The revised edition came into force on April 1, 2003: see the Police and Criminal Evidence Act 1984 (Codes of Practice) (Codes B to E) (No.2) Order 2003 (SI 2003/703). For a discussion of the previous revisions (in force April 1995) (including the requirement in Code D2.0 that the police make a record of the description of a suspect as first given by a potential witness and the requirement in D2.5 that a video-recording or colour photograph be taken of any parade), see Wolchover and Heaton-Armstrong, "Questioning and Identification: Changes under PACE [1995] Crim.L.R. 356, 367–370. For voice identification parades see para.14–48, below.

[71] D:1.1 Code of Practice.

[72] D:1.2 Code of Practice.

(i) test the witness' ability to identify the person they saw on a previous occasion, and

(ii) provide safeguards against mistaken identification.[73]

Code D now provides that video identification is the preferred identification procedure. The identification officer and the officer in charge of the investigation must consult and determine which identification procedure is to be offered. The suspect shall be offered a video identification unless this is not practicable or an identification parade (if a parade is both practicable and more suitable than a video identification).[74] However, a group identification may be offered initially if the officer in charge of the investigation considers that it would be more suitable than either a video identification or identification parade and the identification officer considers it practicable to arrange.[75] Ordinarily, a group identification should only be offered if video identification or identification parade are refused or considered impracticable. If none of these methods are practicable then the identification officer has the discretion to make arrangements for a covert video identification or covert group identification. A confrontation is the last resort.

The various forms of out of court identification are now discussed.

A. Video identification and identification parades

D:3.12 of the Code of Practice provides that whenever a suspect disputes an   **14–17**
identification or purported identification, an identification procedure *shall* be held unless it is not practicable or it would serve no useful purpose in proving or disproving whether the suspect was involved in committing the offence.[76] Moreover, D:3.13 of the Code provides that such a procedure may also be held if the officer in charge of the investigation considers it would be useful. In *Forbes*,[77] the House of Lords held, following a full consideration of the authorities, that under the previous version of the Code an identification parade was necessary where the suspect disputed identification evidence and consented to a parade, the only exception being those expressed in the Code or in a case of "pure recognition of someone well-known to the eye-witness". A prior identification, however complete, was held not to mean that a parade need not be held and a failure to hold a parade in such circumstances could amount to a breach of the Code. Thus,

---

[73] *ibid.*
[74] D:3.14 Code of Practice.
[75] D:3.16 Code of Practice.
[76] An example is given of where the suspect is well known to the witness or where there is no reasonable possibility that the witness would be able to make an identification. See Roberts, "Identification Evidence: Rule, Principle, Discretion and Reform of Code D Following *Forbes*" 66 Jo.Crim.L. 250 in which the author observes the dangerous effect of the subjective nature of this test.
[77] [2001] 1 A.C. 473.

under the version of the Code in force until April 2002, in most cases of disputed identification a parade was mandatory.[78]

Following amendment of the Code, there are conflicting views as to whether *Forbes* remains applicable and whether a formal identification procedure is required where the suspect has already been identified following a street identification pursuant to procedures under para.D:3.2 of the Code (see para.14–24 below).[79] The newly inserted para.D:3.2(d) provides that after a witness makes a positive identification, subject to para.D:3.12 and D:3.13, it is not necessary for the witness to take part in a further procedure.

A street identification is very often a poor test of a witness's ability to recognise an offender, especially where the offender has been detained by police. It is submitted that it cannot have been the intention of the drafters of the current version of Code D to effectively reverse the House of Lords decision in *Forbes* and leave the necessity of a formal identification procedure to the discretion of a police officer. Thus, para.D:3.2(d) clearly stipulates that the decision on whether to hold a formal identification procedure following a street identification is *subject* to paras D:3.12 and D:3.13 which provide only very limited circumstances in which a formal identification need not be held, *i.e.* if is not practicable or it would serve no useful purpose. Given the obvious shortcomings with street identifications, it is submitted that in most circumstances the subsequent holding of a formal identification procedure will be useful. The "no useful purpose" exception is limited to the most exceptional cases.[80]

14–18 Under a previous version of the Code it was held that where the witness to a crime states that they cannot identify the perpetrator, a mere assertion

---

[78] para.2.3 of the version of Code D (in force until April 2002) provided that whenever a suspect disputed an identification, an identification parade would be held if the suspect consented. In even earlier editions of the Code the paragraph had provided that in such cases a parade must be held only if the suspect asked for one and it was practicable to hold one. The version in force until April 2002, therefore, maintained the requirement for holding a parade in a case of a disputed identification, but removed the earlier qualifications. The purpose of the amendment must have been to do away with the sort of difficulties which arose when the police said that they were entitled to refuse a request for a parade, *Conway* (1990) 91 Cr.App.R. 143, or that it was not practicable to hold one, *Penny* (1992) 94 Cr.App.R. 345. Accordingly, in most cases prior to April 2002 the requirement to hold a parade was mandatory, the only exceptions being if the suspect did not consent or it was not practicable to assemble a parade, or a group or video identification takes place. Under earlier versions of para.2.3 it was held that the right to an identification parade arose not only where there was an actual dispute, but also where a dispute might reasonably be anticipated, *Rutherford and Palmer* (1994) 98 Cr.App.R. 191. However, if there was no reasonable possibility of the witness making an identification, no dispute could have be said to arise and there was no right to a parade, *Montgomery* [1996] Crim.L.R. 507.
[79] Wolchover and Heaton-Armstrong, "Farewell to *Forbes*" *Archbold News*, Issue 7, August 5, 2003, argue that following amendment of the Code an identification procedure is no longer required following a street identification. Bogan, "*Forbes* Alive and Well" *Archbold News*, Issue 9, November 3, 2003, argues that the amendment of the Code reinforces the mandatory nature of the requirement to hold an identification procedure.
[80] See *Anastasiou* [1998] Crim.L.R. 67 at para.14–25 below.

by the defendant that he requires an identification parade does not trigger an obligation on the police to hold one.[81] Even where the witness can identify some distinguishing feature, for example a description of the perpetrator's clothes, there is no need for a parade and the judge need not direct the jury that the defendant has lost the benefit of an inconclusive parade.[82]

In cases where it is proposed to hold an identification procedure, the suspect shall initially be offered a video identification unless it is not practicable or or an identification parade is both practicable and more suitable than a video identification.[83] Alternatively, a group identification (see para.14–21 below) may initially be offered if the officer in charge of the investigation considers it is more suitable than either a video identification or parade and the identification officer considers it practicable to arrange.[84] The identification officer and the officer in charge are to consult each other and decide which of the options is most suitable. A video identifaction will normally be more suitable if it can be arranged and completed sooner than an identification parade. Moreover, an identification parade may not be practicable because of factors relating to the witnesses, such as their number, state of health, availability and travelling requirements.[85]

Video identification involves a witness being shown moving images of a known suspect, together with similar images of others who resemble the suspect.[86] Video identifications must be carried out in accordance with Annex A of the Code of Practice.[87] It is the responsibility of the identification officer to obtain a suitable set of images to be used in a video identification. The set of images must include at least eight other people who, so far as possible, resemble the age, height and general appearance and position in life as the suspect. Only one suspect shall appear in any set unless there are two suspects of roughly similar appearance, in which case they may be shown together with at least twelve other people.[88]

The images used to conduct a video identification shall, as far as possible, **14–19** show the suspect and other people in the same positions or carrying out the same sequence of movements. The other people must also be shown under identical conditions as the suspect unless the identification officer reasonably believes that because of the suspect's failure or refusal to co-operate it is not practicable for the conditions to be identical, and any difference in conditions would not direct a witness's attention to any individual image.[89]

---

[81] *Gayle* [1999] 2 Cr.App.R. 130 and *Nicholson (Andrew Robert), The Times*, September 7, 1999.
[82] *Doldur* [2000] Crim.L.R. 178.
[83] D:3.14 Code of Practice.
[84] *ibid.*
[85] *ibid.*
[86] D:3.5 Code of Practice. In certain circumstances still images may be used: D:3.21.
[87] D:3.6 Code of Practice.
[88] Annex A—D:2.
[89] Annex A—D:3.

The suspect, or other appropriate person, must be given an opportunity to see the complete set of images before it is shown to any witness. Steps must be taken to remedy any reasonable grounds of objection.[90] Before the images are shown to the witness, the suspect or his solicitor must be provided with the details of the witness's first description of the suspect. Moreover, the suspect's solicitor should, if practicable, be given a reasonable opportunity to attend the video identification on behalf of the suspect.[91]

An identification parade entails the witness seeing the suspect in a line of other people who resemble the suspect.[92] Identification parades must be carried out in accordance with Annex B of the Code of Practice.[93]

"The object of the identification parade is to test the ability of a witness to pick out from a group the person, if he is present, whom the witness has said that he has seen previously on a specified occasion."[94] Once a witness has picked out a suspect at a parade, he is permitted to identify the suspect in the dock. The conduct of identification parades is governed by rules set out in Code of Practice D. The police must not substitute their own procedure.[95]

A suspect must be given an opportunity to have a solicitor or friend present at an identification parade.[96] The police are responsible for selecting suitable people for the parade—and it must consist of at least eight people, similar to the suspect in the same areas as required for video identification. Similarly, where there are two suspects of roughly similar appearance they may appear in the same parade provided they appear with at least twelve other people.[97] In *Thorne*,[98] the defendant had brought another man with him to the police station and requested through his solicitor that the other man be put on the parade. The officer in charge of the parade did not allow his request and, after an argument, took the view that the defendant was refusing to go on the parade. The defendant was subsequently identified at a confrontation. He appealed on the ground that the identification was so unsafe that the judge should have withdrawn the case from the jury. The Court of Appeal dismissed his appeal and held that it was for the police to decide who to have on an identification parade. The

---

[90] Annex A—D:7.

[91] Annex A—D:9.

[92] D:3.7 Code of Practice.

[93] D:3.8 Code of Practice.

[94] "Report of the Committee On Evidence of Identification", Cmnd. 338 (1976), para.5.89. For a summary of research findings from a psychological study of identification parades, see McKenzie, "Psychology and Legal Practice: Fairness and Accuracy in Identification Parades" [1995] Crim.L.R. 200.

[95] *Quinn* [1995] 1 Cr.App.R. 480.

[96] Annex B—D:1.

[97] Annex B—D:9. As with video identification, the suspect or his solicitor must be provided with details of the first description of the suspect by the witness before any parade takes place: Annex B—D:3.

[98] [1981] Crim.L.R. 702.

Court said that it was the responsibility of the police to make up the panel according to the rules but if they failed in that respect it would be a matter for comment by the judge and might lead to evidence being excluded.

Annex B to the new Code provides that where the suspect has an unusual   **14–20** physical feature, which cannot be replicated on other members of the parade, steps may be taken to conceal the location of that feature.[99] In *Marrin*[1] a case under a previous version of the Code, it was held that sensible and reasonable steps taken in good faith to achieve resemblance to the suspect on the parade were permissible. Accordingly, it had been permissible to apply make-up to members of a parade, although the Court noted that it would be sensible to keep a record of those to whom such make up was applied. Moreover, it had been permissible for all participants to wear hats to minimise differences in hair colour and hair line (no hat having been worn at the time of the offence).[2] By contrast in *Hutton*[3] those participating in the identification parade (again held pursuant to a previous version of the Code) had all worn basebll caps and the lower part of their faces obscured by some sort of scarf. It was held that the manner in which the parade had been conducted was a matter of concern and that it was a mistake to have those taking part in the parade masked. Therefore, in view of the witness's limited opportunity of seeing the assailant, there had been insufficient evidence for the case to have proceeded beyond the end of the prosecution case and the conviction was quashed. If the caps and scarfs in *Hutton* were donned to cover an unusual feature, in light of the ammendments to the Code, a similar case would now perhaps be differently decided. However, the transcript in *Hutton* does not reveal whether the offender, at the time of the offence, had dressed in a similar manner to that adopted by members of the parade. If he had, it is submitted that to present the identifying witness with the same portion of the features as was on display at the time of the offence was neither unreasonable nor unfair.[4]

When an identification procedure is required, in the interests of fairness to both suspects and witnesses, it must be held as soon as practicable.[5] While the suspect is not obliged to take part in the video identification or parade, his attention should be drawn to the consequences of any refusal to do so, including the fact that his refusal may be given in evidence in any

---

[99] Annex B—D.10. Annex B—D.19 provides that if the witness requests that a person they have indicated remove anything used to conceal an unusual feature, that person may be asked to remove it.

[1] *The Times*, March 5, 2002.

[2] The suspect had been asked to remove his hat at the request of the witness. There could be no objection to the request to remove the hat as this was covered by the then para.17 of Annex A to the Code, now replaced by para.18 of Annex B to the Code.

[3] [1999] Crim.L.R. 74

[4] In *Creamer* (1985) 80 Cr.App.R. 248 an identification by a witness after a parade was held to have been correctly admitted when the witness had recognised the defendant on the parade, but had refrained from identifying him because she was frightened.

[5] D:3.11 of the Code of Practice.

subsequent trial or that the police may proceed covertly without the suspect's consent.[6]

B. Identification at a group identification or confrontation

14-21   The officer in charge of an investigation may initially offer a group identification to a suspect if it is more suitable than either a video identification or identification parade.[7] The arrangements for a such group identifications are governed by Annex C of the Code. They may take place either with the suspect's consent and co-operation or covertly.[8] The location of the group identification is a matter for the identification officer, although representations may be made.[9] Group identifications should be held where other people are either passing by or waiting around informally, such that the suspect is able to join them and be capable of being seen by the witness at the same time as others in the group,[10] for example in a shopping centre or at a railway station. In *Tiplady*[11] evidence of a group identification in the foyer of a magistrates' court was held to have been correctly admitted (there had been 20–30 people in the foyer at any one time, including young men in the defendant's age group).

Although the number, age, sex, race and general description and style of clothing of other people present at the location cannot be controlled by the identification officer, in selecting the location they must consider the general appearance and numbers of people likely to be present.[12] A group identification need not be held where, because of the unusual appearance of the suspect, none of the locations would satisfy the requisite requirements of making the identification fair.[13]

As a last resort—and only where none of the other identification procedures are practicable—the identification officer may arrange for the suspect to be confronted by the witness. Such confrontation does not require the suspect's consent.[14] The procedure for confrontations is governed by Annex D of the Code.[15]

14-22   Confrontation refers to a situation where a witness confronts the defendant alone (usually at a police station) for the purpose of identifica-

---

[6] D:3.17 of the Code of Practice.
[7] D:3.16 of the Code of Practice.
[8] Annex C—D:2: Covert procedures should only be resorted to in the event that the suspect does not give his consent (D:3.17 of the Code of Practice).
[9] Annex C—D:3.
[10] Annex C—D:4.
[11] (1995) 159 J.P. 548.
[12] Annex C—D:6.
[13] Annex C—D:7.
[14] D:3.23 Code of Practice.
[15] In Roberts, "Eyewitness Identification: Scene of Crime Confrontations—The Need for a More Cautious Approach" (1999) 63 Jo.Crim.L. 251, the author outlines the limitations of the previous Code (similar to the present version) in providing guidance to police officers conducting them and suggests that the Code should be extended to regulate this type of procedure so as to guard against the possibility of misidentification.

tion. The dangers inherent in such an identification are similar to those inherent in a dock identification. In 1911 the Court of Criminal Appeal disapproved of identification which took place at the police station when the suspect was alone.[16] The Court said that the suspect should be placed with the others for a proper identification and that leading questions should not be asked.

A confrontation must take place in the presence of the suspect's solicitor, where he has one, unless this would cause unreasonable delay. The Privy Council has said that confrontation, if resorted to, should be confined to rare and exceptional circumstances. "Once a suspect is in [police] custody he should be kept apart from eye-witnesses to the incident. Nothing should be done at that stage which might assist the eye-witnesses in their identification of him as the perpetrator ... Unless there are exceptional circumstances, he should be shown to them only by means of an identification parade."[17] In *Johnson*[18] the victim of a robbery was shown a video-recording of the defendant and another woman taken at a petrol station near the scene shortly after the robbery. The victim identified the defendant as one of the robbers. The Court of Appeal held that the identification evidence should have been excluded as it amounted to a confrontation by video.

In *Jones and Nelson*,[19] under a previous version of the Code, the Court of Appeal held that there is no power enabling the police to use reasonable force to make a suspect submit to a confrontation by a witness. There was no express or implied power in Code D to authorise the use of force. The fact that Code C 8.9 permitted the use of reasonable force to "secure compliance with reasonable instructions" did not authorise the use of force to bring about a confrontation. The Court held that use of force, or even the threat of force, amounted to a breach of the Codes of Practice. Accordingly, the identification evidence should have been excluded. Section 3 of Annex D of the Code now stipulates that force may not be used to make the face of the suspect visible to the witness.

The court has a discretion to exclude evidence of identification at a **14–23** confrontation, similar to that in the case of a dock identification.[20] Thus, in *Joseph*[21] the Court of Appeal held that evidence of a confrontation which took place in the cells at court before the trial (at the defendant's insistence and despite warnings from the judge) should have been excluded under s.78 of the Police and Criminal Evidence Act 1984. The Court said that the fact that the confrontation had taken place at the defendant's insistence was a relevant circumstance but it was only one factor and not the decisive factor

---

[16] *Chapman* (1911) 7 Cr.App.R. 53; *William* (1912) 8 Cr.App.R. 84.
[17] *Williams (Noel) v The Queen* [1997] 1 W.L.R. 548, 555.
[18] [1996] Crim.L.R. 504.
[19] *The Times*, April 21, 1999.
[20] *Lamb* (1980) 71 Cr.App.R. 198, 202, CA.
[21] *The Times*, May 25, 1993.

to be taken into account: the balance lay in excluding the evidence of confrontation despite the defendant's persistence in requesting it.

The risk of a mistake is such that the discretion should be exercised in favour of the defendant, it is submitted, unless he has previously refused to go on an identification parade or there are other exceptional circumstances. An example of an exceptional circumstance occurred in *Lamb*[22] where the defendant suggested "somewhat aggressively" to the police that he should be confronted with the man who had identified him as one of a number of assailants. The Court of Appeal said that the confrontation which ensued was "unfortunate in the circumstances, but understandably so". The defendant had been demanding to be confronted with his accuser. If the police had refused to produce him the defendant might have said at his trial that if the accuser had been brought to the police station, he would have failed to identify the defendant and so the defendant would not have been charged.

C. Street identifications

14–24 It sometimes happens that an eye-witness identifies a suspect shortly after an offence has been committed. Typically, the police may take such a witness in a car around the neighbouring area to see if he can pick out the offender. (It may be noted that Code D specifically permits the police to do this in a case where the identity of the suspect is not known.[23]) An identification by the witness in these circumstances is often called a "street identification". Where it is practicable to do so, a record should be made of the witness' description of the suspect before asking the witness to make an identification.[24] Care must be taken not to direct the witness's attention to any individual unless this cannot be avoided.[25] Where there is more than one witness they should be kept separate to determine whether they can identify a person independently.[26] A full record of the procedure must be made.[27]

The rules in relation to the admissibility of such identifications may be summarised as follows:

1. Where a street identification leads to a positive identification and arrest, para.D:3.2(d) provides that, subject to paras D:3.12 and D:3.13, for the witness who makes the identification, it is not necessary for them to

---

[22] Above.
[23] Code D:3.2 provides that a police officer may take a witness to a particular neighbourhood or place to see whether he can identify a person but that care should be taken not to direct his attention to any individual. See Roberts, "Identification Evidence: Rule, Principle, Discretion and Reform of Code D Following *Forbes*", 66 Jo.Crim.L. 250 in which the author welcomes the increased guidance on how street identifications should be conducted.
[24] D:3.2(a) of the Code of Practice.
[25] D:3.2(b) of the Code of Practice.
[26] D:3.2(c) of the Code of Practice.
[27] D:3.2(e) of the Code of Practice.

take part in a further procedure. Paragraphs D:3.12 and D:3.13 provide that no formal identification procedure is required if it is not practicable or would serve no useful purpose (see para.14–17 above).

2. In *Forbes*[28] the House of Lords held that, under a previous version of the Code, an identification parade is necessary where the suspect consented and disputed identification evidence, the only exception being those expressed in Code D.2. For the reasons set out above (para.14–17) it is submitted that the obligation to hold a parade remains even where the suspect has been unequivocally identified, and a prior street identification does not mean that a parade or one of the other identification procedures is not to be held. Accordingly, *Popat*[29] in which the Court of Appeal held that where a person has already made an identification, there is no requirement for a parade, has been overruled.

Lord Bingham held that where an eye-witness of a criminal incident makes plain that (i) he cannot identify the culprit, (ii) may be able to identify clothing of the culprit, but not the culprit himself, or (iii) if the case is one of pure recognition of someone well-known to the eye-witness, it may be futile to hold an identification parade. He stated: **14–25**

"…the effect of paragraph 2.3 [replaced by para.D:3.12, a similar provision under the present Code] is clear: if (a) the police have sufficient information to justify the arrest of a particular person for suspected involvement in an offence, and (b) an eye-witness has identified or may be able to identify that person, and (c) the suspect disputes his identification as a person involved in the commission of that offence, an identification parade must be held if (d) the suspect consents and (e) [the exceptions] of Code D do not apply."[30]

3. At a time when a much earlier edition of the Code was applicable it was held that if a suspect asked for a parade one must be held.[31] This requirement no longer appears in para.D:3.12 of the Code (above), but the paragraph still requires that a parade be held if a suspect disputes an identification. Thus, in *Wait*[32] the Court of Appeal said that the fact that a witness was present at the time of arrest was not a valid reason for declining to hold a parade and it should not be assumed that the victim is to identify the suspect because he had seen him arrested: parades were held for the

---

[28] [2001] 1 A.C. 473.
[29] [1998] 2 Cr.App.R. 208.
[30] Above. See Roberts, above, in which the author calls for fundamental reform in this area of law: Code D should contain only provisions relating to the *conduct* of the procedures and guidance on applicability should be set out in a statute such as s.114 of the Australian Evidence Act 1995.
[31] *Brown* [1991] Crim.L.R. 368.
[32] [1998] Crim.L.R. 68, considering para.2.3 of the previous Code, a similar provision to para.D:3.12 of the present Code.

benefit of the defence as well as the prosecution. On the other hand, in *Anastasiou*[33] the Court of Appeal upheld the trial judge's decision that a parade was unnecessary in these circumstances, particularly as the identifying witnesses were police officers who arrested the suspect after a chase during which they only lost sight of the suspect for a very short period of time with the consequence that there was no room for the possibility that they had caught the wrong man. Thus, a formal identification procedure could reasonably be said to be of no useful purpose.

4. If a person has been arrested and brought to a police station as a known suspect the provisions of Code D apply. Thus, in *Powell*[34] a police sergeant attempted to stop the defendant's car on a motorway. The defendant crashed the car and ran off, but was subsequently caught and arrested. He was taken to a police station where the sergeant identified him at a confrontation. The Crown Court held that the Code was not applicable because identification was not in dispute since the defendant had confessed. However, the Divisional Court held that even if the defendant had confessed (which he had not) the police were not absolved from complying with the Code and holding an identification parade.

14–26   5. Once a suspect at a police station agrees to an identification procedure it should be held unless impracticable. If no identification procedure is held and the suspect is released it is not permissible to allow the complainant to make a street identification outside the station (on the ground that he is no longer a suspect at a police station). The Court of Appeal said that this having occurred in one case, it amounted to "a complete flouting of the Code" and the trial judge should have exercised his discretion to exclude the evidence of identification.[35]

An identification by video-recording[36] has been said to be analogous to a street identification. In *Jones (M.A.)*[37] a doorman at a public house was attacked and wounded by a group of assailants. Subsequently, the owner of the public house installed video equipment and on one evening a recording was made of all the customers at the public house. The doorman viewed the recording and identified four persons shown on it as having taken part in the attack. At trial he gave evidence identifying the four from his own recollection of the attack, but only after seeing the video-recording and after police officers who saw it with him had indicated that they were able to name the four persons he recognised. The Court of Appeal held that the evidence of identification was admissible: the video-recording was equivalent to street or group identification.

---

[33] [1998] Crim.L.R. 67.
[34] [1992] R.T.R. 270.
[35] *Nagah* (1991) 92 Cr.App.R. 344.
[36] Not to be confused with video identification covered by Annex A of the Code. See para.14–17 above.
[37] (1994) 158 J.P. 293.

D. Breaches of the Code of Practice

A breach of Code D may lead to the exclusion of evidence of identification **14–27** in the exercise of the court's discretion under s.78 of the Police and Criminal Evidence Act 1984 if its admission would have an adverse effect on the fairness of the proceedings.[38] This was accepted by the Court of Appeal without argument in *Gall*.[39] In that case a police officer concerned in the investigation came into the parade room, had a look at the parade and then had the opportunity of speaking to a witness who was then introduced to the parade. The Court of Appeal held that there had been a breach of the then para.2.2 of Code D[40] and that evidence of identification should have been excluded. However, in *Jones (M.A.)*,[41] the Court of Appeal emphasised that Code D set out practices to be followed by the police and was not concerned directly with the admissibility of evidence, even though the consequences of a breach of the Code might be the exclusion of the evidence under s.78. Accordingly, the fact that there have been breaches of Code is not conclusive as to whether evidence of identification will be admitted or not.[42] This will depend on the nature of the breach and all the circumstances.

If the police have deliberately flouted the Code so as to make any identification inherently unfair, it is submitted that the evidence of identification should be excluded. In *Finley*[43] the police persistently breached the Code (the Court of Appeal suspected deliberately). The witnesses, who worked together, were shown photographs and one of them purported to identify the defendants. Before the identification parade the police (in breach of the Code) kept the witnesses together and did not warn them not to discuss the case. Three of the witnesses identified the defendant on the parade. The Court of Appeal said that the identification officer was responsible for ensuring that witnesses were not able to communicate with each other about the case but the witnesses in this case had been in a position to do so: it was bound to appear that justice had not been done. The Court held that the judge should have withdrawn the case from the jury at the close of the prosecution. Even in cases of accidental non-compliance with the Code by police, in certain circumstances, it will be right to exclude the identification evidence.[44]

On the other hand, not every breach of the Code will lead to exclusion of **14–28**

---

[38] The exercise of the discretion under s.78 is discussed at para.10–13, above.
[39] (1990) 90 Cr.App.R. 64.
[40] para.2.2 provided that no officer involved in the investigation should take part in the arrangement or conduct of the parade. Para.3.19 of the current Code D contains the same restriction.
[41] (1994) 158 J.P. 293.
[42] While the importance of compliance with the code could not be over-emphasised, failure to comply with it is not necessarily fatal in every case: *Kelly* (1998) 162 J.P. 231.
[43] [1993] Crim.L.R. 50.
[44] *Lennon* (1999) 63 Jo.Crim.L. 459.

the evidence of identification. Thus, in *Grannell*[45] procedures relating to group identification were not followed. As a result there were breaches of Code D. The Court of Appeal said that simply because there was a breach of the Code, it did not mean that the evidence was inadmissible: it was important to see whether any unfairness followed from the evidence. The Court held that in the instant case the trial judge had rightly exercised his discretion under s.78 to admit the evidence. In *DPP v D*[46] a witness identified two suspects before during and after the commission of an offence: he then described them to the police by reference to their clothing and approximate age. Acting on this information the police arrested the defendants at the scene. One suspect asked for an identification parade, but none was held (in breach of the previous Code D2.3, similar provision is now made in Code D3.12—see para.14–17 above). The justices admitted the evidence of this "informal identification". The Divisional Court held that the breach was not of such substance, having regard to the nature of the identification evidence, as to cause unjust prejudice to the defendant. The Court observed that there never was an actual identification to the police and the holding of a parade would serve no useful purpose since nothing of what the witness had seen could usefully be challenged on a parade.

Even if there has been a substantial breach of the Code a judge may admit the evidence of identification in the exercise of his discretion under s.78. Thus, in *Ryan*[47] the trial judge found that there had been a "major" breach of Code D because investigating officers had taken part in the identification procedures. Nonetheless, the judge admitted the evidence in the exercise of his discretion under s.78. The Court of Appeal upheld the exercise of discretion: no unjust prejudice was caused to the defendant thereby.

In exercising discretion under s.78 the court must take into account the relevant provisions of the Code,[48] and all the circumstances of the case.[49] It is otherwise not possible to lay down general rules for the exercise of discretion: it will depend on the nature of the breach and the circumstances of the particular case. A technical breach which had no effect on the reliability of the identification will hardly lead to exclusion. On the other hand, it is submitted that if a breach caused the parade to be so unfair that no identification could be properly relied on, the court should exclude it.[50]

14–29   The Court of Appeal has said that it will not interfere with the exercise of the judge's discretion unless it is satisfied that no resonable judge, having heard the evidence, could have reached the conclusion that he did.[51] The

---

[45] (1990) 90 Cr.App.R. 149.
[46] *The Times*, August 7, 1998.
[47] [1992] Crim.L.R. 187.
[48] Police and Criminal Evidence Act 1984, s.67(11).
[49] *Penny* (1992) 94 Cr.App.R. 345, 349.
[50] See para.10–13, above, for a discussion of s.78.
[51] *Quinn* [1995] 1 Cr.App.R. 480, 489.

Court has also said that the judge should give reasons for admitting the evidence when breaches of code were admitted or proved.[52] This will make easier a review of his decision on appeal.

In *Forbes*[53] the House of Lords held that in any case where a breach of Code D has been established, and the trial judge has refused to exclude the evidence, the judge, in summing up, should (a) explain to the jury that there has been a breach (forcefully if needs be[54]) and how it has arisen, and (b) invite the jury to consider the possible effect of that breach.[55] The terms of the appropriate direction will vary from case to case and breach to breach. But where the breach relates to the failure to hold an identification parade, the jury should ordinarily be told that an identification parade enables a supect to put the reliability of an eye-witness's identification to the test and that the suspect has lost the benefit of that safeguard, so that the jury should take accoint of that failure in its assessment of the case, giving it such weight as it thinks fair.[56]

In a case decided before the passing of the 1984 Act the Court of Appeal deprecated the holding of a trial-within-a-trial to determine the admissibility of evidence relating to an identification parade.[57] However, if an issue is raised under s.78(1) the court may have to determine how evidence was obtained in order to decide whether it should be excluded or not. As a result, the court may be required to decide matters of fact. This has led the Court of Appeal to modify its earlier view. In *Beveridge*[58] the Court said that, when a point is taken on an identification parade, the trial judge in the light of s.78 must consider the depositions, statements and submissions of counsel; but the Court also said that there may be occasions (which will be rare) when the judge will think it desirable to hold a trial-within-a-trial.[59]

E. Prosecution disclosure

It has always been the practice for the prosecution to disclose the notes relating to an identification procedure. (These notes are made by the inspector in charge of the procedure.) It was also normal for the police to disclose any description of an offender given by a witness and any photo-

14–30

---

[52] *Allen* [1995] Crim.L.R. 643.
[53] [2001] 1 A.C. 473. See para.14–24 above.
[54] *Lennon* above.
[55] Citing *Quinn* [1995] 1 Cr.App.R. 480 at 490.
[56] In *Forbes* the trial judge had failed (a) to exercise any discretion pursuant to PACE, s.78 on whether to admit evidence of a street identification, or (b) to direct the jury as to effect of a breach of Code D. Overall, the circumstances of the case were such that the House of Lords did not consider the trial unfair or the conviction unsafe.
[57] *Walshe* (1982) 74 Cr.App.R. 85.
[58] (1987) 85 Cr.App.R. 255.
[59] In *Martin and Nicholls* [1994] Crim.L.R. 218, the Court of Appeal said that the circumstances in which it would be appropriate to hold a *voir dire* must be very rare and generally, the trial judge should not determine issues of fact, but make an objective assessment. However, it is submitted that this comment does not detract from the general force of what was said in *Beveridge*.

graph of the defendant taken on arrest. This material had on occasion to be requested by the defence. It would then usually be forthcoming. The modern emphasis is on the need for such disclosure to be made automatically. Accordingly, the Court of Appeal in *Fergus*[60] held that such photographs and police reports are disclosable under the general common-law duty of disclosure explained in *Ward*.[61] In *Fergus* the defendant, a 13-year-old boy, was on his way to school when he was identified by another boy as the person responsible for an attempted robbery a month previously. At the hearing of the defendant's appeal the prosecution produced a photograph of the defendant taken by the police after his arrest and a crime report containing the first details given to the police by the victim. Neither had previously been disclosed. The Court of Appeal, quashing the defendant's conviction, said that it was imperative that counsel for both prosecution and defence should be alive to the need to disclose photographs and crime reports: if necessary the trial judge ought to be asked for an appropriate order.

The same principles must be taken to apply to the Criminal Procedure and Investigations Act 1996 (which now governs disclosure). Section 3 of that Act requires the prosecutor to disclose undisclosed material to the defence which might in his opinion undermine the prosecution case.[62] It is submitted that all material relating to an identification has the potential of undermining the prosecution case and should be disclosed as a matter of course.

F. Evidence of out of court identification

14–31   Once a witness has made an out-of-court identification on some previous occasion, he is permitted to identify the suspect in the dock. This is by way of exception to the rule that dock identifications should not generally be permitted. The reason for this exception is that it is thought that the dock identification in this instance is safe and reliable since it is confirmed by the earlier out-of-court identification.[63] This evidence is admitted despite the general rule excluding evidence of previous consistent statements. The rationale for admitting evidence of the previous out-of-court identification is to show consistency in the identifications made by the witness: "to show that the [witness] was able to identify at the time to exclude the idea that the identification of the prisoner in the dock was an afterthought or mistake."[64]

In certain circumstances evidence of witnesses other than the witness who

---

[60] (1994) 98 Cr.App.R. 313.
[61] (1993) 96 Cr.App.R. 1.
[62] See para.18–11, below, for a discussion of s.3.
[63] *Christie* [1914] A.C. 545. In *Smith and Doe* (1987) 85 Cr.App.R. 197 the Court of Appeal said that a video tape of an identification at a shopping precinct should not have been shown to a witness before she gave evidence in order to "improve" her evidence as to identification.
[64] *Christie*, above, at 551, *per* Lord Haldane L.C.

has made the identification ("the identifying witness") is admissible. This subject will be considered according to the situations which may arise.

1. If the identifying witness identifies the defendant in court and gives evidence of the out-of-court identification, other witnesses may also give evidence of the out-of-court identification.[65] The rationale of admitting such evidence is the same as that for admitting similar evidence given by the identifying witness himself; to confirm the identification in court by the identifying witness.[66]

14–32

It would appear that such evidence is admitted by way of exception to the hearsay rule. That rule prohibits a witness giving evidence of what another person said, or asserted, if the purpose of the evidence is to prove that what the other person said or asserted is true. In giving evidence of the out-of-court identification, witnesses other than the identifying witnesses are giving evidence of a statement made by the identifying witness and the purpose of their evidence is to show that the identification of the accused as the person responsible for the offence is true. It would therefore appear to be an exception to the rule. However, no mention of the hearsay rule was made in *Christie* and the exception remains unformulated.

The evidence must be limited to the words which accompany and are part of the identification. Words spoken by the identifying witness which do not form part of the identification are not admissible.[67]

2. If the identifying witness identifies the defendant in court, but does not give evidence of the out-of-court identification, other witnesses may still give evidence of the out-of-court identification. Thus, in *Christie* a small boy had been indecently assaulted. Shortly after the incident he identified the accused to his mother and a police constable. At the trial the boy identified the accused in court but was not asked about the previous identification. His mother and the police constable both gave evidence of that identification. The majority of the House of Lords held that the evidence of the mother and the police constable was admissible. It went to confirm the identification made in court by the boy.

3. If the identifying witness cannot remember in court whom he picked out in an identification parade but says that the man he picked out was the man responsible for the offence, another witness may prove that he picked out the defendant.[68] The evidence of the other witness is open to the objection that it is hearsay and that it cannot be admitted for the reasons

14–33

---

[65] *Christie*, above, at 551, *per* Lord Haldane, at 554, *per* Lord Atkinson, at 563, *per* Lord Reading.

[66] *Christie*, above, at 551, *per* Lord Haldane.

[67] *Christie*, above. Evidence of words spoken by the identifying witness may, however, be admissible under rules governing admissions if the defendant's replies amount to an acceptance of the truth of what the witness has said.

[68] *Burke and Kelly* (1847) 2 Cox. C.C. 295; *Osbourne and Virtue* [1973] 1 Q.B. 678. There is no reason why the same practice should not apply to other identifications out of court provided that evidence of the identification is admissible and has not been excluded as a matter of discretion.

given in *Christie*, *i.e.* to confirm an in-court identification. Nonetheless, such evidence is admitted as a matter of practice. Whether those objections are valid or not, there are practical reasons for admitting the evidence, namely:

(a) the delay between an identification parade and trial may cause a witness to forget whom he has identified at the parade;

(b) the possibility that a defendant may change his appearance[69]; and

(c) the defence will have the opportunity of cross-examining the identifying witness as to the truth and accuracy of his identification; thus, the chief mischief against which the hearsay rule is aimed will not be present.[70]

In *McCay*[71] a witness attended an identification parade. The participants in the parade were numbered. The witness, looking at the parade from a separate room through a two-way mirror, identified the defendant by reference to his number. At the trial the witness said that he attended the parade and made an identification, but could not remember the number. A police inspector was allowed to give evidence of the number to which the witness had referred at the parade. The Court of Appeal held that the inspector's evidence was admissible as part of the *res gestae* (see para.8–50, above) and also because the procedure adopted at the parade was sanctioned by Code D and, as a result, there was statutory authority in ss.66 and 67(11) of the Police and Criminal Evidence Act 1984 for the words to be admitted.[72]

In *Osbourne and Virtue*[73] the Court of Appeal held that, even if an identifying witness is not able to identify the defendant in court and does not recall the identification parade, another witness may give evidence that the identifying witness picked out the defendant on a parade. This decision has been criticised on the grounds that: (a) it conflicts with the decision of the House of Lords in *Christie*; and (b) it involves the admission of hearsay evidence as a result of which the defence has no opportunity of cross-examining the person who made the identification.[74]

14–34   It is submitted that these criticisms are valid. The Court said in *Osbourne and Virtue* of *Christie* that "this can be got from the speeches: that evidence of identification other than identification in the witness-box is admis-

---

[69] *Osbourne and Virtue*, above, at 690.
[70] D.F. Libling, "Evidence of Past Identification" [1977] Crim.L.R. 268, 277.
[71] [1990] 1 W.L.R. 645.
[72] Code D provided that a witness (in the procedure adopted in the case) should make an identification by indicating the number of the person concerned a similar procedure is now contained in para.17 of Annex B of Code D).
[73] [1973] 1 Q.B. 678.
[74] *Phipson on Evidence* (14th ed., 1990), para.15–10; Libling, *op.cit.*

sible."[75] However, *Christie* does not support this wide proposition. As has been seen, the evidence of the identifying witness and the other witnesses in *Christie* was admitted to confirm the identification of the defendant in court. In *Osbourne and Virtue* there was no identification in court. The evidence therefore could not be admissible under the principle stated in *Christie*.

The situation where the identifying witness cannot recall the identification *procedure* is to be contrasted with the situation considered in para.14–33 where the witness could remember making an identification. In those circumstances the identifying witness can be cross-examined about his identification.

In the situation considered in this paragraph, the identification is established by the hearsay evidence of another witness with the result that:

(a) the jury is deprived of the opportunity of hearing and observing the identifying witness giving evidence about the identification; and

(b) the defence is deprived of the opportunity of cross-examining the identifying witness.

These circumstances are not consistent with the principle that the defendant should have a fair trial. It is therefore submitted that *Osbourne and Virtue* should not be followed and that if a witness cannot identify the defendant in court and cannot recall making an earlier identification, no other evidence as to that identification should be admitted.

4. THE USE OF PHOTOGRAPHS FOR IDENTIFICATION

Two rules governing the use of photographs must be distinguished, namely: **14–35**

(1) The police may show a witness photographs in order to identify a suspect.[76]

(2) Once a man has been arrested, and there is therefore an opportunity that he can be identified in person, photographs should not be shown to witnesses before an identification parade.[77]

The distinction is that when the police are looking for a culprit, the showing of photographs to witnesses may be essential; indeed, it may be the only way in which the culprit can be identified. Once, however, a man has been arrested and is to be put on an identification parade, it would be

---

[75] Above, at 690.
[76] *Dwyer* [1925] 2 K.B. 799; *Kitchen* [1994] Crim.L.R. 684.
[77] *Dwyer*, above. See para.14–37, below, for Code D:3.3.

dangerous to allow the witnesses to see photographs since they may identify the man in the photograph rather than the man whom they saw committing the offence.

When the police show photographs to a witness in order that the witness can identify a suspect, considerations of fairness must be borne in mind. Therefore, the witness should be shown a number of photographs of different people (one of whom is the accused) rather than one or two photographs only.[78] This makes a photographic identification of the defendant by the witness more effective as evidence.[79]

If a witness has been shown a photograph of the accused, this fact should be disclosed to the defence.[80] The defence may then wish this fact to be brought out at the trial.

Until recently, it had been held that there was a rule that the prosecution could not lead evidence of identification of the defendant from a photograph. This was because it was felt that the jury would infer from the existence of the photographs that the defendant had a criminal record, such photographs usually being taken in a police station. Thus, the Court of Criminal Appeal held that an irregularity had occurred in *Wright*,[81] where a prosecution witness volunteered that he had seen a photograph of the defendant in the "rogues' gallery" at New Scotland Yard. Similarly, in *Lamb*[82] the prosecution produced in court a sheet of prison photographs of a number of men including the defendants. The jury, when then in retirement, asked to see "mug-shots" of the defendants. The Court of Appeal held the production of the photographs to have been an irregularity. Only if the defence was in some way taking unfair advantage of the rule could the photographic identification be referred to. In *Bleakley*[83] the witness, who was a shopkeeper, identified the defendant first from a photograph and then at an identification parade. The evening before the parade the defendant

---

[78] *Dwyer*, above.

[79] "The object of showing a group of photographs to a witness is to test his ability to pick out the photograph, if it is there, of the person whom the witness had said that he has seen previously on a specified occasion": Report of the Departmental Committee on Evidence of Identification, Cmnd.338 (1976), para.5.91.

[80] *Lamb* (1980) 71 Cr.App.R. 198. Para.9 of Annex E of the Code provides that where a witness attending a video identification, identification parade or group identification has previously been shown photographs or computerised or artist's composite likeness or similar likeness, the suspect and his solicitor must be informed of this fact before an identification parade. In *Wright* [1994] Crim.L.R. 131 an identifying witness contributed to the making of an identikit. The defence were not informed of this fact until the closing tages of the trial. However, the Court of Appeal held that there had been no breaching of the Code as it did not apply to a person responsible for making an identikit. The Court pointed out that the theme of the Code was that the suspect should be protected from a person who, having seen a photograph before the parade, tended to identify the person in the photograph rather than the person who committed the crime. On the other hand, in the instant case the witness, having contributed to the making of the identikit, would be identifying his own identification.

[81] (1934) 25 Cr.App.R. 35.

[82] Above.

[83] [1993] Crim.L.R. 203.

came to the witness's shop and tried to speak to him. At the trial the defence suggested that the witness had identified the defendant at the parade because of the defendant's visit to the shop. The trial judge allowed evidence to be given of the identification by photograph by the witness, and the Court of Appeal held that he was right to have done so.

However, in *Allen*,[84] when both *Lamb* and *Bleakley* were applied, the Court of Appeal held that there was no rule that the prosecution could not lead evidence of previous photographic identifications unless the defence took unfair advantage of the rule: there were a number of circumstances in which such evidence could be led before the jury. But it is submitted that the overriding criterion must be that of fairness.

14–36

If it does emerge in evidence that the police showed a witness photographs of a defendant, it is a matter for the discretion of the judge whether to direct the jury that it must not be prejudiced because the police had a photograph of the defendant.[85] It may make matters worse if such a warning is given, as the jury may not realise that the photograph results from a criminal record. It may be better to make no remark at all.[86]

The judge has a discretion to exclude evidence of identification if there is an irregularity in the use of photographs, although any such irregularity need not necessarily lead to exclusion of the evidence or, if admitted, the quashing of any subsequent conviction. The question of exclusion arose in *Maynard*.[87] A witness in that case identified two defendants by photograph. No identification parade took place. The admissibility of the evidence of identification was contested in a trial-within-a-trial which lasted two-and-a-half days. It was contended by the defence that the evidence of identification by photograph was inadmissible because it had not been followed by an identification parade. The judge admitted the evidence. The Court of Appeal held that the evidence was admissible. While identification by photograph not followed by an identification parade may be very weak identification, its weight was a matter for the jury. The Court said: "We would only interfere with the learned judge's exercise of his discretion after a long argument and a trial-within-a-trial if we thought that in some relevant respect the learned judge had exercised his discretion upon some erroneous principle."[88]

The admission of evidence of identification by photograph may be justified by the defendant's conduct. In *Byrne and Trump*[89] a witness was shown photographs by the police six days after a robbery. He picked out B

14–37

---

[84] [1996] Crim.L.R. 426.
[85] *Lawrenson* [1961] Crim.L.R. 398.
[86] *Wright* (1934) 24 Cr.App.R. 35; *cf. Hunjan* (1979) 68 Cr.App.R. 99 (a case in which the Court of Appeal said that a comment should have been made by the judge).
[87] (1979) 69 Cr.App.R. 309, 314–316.
[88] At 315. In *Governor of Pentonville Prison Ex p. Voets* [1986] 1 W.L.R. 470, 473, the Divisional Court said that photographs from police files were admissible to prove identity subject to the judge's discretion to exclude them.
[89] [1987] Crim.L.R. 689.

as a participant in the robbery. He did not pick out B at an identification parade held two days later. B had altered his appearance from that in the photograph. The prosecution was allowed to adduce evidence of B's picking out the photo. The Court of Appeal held that this course was justified in order to defeat B's attempt to avoid being identified.

The Code of Practice lays down rules for the use of photographs. The Code provides that:

(a) photographs must be shown in accordance with Annex E to the Code[90];

(b) photographs should not be shown if there is a suspect whose identity is known to the police and who is available to take part in a video identification, an identification parade or a group identification[91];

(c) once the witness has made an identification from photographs, other witnesses should not be shown photographs but should attend a video identification, an identification parade, or group identification.[92] It sometimes happens, as in *Lamb*,[93] that more than one suspect falls to be identified. In that case, subsequent witnesses will have to see the photographs in an attempt to identify other suspects. If this is done, the photographs of the original suspect (once identified by any witness) should be removed from the album[94];

(d) a witness who has made a firm identification by photograph should always be asked to attend an identification parade unless the person identified is eliminated from inquiries or is unavailable.[95]

5. ADMISSIBILITY OF IDENTIFICATION BASED ON PHOTOGRAPHIC IMAGES

14–38   In some cases it may arise that the defendant is positively identified by a witness from a photograph or video film without subsequently making an identification at one of the identification procedures set out in Code D. The position in relation to the admission of identification evidence involving

---

[90] para.D:3.3.
[91] *ibid.*
[92] Annex E, para.6.
[93] (1980) 71 Cr.App.R. 198, cited at para.14–23.
[94] *Lamb*, above, at 201, 202.
[95] Annex E, para.6.

video films or photographs has now been clarified.[96] There are at least four circumstances in which identification evidence based on such evidence is admissible:

(i) Where the photographic image is sufficiently clear and the jury can compare it with the defendant sitting in the dock.[97]

(ii) Where a witness knows the defendant sufficiently well to recognise him as the offender depicted in the photographic image,[98] this may be so even where the photographic image is no longer available to the jury.[99]

(iii) Where a witness who does not know the defendant has spent substantial time viewing and analysing photographic images from the scene, thereby acquiring special knowledge and skill, he can give evidence of identification based on a comparison between those images and a reasonably contemporary photograph of the defendant, provided that the images and photograph are available to the jury.[1]

(iv) A suitably qualified facial mapping expert can give opinion evidence of identification based on a comparison between images from the scene, whether enhanced or not, and a reasonably contemporary photograph of the defendant, again, provided the images and photograph are available to the jury.[2]

In *Hookway*[3] it was held that evidence of a facial mapping expert alone may be sufficient to establish a prima facie case upon which a jury would be entitled to convict.

6. ADMISSIBILITY OF PHOTOFITS AND SKETCHES

There was doubt for some time as to whether photofit pictures were admissible or not.[4] Although occasionally admitted, it was thought that

14–39

---

[96] *Att-Gen's Reference (Criminal Justice Act 1972, s.36) (No.2 of 2002)*, October 7, 2002, unreported, *Archbold News*, Issue 10, December 18, 2002.
[97] *Dodson and Williams* (1984) Crim.L.R. 220.
[98] *Caldwell and Dixon* (1994) 99 Cr.App.R. 73 and *Blenkinsop* [1995] 1 Cr.App.R. 7.
[99] *Taylor v Chief Constable of Cheshire* (1987) 84 Cr.App.R. 191.
[1] *Clare and Peach* [1995] 2 Cr.App.R. 333.
[2] *Stockwell* (1993) 97 Cr.App.R. 260; *Clarke* [1995] 2 Cr.App.R. 425; and *Hookway* [1999] Crim.L.R. 750.
[3] Above.
[4] See the contrasting decisions of *Okorodu* [1982] Crim.L.R. 747 (in which a photofit was admitted in a trial at Inner London Crown Court) and *O'Brien* [1982] Crim.L.R. 746 (in which a photofit was excluded in a trial at the Central Criminal Court).

they fell foul of the rule against consistent statements. However, in *Cook*[5] the Court of Appeal held that photofits are admissible since they are not statements but (with photographs and sketches) in a class of evidence of their own. The Court said that neither the rule against hearsay nor the rule against consistent statements applied. The Court described the production of a sketch or photofit as a graphic representation of the witness's memory and, as such, another form of the camera at work.

The decision in *Cook* has been criticised as owing more to practical considerations than to logical consistency.[6] If so, it would seem right that practical considerations should prevail over technical rules. In assessing the accuracy of an identification the jury should have access to all relevant information. In this connection the witness's impression in the form of a photofit made soon after the event in question is vital. As such, it should not be withheld from the jury.[7]

The government has also approved a computer-based system known as "electronic facial identification" (E-FIT). In this system a computer is programmed with numerous facial features taken from photographs. The operator uses this program to make a picture of the suspect on a video screen. Technology is thus used to assist the operator in drawing the picture. This would appear to make no difference to the admissibility of the picture. If a picture produced by photofit is admissible, so, it would appear, is a picture produced by means of E-FIT.

14–40 At the time of writing there has been no reported case in which the Court of Appeal has given general guidance as to how a jury should be directed in relation to the significance of photofit evidence. In *Constantinou*[8] the Court of Appeal held that the judge had correctly directed the jury in telling them (a) that no witness had identified the appellant, (b) that witnesses had given descriptions and produced a photofit which the jury may think were consistent with the defendant, but (c) "it does not go further than that". The Court said that it was not necessary to supplement this direction with a "*Turnbull*" warning. Accordingly, it would appear appropriate to remind a jury that (a) the production of a photofit does not amount to an identification, but (b) its significance is to show the witness's impression of the offender made soon after the offence.

It is submitted that the same principles apply to sketches made on the instructions of a witness soon after the event. As has been seen, the Court of Appeal in *Cook*[9] put them in the same category of evidence as photofits.

---

[5] (1987) 84 Cr.App.R. 369. *Cook* was followed by the Court of Appeal in *Constantinou* (1990) 91 Cr.App.R. 74.
[6] Munday, "Photofit pictures and the Law of Evidence" 151 J.P.N. 83. See also commentary by Professor J.C. Smith [1987] Crim.L.R. 403.
[7] See *Okorodu* and Munday, *op.cit.*
[8] (1990) 91 Cr.App.R. 74.
[9] Above.

The question of the admissibility of a sketch was considered in *Smith (Percy)*.[10] In that case a witness had seen a man near the house where a woman was murdered; and at her direction a police officer made a sketch. The sketch was admitted in evidence. The defendant's appeal on the ground that the admission of the sketch involved hearsay was dismissed. The Court said that the witness using her memory had directed the sketching hand of the officer and it was her sketch made through the officer's hand.

7. OTHER FORMS OF IDENTIFICATION

A. Identification by fingerprints

Identification is often made by means of fingerprints.[11] In a typical case, a **14–41** police officer goes to the scene of a crime and finds fingerprints (or palm prints) there.[12] The fingerprints are compared by an expert with those of the defendant. The expert gives evidence that having compared the two sets of prints his opinion is that the fingerprints at the scene were made by the defendant. Since experts usually demand a very high level of correspondence between the two sets (16 similar ridge characteristics is normally quoted), such evidence is very convincing proof of identity. If the evidence is disputed, it will be a matter for the jury to decide whether the identification is correct or not.[13] Juries should be warned that expert evidence is not always conclusive in itself and the issue of guilt would have to be proved in light of all the evidence. In *Buckley*[14] it was held that if there were fewer than eight ridge characteristics matching the fingerprints of an accused with fingerprints found by the police, it was unlikely that a judge would exercise his discretion to admit such evidence and, unless there were exceptional circumstances, the prosecution should not seek to introduce it. Rose L.J. stated that whether fingerprint evidence was admissible as a matter of law tending to prove guilt would depend on:

    (i)   experience and expertise of the witness;

    (ii) number of similar ridge characteristics;

---

[10] [1976] Crim.L.R. 511.

[11] Code of Practice D:1.3 provides that identification by fingerprints applies when a person's fingerprints are taken to compare with fingerprints found at the scene of a crime, check and prove convictions, and help to ascertain a person's identity.

[12] Code of Practice D:4.1 provides that reference to "fingerprints" means any record, produced by any method, of the skin pattern and other physical characteristics or features of a persons fingers or palms. Section D:4 of the Code of Practice is concerned with the taking of fingerprints in connection with a criminal investigation. Annex F of the Code provides for the retention and destruction of such records.

[13] See Campbell, "Fingerprints: A Review" [1985] Crim.L.R. 195 for a discussion of identification by means of fingerprints.

[14] *The Times*, May 12, 1999.

(iii) whether there are dissimilar characteristics;

(iv) size of print relied on; and

(v) quality and clarity of print relied on which might involve consideration of possible injuries to fingers.

Even if there is no other evidence of identity (as is often the case in offences such as burglary) the evidence may well be sufficient to convict the defendant. The Court of Criminal Appeal has dismissed appeals made on the ground that identity was established by fingerprints alone.[15] It does not, of course, follow that by establishing the defendant's presence at a certain place by means of fingerprints that the prosecution will establish the offence charged. Thus, in *Court*,[16] the defendant was convicted of receiving a stolen motor car. His fingerprints had been found on the rear view mirror of the car. The Court of Criminal Appeal held that this was insufficient evidence of his possession of the car. It may well, however, in certain circumstances be sufficient evidence of taking the car without consent, or driving or being carried in it.

B. Identification by DNA

14–42 A defendant may be identified by the technique of DNA profiling, the analysis of the material of which chromosomes are made.[17] This technique has been used successfully for forensic purposes for a number of years.[18] However, problems have arisen concerning the complexity of the evidence and the weight to be attached to it. This led the Court of Appeal in *Gordon*[19] to say that it did not doubt the validity and value of DNA evidence, but the effect of the evidence in the instant case was to raise arguable questions as to whether the match probabilities could be sustained. Lord Taylor C.J. commented that figures running into millions exert a strong influence on a jury. The Court heard additional expert evidence and ordered a retrial. In *Deen*[20] Lord Taylor C.J. warned of the dangers of the "prosecutor's fallacy" in relation to DNA evidence, *i.e.* confusing the answers to the following questions: (1) what is the probability that a person

---

[15] *Castleton* (1909) 3 Cr.App.R. 74; *Bacon* (1915) 11 Cr.App.R. 90.

[16] (1960) 44 Cr.App.R. 242.

[17] Code of Practice D:1.4 provides that identification by body samples and impressions includes taking samples such as blood or hair to generate a DNA profile for comparison with material obtained from the scene of a crime, or a victim. Section D:6 provides procedures for obtaining body samples and impressions from suspects. Code F provides procedures for the retention or destruction of such samples.

[18] In Kelly, Rankin and Wink, "Method and Applications of DNA Fingerprinting" [1987] Crim.L.R. 105, 110 it is claimed that the technique makes positive identification "virtually certain". It must be doubted whether (in the light of subsequent cases) such a claim would be made now (see below). However, the evidence clearly has a very high probative value.

[19] [1995] 1 Cr.App.R. 290.

[20] *The Times*, January 10, 1994.

would match the DNA from the crime sample if he is innocent?; (2) what is the probability of his being innocent given that he matches the DNA profile from the crime sample? The fallacy consists in giving the answer to the first question as the answer to the second: for an example, see para.14–43, below.[21]

Similarly, in *Adams*[22] the defence at trial were allowed to adduce evidence of Bayes Theorem (a formula giving a numerical probability to pieces of evidence) in connection with the statistical evaluation of the DNA profile. The Court of Appeal doubted whether evidence of the Theorem was admissible because it trespassed on an area exclusively within the jury's province, namely the way in which they evaluated the relationship between one piece of evidence and another. The Court also said such evidence (or any similar statistical method of analysis) plunged the jury into inappropriate and unnecessary realms of theory and complexity deflecting them from their proper tasks: it was not appropriate for use in jury trials. This view was reinforced in *Adams (No.2)*[23] (an appeal from the retrial in *Adams*). In *Adams (No.2)* the Court of Appeal said that (in the absence of special features) expert evidence such as that of Bayes Theorem should not be admitted since such evidence was a recipe for confusion, misunderstanding and misjudgment: the instant case was properly approached on conventional lines and the jury would not have been assisted by reference to a complex approach which they were unlikely to understand or apply accurately, and which would distract them from consideration of the real issues.

A further danger has been identified in relation to the calling of DNA **14–43** evidence, *i.e.* that of the expert scientific witness usurping the function of the jury by giving an opinion as to the strength of the DNA evidence (a matter which should be left to the jury). Thus in *Doheny and Adams*[24] scientists had been allowed to comment on the high degree of probability that the defendant had left the crime stain. Indeed, in *Adams* (one of the two similar cases considered by the Court of Appeal) a scientist agreed in answer to a leading question that he was sure it was the defendant. The Court said that all the scientist should do is give evidence of the match in the DNA between the crime stain and the defendant; of his calculation of the frequency with which such matching DNA characteristics are likely to be found in the population at large (the "common occurrence ratio"); and, if appropriate, how many people with the same characteristics are likely to be found in the UK (or some relevant sub-group).

---

[21] For a full discussion, see Balding and Donnelly, "The Prosecutor's Fallacy and DNA Evidence" [1994] Crim.L.R. 711.
[22] [1996] 2 Cr.App.R. 467.
[23] [1998] 1 Cr.App.R. 377.
[24] [1997] 1 Cr.App.R. 369.

"If one person in a million has a DNA profile which matches that obtained from the crime stain and the suspect has such a profile, then the suspect will be one of perhaps 26 men in the UK who share that characteristic. If no fact about the defendant is known other than that he was in the United Kingdom at the time of the crime the DNA evidence tells us no more than that there is a statistical probability that he was the criminal of 1 in 26. The significance of the DNA evidence will depend critically upon what else is known about the suspect."[25]

(The prosecutor's fallacy is to say in the above example that there is a million-to-one probability that the defendant is guilty.) The true position is this: it is for the jury to decide on all the evidence whether they are sure that it was the defendant who left the crime stain rather than one of the other men with the same DNA profile.

The Court in *Doheny and Adams*[26] said that the following procedure should be followed in relation to DNA evidence.

(1) The expert's evidence

14–44   The prosecution scientist should adduce evidence of the DNA comparisons together with his calculations of the "random occurence ratio". Also, the scientist should say, if appropriate, how many people with matching characteristics are likely to be found in the UK population. The scientist should not be asked (and should not use language to suggest) his opinion as to the likelihood that it is the defendant who left the crime stain.

(2) Disclosure

14–45   The prosecution should disclose to the defence suficient details as to how the calculations have been carried out to allow the defence to scutinise the basis of the calculations. The Forensic Sciences Service should make available to the defence expert, if requested, the databases upon which the calculations have been based.[27]

(3) Summing-up

14–46   The judge should explain to the jury the relevance of the "random occur-rence ratio" and draw attention to the extraneous evidence which provides the context which gives the ratio its significance. The judge should also draw attention to the evidence which conflicts with the conclusion that the defendant is responsible for the crime stain. The following direction (tai-lored to the circumstances of the particular case) may be appropriate:

---

[25] *Doheny and Adams*, above, at 373.
[26] Above, at 374–375.
[27] See para.18–10, below, for general discussion concerning disclosure.

"[If] you accept the scientific evidence called by the Crown, this indicates that there are probably only four or five males in the United Kingdom from whom that semen stain could have come. The defendant is one of them. If that is the position, the decision you have to reach, on all the evidence, is whether you are sure that it was the defendant who left that stain or whether it is possible that it was one of that other small group of men who share the same DNA characteristics."[28]

C. Possession of Incriminating Articles as Evidence of Identity

There may be occasions when the possession of incriminating articles will support an identification. Two cases illustrate the proposition.   **14–47**

1. In *Thompson*,[29] the defendant had been charged with gross indecency with two boys. The boys said that after committing the offences the defendant made an appointment to meet them at a public lavatory three days later. The police were informed. When the defendant kept the appointment one of the boys pointed him out. Powder puffs and indecent photographs were found in the defendant's possession. These articles had not been used in the offences. The House of Lords, however, held that the evidence of the accused's possession of such articles had been rightly admitted since it supported the identification of the accused by the witnesses: possession of these articles tended to show that the defendant was a homosexual, and so it was less likely that the identification was mistaken.

2. In *Reading*,[30] lorries had been hijacked. A driver identified the defendant as one of the men involved. Evidence was given that when the defendant's house was searched, a police-type uniform, walkie-talkie and number plates were found. There was no evidence that any of these articles had been used in the robberies. Shoes and stockings of a type carried by one of the hijacked lorries were also found. The Court of Appeal followed *Thompson* and held that this evidence had rightly been admitted. Although the articles had not been used in the perpetration of offences, evidence of the defendant's possession of them tended to negative the possibility of mistaken identification. The possession of articles in

---

[28] *Doheny and Adams*, above, at 375.
[29] [1918] A.C. 221. The House of Lords in *DPP v Boardman* [1975] A.C. 421 rejected the notion expressed by Lord Sumner in *Thompson* that homosexual offences were in a special category of their own. However, the rejection of that notion would not necessarily prevent evidence similar to that adduced in *Thompson* being admitted today, provided that its probative value outweighed its prejudicial effect. See Ch.7, above.
[30] (1966) 50 Cr.App.R. 98.

Reading showed a criminal disposition. Therefore, the identification was less likely to be mistaken.

D. Voice identification

14–48 A suspect may be identified by means of his voice. While Code D of PACE is primarily concerned with visual identification procedures, it does not preclude the police making use of aural identification procedures such as a "voice identification parade", where it is judged appropriate.[31] In *Hersey*[32] the defendant was charged with robbery. The offence involved the robbery of a shop by two men in balaclavas. The shopkeeper thought that he could identify the voice of one of the robbers as being that of a customer. The police arranged a voice identification parade at which the defendant and eleven volunteers read out a passage from a previous unrelated interview with the defendant: the shopkeeper identified the defendant's voice (although two other witnesses failed to do so). At trial the defence submitted that the evidence relating to the parade should be excluded under s.78 of the Police and Criminal Evidence Act 1984, and called an expert to give evidence on the *voir dire*. The expert gave evidence about the readings, the pitch of the voices, and the effect of stress on pitch. The judge in the exercise of his discretion refused to exclude the evidence; and the Court of Appeal held that he was right to have done so. The Court said that one of the purposes of the parade was to give the witness the opportunity to test his identification, and to give the defendant the opportunity to have the evidence excluded: the police must do the best they can with regard to the arrangements for the parade and a judge would exclude the evidence if he considered it unfair.[33] If the evidence is admitted the judge must direct the jury of the risk of a mistaken identification, following the *Turnbull* guidelines (suitably adapted and tailored for voice identification) and dealing with the strengths and weaknesses of the case.[34] Research has indicated that voice identification is even more difficult than visual identification, thus the warning given to jurors should be even more stringent than that given in relation to visual identification. Identification of the voice

---

[31] D:1.2 Code of Practice.

[32] [1998] Crim.L.R. 281. See also *Gummerson and Steadman* [1999] Crim.L.R. 680.

[33] For a call for greater safeguards before evidence is admitted in these circumstances, see commentary at [1998] Crim.L.R. 282.

[34] *Hersey*, above. For the *Turnbull* guidelines, see para.14–03, above. See Ormerod "*Sounds Familiar?—Voice Identification Evidence*" [2001] Crim.L.R. 595 for a full discussion of the dangers of relying on voice identification evidence. Ormerod suggests specific factors relevant to the quality of voice identification which could be adapted to the structure of a *Turnbull* warning. These are for example: the length of exposure, the audibility and variety of speech, and other environmental factors affecting quality. The jury should also be alert to the witness's age and any hearing disability. Particular factors affecting a given case might include the witness's intoxication or drowsiness, whether there was dialogue with the suspect, and most importantly the degree of familiarity the witness claims with the voice. Relevant factors relating to the voice itself include the language and accent.

of a stranger is especially difficult, even where there was a good opportunity to listen to the voice.[35] It is submitted that judges should be alert to the relevant dangers, and be prepared to withdraw cases, by analogy with *Turnbull*, where evidence is of a poor quality.

E. Miscellaneous cases

(a) A defendant may be identified by his handwriting on the evidence of an expert. **14–49**

(b) The analysis of bloodstains may assist in identifying a suspect by means of blood-grouping tests.

(c) A witness may identify an acquaintance by means of a video tape: see paras 2–37 *et seq.*, above.

(d) Photographs taken by a security camera at the time that an offence (for example a bank robbery) is committed are admissible to prove the identity of the offender: see para.2–14, above.

(e) In the 1950s evidence was admitted at first instance that a police dog tracked the defendant from the scene of an arson to a shelter where he was found.[36] There was, until recently, no authority of an appellate court that such evidence was admissible to establish identity.[37] Such evidence has been admitted in New Zealand, provided that the qualifications of the dog-handler and his dog have been established.[38] The Court of Appeal of New Zealand has said that if the evidence is admitted the judge must draw the jury's attention (a) to the nature of the conclusions which they are asked to draw and (b) to the risks of relying on material which has not been the subject of cross-examination.[39]

The Court of Appeal has now held that tracker dog evidence is admissible provided that there is evidence that the dog is properly trained and reliable.[40] The Court stressed that before such evidence was admitted, a proper foundation had to be laid by evidence in detail establishing the reliability of the dog to be able to follow a scent by reason of its training and experience. The Court also said that the judge must direct the jury to consider the

---

[35] *Roberts* [2000] Crim.L.R. 183. For a more detailed comment on the scientific evidence in this area see Bull and Clifford, "*Earwitness Testimony*" in Heaton-Armstrong, Shepherd and Wolchover (eds), *Analysing Witness Testimony* (1999).
[36] *Webb* [1954] Crim.L.R. 49.
[37] For a discussion of the admissibility of such evidence in other jurisdictions, see McCormack, "The Admissibility of Tracker Dog Evidence" [1985] Crim.L.R. 202.
[38] *Lindsay* [1970] 1 N.Z.L.R. 1002.
[39] *McCarthy* [1976] 1 N.Z.L.R. 472.
[40] *Pieterson and Holloway* [1995] 2 Cr.App.R. 11.

evidence with care and circumspection as the dog might not be reliable and could not be cross-examined. (More recently, the Court of Appeal reiterated this guidance and said that the judge should expressly direct the jury that they should look with circumspection at the evidence.[41])

(f) Comparison of ear prints from a crime scene and suspect cannot alone be regarded as a safe basis on which to identify a particular individual for the purpose of trial, they can only properly help to narrow the field by eliminating potential suspects.[42]

(g) In *Allen v Ireland*[43] the Divisional Court held that a magistrate could take judicial notice of the ordinary processes of arrest, charge and bail to raise a prima facie case that the person surrendering to bail was the same person who had been arrested, charged and bailed. In that case about 250 football supporters were arrested under s.5 of the Public Order Act 1936 in Euston Road. They were charged at various police stations and bailed. The 11 defendants surrendered to their bail at the magistrates' court. A submission that there was no evidence identifying the defendants as part of the group in Euston Road was rejected by the court for the reason mentioned above.

(h) Evidence of propensity to commit the crime charged may be admissible to identify the defendant as the person responsible for committing the offence charged: para.7–14, above. However, it is doubtful whether it is permissible to prove identity by the technique known as "psychological profiling". Thus, in a trial at the Central Criminal Court, Ognall J. said that there were considerable dangers in admitting such evidence as proof of identity.[44] This was because (a) such evidence might tend to show propensity and nothing more and (b) it was doubtful whether the evidence was expert evidence.

(i) Section 54A of PACE 1984 allows a detainee at a police station to be searched or examined to establish whether they have any marks, features or injuries that would tend to identify them as a person involved in the commission of an offence and to photograph such marks.[45] Evidence of a descriptive nature, such as describing a man with a large tattoo on his arm, may be highly probative and therefore admissible. In the event that the prose-

[41] *Sykes* [1997] Crim.L.R. 752.
[42] *Dallagher*, July 25, 2002, unreported, *Archbold News*, Issue 8, September 19, 2002.
[43] (1984) 79 Cr.App.R. 206.
[44] *Stagg*, September 14, 1994, unreported, *Archbold News*, Issue 9, November 4, 1994.
[45] Code of Practice D:5 provides procedures for the examination and photographing of such persons.

cution are unable to call identification evidence because of its failure to hold an identification parade, they are not prevented from calling descriptive evidence. In *Byron*,[46] where the appellant had been one of only two adults living in the house, the tattoo evidence—which was descriptive—was of elimination and not identification.

---

[46] *The Times*, March 10, 1999.

CHAPTER 15

Corroboration and Suspect Evidence

1. THE CORROBORATION RULES

A. Common law rules

15–01 In general, the evidence of a single witness is sufficient to prove any issue. Juries or magistrates may, therefore, as a general rule, convict on the evidence of one competent witness alone.[1]

However, until the 1990s, the law required that the evidence of certain witnesses be confirmed by other evidence. This confirming evidence is known as "corroboration" and the rules governing the topic as the "corroboration rules".

It has been said that the word "corroboration" is not a technical term of art but a dictionary word bearing its own meaning.[2] In this sense it means evidence which "confirms", "supports" or "strengthens" other evidence.[3] However, for the purpose of the rules relating to corroboration, it meant independent evidence which implicated the accused in the offence charged in a material particular.[4]

In some cases, statute required that evidence be corroborated: see below. In others, the judge had, as a matter of practice, to warn juries that it was dangerous to convict on the evidence of a particular witness unless it was corroborated. (In these cases magistrates had to direct themselves in the same way as juries were directed.)

Such warnings had to be given in relation to the evidence of children, accomplices and complainants in sexual cases. This was because it was considered that the evidence of these witnesses was inherently unreliable. Thus, it was thought that the evidence of children may be unreliable due to fallibility of memory or susceptibility to influence. In the case of an accomplice there is the risk that he may give false evidence, for instance,

---

[1] *Hester* [1973] A.C. 296, 324 (*per* Lord Diplock); *Kilbourne* [1973] A.C. 729, 739, *per* Lord Hailsham.
[2] *Kilbourne*, above, at 741, *per* Lord Hailsham.
[3] *Hester*, above, at 315 *per* Lord Morris of Borth-y-Gest, at 321, *per* Lord Pearson, at 323, 325, *per* Lord Diplock.
[4] *Baskerville* [1916] 2 K.B. 658, 667, *per* Lord Reading C.J. For the common law rules, see Ch.12 of the second edition of this work.

minimising his own part and exaggerating that of others in order to obtain a lighter sentence; and in the case of complainants in sexual cases it was thought that they may give false evidence as a result of fantasy, neurosis, jealousy or spite (or, if a girl, shame at having to admit to consenting to sexual intercourse). Ideas about these matters have now changed and, as will be seen, the common law rules have been abolished.

B. Statutory provisions

In the following cases, statutes require that evidence should be corroborated before a person is convicted.[5] The same rules apply to attempts to commit these offences: Criminal Attempts Act 1981, ss.2(1) and 2(2)(g). These provisions (apart from those relating to procuration, below) have not been affected by the abolition of the common law rules.[6] 15–02

(1) Perjury

A person may not be convicted of an offence of perjury or subornation of perjury "solely upon the evidence of one witness as to the falsity of any statement alleged to be false": Perjury Act 1911, s.13. The reason for the requirement is historical. Perjury was originally punished in the Star Chamber which usually required a second witness in cases which it tried.[7] 15–03

However, the section does not refer to the need for a second witness to give evidence as to the falsity of the statement. The requirement is for something more than the evidence of one witness on the point. Thus, the evidence of one witness together with proof of some material which confirms the witness's evidence would be sufficient. Denman C.J. said that a letter written by the accused contradicting a statement made by him on oath would suffice.[8] A letter sent on behalf of the defendant which was consistent with subornation of a witness has also been held to be sufficient to comply with the section[9] as has the evidence of two witnesses testifying to having heard the defendant admit the falsity of the statement on the same occasion[10]: "the evidence is evidence of the falsity and there are two witnesses testifying to it."[11]

Once the falsehood of the statement has been established by further

---

[5] The proviso to s.38(1) of the Children and Young Persons Act 1933 (which prevented a person being convicted on the unsworn evidence of a child unless it was corroborated) has been repealed by the Criminal Justice Act 1988, s.34(1) and Sch.16. Accordingly, the unsworn evidence of a child is of the same effect as sworn evidence given by an adult or child.
[6] para.15–05, below.
[7] Criminal Law Revision Committee Eleventh Report, Cmnd. 4991, para.178.
[8] *Mayhew* (1834) 6 C. & P. 315. In Mayhew an account delivered by the defendant which contradicted his statement on oath was held to be sufficient.
[9] *Threlfall* (1914) 10 Cr.App.R. 112, 114.
[10] *Peach* [1990] 2 All E.R. 966.
[11] At 969, *per* Lord Lane C.J.

evidence, there is no need for corroboration that the defendant knew that the statement was false.[12]

Although there is no mention of corroboration in the section, the modern practice is to approach the statutory requirement as one of corroboration.[13] The reason is that prosecution witnesses may have a purpose of their own for giving evidence against the defendant which is not true. This means that juries should be warned of the need for corroboration of the evidence relating to the falsity of the material statement.[14] The jury should, therefore, be directed that it must not convict in the absence of corroboration. Such a direction must always be given in cases where the prosecution alleges that the material statement was false, unless this is not disputed by the defendant.[15] The Court of Appeal described such a direction as a requisite of a summing up, together with a reference to the need for the jury to have before it the evidence (which they accept) of more than one witness, *i.e.* the evidence of another witness or some other supporting evidence.[16] A warning is particularly necessary where the prosecution is relying upon the evidence of any accomplice who has himself committed perjury.[17]

If, of course, there is no evidence capable of amounting to corroboration at the close of the prosecution case, it will be the duty of the judge to stop the case.

(2) Speeding

15–04 A person may not be convicted of exceeding the speed limit solely on the evidence of one witness to the effect that in the opinion of the witness the defendant was exceeding the limit: Road Traffic Regulation Act 1984, s.89(2). (The Law Commission in its Report on Corroboration, below, pointed out that the requirement was not a corroboration requirement properly so called. However, it is convenient to deal with the topic here.)

A person may be convicted under this section on the evidence of the opinion of the police officer corroborated by a speedometer reading by him.[18] Justices may act on the evidence of a reading, notwithstanding that it is not proved that the speedometer has been tested.[19] Once justices have accepted that the reading of a speedometer is capable of providing corroboration of the police officer's opinion, they cannot reject the unchallenged

---

[12] *O'Connor* [1980] Crim.L.R. 43.
[13] *Hamid and Hamid* (1979) 69 Cr.App.R. 324, 328.
[14] *Hamid and Hamid*, above.
[15] *Rider* (1986) 83 Cr.App.R. 207. The rule does not apply in cases where an allegation as to the falsity of the statement is not part of the prosecution case: *ibid.*
[16] *Carroll* (1994) 99 Cr.App.R. 381, 384.
[17] *Atkinson* (1934) 24 Cr.App.R. 123, 127, *per* Lord Hewart C.J.
[18] *Nicholas v Penny* [1950] 2 K.B. 466. The police officers' opinion may also be corroborated by evidence of the reading of a radar gun: *Collinson v Mabbott, The Times,* October 6, 1984; or speed-trap device: *Darby v DPP* [1995] R.T.R. 294.
[19] *Swain v Gillett* [1974] Crim.L.R. 433.

evidence of the reading on the ground that it is of insufficient quality to provide corroboration.[20]

In *Crossland v DPP*[21] the Divisional Court upheld a conviction in a case where the prosecution relied on the evidence of a police officer that in his opinion, based on calculations from skidmarks and tests, the speed was not less than 41 m.p.h. The court said that the officer's opinion was based on objectively determined phenomena and, accordingly, the conviction did not rest merely upon the opinion of one witness. Evidence of the measure of speed by radar is admissible provided the device is of a type approved by the Secretary of State.

(3) Miscellaneous

Procuration. The provisions of ss.2–4, 22 and 23 of the Sexual   15–05
Offences Act 1956 (requiring corroboration of evidence relating to the procuring of women to have sexual intercourse) have been abolished by s.33 of the Criminal Justice and Public Order Act 1994.

Treason. The Treason Act 1795, s.1 requires "the oaths of two lawful and credible witnesses" for conviction for compassing the death of the Sovereign or her heirs. It is to be repealed from a day to be appointed: s.36(3) of the Crime and Disorder Act 1998.

(4) Other rules

The nature of corroboration when required by statute is the same as that at   15–06
common law, namely, independent evidence which implicates the defendant in the offence charged in a material particular.[22]

(5) Functions of judge and jury

   (a) If at the close of the prosecution case, there is no corroborative   15–07
         evidence, the case must be stopped by the judge or magistrates.

   (b) The judge should direct the jury that unless it decides that there is corroborative evidence, as required by the statute, it must not convict.[23]

   (c) A mere warning of the dangers of acting in the absence of corroborative evidence will not suffice.[24]

   (d) If the judge fails to give a direction when it is required by statute an appeal will be allowed, unless the court applies the proviso to

---

[20] *Burton v Gilbert* (1983) 147 J.P. 441.
[21] [1988] 3 All E.R. 712.
[22] *Baskerville* [1916] 2 K.B. 658, 667.
[23] *Shillingford* (1968) 52 Cr.App.R. 188.
[24] *Shillingford*, above.

s.2(1) of the Criminal Appeal Act 1968, on the ground that no miscarriage of justice has actually occurred.[25]

C. Abolition of the common law rules

15–08   The corroboration rules led to a high level of technicality in the law and to the giving of complex and abstruse directions to juries. The law was described as "arcane, technical and difficult to convey".[26] As a result, the common law corroboration rules were abolished. This happened in two stages. The first to go was the requirement to give a corroboration warning in relation to the evidence of children, which was abolished by s.34(2) of the Criminal Justice Act 1988-and which provides:

> "(2) Any requirement whereby at a trial on indictment it is obligatory for the court to give the jury a warning about convicting the accused on the uncorroborated evidence of a child is abrogated."[27]

In 1991 the Law Commission in its Report, "Corroboration of Evidence in Criminal Trials",[28] recommended that the remaining corroboration rules (*i.e.* those requiring a warning) should be abolished, since they were inflexible, complex and productive of anomalies. These views were accepted by the Royal Commission on Criminal Justice which endorsed the recommendation.[29]

Section 32 of the Criminal Justice and Public Order Act 1994 followed the Law Commission's recommendation. The section abolished the requirement to give a warning about convicting the defendant on the uncorroborated evidence of an accomplice or a complainant in a sexual case.

15–09   Section 32 provides:

> "(1) Any requirement whereby at a trial on indictment it is obligatory for the court to give the jury a warning about convicting the accused on the uncorroborated evidence of a person merely because that person is—
>
> (a)   an alleged accomplice of the accused, or
> (b)   where the offence charged is a sexual offence, the person in

---

[25] *Hamid and Hamid* (1979) 69 Cr.App.R. 324, 326–327; see also, *Shillingford*, above.
[26] *Cheema*, (1994) 98 Cr.App.R. 195, 205, *per* Lord Taylor C.J.
[27] As amended by s.32(2) of the Criminal Justice and Public Order Act 1994. The 1988 Act abolished the requirement for a warning only in cases where it was mandatory because the evidence was that of a child. S.32(2) of the Criminal Justice and Public Order Act 1994 repealed this restriction, thereby abolishing the requirement entirely.
[28] Corroboration of Evidence in Criminal Trials, Cm. 1620.
[29] Cm. 2263 (1993), para.8–35.

respect of whom it is alleged to have been committed, is hereby abrogated.

[...]

(3) Any requirement that—

    (a) is applicable at the summary trial of a person for an offence, and

    (b) corresponds to the requirement mentioned in subsection (1) above or that mentioned in section 34(2) of the Criminal Justice Act 1988, is hereby abrogated.

(4) Nothing in this section applies in relation to—

    (a) any trial, or

    (b) any proceedings before a magistrates' court as examining justices, which began before the commencement of this section".

D. The effect of abolition

The effect of the abolition of the rules was that judges were no longer **15–10** required to warn juries that it was dangerous to convict in reliance on the evidence of the witnesses in the above categories and magistrates were not required so to direct themselves.

The Law Commission recommended that the rules should be abolished without replacement. The Commission concluded that no new rules should be introduced because defendants receive adequate protection from the general law and practice of criminal trials and the creation of new rules could lead to unnecessary formalism and the unjustified categorisation of witnesses.[30] The Commission said that the effect of their recommendation would be as follows:

    (a) Witnesses within the corroboration rules would be treated, as other witnesses already are, on their merits.

    (b) The courts would not be prevented from developing new principles for the general guidance of trial judges in relation to particular kinds of witness.[31]

Accordingly, the Commission took the view that judges should be left free to comment on particular evidence in the way that their experience and judgment suggested would most fairly and effectively assist the jury.[32] These views were accepted by the Royal Commission on Criminal Justice

---

[30] *op.cit.*, para.2.23.
[31] *ibid.*, paras 3.12–3.15.
[32] *ibid.*, para.4.12.

which recommended that where a warning from the judge is required it should be tailored to the particular circumstances of the case.[33] (As will be seen, these views anticipated accurately the practice of the courts following the abolition of the rules).

During debates on s.32 in the House of Lords it was suggested that the Lord Chief Justice might issue a Practice Direction as to a revised form of warning. However, it was reported to the House that the Lord Chief Justice had concluded that a Practice Direction was not necessary; if further guidance proved necessary, it would be for the Court of Appeal to provide it.[34]

15–11   That guidance was given by the Court of Appeal in *Makanjuola*[35] where Lord Taylor C.J. said:

> "(1) Section 32(1) abrogated the requirement to give a corroboration direction in respect of an alleged accomplice or a complainant of a sexual offence, simply because a witness falls into one of those categories. (2) It is a matter for the judge's discretion what, if any warning, he considers appropriate in respect of such a witness as indeed in respect of any other witness in whatever type of case. Whether he chooses to give a warning and in what terms will depend on the circumstances of the case, the issues raised and the content and quality of the witness's evidence. (3) In some cases, it may be appropriate for the judge to warn the jury to exercise caution before acting upon the unsupported evidence of a witness. This will not be so simply because the witness is a complainant of a sexual offence nor will it necessarily be so because a witness is alleged to be an accomplice. There will need to be an evidential basis for suggesting that the evidence of the witness may be unreliable. An evidential basis does not include mere suggestion by cross-examining counsel. (4) If any question arises as to whether the judge should give a special warning in respect of a witness, it is desirable that the question be resolved by discussion with counsel in the absence of the jury before final speeches. (5) Where the judge does decide to give some warning in respect of a witness, it will be appropriate to do so as part of the judge's review of the evidence and his comments as to how the jury should evaluate it rather than as a set-piece legal direction. (6) Where some warning is required, it will be for the judge to decide the strength and terms of the warning. It does not have to be invested with the whole florid regime of the old corroboration rules."[36]

This passage from the judgment in *Makanjuola* sets out the modern

---

[33] Above, para.8.35.
[34] *Hansard*, HL, Vol.556, col.1263, Minister of State, Home Office.
[35] [1995] 1 W.L.R. 1348.
[36] At 1351–1352.

practice with regard to the evidence of accomplices and complainants in sexual cases. Thus, it is for the judge to determine in his discretion whether to give a warning in such cases, and if so, what warning to give. The warning or direction will be dependent on the judge's view of the circumstances of the case, the issues raised, and the content and quality of the witness's evidence[37] (The Court of Appeal has said that it is unlikely to interfere with this exercise of discretion unless the exercise was unreasonable.[38]) It should be particularly noted that there must be an evidential basis for saying that the witness's evidence is unreliable before any question of a warning arises. Thus, in *Makanjuola*[39] the Court of Appeal pointed out that there was no evidential basis in that case (as opposed to suggestions by counsel in cross-examination) for the contention that the complainant's allegation of indecent assault was fabricated because she had quarrelled with the defendant. Accordingly, the Court held that there was no need for a warning. On the other hand, in *Walker*[40] there was an evidential basis for questioning the complainant's reliability. The defendant in that case was charged with rape of his step-daughter. Before the trial the complainant made a statement to the police, retracting her allegations against the defendant. A few days later, she withdrew the retraction. The judge in his summing up did not refer to the retraction or its withdrawal. The Court of Appeal in allowing the appeal said that these incidents were important to the witness's credibility and a warning should have been considered.

What is an appropriate warning will depend on the circumstances of the **15–12** particular case. However, once such a warning is given it is incumbent on the trial judge to identify any independent supporting evidence which exists, moreover the jury must be given careful direction on this point.[41] In *B(MT)*[42] the judge's failure to identify supporting evidence was held to give rise to a real risk that the jury improperly treated certain evidence as support for the witnesses' accounts. There were formerly complicated rules as to what evidence was capable of amounting to corroboration.[43] However, in *Makanjuola*[44] the Court of Appeal rejected a suggestion in *Archbold*[45] to the effect that the previous law as to what constituted corroboration continued to apply. As a result, these rules have ceased to have effect; and the judge is free to give a direction to fit the circumstances of the case and not to

---

[37] *L* [1999] Crim.L.R. 489.
[38] *Makanjuola*, above, 1352. The appellant must show that the exercise was unreasonable in the sense of *Associated Provincial Picture Houses v Wednesbury Corporation* [1948] 1 K.B. 223, *i.e.* so unreasonable that no reasonable judge could have exercised his discretion in this way: in *R* [1996] Crim.L.R. 815 this was described as a heavy burden for any appellant to discharge.
[39] Above.
[40] [1996] Crim.L.R 742.
[41] *B(MT)* [2000] Crim.L.R. 181.
[42] Above.
[43] A discussion of these rules is to be found at para.12–68 of the second edition of this work.
[44] Above.
[45] 1995 edition, para.16–36.

fit some prescribed formula. However, the Law Commission (in a passage which, it is submitted, reflects the current practice) said that the judge may wish to speak about the way in which evidence fits together rather than the "corroboration" of one piece of evidence by another because it would be a misdirection to give the impression that evidence which was "corroborative" in the former strict sense continued to have some special legal effect, or should be treated by the jury in some special way.[46]

15–13   The upshot is that witnesses formerly subject to the corroboration rules are no longer witnesses in a special category. As a result, children, accomplices and complainants in sexual cases are to be treated like other witnesses. The following points with regard to the evidence of these witnesses may be noted:

(a)   An accomplice may have no motive for lying, in which case there is no need for a warning of any sort. On the other hand, there may be a danger in some cases that he is lying to save his own skin. If the judge thinks that there is such a danger which may be unperceived by the jury he should point it out to them. In any case, the judge is under an obligation to warn the jury to proceed with caution if there is material to suggest that a witness's evidence may be tainted by an improper motive: *Beck*.[47] The Law Commission anticipated that trial judges would adopt the direction in *Beck* in cases where an accomplice may have an interest to serve in giving evidence.[48]

(b)   As has been seen, there is no longer any obligation on the judge to give a warning to the jury in a sexual case: it is a matter for his discretion.[49] Thus, to suggest in most cases that a woman may be motivated by fantasy, neurosis, jealousy or spite (as the old rules required) is to make an irrelevant comment and one which may sound gratuitously offensive. If such a danger does exist the judge should warn the jury of it. However, there must be an evidential basis for the suggestion. Thus, in *E*[50] it was suggested to the complainant in cross-examination that she had either made up an allegation of indecent assault, or, alternatively, she was fantasising or dreaming. It was submitted that a warning should have been given. This was based on evidence that the complainant had been asleep before the alleged assault. The Court of Appeal rejected this

---

[46] *op.cit.*, para.4.13.
[47] (1982) 74 Cr.App.R. 221, cited at para.15–15 below.
[48] *op.cit.*, para.3–19. The Court of Appeal has said that if an accomplice does give evidence for the Crown his previous convictions should normally be disclosed to the jury at the outset of the trial: *Taylor and Goodman* [1999] 2 Cr.App.R. 163.
[49] See *Makanjuola*, cited at para.15–11, above.
[50] [1995] 1 W.L.R. 1348.

submission and said that there was no evidential basis for regarding the witness as unreliable.

(c) It is wrong for counsel to refer to the old law on corroboration in his speech to the jury. Counsel sometimes try to do this in order to undermine a complainant's evidence. However, in A^{51} the trial judge prevented counsel from doing so. The Court of Appeal upheld this ruling: the Court said that s.32 specifically removed all the pre-existing obligatory requirements and the trend of decisions in the Court of Appeal had been to resist any attempt to reintroduce the old straitjacket.

(d) The Court of Appeal has held that there is no obligation on the court to direct the jury to treat a child's evidence in a sexual case with caution because of her tender years.[52] It is, therefore, anticipated that in the normal case no warning will be necessary. However, if the child shows signs of unusual forgetfulness or unreliability in the witness-box or there is a real possibility of influence having been exerted on him or her by another person, a warning may be necessary.

An appropriate warning might be to invite the jury to look with care at the child's evidence and, in deciding whether to rely on it or not, to see how it fits in with other evidence and to consider if there is any evidence to support it. However, the nature of the warning will depend on the facts of the particular case.[53]

2. The Evidence of Suspect Witnesses

The common law developed rules requiring that a warning (short of a corroboration warning) be given to juries (and applied by magistrates) in order to point out the dangers of convicting in reliance on the evidence of certain witnesses. Some may be potentially unreliable, for example witnesses who purport to identify a defendant: considered in Ch.14, above.[54] Others are suspect because, when giving evidence, they may have a purpose of their own to serve. This category includes co-defendants.

15–14

---

[51] [1997] Crim.L.R. 883.
[52] *Pryce* [1991] Crim.L.R. 379.
[53] Suggestions about this topic were made by the late Judge Leo Clark Q.C. The views expressed are, of course, those of the authors.
[54] para.14–03.

A. Witnesses with a purpose of their own to serve

(1) The rule in Beck's case

15–15   It is sometimes alleged that a prosecution witness is not telling the truth, but is giving evidence with a view to serving some purpose of his own. Then, if there is material to suggest that the witness's evidence may be tainted by such an improper motive, it is the practice for the judge to warn the jury to proceed with caution. In the leading case of *Beck*,[55] the Court of Appeal described the giving of such a warning as an obligation upon the judge. (In that case the defendant was charged with defrauding a finance company. Three directors of the finance company gave evidence for the prosecution. They were not accomplices of the defendant. However, it was alleged that they had a purpose of their own to serve in giving evidence, namely to cover up false representations made or acceded to by them in an insurance claim.)

The Court of Appeal in *Beck* said that the strength of the warning must vary according to the facts of the case. The purpose of the warning is to ensure that all members of the jury understand that they should look with care at possibly tainted evidence before acting on it. The House of Lords in *Spencer*[56] approved the decision in *Beck* and said that the extent to which the trial judge should make reference to any potentially corroborative material depends upon the facts of each case: the overriding rule is that the judge must put the defence fairly and adequately. It is for the trial judge to determine whether a witness had or might have had a purpose of his own to serve in giving evidence and, if so, what warning should be given: there is no need to give such a warning simply because counsel alleges that the witness had such a purpose.[57]

The Law Commission considered that the range of witnesses to whom the rule has so far been applied is less extensive than its verbal formulation might be thought to indicate.[58] The Commission said that it appeared to have been actually applied only to cases involving the witness's own liability for an offence; commonly, but not necessarily, the offence charged.

However, in *Spencer*,[59] the defendants were members of the staff at Rampton Hospital, charged with offences involving the ill-treatment of inmates. The prosecution relied upon the evidence of witnesses who had been detained after conviction and who were suffering from some form of mental disorder. The judge warned the jury that they must approach this evidence with great caution and explained the reasons for doing so. It was submitted that he should have gone further and given a full corroboration warning. The House of Lords did not accept this submission. The House

---

[55] [1991] 74 Cr.App.R. 221, 228.

[56] (1986) 83 Cr.App.R. 277, 289, *per* Lord Ackner, with whom the other members of the House agreed.

[57] *Mouqni, The Times*, April 4, 1994.

[58] Report on Corroboration of Evidence in Criminal Trials, Cm. 1620, Appendix C, para.3.

[59] Above.

said that where the prosecution evidence was solely that of a witness, not in any of the accepted categories of suspect witnesses, but who by his mental condition and criminal connection fulfilled analogous criteria, the judge must warn the jury of the dangers of convicting on such evidence, but that it was not essential that the words "danger" or "dangerous" be used. Accordingly, it will be for the judge in such cases to bring home to the jury the need for caution, before convicting in reliance on the suspect evidence.

(2) Development of the rule

15–16

The Law Commission commented that it is possible that the decision in Spencer, above, is limited to its particular and unusual facts: but that if it was of general application it would seem to have extended the rule in Beck's case; (i) by requiring a particularly strong warning to be given where a prosecutor relies solely on the evidence of a suspect witness; and (ii) by applying the Beck principle to a witness who has an interest in a form other than escaping liability for an offence.[60]

The Commission considered that the abolition of the corroboration rules would not affect the Beck rule or the development of that line of authority.[61] It is submitted that this is correct and that the rule may in future be extended to other potentially unreliable witnesses. For instance, the New South Wales Evidence Bill 1991 sought to replace the corroboration requirements with a list of various categories of potentially unreliable evidence (including hearsay, identification evidence, "verbals", accomplices and children). It was proposed that in these cases the judge, if required, should give a warning associated with the particular evidence. However, it is submitted that this course should not be followed here. This is because it would involve the introduction of categories of witnesses (against which the Law Commission warned[62]) and the re-introduction of the rigidity and technicality associated with the corroboration rules. Accordingly, the rule should be allowed to develop without the constraints of a list of categories. This would mean that the judge would have a wide discretion to warn as to the unreliability of suspect witnesses as he thought fit without the witnesses having to fit into a category and thus attract a set warning.

The rule in Beck's case may have to be reconsidered following Muncaster[63] in which the Court of Appeal held that the rule in Beck had to be looked at afresh in light of s.32 of the Criminal Justice Act 1994[64] and the case of Makanjuola.[65] In the later case of, Causley,[66] however, it was contended by the appellant that despite the abolition of corroboration

---

[60] op.cit., Appendix C, para.12.
[61] ibid., para.3.17.
[62] op.cit., para.3.27.
[63] [1999] Crim.L.R. 409.
[64] para.15–09 above.
[65] Above.
[66] [1999] Crim.L.R. 572.

requirements by s.32, the principles enunciated in *Spencer*[67] remained good. In rejecting the submission, the Court of Appeal held that there was no inconsistency between the decisions in either *Makanjuola*, *Spencer*, or *Muncaster*. It is submitted that for the time being, until there is comprehensive review of the effect of s.32 and *Makanjuola* on corroboration requirements the rule in *Beck* and the decisions that follow retain force.

15–17 An example of a case where a warning has been held to be necessary is to be found in *Chan v R*.[68] The Privy Council in that case held that the evidence of a witness who was under threat of prosecution or sentence for an offence unrelated to that charged against the defendant (and who knew that he would receive favourable treatment as a result of giving evidence) was not inadmissible, provided a warning was given to the jury of the potential fallibility of the witness's evidence. The force of such a warning is a matter for the trial judge and the extent and detail in which it is decided to go is a matter for the judge to decide.[69] The potential fallibility and ulterior motives of the witness must, however, be put squarely before the jury.[70] In *Causley*[71] the accused criticised the failure to warn the jury in sufficiently strong terms of the dangers of relying on confessions to convicts and the unsatisfactory nature of the evidence of such witnesses. The Court of Appeal held that the warning given had, in all the circumstances, been appropriate and stressed that it was not incumbent upon a judge to rehearse all of the evidence which had been heard. However, in *Benedetto*[72] the Privy Council held that whilst it was undesirable to restrict the circumstances and terms in which a judge might urge caution in relation to such witnesses, as a minimum, the judge should (i) draw to the jury's attention any indications, and the significance thereof, that the evidence might be tainted by improper motive, and (ii) advise the jury to be cautious before acting upon such evidence.

B. Co-defendants

15–18 A defendant called in his own defence sometimes gives evidence that implicates a co-defendant in the offence charged or damages the co-defendant's case. The damage to the co-defendant will vary in severity. At one extreme two co-defendants may put forward a "cut-throat" defence, *i.e.* each blame the other for the offence. At the other extreme, relatively minor damage may be inflicted on part of the co-defendant's case. The scale of the attack, however, makes no difference. It is a matter for the judge to decide in his discretion, in the first instance, whether to give any warning,[73]

---

[67] Above.
[68] [1995] 1 W.L.R. 251.
[69] *Muncaster*, above.
[70] *Cairns, Zaidi and Chaudhary* [2003] 1 Cr.App.R. 38.
[71] Above.
[72] *Benedetto v R; Labrador v R* [2003] 1 W.L.R. 1545.
[73] *Burrows* [2000] Crim.L.R. 48.

and if so, what warning to give.[74] In *Burrows*[75] the judge had been right not to give any warning in a case where each of two defendants gave evidence against the other. Any warning would have had to apply to both defendants, and in those circumstances would have meant directing the jury to treat each defendant's essential evidence with caution solely on the basis that it inculpated the other. It was held that this might have led to a complaint that the jury had not been allowed to approach the case with open minds. The convictions were safe as the judge had underlined the "extreme care" with which the jury should approach the allegations against each defendant.

In *Knowlden*[76] a father and his two sons were charged with murder. They all gave evidence. Family loyalty had crumbled. Each gave evidence which damaged the defence of one or more of the others. The Court of Appeal said that in these circumstances the judge in exercising his discretion is at least to be expected to give "the customary clear warning to the jury ... to examine the evidence of each defendant with care because each has or may have an interest of his own to serve."[77]

This rule was reaffirmed by the Court of Appeal in *Cheema*.[78] The Court held in that case that a corroboration warning was not required in respect of a co-defendant's evidence and Lord Taylor C.J. said that what was required was a warning in suitable terms as to the danger that a co-defendant might have an axe to grind: a purpose of his own to serve.[79]

The content and formulation of the warning are matters for the judge. However, the jury should be warned:

(a) to approach the evidence of co-defendants with care, since in giving evidence a particular defendant may have been paying more regard to his own interests and to protecting himself than to telling the truth; and

(b) to have this risk in mind before deciding to accept what one defendant says about another.

C. Procedure

In recent years a practice was developed whereby the judge at the close of **15–19** the evidence in all but the most straightforward cases initiated a discussion with counsel about corroboration directions. This course allowed counsel the opportunity to make submissions as to the appropriate directions to be

---

[74] Knowlden (1991) 77 Cr.App.R. 94.
[75] Above.
[76] (1991) 77 Cr.App.R.48.
[77] At 100.
[78] (1994) 94 Cr.App.R. 195.
[79] At 204.

given to the jury. Thus, in *Ensor*[80] Lord Lane C.J. said that in almost all cases where a direction was required it was desirable that the judge should hear submissions, often brief, from counsel. This view has been reiterated with regard to cases in which it is thought that the judge should give a special warning.[81]

The Law Commission in its Report on Corroboration of Evidence in Criminal Trials[82] recommended that this practice be introduced in any case where issues of fact or the credibility of a witness required special treatment. The purpose of such a discussion would be to ensure that no issues were overlooked and that unnecessary errors were avoided. The Commission described the scheme as a generalisation of the approach in *Ensor*[83] and suggested that it be implemented by Practice Direction. They also said that the scheme should not be used as a means of re-introducing the categorisation of witnesses; and, to this end, courts should resist suggestions that witnesses in a particular category must be subject to a special direction. In the event, the fears of the Commission have proved to be unfounded. No attempt has been made to categorise witnesses and the decision of the Court of Appeal in *Makanjuola* has obviated the need for a Practice Direction.[84]

---

[80] [1989] 1 W.L.R. 497, 505.
[81] *Makanjuola* [1995] 1 W.L.R. 1348, 1352, cited at para.15–11, below.
[82] Cm. 1620, para.4.29.
[83] Above.
[84] Above.

PART 6

Rules Connected with the Trial

CHAPTER 16
Functions of Judge, Jury and Justices

The purpose of this Chapter is to consider the functions (in relation to the **16–01** evidence) of judge, jury and justices. Trials on indictment are, in most circumstances, heard by a judge and jury. In such cases the judge and jury have contrasting functions. However, under the Criminal Justice Act 2003, in certain limited circumstances, trials on indictment may sometimes be heard without a jury (see para.16–25 below). In such cases and in all summary trials the judge and magistrates respectively combine the functions of both judge and jury. Trials on indictment are considered first.

1. TRIALS ON INDICTMENT BY BOTH JUDGE AND JURY: THE FUNCTIONS OF JUDGE AND JURY

The general rule is that in trials on indictment by both judge and jury, all **16–02** matters of law are to be decided by the judge, while all matters of fact are to be decided by the jury. When matters of law are raised the judge must rule on them. He must also instruct the jury on the law. This rule relates to English law. Foreign law is a question of fact, to be determined by the evidence.[1] Moreover, it has been held that foreign law must be proved by expert evidence, it is impermissible to rely on a rebuttable presumption that foreign laws are the same as English laws.[2]

The proper construction of a statute is a matter of law for the judge. However, if words are used in a statute in an ordinary sense, it will be for the jury to apply them to the facts of a particular case. The leading authority is *Brutus v Cozens*.[3] B was charged with insulting behaviour contrary to s.5 of the Public Order Act 1936. He had interrupted a tennis match during the Wimbledon tournament, causing the court to be invaded by demonstrators to the displeasure of the spectators. The House of Lords held that the question of whether his behaviour was insulting was one of fact for the magistrates to decide. Lord Reid said:

---

[1] In *Ofori* (1994) 99 Cr.App.R. 223 the Court of Appeal held that in criminal proceedings questions of foreign law cannot be the subject of judicial notice.
[2] *Okolie, The Times*, June 6, 2000.
[3] [1973] A.C. 854.

"The meaning of an ordinary word of the English language is not a question of law. The proper construction of a statute is a question of law. If the context shows that a word is used in an unusual sense the court will determine in other words what that unusual sense is. But here there is in my opinion no question of the word 'insulting' being used in any unusual sense. It appears to me ... to be intended to have its ordinary meaning. It is for the tribunal which decides the case to consider, not as law but as fact, whether in the whole circumstances the words of the statute do or do not as a matter of ordinary usage of the English language cover or apply to the facts which have been proved. If it is alleged that the tribunal has reached a wrong decision then there can be a question of law but only of a limited character. The question would normally be whether their decision was unreasonable in the sense that no tribunal acquainted with the ordinary use of language could reasonably reach that decision."[4]

Thus, in a trial on indictment, it is for the judge to explain words which may have a technical meaning such as "recklessly", "unlawfully" or "maliciously". He will also explain words with which the jury may be unfamiliar (such as "grievous" in relation to bodily harm). However, the application of the words to the facts is a matter for the jury.

16–03   The construction of a document (*i.e.* the determination of its meaning and effect) may be a matter for the judge or jury depending upon the type of document involved. As a general rule, the construction of ordinary documents is a matter of fact for the jury. This approach was adopted by the Divisional Court in *Clarksons Holidays Ltd.*[5] In that case Roskill L.J. said that the question of what written representations in a holiday brochure meant was "essentially a question of fact for the jury, subject only to this, that if the words relied upon by the Crown were on their true construction incapable of bearing the meaning which the Crown sought to attribute to them" the case ought to be withdrawn from the jury.[6] This approach was followed in *Sunair Holidays*[7] and approved by the House of Lords in *British Airways Board v Taylor.*[8] Similarly, the Court of Appeal has held that in a case of deception, where the crucial issue was whether the defendant had made a representation or not, the issue whether a car-hire form contained a representation that the defendant had not been disqualified was an issue of fact for the jury and not a question of law for the judge.[9]

On the other hand, construction of all forms of legislation is a matter for

---

[4] At 861.
[5] (1973) 57 Cr.App.R. 38.
[6] At 53.
[7] [1973] 2 All E.R. 1233, 1240.
[8] [1976] 1 All E.R. 65, 68.
[9] *Adams, The Times,* January 26, 1993.

the judge. In *Spens*[10] the Court of Appeal held that the City Code on Take-overs and Mergers sufficiently resembled legislation as to require construction of its provisions by a judge. Similarly, the construction of written agreements, intended to have a binding effect between parties, is a matter for the judge to determine. Thus, in *Stephens v R*[11] a majority of the Australian High Court held that it was for the trial judge, as a matter of law, to determine the true meaning of a building agreement. The reason for this rule was explained by Parke B. in *Neilson v Harford*[12] (a case in which it was held that the construction of the specification of a patent was for the court to determine) when he said: "Unless this were so, there would be no certainty in the law, for a misconstruction by the court is the proper subject ... of redress in a Court of Error; but a misconstruction by the jury cannot be set right at all effectually."

A. Functions of the judge

The functions of the judge in relation to the evidence are: **16–04**

(a) to decide all questions concerning the admissibility of evidence (including objections to questions)[13];

(b) to question witnesses called by either the prosecution or defence and, in certain very limited situations take over cross-examination of a witness[14];

(c) to determine whether there is sufficient evidence to be considered by the jury; and

(d) to sum the case up to the jury, directing it as to the law and summing up the evidence to it.

Each of these functions will be considered separately.

(1) Admissibility of evidence

The judge decides all questions relating to the admissibility of evidence.   **16–05**
"The function of a judge at a criminal trial as respects the admissibility of

---

[10] (1991) 93 Cr.App.R. 194, 201.
[11] (1978) 21 A.L.R. 680.
[12] (1841) 8 M. & W. 806, 823.
[13] *Stirland v DPP* [1944] A.C. 315, 324, *per* Lord Simon L.C. It should also be noted that s.82(3) of the Police and Criminal Evidence Act 1984 provides that nothing in Pt VIII of the Act (relating to general evidence in criminal proceedings) shall prejudice any power of a court "to exclude evidence (whether by preventing questions from being put or otherwise) at its discretion."
[14] *Cameron* [2001] Crim.L.R. 587.

evidence is to ensure that the accused has a fair trial according to law."[15] The procedure is as follows.

1. If defence counsel wishes to object to the admissibility of some part of the evidence, he tells prosecuting counsel before the trial starts. Prosecuting counsel does not refer to that part of the evidence when he opens the case to the jury.[16]

2. Objection is normally taken when the evidence is about to be called. In many cases, the evidence to which objection is taken appears clearly on the statements of the prosecution witnesses. In other cases, objections may occur during the course of evidence either to the form of a question or to an anticipated answer. (The fact that the defence did not object to the introduction of inadmissible evidence at trial does not prevent a conviction being quashed on appeal if the introduction of the evidence was prejudicial to the defendant.[17])

3. When the objection is made the judge will hear argument and then rule. If the judge has to decide a question of fact in considering admissibility, a "trial-within-a-trial" will be held: see para.16–07. The judge will normally give his reasons for a ruling (albeit briefly), although there is no rule requiring him to do so. In *Wallace and Fuller*[18] the Privy Council said that while there could be no such rule of general application there were occasions when good practice required a reasoned ruling, such as when a judge decided a question of law, or mixed law and fact, or when he was exercising a discretion: on such occasions, sufficient, but no more, of his reasons or findings should be given to enable a review on appeal. However, the Privy Council emphasised that it was neither stating a general rule as to the giving of reasons, nor recognising categories of situations in which this should be done; it was for the judge to decide whether the interests of justice called for the giving of reasons.

4. In some cases, the objection may be heard earlier than at the stage when it arises in the evidence. It is a matter for the judge's discretion to decide whether to hear it earlier or not.[19] If it would be impossible for prosecuting counsel to open the case properly to a

---

[15] *Sang* (1979) 69 Cr.App.R. 282, 290, *per* Lord Diplock.
[16] *Hammond* (1941) 28 Cr.App.R. 84; *Zielinski* (1950) 34 Cr.App.R. 193; *Patel* (1951) 35 Cr.App.R. 62.
[17] *DPP v Stirland* [1944] A.C. 315, applied in *Gordon* [1995] 2 Cr.App.R. 61, 67.
[18] [1997] 1 Cr.App.R 396, 407–408. If the judge has reached a correct decision on wrong or inadequate reasons but right and adequate reasons are apparent on the evidence, the Court of Appeal may uphold his decision: *Bedi* [1992] Crim.L.R. 299.
[19] *Hammond*, above.

jury without referring to the evidence, the issue of admissibility will be decided before counsel opens the case. This happens most frequently when the admissibility of a confession is in dispute and the confession is the only evidence against a defendant.

5. A judge at a pre-trial hearing of a trial on indictment is now **16–06** empowered to make a ruling as to the admissibility of evidence (or any other question of law relating to the case), thus allowing such matters to be decided before the trial and obviating the need for interruptions during the trial while they are decided: Criminal Procedure and Investigations Act 1996, s.40(1). A ruling under this section has binding effect until the end of the trial, but it may subsequently be varied or discharged if there is a change in the circumstances.[20] It is impossible to lay down rules as to what change in circumstances would justify variation or discharge of a ruling. However, it is submitted that the change would normally need to be significant to justify this course being taken. Thus, s.40(5) provides that no application for variation or discharge shall be made unless there has been a material change in the circumstances.

6. Submissions as to admissibility are heard in open court. Normally they are heard in the absence of the jury. However, it is for the judge to decide whether the jury should be present or not. In *Anderson*,[21] Lord Hewart C.J. said that the jury in that case might have drawn the inference that they had been asked to leave court because circumstances of a character damaging to the accused were to be discussed. Lord Hewart continued: "It is difficult to imagine any circumstances in which, except at the request or with the consent of the defence, a jury can possibly be asked to leave the box in order that statements may be made during their absence." Lord Lane C.J., giving the judgment of the Court of Appeal in *Hendry*,[22] said that the observations of Lord Hewart were no doubt correct in the particular circumstances of the case, but that whatever the position might have been in 1929, at the present day it was for the judge to have the final word whether the jury should remain in court. In *Mitchell*[23] Lord Steyn said that the right of a defendant in appropriate circumstances to require the jury to be absent is "an important rule which exists to protect accused persons and a very important safeguard". However, these words cannot be taken to have detracted from what Lord Lane

---

[20] s.40(3)(4).
[21] (1930) 21 Cr.App.R. 178, 182–183.
[22] (1989) 88 Cr.App.R. 187.
[23] *The Times*, January 24, 1998.

said; and it must remain for the judge to decide whether the jury should be excluded. In practice, since these submissions usually relate to evidence prejudicial to the defendant, the jury is, as a general rule, excluded.

7. On the other hand, there are occasions when the jury is present because either: there is no prejudice to the defendant; or there are matters which the members of the jury should hear to assist them in determining the credibility of a witness, for example, the examination of a person of unsound mind by the judge to decide whether the witness understands the nature of the oath: see para.17–06.[24]

(2) Trial-within-a-trial

16–07   The judge is not normally required to determine questions of fact. However, there are occasions when a disputed question of fact must be determined in order to decide whether an item of evidence should be admitted. On these occasions the judge alone determines questions of fact. He normally hears witnesses in order to do so. This procedure is called a "trial-within-a-trial" or "*voir dire*".[25] It most commonly occurs when the admissibility of confessions is in dispute. This question is now governed by ss.76 and 78 of the Police and Criminal Evidence Act 1984, but the procedure for the trial-within-a-trial remains unchanged.

However, there are other occasions when a trial-within-a-trial is appropriate, for example to determine: the admissibility of tape recordings[26]; or the competence of a witness[27]; or whether evidence of a previous plea of guilty to the charge (tendered but subsequently withdrawn) should be admitted.[28] In *Wright*[29] the Court of Appeal held that it would have been preferable if evidence of the defendant's bad character had first been considered by the judge in a *voire dire* before being put to the jury. Had the evidence been so considered the judge may have prevented cross-examination on the subject by the prosecution.

A trial-within-a-trial is not an appropriate procedure when the question to be determined is not one of fact for the judge but is purely within the province of the jury, for example whether the evidence is true or not,[30] fabricated,[31] or whether the defendant's signature has been forged on notes

---

[24] See *Dunne* (1929) 21 Cr.App.R. 176; *Reynolds* (1950) 34 Cr.App.R. 60, 64.
[25] See para.16–08 (vi).
[26] *Robson; Harris* (1972) 56 Cr.App.R. 450; discussed at para.2–18, above.
[27] *Yacoob* (1981) 72 Cr.App.R. 313, 317.
[28] In *Rimmer* (1972) 56 Cr.App.R. 196, 201, the Court of Appeal said that a trial-within-a-trial was appropriate in all such cases. A differently constituted court in *Hetherington* [1972] Crim.L.R. 703 did not agree that this was so.
[29] [2000] Crim.L.R. 851.
[30] *Terrelonge* [1977] Crim.L.R. 218.
[31] *Drury, Clark* [2001] Crim.L.R. 847.

of an interview.[32] In *Walshe*[33] the Court of Appeal said that a trial-within-a-trial was not an appropriate procedure for deciding the admissibility of evidence relating to an identification parade. In *Flemming*[34] the Court came to the same conclusion when considering the admissibility of a disputed identification. However, the provisions of s.78 of the Police and Criminal Evidence Act 1984 did not apply to either of these cases. (At the material time the Act was not in force.) There may now be occasions, such as those when a court is considering how evidence was obtained, when it may be necessary to hold a trial-within-a-trial to determine whether it should be excluded under s.78. Thus, the Court of Appeal in *Beveridge*[35] said that a judge, when considering under s.78 whether to exclude evidence concerning an identification parade, may on occasion think it desirable to hold a trial-within-a-trial but that such occasions would be rare.

The procedure at a trial-within-a-trial is usually as follows: **16–08**

(i) The objection is made when the evidence is about to be called; for exceptions, see para.16–05, 3.

(ii) The decision on whether to hold a trial-within-a-trial is one entirely at the discretion of the judge.[36]

(iii) The judge should hear the evidence before ruling on admissibility unless the circumstances are very exceptional.[37]

(iv) The jury is normally sent out and the evidence is heard in its absence.[38]

(v) Evidence for both prosecution and defence is usually called. Witnesses are sworn on the *voir dire*, not on the oath taken when giving evidence before the jury.[39]

(vi) Prosecution witnesses may be cross-examined without affecting

---

[32] *Flemming* (1988) 86 Cr.App.R. 32; see para.14–29, above.
[33] (1982) 74 Cr.App.R. 85.
[34] Above.
[35] (1987) 85 Cr.App.R. 255.
[36] *Drury, Clark* [2001] Crim.L.R. 847.
[37] *Sang* (1979) 68 Cr.App.R. 240, 249–250, CA. In *Sang* the judge ruled upon an assumed factual basis. The Court of Appeal said that in the exceptional circumstances of that case, the judge was justified in doing so, but "the fact that we have accepted that this is so must not be taken as in any way encouraging departure from the basic principle that trial judges should not rule upon questions of admissibility of evidence without first hearing the evidence to which exception is sought to be taken" (250).
[38] *Ajodha v The State* (1981) 73 Cr.App.R. 129, 140. See discussion at para.16–06, 6 above. It would only be in the most unusual circumstances, it is submitted, that it would be proper for the jury to be present. See also, Rowe, "The Voir Dire and the Jury" [1986] Crim.L.R. 226.
[39] The oath is: "I swear by Almighty God that I will true answer make to all such questions as the Court shall demand of me."

the right to cross-examination in the substantive trial before the jury.[40]

(vii) The defendant may give evidence himself[41] and may call witnesses on his behalf. If the defendant gives evidence:

    (a) he may be cross-examined (as may his witnesses),[42] and

    (b) his right to remain silent in the substantive trial is not affected.[43]

(vii) When deciding the question of admissibility, the judge should act on admissible evidence.

(viii) For the burden and standard of proof see paras 4–02 *et seq.* and 4–36 *et seq.*, above.

(ix) The judge's decision as to admissibility is not communicated to the jury.[44] To do so would usually result in prejudice to the defendant, since it may reveal the judge's view of the evidence or decision as to the credibility of witnesses.

(3) Questioning witnesses

16–09   A judge may question witnesses called by either the prosecution or defence during the course of a trial.[45] He must, however, exercise restraint when making such interventions. It is most undesirable for a judge to interrupt a witness, in particular the defendant, during evidence in chief or cross-examination.[46] Thus, in normal circumstances it would not be appropriate for the judge to take over the cross-examination of a witness, even in a situation where the witness refuses to answer questions put by counsel. However, in *Cameron*[47] the Court of Appeal held that a judge had not been wrong in taking over the cross-examination of a 14-year-old complainant in a rape trial after she had refused to answer any questions put to her in cross-examination by defence counsel. Such a course may also be appropriate in the case of a witness labouring under a mental handicap or a frightened or traumatised witness in the case of a sexual complaint.

---

[40] *Murray* [1951] 1 K.B. 391.
[41] *Cowell* [1940] 2 K.B. 49.
[42] For questions relating to the truth of a confession see para.9–48, above.
[43] *Brophy* [1981] 3 W.L.R. 103, 108, *per* Lord Fraser of Tullybelton: this right is absolute and not conditional on the exercise of discretion.
[44] *Mitchell* [1998] 2 Cr.App.R. 35, PC.
[45] *Wilson* 18 Cr.App.R. 108, CCA.
[46] *Marsh, The Times,* July 6, 1993.
[47] [2001] Crim.L.R. 587, CA. After the witness refused to answer defence counsel's questions, the judge, in the absence of the jury, invited counsel to provide him with the material he wished to put to the witness. The judge proposed to put only those questions that would not unproductively inflame the witness.

(4) Case for the jury

If, at the close of the prosecution case, there is no evidence upon which a reasonable jury properly directed could convict the defendant, the judge must rule (upon a submission being made) that there is no case to go to the jury. He will then direct the jury to acquit the defendant.

16–10

If experienced counsel does not make a submission the judge is not required to interfere in the absence of improper or irregular conduct.[48] However, judges, on occasion, invite a submission if none appears forthcoming.[49] The time to make the submission is after the evidence has been called, not before.[50] However, in appropriate circumstances a judge may indicate before the prosecution case closes that he has it in mind to accede to a submission. For instance, if the prosecution witnesses have failed to come up to proof and there is no evidence to connect the defendant with the offence charged, the judge might make such an indication before the prosecution called evidence of police interviews which contained no admissions. In *Brown (Davina)*[51] the Court of Appeal held that if, at any time after the conclusion of the prosecution case, the judge is satisfied that there is no case to answer, he has the power to withdraw the case from the jury. The judge must be mindful, however, not to usurp the function of the jury by assessing the credibility of evidence called on behalf of the defendant.

The Court of Appeal held in *Galbraith*[52] that the judge must rule that there is no case where: (i) there is no evidence that the defendant committed the offence charged; or (ii) he decides that, taking the prosecution evidence at its highest, a reasonable jury properly directed could not properly convict on it.

> "Where however the prosecution evidence is such that its strength or weakness depends on the view to be taken of a witness's reliability or other matters which are generally speaking within the province of the jury and when on one possible view of the facts there is evidence upon which a jury could properly come to the conclusion that the defendant is guilty, then the judge should allow the matter to be tried by the jury."[53]

---

[48] *Juett* [1981] Crim.L.R. 113.
[49] In *Brown* [1998] Crim.L.R. 196, it was said *obiter* that if, at the conclusion of the evidence, the judge is of the opinion that no reasonable jury could safely convict, the matter should be raised with counsel and the case withdrawn from the jury if the judge's opinion remained unchanged.
[50] *Leadbeater* [1988] Crim.L.R. 463.
[51] [2002] 1 Cr.App.R. 5, CA.
[52] (1981) 1 W.L.R. 1039.
[53] *Galbraith* [1981] 1 W.L.R. 1039, 1042. For the judge's duty to withdraw a case dependent upon an unconvincing confession made by a mentally-handicapped defendant, see *McKenzie (Note)* [1993] 1 W.L.R. 453, cited at para.9–23 above.

16–11 It had been thought at one stage that the judge could direct an acquittal if he took the view that the prosecution evidence was unsafe or unsatisfactory.[54] It was said that the effect of this practice was that the judge decided questions of the weight and reliability of evidence and thereby took over the functions of the jury.[55] *Galbraith* put an end to such submissions.[56]

(Cases of identification may present acute problems when determining whether a case should be stopped. The Court of Appeal in *Turnbull*[57] held that the judge should withdraw the case from the jury if the quality of the identifying evidence is poor: para.14–06, above. In *Daley v R*[58] the Privy Council said that there was no conflict between *Galbraith* and *Turnbull*. This is because the judge is operating under different rules in each case. Under the ruling in *Galbraith* he may not withdraw the case merely because he thinks the evidence unworthy of credit; whereas, under *Turnbull* the case may be withdrawn since the evidence, even if honest, is too unreliable to found a conviction.[59])

As a general rule, the submission is made in the absence of the jury.[60] If the judge rejects the submission there is no obligation to give a reasoned ruling. However, in *S and C*[61] the Court of Appeal complained that the trial judge in that case had failed to give such a ruling, which would have been of assistance to the Court; and said that if the judge found it inconvenient to give reasons at the time he should have considered doing so after the jury had retired to consider their verdict. It is submitted that in the majority of cases a reasoned ruling is unnecessary (unless a point of law is involved or the case is one of substantial factual complexity). If the submission is successful the judge gives an appropriate direction to the jury on its return to court. On the other hand, if the submission is unsuccessful, no mention of it is made to the jury. This is because it would clearly be prejudicial to the defendant to do so. Thus, in *Smith and Doe*[62] the judge observed in summing-up that if he had not thought that there was sufficient evidence of identification available to the jury he would have withdrawn the case. The Court of Appeal said that he should not have revealed his decision to the jury. For the position when a submission of no case is made in the magistrates' court, see para.16–30.

16–12 If a trial judge errs in law in rejecting a submission of no case the Court of

---

[54] *Young* (1964) 48 Cr.App.R. 292.
[55] *Barker* (1973) 65 Cr.App.R. 287, 288, *per* Lord Widgery C.J.
[56] A dictum in *Mansfield* (1977) 65 Cr.App.R. 276, 281 suggested that a judge could stop a case if the evidence was unsafe. The Court in *Galbraith*, above at 1047 said that if this meant that the judge could stop the case if he thought, *e.g.*, that the main prosecution witness was not to be believed, it was wrong.
[57] [1977] Q.B.224.
[58] [1993] 3 W.L.R. 666.
[59] At 675–676, *per* Lord Mustill.
[60] *Crosdale v R* [1995] 1 W.L.R. 864.
[61] [1996] Crim.L.R. 346.
[62] (1987) 85 Cr.App.R. 197.

Appeal should not take account of the defence evidence and uphold the conviction on the ground that no miscarriage of justice has occurred.[63] However, in *Clarke and Hewins*[64] is was said that as the sole ground for allowing an appeal against conviction is whether the conviction is "unsafe", it is immaterial that a submission of no case to answer is wrongly rejected if the at the time of the appeal the test is not satisfied by virtue of evidence that emerged after the rejection of the submission. It is submitted that, as a matter of principle, the former approach is preferable.

The Royal Commission on Criminal Justice recommended that *Galbraith* be reversed and that the judge should have the power to stop a case if the prosecution evidence is unsafe or unsatisfactory.[65] If followed, the effect of this recommendation would be to restore to judges the power to stop a case where there is evidence, but it is so weak, or comes from such a discredited witness, that it is in the interests of justice to withdraw the case from the jury. This is not a power which, it is anticipated, will very often be exercised. However, it would be a useful addition to the judge's armoury of powers in cases such as those when a witness fails to come up to proof and a prosecution case is much weaker than had at first been thought. Stopping such a case would also involve a useful saving in public time and money.

(5) Summing-up

The law.   During the course of his summing-up, the judge directs the   16–13
jury as to their respective functions. An appropriate direction is for the judge to tell the jury that while his function is to direct it as to the law (and they must act upon his direction) it is the sole judges of fact and it decides which evidence to accept and which to reject. In *Jackson*[66] the Court of Appeal held that the judge's failure to give a clear direction on the respective functions (combined with strong comments on the evidence) amounted to a misdirection. The suggested direction is now as follows:

"Our functions in this trial have been and remain quite different. Throughout this trial the law has been my area of responsibility, and I must now give you directions as to the law which applies in this case. When I do so, you must accept those directions and follow them.

I must also remind you of the prominent features of the evidence. However, it has always been your responsibility to judge the evidence and decide all the relevant facts of this case, and when you come to consider your verdict you, and you alone, must do that.

You do not have to decide every point which has been raised; only such matters as will enable you to say whether the charge laid against

---

[63] *Cockley* (1984) 79 Cr.App.R. 181 and *Smith (Patrick) Joseph* [1999] 2 Cr.App.R. 238.
[64] [1999] 6 *Archbold News* 2, CA (97 04882 W3).
[65] Cm. 2263 (1993), para.4–41.
[66] [1992] Crim.L.R. 214.

the defendant has been proved. You will do that by having regard to the whole of the evidence [including the agreed/admitted evidence] and forming your own judgement about the witnesses, and which evidence is reliable and which is not. [The defendant has chosen to give evidence (and call witnesses). You must judge that evidence by precisely the same fair standards as you apply to any other evidence in the case.]

[Add something along the following lines, if you believe it may be of assistance in the particular case: You must decide this case only on the evidence which has been placed before you. There will be no more. You are entitled to draw inferences, that is come to common sense conclusions based on the evidence which you accept, but you may not speculate about what evidence there might have been or allow yourselves to be drawn into speculation.]

The facts of this case are your responsibility. You will wish to take account of the arguments in the speeches you have heard, but you are not bound to accept them. Equally, if in the course of my review of the evidence, I appear to express any views concerning the facts, or emphasise a particular aspect of the evidence, do not adopt those views unless you agree with them; and if I do not mention something which you think is important, you should have regard to it, and give it such weight as you think fit. When it comes to the facts of this case, it is your judgement alone that counts."[67]

16–14   The judge must also direct the jury on the burden and standard of proof; the law applicable to the offence(s) charged; and other matters of law arising in the case, for example the rules concerned with character. Specimen Directions relating to these matters were first published by the Judicial Studies Board in 1991, with the approval of the Lord Chief Justice.[68] While appropriate in many cases, the directions may well require adaptation to suit the particular circumstances. In *Taylor*[69] the Court of Appeal issued a warning about the use of the Directions. The Court said that while a specimen direction could safely be given verbatim in a straightforward case for which it was designed, great care should be taken to adapt such a direction appropriately in a case where adaptation was required. Similarly, in his foreword to the current edition of the Specimen Directions, the Lord Chief Justice stressed that "the directions should never be used 'mechanistically'". Moreover, he reiterated that the directions are not intended to lay down or develop any principles of criminal law but to reflect in a clear and summary form the law as it stands.[70]

In cases where there may be doubt about whether a direction should be

---

[67] Specimen Directions, published by the Judicial Studies Board (see below).
[68] The Specimen Directions, now in their Sixth Edition (1999), can be found at *www.jsboard.co.uk/criminal_law/index.htm*.
[69] *Taylor, The Times*, June 15, 1993.
[70] Foreword (sixth edition, 1999).

given (or the form the direction should take) it may be prudent for the judge to raise the issue with counsel before closing speeches in order to hear submissions, for example a case where one defendant has a good character while a co-defendant has a bad character, or a case where the defendant has told lies (see below). On the other hand, in *Higgins and Litchfield*[71] the Court of Appeal said that counsel should raise with the judge issues concerning directions about which there was scope for two views (in the instant case, lies told by the defendants and the approach to witnesses who might have reasons of their own to lie).

The facts. The judge usually sums up the evidence to the jury. In **16–15** *Brower*[72] the Court of Appeal said that in the majority of cases the judge should do so in order to assist the jury and to ensure a fair trial: the Court held that in the instant case the judge should have defined the issues and reminded the jury of the evidence. However, the Court did not go so far as to say that there never would be a case when the judge need not sum up the facts; and it is submitted that in a short case where the issue of guilt or innocence can be clearly stated it may not necessarily be a fatal defect in the summing-up if the judge does not sum up the evidence.

In summing up the evidence the judge is not limited to the points made by the prosecution or defence. He is entitled to comment on all the matters given in evidence.[73] He must put the defence to the jury even if the defendant does not give evidence[74] or (provided it arises in evidence) if counsel has not relied on it.[75] For instance, he must put a defence disclosed in interview.[76] In *Curtin*[77] the Court of Appeal said that the way in which the judge puts the defence will depend on the circumstances of the case: where the defendant has given evidence it will usually be desirable to summarise his evidence and to draw attention to consistencies and inconsistencies between the evidence and his replies in interview. Where a defendant has not given evidence or answered questions in interview it will usually be appropriate to remind the jury of counsel's speech. Finally, where the case against a defendant is strong and his defence correspondingly weak, the judge should be scrupulous to ensure that the defence is presented in an even-handed and impartial manner.[78]

---

[71] *The Times*, August 11, 1995.
[72] [1995] Crim.L.R. 746.
[73] *Evans* (1990) 91 Cr.App.R. 173.
[74] *Soames-Waring*, below. *Badjan* (1966) 50 Cr.App.R. 141. The way in which the judge identifies the defence will depend on the circumstances of the particular case. In *Soames-Waring* [1999] Crim.L.R. 89 the trial judge invited the jury to read the whole of the defendant's interview with the police and referred them to the salient parts in relation to each count; a course which the court of Appeal approved. In a short or straight forward case the defence may be identified and summarised in a few words.
[75] *Porritt* (1961) 45 Cr.App.R. 348; *Kachikwu* (1968) 52 Cr.App.R. 538.
[76] *Bass* [1992] Crim.L.R. 647.
[77] [1996] Crim.L.R. 831.
[78] *Reid*, *The Times* August 17, 1999.

The judge is entitled to express a view on the facts and express it in strong terms, provided it is made clear to the jury that it decides the issues of fact. "A judge may of course give his opinion to the jury on a question of fact and express it as strongly as the circumstances permit so long as he gives it as advice and not as a direction."[79] However, comment must be kept within proper bounds. A judge, for instance, is not entitled "to comment in such a way as to make the summing up as a whole unbalanced".[80] In one case the Court of Appeal said that the judge should not make sarcastic and extravagant comments on the evidence.[81] The overall duty is one of fairness. Thus, Lord Lane C.J. has said that it is an inherent principle of our system of trial that:

> "however distasteful the offence, however repulsive the defendant, however laughable his defence, he is entitled to have his case fairly presented to the jury by judge and counsel ... [and] where the cards seemed to be stacked most heavily against [him] the judge should be most scrupulous to ensure that nothing untoward took place which might exacerbate the defendant's difficulties."[82]

16–16   The object of the summing-up is to assist the jury in trying the case. The judge should therefore clarify the issues for it. He should also assist it in assessing the significance of the evidence. Thus, Lawton L.J. giving the judgment of the Court of Appeal in *Sparrow*,[83] said:

> "In our experience a jury is not helped by a colourless reading out of the evidence as recorded by the judge in his notebook. The judge is more than a referee who takes no part in the trial save to intervene when a rule of procedure or evidence is broken. He and the jury try the case together and it is his duty to give them the benefit of his knowledge of the law and to advise them in the light of his experience as to the significance of the evidence."

The Court of Appeal has stated that it could not be too strongly emphasised that when summing up a judge is under no obligation to rehearse all the evidence or all the arguments—brevity is a virtue not a vice.[84] In a trial lasting several days or more it is generally of assistance to the jury if the judge summarises factual issues not in dispute and, where there is significant dispute as to material facts, identify succinctly the factual

---

[79] *Chandler v DPP* [1964] A.C. 763, 804, *per* Lord Devlin.
[80] *Gilbey* (unreported) January 26, 1990, *per* Lloyd L.J., quoted with approval by the Privy Council in *Mears v R* [1993] 1 W.L.R. 818, 822.
[81] *Berrada* (1989) 91 Cr.App.R. 131 (Note).
[82] *Marr* [1989] 90 Cr.App.R. 154, 156.
[83] [1973] 1 W.L.R. 488, 495.
[84] *Farr, The Times*, December 10, 1998.

issues to be resolved. The summing-up should not, however, consist of a mere "safety net" exercise to ensure the jury has been reminded of all the salient points, nor should it be a mere rehearsal of the evidence. It is not acceptable for the judge to fail to give any directions on the evidence and simply tell the jury that they have received sufficient assistance from counsel's closing speeches.[85]

Juries may find it helpful to receive a direction as to how they should approach the examination of the witnesses's evidence. Such a direction is often given. An appropriate direction would be along these lines: to remind the jury that all the witnesses start equal and the fact that the defendant comes from the dock to give his evidence, whereas the prosecution witnesses came from outside the court (and, if it is the case, are police officers)[86] makes no difference. However, the witnesses do not finish equal because the jury has to judge them and in judging the witnesses and evaluating the evidence, the jury should use its common sense, knowledge and experience of the world.

The judge should not, however, state his own views as to whether witnesses have told the truth or not: that is for the jury to decide. Thus, he should not tell the jury that he thought that the defendant was lying.[87]

Lies told by the defendant. The judge was previously under a duty to give an appropriate direction about the significance of lies told by the defendant either to the police or to the court if they were capable of amounting to corroboration[88] or confirming an identification.[89] (For an appropriate direction in identification cases see below.) On the other hand, 16–17

---

[85] *Amado-Taylor* [2000] 2 Cr.App.R. 189.

[86] The Court of Appeal has said that it was undesirable that a judge should make comments which suggested that police witnesses were in a special category or that their careers would be adversely affected if the defendant were acquitted: *Harris* [1986] Crim.L.R. 123; *Culbertson* (1970) 54 Cr.App.R. 310. (This applies to prosecuting counsel as well as judges: *Gale* [1994] Crim.L.R. 208.) In *Bentley* [1999] Crim.L.R. 330 Lord Bingham C.J. said that there was an obvious risk of injustice if a jury were invited to approach the evidence on the assumption that police officers, because they were such, were likely to be accurate and reliable witnesses and defendants, because they were such, likely to be inaccurate and unreliable. On the other hand, in a case where it was suggested that police officers had a personal motive for inventing an interview, the Court of Appeal held that a judge was justified in commenting that anyone who invents an interview runs the risk of severe punishment for perjury and perverting the course of justice (the judge told the jury to weigh that consideration against the alleged motive): *Keane* [1992] Crim.L.R. 306. If a witness mentions such matters as the adverse effect on his career of an acquittal, the judge may have to direct the jury on this evidence. In *Gale, The Times,* June 2, 1993, the Court of Appeal approved the trial judge's direction that an acquittal was not tantamount to a finding of perjury and to scrutinise the police evidence with care, bearing in mind defence criticisms.

[87] *Iroegbu, The Times,* August 2, 1988.

[88] *Lucas (Ruth)* [1981] Q.B. 720. For the abolition of the corroboration rules, see para.15–08, above.

[89] *Penman* (1986) 82 Cr.App.R. 44.

it was not considered necessary to give a direction in other cases[90] and it was held to be a matter for the judge's discretion.[91]

However, in *Goodway*,[92] Lord Taylor C.J. said that there was no reason to distinguish between corroboration and identification cases and any other case where lies are relied on by the prosecution as part of its case. The Court of Appeal, accordingly, held in *Goodway* that if the prosecution relies on lies told by the defendant in or out of court as evidence of his guilt the judge must give a direction based on that in *Lucas*[93] (see below). The reason for this ruling is to be found in the dictum of Lord Devlin in *Broadhurst v R*[94]:

> "It is very important that a jury should be carefully directed upon the effect of a conclusion ... that the accused is lying. There is a natural tendency for a jury to think that if an accused is lying, it must be because he is guilty, and accordingly convict him without more ado. It is the duty of the judge to make clear to them that this is no so ... [If] upon the proved facts two inferences may be drawn about the accused's conduct or state of mind, his untruthfulness is a factor which the jury can properly take into account as strengthening the inference of guilt. What strength it adds depends ... on all the circumstances and especially whether there are reasons other than guilt that might account for untruthfulness."

16–18   However, if the lies told by the defendant amount to an explanation, the rejection of which leaves the jury with no option but to convict, there is no need to give a Lucas direction (as it has come to be called).[95] In *Dehar*,[96] North P. said: "We do not say that in every case in which lies are put forward in aid of the Crown case to reinforce the other evidence it is always necessary for the trial judge to give any specific form of direction. How far a direction is necessary will depend on circumstances. There may be cases ... where the rejection of the explanation given by the accused almost necessarily leaves the jury with no choice but to convict as a matter of logic".

There is, therefore, no need to give a direction if the lies are not relied on as additional evidence of guilt and there is no distinction between the issue

---

[90] *Sharp* (1994) 98 Cr.App.R. 144 (Note).
[91] *Bey* (1994) 98 Cr.App.R. 158 (Note).
[92] (1994) 98 Cr.App.R. 17.
[93] *Lucas*, above, n.88.
[94] [1964] A.C. 441, 453. In *Richens* (1994) Cr.App.R. 43 Broadhurst was cited and it was suggested that Lord Devlin was referring to lies in court but Lord Taylor C.J. said that there was no reason to think that the observations were not equally applicable to lies out of court.
[95] *Dehar* [1969] N.Z.L.R. 763; *Barsoum* [1994] Crim.L.R. 194.
[96] Above, at 765.

of whether the defendant has told lies and the issue of whether he is guilty.[97] Thus, a denial of the offence will not call for a direction.[98]

Similarly, if there is a direct conflict between the evidence of the prosecution witnesses and the evidence of the defendant, no direction will be called for. This is because if the jury accept the prosecution evidence that involves the conclusion that the defendant is lying and there is therefore no distinction between the issue of lies and the issue of guilt. As has been said, the lies must play a part as a separately identifiable feature of the case which the jury would have to take into account separately from their determination of the main issue.[99]

It should also be noted that a direction may well not be necessary if the issue about which the lie was told was purely peripheral and a direction would merely serve to give the lie undue prominence.[1] In *Middleton*[2] it was held that the point of a *Lucas* direction was to warn the jury against adopting the "forbidden reasoning" that a defendant's lies necessarily demonstrated his guilt. Were there was no such risk a direction would not be necessary. This is generally the case in relation to lies told by the defendant in evidence as the position would be covered by the general direction on the burden and standard of proof. In short, whether a direction is necessary will depend on the circumstances.

The need to give a *Lucas* direction only arises if the prosecution invite the   **16–19** jury to draw an inference of guilt from the fact that the defendant has told lies about some collateral matter or changed his account (or there is a danger that the jury may think that they can do so).[3] It will be for the judge to determine in the circumstances of the particular case whether a direction is necessary. However, in *Burge and Pegg*[4] the Court of Appeal sought to summarise four circumstances in which a direction is required, namely:

(1)   where the defendant relies on alibi;

(2)   where lies are relied on to corroborate or support other evidence;

(3)   where the prosecution seek to rely on lies in relation to a separate and distinct issue as evidence of guilt in relation to the offence charged;

---

[97] *Landon* [1995] Crim.L.R. 338; *Harron* [1996] 2 Cr.App.R. 457, 463.
[98] *Mussell and Dalton* [1995] Crim.L.R. 887.
[99] *House and Meadows* [1994] Crim.L.R. 682.
[1] *Keeton* [1995] 2 Cr.App.R. 241.
[2] [2001] Crim.L.R. 251.
[3] *Landon* [1995] Crim.L.R. 338; *Harron* [1996] 2 Cr.App.R. 457, 463; and *Faryab* [2000] Crim.L.R. 180. In the commentary on *Landon* there is reference to this sort of evidence amounting to an implied admission (an observation quoted with approval in *Harron*). It is difficult, however, to see how a lie can ever amount to an admission of an offence (implied, or otherwise). In *Faryab* the Court of Appeal held that where lies are told by the accused during an examination by the Official Reciever under the Insolvency Act 1986, the jury should be told that such lies do not necessarily indicate guilt. But see para.11–09 above for the present law.
[4] [1996] 1 Cr.App.R. 163, 173.

(4) where the judge envisages that the jury may adopt the approach in (3), above, although the prosecution have not done so.

However, it is submitted that it is not possible to categorise cases in which a direction should be given because the circumstances of each case will vary. This is illustrated by two decisions of the Court of Appeal in relation to special directions which should be given when the defendant puts forward a defence of alibi. In *Lesley*[5] the Court said that in these cases the judge should direct the jury that even if they conclude that the alibi is false that does not entitle them to convict the defendant, because an alibi may sometimes be invented to bolster a genuine defence: the Court said that this direction should routinely be given. On the other hand, in *Harron*[6] a differently constituted Court of Appeal held that no special direction was required in that case because (distinguishing *Lesley*) the lies in the instant case played no part in the prosecution case (*i.e.* were not relied on by the prosecution) and did not constitute a matter which the jury might have to take into account separately from the main issue in the case.

16–20   The Court of Appeal in *Burge and Pegg*[7] pointed out that if a *Lucas* direction is given in a case where there is no need for such a direction (for example in a case where there is a straight conflict of evidence) it will add to the complexity of the case and do more harm than good. Therefore, in cases where the judge envisages a danger that the jury may infer guilt from a lie (even though the prosecution have not invited them to do so), before speeches and summing-up he should always consider with counsel whether a direction is required.[8] (It is submitted that in any case where there may be doubt about whether a direction should be given it may be prudent for the judge to discuss matters with counsel.) In *McGuinness*,[9] a case in which a *Lucas* direction should have been given, the judge did not seek the assistance of counsel as to appropriate directions and counsel had not thought it necessary to bring the omission to to his attention. The Court of Appeal held that as the judge placed no emphasis on the lies in the summing-up and as the lies were not a large feature of the case, the absence of the usual direction did not make the verdict unsafe.

An appropriate direction would be along these lines:

"It is alleged [admitted] that the defendant lied to the police [or X] in saying [that ...], and you are entitled to consider whether this sup-

---

[5] [1996] 1 Cr.App.R. 39.
[6] [1996] 2 Cr.App.R. 457.
[7] [1996] 1 Cr.App.R. 163, 173.
[8] The Court said that if the matter were dealt with in this way it would be slow to interfere with the exercise of the judge's discretion and would not be inclined to find that there was a danger that the jury would treat a lie as evidence of guilt unless defence counsel had asked the judge to give a direction.
[9] [1999] Crim.L.R. 318.

ports the case against him. In this regard you should consider two questions:

1. You must decide whether the defendant did in fact tell [these] lies. If you are not sure he did, ignore this matter. If you are sure, consider:

2. Why did the defendant lie? The mere fact that a defendant tells a lie is not in itself evidence of guilt. A defendant may lie for many reasons, and they may possibly be 'innocent' ones in the sense that they do not denote guilt, for example, lies to bolster a true defence, to protect somebody else, to conceal some disgraceful conduct [other than] [short of] the commission of the offence, or out of panic or confusion. In this case the explanation for his lies is [. . .]. If you think that there is, or may be, an innocent explanation for his lies then you should take no notice of them. It is only if you are sure that he did not lie for an innocent reason that his lies can be regarded by you as evidence [going to prove guilt] [supporting the prosecution case]."[10]

The jury must also be satisfied that the lie was deliberate and related to a material issue; and it must be so directed in an appropriate case.[11] However, in most cases these issues will not arise: it will usually be clear whether the lie was deliberate or not; and if the lie does not relate to a material issue it will be simple to disregard it.

Failure to call witnesses. The judge may comment on the failure of   **16–21** the defendant to call potential witnesses and, in an appropriate case, make a strong comment.[12] However, he must exercise care in doing so[13]: there may, for instance, be perfectly innocent reasons for not calling a witness. The Court of Appeal has said that comment is undesirable when a witness could have been called by either side and that in these circumstances the judge should tell the jury not to speculate as to what inference should be drawn.[14] In *Wilmot*[15] the judge commented on the defendant's failure to call his solicitor to rebut a suggestion that he had recently fabricated his

---

[10] This suggested direction is based on the Specimen Directions published by the Judicial Studies Board. This is a basic direction to be given only when the need arises. It must be "tailored to the circumstances of the case". See *R v Sutton*, unreported (96/8551/Z5). As with other directions, there is no rule as to where in the summing-up this direction should be given. It is often convenient for the judge to give it when dealing with the defendant's evidence, but he does not have to do so. In *Friend* [1997] 2 All E.R. 1012 the Court of Appeal rejected a submission that the trial judge had wrongly separated a *Lucas* direction in his summing-up from the evidence relating to the defendant: the Court held that the direction had been clearly and correctly included in the directions on the law rather than during the analysis of the evidence.
[11] *Lucas*, above, n.88.
[12] *Robertson*; *Golder* (1987) 85 Cr.App.R. 304, 312–313.
[13] See *Gallagher* [1974] 1 W.L.R. 1204, 1211, cited para.17–37, below; *Couzens and Frankel* [1992] Crim.L.R. 822.
[14] *Wheeler* (1967) 52 Cr.App.R. 28.
[15] (1989) 89 Cr.App.R. 341.

story. The Court of Appeal held that the comment was proper, but said that such a comment should only be made where there is a strong case for suggesting that the story had been recently fabricated and, if it was not, where there would be witnesses to substantiate the defendant's account. From the foregoing, it would appear that a comment should only be made in a clear case where the only reasonable inference to be drawn from the defendant's failure to call the witness is that his story is not true.

In *Khan (Shakeel)*[16] it was observed that a jury might sometimes be entitled to ask themselves why a witness had not been called. A universal requirement to direct the jury not to speculate would be unfair. Similarly, to give no direction could invite speculation and thereby work injustice. Commenting adversely, however, could also be unfair in cases where there might be good reason for not calling the witness. It is ultimately a matter dependent upon the judge's sense of fairness. When the judge proposes to comment upon the defendant's failure to call a witness he should usually invite submissions from counsel and should, when commenting on the failure, remind the jury of the burden of proof.

(5) Directions to convict

16–22 May the judge direct the jury to convict the defendant if there are undisputed facts which clearly point to his guilt? Dicta in the House of Lords indicate that he cannot. Lord Sankey, for instance, said that for the judge to do this would be to make him "decide the case and not the jury which is not the common law."[17] Similarly, Lord Devlin, in *Chandler v DPP*,[18] said: "I cannot accept that the judge is entitled to direct the jury how to answer a question of fact however obvious he may believe the answer to be and although he may be satisfied that any other answer would be perverse."

On the other hand, the Court of Appeal has said on a number of occasions that in exceptional cases the judge is entitled to direct a jury to convict upon undisputed facts.[19] Such directions have been approved[20] and supported by academic writers.[21]

The matter came before the House of Lords in *DPP v Stonehouse*.[22] The defendant in that case was charged with attempting to obtain money on life insurance policies by faking his death by drowning. The judge directed the

---

[16] [2001] Crim.L.R. 673.

[17] *Woolmington v DPP* [1935] A.C. 462, 480.

[18] [1964] A.C. 763, 803.

[19] *Vickers* (1975) 61 Cr.App.R. 48, 51; *Kelly* [1970] 1 W.L.R. 1050, 1052; *Morris* [1973] R.T.R. 171, 174.

[20] *Eastwood* [1961] Crim.L.R. 414; *Draper* [1962] Crim.L.R. 107; *Collinson* (1931) 23 Cr.App.R. 49; *Pico* [1971] Crim.L.R. 599; *per contra, Gutteridge* [1973] R.T.R. 135; *Clemo (Note)* [1973] R.T.R. 176n; *Martin* (1973) 57 Cr.App.R. 279.

[21] Griew, "Directions to Convict" [1972] Crim.L.R. 204; Glanville Williams, "Law and Fact" [1976] Crim.L.R. 472, 475. For an opposite view see Lord Devlin, *Trial by Jury* (revised ed., 1966), p. 84, App. II.

[22] [1978] A.C. 55.

jury that the offence was committed if the defendant falsely staged his death dishonestly intending that money should be obtained from the insurance company. The judge thereby failed to leave to the jury an issue of fact, namely whether the acts of the defendant were sufficiently proximate to constitute an attempt. The majority of the House of Lords held that the judge's direction was wrong. They took the view that the judge must leave issues of fact to the jury even where any reasonable jury properly directed must convict upon the facts. This is because, in every case where a jury may be entitled to convict, the application of the law to the facts is a matter for the jury and not for the judge.[23]

The decision of the House of Lords in *Stonehouse* disposed of the con- **16–23** troversy and restored the position to that set out by Lord Sankey. In a series of cases the Court of Appeal has applied *Stonehouse* and held that it is wrong for a judge to withdraw an issue of fact from the jury and direct them to convict (even if the evidence, including the defendant's own evidence, makes conviction inevitable).[24] The Court in *Gent*[25] said that if there was a category of cases where the judge was justified in directing a conviction it must be confined to wholly exceptional cases where, for example, there had been something in the nature of a formal admission of guilt. Such an occurrence will be rare. However, as a matter of principle it must be correct that if the jury are the sole judges of the facts, the right to decide the facts cannot be removed from them, however perverse a verdict of not guilty would seem. This does not prevent the judge pointing out to the jury in the strongest terms that in his view there is only one possible verdict on the evidence.[26]

If, on the other hand, as a matter of law, the defendant has no defence, the judge is entitled to direct the jury to convict. Thus, the Court of Appeal has held that judges were correct in directing juries to convict in two cases of possessing articles with intent to damage property where the judges had correctly ruled that there was no evidence capable of constituting a defence.[27] Indeed, in this situation the judge has no option but to direct the jury to convict: nothing is removed from its decision, because there is nothing left to decide. This may be contrasted with the situation in *Stonehouse* where the judge removed part of the affirmative prosecution case from the jury's decision.

---

[23] At 94, *per* Lord Keith.
[24] *Challinor* (1985) 80 Cr.App.R. 253; *Thompson* [1984] 1 W.L.R. 962; *Gordon* (1987) 92 Cr.App.R. 50 (Note); *Gent* (1989) 89 Cr.App.R. 247.
[25] Above, at 250.
[26] *Stonehouse*, above, at 80, *per* Lord Salmon; *Gent*, above.
[27] *Hill and Hall* (1989) 89 Cr.App.R. 74.

B. Functions of the jury

16–24 The jury's function is to decide all matters of fact. It therefore decides all questions:

> (i) of primary fact, *i.e.* "facts observed by the witnesses and proved by testimony";[28]
>
> (ii) of inferential fact, *i.e.* what inferences to draw from the primary facts[29];
>
> (iii) of the reliability and credibility of witnesses and the weight of evidence; and
>
> (iv) of the application of ordinary words in a statute to the particular case.[30]

Thus, whether a person behaved dishonestly is a matter for the jury to determine[31]; or whether he was reckless; or whether the facts proved amount to an attempt[32]; or whether the defendant had a reasonable excuse for his possession of an offensive weapon.

If a judge rules evidence admissible, it is for the jury to decide whether to accept it. For instance, once a confession is admitted it is for the jury to decide whether it is true or not. Such an issue must not be withdrawn from them. In *Beckford*[33] the trial judge ruled on a *voir dire* that evidence of a police search was admissible, the defendant having submitted that the search was unlawful. The judge directed the jury that the police were entitled to search. The Court of Appeal held that this was a misdirection because it withdrew from the jury the question whether the police were being truthful in their account of dealings with a witness and genuine in their stated reason for entering the premises. The Court said that it was for the judge to rule on the admissibility of evidence, but, once it was admitted, it was for the jury to say whether they accepted it as true or not. This is because issues relating to the credibility of witnesses are solely a matter for the jury to determine.

---

[28] *Bracegirdle v Oxley* [1947] K.B. 349, 358, *per* Denning J.
[29] "[The] drawing of the inference is a matter for the jury not the judge," *Clemo (Note)* [1973] R.T.R. 176, 177, *per* Chapman J.
[30] para.16–02.
[31] *Feely* [1973] 1 Q.B. 530; *Ghosh* [1982] 2 W.L.R. 110.
[32] *DPP v Stonehouse* [1978] A.C. 55; cited at para.16–22, above.
[33] (1992) 94 Cr.App.R. 43.

2. TRIALS ON INDICTMENT WITHOUT A JURY

Lord Justice Auld's "Review of the Criminal Courts of England and **16–25** Wales"[34] recommended that trial by jury should remain the main form of trial for more serious offences triable on indictment. However, it was suggested that defendants should be entitled, with the court's consent, to opt for trial by judge alone. Moreover, in serious and complex frauds the nominated trial judge should have the power to direct trial by judge with two lay members drawn from a panel established for the purpose (or, if the defendant requests, by judge alone). These recommendations were followed, in a limited way, in the Criminal Justice Act 2003.

Part 7 of the Criminal Justice Act 2003 makes provision for trials on indictment to be heard, in certain limited circumstances, without a jury. At the time of writing, Pt 7 had not yet entered into force.[35] The prosecution may apply to a judge of the Crown Court for a trial to be conducted without a jury in cases of (i) serious or complex fraud (s.43), and (ii) where there is a danger of jury tampering (s.44).

In cases of serious or complex fraud (where a notice has been given under s.51B of the Crime and Disorder Act 1998) the judge *may* order that the trial be conducted without a jury if he is satisfied that the complexity or length of the trial (or both) is likely to make the trial so burdensome to the members of the jury that the interests of justice require trial without a jury.[36] In making his determination the judge must consider any steps which might reasonably be taken to reduce the complexity or length of trial.[37] Such steps, however, must not significantly disadvantage the prosecution.[38] A judge may only order a trial without jury in such cases with the approval of the Lord Chief Justice or a judge nominated by him.[39]

In cases where there is a danger of jury tampering, a judge *must* order that the trial be tried without a jury if he is satisfied that:

(i) there is evidence of a real and present danger that jury tampering would take place,[40] and

(ii) notwithstanding any steps (including provision of police protec-

---

[34] September 2001. Auld L.J. made a number of recommendations aimed at a fundamental restructuring of both trials on indictment and summary trial by justices. He recommended replacing the Crown Court and magistrates' courts with a "unified Criminal Court" consisting of three divisions: the Crown Division, constituted as the Crown Court now is; the District Division, constituted by a judge, normally a District Judge or Recorder, and at least two lay magistrates; and the Magistrates' Division, constituted as the current magistrates' courts.

[35] s.336(3) of the Criminal Justice Act 2003 provides that Pt 7 will come into force in accordance with provision made by the Secretary of State by order.

[36] s.43(5) of the Criminal Justice Act 2003.

[37] s.43(6) of the Criminal Justice Act 2003.

[38] s.43(7) of the Criminal Justice Act 2003.

[39] s.43(4) of the Criminal Justice Act 2003.

[40] s.44(4) of the Criminal Justice Act 2003.

tion) which might reasonably be taken to prevent jury tampering, the likelihood that it would take place would be so substantial as to make it necessary in the interests of justice for the trial to be conducted without a jury.[41]

16–26   Examples of real and present danger of jury tampering are given as a case where: (i) the trial is a retrial and the jury in the previous trial was discharged because jury tampering had taken place, (ii) jury tampering has occurred in previous criminal proceedings involving the defendant, and (iii) there has been intimidation or attempted intimidation of any person who is likely to be a witness in the trial.[42]

If, after a trial on indictment has commenced with a jury, the judge discharges the jury because jury tampering has taken place, he may continue without a jury if he is satisfied that to do so would be fair to the defendant.[43] The trial must, however, be terminated if this is necessary in the interests of justice.[44] If the trial is terminated, the judge may order that any new trial be conducted without a jury if he is satisfied that both the conditions set out above are satisfied.[45]

Where a trial is conducted or continued without a jury, the court is to have all the powers, authorities and jurisdiction which the court would have had if the trial had been conducted with a jury, including the determination of any question or the making of any finding which would normally be required to be made by a jury.[46] Where the court convicts the defendant in a trial without a jury, the court must give a judgment which states the reasons for the conviction at, or as soon as reasonably practicable after, the time of the conviction.[47] (For the potential problems on public interest immunity application in such cases, see para.12–18 above.)

3. SUMMARY TRIALS: FUNCTIONS OF JUSTICES

A. Admissibility of evidence

16–27   Justices have to perform the functions of both judge and jury in relation to the evidence. Both fact and law are matters for them. They are therefore responsible for deciding questions of admissibility as well as weight of evidence. They also have a discretion to exclude relevant evidence.[48] This leads to the complication that if, having heard the evidence, they rule it

---

[41] s.44(5) of the Criminal Justice Act 2003.
[42] s.44(6) of the Criminal Justice Act 2003.
[43] s.46(3) of the Criminal Justice Act 2003.
[44] s.46(4) of the Criminal Justice Act 2003.
[45] s.46(5) of the Criminal Justice Act 2003.
[46] s.48(3) of the Criminal Justice Act 2003.
[47] s.48(5)(a) of the Criminal Justice Act 2003.
[48] *Sang* [1979] 69 Cr.App.R. 282, 307, *per* Lord Scarman; *Jeffrey v Black* [1978] 1 Q.B. 490, 497, *per* Lord Widgery C.J.

inadmissible, they must thereafter ignore it. When considering admissibility of evidence, justices:

(i) ought not to rule until the evidence has been tendered and objection taken[49];

(ii) should know what the evidence is before ruling on it[50];

(iii) do not have powers to delegate their function of determining admissibility to another bench.[51]

In *F v Kent Chief Constable*[52] the Divisional Court said that a trial-within-a-trial was not an appropriate procedure in a magistrates' court. The Court said that incidental matters, such as the admissibility of evidence, should be decided as separate issues from the question of guilt and innocence, but not as trials-within-trials; and there was no need for evidence to be repeated after the issue of admissibility had been determined. The court declined to lay down rules as to when justices should announce their decisions as to admissibility, but said that they must ensure that what was done was fair to the defendant and just to the prosecution.

However, this principle does not apply where the court has to determine whether a confession should be admitted under s.76(2) of the Police and Criminal Evidence Act 1984. Section 76(2) provides that if it is represented that the confession has or may have been obtained in either of the two ways set out in the subsection, the court shall not allow it to be given in evidence except insofar as the prosecution prove beyond reasonable doubt that it was not so obtained. Accordingly, the Divisional Court in *Liverpool Juvenile Court Ex p. R*[53] held that s.76(2) obliged magistrates to hold a trial-within-a-trial in these circumstances. The Court said that a trial-within-a-trial will only take place if it is represented that the confession was obtained in one of the ways set out in s.76(2). The Court also said that for this purpose a suggestion in cross-examination did not amount to a representation.

It would appear that this rule applied in committal proceedings. Thus, in **16–28** *Oxford City Justices Ex p. Berry*[54] the Divisional Court held that judicial review could go to quash a committal where the justices had refused to undertake the enquiry contemplated by s.76(2) but added the rider that, save in the exceptional case, the court should not quash any committal on that ground alone. On the other hand, if an application to exclude evidence

---

[49] *Sang* [1979] 69 Cr.App.R. 282, 307, *per* Lord Scarman; *Williams v Mohamed* [1977] R.T.R. 12.
[50] *Turner v Underwood* [1948] 2 K.B. 284; *Sang* [1979] 69 Cr.App.R. 282, 294, *per* Lord Dilhorne.
[51] *Ormskirk JJ. Ex p. Davies* (1994) 158 J.P. 1145.
[52] [1982] Crim.L.R. 682.
[53] [1988] Q.B. 1.
[54] [1988] Q.B. 507.

is made under s.78 of the 1984 Act there is no obligation upon the magistrates to hold a trial-within-a-trial. The Divisional Court held in *Vel v Owen*[55] that the defendant has no right in the magistrates' court to have the admissibility of evidence determined under s.78 in advance of the evidence being given. This is because the court under s.78 has a discretion to exclude evidence if it would bear unfairly on the proceedings: and there is no burden on the prosecution to disprove unfairness. However, there may be cases where, in order to secure a trial which is just and fair to both sides, magistrates may decide that if the accused wishes to proceed by way of a trial-within-a-trial, he should be allowed to do so, in order to have the opportunity to secure the exclusion of the unfair evidence before giving evidence on the main issue, thereby maintaining his right to remain silent on the main issue: *Halawa v F.A.C.T.*[56]

It is sometimes suggested that if justices hear evidence which they subsequently rule is inadmissible, they should adjourn the trial in order that the case may be heard by another bench. In most cases this would appear unnecessary since the justices are quite capable of ignoring the inadmissible evidence (as they must). Indeed, in *Ormskirk JJ. Ex p. DPP*,[57] the Divisional Court said that it was the duty of magistrates to put out of their minds evidence which they have ruled inadmissible.

16–29 However, if justices hear of a defendant's convictions or charges pending against him, other than as a result of admissible evidence, it may well be necessary to adjourn the case for hearing by a new bench. The test to be applied in these circumstances was established by the Divisional Court in *Liverpool JJ. Ex p. Topping*[58] "Would a reasonable and fair-minded person sitting in court and knowing all the relevant facts have a reasonable suspicion that a fair trial for the (defendant) was not possible?" For the position following public interest immunity applications, see para.12–25, above.

(Justices may reverse a previous decision as to inadmissibility provided that there is a good reason to do so and that no injustice is caused thereby, but "such reversals ... cannot be treated as routine."[59])

---

[55] [1987] Crim.L.R. 496. See paras 10–13 *et seq.*, above, for a discussion of the exclusion of evidence under s.78.

[56] [1995] 1 Cr.App.R. 21, 35. It should be noted that *Halawa* was decided before the enactment of s.35 of the Criminal Justice and Public Order Act 1994 which considerably resticted the right of the accused to remain silent at trial, see para.17–16, below. Accordingly, the effect of this decision may well be reduced as a result of s.35.

[57] (1995) 158 J.P. 1145.

[58] [1983] 76 Cr.App.R. 170, 175.

[59] *Sittingbourne JJ. Ex p. Stickings* (1996) 160 J.P. 801, 806

B. Submission of no case

Magistrates may dismiss a case at the close of the prosecution evidence on a submission being made. In 1962 the following Practice Direction[60] was laid down for the guidance of magistrates considering such a submission:

16–30

> "A submission that there is no case to answer may properly be made and upheld:
>
> (a) when there has been no evidence to prove an essential element in the alleged offence;
> (b) when the evidence adduced by the prosecution has been so discredited as a result of cross-examination or is so manifestly unreliable that no reasonable tribunal could safely convict on it.
>
> Apart from these two situations a tribunal should not in general be called on to reach a decision as to conviction or acquittal until the whole of the evidence which either side wishes to tender has been placed before it. If, however, a submission is made that there is no case to answer, the decision should depend not so much on whether the adjudicating tribunal (if compelled to do so) would at that stage convict or acquit but whether the evidence is such that a reasonable tribunal might convict. If a reasonable tribunal might convict on the evidence so far laid before it, there is a case to answer."

It is to be noted that:

(a) The test may be contrasted with that laid down for judges in trials on indictment in *Galbraith*.[61] Allowance is made for the fact that justices are judges of fact. In consequence they may consider the reliability of the prosecution evidence (which the judge may not).

(b) The distinction is made between the decision facing justices at the close of the whole of the evidence and that facing them if a submission is made at the close of the prosecution. (In the former case they may convict only if the prosecution have proved their case beyond reasonable doubt. In the latter case the prosecution have only to satisfy the justices that a reasonable tribunal might safely convict.)

---

[60] [1962] 1 All E.R. 448. Justices' clerks should keep a copy of the Practice Direction in court and put it before the justices for guidance in every submission of no case: *Stoneley v Coleman* [1974] Crim.L.R. 254, *per* Lord Widgery C.J. This advice was reiterated in *Barking JJ. Ex p. DPP* (1995) 159 J. P. 373.
[61] (1981) 73 Cr.App.R. 124; para.16–10, above.

(c) If an unsuccessful submission is made on behalf of a defendant, the defence still has the right to call evidence. To avoid confusion, therefore, when a submission is made the justices should ask whether the advocate is making a final speech or a submission, reserving the right to call evidence.[62]

(d) Justices, if minded to stop a case (either on a defence submission or of their own motion), should always give the prosecution the opportunity to make submissions before they give their final ruling.[63] Such a course is in the interests of justice and in order to avoid some matter being overlooked.

C. Review of justices' findings of fact

16–31 The Divisional Court will not interfere with justices' findings of "primary fact", *i.e.* facts observed by witnesses and proved by testimony since these are matters essentially for the tribunal of fact which sees and hears the witnesses.[64] However, the Court will intervene if the conclusions drawn from these facts are such that no reasonable bench could have drawn them. Thus, in *Bracegirdle v Oxley* justices had dismissed two cases of dangerous driving in similar circumstances and in the face of overwhelming evidence. A Court of five judges directed that the justices should convict in both cases. Humphreys J. said: "For a very great number of years, whenever justices have found facts from which only one conclusion can be drawn by reasonable persons honestly applying their minds to the question, and have refused to draw that only conclusion, this court has invariably upset the justices in the appropriate manner."[65] The court will interfere in these circumstances because the position is the same as if the justices had come to a decision of fact without evidence to support it.[66]

The Court has also been prepared to reverse the findings of justices on issues as to the meaning of words which amount to findings of fact. For instance, the Court has held that an air rifle was a firearm for the purpose of the Licensing Act 1872[67]; that a mobile snack bar (which was towed by a separate van) parked in a lay-by was "pitched" for the purposes of s.127 of the Highways Act 1959[68] and that certain firearms did not amount to antiques for the purposes of s.58(2) of the Firearms Act 1968.[69] These decisions appear to be a far cry from *Brutus v Cozens*. The rationale,

---

[62] *Gravesend JJ. Ex p.* Sheldon [1968] 1 W.L.R. 1699.

[63] *Barking JJ. Ex p. DPP* (1995) 159 J.P. 373.

[64] *Bracegirdle v Oxley* [1947] K.B. 349, 358, *per* Denning J. There may, of course, be an appeal to the Crown Court against a conviction by justices. Such an appeal involves a complete rehearing of the case.

[65] Above, at 357.

[66] *Bracegirdle v Oxley*, above, at 353, *per* Lord Goddard C.J.

[67] *Seamark v Prouse* (1980) 70 Cr.App.R. 236.

[68] *Waltham Forest B.C. v Mills* (1979) 78 L.G.R. 248.

[69] *Bennett v Brown* (1980) 71 Cr.App.R. 109; *cf. Richards v Curwen* (1977) 65 Cr.App.R. 95.

however, may be the need to ensure a uniformity of approach on the meaning of a particular word in order to avoid inconsistent findings from different benches.

CHAPTER 17

Competence and Compellability of Witnesses

1. THE GENERAL RULE

17–01   A witness is competent if he may lawfully give evidence. He is compellable if he may lawfully be required to do so.

The Youth Justice and Criminal Evidence Act 1999 (YJCEA 1999) provides a new statutory regime governing the competence and compellability of witnesses. It replaces the former mix of common law and statutory rules.[1] The general rule, contained in s.53(1) of the YJCEA 1999 provides:

> "At every stage in criminal proceedings all persons are (whatever their age) competent to give evidence."

Section 53(3) of the YJCEA 1999 provides:

> "A person is not competent to give evidence in criminal proceedings if it appears to the court that he is not a person who is able to—
>
> (a) understand questions put to him as a witness, and
> (b) give answers to them which can be understood."

This puts on a clear statutory basis the old common law rule that any person is competent and compellable as a witness provided that he or she is capable of coherent communication.[2] The most likely categories of witness

---

[1] The following acts are repealed: the Criminal Evidence Act 1898, s.1 (up to the proviso); the Children and Young Persons Act 1933, s.38; and the Criminal Justice Act 1988, s.33A. S.80 of the Police and Criminal Evidence Act 1984 is amended.

[2] See *Ex p. Fernandez* [1861] 10 C.B. (N.S.) 3, 39, *per* Willes J. The Sovereign and foreign ambassadors and their suites (Diplomatic Privileges Act 1964) are exceptions to the rule. They are not compellable. Bankers and officers of banks are not compellable to produce any bankers' book or to appear as witnesses to prove matter recorded therein unless by order of a judge for special cause: Bankers' Books Evidence Act 1879, s.6. Expert witnesses are in the same position as witnesses of fact. They are compellable: *Harmony Shipping Co. v Davis* [1979] 3 All E.R. 177, 181, *per* Lord Denning M.R. Judges are competent but not compellable in relation to their judicial functions; however, it appears that a judge would be compellable to give evidence of a collateral matter occurring in his presence, *e.g.* a murder in court: *Warren v Warren* [1996] 3 W.L.R. 1129.

to be held incompetent pursuant to s.53(3) are children and persons of unsound mind. The exceptions to the rule remain, in certain circumstances, the defendant[3] and his or her spouse.[4]

The competence of a witness is determined by the court. Section 54(1) of the YJCEA 1999 replaces the old common law rules[5] and provides: **17–02**

> "Any question whether a witness in criminal proceedings is competent to give evidence in the proceedings, whether raised—
>
> (a) by a party to the proceedings, or
> (b) by the court of its own motion,
>
> shall be determined by the court in accordance with this section."

Once the question of a witness' competence has been raised, either by a party to the proceedings or the court of its own motion, it is for the party calling the witness to satisfy the court that, on a balance of probabilities, the witness is competent to give evidence.[6] Such determination is to be made in the absence of the jury (if there is one)[7] and expert evidence may be called on the issue.[8] Thus, the old common law requirement that the prosecution must satisfy the court of a witness's competence beyond reasonable doubt has been removed.[9] It is submitted that, ideally, the competence of prosecution witnesses should still be decided at the outset of the trial.[10]

2. CHILDREN

The testimony of children is now governed by Chapter V of the YJCEA   **17–03**
1999. Thus, pursuant to s.53 of the YJCEA 1999, all children, whatever their age, are competent to give evidence if they can understand the questions put to them as a witness and give answers which can be understood. It is for the party wishing to call the child witness that must satisfy the court on a balance of probabilities of the child's competence. Thus, the extreme

---

[3] s.53 (4) and (5) of YJCEA 1999.
[4] s.80 of the Police and Criminal Evidence Act 1984, as amended by Sch.4 to the YJCEA 1999.
[5] The law of evidence was formerly much concerned with questions of the competence of witnesses. However, disqualifications on the grounds of interest, want of religion and crime were all abolished in the nineteenth century. Thus, incompetence through interest or by reason of conviction of crime was abolished by the Evidence Act 1843, s.1. The Oaths Act 1978, s.5 permits a person who objects to being sworn to affirm instead of taking an oath (para.19–08).
[6] s.54(2) of the YJCEA 1999.
[7] s.54(4) of the YJCEA 1999. See para.16–07 above on trial-within-a-trial.
[8] s.54(5) of the YJCEA 1999.
[9] *Yacoob* (1981) 72 Cr.App.R. 313.
[10] Yacoob above, 316–317. See, however, para.17–08 for incapacitated witnesses.

youth of a witness does not of itself demonstrate that a child is incompetent.[11] It is submitted that if an issue as to a child's competence arises, the issue can best be determined by the judge watching the video-recording of the child and, if appropriate, then asking questions of the child. This should take place in the absence of any jury.[12] Expert evidence *may* be received on the question of competence[13]; however, in *G v DPP*[14] the Divisional Court held that it is not *necessary* to hear expert evidence as to a witness's competence since the test is well within the capacity of a judge or magistrate.

Pursuant to s.55(2) of the YJCEA 1999, a child may not be sworn for the purpose of giving evidence unless he:

(i) has attained the age of 14, and

(ii) has attained a sufficient appreciation of the solemnity of the occasion and of the particular responsibility to tell the truth which is involved in taking an oath.

Thus, children over 14 will be treated as adults and will give sworn evidence.[15] No competency examination is required, except in similar circumstances as those applying to an adult. It is for the party seeking to have the witness sworn to satisfy the court that, on a balance of probabilities, the witness has attained the age of 14 and has sufficient appreciation of the solemnity of the occasion, etc.[16] A child under 14, who is otherwise competent to give evidence, must give evidence unsworn. The court will receive a deposition of unsworn evidence of such a child as if that evidence had been given on oath.[17] Since the witness is giving evidence unsworn, it will be necessary for the judge to ensure that the child understands the importance of telling the truth. This procedure is best carried out before the witness gives evidence and in the presence of the jury. The Pigot Report (para.17–04 below) recommended that judges should admonish child wit-

---

[11] See also *DPP v M* [1997] 2 Cr.App.R. 70 decided under legislative the regime preceding YJCEA 1999.

[12] *Hampshire* [1995] 2 Cr.App.R. 319 had required the investigation of a child's competence to take place in the presence of the jury.

[13] s.54(5) of the YJCEA 1999.

[14] [1997] 2 Cr.App.R. 78.

[15] The child must be sworn before giving evidence. There is a danger that this necessity may be overlooked if a video-recording is played as the child's evidence in chief. The normal practice then is for the oath to be administered before the witness is cross-examined. This may be forgotten. This is what happened in *Simmonds* [1996] Crim.L.R. 816. The Court of Appeal held that in the circumstances of that case the situation had not been rectified by the witness taking the oath after giving evidence and being asked whether her answers had been true. If such a course is followed, the judge must explain to the jury what has happened. Similarly, in *Sharman* [1998] 1 Cr.App.R. 406, the Court of Appeal held that failure to administer the oath was not a mere technicality but amounted to a material irregularity in the trial.

[16] s.55(4) of the YJCEA 1999.

[17] s.56 of the YJCEA 1999.

nesses to give a full and truthful account of what occurred in terms suitable to their age and understanding. The suggested procedure will assist to serve that purpose; the procedure need not be lengthy or oppressive and may also help to put the child at its ease. Thus, in *Hampshire*[18] (a case under the Criminal Justice Act 1988) the Court of Appeal said that a softly worded and spoken remark would do.

Section 55(4) and (8)

The position at common law had been that a child of tender years could be sworn in any proceedings provided that he or she understood the nature of the oath and the obligation of telling the truth.[19] Until the repeal of the sections by the YJCEA 1999, the testimony of children was governed by s.38(1) of the Children and Young Persons Act 1933 and s.33A of the Criminal Justice Act 1988. Prior to the Criminal Justice Act 1988, while the evidence of children under the age of 14 was heard, the practice of the courts was not to hear the evidence of very young children. In *Wallwork*,[20] Lord Goddard C.J. said that it was most undesirable that a child as young as five should be called as a witness. This view remained unchallenged for 30 years and was reiterated by the Court of Appeal as recently as 1987.[21] However, it came to be recognised that the practice of the courts failed to take account of modern research which showed that very young children are capable of giving reliable evidence and that they are no more likely to give untrue or inaccurate evidence than any other witness. It was further recognised that the practice impeded the prosecution of perpetrators of offences against children.

17–04

The above points were forcefully made by the Advisory Group on Video Evidence which commented in its Report (the "Pigot Report")[22] that the approach of the courts appeared to be founded on an archaic belief concerning the inability of children to give honest and coherent evidence. The Report proposed (a) that the competence requirement should be abolished, and (b) that children over 14 should always be sworn while those under that age should always give unsworn evidence.[23] The Report also recommended that a video-recorded interview with a child about an offence

---

[18] [1995] 2 Cr.App.R. 319.
[19] *Brasier* (1779) 1 Leach 199.
[20] (1958) 42 Cr.App.R. 153, 160.
[21] *Wright and Ormerod* (1990) 90 Cr.App.R. 91, 94–95.
[22] (1989) Home Office, London (so-called after the Group's Chairman, His Honour Judge Thomas Pigot Q.C.).
[23] The latter proposal was also recommended by the Criminal Law Revision Committee in its Eleventh Report: Cmnd. 4991, para.206.

should be admissible in evidence.[24] These recommendations were given effect by ss.52 to 55 of the Criminal Justice Act 1991, which came into force in October 1992.[25]

The particular care needed to safeguard the welfare of young witnesses has been highlighted by guidelines for the treatment of child witness drawn up by the National Society for the Prevention of Cruelty of Children, the Home Office, the Lord Chancellor's Department, and the Crown Prosecution Service.[26]

17-05   Section 53(1) of the YJCEA 1999 provides that children of *any* age are competent to give evidence. It is submitted that the following three cases under the previous legislative regimes are illustrative of the approach to be taken in relation to the proposed testimony of extremely young children:

1.   In *C.A.Z.*[27] Lord Lane C.J. said that the decision in *Wallwork* had to some extent been overtaken by events relating to children's evidence, namely the introduction of television links and the abolition of the corroboration requirement, the latter reflecting a change in public attitude and an increasing belief that the evidence of children is just as reliable as that of their elders. Accordingly, in *C.A.Z.* the Court of Appeal upheld the trial judge's decision to allow a six-year-old child to give evidence against her father on a charge of incest. The Court said that no minimum age was laid down by statute and the discretion whether to allow a child to give evidence was to be exercised according to well-known criteria and was unfettered save that the younger the child, the greater the care that had to be taken before admitting the evidence.

2.   Similarly, in *D.J.N.*[28] the trial judge, having seen video tapes of interviews with the child and heard evidence from the social worker and police officers present at the interview, admitted the evidence of a six-year-old girl in a case of attempted rape. The

---

[24] See para.19–24, below, for a discussion of video recordings of interviews as evidence. The Pigot Committee recommended that the child's evidence be given and cross-examination take place at a preliminary hearing. This recommendation was reiterated by a Working Party of the Royal College of Psychiatrists in their Report, "The Evidence of Children" (1996). The Working Party identified delay before the trial as one of the worst features of the present system and pointed out that the effect of delay upon a child can be serious. To date, this recommendation has not been implemented: no doubt, because of the considerable practical difficulties of arranging such hearings prior to trial.

[25] See *McAndrew Bingham*[1999] 2 Cr.App.R. 293 at para.19–15 below and para.21–20 on video recordings as previous inconsistent statements.

[26] Reported in *The Times*, November 22, 1999. See also two further publications aimed at improving the quality of evidence of child witnesses: (i) "Interviewing Child Witnesses under the *Memorandum of Good Practice*: A research review", Home Officer Police Research Paper 115, and (ii) Court Service Checklist for use at Plea and Direction Hearings as a supplementary checklist for cases involving young witnesses.

[27] (1990) 91 Cr.App.R. 203.

[28] (1992) 95 Cr.App.R. 256.

Court of Appeal, upholding the judge's ruling, said the fact that the child was too young to be prosecuted for perjury was not a reason for excluding her evidence. The Court also said that s.78 of the Police and Criminal Evidence Act 1984 had not changed the established practice: "if there were material which suggested that the evidence of the child had been wrongfully obtained or that the child had been improperly coached or encouraged [the judge] ... would take all such matters into account when deciding whether to permit the reception of the child's evidence...".[29]

3. In *DPP v M*[30] a boy was convicted in a youth court of indecently assaulting a girl aged four. She was aged five-and-a half at the time of the hearing of the boy's appeal to the Crown Court. That court decided that by reason of her age she was not a witness on whom the court could rely. The Divisional Court (allowing the appeal by the prosecution) held that, although the extreme youth of the complainant was a matter which raised concern as to whether the child was competent, it did not demonstrate, of itself, that she was not.

Whether a child should give evidence or not is a matter for the judge's discretion depending upon the circumstances and type of case and the circumstances of the particular child.[31]

For evidence by television link or video-recording see paras 19–20 and 19–24, below.

3. PERSONS OF UNSOUND MIND

The testimony of persons of unsound mind, like that of children, is governed by Chapter V of the YJCEA 1999. Thus, provided the witness can (i) understand questions put to him as a witness, and (ii) give answers to them which can be understood, he will be competent to give evidence.[32]   **17–06**

The position at common law had been that persons of unsound mind who were not capable of understanding the nature of the oath and giving rational evidence were not competent witnesses. It was for the court to decide whether such a person was competent or not. The test was whether the witness understood the nature and sanction of the oath. The test was

---

[29] At 261–262, *per* Judge J.
[30] [1997] 2 Cr.App.R. 70.
[31] It is not necessary to seek the leave of the High Court in order to call a Ward of Court who has been interviewed by the police in connection with contemplated criminal proceedings: *Re K (Minors) (Wardship: Criminal Proceedings)* [1988] 1 Fam. 1. However, leave from the wardship court is required before a ward is interviewed by anyone: *Practice Direction (Ward: Witness at Trial)* [1987] 1 W.L.R. 1739; *Practice Direction (Ward: Witness at Trial (No.2))* [1988] 1 W.L.R. 989; In *Re R (A Minor)*, *The Times*, January 1, 1991.
[32] s.53(3) of the YJCEA 1999.

established in 1851 in *Hill*.[33] A witness in that case was an inmate of a lunatic asylum who suffered from the delusion that he had numerous spirits who talked to him. However, medical evidence was given that the witness was capable of giving an account of any transaction of which he was an eye-witness. The judge ruled that the witness was competent. This ruling was upheld.

Under the YJCEA 1999 it would appear that the modern emphasis is on whether the witness is competent as a witness or not, rather than on whether he is aware of the divine sanction of the oath. Thus, pursuant to s.56 of the YJCEA 1999, evidence of a person of any age who is competent to give evidence, but does not have sufficient appreciation of the solemnity of the occasion and of the particular responsibility to tell the truth, may give their evidence unsworn. In *Bellamy*[34] the Court of Appeal held that the cases relating to the swearing of children applied in the case of a complainant in a rape case who was aged 33 but had a mental age of 10. The Court said that it was no longer necessary that a witness should have an appreciation of the divine sanction of the oath. Accordingly, once the judge had found that she was competent to give evidence she should have been sworn.

17–07   The credibility and weight of evidence given by persons of unsound mind is a matter for the jury to decide. The determination, however, of the competence of such witnesses must take place in the absence of the jury.[35] The previous common law requirement, therefore, that the jury be present when the witness is examined (or evidence given on the *voir dire*) to determine whether he is competent or not no longer applies.[36] Expert evidence may, and should normally, be received on the question. In *Barratt and Sheehan*[37] the Court of Appeal said that the proper course was to present appropriate medical evidence, so that it would not normally be necessary to call the witness. In *Barratt and Sheehan* the cross-examination on the *voir dire* had concentrated on the witness's private life and beliefs and she was not asked about her recollection of the events, her ability to answer questions, or her knowledge that she ought to tell the truth. This cross-examination was deplored by the Court of Appeal. However, it is submitted that in some cases it will be necessary to cross-examine the witness because no other means will be available by which to ascertain whether the witness is competent or not. Such cross-examination must be on relevant matters and conducted with a proper restraint, having regard to the potential vulnerability of the witness.

It should also be borne in mind as a separate but related issue that

---

[33] (1851) 2 Den. 254. The test was also applied to *Dunning* [1965] Crim.L.R. 372
[34] (1986) 82 Cr.App.R. 222.
[35] s.54(4) of the YJCEA 1999.
[36] *Deakin* [1994] 4 All E.R. 769; *Dunne* (1929) 21 Cr.App.R. 176; *Reynolds* [1950] 1 K.B. 606.
[37] [1996] Crim.L.R. 495.

medical evidence may in any case be called to show that a witness suffers from some disease of the mind which affects the reliability of his evidence.[38]

4. INCAPACITATED WITNESSES

The competence of incapacitated witnesses is, like all witnesses, governed by Chapter V of the YJCEA 1999. Thus, provided that the witness (i) can understand the questions put to him as a witness and giver answers to them which can be understood,[39] and (ii) has sufficient apprehension of the solemnity of the occasion and of the particular responsibility to tell the truth,[40] he is competent.

17–08

The cases below, although decided prior to the YJCEA 1999, are helpful in setting out the various considerations for a court when considering the competence of incapacitated witnesses.

A deaf and dumb witness is competent provided that (a) he can be made to understand the nature of the oath; and (b) through signs, understand questions and give answers.[41] This may be easily achieved through an interpreter, the use of an intermediary, or an aid to communication.[42]

On occasion a witness goes into the box who is so much the worse for drink that he cannot give coherent evidence. It is then a matter for the judge whether to rule then and there that the witness is incompetent or whether his evidence should be adjourned until such time as he is sober. In *Baines*[43] the Court of Appeal held that the judge had rightly exercised his discretion in adjourning a case over the weekend because a witness was too affected by drugs to comprehend the proceedings.

If a witness who has been sworn appears, while attempting to give evidence, to be of unsound mind or too incoherent or incapable of communication to make sense the judge may rule the witness incompetent.[44] The judge may then continue the hearing, having directed the jury to ignore any evidence which the witness may have given.

In *Stretton*[45] the Court of Appeal held that the trial judge had a discretion to allow a trial to continue where a witness (who was epileptic and mentally handicapped), having been cross-examined for some time, became ill and could not give evidence further (and where medical evidence showed it would be undesirable and forensically unfair to have the witness back into the witness-box or to have her called in a new trial).

17–09

---

[38] *Toohey v Metropolitan Police Commissioner* [1965] A.C. 595; 49 Cr.App.R. 148; para.6–25, above.
[39] s.53(3) of the YJCEA 1999.
[40] s.55(2) of the YJCEA 1999.
[41] *Ruston* (1786) 1 Leach 408.
[42] See ss.29 and 30 of the YJCEA 1999 considered at para.19–32.
[43] [1987] Crim.L.R. 508.
[44] *Whitehead* (1866) L.R. 1 C.C.R. 33.
[45] (1986) 86 Cr.App.R. 7.

However, it may be necessary to discharge the jury if a witness becomes incapacitated and a fair trial is not possible. The Court of Appeal held that this should have happened in *Lawless*[46] when a crucial prosecution witness (an accomplice) suffered a heart attack after giving evidence in chief.

In practice, if the incapacity is temporary the judge may adjourn the evidence until the incapacity is over. Thus, when a witness is too overcome with emotion to continue giving evidence there will usually be a short adjournment.

If there is then no improvement in a witness who has become ill or seriously distressed the judge may allow the trial to continue. In *Wyatt*[47] a seven-year-old witness became so distressed during cross-examination that the judge allowed a 15–20-minute adjournment for her to compose herself. After the adjournment the witness was still distressed and the judge terminated the cross-examination. The Court of Appeal held that the judge had a discretion to adjourn the case for the length of time he did and rejected an argument that he had not allowed the witness enough time to compose herself.

If cross-examination is cut short because of a witness's incapacity it will be necessary for the judge in summing up to remind the jury of this fact and direct them to bear in mind the curtailment of cross-examination when considering whether they believe the witness's evidence or not.

17–10   The decision whether to discharge the jury will depend on the circumstances of each case. However, some guidance may be gained from the decision of the Court of Appeal in *Simpson*.[48] In that case a child witness became very distressed when giving evidence of sexual abuse. The distress was so deep that it may have had a profound effect on the jury: the trial judge spoke of the "discomfort" of others. An application was made to discharge the jury because of the prejudicial effect of the evidence. However, the judge refused to discharge the jury. The Court of Appeal upheld this refusal and said that it would be intolerable if the distress of a witness, however acute when describing sexual abuse, should be regarded as making the evidence unfit for the ears of a jury. The Court said that what was needed in these circumstances was a reminder by the judge to the jury of the possibility that the witness's distress was caused by the knowledge that she was not telling the truth rather than the recollection of the incident.[49] (It is submitted that in deciding applications of this kind the court is entitled to have regard to the effect on the child of having to give evidence a second time. For instance, if the jury were discharged in some cases, the prosecution might be faced with the dilemma of either putting the child through the ordeal of giving evidence again or of offering no evidence.)

---

[46] (1994) 98 Cr.App.R. 342.
[47] (1990) Crim.L.R. 343.
[48] (1994) 99 Cr.App.R. 48.
[49] At 53–54.

5. THE DEFENDANT

A. The Youth Justice and Criminal Evidence Act 1999, s.53 and the Criminal Evidence Act 1898, s.1 (as amended)

The defendant is not a competent witness for the prosecution. Section 53(4)   **17–11**
of the YJCEA 1999 provides:

> "A person charged in criminal proceedings is not competent to give
> evidence in the proceedings for the prosecution (whether he is the only
> person, or is one of two or more persons, charged in the proceedings)."

This was always the rule at common law which also included anyone
jointly charged.[50]

Section 1(1) of the Criminal Evidence Act 1898 (as amended by s.67(1)
and Sch.4, para.1 to the YJCEA 1999) provides:

> "A person charged in criminal proceedings shall not be called as a
> witness in the proceedings except upon his own application."

Thus, on the application of the defendant, or by his counsel with his
consent, the defendant is a competent witness for the defence.

The following general points should be noted.

1. Despite the removal of the reference to the defendant's competence to
give evidence at "every stage of the proceedings" from s.1 of the Criminal
Evidence Act 1898, it is submitted that the defendant is clearly still so
competent and may give evidence at a trial-within-a-trial[51] or in mitigation
of sentence after a plea of guilty.[52] The right of the defendant to give
evidence in his own defence has been described as "fundamental", so that
where a male defendant was prevented from exercising the right because he
was dressed in a frock, the Court of Appeal quashed the conviction.[53]

2. If the defendant gives evidence, he must do so on oath (subject of
course to the application of ss.55 and 56 of the YJCEA 1999)[54] and be
liable to cross-examination.[55] Until 1983 the defendant had the right to
make an unsworn statement from the dock about the facts of the case
instead of giving evidence on oath. This right existed at the time that the

---

[50] *Grant* (1944) 30 Cr.App.R. 99; *Sharrock* (1974) 32 Cr.App.R. 124.
[51] *Cowell* [1940] 2 K.B. 49.
[52] *Wheeler* [1917] 1 K.B. 283.
[53] *Cunningham* [1988] Crim.L.R. 543. To preserve the fundamental right to give evidence, a
defendant was even permitted to attend trial and give evidence naked (subject to a requirement
that he not rise upon the entry of the judge into court): *R v Bethall* Southwark Crown Court,
January 10, 2001.
[54] See paras 17–03 and 17–06, above.
[55] Criminal Justice Act 1982, s.72. (Although the section does not mention it, oath must
include affirmation.)

Criminal Evidence Act 1898 was passed and was preserved by s.1(h) of that Act. However, the practice of making a statement from the dock was anomalous and it was abolished by s.72 of the Criminal Justice Act 1982.

17–12   3. When the defendant does give evidence, that evidence is "evidence for all the purposes of the case including the purpose of being evidence against his co-defendant."[56] This may be contrasted with a defendant's out of court statements which are not admissible evidence against a co-defendant, save in exceptional circumstances. Once, however, the defendant goes into the witness-box and gives evidence, anything he says may be evidence against a co-defendant. It is on a similar footing to any other evidence in the case. However, if it appears that the co-defendant has a purpose of his own to serve in giving evidence, for example to exculpate himself or minimise his involvement, rather than telling the truth, the judge should warn the jury of the danger of relying on his uncorroborated evidence.[57]

4. If the defendant goes into the witness-box and gives evidence for the defence, he becomes subject to cross-examination.[58] He may be cross-examined:

    (a)   as to the offence charged,[59]

    (b)   to incriminate a co-defendant,[60] and

    (c)   on behalf of a co-defendant, whether he has given evidence against the co-defendant or not.[61]

The defendant who gives evidence is thus in the same position as an ordinary witness in relation to cross-examination, save that he may not be cross-examined as to his bad character, unless in exceptional circumstances as provided for in the Criminal Justice Act 2003, ss.101–108 (paras 7–33 *et seq.*).

Section 1(4) of the Criminal Evidence Act 1898 provides that every person charged in criminal proceedings who is called as a witness shall, unless otherwise ordered by the court, give his evidence from the witness-

---

[56] *Rudd* (1948) 32 Cr.App.R. 138, 140, *per* Humphreys J.

[57] paras 15–18 *et seq.* above.

[58] If the accused gives evidence "he shall do so on oath and be liable to cross-examination": Criminal Justice Act 1982, s.72.

[59] Criminal Justice Act 2003, s.98, discussed at para.7–32 above.

[60] *Paul and McFarlane* [1920] 2 K.B. 183 (in which the CCA held that the prosecution had rightly been allowed to cross-examine a defendant in order to incriminate his two co-defendants, although the defendant had only said in examination-in-chief that he was guilty and had nothing more to say). *Paul and McFarlane* was followed by the House of Lords in *R v Bingham* [1999] 1 W.L.R. 598.

[61] *Hilton* [1972] 1 Q.B. 421. The rationale of allowing cross-examination in these circumstances is as follows: if the co-defendant has implicated the defendant in the offence charged, the defendant should clearly have the right (and perhaps the duty) to challenge the evidence implicating him. If, on the other hand, the co-defendant does not implicate him, there may well be facts which the defendant wishes to elicit from the co-defendant.

box or other place from which other witnesses give their evidence. In
Symonds,[62] the Court of Criminal Appeal said that unless there were circumstances such as that the accused was too infirm to walk to the witness-
box or too violent to be controlled there, this right should not be interfered
with. Swift J. said that the intention of the provision is that the accused
"shall have an opportunity of giving evidence on his own behalf in the same
way and from the same place as the witnesses for the prosecution."[63] Thus,
judges very often direct juries that the fact that the defendant comes from
the dock to give his evidence, while the prosecution witnesses come from
outside the court, makes no difference when it comes to assessing the
defendant's evidence. The same rule applies to magistrates' courts.[64]

(1) As a witness for a co-defendant

A defendant is a competent but not a compellable witness for any co-
defendant who is indicted and tried jointly with him.[65] This is because
s.53(1) of the YJCEA 1999 states that all persons are competent to give
evidence and s.1(1) of the Criminal Evidence Act 1898 provides that every
person charged with an offence may only be called on his own application.

  On the other hand, a co-defendant who is not in the charge of the jury,
that is, is not on trial, is both competent and compellable as a witness for a
co-defendant. This is because the defendant has ceased to be a person
"charged in criminal proceedings " for the purposes of the Criminal Evidence Act 1898, s.1 (as amended). The common law therefore applies to
him. A person "charged with an offence" (in a case prior to the amendment
of s.1 from "charged with an offence" to be "charged in criminal proceedings") was held to mean a person charged with an offence actually
within the consideration of the jury at the trial.[66] It is submitted that the
same considerations will apply to the amended s.1. Thus, if one or more
defendants are charged jointly in an indictment and one defendant pleads
guilty[67] or is discharged as a result of a successful submission of no case[68]
or is tried separately[69] he is both competent and compellable as a witness
for a co-defendant.

17–13

---

[62] (1924) 18 Cr.App.R. 100.
[63] At 101.
[64] It was the policy of a bench of justices that the defendant should give evidence from the
dock. The Divisional Court held this policy to be unlawful: *Farnham JJ. Ex p. Gibson* [1991]
R.T.R. 309. The court said that the justices had no discretion to deny the defendant the right to
give evidence from the witness-box unless there was misconduct or other consideration in
relation to a particular defendant which entitled them to do so: there had to be "some striking,
particular, unusual reason for preventing him from leaving the dock".
[65] *Macdonnell* (1909) 2 Cr.App.R. 322.
[66] *Boal* [1965] 1 Q.B. 402; (1964) 48 Cr.App.R. 342, 345.
[67] *Boal*, above.
[68] *Conti* (1974) 58 Cr.App.R. 387.
[69] *Richardson* (1967) 51 Cr.App.R. 381.

(2) As a witness for the prosecution

17–14 As has been seen above, the rule is that the defendant is neither a competent nor a compellable witness for the prosecution. However, where two or more persons are charged jointly in an indictment, a defendant is competent and compellable to give evidence for the prosecution where the person is no longer liable to be convicted of any offence in the proceedings, whether as a result of having pleaded guilty, or for any other reason,[70] such as:

> (i)   no evidence has been offered against him and he has been acquitted; or
>
> (ii) a *nolle prosequi*[71] has been entered; or
>
> (iii) he is not tried with the defendant against whom he gives evidence.[72]

The most usual circumstance in which a co-defendant gives evidence for the prosecution is after a plea of guilty. This plea normally occurs at arraignment.[73] The usual practice used to be to sentence the co-defendant before he gave evidence. This was so that he might give evidence free of any temptation to try to ingratiate himself with the court and prosecution at the expense of the defendant.[74] However, it is not obligatory to pass sentence before the co-defendant gives evidence there is no rule of law to this effect[75] and it is no longer the general practice. It is a matter to be decided in the judge's discretion.[76] A reason for not sentencing the co-defendant would be, for instance, if it were impossible to judge the respective roles played by the participants in an offence until all the evidence had been heard. Indeed, it is better, as a matter of sentencing policy, not to sentence the defendant before he gives evidence: but to sentence all the defendants at the same time.[77] Accordingly, the modern (but not invariable) practice is for the court to permit the co-defendant to give evidence and to pass sentence later.[78]

The Court of Appeal has stressed the need for prosecutors to think

---

[70] s.53(5) of the YJCEA 1999.

[71] A *nolle prosequi* stays the proceedings. It may only be entered on the direction of the Att-Gen.

[72] *Winsor* (1866) L.R. 1 Q.B. 289.

[73] It may occur later in the trial (when a defendant having pleaded not guilty at the outset of a trial, changes his plea during the course of the trial): *Tomey* (1909) 2 Cr.App.R. 329.

[74] *Winsor* (1866) L.R. 1 Q.B. 289, 312, *per* Cockburn C.J.; *Turner* (1975) 61 Cr.App.R. 67, 78, *per* Lawton L.J.

[75] *Chan v R*, *The Times*, December 21, 1994.

[76] *Palmer*, below.

[77] *Weekes* (1982) 74 Cr.App.R. 161, 166, CA.

[78] *Palmer* (1994) 99 Cr.App.R. 83. The Court of Appeal in *Palmer* described the practice as that of "the 80s and 90s". The Privy Council has described it as often the better practice: *Chan v R*, above.

carefully before calling co-defendants.[79] Caution is necessary because a co-defendant may well not be prepared to give evidence against a fellow offender from a sense of loyalty or out of fear of reprisal in prison. Experience also shows that such evidence has a habit of back-firing on the party calling it.

(3) Accomplices

Accomplices are competent witnesses for the prosecution. They are fre-   **17–15**
quently co-defendants and the rules mentioned in the last paragraph apply to them when they are. However, it is sometimes proposed to call an accomplice who is not a co-defendant in the offence charged. If it is proposed to call such an accomplice, the practice is:

(a) to omit him from the indictment; or

(b) to take his plea of guilty on arraignment; or

(c) before calling him, either offer no evidence and permit his acquittal; or

(d) to enter a *nolle prosequi*.

This practice was approved by the Court of Appeal in *Pipe*.[80] In that case a receiver of stolen goods, against whom proceedings were about to start, was called as a witness for the prosecution in the trial of the thief of the goods. The Court of Appeal held that this was wholly irregular in the absence of any indication that the proceedings against the accomplice were to be discontinued.

Later, in *Turner*[81] the Court appeared to take a different view. In that case, the Court rejected a submission that the evidence of an accomplice, who could still be influenced by continuing inducements, should not be admitted. The Court said that "it does not follow, in our judgment, that in all cases calling a witness who can benefit from giving evidence is 'wholly irregular'". However, the Court said that the judge had a discretion to exclude the accomplice's evidence if the inducement to ingratiate himself with the prosecution and the court was powerful: but when exercising the discretion the judge must take into consideration all factors including those affecting the public.

The rule would therefore appear to be that:

---

[79] *Moran* (1985) 81 Cr.App.R. 51, 52.
[80] (1967) 51 Cr.App.R. 17, 21.
[81] (1975) 61 Cr.App.R. 67, 78.

(a) an accomplice is a competent witness for the prosecution unless he is both indicted and tried with the defendant[82];

(b) the judge has a discretion to exclude an accomplice's evidence if it is in the interests of justice to do so, for example if it appears to the judge that there is a real danger that because of powerful inducements the accomplice will give false evidence against a co-defendant in order to curry favour with the court.

(For an appropriate direction to be given to the jury when an accomplice gives evidence, see para.15–18, above.)

(2) The Criminal Justice and Public Order Act 1994, s.35

17–16   Section 35 of the Criminal Justice and Public Order Act, 1994[83] provides:

"(1) At the trial of any person for an offence subsections (2) and (3) below shall apply unless—

(a)   the accused's guilt is not in issue; or
(b)   it appears to the court that the physical or mental condition of the accused makes it undesirable for him to give evidence.

But subsection (2) below does not apply if, at the conclusion of the evidence for the prosecution, his legal representative informs the court that the accused will give evidence or, where he is unrepresented, the court ascertains from him that he will give evidence.

(2) Where this subsection applies, the court shall, at the conclusion of the evidence of the prosecution, satisfy itself (in the case of proceedings on indictment, in the presence of the jury) that the accused is aware that the stage has been reached at which evidence can be given for the defence and that he can, if he wishes, give evidence and that, if he chooses not to give evidence, or having been sworn, without good cause refuses to answer any question, it will be permissible for the court or jury to draw such inferences as appear proper from him failure to give evidence or his refusal, without good cause, to answer any question.

(3) Where this subsection applies, the court or jury, in determining whether the accused is guilty of the offence charged, may draw such inferences as appear proper from the failure of the accused to give evidence or his refusal, without good cause, to answer any question.

(4) This section does not render the accused compellable to give evidence on his own behalf, and he shall accordingly not be guilty of contempt of court by reason of a failure to do so.

---

[82] *Governor of Pentonville Prison Ex p. Schneider* (1981) 73 Cr.App.R. 200, 212.
[83] As amended by the Crime and Disorder Act 1998, s.35.

(5) For the purpose of this section a person who, having been sworn, refuses to answer any question shall be taken to do so without good cause unless—

    (a) he is entitled to refuse to answer the question by virtue of any enactment, whenever passed or made, or on the ground of privilege; or

    (b) the court in the exercise of its general discretion excuses him from answering it.[84]

(7) This section applies—

    (a) in relation to proceedings on indictment for an offence, only if the person charged with the offence is arraigned on or after the commencement of this section;

    (b) in relation to proceedings in a magistrates' court, only if the time when the court begins to receive evidence in the proceedings falls after the commencement of this section."

Section 35(3) of the 1994 Act permits the court or jury, in determining whether the accused is guilty of the offence charged, to draw such inferences as appear proper from the failure of the defendant to give evidence or, having been sworn, his failure to answer questions without good cause. However, unless informed that the accused will give evidence, the court must first satisfy itself that the accused is aware that he can give evidence and that if he does not do so (or refuses to answer questions) inferences may be drawn. This must be done in the presence of the jury in trials on indictment: s.35(2).[85] It is submitted that in cases where it is not likely that a direction to draw an adverse inference will be given (despite the accused's failure to testify) or where the jury are to be directed that no inference should be drawn, the trial judge should not conduct the requirements of section 35(2) in the presence of the jury as this may serve to confuse them.[86]

    17–17

Section 35 applies both to proceedings on indictment and in the magistrates' court. However, the section does not render the accused compellable to give evidence on his own behalf and it provides that the accused shall not be guilty of contempt by reason of his refusal to be sworn: s.35(4).[87] The Crown Court is required to satisfy itself by inquiry of the defendant's legal representative that the defendant is aware of the consequences of not giving

---

[84] subs.(6) was deleted by the Crime and Disorder Act 1998, s.35.

[85] See *Practice Direction: Crown Court (Defendant's Evidence)* [1995] 2 Cr.App.R. 192 on the form of words to be used pursuant to s.35 in cases where the accused is either legally represented or not legally represented.

[86] See commentary to *Taylor* [1999] Crim.L.R. 77.

[87] Thus, expessly preserving the defendant's right to silence: *Cowan* [1996] 1 Cr.App.R. 1, 4, *per* Lord Taylor C.J. The subsection does not apply once the defendant has elected to give evidence, gone into the witness-box and been sworn: *Ackinclose* [1996] Crim.L.R. 747.

evidence, or (if he is unrepresented) by itself telling the defendant of the consequences.[88] In *Price*[89] it was held (in the circumstances of that case) to have been a material irregularity for the judge to have directed the jury that they were entitled to draw inferences when he had not ascertained under s.35(2) that the defendant had been aware of the consequences of not giving evidence. Similarly, justices in the magistrates' court must so satisfy themselves. In *Radford v Kent C.C.*[90] the Divisional Court said that a failure to do so would normally render a verdict unsafe, although in the instant case (the justices' attention not having been drawn to the section) they drew no adverse inference and the Divisional Court held that the conviction was not unsafe.

(1) Application of the section

17–18   The section does not apply if it appears to the court that the mental or physical condition of the accused makes it undesirable for him to be called. It will be for the court to determine as a matter of discretion whether this consideration applies. However, it is submitted that it will be unusual for it to apply; since, if it did, the accused should not normally be on trial at all.

In *Friend*[91] the defendant (who was aged 14 at the time of the offence and 15 at the time of the trial) was charged with murder. In a trial-within-a-trial a clinical psychologist gave evidence that the defendant had a low I.Q. and a mental age of nine. It was argued on appeal that his low mental age entitled him to immunity from adverse comment under the section. In dismissing the appeal the Court of Appeal held that the fact that the defendant had the mental age of a person under 14 did not mean that he had the same immunity from adverse inference as a person under 14[92]: the jury were entitled to draw such inferences as appeared proper from the failure to give evidence, taking account of the medical and other evidence. The Court held that there was no correct test laid down as to the exercise of judicial discretion under s.35 and said:

> "Indeed we do not consider it appropriate to spell out a test to be applied in such a situation. The language of the section is simple and clear. It is for the judge in a given case to determine whether or not it is undesirable for the accused to give evidence. A physical condition might include risk of an epileptic attack; a mental condition, latent schizophrenia where the experience of giving evidence might trigger a florid state. If it appears to the judge on the voir dire that such a

---

[88] *Practice Direction: Crown Court (Defendant's Evidence)* [1995] 2 Cr.App.R. 192.
[89] [1996] Crim.L.R. 738.
[90] *The Times*, March 11, 1998.
[91] [1997] 2 All E.R. 1012.
[92] s.35(1) originally conferred immunity from adverse influence on children under 14. This immunity was abolished by the Crime and Disorder Act 1998, s.35, with application to offences committed after the commencement of the section: Sch.9, *ibid.*

physical or mental condition of the accused makes it undesirable for him to give evidence he will so rule, the inference cannot thereafter be drawn and he will so direct the jury ... Thus we consider that the the the clarity of the language of the section is such that it is not necessary to supplement the 1994 Act with a test. The section itself is a practical framework within which the provision and purpose of the statue can be put into effect and no formal guidelines are called for."[93]

If, after a *voir dire*, the judge declines to make an advance ruling that the case comes within s.35(1), the defence must adduce evidence before the jury, failure to do so will mean that the judge is under no duty to direct the jury in relation to it.[94]

In addition to the mandatory exceptions in s.35(1), the Court of Appeal in *Cowan*[95] held that there might be cases, other than those identified in s.35 itself, in which it would be justified for a direction that no inferences should be drawn. The Court of Appeal did not give examples of the sort of circumstances in which such a direction would be appropriate.[96] The Court stressed, however, that the application of s.35 is not confined to "exceptional cases". Lord Taylor C.J. said that while it was open to a court to decline to draw an adverse inference, there would have to be some evidential basis or some exceptional factors in the case to make it a proper course to take.[97] Thus, the possibility of an accused, because of attacks on a co-accused, being cross-examined on his previous convictions if he gave evidence is not amoung the reasons for not applying s.35.[98]   **17–19**

Section 35 may also apply if an accused, having been sworn, without good cause refuses to answer any question. The section further provides that a person shall not be taken to have refused to answer a question without good cause if he is entitled to refuse to answer on the ground of privilege or the court, in the exercise of its general discretion, excuses him from doing so: s.35(5). Thus, the judge's power to restrain unfair, oppressive or inadmissible questioning remains intact, but if the accused refuses to answer a question for some other alleged reason (for example fear of reprisal or unwillingness to incriminate another) it will be open to the

---

[93] At 1020, *per* Otton L.J.
[94] *A* [1997] Crim.L.R. 883.
[95] *Cowan* [1996] 1 Cr.App.R. 1.
[96] In *Chadwick* [1998] 7 *Archbold News* 3, CA, it was held that if it is submitted that no inference should be drawn against the accused on the basis that his failure to give evidence is due to fear or duress, it is a matter for the trial judge as to whether he hears evidence on a *voir dire*.
[97] In *A*, above the Court of Appeal reiterated this point, commenting that in the instant case there was no evidential basis for a departure from the usual position and there was no obligation on the court to investigate whether there was such a basis.
[98] *Taylor* [1999] Crim.L.R. 77. The Court of Appeal held that the judge was not bound to proceed on the basis that there were not other reasons, in addition to the possible revelation of his previous convictions, for the accused's failure to give evidence.

jury to draw an inference from the refusal. In *Ackinclose*[99] the defendant was charged with possessing drugs with intent to supply. When he was arrested he was in possession of the drugs and was with another man who escaped. At his trial the defendant alleged in evidence that the other man was the drug dealer, but refused to name him. The judge told him he had no choice but to name the man: the defendant again declined to do so. The Court of Appeal held that s.35(5) applied, there was no statutory right or protection and no question of privilege arose; and since the question was relevant, it was not so oppressive that it amounted to a material irregularity.

(2) Operation of the section

17–20   Section 35 represents a significant departure from the practice under the common law which prevented the drawing of an adverse inference from the failure of the accused to give evidence. The section is based on a recommendation of the the Criminal Law Revision Committee.[1] When first published in 1972 this recommendation met much opposition and was not then implemented.

The Committee stressed that their proposal depended on there being a prima facie case against the accused: "failure to give evidence may be of little or no significance if there is no case against him or a weak one. But the stronger the case is the more significant will be his failure to give evidence."[2]

Accordingly, s.38(3) of the 1994 Act provides that a defendant shall not be be convicted solely on an inference drawn under s.35. This requirement was underlined by Lord Taylor C.J., giving the judgment of the Court of Appeal in *Cowan*,[3] the leading case on this topic:

> "The effect of section 35 is that the court or jury may regard the inference from failure to testify as, in effect, a further evidential factor in support of the prosecution case. It cannot be the only factor to justify a conviction and the totality of the evidence must prove guilt beyond reasonable doubt."

17–21   Therefore, provided that an inference under s.35 is not the only evidence against the defendant, the section will usually operate. Thus, the Court of Appeal in *Cowan* emphasised that the operation of s.35 was not confined to exceptional cases. Similarly, in *Napper*,[4] Lord Taylor C.J. said that attempts to minimise or marginalise the operation of s.35 were contrary to

---

[99] [1997] Crim.L.R. 747.
[1] Eleventh Report, Cmnd. 4991, para.28.
[2] *op.cit.*, para.110.
[3] [1996] 1 Cr.App.R. 1, 5.
[4] [1996] Crim.L.R.591; 161 J.P. 16.

the spirit of the statutory provisions: it was clear that Parliament had intended the general rule to be that it was open to the jury to draw adverse inferences where a defendant had declined to give evidence. (In *Napper* it was argued that the judge should not have allowed the jury to draw inferences from the defendant's failure to give evidence because police officers had failed to interview him about a number of transactions involved in an alleged fraud, thereby depriving him of the opportunity to give his account at a time when his memory was fresh, and at the time of the trial it was unreasonable to expect him to remember the details. The Court of Appeal rejected this argument, pointing out that that the defendant could have recorded a statement for his legal advisers from which he could have refreshed his memory.)

On the other hand, as was pointed out in *Cowan*, the use of the expression "as appear proper" in s.35(3) (in relation to the inferences to be drawn) leaves the trial judge with a broad discretion to decide in all the circumstances whether any proper inference is capable of being drawn by the jury. If not, the judge should tell them so; otherwise it is for the jury to decide whether in fact an inference should be drawn.

If the jury do decide to draw an inference, they are not limited as to what inferences may be drawn. In *Murray v DPP*[5] the House of Lords held that the inferences which may be drawn under art.4 of the Criminal Justice (Evidence) (Northern Ireland) Order 1988 (a provision in similar terms to s.35) are not limited to specific inferences from specific facts but include an inference that the defendant is guilty of the offence charged.

(3) Summing-up

In *Cowan*[6] Lord Taylor C.J. said thatthere were certain "essentials" upon **17–22**
which the judge must direct the jury in his summing-up, namely:

(a) the burden of proof remains on the prosecution throughout;

(b) the defendant is entitled to remain silent: that is his right; and that an inference from failure to give evidence cannot on its own prove guilt;

(c) the jury must find there to be a case to answer on the prosecution evidence before drawing an adverse inference from the defendant's silence[7];

(d) if, despite any evidence relied upon to explain his silence or in the absence of any such evidence, the jury conclude that the silence

---

[5] (1993) 97 Cr.App.R. 151.
[6] Above.
[7] This direction was described as essential by Lord Bingham C.J. in *Birchall* [1999] Crim.L.R. 311: failure to give it would give rise to a clear risk of injustice.

can only sensibly be attributed to the defendant's having no answer or none that would stand up to cross-examination, they may draw an adverse inference.

The Court in *Cowan*, also, approved a specimen direction put forward by the Judicial Studies Board containing the above points.[8]

Dealing with the circumstances in which a judge might think it right to direct or advise a jury against drawing an adverse inference, the Court of Appeal in *Cowan* said that it would be impossible to anticipate all such circumstances and declined to give examples as each case turned on its own facts. The Court quoted with approval the dictum of Kelly L.J. in the Northern Ireland case of *McLernon*[9]:

> "the court then has a complete discretion as to whether inferences should be drawn or not. In these circumstances it is a matter for the court ... (1) to decide whether to draw inferences or not: and (2) if it decides to draw inferences what their nature, extent and degree of adversity, if any, may be. It would be improper and indeed quite unwise for any court to set out the bounds of either steps (1) or (2). Their application will depend on factors peculiar to the individual case."

17–23   (The Court in *Cowan* said that although these remarks were made in relation to a trial without a jury, they applied equally to the direction which a judge gives in summing-up to the jury.)

The Court of Appeal in *Cowan*[10] said that provided the judge gives the jury adequate directions of law and leaves the decision whether to draw an inference to them, the Court of Appeal would be slow to interfere with the exercise of his discretion to direct and advise the jury as to the drawing of inferences and as to the nature, extent and degree of such inferences.

(4) Convention rights

17–24   In *Murray v UK*[11] (a case under art.4 of the Criminal Justice (Evidence) (Northern Ireland) Order 1988, a provision in similar terms to s.35) the European Court of Human Rights held that there had been no breach of Art.6(1) of the Convention (which provides for the right to "a fair ... hearing") arising from the drawing of adverse inferences due to the defendant's failure to answer questions during interrogation and his failure to give evidence during his trial. The Court said that whether the drawing of adverse inferences amounted to an infringement of Art.6 was a matter to

---

[8] See *www.jsboard.co.uk* for full, current version of specimen direction.
[9] [1990] N.I.J.B. 91, 102.
[10] Above, at 9.
[11] (1996) 22 E.H.R.R. 29.

be determined in the light of all the circumstances of the case, having regard to the situations where inferences might be drawn, the weight attached to them by the national courts in their assessment of the evidence and the degree of compulsion inherent in the situation. The Court noted that "the drawing of inferences under the 1988 Order was subject to an important series of safeguards designed to respect the rights of the defence and limit the extent to which reliance be placed on inferences", *i.e.* (a) under art.4 of the Order the defendant was a non-compellable witness, (b) silence, in itself, could not be regarded as an indication of guilt, (c) the prosecution had, first, to establish a prima facie case and (d) the trial judge had a discretion whether, on the facts, an inference should be drawn. In these circumstances the Court found that the drawing of inferences, having regard to the weight of the evidence, was a matter of common sense and could not be regarded as unfair or unreasonable.

The safeguards to which the Court referred are, of course, present under s.35 of the 1994 Act. Accordingly, it is submitted that the Court would be unlikely to find that the drawing of inferences under that section amounts to a violation of Art.6. However, it may be pointed out that *Murray* involved a trial by judge alone, a fact to which the Court referred when it said that it was concentrating its attention on the role played by inferences in the proceedings against the applicant and, in that context, it was recalled that the trier of fact was an experienced judge. It is submitted that the fact that a jury is ultimately responsible for drawing inferences under s.35 makes no difference because they cannot do so unless a judge has ruled that they are entitled to do so.[12] However, the dangers were emphasised by Lord Bingham C.J. when warning that a failure by a judge to give a carefully framed direction relating to s.35 and the sister sections could lead to decisions adverse to the UK at Strasbourg.[13]

Now that the Convention has been incorporated into English law by the **17–25** Human Rights Act 1998 (see Ch.13, above), courts in determining whether an inference may be drawn in a particular case, may have to determine whether to do so would violate the defendant's rights under Art.6. It is submitted that normally this will not be so (see para.13–14, above for a discussion of Art.6), but that courts must heed the warning of Lord Bingham C.J., above.

The prohibition under s.1 of the Criminal Evidence Act 1898 on comment by the prosecution on the defendant's failure to give evidence has been abolished by s.168 of and Sch.11 to the 1994 Act. As a result, comment by the prosecution is now permissible. It is submitted that such comment

---

[12] See, however, Munday, "Inferences from Silence and European Human Rights Law" [1996] Crim.L.R. 370 for a discussion of *Murray v UK* to the effect that it was not a test case for the 1994 Act and that the European Court's tolerance of convictions based on silence has definite limits.
[13] *Birchall*, above.

should be restrained and should not extend to an invitation to convict solely on this ground.

The common law permitted the judge to comment on the defendant's failure to give evidence. However, that right was latterly much circumscribed and the conventional direction required the judge to stress that the jury must not assume that the defendant was guilty because he had not given evidence.[14] The judge is now free to comment as he thinks fit.

6. The Defendant's Spouse

17–26 The law relating to the competence and compellability of the defendant's spouse used to be a confusing mixture of common law and statute. In 1972, the Criminal Law Revision Committee recommended a complete overhaul.[15] Parliament largely, but not entirely, followed the Committee's recommendations. The result was s.80 of the Police and Criminal Evidence Act 1984, which now governs the law on this subject.[16] The relevant parts of s.80 (as amended) provide:

"(2) In any proceedings the wife or husband of a person charged in the proceedings shall, subject to subsection (4) below, be compellable to give evidence on behalf of that person.

(2A) In any proceedings the wife or husband of a person charged in the proceedings shall, subject to subsection (4) below, be compellable—

(a) to give evidence on behalf of any other person charged in the proceedings but only in respect of any specified offence with which that other person is charged; or

(b) to give evidence for the prosecution but only in respect of any specified offence with which any person is charged in the proceedings.

(3) In relation to the wife or husband of a person charged in any criminal proceedings, an offence is a specified offence for the purpose of subsection (2A) above if—

(a) it involves an assault on, or injury or a threat of injury to, the wife or husband or a person who was at the material time under the age of 16;

(b) it is a sexual offence[17] alleged to have been committed in

---

[14] *Bathurst* [1968] 2 W.L.R. 1092; *Martinez-Tobon* (1994) 98 Cr.App.R. 375.
[15] Eleventh Report, Cmnd. 4991, paras 14.3–15.7; cl.9 of the draft Bill.
[16] s.80 has been amended and repealed by s.67(1) and (3) and Sch.4, para.13 and Sch.6 to the YJCEA 1999.
[17] s.80(7) provides in subs.(3)(b) "sexual offence" means an offence under the Sexual Offences Act 1956, the Indecency with Children Act 1960, the Sexual Offences Act 1967, s.54 of the Criminal Law Act 1977 or the Protection of Children Act 1978.

respect of a person who was at the material time under that age; or

(c) it consists of attempting or conspiring to commit, or of aiding, abetting, counseling, procuring or inciting the commission of, an offence falling within paragraph (a) or (b) above.

(4) No person who is charged in any proceedings shall be compellable by virtue of subsection (2) or (2A) above to give evidence in the proceedings.

(4A) References in this section to a person charged in any proceedings do not include a person who is not, or is no longer, liable to be convicted of any offence in the proceedings (whether as a result of pleading guilty or for any other reason).

(5) In any proceedings a person who has been but is no longer married to the accused shall be compellable to give evidence as if that person and the accused had never been married.

(6) Where in any proceedings the age of any person at any time is material for the purposes of (3) above, his age at the material time shall for the purposes of that provision be deemed to be or to have been that which appears to the court to be or to have been his age at that time.

[...]"

In *Pearce*[18] it was held that s.80 and the terms "wife" and "husband" did not include the co-habitee of a defendant even though they had lived together for 19 years and had three children together.   **17–27**

A discussion of the effect of this section follows. In the discussion it will be convenient to treat the husband as the defendant: however, the law is similar if the wife is the defendant.

A. As a witness for the prosecution

A wife is competent to give evidence for the prosecution against her husband in all cases unless she is jointly charged with him: s.80(2A) and (4).   **17–28**
Thus the old common law rule that a wife was only competent in cases of personal violence against herself has been overturned. Various statutes made a spouse competent for the prosecution in respect of certain offences, for example, failing to maintain wife and family; offences relating to children or to the property of the spouse; child destruction; bigamy; and sexual offences.[19] Parliament has now abolished this partial competence in favour

---

[18] [2002] 1 Cr.App.R.39.
[19] There were also possible, but unimportant exceptions, in the case of treason and abduction.

of a general rule of competence.[20] The law on this topic has to balance two competing interests: (i) the preservation of marriages, which are put in jeopardy when wives give evidence against their husbands; and (ii) the investigation of crime which may be impossible without the evidence of a wife in the case of a crime committed in the home. In *Pearce*[21] it was argued that failure to provide the same protections from testimony afforded wives and husbands to co-habitees and long term partners amounted to a violation of Art.8 of the ECHR (right to privacy and family life). The Court of Appeal held that Art.8(1) did not require that a co-habitee should not be compelled to give evidence. In short the interests of the family must be weighed against those of the community at large.

The common law rule was based on the first consideration, the need to preserve marriage. However, it must be the case that if a wife is prepared to give evidence against her husband, it is likely that the marriage will already have substantially broken down. For this reason it cannot be said that the new rule will in fact lead to marriages being put in jeopardy.

As a general rule, a wife, although competent, is not compellable against her husband. This is no doubt because of the repugnance felt at forcing a wife to give evidence in these circumstances and the likely effect upon the marriage.

17–29 Thus, except in the cases mentioned below, the wife has a right to refuse to give evidence against her husband. She retains this right until she waives it by going into the witness-box and taking the oath. Once, however, she starts to give evidence she becomes an ordinary witness. She may therefore be treated as hostile.[22]

In *Pitt*,[23] the Court of Appeal stressed that the waiver of the right of refusal was only effective if made with full knowledge of the right. Accordingly, the Court said:

> "It seems to us to be desirable that where a wife is called as a witness for the prosecution of her husband, the judge should explain to her, in the absence of the jury, that before she takes the oath she has the right to refuse to give evidence, but that if she chooses to give evidence she may be treated like any other witness."

---

[20] The Theft Act 1968, s.30(2) provides that (subject to the consent of the Director of Public Prosecutions in certain cases) a person has the same right to bring proceedings against his or her spouse as if they were not married and a person bringing such proceedings is competent to give evidence for the prosecution at every stage of the proceedings. This section has not been repealed by the 1984 Act, presumably in order to retain the right of a person to bring proceedings against his or her spouse. However, the provisions relating to competence are no longer of any importance in the light of the 1984 Act.

[21] Above.

[22] *Pitt*, below.

[23] (1983) 75 Cr.App.R. 254, 258.

The Court said in *Pitt* that such an explanation was not required as a matter of law and the Court was not seeking to lay down a rule of practice. However, now that the 1984 Act has made wives generally competent as witnesses for the prosecution, it seems proper that such a warning should generally be given when the wife is not a compellable witness. This is for the following reasons: (a) The consequences for the marriage of the wife's giving evidence against her husband may be very grave. She may, for instance, have become reconciled to her husband since giving a statement to the prosecution. If she gave evidence adverse to her husband, the reconciliation might well be undone. (b) There is a risk that the true position may never have been explained to her or she may not have fully understood it. Accordingly, she should hear an explanation from the judge himself.

The same rule applies in magistrates' courts. This is illustrated by *Birmingham Justices Ex p. Shields.*[24] In that case a witness spoke to the prosecutor outside court and told him that (a) she did not wish to give evidence against her husband and (b) her statement was inaccurate. The Divisional Court held that in these circumstances the prosecutor was under a duty to disclose the conversation and inform the court so that the witness could be warned that she did not have to give evidence.   **17–30**

The general rule that a wife is not compellable against her husband is subject to two exceptions, *i.e.* cases where a husband is charged with

(a) personal violence against his wife or against a child under 16: 1984 Act, s.80(3)(a); or

(b) a sexual offence against a child under 16[25]: s.80(3)(b).

(1) Violence against a wife

Until the decision of the House of Lords in *Hoskyn v Metropolitan Police Commissioner*[26] it had been thought that a wife was compellable at common law where a husband was charged with personal violence against her. However, in *Hoskyn* the House of Lords held by a majority that a wife was not compellable in such a case. The view of Parliament was that the public interest in the investigation of crime required that the wife's evidence should be available to the court. This may not be surprising given (a) the continued prevalence of violence towards wives and the consequent public interest in the detection, punishment and resulting deterrence of that violence; and (b) the fact that very often the only available evidence is that of the wife herself.   **17–31**

---

[24] *The Times*, August 3, 1994.
[25] Or attempting or aiding and abetting these offences: s.80(3)(c).
[26] [1979] A.C. 474.

(2) Offences against children

17-32 The provision that a wife should be compellable to give evidence against her husband when he is charged with an offence of violence or sexual offences against children under the age of 16 reflects the serious public concern at the high incidence of physical and sexual abuse of children. The Criminal Law Revision Committee was of the view that compellability in the case of violence towards children was more important than in the case of violence towards the wife herself.[27] That view was expressed in 1972. The experience of the intervening years has done nothing to lessen the impact of that observation.

Similar considerations apply in the case of sexual offences against children. The section protects all children. Thus, a visitor to the defendant's household will be protected, for example, a 15-year-old babysitter against whom an offence is committed.

B. As a witness for the defence

17-33 A wife is both competent and compellable as a witness for her husband unless she is jointly charged and tried with him: s.80(2) and (4). While previously competent to give evidence, a wife was not compellable. Whether the change will make much practical difference must be doubtful. Most wives will no doubt willingly give evidence on behalf of their husbands. It would be an exceptional case for the defence to call a wife who required compulsion to make her attend.

The wife of one defendant is competent to give evidence on behalf of another defendant: 1984 Act, s.80(2A)(a). However, a wife will only be a compellable witness on behalf of a co-defendant in the same circumstances as those in which she is compellable for the prosecution, *i.e.* personal violence on herself or sexual offences or violence against children under 16: s.80(3).[28] The reason that the wife is compellable for the co-accused only in these cases is that since the prosecution cannot compel the wife to give evidence, it would be wrong to compel her to give evidence and thereby give the prosecution the opportunity to incriminate her husband by cross-examining her. Section 80(2A)(a) refers to "any person jointly charged in the proceedings". The Court of Appeal in *Woolgar*[29] held that the wife of a co-defendant jointly indicted, but not jointly charged in the same count as the defendant, was compellable.

C. Former spouses

17-34 When spouses have been divorced or a marriage annulled, the former spouse is both competent and compellable as if the parties had never been

---

[27] Eleventh Report, Cmnd. 4991, para.150.
[28] Or attempting or aiding and abetting such offences: s.80(3)(c).
[29] [1991] Crim.L.R. 545.

married (1984 Act, s.80(5)). This provision abolished the former rule, *i.e.* that a spouse was incompetent to give evidence for the prosecution concerning matters which occurred during marriage.[30] (A witness married to a defendant at the time s.80 came into force, but divorced at the time of trial, has been held to be compellable to give evidence about events before s.80 came into force.[31]) The provision has not affected the position where the parties are judicially separated, *i.e.* the usual rules as to the competence and compellability of spouses apply.[32]

D. Polygamous marriages

In *Khan*[33] the Court of Appeal held that a woman who had undergone a Muslim marriage ceremony with a defendant (who had already married under English law) was a competent witness for the prosecution against the defendant and his co-defendant. This case was decided before s.80 of the 1984 Act came into force. However, there appears to be no reason why the same principle should not be applied when questions of compellability under s.80 arise. The Court in *Khan* said that the same principle applies in the case of a spouse of a second polygamous marriage as applies to a woman who has not been through a ceremony of marriage or as applies to the spouse of a bigamous marriage.

17–35

E. Comment on the failure of a spouse to give evidence

(1) By the prosecution

Section 80A of the 1984 Act[34] forbids comment by the prosecution on the failure of a defendant to call his or her spouse. This provision originally appeared in s.80(8) of the 1984 Act, and prior to that, s.1(b) of the 1898 Act.

17–36

The unamended provisions of s.1(b) have been held to be mandatory and breach of them a material irregularity.[35] Thus in *Naudeer*[36] a conviction was quashed in a shoplifting case because prosecuting counsel told the jury that they had been deliberately deprived of material evidence as the defendant had not called his wife (who had been in the shop at the relevant time). However, the damage done by a comment may be remedied by a correction by the court.[37]

---

[30] *Algar* [1954] 1 Q.B. 279; 37 Cr.App.R. 200.
[31] *Cruttenden* (1991) 93 Cr.App.R. 119.
[32] *Moss v Moss* [1963] 2 Q.B. 799; 47 Cr.App.R. 222.
[33] (1987) 84 Cr.App.R. 44.
[34] As inserted by s.67(1) and Sch.4, para.14 of the YJCEA 1999.
[35] *Brown and Routh* [1983] Crim.L.R. 38.
[36] Below.
[37] *e.g. Whitton* [1998] Crim. L. R. 492 where the Court of Appeal said that in the case of a clear breach of the subsection the judge ought to stop counsel after his comment and point out the error.

(2) By the judge

17–37 A judge may, in an appropriate case, comment upon the failure of a defendant to call his wife.[38] He may make such a comment in relation to any witness who might have been called.[39] A spouse is no exception. However, care should be exercised when making this comment.

> "It is permissible for a judge in an appropriate case to tell the jury that they are entitled to take into account the fact that a potential witness who has not been called has not indeed been called. . . . [In] making any such comment, the judge must exercise care, [just as he] has got to exercise care when he thinks it right to make a comment in respect of the failure of a defendant himself to give evidence. . . . [The] same general approach is right in respect of a comment on the failure to call a witness as is right in respect of a comment by a judge on the failure of an accused person to give evidence."[40]

---

[38] *Gallagher* [1974] 1 W.L.R. 1204.

[39] See para.16–21. In *Wright* [2000] Crim.L.R. 510, the Court of Appeal deprecated a judge's comments on the defendant's failure to call her boyfriend as a witness "dangerous" because they detracted from the burden of proof.

[40] *ibid.*, 1211. In *Naudeer* (1984) 80 Cr.App.R. 9, 13 the Court of Appeal said that save in exceptional circumstances a judge must make such a comment with a great deal of circumspection.

CHAPTER 18
Disclosure

1. TRIALS ON INDICTMENT

The prosecution must disclose its case against a person to be tried on 18–01
indictment at an early stage in the proceedings. Before a person is tried on
indictment he or she will normally be either "sent" to the Crown Court for
trial for indictable only matters or committed for trial by examining
magistrates for either way offences to be tried in the Crown Court.

Section 51 of the Crime and Disorder Act 1998 abolished committal
proceedings for offences triable only on indictment. In such cases an adult
offender must be sent forthwith to the Crown Court for trial: copies of the
documents containing the evidence on which the charge is based must be
disclosed within 42 days of the first hearing in the Crown Court.[1] Section
41 of and Sch.3 to the Criminal Justice Act 2003, not yet in force at the time
of writing, amends s.51 of the 1998 Act so as to make provision for "either
way offences", to be tried on indictment, to be similarly "sent" to the
Crown Court.

When a matter is committed to the Crown Court, the prosecution is
required to show that there is sufficient evidence to put the defendant on
trial by jury. It is for the prosecution to decide which witnesses to rely upon
for the purposes of committal proceedings.[2] Under the modified committal
proceedings introduced by s.47 and Sch.1 to the Criminal Procedure and
Investigations Act 1996 (amending the Magistrates' Courts Act 1980), the
evidence at committal is limited to documentary evidence, *i.e.* written
statements and depositions, tendered by the prosecution, together with any

---

[1] Crime and Disorder Act 1998 (Service of Prosecution Evidence) Regulations 2000 (SI 2000/
3305), made under the Crime and Disorder Act 1998, Sch.3, para.1, came into force on
January 15, 2001.
[2] *Wilkinson v Crown Prosecution Service* [1998] Crim.L.R. 743. The prosecutor need tender
only a portion of the evidence provided it is sufficient to commit. However, the court may
intervene if there is compelling evidence to show that improper behaviour has taken place if the
prosecutor has mislead the court in the selection of evidence for committal. See also *DPP Ex p.
Lee* [1999] 2 Cr.App.R. 304 on the prosecution's disclosure obligations between arrest and
committal.

exhibits (s.5A of the 1980 Act, inserted by Pt I of Sch.1 to the 1996 Act).[3] As a result, no witnesses may be called to give oral evidence and, thus, there is no possibility of cross-examination. For the purposes of committal, a witness statement tendered by the prosecution must comply with the requirements of s.5A(3)(a) of the Magistrates' Courts Act 1980. In *Raynor*[4] it was held that, where a witness does not speak English, to comply with s.5A(3)(a) the prosecution must serve the actual statement of the witness rather than a translation prepared by a translator.[5] The parties may make oral representation to the magistrates as to whether to commit a case to the Crown Court or to discharge the defendant: s.6(2) of the 1980 Act, inserted by Pt I of Sch.1 to the present Act.[6]

18–02 Section 1 of the Criminal Procedure (Attendance of Witnesses) Act 1965 provided for the making of witness orders by examining justices, *i.e.* orders for the attendance of witnesses for trials which had been committed to the Crown Court. Such orders were either "full" orders, *i.e.* requiring the attendance of the witness, or "conditional" orders, *i.e.* requiring the witness to attend only if notice was given to him. Section 65 of and Sch.5 to the Criminal Procedure and Investigations Act 1996 repealed s.1. Now, the statements of the prosecution witnesses having been served at the committal proceedings, arrangements as to which of the witnesses are to be called at trial are made at plea and directions hearings at the Crown Court.

The Criminal Justice Act 1987 has placed additional obligations upon the prosecution in cases of serious and complex fraud. Section 9(4) of the Act provides that in such cases the judge may order the prosecution to supply the court and defence with a case statement setting out, *inter alia*, the principal facts relied on by the prosecution and identifying the witnesses to be called to prove them. The Act provides sanctions for failure to comply

---

[3] For the admissibility of such written statements and depositions at trial, see para.8–79, above. In *DPP Ex p. J* [2000] 1 W.L.R. 1215, the prosecution was only prepared to disclose transcripts of surveillance tapes to the defence instead of copies of the actual surveillance tapes. The Divisional Court held that the provision of copies of copiable exhibits, although the norm, is not an absolute entitlement. There is a strong presumption in favour of such provision which it is for the prosecution to displace. It must normally be for the trial judge to determine in the circumstances of each case whether fairness could be achieved. In deciding whether to provide copies of audio and video surveillance tapes the Crown Prosecution Service was entitled to take into consideration the protection and safety of an undercover police officer.

[4] *The Times*, September 19, 2000.

[5] The Court of Appeal held that there is no doubt that the Crown Court has jurisdiction to consider the extent to which any deficiency in a committal should result in the quashing of an indictment. Following *Neill v North Antrim Magistrates' Court* (1993) 97 Cr.App.R. 121, the Court held that the accused's committal should not have been quashed as there was a strong prima facie case against him and he had not suffered a demonstrable injustice despite the irregularity at committal caused by the inclusion in the committal papers of statements that did not meet all the requirements.

[6] The system of committal remains largely unchanged from the previous system, apart from the exclusion of oral evidence. The object of this change was said to be to prevent witnesses having to go through the ordeal of having to give evidence twice. Another effect is to prevent the unnecessary wastage of time and expense involved in longer hearings in magistrates' courts necessitated by the calling of evidence.

with such an order (or departure from the case disclosed), namely (a) comment by the judge; (b) (with leave) comment by the defence and (c) the drawing of an adverse inference by the jury (s.1(1)). Failure to comply with the order will not necessarily produce these consequences but may do so. In *Re Case Statements*[7] the Divisional Court said that it was of prime importance that the prosecution case statement was in the hands of the court and the defence at least seven days before a preparatory hearing under s.9 of the Criminal Justice Act 1987 in order to give the defence the opportunity of examining it and arguing such points as are raised by the Crown at the hearing. (The Court also said that any order of the court under s.9 should be "clarity itself".[8])

Similar powers are now exercisable under s.31 of the Criminal Procedure and Investigations Act 1996. Section 29 of that Act permits the judge in a long and complex case in the Crown Court to order and hold a preparatory hearing if it appears that substantial benefits are likely to accrue. (This provision gave effect to proposals in a government consultation paper on pre-trial hearings, following a recommendation of the Royal Commission on Criminal Justice.[9]) Under s.31 of the Act the judge may exercise a range of powers with the purpose of identifying and clarifying the issues in the case. To this end, he may order either party to serve a written statement of its case, beginning with the prosecution. Departure from the statement may entitle the judge (or, with leave, the other party) to comment and the jury to draw inferences (s.34).

2. SUMMARY TRIAL

Originally, there was no rule requiring that the defendant in a summary trial should have any notice of the evidence on which the prosecution intended to rely. However, in May 1985 the Magistrates' Courts (Advance Information) Rules 1985 (made under s.48 of the Criminal Law Act 1977) came into force. The effect of these rules is that a defendant in proceedings for an offence "triable either way" (*i.e.* a case in which the defendant may choose whether to be tried by justices or on indictment) may now ask for information about the prosecution case and, if such a request is made, the prosecution is obliged to provide the information either by supplying the relevant witness statements or by supplying a summary of the case. Disclosure may be withheld if, in the prosecutor's opinion, it might lead to the intimidation of witnesses or interference with the course of justice. If the prosecutor fails to provide the information as required by the Rules, justices have no power under s.7 to dismiss the information: they should either

18–03

---

[7] (1993) 97 Cr.App.R. 417, 420.
[8] *ibid.*
[9] (1993) Cm. 2263, para.7.4.

adjourn the case or, if they are satisfied that the defendant is not prejudiced, hear it.[10]

The prosecution is not obliged to provide advance information beyond the case summary if the case summary does not refer to a document on which the prosecution propose to rely within the meaning of r.4(3) of the 1985 Rules. Thus, in *Croydon Magistrates' Court Ex p. DPP*,[11] it was held that reference in a case summary to DNA profiles could not by itself be a reference to a document and the prosecution were not obliged therefore to disclose it. The Divisional Court stated that there could be serious implications for the administration of justice if scientific evidence had to form part of the advance information in view of the potential for significant delays.

There is no general duty on a prosecuting authority to disclose in advance evidence and other material, for example before transfer of a serious fraud case to the Crown Court: the performance of the duty has to depend on the standard procedures applicable to the particular case.[12]

18–04 The 1985 Rules do not apply to cases which are only triable summarily. Thus, there is no requirement of disclosure of statements of prosecution witnesses in such a case. In *Kingston upon Hull JJ. Ex p. McCann*[13] the Crown prosecutor refused requests for disclosure because the witnesses were in fear of the defendant who had a record for violence. The Divisional Court held that there is no obligation on the prosecution to disclose the statements of evidence in a summary trial. Bingham L.J. said that, although ordinarily Crown prosecutors are well advised to adopt a policy of disclosing the material on which they intend to rely (and in some circumstances fairness required disclosure), where a prosecutor reasonably believes that disclosure may lay a witness open to reprisal, that apprehension justifies non-disclosure, whether or not it is seen to be justified by the facts.

In *Imbert*[14] the Divisional Court held that *McCann* remained in force and that there was no requirement of disclosure of witness statements in summary trials. The advance disclosure of statements in summary trials was neither required pursuant to the Criminal Procedure and Investigations Act 1996 ("CPIA 1996") nor Art.6 of the ECHR. It was held, however, that failure to provide advance disclosure could not affect the fairness of the trial provided that justices appreciated the need to grant adjournments to enable a defendant or his representatives to deal with the evidence when it was adduced, to cross-examine a witness and, if necessary, to obtain evidence to show that the witness was wrong. It is submitted that the prosecution should in practice, to avoid unnecessary delays in summary trials, make

---

[10] *King v Kucharz, The Times*, February 2, 1989.
[11] [2001] Crim.L.R. 980.
[12] *Serious Fraud Office Ex p. Maxwell, The Times*, October 9, 1992.
[13] (1991) 155 J.P. 569.
[14] [1999] 2 Cr.App.R. 276.

advance disclosure to the defence. Indeed, the Attorney-General's Guide-lines on Disclosure require that the prosecutor should, in addition to complying with the requirements under the CPIA 1996, provide the defence with all evidence upon which the prosecution propose to rely in a summary trial.[15] Lord Justice Auld's "Review of Criminal Courts in England and Wales" ("Auld Review") recommended that there should be a single set of statutory rules imposing on the prosecution *in all cases* a duty to provide proposed evidence in sufficient time to enable the defence to prepare for trial.[16]

3. UNUSED MATERIAL: THE CRIMINAL PROCEDURE AND INVESTIGATION ACTS 1996, PTS I AND II UNUSED MATERIAL

Part I of the 1996 Act introduced a new scheme for disclosure of "unused material" by the prosecution, *i.e.* material which has not been disclosed as part of the prosecution case. Thus, s.21 enacted that (with one exception) the common law rules as to disclosure no longer applied after the provisions of this Part came into force.[17] The exception concerns the common law rules relating to whether disclosure is in the public interest: these rules are not affected by s.21.[18] It should also be noted that the effect of s.20(1) of the Act is to permit the disclosure scheme in Pt I to operate unaffected by the existing statutory rules as to disclosure. (The statutory rules referred to are those in the Criminal Justice Act 1987, s.9, relating to serious or complex fraud and those in the Police and Criminal Evidence Act 1984, s.81, relating to expert evidence.[19]) The 1996 Act has not worked well.[20] Accordingly, wide-ranging amendments have been made to the disclosure regime under Pt I of the 1996 Act by the Criminal Justice Act 2003. The consideration of the 1996 Act below is of the Act as amended by the 2003

18–05

---

[15] *Disclosure of Information in Criminal Proceedings*, November 29, 2000, at para.43.
[16] "Review of Criminal Courts in England and Wales", Report by Lord Justice Auld (2001, Stationery Office, London), Ch.10—Disclosure.
[17] The appointed day on which Pt I came into force was April 1, 1997. s.1(3) of the Act provides that Pt I should only apply to alleged offences into which no criminal investigation had begun before the appointed day. In *Norwich Stipendiary Magistrate Ex p. Keable* [1998] Crim.L.R. 510 the Divisional Court held that this meant that Pt I applied only to offences allegedly committed after the appointed day, notwithstanding that the investigation had begun before that day. *Keable* was not followed in *Uxbridge Magistrates' Court Ex p. Patel* [2000] Crim.L.R. 383, in which it was held that a criminal investigation could begin into an offence before it was committed and that, if the investigation had began before April 1, 1997, Pt I would not apply.
[18] These rules require that if the prosecution makes a claim that material should be withheld on the ground of public interest immunity it is for the court to decide whether the material should be disclosed: Ward [1993] 1 W.L.R. 619; 96 Cr.App.R. 1.
[19] These rules are discussed at para.18–31 *et seq.*, below.
[20] "Review of Criminal Courts in England and Wales", Report by Lord Justice Auld (2001, Stationery Office, London), Ch. 10—Disclosure.

Act. However, at the time of writing, the amendments made by the 2003 Act were not yet in force. (It is anticipated that such amendments will enter into force in April 2005.)

Before considering the revised scheme under Pt I of the 1996 Act, it is first necessary to consider the background against which it was originally devised.

A. Disclosure at common law

18–06   The common law developed its own rules relating to disclosure in trials on indictment. In accordance with those rules, the prosecution was under an obligation to disclose any inconsistent statement made by a prosecution witness and any previous convictions of such a witness. The prosecution had also for many years been under an obligation to disclose the name and address of any person from whom they had taken a statement and whom they decided not to call as a witness: *Bryant and Dickson*.[21] The usual (and preferable) practice was also to disclose the statement: *Dallison v Caffery*[22]; *Lawson*.[23]

In 1981 the Attorney-General issued Guidelines to prosecuting authorities relating to the disclosure of information to the defence in trials on indictment.[24] The Guidelines called for the disclosure to the defence of all "unused material" (*i.e.* material not disclosed as part of the prosecution case at committal) if it had some bearing on the offences charged or the surrounding circumstances. "Unused material" was defined in the Guidelines as including all witness statements and documents (not served as part of the prosecution at committal and the unedited version of any such statements). The Guidelines permitted the prosecuting authority not to disclose material in circumstances (a) where it was not in the public interest to make disclosure (such as matters of national security or to protect the identity of an informant); or (b) where it was feared that the witness might be persuaded to change his story or might give an untrue account and the statement could be used in cross-examination.

In 1997, the House of Lords in *Mills and Poole*[25] decided that the rule in *Bryant and Dickson* (*i.e.* that it was sufficient merely to disclose the name and address of a witness) should no longer be applied since it was not in conformity with the modern principles of disclosure, established by the Court of Appeal (see below). Accordingly the House held that the non-disclosure of the two statements (which were described as "highly material" to the issues at the trial but which were not disclosed on the ground that they were not accepted by the prosecution to be credible) amounted to

---

[21] (1946) 31 Cr.App.R. 146.
[22] [1965] Q.B. 348, 349 *per* Lord Denning M.R.
[23] (1990) 90 Cr.App.R. 107.
[24] (1982) 74 Cr.App.R. 302.
[25] [1998] 1 Cr.App.R. 43.

a material irregularity. Lord Hutton said that the risk that disclosure might assist the defence to tailor its evidence was not a consideration that should outweigh the risk that the operation of the rule might result in injustice.

On the other hand, the House of Lords in *Brown (Winston)*[26] held that the prosecution's duty of disclosure did not extend to the disclosure of material relating solely to the credibility of defence witnesses. Lord Hope said that the defendant's entitlement to a fair trial did not require that his witnesses should be immune from challenge as to their credibility: material which may assist the defence case can be distinguished from material which may undermine it and to insist on the disclosure of the latter would weaken cross-examination and would protect from challenge those disposed to give false evidence in support of a fabricated defence.[27]

18–07

The ambit of "unused material" has been much extended, particularly by the pronouncements and decisions of courts in two cases. These cases were: (a) *Saunders*[28] (the "Guinness" case) where Henry J. ruled that the defence was entitled to see all the preparatory notes and tape recordings which led to the making of witness statements; and (b) *Ward*[29] where Glidewell L.J. said that the defence should have the opportunity of considering all the material evidence which the prosecution had gathered and from which it had made its own selection of evidence to be led. The result of these cases was to broaden the scope of disclosure to include all material gathered by the prosecution including statements, documents and computer entries.

The question of what material should be disclosed was ultimately considered by the Court of Appeal in *Keane*.[30] The Court of Appeal in that case said that the test of what was discloseable was to determine whether the material was relevant (or possibly relevant) to an issue in the case, or raised (or possibly raised) a new issue the existence of which was not apparent from the prosecution evidence, or held out a real prospect of providing a lead on evidence relevant to these matters. The Court said in *Keane* that, having identified material according to these criteria, the prosecution should disclose it unless they intend to claim public interest immunity. If the prosecution was in doubt about the materiality of information, the court should be asked to rule.

Four other matters should be noted:

18–08

(a) Failure to disclose evidence which ought to have been disclosed was held to amount to a material irregularity in the course of the trial: *Maguire*.[31]

---

[26] [1998] 1 Cr.App.R. 66.
[27] At 75–76.
[28] Unreported, CCC, September 1990.
[29] (1993) 96 Cr.App.R. 1, 2.
[30] (1994) 99 Cr.App.R. 1.
[31] (1992) 94 Cr.App.R. 13.

(b) In a later development the Court of Appeal in *Brown (Winston)*[32] said that the Attorney-General's Guidelines did not have the force of law and did not conform to the modern law of disclosure[33]: it was thus for the court (and not prosecuting counsel) to decide what material to disclose. (In practice, it was prosecuting counsel who made the decision: it was only if there was any doubt about it that the court was called on to decide.)

(c) The Divisional Court held that in summary proceedings the prosecution was under a similar duty in relation to disclosure as in trials on indictment and that magistrates had jurisdiction to rule in disputes: *Bromley JJ. Ex p. Smith*.[34]

(d) At common law the defence was under no obligation to disclose any part of its case before trial. This rule was based on principles relating to the right of silence, the privilege against self-incrimination and the duty of the prosecution to prove its case. However, inroads were made by statute upon this rule. As a result, the defence were obliged to disclose: (i) evidence of alibi (Criminal Justice Act 1967, s.11(1)); (ii) expert evidence (Police and Criminal Evidence Act 1984, s.81, Crown Court (Advance Notice of Expert Evidence) Rules 1987); and (iii) the nature of the defence in cases of serious or complex fraud (Criminal Justice Act 1987, s.9(5)[35]).

B. Recommendations and proposals for reform

18–09   Following the decisions in the "Guinness" and Ward cases, above the requirements for disclosure placed a substantial burden on the police and provided the defence with opportunities for mounting "fishing expeditions". Accordingly, the Royal Commission on Criminal Justice devised a new regime for disclosure with the aim of striking a balance between the duties of the prosecution and the rights of the defence.[36] The Commission proposed a statutory scheme of disclosure, supported by subordinate legislation or a code of practice. The Commission recommended that the prosecution should be obliged to make disclosure in two stages. Initially, the prosecution would be required: (a) to supply to the defence copies of all material relevant to the offence, the offender or the surrounding circumstances (whether or not the prosecution intended to rely on it); and (b) to inform the defence by lists or schedules of any other material obtained during the course of investigation (except internal working documents such

---

[32] [1994] 1 W.L.R. 1599.
[33] On appeal this view was supported by the House of Lords (1988) 1 Cr.App.R. 66, 70.
[34] [1995] 2 Cr.App.R. 285.
[35] Repealed by the Criminal Justice Act 2003.
[36] Cm. 2266 (1993), paras 6.50–6.56.

as police documents and legal advice). Secondary or further disclosure would be made if the defence could establish its relevance to the case. If the parties disagreed then the court would rule. The defence would be in a position to relate the material requested to its case when the substance of that case had been disclosed.

In May 1995 the Government published a Paper on this topic: Home Office, "Disclosure, a Consultation Document".[37] The Paper stated that the effect of the then-current requirements on disclosure had been to place heavy burdens on the investigating and prosecuting authorities, which may not be in the interests of justice. As examples the Paper referred to cases (a) in which an inordinate volume of material had to be prepared and copied by the police in order to meet defence requests, and (b) in which the authorities had to abandon the prosecution rather than comply with rulings to disclose sensitive material, for example to disclose the identity of an informant. The Government agreed with the Royal Commission that disclosure should be in stages, but thought that the Commission's scheme would not significantly reduce the burdens on the police and prosecution and that the proposals for defence disclosure would not sufficiently narrow the issues in dispute.[38] They produced a scheme which is largely embodied in the original Pt I of the 1996 Act.

After a number of years of operation, the disclosure regime under Pt I of the 1996 Act was found to have a number of shortcomings and was, in short, not working well. The Auld Review highlighted a number of concerns in relation to the operation of the regime. The Review recommended, amongst other things, a single test of disclosability at both stages of prosecution disclosure. The single test proposed was that the prosecutor must disclose material which, in his opinion, "might weaken the prosecution case or assist that of the defence."[39] Part I of the 1996 Act has been substantially amended by the Criminal Justice Act 2003. The regime, as amended by the 2003 Act, is considered below.

C. Disclosure under Part I of the 1996 Act

Disclosure under Part I, as revised by Pt 5 of the Criminal Justice Act 2003 (not in force at time of writing but anticipated to enter into force in April 2005) is now governed by a single objective test for the disclosure of unused material to the defence, replacing the previous two-stage test. (As already noted in para.18–05, above, s.21 of the 1996 Act abolished the common law rules as to disclosure, save for those relating to public interest immunity.)

In November 2000—after the operation of the CPIA 1996 for three

18–10

---

[37] HMSO.
[38] paras 22 and 23.
[39] "Review of Criminal Courts in England and Wales", Report by Lord Justice Auld (2001, Stationery Office, London), Ch.10—Disclosure.

years—in order to meet the concerns of judges, prosecutors and defence practitioners, the Attorney-General published guidelines concerning the role of participants in the disclosure process, pending any review by the Government of the legislative scheme.[40] The guidelines contain a number of changes addressing areas not covered by the CPIA 1996 (see para.18–12 below). The guidelines aim to clarify the responsibilities of investigators, disclosure officers, prosecutors and defence practitioners and generally improve the operation of the CPIA 1996.

(1) Primary prosecution disclosure: s.3

18–11 Section 3(1) and (2) of the CPIA 1996, as amended by s.32 of the Criminal Justice Act 2003, provide:

> "(1) The prosecutor must—
>
> (a) disclose to the accused any prosecution material which has not previously been disclosed to the accused and which might reasonably be considered capable of undermining the case for the prosecution against the accused or of assisting the case for the accused, or
>
> (b) give to the accused a written statement that there is no material of a description mentioned in paragraph (a).
>
> (2) For the purpose of this section prosecution material is material—
>
> (a) which is in the prosecutor's possession, and came into his possession in connection with the case for the prosecution against the accused, or
>
> (b) which, in pursuance of a code operative under Part II, he has inspected in connection with the case for the prosecution against the accused."

This section requires the prosecutor to disclose undisclosed prosecution material to the defence which might reasonably be considered capable of undermining the prosecution case or might assist the case for the accused. If there is no such material, the prosecution must give the defence a written statement to that effect.[41] The new test in s.3, following amendment by the Criminal Justice Act 2003, introduces an objective element in determining the disclosure of unused material to the defence. The same test is applied throughout proceedings and replaces the two-stage "primary" and "secondary" disclosure regime. Prior to the amendment of s.3 by the 2003 Act,

---

[40] *Disclosure of Information in Criminal Proceedings*, November 29, 2000.
[41] The Attorney-General's Guidelines (above) stipulate that, in the interests of justice and fairness, prosecutors must always be alive to the need to make disclosure of material after the commencement of proceedings but before the prosecutor's duty arises under s.3, *i.e.* for the purpose of bail or committal proceedings (para.34). See also *DPP v Lee* (n.2 above).

the prosecutor was only required, at the "primary" disclosure stage, to disclose material which in "the prosecutor's opinion" might undermine the prosecution case. The amendment followed concerns about the extent to which prosecutors had been carrying out their disclosure obligations. Surveys conducted by the Law Society and Criminal Bar Association revealed that in more than 200 cases crucial evidence had been withheld in breach of the CPIA 1996. In response to the surveys the Director of Public Prosecutions issued a warning to Chief Crown Prosecutors to stop withholding evidence before trials and thereby increasing the risk of miscarriages of justice.[42] Moreover, the Crown Prosecution Service Inspectorate found that the 1996 Act was not working as Parliament had intended: poor practice in relation to disclosure was widespread.[43] The effect of the amendment to s.3 of the 1996 Act is to move away from prime responsibility for disclosure being upon the prosecutor.[44]

The new test in s.3, following amendment by the 2003 Act,[45] introduces **18-12** a requirement to disclose material which might assist the case of the defence as well as material capable of undermining the prosecution case. Thus, the prosecutor is now required to disclose a broader range of material. It is not, however, as broad as the common law test of "relevance". Accordingly, there is still a great responsibility on the prosecutor as he must make a judgment as to whether material might reasonably be considered capable of either undermining the prosecution or assisting the accused. In many cases this will be obvious, for example inconsistent or contradictory statements made by a witness, conflicting descriptions of an offender, or the previous convictions of witnesses.[46] In other cases it might be more finely balanced. It is submitted that in determining what material might reasonably be capable of undermining the prosecution case or assisting the accused, the prosecutor must take a broad, common-sense approach. In such situations a sensible maxim may be "if in doubt, disclose".

"Prosecution material" is defined in s.3(2) as material connected to the case which is in the possession of the prosecutor or material in the possession of the police which the prosecutor has inspected. The words "in connection with the case for the prosecution against the accused" in s.3(2)(a) are to be widely construed in relation to the prosecutor's duty of

---

[42] *The Times*, May 21, 1999.
[43] Crown Prosecution Service Inspectorate, *Report on the Thematic Review of the Disclosure of Unused Matrial*, 2/2000 (March 2000).
[44] See, *e.g.*, *B* [2000] Crim.L.R. 50, in which the question of whether a social worker's report (of relevance to the credibility of a complainant in a case of sexual abuse) should be disclosed under s.3 was held to be a matter entirely for the prosecution and not the judge.
[45] s.32.
[46] Such disclosure must include relevant misconduct by police witnesses, *e.g.* disciplinary findings or details of cases stopped or quashed on appeal due to their misconduct: *Guney* [1998] 2 Cr.App.R. 242. In *McCartney* [2003] 6 *Archbold News* 2, the Court of Appeal held that, where crucial prosecution evidence comes from a witness with a prison record, the prosecution should seek out matters which are relevant to his conviction at an early stage, including seeking out prison records.

primary disclosure.[47] Moreover, the route by which material comes into the possession of the prosecutor is irrelevant.[48]

There is an increasing duty on the prosecution to actively seek out relevant material from third parties, especially if such third parties are government departments. The Attorney-General's Guidelines stipulate that, where it appears to an investigator, disclosure officer or prosecutor that a government department has material that may be relevant to an issue in the case, reasonable steps should be taken to identify and consider such material.[49] Moreover, where it is suspected that a non-government agency has material or information which might be disclosable if it were in the possession of the prosecution, consideration should be given as to whether it is appropriate to seek access to the material. It will be important to seek access to such material if the material or information is likely to undermine the prosecution case or assist a known defence.[50] However, in *Shannon*[51] police took over an investigation, and the investigative material obtained, from a newspaper. It was accepted that the procedure for primary disclosure did not apply to the newspaper investigation with the result that the prosecution were not under a duty to disclose the identity of the newspaper's informant (which the prosecution did not know). The Auld Review recommended consideration of a new statutory scheme for third party disclosure to operate alongside and more consistently with the general provisions for disclosure of unused material.[52]

18–13   There is a special duty of disclosure in cases where the prosecution rely on the evidence of a cellmate or fellow prisoner of the accused.[53] It has been generally recognised that such witnesses may, due to possible improper motives, be unreliable. Thus, in *Molloy*,[54] Lord Justice Roche said that there was a duty to research and disclose the history of any fellow prisoners called by the prosecution to give evidence of a confession.

Under the common law, the Court of Appeal held that failure to make disclosure was capable of amounting to a material irregularity in the trial, which was in the course of the trial because the obligation was a continuing one, for example in *Ward*[55] the failure to disclose the defendant's proclivity

---

[47] *Reid* [2002] 1 Cr.App.R. 21.

[48] Above. In *Reid* the material was the psychiatric report of one of the co-accused which came to the prosecution by virtue of an order of the trial judge. The Court of Appeal held that this was disclosable material within the meaning of s.3(2).

[49] para.29.

[50] para.30. See *Re Z (Children) (Disclosure: Criminal Proceedings)* [2003] 1 F.L.R. 1194, a decision of the Family Division in respect of statements made in family proceedings by a wife who was to give evidence in a criminal trial.

[51] [2001] 1 Cr.App.R. 168.

[52] "Review of Criminal Courts in England and Wales", Report by Lord Justice Auld (2001, Stationery Office, London), Ch.10—Third party disclosure.

[53] *Molloy*, unreported, July 30, 1997; *Pollit* (1992) 174 C.L.R. 558; *Bevan* (1993) 82 C.C.C. (3d) 310; and *Dodds v State of Oklahoma* 993 P2d 778.

[54] Above.

[55] (1993) 96 Cr.App.R. 1.

for attention-seeking, fantasy and the making and withdrawal of untrue confessions; in *Phillipson*[56] material relied upon by the prosecution in cross-examination of the defendant, but not revealed before then; in *Maguire*[57] the failure by a forensic scientist advising the prosecuting authority to reveal the results of certain tests which might have some bearing on the offence charged and the surrounding circumstances of the case. The Court has taken a similar approach to breaches of s.3. In both *Vasiliou*[58] (failure to disclose a prosecution witness's previous convictions) and *Langley*[59] (failure to disclose existence of records suggesting that the defendant had offered to act as an informant) such breaches led to the quashing of the convictions by the Court. In *Underwood*,[60] however, the Court of Appeal held that the non-disclosure of a witness's convictions did not affect the safety of the conviction because, even without the witness's evidence, the jury would inevitably have convicted. (See para.14–30, above, for rules on disclosure in identification cases, and para.14–45 for DNA cases.)

(2) Defence disclosure

Content of defence statement: ss.5 and 6A. After the prosecutor 18–14 complies, or purports to comply with, s.3 of the CPIA, the accused must prepare a defence statement. The relevant subsections of s.5 of the CPIA 1996 (as amended by the Criminal Justice Act 2003[61]) provide:

> "(5) Where this section applies, the accused must give a defence statement to the court and the prosecutor.
>
> (5A) Where there are other accused in the proceedings and the court so orders, the accused must also give a defence statement to each other accused specified by the court.
>
> (5B) The court may make an order under subsection (5A) either of its own motion or on the application of any party."

Section 6A provides:

> "(1) For the purposes of this Part a defence statement is a written statement—
>
> > (a) setting out the nature of the accused's defence, including any particular defences on which he intends to rely,

---

[56] (1990) 91 Cr.App.R. 226.
[57] (1992) 94 Cr.App.R. 13.
[58] [2000] Crim.L.R. 845.
[59] [2001] Crim.L.R. 651.
[60] (2003) 147 SJ 657.
[61] s.33 and Sch.37.

    (b) indicating the matters of fact on which he takes issue with the prosecution,

    (c) setting out, in the case of each such matter, why he takes issue with the prosecution, and

    (d) indicating any point of law (including any point as to the admissibility of evidence or an abuse of process) which he wishes to take, and any authority on which he intends to rely for that purpose.

(2) A defence statement that discloses an alibi must give particulars of it, including—

    (a) the name, address and date of birth of any witness the accused believes is able to give evidence in support of the alibi, or as many of those details as are known to the accused when the statement is given;

    (b) any information in the accused's possession which might be of material assistance in identifying or finding any such witness in whose case any of the details mentioned in paragraph (a) are not known to the accused when the statement is given.

(3) For the purposes of this section evidence in support of an alibi is evidence tending to show that by reason of the presence of the accused at a particular place or in a particular area at a particular time he was not, or was unlikely to have been, at the place where the offence is alleged to have been committed at the time of its allegation.

(4) The Secretary of State may by regulations make provision as to the details of the matters that, by virtue of subsection (1), are to be included in defence statements."

18–15   Under s.5 defence disclosure is made mandatory in trials on indictment. (Section 6 allows for voluntary disclosure by the defence in summary trials.[62]) Section 6A requires the defence to provide a more detailed statement than under s.5 of the CPIA 1996 before amended by the Criminal Justice Act 2003. The accused is required to set out the nature of his defence, including any specific defences on which he intends to rely and indicate any points of law he intends to take.

The defendant in a trial on indictment (after prosecution disclosure pursuant to s.3 has been made) is required to serve on the court, the prosecution, and to any other accused in the proceedings if the court so orders, a written defence statement setting out the nature of the defence and indicating the matters on which he takes issue with the prosecution and the reasons why he does so. When first introduced under the CPIA 1996, the

---

[62] Where the prosecutor complies, or purports to comply, with s.3 of the CPIA in summary proceedings, s.6(2) provides: "The accused—(a) may give a defence statement to the prosecutor, and (b) if he does so, must also give such a statement to the court."

requirement to provide a defence case statement amounted to a radical departure from previous practice. At common law the defendant was required to reveal nothing. As already noted, this rule was based on principles relating to the right of silence, the privilege against self-incrimination and the duty of the prosecution to prove its case.

In *Tibbs*,[63] a case prior to amendment by the 2003 Act, it was held that as the provisions in s.5 diminish the accused's right to silence and privilege against self-incrimination they should be strictly construed. The aim of the CPIA 1996 was to introduce a procedure to ensure that the defence and the prosecution should have an opportunity to investigate facts relied upon by the opposite party and so to reduce the risk of a miscarriage of justice by wrongful conviction or wrongful acquittal. Accordingly, it was held that the meaning of "defence statement" was not restricted to a description of the defence in very general terms but included the nature of the defence, the matters on which issue was taken, and the reasons for taking issue.

There is no discretion to waive the requirements under this section which is mandatory, whatever the case. These requirements were criticised by Lord Ackner in the debates on this Act in the House of Lords as assimilating criminal to civil procedure.[64] Accordingly, it is submitted that the provisions should be interpreted in a broad way in order to avoid the introduction of the technicalities of civil pleading into criminal trials. Thus, it is submitted that a statement such as "confession disputed due to oppression and inducement by police officers X and Y promising bail" should suffice for these purposes.

Sections 6A(2) and 6A(3) are similar to the provisions of ss.5(7) and 5(8) **18–16** of the CPIA, and provide for the regime for the disclosure of alibi evidence, which, prior to the 1996 Act, was governed by s.11 of the Criminal Justice Act 1967 (repealed by s.74 of the 1996 Act). Section 6A(2) provides that, if the defence statement discloses an alibi, particulars of the alibi must be given, including the names and addresses (if known) of any witness who the defendant believes is able to give evidence in support of the alibi and (if not known) any information in the defendant's possession which might be of material assistance in finding the witness. The purpose of these requirements is to enable the prosecution to interview the alibi witnesses in order not to be surprised by fresh evidence at trial. Accordingly, sufficient particularity must be given for this purpose, for example "the defendant will say that between ... and ... he was in the Dog and Duck public house and thereafter at home."

Section 11 of the 1967 Act provided that evidence of alibi could not be given without leave if the requirements of the section, *i.e.* to give notice of the particulars of alibi, were not complied with. Section 6A(2) does not contain any such provision. However, if the provisions of that subsection

---

[63] [2001] Crim.L.R. 759.
[64] *Hansard*, HL, Vol.667, col.1458.

are not complied with and evidence of the alibi is called, comment may be made and inferences drawn under s.11 of the Act; see para.18–20, below.

The wording of s.6A(3) in defining what is "evidence in support of an alibi" follows that in s.11(8) of the 1967 Act, *i.e.* "evidence tending to show that by reason of the presence of the accused at a particular place ... at a particular time he was not ... at the place where the offence is alleged to have been committed. ...." The Court of Appeal held that questions under s.11(8) as to the place at or date on which the offence is alleged to have been committed must be resolved by reference to the committal charges and the depositions: *Lewis*.[65] Reference must now be made to the statements and any other documentary evidence tendered at the committal. (For a direction by the judge in summing up cases, see para.16–19, above.)

18–17 Section 6B of the CPIA 1996, inserted by s.33 of the Criminal Justice Act 2003 (not yet in force at the time of writing), stipulates that where the accused has given a defence statement under either s.5 or 6 of the CPIA 1996, he must thereafter give the court and prosecutor an updated defence case statement.[66] The updated defence statement must comply with the requirements under s.6A by reference to the state of affairs at the time when the statement is given.[67] Instead of giving an updated defence statement, the accused may alternatively give a written statement to the effect that he has no changes to make to the defence statement originally given under either s.5 or 6.[68]

18–18 **Notification of intention to call defence witnesses: s.6C.** Section 6C(1) of the CPIA 1996, as amended by s.34 of the Criminal Justice Act 2003 (not yet in force at the time of writing), provides:

"(1) The accused must give to the court and the prosecutor a notice indicating whether he intends to call any persons (other than himself) as witnesses at his trial and, if so—

(a) Giving the name, address and date of birth of each such proposed witness, or as many of those details as are known to the accused when the notice is given;

(b) Providing any information in the accused's possession which might be of material assistance in identifying or finding any such proposed witness in whise case any of the details mentioned in paragraph (a) are not known to the accused when the notice is given."

This is a new requirement under the CPIA 1996, inserted by the 2003

---

[65] [1969] 2 Q.B. 1.
[66] s.6B(1)(a) of CPIA 1996.
[67] s.6B(3) of CPIA 1996.
[68] s.6B(4) of CPIA 1996.

Act. It requires the accused to serve, before trial, a notice giving the details of any witness he intends to call at his trial. The accused need not provide such details if they have already been provided pursuant to s.6A(2) as alibi witnesses.[69] If the accused decides to call additional witness to those on the notice, or decides not to call witnesses on the notice, he must give an appropriately amended notice to the court and prosecutor.[70] Section 21A (as inserted by the 2003 Act) provides that the Secretary of State shall prepare a code of practice giving guidance to police officers, and other persons charged with investigating offences, in relation to arranging and conducting interviews of witnesses disclosed by the defence pursuant to ss.6C and 6A(2) (alibi witnesses). There is no requirement that the defence identify the issue to which the witness relates or to disclose the evidence which the witness will give. The purpose of such disclosure is to enable the prosecution investigators to run checks on proposed defence witnesses, *i.e.* whether they have a criminal record, relevant antecedents, or, in the case of alibi, the exact location at the time of the offence. It is aimed at deterring "surprise witnesses" and "ambush defences".[71] Failure to give notice pursuant to s.6C does not prevent a witness from being called, this would clearly violate Art.6(3)(d) of the European Convention (see para.13–23 above). It does, however, create a risk of adverse comment under s.11 (see para.18–20 below). The danger with advance disclosure of defence witnesses is that such witnesses may feel inhibited about coming forward and may be subject to interference. Section 6C statements are to be provided by the defence to the prosecution and the court. There is no requirement for them to be served upon co-defendants. However, in *Cairns*[72] it was held that where a defendant intends to run a "cut throat" defence against another, the latter is entitled to a copy of any defence statement provided to the Crown. Similarly, it is likely that the details of any witnesses to be called on the defendant's behalf will similarly be the subject of disclosure to co-defendants, thus leaving them open to potential intimidation.

Notification of names of experts instructed by defendant: s.6D. Section 6D(1) of the CPIA, as amended by s.34 of the Criminal Justice Act 2003 (not yet in force at the time of writing), provides: 18–19

> "(1) If the accused instructs a person with a view to his providing any expert opinion for possible use as evidence at the trial of the accused, he must give to the court and the prosecutor a notice specifying the person's name and address."

[69] s.6C(2) of CPIA 1996.
[70] s.6C(4) of CPIA 1996.
[71] Standing Committee B, col.247, January 9, 2003.
[72] [2003] 1 Cr.App.R. 38.

Such notice need not be given if the expert's name and address have already been provided pursuant to s.6C. The requirement to provide details of any expert instructed by the defence is a new requirement under the CPIA 1996. Prior to s.6D, the defence could instruct an expert confident that if the expert's conclusion was adverse to the defendant, there would be no need to call the expert as a witness or disclose the expert's conclusion to the prosecution. The consequence of s.6D may be that, where the defence instructs an expert whom the defence decide not to call due to the adverse nature of his conclusion, the prosecution may subsequently be able to approach such witness as a potential prosecution witness, there being no property in a witness. Accordingly, s.6D may serve to hamper defence investigations and preparation for trial in that the defence may be reluctant to explore certain lines of investigation with an expert unless confident of the likely conclusion prior to instruction. (See paras 6–29 and 11–33 on privilege and compellability of experts.)

18–20   **Faults in defence disclosure: s.11.** Section 11 of the CPIA 1996, as amended by s.39 of the Criminal Justice Act 2003 (not in force at the time of writing), provides that the court or any other party may make such comment as appears appropriate, and that the court or jury may draw such inferences as appear proper in deciding whether the accused is guilty,[73] if the defendant fails to give a defence statement or an updated defence statement, or gives either out of time. Moreover, comment may be made and inferences drawn if the accused sets out inconsistent defences in his defence statement or at trial puts forward a defence which was not mentioned or is different from any defence set out in the statement. Similar provisions apply to alibis.

Leave of the court is required before a party may comment on the accused's reliance on a matter which was not mentioned in the defence statement, but which should have been pursuant to s.6A.[74] Comment may also be made and inferences drawn by the court (or by a party with leave of the court) if the accused calls witnesses at trial not identified in the witness notice or if the witness notice is not provided within the requisite time-limit.[75]

The provisions of s.11 were originally recommended by the Royal Commission on Criminal Justice.[76] The Commission said that the defendant will no doubt usually give reasons for late production of a defence, or for any difference between the defence raised at trial and that disclosed before trial. "[It] is then for the jury, aided by the judge in the summing-up,

---

[73] s.11(5) of CPIA 1996.
[74] s.11(6) of CPIA 1996.
[75] s.11(7) of CPIA 1996.
[76] Report (1993) Cm. 2263, para.6–70.

to decide whether or not they accept those reasons and to reach their verdict in the light of the evidence."[77]

In cases where a defendant puts forward a defence that is different from that in the defence statement, the court (when deciding whether to comment or draw an inference) is required to have regard to the extent of the difference and any jusitification for it (s.11(8)). This subsection would apply where the prosecution has changed its case or called new evidence. In these circumstances it would appear unlikely that the court would allow an inference to be drawn. On the other hand, if no such reason existed, the court is likely to permit an inference to be drawn. In a trial on indictment it will then be for the jury to determine whether to draw an inference or not. Similarly, before comment or drawing of an inference for an accused's failure to adequately include or identify witnesses in a witness notice, the court must have regard to any justification for such failure (s.11(9)).

In *Tibbs*,[78] (a case decided prior to amendment of s.11 by the 2003 Act) **18–21** it was held that s.11 did not disallow or require leave for cross-examination of an accused on differences between a defence at trial and a defence statement. Leave was, however, required before comment or invitation to the jury to draw inferences from the differences could be made by either the prosecution or co-defendants. The amendments to s.11 by the 2003 Act result in such leave no longer being required.

In *Wheeler*[79] the defendant attributed discrepancies between his evidence and the contents of his defence case statement to an error on the part of his solicitors. The prosecution did not seek leave to comment on the matter (thereby apparently accepting the explanation). The judge, however, in his summing-up, proceeded to comment on the discrepancy between the defence at trial and the defence case statement. On appeal the conviction was quashed. The Court of Appeal stated that, while there was no statutory requirement that defence case statements be signed by defendants as an acknowledgment of their accuracy, it was, however, wise that a signature be obtained to prevent any errors or discrepancies. Thus, a local practice direction requiring that defendants sign defence case statements was declared unlawful by the Divisional Court.[80] In practice, however, it is preferable for such statements to be signed.[81] Section 6E of the CPIA 1996, inserted by the Criminal Justice Act 2003 (not in force at the time of writing), provides that where an accused's solicitor purports to give either a

---

[77] *ibid.*
[78] Above.
[79] [2001] 1 Cr.App.R. 10.
[80] *R (Sullivan) v Crown Court at Maidstone* [2002] 1 W.L.R. 2747.
[81] In *Crown Court at Maidstone* it was stated *per curiam* that if a defence case statement is not signed it would be within the powers of the Crown Court to require the defendant to satisfy the court that he had complied with s.5 and the document tendered really was his defence statement. If that involved extra cost which need not have been incurred it might be necessary to consider whether those costs should be paid by the defendant or those who advised him not to sign.

defence case statement or an updated defence statement, it shall be deemed to be given with the authority of the accused unless the contrary is proved.

Under s.11(5), if the section applies, the jury may draw "such inferences as appear proper". In *Cowan*[82] (a case concerned with similar provisions in s.35 of the Criminal Justice and Public Order Act 1994) Lord Taylor C.J. said that the phrase "such inferences as appear proper" was doubtless intended to leave a broad discretion to a trial judge to decide in all the circumstances whether any proper inference was capable of being drawn: if not, he should tell the jury so; otherwise it was for the jury to decide whether in fact an inference should properly be drawn.[83] The jury must be told that an inference alone could not prove guilt.[84] Section 11(10) provides that a person shall not be convicted of an offence solely on the basis of any adverse inference drawn.

(3) Prosecutor's continuing duty of disclosure: s.7A

18–22   Section 7A is inserted into the CPIA 1996 by the Criminal Justice Act 2003 (not in force at the time of writing). It replaces the previous s.7 (secondary disclosure) and s.9 (continuing duty), which are repealed. Thus, the secondary disclosure stage is removed from the disclosure process and the prosecutor is now simply under a continuing duty of disclosure. Section 7A applies at all times after the prosecutor has provided initial prosecution disclosure under s.3 or purported to do so (s.7A(1)). The duty under this section continues until the trial is over as a result of acquittal or conviction or because prosecutor abandons the case. This duty reflects the common law where it was held that the duty of disclosure upon the prosecution was a continuing one. Thus, in *Maguire*[85] the Court of Appeal said:

> "The Court has now consistently taken the view that a failure to disclose what is known or possessed and which ought to have been disclosed, is an 'irregularity in the course of the trial'. Why there was no disclosure is an irrelevant question, and if it be asked how the irregularity was 'in the course of the trial' it can be answered that the duty of disclosure is a continuing one."

The prosecutor must keep under review, in particular following the provision of a defence statement, the question of whether there is any prosecution material that meets the disclosure requirements set out in s.3 (material which might reasonably be considered capable of undermining the case for the prosecution against the accused or of assisting the case for the accused which has not already been disclosed to the accused) (s.7A(2)).

[82] [1995] 3 W.L.R. 818.
[83] At 823–824.
[84] *Tibbs*, above.
[85] (1992) 94 Cr.App.R. 133, 146.

Such material must be disclosed as soon as is practicable. When reviewing the disclosure, the prosecutor must take account of the state of affairs at the time, including the prosecution case (s.7A(4)). "Prosecution material" is defined as material which is in the prosecutor's possession and came into his possession in connection with the case for the prosecution against the accused or which he has been allowed to inspect under Pt 2 (s.7A(6)). Where the prosecutor receives a defence statement pursuant to ss.5, 6 or 6B, he must make any further disclosure required within the time-limits specified in regulations made under s.12 of the CPIA 1996 or provide a written notice that no such further disclosure is required (s.7A(5)).

Material must not be disclosed under the section if there is an order of the court forbidding it on the grounds of public interest immunity (s.7A(8)) (see Ch.12) or where the disclosure of material is prohibited by s.17 of the Regulation of Investigatory Powers Act 2000 (s.7A(9)).

(4) Disputes about disclosure: s.8

Sections 8(1) and (2) of the CPIA 1996, as amended by the Criminal Justice Act 2003, provide: **18–23**

> "(1) This section applies where the accused gives a defence statement under section 5, 6 or 6B and the prosecutor has complied with section 7A(5) or has purported to comply with it or has failed to comply with it.
>
> (2) If the accused has at any time reasonable cause to believe that there is prosecution material which is required by section 7A to be disclosed to him and has not been, he may apply to the court for an order requiring the prosecutor to disclose it to him."

Any dispute about disclosure is to be resolved by the court. Thus, s.8 permits the defendant to apply to the court for the disclosure of undisclosed material which he has reasonable cause to believe might reasonably be expected to assist the defence disclosed in the defence statement or updated defence statement. The section only applies where the defendant has given a defence statement and the prosecutor has made disclosure under s.7A(5) or has failed to comply with that section. The section does not apply to material for which the prosecution successfully make a claim for public interest immunity.[86]

The effect of the section is to give the court power to order disclosure in cases where there is dispute. Under the common law the court had such a power which extended to a power to order disclosure of any relevant material. This section represents the residue of the common law power

---

[86] See para.12–12, above, for a discussion of claims for public interest immunity.

under the new disclosure regime. In *Law*[87] the Court of Appeal held that under the common law a judge, when deciding whether to order disclosure, was not restricted to considering admissible evidence but could himself decide what material he required in order to make the decision.

It will be for the defence to establish why the material might be expected to assist them. The requirement that it might "reasonably be expected" to assist means that fishing expeditions or fanciful possibilities will not suffice as reasons for an order for disclosure. On the other hand, if proper explanation of the relevance of the material and as to how it might assist is given, the court will be under a duty to order disclosure in the interests of a fair trial.

D. Code of Practice: Part II of the 1996 Act

18–24   Detailed procedures for prosecution disclosure are contained in a Code of Practice, prepared by the Home Secretary and laid before Parliament. (The Code came into force on April 1, 1997.) Section 23 requires the Home Secretary to prepare a Code of Practice to guide the police (and others conducting criminal investigations) in relation to unused material obtained in such investigations.[88] The purpose of the Code is to ensure that: (a) the police record, retain and make this material available to the prosecutor; (b) if disclosure is requested by the prosecutor, the defence is given the material; and (c) the prosecutor is given a written statement that the activities prescribed by the Code have been carried out: s.23(1). The police are required to record and retain only relevant material. Therefore, material which has no bearing on the case which may have been seized by the police during a search does not have to be retained. The duty to obtain and/or retain material under both the Code and Attorney-General's Guidelines was considered in detail by the Divisional Court in *Ebrahim*.[89] The effects of a breach of the Code are considered at para.18–27 below.

The Royal Commission on Criminal Justice recommended that the detailed procedures for prosecution disclosure should be governed by subordinate legislation or codes of practice.[90] Section 23 follows that recommendation. (The Code also resembles those issued by the Home Secretary under s.66 of the Police and Criminal Evidence Act 1984.)

18–25   Under the Code, the disclosure scheme operates as follows:

---

[87] *The Times*, August 15, 1996.
[88] The definition of "criminal investigation" in the Code of Practice includes investigations in the belief that an offence might have been committed. It is possible for an investigation to have begun before the alleged commission of an offence, particularly where surveillance on a series of offences take place over a period of time. It is a question of fact in each case for the court to determine whether a series of offences formed part of an investigation and when the investigation began. *R v Uxbridge Magistrates Court Ex p. Patel* [2000] Crim.L.R. 383.
[89] *R (Ebrahim) v Feltham Magistrates' Court* [2001] 1 W.L.R. 1293.
[90] Report (1993) Cm. 2263, para.6.53.

(a) the appointment in a criminal investigation of an "officer in charge" of the investigation and of a "disclosure officer" who is responsible for the administration of the investigation, including the operation of the disclosure scheme;

(b) "the investigator" (*i.e.* any police officer involved in the conduct of the investigation) is responsible for retaining any material obtained or generated in the investigation (such material to include crime reports, differing versions of statements, interview records, experts' reports and material casting doubt on the reliability of witnesses or confessions);

(c) the disclosure officer prepares a schedule of the unused material which has been retained and a separate schedule of sensitive material (to include material relating to national security or informants, material given in confidence, material liable to reveal either the location of premises used for police surveillance or police techniques, and material which might facilitate the commission of offences or hinder the detection of crime);

(d) the disclosure officer must then send the schedules to the prosecutor, together with copies of any material either showing conflicting descriptions or the unreliability of witnesses or confessions, or containing any explanation by the accused for the offence;

(e) after the defence statement is filed, the disclosure officer must look again at the retained material and draw the prosecutor's attention to any which might reasonably be expected to assist the defence disclosed;

(f) the disclosure officer must then certify to the prosecutor that to the best of his knowledge and belief the duties imposed by the Code have been complied with.

Section 23(1)(a) of the 1996 Act ensures that the Code must require an **18–26** investigator to take all reasonable steps for the purposes of the investigation and must pursue all reasonable lines of inquiry. This provision follows recommendations made in the "Scott Report" (*i.e.* the *Report of the Inquiry into the Export of Defence Equipment and Dual-Use Goods to Iraq and Related Prosecutions*[91]). However, according to the Minister of State (speaking in the debates on this Act in the House of Lords), it was felt that something more was needed: it was thought that the code of practice should require the investigator to pursue all reasonable lines of inquiry in a criminal investigation, whether these point towards or away from the

---

[91] HMSO (1996) 115 at para.K5.1.

suspect (and para.3.4 of the Code so provides). The Minister said: "This should help to ensure that relevant material is not overlooked. It also provides statutory backing for what is already regarded as good investigative practice."[92] What constitute "reasonable steps" and "reasonable lines of inquiry" will depend on the circumstances of each case and the subjective judgment of the officer in charge.

Section 26(1) requires persons other than police officers, charged with the duty of conducting criminal investigations, to have regard to the provisions of the Code of Practice. A similar (although differently worded and less widely drawn) provision appears in s.67(9) of the Police and Criminal Evidence Act 1984. That subsection has been held to apply the Code (implemented under the 1984 Act), *inter alia*, to customs officers, store detectives, commercial investigators and employees of a private company investigating copyright offences: see para.9–28, above. Thus, in *Smith*,[93] the Court of Appeal said that the question whether a person is charged with the duty of investigating offences under s.67(9) of the 1984 Act is a question of mixed law and fact, involving an examination of the statute, contract or other authority under which he carries out his functions, and a consideration of his actual work.

18–27   The effect of s.26(3) is to make the provisions of the Code admissible in evidence, while under s.26(4) a court must take a breach of the Code into account in deciding any question to which it is relevant. (These subsections follow s.67(11) of the 1984 Act.) Thus, a court—in deciding a question of admissibility of evidence where it is alleged that this Code has been breached—must, first, determine whether there has been a breach and then, if so, what effect it has upon admissibility. While the courts have tended to ignore technical or trivial breaches of the Code when determining questions of admissibility under the 1984 Act, "significant and substantial" breaches have led to the exclusion of evidence: *Absolam*[94]; *Keenan*[95]; *Walsh*.[96] Similarly, in *Ebrahim*[97] the Divisional Court held that where there had been a breach of the Code any unfairness resulting from it should normally be dealt with in the course of the trial. A stay of proceedings as an abuse of process would, however, be appropriate if the defendant could show, on the balance of probabilities, either (i) that by reason of such a breach he would suffer serious prejudice to the extent that it was impossible for a fair trial to be held; or (ii) that there had been such bad faith or serious fault on the part of the police or prosecutor that it was not fair that the defendant should be tried.

---

[92] *Hansard*, HL, Vol.573, col.963.
[93] (1994) 99 Cr.App.R. 233, 240.
[94] (1989) 88 Cr.App.R. 332; cited at para.9–31, above.
[95] (1990) 90 Cr.App.R. 1.
[96] (1991) 91 Cr.App.R. 161.
[97] Above.

E. Conclusion

The significance of the CPIA 1996 disclosure scheme, as amended by the **18–28**
Criminal Justice Act 2003, is fourfold:

(a) the prosecutor has the prime responsibility of deciding what material should be disclosed: this would no longer be the responsibility of the court (except in cases of dispute);

(b) the responsibility is no longer to disclose all "relevant" material but only that which undermines the prosecution case or assists the case of the accused;

(c) this duty on the prosecution is now statutory;

(d) the defence is required (in the generality of cases) to make disclosure of its case and identify defence witnesses and experts before the trial commences.

During debates on the CPIA 1996, the Minister of State at the Home Office said that the Government believed that the scheme would prove more effective in convicting the guilty, while not prejudicing the acquittal of the innocent.[98] The scheme was also welcomed in principle by Lord Taylor C.J. who, during the debate on this Act in the House of Lords, said that he believed that the House could endorse the wisdom of clarifying by statute what had become a complex and, in a number of respects, unsatisfactory area of the law.[99] However, the scheme did not receive a universal welcome, and (according to a newspaper report) the Bar Council, the Law Society, Justice and Liberty said that it went too far in lightening the burden of disclosure on the prosecution.[1] The changes made by the Criminal Justice Act 2003 go some way in addressing such concerns.

The 1996 Act reflected recommendations made in the Scott Report[2]   **18–29**
(which was published during the passage of the 1996 Act through Parliament). These recommendations related to the duties upon the prosecution to obtain and disclose relevant material from government departments and other agencies and to refer any dispute as to the adequacy of disclosure to the court (it being incumbent on the defence in seeking additional disclosure to specify the lines of defence rendering the disclosure relevant). The regime established by the Act and Code of Practice represents the Government's response: according to the Minister of State, Home Office, it provides a clear audit trail whenever requests for documents elicit items which may be relevant to the investigation and imposes specific new disclosure duties on

---

[98] *Hansard*, HL, Vol.567, col.465.
[99] *Hansard*, HL, Vol.567, col.476, 477.
[1] *The Times*, November 27, 1995.
[2] *Report of the Inquiry into the Export of Defence Equipment and Dual-Use Goods to Iraq and Related Prosecutions*, HMSO (1996) 115 at para.K5.1.

the prosecutor and the accused which are designed to clarify the issues in dispute.[3]

F. The European Convention on Human Rights

18–30   The European Court of Human Rights has issued strong statements on the accused's right to disclosure at all stages of the proceedings.[4] In *Edwards v UK*[5] the European Court said that (a) it is a requirement of fairness under Art.6(1) of the Convention (which guarantees the right to a fair trial) that prosecuting authorities disclose to the defence all material evidence for or against the accused and (b) failure to do so gave rise to a defect in the trial proceedings. (*Edwards* was decided under the common law rules which (the Court acknowledged) recognised disclosure as a requirement of fairness.)

The question whether failure to make proper disclosure will be held to have deprived a defendant of a fair trial under Art.6 will depend on the circumstances of the particular case. In *Edwards*, the Court said that its task is to ascertain whether the proceedings in their entirety, including the way in which the evidence was taken, were fair. Thus, in *Miailhe v France (No.2)*[6] the applicant complained of a breach of Art.6 because he was denied access to documents seized from him in violation of Art.8 and which he needed in order to contest fraud charges. The Court said that it had to satisfy itself that the proceedings as a whole were fair: (a) having regard to any possible irregularities before the case was brought before the courts; and (b) checking whether the courts were able to remedy them.[7] Accordingly, it would be open to a court to find that, if some material was not disclosed (although lawful under the present scheme), the defendant was deprived of a fair trial in violation of Art.6.

The decisions of the European Court in relation to disclosure and public interest immunity will potentially have far-reaching consequences for the public immunity procedure in criminal proceedings.[8] These cases, and their potential impact, are considered at paras 12–18 and 12–22 above.

Now that the European Convention on Human Rights has been incorporated into domestic law, it is especially important that courts (and

---

[3] *Hansard*, HL, Vol.573, col.963. It may be noted that in *Blackledge*, *The Times*, November 8, 1995, Lord Taylor C.J. said that documents in the possession of one or other government departments involved in granting export licences were to be regarded as in the possession of the Crown as an "indivisible entity".
[4] The European Court found a violation of Art.5(4) where material from an anonymous witness had been shown to the judge, but not the defence, leading to a decision withholding bail: *Garcia Alva v Germany* (2003) 37 E.H.R.R. 12.
[5] (1993) 15 E.H.R.R. 417, para.36.
[6] (1997) 23 E.H.R.R. 491.
[7] para.43.
[8] *Rowe and Davis v UK* 30 E.H.R.R. 1; *Jasper v UK* 30 E.H.R.R. 441; *Fitt v UK* 30 E.H.R.R. 480; and *Edwards and Lewis v UK* (Application Nos 39647/98 and 40461/98) Judgment of July 22, 2003.

prosecutors), when determining issue of disclosure, have Art.6 in mind.[9] (See Ch.13, above, for the effect of incorporation of the Convention into English Law and paras 13–14 *et seq.* for Art.6, in particular para.13–18 for the rights necessary for the preparation and conduct of the defence.)

4. OTHER STATUTORY RULES[10]

A. Expert evidence

Provision is made in s.81 of the Police and Criminal Evidence Act 1984 for Crown Court rules to require any party to proceedings before the Crown Court to disclose expert evidence which the party seeks to adduce. The Crown Court (Advance Notice of Expert Evidence) Rules 1987 have been made under this section. (Section 20 of the Criminal Procedure and Investigations Act 1996 permitted these rules to be extended to apply to magistrates' courts also.) These rules are discussed at para.8–35, above. For disclosure in identification cases, see para.14–30 above, and para.14–45 for disclosure in DNA cases.

18–31

B. The defence in serious fraud cases

Section 9(5) of the Criminal Justice Act 1987 permits the judge to order a defendant in a case of serious and complex fraud to provide a statement in writing setting out in general terms the nature of the defence.[11] Such a statement need not disclose the identity of defence witnesses (except in so far as disclosure is required in relation to alibi witnesses and experts, above). When ordering disclosure the judge must warn the defendant of the possible consequences under s.10(1) of not complying with it, *i.e.* possible comment by the judge and prosecution and the drawing of an adverse inference by the jury (s.9(7)).

18–32

These provisions are based on recommendations made by the Fraud Trials Committee in their report.[12] The Committee gave these reasons for recommending disclosure: to shorten trials and clarify issues for the jury. While these provisions should have that effect, they will apply in a very small number of cases.

As has been seen, s.10(1) of the Act provides the court with a sanction if

---

[9] For an analysis of whether the disclosure provisions of the CPIA 1996 are likely to be successfully challenged at the ECHR, see S.D. Sharpe, "Article 6 and the Disclosure of Evidence in Criminal Trials" [1999] Crim.L.R. 273; and, for argument that the CPIA 1996 increases the imbalance between the state and the individual but that incorporation will not necessarily lead to a "declaration of incompatibility", see S.D. Sharpe, "Disclosure, Immunity and Fair Trials" (1999) 63 Jo.Crim.L. 67.
[10] See para.2–21 above for effect of ss.17 and 18 of Regulation of Investigatory Powers Act 2000.
[11] Such an order can only be made where the prosecution have supplied the court and defence with a case statement.
[12] (1986) paras 6.71 *et seq.*

the defence fails to make disclosure under s.9(3). As the Committee pointed out, such a failure may be relevant to the credibility of the defence. Whether it is relevant or not will depend upon the circumstances of the particular case. The defendant's lawyers may be responsible for the failure, in which case the defendant's credibility is not in issue. On the other hand, a strong comment might be expected where the defendant himself is responsible for the failure to make disclosure and the defence only emerges at trial. In these circumstances, the jury would be entitled to ask itself why the defence had not been put forward earlier. Is there an explanation other than the defendant's failure to think of it until the last minute?

18–33   The following limits on the judge's power should be noted.

(a) A judge exercising powers under s.9(5) of the Act at a preparatory hearing may not order that a defendant disclose a statement of his defence to a co-defendant or that defendants have leave to inspect the statement of a co-defendant.[13]

(b) A judge does not have power to prevent the prosecution re-interviewing their witnesses and asking further questions arising out of a defence case statement.[14]

---

[13] *Re Tariq* [1991] 1 W.L.R. 101.
[14] *Nadir* [1993] 1 W.L.R. 1322.

CHAPTER 19

Course of Evidence

1. CALLING WITNESSES

A. Obligation on the parties

(1) Prosecution

The usual practice at trials on indictment is for the prosecution either to call   **19–01**
all the witnesses whose statements were served at the committal proceedings to give evidence, or to tender such witnesses for cross-examination, or
to read their statements. (The same principles apply in the magistrates'
court.[1])

However, prosecution counsel does have a discretion not to call witnesses
in certain circumstances: and the judge has no power to order him to call
the witnesses.[2] This discretion was outlined by Lord Parker C.J. in *Oliva*[3]
where he said:

> "The prosecution must of course have in the court witnesses whose
> names are on the back of the indictment,[4] but there is a wide discretion
> in the prosecution whether they should call them either calling and
> examining them, or calling and tendering them for cross-examination.
> The prosecution does not, of course, put forward every witness as a
> witness of truth, but where the witness's evidence is capable of belief,
> then it is their duty, well recognised, that he should be called, even
> though the evidence that he is going to give is inconsistent with the case
> sought to be proved. Their discretion must be exercised in a manner
> which is calculated to further the interests of justice, and at the same
> time be fair to the defence. If the prosecution appear to be exercising
> that discretion improperly, it is open to the judge of trial to interfere
> and in his discretion in turn to invite the prosecution to call a particular

---

[1] *Haringey JJ. Ex p. DPP* [1996] 2 Cr.App.R. 119. For the substitution of a new system for committal proceedings in the case of offences triable only on indictment, see para.18–01, n.1, above.
[2] *Baldwin* [1978] Crim.L.R. 104; *Roberts* (1984) 80 Cr.App.R. 89, 93.
[3] (1965) 49 Cr.App.R. 298, 309–310.
[4] It was formerly the practice to place the names of prosecution witnesses on the back of the indictment.

witness, and, if they refuse, there is the ultimate sanction in the judge himself calling that witness."[5]

Consequently, if a witness is capable of belief, the prosecution is bound to call him, albeit that his evidence is inconsistent with the prosecution case.[6] For instance, in a case of wounding, some witnesses may give an account of the offence which does not coincide with that given by the victim. The prosecution is not entitled to refuse to call the witnesses merely for that reason. On the other hand, if it is considered that the witnesses are not telling the truth in the account which they have given, other considerations may apply. Thus, it may happen that the witnesses are close friends or relatives of the defendant and are deliberately telling an untrue story, in order to provide him with a defence. In these circumstances, the prosecution is not obliged to call the witnesses.[7] A *fortiori*, the prosecution is under no obligation to call witnesses whose statements form part of the unused material and have never formed part of the prosecution case.[8]

19–02   In giving guidance on the exercise of the prosecutor's discretion in these circumstances, the Court of Appeal in *Russell-Jones*[9] said that the prosecutor ought normally to call all the witnesses who give direct evidence of the primary facts of the case, unless for good reason the prosecutor regards the witness's evidence as unworthy of belief. This is so that the jury have available all the evidence of what actually happened, which the prosecution

---

[5] Authority for the rule that the prosecution is not bound to call all its witnesses, in the above circumstances, is also to be found in *Seneviratne v R* [1936] 3 All E.R. 36 P.C.; *Adel Muhammed El Dabbab v Att-Gen for Palestine* [1944] A.C. 156, P.C.; *Woodhead* (1847) 2 C. & K. 520 (Alderson B.); *Edwards* (1848) 3 Cox. C.C. 82, 83 (Erle J.); *Cassidy* (1858) 1 F. & F. 79 (Parke B.).

[6] The same rule applies in the magistrates' court. Thus in *Wellingborough JJ. Ex p. Francois* (1994) 158 J.P. 813 the Divisional Court held that in a summary trial a prosecutor had failed to exercise her discretion properly (and the justices had failed to do so at all) when the prosecutor did not call two prosecution witnesses (at court at the request of the defence) or tender them for cross-examination because she was due to prosecute another case in another court.

[7] See, *e.g.*, *Nugent* (1977) 65 Cr.App.R.40, in which Park J. ruled that there was no obligation to call eight witnesses whose statements had been rendered in committal proceedings and supported the defendant's alibi; and *Tregear* [1967] 2 Q.B. 574, in which the Court of Appeal held that the judge was right in deciding that the prosecution were entitled not to call two witnesses who could not be put forward as truthful witnesses. On the other hand, in *Balmforth* [1992] Crim.L.R. 825 the prosecutor, having been referred by the judge to *Nugent*, decided not to tender a witness for cross-examination, although he had originally considered the witness to be capable of belief and intended to tender him. The Court of Appeal held that the witness should have been tendered because there was a duty to tender any witness capable of belief. The Court said that if such a witness causes inconvenience to the prosecution the solution may be not to include his statement in the committal bundle. It is submitted with respect that this must be right. If this difficulty is to be avoided, proper vetting of the statements before committal is required. If this is done the prosecution will not find themselves in the position of the prosecutor in *Balmforth*. (The statement will then have to be handed to the defence as part of the unused material.) Note, also, *Anderson* [1995] Crim.L.R. 831 where the Court of Appeal said that *Nugent* was merely an example of the principle laid down in *Oliva* that the prosecutor does not have the duty of calling a witness whose evidence is not capable of belief.

[8] *Richardson* (1994) 98 Cr.App.R. 174.

[9] [1995] 1 Cr.App.R. 538, 544–555.

(when serving the statements) considered material, even if there are inconsistencies between one witness and another. The Court said that it is for the prosecutor to decide which witnesses give direct evidence of the primary facts of the case and, also, to determine whether a witness is incredible or unworthy of belief. In carrying out the latter task, the prosecutor should not condemn a witness as incredible merely because his evidence is at variance with that of a large number of other witnesses, but the prosecutor is not obliged to proffer a witness merely in order to give the defence material to attack the credit of other prosecution witnesses. In determining whether a witness is worthy of belief the prosecutor should have regard to the content of evidence rather than credit generally (unless the witness has been convicted of perverting the course of justice): a collateral act of dishonesty would not mean that a witness's evidence on an unrelated matter was not true.[10] Thus, the Divisional Court held that the prosecution should have called a police officer in a case where the witness gave evidence of an assault on himself and another officer and where his evidence was central to the case, although he was suspended at the time pending a disciplinary hearing on matters unrelated to the case.[11] In *Brown and Brown*[12] the Court of Appeal said that nowadays "the primary time" when the prosecution should decide whether to call a witness was at the Plea and Directions Hearing in the Crown Court, although the decision may have to be reconsidered in the light of changed circumstances.

The fact that the prosecution has a discretion not to call a witness does not affect the rule that the prosecution must have all witnesses (who are required to attend) available at the trial.[13] Where, however, the prosecution is not able to secure the attendance of a witness by circumstances beyond its control, for example the witness has disappeared and cannot be traced, the prosecution must take all reasonable steps to secure the attendance of the witness; but if it proves impossible to secure his attendance, the court may in its discretion permit the trial to proceed in the absence of the witness, provided that no injustice will be done thereby.[14]

(2) Defence

The defence is not obliged to call any witnesses. The defendant himself is   **19–03** not obliged to give evidence. However, if he fails to do so the court or jury (under s.35 of the Criminal Justice and Public Order Act 1994) may draw such inferences as appear proper. See para.17–16, above, for discussion.

---

[10] *Haringey JJ. Ex p. DPP* [1996] 2 Cr.App.R. 119.
[11] *ibid.*
[12] [1997] 1 Cr.App.R. 112, 113.
[13] *Woodhead*, above.
[14] *Cavanagh and Shaw* (1972) 56 Cr.App.R. 407; *Gallagher* [1983] Crim.L.R. 335.

B. Order of witnesses

19–04 In general, counsel has a discretion as to the order in which he calls witnesses. There would appear to be no authority for this principle in criminal proceedings. However, the Divisional Court held in *Briscoe v Briscoe*[15] that counsel had such a discretion in a matrimonial suit.

This practice is followed in criminal trials. This practice is subject to one important exception: evidence given by the defendant. Section 79 of the Police and Criminal Evidence Act 1984 provides that the defendant must give evidence before any witness he intends to call to the facts of the case "unless the court in its discretion otherwise directs." This section made the common law statutory.[16] The reasons for the rule would appear to be twofold: (a) so that the defendant gives his evidence without being able to tailor it to fit in with what he has heard his witness say; and (b) so that the defendant gains no advantage over the witnesses for the prosecution, who are normally kept out of court until they give evidence.[17]

In *Smith*[18] the Court of Criminal Appeal said that there were only rare exceptions to the rule, for example, a formal witness or a witness about whom there is no controversy. The Criminal Law Revision Committee (on whose recommendation s.79 is based) considered that this view was too restricted and that the court should have a wider discretion to allow a witness to be called before the defendant, for example a witness who is to give evidence about events before those about which the defendant is to give evidence. Section 79 does give the court a wide discretion. However, it was unusual under the common law for a witness to be called before the defendant; and and has remained so under s.79.

C. Witnesses remain out of court until called

19–05 The general rule is that witnesses remain out of court until they are called.[19] The only exception to this rule is in the case of experts. The rule applies equally to witnesses for the prosecution and witnesses for the defence. (Witnesses as to the defendant's character are sometimes also allowed to remain in court; but this is by no means a universal practice and is only permitted with the consent of the prosecution.)

The reason for the rule is to avoid the risk that witnesses will tailor their evidence because of what they have heard other witnesses say. On the other hand, the expert needs to hear the evidence of the witnesses because his opinion is based on the facts. This, however, is a rule of practice not a rule

---

[15] [1968] P. 501.
[16] *Morrison* (1911) 6 Cr.App.R. 159 at 165, *per* Lord Alverstone C.J.; *Smith* [1968] 1 W.L.R. 636; (1968) 52 Cr.App.R. 224.
[17] Criminal Law Revision Committee, Eleventh Report, Cmnd. 4991, para.107.
[18] (1968) 52 Cr.App.R. 224, 225.
[19] For a general statement of the practice, see *Bexley JJ. Ex p. King* [1980] R.T.R. 49, 50–51, *per* Waller L.J.

of law.[20] Accordingly, a judge may not prohibit a witness from giving evidence because he has been in court, if no order has been made excluding witnesses.[21]

D. Power of judge to call witnesses

A judge cannot order the prosecution to call a witness.[22] However, in criminal proceedings the judge has power to call a witness himself[23] but it is a power which should be exercised sparingly. Thus, in *Cleghorn*,[24] Lord Parker C.J. said:

19–06

> "It is abundantly clear that a judge in a criminal case where the liberty of the subject is at stake and where the sole object of the proceedings is to make certain that justice should be done as between the subject and the state should have the right to call a witness who has not been called by either party. It is clear, of course, that the discretion to call such a witness should be carefully exercised, and indeed, as it was said in *Edwards*[25] by Erle J.: 'There are, no doubt, cases in which a judge might think it a matter of justice so to interfere, but generally speaking, we ought to be careful not to overrule the discretion of counsel who are, of course, more fully aware of the facts of the case than we can be.'"

It is, accordingly, exceptional for a judge to call a witness. Whether he does so or not is a matter for his discretion[26] which should be exercised for achieving the ends of justice and fairness.[27] In any case, the judge should not call a witness after the close of the defence case, unless a matter has arisen unexpectedly which could not have been foreseen.[28] However, the rule may be departed from in an exceptional case.[29] The same rules apply to magistrates' courts.[30]

If a witness appears reluctant to give evidence, the judge in an appropriate case may warn him of the consequences of his refusing to do so

---

[20] *Bexley JJ. Ex p. King*, above, *per* Waller L.J.; *Moore v Registrar of Lambeth County Court* [1969] 1 W.L.R. 141, 142, *per* Edmund Davies L.J.
[21] *Briggs* [1930] 22 Cr.App.R. 68; *Thomson (No.2)* [1967] Crim.L.R. 62; *Moore v Registrar of Lambeth County Court*, above, *per* Edmund Davies L.J.
[22] *Baldwin* [1978] Crim.L.R. 104.
[23] *Chapman* (1838) 8 C. & P. 558; *Holden* (1838) 8 C. & P. 606; *Harris* [1927] 2 K.B. 587, 594, *per* Avory J.; *Cleghorn*, below, *per* Lord Parker C.J.; *Roberts* (1985) 80 Cr.App.R. 89; *Wallwork* (1958) 42 Cr.App.R. 153, 159.
[24] [1967] 2 Q.B. 584, 587.
[25] (1848) 3 Cox C.C. 82, 93.
[26] *Roberts*, above.
[27] *Grafton* [1992] 3 W.L.R. 532, 536.
[28] *Harris*, above; *Day* (1940) 27 Cr.App.R. 168.
[29] *Tregear* [1967] 2 Q.B. 574.
[30] *Webb v Leadbetter* [1966] 1 W.L.R. 245, 247; *Phelan v Back* (1972) 56 Cr.App.R. 257.

(including the consequence of punishment to himself), but should not ask him whether his witness statement is true.[31]

19–07   These rules do not affect the power of a judge at any stage of the trial to recall a witness who has already given evidence to put such questions as the interests of justice require.[32] Thus, for instance, a witness may be recalled to deal with matters which should have been put to him in cross-examination.

The judge may also question witnesses during the course of their examination by counsel. This is sometimes necessary in order to clarify a point. However, the judge should not generally descend into the arena and his questioning should not amount to an invitation to disregard what was being said or active interference with counsel in pursuit of their task.[33] (Lord Taylor C.J. emphasised that it was most undesirable for a judge to interrupt a witness, particularly a defendant, when giving evidence since it was for counsel to conduct examination and cross-examination of witnesses and for the judge to see that they did it fairly.)[34] In *Cameron*,[35] however, the Court of Appeal held that a judge had been right to take over the cross-examination of a 14-year-old complainant in a rape trial after she refused to answer questions put to her by defence counsel.[36]

The Court of Appeal supported the recommendation of the Royal Commission on Criminal Justice to the effect that judges should become more interventionist in order to curb prolixity, repetition or irrelevance and to exclude discursiveness and the oppression of witnesses.[37] However, the Court in the same case reiterated that the judge should not intervene with such frequency and hostility as to deny a defendant a fair hearing and to convey to the jury the judge's disbelief of the defendant's evidence.

2. SWEARING WITNESSES

19–08   The general rule is that the oral evidence of a witness is not admissible unless he has sworn to tell the truth or made an affirmation to the like effect. This is not a mere technicality and failure to have the witness sworn (or make an affirmation) is capable of amounting to a material irregularity

---

[31] *Darby* [1989] Crim.L.R. 817.
[32] *Sullivan* [1923] 1 K.B. 47, CCA.
[33] *Leggett* [1970] 1 Q.B. 67; *Clewer* (1953) 37 Cr.App.R. 37; *Jones v N.C.B.* [1957] 2 Q.B. 55; *Hulusi and Purvis* (1974) 58 Cr.App.R. 378.
[34] *Marsh, The Times*, July 6, 1993. "The judge is not an advocate ... he is much more like an umpire at a cricket match ... [If he] descends into the forum and asks great numbers of pointed questions of the accused when he is giving evidence in chief, the jury may very well get the impression that the judge does not believe a word that the witness is saying ...", *Gunning* (1994) 98 Cr.App.R. 303 (Note), 306, *per* Cumming-Bruce L.J.
[35] [2001] Crim.L.R. 587.
[36] See para.16–09.
[37] *Whybrow, The Times*, February 14, 1994.

in the trial.[38] The only significant exceptions to this are children under 14 years of age and witnesses who do not appear to understand the solemnity of the occasion and the particular responsibility to tell the truth which is involved in taking the oath. Such persons may give evidence unsworn.[39] If the witness is able to give intelligible testimony, namely understand questions and give answers to them which can be understood, they will be presumed able to give sworn evidence unless there is evidence to the contrary.[40] The purpose of the oath or solemn affirmation is to emphasise to the witness the duty of telling the truth in the proceedings. A witness is sworn in silence and movement about the court is forbidden. This serves to underline the solemnity of the occasion. A majority of the Criminal Law Revision Committee were of the view that the oath should be abolished and replaced by a form of declaration.[41] There has, however, been no recent sign of any such change. It would, therefore, seem likely that the oath will remain for the foreseeable future.

Forms of oath and affirmation are prescribed by the Oaths Act 1978. However, the central rule is that a witness should be sworn in a way which he regards as binding. The Oaths Act 1978, s.1(1), provides that any oath may be administered to Christians and Jews in the following form: "The person taking the oath shall hold the New Testament or, in the case of a Jew, the Old Testament, in his uplifted hand, and shall say or repeat after the officer administering the oath the words 'I swear by Almighty God that ...,' followed by the words of the oath prescribed by law."

In the case of a witness these words are "the evidence which I shall give shall be the truth, the whole truth and nothing but the truth".[42] In the case of children in any court or witnesses in a juvenile court the words "I promise before Almighty God" are substituted for the words "I swear by Almighty God that".[43]

The words in s.1 are directive. Thus, although they should be complied with, failure to comply with them does not necessarily invalidate the taking of an oath.[44] This is because the efficacy of an oath must depend upon it being taken in a way intended to be binding upon the conscience of the intended witness. Thus, in *Kemble*[45] the Court of Appeal said that the

---

[38] *Sharman* [1998] 1 Cr.App.R. 406.
[39] s.56 of the Youth Justice and Criminal Evidence Act 1999. See paras 17–03 and 17–06 above.
[40] s.55 of the Youth Justice and Criminal Evidence Act 1999.
[41] Eleventh Report, Cmnd. 4991, paras 279–281.
[42] These words were approved by a resolution of the judges of the King's Bench Division on January 11, 1927. When a witness gives evidence at a trial-within-a-trial, he takes the oath on the *voir dire*.
[43] Children and Young Persons Act 1963, s.28(1). However, if either form of words is used in an oath otherwise duly administered, the oath shall be deemed to have been duly administered and taken: s.28(2).
[44] *Chapman* [1980] Crim.L.R. 42 (leave to appeal refused when witness failed to take the Testament in his hand).
[45] (1990) 91 Cr.App.R. 178.

administration of an oath was lawful within s.1 if it appeared to the court to be binding on the witness's conscience and was an oath which the witness considered binding: it did not depend on the intricacies of the religion adhered to by the witness.

19–09   Section 1(2) of the Oaths Act 1978 provides that "in the case of a person who is neither a Christian nor a Jew the oath shall be administered in any lawful form." Accordingly, believers in non-Christian religions may be sworn on books which they regard as holy. Thus, Muslims are sworn on the Koran and Sikhs on their holy book. The practice is to ask the witness what his religion is or what oath he accepts as binding and swear him accordingly.

If an oath has been administered to a person in a form other than that prescribed by law, he is bound by it if it has been administered in a form which he has declared to be binding: s.5(3).

However, if it is not "reasonably practicable without inconvenience or delay to administer an oath in the manner appropriate to his religious belief" to a witness, he is permitted to affirm: s.5(2). He may also be required to do so: s.4(1). This course is followed if the appropriate book is not available or, as sometimes happens, the witness appears unsure as to what his religion is.

If it transpires that a person to whom an oath has been administered has no religious belief, the validity of the oath is not affected: s.4(2).

A person who objects to being sworn is permitted (or may be required) to make an affirmation instead of taking an oath: Oaths Act 1978, s.5.

19–10   The form of the affirmation is as follows: "I [name] do solemnly, sincerely and truly declare and affirm" and then proceed with the words of the oath prescribed by law, omitting any words of imprecation or calling to witness.

It may sometimes be permissible to cross-examine a witness as to their reasons for affirming, for example where someone with religious beliefs decides to affirm instead of taking the oath on a holy book.[46] The trial judge has a discretion to allow such cross-examination when the ground has been properly laid for an expectation that the witness would normally take the oath on a holy book relevant to their religious belief. No such questions should be put, however, without the matter first being raised in the absence of the jury.

3. VULNERABLE AND INTIMIDATED WITNESSES

19–11   Vulnerable and intimidated witnesses are those who are thought to require the protection of the court when giving evidence, due to their youth, incapacity, fear or distress at the prospect of testifying. Such protection used not to be considered necessary and all witnesses gave their evidence

---

[46] *Mehrban* [2002] 1 Cr.App.R. 561.

from the witness-box in the normal way. However, with the growing practice of calling child witnesses, and the recognition of the need to protect certain classes of adult witnesses, protection for them was sought. The purpose is to protect the witness from (a) having to give evidence in the presence of the accused and (b) having to do so in potentially intimidating surroundings. Chapter I of Pt II of the Youth Justice and Criminal Evidence Act 1999 ("YJCEA 1999") came into force on July 24, 2002.[47] It implements proposals made in the interdepartmental review, *Speaking Up for Justice*, and makes important changes to the law as it relates to vulnerable and intimidated witnesses. It introduces a new statutory regime of assistance for all those who come within the categories of witnesses protected by the Act by means of special measures directions, that is, a direction given under s.19 of the Act. (See para.19–14 below.)[48]

A. Witnesses eligible for assistance

Sections 16 and 17 of the YJCEA 1999 identify the categories of witnesses (other than the accused) eligible for assistance by way of special measures. They are as follows: **19–12**

(a) Witnesses under 17 at the time of hearing,[49] *i.e.* at the time when it falls to the court to make a determination on whether any special measures would be likely to improve the quality of evidence.[50]

(b) Witnesses suffering from (i) a mental disorder within the meaning of the Mental Health Act 1983[51]; (ii) a significant impairment of intelligence and social functioning[52]; or (iii) a physical disability or physical disorder[53]; if the court considers that the quality of evidence given by the witness is likely to be diminished as a result of the relevant impairment, disability or disorder.[54] In making this determination the court must consider any views expressed by the witness.[55]

(c) Witnesses in fear or distress about testifying if the court is satisfied that the quality of evidence given by the witness is likely to be

---

[47] Youth Justice and Criminal Evidence Act 1999 (Commencement No.7) Order 2002 (SI 2002/1739).
[48] The Act repeals and replaces ss.32 (to the extent that it relates to child witnesses), 32A, and 34A of the Criminal Justice Act 1988.
[49] s.16(1)(a) of the YJCEA 1999.
[50] s.16(3) of the YJCEA 1999.
[51] s.16(2)(a)(i) of the YJCEA 1999.
[52] s.16(2)(a)(ii) of the YJCEA 1999.
[53] s.16(2)(b) of the YJCEA 1999.
[54] s.16(1)(b) of the YJCEA 1999.
[55] s.16(4) of the YJCEA 1999

diminished.[56] In making such a determination the court must take into account (i) the nature and alleged circumstances of the offence to which the proceedings relate[57]; (ii) the age of the witness[58]; (iii) if the court thinks relevant, the witness's social and cultural background, their ethnic origins, domestic and employment circumstances, and any religious or political beliefs they may hold[59]; and (iv) the behaviour of the accused, the accused's family members or associates, or any other person likely to be an accused or witness in the proceedings, towards the witness.[60] The court should also consider any views expressed by the witness.[61]

In determining whether a witness falls into any of the above categories the court must consider the effect of any special measures on the "quality of evidence" of the witness. This means its quality in terms of completeness, coherence, and accuracy. Coherence means a witness's ability when giving evidence to give answers which address the questions put and which can be understood both individually and collectively.[62]

19–13   Complainants in proceedings for sexual offences are automatically eligible for assistance as a witness in relation to those proceedings unless the witness informs the court that he or she does not wish to be so eligible.[63]

There is no power to give a "special measures direction" to a vulnerable accused pursuant to the YJCEA 1999. However, in *H (Special Measures)*[64] the Court of Appeal said that at common law a trial judge has the power to direct the taking of measures to assist the accused with learning difficulties. Such measures could include (i) the assistance of an interpreter whilst giving evidence; (ii) reading a detailed defence statement to the jury; and (iii) allowing leading questions based on a statement in examination-in-chief where it is apparent that the accused is having difficulty recalling the facts.

B: Special measures directions

19–14   Where a court (either on its own motion or on application by a party to the proceedings)[65] determines that a witness is eligible for assistance by virtue

---

[56] s.17(1) of the YJCEA 1999.
[57] s.17(2)(a) of the YJCEA 1999.
[58] s.17(2)(b) of the YJCEA 1999.
[59] s.17(2)(c) of the YJCEA 1999.
[60] s.17(2)(d) of the YJCEA 1999.
[61] s.17(3) of the YJCEA 1999.
[62] s.16(5) of the YJCEA 1999.
[63] s.17(4) of the YJCEA 1999.
[64] *The Times*, April 15, 2003.
[65] s.19(1) of the YJCEA 1999. In most cases the party calling the witness will make the application for a special measures direction. However, where the court makes a direction on its own motion it should consult the party calling the witness, the witness themselves, and it may also consult the witness's parents, social workers and other source of expert advice (H.C. Stand. Comm., June 17, 1999).

of s.16 or 17, it must then determine, under s.19 of the YJCEA 1999, whether or not the quality of the evidence of the witness would be improved by one or more of the special measures available.[66] If the evidence would be so improved the court must determine which of those measures would in its opinion be likely to maximise the quality of such evidence and give a direction, known as the "special measures direction", to that effect.[67] In determining whether to give a special measures direction the court must consider any views expressed by the witness and whether the measure or measures might tend to inhibit the evidence being effectively tested by a party to the proceedings.[68]

It should be noted that in relation to those witnesses who are not eligible for special measures, the court retains its inherent jurisdiction or otherwise to make an appropriate order or give leave of any description.[69] Moreover, a court is able to make directions over and above those falling within the YJCEA 1999, for example relating to a foreign language interpreter.[70]

A special measures order may be varied or discharged, either on application by a party or by the court of its own motion, where it appears to the court to be in the interests of justice to do so.[71] The court must state its reasons for giving, varying, refusing, or discharging a special measures direction in open court. In the magistrates court the reasons must be entered in the register of its proceedings.[72] The Crown Court (Special Measures Directions and Directions Prohibiting Cross-Examination) Rules 2002[73] make detailed provision as to the measures: in particular as to the giving of expert evidence in connection with directions and to the disclosure or withholding of sensitive or confidential information.

The courts discretion over whether to make certain special measures **19–15** directions for child witnesses, in particular those giving evidence on allegations of sexual and other certain offences, is limited by ss.21 and 22 of the YJCEA 1999. These provisions replace s.32A of the Criminal Justice Act 1988 which only applied to offences of violence (children under 14) and sexual offences (children under 17). The new provisions in the YJCEA 1999 are general in application and do not repeat the provisions in s.32A as to who interviews the child, and the need for the court, where it considers whether part of an interview should be excluded, to take account of the effect of the whole interview.

Section 21 of the YJCEA 1999 qualifies the court's discretion in relation to certain special measure for child witnesses, as defined by s.16(1)(a). The

---

[66] s.19(2)(a) of the YJCEA 1999.
[67] s.19(2)(b) of the YJCEA 1999.
[68] s.19(3) of the YJCEA 1999.
[69] s.19(6)(a) of the YJCEA 1999.
[70] s.19(6)(b) of the YJCEA 1999.
[71] s.20(2) of the YJCEA 1999.
[72] s.20(5) of the YJCEA 1999.
[73] (SI 2002/1688). See also the Magistrates' Courts (Special Measures Directions) Rules 2002 (SI 2002/1687) for the rules pertaining to special measures directions in the Magistrates' Court.

primary rule in relation to child witnesses is that the court *must* provide that any video recording of an interview of the witness made with a view to its admission as evidence in chief is admitted pursuant to s.27 of the YJCEA 1999 (see para.19–24 below).[74] The court must also provide that any evidence which is not given by way of a video recording (whether in chief or otherwise) is given by means of a live link in accordance with s.24 of the YJCEA 1999 (see para.19–20 below).[75] This rule does not, however, apply if the special measures in question are not available or if the court is satisfied that their provision would not be likely to maximise the quality of the witness's evidence.[76] Moreover, such measures will, normally, cease to have effect when the witness attains the age of 17.[77] Child witnesses in proceedings relating to certain types of offences, such as sexual offences, kidnapping, and assaults,[78] are deemed to be "in need of special protection" and are accordingly afforded additional protection.[79] It is irrelevant whether the assault or injury is to the child in question or another person.[80] The court must provide for the special measure under s.28 of the YJCEA 1999, namely video recorded cross-examination and re-examination.[81] Section 28 is, however, not yet in force (see para.19–31 below). The protections contained in s.28 will be subject to availability and will not be required if the witness informs the court that he or she does not require such protection.[82]

19–16   Section 22 of the YJCEA 1999 extends the protections contained in s.21 of the Act to certain witnesses over 17 at the time of the hearing, but who were under 17 at the time that any video recording was made for the purpose of its admission into evidence as evidence in chief.

The special measures regime for child witness (*i.e.* primary rule for video recorded evidence in chief and otherwise evidence by live link) has been held compatible with the rights guaranteed in Art.6 of the European Convention of Human Rights.[83]

---

[74] s.21(3)(a) of the YJCEA 1999.
[75] s.21(3)(b) of the YJCEA 1999.
[76] s.21(4) of the YJCEA 1999.
[77] s.21(8) of the YJCEA 1999.
[78] See further s.35 of the YJCEA 1999 at para.21–18, n.80.
[79] s.21(1)(b) of the YJCEA 1999.
[80] *Lee* [1996] 2 Cr.App.R 266. *Lee*, a case under s.32 of the Criminal Justice Act 1988, the Court of Appeal held that s.32 applied in a case where the defendant was charged with arson, being reckless as to whether life was endangered. S.32 was also held to apply to attempted child abduction under s.2 of the Child Abduction Act 1984 since, on a purposive construction, it was clearly within the scope of the section: *McAndrew-Bingham* [1999] 2 Cr.App.R. 293.
[81] s.21(6) of the YJCEA 1999.
[82] s.21(7) of the YJCEA 1999.
[83] *D v Camberwell Green Youth Court; R v Balham Youth Court; N v Camberwell Green Youth Court; DPP v Same and G; DPP v Same and I; DPP v Same and K.E.* 167 J.P. 210.

C: The special measures available

(1) Screens

Section 23 of the YJCEA 1999 provides that a special measures direction   **19–17**
may provide for the witness, while giving testimony or being sworn in
court, to be prevented by means of a screen or other arrangement from
seeing the accused. The witness must, however, be able to see and be visible
to, the judge or justices (or both), jury, legal representatives acting in the
proceedings (where two or more legal representatives are acting only one
representative need be able to see and be seen the witness), and any interpreter or other person appointed to assist the witness.[84]

It should be noted that s.23 only requires that the witness be prevented
from seeing the accused. There is no requirement that the accused not be
able to see the witness. Thus, if it is possible to protect the witness from
seeing the accused while at the same time ensuring that the accused can see
the witness this would satisfy the requirements of a special measures
direction pursuant to s.23. In practice, however, this may be difficult to
achieve.

The following cases, decided before the YJCEA 1999, may still prove
useful in determining how courts should exercise their discretion pursuant
to s.23 in allowing the use of screens.

In XYZ,[85] the Court of Appeal upheld a trial judge's decision to allow
screens to be placed between the child witnesses and the defendants. The
Court said that the necessity of trying to ensure that the children gave
evidence without intimidation outweighed any possible prejudice to the
defendants.

It is a matter for the judge's discretion whether screens are used. The
judge must balance the interests of the public (represented by the prosecution) in the witnesses giving evidence free from any fear of intimidation
against the interest of the defendant in avoiding the risk of prejudice. In
practice, if they request to do so or a request is made on their behalf,
witnesses are usually permitted to give evidence in this way. Any risk of
prejudice can be overcome by a suitable warning from the judge (see
para.19–33 below). In XYZ the trial judge told the jury that the purpose of
providing the screens was to prevent the children from being intimidated by
their surroundings, since they may find coming before a court frightening;
and the jury should not allow the presence of the screen to prejudice them
against the defendants. It is submitted that a warning along these lines
(together, if thought appropriate, with an explanation that the provision of
screens represents the modern practice for the protection of children) will
be sufficient to counteract any prejudice.

The use of screens to protect adult witnesses will be much more unusual   **19–18**

---

[84] s.23(2) of the YJCEA 1999.
[85] (1990) 91 Cr.App.R. 40.

and until relatively recently it was virtually unknown. The Court of Appeal in *Cooper and Schaub*[86] said that screens to protect such a witness from eye contact with a defendant should only be used in very exceptional circumstances and by no means in every case involving rape or other sexual offences. In that case the Court did not criticise the use of screens for a 21-year-old witness giving evidence of an exceptionally unpleasant kind involving multiple rape. The Court of Appeal returned to this topic in *Foster*.[87] The trial judge in that case permitted a 20-year-old woman to give evidence from behind a screen against her stepfather, who was charged with raping her. The Court of Appeal upheld this decision and said that the test had been set out in *XYZ*, namely that it was the duty of the judge to see that justice was done, and that what was said in *Cooper and Schaub* was not intended to put a gloss on that test. The Court said that it was pre-eminently a matter for the trial judge and in the instant case his warning to the jury not to read anything adverse to the defendant in the use of screens was exemplary. However, it is submitted that for adults, notwithstanding s.23, screens should be very much the exception rather than the rule because of the prejudice which may be occasioned to a defendant.

Different considerations may apply if witnesses are in fear of violence from a defendant. Thus, in *Watford Magistrates' Court Ex p. Lenman*,[88] decided prior to the YJCEA 1999, the Divisional Court upheld the decision of a magistrate to allow witnesses to give evidence anonymously because they were afraid of reprisals. The Court said that it was a matter for the discretion of the magistrates and, applying *XYZ*, a balance must be struck between the risk of prejudice to the defendant and risks to the interests of justice. This decision was approved in *Taylor*[89] where the Court of Appeal upheld the decision of the trial judge to allow a schoolgirl witness in a murder trial to give evidence anonymously and from behind a screen because it was feared there might be reprisals against her. Similarly, in *HM Coroner for Newcastle upon Tyne Ex p. A*,[90] another case prior to the YJCEA 1999, it was held that the principles applicable in the Crown Court should apply to inquests in the coroner's court. It was therefore not inappropriate for a police officer who had shot someone dead during a burglary to give evidence from behind a screen. The Court in *Taylor* set out the relevant factors for the exercise of the Court's discretion in these circumstances, *i.e.* there should be real grounds for fear of the consequences if the witness's identity were revealed[91]; the evidence must be sufficiently relevant

---

[86] [1994] Crim.L.R. 531 (decided prior to the YJCEA 1999).
[87] [1995] Crim.L.R. 333 (decided prior to the YJCEA 1999).
[88] [1993] Crim.L.R. 388
[89] [1995] Crim.L.R. 253.
[90] (1998) 162 J.P. 387.
[91] The Court said that it is not necessary for the witness himself to be fearful: it could be concern expressed by others (in the instant case, by the witness's mother) and the consequences may not be limited to the witness himself, but could include others.

and important to make it unfair to the prosecution to proceed without it; the prosecution must satisfy the court of the creditworthiness of the witness; there must be no undue prejudice to the defendant; and the court must balance the need for anonymity and protection against the unfairness or appearance of unfairness in the particular case.[92] It is submitted that (with these considerations in mind) courts should be prepared to take a robust attitude and allow witnesses protection in appropriate cases in order to counter what appears to be a growing trend towards intimidation of witnesses.

The use of screens may also be justified because of the need to protect **19–19** witnesses from identification for security reasons. This matter has not been tested in an appellate court. However, it is submitted that the court has the power to order the use of screens in these circumstances in order to receive evidence which would not otherwise be available to it. A newspaper report claimed that with the passage of the Intelligence Services Act 1994 more agents will give evidence behind screens in ordinary criminal trials.[93] Whether they do or not will depend on the circumstances of each case, including the nature of the danger faced by the witness and the importance of the evidence to be given.

It may be noted that the Law Commission discussed these issues in its Consultation Paper on Hearsay.[94] The Commission concluded that there is no "right of confrontation" in English law, but that it was desirable that witnesses give their evidence in the presence of the accused if possible. However, the Commission recognised that there may be other factors which may outweigh the need for this to happen.

(2) Live link

The court may make a special measures direction for a vulnerable witness **19–20** to give evidence by means of a live link. Section 24(8) of the YJCEA 1999 provides that this will be in the form of a live television link or other arrangement whereby a witness, while absent from the courtroom or place where the proceedings are being held, is able to see and hear them and be able to be seen and heard by the judge, justices (or both), jury, legal representatives of the parties, any interpreter or other person appointed to assist the witness. Where such a direction is given the witness may only give evidence by way of live link unless the court permits otherwise.[95] If, in a magistrates' court, live link facilities are not available, the court may sit, for such purposes, at some other place where they are.[96]

---

[92] The Court said that there was no reason in principle why the same considerations should not apply when the defence sought to call a witness whose identity is not revealed.
[93] *Guardian*, January 20, 1994.
[94] Law Commission Consultation Paper No.138, "Evidence in Criminal Proceedings: Hearsay and Related Topics", HMSO, 1995, paras 6.88–6–94.
[95] s.24(2) of the YJCEA 1999.
[96] s.24(5) of the YJCEA 1999.

Section 32(1)(a) of the Criminal Justice Act 1988, not repealed by the YJCEA 1999, permits evidence to be given by live television link by witnesses abroad in cases of murder, manslaughter and serious and complex fraud. (Section 32(3) applies the law of perjury to such evidence.) The fact that there is no extradition treaty with the country from which the witness is to give evidence does not render his evidence inadmissible.[97] "In general, once it is shown that there is difficulty in obtaining the attendance of witnesses abroad whose evidence is relevant to the defence ... the court should then lean in favour of permitting evidence to be given in this way though in particular cases there may be reasons to refuse it."[98] The procedure for applications under s.32(1)(a) is governed by rules of the Crown Court.[99] The rules permit the court to impose a condition that the witness gives evidence in the presence of a specified person who is able and willing to answer under oath any questions which the court may put as to the circumstances in which the evidence is given.[1]

19–21 Part 8 of the Criminal Justice Act 2003 (not in force at the time of writing)[2] makes provision for more extensive use of live links.[3] Section 51 of the Criminal Justice Act 2003 provides that *any* witness may, upon direction of the court, give evidence through live link in criminal proceedings if the court is satisfied that "it is in the interests of the efficient or effective administration of justice".[4] In deciding whether to give such a direction the court must consider all the circumstances of the case.[5] Those circumstances include in particular:

(i) the availability of the witness,

(ii) the need for the witness to attend in person,

(iii) the importance of the witness's evidence to the proceedings,

(iv) the views of the witness,

(v) the suitability of the facilities at the place where the witness would give evidence through live link,

(vi) whether a direction might tend to inhibit any party to the proceedings from effectively testing the witness's evidence.[6]

---

[97] *Forsyth* [1997] 2 Cr.App.R. 299.
[98] *ibid.*, 311.
[99] Crown Court Rules 1982, r.23B.
[1] r.23B(10).
[2] s.336(3) of the Criminal Justice Act 2003 provides that the provision will come into force in accordance with provision made by the Secretary of State by order.
[3] Rules of Court may make such provision as appears to be necessary or expedient for the purposes of Pt 8: s.55 of the Criminal Justice Act 2003.
[4] s.51(4)(a) of the Criminal Justice Act 2003.
[5] s.51(6) of the Criminal Justice Act 2003.
[6] s.51(7) of the Criminal Justice Act 2003.

A direction may be given on the court's own motion or on application by a party to the proceedings.[7] If an application is refused the court must state its reasons for such refusal in open court.[8] Where evidence is given through live link during a trial on indictment, the judge may give the jury (if there is one) such direction as he thinks necessary to ensure that the jury gives the same weight to the evidence as if it had been given by the witness in the courtroom or other place where the proceedings are held.[9]

(3) Evidence in private

Section 25 of the YJCEA 1999 provides for the exclusion from court of persons of any description specified in the order during the testimony of a vulnerable witness's evidence. The section only applies to witnesses testifying in proceedings for sexual offences or where it appears to the court that there are reasonable grounds for believing that any person other than the accused has sought, or will seek, to intimidate the witness in connection with testifying in the proceedings.[10] Certain persons may not be excluded from court during such testimony, the accused, legal representatives, interpreters, or any other person appointed to assist the witness.[11] If the media are to be excluded by such a special measures direction, one nominated media representative must be allowed to remain in court.[12]

When exercising a discretion to exclude persons from court pursuant to the YJCEA 1999 it is submitted that the court should be mindful of the balance between public hearings and the "interests of justice" as set out in Art.6(1) of the European Convention of Human Rights which provides:

> "...Judgment shall be pronounced publicly but the press and public may be excluded from all or part of the trial in the interests of morals, public order or national security in a democratic society, where the interests of juveniles or the protection of private lives of the parties so require, or to the extent strictly necessary in the opinion of the court in special circumstances where publicity would prejudice the interests of justice."

(4) Removal of wigs and gowns

Section 26 of the YJCEA 1999 provides that the court may direct that wigs and gowns need not be worn during the giving of a witness's evidence. It is not clear why it was necessary for an Act of Parliament to this effect as the common law has permitted this practice for many years.

19–22

19–23

---

[7] s.51(3) of the Criminal Justice Act 2003.
[8] s.51(8) of the Criminal Justice Act 2003.
[9] s.54 of the Criminal Justice Act 2003.
[10] s.25(4) of the YJCEA 1999.
[11] s.25(2) of the YJCEA 1999.
[12] s.25(3) of the YJCEA 1999.

(5) Video-recorded evidence in chief

19–24   **Admissibility.**   As noted above, the YJCEA 1999 repeals s.32 of the Criminal Justice Act 1988 (video recorded evidence by children) and replaces it with the provisions in s.27 of the YJCEA 1999 which allows for a special measures direction to provide for *any* vulnerable witness (not just a child) to give evidence-in-chief on a video recording. The purpose of s.27 is first, to lessen the distress which a witness may feel at giving evidence in the intimidating atmosphere of a court; and secondly, as a means of having the witness's earliest (and presumably, best) recollection put in evidence before the court. Evidence of children under 17 will automatically be given on video unless the court determines otherwise (see para.19–15 above). However, for other vulnerable witnesses, *i.e.* non-child witnesses, the court may not admit such recording, or part of it, where it would not be in the interests of justice to do so.[13] In making such determination, the court must consider whether any prejudice to the accused might result from any part of the recording being admitted is outweighed by the desirability of showing the whole, or substantially the whole, of the recorded interview.[14]

Section 137 of the Criminal Justice Act 2003 (not in force at the time of writing)[15] provides for the use, in certain circumstances, of video recordings to be admitted as evidence in chief of a witness in proceedings for an offence triable only on indictment, or for a prescribed offence triable either way.[16] Persons, other than the defendant,[17] who claim to have witnessed (whether visually or in any other way) events alleged by the prosecution to include either (i) conduct constituting the offence or part of the offence, or (ii) events closely connected with such events, may give evidence in chief by video recording.[18] To be admissible, the video recording must have been made at a time when the events were fresh in the person's memory.[19]

19–25   A video recording may only be admitted as a witness's evidence in chief if it appears to the court that the witness's recollection of the events in question is likely to have been significantly better when he gave the recorded account than it will be when he gives oral evidence in the proceedings.[20] Moreover, it must appear to the court to be in the interests of justice for such recording to be admitted, having particular regard to the following matters:

---

[13] s.27(2) of the YJCEA 1999.
[14] s.27(3) of the YJCEA 1999.
[15] s.336(3) of the Criminal Justice Act 2003 provides that the provision will come into force in accordance with provision made by the Secretary of State by order.
[16] s.137(1)(a) and (f) of the Criminal Justice Act 2003. Subject to notification by the Secretary of State: s.138(4) of the Criminal Justice Act 2003.
[17] s.137(3)(a) of the Criminal Justice Act 2003.
[18] s.137(1)(b) of the Criminal Justice Act 2003.
[19] s.137(1)(d) of the Criminal Justice Act 2003.
[20] s.137(3)(b)(i) of the Criminal Justice Act 2003.

(i) the interval between the time of the events in question and the time when the recording was made;

(ii) any other factors that might affect the reliability of what the witness said in the recorded account;

(iii) the quality of the recording; and

(iv) any views of the witness as to whether his evidence in chief should be given orally or by means of the recording.[21]

When a video recording is admitted under s.137, the witness may not give evidence in chief otherwise than by means of the recording as to any matter which, in the opinion of the court, has been dealt with adequately in the recorded account.[22] In considering whether any part of a recording should not be admitted under s.137, the court must consider any risk of prejudice to the defendant and, if such risk exists, whether the interests of justice nevertheless require it to be admitted in view of the desirability of showing the whole, or substantially the whole, of the recorded interview.[23]

Procedure. 1. The procedure for making an application for leave to tender a video recording in evidence under s.27 is governed by the Consolidated Criminal Practice Direction (para.40) Video Recorded Evidence in Chief.[24]   **19–26**

2. Where a special measures direction is made for the use of video recorded evidence in chief, the court may subsequently direct that it is not to be admitted where it appears that the witness will not be available for cross-examination and the parties have not agreed that that there is no need for the witness to be so available.[25] Accordingly, where a recording is admitted, unless the parties agree otherwise, the witness must be called by the party tendering the evidence unless a special measures direction provides for the witness's evidence on cross-examination and re-examination to be given otherwise than by testimony in court. Moreover, where a witness gives video recorded evidence in chief they cannot give evidence in chief by other means so long as the video recorded evidence is, in the opinion of the court, adequate.[26] If the court decides to admit further evidence in chief from the witness, it may direct that such evidence is given by way of live link (see para.19–20 above).[27]

3. Where only part of the video recording is admitted into evidence, it is for the party calling the evidence to edit the recording in accordance with

---

[21] s.137(4) of the Criminal Justice Act 2003.
[22] s.138(1) of the Criminal Justice Act 2003.
[23] s.138(3) of the Criminal Justice Act 2003.
[24] *Consolidated Criminal Practice Direction* [2002] 1 W.L.R. 2870.
[25] s.27(4) of the YJCEA 1999.
[26] s.27(5) of the YJCEA 1999.
[27] s.27(9) of the YJCEA 1999.

the judge's directions.[28] Video evidence to be adduced pursuant to s.27 must be produced and proved at trial by the interviewer or any other person present at the interview. The party wishing to adduce the evidence should ensure that such a person is available for this purpose unless the parties accept a written statement in lieu of attendance.[29]

4. If any issue arises as to the competence of a witness the judge will, almost inevitably, have to watch the video-recording. Thus, in *Hampshire*,[30] a case under s.32A of the Criminal Justice Act 1988, the Court of Appeal said that in order to determine, under s.32A(3)(c), whether "in the interests of justice" the recording ought not to be admitted, the judge in most, if not all cases, must watch the recording. The Court said that such a determination must necessarily include a determination as to competence, and, if on viewing the recording the judge considers that the child is incompetent, he should conclude that the evidence in that form should be excluded: on the other hand, if the judge, on viewing the recording, considers that there is no reason to refuse leave, he is bound by s.32(A)(3) to grant leave.

19–27 5. If the child changes his or her mind about giving evidence and seeks to retract the allegations made in the video-recording (a not altogether uncommon occurrence) the court should not permit the recording to be admitted as evidence. Thus, in *Parker*,[31] a case prior to the YJCEA 1999, the Court of Appeal held that it was a wrong exercise of the judge's discretion to allow a video-recording of a child's evidence to be played after the child had made a statement retracting the allegations: the child should have given evidence live, if necessary via the television link.

6. It is not the normal practice for the jury to be supplied with a transcript of a witness's interview on a video-recording: indeed in many cases no transcripts are available. The reasons for not supplying a transcript are (a) the danger that the jury will give disproportionate weight to the evidence and (b) the danger that the jury will concentrate on the transcript, rather than watching the witness. However, in exceptional circumstances, it may be necessary to provide a transcript because, for instance, the quality of the tape is poor, or because the witness's voice is indistinct. The Court of Appeal has said that the jury may have a transcript provided that: (a) it was likely to assist in understanding the evidence; (b) it was made clear to the jury that they had it for that limited purpose; and (c) the judge gave them such directions as would be likely to be effective safeguards against the risk of giving disproportionate weight to the transcript.[32] However, if the jury do have a transcript, they should not normally take it with them when they retire to consider their verdict, unless the prosecution and defence consent

---

[28] Consolidated Criminal Practice Direction (para.40.2).
[29] Consolidated Criminal Practice Direction (para.40.3).
[30] [1995] 2 Cr.App.R. 319, 324.
[31] [1996] Crim.L.R. 511.
[32] *Welstead* [1996] 1 Cr.App.R. 59, 69. Decided prior to the YJCEA 1999.

and the jury are reminded of the other evidence and the status of the transcript.[33]

7. If the witness becomes hostile while giving evidence live or through the television link, it would appear that the video-recording should not be shown during cross-examination of the witness by the prosecution.[34] In R,[35] decided prior to the YJCEA 1999, the defendant was charged with indecent assault upon his daughter. She became hostile; the prosecution were allowed to treat her as a hostile witness and to show the jury a video-recording of a police interview with her. The Court of Appeal refused the appeal because the defence had not objected at the time and the judge had directed the jury to place no reliance on the witness's evidence. However, the Court said that this should not be taken as a precedent and it was the better practice for the jury not to see the video-recording. It is submitted, with respect, that this must be right since it will be difficult for the jury to rid their minds of what they have heard on the video-recording.

Replaying the video. In *John M*,[36] decided before the YJCEA 1999, **19–28** the Court of Appeal said that in normal circumstances it is not appropriate to replay the video unless there has been a specific request from the jury, since it involves replaying one aspect of the evidence. Such a departure from the normal practice could only be justified for an exceptional reason. However, in *Rawlings and Broadbent*,[37] also decided prior to the YJCEA 1999, the Court of Appeal held that if the jury request that a video-recording be replayed after they have retired, it was a matter for the judge's discretion whether to allow a replay or not. Lord Taylor C.J. said that the judge should bear in mind the need to guard against unfairness due to the replay of only the evidence in chief of the complainant; accordingly, if the jury only wishes to be reminded of what the witness said, a reading of the judge's note would suffice. On the other hand, if the circumstances indicate that how the words were spoken was of importance to the jury, the judge might allow the video (or the relevant part) to be played. The Court held that if the judge did allow the video to be replayed it should be subject to the following requirements:

(a)   the video should be replayed in court in the presence of the judge, counsel and defendant;

(b)   the judge should warn the jury to guard against the risk of giving

---

[33] *Coshall, The Times*, February 17, 1995. In *Morris* [1998] Crim.L.R. 416 the Court of Appeal said that it was rare that the jury should be allowed to take the transcript. Both decided prior to the YJCEA 1999.
[34] For the procedure in relation to hostile witnesses, see para.21–09, below.
[35] Unreported, CA, February 6, 1995.
[36] [1996] 2 Cr.App.R. 56, 61.
[37] [1995] 2 Cr.App.R. 222.

disproportionate weight to this evidence because it was hearing it a second time and to bear in mind the other evidence in the case;

(c) after the replay the judge should remind the jury of the cross-examination of the complainant.[38]

The decision of the court in *Rawlings and Broadbent* may also serve as some guidance as to how the discretion should be exercised. The Court in that case heard two appeals, the results of which may be usefully contrasted. In *Rawlings* it was suggested that the complainant had been play-acting: therefore, how he deported himself in interview was important. The trial judge allowed the video to be replayed in court; he reminded the jury of cross-examination and warned it against giving disproportionate importance to the video by reason of hearing it a second time. In these circumstances the appeal was dismissed. On the other hand in *Broadbent* there was no obvious reason for the jury to wish to hear the manner of the complainant's evidence as opposed to its content. The trial judge took the view that the jury was entitled to have the video because it had been made an exhibit (the Court of Appeal commented that it did not appear that he had exercised his discretion). The judge allowed the jury to have the video in its room and, in response to a later request, allowed a further replay of the video. The appeal in that case was allowed.

19–29   If the judge decides (as he may) that the video should not be replayed, but that he will remind the jury of the complainant's evidence by reading from the transcript of the recording, he should warn the jury not to give the complainant's evidence disproportionate weight because it is being repeated; and he should remind the jury of the cross-examination of the complainant and, where relevant, any part of the defendant's evidence.[39]

In *L and B v DPP*[40] it was held that where a month's gap had occurred in case in the magistrates' court between the evidence in chief of a complainant given by way of video recordings of interviews and the case being resumed, it would have been wrong for the justices to have seen the recording again with a view to reminded themselves of the evidence, as this might have had the effect (as observed in *Rawlings and Broadbent*) of

---

[38] In *S* [1995] 2 Cr.App.R. 313, 318 the Court of Appeal said that Lord Taylor C.J. could not have intended to require a judge, having reminded the jury of the cross-examination of the complainant in summing-up and permitted the video to be replayed during the retirement, to remind the jury again of the cross-examination after he had taken the care which the judge in the instant case had. It is submitted that *S* is to be taken as a decision on its own facts and that the safer course normally is for the judge to remind the jury of the relevant cross-examination, thereby ensuring that they have all the complainant's evidence in mind. Thus in *M* [1995] Crim.L.R. 336 the judge did not remind the jury of the cross-examination. The Court of Appeal described this as a material omission which might have altered the balance of the trial since it was especially important because the cross-examination established a motive for lying by the complainant.
[39] *McQuiston* [1998] 1 Cr.App.R. 139, 141.
[40] [1998] 2 Cr.App.R. 69.

doubling the effect of the evidence, Thus, the justices had been correct to simply ask the prosecutor to repeat the opening.

Conduct of interviews. Since children, and some adult vulnerable 19–30 witnesses, may be more open to suggestion and also more vulnerable to oppression than ordinary witnesses, particular care must be exercised in the conduct of any interviews with them. The mishandling of such an interview may affect a trial at which the witness subsequently gives evidence. Advice is now to be found in *Achieving Best Evidence in Criminal Proceedings: Guidance for Vulnerable or Intimidated Witnesses, including Children,*[41] which expands and replaces two publications, the "Cleveland" guidelines and the Memorandum of Good Practice. The new guidance sets out best practice in preparing for and conducting interviews with children and vulnerable witnesses. It also provides guidance on supporting and preparing such witnesses for court.

Failure to follow the guidance contained in *Achieving Best Evidence in Criminal Proceedings* will not necessarily result in a recording being excluded. However, it will be a matter which a judge may wish to take into account when deciding whether to admit or exclude a recording under either s.27 of the YJCEA 1999 or s.78 of the Police and Criminal Evidence Act 1984. In *G v DPP*[42] the Divisional Court emphasised the importance of following the previous Memorandum, but said that the question whether failure to comply with it should lead to exclusion will not necessarily depend on the nature and extent of the breaches, but may depend on other evidence in the case and the extent to which that evidence corroborates the video interview. (The Court also said in *G* that this is a legitimate area for expert evidence. However, such evidence must be kept within its proper boundaries and the expert must not attempt to usurp the functions of the court.) Similarly in *D and S,*[43] a case under s.32A of the Criminal Justice Act 1988, it was held that failure to comply with the guidance by virtue of an "appropriate adult" being present at the complainant's second interview when she had herself informally interviewed the complainant since her first interview, did not render the interview and video recording inadmissible. Moreover, failure to follow procedures to the letter can, in some circumstances, be remedied with appropriate directions. In *B(K),*[44] it was held that where an interviewer told a child witness "You're doing really well" during the course of an interview that had been played to the jury, the judge should have directed the jury to disregard such comment for the purpose of their assessment.

---

[41] HMSO.
[42] [1997] 2 Cr.App.R. 78, 87.
[43] 166 J.P. 792.
[44] [2002] 10 *Archbold News* 1.

(6) Video-recorded cross-examination or re-examination.

19–31 Section 28 of the YJCEA 1999 (not in force at the time of writing) will permit the court to make similar provision for the admission of video recordings of the cross-examination and re-examination of a witness as provided for under s.27 of the YJCEA 1999.

(7) Intermediaries and communication aids

19–32 Section 29 of the YJCEA 1999 (not in force at the time of writing) will permit the court to provide for the witness to be examined with the assistance of an "intermediary" or other person approved by the court. The intermediary will be someone who may be trained in the necessary skills or who may have unique knowledge of the witness. The function of the intermediary is to communicate questions put to the witness and any response thereto to the party asking the question. The intermediary may explain such questions or answers to the witness or the person asking the question so far as necessary to enable them to be understood.[45] Section 29 does not alter existing arrangements for the provision in court of interpreters for the deaf who can choose either such an interpreter or an intermediary pursuant to s.29.

Section 30 of the YJCEA 1999 authorises the use of aids to overcome physical difficulties by a witness. Such aids might include signboards or communication aids for the disabled, but not devices for disguising speech.

D: Status of evidence and warning to jury

19–33 By s.31 of the YJCEA 1999 all evidence given under a special measures direction shall be treated as if made by the witness in direct oral testimony.[46] Evidence given by video recording pursuant to ss.27 and 28 which is unsworn shall be treated as if sworn.[47] In estimating the weight (if any) to be attached to such recording, the court must have regard to all the circumstances from which an inference can reasonably be drawn (as to the accuracy of the statement or otherwise).[48]

Where, on a trial on indictment, evidence is given in accordance with a special measures direction, s.32 of the YJCEA 1999 provides that the judge must give the jury such warning (if any) as he or she considers necessary to ensure that the jury do not allow the existence of the special measures direction to prejudice them against the accused. This follows the common law practice.

---

[45] s.29(2) of the YJCEA 1999.
[46] s.31(2) of the YJCEA 1999.
[47] s.31(3) of the YJCEA 1999. On the new provisions relating to sworn and unsworn evidence see para.19–08 above.
[48] s.31(4) of the YJCEA 1999.

4. THE ORDER OF EVIDENCE

A. Procedure

In order to discuss the rules relating to the order of evidence it is necessary
first to indicate the framework within which evidence is given,[49] *i.e.* the
procedure governing the course of a trial. This procedure is as follows: **19–34**

- (i) opening speech on behalf of the prosecution[50];
- (ii) calling of evidence by the prosecution;
- (iii) close of prosecution case;
- (iv) calling of evidence by the defence[51];
- (v) close of defence case;
- (vi) (in trials on indictment) closing speech on behalf of the prosecution[52];

---

[49] It should be noted that evidence is normally given orally in English in open court, in the
presence of the defendant and (in trials on indictment) in the presence of the jury. Evidence
given in a foreign language must be interpreted: *Lee Kun* [1916] 1 K.B. 337, 343, *per* Lord
Reading C.J., applied by the Privy Council in *Kunnath v The State* [1993] 1 W.L.R. 1315. An
oral statement cannot be proved without translation into English: *Fakisandhla Nkambule v R*
[1940] A.C. 760, 771. Double translation is permissible where a single translator cannot be
found (using two interpreters sharing a common language other than English) but both must be
impartial and not connected with the accused or witness: *West London Youth Court Ex p. N*
[2000] 1 W.L.R. 2368. When a person is interviewed through an interpreter, the latter should
give evidence of the interview: *Attard* (1958) 43 Cr.App.R. 90. Similar rules may be applied to
a physically handicapped witness. In *Duffy* [1999] Q.B. 919, a witness with very poor powers
of speech witnessed the killing of his father. The only person capable of understanding him was
a social worker. The witness was interviewed at a police station: the social worker asked him
questions and interpreted the answers. The interview was video-recorded and the social worker
compiled a transcript of the interview. The trial judge held that the video amounted to a
document within s.23(1) of the Criminal Justice Act 1988 as the witness was not able to attend
court to give evidence: however, he refused to permit the recording or the transcript, on the
grounds that the recording was of poor quality and the fact that it was interpreted meant that it
was effectively the evidence of the interpreter. The Court of Appeal held that the recording
should have been admitted since it was a document within s.23(1) and the social worker was in
a position akin to that of a translator who could have given admissible evidence of what the
witness said in interview; the transcript was akin to the notes made by a witness at the time of
an event: as a result, the video and transcript would have been admitted together.
[50] It may sometimes be appropriate for prosecution counsel to repeat the opening where there
has been a substantial gap in time between the evidence of a witness and the resumption of
proceedings so as to remind the bench of the evidence given. If the prosecution opening is
repeated, the defence should be allowed to address the court in reply so as to correct any errors
or draw attention to any differences of recollection which might occur: *L and B v DPP* [1998]
2 Cr.App.R. 69. In *L and B* there had been a one month adjournment of proceedings mid-way
through the prosecution case.
[51] In trials on indictment defence counsel may make an opening speech to the jury if he is
calling evidence as to the facts other than that of the defendant himself: *Hill* (1912) 7
Cr.App.R. 1.
[52] In certain cases prosecuting counsel does not make a closing speech, *e.g.* where an unrepresented defendant calls no witnesses to the facts.

(vii)   speech on behalf of the defence;

(viii) (in trials on indictment) summing up by judge;

(ix)   retirement of the jury or justices.

As a general rule, evidence is given either for the prosecution or defence at the stages of the trial indicated above. There are, however, circumstances in which evidence may be given at later stages in the trial. Two such stages are discussed:

(a)   evidence called after the closing of the prosecution case; and

(b)   evidence called after speeches.

B. Evidence after the close of the prosecution case

19–35   As a general rule, the prosecution must call all the evidence on which it intends to rely before the close of its case.[53] However, the court has a discretion to allow the prosecution to call evidence after the close of its case and before the jury or justices retire. Three well-known examples are discussed below:

(a)   where there has been an omission to call technical evidence;

(b)   where the evidence has become available after the close of the case;

(c)   where the evidence is called in rebuttal.

However, the Court of Appeal in *Francis*[54] held that the judge's discretion to admit evidence in these circumstances is wider than that illustrated in the above examples. For instance, the Court in *Francis* held that the discretion extended to evidence not adduced as a result of a misunderstanding between counsel. Similarly, in *James v South Glamorgan C.C.*[55] the Divisional Court held that an unusual combination of circumstances, including a change of court location (of which witnesses had not been notified), entitled justices to allow the prosecution to call evidence after the close of its case.

The Court in *Francis* refrained from defining precisely the limits of the discretion since all the circumstances in which it would fall to be exercised could not be foreseen. As Mustill L.J. said in *Munnery*,[56] the trial judge

---

[53] *Rice* (1963) 47 Cr.App.R. 79, 85, *per* Winn J. The rule is one of practice and not one of law, *per* Winn J.
[54] (1990) 91 Cr.App.R. 271.
[55] (1994) 99 Cr.App.R. 321.
[56] (1992) 94 Cr.App.R. 164.

must be left with some degree of freedom to meet the various and unpredictable problems which may arise during a trial.

The following principles for the exercise of the discretion may be distilled from the authorities mentioned above:　　　　　　　　　　　　　　　19–36

1.　The discretion should be exercised rarely and with caution.

2.　The earlier the application is made after the close of the prosecution case the better for the prosecution.

3.　The judge should have in mind the adversarial nature of the process and that "to depart substantially from the normal order of events, unless justice really demands, is liable to cause confusion and hardship."[57]

4.　The judge should also have in mind that the defendant may be prejudiced if the judge allows the prosecution to fill a gap in its evidence to which the defence had drawn attention by a submission of no case.

5.　These considerations are not necessarily conclusive. "[J]ustice is what matters: justice to the public, represented by the prosecution, as well as to the defendant."[58]

Accordingly, it is submitted that courts are seldom justified in admitting evidence in these circumstances, other than in the examples mentioned below; and that such evidence may only be admitted for the most cogent reasons.

(1) Omission to call technical evidence

The prosecution may not re-open its case and call further evidence if it concerns matters of real substance.[59] Thus, it may not re-open its case in order to meet a submission of no case: it should not be allowed an adjournment in order to call evidence for this purpose.[60]

On the other hand, the court in both a trial on indictment and summary trial has a discretion to allow the prosecution in such circumstances to call further evidence if it concerns matters which are purely technical. Thus, the judge in a trial on indictment may allow the prosecution to call such evidence after the close of its case[61] and justices have a similar discretion.[62] For instance, if the evidence relates to a technicality such as the proof of a

19–37

---

[57] *Munnery*, above, at 173, *per* Mustill L.J.
[58] *ibid.*
[59] *Day* (1940) 27 Cr.App.R. 168; *Middleton v Rowlett* [1954] 1 W.L.R. 831; *Gainsborough J. Ex p. Green* (1984) 78 Cr.App.R. 9.
[60] *Central Criminal Court Ex p. Garnier* [1988] R.T.R. 42.
[61] *McKenna* (1956) 40 Cr.App.R. 65.
[62] *Middleton v Rowlett*, above; *Royal v Prescott-Clark* [1966] 1 W.L.R. 788.

statutory rule or order, justices should allow the prosecution to re-open its case.[63] Thus, the Divisional Court held that the justices in a case of unlawful driving on a motorway should have allowed the prosecution to re-open its case to prove that a notice of the opening of the motorway had been published.[64] Similarly, where it was alleged that a defendant's counsel had been pressed into revealing the purely technical defence that prosecution statements did not disclose a complete chain of evidence at the time of plea, the Divisional Court held that there had been no prejudice as the matter would have been adjourned in any event once the issue had come to the prosecution's attention for them to remedy the defect.[65]

It has also been held that the court's discretion extends to admitting evidence relating to some matters of substance such as evidence which had not been adduced through an oversight.[66] Thus, in *Matthews v Morris*,[67] the Divisional Court held that the justices had correctly allowed the prosecution to re-open its case to tender a statement which by mistake had not been tendered as part of the prosecution case, but which had been served on the defence under s.9 of the Criminal Justice Act 1967. The court observed that no injustice was done to the defendant by the admission of the evidence after the close of the prosecution case. It is submitted that if there is any risk of such injustice the evidence should not be admitted.

(2) Evidence not available before

19–38   If evidence becomes available for the first time after the close of the prosecution case the court may admit it as a matter of discretion even if it is not strictly of a rebutting character. Thus, Winn J. said that the question of whether or not such evidence should be admitted is: "a matter to be determined by the trial judge in his discretion, exercised in such a way that subject to such safeguards as seems to him best suited to achieve justice between the Crown and the defendant and between the defendants."[68]

However, the admission of such evidence is extremely rare. An example is to be found in *Doran*.[69] In that case the judge allowed the prosecution to call two witnesses after the close of its case. The witnesses were members of the public who had been present at the trial. During the course of the defence case they realised that they could give material evidence. The prosecution had not been aware that the evidence was available. The Court of Appeal upheld the judge's ruling. The Court said:

---

[63] *Duffin v Markham* [1918] 88 L.J.K.B. 581.
[64] *Royal v Prescott-Clark*, above.
[65] *Horseferry Road Magistrates Court Ex p. Hillier* (1998) 162 J.P. 783.
[66] *Piggott v Sims* [1973] R.T.R. 15.
[67] [1981] Crim.L.R. 495.
[68] *Rice* (1963) 47 Cr.App.R. 79, 85.
[69] (1972) 56 Cr.App.R. 429.

(a) that the question in every case was whether it was right to serve the ends of justice that the evidence should be admitted; and

(b) that in such a case the court must be vigilant to ensure that no injustice is done to the defendants.

If the evidence is admitted, the court should ensure that proper notice of it has been given to the defence and that they have sufficient time to consider it and take instructions. Accordingly, the general practice is for the prosecution to serve it by way of notice of additional evidence and for the court to grant an adjournment if needed.[70] It may also be necessary to adjourn the case to allow the defence to call rebutting evidence. The Court of Appeal quashed a conviction in a case where the judge called a police witness after the close of the prosecution case and then refused the defence an adjournment to call evidence in rebuttal.[71]

(3) Evidence in rebuttal

In cases where the defendant or his witnesses give evidence of some new matter which the prosecution could not have foreseen the court may allow the prosecution to call evidence in reply. Such evidence is called evidence in rebuttal. Tindal C.J. stated the principle:

19–39

> "There can be no doubt about the general rule, that where the Crown begins a case (as it is with an ordinary plaintiff), they bring forward their evidence, and cannot afterwards support their case by calling fresh witnesses, because there may be evidence in the defence to contradict it. But if any matter arises *ex improviso*, which the Crown could not foresee, supposing it to be entirely new matter, which they may be able to answer only by contradictory evidence, they may give evidence in reply."[72]

Lord Goddard C.J. said that this observation was in wider language than would be used today.[73] The modern test is to ask whether the prosecution could reasonably have foreseen that the matter would arise.[74] If the evidence is clearly relevant, it should be called before the close of the prosecution case.[75]

> "Where the evidence sought to be introduced in rebuttal is itself evidence probative of the guilt of the defendant and where it is reasonably

---

[70] *Dartey* (1987) 84 Cr.App.R. 352, 355.
[71] *Coleman, The Times*, November 21, 1987.
[72] *Frost* [1839] 9 C. & P. 129, 159.
[73] *Owen* [1952] 2 Q.B. 362, 367.
[74] *Scott* (1984) 79 Cr.App.R. 49.
[75] *Levy and Tait* (1966) 50 Cr.App.R. 198.

foreseeable by the prosecution that some gap in the proof of guilt needs to be filled by evidence called by the prosecution then, generally speaking, the court is likely to rule against the closing of any such gap by rebuttal evidence."[76]

The question whether a matter is reasonably foreseeable will be a matter for the judge to determine in the circumstances of the particular case. In some cases the line to be taken by the defence is apparent from the defendant's statements to the police in interview: in others, it is revealed during cross-examination of prosecution witnesses. In such cases, it will be difficult for the prosecution to say that it has been taken by surprise. On the other hand, there may be matters which the prosecution could not possibly have foreseen, for instance allegations that police officers have fabricated evidence when those allegations are made for the first time during the defendant's evidence. In *Mendy*[77] a man left court and spoke to the husband of the accused. When the husband gave evidence he denied that he had spoken to the man. The Court of Appeal held that evidence in rebuttal had properly been given because the episode indicated that the husband was prejudiced and was prepared to cheat in furtherance of the wife's cause.

19–40   The prosecution cannot be expected to anticipate the extraordinary or bizarre, as the case of *Hutchinson*[78] illustrates. The defendant in that case was charged with offences of murder. Before trial he wrote a letter to the Director of Public Prosecutions in which he mentioned a particular family by name. When giving evidence at the trial he accused a journalist sitting in the press gallery of committing the murders. The journalist bore the same name as the family mentioned in the letter. The prosecution was allowed to call the journalist in rebuttal. The defendant appealed on the ground, *inter alia*, that the journalist's evidence should have been excluded because the letter should have warned the prosecution of the possibility of the accusation being made. The Court of Appeal held that the evidence was admissible because the letter contained so many obviously untrue allegations that the prosecution was entitled to disregard it, and it would be unreasonable to say that it should have anticipated that anything in it would be repeated. The Court said that the prosecution is not expected to take notice of fanciful and unreal statements no matter from what source they emanate.

Whether the evidence is admitted or not is a matter for the discretion of the judge, which should be applied with caution.[79]

---

[76] *Milliken* (1969) 53 Cr.App.R. 330, 333, *per* Winn L.J.
[77] (1977) 64 Cr.App.R.4.
[78] (1986) 82 Cr.App.R. 51.
[79] *Owen* [1952] 2 Q.B. 362, 368.

C. Evidence after speeches

Evidence may be given until the time when the jury or justices retire. Thus, **19–41**
evidence may be given after counsel have made their speeches.[80] There is a
general discretion to permit the calling of evidence after closing speeches.
Before exercising this discretion the court should look carefully at the
interests of justice overall, and in particular, the risk of any prejudice
whatsoever to the defendant. Each case should be considered on its own
facts and the discretion sparingly used.[81] However, such a course may be
justified because counsel in a closing speech raises matters which should
have been the subject of evidence; in these circumstances the other side may
well be entitled to call evidence in rebuttal. The Court of Appeal upheld the
trial judge's decision to allow the prosecution to call rebuttal evidence after
defence counsel's closing speech, since no questions had been asked of
prosecution witnesses, the defendant had not given evidence, and the prosecution could not reasonably have been expected to foresee the argument
raised in the speech which contained evidential implications.[82] Similarly, in
summary proceedings, the prosecution were allowed to recall an expert
witness to provide evidence, as required by statute, that equipment used
during breath test procedures in a drink-drive case had been correctly
working at all times where defence counsel had failed to lay the ground for
his submission either by cross-examination or by calling evidence.[83]

The usual rule is that no evidence may be given after the summing-up.[84]
The rule applies to the prosecution, although it would appear that some
latitude may be extended to the defence. Thus, in *Sanderson*,[85] an exception
to the rule was made in favour of the defence when a witness arrived late
for the hearing and was allowed to give evidence after the summing-up. The
Court of Criminal Appeal said that this course was right because the extra
leave was extended to the defence but it was not a course which should be
taken often.

Once the jury has retired in a trial on indictment, no further evidence **19–42**
should be given.[86] This has been described as a strict rule[87] and if evidence
is allowed after the jury has retired even in a matter which appears irrelevant to the issues raised in the trial, the conviction will be quashed. Thus, in
Owen,[88] the jury, after retiring, sent a message saying that it wanted some
further evidence. The judge allowed this request and further evidence was

---

[80] *Jolly v DPP* [2000] Crim.L.R. 471 and *Morrison* (1911) 75 J.P. 272.
[81] *Jolly, ibid.*
[82] *O'Hadhmaill* [1996] Crim.L.R. 509.
[83] *Jolly, ibid.*
[84] *Owen* [1952] 2 Q.B. 362, 368–369, *per* Lord Goddard C.J.
[85] (1953) 37 Cr.App.R. 32.
[86] *Browne* (1943) 29 Cr.App.R. 106; *Wilson* (1957) 41 Cr.App.R. 226; *Corless* (1972) 56 Cr.App.R. 341.
[87] *Gearing* (1966) 50 Cr.App.R. 18, 21, *per* Lord Parker C.J.
[88] [1952] 2 Q.B. 362.

given. The Court of Criminal Appeal held that this was wrong and quashed the conviction. Lord Goddard C.J. said:

> "The theory of our law is that he who affirms must prove and therefore it is for the prosecutor to prove his case, and if there is some matter which the prosecution might have proved but have not, it is too late after summing up to allow further evidence to be given, and that whether it might have been given by one of the witnesses already called or whether it would necessitate ... the calling of a fresh witness. If this were allowed, it is difficult to see what limitation could be put on it."[89]

If in extremely unusual circumstances the defence invites the judge to allow the trial to continue, it may do so. Thus, in *Kaul and Collin*[90] the jury, after retiring, discovered articles inside a rucksack which had been empty when counsel examined it at the start of the trial. Fresh evidence was introduced. Counsel invited the judge to allow the trial to continue; which he did and directed the jury that the rucksack was to be treated as empty. The Court of Appeal, allowing the appeal, said that the introduction of fresh evidence after the jury had retired should almost inevitably lead to the jury being discharged; in certain circumstances the defence might properly invite the judge to allow the trial to continue, but if they did so, and the defendant was convicted, they could be regarded as having given up the right to carry out further investigation which the discovery of fresh evidence might have necessitated.

19–43   The rule extends to the inspection by the jury of objects referred to in the evidence.[91] In *Lawrence*,[92] the Court of Appeal quashed the conviction because the jury was allowed, after retirement, to leave the court to inspect a car which had been mentioned in the evidence. A similar incident occurred in *Nixon*,[93] but the inspection of the car in that case took place at the express wish of the defence. The Court of Appeal held that there had been an irregularity but dismissed the appeal on the ground that there had been no miscarriage of justice.

A fortiori, the jury may not be provided in its room with something which was not part of the evidence in the trial.[94] As a result, the Court of Appeal has held that a judge was wrong to allow a jury to have a map which had not been adduced in evidence.[95] Similarly, if the jury wishes to

---

[89] At 368–369.
[90] *The Times*, November 10, 1997.
[91] This rule does not, of course, prevent the jury from examining exhibits in their retiring room.
[92] (1968) 52 Cr.App.R. 163.
[93] (1968) 52 Cr.App.R. 218.
[94] See *Davis* (1976) 62 Cr.App.R. 194, 201.
[95] *Thomas (Horatio Gerald), The Times*, February 9, 1987. It is an irregularity for an usher to supply the jury with a dictionary at their request without informing the trial judge: *Wallace* [1990] Crim.L.R. 433.

conduct an experiment such as weighing or measuring an exhibit, it must be done in open court.[96] This is to avoid the danger of the jury relying on material which was not subject to cross-examination, argument by counsel or direction by the judge.

This rule also applies to any reconstruction which the jury might be minded to carry out in their room. Thus, in *Crees*[97] (a murder trial) the jury called for "something like a kitchen knife to re-enact the situation." They were provided with a ruler, but were given no further direction. The Court of Appeal, quashing the conviction, said that the real objection lay in the lack of warning since the jury might have drawn conclusions from the re-enactment rather than from the evidence.

In *Stewart and Sappleton*[98] the Court of Appeal held that there had been **19–44** a material irregularity when the judge allowed the jury to be provided with scales in the jury room in order to clarify evidence relating to the weight of certain exhibits. The Court said that to provide the jury with a magnifying glass or ruler would be to give them something new. However, in *Maggs*,[99] another division of the Court said that this observation was obiter, and so far as it sought to lay down a general principle, was too wide. In *Maggs*, a sketch-plan had been produced in evidence with measurements in metres. The jury asked for a measuring-tape. A surveyor's tape was available and the jury were provided with it. The Court of Appeal held that no material irregularity had occurred. The Court said that equipment that was required to enable a jury to carry out unsupervised scientific experiments in their room was not admissible, but that a magnifying glass, or a ruler, or a tape did not normally raise the possibility of such an experiment. If the jury wishes to have a question resolved relating to an exhibit (for example clarifying something on a photograph), the answer should be given in open court. On the other hand, it is submitted that if the question relates to something not in evidence, for example the weight of an exhibit, it is usually safer for the judge to tell the jury that there is no evidence about it.

For the playing of tape recordings of interviews after retirement, see para.2–25, above.

If the jury asks a question of the judge after he has finished his summing-up, the practice is to tell the jury, if it be the case, that no evidence on the point has been given and it must take it that there is no evidence upon it.[1] On the other hand, if the jury asks a question on a point about which evidence has been given, the practice is for the judge to remind it of the evidence.

The same general rule applies to magistrates' courts. In the absence of special circumstances, justices should not allow evidence to be called once

---

[96] *Higgins, The Times,* February 16, 1989.
[97] [1996] Crim.L.R. 830.
[98] (1989) 89 Cr.App.R. 273.
[99] [1990] Crim.L.R. 654.
[1] *Owen,* above, at 368.

they have retired.[2] Thus, convictions have been quashed where prosecution witnesses have been called after the bench has retired.[3]

---

[2] *Webb v Leadbetter* [1966] 1 W.L.R. 245, *per* Lord Parker C.J.
[3] *Webb v Leadbetter*, above; *French's Dairies v Davis* [1973] Crim.L.R. 630, DC.

CHAPTER 20

Previous Consistent Statements

This Chapter discusses the rules in relation to a previous consistent statement made by a witness, *i.e.* a statement which conforms with the witness's evidence given at trial. The general rule is that a witness's previous consistent statement is not admissible in evidence. There are, however, a number of exceptions to the rule; and the rule and exceptions play an important part in the criminal trial. A discussion of these topics forms the subject of Part I of this Chapter. A similar (but unrelated) rule permits a witness to refresh his or her memory from a statement made-prior to trial. This rule forms the subject-matter of Part II.

20–01

1. THE RULE AGAINST PREVIOUS CONSISTENT STATEMENTS

A. The General Rule

A witness may not seek to confirm or strengthen his evidence by saying in the witness-box that he had made a similar statement on a previous occasion.[1] Nor may he, if the statement is in writing, refer to it for the same purpose.[2] The rule against previous consistent statements, sometimes called "the rule against narrative" or "the rule against self-serving statements" prevents the witness giving such evidence.

20–02

The rule applies both when the witness is answering his own counsel, and when he is being cross-examined by the opposing party. "(The) evidence of a witness cannot be corroborated by proving statements to the same effect made by him; nor will the fact that his testimony is impeached in cross-examination render such evidence admissible."[3]

The rule also prevents other witnesses being called to prove such statements. Thus, in *Roberts*,[4] the defendant was charged with the murder of a girl by shooting. The defence was accident. While the defendant was in custody after his arrest, he told his father about his defence. At the trial, the

---

[1] *Roberts* (1942) 28 Cr.App.R. 102; *Larkin* [1943] 1 K.B. 174; *Jones v S.E. & Chatham Ry Co.* (1918) 87 L.J.K.B. 775, 778–779; *Gillie v Posho* [1939] 2 All E.R. 196; *Corke v Corke and Cooke* [1958] P. 93; *Fox v General Medical Council* [1960] 1 W.L.R. 1017, 1025.
[2] *Gillie v Posho*, above.
[3] *Coll* (1889) 24 I.R. 522, 541, *per* Holmes J.
[4] Above.

judge refused to allow the father to give evidence of what his son had told him. The Court of Criminal Appeal upheld this ruling. Humphreys J. said: "The rule is sometimes expressed as being that a party is not permitted to make evidence for himself. ... So, in a criminal case an accused person is not permitted to call evidence to show that, after he has been charged with an offence, he told a number of persons what his defence was going to be."[5] The reasons for the rule appear to be that such evidence (a) may be easily manufactured; and (b) is of no evidential value, since a witness's evidence is not confirmed by the fact that he said the same thing to somebody else on a previous occasion.[6]

B. Exceptions

20–03   Three exceptions to the rule are well known and recognised:

  (i)   complaints in sexual cases made at the first opportunity and known as "recent complaints";

  (ii)   statements forming part of the "*res gestae*"; and

  (iii) statements to rebut allegations of recent invention.

Mr R.N. Gooderson identified two further exceptions: (a) statements relating to a previous identification; and (b) previous statements by accused persons.[7] These statements have not have been recognised generally as exceptions to the rule. However, in both cases previous consistent statements may be admitted. Accordingly, it is convenient to discuss them here.

(1) Recent complaints

20–04   In cases of rape, indecent assault and other sexual offences against women or girls, evidence that the victim made a complaint is admissible to show that her conduct in complaining was: (a) consistent with her evidence in the witness-box; and (b) (if consent is in issue) inconsistent with her consent to the actions complained of.[8] Such evidence has also been held to be admissible in a case of indecency against a boy under 16 years of age[9] and

---

[5] At 105.
[6] *Roberts* (1942) 28 Cr.App.R. 102, 105–106; *Fox v General Medical Council* [1960] 1 W.L.R. 1017, 1025, *per* Lord Radcliffe.
[7] "Previous Consistent Statements" [1968] C.L.J. 64.
[8] *Lillyman* [1896] 2 Q.B. 167; *Osborne* [1905] 1 K.B. 551. The evidence is admissible whether consent is in issue or not: *Osborne*, above. In *Wink* (1834) 6 C. & P. 397, evidence of complaint was admitted in a case of robbery. *Wink* was not expressly overruled in *Lillyman* and *Osborne*. However, the dicta in those cases confined the admissibility of complaints to sexual cases. It would be very surprising if this limitation were now not held to exist and evidence of complaint was admissible in other types of case.
[9] *Camelleri* [1922] 2 K.B. 122; *Coulthread* (1933) 24 Cr.App.R. 4.

buggery with a youth of 19.[10] It would appear that it is admissible in the case of such offences against a male of any age.[11]

It should be borne in mind that evidence of complaint is only admissible for the purpose mentioned above, *i.e.* to show consistency. Such evidence is not admissible as evidence of the facts complained of.[12] Thus, in *Brasier*,[13] the accused was charged with assaulting a girl under seven years of age with intent to rape her. After the incident the girl complained to her mother. At the trial the child was not permitted to give evidence. However, the mother gave evidence of the child's complaint and the judge left the evidence to the jury as evidence of the facts complained of. It was held that the evidence of complaint should not have been admitted because there was no evidence of the commission of the offence.

It follows that the judge must direct the jury that the evidence should not be treated as evidence of the facts complained of, but used only for the purpose mentioned.[14] The Judicial Studies Board standard direction[15] (which was approved by the Court of Appeal in *Islam*[16]) is to the effect that the evidence may help the jury decide whether the complainant has told them the truth, but it cannot be independent confirmation of their evidence since it does not come from a source independent of them. In *K*[17] evidence from a mother who had elicited details of an assault from her young daughter that corroborated the daughter's complaint, as well as a letter written by the daughter containing details of that assault and others, were put before the jury. It was held that a "full and careful" direction should have been given to the effect that the corroborative evidence of the mother and the letter were not independent support for the complainant's evidence. Moreover, as the complainant was a young child from whom evidence had been elicited, the jury should have been warned of her suggestibility.

Both the fact of the complaint and the terms in which it was made may be proved. Until the decision of the Court of Crown Cases Reserved in *Lillyman*[18] the practice was to limit such evidence to the fact that a complaint was made. However, in *Lillyman* the defendant was charged with indecent assault and connected offences against a girl aged under 16. Shortly after the incidents the girl complained to her school mistress. At the trial the judge ruled that the school mistress should be asked to state the details of

20–05

---

[10] *Warnell* (1923) 17 Cr.App.R. 53.

[11] See *Camelleri*, above, *per* Lord Hewart C.J. These offences now include male rape, made an offence by the Criminal Justice and Public Order Act 1994, s.142.

[12] *Brasier* (1779) 1 Leach 199; *Wood* (1877) 14 Cox 46; *Lillyman*, *op.cit.*, at 170, *per* Hawkins J.; *Wallwork* (1958) 42 Cr.App.R. 153, 161, *per* Lord Goddard C.J.

[13] Above.

[14] *Lillyman*, above, at 178; *Wallwork* (1958) 42 Cr.App.R. 153, 162, *per* Lord Goddard C.J.

[15] www.jsboard.co.uk.

[16] [1999] 1 Cr.App.R. 22. In *Islam* the Court of Appeal said that such a direction was essential since the matter was one of law and not of judgment or discretion. *Islam* was followed in *K* [1999] Crim.L.R. 980.

[17] Above.

[18] Above.

the complaint in the language used by the girl. The Court upheld the judge's ruling and held that the whole statement of a woman containing her alleged complaint should be given:

> "for the purpose of enabling the jury to judge for themselves whether the conduct of the woman was consistent with her testimony on oath given in the witness-box negativing her consent, and affirming that the acts complained of were against her will, and in accordance with the conduct they would expect in a truthful woman under the circumstances detailed by her. The jury, and they only, are the persons to be satisfied whether the woman's conduct was so consistent or not. Without proof of her condition, demeanour, and verbal expressions, all of which are of vital importance in the consideration of that question, how is it possible for them satisfactorily to determine it?"[19]

As the court pointed out, if evidence of the terms of the complaint were not admitted, it would be left to the witness to whom the statement was made to determine whether a real (as opposed to a feigned) complaint had been made.

Evidence of a complaint is not admissible if the victim gives no evidence about the matter complained of.[20] Thus, in *Wallwork*, the defendant was charged with incest with his daughter, aged five. The child was called to give evidence, but said nothing. Her grandmother, however, gave evidence that the child had made a complaint about the defendant's conduct. The Court of Criminal Appeal held that the evidence concerning the complaint should not have been admitted because there was no evidence given by the complainant with which the complaint could be shown to be consistent.

20–06 Conversely, evidence of a previous complaint is not admissible from the victim unless the person to whom the complaint was made gives evidence. In *White*,[21] the Privy Council held that the complainant's own evidence that she made complaints to her parents, aunt, friend, and neighbour, in a case where those to whom the complaints were made did not give evidence, would not assist in proving consistency or negative consent. The danger being that the jury was bound to infer that she had made complaints in terms substantially the same as her evidence in court. Accordingly, not only must the complainant testify as to the making of the complaint but the recipient should prove its terms.

In order to be admissible, the complaint must have been made at the first reasonable opportunity.[22] It is thus said that the complaint must be "recent". It is a matter for the court to determine whether the complaint

---

[19] At 177, *per* Hawkins J.
[20] *Wallwork* (1958) 42 Cr.App.R. 153; *Guttridge* (1840) 9 C. & P. 471; *Brasier* (1779) 1 Leach 199, cited para.20–04, above; *Wright and Ormerod* (1987) 90 Cr.App.R. 91.
[21] [1999] 1 A.C. 210.
[22] *Lillyman*, above, at 171; *Osborne* [1905] 1 K.B. 551, 561.

was made as speedily as could reasonably be expected.[23] Circumstances in this sort of case will vary. Thus, in one case a complaint made after a day had elapsed was rejected[24]; in another, a complaint made after a week had elapsed was admitted.[25] Generally, however, complaints of more than a week old will not be held admissible.[26]

The fact that there was opportunity to make the complaint to others before it was made to the witness to whom it was made does not make it inadmissible.[27]

To be admissible the complaint must be made at the first reasonable opportunity. Thus in *Valentine*[28] the complainant had been raped at knife-point one night by the defendant whom she had met while she was making her way home. After the rape, she returned home where her parents and brother were asleep. The next morning she told her brother that she had been attacked with a knife, but she added that she did not want to tell her parents. She went to work that afternoon, but made no complaint until the evening when she complained to a friend that she had been raped. It was argued that this complaint was inadmissible because it was not made at the first opportunity which presented itself after the offence. The Court of Appeal, noting that we now have a greater understanding that victims of sexual offences often need time before they can bring themselves to complain and that some feel they can complain to a member of their family (and nobody else) while others feel they can only complain to somebody who is not a member of their family, rejected this argument and held that the complaint was admissible. The Court said that a complaint can be recent and admissible, although not made at the first opportunity which presented itself, provided it is made at the first reasonable opportunity. "What is the first reasonable opportunity will depend on the circumstances including the character of the complainant and the relationship between the complainant and the person to whom she complained and the persons to whom she might have complained but did not do so."[29]

There is no reason to prevent more than one complaint being admitted if **20–07** both were made within a reasonable time.[30] However, this does not allow the prosecution to adduce evidence of several complaints made in similar terms, where to do so would be prejudicial since it might lead a jury to consider the contents of the complaints to be evidence of the truth of what they asserted.[31]

The complaint must be voluntary in the sense that it was not made as a

---

[23] *Cummings* [1948] 1 All E.R. 551.
[24] *Rush* (1896) 60 J.P. 777.
[25] *Hedges* (1909) 3 Cr.App.R. 262.
[26] *Birks* [2003] Crim.L.R. 401.
[27] *Wilbourne* (1917) 12 Cr.App.R. 279.
[28] [1996] 2 Cr.App.R. 213.
[29] At 223.
[30] *Lee* (1911) 7 Cr.App.R. 31.
[31] *Valentine*, above.

result of "leading, inducing or intimidating questions".[32] Thus, it has been said that questions such as "Did X assault you?" "Did X do this and that to you?" would render the answers inadmissible.[33] On the other hand, the fact that the questioner speaks first does not necessarily make the reply inadmissible.[34] Thus, neutral questions such as "why are you crying?" or "what is the matter?" will not make the replies inadmissible. Whether or not the complaint is voluntary is a matter to be determined by the trial judge.[35]

The evidence of the recent complaint is usually given by the person to whom it was made: the complainant's own evidence to this effect is of little value in showing consistency. If such evidence is given by the complainant, the judge must give the jury a careful direction as to its limited value.[36]

(2) Statements forming part of the res gestae

20–08 A witness's previous consistent statement may be admissible because it is part of the *res gestae*, meaning part of the transaction or story.[37] Thus, in *Fowkes*,[38] the defendant was charged with murder. He was known as "Butcher". A witness gave evidence that he was in a room with a police officer and the deceased when the latter was shot through the window. Just before the shot was fired, the witness saw a face at the window which he thought was that of "Butcher". He was allowed to say that on seeing the face, he had shouted "There's Butcher"; and the police officer was allowed to give evidence to the same effect.

(3) Statements to rebut allegations of recent invention

20–09 A witness's previous consistent statement is admissible to rebut an allegation in cross-examination that his evidence has been invented or fabricated after the events in question and, thus, is a "recent" invention or fabrication. The principle of admissibility was stated by Dixon C.J. as follows:

> "If the credit of a witness is impugned as to some material fact to which he deposes upon the ground that his account is a late invention or has been lately devised or reconstructed, even though not with conscious dishonesty, that makes admissible a statement to the same effect as the account he gave as a witness, if it was made contemporaneously with the event or at a time sufficiently early to be

---

[32] *Osborne* [1905] 1 K.B. 551, *per* Ridley J; *Norcott* [1917] 1 K.B. 347.
[33] *Osborne*, above, at 561.
[34] *Norcott*, above.
[35] *Osborne*, above, at 556.
[36] *White, The Times*, September 25, 1998.
[37] *Roberts* (1942) 28 Cr.App.R. 102, 105–106, *per* Humphreys J. See para.8–50, for a discussion of the meaning of *res gestae* and for exceptions to the hearsay rule connected therewith.
[38] Stephen, *Digest of the Law of Evidence* (12th ed., 1948), p.8. This example may also be admissible as a result of the exception discussed below, relating to a previous identification of the defendant para.20–12.

inconsistent with the suggestion that his account is a later invention or reconstruction."[39]

This was demonstrated in *Oyesiku*,[40] where the defendant was charged with assaulting a police officer. The officer was attempting to arrest the defendant for non-payment of rates. After the alleged assault, the defendant was arrested and detained in custody. While he was in custody, the defendant's wife made a statement to a solicitor about the alleged assault. She said in the statement that the police officer was the aggressor. At the defendant's trial she gave evidence according to her statement. When she was cross-examined, prosecuting counsel suggested that she had made up her evidence. In re-examination, defending counsel was allowed to adduce evidence that she had made the statement and that it was consistent with her evidence. The judge refused to allow the jury to see the statement. However, the Court of Appeal held that the jury should have been allowed to see the statement to assess the extent to which it rebutted the allegation of recent invention.

A further example is to be found in *Flanagan v Fahy*[41] where a witness gave evidence about the forging of a will. In cross-examination it was put to him that he had invented the story because of hostility which existed between him and the accused. Evidence was then admitted to establish that the witness had given an account consistent with his evidence to a third party before the cause of hostility had arisen.

The mere fact that the witness's testimony is impeached in cross-examination will not make such evidence admissible[42] and the fact that his consistency is challenged will not necessarily have this effect. Thus: **20–10**

> "even if the impeachment takes the form of showing a contradiction or inconsistency between the evidence given at the trial and something said by the witness on a former occasion it does not follow that the way is open for proof of other statements made by him for the purpose of sustaining his credit. There must be something either in the nature of the inconsistent statement, or in the use made of it by the cross-examiner, to enable such evidence to be given."[43]

This principle is sometimes overlooked and attempts are made to have an earlier consistent statement put before the jury. The Court of Appeal has reiterated that there is no general exception to the rule to the effect that

---

[39] *Nominal Defendant v Clements* (1961) 104 C.L.R. 476, 479, approved by the Court of Appeal in *Oyesiku* (1972) 56 Cr.App.R. 240.
[40] Above.
[41] [1918] 1 I.R. 361.
[42] *Fox v General Medical Council* [1960] 1 W.L.R. 1017; *Coll*, below.
[43] *Coll* (1889) 24 I.R. 522, 541, *per* Holmes J.

where counsel cross-examined to show inconsistency the witness could be re-examined to show consistency.[44]

20–11   It will be a matter for the judge to determine in the circumstances of the particular case whether as a matter of discretion the evidence should be admitted. Evidence of recent complaint ruled inadmissible because it was not made at the earliest opportunity may become admissible in order to rebut suggestions put to a witnesses in cross-examination that the complainant's allegations were of recent fabrication.[45] Before admitting the evidence he must exercise care in ensuring that:

(i)   the witness's account had been attacked on the ground of recent invention;

(ii)   the statement is consistent with the witness's evidence; and

(iii) having regard to the time and circumstances in which the statement was made, it tends to answer the attack.[46]

The purpose of admitting such evidence is to show that the witness has been consistent in his account and, thus, to rebut the allegation of recent invention or fabrication.[47] Accordingly, it is not admissible as evidence of the facts stated.

(4) Statements relating to a previous identification

20–12   Evidence that a witness identified the defendant at the time of or soon after the offence is admissible, together with any statement forming part of the identification.[48] The purpose of such evidence is to show consistency in the identification made by the witness, *i.e.* to confirm the identification of the defendant in court and to show that the witness "was able to identify at the time and to exclude the idea that the identification of the prisoner in the dock was an afterthought or mistake."[49] For a discussion of the admissibility of evidence relating to an out of court identification, see para.14–16 *et seq.*, above.

(5) Previous statements by accused persons

20–13   It is the practice for the prosecution to adduce in evidence oral or written statements made by defendants to the police, whether they contain admissions of guilt or denials. To the extent that the statements consist of

---

[44] *Beattie* (1989) 89 Cr.App.R. 302, 307, *per* Lord Lane C.J.; *Weekes* [1988] Crim.L.R. 245.
[45] *Tyndale* [1999] Crim.L.R. 320.
[46] *Nominal Defendant v Clements*, above, at 479, *per* Dixon C.J., approved by the Court of Appeal in *Oyesiku*, above.
[47] *Benjamin* (1913) 8 Cr.App.R. 146.
[48] *Christie* [1914] A.C. 545.
[49] *Christie*, above, at 551, *per* Lord Haldane L.C.

denials they are previous consistent statements and admissible when adduced by the prosecution, despite the rule prohibiting such statements.[50] However, this rule is subject to qualification. Accordingly, it is necessary to analyse the contents of statements made in these circumstances to the police.

Admissions and exculpatory statements.   A statement containing an   **20–14** admission is admissible as evidence of the facts stated.[51] Nothing further need be said here about this rule: see paras 9–01 *et seq.*, for a discussion.

An exculpatory statement is not evidence of the facts stated since (with the exception of an admission) "a statement made by an accused person is never evidence of the facts in the statement".[52] Thus, the judge does not have to take such a statement into account if there is a submission of no case[53] or remind the jury of its terms if the defendant does not give evidence.[54] (See, however, para.16–15 on judge's summing-up where defendant does not give evidence.)

However, such a statement is admissible as showing the attitude of the accused when questioned[55] or "the reaction of the accused when first taxed with incriminating facts"[56] (provided that the reference to the reaction of the accused when "first taxed" is not read as circumscribing the limits of admissibility).[57]

Accordingly, (a) it is a misdirection to tell the jury that anything which the defendant may have said is not evidence save in so far as it may consist of admissions[58] and (b) evidence which shows such a reaction should not be excluded.

In *McCarthy*[59] the defendant was charged with burglary. He was arrested three days after the offence and interviewed. He denied the charge and gave details of an alibi orally and in writing. The Judge refused to admit evidence of the interview and statement. The Court of Appeal held that this evidence had been wrongly excluded and said that one of the best pieces of evidence that an innocent man can produce is his reaction to an accusation of a crime.

Thus, the defence may rely on the earlier statement in order to show consistency between the defendant's immediate reaction on being questioned and his evidence at the trial.

---

[50] The defence may not adduce evidence of a previous consistent statement.
[51] *Pearce* (1979) 69 Cr.App.R. 365, 369.
[52] *Pearce* (1979) 69 Cr.App.R. 365, 369; *Donaldson* (1977) 64 Cr.App.R. 59, 64; *Kurshid* [1984] Crim.L.R. 288. See, however, "mixed" statements, para.20–17 below.
[53] *Storey*, below.
[54] *Barbery* (1975) 62 Cr.App.R. 248.
[55] *Pearce*, above; *Storey*; *McCarthy*, below.
[56] *Storey* (1968) 52 Cr.App.R. 334, 337–338, *per* Lord Widgery C.J. below.
[57] See *Pearce*, above, at 369.
[58] *McCarthy*, below.
[59] (1980) 71 Cr.App.R. 142.

20–15   The Court of Appeal in *Pearce*[60] summarised the principles relating to admissions and exculpatory statements as follows:

> "(1)   A statement which contains an admission is always admissible as a declaration against interest and is evidence of the facts admitted. With this exception a statement made by an accused person is never evidence of the facts in the statement.
>
> (2)   (a) A statement that is not an admission is admissible to show the attitude of the accused at the time when he made it. This however is not to be limited to a statement made on the first encounter with the police. The reference in *Storey* to the reaction of the accused 'when first taxed' should not be read as circumscribing the limits of admissibility. The longer the time that has elapsed after the first encounter the less the weight which will be attached to the denial. (b) A statement that is not in itself an admission is admissible if it is made in the same context as an admission, whether in the course of an interview or in the form of a voluntary statement. It would be unfair to admit only the statements against interest while excluding part of the same interview or series of interviews. It is the duty of the prosecution to present the case fairly to the jury; to exclude answers which are favourable to the accused while admitting those unfavourable would be misleading. (c) The prosecution may wish to draw attention to inconsistent denials. A denial does not become an admission because it is inconsistent with another denial. There must be many cases however where convictions have resulted from such inconsistencies between two denials.
>
> (3)   Although in practice most statements are given in evidence even when they are largely self-serving, there may be a rare occasion when an accused produces a carefully prepared written statement to the police, with a view to it being made part of the prosecution evidence. The trial judge would plainly exclude such a statement as inadmissible."

20–16   Two glosses on the judgment in *Pearce* should be noted:

1. Lord Lane C.J. said in *Tooke*[61] that the test to be applied to determine whether a statement should be admitted, under para.(2)(a) in *Pearce*, was partly that of spontaneity, partly that of relevance and partly that of asking whether the statement which was sought to be admitted added any weight to the other testimony which had been given in the case. (In *Tooke*, immediately after a wounding in a public house, the defendant blamed the

[60] (1979) 69 Cr.App.R. 365, 369–370.
[61] (1990) 90 Cr.App.R. 417.

complainant both to the licensee and a police constable. About 40 minutes later he went to a police station and made a witness statement. The Court of Appeal held that the Judge had rightly refused to admit the statement which was not relevant, since it added nothing to the evidence of the licensee and the police constable.)

2. With regard to para.(3) in *Pearce*, it may be difficult to determine whether a statement is "carefully prepared" or not; but an example of such a statement might be as follows. Suppose a defendant to have left the police station, having been interviewed by the police about an offence. He goes to see a solicitor and makes an exculpatory statement. He then goes to the police station and hands the statement to the police with a request that it form part of the prosecution case. Such a statement forms no part of the defendant's immediate reaction to questions about the offence and accordingly, it is submitted, should be excluded.

This principle was applied in *Newsome*.[62] The defendant in that case was charged with rape. He was interviewed twice by police officers. He then saw his solicitor. He was interviewed a third time by the police and on legal advice refused to answer any questions. Later (some 13 hours after the offence) the defendant made an exculpatory statement in the presence of his solicitor. The Court of Appeal held, following *Pearce*, that the statement had been rightly excluded since it revealed nothing relevant about the attitude of the accused, because it was coloured by the circumstances in which it was made.[63]

Partly adverse and partly favourable statements. When such a "mixed" statement is adduced the whole statement is admissible and should be put before the jury,[64] since both the admissions and the favourable parts are evidence of the facts stated, although the latter are of less weight.[65] It will be a matter for the jury to decide whether, having considered the whole statement, it does amount to an admission.[66]   20–17

This may lead to problems in summing up, particularly in a case where the defendant does not give evidence. For some time there was doubt about how the jury should be directed in such a case. These doubts arose over the self-exculpatory part of the statement. One approach was to direct the jury that this part was not evidence of the facts related but was only admitted to show the context in which the admission was made. The other approach,

---

[62] (1980) 71 Cr.App.R. 325.
[63] The fact that the police have initially denied the defendant's right of access to a solicitor under s.58 of the 1984 Act does not mean that a statement made after consultation with the solicitor becomes admissible as showing the defendant's immediate reaction. It will be a question of fact for the court to determine whether the statement is admissible or not within the principles stated in *Hutton, The Times*, October 27, 1988.
[64] *Pearce* (1979) 69 Cr.App.R. 365.
[65] *Duncan* (1981) 73 Cr.App.R. 359; *Hamand* (1986) 82 Cr.App.R. 65.
[66] *Donaldson* (1977) 64 Cr.App.R. 59, 65; *Duncan*, above.

adopted by the Court of Appeal in *Duncan*[67] and followed by the Court in *Hamand*,[68] was that the whole statement should be considered by the jury as evidence of the facts related in it, but that their attention should be drawn, where appropriate, to the different weight that they may think it right to attach to the admission in contrast to the explanation:

> "It is ... not helpful to try to explain to the jury that the exculpatory parts of the statement are something less than evidence of the facts they state. Equally, where appropriate, as it will usually be, the judge may and should point out that the incriminating parts are likely to be true (otherwise why say them?) whereas the excuses do not have the same weight."[69]

20–18   These doubts were resolved by the House of Lords in *Sharp*.[70] In that case police officers, investigating a burglary, came across the defendant running from the scene. They tried to apprehend him, but without success. Three days later, he went to a police station. When interviewed, he said that he had been in the area at the material time, but gave an innocent explanation for his being there. He did not give evidence at the trial. The judge directed the jury according to the first approach, mentioned above, *i.e.* that the defendant's account that he had been in the area was an admission and therefore evidence of the fact that he had been there, but that the other parts were exculpatory and not evidence of the facts related. The House of Lords held that this was a misdirection and said that the direction formulated in *Duncan* was to be followed. The House pointed out that, as a matter of common sense, this approach was to be preferred to an attempt to deal differently with different parts of the same statement. Lord Havers said:

> "How can a jury fairly evaluate the facts in the admission unless they can evaluate the facts in the excuse or explanation? It is only if the jury think that the facts set out by way of excuse or explanation might be true that any doubt is cast on the admission, and it is surely only because the excuse or explanation might be true that it is thought fair that it should be considered by the jury."[71]

---

[67] Above.

[68] The same approach had been adopted by the Court in Donaldson, above, at 65 and was adopted by the Privy Council in *Leung Kam-Kwok v R* (1985) 81 Cr.App.R. 83, 91.

[69] *Duncan*, above, at 365, *per* Lord Lane C.J. In *Downes, The Times*, December 10, 1993 the Court of Appeal said that an appropriate direction would be to tell the jury that they should regard everything they have heard from the witness-box and said by the accused to others, including the police, as evidence in the case, but they should not attach equal weight both to sworn evidence and to what was said out of court.

[70] (1988) 86 Cr.App.R. 274.

[71] At 281.

In *Aziz*[72] the House of Lords refused to reconsider the the correctness of the decision in *Sharp*. Lord Steyn, restating the principle that both the inculpatory and the exculpatory parts of a mixed statement are evidence of their truth, rejected an argument that the decision in *Sharp* was unduly favourable to defendants who do not testify, pointing out that a judge is entitled to comment adversely on the quality of the exculpatory parts untested by cross-examination.[73]

How should a "mixed" statement be identified? In *Garrod*[74] the Court of Appeal said that, where a statement contains an admission of fact which was relevant (meaning capable of adding some degree of weight to the prosecution case on an issue which was relevant to guilt), the statement must be regarded as "mixed" for the purposes of the rule. This test has been subjected to academic criticism as being more open to misunderstanding and manipulation than the simple test of whether the prosecution relies on the statement.[75] However, it is submitted that the nature of the statement can only be ascertained by looking at it and not inquiring of the prosecution what their view of it is. Thus, the Divisional Court said that, whether a statement was mixed or not depends upon an examination of the statement, and not on whether the prosecution relies on it.[76]

20–19

The same rules apply in magistrates' courts. Thus, the Divisional Court in *Western v DPP*[77] held that justices should take into consideration a "mixed" statement containing both admissions and excuses (in the instant case, an assertion that the defendant, while fighting, was acting in self-defence).

C. Proposals for reform

In its Consultation Paper on Hearsay[78] the Law Commission criticised the present rule as producing anomalies, for example a witness can give evidence of a previous identification but not a previous description; and producing arbitrary results, for example a previous inconsistent statement can be used to discredit a witness, but he cannot rely on his previous consistent statement. The Commission proposed that a witness's previous statement should be admissible as evidence of the truth of its contents in order (a) to rebut any suggestion of afterthought, (b) as evidence of a previous identification or description of a person, object or place, (c) on accusation (save for prepared self-serving statements), or (d) where the

20–20

---

[72] [1995] 2 Cr.App.R. 478
[73] At 485.
[74] [1997] Crim.L.R. 445.
[75] Birch, "The Sharp End of the Wedge: Use of Mixed Statements by the Defence" [1997] Crim.L.R. 416, 426.
[76] *Western v DPP* [1997] 1 Cr.App.R. 474, 484–485.
[77] Above.
[78] "Evidence in Criminal Proceedings: Hearsay and Related Topics" (1995) Law Comm. Consultation Paper No.138, Pt XIII.

witness cannot remember details in a statement which he made or adopted when the details were fresh in his memory and the details are such that the witness cannot reasonably be expected to remember them. (The Commission suggested that the statement should be read as evidence rather than relating merely to the credibility of the witness, since the witness could then be cross-examined about the account in the statement and the jury could decide which parts to accept.) These proposals now form part of the Law Commission's Paper on Hearsay, published in 1997.[79]

However, it is submitted that the criticisms of the present rule are not justified. If a witness is cross-examined about a previous inconsistent statement (an incident of practically every criminal trial), he or she can be re-examined about the relevant part of the statement and (very occasionally) the statement may be exhibited under the Criminal Procedure Act 1865. To encourage statements to be exhibited in these circumstances as a matter of course can only lead to trial by statement, since the whole statement would be admissible to rebut a suggestion of afterthought of part. As a result, much other information would be before the jury, although the part of the statement challenged might be small. In fact, it was apparently the nineteenth-century practice (and 20 or 30 years ago it was still the practice) that if any part of a witness's statement was put to him or her, then the whole statement became admissible and was exhibited. However, this does not represent the modern practice.[80] On the other hand, there is a strong argument from the point of view of consistency for allowing evidence of a previous description to be given in the same way as evidence of a previous identification, thus avoiding the anomalous situation of a witness being unable to refer to a car registration number because it had been given to someone else.

20–21   More recently, in his report, "Review of the Criminal Courts of England and Wales" ("The Auld Report"), Sir Robin Auld recommended that all previous statements of a witness should be admissible regardless of the existence or extent of the witness's memory, leaving weight—along with the oral evidence of the witness after testing in cross-examination—to be a matter of determination by the tribunal.[81] He concluded that where a witness has made a prior statement, in written or recorded form, it should be admissible as evidence of any matter stated in it of which his direct oral evidence in the proceedings would be admissible provided that he authenticates his statement. He also recommended that witnesses should be permitted, where appropriate, to adopt the statement in the witness-box as their evidence in chief.[82] Thus, making the practice in criminal proceedings

---

[79] "Evidence in Criminal Proceedings: Hearsay and Related Topics" (1995) Law Comm. Report No.245, paras 10.2–10.86.
[80] See para.20–33, below.
[81] The Auld Report.
[82] Above.

much the same as currently exists in civil proceedings under the Civil Evidence Act 1995.

The problem with undertaking such proposals would, again, be to encourage trial by statement. The Criminal Justice Act 2003 does not put into effect these recommendations contained in the Auld Report. The new Act does, however, make provision for a witness to refresh his or her memory by making reference to the witness's written statement or transcript of recording. (See para.20–26 below).

2. MEMORY REFRESHING

Before a witness gives evidence he may refresh his memory from a statement or other document made at a time reasonably close to the events in question. Stricter rules apply to the circumstances in which the witness may refresh his memory while he is giving evidence. However, upon entry into force of s.139 of the Criminal Justice Act 2003, a witness will be permitted to use documents to refresh their memory when giving evidence. The rules governing memory refreshing in both these situations are now discussed.

20–22

A. Before the witness gives evidence

A witness is normally entitled to refresh his memory before going into the witness-box from a statement or note made at a time reasonably close to the events in question.[83] This practice applies to both witnesses for the defence and witnesses for the prosecution. Thus, the practice in the case of witnesses for the defence is that they are entitled to have copies of their statements and refresh their memories at any time up to the moment when they go into the witness-box.[84]

20–23

The practice in relation to prosecution witness is that they are normally (though not in all circumstances) entitled, if they so request, to copies of any statements taken from them by police officers.[85] The leading authority on this topic is *Richardson*.[86] In that case the defendant was charged with an offence of burglary in April 1969 and another offence of burglary in May 1969. The trial took place in November 1970. Shortly before giving evidence, each of five prosecution witnesses refreshed his or her memory from a statement which each had made to the police in July 1969. The Court of Appeal held that this was a proper course. Sachs L.J., giving the judgment of the Court, said:

---

[83] *Richardson* [1971] 2 Q.B. 484; 55 Cr.App.R. 244.
[84] This practice was recognised by the Court of Appeal in *Richardson*, above, at 250.
[85] It should also be noted that the witness may see the statement whether he makes a request to do so or merely accepts an offer to allow him to do so: *Westwell* (1976) 62 Cr.App.R. 251, 253.
[86] Above.

"There can be no absolute rule (which incidentally would be unenforceable unlike the rule as to what can be done in the witness-box) that witnesses may not before trial see the statements they made at some period reasonably close to the time of the event which is the subject of the trial. Indeed one can imagine many cases, particularly those of a complex nature, when such a rule would militate very greatly against the interests of justice."[87]

The reason for this practice is that the interests of justice are more likely to be best served if the witness has the opportunity of refreshing his memory by looking at a statement made close to the relevant events, particularly if a long time has elapsed between the events and the trial. The Supreme Court of Hong Kong commented that if a witness is deprived of this opportunity, his testimony becomes more a test of memory than truthfulness; and so to deprive witnesses tends to create difficulties for honest witnesses while doing little to hamper dishonest witnesses.[88]

20–24   If witnesses are shown statements, it should not be done in circumstances which permit the witnesses to compare with one another what each has said.[89] It follows that no form of conference between witnesses should take place before trial and there should be no discussion between them concerning the evidence to be given.[90] Thus, in *Lau Pak Ngam v R*,[91] the day before the trial the police officer in charge of the case read over to the principal witnesses in the presence of all of them the statements they had made about the case. The Supreme Court of Hong Kong dismissed the defendant's appeal but commented that statements should not be read to witnesses in each other's presence and that a better practice would be to give the witnesses a copy of their statements. This is, in fact, the practice which is normally followed. In *Arif*,[92] it was held that pre-trial discussions between witnesses would not necessarily make such evidence so unsafe that it ought to be excluded. In certain circumstances it may be sufficient to stress to the jury, in the course of summing up, the implications such collusion may have for the reliability of the evidence concerned.

There may be certain circumstances when it is undesirable for a witness to see his statement. Thus, in *Graham*,[93] the Court of Appeal said that the cases must be rare when an accomplice, the testing of whose evidence was particularly important, should be allowed to refresh his memory. Similarly, if it is supposed that the witness has some improper motive for wanting to

---

[87] At 251.
[88] *Lau Pak Ngam*, below, quoted with approval by the Court of Appeal in *Richardson*.
[89] *Richardson*, above.
[90] *Skinner* (1994) 99 Cr.App.R. 212, 215–218.
[91] [1966] Crim.L.R. 443.
[92] *The Times*, June 17, 1993.
[93] [1973] Crim.L.R. 628

see his statement he should not be shown it.[94] It has been said that it is undesirable for a young child (aged eight in the instant case) to see her witness statement.[95] It has been pointed out this may be because a child of this age may not appreciate that her evidence should relate to what she remembered of the incident, not to what she had read in her statement.[96]

Two further points should be noted: 20–25

(a) If prosecution witnesses are allowed to see their statements it is desirable but not essential that the defence should be informed.[97] It is submitted that this should be the normal practice. The fact that a witness has seen his statement may affect the weight of his evidence. Accordingly, the defence should be informed so that the witness may be tested as to what effect seeing the statement has had.

(b) The opposing party is entitled to see the document used by the witness to refresh his memory. Thus, if a police officer uses his notebook to refresh his memory out of court (but not in the witness-box), counsel for the defence is entitled to see the notebook and cross-examine upon the relevant parts.[98]

In an apparent exception to the general rule the Court of Appeal held in *Da Silva*[99] that, provided certain conditions are fulfilled, a judge in the exercise of his discretion and in the interests of justice may allow a witness who has begun to give evidence to refresh his memory from a statement made close in time to the events in question even though it was not contemporaneous. The witness in that case had made a statement a month after a certain conversation. He did not see his statement before giving evidence. When he gave evidence he said he could not remember the conversation but he had made a statement at the time. The judge allowed the witness to withdraw and read his statement. The Court of Appeal held that the judge was entitled to do this provided: (a) the witness indicated that he could not recall the events because of the lapse of time; (b) had made a statement much nearer the events in question; (c) had not read the statement before coming into the witness-box; and (d) wished to have an opportunity to read it before he continued to give evidence. It is submitted that it will only be in an exceptional case that the court will have to exercise this discretion because this sort of difficulty is usually avoided by allowing the witness to read his statement before he gives evidence.

---

[94] *Westwell* (1976) 62 Cr.App.R. 251, 253, CA.
[95] *Thomas* [1994] Crim.L.R. 745.
[96] See Commentary by Sir John Smith at [1994] Crim.L.R. 746.
[97] *Worley v Bentley* [1976] 62 Cr.App.R. 239; *Westwell*, above.
[98] *Owen v Edwards* (1983) 77 Cr.App.R. 191.
[99] (1990) 90 Cr.App.R. 233.

B. While the witness is giving evidence

20–26 The question of whether a witness may refresh his or her memory while giving evidence will, when it comes force,[1] be governed by s.139 of the Criminal Justice Act 2003. Section 139 provides:

> "(1) A person giving oral evidence in criminal proceedings about any matter may, at any stage in the course of doing so, refresh his memory from it from a document made or verified by him at an earlier time if—
>
> (a) he states in his oral evidence that the document records his recollection of the matter at that earlier time, and
> (b) his recollection of the matter is likely to have been significantly better at that time than it is at the time of his oral evidence.
>
> (2) Where—
>
> (a) a person giving oral evidence in criminal proceedings about any matter has previously given an oral account, of which a sound recording was made, and he states in that evidence that the account represented his recollection of the matter at that time,
> (b) his recollection of the matter is likely to have been significantly better at the time of the previous account than it is at the time of his oral evidence, and
> (c) a transcript has been made of the sound recording,
> he may, at any stage in the course of giving his evidence, refresh his memory of the matter from that transcript."

The purpose of s.139 is to make it easier for witnesses to give evidence by making their previous and original statements, often made at the time of or shortly after the incident, more widely admissible at trial. The government White Paper stressed the importance of ensuring that when a witness testifies, rules of evidence do not artificially prevent the true and full story from being presented to the court.[2] Thus, s.139 provides that a witness may refresh his or her memory from a document or transcript when giving evidence if the witness's recollection would have been "significantly better" at the time of the previous account. It is submitted, therefore, that in most cases where witnesses are unable to recall a matter dealt with by them in a previous account, they should be permitted to refresh their memory from it as their recollection at that time was clearly significantly better than at the time of testimony at trial. Reference to a previous account should not be

---

[1] s.336(3) of the Criminal Justice Act 2003 provides that s.139 will come into force in accordance with provision made by the Secretary of State by order.
[2] *Justice for All* (2002), Cm. 5563, para.4.62.

permitted, however, where a witness is able to recall matters unaided; reference to previous accounts in documents or transcripts should not become routine.

Until s.139 of the Criminal Justice Act 2003 enters into force, the common law rules on the use of memory refreshing documents will apply. Moreover, the common law rules, although slightly different to the regime pursuant to s.139, may prove useful in defining the application of s.139. Accordingly, they are dealt with here. **20–27**

Under the common law, as a general rule, a witness may refresh his memory when giving evidence from any writing made or verified by himself concerning the facts to which he testifies, provided that the writing was made or verified at the time when the facts were still fresh in his memory. Thus, in order that the witness should be allowed to refresh his memory from any writing, it must:

(a) have been written by the witness or, if written by another, it must have been verified by the witness; and

(b) the witness must have written or verified the writing while the facts were still fresh in his memory.

The witness may refresh his memory at any time while giving evidence. He usually does so in evidence in chief, but he may also do so in cross-examination and in re-examination.[3]

The court also has a discretion to permit a witness who has begun to give evidence to refresh his memory from a non-contemporaneous statement which he has read before giving evidence: the court may permit memory refreshing even if the criteria in *Da Silva*, above, are not met.[4]

(1) The writing

The most common form of such writing is the note kept in a police officer's notebook. It was the practice for police officers to record all interviews with defendants in such notebooks. Some interviews are still recorded in this way. Thus, it is common for a police witness to seek leave to refresh his memory from his notebook. Another common example is a note made by a witness of a car registration number. Thus, if a witness to a robbery records the number of the getaway car on a piece of paper which he hands to the police, he may, when giving evidence, use it to refresh his memory. **20–28**

A witness may refer to a statement which he made to the police,[5] or some other record kept by himself, for example a diary or a note made from a

---

[3] *Sutton* (1992) 94 Cr.App.R.70.
[4] *South Ribble Stipendiary Magistrate Ex p. Cochrane* [1996] 2 Cr.App.R. 544.
[5] *Mullins*, below; *Lau Pak Ngam v R* [1966] Crim.L.R.443 (Supreme Court of Hong Kong); *Richardson*, below. A witness may refer to a deposition if contemporaneous: *Edwards* (1837) 8 C. & P. 26, 31; *Williams* (1853) 6 Cox 343; *Mullins* (1848) 32 Cox 526, 527–528.

tape recording of a conversation.[6] Thus, a solicitor was allowed to refer to notes which he had dictated to a shorthand clerk who had transcribed them into longhand which the solicitor had checked shortly afterwards.[7] Similarly, the Court of Appeal held that a police officer who had taken notes in the form of jottings during an interview should have been allowed to refer to the full note which he made in his notebook shortly after the interview.[8]

If the note is written by somebody else, the witness may refer to it if he has verified it when the facts were still fresh in his recollection.[9] This is because if the witness verifies the note in such circumstances "it is as good as if he had written it with his own hand".[10]

20–29   The witness may verify the writing by seeing it, reading it and adopting it as accurate.[11] Thus, suppose two police officers, A and B, conduct an interview with a defendant and afterwards pool their recollection of what was said.[12] However, only A makes a note of what was said. B then reads through the note to ensure that it accords with his recollection. He then signs the note and adopts it as accurate. In these circumstances both A and B may refresh their memories from the note while in the witness-box.

Alternatively, the witness may verify the writing by hearing it, *i.e.* the maker reads the note back to the witness for confirmation at the time that it was made.[13]

In *Kelsey*,[14] a witness saw a car at the scene of the burglary. Twenty minutes later, he related the number to a police officer who wrote it down. The witness did not read what the officer had written but the officer read it back aloud to him. The witness confirmed that the number was correct. The Court of Appeal held that the witness was entitled to refresh his memory from the note made by the officer.

On the other hand, a witness may not refer to a note if he has not verified it. In *Eleftheriou*[15] the Court of Appeal held that two customs officers were not entitled to refresh their memories from schedules made by one of them calling out what he saw during an observation and the other writing it down. This was because the observer had not verified the note.

20–30   A witness may refer to a copy of an original document if it is an accurate copy[16] or if it substantially reproduces the contents of the original. In *Horne v Mackenzie*[17] a surveyor was allowed to refer to a printed copy of a

[6] *Mills and Rose* (1962) 46 Cr.App.R. 336.
[7] *Dexter* (1899) 19 Cox 360.
[8] *Att-Gen's Reference (No.3 of 1979)* (1979) 69 Cr.App.R. 411.
[9] *Burrough v Martin* (1809) 2 Camp. 112.
[10] *ibid.*, above, *per* Lord Ellenborough.
[11] *Mills and Rose* (1962) 46 Cr.App.R. 336, 342, *per* Winn L.J.
[12] They are entitled to do so: *Bass* [1953] 1 Q.B. 680, 686, *per* Byrne J.
[13] *Kelsey* (1982) 74 Cr.App.R. 213.
[14] Above.
[15] [1993] Crim.L.R. 947.
[16] *Burton v Plummer* (1834) 2 A. & E. 341.
[17] (1839) 6 Cl. & F. 628.

written report made to his employers which was substantially, but not literally, transcribed from original notes made by him at the time of the survey. Similarly, in *Cheng*,[18] a police officer kept notes of observations made on certain drug dealers in Soho in February 1972. He later made a statement by transcribing from the notes those parts which dealt with the men who had been arrested as a result of the observations. These men included the defendant. The officer left out of the statement entries in the notes relating to men who had never been identified. After the committal proceedings the defendant absconded to Hong Kong. He was extradited and his trial took place in 1975. The Court of Appeal held that the officer was entitled to refresh his memory from the statement. The Court said that if the statement or transcription is substantially what is in the notes the judge should allow the witness to refresh his memory from it, but if the statement or transcription bears little relation to the original note the judge would be entitled to refuse to allow a witness to refresh his memory from such an imperfect source of information.

Likewise, a police officer who has taken jottings during the course of an interview and within a short time makes a full note in his notebook incorporating the jottings should be permitted to refer to his notebook.[19]

It sometimes happens that a witness in the box asks to see his statement to refresh his memory. Leave is granted. The original is then sought but cannot be found. The only copy is typewritten (the original being hand-written). It would appear in these circumstances that provided the judge is satisfied from investigation that the typewritten statement is an accurate copy of the original, the witness should be allowed to refresh his memory from it. This may require both the witness and the police officer who took the original statement to testify that the typewritten statement was an accurate copy of the original.

(2) Contemporaneity

A witness is only entitled to refresh his memory from some writing if it was made or verified at a time when the facts to which it refers were still fresh in the witness's memory or, as is often said, the note was made "contemporaneously" with the facts to which he testifies.[20]

Thus, the document must have been written or verified either at the time of the transaction or so shortly afterwards that the facts were fresh in the

20–31

---

[18] (1976) 63 Cr.App.R. 20.

[19] *Att-Gen's Reference (No.3 of 1979)* (1979) 69 Cr.App.R. 411.

[20] In *Att-Gen's Reference (No.3 of 1979)* (1979) 69 Cr.App.R. 411, 414, the Court of Appeal approved a passage in *Archbold: Criminal Pleading, Evidence and Practice* (40th ed.), para.515 which included the following: "Contemporaneously" is somewhat misleading in the context of the memory refreshing rule. It is sufficient for the purpose of the rule, if the writing was made or verified at a time when the facts were still fresh in the witness's memory."

witness's recollection.[21] In *Richardson* Sachs L.J. said that the definition provided a measure of elasticity and should not be taken to confine witnesses to an over-short period. Thus, periods of a fortnight[22] or 22 days have not been held to be too long.[23] On the other hand, periods of three months[24] and six months[25] have been held to be too long. In *Graham*[26] the Court of Appeal said that a period of 27 days should lead a judge to hesitate before giving leave.

(3) Producing the document for inspection

20–32   A witness who has used a document to refresh his memory must produce it for the inspection of the opposing party.[27] That party may then cross-examine the witness upon it.[28] However, the only part of the document which the opponent has the right to inspect is that relating to the subject-matter of his evidence.[29] Thus, if a police officer refers to a notebook to refresh his memory of an interview with the defendant, defence counsel may inspect the book. However, he may inspect only that part of the book which relates to the interview in question.

(4) Exhibiting the document

20–33   The rules on this complex topic have been restated and clarified. They may be summarised as follows.

   1. The fact that counsel inspects and cross-examines a witness upon parts of a document used by the witness to refresh his memory does not make the document an exhibit in the case.[30]

   2. However, if counsel cross-examines upon parts of the document which have not been used to refresh the witness's memory, the document may be exhibited.[31] In *Britton*[32] the defendant was a trade union official, charged with assault during a demonstration. When he was released from the police station he typed an aide-memoire of the events of the evening. He was allowed to refresh his memory from the aide-memoire when giving evidence in chief about the circumstances leading to his arrest. Cross-examination on the aide-memoire went outside those parts which the defendant had used to

---

[21] *Burrough v Martin*, above; *Att-Gen's Reference (No.3 of 1979)*, above; *Richardson* [1971] 2 Q.B. 484; *Kelsey*, above.

[22] *Langton* (1877) 2 Q.B.D. 296.

[23] *Fotheringham* (1975) 119 S.J. 613.

[24] *Woodcock* [1963] Crim.L.R. 273.

[25] *Jones v Stroud* (1825) 2 C. & P. 196.

[26] [1973] Crim.L.R. 628.

[27] *Beech v Jones* (1848) 5 C.B. 696.

[28] *Gregory v Tavernor* (1836) 6 C. & P. 280.

[29] *Burgess v Bennett* (1872) 20 W.R. 720; see also, *Bass*, below.

[30] *Gregory v Tavernor* (1836) 6 C. & P. 280. *Senat v Senat* [1965] P. 172, 17, *per* Sir Jocelyn Simon P.

[31] *Gregory v Tavernor*, above; *Stephens v Foster* (1833) 6 C. & P. 289; *Senat v Senat*, above.

[32] (1987) 85 Cr.App.R. 14.

refresh his memory. An application by the defence to make the aide-memoire an exhibit was rejected. The Court of Appeal, applying the common law rule, held that it should have been exhibited because cross-examination had not been confined to the matters upon which the defendant had refreshed his memory.

Application to make an aide-memoire an exhibit in these circumstances is perhaps more commonly made by the prosecution, in which case the court has a discretion to exclude it if prejudice would be occasioned to the defendant.[33] Accordingly, if the aide-memoire contained material unfavourable to the defendant which had not been given in evidence because it was irrelevant or inadmissible the court might well exclude the aide-memoire or limit production to an extract. The effect of exhibiting the document is to show consistency on the part of the witness producing it: it is not exhibited as evidence of the facts stated in it.[34]

3. If the document is relevant to the witness's credibility it may be exhibited. Thus, if it is inconsistent with the witness's evidence, it may be admitted as evidence of the inconsistency. Similarly, if it is suggested expressly or by implication that the document is concocted, it may be admitted to rebut this suggestion. This led the Court of Criminal Appeal to hold in *Bass*[35] that if the state of the police officer's notebook is relevant to his credibility the notebook should be exhibited so that the jury may examine it.

20–34

In *Sekhon*[36] a detective inspector had compiled a log of his own observations of the defendant and his co-defendant and those of other officers as reported to him. The other officers verified the entries by signing them. The inspector and the other officers used the log to refresh their memories. The defendant did not give evidence, but it was suggested in cross-examination that the evidence of observation was untrue and the log was a concoction. The jury asked to see the log and the judge permitted them to do so. The Court of Appeal upheld this ruling because the log would assist the jury in deciding whether it was genuine or not.

The judge has a discretion to exclude the document even if it is technically admissible, if the interests of justice so require.[37]

The document is not admitted as evidence of the truth of its contents but to assist the jury in evaluating the evidence given by the witness. During the course of his summing-up the judge should explain this to the jury.[38]

---

[33] *Virgo* (1978) 67 Cr.App.R. 323, 328; *Britton* (1987) 85 Cr.App.R. 14, 19. The evidence may also be excluded in the judge's discretion under s.78 of the Police and Criminal Evidence Act 1984, discussed at para.10–13, above.

[34] *Virgo*, above, at 328–329, *Britton*, above, at 18.

[35] [1953] 1 Q.B. 680.

[36] (1987) 85 Cr.App.R. 19.

[37] *Sekhon* (1987) 85 Cr.App.R. 19, 23; s.78, above.

[38] *Sekhon*, above, at 27. In some cases it will be necessary to warn the jury that the document has only a limited use and they must not think that it is evidence: *Virgo* (1978) 67 Cr.App.R. 323.

However, in a limited number of cases, the document itself may become evidence, for example where the nature of the document provides material by which its authenticity can be judged.[39]

20–35   4. Notes made contemporaneously by police officers during an interview with a suspect may be exhibited and put before the jury provided that the defendant has signed or initialled them or otherwise adopted them as a correct record of the interview, *i.e.* he has had the notes read to him by someone other than the interviewing officers and has told them that they are correct.[40] In the ordinary course of events such notes are put before the jury without dispute. However, unsigned contemporaneous notes of which the authenticity is in dispute and which do not assist the jury in determining authenticity should not be put before the jury as an aide-memoire.[41] (For the effect of the Code of Practice upon such interviews, see paras 9–27 *et seq.*, above.)

5. In *Sekhon* the Court of Appeal said that it was appropriate for a record to be put before the jury where it is difficult to follow cross-examination of the witness who has refreshed his memory without having the record before them or to use as an aide-memoire where the evidence is long and involved. However, while this may be an eminently practical course, care should be taken, as the Court pointed out, in cases where the evidence is contested because of the danger that the jury may wrongly regard the record as evidence. If the record is admitted, the jury will have to be directed that it is only to be used as an aide-memoire and not to be used as a substitute for the evidence given in the witness-box.

---

[39] *Sekhon*, above, at 23.
[40] See *Fenlon and Neal* (1980) 71 Cr.App.R. 307, 311–312.
[41] *Dillon* (1987) 85 Cr.App.R. 29 (Note).

CHAPTER 21
Examination of Witnesses

1. INTRODUCTION

The stages of the examination of witnesses are as follows: 21–01

- (a) The witness is first examined by the party calling him ("examination-in-chief");

- (b) he is then cross-examined by the opposing party ("cross-examination");

- (c) he is then examined again by the party calling him (as to matters arising from cross-examination) ("re-examination").

These stages are separately discussed. Before embarking on this discussion, it is first necessary to mention two general matters: these are concerned with the naming of witnesses and the effect of the fact that a witness has undergone sessions of hypnosis.

Witnesses normally begin their evidence by giving their names.[1] It is also normal practice for a witness to be asked his or her occupation. Thus, in D.S.[2] the prosecution were permitted to adduce evidence that the complainant was a senior Church of England clergyman. It is, however, impermissible to call further evidence in order to bolster the credibility of a witness.

In very exceptional circumstances a witness may be allowed to give 21–02
evidence anonymously. Most commonly, this occurs in cases of witnesses whose occupations require anonymity, for example undercover police officers. However, because of increasing levels of violence against witnesses, the courts may be more prepared than previously to allow witnesses to give their evidence anonymously. If such an application is made the court must

---

[1] Until recently, witnesses also gave their addresses. In 1996 the practice was changed; and a witness is now only asked for his or her address in exceptional circumstances and if it is relevant to an issue in the trial. This change came about after the Lord Chief Justice approved the Trial Issue Group's Statement of National Standards of Witness Care in the Criminal Justice Systems (July 1996), para.17.1 of which states: "Unless it is necessary for evidential purposes, defence and prosecution witnesses should not be required to disclose their addresses in open court. Exceptionally, it will be appropriate for the defence and prosecution to make application for the non-disclosure, in open court, of the names of witnesses."
[2] [1999] Crim.L.R. 911.

decide whether to allow this course to be taken in the circumstances of the particular case. In *Taylor*[3] the Court of Appeal held that this was pre-eminently a question for the exercise of the judge's discretion. The Court set out the relevant factors for that exercise, as follows:

(1) Were there real grounds for fear of the consequences if evidence were given and the identity of the witness were revealed (not necessarily restricted to the witness himself)?

(2) The evidence must be sufficiently relevant and important to make it unfair for the prosecution to proceed without it.

(3) The prosecution must satisfy the court that the credit worthiness of the witness has been fully investigated.

(4) There must be no undue prejudice to the accused.

(5) The court must balance the need for protection of the witness against the unfairness or appearance of unfairness to the accused.

Any decision to allow a witness to give evidence anonymously is bound to involve a degree of unfairness to the accused since it will suggest the defendant is the type of person who is willing and able to take reprisals against those who give evidence against him. On the other hand, this risk will be outweighed in some cases by the public interest in making the evidence of serious crime available to the court. Moreover, allowing a witness to testify anonymously must comply with the requirements of Art.6 of the European Convention on Human Rights (see para.13–14 above). The European Court has held that depriving the defence of information neces-sary to challenge a witness's credibility could amount to a violation of the right to fair trial.[4] If there is a threat to the safety of a witness, anonymity may be justified if safeguards are put in place to protect the accused from any resulting unfairness. Thus, the interests of the witness must be balanced against those of the accused.[5] Consideration must be given to alternative witness protection methods and the least intrusive followed.[6]

21–03 The fact that a witness has undergone sessions of hypnosis in order to help him recall details of the events in question will not necessarily lead to his evidence being excluded, provided full disclosure of the sessions is made to the defence and the Home Office guidelines on hypnosis are complied with. In *Browning*[7] an attempt was made to help a witness recall features of a car, but there had not been compliance with some of the guidelines and

[3] [1995] Crim.L.R. 253. *Taylor* is also discussed at para.19–18, above, where reference is made to the facts of the case.
[4] *Kostovski v Netherlands* 12 E.H.R.R. 434 and *Windisch v Austria* 13 E.H.R.R. 281.
[5] *Doorson v Netherlands* 22 E.H.R.R. 330.
[6] *Van Mechelen v Netherlands* 25 E.H.R.R. 647.
[7] [1995] Crim.L.R. 227.

the defence were not informed that these sessions had taken place. The Court of Appeal held that the failure to comply with the guidelines and to make disclosure amounted to a material irregularity in the trial. (The guidelines require a video-recording of the session to be made, together with a resume of the witness's recollection before the session, and statements from the hypnotherapist and the witness relating to any additional information obtained under hypnosis: full details must be given to the CPS.)

2. EXAMINATION-IN-CHIEF

The object of examination-in-chief is that the party calling the witness should elicit from him all the relevant facts which he can prove in support of the party's case.   21–04

In general, the witness must give evidence from his personal knowledge. He should tell the court what he saw or heard or did. The usual exclusionary rules apply.

No form of rehearsal of a witness should take place. There have, however, been calls for witnesses, especially in relation to allegations of sexual abuse, to be "trained", as opposed to coached, before testifying at trial.[8] Such training would have to be strictly monitored and only prepare a witness for the courtroom experience and not cover the specific facts of the witness's testimony. In *Dye and Williamson*[9] the Court of Appeal condemned the interviewing of three prosecution witnesses before trial by a television company. The interviewing took place as if the witnesses were giving evidence in chief. The Court said that the prosecution should have forbidden any co-operation in the making of the film, amounting as it did to a dress rehearsal for the witnesses.

There has been much concern about the potentially harmful effect upon   21–05
criminal trials of "chequebook journalism", *i.e.* the practice of certain newspapers of making payments to witnesses and buying their stories before they give their evidence (or entering into contracts to do so). In *West*[10] a number of prosecution witnesses had been paid or promised payment by newspaper companies in return for their stories. The defence argued on appeal that these contracts rendered the evidence of these witnesses tainted and unsafe because (a) there would be a temptation for the witnesses to exaggerate to make their accounts more valuable to the press or a desire in them to fulfil their agreements with the media, (b) there was a danger of rehearsals before trial with journalists, and (c) there could be no question of monitoring, recording and disclosing statements given to jounalists in the same way that statements to the police were monitored,

---

[8] "Time to Give Witnesses the Right to a Fair Trial", *The Times Law Section*, October 7, 2003.
[9] *The Times*, December 19, 1991.
[10] [1996] 2 Cr.App.R. 374.

recorded and disclosed.[11] The Court of Appeal held that in the circumstances of the particular case the contracts with the media did not render the verdicts unsafe. However, Lord Taylor C.J. condemned the practice of buying the stories of witnesses and said that in some circumstances it could put justice at risk. The Lord Chief Justice called for a review to determine whether such payments should be prohibited, or if allowed, at what stage of the proceedings and subject to what control.[12] A Consultation Paper from the Lord Chancellor's Department recommended that this practice be made a criminal offence or contempt.[13] The Paper pointed out the danger that a witness might omit something from his evidence in order to leave something exclusive for the media, or might exaggerate in order to make his story more newsworthy: he may rehearse his story with a journalist or may become so committed to a particular account as to be unwilling to examine objectively points put in court. No action has been taken upon this recommendation.

Examination-in-chief must be conducted according to rules relating to:

(a) the prohibition of leading questions; and

(b) the discrediting of a party's own witness.

These rules are now discussed.

A. Leading questions

(1) General rule

21–06   As a general rule a party should not seek to elicit evidence from a witness during examination-in-chief by means of "leading" questions. A leading question is one which either:

(a) suggests the desired answer; or

(b) assumes the existence of a disputed fact.

Thus, the witness to a shooting should not be asked. "Did you see A shoot B?" Instead, he should be asked what happened at the time and place in question. Similarly, if the fact that the shooting took place is in dispute, the witness should not be asked, "What did you see A do after the shooting?" because that assumes that there was a shooting.

The reason for the prohibition, it is submitted, is twofold:

---

[11] *Shannon* [2001] 1 Cr.App.R. 168 at paras 10–15 and 18–12, above.
[12] At 389.
[13] Lord Chancellor's Department, October 1996.

(a) the witness should not be prompted by the party calling him, but should give his evidence unaided; and

(b) it is improper and misleading to misrepresent the evidence by assuming a disputed fact.

However, if evidence is given as a result of a leading question, it is not per se inadmissible, although the weight to be attached to it may be substantially reduced.[14] See para.20–28 above for proposals on the use of written documents and statements as evidence at trial.

(2) Exceptions

It is not possible to formulate an exhaustive list of exceptions to the general rule, as leading questions may be allowed in varying circumstances, and the court may relax the rules in the interests of justice.[15] However, three general exceptions may be mentioned.

21–07

Introductory questions; or questions about matters not in dispute. Leading questions are commonly asked about such matters without objection.[16] Thus, there can be no objection to bringing the witness to the material point as quickly as possible, or directing his attention to a particular topic, by means of leading questions. Similarly, there can be no objection to leading a witness if a fact or issue is not in dispute. Indeed, much time would be wasted if objection were taken to such questions.

Contradiction. A witness called to contradict evidence about a conversation given by another witness may be asked if a particular expression was used.[17] Thus, suppose a witness, X, says, "I told Y so and so." Then Y may be asked, "Did X tell you so and so?"

Hostile witness. Where a witness shows himself to be hostile to the party calling him, the judge may allow that party to treat him as hostile, in which case he may be asked leading questions: see paras 21–09 *et seq.,* below.

B. Discrediting a party's own witness

(1) Common law

As a general rule, a party is not allowed to impeach his own witness. Thus, **21–08**

---

[14] *Moor v Moor* [1954] 1 W.L.R. 927; *Wilson* (1913) 9 Cr.App.R. 124.
[15] *Ex p. Bottomley* [1909] 2 K.B. 14, 21.
[16] *Robinson* (1897) 61 J.P. 520.
[17] *Courteen v Touse* (1807) 1 Camp. 43.

for instance, he may not cross-examine the witness or call evidence to show that the witness is of bad character or of bad disposition.

However, if the witness is unfavourable to the party calling him, *i.e.* he fails to prove relevant facts which he was called to prove, that party may call other evidence to contradict him[18]; but he may not cross-examine him or put a previous inconsistent statement to him. In *Sumner v John Brown & Co.*,[19] Hamilton J. said that if two credible witnesses gave contradictory evidence, the testimony of both must be disregarded. This statement was held to be inapplicable to criminal proceedings because of the duty on the Crown to call all relevant evidence: *Brent*.[20] Thus, it sometimes happens that two prosecution witnesses give conflicting accounts of the same incident. In these circumstances, the jury must decide which account, if either, to believe.

(2) Criminal Procedure Act 1865, s.3

21–09 On the other hand, if the witness is hostile, *i.e.* he bears a hostile animus to the party calling him and does not give his evidence fairly and with a desire to tell the truth,[21] the party calling him may, in certain circumstances, cross-examine him and put a previous inconsistent statement to him. Those circumstances are governed by s.3 of the Criminal Procedure Act 1865 (also known as "Lord Denman's Act"). The section provides:

> "A party producing a witness shall not be allowed to impeach his credit by general evidence of bad character; but he may, in case the witness shall, in the opinion of the judge, prove adverse, contradict him by other evidence, or by leave of the judge, prove that he has made at other times a statement inconsistent with his present testimony; but before such last-mentioned proof can be given, the circumstances of the supposed statement, sufficient to designate the particular occasion, must be mentioned to the witness, and he must be asked whether or not he has made such statement".[22]

Thus, the judge has a discretion whether to allow a witness to be cross-

---

[18] *Ewer v Ambrose* (1825) 3 B. & C. 746; *Greenough v Eccles* (1859) 5 C.B. (N.S.) 786.
[19] (1909) 25 T.L.R. 745.
[20] [1973] Crim.L.R. 295.
[21] Stephen, *Digest of the Laws of Evidence* (12th ed., 1948), art.147. For a review of the law and procedure relating to hostile witnesses, see Newark, "The Hostile Witness and the Adversary System" [1986] Crim.L.R. 441.
[22] For a suggestion that the statements by such witnesses may also be admissible under s.23 of the Criminal Justice Act 1988 (now replaced by s.116 of the Criminal Justice Act 2003—see para.8–19, above) see Munday, "Hostile Witnesses and the Admission of Statements" [1993] Crim.L.R. 349.

examined as to a previous inconsistent statement. Leave may only be granted if, in the opinion of the judge, the witness is adverse.[23] In the context of this section "adverse" means "hostile".[24] Accordingly, it is not enough for the witness to give evidence unfavourable to the party calling him: he must have proved hostile in the sense that he is unwilling to tell the truth. There is, therefore, a distinction between a witness who is, for instance, merely forgetful and one who is recalcitrant and does not wish to give evidence for the party calling him. An example of a hostile witness of the latter sort is a friend or relative of the accused who is called for the Crown.[25] It is not an uncommon experience for such a witness to refuse to give evidence against the accused or, contrary to his statement made to the police, to give only evidence that is favourable to the accused.[26]

If a witness proves to be hostile the usual procedure is as follows: **21–10**

1. Prosecuting counsel should show the witness's statements to the judge and to apply (in the absence of the jury)[27] to treat the witness as hostile.[28] The Court of Appeal has said that the application should be made when the witness first shows unmistakeable signs of hostility.[29] Normally, these signs will appear in the evidence in chief. Lord Goddard C.J. said that if counsel for the Crown has a statement from a prosecution witness contradicting his evidence that he is unable to identify the accused, he should at once show the statement to the judge and ask for leave to cross-examine the witness as hostile.[30] The witness in these circumstances may be showing clear signs of hostility. However, in other cases a witness may genuinely have forgotten. The Court of Appeal has said that the prosecutor and trial judge should first

---

[23] The exercise of the judge's discretion will only be disturbed by the Court of Appeal if it is clearly shown that either there was no real exercise of discretion or that it was improperly exercised: *Booth* (1982) 74 Cr.App.R. 123, 130.

[24] *Greenough v Eccles*, above.

[25] If a wife chooses to give evidence against her husband, she may be treated as hostile, but before she gives evidence, it is desirable that the judge should explain to her, in the absence of the jury, that she has the right to refuse to give evidence, but if she does, she may be treated like any other witness: *Pitt* [1983] Q.B. 25. See para.17–29, above.

[26] The prosecution are not prevented from calling such a witness simply because they know or suspect the witness is hostile: for discussion, see Munday, "Calling a Hostile Witness" [1989] Crim.L.R. 866.

[27] Questioning to determine whether the witness is hostile should normally take place in the presence of the jury: *Darby* [1989] Crim.L.R. 817. This does not prevent a judge examining (outside the presence of the jury) a witness, who is unwilling to go into the witness-box, if such examination is aimed at excluding a possibility that she could not say on oath that her statement was true: *Jones (Kerry Michael)* [1988] Crim.L.R. 579. In *Honeyghon and Sayles* [1999] Crim.L.R. 221 it was held that the judge has a discretion whether to hold a *voir dire* in order to determine whether a witness is wrong to persist in a refusal to give evidence. *Darby* was not read as denying the existence of such a discretion. However, in *Khan, Dad, and Afsar* [2003] Crim.L.R. 428, it was held that a *voir dire* would only be appropriate in exceptional circumstances and that it was difficult to determine in advance what a witness may do when confronted with his statement.

[28] The fact that the previous inconsistent statement is oral rather than written does not affect the principle: *Prefas and Pryce* (1988) 86 Cr.App.R. 111.

[29] *Pestano* [1981] Crim.L.R. 397.

[30] *Fraser and Warren* (1956) 40 Cr.App.R. 160.

consider inviting the witness to refresh his memory from his statement; it was undesirable to treat the witness as hostile immediately upon not getting the expected answer.[31] (This may be dealt with more expeditiously by asking the witness if he has had the opportunity of reading his statement before giving evidence.) Then, if the witness has had the chance to read his statement (or declines to do so), the court may be in a better position to determine whether he is hostile or not.

2. If the application is granted the witness must be asked whether or not he has made the inconsistent statement: s.3. To this end, the witness is asked whether he made the statement. Once he accepts that he made the statement, he may be cross-examined upon it.

3. If the witness denies making the statement the judge will have to decide on the evidence whether he did make it or not. The Court of Appeal in *Baldwin*[32] said that whether an earlier statement could be used depends upon the facts of the particular case. In that case the witness accepted that he had made some parts of the statement and that the signatures on it were his. As a result the Court held that there was evidence entitling the judge to decide that the witness had made the statement and cross-examination upon it was permissible.

Suppose, however, the witness were to deny that he had made any part of the statement and to deny that the signature was his: does this bring the application to an end? Section 3 does not appear to anticipate that this should be so. The witness's admission is merely the most convenient way of proving that he has made an earlier inconsistent statement. It is not the only way of doing so. Accordingly, it would appear that with leave, the prosecution could call the person who took the statement from the witness to prove that he made it. The witness could then be re-called and cross-examined upon the statement.

21–11   4. Section 3 restates the common law prohibition against impeaching the credit of a party's own witness. This rule applies to all witnesses. Accordingly, a hostile witness may not be cross-examined about his previous convictions, bad character or disposition.

5. A defence witness who proves to be hostile is treated in the same way as a prosecution witness and if leave is given, he may be cross-examined about an inconsistent statement: s.3. In *Booth*[33] the trial judge allowed the defence to treat a defence witness as hostile and cross-examine him.

6. The procedure in summary trials is similar to that on indictment.[34] However, there is this distinction. The magistrates are judges of both fact and law and will have to see the witness's statement when determining

---

[31] *Maw* [1994] Crim.L.R. 841.
[32] [1986] Crim.L.R. 681.
[33] (1982) 74 Cr.App.R. 123.
[34] *Hart* (1958) 42 Cr.App.R. 47, 50, *per* Devlin J.

whether the witness should be treated as hostile.[35] If they refuse the application, they must put the contents of the statement out of their minds. In committal proceedings the prosecution were not obliged to treat a witness as hostile, but could wait to see what happened at trial.[36]

7. If the prosecution has been permitted to treat a child witness as hostile, the jury should not be shown a video-recording of the child's interview with the police: cross-examination should be confined to the written text of the transcript of the interview and limited to discrediting the child's latest version of what happened.[37]

Section 3 does not affect the right of a party, without the leave of the judge, to call evidence contradicting: **21–12**

(a) a hostile witness[38]; and

(b) (it would appear) an unfavourable witness[39] on matters relevant to the offence charged.

The section does not affect the power of the judge at common law to allow a hostile witness to be examined by means of leading questions or with reference to a previous statement.[40] Thus, in *Thompson*,[41] a father was charged with incest with his daughter. She was called as a witness for the prosecution but refused to give evidence. The judge allowed her to be treated as hostile and she was cross-examined on a statement which she had given to the police. It was argued on appeal that s.3 did not apply because her testimony was not "inconsistent with her present testimony." The Court of Appeal upheld the judge's ruling and said: "(There) is no reason to suppose that the subsequent statutory intervention has in any way destroyed or removed the basic common law right of the judge in his discretion to allow cross-examination when a witness proves to be hostile."[42]

If a witness is cross-examined on an inconsistent statement, that statement does not become evidence of the facts stated in it[43] and the statement should not be put before the jury.[44] The fact that he has made an incon-

---

[35] See Samuels, "Hostile Witness in the Magistrates' Court—Practice and Procedure examined" (1980) 144 J.P.N. 497, 498.
[36] *Mann* (1972) 56 Cr.App.R. 750.
[37] *R*, unreported, CA, February 6, 1995.
[38] *Booth*, above, at 131.
[39] *Greenough v Eccles*, above.
[40] *Clarke v Saffery* (1824) Ry. & M. 126; *Bastin v Carew* (1825) Ry. & M. 127.
[41] (1976) 64 Cr.App.R. 96.
[42] At 97.
[43] *White*, below; *Golder*, below; *Harris*, below; *Dibble* (1908) 1 Cr.App.R. 155; *Birch* (1924) 18 Cr.App.R. 26; *Oliva* (1965) 49 Cr.App.R. 298; *Newton and Dyer* [1987] Crim.L.R. 687.
[44] *Darby* [1989] Crim.L.R. 817. The statement cannot go before the jury because it is not evidence of anything. However, the Court of Appeal in *Darby* contemplated the possibility of an exception to this rule and gave as an example a case where for tactical reasons the defence wished the jury to see the statement. This is unlikely to be a common occurrence because of the risks involved for the defence.

sistent statement is, however, relevant to the witness's credibility because it may serve to destroy the effect of his evidence. Thus, the jury may be directed as to the effect of the statement on the witness's credibility but must not be directed that the witness's testimony may be disbelieved and his statement substituted for it.[45] In *Golder*[46] the Court of Criminal Appeal said,

> "When a witness is shown to have made previous statements inconsistent with the evidence given by that witness at the trial, the jury should not merely be directed that the evidence given at the trial should be regarded as unreliable; they should also be directed that the previous statements, whether sworn or unsworn, do not constitute evidence upon which they can act."

21–13   This statement was criticised by the High Court of Australia in *Driscoll v R*[47] where the Court said that it could not be accepted that there was an inflexible rule that the jury should be directed in the circumstances that the evidence should be regarded as unreliable.

It is submitted that, if the witness gives an explanation for the inconsistency which the jury accept, it may rely on his evidence, since weight of evidence is a matter for the jury to determine.[48] It may, for instance, accept one part and reject another. In some cases it may be a misdirection to tell it to disregard the witness's evidence. The appropriateness or otherwise of such a direction will depend on the facts of the case. However, in many cases the value of the evidence given by a witness who has been treated as hostile is nil. As a result, in *Maw*,[49] the Court of Appeal said that if a witness has been treated as hostile it will be necessary for the jury to consider whether he or she can be regarded as creditworthy at all; and it must be directed accordingly. It was only if it thought it could give the witness credence that it could consider which part of his evidence should be accepted and which rejected. In *Ugorji*[50] the Court of Appeal held that it was essential for a jury to be directed as to the weight to be accorded the

---

[45] *White* (1922) 17 Cr.App.R. 60, 64. In *Nelson* [1992] Crim.L.R. 653 the Court of Appeal held that it was a serious misdirection not only to fail to warn the jury not to act on the witness statement of a hostile witness, but also to suggest that her evidence was unreliable when compared with the statement.

[46] (1961) 45 Cr.App.R. 5, 11.

[47] (1977) 51 A.L.J.R. 731.

[48] In *Maw* [1994] Crim.L.R. 841 the Court of Appeal said that it was the task of the prosecution or the party seeking to rely on the witness's evidence to explore the inconsistencies and the reluctance to testify in order to provide an explanation (if there is one) for the inconsistencies. However, as is pointed out in the commentary on this case in the Criminal Law Review, there is a considerable danger of undue prejudice to the accused if this course is followed. There is also a danger of side issues being raised which would distract the jury.

[49] Above.

[50] *Independent*, July 5, 1999.

evidence of a witness turned hostile even where the standard direction was unsuitable.

Section 3 provides that if, in the opinion of the judge, a witness proves   **21–14**
adverse, the party calling him may contradict him by other evidence. Two matters may be noted about this provision:

(i)   It does not, despite its wording, affect the right of a party at common law to call evidence contradicting an unfavourable witness[51] (see para.21–12, above).

(ii) The party does not need the leave of the judge to call contradictory evidence. On the other hand, the leave of the judge is required in order to prove a previous inconsistent statement. If leave is refused, the party cannot prove the statement under s.4 of the Act (see para.21–25, below).[52]

The section specifically provides that the party cannot impeach the witness's credit by evidence of bad character. This means that he cannot lead evidence as to the witness's previous convictions or bad character or disposition. However, suppose a hostile witness, when cross-examined about a previous inconsistent statement, says that he made it as a result of improper pressure from a police officer. May the prosecution call evidence from the police officer to rebut the witness's allegations? It is submitted that since s.3 simply provides that the party may "contradict him by other evidence", the police officer's evidence would be admissible.

3. CROSS-EXAMINATION

The object of cross-examination is: **21–15**

(a)   to destroy or weaken the effect of the evidence given by the witness in chief; and

(b)   to elicit from the witness information favourable to the cross-examining party.[53]

Before considering the rules governing cross-examination it is necessary to consider when the right to cross-examine arises.

---

[51] *Greenough v Eccles* (1859) 5 C.B. (N.S.) 786, 805–806, *per* Willes J.
[52] *Booth* (1982) 74 Cr.App.R. 123, 130.
[53] The Law Commission in its Consultation Paper on Hearsay (1995) (Law Comm. No.138) discussed cross-examination and cast doubt upon its effectiveness as a tool for testing the veracity of evidence. The Commission also commented upon the unwelcome effect of cross-examination upon witnesses who are subject to aggressive questioning (paras 6.36–6.62). These discussions are outside the scope of this work, but it may be taken that cross-examination will be the principal tool for testing a witness's evidence for the foreseeable future.

Once a witness has been called by a party and sworn, all other parties with a legitimate interest in putting questions have the right to cross-examine him.[54] Usually a witness is examined-in-chief before he is cross-examined, but this is not a necessary pre-condition of cross-examination. Thus, witnesses are sometimes tendered by the prosecution for cross-examination, in which case the witness is sworn; there is no examination-in-chief; and the witness is then cross-examined by the defence.

Two further points should be noted:

(a) A defendant has the right to cross-examine a co-defendant, whether the co-defendant has given evidence against him[55] or not.[56] The same rule applies to witnesses called by a co-defendant.

(b) A witness called by the judge is liable to cross-examination by all parties.[57]

A. General rule

21–16   The following rules should be mentioned.

1. Cross-examination is not confined to the issues raised in evidence in chief; but it must relate either (i) to the issues in the case or (ii) to the credit of the witness.[58] If it does not relate to these matters, the judge should step in and should disallow questions which are irrelevant or vexatious.[59]

2. Leading questions may be asked.[60] However, questions should not be asked in the form of a comment or invitation to argument, since the purpose of cross-examination should be to elicit matters of fact.[61] Nor should the advocate state what somebody else has said or will say. Thus, a statement such as "the defendant will say ..." or "the defendant's recollection is ..." should not be made.[62] Nowadays, this rule seems often to be overlooked. Presumably, by putting to a witness what another witness has said

---

[54] *Bingham* [1999] 1 W.L.R. 598. There is no rule which prevents a witness who has been sworn, but not asked questions by the party calling him, being questioned by other parties (*per* Lord Hope, at 603). In exceptional circumstances a witness is not liable to cross-examination, *e.g.* a witness called merely to produce a document; or a witness sworn by mistake (*Wood v Mackinson* (1840) 2 M. & R. 273); or in circumstances where the judge has stopped the examination-in-chief before a material question was asked (*Creevy v Carr* (1835) 7 C. & P. 64). A witness who has given no evidence in chief may not be asked questions as to credit: *Coulson v Disborough* [1894] 2 Q.B. 316; *Re Enoch and Zarestsky* [1901] 1 K.B. 32.
[55] *Hadwen* [1902] 1 K.B. 882; *Paul* [1920] 2 K.B. 183.
[56] *Hilton* [1972] 1 Q.B. 421; *Murdoch v Taylor* [1965] A.C. 574.
[57] *Bingham*, above.
[58] *Treacey* [1944] 2 All E.R. 229.
[59] *Kalia* (1974) 60 Cr.App.R. 200; *Simmonds* [1969] 1 Q.B. 685; *Maynard* (1979) 69 Cr.App.R. 309.
[60] *Parkin v Moon* (1836) 7 C. & P. 409.
[61] *Baldwin* (1925) 18 Cr.App.R. 173, 178–179, *per* Lord Hewart C.J. and *Randall* [2002] 2 Cr.App.R. 17.
[62] *Baldwin, ibid.*; *North Australian Territory Co. v Goldsborough Mort & Co.* [1893] 2 Ch. 381.

or what the defendant will say, the cross-examiner intends to shake the witness's testimony in the hope that he will retract what he has said. In fact, it is no more than a comment on the part of the cross-examiner and, as such, should not be made to the witness, but to the jury. The rule applies equally to questions in the form of statements, along these lines: "The police officer must be lying if your evidence is true." A defendant in a case of an alleged sexual offence may, however, be asked in cross-examination whether he knows any reason why the complainant might be lying.[63]

3. A witness must not be asked about inadmissible evidence, for example hearsay[64] (as to the admissibility of hearsay, see Ch.8) or an inadmissible confession.[65] However, the Court of Appeal has held that a defendant may be cross-examined on behalf of a co-defendant on the contents of an inadmissible statement made by the defendant if he gives evidence inconsistent with the statement.[66]

4. The cross-examining party should put as much of his own case as concerns the witness to him. Thus, if the cross-examining party intends to adduce evidence which contradicts evidence given by the witness, he should put his version to the witness, so that the witness may have the opportunity of explaining the contradiction.[67] If a party fails to do this, he is generally taken to have accepted the witness's evidence. Accordingly, counsel should not in his closing speech attack that part of a witness's evidence which he has not challenged in cross-examination.[68] However, this rule has been held not to apply to a case tried by lay justices in that justices do not have to accept a witness's evidence merely because it is unchallenged.[69] A strict application of the rule may also not be necessary where a witness is called whose evidence is corroborative of evidence already given by another witness who has himself been cross-examined, for example a police officer who gives evidence about an interview with the defendant. In this situation a second cross-examination is frequently unnecessary. It is the duty of defence counsel to cross-examine a co-defendant if he intends to suggest that the co-defendant has not given truthful evidence.[70]

5. Cross-examination should be conducted with restraint and with the courtesy and consideration which a witness is entitled to expect in a court of law.[71]

21–17

---

[63] *Brook, The Times*, March 31, 2003.
[64] *Thompson* [1912] 3 K.B. 19.
[65] *Treacey*, above; *Rice* [1963] 1 Q.B. 857.
[66] *Rowson* (1985) 80 Cr.App.R. 218; approved by the Privy Council in *Lui Mei Lin v R* [1989] 2 W.L.R. 175. S.76A(i) of PACE now provides that a confession may be given in evidence on behalf of a co-accused in certain circumstances. See para.9–53, above.
[67] *Brown v Dunn* (1869) 6 R. 67; *Hart* (1932) 23 Cr.App.R. 202.
[68] *Bircham* [1972] Crim.L.R. 430.
[69] *O'Connell v Adams* [1973] R.T.R. 150.
[70] *Fenlon and Neal* (1980) 71 Cr.App.R. 307, 312–313.
[71] *Mechanical and General Inventions Co. Ltd v Austin* [1935] A.C. 346, 360, *per* Lord Sankey L.C.

6. In rules which, it is submitted, should be followed by all advocates, the Code of Conduct for the Bar provides that it is the duty of a barrister to guard against being made the channel for questions which are only intended to insult or annoy the witness or some other person; that a barrister may only suggest that a witness is guilty of fraud, misconduct or crime if such allegations go to a matter in issue which is material to his client's case: where the only such matter is the credibility of the witness the barrister must be satisfied as to the reasons for such allegations being made and that they are supported by reasonable grounds.[72]

7. In *Callaghan*,[73] Waller L.J. said that it was not a proper practice for counsel for the defence to make an attack on the honesty of police officers in taking a voluntary statement and then fail to call the defendant to substantiate the allegations. This statement follows a similar dictum by Lord Goddard C.J. in *O'Neill and Ackers*.[74] Waller L.J. modified this view in a rider to the effect that it was permissible in exceptional circumstances to conduct such a cross-examination if the defendant refuses to go into the witness-box to support the challenge because of his very bad record.[75] However, it is submitted that counsel should not be prevented in any circumstances from attacking a witness because the defendant is not giving evidence. If this were not the position, the defence would be put in an impossible situation. Either the defendant would have to give up his right not to give evidence or his case could not be put.[76] It is submitted that a defendant should not as a matter of principle be put in the position of having to make such a choice. However, failure to call evidence in support of allegations of this kind may well lead to adverse comments from the judge. After all, a jury may expect to hear from the person making the allegations.

B. Cross-examination by accused in person

21–18   A person accused of a criminal offence may choose to represent him or herself at trial with the consequence that they themself must conduct the cross-examination of prosecution witnesses. It is the duty of the court (consistent with its duty to give the defendant a fair trial) to protect the complainant and, it is submitted, all other witnesses, from intimidation or abuse by the manner of the defendant's cross-examination or by irrelevant and repetitious questioning.[77] Accordingly, it is desirable, before cross-

---

[72] The Court of Appeal said of the Bar Council Rules (which were superseded by the Code of Conduct) that, although of persuasive force, they do not bind the court: *McFadden* (1976) 62 Cr.App.R. 187.
[73] (1979) 69 Cr.App.R. 88.
[74] (1950) 34 Cr.App.R. 108.
[75] *The Times*, February 20, 1980.
[76] See the Report of the Professional Conduct Committee of the Bar Council dated December 7, 1983 which may be found at [1984] L.S. Gaz. 277.
[77] *Brown (Milton)* [1998] 2 Cr.App.R. 364.

examination, for the judge to discuss the course of proceedings with the defendant in the absence of the jury. If judges intervene (exercising their best judgment) to ensure that witnesses are not subject to inappropriate pressure, the Court of Appeal will be slow, in the absence of injustice, to allow an appeal.[78]

Special considerations arise in respect of certain vulnerable witnesses, such as children and the complainant in relation to sexual offences. Accordingly, Chapter II of Pt II of the Youth Justice and Criminal Evidence Act 1999 ("YJCEA 1999") makes provision for the protection of certain witnesses from cross-examination by the accused in person.[79]

Section 34 of the YJCEA 1999 provides that no person accused of a sexual offence may cross-examine the complainant in person either in connection with that offence or any other offence (of whatever nature). Similarly, s.35 of the YJCEA 1999 provides that no person charged with an offence specified in the section may cross-examine a "protected witness" in person.[80] A "protected witness" is defined as a witness who is (i) a child, or (ii) a person who falls to be cross-examined after giving evidence in chief by means of a video-recording at a time when the witness was a child or in any other way at any such time.[81] For the purpose of s.35, "witness" includes a witness who is charged with an offence in the proceedings.[82]

Section 36 of the YJCEA 1999 makes provision to give the court power **21–19** to prohibit an accused from cross-examining other witnesses, not covered by ss.34 or 35, in person if the court is satisfied that the quality of their evidence would be diminished by such cross-examination or improved as a result of prohibiting such cross-examination.[83] The prosecutor may apply for such a direction or the court may raise the issue of its own motion.[84] The court must be satisfied that it would not be contrary to the interests of justice to give such a direction.[85] In determining whether a witness's evi-

---

[78] *ibid.*
[79] ss.34, 35, and 38 came into force on September 4, 2000: SI 2000/2091. Ss.36 and 37 came into force on July 24, 2002: Youth Justice and Criminal Evidence Act 1999 (Commencement No.7) Order 2002 (SI 2002/1739). Crown Court Rules 1982, rr.24B–24D pertaining to the restrictions on the cross-examination of witnesses, appointment of counsel by the court, and appointment of counsel by the accused, were inserted by the Crown Court (Amendment) Rules 2000 (SI 2000/2093). These were amended by Crown Court (Special Measures and Directions Prohibiting Cross-Examination) Rules 2002 (SI 2002/1688). Crown Court Rule 22E was inserted by Crown Court (Special Measures and Directions Prohibiting Cross-Examination) Rules 2002 (SI 2002/1688).
[80] s.35(3) stipulates that s.35 applies to any offence under: (i) the Sexual Offences Act 1956; (ii) the Indecency with Children Act 1960; (iii) the Sexual Offences Act 1967; (iv) s.54 of the Criminal Law Act 1977; or (v) the Protection of Children Act 1978. It also applies to kidnapping, false imprisonment or an offence under s.1 or 2 of the Child Abduction Act 1984; any offence under s.1 of the Children and Young Person Act 1933; and any offence which involves an assault on, or injury or a threat of injury, to any person.
[81] s.35(2) of the YJCEA 1999.
[82] s.35(5) of the YJCEA 1999.
[83] s.36(2) of the YJCEA 1999.
[84] s.36(1) of the YJCEA 1999.
[85] s.36(2)(b) of the YJCEA 1999.

dence would be improved or diminished, the court must have regard to any views expressed by the witness, the nature of the questions likely to be asked, any behaviour of the accused at any stage of the proceedings, any relationship between the witness and the accused, whether any person (other than the accused) is or has been charged in the proceedings with a sexual offence or an offence to which s.35 applies, and whether any special measures directions pursuant to s.19 of the YJCEA 1999 (see para.19–16 above) have been, or are proposed to be, given.[86] The court may discharge a direction where it appears in the interests of justice to do so.[87] The court must state its reasons for giving any direction or otherwise in open court.[88]

Where an accused is prevented from cross-examining a witness in person by virtue of ss.34, 35, or 36 of the YJCEA 1999, the court must invite the accused to arrange for a legal representative to act from him for the purpose of cross-examining the witness.[89] If the accused fails to instruct such legal representative, the court must consider whether it is necessary in the interests of justice for the witness to be cross-examined by a legal representative appointed by the court to represent the interests of the accused.[90] If it is so necessary, the court must then choose and appoint such qualified legal representative.[91] The legal representative will not, however, be responsible to the accused.[92] Where an accused is prevented from cross-examining a witness in person on a trial on indictment, the judge is under a duty, if he thinks it necessary, to warn the jury as to the risk of prejudice.[93]

C. Cross-examination on documents

21–20 If a document written by another person is put to a witness and he accepts what it purports to record as true, the contents of the document become admissible as evidence, but if he does not accept what it purports to record as true, the document is inadmissible, since it is hearsay.[94] Thus, a hearsay document cannot be made evidence by putting it to a witness in cross-examination[95] or by requiring him to read it aloud.[96]

---

[86] s.36(3) of the YJCEA 1999.
[87] s.37(2) of the YJCEA 1999.
[88] s.37(4) of the YJCEA 1999.
[89] s.38(2) of the YJCEA 1999.
[90] s.38(3) of the YJCEA 1999.
[91] s.38(4) of the YJCEA 1999.
[92] s.38(5) of the YJCEA 1999.
[93] s.39 of the YJCEA 1999.
[94] *Gillespie and Simpson* (1967) 51 Cr.App.R. 172. See paras 8–30 *et seq.*, above, for the hearsay rule in relation to documents.
[95] *Treacey* (1944) 30 Cr.App.R. 93.
[96] *Gillespie and Simpson*, above.

The principle is illustrated by *Cooper (Warwick)*.[97] The defendant in that case was charged with an offence connected with the importation of drugs found in a television set delivered to his house. When customs officers searched the house they found two letters written by the defendant's wife and signed in the names of the defendant and his wife. The letters contained passages relating to a shortage of drugs in the house. The wife did not give evidence, but the letters were put before the jury. The Court of Appeal held that the letters were inadmissible as hearsay. The Court indicated that the correct procedure should have been as follows. The prosecution ought to have proved the finding of the letters, but given no indication of their contents. When the defendant was cross-examined the letters should have been put before him and he should have been asked whether he was aware of their contents. If he said yes, he should have been cross-examined about the passages relating to the shortage of drugs.[98]

It is improper for an advocate to describe the nature of an inadmissible document while asking the witness to look at it and say whether he still adheres to his answer. The proper course is for the advocate to give the document to the witness and tell him to look at it; and then ask if he still adheres to his answer.[99]

It is also improper for an advocate to cross-examine a witness about an **21–21** inadmissible document and ask him to explain the meaning of the document. In *Windass*,[1] W and F were tried together on an indictment containing counts relating to shoplifting activities. F's diary was admitted in evidence (with a warning to the jury from the judge that it was only evidence against F). The diary contained entries by F showing that she had been concerned in shoplifting with W. Prosecution counsel cross-examined W about these entries and asked him to explain what the writer meant. The Court of Appeal held that the judge had been wrong to allow prosecution counsel to cross-examine in this way. Lord Lane C.J. said that it is quite improper for prosecuting counsel to take in his hand a statement inadmissible *vis-à-vis* the witness and then ask the witness to explain the highly

---

[97] (1985) 82 Cr.App.R. 74. On the other hand, in *Madden* [1986] Crim.L.R. 804, the defendant was charged with importation of cannabis. A trunk containing cannabis was delivered to her home. Customs officials found letters at her house, written by the father of the defendant's children, referring to the use and smuggling of cannabis. In interview the defendant admitted that she knew that the letters referred to cannabis and its importation. The Court of Appeal upheld the admission of the letters to rebut the defence that the receipt of the trunk was unsolicited and without her knowledge of its contents.

[98] Further illustration is to be found in *Cross* (1990) 91 Cr.App.R. 115. In that case, prosecuting counsel was permitted to cross-examine the defendant about a statement made by a person not called as a witness. The statement was handed to the defendant; he was invited to read it and questioned about it, although he had not seen it before and did not agree that it was true. The Court of Appeal commented that the effect of this cross-examination was likely to have been to persuade the jury that the person had made a statement contradicting the defendant's account. The Court held that this amounted to a material irregularity.

[99] *Yousry* (1916) 11 Cr.App.R. 13; *Tompkins* (1978) 67 Cr.App.R. 181.

[1] (1989) 89 Cr.App.R. 258.

damaging statements, inadmissible against him, which the maker of the document had written. Such cross-examination is objectionable because:

(a) the witness is asked about another's intention or state of mind and

(b) it suggests that the statement is evidence against the witness. It is not improper for an advocate to cross-examine the witness about information which may be obtained from such a document, for example "were you in the Pig and Whistle on the 1st January with X and Y?" However, the cross-examination must not be linked to the inadmissible document and the witness must not be asked questions about it.[2]

If a party calls for and inspects a document held by the other party, he is bound to put it in evidence if the other party so requires.[3] This is an old rule, rarely invoked. There is no modern authority dealing with it in relation to criminal trials. It might be applied in circumstances where the prosecution called for a document held by a defence witness. Whether it would now be applied to documents held by prosecution witnesses must be more doubtful, having regard to the obligation on the prosecution to disclose material in its possession under the Criminal Procedure and Investigation Act 1996 (provided, of course, that the obligation had been fulfilled).[4]

21–22   There is a clear exception to the rule in relation to memory refreshing documents: paras 20–32 *et seq*, above. Similarly, records made during a defendant's detention at a police station are not usually exhibited. However, in *Hackney*[5] the Court of Appeal said that judges should control the use made of these records and ensure that cross-examination is directly confined to an issue in the case, that the time spent on them is not inordinate, and that indiscriminate use of them is not made by counsel or by a defendant in person.

D. Proof of previous inconsistent statements

21–23   The proof of a previous statement made by a witness under cross-examination which is inconsistent with his evidence is governed by ss.4 and 5 of the Criminal Procedure Act 1865.

Section 4 of the Criminal Procedure Act 1865 provides:

---

[2] At 263. *Windass* was applied in *Gray and Evans* [1998] Crim. L.R. 570 where the Court of Appeal said that it is inappropriate to do so if the effect is to use what is said in the document as if it were evidence against the witness.
[3] *Wharam v Routledge* (1805) 5 Esp. 235; *Calvert v Flower* (1836) 7 C. & P. 386; *Palmer v Maclear and M'Grath* (1858) 1 Sw. & Tr. 149; *Stroud v Stroud* [1963] 1 W.L.R. 1080 (Wrangham J.); *Senat v Senat* [1965] P. 172, 177.
[4] See paras 18–11 *et seq.*, above, for a discussion of the obligation on the prosecution.
[5] (1982) 74 Cr.App.R. 194, 198.

"If a witness, upon cross-examination as to a former statement made by him relative to the subject-matter of the indictment or proceeding, and inconsistent with his present testimony, does not distinctly admit that he has made such statement, proof may be given that he did in fact make it; but before such proof can be given the circumstances of the supposed statement, sufficient to designate the particular occasion, must be mentioned to the witness, and he must be asked whether or not he has made such statement."

The terms of the section are wide enough to cover both oral statements and statements in writing, but since s.5 relates specifically to written statements, it had been thought that s.4 applied particularly to oral statements. However, in *Derby Magistrates' Court Ex p. B*[6] the House of Lords said that there was no reason to confine s.4 to oral statements since the wording of the section does not do so and its content is apt to cover both oral and written statements. Video-recordings of the evidence of children should not be treated as previous inconsistent statements as the situation does not strictly fall into the law concerning previous inconsistent statements.[7] It is submitted that statutory guidance may of assistance on the treatment of previous recordings within the rules on previous consistent and inconsistent statements.

The following rules should be noted: **21–24**

(a)   Before the statement is proved the circumstances (sufficient to designate the occasion) must be mentioned to the witness and he must be asked whether he made the statement: s.4.

(b)   The statement must relate to the "subject-matter of the indictment or proceeding" before the section applies: s.4. It will be for the court to determine whether it does or not. In practice, this decision has not presented any difficulty. However, it would appear that the court has a discretion when so deciding.[8]

(c)   Section 4 is not applicable to cross-examination as to credit, which is governed by common law rules (para.21–28, below).[9]

(d)   The section is not confined to previous statements on oath or in a deposition.[10] Thus, in *O'Neill*,[11] two defendants, M and O, were tried together. M pleaded guilty to the first two counts in the indictment to which O pleaded not guilty. M gave evidence and

---

[6] [1995] 3 W.L.R. 681, 687.
[7] *Eldridge and Salmon* [1999] Crim.L.R. 166.
[8] *Bashir* (1970) 54 Cr.App.R. 15.
[9] *Funderburk* (1990) 90 Cr.App.R. 466.
[10] *Hart* (1958) 42 Cr.App.R. 47, 50.
[11] [1969] Crim.L.R. 260.

denied in cross-examination that O had committed with him the offence alleged in count one. The judge then allowed the prosecution to put to M an oral statement which he had made to the police, in which he said that O was involved in committing the offence with him. The Court of Criminal Appeal upheld this ruling.

(e) Where, however, a witness is treated as hostile by leave of the judge under s.3 of the Act, evidence may not be called under s.4 to show that the witness had made a previous inconsistent statement.[12]

(f) The cross-examiner must have the statement available to put to the witness: if he does not have the statement in his hand the procedure under the section cannot begin.[13] This is because the statement only becomes admissible under the section when it is shown to the witness and he does not "distinctly admit" making it.

21–25   Section 5 of the Criminal Procedure Act 1865 provides:

"A witness may be cross-examined as to previous statements made by him in writing, or reduced into writing, relative to the subject-matter of the indictment or proceeding, without such writing being shown to him; but if it is intended to contradict such witness by the writing, his attention must, before such contradictory proof can be given, be called to those parts of the writing which are to be used for the purpose of so contradicting him: provided always, that it shall be competent for the judge, at any time during the trial, to require the production of the writing for his inspection, and he may thereupon make such use of it for the purposes of the trial as he may think fit."

The rules relating to cross-examination under this section may be summarised as follows.

(a) A witness may be cross-examined about a previous statement in writing without being shown the statement: s.5. Hence, he can be asked if he made a statement to the police and when and where he made it. If the cross-examiner adopts this course he must have the statement available even if he does not intend to contradict the witness with it.[14] However, if the purpose of the cross-examina-

---

[12] *Booth* (1982) 74 Cr.App.R. 123. See paras 21–09 *et seq.*, above for s.3.
[13] *Derby Magistrates' Court Ex p. B* [1995] 3 W.L.R. 681, HL: see at 687, *per* Lord Taylor C.J.
[14] *Anderson* (1930) 21 Cr.App.R. 178. In *Derby Magistrates' Court Ex p. B*, above, the House of Lords held this to be the law, applying to both ss.4 and 5 of the Act.

tion is to point out inconsistency it is not a course which can be followed.

(b) The cross-examiner may show the statement to the witness without making it evidence. Thus, he may refer the witness to a particular passage without reading it out and ask the witness if he adheres to his evidence. This is a course with much to recommend it, because the witness, faced with his statement, often retracts, alters or explains his evidence. It also has the advantage that the statement will not be exhibited. However, if the cross-examiner follows this course, he is bound by the witness's answers.[15]

(c) If the cross-examiner wishes to use the statement to contradict the witness's evidence he must draw the witness's attention to the relevant parts: s.5. For this purpose, the witness ought to have a copy of the statement before him. The passages may be read aloud and the witness cross-examined about inconsistencies between his evidence and the contents of his statement.

(d) If the cross-examiner adopts this course ((c) above) and uses the statement to contradict the witness, the nineteenth-century authorities say that he must put it in evidence,[16] *i.e.* it will be exhibited and put before the jury. Channell B. explained that this should be done so that the whole statement may be read: "and then it will appear how far the suggested contradiction exists, and the absence of a particular statement may be explained by the context, or, even if there is a discrepancy on one point, it may appear that it is only one minute point and that in all the rest of the evidence there is perfect consistency, so that the general result of the comparison may be confirmation rather than contradiction."[17]

(e) However, the section provides that the judge may make such use of the statement for the purposes of the trial as he may think fit. Accordingly, he has a discretion in determining whether the statement should be exhibited or not.[18] In exercising the discretion the court may have to consider a number of factors, including the scope of the cross-examination in relation to the contents of the statement (in particular, the contents unconnected with cross-

---

[15] *Riley* (1866) 4 F. & F. 964.

[16] *Riley*, above; *Wright* (1866) 4 F. & F. 967.

[17] *Riley*, above.

[18] In *Longden, The Times*, May 31, 1995, the Court of Appeal emphasised that this was a matter of discretion, and not a matter of policy as the trial judge in the instant case seems to have thought. It may be noted that 20–30 years ago it was a commonly held view that the whole statement should be exhibited in these circumstances. Such a view no longer represents the law.

examination) and prejudice to the accused if the statement is admitted, particularly if it contains material unconnected with cross-examination.

21–26 If it is proper for the jury to have the relevant parts of a statement which contains prejudicial matter, it may be necessary to provide them with only part of the statement. Thus, in *Beattie*[19] the Court of Appeal criticised the trial judge's decision to allow the jury to have the whole of a statement where two small matters had been the subject of cross-examination and the statement contained much other matter. The Court said it would have been better to have confined the jury's view of the statement to the matters subject to cross-examination.

If a statement is admitted in evidence under ss.4 or 5, it is not evidence of the facts stated in it, but may be used to impugn the credibility of the witness.[20]

The fact that s.5 provides that the judge may make such use of the statement as he may think fit does not mean that he may treat the witness's previous statement as evidence of its contents,[21] although he may call attention to parts to which no reference has been made.[22]

E. Cross-examination as to credit

21–27 The purpose of cross-examination as to credit is to show that the witness should not be believed on his oath. "Generally speaking questions may be put to a witness as to any improper conduct of which he may have been guilty for the purpose of testing his credit."[23]

Accordingly, a witness may be cross-examined about his previous convictions and antecedents.[24] However, such cross-examination may not be conducted without restriction. For instance, a witness must not be asked to draw an inference of fact discreditable to himself[25]; nor asked questions about his religious belief in order to discredit him[26]; nor asked about disparaging comments made by the court about his conduct and testimony in other trials.[27] The cross-examination must be relevant to the standing of the

---

[19] (1989) 89 Cr.App.R. 302.
[20] *O'Neil*, above; *Birch*, below; *North Australian Territory Co. v Goldsborough, Mort & Co.* [1893] 2 Ch. 381, 386.
[21] *Birch* (1924) 18 Cr.App.R. 26. In *Martin and White* [1998] Cr.App.R. 385 the Court of Appeal held that, although the prosecution was not prevented from cross-examining (in order to demonstrate inconsistency) upon the contents of a disclosure affidavit sworn by an accused pursuant to a High Court restraint order, the affidavit is not admissible in evidence.
[22] *Birch*, above, at 28, *per* Avory J.
[23] *Edwards* (1991) 93 Cr.App.R. 48, 55, *per* Lord Lane C.J.
[24] For a discussion of cross-examination on these subjects, including cross-examination of complainants in rape cases, see paras 7–73 *et seq.*, above.
[25] *Bernard* (1858) 1 F. & F. 240.
[26] *Darby v Ouseley* (1856) 1 H. & N. 1. No doubt the same rule should apply to political beliefs.
[27] *Seaman v Netherclift* (1877) 2 C.P.D. 53.

witness with the tribunal of fact.[28] The judge will stop questioning which has no such relevance and which is purely vexatious.

Guidance as to when such questioning is proper is to be found in the judgment of Sankey L.J. in *Hobbs v Tinling*.[29]

"The Court can always exercise its discretion to decide whether a question as to credit is one which the witness should be compelled to answer ... in the exercise of its discretion the Court should have regard to the following considerations:

'(1) Such questions are proper if they are of such a nature that the truth of the imputation conveyed by them would seriously affect the opinion of the Court as to the credibility of the witness on the matter to which he testifies.

(2) Such questions are improper if the imputation which they convey relates to matters so remote in time, or of such a character, that the truth of the imputation would not affect, or would affect in a slight degree the opinion of the Court as to the credibility of the witness on the matter to which he testifies.

(3) Such questions are improper if there is a great disproportion between the importance of the imputation made against the witness's character and the importance of his evidence.'"

The general rule is that an answer to a question relating to credit or other **21–28** collateral matter is final. The answer must be accepted and the other party may not call evidence to contradict the answer.[30] The reason for the rule is to avoid a multiplicity of side issues which might blur the issue which the jury has to decide. Thus, for example, in a case of rape before the Sexual Offences(Amendment) Act 1976, the complainant might be asked if she had had sexual intercourse with other men. However, her answers to such questions would be final and could not be contradicted by other evidence.[31]

The test as to whether a matter is collateral or not was put by Pollock C.B. in *Att-Gen v Hitchcock*[32] as follows: "[If] the answer of a witness is a matter which you would be allowed on your own part to prove in evidence—if it had such a connection with the issues that you would be allowed to give it in evidence—then it is a matter on which you may contradict him."

A distinction must thus be made between matters in issue and matters

---

[28] *Sweet-Escott* (1971) 55 Cr.App.R. 316, 320 *per* Lawton J.
[29] [1929] 2 K.B. 1, 51. This passage was quoted above with approval by Lord Lane C.J. in *Edwards*, above.
[30] *Harris v Tippett* (1811) 2 Camp. 637; *Palmer v Trower* (1852) 8 Exch. 247.
[31] *Holmes* (1871) L.R. 1 C.C.R. 334.
[32] (1847) 1 Ex. 91, 99.

going to credit only. Examples of the distinction are to be found in *Busby*[33] and *Marsh*.[34]

In *Busby* allegations were made in cross-examination that two police officers had fabricated statements attributed to the defendant. The police officers were also cross-examined to the effect that they had threatened a potential witness to prevent him from giving evidence. The judge would not allow the defence to call the witness to give evidence about the threats since, in the judge's view, the cross-examination was an attack on credit. The Court of Appeal held that the judge was wrong because the evidence went to an issue in the case, namely as to whether the officers had fabricated the statements. The court said that the witness's evidence went to the issue for the following reason. If the jury had accepted the witness's evidence, it would show that the police officers were prepared to go to improper lengths to secure a conviction. Accordingly, the jury would be more prepared to accept that the officers had fabricated the statements.

21–29   In *Marsh* the defendant was charged with various offences arising out of incidents involving himself and A. The defence sought to call a witness to say that A had uttered threats to the defendant. The trial judge refused to admit the evidence on the ground that it went to credit. The Court of Appeal disagreed and held that the evidence should have been admitted because it was relevant to the most important issue in the case, *i.e.* whether the defendant or A was the aggressor.

In *Funderburk*[35] it was said that *Busby* had provided a further exception to the general rule relating to the admissibility of evidence as to credit, namely to show that the police are prepared to go to improper lengths to secure a conviction. However, in *Edwards*[36] Lord Lane C.J. said that the true basis of the decision in *Busby* may have been the suggestion of bias against a particular defendant in a particular case: accordingly, cross-examination was permissible to show that the witness was biased or partial. (While it is submitted that the decision in *Busby* created no new exception to the general rule, it is also submitted that such allegations of fabrication of statements and threats by witnesses are very much matters in issue.)

Another example is to be found in *Nagrecha*.[37] The defendant in that case was charged with indecent assault. The defence was that no such assault had occurred. The only witnesses were the complainant and the defendant. The complainant was cross-examined about allegations of indecency she had made against other men. She denied making the allegations. The defence applied to call a witness to give evidence about the complainant's making of these allegations. The judge refused the application on the ground that the evidence related only to credit. The Court of

---

[33] (1982) 75 Cr.App.R. 79.
[34] (1986) 83 Cr.App.R. 165.
[35] (1990) 90 Cr.App.R. 466, 470.
[36] (1991) 93 Cr.App.R. 48, 56.
[37] [1997] 2 Cr.App.R. 401.

Appeal, quashing the conviction, held that the judge ought to have permitted the evidence to be called. Rose L.J. said: "[S]uch evidence went not merely to credit, but to the heart of the case, in that it bore on the crucial issue as to whether or not there had been an indecent assault. As to that matter, only the complainant and appellant were able to give evidence. In our judgment, that being so, the learned judge ought to have permitted the evidence to be called because it might well have led the jury to take a different view of the complainant's evidence."[38] Similarly, in *David R*[39] the Court of Appeal held that although the general rule was that evidence was not admissible to contradict answers given by a witness when cross-examined as to credit, where the evidence sought to be adduced goes to the "heart of the case", *i.e.* a sexual case where collusion is advanced, derogation from the rule is acceptable. Moreover, in *Elahee*[40] it was held that where the issue in a sexual case was not one of consent, but who had made an improper approach to whom, the evidence of a complainant's previous sexual experience was a matter which was relevant to an issue in the trial and therefore one which the jury could properly take into account in assessing the plausibility of the account given by the defendant.

Complaints are sometimes made about the usefulness in practice of the test in *Att-Gen v Hitchcock*. For instance, in *Funderburk*[41] the defendant was charged with having unlawful sexual intercourse with a 13-year-old girl. In chief, the complainant gave evidence which suggested that she was a virgin prior to having sexual intercourse with the defendant. The judge refused the defence leave to cross-examine the complainant about a conversation in which she discussed her previous sexual experience. The judge also prevented the defence from calling a witness to give evidence about the conversation. The Court of Appeal held that the cross-examination and the evidence were admissible in relation to the central issue of the complainant's credit. Henry J. commented that Pollock C.B.'s test was difficult to apply, but its utility lay in the fact that it was based on the court's sense of fair play rather than any philosophic or analytic basis.[42] Thus, the Court in *Funderbank* urged a flexible approach so that a general rule designed to serve the interests of justice should not be used to defeat justice by an over-pedantic approach. Following the decision in *Funderbank* there have been suggestions of a more relaxed approach to the finality rule.[43]

21–30

In *Somers*[44] the Court of Appeal re-iterated the general rule that evidence was not admissible to contradict answers given by a witness to questions

---

[38] At 410.
[39] [1999] Crim.L.R. 909.
[40] [1999] Crim.L.R. 399.
[41] Above.
[42] Above, at 476.
[43] S. Seabrooke, "The Vanishing Trick—blurring the line between credit and issue" [1999] Crim.L.R. 387; *Nagrecha* above; and *Neale* [1998] Crim.L.R. 737.
[44] [1999] Crim.L.R. 744.

put in cross-examination which concerned collateral matters, *i.e.* matters going merely to credit but otherwise irrelevant to the issues in the case. The issue of sufficient relevance was held to be a matter for the trial judge and the Court of Appeal will therefore only interfere where it concludes that the decision to exclude the evidence as insufficiently relevant was either wrong in principle or plainly wrong as being outside that wide ambit.

Facts showing that the witness is biased or partial in relation to the parties may be elicited in cross-examination. If such allegations are denied, evidence may be called to prove them.[45] For instance in *Phillips*,[46] the defendant was charged with incest. His daughters gave evidence for the prosecution. In cross-examination they denied that they had been "schooled" in their evidence by their mother. The Court of Criminal Appeal held that the defence should have been allowed to call two women to say that the daughters had made statements to them to that effect.

21-31   A further example is to be found in *Mendy*.[47] During the course of the trial in that case a police constable saw a man taking notes in the public gallery during the evidence of a prosecution witness. The constable and a court official then saw the man talking outside the court to the defendant's husband, apparently describing the witness's evidence to him. When the husband gave evidence he denied that the incident had taken place. The Court of Appeal upheld the judge's ruling allowing the prosecution to call the constable and court official to give evidence of what they had seen.

If a witness denies a conviction when it is put to him in cross-examination or refuses to answer, the conviction may be proved against him: Criminal Procedure Act 1865, s.6.

4. RE-EXAMINATION

21-32   After the close of cross-examination, the party calling the witness may re-examine him. However:

(a)   if there has been no cross-examination, there is no right to re-examine; and

(b)   re-examination is confined to matters arising out of cross-examination.

Thus, a witness may be asked to explain or expand an answer given in cross-examination, but no new matter may be introduced without leave of

---

[45] *Att-Gen v Hitchcock*, above; *Thomas v David* (1836) 7 C. & P. 350; *Dunn v Aslett* (1828) 2 M. & R. 122; *Shaw* (1888) 16 Cox 503.
[46] (1936) 26 Cr.App.R. 17.
[47] (1977) 64 Cr.App.R. 4.

the judge. The same facility with regard to demonstrations by the witness should be granted.[48] Leading questions may not be asked.

However, as a matter of indulgence, the judge may allow re-examination of a witness on matter about which counsel has forgotten to ask (subject to the right of the other party to cross-examine).

In *Reading and West Berkshire Stipendiary Magistrate*,[49] it was held that while a defendant should not normally be denied his right to give evidence in re-examination, where an accused has been allowed to consult his solicitor after examination-in-chief and cross-examination, the court may be entitled to refuse to allow him to give evidence in re-examination.

The following rules relating to re-examination on a witness's statements may be noted:

21–33

(i) The witness may not be asked about a previous consistent statement (whether he has been cross-examined to show inconsistency or otherwise), unless it be to rebut an allegation of recent invention: paras 20–09 *et seq.*, above. "[There] is no general exception [to the rule against previous consistent statements] to the effect that where counsel cross-examined to show inconsistencies, the witness can be re-examined to show consistency".[50] The same rule applies to video recordings of police interviews with child witnesses admitted under s.32(A) of the Criminal Justice Act 1988.[51] The same will apply to video recordings made under s.27 of the Youth Justice and Criminal Evidence Act 1999 (see para.19–24 above).

(ii) If the witness has been cross-examined about his witness statement, he may be re-examined about it to clarify or explain the part on which he was cross-examined: were the rule otherwise, there is a danger of the jury being misled.

(iii) A witness's evidence in cross-examination of part of a conversation does not entitle the party calling him to re-examine him on all that was said: new matter relating to the conversation may not be

---

[48] In *Marr* [1989] Crim.L.R. 743, the defendant was asked in cross-examination to demonstrate how he said an incident had happened. The judge refused to allow counsel to adopt the same procedure in re-examination. The Court of Appeal said that the judge was wrong and that the same facility should have been allowed to the defence as had been allowed to the prosecution.

[49] (2000) 164 J.P. 117.

[50] *Beattie* (1989) 89 Cr.App.R. 302, 307, *per* Lord Lane C.J.

[51] In *P(GR)* [1988] Crim.L.R. 667 the video recording of a police interview with a child witness was excluded by the trial judge. The witness was cross-examined about the inconsistencies between her evidence and the interview, and a small part of the video recording was played. The judge permitted the prosecution to play other parts of the recording to the jury in order to show the witness's consistency. The Court of Appeal held this to have been an error and ordered a retrial. S.32(A) of the Criminal Justice Act 1988 has now been repealed.

introduced.[52] It would appear that the same rule should apply to previous inconsistent statements used by some other party to cross-examine the witness under s.5 of the Criminal Procedure Act 1865, para.21–33, above. However, if the statement has been exhibited under that section there can be nothing to prevent re-examination upon it. Otherwise, it would appear that re-examination is not permissible except to clarify the part subject to cross-examination.

A witness is entitled to refresh his memory from a contemporaneous statement in re-examination. In *Sutton*[53] the Court of Appeal held that a witness may refresh his memory in these circumstances from a police record of an interview made the day after an incident. However, in *Harman*[54] the Court of Appeal said that while there was nothing wrong with this practice the witness should not be shown his statement and under the guise of refreshing his memory be asked if the account in the statement was more likely to be reliable than that given in cross-examination.

21–34   There is doubt as to whether a party calling a hostile witness may re-examine him. The Court of Appeal has said that the right to do so is by no means well established.[55] In a Crown Court case the prosecution was allowed to re-examine a hostile witness on new matters which had arisen during cross-examination.[56] While the matter has yet to be decided, it would appear to require very exceptional circumstances to justify a party, having cross-examined the witness once to subject him to further examination after the other party have completed their cross-examination.

On the other hand, an application may be made in re-examination to treat as hostile a witness who in cross-examination has shown his hostility to the party calling him. In *Powell*[57] the Court of Appeal described such an application as a little unusual but said that it was a matter for the judge's discretion. In *Norton and Driver*[58] a prosecution witness said he could not remember incidents relating to the offence charged. In cross-examination he gave evidence about them exculpating the defendants. The prosecution was allowed to treat him as hostile. The Court of Appeal commented that there is no distinction between hostility arising in evidence in chief and hostility arising in cross-examination.

The Royal Commission on Criminal Justice reported that many expert witnesses feel that they are not given sufficient opportunity to explain the

---

[52] *Prince v Samo* (1837) 7 L.J.Q.B. 123.
[53] (1992) 94 Cr.App.R. 70.
[54] [1985] Crim.L.R. 326.
[55] *Booth*, above, at 131.
[56] *Wong* [1986] Crim.L.R. 683.
[57] [1985] Crim.L.R. 592.
[58] [1987] Crim.L.R. 687.

full meaning of scientific evidence.[59] The Commission recommended that in the absence of the jury the trial judge should ask an expert before he leaves the box if there is anything he wishes to add; and then, providing that the answer is admissible, it should be repeated in the presence of the jury. While this may be a sensible proposal in the interests of clarifying technical evidence, it is to be hoped that such a cumbersome procedure could be avoided.

---

[59] Cm. 2263 (1993), para.9.73.

Index

ACCIDENT
  burden of proof, 4–07
ACCOMPLICES
  corroboration evidence, from,
      15–01, 15–13
  witnesses, as, 17–15
ACCUSATIONS
  failure to reply, 9–06, 9–08
  indignant rebuttal, 9–07
  parties on even terms, 9–08
  right to silence, 9–06, 9–07
    and see RIGHT TO SILENCE
ACCUSED
  cross-examination, conducted by,
      21–18, 21–19
  lies
    alibi defences, 16–19
    conflict of evidence, 16–20
    deliberate lies, 16–20
    inference of guilt, 16–19
    judge's directions, 16–17, 16–18
    previous consistent statements, by,
        20–13
  witness, as, 17–18, 17–19
ACQUITTAL
  admissibility of, 5–21, 5–25, 5–26
  burden of proof, 3–28
  certificate of, 3–23
  challenges to, 5–14
  double jeopardy, and, 5–14, 5–15,
      5–17
  evidential effect of, 5–13
  jury directions, as to, 16–10, 16–11
  PACE provisions, concerning, 3–23
  previous acquittal
    character evidence, 7–28
    confession, effect on, 5–24
    defence reliance, on, 5–21
    references permitted, to, 5–22,
        5–24
    relevance of, 5–22, 5–23
    validity of, 5–14
    witness credibility, and, 5–24,
        5–25

ACQUITTAL—*cont.*
  proof of, 3–23, 3–24
  subsequent prosecutions
    evidence admissible, in, 5–14—
        5–16, 5–18
    issue estoppel, and, 5–19, 5–20
    proof of guilt, in, 5–16
    same incident, based on, 5–16
    similar facts rule, 5–15
  validity of, 5–14
  verdict conclusive, 5–14
ADJOURNMENT
  magistrate's decision, on, 16–28,
      16–29
ADMISSIBILITY
  acquittals, and, 5–21, 5–25, 5–26
  character evidence, 7–02—7–04
    and see CHARACTER EVIDENCE
  confessions, 4–33, 9–02, 9–15,
      9–16, 9–25, 9–47—9–50
    and see CONFESSIONS
  convictions, and, 5–27, 5–33
    and see CONVICTIONS
  depositions, 8–77
  documents, 2–05, 3–01, 3–06, 3–07,
      3–12, 21–20
    and see DOCUMENTS
  dying declarations, 4–35
  evidence, of, 1–12, 4–33, 4–48,
  expert evidence, 6–12, 6–16
  hearsay evidence, 8–12, 8–13, 8–17,
      8–19
    and see HEARSAY
  identification evidence, 14–37
  intercepts, and, 2–21
  judicial decisions, as to, 1–12,
      16–05, 16–06, 16–08
  magistrate's decision, as to, 16–27
  opinion evidence, 6–02, 6–05, 6–06
    and see OPINION EVIDENCE
  photographs, 2–09, 2–10
  previous consistent statements,
      20–04—20–06, 20–09–20–11
  recordings, 2–09, 2–10

ADMISSIBILITY—*cont.*
  res gestae
    see RES GESTAE
  relevance, and, 1–12, 1–16, 1–18
  similar fact evidence, 7–03
  standard of proof, and, 4–48
  summary trials, in, 16–27
  video recordings, 2–31, 19–24, 19–25
  video tapes, 2–09
ADMISSIONS
  see also CONFESSIONS
  admission of fact, 1–02, 9–59
  agents, by, 8–63
  conduct, by, 9–05
  conviction, proved by, 3–26
  counsel, by, 8–63, 9–11, 9–12
  defendant's belief, supporting, 9–59
  formal
    evidence, as to, 5–07
    jury directions, 5–07
    oral, 5–07
    statutory provisions, 5–07
    written, 5–07
  guilt, of, 9–54
  personal knowledge, supporting,
      9–59
  previous consistent statements,
      involving, 20–14—20–16,
      20–18
  right to silence, 9–06, 9–07
    and see RIGHT TO SILENCE
  solicitors, involving, 9–11
  vicarious, 9–11
ADVERSE INFERENCE
  defence statement, liable to, 18–21
  failure to answer questions, 17–16,
      17–17, 17–19
  failure to be sworn, 17–17
  failure to give evidence, 17–16,
      17–17, 17–25, 19–03
  failure to reply, 9–08,
  human rights, and, 17–24
  judge's directions, on, 17–22
AFFIRMATION
  form of, 19–10
  practice, relating to, 19–09
  purpose of, 19–08
  witness, by, 17–02
AGENT PROVOCATEUR
  evidence of, 10–11, 10–14, 10–15
ALIBI
  accused lying, where, 16–19
  burden of proof, 4–07, 4–27

ALIBI—*cont.*
  defence, as, 18–14, 18–16
  defence statement, within, 18–14,
      18–16
  evidence of, 18–16
  visual identification, and, 14–09
  witness, as to, 18–14, 18–18
ALLEGATIONS
  failure to reply, 9–10
ANTI-SOCIAL BEHAVIOUR
  character evidence, and, 7–30
ARREST
  human rights, and, 13–11
  marks found, on, 11–24, 11–25
  objects found, on, 11–24, 11–25
  police caution, 9–33, 9–43, 9–45
  right to silence, on, 11–24
    and see RIGHT TO SILENCE
  substances found, on, 11–24, 11–25
  suspect of, 9–38, 9–45
AULD REPORT (REVIEW OF CRIMINAL
    COURTS)
  recommendations
    character evidence, on, 7–04
    disclosure of evidence, 18–09
    evidence, relevance of, 1–18
    exclusion of evidence, 10–33
    hearsay evidence, 8–11
    jury trial, on, 16–25
    previous consistent statements,
        20–21
AUTOMATIC RECORDINGS
  evidence, as, 2–43
AUTOMATISM
  burden of proof, 4–07, 4–30

BANKERS' BOOKS
  admissibility, 3–15
  copies, taken from, 3–15, 3–16
  evidence of transactions, 3–15
  inspection orders, 3–16, 3–17
BEHAVIOUR
  see also ADVERSE INFERENCE
  guilt, inferred from, 1–09
BEST EVIDENCE RULE
  application of, 1–11
  documents, involving, 3–06
  significance diminished, 1–11
BURDEN OF PROOF
  defence
    defences in law, 4–07, 4–08
    disproving, 4–07, 4–08
    putting in issue, 4–08, 4–09

BURDEN OF PROOF—*cont.*
  defendant, position as to, 4–07,
    4–08, 4–13, 4–20, 4–21
  evidential burden
    automatism, cases involving,
      4–30
    confessions, 4–33, 4–47
    defence, on, 4–26, 4–27, 4–28,
      4–32
    dying declarations, 4–35
    guilty knowledge, 4–26
    jury, considered by, 4–28, 4–30
    meaning of, 4–26
    "prima facie case", distinguished,
      4–26
    self-defence, cases involving, 4–27
    "shifted to defence", 4–27, 4–28
    unexplained facts, 4–26
    witnesses, competence of, 4–34
  fair trial, and, 13–20, 13–21
  human rights, and, 4–13, 4–14,
    13–20, 13–21
  judge's directions, on, 16–14
  meaning of, 4–02
  persuasive burden
    controlled drugs, knowledge of,
      4–12
    corruption, cases involving, 4–12
    diminished responsibility, 4–12
    drink driving offences, 4–12
    evidential burden, 4–02
    exceptions to rule, 4–10
    extent of proof, 4–04
    immoral earnings, living off, 4–12
    insanity, cases involving, 4–11
    jury directions, 4–03— 4–06
    legal burden, 4–02
    presumption of innocence, 4–03,
      4–13, 4–14
    prosecution, on, 4–03, 4–07
    reverse burden, where, 4–13—
      4–15
    rule, relating to, 4–03, 4–07
    significance of, 4–02
    statutory exceptions, 4–12
  presumptions, regarding, 5–04,
    5–05
    and see PRESUMPTIONS
  self-defence, cases involving, 4–07,
    4–26
  statutory exceptions
    express, 4–12
    implied, 4–19, 4–20

BURDEN OF PROOF—*cont.*
  statutory exceptions—*cont.*
    statutory interpretation, 4–23,
      4–24
    summary trials, 4–19, 4–20
    trial on indictment, 4–21
  terrorism, cases involving, 4–13,
    4–18
BUSINESS RECORDS
  admissibility, 8–30, 8–31, 8–67
  computer records, 8–32
  standard of proof, concerning, 8–32

CHARACTER
  anti-social behaviour, 7–30
  bad character
    crime charged, propensity
      towards, 7–41, 7–42
    definition of, 7–28–7–30
    evidence of, 7–03, 7–04, 7–27,
      7–33, 7–35, 9–54
    false impression, correcting,
      7–60–7–62
    jury directions, 7–63, 7–68
    previous acquittal, where, 7–28
    previous convictions, where,
      7–28, 7–31, 7–47
    same category offences, 7–45—
      7–47
    similar convictions, 7–45, 7–46,
      7–47
    untruthfulness, 7–43, 7–44, 7–55
    witness character, 7–73
    witness credibility, 7–65, 7–67,
      7–76
  evidence
    see CHARACTER EVIDENCE
  false impression, as to, 7–60—7–62
  general conduct, 7–29
  good character
    asserting, 7–60, 7–61
    defence, used as, 7–17
    defendant's credibility, 7–12,
      7–13
    employer, evidence from, 7–08
    evidence in rebuttal, 7–11
    evidence permitted, 7–06—7–08,
      7–10
    fairness and balance, concerning,
      7–19
    general reputation, 7–01, 7–07,
      7–08

CHARACTER—*cont.*
  good character—*cont.*
    isolated conviction, where, 7–14
    jury directions, 7–12, 7–14—7–18
    offence incompatible, with, 7–12
    police caution, effect of, 7–19
    spent convictions, 7–21, 7–23
  indivisible nature, of, 7–63
  jury directions, as to, 7–12,
      7–14—7–18, 7–63, 7–68
  misconduct, disposition towards,
      7–29
  young persons, 7–31
CHARACTER EVIDENCE
  see also CHARACTER
  adduced
    co-defendant, by, 7–55, 7–56,
      7–54
    defendant, by, 7–36
  admissibility
    judge's discretion, as to, 7–04,
      7–47—7–49
    previous acquittal, 7–28
    previous convictions, 7–04, 7–05,
      7–28, 7–31, 7–47
    probative force, 7–03, 7–04
    relevant evidence, 7–03, 7–04
    rules, as to, 7–02—7–04, 7–27,
      7–33, 7–35, 9–54
    similar fact evidence, 7–03
  assumptions, as to, 7–71
  attacking another's character, 7–64,
      7–65, 7–68, 7–73
  co-defendants, position regarding,
      7–19, 7–20, 7–46, 7–54, 7–55,
      7–56
  contaminated evidence, 7–69
    and see CONTAMINATED
      EVIDENCE
  court ruling, on, 7–72
  cross-examination, in, 7–36
  disposition, as to, 7–01—7–03
  exclusionary rules
    application for exclusion,
      7–49—7–51, 7–68
    basis for, 7–02
    effect of, 7–03
    multiple offences, 7–51
    prejudicial effect, 7–68
    severance of indictment,
      7–52—7–54
  general reputation, as to 7–01,
      7–02, 7–07, 7–08

CHARACTER EVIDENCE—*cont.*
  important explanatory evidence,
      7–37, 7–38, 7–73—7–75
  impropriety, allegations of, 7–66
  jury directions, 7–12, 7–14—7–18
  misconduct, allegations of, 7–66
  parties agreement, over, 7–35
  prejudicial effects, 7–39, 7–44,
      7–45, 7–47, 7–68
  probative value, 7–41, 7–45, 7–55,
      7–56, 7–73, 7–74, 7–76
  quality of, 7–71
  rebuttal, evidence in, 7–77
  reform, proposals for, 7–04
  sexual offences, 7–78, 7–79
    and see SEXUAL OFFENCES
  statutory provisions, governing,
      7–27, 7–33, 7–34, 7–49
    see also CRIMINAL JUSTICE ACT
      2003
  "tit for tat" evidence, 7–65
CHATTELS
  court exhibits, as, 2–03
  real evidence, as, 2–02
CHILDREN
  accused
    cross-examination by, 21–18
    presence of, 19–11
  competence as witness
    appreciation of occasion, 17–04
    burden of proof, 17–03
    cases, relating to, 17–05
    common law position, 17–04
    expert evidence, as to, 17–03
    statutory provisions, 17–05
    truthfulness, 17–04
    very young children, 17–04,
      17–05
  cross-examination of, 19–15, 21–18
  evidence
    accused, presence of, 19–11
    admissibility of, 19–24
    age considerations, 17–03, 17–04
    change of mind, where, 19–27
    corroboration evidence, 15–01,
      15–13, 17–05
    exclusion of, 17–05
    extremely young children, 17–04,
      17–05
    intimidation, 19–11, 19–17,
      19–24
    judge's warning, as to, 17–03
    live link, use of, 19–15

CHILDREN—*cont.*
evidence—*cont.*
previous convictions, of, 7–31
quality of evidence, from, 19–15
screens, use of, 19–17
sexual offences, involving, 19–15
statutory provisions, 17–03—
17–05, 19–15
unsworn evidence, 17–03
hostile witness, as, 21–11
interviews, best practice, 19–30
judicial discretion, regarding, 17–05
NSPCC Guidelines, 17–04
previous convictions, 7–31
previous inconsistent statements,
21–23
protection of, 19–11
re-examination of, 19–15
special measures directions, and,
19–11, 19–15, 19–16, 19–24
and see SPECIAL MEASURES
television links, use of, 17–05
video recorded interviews, 17–04,
17–05, 19–15, 19–24, 19–27,
21–11, 21–23
vulnerable witness, as, 19–11,
19–12, 19–15, 19–30, 21–18
witness, as, 17–03—17–05, 19–11,
19–15
CIRCUMSTANTIAL EVIDENCE
fingerprints, as, 1–07
lies, as 1–08
motive, evidence of, 1–07
preparatory acts, 1–07
stolen goods, 1–08, 1–09
CLOSING SPEECHES
evidence, following, 19–41
CO-DEFENDANTS
character evidence,
adduced by, 7–55, 7–56
provisions, relating to, 7–19,
7–20, 7–24, 7–46
reform proposals, 7–57, 7–58
confessions, and, 9–53, 9–53, 9–54
cross-examination, and, 21–15
exclusion of evidence, 10–11
informants, as, 12–08
meaning of, 7–55
suspect evidence, involving, 15–18
witnesses, as, 17–13, 17–14
CODES OF PRACTICE
confessions, regarding, 9–27

CODES OF PRACTICE—*cont.*
disclosure of evidence, 18–24,
18–25—18–27
identification, under, 14–16, 14–27
police interviews, under, 9–37—
9–39, 9–41
protection, afforded by, 9–27
tape recordings, under, 2–22
COMMITTAL PROCEEDINGS
evidence from, 8–77
COMPELLABILITY OF WITNESSES
see also COMPETENCE OF WITNESSES
accused
mental condition, of, 17–18
physical condition of, 17–18
privileged, where, 17–19
bankers, position regarding, 17–01
co-defendants, where, 17–13
defendant
failure to answer questions,
17–16, 17–17, 17–19
failure to be sworn, 17–17
failure to give evidence, 17–16,
17–17, 17–25
position regarding, 17–13, 17–14
diplomatic privileges, and, 17–01
expert witnesses, 6–29, 17–01
judge's position, regarding, 17–01
meaning of, 17–01
polygamous marriage, where, 17–35
spouses, position regarding, 17–26,
17–29, 17–30, 17–33, 17–34
and see SPOUSES
statutory provisions, 17–01
COMPETENCE OF WITNESSES
accomplices, 17–15
burden of proof, 17–02
coherent communication,
requirement for, 17–01
court decision, as to, 17–02
defendant
co-defendants, as to, 17–12,
17–13
cross-examination, in, 17–12
evidence on oath, 17–11
mitigation of sentence, in, 17–11
own defence, in, 17–11
prosecution witness, as, 17–14
statutory provisions, 17–11
trial within a trial, as to, 17–11
incapacitated witness, 17–08—
17–10
and see INCAPACITATED WITNESS

COMPETENCE OF WITNESSES—*cont.*
  judge's position, regarding, 17–01
  meaning of, 17–01
  persons of unsound mind
    see PERSONS OF UNSOUND MIND
  polygamous marriage, where, 17–35
  spouses, position as to, 17–26,
      17–28, 17–33, 17–34
    and see SPOUSES
  statutory provisions, 17–01
COMMON ENTERPRISE
  common purpose, evidence of, 8–64
  conversation, evidence as, 8–64
  hearsay evidence, concerning, 8–64
  multiple offences, involving, 8–64
  subsequent acts and declarations,
      8–64
COMPUTER INFORMATION
  evidence, as, 3–02, 8–32, 8–75
COMPUTER RECORDINGS
  evidence, as, 2–44
CONFESSIONS
  see also ACCUSATIONS
  acquittal, effect of, 5–24
  admissibility
    facts, relating to, 9–53, 9–59, 9–60
    general rule, as to, 9–15
    judicial decisions, as to, 16–07
    judicial powers, 9–49, 9–50
    magistrate's decision, on, 16–27
    PACE provisions, 9–02, 9–15, 9–16,
        9–25
    procedure for determining, 9–47—
        9–49
    provisions governing, 4–33, 9–02
    restrictions on, 9–15
  admissions
  and see ADMISSIONS
    conduct, by, 9–05
    guilt, admissions of, 9–54
    vicarious admissions, 9–11
  breach of statute and code
    apparent breach, 9–29
    charging powers, 9–28
    consequences of, 9–28
    court, determined by, 9–29, 9–32,
        9–35
    dispute, as to, 9–29
    exclusion, owing to, 9–27, 9–29,
        9–31
    general rules, regarding, 9–27
    investigating powers, 9–28

CONFESSIONS—*cont.*
  breach of statute and code—*cont.*
    legal advice, access to, 9–33—
        9–35
    oppression, amounting to, 9–30
    police interview, during, 9–36,
        9–38, 9–39, 9–41
    prima facie breach, 9–29
    "significant and substantial",
        where, 9–31, 9–32, 9–35,
        9–38, 9–39
    trivial breaches, 9–30, 9–35
  "cell" confessions, 9–24
  co-accused, involving, 9–03, 9–15
  co-defendant
    confession of, 9–53
    evidence of, 9–52, 9–54
  common law position, 9–01, 9–04
  conduct, admission by, 9–05
  defendant
    fit for interview, 9–23
    medical condition, of, 9–21, 9–22
    mental condition, of, 9–22, 9–23
  exclusion of evidence
    breach of statute, where, 9–27,
        9–29, 9–31
    court discretion, as to, 9–25
    deceit, where, 9–26
    discretionary powers, 9–46
    hearsay evidence, 9–46
    PACE provisions, 9–25
    police impropriety, where, 9–26
  exculpatory statements, 9–13, 9–14
  expert evidence, regarding, 6–18
  facts, proved by, 9–53, 9–59, 9–60
  failure to reply
    questioning, to, 9–08
    written allegations, to, 9–10
  form of, 9–04
  hearsay evidence, 9–46
    and see HEARSAY
  human rights provisions,
      concerning, 9–33, 13–10
  identification parade, following,
      14–25
  inducement, resulting from, 9–01
  jury function, regarding, 9–58,
      16–24
  legal advice
    access to, 9–33, 9–34
    human rights provisions, 9–33
    PACE provisions, 9–33
  meaning of, 9–04

CONFESSIONS—*cont.*
mentally handicapped persons,
9–56, 9–57
obtaining
"causal links", 9–21
deceit, by, 9–26
defendant, condition of,
9–21—9–23
"grounds for suspicion", 9–28
inhuman and degrading
treatment, 13–10
oppression by, 9–02, 9–16, 9–17,
9–53
rendered unreliable, 9–02, 9–16,
9–20, 9–24, 9–53
social workers' advice, on, 9–20
solicitors' advice, on, 9–20
"off the record" conversations,
9–14
oppression
breach of statute, where, 9–30
conduct, amounting to, 9–17,
9–18
meaning of, 9–02, 9–17
police impropriety, 9–18, 9–19,
9–24
PACE provisions, governing, 4–33,
4–47, 9–02, 9–15, 9–16, 9–25
police interviews, and, 9–36—9–39,
9–41, 9–42
police officer, to, 9–01, 9–04
probation officer, to, 9–26
psychiatrist, to, 9–26
reliability of, 5–24, 9–01, 9–02,
9–16, 9–20, 9–21, 9–36
rendered unreliable, 9–02, 9–16,
9–20, 9–24, 9–53
silence, 9–06, 9–07
and see RIGHT TO SILENCE
standard of proof, 4–47, 9–17
use
admissible confessions, 9–54
co-defendant's confession, 9–53
general rules, 9–52
inadmissible confessions, 9–52,
9–53, 9–60
voluntary nature, of, 9–01
young persons, from, 9–30
CONFRONTATION
identification evidence, as,
14–21—14–23
and see IDENTIFICATION

CONSISTENCY
see PREVIOUS CONSISTENT
STATEMENTS
CONTAMINATED EVIDENCE
collusion, over, 7–70
effect of, 7–69
exclusion of, 7–70
"group objection", 7–69
instances of, 7–69
jury directions, 7–70
remaining evidence assessed, 7–70
witnesses, agreement between,
7–69
CONVENTION RIGHTS
see also EUROPEAN CONVENTION ON
HUMAN RIGHTS (ECHR), *and*
HUMAN RIGHTS
arrest, and, 13–11
definition of, 13–04
detention, and, 13–12, 13–13
ECJ judgments, concerning, 13–06
fair trial, 10–09, 10–26, 11–10,
11–11, 11–23, 11–26, 12–23,
13–14
and see FAIR TRIAL
family life, respect for, 13–24,
13–25
inhuman and degrading treatment,
13–10
judicial interpretation, and, 13–07,
13–08
legal assistance, right to, 9–33
liberty and security, 13–11, 13–12
"margin of appreciation", doctrine
of, 13–28
national courts, and, 13–28, 13–29
national legislation, and, 13–01,
13–03, 13–07, 13–08
privacy, 10–26, 13–25, 13–26
and see PRIVACY
private life, respect for, 13–24
protection of, 13–05
reliance on, 13–05
remedies available, 13–05
rights and freedoms, unaffected by,
13–05
self-incrimination, right against,
11–10—11–12, 11–26, 13–17
and see SELF-INCRIMINATION
silence, right to, 11–10, 11–12,
11–21, 13–17
torture, prohibition of, 13–10

CONVENTION RIGHTS—*cont.*
trial
  entitlement to, 13–13
  release pending, 13–13
  UK law, compatible with, 13–01,
    13–03
  see also HUMAN RIGHTS ACT
    1998
unlawful acts, victims of, 13–05
violations of, 13–27—13–29
CONVICTION
admissibility
  common law position, 5–27
  Criminal Justice Act 2003, under,
    5–30
  offence charged, as to, 5–27
  offence denied, where, 5–31
  PACE provisions, 5–27, 5–28
  relevance, and, 5–30, 5–32
  third party convictions, 5–32
date of, 7–50
evidence
  character evidence, 7–28, 7–31,
    7–47, 7–50
  discretion to exclude, 5–33
  evidential effect, of, 5–13, 5–27
  jury directions, 5–35, 16–22,
    16–23
judge sitting alone, where, 16–26
probative value, 7–50
proof
  admission, by, 3–26
  burden of proof, 3–28
  certificate of, 3–23
  foreign convictions, 3–26
  PACE provisions, 3–23
spent convictions
  see SPENT CONVICTIONS
CORROBORATION
accomplices, evidence from, 15–01,
  15–13
children, evidence from, 15–01,
  15–13
common law rules, 15–01, 15–08,
  15–10
driving offences, concerning, 15–04
evidence amounting to, 15–12
judge's warning, on, 15–01, 15–07,
  15–10, 15–11
jury directions, 15–01, 15–07,
  15–09, 15–11, 15–19
meaning of, 15–01, 15–06
need for, 15–01

CORROBORATION—*cont.*
perjury, cases involving, 15–03
procuring offences, 15–05
sexual offences, cases involving,
  15–01, 15–08, 15–09, 15–13
statutory requirements, as to,
  15–01, 15–02, 15–06
summary trials, in, 15–09
treason, as to, 15–05
CORRUPTION
burden of proof, 4–12
COUNSEL
admissions by, 8–63
COURT INSPECTION
defendant present, at, 2–06
judge present, at, 2–06
jury, rules concerning, 2–07
timing of, 2–06
COURT VIEW
information obtained, by, 2–06,
  2–08
locus in quo, rules regarding, 2–07
situations requiring, 2–06
CRIMINAL JUSTICE ACT 2003
character evidence
  adduced by defendant, 7–36
  admissible, under, 7–33, 7–34,
    7–49
  attacking another's character,
    7–73, 7–74
  convictions, as to, 7–50
  exclusion of, 7–49, 7–50, 7–51,
    7–68
  important explanatory evidence,
    7–37, 7–75
  parties agreement, over, 7–35
  previous convictions, 7–05, 7–28
  probative value, 7–76
  provisions, as to, 7–28–7–30
  same category offences, 7–45—
    7–47
  similar convictions, 7–45—7–47
  similar offences, 7–45, 7–46
confessions, provisions under, 9–02
convictions, admissibility of, 5–30
disclosure
  defence case, and, 18–20
  unused material, 18–10
documents, admissibility of,
  8–30—8–34
evidence
  exclusion of evidence, under,
    8–73

CRIMINAL JUSTICE ACT 2003—*cont.*
evidence—*cont.*
expert evidence, under, 18–19
live links, use of, 19–21
unconvincing, where, 8–71
hearsay evidence
admissibility, 8–12—8–14, 8–17,
8–68, 8–75, 8–87
multiple hearsay, 8–66
provisions, as to, 8–01, 8–02
jury
tampering, where, 16–25
trial, without, 16–25
memory refreshing, 20–22, 20–26,
20–27
statements
admissibility, under, 8–38, 8–68,
8–69, 8–73
doubtful statements, 8–36
trial on indictment, cases sent for,
18–01
video recordings, use of, 19–24,
19–25
witnesses
calling of, 18–18
expert evidence, 18–19
CROSS-EXAMINATION
accused, conducted by, 21–18,
21–19
co-defendants, 21–15
conduct of, 21–17
documents
admissibility, 21–20
explanation of, 21–21
memory refreshing, 21–22
and see MEMORY REFRESHING
evidence
contradictory, 21–16
inadmissible evidence, 21–16
general rule, as to, 21–16
hostile witness, 21–10, 21–11
object of, 21–15
leading questions, and, 21–16
and see LEADING QUESTIONS
previous convictions, as to, 7–73,
21–27, 21–30
previous inconsistent statement, as
to, 21–08, 21–09, 21–12,
21–23—21–25
and see PREVIOUS INCONSISTENT
STATEMENTS
relevant issues, on, 21–16, 21–28
right of, 21–15

CROSS-EXAMINATION—*cont.*
sexual offences, cases involving,
21–18
video recordings, shown in, 19–31
witness
biased, where, 21–30
called by judge, where, 21–15
credit, as to, 21–16, 21–27, 21–28
guidance on, 21–27
impartiality, 21–30
previous convictions, as to,
21–27, 21–30
restrictions on, 21–27
vulnerable witness, 21–18

DEFENCE
alibi
defence, as, 18–14, 18–15
evidence of, 18–16
witness, as to, 18–14, 18–18
defence disclosure
and see DISCLOSURE OF EVIDENCE
mandatory, where, 18–14
statutory provisions, 18–14
voluntary, where, 18–15
defence statement
accuracy of, 18–21
adverse inference, from, 18–21
alibi defence, within, 18–14,
18–16
contents of, 18–14, 18–20
continuing duty, regarding, 18–22
defence differs, from, 18–20,
18–21
failure to provide, 18–20
inconsistent defence, within,
18–20
matters omitted, from, 18–20
meaning of, 18–15
service of, 18–15
updating of, 18–17, 18–20
previous acquittal, reliance on, 5–21
witnesses
alibi, for, 18–14, 18–18
details of, 18–18
expert witnesses, 18–19
intention to call, 18–18
notice to call, 18–20
DEPOSITIONS
admissibility, of, 8–77, 8–79, 8–80
committal proceedings, involving,
8–77

DEPOSITIONS—*cont.*
hearsay rules, and, 8–76, 8–77
previous inconsistent statements, in,
21–24
DETECTION OF CRIME
informants, protection of, 12–02,
12–04—12–07, 12–09
public interest, and, 12–02, 12–03
see also PUBLIC INTEREST
IMMUNITY
DETENTION
human rights, and, 13–12
police interviews
see POLICE INTERVIEWS
reasonable suspicion, on, 13–12,
13–13
DIMINISHED RESPONSIBILITY
burden of proof, 4–12
DISCLOSURE OF EVIDENCE
committal proceedings, 18–01
court's powers, concerning, 18–23
defence case, relating to, 18–08,
18–14, 18–28
and see DEFENCE
disclosure scheme
Code of Practice, and, 18–24,
18–25—18–27
disclosure officer, role of, 18–25
investigators, role of, 18–25,
18–26
officer in charge, role of, 18–25
significance of, 18–28
disputes, concerning, 18–23
documentary evidence, 18–01
expert evidence, 6–35—6–37,
18–31
fellow prisoners, evidence of, 18–13
fraud, cases involving, 18–02,
18–03, 18–32
Government proposals, concerning,
18–09
human rights, and, 18–30
material evidence, 18–07
official documents, 18–29
preparatory hearings, 18–02
primary disclosure, 18–11
primary prosecution material,
18–11, 18–12
procedure, involving, 18–24, 18–26,
18–27
prosecution disclosure, 14–30,
14–45,18–01, 18–24, 18–28

DISCLOSURE OF EVIDENCE—*cont.*
public interest immunity, 18–22,
18–30
and see PUBLIC INTEREST
IMMUNITY
requirement for, 18–01
right to silence, and, 18–08, 18–15
and see RIGHT TO SILENCE
secondary disclosure, 18–09, 18–11,
18–22
self-incrimination, and, 18–08,
18–15
and see SELF-INCRIMINATION
summary trials, 18–03, 18–04,
18–08
trials on indictment, 18–01
unused material
Attorney-General's Guidelines,
18–06, 18–08, 18–10,
18–12
Code of Practice, and, 18–24,
18–27
common law position, 18–06
court's discretion, as to, 18–08
disclosure scheme, involving,
18–25
failure to disclose, 18–08, 18–13
fair trial, ensuring, 18–07
material evidence, 18–07
preparatory notes, 18–07
public interest considerations,
18–05, 18–06
relevant material, 18–07, 18–09,
18–12, 18–24, 18–28
statutory provisions, 18–05,
18–10
summary cases, in, 18–08
tape recordings, 18–07
third parties, from, 18–12
undermining prosecution case,
18–11, 18–12, 18–28
witness statements, 18–07
witness credibility, 18–07
witness orders, 18–02
witness statements, 18–01, 18–04,
18–07
DISCRETION TO EXCLUDE EVIDENCE
see also EXCLUSION OF EVIDENCE
case law, relating to, 10–03, 10–04
common law position, 10–02
dock identification, 10–11
entrapment, where, 10–15, 10–23

DISCRETION TO EXCLUDE EVIDENCE—
cont.
evidence
admissibility test, 10–05
agent provocateur, 10–11, 10–14,
10–15
co-defendant, 10–11
improperly obtained, 10–05,
10–06, 10–09, 10–11, 10–13,
10–19
misconduct, of, 10–11
obtained abroad, 10–21
prejudicial effect, of, 10–03,
10–12
probative value, 10–03, 10–12
rebuttal, in, 10–11
relevance of, 10–05
self-incrimination, leading to,
10–07
undercover officers, from, 10–25
unfair evidence, 10–06, 10–13
exercise criteria
breach of code, where, 10–20
breach of statute, where, 10–20
consideration of evidence, 10–17
fairness of proceedings, 10–17,
10–18, 10–22, 10–28
general principle, 10–17
improperly obtained evidence,
10–19
police bad faith, 10–21
police impropriety, 10–19, 10–23,
10–24
fairness
fair trial, requirement for, 10–01,
10–02, 10–10, 10–13
proceedings, of, 10–13, 10–14,
10–17, 10–18, 10–22, 10–28
hostile witness, where, 10–11
and see HOSTILE WITNESS
human rights
case law, involving, 10–09,
10–10, 10–16, 10–26, 10–27
provisions, concerning, 10–09,
10–26
judge's discretion, 10–02, 10–05,
10–12, 10–13, 10–29
magistrate's discretion, 10–08
PACE provisions, and, 10–11, 10–13
procedures, governing, 10–30, 10–31
rationale, for, 10–04
review, provisions enabling, 10–29
statutory powers, extent of, 10–11

DNA
"common occurrence ratio", 14–43
expert evidence, as to, 14–44
jury directions, concerning, 14–46
identification, using, 14–42, 14–43
prosecution disclosure, regarding,
14–45
"random occurrence ratio", 14–43
DOCUMENTS
accuracy of, 20–30
admissibility of, 2–05, 3–01, 3–06,
3–07, 3–12, 3–14, 11–35,
11–36, 21–20
and see ADMISSIBILITY
bankers' books, 3–15
and see BANKERS' BOOKS
best evidence rule, 3–06
business records, 8–30, 8–31, 8–67
classification of, 3–03
computer information, 3–02, 8–32
copies, position regarding, 3–08,
3–09, 20–30
criminal investigation, for, 8–33—
8–35
criminal proceedings, for, 8–33—
8–35
electronic communications, 3–03
electronic data, 3–03
electronic signatures, 3–03
evidence, as, 1–02, 1–05, 2–05,
3–01, 3–06, 3–07, 3–12,
3–14, 8–05, 8–35—8–37,
21–20
exhibits, as, 20–33, 20–34
foreign language, in, 3–03
hearsay rules, and, 3–07, 3–11,
8–05, 8–30, 8–31, 8–36, 8–37,
8–41, 8–42
identification evidence, as, 3–06
information, conveyed by, 3–02
judicial documents
see JUDICIAL DOCUMENTS
meaning of, 3–02, 3–03
memory refreshing, from, 20–26,
20–32, 21–22
and see MEMORY REFRESHING
microfilm copies, 3–10
notice to produce, 3–12—3–14
oral evidence, regarding, 3–07
PACE definition, of, 3–02
primary evidence, of, 3–01, 3–04
private documents, 3–04
proof of, 3–01, 8–86

DOCUMENTS—*cont.*
public documents, 3–18, 3–19,
8–41, 8–42
public interest immunity, affecting,
12–13
and see PUBLIC INTEREST
IMMUNITY
real evidence, as, 3–06
secondary evidence, of, 3–07
statements, contained in, 8–35, 8–36
translations of, 3–03
unreliable, where, 8–37
writing, significance of, 3–02
DOUBLE JEOPARDY
rule against, 5–14, 5–15, 5–17
DRIVING OFFENCES
burden of proof, 4–12
DRUGS
offences
burden of proof, 4–12
DURESS
burden of proof, 4–07
DYING DECLARATIONS
admissibility of, 4–35

ELECTRONIC FACIAL IDENTIFICATION
(E-FIT)
use of, 14–39
ENTRAPMENT
exclusion of evidence, where,
10–15, 10–23
EUROPEAN COMMISSION
human rights, opinions on, 13–06
EUROPEAN CONVENTION ON HUMAN
RIGHTS (ECHR)
see also CONVENTION RIGHTS
burden of proof, and, 4–13, 4–14
disclosure of evidence, and, 18–30
exclusion of evidence, and, 10–09,
10–26, 10–27, 10–33
fair trial, right to, 10–09, 10–26,
11–10, 11–11, 11–23, 11–26,
12–23, 18–30
legal assistance, right to, 9–33
national law, compatible with,
4–14—4–16
origins of, 13–01
press freedom, and, 11–38
presumption of innocence, under,
4–03, 4–13, 5–02
privacy, right to, 10–26
and see PRIVACY

EUROPEAN CONVENTION ON HUMAN
RIGHTS (ECHR)—*cont.*
purpose of, 13–01
self-incrimination, right against,
11–10—11–12, 11–26
and see SELF-INCRIMINATION
silence, right to, 11–10, 11–12,
11–21, 11–26
and see RIGHT TO SILENCE
statutory interpretation, and, 4–14,
4–15
UK law, and, 13–02
see also HUMAN RIGHTS ACT
1998
EUROPEAN COURT OF HUMAN RIGHTS
disclosure of evidence, and, 18–30
influence of, 13–06
interpretation methods, 13–27
EUROPEAN COURT OF JUSTICE (ECJ)
disclosure of evidence, decisions on,
12–18, 18–30
human rights judgments, 13–06,
13–28
"margin of appreciation" doctrine,
13–28
public interest immunity, decisions
on, 12–18, 18–30
EVIDENCE
acquittal, of, 5–13, 5–15, 5–16,
5–18, 5–21
admissibility
see ADMISSIBILITY
admission of fact, 1–02
anonymously, given, 19–18
best evidence
see BEST EVIDENCE RULE
circumstantial
see CIRCUMSTANTIAL EVIDENCE
classification
circumstantial, 1–03, 1–06
direct, 1–03
hearsay, 1–03, 1–04
indirect, 1–03
original, 1–04
primary, 1–05
secondary, 1–05
closing speeches, following, 19–41
compulsion, obtained by, 11–10,
11–11
contaminated evidence, 7–69, 7–70
and see CONTAMINATED
EVIDENCE
conviction, of, 5–13, 5–27, 5–33

EVIDENCE—*cont.*
corroboration, 15–01, 15–06,
15–09
and see CORROBORATION
disclosure
see DISCLOSURE OF EVIDENCE
documents, as, 1–02, 8–05, 8–35—
8–37, 8–41, 8–42, 11–35,
11–36
and see Documents
exclusion
see EXCLUSION OF EVIDENCE
expert evidence, 6–12, 6–16
and see EXPERT EVIDENCE
facts in issue, 1–02, 1–14
foreign language, in, 19–34
foreseeable matters, 19–39, 19–40
hearsay rules, 1–03, 1–04, 8–03,
8–70—8–73
see also HEARSAY
identification evidence, 14–03,
14–13, 14–16, 14–17, 14–37
improperly obtained, 10–05, 10–06,
10–09, 10–11, 10–13, 10–19,
11–36
intercepts, as, 2–21
judicial decisions, concerning,
16–02, 16–03, 16–05, 16–11,
16–12
jury
following retirement, of, 19–42,
19–43
objects, provided to, 19–43, 19–44
live link, using, 19–16, 19–15
meaning of, 1–01
motive, as to, 1–07
opinion, 6–01–6–03
and see OPINION EVIDENCE
oral evidence
detection of crime, and, 12–02,
12–03
documents, as to, 3–07
order of, 19–34
original evidence
examples of, 8–04
hearsay, distinguished from,
8–03
prejudicial evidence, 8–20, 10–03,
10–12
private, given in, 19–22
probative force, 7–03, 7–04
probative value, 10–03, 10–12

EVIDENCE—*cont.*
prosecution, for, 18–01, 18–11,
18–12, 18–28, 19–01, 19–02,
19–35—19–37
and see PROSECUTION
real evidence, 1–02, 2–01, 2–02,
2–05
and see REAL EVIDENCE
relevance, 1–12, 1–13, 7–03, 7–04,
10–05
self-incrimination
see SELF-INCRIMINATION
similar fact evidence, 7–03, 14–49
special measures
see SPECIAL MEASURES
spouses, from, 17–26, 17–28,
17–29, 17–30, 17–33, 17–36,
17–37
summing up, following, 19–41,
19–42
suspect evidence, 15–14—15–16
and see SUSPECT EVIDENCE
testimony, 1–02
unconvincing evidence, 8–71, 8–72
unfair evidence, 8–20, 10–06, 10–13
unnecessary evidence, 8–73
unsafe evidence, 16–11, 16–12
unused material, 6–37
and see UNUSED MATERIAL
video recordings, as, 2–33, 19–16,
19–24—19–26
EXAMINATION IN CHIEF
"chequebook journalism", effect of,
21–05
contradicting evidence, 21–12,
21–14
discrediting own witness
common law position, 21–08,
21–11
contradictory evidence, 21–08
statutory provisions, 21–09
hostile witness, 21–07, 21–09,
21–10
and see HOSTILE WITNESS
object of, 21–04
leading questions, 21–06, 21–07
and see LEADING QUESTIONS
personal knowledge, from, 21–04
rehearsing a witness, 21–04
EXCLUSION OF EVIDENCE
acquittals, involving, 5–21, 5–25,
5–26

EXCLUSION OF EVIDENCE—*cont.*
  character evidence, 7–02, 7–03,
    7–49, 7–50, 7–51, 7–68
    and see CHARACTER EVIDENCE
  confessions, involving, 9–25, 9–27,
    9–29, 9–31, 9–46
    and see CONFESSIONS
  contaminated evidence, 7–70
  convictions, relating to, 5–33
  court's discretion, as to, 1–17
  defendant's character, 1–16
  discretion to exclude
    see DISCRETION TO EXCLUDE
      EVIDENCE
  hearsay statements, 1–16
    and see HEARSAY
  human rights, and, 10–09, 10–26
  identification evidence, 14–23
  improperly obtained, 10–05, 10–06,
    10–09, 10–11, 10–13, 10–19
  jury, position regarding, 1–17
  magistrate's decision, on, 16–27,
    16–28
  multiple offences, involving, 7–51
  opinion evidence, 6–03
    and see OPINION EVIDENCE
  prejudicial evidence, 8–20, 10–03,
    10–12
  privilege, 1–16
    and see PRIVILEGE
  probative value, 10–03, 10–12
  public interest, 1–16
    and see PUBLIC INTEREST
  rules, as to, 1–16—1–18
  severance of indictment, 7–52—
    7–54
  sexual offences, 7–80—7–82
  unconvincing evidence, 8–71, 8–72
  unfair evidence, 8–20
  unnecessary evidence, 8–73
  witness, opinion of, 1–16
EXCULPATORY STATEMENTS
  confessions, as to, 9–13, 9–14
  previous consistent statements,
    20–14, 20–15, 20–18
EXHIBITS
  chattels, as, 2–02, 2–03
  court jurisdiction, over, 2–02
  documents, as, 2–05, 20–33, 20–34
  failure to produce, 2–04
  goods destroyed, where, 2–03
  goods lost, where, 2–03
  perishable articles, 2–03

EXHIBITS—*cont.*
  responsibility for, 2–02
  tape recordings, as, 2–26
  video recordings, as, 2–32
EXPERT EVIDENCE
  admissibility of, 6–12, 6–16
  categories of, 6–17
  challenges to, 6–34, 6–43
  confessions, concerning, 6–18
  contradictory evidence, 6–44
  credibility of witness, 6–25
  disclosure
    advance notice, 6–35, 6–36
    limits on, 6–37
    PACE provisions, 18–31
    records of experiments, 6–37
    unused material, 6–37
  experiments, based on, 6–37, 6–38
  expert reports, 6–31, 6–32, 6–34
  expert witness
    see EXPERT WITNESS
  facts, evidence of, 6–15, 6–16, 6–40
  function of, 6–42
  hearsay, and, 6–12, 6–41
  jury
    assessment, of, 6–40, 6–43
    directions, on, 6–43—6–45
  medical evidence, 6–25
  need for, 6–13, 6–14
  obscenity cases, in, 6–22, 6–23
  opinion evidence, and, 6–05, 6–06,
    6–15, 6–40
  personal experience, based on, 6–39
  personality disorder, as to, 6–18
  polygraph, use of, 6–26
  preparatory work, based on, 6–33,
    6–34
  proof of, 6–40, 6–41
  psychiatric evidence, 6–18—6–20
  purpose of, 6–12
  reform, proposals for, 6–46
  scientific expertise, 6–12, 21–34
  special measures directions, 6–24
    and see SPECIAL MEASURES
  statistics, use of, 6–38
  weight of, 6–42, 6–43
  written materials, 6–38
EXPERT WITNESS
  appearance in court, 6–30, 6–32
  compellability of, 6–29
  confidential communications, 6–29
  cross-examination, of, 6–41
  defence, for, 18–19

EXPERT WITNESS—*cont.*
　details of, 18–19
　duty of, 6–42
　expert evidence
　　see EXPERT EVIDENCE
　opinion evidence, and, 6–05, 6–06,
　　6–11, 6–12
　police officers, as, 6–27
　professional privilege, and, 6–29,
　　11–33
　　see also PRIVILEGE
　qualifications of, 6–27, 6–28
　recalling of, 19–07
　re-examination, and, 21–34
　swearing of, 19–08

FACTS
　collateral facts, 1–15
　facts in issue, 1–02, 1–14
　res gestae, as part of, 1–15
　　and see RES GESTAE
FAILURE TO REPLY
　see also RIGHT TO SILENCE
　accusations, to, 9–06
　adverse inference
　　see ADVERSE INFERENCE
　police questioning, to, 9–08, 9–55
　written allegations, to, 9–10
FAIR TRIAL
　criminal charges, relating to,
　　13–14
　criminal proceedings, in, 13–14
　defence
　　burden of proof, 13–20, 13–21
　　conduct of, 13–18, 13–23
　　preparation of, 13–18, 13–22
　　public hearing, 13–19
　disclosure of evidence, ensuring,
　　18–07, 18–30
　equality of arms, 13–16
　exclusion of evidence, and, 10–01,
　　10–02, 10–10, 10–13
　human rights provisions, 10–09,
　　10–26, 13–14
　innocence, presumption as to,
　　13–14, 13–20
　proceedings, fairness of, 13–15
　right to, 10–09, 10–26, 11–10,
　　11–11, 11–23, 11–26, 12–23,
　　13–14
　self-incrimination, and, 13–17
　　and see SELF-INCRIMINATION

FAIR TRIAL—*cont.*
　silence, right to, 13–17
　　and see RIGHT TO SILENCE
　witnesses, attendance of, 13–23
FAMILY LIFE
　respect for, 13–24, 13–25
FINGERPRINTS
　circumstantial evidence, as, 1–07
　identification, using, 1–07, 14–41
FITNESS TO PLEAD
　standard of proof, 4–47
FRAUD TRIALS
　disclosure of evidence, in, 18–32
　hearsay evidence, 8–84
　judge sitting alone, in, 16–25

HANDWRITING
　disputes, involving, 4–48
　identification, from, 14–49
　opinion evidence, as to, 6–10
HEARSAY
　admissible statements
　　automatic recordings, 8–14
　　business records, 8–30, 8–31
　　conditions governing, 8–13, 8–17,
　　　8–19
　　criminal proceedings, concerning,
　　　8–79, 8–86
　　depositions, 8–76, 8–77, 8–79,
　　　8–80
　　documents, 8–30, 8–31
　　general rule, 8–12
　　glossaries, provision of, 8–84
　　identification requirements, 8–18
　　negative hearsay, 8–14
　　oral evidence, 8–17, 8–18
　　schedules, provision of, 8–84
　　standard of proof, 8–19
　　statutory requirements, 8–19
　　unintentional communications,
　　　8–14
　　young persons, position
　　　regarding, 8–82
　admissions
　　agents, by, 8–63
　　counsel, 8–63
　common enterprise, as to, 8–64
　computer information, 8–75
　confessions
　　see CONFESSIONS
　criminal appeals, and, 8–81

HEARSAY—*cont.*
  criminal proceedings, involving,
      8–79, 8–86
  depositions, provisions governing,
      8–76, 8–77, 8–79, 8–80
  documents, and, 8–05, 8–30, 8–31,
      8–37, 8–86
  expert evidence, and, 8–65
      and see EXPERT EVIDENCE
  fraud, cases involving, 8–84
  identity, evidence of, 14–32, 14–33
  international crimes, 8–83
  jury directions, 8–74
  machine generated information,
      8–75
  matters stated, meaning of, 8–14
  meaning of, 8–01
  multiple hearsay, 8–66
  original evidence, distinguished
      from, 8–03
  personal details
      age, 8–44
      place of birth, 8–44
  previous consistent statements, and,
      8–02
      and see PREVIOUS CONSISTENT
          STATEMENTS
  procedural requirements, 8–87
  reform, proposals for, 8–10, 8–11
  reputation, evidence as to, 8–45,
      8–46
  res gestae
      see RES GESTAE
  retrial
      evidence, at, 8–85
      transcripts, at, 8–85
  safeguards
      additional evidence, 8–70
      exclusion of evidence, 8–73
      unconvincing evidence, 8–71,
          8–72
      witness capability, 8–68
      witness credibility, 8–69
  statements,
      doubtful statements, 8–36, 8–37
      meaning of, 8–14
      position regarding, 8–04, 8–07—
          8–09
      public information, contained in,
          8–39
      published works, contained in,
          8–40
      words, contained in, 8–06

HEARSAY—*cont.*
  statutory provisions, governing,
      8–01, 8–12, 8–13, 8–19
  theft, cases involving, 8–80
  unnecessary evidence, 8–73
  witness,
  cannot be found, 8–25
  dead, where, 8–21
  fear, in, 8–26—8–28
  non-appearance of, 8–20
  resident abroad, 8–23, 8–24
  unavailable, where, 8–17, 8–20
  unfit, 8–22
HOSTILE WITNESS
  application to treat, as, 21–10
  bad character, of, 21–11
  children, as, 21–11
  contradicting evidence, 21–12
  cross-examination of, 21–09—
      21–11
  defence witness, as, 21–11
  examination in chief, 21–07, 21–09,
      21–10
  exclusion of evidence, 10–11, 19–27
  leading questions, addressed to,
      21–07, 21–12
  previous convictions, 21–11, 21–14
  previous inconsistent statements,
      and, 21–09—21–11, 21–14,
      21–24
  previous statements, questions
      regarding, 21–12
  re-examination of, 21–34
  summary trials, in, 21–11
HUMAN RIGHTS
  adverse inference, and, 17–24,
      17–25
  arrest, and, 13–11
  burden of proof, and, 4–13, 4–14
  confessions, and, 9–33, 13–10
  detention and, 13–12
  disclosure of evidence, and, 18–30
  judicial review, and, 13–04
  legal advice, access to, 9–33
  press freedom, and, 11–38
  presumption of innocence, 4–03,
      4–13
  public authorities, position of,
      13–03, 13–04
  public interest, and, 12–17, 12–18,
      12–22
  right to silence, and, 11–10, 11–12,
      11–21—11–23

HUMAN RIGHTS—*cont.*
  right to silence, and—*cont.*
    and see RIGHT TO SILENCE
  vulnerable witness, and, 19–16,
    19–22
HUMAN RIGHTS ACT 1998
  adverse inference, and, 17–25
  Convention rights, and, 13–03,
    13–05
    and see CONVENTION RIGHTS
  impact of, 13–01
  judicial review, under, 13–04
  legal proceedings
    limitation period, 13–04
    public authority, against, 13–04
    statutory meaning, 13–04
  public authority
    proceedings against, 13–04
    statutory meaning, 13–03
    statutory provisions, governing,
      13–03
  rights, protected by,13–05

IDENTIFICATION
  arrest process, through, 14–49
  bloodstains, from, 14–49
  confrontation
    exclusion of evidence, 14–23
    procedure, for, 14–21, 14–22
    risk of mistake, 14–23
    solicitor present, at, 14–22
  dock identification
    dangers of, 14–13, 14–15
    exclusion of evidence, 10–11,
      14–14
    general principle, 14–13
    identification parade, following,
      14–15
    magistrates discretion, 14–14
    meaning of, 14–13
    previous identification, following,
      14–31
    summary cases, in, 14–14
  DNA, using, 14–42, 14–43
    and see DNA
  documents, involving, 3–06
  ear prints, from, 14–49
  electronic facial identification
    (E-FIT), 14–39
  fingerprints, use of, 1–07, 14–41
  handwriting, from, 14–49
  incriminating articles, possession of,
    14–47

IDENTIFICATION—*cont.*
  informants
    see INFORMANTS
  judge's discretion, on, 14–28, 14–29
  jury directions, as to, 14–29
  out of court
    disputed evidence, 14–17
    group identification, 14–21,
      14–28
    hearsay rule, 14–32, 14–33
    identification parades, at, 14–17
    PACE provisions (Code D),
      14–16, 14–27
    police practice, as to, 14–16,
      14–17
    street identification, 14–17,
      14–24, 14–26
    video identification, 14–17,
      14–18, 14–19
    witness evidence, 14–31—14–33
  parade
    see IDENTIFICATION PARADE
  photofits, using, 14–39, 14–40
  photographic evidence, 2–13—
    2–15, 14–35—14–38
  physical features, from, 14–49
  procedure
    failure to remember, where,
      14–33, 14–34
    prosecution disclosure, 14–30
    suspect's agreement, 14–26
    timing, 14–20
  security cameras, using, 14–49
  similar fact evidence, from, 14–49
  sketches, using, 14–39, 14–40
  tracker dogs, using, 14–49
  video film, from, 14–38, 14–49
  video identification
    images, used for, 14–19
    procedure governing, 14–18
  video recordings, involving, 2–38,
    2–39, 14–26
  visual identification
    alibi defence, where, 14–09
    case withdrawn, where, 14–06,
      14–07
    caution, need for, 14–04
    general rules, 14–03
    imperfect nature, of, 14–02
    judge's warning, on, 14–03—
      14–05, 14–09
    jury directions, 14–03, 14–08,
      14–09

IDENTIFICATION—*cont.*
visual identification—*cont.*
mistaken identification, 14–08,
14–11
quality of evidence, 14–06, 14–07
supporting evidence, 14–08
Turnbull guidelines, 14–03,
14–04, 14–10
voice identification, 14–48
witness
credibility of, 14–11
failure to remember, 14–33,
14–34
IDENTIFICATION PARADE
composition of, 14–19
conduct of, 14–19
confession, following, 14–25
dock identification, following,
14–15
need for, 14–18, 14–25
object of, 14–19
physical features concealed, at,
14–20
procedure for, 14–19
refusal to participate, 14–15, 14–20
solicitor present, at, 14–19
IMMORAL EARNINGS
burden of proof, 4–12
INCAPACITATED WITNESS
adjournment permitted, where,
17–09
drunkenness, though, 17–08
interpreter, use of, 17–08
judge's ruling, on, 17–08, 17–09
jury discharged, where, 17–10
temporary incapacity, 17–09, 17–10
witness distressed, where, 17–10
INCONSISTENCY
see PREVIOUS INCONSISTENT
STATEMENTS
INDICTMENT
severance of, 7–52, 7–53
INFORMANTS
co-defendants, as, 12–08
detection of crime, and, 12–02
identity, withholding of, 12–02,
12–06, 12–07
police surveillance, and, 12–09,
12–10
protection of, 12–04—12–07,
12–09
public interest
see PUBLIC INTEREST

INDICTMENT—*cont.*
public interest immunity, and,
12–14
and see PUBLIC INTEREST
IMMUNITY
INSANITY
burden of proof, 4–11
standard of proof, 4–46
INTERCEPTS
admissibility, 2–21
disclosure permitted, 2–21
evidence, as, 2–21
foreign intercepts, 2–21
privacy, and, 13–25, 13–26
and see PRIVACY
statutory provisions, 2–21
unlawful, 2–21
INTIMIDATION
witness, of, 18–03, 19–11

JOURNALISTS
"chequebook journalism", effect of,
21–05
press freedom, 11–38
privilege, and, 11–37, 11–38
sources of information, 11–37—
11–39
JUDGE
admissibility
confessions, of, 16–07
evidence, of, 16–05, 16–06,
16–08
tape recordings, of, 16–07
case stopped, by, 16–10—16–12
court inspections, presiding over,
2–06
directions to jury
see JURY
discretion
exclusion of evidence, 10–02,
10–05, 10–12, 10–13,
10–29
identification evidence, 14–28,
14–29
tape recordings, 2–20
video recordings, 2–31
evidence
admissibility, dealing with, 16–05
disputed facts, 16–07
objections, relating to, 16–05,
16–08
pre-trial hearings, on, 16–06

JUDGE—*cont.*
  evidence—*cont.*
    ruling on, 16–05, 16–08
    submissions, on, 16–06
    unsafe evidence, 16–11, 16–12
  functions
    documents, construction of,
      16–03
    evidence, dealing with,
      16–04—16–06, 16–08
    matters of law, dealing with,
      16–02
    statutory construction,
      concerning, 16–02, 16–03
  public interest immunity
    judge's role, 12–16, 12–17
    undisclosed material, reliance on,
      12–18, 12–20
  sitting alone
    convictions, where, 16–26
    fraud cases, in, 16–25
    jury tampering, where, 16–25,
      16–26
  summing up
    burden of proof, on, 16–14
    evidence, summary of, 16–15,
      16–16
    fact, issues of, 16–15
    jury's function, as to, 16–13
    law, issues of, 16–13
    object of, 16–16
    standard of proof, on, 16–14
    trial-within-a-trial (*voir dire*), held
      by, 16–07, 16–08
  warnings
    corroboration evidence, on,
      15–01, 15–07, 15–10,
      15–11
    identification evidence, on,
      14–03—14–05, 14–09
    suspect evidence, 15–14—15–16,
      15–18
  witnesses
    competence of, 16–07
    failure to call, where, 16–21
    powers, concerning, 19–01,
      19–06, 19–07
    questioning of, 16–09, 19–07
JUDICIAL DOCUMENTS
  acquittals, concerning, 3–24
  civil proceedings, involving, 3–22
  convictions, concerning, 3–23
  proof of, 3–21, 3–22

JUDICIAL NOTICE
  case law, and, 5–09
  doctrine of, 5–08
  established facts, 5–08
  general knowledge, and, 5–10
  jury directions, 5–10
  local knowledge, and, 5–11
  personal knowledge, and, 5–10—
    5–12
  special knowledge, and, 5–10
JUDICIAL REVIEW
  human rights, and, 13–04
JURY
  admissible evidence, accepted by,
    16–24
  confessions, function as to, 9–58,
    16–24
  crime scene, visited by, 2–07
  directions
    accused lying, where, 16–17,
      16–18
    acquittal, on, 16–10, 16–11
    admissions, on, 5–07
    burden of proof, 4–03—4–05
    character evidence, on, 7–12,
      7–14—7–18
    contaminated evidence, on, 7–70
    convictions, as to, 5–35
    corroboration evidence, 15–01,
      15–07, 15–09, 15–11, 15–19
    function, as to, 16–13
    judicial notice, and, 5–10
    hearsay evidence, as to, 8–74
    identification evidence, on,
      14–03, 14–08, 14–09, 14–29
    previous consistent statements,
      on, 20–04
    right to silence, as to, 11–20—
      11–23
    standard of proof, 4–39, 4–40,
      8–19
    suspect evidence, on, 15–19
    witness evidence, 16–16
  evidence considered
    admissible evidence, 16–24
    character evidence, 7–12,
      7–14—7–18, 7–63, 7–68
    evidential burden, 4–28, 4–30
    expert evidence, 6–40, 6–43—
      6–45
    objects, referred in evidence,
      19–43, 19–44
    opinion evidence, 6–03

JURY—*cont.*
  evidence considered—*cont.*
    retirement, subsequent to, 19–42,
      19–43
    witness evidence, 16–16
  function
    construction of documents, by,
      16–02
    matters of fact, decided by,
      16–02, 16–07, 16–24
    no case to answer, 16–10—16–12
    re-constructions, by, 19–43
    spent convictions, knowledge of,
      7–26
    tampering, where, 16–25, 16–26
    tape recordings, played to, 2–26,
      2–27
    trials, without, 16–25
JUSTICES
  see MAGISTRATES

LEADING QUESTIONS
  contradiction, 21–07
  cross-examination, and, 21–16
  general rule, as to, 21–06
  hostile witness, involving, 21–07,
    21–12,
  introductory questions, 21–07
LEGAL ADVICE
  access,
    arrest, on, 11–24
    human rights provisions, 9–33
    information regarding, 9–35
    police interviews, and, 9–30,
      9–33, 9–35
    statutory provisions, 9–33, 9–35
  confessions, regarding, 9–20, 9–33
  facilitating crime, 11–31
  unlawful purpose, 11–31
LEGAL PROFESSIONAL PRIVILEGE
  absolute nature, of, 11–32
  advice
    facilitating crime, 11–31
    unlawful purpose, 11–31
  communications
    client, belonging to, 11–28, 11–34
    confidential, 11–28, 11–37,
      11–38
    criminal proceedings, involving,
      11–30
    privileged communications,
      11–28

LEGAL PROFESSIONAL PRIVILEGE—
    cont.
  communications—*cont.*
    unlawful proceedings,
      concerning, 11–30
  documents
    admissibility of, 11–35, 11–36
    evidence improperly obtained,
      11–36
    lawyer's possession, in, 11–34
  expert witnesses, and, 11–33
  general rule, as to, 11–28
  waiver of, 11–29
LIVE LINK
  evidence, given by, 19–15, 19–16,
    19–20, 19–21

MAGISTRATES
  adjournment, decisions as to,
    16–28, 16–29
  admissibility
    confessions of, 16–27
    evidence of, 16–27
  dismissal of case, by, 16–30
  evidence
    exclusion of, 10–08, 16–27,
      16–28
    identification evidence, 14–14
  findings of fact, 16–31
  functions of, 16–27
  no case, submission of, 16–30
MECHANICAL INSTRUMENTS
  presumptions, as to, 5–06, 5–07
MEDICAL EVIDENCE
  witness competence, and, 17–07
  witness credibility, 6–25
MEMORY REFRESHING
  common law rules, 20–27
  contemporaneous, 20–31
  documents
    accurate copies, 20–30
    evidence from, 20–26, 21–22
    exhibits, as, 20–33, 20–34
    production of, 20–32
  evidence
    before giving, 20–23
    documents, from, 20–26
    transcripts, from, 20–26
    while giving, 20–26
    written records, from,
      20–27—20–29
  notice to defence, 20–25

MEMORY REFRESHING—*cont.*
  police notebooks, and, 20–28, 20–35
  rule, as to, 20–22, 20–23
  witness
    conferences, between, 20–24
    defence, for, 20–23
    improper motive, 20–24
    prosecution, for, 20–23
    statements, shown to, 20–24
MENTALLY HANDICAPPED PERSONS
  confessions, and, 9–56, 9–57
MOTIVE
  evidence of, 1–07
  improper, where, 20–24
  witness of, 20–24

OATH
  children, position as to, 17–03,
    17–04,
  defendant, under, 17–11
  divine sanction, understanding of,
    17–06
  incapacitated witnesses, 17–08
  persons of unsound mind, 17–06
  prescribed forms, 19–08, 19–09
  purpose of, 19–08
  religious observance, relating to,
    19–09
  spouses, under, 17–29
  words accompanying, 19–08
OBSCENITY
  expert evidence, and, 6–22, 6–23
OBSERVATION POSTS
  practice regarding, 12–09, 12–10
  and see POLICE SURVEILLANCE
OFFENCE
  preparatory acts, 1–07
OPINION EVIDENCE
  admissible, whether, 6–02, 6–05,
    6–06
  exclusion of, 6–03
  expert witness, and, 6–05, 6–06,
    6–11, 6–12
  general rule, as to, 6–02
  handwriting, on, 6–10
  impression and narrative, 6–08
  jury's position, regarding, 6–03
  non-expert opinion, 6–03
  opinion, definition of, 6–01
  "ultimate issue", questions as to,
    6–04, 6–05
  witness opinion, 6–03, 6–04, 6–06

PATENT AGENTS
  privilege, and, 11–37
PERJURY
  corroboration evidence, for, 15–03
PERSONS OF UNSOUND MIND
  evidence, given by, 17–07
  medical condition of, 17–07
  oath, understanding of, 17–06
  witness, competence as, 17–06,
    17–07
PHOTOGRAPHS
  authenticity of, 2–11
  identification, and, 2–13—2–15,
    14–35—14–37
  judge's discretion, regarding, 2–11
  PACE provisions, concerning, 2–11
  real evidence, as, 2–11, 2–12
POLICE INTERVIEWS
  children, involving, 9–31
  Code of Practice, and, 9–37—9–39,
    9–41
  conduct of, 9–36, 9–38
  confessions, during, 9–33, 9–36,
    9–38, 9–39, 9–41
    and see CONFESSIONS
  custody officer, responsibility of,
    9–33
  defendant
    condition of, 9–21—9–23
    failure to reply, 9–08
    fit for interview, 9–23
  human rights provisions, 9–33
  impropriety, involving, 9–18, 9–19,
    9–24, 9–26
  interview, meaning of, 9–42
  legal advice, access to, 9–33—9–35
  questioning
    caution, giving of, 9–43, 9–45
    "co-operation conversations",
      9–45
    failure to answer, 9–08, 9–55
    parties on even terms, 9–08
    request for information, 9–43
    right to silence, 11–17
  recording of, 9–36, 9–37, 9–39
  statutory requirements, compliance,
    9–35
  tape recordings
    access to, 2–23
    PACE provisions, governing,
      2–22
    summaries of, 2–23, 2–25
    translations of, 2–24, 2–30

POLICE INTERVIEWS—*cont.*
  tape recordings—*cont.*
    use of, 2–09, 2–16, 9–36, 9–40
    written record, supporting, 2–23,
      2–24
  video recordings, and, 2–31, 2–42
  visual recordings, 2–22
  written record, of, 9–39
POLICE OFFICER
  bad faith, involving, 10–21
  caution, given by, 9–33, 9–43,
    9–45
  confession, made to, 9–01, 9–04
  expert witness, as, 6–27
  impropriety, involving, 9–18, 9–19,
    9–24, 9–26, 10–19, 10–23,
    10–24
  interviews
    see POLICE INTERVIEWS
  undercover officers
    evidence of, 10–25
    questioning by, 9–44, 21–02
POLICE SURVEILLANCE
  evidential requirements, regarding,
    12–09
  observation posts, 12–09, 12–10
  police cars, used for, 12–11
  premises used for, 12–09, 12–10
POLYGAMOUS MARRIAGE
  witness evidence, where, 17–35
POLYGRAPH
  use of, 6–26
POSTAL COMMUNICATIONS
  intercepts
    see INTERCEPTS
PRESS FREEDOM
  human rights, and, 11–38
PRESUMPTIONS
  burden of proof, resulting from,
    5–04, 5–05
  "conclusive" presumptions, 5–03
  fact, of, 5–02
  innocence
    evidential burden, applied, 4–15,
      4–16
    fair trial, and, 13–14, 13–20
    human rights, and 4–03, 4–13,
      5–02, 13–14, 13–20
    legislative interference, with, 4–14
  law
    irrebuttable, 5–03
    rebuttable, 5–03

PRESUMPTIONS—*cont.*
  mechanical instruments, as to, 5–06,
    5–07
  omnia praesumuntur rite esse acta,
    5–05
  regularity, as to, 5–05, 5–06
  sanity, of, 5–02
  sexual offences, involving, 5–04
PREVIOUS ACQUITTAL
  see also ACQUITTAL
  defence reliance, on, 5–21
  evidence
    admissibility, 5–21, 5–25, 5–26
    character evidence, 7–28
    subsequent prosecution, in, 5–15,
      5–16, 5–18
  relevance of, 5–22, 5–23
  similar facts rule, 5–15
  validity of, 5–14
PREVIOUS CONSISTENT STATEMENTS
  accused persons, by, 20–13
  admissions, 20–14—20–16, 20–18
  exculpatory statements, 20–14,
    20–15, 20–18
  general rule, as to, 20–02
  hearsay, distinguished from, 8–02
  inconsistent denials, 20–15
  meaning of, 20–01
  mixed statements
    identification of, 20–19
    interpretation of, 20–18
    magistrates courts, in, 20–19
    partly adverse, 20–17
    partly favourable, 20–17
  previous identification, concerning,
    20–12
  "recent complaints"
    admissibility of, 20–04—20–06,
      20–10
    consistency, showing, 20–04
    earliest opportunity, 20–06,
      20–10, 20–11
    evidence of, 20–05—20–07
    jury directions, on, 20–04
    multiple complaints, 20–07
    proof of, 20–05
    voluntary nature, 20–07
  recent invention, statements of,
    20–09—20–11
  reform, proposals for, 20–20
  res gestae, as part of, 20–08
    and see RES GESTAE
  sexual offences, involving, 20–04

Previous consistent statements—
    cont.
  witness, examination of, 20–02
Previous convictions
  see also Conviction
  evidence,
    admissibility, 5–13, 5–27
    character evidence, 7–04, 7–05,
      7–28, 7–31, 7–47
    exclusion of, 5–33
    jury directions, on, 5–35
    statutory provisions, 5–27
  relevance of, 5–30, 5–32
Previous inconsistent statements
  availability of statement, 21–24
  cross-examination, as to, 21–08,
    21–09, 21–12, 21–23—21–25
  deposition, contained in, 21–24
  explanation given, where, 21–13
  hostile witness, where, 21–09,
    21–10, 21–11, 21–14, 21–24
    and see Hostile witness
  jury directions, 21–12, 21–13
  oral statements, 21–23
  proof of, 21–23, 21–24
  relevant statements, 21–24
  statements on oath, 21–24
  statutory provisions, 21–23,
    21–25
  witness credibility, 21–12
  written statements, 21–23
Privacy
  intercepts, and, 13–25, 13–26
  right to, 10–26, 13–25
  surveillance, and, 13–25
Privilege
  doctors, position regarding, 11–37
  expert witnesses, involving, 6–29
  forfeiture of property, 11–03
  legal professional privilege
    see Legal professional
      privilege
  meaning of, 11–01
  media privilege, 11–37, 11–38
  patent agents, involving, 11–37
  personal right, as, 11–01
  priests, position as to, 11–37
  public interest, and, 11–01
  removal of, 11–08, 11–09
  self-incrimination
    see Self-incrimination
Procuring
  corroboration evidence, for, 15–05

Proof
  see Burden of proof, Standard
    of proof
Prosecution
  disclosure of evidence
    DNA evidence, 14–45
    identification evidence, 14–30
    prosecution material, definition
      of, 18–12
    requested by, 18–24
    undermining prosecution case,
      18–11, 18–12, 18–28
    unused material, 18–11, 18–12,
      18–24
  evidence
    closure of case, following, 19–35,
      19–36
    failure to call, 19–37
    notice of, 19–38
    previously not available, 19–38
    rebuttal, in, 19–39
    technical evidence, 19–37
    re-opening of case, by, 19–35,
      19–36
  witnesses
    co-defendants, as, 17–14
    defendant, as, 17–14
    prosecution, for, 19–01, 19–02
    spouses, as, 17–28, 17–29
Public authority
  see also Human Rights Act 1998
  human rights
    proceedings, against, 13–04
    statutory provisions, involving,
      13–03
  meaning of, 13–03
Public documents
  see also Documents
  definition of, 8–41
  hearsay rules, and, 8–41
  provisions governing, 8–42
  statements in, 8–41
Public interest
  see also Public interest immunity
  defendant's innocence, protecting,
    12–05, 12–06
  detection of crime
    informant's identity, withholding,
      12–02, 12–06, 12–07
    information sources, withholding,
      12–02, 12–11
    oral evidence, relating to, 12–02,
      12–03

PUBLIC INTEREST—*cont.*
  detection of crime—*cont.*
    pre-trial disclosure, 12–02, 12–03
    sensitive information,
        withholding, 12–03
  disclosure of evidence, and, 18–05,
      18–06
  and see DISCLOSURE OF EVIDENCE
  disclosure of information
    co-defendants, regarding, 12–08
    order for, 12–07, 12–08
    pre-trial disclosure, 12–02, 12–03
  exclusion of evidence, involving,
      1–16, 12–02—12–05
  and see EXCLUSION OF EVIDENCE
  privilege, and, 11–01
  public order, maintenance of, 12–04
PUBLIC INTEREST IMMUNITY
  "class based" claims, 12–13
  confidentiality, and, 12–14
  "content based" claims, 12–13
  court decision, as to, 12–12, 12–20,
      12–22
  criminal proceedings, involving,
      12–16
  Crown privilege, 12–12, 12–14
  disclosure
    evidence, of, 18–22, 18–30
    information, of, 12–12
  documents, affected by, 12–13
  exclusionary rules, 12–12, 12–14,
      12–16
  human rights, and, 12–17, 12–18,
      12–22
  informants, identity of, 12–14
  interests of justice, and, 12–16,
      12–17, 12–20
  judge's role, as to, 12–16, 12–17
  materiality, and, 12–13
  procedure
    application, for, 12–21
    conduct of hearing, 12–21
    ex parte application, 12–21,
        12–23
    notice requirements, 12–21
    ruling under review, 12–24
    summary trials, 12–25
  relevance, and, 12–13
  scope of, 12–14
  special counsel, use of, 12–19,
      12–23
  third party applications, 12–15
  undisclosed material

PUBLIC INTEREST IMMUNITY—*cont.*
  undisclosed material—*cont.*
    judicial reliance on, 12–18,
        12–20
    significance of, 12–22, 12–23
PUBLIC ORDER
  maintenance of, 12–04

REAL EVIDENCE
  automatic recordings, 2–43
  chattels, as, 2–02
  computer recordings, 2–44
  documents, as, 2–05, 3–06
  obtaining
    court inspection by, 2–06
    court view, by, 2–06
  video recordings, as, 2–31
  and see VIDEO RECORDINGS
RE-EXAMINATION
  cross-examination evidence, 21–33
  hostile witness, of, 21–34
  and see HOSTILE WITNESS
  matters eligible, for, 21–32
  memory refreshing, and, 21–33
  and see MEMORY REFRESHING
  previous consistent statements,
      21–33
  and see PREVIOUS CONSISTENT
      STATEMENTS
  right of, 21–32
  witness of, 21–32
  witness statements, rules regarding,
      21–33
RELEVANCE
  meaning of, 1–13
REPUTATION
  character evidence, involving, 7–07,
      7–08
  and see CHARACTER EVIDENCE
  evidence, as to, 8–45, 8–46
RES GESTAE
  see also HEARSAY
  additional evidence available, 8–56
  admissible statements
    accompanying an act, 8–58
    actor, responsible for, 8–58
    bystanders, from, 8–52
    "concoction or distortion",
        unlikely, 8–52, 8–55
    contemporaneous with act, 8–58
    explaining an act, 8–58
    extent of, 8–50, 8–51

RES GESTAE—*cont.*
  admissible statements—*cont.*
    mental state, relating to, 8–60
    person emotionally overpowered,
      8–52
    physical sensation, as to, 8–59
    relating to act, 8–58
    spontaneous exclamation, 8–52,
      8–54, 8–55
    victims, from, 8–52
  contradicted statements, 8–57
  criticisms of, 8–61
  jury directions, regarding, 8–56
  meaning of, 8–50
  previous consistent statements,
    20–08
  relevant evidence, as, 8–50, 8–51
RETRIAL
  evidence admissible, at, 8–85
  transcripts, available at, 8–85
RIGHT TO SILENCE
  adverse inference, and, 9–08
  arrest
    following on, 11–24
    marks found on, 11–24, 11–25
    objects found, on, 11–24, 11–25
    substances found, on, 11–24,
      11–25
  common law, at, 11–15
  confessions, 9–06, 9–07
  defendant's silence
    facts not mentioned, significance
      of, 11–20
    inferences drawn from, 11–16,
      11–17, 11–19, 11–20
    jury directions, 11–20—11–23
    jury's interpretation, of, 11–23
    legal advice, acting on, 11–19,
      11–21, 11–22,
    police questioning, during, 11–17,
      11–19
    statutory provisions, as to,
      11–16
  disclosure of evidence, and, 18–08,
    18–15
  fair trial, and, 13–17
    and see FAIR TRIAL
  human rights, and, 11–10, 11–12,
    11–21—11–23, 11–26, 13–17
    and see HUMAN RIGHTS
  legal advice
    access to, 11–24
    acting on, 11–19, 11–21, 11–22

RIGHT TO SILENCE—*cont.*
  protection, afforded by, 11–18
  self-incrimination, and, 11–14
    and see SELF-INCRIMINATION
ROYAL COMMISSION ON CRIMINAL
    JUSTICE
  recommendations
    confessions, 9–38
    disclosure of evidence, 18–09,
      18–24
    exclusion of evidence, 10–32
    expert evidence, 6–46
    judge's intervention, 19–07
    right to silence, 11–18
ROYAL COMMISSION ON CRIMINAL
    PROCEDURE
  tape recordings, recommendations
    on, 2–16, 2–23

SCREENS
  evidence, given behind, 19–17—
    19–19
SECURITY CAMERAS
  use of, 14–49
SELF-DEFENCE
  burden of proof, 4–07, 4–26, 4–27
SELF-INCRIMINATION
  absolute right, whether, 11–11,
    11–12
  children, cases involving, 9–30,
    11–09
  compulsion, evidence obtained by,
    11–10, 11–11
  court, duty of, 11–06
  cross-examination, during, 11–02,
    11–08
  disclosure of evidence, and, 18–08,
    18–15
  evidence, leading to, 10–07
  exceptions to rule, 11–02
  fair trial, and, 13–17
    and see FAIR TRIAL
  general rule, against, 11–02
  human rights, and, 11–10—11–12 ,
    11–26, 13–17
    and see HUMAN RIGHTS
  real and appreciable danger, of,
    11–06
  recovery of property, involving,
    11–08
  risk of proceedings, 11–05, 11–07

SELF-INCRIMINATION—*cont.*
spouses, position regarding, 11–02, 11–09
statutory provisions, 11–08
"taking the objection", 11–04, 11–05
witness, rights as to, 11–04, 11–05, 11–07
SEXUAL OFFENCES
accused, cross-examination by, 21–18
character evidence, and, 7–78, 7–79
complainant
behaviour of, 7–78, 7–79
consent, issues involving, 7–78, 7–79
credibility, 7–80, 7–81
human rights provisions, 7–80
corroboration evidence, concerning, 15–01, 15–08, 15–09, 15–13
cross-examination, relating to, 21–18
evidence, exclusion of, 7–80, 7–81, 7–82
presumptions, involving, 5–04
previous consistent statements, concerning, 20–04
witnesses, position regarding, 19–13, 19–15
SILENCE
see RIGHT TO SILENCE
SOLICITOR
admissions, involving, 9–11
confessions, advice on, 9–20
SPECIAL MEASURES
child witnesses, involving, 19–11, 19–15, 19–16, 19–24
communication aids, use of, 19–32
court discretion, as to, 19–15
directions, on, 19–14, 19–15, 19–20, 19–26
evidence in private, 19–22
intermediaries, use of, 19–32
live link, use of, 19–16, 19–20, 19–21
practice, relating to, 19–14
screens, use of, 19–17—19–19
security considerations, 19–19
wigs and gowns, removal of, 19–23
witnesses, eligible for, 19–12, 19–14
SPEEDING
corroboration evidence, for, 15–04

SPENT CONVICTIONS
co-defendants, position regarding, 7–24
disclosure, as to, 7–23, 7–24
evidence relating to, 7–21, 7–25
judicial discretion, regarding, 7–23, 7–24
jury's knowledge, of, 7–26
prejudicial effect, of, 7–23, 7–24
rehabilitation period, 7–21
SPOUSE
refusal to give evidence, 17–29, 17–36, 17–37
self-incrimination, and, 11–02, 11–09
witness
child offences, where, 17–32
co-defendants, where, 17–33
compellable, as, 17–26, 17–28, 17–29, 17–30, 17–33
competent, as 17–26, 17–28, 17–33
defence, for, 17–33
former spouses, as, 17–34
magistrates court, in, 17–30
PACE provisions, 17–26
prosecution, for, 17–28, 17–29
violence against wife, where, 17–31
STANDARD OF PROOF
admissibility of evidence, and, 4–48
balance of probabilities, 4–45, 4–46, 8–19
beyond reasonable doubt, 4–37, 4–42, 4–43, 8–19
confessions, and, 4–47, 9–17
counsel, responsibility of, 4–40
"criminal standard", 4–37, 4–38, 4–48
fitness to plead, 4–47
handwriting disputes, 4–48
hearsay evidence, 8–19, 8–32
and see HEARSAY
insanity cases, 4–46
judge's directions, on, 16–14
jury directions, 4–39, 4–40, 4–41
STOLEN GOODS
possession of, 1–08, 1–09
SUMMARY TRIAL
corroboration of evidence, in, 15–09
disclosure of evidence, 18–03, 18–04, 18–08
hostile witness, in, 21–11

SUMMARY TRIAL—*cont.*
  identification evidence, in, 14–14
  unused materials, in, 18–08
  witness statements, 18–04
SUMMING UP
  evidence, following, 19–41, 19–42
  judge
    burden of proof, on, 16–14
    evidence, summary of, 16–15,
      16–16
    fact, issues of, 16–15
    jury's function, as to, 16–13
    law, issues of, 16–13
    object of, 16–16
    standard of proof, on, 16–14
SUSPECT
  arrest of, 9–38, 9–45
  police interviews, involving, 9–36,
    9–38, 9–40
  and see POLICE INTERVIEWS
  questioning of, 9–43—9–45, 11–17
SUSPECT EVIDENCE
  Becks case, rule in, 15–15, 15–16
  co-defendants, involving, 15–18
  judge's warning, as to, 15–14—
    15–16, 15–18
  jury directions, 15–19
  witness, from, 15–14, 15–15

TAPE RECORDINGS
  accuracy of, 2–18
  admissibility of, 2–17, 2–19, 2–22,
    16–07
  authenticity, 2–18, 2–26
  Code of Practice, concerning, 2–22
  copies, position regarding, 2–28
  court exhibit, as, 2–26
  interpretation of, 2–28
  judge's discretion, regarding, 2–20
  jury, listening to, 2–26, 2–27
  PACE provisions, governing, 2–20
  police interviews, at, 2–09, 2–16,
    2–22
  and see POLICE INTERVIEWS
  procedure at trial, 5–25—5–27
  real evidence, as, 2–16
  secondary evidence of, 2–28
  summaries of, 2–25
  transcripts, 2–25, 2–29, 2–30
  translations of, 2–24, 2–30
TELEPHONE COMMUNICATIONS
  intercepts
    see INTERCEPTS

TERRORISM
  burden of proof, 4–13, 4–18
TORTURE
  prohibition of, 13–10
TRANSCRIPTS
  memory refreshing, from, 20–26
  retrial, available at, 8–85
  tape recordings, of, 2–25, 2–29,
    2–30
  video recordings, of, 19–27
TREASON
  corroboration evidence, need for,
    15–05
TRIAL-WITHIN-A-TRIAL (*VOIR DIRE*)
  evidence, at, 16–08
  matters decided by, 16–07
  procedure, at, 16–08
  witness competence, 17–11

UNUSED MATERIAL
  common law position, 18–06
  court's discretion, as to, 18–08
  defence case, concerning, 18–08,
    18–14, 18–28
  disclosure of evidence
    see DISCLOSURE OF EVIDENCE
  failure to disclose, 18–08, 18–13
  fellow prisoners, evidence of, 18–13
  material evidence, whether, 18–07
  primary prosecution material,
    18–11, 18–12
  relevant material, 18–07, 18–09,
    18–12, 18–28
  right to silence, and, 18–08, 18–15
    and see RIGHT TO SILENCE
  self-incrimination, and, 18–08,
    18–15
    and see SELF-INCRIMINATION
  statutory provisions, concerning,
    18–05, 18–10
  summary trials, in, 18–08
  third parties, from, 18–12
  undermining prosecution case,
    18–11, 18–12, 18–28
  witness credibility, and, 18–07

VIDEO RECORDINGS
  admissibility of, 2–31, 19–24,
    19–25
  authenticity, 2–31
  children, involving, 19–27, 19–30

VIDEO RECORDINGS—*cont.*
  commentary of, 2–39, 2–40
  conduct of interview, 19–30
  copies, position regarding, 2–31
  court exhibit, as, 2–32
  cross-examination, dealing with,
    19–31
  evidence, as, 2–33
  hearsay rules, and, 2–32
  hostile witness, where, 19–27
  interpretation of, 2–34, 2–36, 2–37,
    2–38
  judge's discretion, as to, 2–31
  PACE provisions, covering, 2–31
  procedural matters, 2–32, 19–26
  re-enactments, 2–41, 2–42
  re-examination, dealing with, 19–31
  relevance of, 2–31
  replay of, 19–28, 19–29
  status of evidence, 19–33
  transcripts, of, 19–27
VIDEOTAPES
  use of, 2–09
VOIR DIRE
  evidence, at, 16–08
  procedure, at, 16–08
  trial-within-a-trial, 16–07
  witness competence, 17–11
VULNERABLE WITNESSES
  children, as, 19–11, 19–12, 19–15
  cross-examination of, 21–18
  distressed, where, 19–12
  fear, in, 19–12, 19–18
  human rights, and, 19–16, 19–22
  interviews, involving, 19–30
  intimidation of, 19–11
  learning difficulties, with, 19–13
  mental disorder, with, 19–12
  physical disability, with, 19–12,
    19–32
  quality of evidence, from, 19–12
  special measures
    see SPECIAL MEASURES

WITNESS
  absence of, 1–06
  alibi, as to, 18–14, 18–18
  attendance of, 13–23
  bad character, of, 7–73
  calling
    expert witness, 19–05

WITNESS—*cont.*
  calling—*cont.*
    judge's powers, as to, 19–01,
      19–06, 19–07
    intention to call, 18–18
    out of court, remaining, 19–05
    procedure for, 19–04
  cannot be found, 8–25
  capability of, 8–68
  co-habitees, as, 17–27
  committal proceedings, at, 18–01
  compellability
    see COMPELLABILITY OF
      WITNESSES
  competence of, 4–34, 16–07, 17–01,
    17–02
    and see COMPETENCE OF
      WITNESSES
  credibility of, 5–24, 5–25, 6–25,
    7–65, 7–67, 7–76, 8–69,
    14–11, 21–12
  cross-examination, 1–15, 1–17,
    7–73, 21–16, 21–27
    and see CROSS-EXAMINATION
  dead, where, 8–21
  defence, for, 18–18, 19–03
    and see DEFENCE
  defendant, as, 19–03, 19–04
  evidence
    anonymously, given, 19–18
    contaminated evidence, 7–69
    inconsistent evidence, from, 19–01
    identification evidence,
      14–31—14–33
    live link, use of, 19–16
    opinion evidence, from, 6–03,
      6–04, 6–06
    private, given in, 19–22
    status of, 19–33
    suspect evidence, from, 15–14,
      15–15
    video recordings, use of, 19–16,
      19–24—19–26
  examination
    anonymously, where, 21–02
    hypnosis used, where, 21–03
    naming of, 21–01
    undercover officers, by, 21–02
  examination in chief
    see EXAMINATION IN CHIEF
  expert witness, 6–27, 6–28, 6–42,
    11–33, 18–19, 19–05, 19–07,
    19–08

WITNESS—*cont.*
  examination in chief—*cont.*
    and see EXPERT WITNESS
  failure to call, 16–21
  fear
    see WITNESS IN FEAR
  fellow prisoner, as, 18–13
  hostile
    see HOSTILE WITNESS
  incapacitated, where, 17–08—
    17–10
  intimidation of, 18–03, 19–11
  judge's intervention, and, 19–07
  memory refreshing, 20–22, 20–23,
    20–27
    and see MEMORY REFRESHING
  non-appearance of, 8–20
  opinion, statements involving, 2–39
  and see OPINION EVIDENCE
  persons of unsound mind, as, 17–06,
    17–07
  police officers, as, 6–27
  previous consistent statement,
    20–02
    and see PREVIOUS CONSISTENT
      STATEMENTS
  previous convictions, where, 7–73
  prosecution, for, 19–01, 19–02
  questioning of, 16–09, 19–07
  re-examination of, 21–32, 21–33
  resident abroad, 8–23, 8–24
  serving own purpose, where, 15–15
  sexual offences, cases concerning,
    19–13, 19–15
  special measures
    see SPECIAL MEASURES

WITNESS—*cont.*
  spouse, as, 17–26, 17–28, 17–33
    and see SPOUSE
  unavailable, where, 8–17, 8–20
  unfit, where, 8–22
  unreliable, where, 15–15, 15–16
  untruthful, where, 19–01
  vulnerable
    see VULNERABLE WITNESSES
  worthy of belief, 19–01, 19–02
WITNESS IN FEAR
  evidence partially given, 8–28
  hearsay evidence, where, 8–26—
    8–28
  offence related fear, 8–28
  vulnerable witness, 19–12, 19–18
  and see VULNERABLE WITNESS

YOUNG PERSONS
  see also CHILDREN
  character evidence, and, 7–31
  confessions, involving, 9–30
  evidence
    attendance in court, 8–82
    exclusion of, 8–82
    prejudicial material, 8–82
    previous convictions, 7–31
  hearsay evidence, and, 8–82
  interviews
    adult present, at, 9–30
    legal representative present, at,
      9–30
    police questioning, 9–31
    self-incrimination, at, 9–30
  witness, as, 19–16